Frank M. Howland
Stanford Univ.
June 15, 1984

PRINCIPLES OF ECONOMETRICS

PRINCIPLES OF ECONOMETRICS

HENRI THEIL

Center for Mathematical Studies in Business and Economics

The University of Chicago

JOHN WILEY & SONS, INC.

New York / London / Sydney / Toronto

Sole distributors outside the Western Hemisphere:
North-Holland Publishing Company--Amsterdam

Library of Congress Catalogue Card Number: 78-118626

ISBN 0-471-85845-5

Printed in the United States of America

10 9 8 7 6 5 4 3 2

PREFACE

Nobody believes that he can become a chemist by attending lectures and reading textbooks and journal articles. He should also devote time and energy to the real work in a laboratory. In the same way, nobody should believe that he will be able to handle statistical data in economics without touching actual data. A description of techniques that are available to handle these data is obviously needed; such a description is more useful when it is accompanied by applications at every step, and I have tried to follow this rule as much as possible. It is equally true that reading applied texts such as KARL FOX's *Intermediate Economic Statistics* and J. S. CRAMER's *Empirical Econometrics* is of considerable value. But only by working with data is it possible to acquire a feeling of what should and what should not be done, and no textbook is able to provide this kind of guidance.

It occurs too frequently that a student is unaware of this until he is at an advanced stage of his study. He then wants to do research in a certain area and computes a number of regressions, knowing only vaguely what the technique is supposed to perform. The computer output forces him to look at F ratios, partial correlation coefficients, and many more things which convince him that it is better to know what they mean. If he responds by attending an introductory econometrics course, he may find out that his general statistics background is weak and that some knowledge of matrix algebra might have been useful. He is much better off taking an introductory econometrics course at an earlier stage of the study, thus devoting part of his time and energy to techniques rather than substantive problems while his mind is still young, so that he has these techniques available for the analysis of problems and of the data on which their solutions are to be based when his mind is more mature. It does require maturity to realize that models are to be used but not to be believed.

Prerequisites

The use of this book presupposes some knowledge of elementary mathematical statistics and matrix algebra. The advice given in the preceding paragraph thus implies that courses in these areas should be taken at a very early stage.

I am well aware of the fact that matrix algebra is a stumbling block for many students, and I have tried to take this into account by minimizing the requirements in this regard. An alternative strategy is to design a textbook in which the matrix algebra is developed from scratch. There was something to be said in favor of this strategy at an earlier stage of the development of econometrics, but the approach is less desirable now that there are other areas in economics that require the use of matrices, such as input-output analysis and mathematical programming. An econometrics course was never an ideal place for the teaching of linear algebra, and given these new developments it is much better to arrange for a general introductory course on matrix algebra to be taken before the econometrics course.

As far as statistics is concerned, it is assumed that the reader is aware of elementary normal distribution theory (χ^2, t, F) and that he knows the first principles of point and interval estimation and of hypothesis testing.

The Organization of the Book

The book is divided into chapters; chapters are divided into sections (for example, Section 3.2 is the second section of the third chapter), and sections are divided into (unnumbered) subsections. The first two chapters summarize the algebra and statistics prerequisites. Chapter 3 on least squares and the standard linear model is the starting point of the econometrics treatment. It is followed by Chapter 4 on partial and multiple correlation and Chapter 5 on the use of various forms of residuals for testing the assumptions of the standard linear model. Thereafter the model is extended by the formulation of weaker assumptions. In Chapter 6 the generalized least-squares method is developed, and it is applied in Chapter 7 to the case in which not one but several economic relations are under investigation. Many of the results in this area have only large-sample validity. Since I do not believe in a teaching approach that handles all complications at the same time, I decided to collect the basic results of asymptotic distribution theory as well as its applications to this area in one chapter, Chapter 8.

Chapter 9 extends the theory of Chapter 7 on several equations to the case in which these equations are "simultaneous." That chapter has an introductory character; it is followed by Chapter 10 in which the large-sample properties of simultaneous equation estimators are developed. Chapter 11 concerns specification and aggregation problems. The last (twelfth) chapter has unavoidably a mixed character and includes such topics as regression strategies, distribution-free estimation, informational measures, and Bayesian inference. I originally planned to include advanced topics of time series analysis, but I decided not to do this because areas such as spectral analysis require a level of analysis which exceeds that of the rest of the book.

The organization as described here is a logical one, although I recognize that the term "logical" in this context is necessarily somewhat subjective. I think that such a presentation has, in principle, great merits when the book is used for reference purposes. However, this organization does imply that reading the book from cover to cover is not the optimal method when it is used as a textbook. To facilitate the selection of sections for an introductory course, I marked them by A, B, or C depending on whether the section is recommended, optional, or not recommended for an introductory course. The arrangement is such that no A section depends on previous B or C material and no B section depends on previous C material.[1] A few sections are marked AB, AC, or BC, which means that the material is heterogeneous in this regard. In such cases the separate subsections are marked A, B, or C.

A Suggested Introductory Course

A specific course is described below, based on this book, which I have found to be useful in my teaching at The University of Chicago. It is designed both for students who want to be practitioners in the art of data analysis and for whom this is the only econometrics course, and also for students who want to specialize in econometrics by taking more advanced courses at a later stage. The course is exclusively based on material which is marked A; if a recommended section is AB or AC, the subsections marked B or C are to be omitted.

I have found it very useful to teach according to a two-track system. The main track consists of about 60 percent of the available time in class; it is followed in each session by the second track which may either be handled by the instructor himself or by a teaching assistant. The material of the second

[1] There are some footnotes and problems at the end of the sections that are exceptions to this rule, but these can be easily identified.

track consists in the beginning of the course mainly of a review of the statistics prerequisites (Chapter 2); later it is devoted to applications of the more general ideas which are considered in the main track. One of the advantages of this two-track system is that the class sessions are livelier; each session is devoted to at least two topics, which induces the students to be more alert. Another advantage is that there is less accumulation of new and unfamiliar concepts in each class session, which may be illustrated by means of the following example. It is easily possible to treat Sections 9.1 and 9.2 in one session of $1\frac{1}{2}$ hours, but this would imply that the student is successively exposed to the concepts of endogenous and exogenous variables, to the completeness of an equation system, to structural equations and the reduced form, to Klein's Model I, to current and lagged variables and jointly dependent and predetermined variables, and to the extension of the reduced form concept for the case in which there are lagged variables. This is clearly more than even a bright student can digest in $1\frac{1}{2}$ hours; the reduced form without lagged variables has had no chance to sink in, and its generalization is hardly appropriate at this stage. Therefore it is much better to divide Sections 9.1 and 9.2 over two successive sessions and to use the balance of the available time in these sessions for the second track.

The second track may also be used to review the problems assigned to the students (which are given at the end of the sections), particularly those which appear to be difficult. I made a special effort to provide a good collection of problems. There are more than 400 in the book as a whole, partly theoretical and partly applied. In a few cases I used a set of three or four successive problems to outline a proof which would have been rather lengthy if it had been put into the text. An example is Problems 5.2 to 5.5 at the end of Section 3.5; it is quite possible that the instructor will regard such a proof as a suboptimal use of the available time for an introductory course such as the one which will now be described.

PRIOR TO THE COURSE

Students are asked to study, in the week before the beginning of the course, Sections 0.1 and 0.2 (Introduction), 1.1 to 1.4 (the elementary matrix material through quadratic forms), and 2.1 to 2.4. This should cause no difficulties for students who satisfy the prerequisites. Section 1.5 on latent roots and characteristic vectors is not part of the course; this material typically does cause difficulties.

FIRST ROUND

Main track: The instructor quickly reviews Sections 1.1 to 1.4; he stresses the importance of idempotent matrices (Section 1.1) and of the theorem which states that any symmetric positive definite matrix **A** can be written as the product $\mathbf{P}'\mathbf{P}$ for some nonsingular $\mathbf{P}$ (Section 1.4). He then proceeds to Sections 1.6 on matrix differentiation and 1.7 on maximization and minimization. The last section contains least squares as an adjustment procedure, so that the students become familiar with this method at an early stage of the course.

Second track: The instructor reviews briefly Sections 2.1 to 2.4, stressing particularly the use of matrix algebra in multivariate distribution theory (Section 2.2) and in the algebra of expectations (Section 2.4). Thereafter he considers the moment-generating functions of Section 2.5 and the χ^2, F, and t distributions described in Section 2.6.

SECOND ROUND

First track: Immediately after the least-squares exposition of Section 1.7 the instructor moves to Chapter 3 on least squares and the standard linear model, where he treats the material of Sections 3.1 through 3.7.

Second track: The instructor goes through Sections 2.7 to 2.9, which provide an elementary account of statistical inference that serves as a base for the corresponding material in Sections 3.3 to 3.7. He then proceeds to Section 3.8 on multicollinearity. It is advantageous to teach this subject in the second track because it is mentioned on several occasions in Chapter 4 which is also part of this track (see below).

THIRD ROUND

Main track: The instructor goes quickly through Section 3.9 on the limitations of the standard linear model.[2] He then moves to Section 6.1 on the generalized least-squares estimation technique, which he subsequently applies to problems of heteroscedasticity (Section 6.2) and joint estimation of seemingly unrelated equations (Section 7.1).

Second track: The instructor discusses Sections 4.1 through 4.5, which concern mainly elementary material on correlation coefficients as a descriptive device. Thereafter he treats Section 5.1 on least-squares residuals and their use in testing against heteroscedasticity and autocorrelation.

FOURTH ROUND

Main track: After completing Section 7.1 the instructor proceeds to Chapter 9 on simultaneous equation models. He covers Sections 9.1 through 9.5, which deal with a number of basic concepts in that area including the elements of identification analysis and of two-stage least-squares estimation.

[2] It is unlikely that the student will understand all details of this section when he reads it for the first time, but he will develop a more positive appreciation when he uses the section for reviewing purposes later on.

Second track: The instructor discusses Section 6.3 on correlated disturbances and autoregressive transformations.[3] He then moves to the distributed lags of Section 6.4, after which he turns to the A material of Chapter 8 (Section 8.1 and parts of Sections 8.2 and 8.9), which should give the student an idea of what is meant when it is stated that certain results have only large-sample validity.

FIFTH ROUND

Main track: The instructor covers Sections 11.1 and 11.2, which contain an elementary account of specification problems.

Second track: The instructor proceeds to Section 9.7 (impact and interim multipliers of dynamic equation systems) and then to Sections 9.8 and 9.9. The last two sections concern the Klein-Goldberger model, which is useful material for the student who is interested in the operation of a medium-size econometric model of the simultaneous-equation type.

Alternative Introductory Courses

Since there are many sections marked B, a substantial number of different introductory courses can be designed on the basis of this book. This amounts to adding certain material and probably also deleting some of the suggested topics above. It obviously makes no sense to try to be exhaustive with regard to the set of all alternative introductory courses, but three possibilities may be mentioned.

1. The introductory course suggested above is based on the assumption that a substantial proportion of the students takes only one introductory econometrics course. If, on the other hand, most of them take two econometrics courses, the first of these may concentrate on single-equation models and the second on equation systems. In that case the first course may dispense with Section 7.1 and Chapter 9, and the instructor may want to substitute for these Sections 12.2 to 12.4 on errors in the variables, robust and distribution-free procedures, and models with random coefficients. The course on equation systems can be organized along the lines of the suggested second course described below, but Section 7.1 and Chapter 9 should be added; the instructor in charge of this course may then want to delete certain other subjects such as the BLUS residuals.

2. If the instructor can rely on a higher level of mathematical sophistication of his students, he may include Section 1.5 on latent roots and characteristic vectors, which enables him to derive the chi-square distribution of idempotent

[3] This is also a convenient point for the discussion of a regression computer program. An example is the B34E-BLUS program of the Center for Mathematical Studies in Business and Economics of The University of Chicago, about which information can be obtained on request.

quadratic forms in normal variates (Section 2.6). He may also want to include the extrema under constraints of Section 1.8 and the parameter spaces and likelihood ratio tests of Section 2.9, which would give him the opportunity of covering most of the material which is marked B in Chapters 1 through 4. Details are provided in the discussion of a second course below.

3. If the instructor wants to include the elements of Bayesian inference, he is advised to treat Section 7.8 on mixed estimation immediately after Section 7.1 and then to proceed directly to Section 12.9.

A Suggested Second Course

For the second course, too, I have found it useful to proceed according to the two-track system. The course is based on the assumption that the students went through the five rounds of the suggested introductory course described above, and its contents may be briefly summarized as follows.

The main track starts with a review of Section 5.1 on least-squares residuals, followed by the remainder of Chapter 5 (except Section 5.6) which deals with BLUS residuals. Next is a review of Section 6.1 followed by Sections 6.6 through 6.8 on generalized inverses and generalized least squares based on a singular disturbance covariance matrix. After a review of Section 7.1 the remainder of Chapter 7 can then be treated, but the instructor will prefer to delete Sections 7.5 through 7.7 if he plans to teach the special topics course which is described below. The last part of the main track is Chapter 10 on simultaneous equation estimation.[4]

The second track starts with the material of the first four chapters that was deleted in the introductory course. This amounts to the following sections:

- 1.5 on latent roots and characteristic vectors
- 1.6 (subsection) on the derivatives of the elements of an inverse
- 1.8 on extrema under constraints
- 1.9 on principal components
- 2.6 (subsection) on the chi-square distribution of idempotent quadratic forms in normal variates
- 2.9 (subsections) on parameter spaces and likelihood ratio tests
- 3.7 (subsections) on likelihood ratio tests for linear constraints on the coefficient vector of the standard linear model
- 3.8 (subsection) on minimum-variance estimation of linear combinations of the coefficients under conditions of multicollinearity
- 4.6 on the relation between R^2 and the analysis of variance
- 4.7 on regression and correlation in the multivariate normal model

After this material has been discussed the instructor goes through Chapter 8

[4] Note that Section 9.6 is to be inserted before Section 10.7.

on asymptotic distribution theory insofar as this chapter was not covered by the introductory course.[5] This theory forms the statistical base of Chapter 10 of the main track. The second track concludes with those parts of Chapters 5 and 6 that were not included in the main track (Sections 5.6 and 6.9).

It may seem that the topics of the second track, especially those of the first four chapters, are quite heterogeneous. In fact, however, it is readily seen that they are characterized by a considerable mathematical coherence, in particular when they are regarded (as they should be) in conjunction with the main track. For example, the characteristic roots and vectors of Section 1.5 are needed almost immediately in Sections 5.2 through 5.5 of the main track, and very soon in Sections 1.9, 2.6, and 3.8 of the second track, and later in Sections 6.6 to 6.8 and 7.2 to 7.4 of the main track, and so on. Similarly, the constrained minimization procedure of Section 1.8 is used in Sections 1.9, 3.7, 3.8, and 4.6 of the second track and on several occasions in the main track, and the principal components of Section 1.9 are used in Section 5.6. Analogous statements can be made on the likelihood ratio tests of Sections 2.9 and 3.7.

A Special Topics Course

I have used parts of this book for a special topics course centered around consumer demand theory. The demand specification which is considered in particular is that of the model developed by BARTEN and myself. From the standpoint of an advanced econometrics course this model has the attractive feature of being linear in the unknown parameters when the absolute price version is adopted but nonlinear when the relative price version is used. The course is taught according to the conventional single-track system; it is described in the two paragraphs which follow. Reading assignments include articles by FRISCH, HOUTHAKKER, and STONE on the addilog, linear expenditure, and related systems, articles on preference independence and utility trees, WOLD'S and JUREEN'S *Demand Analysis*, and my *Economics and Information Theory*.

The starting point is the absolute price version of the model described in Sections 7.5 to 7.7, which presuppose knowledge of the joint generalized least-squares technique of Sections 7.1 to 7.3. The instructor then moves to Appendix A and to Section 11.6 in which the relative price version is derived. Section 11.7 on aggregation over consumers requires that Section 11.5 on the convergence approach to the aggregation problem be read before. (Some instructors will find it advantageous to cover Sections 11.3 and 11.4 on aggregation also.) Sections 11.8 and 11.9 complete the estimation of the relative price version.

[5] Section 6.5 can be treated jointly with Section 8.8. The proof of the convergence of BLUS residuals in Section 8.3 should be postponed until Section 5.6 has been treated.

The instructor then proceeds to Section 12.6 on informational measures in one dimension and to the application of these measures to demand equation systems in Section 12.7. Next he moves to Section 12.1 on regression strategies, which should give the student an impression of the implications of procedures which use the same data for testing and estimation several times. The instructor finally proceeds to Section 12.5 (probit and logit analysis), which enables him to complete the course with the multivariate informational measures of Section 12.8. Discussions of the reading assignments will serve to make the course a lively one.

Acknowledgments

Franklin M. Fisher of the Massachusetts Institute of Technology read an earlier draft of this book and provided many comments that led to several improvements of the exposition. J. C. Gupta, a graduate student in the Department of Statistics in Chicago, spent two summers reading successive drafts and made many valuable suggestions. Other persons, who contributed to the book in its final form, are my colleagues Harry V. Roberts (particularly Chapters 1–4 and Section 12.9) and Marc Nerlove, and my former Rotterdam colleague Teun Kloek. I am grateful to all of them.

I am indebted to the editors of *Biometrika* and the *Annals of Mathematical Statistics;* to the Syndics of the Cambridge University Press and The Collegiate Press, Ames, Iowa; and to Messrs. Durbin, Press, and Brooks for permission to use the tables that appear at the end of this book. I am also grateful to the editors of the *International Economic Review*, the *Journal of the Royal Statistical Society*, and *Econometrica;* and to authors Boot, Stone, and Adelman for their permission to use elsewhere in this book materials that were originally published in these journals.

The completion of this book was a long and arduous task. Much of the credit should go to my secretary, Mrs. Sharon R. Massie, who typed several successive drafts, checked and rechecked galleys and page proofs, and remained cheerful despite the obstacles. In the last stages of the work she was competently assisted by Mrs. Pat Mackay. I also appreciate the help that I received from the University's Graduate School of Business.

Several generations of my students in Chicago were exposed to the successive drafts. Their reactions led to many changes, which usually amounted to simpler or more lucid expositions. I have not maintained an accurate record of who said what, so these contributors must remain anonymous, but they do deserve the reader's gratitude.

Finally, I thank my wife, Lore, for her help, which was of a different nature but at least equally valuable.

H. T.

CONTENTS

LIST OF TABLES

CHAPTER *12*

(For the tables at the end of the book, see page xix.)

LIST OF FIGURES

LIST OF ASSUMPTIONS

LIST OF THEOREMS

CHAPTER *3*

CHAPTER *5*

CHAPTER *6*

ABBREVIATIONS AND OTHER TECHNICAL NOTES

LS:	least squares
GLS:	generalized least squares
2SLS:	two-stage least squares
3SLS:	three-stage least squares
BLUS residual vector:	a best linear unbiased residual vector with a scalar covariance matrix

Formulas and problems are indicated by two numbers, the first of which refers to the section and the second to the order in which they occur. Thus, eq. (3.2) is the second equation of the third section of some chapter. When reference is made to eq. (3.2), it is always the equation in the same chapter except when the contrary is stated explicitly. Similarly, Problem 7.4 (no parentheses) is the fourth problem of the seventh section of some chapter, to be found in the same chapter unless otherwise indicated.

Tables, figures, assumptions, and theorems are indicated by two numbers, the first of which refers to the *chapter* and the second to the order of occurrence: Table 5.1 is the first table of Chapter 5, Assumption 10.2 is the second assumption of Chapter 10. To facilitate finding a table, figure, assumption, or theorem when it is not in the same chapter, the section in which it occurs is usually indicated. Thus, Assumption 3.3 is simply "Assumption 3.3" in Chapter 3, but it is "Assumption 3.3 of Section 3.2" in other chapters.

INTRODUCTION

Econometrics is concerned with the empirical determination of economic laws. The word "empirical" indicates that the data used for this determination have been obtained from observation, which may be either controlled experimentation designed by the econometrician for the particular purpose of the law in which he is interested, or "passive" observation. The latter type is as prevalent among economists as it is among meteorologists.

0.1 Typology of Economic Relations[A]

Behavioral and Technical Relations

In most cases, economic laws are expressed in a relatively simple mathematical form. An example that will be discussed in detail in Chapter 3 as well as in later chapters is

$$\log C = \beta_0 + \beta_1 \log Y + \beta_2 \log p \tag{1.1}$$

where C is the consumption of textiles per capita in a certain year, Y real income per capita in the same year, p an index of textile prices deflated by a general cost of living index, and β_0, β_1, and β_2 are constants. This equation is known as a *behavioral relation*. It describes how consumers behave, on the average, with regard to their purchases of texile goods, given the relative price level of these goods as well as real income per capita. The law (1.1) is determined as soon as we know the coefficients β_0, β_1, and β_2. Accordingly, the econometric problem is to draw inferences about these coefficients from an appropriate set of observations.

Not all economic laws are concerned with the behavior of households or of other economic agents (such as entrepreneurs or trade unions). A counterexample is

$$P = cK^{\alpha}L^{1-\alpha} \tag{1.2}$$

where P is the maximum output of a factory during a certain year (measured in physical units) that can be attained when the average capital stock during the year is K and the total number of man-hours employed is L; c and α are constants. Equation (1.2) is a *technical relation* describing how any input combination (K, L) leads to a particular (maximum) numerical value of the output P. Specifically, it is a production function of the Cobb-Douglas type with constant returns to scale.[1]

Micro- and Macrorelations

Note that there is another difference between (1.1) and (1.2). The latter equation is concerned with inputs and output of an individual factory, whereas the former deals with a "per capita consumer"; that is, it is an equation describing the "average" behavior of a large number of consumers. In this case we speak about a *macrorelation*, whereas (1.2) is a *microrelation*. Both types can be found for behavioral equations as well as for technical relations. For example, in Section 7.1 we shall examine equations for individual firms describing how much they invest each year, given certain determining factors. These are behavioral microequations. Similarly, we may have the following interpretation for the variables in (1.2): P is the total industrial output of a country in any given year,[2] K is total capital stock in industry, and L is the total number of man-hours employed in industry. This is evidently a technical macroequation. The analysis of the relationship between micro- and macrorelations—usually known as aggregation theory—is important and will be pursued in Chapter 11.

[1] The phrase "constant returns to scale" indicates that if the inputs are all increased by a factor k (any positive number), output is raised in the same porportion. In the case of (1.2) this is guaranteed by the fact that the exponents α and $1 - \alpha$ add up to one.

[2] In this case, P is usually measured in dollars per year at constant prices, not in physical units.

Static and Dynamic Relations

There is another distinction which also applies equally to behavioral as well as technical equations. Imagine that our textile consumers do not only react to the income earned in the same year but also to last year's income. Specifically, suppose that (1.1) is replaced by

$$\log C = \beta_0 + \beta_1 \log Y + \beta_1' \log Y_{-1} + \beta_2 \log p \tag{1.3}$$

where Y_{-1} stands for last year's per capita real income. (In a more explicit time series notation this would be Y_{t-1} when Y_t is per capita real income in year t.) The modification implies that consumers no longer react immediately (in the same year) to changes in income, but that part of the effect takes place one year later. When variables dated differently occur in the same equation, as is the case in (1.3), we speak about a *dynamic* relation. Otherwise the relation is said to be *static*, and (1.1) and (1.2) are examples of that category.

Technical relations may be dynamic, too. We can imagine, for example, that capital goods bought in different years have different productivities. If we write $K, K_{-1}, K_{-2}, \ldots$ for the presently existing capital stock insofar as it was bought in the current year, one year ago, two years ago, and so on, our production function may be of the form

$$P = cK^{\alpha_0}K_{-1}^{\alpha_1}K_{-2}^{\alpha_2} \cdots L^{1-\alpha} \tag{1.4}$$

which is indeed a dynamic technical relation. The static/dynamic dichotomy will prove to be important on several occasions, particularly in the framework of systems of simultaneous equations.

Definitional and Institutional Relations

Returning to the distinction between behavioral and technical relations, we should mention that these two groups do not exhaust the set of all relations that we shall meet in this book. There are two other groups, both of which are much less interesting from an econometric point of view because they normally do not contain any unknown coefficients. Nevertheless, they should be mentioned in view of the role that they play in the analysis of systems of equations. One type is the *identity* (or *definitional equation*), an equation that holds identically in its variables simply because these variables are defined so that the equation must hold. Examples: price × quantity = value (for any commodity in any period); the totals of each side of a balance sheet are equal; the change in capital stock is equal to net investment. The other type is the *institutional equation*, of which the following is an example. The government imposes a 20 percent excise tax on the sales of a certain group of commodities; hence $T = .2S$, where S = sales and T = excise tax revenue. As in the case of the identity, there is no unknown coefficient, but the situation is different because the (known) coefficient may change: the relation is modified to $T = .15S$ when the government decides to lower the tax rate to 15 percent. More generally, institutional relations describe the behavior of variables in terms of other variables in a way prescribed by the institutional arrangements of the society. Another example is the amount of income tax to be paid by an individual as a function of his net income and the number of dependants.

Problems

1.1 Would you regard a numerical value of $\alpha < 0$ or > 1 plausible for the production function (1.2)? Explain your answer.

1.2 What is the condition to be imposed on the production function (1.4) if it is to have constant returns to scale?

1.3 The last paragraph contains three examples of identities. Indicate which of the three are static and which are dynamic. Can the examples be specified so that they are micro and also so that they are macro?

1.4 Does the identity "price × quantity = value" always hold when we work with index numbers for composite commodities rather than with the price and the quantity of a single commodity?

0.2 Data and Theoretical Relations[A]

The determination of the coefficients of behavioral and technical relations would be a simple problem if the observations were in exact agreement with the relation postulated, but that is a very rare phenomenon. To show what happens in the usual case, imagine that real per capita income remains unchanged in (1.1), so that the relative price of textile goods is the only determining variable that really varies. For seven annual observations we may then have a picture like that in Figure 0.1*a*. The equation states that the relation should be linear with slope β_2, but there is evidently no straight line which fits all seven observations. If one insists on a curve which does fit all seven, it will be something like the one shown in Figure 0.1*b*. It should be clear, however, that it is not really satisfactory to regard this curve as the correct representation of the relationship between textile consumption and textile price. First, it is seen that the curve moves upward in at least one price interval, thus indicating that a price increase stimulates rather than reduces consumption. Second, no one will believe that if an eighth observation becomes available, it will be exactly on the curve except by chance. This

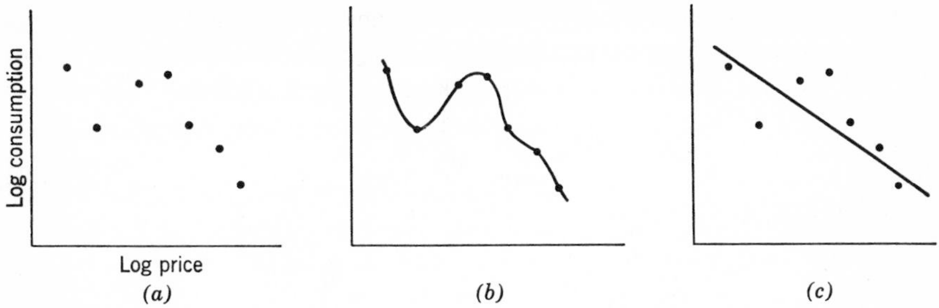

Fig. 0.1 Analysis of a scatter of observation points.

means that the curve would have to be refitted each time a new observation becomes available, and that one can never be sure that the curve which one uses will agree with the next observation.

The Method of Least Squares

It seems much more plausible to accept the fact that there are deviations and to fit a straight line as is shown in Figure 0.1*c*. Let us simplify the notation of (1.1) and write x_1 for the logarithm of the price of the first observation, x_2 for that of the second, and so on, and similarly $y_1, \ldots, y_7$ for the logarithm of textile consumption of the successive observations. The data thus consist of seven pairs of real numbers:

$$(x_1, y_1) \quad (x_2, y_2) \quad \cdots \quad (x_7, y_7) \tag{2.1}$$

A linear relation expressing y in terms of x is of the form $y = b_0 + bx$. The data (2.1) may then be used to determine the coefficients b_0 and b. One line of argument is the following. For the first observation we have $x = x_1$, so that the y value which is implied by the linear relation is $b_0 + bx_1$. But the observed y value is y_1; hence there is a discrepancy equal to $y_1 - b_0 - bx_1$. The sum of the squares of all seven such discrepancies is

$$(y_1 - b_0 - bx_1)^2 + (y_2 - b_0 - bx_2)^2 + \cdots + (y_7 - b_0 - bx_7)^2 \tag{2.2}$$

Suppose we are interested in the values of b_0 and b which minimize this sum of squares. We differentiate (2.2) with respect to b_0 and equate the result to zero:

$$-2(y_1 - b_0 - bx_1) - 2(y_2 - b_0 - bx_2) - \cdots - 2(y_7 - b_0 - bx_7) = 0$$

This can be written in the simple form

$$b_0 = \bar{y} - b\bar{x} \tag{2.3}$$

where $\bar{y} = \frac{1}{7}\sum y_i$ and $\bar{x} = \frac{1}{7}\sum x_i$ are the means of the y and the x observations, respectively. Equation (2.3) determines b_0 as soon as b has been found. To find b we differentiate (2.2) with respect to that coefficient:

$$-2x_1(y_1 - b_0 - bx_1) - 2x_2(y_2 - b_0 - bx_2) - \cdots - 2x_7(y_7 - b_0 - bx_7) = 0$$

Substituting $\bar{y} - b\bar{x}$ for b_0 in accordance with (2.3) we conclude that this equation can be written as

$$-2\sum_{i=1}^{7} x_i[y_i - \bar{y} - b(x_i - \bar{x})] = 0$$

from which we derive

$$b = \frac{\sum_{i=1}^{7} x_i(y_i - \bar{y})}{\sum_{i=1}^{7} x_i(x_i - \bar{x})} \tag{2.4}$$

Our problem has thus been solved in a well-defined manner. However, the solution raises several other questions. Why should we minimize the sum of the squares of the discrepancies and not, say, the sum of their absolute values? How should we interpret these discrepancies? Why should the line be straight? Intuitively, it seems reasonable to adjust a line or a curve of some simple form, so that the discrepancies are as small as possible in some well-defined sense, but what is the justification of this procedure? Is there a general law in economics which states that such discrepancies (whatever they may stand for) are small or as small as possible?

These are among the questions to which we shall have to address ourselves in this book. We shall examine a series of models of successively increasing complexity, all of which are of a statistical nature. This explains why the book has a sizable statistical component.

Problems

2.1 Consider Figure 0.1*b* and suppose that somebody insists on the use of a polynomial which fits all seven observations. Of which degree should this polynomial be?

2.2 Prove that b given in (2.4) also satisfies

$$b = \frac{\sum_{i=1}^{7} (x_i - \bar{x})(y_i - \bar{y})}{\sum_{i=1}^{7} (x_i - \bar{x})^2} \tag{2.5}$$

2.3 When deriving b_0 and b, we equated two first-order derivatives to zero. Does this really guarantee that the sum of the squares of the discrepancies is minimized?

CHAPTER 1

MATHEMATICAL TOOLS: MATRIX ALGEBRA

An excellent textbook in matrix algebra is HADLEY (1961). GRAYBILL'S textbook (1969) is more advanced, but it is very useful for statistical applications. BIRKHOFF and MAC LANE (1965) and HALMOS (1958) are recommended for those who prefer a more abstract treatment. Students who want to combine algebra with mathematical economics should consult ALLEN (1965). Chapter 1 of GRAYBILL (1961) gives a concise summary of a large number of matrix properties. For maximization and minimization techniques (Sections 1.7–1.8 of this chapter), see Chapter 3 of HADLEY (1964).

All sections of this chapter are recommended for an introductory econometrics course with the exception of Sections 1.5, 1.8, and 1.9 and a subsection of Section 1.6, which are optional.

1.1 Matrices, Vectors, and Their Elementary Operations[A]

A *matrix* $\mathbf{A}$ is a rectangular array consisting of m rows and n columns. The element in the ith row and jth column is denoted by a_{ij} and the matrix itself is frequently indicated by its typical element: $\mathbf{A} = [a_{ij}]$. By interchanging the role of rows and columns we obtain the *transpose* of **A**, written as **A**′, the (i, j)th element of which is a_{ji}. A *square matrix* has as many rows as columns: $m = n$. If, moreover, we have $\mathbf{A} = \mathbf{A}'$, the matrix is said to be *symmetric*. Special cases of symmetric matrices are the *unit matrix*, the *scalar matrix*, and the *diagonal matrix*:

$$\begin{bmatrix} 1 & 0 & \cdots & 0 \\ 0 & 1 & \cdots & 0 \\ \cdot & \cdot & & \cdot \\ \cdot & \cdot & & \cdot \\ \cdot & \cdot & & \cdot \\ 0 & 0 & \cdots & 1 \end{bmatrix} \quad \begin{bmatrix} c & 0 & \cdots & 0 \\ 0 & c & \cdots & 0 \\ \cdot & \cdot & & \cdot \\ \cdot & \cdot & & \cdot \\ \cdot & \cdot & & \cdot \\ 0 & 0 & \cdots & c \end{bmatrix} \quad \begin{bmatrix} d_1 & 0 & \cdots & 0 \\ 0 & d_2 & \cdots & 0 \\ \cdot & \cdot & & \cdot \\ \cdot & \cdot & & \cdot \\ \cdot & \cdot & & \cdot \\ 0 & 0 & \cdots & d_n \end{bmatrix}$$

On the left we have a unit matrix (written **I**), in the middle a scalar matrix (all diagonal elements equal but not necessarily equal to 1), and on the right a diagonal matrix (zero off-diagonal elements but no restrictions on the diagonal elements). A matrix is called a zero matrix (written **0**) when all its elements are zero; such a matrix need not be square.

The order of a matrix is indicated by $m \times n$, where m is the number of rows and n the number of columns. An $m \times 1$ matrix is called a *column vector*, which will be denoted by a lowercase letter. For example, $\mathbf{x} = [x_i]$ where x_i is the ith element of the vector. A $1 \times n$ matrix is a *row vector*, which will be denoted by lowercase with a prime added to indicate that it is the transpose of a column vector (for example, $\mathbf{x}'$).

Summation and Multiplication

Given two $m \times n$ matrices $\mathbf{A} = [a_{ij}]$ and $\mathbf{B} = [b_{ij}]$ (of the same order!), their *sum* $\mathbf{S} = [s_{ij}]$ is defined as an $m \times n$ matrix whose elements are equal to the sum of the corresponding elements of **A** and **B**: $s_{ij} = a_{ij} + b_{ij}$. If k is a scalar (an ordinary number) and **A** a matrix of arbitrary order, then $k\mathbf{A}$ is the matrix whose elements are equal to the corresponding element of **A** multiplied by k. This is *scalar multiplication*. If $\mathbf{A} = [a_{ij}]$ is an $m \times n$ matrix and $\mathbf{B} = [b_{jh}]$ an $n \times p$ matrix, the product $\mathbf{C} = \mathbf{AB}$ is an $m \times p$ matrix whose (i, h)th element is

$$c_{ih} = \sum_{j=1}^{n} a_{ij} b_{jh}$$

This is *matrix multiplication*. The product **AB** is defined if and only if the number of columns of **A** is equal to the number of rows of **B**. In general, $\mathbf{AB} \neq \mathbf{BA}$ even if both product matrices exist. **AB** means: **A** postmultiplied by **B** or, equivalently, **B** premultiplied by **A**.

Length, Inner Product, and Orthogonality of Vectors

If we premultiply a column vector **x** by its own transpose we obtain

$$\mathbf{x}'\mathbf{x} = \sum_{i=1}^{n} x_i^2 \tag{1.1}$$

where x_i is the ith element of **x** and n is the number of its elements. The positive square root of $\mathbf{x}'\mathbf{x}$ is known as the *length* of the vector **x** (and also of its transpose $\mathbf{x}'$). Consider now two vectors consisting of the same number (n) of elements, **x** and **y**. Then

$$\mathbf{x}'\mathbf{y} = \mathbf{y}'\mathbf{x} = \sum_{i=1}^{n} x_i y_i \tag{1.2}$$

is known as the *inner product* of **x** and **y**. If we divide the inner product by the product of the lengths of **x** and **y**, we obtain a ratio which is less than 1 in view of Schwarz's inequality:

$$\cos\theta = \frac{\mathbf{x}'\mathbf{y}}{(\mathbf{x}'\mathbf{x})^{\frac{1}{2}}(\mathbf{y}'\mathbf{y})^{\frac{1}{2}}} \tag{1.3}$$

$$-1 \leq \cos\theta \leq 1$$

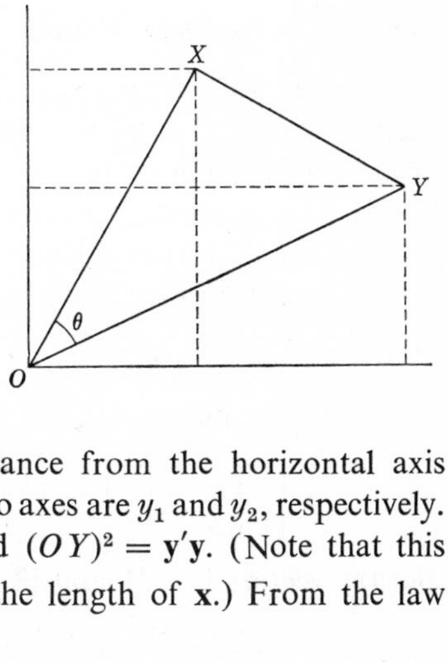

The geometric interpretation can be given easily for $n = 2$. Consider the figure on the right, where the distance of the point X from the vertical axis is equal to x_1 (the first element of the vector **x**) and the distance from the horizontal axis is x_2. Similarly, the distances of Y from the two axes are y_1 and y_2, respectively. It is seen immediately that $(OX)^2 = \mathbf{x}'\mathbf{x}$ and $(OY)^2 = \mathbf{y}'\mathbf{y}$. (Note that this justifies the terminology of $OX = \sqrt{\mathbf{x}'\mathbf{x}}$ as the length of **x**.) From the law of cosines we have

$$\begin{aligned}(XY)^2 &= (OX)^2 + (OY)^2 - 2(OX)(OY)\cos\theta \\ &= \mathbf{x}'\mathbf{x} + \mathbf{y}'\mathbf{y} - 2(\mathbf{x}'\mathbf{x})^{\frac{1}{2}}(\mathbf{y}'\mathbf{y})^{\frac{1}{2}}\cos\theta\end{aligned} \tag{1.4}$$

But, also,

$$\begin{aligned}(XY)^2 &= (x_1 - y_1)^2 + (x_2 - y_2)^2 \\ &= (\mathbf{x} - \mathbf{y})'(\mathbf{x} - \mathbf{y}) \\ &= \mathbf{x}'\mathbf{x} + \mathbf{y}'\mathbf{y} - 2\mathbf{x}'\mathbf{y}\end{aligned}$$

On substituting this result into (1.4), we obtain (1.3) immediately. When the inner product $\mathbf{x}'\mathbf{y}$ vanishes, the angle θ is equal to 90 degrees ($= \frac{1}{2}\pi$ radians), in which case the vectors $\mathbf{x}$ and $\mathbf{y}$ are said to be *orthogonal*. This geometric terminology is also applied when $n > 2$; each n-element vector is then regarded as a point in the n-dimensional Euclidean space.

We mention some simple theorems:[3]

A1 Each matrix is equal to the transpose of its own transpose: $\mathbf{A} = (\mathbf{A}')'$.

A2 The transpose of a product matrix is equal to the product of the transposes but in reverse order: $(\mathbf{AB})' = \mathbf{B}'\mathbf{A}'$.

A3 Diagonal matrices of the same order are commutative in multiplication: $\mathbf{D}_1\mathbf{D}_2 = \mathbf{D}_2\mathbf{D}_1$ if $\mathbf{D}_1$ and $\mathbf{D}_2$ are diagonal $n \times n$ matrices. The product matrix is also diagonal.

A4 For any matrix $\mathbf{A}$ we have $\mathbf{IA} = \mathbf{AI} = \mathbf{A}$ (are the two unit matrices of the same order?) and $\mathbf{0} + \mathbf{A} = \mathbf{A} + \mathbf{0} = \mathbf{A}$ (same question for $\mathbf{0}$).

A5 If $\mathbf{A}'\mathbf{A} = \mathbf{0}$, then $\mathbf{A} = \mathbf{0}$. (*Hint*. Consider the diagonal elements of $\mathbf{A}'\mathbf{A}$.)

Linearly Independent Vectors

Consider K vectors, $\mathbf{x}_1, \ldots, \mathbf{x}_K$, each consisting of n elements. The vector $c_1\mathbf{x}_1 + \cdots + c_K\mathbf{x}_K$, where $c_1, \ldots, c_K$ are real numbers, is called a linear combination of the vectors $\mathbf{x}_1, \ldots, \mathbf{x}_K$. Such vectors are said to be linearly independent if no linear combination exists that is a zero vector except (trivially) when all c's are taken to be zero. Equivalently, the vectors $\mathbf{x}_1, \ldots, \mathbf{x}_K$ are called linearly independent if

$$(1.5) \qquad c_1\mathbf{x}_1 + \cdots + c_K\mathbf{x}_K = \mathbf{0} \qquad \text{implies} \qquad c_1 = \cdots = c_K = 0$$

Thus, $[1 \quad 0]'$ and $[0 \quad 1]'$ are linearly independent:

$$c_1\begin{bmatrix}1\\0\end{bmatrix} + c_2\begin{bmatrix}0\\1\end{bmatrix} = \begin{bmatrix}c_1\\c_2\end{bmatrix} = \begin{bmatrix}0\\0\end{bmatrix} \qquad \text{implies} \qquad c_1 = c_2 = 0$$

but the vectors $[1 \quad 2]'$ and $[2 \quad 4]'$ are not linearly independent:

$$c_1\begin{bmatrix}1\\2\end{bmatrix} + c_2\begin{bmatrix}2\\4\end{bmatrix} = \begin{bmatrix}c_1 + 2c_2\\2c_1 + 4c_2\end{bmatrix} = \begin{bmatrix}0\\0\end{bmatrix} \quad \text{if (for example)} \quad c_1 = -2c_2 = 1$$

The Rank of a Matrix

Let $\mathbf{A}$ be an $m \times n$ matrix. The row rank of $\mathbf{A}$ is defined as the largest number of linearly independent rows; if all rows of $\mathbf{A}$ are linearly independent, $\mathbf{A}$ is said to have full row rank. The column rank of $\mathbf{A}$ is defined as

[3] The theorems are combined in groups and numbered (A1, A2, . . . , B1, B2, . . . , etc.) for easy reference. Most of them will not be proved but some will be, particularly those that are not found in most of the elementary textbooks but that are, nevertheless, used on a large scale in this book.

the largest number of linearly independent columns; if all columns are linearly independent, **A** is said to have full column rank. It can be shown that the row rank and the column rank of any $m \times n$ matrix **A** are equal, so that we may speak about "the" rank of **A**. Obviously, $r \leq m$ and $r \leq n$ if r is the rank of **A**.

B1 Each zero matrix has zero rank.
B2 The rank of an $m \times n$ matrix **A** is equal to the largest number r such that at least one subdeterminant of **A** of order r is nonzero, while all higher-order subdeterminants (if any) vanish.[4]
B3 The rank of the product matrix **AB** is at most equal to the rank of **A** and also at most equal to the rank of **B**.
B4 For any matrix **A** there is equality of the rank of **A**, of **A**′, of **AA**′, and of **A**′**A**.

The Nonsingular Matrix and Its Inverse

A square ($n \times n$) matrix **A** is said to be nonsingular if it has full rank (i.e., rank n); otherwise it is called singular. (The notion of singularity or nonsingularity applies to square matrices only, so that we may delete "square" in the expression "a nonsingular square matrix.") If an $n \times n$ matrix **A** is nonsingular, there exists an $n \times n$ matrix **B** which satisfies $\mathbf{AB} = \mathbf{BA} = \mathbf{I}$. This **B** is called the inverse of **A** and is denoted by $\mathbf{A}^{-1}$. If the inverse exists (i.e., if **A** is nonsingular), then it is unique, because it can be shown that $\mathbf{AB} = \mathbf{BA} = \mathbf{I}$ and $\mathbf{AC} = \mathbf{CA} = \mathbf{I}$ imply $\mathbf{B} = \mathbf{C}$. The (i, j)th element of $\mathbf{A}^{-1}$, usually written as a^{ij}, is equal to $c_{ji}/|\mathbf{A}|$, where $|\mathbf{A}|$ is the determinant of **A** and c_{ji} is the cofactor of a_{ji} in **A**.[5]

C1 Each nonsingular matrix is equal to the inverse of its own inverse: $\mathbf{A} = (\mathbf{A}^{-1})^{-1}$.
C2 The inverse of the transpose of a matrix is equal to the transpose of the inverse: $(\mathbf{A}')^{-1} = (\mathbf{A}^{-1})'$.
C3 A diagonal matrix is nonsingular if and only if all diagonal elements differ from zero. If this condition is satisfied, the inverse is also diagonal and its diagonal elements are equal to the reciprocals of the corresponding elements of the original matrix.

[4] Definitions of and elementary operations on determinants, minors, and cofactors are assumed to be known.

[5] The inverse is thus only defined for nonsingular matrices. A generalized inverse will be defined in Section 6.6 for singular matrices and also for matrices which are not even square.

C4 If **A** is an $n \times n$ matrix and $|\mathbf{A}| = 0$, then the rank of **A** is less than n (**A** is singular).

C5 If **A** and **B** are both $n \times n$, then $|\mathbf{AB}| = |\mathbf{A}|\,|\mathbf{B}|$.

C6 The rank of a matrix is unaltered by pre- or postmultiplication by a nonsingular matrix: **AB** and **CA** have the same rank as **A** if **B** and **C** are nonsingular. (What can be said about the order of **B** and **C**?)

C7 If **A** and **B** are nonsingular and of the same order, then $(\mathbf{AB})^{-1} = \mathbf{B}^{-1}\mathbf{A}^{-1}$.

Idempotent Matrices; Deviations from Means

Any square matrix **A** which satisfies $\mathbf{A}^2 = \mathbf{A}$ is called idempotent. In this book all idempotent matrices that will be met are also symmetric, so that it is convenient to make the implicit assumption $\mathbf{A}' = \mathbf{A}$ when speaking about idempotent matrices. The simplest examples are the unit matrix and the square zero matrix. Another example is

$$\mathbf{A} = \mathbf{I} - \frac{1}{n}\boldsymbol{\iota\iota}' \tag{1.6}$$

where **I** is the $n \times n$ unit matrix and $\boldsymbol{\iota}$ a column vector consisting of n unit elements. *Check*:

$$\left(\mathbf{I} - \frac{1}{n}\boldsymbol{\iota\iota}'\right)\left(\mathbf{I} - \frac{1}{n}\boldsymbol{\iota\iota}'\right) = \mathbf{I} - \frac{1}{n}\boldsymbol{\iota\iota}' - \frac{1}{n}\boldsymbol{\iota\iota}' + \frac{1}{n^2}\boldsymbol{\iota}(\boldsymbol{\iota}'\boldsymbol{\iota})\boldsymbol{\iota}'$$

$$= \mathbf{I} - \frac{1}{n}\boldsymbol{\iota\iota}'$$

because $\boldsymbol{\iota}'\boldsymbol{\iota} = n$. The matrix (1.6) plays a role when we transform observations on variables to deviations from the means. Suppose we have three variables, x, y, and z, and n triples of observations, $(x_\alpha, y_\alpha, z_\alpha)$, $\alpha = 1, \ldots, n$. They can be arranged in an $n \times 3$ matrix:[6]

$$\mathbf{B} = \begin{bmatrix} x_1 & y_1 & z_1 \\ x_2 & y_2 & z_2 \\ \cdot & \cdot & \cdot \\ \cdot & \cdot & \cdot \\ \cdot & \cdot & \cdot \\ x_n & y_n & z_n \end{bmatrix} \begin{matrix} \text{first observation} \\ \text{second observation} \\ \\ \\ \\ n\text{th observation} \end{matrix} \tag{1.7}$$

[6] For a numerical example of such an observation matrix, see Table 1.1 in Section 1.9 below.

We premultiply **B** by the **A** of (1.6):

$$\mathbf{AB} = \mathbf{B} - \boldsymbol{\iota}\left(\frac{1}{n}\boldsymbol{\iota}'\mathbf{B}\right) \tag{1.8}$$

$$= \begin{bmatrix} x_1 & y_1 & z_1 \\ x_2 & y_2 & z_2 \\ \cdot & \cdot & \cdot \\ \cdot & \cdot & \cdot \\ \cdot & \cdot & \cdot \\ x_n & y_n & z_n \end{bmatrix} - \begin{bmatrix} 1 \\ 1 \\ \cdot \\ \cdot \\ \cdot \\ 1 \end{bmatrix} [\bar{x} \quad \bar{y} \quad \bar{z}]$$

$$= \begin{bmatrix} x_1 - \bar{x} & y_1 - \bar{y} & z_1 - \bar{z} \\ x_2 - \bar{x} & y_2 - \bar{y} & z_2 - \bar{z} \\ \cdot & \cdot & \cdot \\ \cdot & \cdot & \cdot \\ \cdot & \cdot & \cdot \\ x_n - \bar{x} & y_n - \bar{y} & z_n - \bar{z} \end{bmatrix}$$

where

$$\bar{x} = \frac{1}{n}\sum_{\alpha=1}^{n} x_\alpha \qquad \bar{y} = \frac{1}{n}\sum_{\alpha=1}^{n} y_\alpha \qquad \bar{z} = \frac{1}{n}\sum_{\alpha=1}^{n} z_\alpha \tag{1.9}$$

Thus **AB** differs from **B** to the extent that the values taken by the three variables are all measured as deviations from their respective means.

Continuing the example, suppose that we are interested in the matrix of sums of squares and products of the values of the three variables:

$$\mathbf{B}'\mathbf{B} = \begin{bmatrix} \sum x_\alpha^2 & \sum x_\alpha y_\alpha & \sum x_\alpha z_\alpha \\ \sum y_\alpha x_\alpha & \sum y_\alpha^2 & \sum y_\alpha z_\alpha \\ \sum z_\alpha x_\alpha & \sum z_\alpha y_\alpha & \sum z_\alpha^2 \end{bmatrix} \tag{1.10}$$

where all summations are over α from 1 through n. Suppose that we are also interested in the sums of squares and products of these values when the latter are all measured as deviations from the means:

$$\begin{bmatrix} \sum (x_\alpha - \bar{x})^2 & \sum (x_\alpha - \bar{x})(y_\alpha - \bar{y}) & \sum (x_\alpha - \bar{x})(z_\alpha - \bar{z}) \\ \sum (y_\alpha - \bar{y})(x_\alpha - \bar{x}) & \sum (y_\alpha - \bar{y})^2 & \sum (y_\alpha - \bar{y})(z_\alpha - \bar{z}) \\ \sum (z_\alpha - \bar{z})(x_\alpha - \bar{x}) & \sum (z_\alpha - \bar{z})(y_\alpha - \bar{y}) & \sum (z_\alpha - \bar{z})^2 \end{bmatrix}$$

This is $(\mathbf{AB})'\mathbf{AB}$ in view of (1.8), which can be simplified to $\mathbf{B}'\mathbf{AB}$ because $\mathbf{A}'\mathbf{A} = \mathbf{A}^2 = \mathbf{A}$. Similarly, if we have another set of, say, two variables u

and v with corresponding observations:

$$\mathbf{C} = \begin{bmatrix} u_1 & v_1 \\ u_2 & v_2 \\ \cdot & \cdot \\ \cdot & \cdot \\ \cdot & \cdot \\ u_n & v_n \end{bmatrix} \begin{matrix} \text{first observation} \\ \text{second observation} \\ \\ \\ \\ n\text{th observation} \end{matrix} \tag{1.11}$$

then $\mathbf{B'C}$ contains the sums of products of the x, y, z variables on the one hand and the u, v variables on the other hand, while $(\mathbf{AB})'\mathbf{AC} = \mathbf{B'AC}$ does so in terms of deviations from the means:

$$\mathbf{B'C} = \begin{bmatrix} \sum x_\alpha u_\alpha & \sum x_\alpha v_\alpha \\ \sum y_\alpha u_\alpha & \sum y_\alpha v_\alpha \\ \sum z_\alpha u_\alpha & \sum z_\alpha v_\alpha \end{bmatrix} \tag{1.12}$$

$$(\mathbf{AB})'\mathbf{AC} = \begin{bmatrix} \sum (x_\alpha - \bar{x})(u_\alpha - \bar{u}) & \sum (x_\alpha - \bar{x})(v_\alpha - \bar{v}) \\ \sum (y_\alpha - \bar{y})(u_\alpha - \bar{u}) & \sum (y_\alpha - \bar{y})(v_\alpha - \bar{v}) \\ \sum (z_\alpha - \bar{z})(u_\alpha - \bar{u}) & \sum (z_\alpha - \bar{z})(v_\alpha - \bar{v}) \end{bmatrix} \tag{1.13}$$

where

$$\bar{u} = \frac{1}{n}\sum_{\alpha=1}^{n} u_\alpha \qquad \bar{v} = \frac{1}{n}\sum_{\alpha=1}^{n} v_\alpha \tag{1.14}$$

The equality of $(\mathbf{AB})'\mathbf{AC}$ and $\mathbf{B}'(\mathbf{AC})$ implies that the right-hand matrix in (1.13) is the same as the right-hand matrix in

$$\mathbf{B}'(\mathbf{AC}) = \begin{bmatrix} \sum x_\alpha(u_\alpha - \bar{u}) & \sum x_\alpha(v_\alpha - \bar{v}) \\ \sum y_\alpha(u_\alpha - \bar{u}) & \sum y_\alpha(v_\alpha - \bar{v}) \\ \sum z_\alpha(u_\alpha - \bar{u}) & \sum z_\alpha(v_\alpha - \bar{v}) \end{bmatrix} \tag{1.15}$$

Similarly, the matrix in (1.13) is also the same as

$$(\mathbf{AB})'\mathbf{C} = \begin{bmatrix} \sum (x_\alpha - \bar{x})u_\alpha & \sum (x_\alpha - \bar{x})v_\alpha \\ \sum (y_\alpha - \bar{y})u_\alpha & \sum (y_\alpha - \bar{y})v_\alpha \\ \sum (z_\alpha - \bar{z})u_\alpha & \sum (z_\alpha - \bar{z})v_\alpha \end{bmatrix} \tag{1.16}$$

In words: to get the sums of the cross-products of the values taken by two sets of variables, all taken as deviations from the respective means, it is sufficient to measure only one of the two sets as deviations from the means. This is due to the symmetry and the idempotency of the transformation matrix $\mathbf{A}$ of (1.6).

The Trace of a Square Matrix

The trace of an $n \times n$ matrix is defined as the sum of its diagonal elements:

$$\text{tr}\,\mathbf{A} = \sum_{i=1}^{n} a_{ii} \tag{1.17}$$

Some properties are:

D1 The trace of the scalar product $k\mathbf{A}$ is equal to k times the trace: $\text{tr}\,k\mathbf{A} = k\,\text{tr}\,\mathbf{A}$ ($\mathbf{A}$ square).

D2 The trace of the sum matrix $\mathbf{A} + \mathbf{B}$ is equal to the sum of the separate traces: $\text{tr}\,(\mathbf{A} + \mathbf{B}) = \text{tr}\,\mathbf{A} + \text{tr}\,\mathbf{B}$ ($\mathbf{A}$ and $\mathbf{B}$ square of the same order).

D3 The traces of the product matrices $\mathbf{AB}$ and $\mathbf{BA}$ are equal: $\text{tr}\,\mathbf{AB} = \text{tr}\,\mathbf{BA}$ ($\mathbf{A}$ and $\mathbf{B}$ of such orders that both product matrices exist). [*Hint.* Both traces are equal to $\sum\sum a_{ij}b_{ji}$, where the summation over i is from 1 through the number of rows of $\mathbf{A}$ (= the number of columns of $\mathbf{B}$) and the summation over j is from 1 through the number of columns of $\mathbf{A}$ (= the number of rows of $\mathbf{B}$).]

D4 The trace of an idempotent matrix is equal to its rank. This will be proved at the end of Section 1.5.

With the help of these properties we can find the trace of the matrix defined in (1.6):

$$\begin{aligned} \text{tr}\left(\mathbf{I} - \frac{1}{n}\boldsymbol{\iota\iota}'\right) &= \text{tr}\,\mathbf{I} + \text{tr}\left(-\frac{1}{n}\boldsymbol{\iota\iota}'\right) && \text{(using D2)} \\ &= n - \frac{1}{n}\,\text{tr}\,\boldsymbol{\iota\iota}' && \text{(using D1)} \\ &= n - \frac{1}{n}\,\text{tr}\,\boldsymbol{\iota}'\boldsymbol{\iota} && \text{(using D3)} \\ &= n - 1 \end{aligned} \tag{1.18}$$

The last step is based on the fact that $\boldsymbol{\iota}'\boldsymbol{\iota}$ is a scalar (a 1×1 matrix) and hence equal to its own trace. Since the matrix (1.6) is idempotent, its rank is thus equal to $n - 1$ in view of proposition D4. Actually, it follows directly from (1.6) that this matrix cannot have a rank larger than $n - 1$, because we obtain a zero vector when we postmultiply it by $\boldsymbol{\iota}$. The statement that the rank is equal to $n - 1$ thus implies that *there exists no nonzero vector other than* $\boldsymbol{\iota}$ (except trivially $c\boldsymbol{\iota}$ where c is a scalar $\neq 0$) which gives a zero vector when it is premultiplied by the matrix (1.6).

Problems

1.1 Prove $\mathbf{A}(\mathbf{B}+\mathbf{C}) = \mathbf{AB} + \mathbf{AC}$. What are the restrictions on the orders of $\mathbf{A}$, $\mathbf{B}$, and $\mathbf{C}$ in order that the multiplications and summations be permissible? Also prove $(\mathbf{AB})\mathbf{C} = \mathbf{A}(\mathbf{BC})$.

1.2 Prove that the inverse of a symmetric nonsingular matrix is also symmetric.

1.3 Prove that $\mathbf{A}$ defined in (1.6) is symmetric.

1.4 Consider the least-squares coefficient b in eqs. (2.4) and (2.5) of Section 0.2. Prove the equivalence of these two expressions by means of the transformation matrix $\mathbf{A}$ of (1.6).

1.5 Prove $\text{tr}\,\mathbf{ABC} = \text{tr}\,\mathbf{CAB} = \text{tr}\,\mathbf{BCA}$ and specify the restrictions on the orders of $\mathbf{A}$, $\mathbf{B}$, and $\mathbf{C}$.

1.6 Prove that

$$\frac{1}{4}\begin{bmatrix} 2 & 4 \\ 1 & 2 \end{bmatrix}$$

is a nonsymmetric idempotent matrix.

1.2 Partitioned Matrices[A]

We shall frequently have to break up a matrix into submatrices. For example, the $n \times n$ unit matrix can be partitioned into n column vectors, each of which contains one unit element, all others being zero:[7]

$$(2.1)\quad \mathbf{I} = [\mathbf{i}_1 \quad \mathbf{i}_2 \quad \cdots \quad \mathbf{i}_n] \qquad \mathbf{i}_1 = \begin{bmatrix} 1 \\ 0 \\ \cdot \\ \cdot \\ \cdot \\ 0 \end{bmatrix} \quad \mathbf{i}_2 = \begin{bmatrix} 0 \\ 1 \\ \cdot \\ \cdot \\ \cdot \\ 0 \end{bmatrix} \quad \cdots \quad \mathbf{i}_n = \begin{bmatrix} 0 \\ 0 \\ \cdot \\ \cdot \\ \cdot \\ 1 \end{bmatrix}$$

Another example is

$$(2.2)\qquad [\mathbf{B} \quad \mathbf{C}] = \left[\begin{array}{ccc|cc} x_1 & y_1 & z_1 & u_1 & v_1 \\ x_2 & y_2 & z_2 & u_2 & v_2 \\ \cdot & \cdot & \cdot & \cdot & \cdot \\ \cdot & \cdot & \cdot & \cdot & \cdot \\ \cdot & \cdot & \cdot & \cdot & \cdot \\ x_n & y_n & z_n & u_n & v_n \end{array}\right]$$

[7] It is more usual to write $\mathbf{e}_1, \mathbf{e}_2, \ldots$ for such vectors, but these symbols will be needed for residual vectors in Chapter 3 and later.

This is the $n \times 5$ matrix of values taken by all five variables x, y, z, u, v. We introduced $\mathbf{B}$ and $\mathbf{C}$ in (1.7) and (1.11) as separate matrices, but we can also regard them as submatrices of the complete $n \times 5$ matrix which refers to all variables jointly.

Partitioned Summation and Multiplication

Partitioning may take place both by sets of rows and by sets of columns. The addition rule can be applied in partitioned form:

$$(2.3) \qquad \begin{bmatrix} \mathbf{A}_{11} & \mathbf{A}_{12} \\ \mathbf{A}_{21} & \mathbf{A}_{22} \\ \mathbf{A}_{31} & \mathbf{B}_{32} \end{bmatrix} + \begin{bmatrix} \mathbf{B}_{11} & \mathbf{B}_{12} \\ \mathbf{B}_{21} & \mathbf{B}_{22} \\ \mathbf{B}_{31} & \mathbf{B}_{32} \end{bmatrix} = \begin{bmatrix} \mathbf{A}_{11} + \mathbf{B}_{11} & \mathbf{A}_{12} + \mathbf{B}_{12} \\ \mathbf{A}_{21} + \mathbf{B}_{21} & \mathbf{A}_{22} + \mathbf{B}_{22} \\ \mathbf{A}_{31} + \mathbf{B}_{31} & \mathbf{A}_{32} + \mathbf{B}_{32} \end{bmatrix}$$

provided that each $\mathbf{A}_{ij}$ is of the same order as the corresponding $\mathbf{B}_{ij}$. The same applies to multiplication:

$$(2.4) \qquad \begin{bmatrix} \mathbf{P}_{11} & \mathbf{P}_{12} \\ \mathbf{P}_{21} & \mathbf{P}_{22} \end{bmatrix} \begin{bmatrix} \mathbf{Q}_{11} & \mathbf{Q}_{12} \\ \mathbf{Q}_{21} & \mathbf{Q}_{22} \end{bmatrix} = \begin{bmatrix} \mathbf{P}_{11}\mathbf{Q}_{11} + \mathbf{P}_{12}\mathbf{Q}_{21} & \mathbf{P}_{11}\mathbf{Q}_{12} + \mathbf{P}_{12}\mathbf{Q}_{22} \\ \mathbf{P}_{21}\mathbf{Q}_{11} + \mathbf{P}_{22}\mathbf{Q}_{21} & \mathbf{P}_{21}\mathbf{Q}_{12} + \mathbf{P}_{22}\mathbf{Q}_{22} \end{bmatrix}$$

provided that the number of columns of $\mathbf{P}_{11}$ and $\mathbf{P}_{21}$ is equal to the number of rows of $\mathbf{Q}_{11}$ and $\mathbf{Q}_{12}$ and that the number of columns of $\mathbf{P}_{12}$ and $\mathbf{P}_{22}$ is equal to the number of rows of $\mathbf{Q}_{21}$ and $\mathbf{Q}_{22}$. As an example we take $\mathbf{A}$, $\mathbf{B}$, and $\mathbf{C}$ of (1.6), (1.7), and (1.11), respectively:

$$(2.5) \qquad \begin{bmatrix} \mathbf{B}' \\ \mathbf{C}' \end{bmatrix} \mathbf{A}[\mathbf{B} \quad \mathbf{C}] = \begin{bmatrix} \mathbf{B}' \\ \mathbf{C}' \end{bmatrix} [\mathbf{AB} \quad \mathbf{AC}] = \begin{bmatrix} \mathbf{B}'\mathbf{AB} & \mathbf{B}'\mathbf{AC} \\ \mathbf{C}'\mathbf{AB} & \mathbf{C}'\mathbf{AC} \end{bmatrix}$$

$$= \left[\begin{array}{ccc|cc} \sum X_\alpha^2 & \sum X_\alpha Y_\alpha & \sum X_\alpha Z_\alpha & \sum X_\alpha U_\alpha & \sum X_\alpha V_\alpha \\ \sum Y_\alpha X_\alpha & \sum Y_\alpha^2 & \sum Y_\alpha Z_\alpha & \sum Y_\alpha U_\alpha & \sum Y_\alpha V_\alpha \\ \sum Z_\alpha X_\alpha & \sum Z_\alpha Y_\alpha & \sum Z_\alpha^2 & \sum Z_\alpha U_\alpha & \sum Z_\alpha V_\alpha \\ \hline \sum U_\alpha X_\alpha & \sum U_\alpha Y_\alpha & \sum U_\alpha Z_\alpha & \sum U_\alpha^2 & \sum U_\alpha V_\alpha \\ \sum V_\alpha X_\alpha & \sum V_\alpha Y_\alpha & \sum V_\alpha Z_\alpha & \sum V_\alpha U_\alpha & \sum V_\alpha^2 \end{array}\right]$$

where capitals are used for deviations from means ($X_\alpha = x_\alpha - \bar{x}$, etc.) to obtain a more compact notation.

Partitioned Inversion

Consider the following nonsingular matrix:

$$(2.6) \qquad \mathbf{D} = \begin{bmatrix} \mathbf{P}_1 & \mathbf{R}_1 \\ \mathbf{R}_1' & \mathbf{Q}_1 \end{bmatrix}$$

where $\mathbf{P}_1$ and $\mathbf{Q}_1$ are nonsingular symmetric submatrices. Let the inverse of $\mathbf{D}$ be

$$\mathbf{E} = \begin{bmatrix} \mathbf{P}_2 & \mathbf{R}_2 \\ \mathbf{R}_2' & \mathbf{Q}_2 \end{bmatrix} \tag{2.7}$$

the submatrices of $\mathbf{E}$ being of the same order as the corresponding submatrices of $\mathbf{D}$. The problem is to express the former submatrices in terms of the latter. For this purpose we write $\mathbf{ED} = \mathbf{I}$ as follows:

$$\begin{bmatrix} \mathbf{P}_2 & \mathbf{R}_2 \\ \mathbf{R}_2' & \mathbf{Q}_2 \end{bmatrix} \begin{bmatrix} \mathbf{P}_1 & \mathbf{R}_1 \\ \mathbf{R}_1' & \mathbf{Q}_1 \end{bmatrix} = \begin{bmatrix} \mathbf{I} & \mathbf{0} \\ \mathbf{0} & \mathbf{I} \end{bmatrix}$$

which amounts to four equations in submatrices:

$$\mathbf{P}_2\mathbf{P}_1 + \mathbf{R}_2\mathbf{R}_1' = \mathbf{I} \tag{2.8}$$

$$\mathbf{P}_2\mathbf{R}_1 + \mathbf{R}_2\mathbf{Q}_1 = \mathbf{0} \tag{2.9}$$

$$\mathbf{R}_2'\mathbf{P}_1 + \mathbf{Q}_2\mathbf{R}_1' = \mathbf{0} \tag{2.10}$$

$$\mathbf{R}_2'\mathbf{R}_1 + \mathbf{Q}_2\mathbf{Q}_1 = \mathbf{I} \tag{2.11}$$

We obtain $\mathbf{R}_2 = -\mathbf{P}_2\mathbf{R}_1\mathbf{Q}_1^{-1}$ from (2.9) and substitute this into (2.8):

$$\mathbf{P}_2(\mathbf{P}_1 - \mathbf{R}_1\mathbf{Q}_1^{-1}\mathbf{R}_1') = \mathbf{I}$$

Hence:

$$\mathbf{P}_2 = (\mathbf{P}_1 - \mathbf{R}_1\mathbf{Q}_1^{-1}\mathbf{R}_1')^{-1} \tag{2.12}$$

$$\mathbf{R}_2 = -(\mathbf{P}_1 - \mathbf{R}_1\mathbf{Q}_1^{-1}\mathbf{R}_1')^{-1}\mathbf{R}_1\mathbf{Q}_1^{-1} \tag{2.13}$$

Combining (2.11) and (2.13), we find

$$-\mathbf{Q}_1^{-1}\mathbf{R}_1'(\mathbf{P}_1 - \mathbf{R}_1\mathbf{Q}_1^{-1}\mathbf{R}_1')^{-1}\mathbf{R}_1 + \mathbf{Q}_2\mathbf{Q}_1 = \mathbf{I}$$

which gives

$$\mathbf{Q}_2 = \mathbf{Q}_1^{-1} + \mathbf{Q}_1^{-1}\mathbf{R}_1'(\mathbf{P}_1 - \mathbf{R}_1\mathbf{Q}_1^{-1}\mathbf{R}_1')^{-1}\mathbf{R}_1\mathbf{Q}_1^{-1} \tag{2.14}$$

Therefore the partitioned inverse is

$$\begin{bmatrix} \mathbf{P}_1 & \mathbf{R}_1 \\ \mathbf{R}_1' & \mathbf{Q}_1 \end{bmatrix}^{-1} \tag{2.15}$$

$$= \begin{bmatrix} (\mathbf{P}_1 - \mathbf{R}_1\mathbf{Q}_1^{-1}\mathbf{R}_1')^{-1} & -(\mathbf{P}_1 - \mathbf{R}_1\mathbf{Q}_1^{-1}\mathbf{R}_1')^{-1}\mathbf{R}_1\mathbf{Q}_1^{-1} \\ -\mathbf{Q}_1^{-1}\mathbf{R}_1'(\mathbf{P}_1 - \mathbf{R}_1\mathbf{Q}_1^{-1}\mathbf{R}_1')^{-1} & \mathbf{Q}_1^{-1} + \mathbf{Q}_1^{-1}\mathbf{R}_1'(\mathbf{P}_1 - \mathbf{R}_1\mathbf{Q}_1^{-1}\mathbf{R}_1')^{-1}\mathbf{R}_1\mathbf{Q}_1^{-1} \end{bmatrix}$$

$$= \begin{bmatrix} \mathbf{P}_1^{-1} + \mathbf{P}_1^{-1}\mathbf{R}_1(\mathbf{Q}_1 - \mathbf{R}_1'\mathbf{P}_1^{-1}\mathbf{R}_1)^{-1}\mathbf{R}_1'\mathbf{P}_1^{-1} & -\mathbf{P}_1^{-1}\mathbf{R}_1(\mathbf{Q}_1 - \mathbf{R}_1'\mathbf{P}_1^{-1}\mathbf{R}_1)^{-1} \\ -(\mathbf{Q}_1 - \mathbf{R}_1'\mathbf{P}_1^{-1}\mathbf{R}_1)^{-1}\mathbf{R}_1'\mathbf{P}_1^{-1} & (\mathbf{Q}_1 - \mathbf{R}_1'\mathbf{P}_1^{-1}\mathbf{R}_1)^{-1} \end{bmatrix}$$

The expression in the last line is obtained when we start by solving $\mathbf{Q}_2$ rather than $\mathbf{P}_2$, which can be done by means of (2.10) and (2.11).

Problems

2.1 Prove that the nonsingularity of $\mathbf{P}_1 - \mathbf{R}_1\mathbf{Q}_1^{-1}\mathbf{R}_1'$, whose inverse occurs as a submatrix in (2.15), follows from the nonsingularity of $\mathbf{D}$ defined in (2.6). [*Hint*. Prove that $(\mathbf{P}_1 - \mathbf{R}_1\mathbf{Q}_1^{-1}\mathbf{R}_1')\mathbf{x} = \mathbf{0}$ implies

$$\begin{bmatrix} \mathbf{P}_1 & \mathbf{R}_1 \\ \mathbf{R}_1' & \mathbf{Q}_1 \end{bmatrix} \begin{bmatrix} \mathbf{x} \\ -\mathbf{Q}_1^{-1}\mathbf{R}_1'\mathbf{x} \end{bmatrix} = \mathbf{0}$$

where $\mathbf{x}$ is a column vector whose number of elements is equal to the number of columns of $\mathbf{P}_1$.]

2.2 Prove that the inverse of the matrix (2.6) is equal to the partitioned matrix after the second equality sign of (2.15).

2.3 Prove that the upper-left and lower-right submatrices occurring in (2.15) are all symmetric when $\mathbf{P}_1$ and $\mathbf{Q}_1$ are symmetric.

1.3 The Solution of Linear Equation Systems[A]

A linear equation system is of the form $\mathbf{Ax} = \mathbf{h}$, where $\mathbf{A}$ is an $m \times n$ matrix and hence $\mathbf{x}$ and $\mathbf{h}$ are column vectors consisting of n and m elements, respectively. Written in full:

$$\begin{aligned} a_{11}x_1 + a_{12}x_2 + \cdots + a_{1n}x_n &= h_1 \\ a_{21}x_1 + a_{22}x_2 + \cdots + a_{2n}x_n &= h_2 \\ &\;\;\vdots \\ a_{m1}x_1 + a_{m2}x_2 + \cdots + a_{mn}x_n &= h_m \end{aligned} \tag{3.1}$$

The problem is: can we find a solution $(x_1, \ldots, x_n)$ which satisfies these equations? It is easily seen that this is not necessarily true. Take $x_1 + x_2 = 2$, $2x_1 + 2x_2 = 3$, which is an inconsistent equation system. Note that this situation cannot occur for a homogeneous system ($\mathbf{h} = \mathbf{0}$) because $\mathbf{Ax} = \mathbf{0}$ always has $\mathbf{x} = \mathbf{0}$ as a solution.

Even if the system is not inconsistent, so that a solution does exist, then this solution need not be unique. In fact, when there are two different solutions, there are always infinitely many, which is shown as follows. Let $\mathbf{y}$ and $\mathbf{z}$ be two solutions, so that $\mathbf{Ay} = \mathbf{Az} = \mathbf{h}$ and $\mathbf{y} \neq \mathbf{z}$. Then for any scalar θ the vector $\theta\mathbf{y} + (1 - \theta)\mathbf{z}$ is also a solution:

$$\mathbf{A}[\theta\mathbf{y} + (1 - \theta)\mathbf{z}] = \theta\mathbf{Ay} + (1 - \theta)\mathbf{Az} = \theta\mathbf{h} + (1 - \theta)\mathbf{h} = \mathbf{h}$$

To verify which of the three possibilities applies we introduce the *augmented matrix*, which is an $m \times (n + 1)$ matrix that can be partitioned into the coefficient matrix $\mathbf{A}$ and the right-hand vector $\mathbf{h}$:

$$\mathbf{B} = [\mathbf{A} \quad \mathbf{h}] = \begin{bmatrix} a_{11} & a_{12} & \cdots & a_{1n} & h_1 \\ a_{21} & a_{22} & \cdots & a_{2n} & h_2 \\ \cdot & \cdot & & \cdot & \cdot \\ \cdot & \cdot & & \cdot & \cdot \\ \cdot & \cdot & & \cdot & \cdot \\ a_{m1} & a_{m2} & \cdots & a_{mn} & h_m \end{bmatrix} \tag{3.2}$$

The rules are the following:

E1 A necessary and sufficient condition that the system $\mathbf{Ax} = \mathbf{h}$ be consistent (have at least one solution $\mathbf{x}$) is that the rank of the coefficient matrix $\mathbf{A}$ be equal to the rank of the augmented matrix $\mathbf{B}$. Thus, if the occurrence of $\mathbf{h}$ besides $\mathbf{A}$ in $\mathbf{B}$ raises the rank of $\mathbf{B}$ above that of $\mathbf{A}$, the system is inconsistent.

E2 The system has a unique solution if and only if the rank of $\mathbf{A}$ and that of $\mathbf{B}$ are both equal to n. The simplest case is $m = n$ and $\mathbf{A}$ nonsingular; the solution is then $\mathbf{x} = \mathbf{A}^{-1}\mathbf{h}$.

E3 If the rank of $\mathbf{A}$ and that of $\mathbf{B}$ are both equal to r and if $r < n$, there is an infinite number of solutions. Specifically, there are then $n - r$ of the unknown x's which can be assigned any desired values and the remaining r will be uniquely determined. It is to be understood that the r columns of $\mathbf{A}$ which correspond to the latter x's should be linearly independent.

Example 1

Consider the system

$$\begin{aligned} x_1 + 3x_2 &= 0 \\ x_1 + x_2 &= 1 \\ 2x_1 + 4x_2 &= 1 \end{aligned}$$

Here $m = 3$, $n = 2$. The rank of $\mathbf{A}$ is 2, since the determinant value of the matrix consisting of the first two rows is $1 \times 1 - 3 \times 1 = -2 \neq 0$. But the rank of the 3×3 augmented matrix is also 2, since its last row is equal to the sum of the first two rows. Hence we have case E2 and the unique solution is $x_1 = 1\frac{1}{2}$, $x_2 = -\frac{1}{2}$.

Example 2

Consider the system

$$\begin{aligned} 2x_2 + 7x_3 &= 4 \\ 3x_1 + 3x_2 + 6x_3 &= 3 \\ x_1 + x_2 + 2x_3 &= 1 \end{aligned}$$

The ranks of **A** and **B** are equal to 2. The determinant of the coefficient submatrix of the first two equations and the first two variables is $0 \times 3 - 2 \times 3 = -6 \neq 0$ and the second rows of **A** and **B** are three times the last row, so that the rank cannot be 3. Therefore we have case E3 and we can express x_1 and x_2 in x_3:

$$x_1 = -1 + \frac{3}{2}x_3 \qquad x_2 = 2 - \frac{7}{2}x_3$$

The value of x_3 can be chosen arbitrarily. We may also express x_1 and x_3 in x_2:

$$x_1 = -\frac{1}{7} - \frac{3}{7}x_2 \qquad x_3 = \frac{4}{7} - \frac{2}{7}x_2$$

Similarly,

$$x_2 = -\frac{1}{3} - \frac{7}{3}x_1 \qquad x_3 = \frac{2}{3} + \frac{2}{3}x_1$$

Problems

3.1 Find the solution, if any, of the equation system $3x - y = 5$, $x + y = 0$. What happens if $x - y = 2\frac{1}{2}$ is added as a third equation? Same question for $x - y = 2$.

3.2 Use proposition E1 to prove that the homogeneous equation system $\mathbf{Ax} = \mathbf{0}$ can never be inconsistent.

1.4 Quadratic Forms[A]

A quadratic form is defined as a square matrix postmultiplied by a column vector and premultiplied by the transpose of that vector:

$$\mathbf{x}'\mathbf{A}\mathbf{x} = \sum_{i=1}^{n}\sum_{j=1}^{n} a_{ij}x_i x_j \tag{4.1}$$

It can be assumed without loss of generality that the matrix of a quadratic form is symmetric, because the value of the form remains unchanged if we replace its matrix **A** by the symmetric matrix $\frac{1}{2}(\mathbf{A} + \mathbf{A}')$:

$$\frac{1}{2}\mathbf{x}'(\mathbf{A} + \mathbf{A}')\mathbf{x} = \frac{1}{2}\mathbf{x}'\mathbf{A}\mathbf{x} + \frac{1}{2}\mathbf{x}'\mathbf{A}'\mathbf{x} = \mathbf{x}'\mathbf{A}\mathbf{x}$$

the scalar $\mathbf{x}'\mathbf{A}'\mathbf{x}$ being equal to its transpose $\mathbf{x}'\mathbf{A}\mathbf{x}$. It will from now on always be assumed (except when the contrary is stated explicitly) that the matrix of a quadratic form is symmetric.

Definite and Semidefinite Quadratic Forms and Matrices

Some quadratic forms $\mathbf{x}'\mathbf{A}\mathbf{x}$ are always positive for whatever vector $\mathbf{x} \neq \mathbf{0}$. A simple example is a quadratic form with a diagonal matrix whose diagonal elements are all positive: $\mathbf{x}'\mathbf{D}\mathbf{x} = d_1x_1^2 + \cdots + d_nx_n^2$, where $d_i > 0$ is the ith diagonal element of $\mathbf{D}$. Sometimes a quadratic form $\mathbf{x}'\mathbf{A}\mathbf{x}$ is never negative (i.e., it is either positive or zero) for whatever vector $\mathbf{x}$. This applies to the diagonal form $\mathbf{x}'\mathbf{D}\mathbf{x}$ when all diagonal elements of $\mathbf{D}$ are nonnegative. Another example is the quadratic form $4x^2 + y^2 - 4xy + z^2$, because it can be written as $(2x - y)^2 + z^2$ and is thus never negative; it vanishes when $y = 2x$, $z = 0$.

The quadratic form $\mathbf{x}'\mathbf{A}\mathbf{x}$ and the associated symmetric matrix $\mathbf{A}$ are said to be *positive definite* if $\mathbf{x}'\mathbf{A}\mathbf{x} > 0$ holds for any $\mathbf{x} \neq \mathbf{0}$, and they are called *positive semidefinite* if $\mathbf{x}'\mathbf{A}\mathbf{x} \geq 0$ holds for any $\mathbf{x}$. (Positive definiteness is thus a special case of positive semidefiniteness.) We also have *negative definite*, *negative semidefinite*, and *indefinite* matrices and quadratic forms. The first is the case $\mathbf{x}'\mathbf{A}\mathbf{x} < 0$ for any $\mathbf{x} \neq \mathbf{0}$, the second $\mathbf{x}'\mathbf{A}\mathbf{x} \leq 0$ for any $\mathbf{x}$ (without restriction), and the third $\mathbf{x}'\mathbf{A}\mathbf{x} < 0$ and $\mathbf{y}'\mathbf{A}\mathbf{y} > 0$ for two (obviously different) vectors $\mathbf{x}$ and $\mathbf{y}$.

Example

The 2×2 matrix

$$\begin{bmatrix} a & b \\ b & a \end{bmatrix} \tag{4.2}$$

is positive definite when $a > |b|$, positive semidefinite when $a \geq |b|$, negative definite when $a < -|b|$, negative semidefinite when $a \leq -|b|$, and indefinite when $|a| < |b|$.

F1 If $\mathbf{x}$ and $\mathbf{y}$ are related by $\mathbf{x} = \mathbf{P}\mathbf{y}$, the quadratic form $\mathbf{x}'\mathbf{A}\mathbf{x}$ is identical with a quadratic form in $\mathbf{y}$ with $\mathbf{P}'\mathbf{A}\mathbf{P}$ as matrix.

F2 If $\mathbf{A}$ is a positive definite matrix, then it is nonsingular. (*Hint.* Suppose it were singular, so that $\mathbf{A}\mathbf{c} = \mathbf{0}$ for some $\mathbf{c} \neq \mathbf{0}$. What can be said about the quadratic form $\mathbf{c}'\mathbf{A}\mathbf{c}$?) The inverse of $\mathbf{A}$ is also positive definite.

F3 If $\mathbf{P}$ is a nonsingular matrix and if $\mathbf{A}$ is positive definite (semidefinite), then $\mathbf{P}'\mathbf{A}\mathbf{P}$ is positive definite (semidefinite).

F4 A necessary and sufficient condition for the $n \times n$ symmetric matrix $\mathbf{A}$ to be positive definite is that the following inequalities hold:

$$a_{11} > 0 \qquad \begin{vmatrix} a_{11} & a_{12} \\ a_{21} & a_{22} \end{vmatrix} > 0 \quad \cdots \quad \begin{vmatrix} a_{11} & a_{12} & \cdots & a_{1n} \\ a_{21} & a_{22} & \cdots & a_{2n} \\ \cdot & \cdot & & \cdot \\ \cdot & \cdot & & \cdot \\ \cdot & \cdot & & \cdot \\ a_{n1} & a_{n2} & \cdots & a_{nn} \end{vmatrix} > 0$$

F5 If $\mathbf{A}$ is an $m \times n$ matrix of rank $m < n$, then $\mathbf{AA}'$ is positive definite and $\mathbf{A}'\mathbf{A}$ is positive semidefinite but not positive definite.

F6 If $\mathbf{A}$ is an $m \times n$ matrix of rank r and if $r < m$ and $r < n$, then $\mathbf{AA}'$ and $\mathbf{A}'\mathbf{A}$ are both positive semidefinite and neither is positive definite.

Positive Semidefinite Matrices Written as Matrix Products

It is known from elementary algebra that for any nonnegative real number A there exists a number P such that $P^2 = A$, and that there are two solutions: $P = \sqrt{A}$ and $P = -\sqrt{A}$. An analogous theorem, to be proved in Section 1.5 (see proposition H4), holds for positive semidefinite matrices. Consider first a symmetric positive definite matrix $\mathbf{A}$ of order $n \times n$. The theorem states that there exists a nonsingular matrix $\mathbf{P}$ of the same order such that $\mathbf{P}'\mathbf{P} = \mathbf{A}$.

Example

$$\begin{bmatrix} a^2 & ab \sin 2\phi \\ ab \sin 2\phi & b^2 \end{bmatrix} = \mathbf{P}'\mathbf{P} \tag{4.3}$$

where

$$\mathbf{P} = \begin{bmatrix} a \sin (\phi + \theta) & b \cos (\phi - \theta) \\ a \cos (\phi + \theta) & b \sin (\phi - \theta) \end{bmatrix}$$

The matrix in eq. (4.3) is positive definite when $a \neq 0 \neq b$ and $|\sin 2\phi| \neq 1$. Since the result holds for any value of the angle θ, there are evidently infinitely many matrices $\mathbf{P}$ for which $\mathbf{P}'\mathbf{P} = \mathbf{A}$.

Next, consider the case of a symmetric positive semidefinite $n \times n$ matrix $\mathbf{A}$ with rank r. The theorem is then: there exists an $r \times n$ matrix $\mathbf{P}$ of full row rank such that $\mathbf{P}'\mathbf{P} = \mathbf{A}$. The following example illustrates this proposition for $n = 3$, $r = 2$:

$$\begin{bmatrix} 2 & 0 & 0 \\ 0 & 1 & 0 \\ 0 & 0 & 0 \end{bmatrix} = \mathbf{P}'\mathbf{P} \qquad \text{where} \qquad \mathbf{P}' = \begin{bmatrix} \sqrt{2} \sin \theta & \sqrt{2} \cos \theta \\ \cos \theta & -\sin \theta \\ 0 & 0 \end{bmatrix} \tag{4.4}$$

Again, the angle θ is arbitrary, so that there are infinitely many $\mathbf{P}$'s satisfying $\mathbf{P}'\mathbf{P} = \mathbf{A}$.

Problems

4.1 Write the following quadratic forms in matrix notation with a symmetric matrix: (1) $x^2 + y^2 - xy$, (2) $4x^2 + 5y^2 + z^2 + 2xy + 2yz$, (3) $-x^2 + 2y^2 + xy$. Verify whether these forms are positive (or negative) definite, semidefinite, or indefinite.

4.2 Consider the matrix (4.2) and prove the statements made below that matrix.

4.3 Prove that if $\mathbf{A}$ is negative definite (semidefinite), $-\mathbf{A}$ is positive definite (semidefinite).

4.4 Can a matrix be both positive semidefinite and negative semidefinite?

4.5 Verify the statements (4.3) and (4.4).

1.5 Latent Roots and Characteristic Vectors[B]

Consider a square ($n \times n$) matrix $\mathbf{A}$ as well as a scalar λ which has the property that, for some n-element vector $\mathbf{x}$, the vector $\mathbf{Ax}$ is equal to the multiple λ of this same $\mathbf{x}$: $\mathbf{Ax} = \lambda\mathbf{x}$. This is trivially true for any λ if $\mathbf{x} = \mathbf{0}$, and we therefore impose $\mathbf{x} \neq \mathbf{0}$. Since $\mathbf{A}(c\mathbf{x}) = \lambda(c\mathbf{x})$ holds for any scalar c if $\mathbf{Ax} = \lambda\mathbf{x}$ is true, the vector $\mathbf{x}$ has one multiplicative degree of freedom, which we shall use to impose the unit-length constraint: $\mathbf{x}'\mathbf{x} = 1$. The equation $\mathbf{Ax} = \lambda\mathbf{x}$ may be written in the equivalent form $(\mathbf{A} - \lambda\mathbf{I})\mathbf{x} = \mathbf{0}$; we thus have

$$(5.1) \qquad (\mathbf{A} - \lambda\mathbf{I})\mathbf{x} = \mathbf{0} \qquad \mathbf{x}'\mathbf{x} = 1$$

which means that the columns of $\mathbf{A} - \lambda\mathbf{I}$ are linearly dependent. Hence the determinant value of this $n \times n$ matrix is zero:

$$(5.2) \qquad |\mathbf{A} - \lambda\mathbf{I}| = 0$$

which is known as the *characteristic equation* of the matrix $\mathbf{A}$. The scalar λ of (5.1)–(5.2) is called a *latent root* (or characteristic root or value) of $\mathbf{A}$, and $\mathbf{x}$ is a *characteristic vector* of $\mathbf{A}$ corresponding to root λ.

When $\mathbf{A}$ is of order 2×2, the characteristic equation (5.2) becomes

$$\begin{vmatrix} a_{11} - \lambda & a_{12} \\ a_{21} & a_{22} - \lambda \end{vmatrix} = 0$$

or

$$\lambda^2 - (a_{11} + a_{22})\lambda + a_{11}a_{22} - a_{12}a_{21} = 0$$

This is a quadratic equation with two solutions:

$$(5.3) \qquad \lambda_1, \lambda_2 = \frac{1}{2}(a_{11} + a_{22}) \pm \frac{1}{2}\sqrt{(a_{11} - a_{22})^2 + 4a_{12}a_{21}}$$

More generally, when $\mathbf{A}$ is of order $n \times n$, its characteristic equation (5.2) is an nth degree polynomial in λ and, therefore, there are n solutions: $\lambda_1, \lambda_2, \ldots, \lambda_n$. It is easily verified from (5.3) that in the 2×2 case, $\lambda_1 + \lambda_2 = a_{11} + a_{22}$ (the trace of $\mathbf{A}$), and that the product $\lambda_1\lambda_2$ is equal to the determinant of $\mathbf{A}$. This, in fact, holds generally for arbitrary n. The *sum* $\lambda_1 + \lambda_2 + \cdots + \lambda_n$ of the latent roots of an $n \times n$ matrix $\mathbf{A}$ is equal to its *trace* and the *product* $\lambda_1\lambda_2 \cdots \lambda_n$ of these roots is equal to its *determinant*.

A simple example is that of a diagonal matrix, for which the characteristic equation is

$$\begin{vmatrix} d_1 - \lambda & 0 & \cdots & 0 \\ 0 & d_2 - \lambda & \cdots & 0 \\ \cdot & \cdot & & \cdot \\ \cdot & \cdot & & \cdot \\ \cdot & \cdot & & \cdot \\ 0 & 0 & \cdots & d_n - \lambda \end{vmatrix} = 0$$

which amounts to

$$(d_1 - \lambda)(d_2 - \lambda) \cdots (d_n - \lambda) = 0$$

The n latent roots are thus simply equal to the n diagonal elements, from which it follows immediately that their sum and product are indeed equal to the trace and the determinant, respectively.

Characteristic Roots and Vectors of Symmetric Matrices

Even if $\mathbf{A}$ consists of real elements, its roots need not be real. But the roots are real when $\mathbf{A}$ is symmetric, which is shown as follows. Let λ be a complex root and write $\mathbf{x} + i\mathbf{y}$ for a characteristic vector corresponding to this root, where $i = \sqrt{-1}$ is the imaginary unit. Hence $\mathbf{A}(\mathbf{x} + i\mathbf{y}) = \lambda(\mathbf{x} + i\mathbf{y})$. Premultiply both sides by $(\mathbf{x} - i\mathbf{y})'$:

$$\mathbf{x}'\mathbf{A}\mathbf{x} + \mathbf{y}'\mathbf{A}\mathbf{y} + i(\mathbf{x}'\mathbf{A}\mathbf{y} - \mathbf{y}'\mathbf{A}\mathbf{x}) = \lambda(\mathbf{x}'\mathbf{x} + \mathbf{y}'\mathbf{y})$$

But $\mathbf{x}'\mathbf{A}\mathbf{y} = \mathbf{y}'\mathbf{A}\mathbf{x}$ if $\mathbf{A}$ is symmetric, so that λ is equal to the ratio of $\mathbf{x}'\mathbf{A}\mathbf{x} + \mathbf{y}'\mathbf{A}\mathbf{y}$ to $\mathbf{x}'\mathbf{x} + \mathbf{y}'\mathbf{y}$, which is real, not complex.

It is also easily seen that the characteristic vectors of any symmetric matrix are orthogonal if they correspond to *different* latent roots.[8] Write λ_1, λ_2 for the two roots and $\mathbf{x}$, $\mathbf{y}$ for the corresponding vectors: $\mathbf{A}\mathbf{x} = \lambda_1\mathbf{x}$, $\mathbf{A}\mathbf{y} = \lambda_2\mathbf{y}$. Premultiply the first equation by $\mathbf{y}'$ and the second by $\mathbf{x}'$ and subtract:

$$\mathbf{y}'\mathbf{A}\mathbf{x} - \mathbf{x}'\mathbf{A}\mathbf{y} = (\lambda_1 - \lambda_2)\mathbf{x}'\mathbf{y}$$

This implies $\mathbf{x}'\mathbf{y} = 0$ if $\mathbf{A} = \mathbf{A}'$ and $\lambda_1 \neq \lambda_2$.

G1 If $\mathbf{x}$ is a characteristic vector of the matrix $\mathbf{A}$ corresponding to root λ, then the quadratic form $\mathbf{x}'\mathbf{A}\mathbf{x}$ is equal to this root. [*Hint*. See (5.1).]

G2 If $\mathbf{x}$ is a characteristic vector of $\mathbf{A}$ corresponding to root λ, so is $-\mathbf{x}$.

G3 The latent roots of the square of $\mathbf{A}$ are the squares of those of $\mathbf{A}$ and the characteristic vectors are the same as those of $\mathbf{A}$. (*Proof.* $\mathbf{A}^2\mathbf{x} = \lambda\mathbf{A}\mathbf{x} = \lambda^2\mathbf{x}$.)

[8] For the case of equal roots see the first paragraph of p. 28.

G4 If $\mathbf{A}$ is nonsingular, the latent roots of $\mathbf{A}^{-1}$ are the reciprocals of those of $\mathbf{A}$ and the characteristic vectors are the same as those of $\mathbf{A}$. (*Hint.* Premultiply both sides of $\mathbf{Ax} = \lambda\mathbf{x}$ by $\mathbf{A}^{-1}$.)

G5 The latent roots of a positive definite (semidefinite) matrix are all positive (nonnegative). (*Hint.* Use G1.) Similarly, the latent roots of a negative definite (semidefinite) matrix are all negative (nonpositive).

G6 The number of nonzero roots of a symmetric matrix $\mathbf{A}$ is equal to the rank of $\mathbf{A}$. This, however, does not always hold true for nonsymmetric square matrices:

$$\begin{bmatrix} 1 & 1 \\ -1 & -1 \end{bmatrix}$$

has two zero roots and unit rank.

G7 If all roots of a symmetric matrix are positive (nonnegative), the diagonal elements of this matrix are all positive (nonnegative). But if the matrix is not symmetric, we can have negative diagonal elements despite positive roots:

$$\mathbf{A} = \begin{bmatrix} 20 & 5 \\ -21 & -2 \end{bmatrix} \qquad \lambda_1 = 5 \qquad \lambda_2 = 13 \tag{5.4}$$

G8 The roots of $\mathbf{AA}'$ and $\mathbf{A}'\mathbf{A}$ are equal except for an additional set of zero roots of the matrix of larger order. [*Hint.* Premultiplication of both sides of $(\mathbf{AA}' - \lambda\mathbf{I})\mathbf{x} = \mathbf{0}$ by $\mathbf{A}'$ gives $(\mathbf{A}'\mathbf{A} - \lambda\mathbf{I})\mathbf{A}'\mathbf{x} = \mathbf{0}$. If $\mathbf{A}$ is $m \times n$, then $\mathbf{AA}'$ has $m - n$ additional zero roots if $m > n$, and $\mathbf{A}'\mathbf{A}$ has $n - m$ additional zero roots if $n > m$.]

G9 Continuing the case of G8, if $\mathbf{x}_1, \mathbf{x}_2, \ldots$ are characteristic vectors of $\mathbf{AA}'$ corresponding to the roots $\lambda_1, \lambda_2, \ldots$, and if these vectors are pairwise orthogonal and have unit length, then the corresponding characteristic vectors $\mathbf{A}'\mathbf{x}_1, \mathbf{A}'\mathbf{x}_2, \ldots$ of $\mathbf{A}'\mathbf{A}$ are also orthogonal but they do not have unit length unless the corresponding root is equal to one. [*Proof.* Premultiply both sides of $\mathbf{AA}'\mathbf{x}_1 = \lambda_1\mathbf{x}_1$ by $\mathbf{x}_1'$ to find $(\mathbf{A}'\mathbf{x}_1)'\mathbf{A}'\mathbf{x}_1 = \lambda_1$, and premultiply by $\mathbf{x}_2'$ to find $(\mathbf{A}'\mathbf{x}_2)'\mathbf{A}'\mathbf{x}_1 = \lambda_1\mathbf{x}_2'\mathbf{x}_1 = 0$.]

Orthogonal Matrices and the Diagonalization of Symmetric Matrices

An orthogonal matrix $\mathbf{C}$ is a square matrix whose inverse is equal to its transpose: $\mathbf{C}^{-1} = \mathbf{C}'$ or, equivalently, $\mathbf{CC}' = \mathbf{C}'\mathbf{C} = \mathbf{I}$. The diagonal elements of the matrix equation $\mathbf{CC}' = \mathbf{I}$ indicate that all rows of this matrix have unit length, and the off-diagonal elements indicate that these rows are pairwise orthogonal. The matrix equation $\mathbf{C}'\mathbf{C} = \mathbf{I}$ shows that the columns of $\mathbf{C}$ have the same properties. Trivial examples of an orthogonal matrix are

I and $-$**I**. A less trivial example is

$$\mathbf{C} = \frac{1}{\sqrt{2}}\begin{bmatrix} 1 & -1 \\ 1 & 1 \end{bmatrix} \text{ implying } \mathbf{CC}' = \frac{1}{2}\begin{bmatrix} 1 & -1 \\ 1 & 1 \end{bmatrix}\begin{bmatrix} 1 & 1 \\ -1 & 1 \end{bmatrix} = \begin{bmatrix} 1 & 0 \\ 0 & 1 \end{bmatrix}$$

Consider an arbitrary symmetric $n \times n$ matrix **A** with latent roots $\lambda_1, \ldots, \lambda_n$ and characteristic vectors $\mathbf{c}_1, \ldots, \mathbf{c}_n$. Hence $\mathbf{Ac}_i = \lambda_i \mathbf{c}_i$, $\mathbf{c}_i'\mathbf{c}_i = 1$ for $i = 1, \ldots, n$. If the roots are all different, the characteristic vectors are orthogonal: $\mathbf{c}_i'\mathbf{c}_j = 0$ for $i \neq j$. It follows that $\mathbf{C} = [\mathbf{c}_1 \cdots \mathbf{c}_n]$, the $n \times n$ matrix whose columns are characteristic vectors of **A**, satisfies $\mathbf{C}'\mathbf{C} = \mathbf{I}$ and is hence an orthogonal matrix. Consider, then,

$$\begin{aligned} \mathbf{AC} &= \mathbf{A}[\mathbf{c}_1 \quad \mathbf{c}_2 \quad \cdots \quad \mathbf{c}_n] = [\mathbf{Ac}_1 \quad \mathbf{Ac}_2 \quad \cdots \quad \mathbf{Ac}_n] \\ &= [\lambda_1 \mathbf{c}_1 \quad \lambda_2 \mathbf{c}_2 \quad \cdots \quad \lambda_n \mathbf{c}_n] \\ &= [\mathbf{c}_1 \quad \mathbf{c}_2 \quad \cdots \quad \mathbf{c}_n]\begin{bmatrix} \lambda_1 & 0 & \cdots & 0 \\ 0 & \lambda_2 & \cdots & 0 \\ \cdot & \cdot & & \cdot \\ \cdot & \cdot & & \cdot \\ \cdot & \cdot & & \cdot \\ 0 & 0 & \cdots & \lambda_n \end{bmatrix} = \mathbf{C\Lambda} \end{aligned} \tag{5.5}$$

In words: if we postmultiply a symmetric matrix **A** by the orthogonal matrix of its characteristic vectors, then we obtain the latter matrix postmultiplied by the diagonal matrix whose diagonal elements are the latent roots of **A**. Next we premultiply both sides of $\mathbf{AC} = \mathbf{C\Lambda}$ by $\mathbf{C}'$ and use $\mathbf{C}'\mathbf{C} = \mathbf{I}$:

$$\mathbf{C}'\mathbf{AC} = \mathbf{\Lambda} \tag{5.6}$$

Thus, by postmultiplying a symmetric matrix **A** by a matrix whose columns are characteristic vectors of **A**, and by premultiplying by the transpose of that matrix, we obtain a diagonal matrix, and the elements along the diagonal are the latent roots of **A**. Now postmultiply both sides of $\mathbf{AC} = \mathbf{C\Lambda}$ by $\mathbf{C}'$ and use $\mathbf{CC}' = \mathbf{I}$:

$$\mathbf{A} = \mathbf{C\Lambda C}' = [\mathbf{c}_1 \quad \mathbf{c}_2 \quad \cdots \quad \mathbf{c}_n]\begin{bmatrix} \lambda_1 & 0 & \cdots & 0 \\ 0 & \lambda_2 & \cdots & 0 \\ \cdot & \cdot & & \cdot \\ \cdot & \cdot & & \cdot \\ \cdot & \cdot & & \cdot \\ 0 & 0 & \cdots & \lambda_n \end{bmatrix}\begin{bmatrix} \mathbf{c}_1' \\ \mathbf{c}_2' \\ \cdot \\ \cdot \\ \cdot \\ \mathbf{c}_n' \end{bmatrix} = \sum_{i=1}^{n} \lambda_i \mathbf{c}_i \mathbf{c}_i' \tag{5.7}$$

This means that any symmetric $n \times n$ matrix **A** can be written as the sum of n matrices of the form $\lambda_i \mathbf{c}_i \mathbf{c}_i'$, where λ_i is a latent root of **A** and $\mathbf{c}_i$ a characteristic vector corresponding to this root. When **A** has rank r, $n - r$ roots vanish (see G6), so that there are then only r nonzero matrices $\lambda_i \mathbf{c}_i \mathbf{c}_i'$. Note that each of these r matrices has unit rank.

The above development is based on the assumption that the roots of $\mathbf{A}$ are all different, because this guarantees that the characteristic vectors are pairwise orthogonal. The results can be extended to the multiple root case as follows. For *any* symmetric $n \times n$ matrix $\mathbf{A}$ there exists an orthogonal matrix $\mathbf{C}$ such that $\mathbf{AC} = \mathbf{C\Lambda}$, $\mathbf{C'AC} = \mathbf{\Lambda}$ and $\mathbf{A} = \mathbf{C\Lambda C'}$, where $\mathbf{\Lambda}$ is diagonal and contains the latent roots of $\mathbf{A}$ along the diagonal. As before, the columns of $\mathbf{C}$ are characteristic vectors of $\mathbf{A}$. However, this orthogonal matrix is not unique when there are multiple roots.[9] Take for $\mathbf{A}$ the 2×2 unit matrix; it has a two-fold unit root because $|\mathbf{I} - \lambda\mathbf{I}| = 0$ is satisfied by $\lambda_1 = \lambda_2 = 1$. Then $\mathbf{AC} = \mathbf{C\Lambda}$ is simply $\mathbf{C} = \mathbf{C}$, so that any orthogonal 2×2 matrix $\mathbf{C}$ can be used. It is easily seen that

$$\mathbf{C} = \begin{bmatrix} \sin\theta & \cos\theta \\ \cos\theta & -\sin\theta \end{bmatrix} \tag{5.8}$$

is orthogonal for any angle θ, and that both columns of this $\mathbf{C}$ (for any θ) are characteristic vectors of the 2×2 unit matrix.

H1 If $\mathbf{C}$ is orthogonal, so is $\mathbf{C}'$ and so is $\mathbf{C}^{-1}$.

H2 If $\mathbf{C}$ is orthogonal, its determinant is 1 or -1.

H3 Real roots of an orthogonal matrix are always ± 1. [*Proof.* Write λ for a real root of an orthogonal matrix $\mathbf{C}$ and $\mathbf{x}$ for a corresponding characteristic vector, so that $\mathbf{Cx} = \lambda\mathbf{x}$; premultiply the left-hand side by $(\mathbf{Cx})'$, which gives $\mathbf{x}'\mathbf{x} = 1$, and the right-hand side by $\lambda\mathbf{x}' = (\mathbf{Cx})'$, which gives $\lambda^2\mathbf{x}'\mathbf{x} = \lambda^2$.]

H4 Let $\mathbf{A}$ of (5.7) be a positive semidefinite matrix of rank r, so that $\lambda_i > 0$ for $i \leq r$ and $\lambda_i = 0$ for $i > r$. Then $\mathbf{P}' = [\sqrt{\lambda_1}\mathbf{c}_1 \quad \cdots \quad \sqrt{\lambda_r}\mathbf{c}_r]$ is an $n \times r$ matrix of rank r satisfying $\mathbf{P'P} = \mathbf{A}$.

Properties of Idempotent Matrices

The latent roots of an idempotent matrix are all either zero or one. This follows from $\mathbf{A}^2 = \mathbf{A}$, which implies $\lambda^2 = \lambda$ in view of G3. Since the number of nonzero roots of a symmetric matrix is equal to its rank (G6), the rank of an idempotent matrix is thus equal to the sum of its roots; and since the sum of the latent roots of a matrix is equal to its trace, the rank and the trace of an idempotent matrix are always equal. This proves the proposition D4 of Section 1.1.

[9] Note that the uniqueness in the case of different roots must be interpreted in the limited sense of unique except for the sign of each column of $\mathbf{C}$. This is true because if $\mathbf{c}_i$ is a characteristic vector of $\mathbf{A}$, so is $-\mathbf{c}_i$ (see G2); the change in sign affects neither the length of the vector nor its orthogonality with any other vector. The lack of uniqueness in the multiple root case is much more fundamental, however.

The fact that the roots of an idempotent matrix are all zero or one enables us to obtain the following result, which will prove to be important for normal distribution theory: if **A** is an $n \times n$ idempotent matrix of rank r, there exists an orthogonal matrix **C** such that **C′AC** is a diagonal matrix with r diagonal elements equal to 1 and all other diagonal elements equal to 0. This follows directly from (5.6) with $\boldsymbol{\Lambda}$ specified appropriately. Note that idempotent matrices have multiple roots as soon as r or $n - r$ exceeds 1, in which case **C** is not unique.

I1 Each idempotent matrix is positive semidefinite. [*Proof.* Since $\mathbf{A}'\mathbf{A} = \mathbf{A}$ in view of $\mathbf{A}' = \mathbf{A} = \mathbf{A}^2$, any quadratic form $\mathbf{x}'\mathbf{A}\mathbf{x} = (\mathbf{A}\mathbf{x})'\mathbf{A}\mathbf{x}$ is equal to the sum of the squares of the elements of $\mathbf{A}\mathbf{x}$.] Conclude that the diagonal elements of an idempotent matrix are all nonnegative.

I2 If **A** is both idempotent and nonsingular, then $\mathbf{A} = \mathbf{I}$. (*Proof.* Premultiply both sides of $\mathbf{A}^2 = \mathbf{A}$ by $\mathbf{A}^{-1}$.)

I3 If **A** is idempotent and **C** orthogonal of the same order, then **C′AC** is idempotent. (*Proof.* $\mathbf{C}'\mathbf{A}\mathbf{C}\mathbf{C}'\mathbf{A}\mathbf{C} = \mathbf{C}'\mathbf{A}^2\mathbf{C} = \mathbf{C}'\mathbf{A}\mathbf{C}$.)

I4 If **A** is idempotent, then $\mathbf{I} - \mathbf{A}$ is also idempotent. [*Proof.* $(\mathbf{I} - \mathbf{A})^2 = \mathbf{I} - 2\mathbf{A} + \mathbf{A}^2 = \mathbf{I} - \mathbf{A}$.] Note that the product of **A** and $\mathbf{I} - \mathbf{A}$ is a zero matrix.

I5 If $\mathbf{A} = [a_{ij}]$ is idempotent and if $a_{ii} = 0$, then the ith row and the ith column of **A** are zero vectors. [*Proof.* The ith diagonal element of $\mathbf{A}^2$ is $\sum_j a_{ij}a_{ji} = \sum_j a_{ij}^2$ (symmetry: $a_{ij} = a_{ji}$); this gives $a_{ii} = \sum_j a_{ij}^2$ because the ith diagonal elements of **A** and $\mathbf{A}^2$ are equal.]

Problems

5.1 Verify the statements on nonsymmetric matrices in propositions G6 and G7.

5.2 Prove that $\mathbf{C} = \frac{1}{\sqrt{2}}\begin{bmatrix} 1 & 0 & 1 \\ -1 & 0 & 1 \\ 0 & \sqrt{2} & 0 \end{bmatrix}$ is an orthogonal matrix.

5.3 For a nonsingular matrix to be orthogonal it is necessary and sufficient that its columns be pairwise orthogonal and that its rows be pairwise orthogonal. True or false?

5.4 Prove that **AB** is an orthogonal matrix when **A** and **B** are both orthogonal.

5.5 Prove that $\begin{bmatrix} \mathbf{C}_1 & \mathbf{0} & \mathbf{0} \\ \mathbf{0} & \mathbf{C}_2 & \mathbf{0} \\ \mathbf{0} & \mathbf{0} & \mathbf{C}_3 \end{bmatrix}$ is orthogonal when $\mathbf{C}_1$, $\mathbf{C}_2$, and $\mathbf{C}_3$ are all orthogonal.

5.6 Verify proposition H2 for the matrix (5.8).

5.7 Consider the matrix

$$\mathbf{A} = \begin{bmatrix} .25 & .25 & .25 & .25 \\ .25 & .25 & .25 & .25 \\ .25 & .25 & .25 & .25 \\ .25 & .25 & .25 & .25 \end{bmatrix}$$

Prove that **A** is idempotent and find the roots of **A**, the trace of **A**, and the rank of **A**.

5.8 Prove that the diagonal elements of an $n \times n$ idempotent matrix are at most equal to 1. (*Hint.* Consider I5 to prove that $a_{ii} = a_{ii}^2 + \sum_j a_{ij}^2$, where the summation over j is from 1 through n excluding i.) Combine this with I1 to conclude that the diagonal elements are all in the interval from zero to one, including the endpoints.

1.6 Vector and Matrix Differentiation[AB]

Gradient and Hessian Matrix[A]

For the development that follows it is important to use a matrix notation for certain concepts in differential calculus. Consider a function of an n-element vector $\mathbf{x}$:

$$y = f(\mathbf{x}) = f(x_1, \ldots, x_n) \tag{6.1}$$

Supposing that all n partial first-order derivatives exist, we can arrange them in an n-element column vector, written $\partial f/\partial \mathbf{x}$ and known as the *gradient* of the function $f(\ )$. Its transpose is the following row vector:

$$\frac{\partial f}{\partial \mathbf{x}'} = \begin{bmatrix} \dfrac{\partial f}{\partial x_1} & \dfrac{\partial f}{\partial x_2} & \cdots & \dfrac{\partial f}{\partial x_n} \end{bmatrix} \tag{6.2}$$

Suppose also that all n^2 second-order derivatives exist. They can be arranged in a square matrix, known as the *Hessian matrix* of the function $f(\ )$:

$$\frac{\partial^2 f}{\partial \mathbf{x}\, \partial \mathbf{x}'} = \begin{bmatrix} \dfrac{\partial^2 f}{\partial x_1^2} & \dfrac{\partial^2 f}{\partial x_1\, \partial x_2} & \cdots & \dfrac{\partial^2 f}{\partial x_1\, \partial x_n} \\ \dfrac{\partial^2 f}{\partial x_2\, \partial x_1} & \dfrac{\partial^2 f}{\partial x_2^2} & \cdots & \dfrac{\partial^2 f}{\partial x_2\, \partial x_n} \\ \vdots & \vdots & & \vdots \\ \dfrac{\partial^2 f}{\partial x_n\, \partial x_1} & \dfrac{\partial^2 f}{\partial x_n\, \partial x_2} & \cdots & \dfrac{\partial^2 f}{\partial x_n^2} \end{bmatrix} \tag{6.3}$$

It is well known that this matrix is symmetric if the second-order derivatives are continuous functions of the x's (Young's theorem).

Derivatives of Linear and Quadratic and Related Forms[A]

As an example we take the linear function $\mathbf{a}'\mathbf{x}$. Its derivative with respect to x_i is a_i, which are the ith elements of $\mathbf{x}$ and $\mathbf{a}$, respectively, so that the gradient is

$$\frac{\partial(\mathbf{a}'\mathbf{x})}{\partial \mathbf{x}} = \mathbf{a} \tag{6.4}$$

As a second example we take the quadratic form $\mathbf{x}'\mathbf{A}\mathbf{x} = \sum\sum a_{ij}x_ix_j$. Its derivative with respect to x_h is

$$\begin{aligned}\frac{\partial}{\partial x_h}\left(\sum_{i=1}^{n}\sum_{j=1}^{n} a_{ij}x_ix_j\right) &= 2a_{hh}x_h + \sum_{j\neq h} a_{hj}x_j + \sum_{i\neq h} a_{ih}x_i \\ &= \sum_{j=1}^{n} a_{hj}x_j + \sum_{i=1}^{n} a_{ih}x_i\end{aligned} \tag{6.5}$$

This is the hth element of $\mathbf{A}\mathbf{x} + \mathbf{A}'\mathbf{x}$. Hence

$$\frac{\partial(\mathbf{x}'\mathbf{A}\mathbf{x})}{\partial \mathbf{x}} = (\mathbf{A} + \mathbf{A}')\mathbf{x} \tag{6.6}$$

Next, suppose that we differentiate the derivative (6.5) with respect to x_k to obtain the second-order cross-derivative with respect to x_h and x_k. The result is $a_{hk} + a_{kh}$, which is the (h, k)th element of $\mathbf{A} + \mathbf{A}'$. Hence

$$\frac{\partial^2(\mathbf{x}'\mathbf{A}\mathbf{x})}{\partial \mathbf{x}\,\partial \mathbf{x}'} = \mathbf{A} + \mathbf{A}' \tag{6.7}$$

Note that the quadratic form $\mathbf{x}'\mathbf{A}\mathbf{x}$ can also be regarded as a function of the elements a_{ij} of the matrix $\mathbf{A}$. The partial derivative with respect to a_{ij} is x_ix_j, which is the (i, j)th element of the matrix $\mathbf{x}\mathbf{x}'$. Hence

$$\frac{\partial(\mathbf{x}'\mathbf{A}\mathbf{x})}{\partial \mathbf{A}} = \mathbf{x}\mathbf{x}' \tag{6.8}$$

where the left-hand side is to be interpreted as the $n \times n$ matrix of first-order derivatives of the scalar $\mathbf{x}'\mathbf{A}\mathbf{x}$ with respect to the elements of the matrix $\mathbf{A}$.

As a third example we take the so-called *bilinear form*:

$$\mathbf{y}'\mathbf{B}\mathbf{z} = \sum_{i=1}^{m}\sum_{j=1}^{n} b_{ij}y_iz_j \quad (\mathbf{B} \text{ not necessarily square}) \tag{6.9}$$

where $y_1, \ldots, y_m, z_1, \ldots, z_n$ are $m + n$ variables. The following results are easily verified:

$$\frac{\partial(\mathbf{y}'\mathbf{Bz})}{\partial \mathbf{y}} = \mathbf{Bz} \qquad \frac{\partial(\mathbf{y}'\mathbf{Bz})}{\partial \mathbf{z}} = \mathbf{B}'\mathbf{y} \qquad \frac{\partial(\mathbf{y}'\mathbf{Bz})}{\partial \mathbf{B}} = \mathbf{yz}' \tag{6.10}$$

Another very simple result is

$$\frac{\partial \operatorname{tr} \mathbf{A}}{\partial \mathbf{A}} = \mathbf{I} \tag{6.11}$$

where **A** is any square matrix and **I** the unit matrix of the same order.

The Derivative of a Determinant[A]

The familiar expansion of a determinant according to cofactors is

$$|\mathbf{A}| = a_{i1}c_{i1} + \cdots + a_{ij}c_{ij} + \cdots + a_{in}c_{in} \tag{6.12}$$

where c_{ij} is the cofactor of a_{ij} in **A**. The only term in (6.12) which depends on a_{ij} is $a_{ij}c_{ij}$, and c_{ij} does not depend on a_{ij}. Hence $\partial |\mathbf{A}|/\partial a_{ij} = c_{ij} = a^{ji} |\mathbf{A}|$, where a^{ji} is the (i, j)th element of $(\mathbf{A}')^{-1}$. We thus find

$$\frac{\partial |\mathbf{A}|}{\partial \mathbf{A}} = |\mathbf{A}| \, (\mathbf{A}')^{-1} \tag{6.13}$$

and, in the case of an **A** with a positive determinant,

$$\frac{\partial \log |\mathbf{A}|}{\partial \mathbf{A}} = (\mathbf{A}')^{-1} \qquad (|\mathbf{A}| > 0) \tag{6.14}$$

where log stands for natural logarithm.

Derivatives Involving Symmetric Matrices[A]

We have not imposed symmetry on the matrix **A** of the quadratic form in (6.6) through (6.8). If we do, the right-hand side of (6.6) is simplified to $2\mathbf{Ax}$ and that of (6.7) to $2\mathbf{A}$. The case of (6.8) is more complicated, because imposing symmetry on **A** implies that a_{ij} and a_{ji} are no longer two different independent variables. The derivative of $\mathbf{x}'\mathbf{Ax}$ with respect to a_{ij} is then x_i^2 if $i = j$ (as before) but it becomes $2x_ix_j$ if $i \neq j$. Similarly, if we impose **A** to be symmetric in (6.13)—supposing that it is indeed symmetric—then the derivative of $|\mathbf{A}|$ with respect to a_{ij} is $a^{ii} |\mathbf{A}|$ for $i = j$ and $2a^{ij} |\mathbf{A}|$ for $i \neq j$. These expressions are less attractive than (6.8) and (6.13). Therefore it is preferable not to impose symmetry in this manner. If **A** is symmetric and if its elements a_{ij} change infinitesimally by da_{ij} such that the matrix remains symmetric, the simplest procedure is to use (6.8) and (6.13) and to impose $da_{ij} = da_{ji}$ afterwards.

The Derivatives of the Elements of an Inverse[B]

Consider the product $\mathbf{C} = \mathbf{AB}$ of two $n \times n$ matrices $\mathbf{A}$ and $\mathbf{B}$, and imagine that the elements of these matrices are functions of some scalar variable x. Using $c_{ij} = \sum_k a_{ik}b_{kj}$, we obtain

$$\frac{\partial c_{ij}}{\partial x} = \sum_{k=1}^{n} a_{ik} \frac{\partial b_{kj}}{\partial x} + \sum_{k=1}^{n} \frac{\partial a_{ik}}{\partial x} b_{kj}$$

which can be regarded as the (i,j)th element of the $n \times n$ matrix equation

$$\frac{\partial(\mathbf{AB})}{\partial x} = \mathbf{A}\frac{\partial \mathbf{B}}{\partial x} + \frac{\partial \mathbf{A}}{\partial x}\mathbf{B} \tag{6.15}$$

Note that we now have a matrix ($\mathbf{C} = \mathbf{AB}$, $\mathbf{B}$, or $\mathbf{A}$) of dependent variables, each element of which is differentiated with respect to a scalar. This is in contrast to the left-hand sides of (6.8) and (6.11), where we have a scalar dependent variable which is differentiated with respect to a matrix of independent variables.

Suppose that $\mathbf{B}$ in (6.15) is $\mathbf{A}^{-1}$ so that $\mathbf{C} = \mathbf{AB} = \mathbf{I}$, independent of x. Then the left-hand side of (6.15) becomes a zero matrix, which gives

$$\frac{\partial \mathbf{A}^{-1}}{\partial x} = -\mathbf{A}^{-1}\frac{\partial \mathbf{A}}{\partial x}\mathbf{A}^{-1} \tag{6.16}$$

We now interpret x as a_{hk}, the (h, k)th element of $\mathbf{A}$, and proceed under the assumption that all n^2 elements of this matrix can be regarded as independent variables. The derivative of $\mathbf{A}$ with respect to a_{hk} is then an $n \times n$ matrix whose (h, k)th element is 1 and all others are 0. This matrix of derivatives can therefore be written as $\mathbf{i}_h\mathbf{i}'_k$, where $\mathbf{i}_1, \mathbf{i}_2, \ldots$ are columns of the $n \times n$ unit matrix [see (2.1)]. We conclude from (6.16) that the derivative of $\mathbf{A}^{-1}$ with respect to a_{hk} takes the form $-(\mathbf{A}^{-1}\mathbf{i}_h)(\mathbf{i}'_k\mathbf{A}^{-1})$. Now $\mathbf{A}^{-1}\mathbf{i}_h$ is the hth column of $\mathbf{A}^{-1}$ and $\mathbf{i}'_k\mathbf{A}^{-1}$ is the kth row of $\mathbf{A}^{-1}$. Therefore the derivative of a^{ij} [the (i,j)th element of $\mathbf{A}^{-1}$] with respect to a_{hk} is[10]

$$\frac{\partial a^{ij}}{\partial a_{hk}} = -a^{ih}a^{kj} \qquad i, j, h, k = 1, \ldots, n \tag{6.17}$$

Problems

6.1 Prove that the Hessian matrix of any quadratic function is a symmetric matrix consisting of constant elements.

[10] The easiest way to remember eq. (6.17) is by means of the familiar American traffic sign NO U TURN ANYTIME. The "no" is represented by the minus sign in the right-hand side, the U indicates the order in which the left-hand indices appear on the right: down from i to h, to the right from h to k, up from k to j.

6.2 Prove $\partial(\text{tr}\,\mathbf{AY})/\partial x = \text{tr}\,\mathbf{A}\,\partial\mathbf{Y}/\partial x$ when $\mathbf{A}$ is an $m \times n$ matrix of constant elements and $\mathbf{Y}$ is an $n \times m$ matrix of elements which are functions of x.

1.7 Unconstrained Extremum Problems; Least-Squares Adjustment[A]

An important problem which arises on many occasions is the maximization or minimization of some function $y = f(\mathbf{x})$, where $\mathbf{x}$ is an n-element column vector of real-valued variables. It is well known that, if all partial derivatives $\partial f/\partial x_i$ are continuous, the function takes its stationary values (maximum, minimum, or saddle point) at those points where all n derivatives vanish. This amounts to a zero value of the gradient:

$$\frac{\partial f}{\partial \mathbf{x}} = \mathbf{0} \tag{7.1}$$

If, in addition, all first and second-order derivatives are continuous, then we have a local maximum at a point which satisfies (7.1) if the Hessian matrix $\partial^2 f/\partial\mathbf{x}\,\partial\mathbf{x}'$ is negative definite, and a local minimum at a point satisfying (7.1) if the Hessian matrix is positive definite. This is the second-order extremum condition.

These results can be illustrated conveniently when we consider the Taylor expansion of $f(\ )$ around a point $\mathbf{x} = \bar{\mathbf{x}}$:

$$\begin{aligned} f(\mathbf{x}) - f(\bar{\mathbf{x}}) &= \sum_{i=1}^{n} \frac{\partial f}{\partial x_i}(x_i - \bar{x}_i) + \frac{1}{2}\sum_{i=1}^{n}\sum_{j=1}^{n} \frac{\partial^2 f}{\partial x_i\,\partial x_j}(x_i - \bar{x}_i)(x_j - \bar{x}_j) + \cdots \\ &= \frac{\partial f}{\partial \mathbf{x}'}(\mathbf{x} - \bar{\mathbf{x}}) + \frac{1}{2}(\mathbf{x} - \bar{\mathbf{x}})'\frac{\partial^2 f}{\partial\mathbf{x}\,\partial\mathbf{x}'}(\mathbf{x} - \bar{\mathbf{x}}) + \cdots \end{aligned}$$

where the gradient $\partial f/\partial\mathbf{x}'$ (written in the form of a row vector) and the Hessian matrix $\partial^2 f/\partial\mathbf{x}\,\partial\mathbf{x}'$ are both evaluated at $\bar{\mathbf{x}}$. If the gradient vanishes in accordance with (7.1), the difference $f(\mathbf{x}) - f(\bar{\mathbf{x}})$ is equal to the quadratic form

$$\frac{1}{2}(\mathbf{x} - \bar{\mathbf{x}})'\frac{\partial^2 f}{\partial\mathbf{x}\,\partial\mathbf{x}'}(\mathbf{x} - \bar{\mathbf{x}})$$

apart from higher-order terms. Clearly, if the Hessian matrix is negative definite, the value of the function, $f(\mathbf{x})$, will be less than $f(\bar{\mathbf{x}})$ for all $\mathbf{x} \neq \bar{\mathbf{x}}$ if the elements of the difference vector $\mathbf{x} - \bar{\mathbf{x}}$ are small. The higher-order terms play a role when these elements take larger values; this aspect is responsible for the fact that we have only a local extremum.

Least-Squares Adjustment

Consider $K + 1$ variables: $x_1, \ldots, x_K, y$. The objective is to describe the last variable linearly in terms of the K other variables:

$$y = b_1 x_1 + b_2 x_2 + \cdots + b_K x_K \tag{7.2}$$

We assume that n observations on these variables are available, each of which consists of one value taken by each of the $K + 1$ variables:

$$(x_{\alpha 1} \quad x_{\alpha 2} \quad \cdots \quad x_{\alpha K} \quad y_\alpha) \qquad \alpha = 1, \ldots, n$$

Hence the observations can be arranged in the form of two matrices with n rows [similar to (1.7) and (1.11)]:

$$\mathbf{X} = \begin{bmatrix} x_{11} & x_{12} & \cdots & x_{1K} \\ x_{21} & x_{22} & \cdots & x_{2K} \\ \cdot & \cdot & & \cdot \\ \cdot & \cdot & & \cdot \\ \cdot & \cdot & & \cdot \\ x_{n1} & x_{n2} & \cdots & x_{nK} \end{bmatrix} \qquad \mathbf{y} = \begin{bmatrix} y_1 \\ y_2 \\ \cdot \\ \cdot \\ \cdot \\ y_n \end{bmatrix} \tag{7.3}$$

Then equation (7.2) for all n observations takes the form

$$\begin{bmatrix} y_1 \\ y_2 \\ \cdot \\ \cdot \\ \cdot \\ y_n \end{bmatrix} = \begin{bmatrix} x_{11} & x_{12} & \cdots & x_{1K} \\ x_{21} & x_{22} & \cdots & x_{2K} \\ \cdot & \cdot & & \cdot \\ \cdot & \cdot & & \cdot \\ \cdot & \cdot & & \cdot \\ x_{n1} & x_{n2} & \cdots & x_{nK} \end{bmatrix} \begin{bmatrix} b_1 \\ b_2 \\ \cdot \\ \cdot \\ \cdot \\ b_K \end{bmatrix} \qquad \text{or} \quad \mathbf{y} = \mathbf{X}\mathbf{b}$$

where **b** is the K-element column whose elements are $b_1, \ldots, b_K$.

It is usually not true that a solution **b** of the equation system $\mathbf{y} = \mathbf{X}\mathbf{b}$ exists. We know from proposition E1 in Section 1.3 that a solution exists only if the rank of **X** and that of the augmented matrix $[\mathbf{X} \quad \mathbf{y}]$ are the same. It will be assumed here that $n > K$ (more observations than coefficients to be adjusted), that the rank of **X** is K, and that the rank of $[\mathbf{X} \quad \mathbf{y}]$ is $K + 1$. So there exists no **b** satisfying $\mathbf{y} = \mathbf{X}\mathbf{b}$, which means that there is a nonzero discrepancy vector $\mathbf{y} - \mathbf{X}\mathbf{b}$ whatever **b** may be. We shall adjust **b** according to the principle of least squares (to be abbreviated as LS from now on): select the vector **b** which minimizes the length of the discrepancy vector or, equivalently, which minimizes the sum of the squares of the n discrepancies. So we minimize the following function of **b**:

$$f(\mathbf{b}) = (\mathbf{y} - \mathbf{X}\mathbf{b})'(\mathbf{y} - \mathbf{X}\mathbf{b}) = \mathbf{y}'\mathbf{y} - 2\mathbf{y}'\mathbf{X}\mathbf{b} + \mathbf{b}'\mathbf{X}'\mathbf{X}\mathbf{b} \tag{7.4}$$

the gradient of which is

$$\frac{\partial f}{\partial \mathbf{b}} = -2\mathbf{X}'\mathbf{y} + 2\mathbf{X}'\mathbf{X}\mathbf{b} \tag{7.5}$$

in view of (6.4) and (6.6). If we put the gradient equal to a zero vector in accordance with (7.1), we obtain

$$\mathbf{X}'\mathbf{y} = \mathbf{X}'\mathbf{X}\mathbf{b} \tag{7.6}$$

or, in scalar form,

$$\begin{aligned}
\sum x_{\alpha 1}y_\alpha &= b_1 \sum x_{\alpha 1}^2 + b_2 \sum x_{\alpha 1}x_{\alpha 2} + \cdots + b_K \sum x_{\alpha 1}x_{\alpha K} \\
\sum x_{\alpha 2}y_\alpha &= b_1 \sum x_{\alpha 2}x_{\alpha 1} + b_2 \sum x_{\alpha 2}^2 + \cdots + b_K \sum x_{\alpha 2}x_{\alpha K} \\
&\;\;\vdots \\
\sum x_{\alpha K}y_\alpha &= b_1 \sum x_{\alpha K}x_{\alpha 1} + b_2 \sum x_{\alpha K}x_{\alpha 2} + \cdots + b_K \sum x_{\alpha K}^2
\end{aligned} \tag{7.7}$$

where all summations are over α from 1 through n. The K equations (7.7) are known as the *normal equations* of the LS procedure.

If $\mathbf{X}$ has full-column rank, the matrix $\mathbf{X}'\mathbf{X}$ is nonsingular (proposition B4 in Section 1.1) and hence the solution $\mathbf{b}$ obtained from (7.6) is

$$\mathbf{b} = (\mathbf{X}'\mathbf{X})^{-1}\mathbf{X}'\mathbf{y} \tag{7.8}$$

The Hessian matrix is found by differentiating the gradient (7.5) with respect to $\mathbf{b}'$:

$$\frac{\partial^2 f}{\partial \mathbf{b}\, \partial \mathbf{b}'} = 2\mathbf{X}'\mathbf{X} \tag{7.9}$$

This matrix is positive definite when $\mathbf{X}$ has full column rank, which implies that the solution (7.8) does indeed minimize the sum of squares of the discrepancies. Note that $f(\;)$ is quadratic in $\mathbf{b}$, so that in this case there are no third and higher-order terms in the Taylor expansion. The $\mathbf{b}$ of (7.8) thus corresponds to an absolute minimum.

The LS method plays a central role in econometrics. The equation

$$y = b_1x_1 + \cdots + b_Kx_K + \text{discrepancy} \tag{7.10}$$

[with the b's specified as the elements of the vector (7.8)] is known as an LS *regression equation*, in this case the regression of y on the K variables $x_1, \ldots, x_K$. The latter variables are sometimes called the "regressors," the former the "regressand."

The Geometry of Least Squares

We return to the geometric approach outlined in the beginning of Section 1.1 and consider the n-dimensional Euclidean space, in which each of the $K + 1$ columns of the observation matrix $[\mathbf{y} \quad \mathbf{X}]$ is represented by one point. This is illustrated in Figure 1.1a for the left-hand variable (indicated by the point Y) in the case of three observations. Note that this picture implies

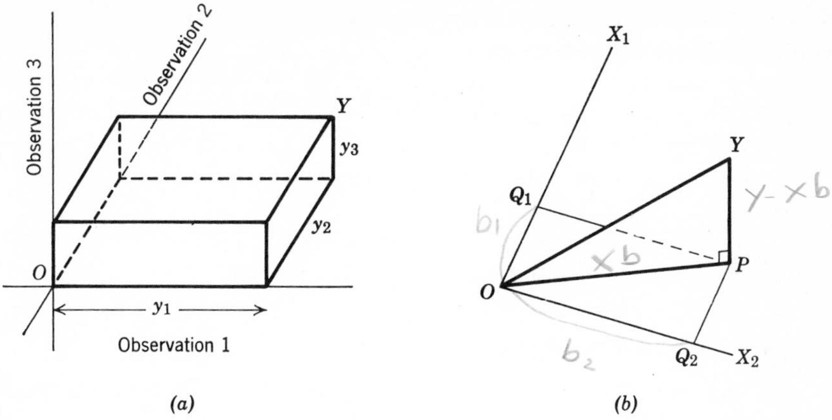

Fig. 1.1 A geometric picture of least-squares adjustment.

that, for each variable, the first observation is measured along the first axis, the second along the second axis, and so on.

The regression equation implies that $\mathbf{y}$ is decomposed in terms of $\mathbf{Xb}$ and the discrepancy vector $\mathbf{y} - \mathbf{Xb}$, where $\mathbf{b}$ is defined in (7.8). Equation (7.6) can be written in the equivalent form $\mathbf{X}'(\mathbf{y} - \mathbf{Xb}) = \mathbf{0}$, which means that *the LS discrepancy vector* $\mathbf{y} - \mathbf{Xb}$ *is orthogonal to each of the K columns of* $\mathbf{X}$. Hence the geometric representation of this vector must be perpendicular to those of the K vectors which represent the right-hand variables of the regression. This is pursued in Figure 1.1*b* for $K = 2$. The three axes are deleted to obtain a clearer picture; what is shown are the points X_1 and X_2 (corresponding to the two right-hand variables) and Y for the dependent variable and the origin O. The orthogonality condition forces the discrepancy vector to be perpendicular to the OX_1X_2-plane; and since $\mathbf{Xb}$ is a linear combination of the columns of $\mathbf{X}$, this vector must be located in the OX_1X_2-plane. Consequently, $\mathbf{Xb}$ is represented by OP and $\mathbf{y} - \mathbf{Xb}$ by YP, P being the projection of Y in the OX_1X_2-plane, in exactly the same way as $\mathbf{y}$ is represented by OY. In other words, the decomposition of $\mathbf{y}$ in terms of $\mathbf{Xb}$ and $\mathbf{y} - \mathbf{Xb}$ is equivalent to the decomposition of OY in terms of OP and YP.

The vector $\mathbf{Xb}$, which represents the part of $\mathbf{y}$ which is accounted for by the K right-hand variables of the regression, can in turn be decomposed in terms of the contributions of these variables separately. This is pursued in Figure 1.1*b* by means of the parallelogram OQ_1PQ_2, which shows that the vector OP is the sum of the vectors OQ_1 and OQ_2. This is the geometric picture of $\mathbf{Xb} = b_1\mathbf{x}_1 + b_2\mathbf{x}_2$, where $\mathbf{x}_1$ and $\mathbf{x}_2$ are the two columns of $\mathbf{X}$. The coefficient b_1 is equal to the ratio of the length of OQ_1 to that of OX_1; if Q_1 is on the same side of the origin as X_1 (as in this figure), then b_1 is positive.

The LS decomposition of OY in terms of OP and YP should be intuitively obvious. Given that $\mathbf{y}$ is approximated linearly in $\mathbf{X}$ by means of $\mathbf{Xb}$, the point Y is approximated by some point in the OX_1X_2-plane. The approximation error is the vector from Y to that point. If the criterion amounts to the minimization of the length of this vector (which is the LS criterion), then the obvious choice of the point in the OX_1X_2-plane is the projection of Y in this plane.

The remainder of this section serves to clarify some special cases and to provide certain results that will be needed in Chapter 3.

Simple and Multiple Regression

In the case $K = 1$ (one right-hand variable) there is only one normal equation with the following solution:

$$b = \frac{\sum x_\alpha y_\alpha}{\sum x_\alpha^2} \qquad \text{(sums over } \alpha \text{ from 1 through } n\text{)} \tag{7.11}$$

where the subscript 1 is deleted from b_1 and $x_{\alpha 1}$ for notational simplicity. When the equation contains one variable plus a constant term on the right, we may write it as $y_\alpha = b_0 + bx_\alpha$ (+ discrepancy) for the αth observation. The two normal equations are then

$$\begin{aligned} \sum y_\alpha &= b_0 n + b \sum x_\alpha \\ \sum x_\alpha y_\alpha &= b_0 \sum x_\alpha + b \sum x_\alpha^2 \end{aligned} \tag{7.12}$$

If we solve this for b and b_0, we obtain

$$b = \frac{\sum (x_\alpha - \bar{x})(y_\alpha - \bar{y})}{\sum (x_\alpha - \bar{x})^2} \qquad b_0 = \bar{y} - b\bar{x} \tag{7.13}$$

where $\bar{x}$ and $\bar{y}$ are the averages of the observations on the two variables:

$$\bar{x} = \frac{1}{n} \sum x_\alpha \qquad \bar{y} = \frac{1}{n} \sum y_\alpha \tag{7.14}$$

The result (7.13) is equivalent to that of eqs. (2.3)–(2.5) of Section 0.2.

Regressions on one variable (with or without constant term) are known as *simple* regressions, those on more variables as *multiple* regressions.

Constant Terms and Deviations from Means

On comparing the b of (7.13) with the b of (7.11) we note that they have the same form except that in the case of (7.13) the two variables are measured as deviations from their means. Thus the addition of a constant term to the right-hand side of the equation leaves the formula for the LS multiplicative coefficient unchanged except for this modification. This result holds generally for any number of right-hand variables. Take the case of a constant term plus three such variables, so that the right-hand side of the regression equation becomes $b_0 \times 1 + b_1 x_{\alpha 1} + b_2 x_{\alpha 2} + b_3 x_{\alpha 3}$. (The notation $b_0 \times 1$ serves to make the constant term b_0 the coefficient of a "constant-term variable" which takes the unit value for each observation.) The observation matrix $\mathbf{X}$ is then

$$\mathbf{X} = \begin{bmatrix} 1 & x_{11} & x_{12} & x_{13} \\ 1 & x_{21} & x_{22} & x_{23} \\ \cdot & \cdot & \cdot & \cdot \\ \cdot & \cdot & \cdot & \cdot \\ \cdot & \cdot & \cdot & \cdot \\ 1 & x_{n1} & x_{n2} & x_{n3} \end{bmatrix} = [\boldsymbol{\iota} \quad \mathbf{Z}] \tag{7.15}$$

where the first column ($\boldsymbol{\iota}$) represents the constant-term variable and $\mathbf{Z}$ consists of the last three columns of $\mathbf{X}$. Next consider

$$\mathbf{X}'\mathbf{y} = \begin{bmatrix} \boldsymbol{\iota}'\mathbf{y} \\ \mathbf{Z}'\mathbf{y} \end{bmatrix} \qquad \mathbf{X}'\mathbf{X} = \begin{bmatrix} n & \boldsymbol{\iota}'\mathbf{Z} \\ \mathbf{Z}'\boldsymbol{\iota} & \mathbf{Z}'\mathbf{Z} \end{bmatrix} \tag{7.16}$$

Using (2.15), we obtain the following partitioned matrix for $(\mathbf{X}'\mathbf{X})^{-1}$:

(7.17) $(\mathbf{X}'\mathbf{X})^{-1}$

$$= \begin{bmatrix} \frac{1}{n} + \frac{1}{n^2}\boldsymbol{\iota}'\mathbf{Z}\left(\mathbf{Z}'\mathbf{Z} - \frac{1}{n}\mathbf{Z}'\boldsymbol{\iota}\boldsymbol{\iota}'\mathbf{Z}\right)^{-1}\mathbf{Z}'\boldsymbol{\iota} & -\frac{1}{n}\boldsymbol{\iota}'\mathbf{Z}\left(\mathbf{Z}'\mathbf{Z} - \frac{1}{n}\mathbf{Z}'\boldsymbol{\iota}\boldsymbol{\iota}'\mathbf{Z}\right)^{-1} \\ -\frac{1}{n}\left(\mathbf{Z}'\mathbf{Z} - \frac{1}{n}\mathbf{Z}'\boldsymbol{\iota}\boldsymbol{\iota}'\mathbf{Z}\right)^{-1}\mathbf{Z}'\boldsymbol{\iota} & \left(\mathbf{Z}'\mathbf{Z} - \frac{1}{n}\mathbf{Z}'\boldsymbol{\iota}\boldsymbol{\iota}'\mathbf{Z}\right)^{-1} \end{bmatrix}$$

$$= \begin{bmatrix} \frac{1}{n} + \frac{1}{n^2}\boldsymbol{\iota}'\mathbf{Z}(\mathbf{Z}'\mathbf{A}\mathbf{Z})^{-1}\mathbf{Z}'\boldsymbol{\iota} & -\frac{1}{n}\boldsymbol{\iota}'\mathbf{Z}(\mathbf{Z}'\mathbf{A}\mathbf{Z})^{-1} \\ -\frac{1}{n}(\mathbf{Z}'\mathbf{A}\mathbf{Z})^{-1}\mathbf{Z}'\boldsymbol{\iota} & (\mathbf{Z}'\mathbf{A}\mathbf{Z})^{-1} \end{bmatrix}$$

where $\mathbf{A} = \mathbf{I} - (1/n)\boldsymbol{\iota}\boldsymbol{\iota}'$ is the idempotent matrix that was introduced in (1.6) to transform variables to deviations from their means. We now postmultiply $(\mathbf{X}'\mathbf{X})^{-1}$ by the $\mathbf{X}'\mathbf{y}$ of (7.16) to obtain the LS coefficient vector:

$$\mathbf{b} = \begin{bmatrix} \frac{1}{n}\boldsymbol{\iota}'\mathbf{y} + \frac{1}{n}\boldsymbol{\iota}'\mathbf{Z}(\mathbf{Z}'\mathbf{A}\mathbf{Z})^{-1}\mathbf{Z}'\left(\frac{1}{n}\boldsymbol{\iota}\boldsymbol{\iota}' - \mathbf{I}\right)\mathbf{y} \\ (\mathbf{Z}'\mathbf{A}\mathbf{Z})^{-1}\mathbf{Z}'\left(-\frac{1}{n}\boldsymbol{\iota}\boldsymbol{\iota}' + \mathbf{I}\right)\mathbf{y} \end{bmatrix} \tag{7.18}$$

$$= \begin{bmatrix} \frac{1}{n}\boldsymbol{\iota}'\mathbf{y} - \frac{1}{n}\boldsymbol{\iota}'\mathbf{Z}(\mathbf{Z}'\mathbf{A}\mathbf{Z})^{-1}\mathbf{Z}'\mathbf{A}\mathbf{y} \\ (\mathbf{Z}'\mathbf{A}\mathbf{Z})^{-1}\mathbf{Z}'\mathbf{A}\mathbf{y} \end{bmatrix}$$

The last three elements of this vector are the LS multiplicative coefficients. Since $\mathbf{A}$ transforms any variable to the deviation from the mean, the expression $(\mathbf{Z}'\mathbf{A}\mathbf{Z})^{-1}\mathbf{Z}'\mathbf{A}\mathbf{y}$ is equivalent in form to $(\mathbf{X}'\mathbf{X})^{-1}\mathbf{X}'\mathbf{y}$ after this transformation and after the constant-term variable [represented by $\boldsymbol{\iota}$ in (7.15)] is deleted from $\mathbf{X}$.

Recall that the discrepancy vector is orthogonal to each column of $\mathbf{X}$: $\mathbf{X}'(\mathbf{y} - \mathbf{X}\mathbf{b}) = \mathbf{0}$. If the regression has a constant term, so that $\mathbf{X}$ is of the form (7.15), one of the elements of this vector equation is $\boldsymbol{\iota}'(\mathbf{y} - \mathbf{X}\mathbf{b}) = 0$, which means that the LS discrepancies have zero sum. They do not, in general, have this property when there is no constant term.

A Fundamental Idempotent Matrix in Least-Squares Theory

Since the original objective was to minimize the sum of the squares of the discrepancies, it is interesting to see what the minimum value actually is. It is readily found that this minimum is a quadratic form with $\mathbf{y}$ as vector:

$$\begin{aligned}(\mathbf{y} - \mathbf{X}\mathbf{b})'(\mathbf{y} - \mathbf{X}\mathbf{b}) &= \mathbf{y}'[\mathbf{I} - \mathbf{X}(\mathbf{X}'\mathbf{X})^{-1}\mathbf{X}']'[\mathbf{I} - \mathbf{X}(\mathbf{X}'\mathbf{X})^{-1}\mathbf{X}']\mathbf{y} \\ &= \mathbf{y}'\mathbf{M}'\mathbf{M}\mathbf{y}\end{aligned}$$

where $\mathbf{M}$ is the symmetric matrix

$$\mathbf{M} = \mathbf{I} - \mathbf{X}(\mathbf{X}'\mathbf{X})^{-1}\mathbf{X}' \tag{7.19}$$

This quadratic form can be simplified to

$$(\mathbf{y} - \mathbf{X}\mathbf{b})'(\mathbf{y} - \mathbf{X}\mathbf{b}) = \mathbf{y}'\mathbf{M}\mathbf{y} \tag{7.20}$$

because $\mathbf{M}$ is idempotent:

$$\begin{aligned}[\mathbf{I} - \mathbf{X}(\mathbf{X}'\mathbf{X})^{-1}\mathbf{X}']^2 &= \mathbf{I} - \mathbf{X}(\mathbf{X}'\mathbf{X})^{-1}\mathbf{X}' - \mathbf{X}(\mathbf{X}'\mathbf{X})^{-1}\mathbf{X}' \\ &\quad + \mathbf{X}(\mathbf{X}'\mathbf{X})^{-1}\mathbf{X}'\mathbf{X}(\mathbf{X}'\mathbf{X})^{-1}\mathbf{X}' \\ &= \mathbf{I} - \mathbf{X}(\mathbf{X}'\mathbf{X})^{-1}\mathbf{X}'\end{aligned}$$

Furthermore, the trace of $\mathbf{M}$ is equal to the excess of the number (n) of rows of $\mathbf{X}$ over the number (K) of its columns:

$$\begin{aligned}\operatorname{tr} \mathbf{M} &= \operatorname{tr} \mathbf{I} - \operatorname{tr} \mathbf{X}(\mathbf{X}'\mathbf{X})^{-1}\mathbf{X}' \\ &= n - \operatorname{tr} (\mathbf{X}'\mathbf{X})^{-1}\mathbf{X}'\mathbf{X} \\ &= n - K\end{aligned} \tag{7.21}$$

Since the rank of an idempotent matrix is equal to its trace (proposition D4 at the end of Section 1.1), the rank of $\mathbf{M}$ is thus also $n - K$. Hence the n columns of $\mathbf{M}$ are subject to K linear dependencies. In fact, postmultiplication of $\mathbf{M}$ by each of the K columns of $\mathbf{X}$ gives a zero column vector:

$$\mathbf{M}\mathbf{X} = \mathbf{X} - \mathbf{X}(\mathbf{X}'\mathbf{X})^{-1}\mathbf{X}'\mathbf{X} = \mathbf{0} \tag{7.22}$$

Since the problem of minimizing the sum of squares of the discrepancies has a unique solution when $\mathbf{X}$ has full column rank, any coefficient vector which differs from the LS vector $\mathbf{b}$ must lead to a larger sum of squares. In Chapter 3, we shall see that this excess is important for statistical testing procedures, so that it is convenient to evaluate it here. Consider, then, any coefficient vector $\mathbf{z}$ and the associated discrepancy vector

$$\mathbf{y} - \mathbf{X}\mathbf{z} = \mathbf{y} - \mathbf{X}\mathbf{b} - \mathbf{X}(\mathbf{z} - \mathbf{b}) \tag{7.23}$$

The sum of squares of the discrepancies is

$$\begin{aligned}(\mathbf{y} - \mathbf{X}\mathbf{z})'(\mathbf{y} - \mathbf{X}\mathbf{z}) &= (\mathbf{y} - \mathbf{X}\mathbf{b})'(\mathbf{y} - \mathbf{X}\mathbf{b}) + (\mathbf{z} - \mathbf{b})'\mathbf{X}'\mathbf{X}(\mathbf{z} - \mathbf{b}) \\ &\quad - 2(\mathbf{z} - \mathbf{b})'\mathbf{X}'(\mathbf{y} - \mathbf{X}\mathbf{b}) \\ &= \mathbf{y}'\mathbf{M}\mathbf{y} + (\mathbf{z} - \mathbf{b})'\mathbf{X}'\mathbf{X}(\mathbf{z} - \mathbf{b})\end{aligned} \tag{7.24}$$

where the second equality sign is based on (7.20) and on $\mathbf{X}'(\mathbf{y} - \mathbf{X}\mathbf{b}) = \mathbf{0}$. The conclusion is that, for any coefficient vector $\mathbf{z}$, the sum of squares of the associated discrepancies is equal to the minimum value (corresponding to the LS vector $\mathbf{b}$) plus a positive definite quadratic form with $\mathbf{X}'\mathbf{X}$ as matrix and $\mathbf{z} - \mathbf{b}$ as vector.

Problems

7.1 Consider a linear regression on time: $y_t = b_0 + bt$ (+ discrepancy), where t is calendar time. Suppose that the number of observations (n) is odd and write $n = 2T + 1$. Specify the transpose of the $\mathbf{X}$ matrix as follows:

$$\mathbf{X}' = \begin{bmatrix} 1 & 1 & \cdots & 1 & 1 \\ -T & -T+1 & \cdots & T-1 & T \end{bmatrix} \tag{7.25}$$

Prove that in this case $b_0 = \bar{y}$ (the average of the y_t's) and

$$b = \frac{T(y_n - y_1) + (T-1)(y_{n-1} - y_2) + \cdots + (y_{T+2} - y_T)}{\frac{1}{3}T(T+1)(2T+1)} \tag{7.26}$$

making use of

$$\sum_{i=1}^{k} i^2 = \frac{1}{6}k(k+1)(2k+1) \tag{7.27}$$

The last equation is to be proved by mathematical induction. (That is, prove first that it is true for $k = 1$; second, that if it is true for some positive integer k, it is also true for $k + 1$.)

7.2 Write (7.18) in the form $\mathbf{b}' = [b_0 \quad \mathbf{b}_Z']$, where b_0 is the constant term and $\mathbf{b}_Z = (\mathbf{Z}'\mathbf{A}\mathbf{Z})^{-1}\mathbf{Z}'\mathbf{A}\mathbf{y}$. Prove $nb_0 = \boldsymbol{\iota}'(\mathbf{y} - \mathbf{Z}\mathbf{b}_Z)$ and prove also that the inner product of $\boldsymbol{\iota}$ and the discrepancy vector $\mathbf{y} - b_0\boldsymbol{\iota} - \mathbf{Z}\mathbf{b}_Z$ vanishes.

7.3 Prove that the matrix **A** defined in (1.6) is a special case of **M** given in (7.19).

7.4 Prove that, if the columns of **X** defined in (7.3) are all pairwise orthogonal, the hth element of **b** of (7.8) is equal to $\mathbf{x}_h'\mathbf{y}/\mathbf{x}_h'\mathbf{x}_h$, where $\mathbf{x}_h$ is the hth column of **X** ($h = 1, \ldots, K$). Conclude that orthogonality of the **X** columns implies that the K-variable multiple regression (without constant term) is reduced to K simple regressions (without constant terms).

7.5 (*Continuation*) Suppose that **Z** defined in (7.15) is such that the columns of **AZ** are all pairwise orthogonal, where $\mathbf{A} = \mathbf{I} - (1/n)\boldsymbol{\iota}\boldsymbol{\iota}'$. Prove that the elements of $\mathbf{b}_Z$ defined in Problem 7.2 can be obtained from simple regressions (with constant terms). Also prove that the condition amounts to zero correlations of the three right-hand variables in the sense

$$\sum_{\alpha=1}^{n}(x_{\alpha h} - \bar{x}_h)(x_{\alpha k} - \bar{x}_k) = 0 \qquad h, k = 1, 2, 3 \quad h \neq k \tag{7.28}$$

where $\bar{x}_h$ is the average of $x_{\alpha h}$ over α.

1.8 Constrained Extremum Problems; Least Squares under Linear Constraints[B]

We return to the maximization or minimization of a general function $f(\mathbf{x})$ and suppose that the arguments of this function are subject to certain constraints. Let there be q such constraints ($q \leqslant n$) and let us write them in the following form:

$$g_h(x_1, \ldots, x_n) = 0 \quad \text{or} \quad g_h(\mathbf{x}) = 0 \qquad h = 1, \ldots, q \tag{8.1}$$

One procedure is to use these constraints to eliminate q of the x's and to determine the extremum of $f(\ )$ by varying the other $n - q$ independent variables. However, in many cases this is less elegant and even cumbersome compared with the following method. We construct the function

$$F(\mathbf{x}, \boldsymbol{\lambda}) = f(\mathbf{x}) - \sum_{h=1}^{q}\lambda_h g_h(\mathbf{x}) \tag{8.2}$$

where $\lambda_1, \ldots, \lambda_q$ are Lagrangian multipliers and $\boldsymbol{\lambda}$ is the column vector of these multipliers in this order. For $f(\ )$ to have a stationary value subject to the constraints (8.1) at some point it is—under certain conditions to be stated immediately—necessary and sufficient that all derivatives of $F(\ )$ vanish:

$$\frac{\partial F}{\partial \mathbf{x}} = \mathbf{0} \qquad \frac{\partial F}{\partial \boldsymbol{\lambda}} = \mathbf{0} \tag{8.3}$$

These are $n + q$ equations, their number being equal to that of the unknowns (the x's and the λ's). The condition under which (8.3) is indeed necessary and sufficient is that the partial derivatives of f and g_h, $h = 1, \ldots, q$, with respect to all x's be continuous, and that the matrix

$$\frac{\partial \mathbf{g}}{\partial \mathbf{x}'} = \begin{bmatrix} \frac{\partial g_1}{\partial x_1} & \frac{\partial g_1}{\partial x_2} & \cdots & \frac{\partial g_1}{\partial x_n} \\ \frac{\partial g_2}{\partial x_1} & \frac{\partial g_2}{\partial x_2} & \cdots & \frac{\partial g_2}{\partial x_n} \\ \cdot & \cdot & & \cdot \\ \cdot & \cdot & & \cdot \\ \cdot & \cdot & & \cdot \\ \frac{\partial g_q}{\partial x_1} & \frac{\partial g_q}{\partial x_2} & \cdots & \frac{\partial g_q}{\partial x_n} \end{bmatrix} \tag{8.4}$$

have full row rank. It is to be understood that the derivatives in (8.4) are evaluated at the point under consideration. Note also that $\partial\mathbf{g}/\partial\mathbf{x}'$ is to be interpreted as the $q \times n$ matrix of derivatives of the functions $g_1(\ ), \ldots, g_q(\ )$, written as a column vector, with respect to the variables $x_1, \ldots, x_n$, the latter being written as a row vector ($\mathbf{x}'$).

Least Squares under Linear Constraints

This result will now be applied to LS adjustment under the linear constraint

$$\mathbf{r} = \mathbf{R}\mathbf{z} \tag{8.5}$$

where $\mathbf{z}$ stands for the coefficient vector[11] and $\mathbf{r}$ and $\mathbf{R}$ are given matrices of order $q \times 1$ and $q \times K$, respectively. Equation (8.5) in the form (8.1) becomes $\mathbf{r} - \mathbf{R}\mathbf{z} = \mathbf{0}$, so that the matrix (8.4) is simply $-\mathbf{R}$. The condition mentioned below (8.4) thus implies that $\mathbf{R}$ should have rank q. If its rank is less than q, the constraints (8.5) are linearly dependent or inconsistent. An

[11] To avoid confusion, we shall reserve the symbol $\mathbf{b}$ for the unconstrained LS coefficient vector (7.8) from now on.

example (with an **R** having full row rank) follows:

$$\begin{bmatrix} 1 \\ 0 \end{bmatrix} = \begin{bmatrix} 1 & 1 & 0 & 0 \\ 1 & 0 & 1 & 0 \end{bmatrix} \begin{bmatrix} z_1 \\ z_2 \\ z_3 \\ z_4 \end{bmatrix}$$

The first constraint implies that z_1 and z_2 add up to 1, the second that z_1 and z_3 are equal apart from sign. This case is very simple; it can be reduced to a two-variable problem by writing $z_2 = 1 - z_1$, $z_3 = -z_1$, so that only z_1 and z_4 have to be determined. However, one can easily conceive of more complicated situations in which such an elimination procedure is less attractive.

We construct the function $F(\ )$ of (8.2) with $f(\ )$ as specified in (7.4): $f(\mathbf{z}) = \mathbf{y}'\mathbf{y} - 2\mathbf{y}'\mathbf{X}\mathbf{z} + \mathbf{z}'\mathbf{X}'\mathbf{X}\mathbf{z}$. The result is

(8.6) $$F(\mathbf{z}, \boldsymbol{\lambda}) = \mathbf{y}'\mathbf{y} - 2\mathbf{y}'\mathbf{X}\mathbf{z} + \mathbf{z}'\mathbf{X}'\mathbf{X}\mathbf{z} - \boldsymbol{\lambda}'(\mathbf{r} - \mathbf{R}\mathbf{z})$$

We differentiate $F(\ )$ with respect to $\mathbf{z}$ and $\boldsymbol{\lambda}$ and put the results equal to zero:

(8.7) $$\frac{\partial F}{\partial \mathbf{z}} = -2\mathbf{X}'\mathbf{y} + 2\mathbf{X}'\mathbf{X}\mathbf{z} + \mathbf{R}'\boldsymbol{\lambda} = \mathbf{0}$$

(8.8) $$\frac{\partial F}{\partial \boldsymbol{\lambda}} = -\mathbf{r} + \mathbf{R}\mathbf{z} = \mathbf{0}$$

Next we premultiply both sides of (8.7) by $\mathbf{R}(\mathbf{X}'\mathbf{X})^{-1}$:

$$-2\mathbf{R}(\mathbf{X}'\mathbf{X})^{-1}\mathbf{X}'\mathbf{y} + 2\mathbf{R}\mathbf{z} + \mathbf{R}(\mathbf{X}'\mathbf{X})^{-1}\mathbf{R}'\boldsymbol{\lambda} = \mathbf{0}$$

We note that $\mathbf{R}\mathbf{z} = \mathbf{r}$ in view of (8.8) and that $\mathbf{R}(\mathbf{X}'\mathbf{X})^{-1}\mathbf{R}'$ is nonsingular because **R** has full row rank. [*Hint.* Consider a quadratic form with $\mathbf{R}(\mathbf{X}'\mathbf{X})^{-1}\mathbf{R}'$ as matrix and an arbitrary vector $\mathbf{x} \neq \mathbf{0}$.] Hence

$$\boldsymbol{\lambda} = -2[\mathbf{R}(\mathbf{X}'\mathbf{X})^{-1}\mathbf{R}']^{-1}[\mathbf{r} - \mathbf{R}(\mathbf{X}'\mathbf{X})^{-1}\mathbf{X}'\mathbf{y}]$$

We substitute this into (8.7):

$$-\mathbf{X}'\mathbf{y} + \mathbf{X}'\mathbf{X}\mathbf{z} - \mathbf{R}'[\mathbf{R}(\mathbf{X}'\mathbf{X})^{-1}\mathbf{R}']^{-1}[\mathbf{r} - \mathbf{R}(\mathbf{X}'\mathbf{X})^{-1}\mathbf{X}'\mathbf{y}] = \mathbf{0}$$

After premultiplying both sides by $(\mathbf{X}'\mathbf{X})^{-1}$ we obtain the constrained LS solution, to be denoted by $\mathbf{b}^*$:

$$\mathbf{b}^* = (\mathbf{X}'\mathbf{X})^{-1}\mathbf{X}'\mathbf{y} + (\mathbf{X}'\mathbf{X})^{-1}\mathbf{R}'[\mathbf{R}(\mathbf{X}'\mathbf{X})^{-1}\mathbf{R}']^{-1}[\mathbf{r} - \mathbf{R}(\mathbf{X}'\mathbf{X})^{-1}\mathbf{X}'\mathbf{y}]$$

This result can be simplified if we write $\mathbf{b} = (\mathbf{X}'\mathbf{X})^{-1}\mathbf{X}'\mathbf{y}$ for the unconstrained coefficient vector in accordance with (7.8):

(8.9) $$\mathbf{b}^* = \mathbf{b} + (\mathbf{X}'\mathbf{X})^{-1}\mathbf{R}'[\mathbf{R}(\mathbf{X}'\mathbf{X})^{-1}\mathbf{R}']^{-1}(\mathbf{r} - \mathbf{R}\mathbf{b})$$

We conclude that the difference between the constrained and the unconstrained LS coefficient vectors is a linear function of the vector $\mathbf{r} - \mathbf{Rb}$, which measures the degree to which the latter coefficient vector fails to satisfy the constraints. Thus, if it happens that $\mathbf{b} = (\mathbf{X}'\mathbf{X})^{-1}\mathbf{X}'\mathbf{y}$ satisfies the constraints $\mathbf{r} = \mathbf{Rz}$ in spite of the fact that they were not imposed, then $\mathbf{b}^* = \mathbf{b}$.

It is obvious from the previous section [see eq. (7.24)] that the sum of squares of the discrepancies associated with $\mathbf{b}^*$ must exceed that of $\mathbf{b}$ except when $\mathbf{b}^* = \mathbf{b}$. The following result is easily verified:

$$(8.10)\qquad (\mathbf{y} - \mathbf{Xb}^*)'(\mathbf{y} - \mathbf{Xb}^*) = \mathbf{y}'\mathbf{My} + (\mathbf{r} - \mathbf{Rb})'[\mathbf{R}(\mathbf{X}'\mathbf{X})^{-1}\mathbf{R}']^{-1}(\mathbf{r} - \mathbf{Rb})$$

which means that the excess of the sum of squares caused by the constraints is a positive definite quadratic form whose vector is $\mathbf{r} - \mathbf{Rb}$, which we just discussed, and whose matrix is the inverse of $\mathbf{R}(\mathbf{X}'\mathbf{X})^{-1}\mathbf{R}'$.

Second-Order Conditions of a Constrained Extremum

Does the solution (8.9) correspond to a minimum of $f(\ )$ subject to the constraints (as we want it), or perhaps to a maximum or a saddle point? To answer this question we return to the general function $f(\mathbf{x})$ and the q constraints (8.1). Consider the quadratic form

$$(8.11)\qquad \sum_{i=1}^{n}\sum_{j=1}^{n} \frac{\partial^2 F}{\partial x_i\, \partial x_j}\, dx_i\, dx_j$$

where $F(\ )$ is the Lagrangian function (8.2) and $dx_1, \ldots, dx_n$ are infinitesimal changes in the arguments of $f(\ )$. Let these changes satisfy

$$(8.12)\qquad \sum_{i=1}^{n} \frac{\partial g_1}{\partial x_i}\, dx_i = \cdots = \sum_{i=1}^{n} \frac{\partial g_q}{\partial x_i}\, dx_i = 0$$

It can be shown that[12] if the first-order condition (8.3) is satisfied at a particular point, the function $f(\ )$ has a local minimum at this point subject to the constraints (8.1) if the quadratic form (8.11) is positive for all values of the dx's which satisfy two conditions: (1) they are not all zero and (2) they satisfy (8.12). Similarly, we have a local maximum subject to the constraints if (8.11) is negative for all dx's not all zero and satisfying (8.12). The derivatives in (8.11) and (8.12) should all be evaluated at the point under consideration.

In the constrained LS case this second-order condition is very simple. Equation (8.7) shows that $\partial^2 F/\partial \mathbf{z}\, \partial \mathbf{z}' = 2\mathbf{X}'\mathbf{X}$, which is positive definite. The quadratic form (8.11) is thus positive for all infinitesimal changes (not

[12] See, for example, HADLEY (1964, pp. 101–102).

Table 1.1

Data on Income and Outlay in the United States, 1922-1938 (in 10^7 Dollars)

Year	Employee Compensation (x_1)	Consumer Perishables Plus Producer Durables (x_2)	Unadjusted Net Savings of Enterprises (x_3)	Consumer Durables and Semi-durables (x_4)	Consumer Services (x_5)	Construction (x_6)	Net Public Outlay (x_7)	Net Increase in Inventories (x_8)
1922	3700	2496	142	1620	2032	532	39	3
1923	4334	2795	313	1927	2229	688	−14	313
1924	4332	2844	182	1864	2351	759	4	−47
1925	4502	3042	339	2042	2434	825	10	163
1926	4802	3254	322	2136	2518	881	−29	141
1927	4843	3181	141	2092	2580	858	−21	81
1928	4936	3281	223	2137	2638	818	12	−66
1929	5221	3504	244	2230	2716	788	1	229
1930	4777	3151	−513	1828	2589	594	47	71
1931	4047	2476	−833	1477	2338	371	227	−92
1932	3170	1997	−1005	1053	1970	177	303	−271
1933	3005	2002	−445	1040	1767	109	226	−144
1934	3489	2371	−219	1220	1819	123	446	−122
1935	3793	2681	−113	1407	1928	160	359	115
1936	4248	3050	87	1654	2095	255	474	182
1937	4657	3323	24	1738	2242	333	127	314
1938	4323	3035	−100	1440	2228	293	185	−108

all zero), including those which satisfy (8.12), so that the solution (8.9) is a constrained minimum.

Problems

8.1 Prove that the condition $\partial F/\partial \boldsymbol{\lambda} = \mathbf{0}$ of (8.3) is always equivalent to the set of q constraints (8.1).

8.2 Prove eq. (8.10).

1.9 Principal Component Analysis[B]

The LS procedure was introduced in the previous sections as a *descriptive* device. Given a certain set of observations, how do we fit a linear relation as well as possible? The method answers this question by minimizing the sum of squares of the discrepancies. We shall meet LS very frequently in later chapters, but its role will be different because it will be based on a statistical model. Here, however, we shall continue with the descriptive interpretation and discuss the so-called principal component technique.

Our starting point consists of n observations on K variables, which will be arranged in an $n \times K$ matrix $\mathbf{X}$. An example is given in Table 1.1, which contains time series data on 17 components of total income and outlay in the

Inventory Revaluation Adjustment (x_9)	Net Rent Received by Individuals (x_{10})	Entrepreneurial Withdrawals (x_{11})	Dividends (x_{12})	Adjustment for Depreciation (x_{13})	Interest (x_{14})	Dividends and Interests from Abroad, etc. (x_{15})	Adjustment for Depreciation and Depletion (x_{16})	Foreign Balance (x_{17})
−88	490	1079	296	−751	398	−105	−41	51
−16	516	1134	374	−839	421	−95	−85	25
16	563	1194	368	−834	437	−96	−68	78
−35	546	1250	427	−848	458	−96	−60	36
170	514	1245	462	−918	470	−105	−55	8
78	508	1262	492	−917	494	−104	−55	42
6	494	1288	534	−941	527	−114	−46	63
70	492	1338	612	−1000	560	−127	−55	35
412	426	1277	577	−953	572	−109	−29	56
323	303	1121	434	−842	571	−61	−1	9
147	209	975	275	−726	552	−37	35	16
−227	211	902	225	−682	500	−45	36	22
−149	190	910	290	−718	485	−75	4	35
−72	214	952	373	−738	465	−110	−2	−27
−16	219	1012	486	−768	461	15	−18	−47
−64	258	1123	502	−850	469	−221	−57	−26
110	258	1106	353	−857	459	−175	−52	61

United States in the 17 years, 1922 to 1938.[13] Hence $n = K = 17$, but the equality of n and K should be regarded as accidental. The problem is: can we describe each of these K variables by a linear function of a small number of other variables with a high degree of accuracy? This would be trivially true if all variables moved proportionally; one single variable would then suffice to describe the behavior of all K variables. Let us start with one variable.

The First Principal Component

Our single variable takes n values, to be arranged in a column vector $\mathbf{p}$. At this stage $\mathbf{p}$ is not yet determined, but we proceed as if it were. If all variables behave proportionally, each column of $\mathbf{X}$ is equal to some scalar multiple of $\mathbf{p}$. This implies $\mathbf{X} = \mathbf{pa}'$, where $\mathbf{a}'$ is the K-element row vector consisting of these scalar multiples, one for each column of $\mathbf{X}$. Note that the product $\mathbf{pa}'$ remains unchanged when $\mathbf{p}$ is multiplied by some scalar $c \neq 0$ and $\mathbf{a}$ by $1/c$. By imposing

$$\mathbf{p}'\mathbf{p} = 1 \tag{9.1}$$

we shall be able to obtain uniqueness except for sign (i.e., $\mathbf{p}$ and $\mathbf{a}$ may still be replaced by $-\mathbf{p}$ and $-\mathbf{a}$, respectively).

Obviously, one should expect that $\mathbf{X} = \mathbf{pa}'$ will not hold exactly in general,

[13] The numerical example is based on R. STONE (1947). Tables 1.1 through 1.5 are derived from this article, but the figures reproduced here have fewer decimal places.

so that there will be a nonzero matrix of discrepancies, $\mathbf{X} - \mathbf{pa}'$, for whatever vectors $\mathbf{p}$ and $\mathbf{a}$. Our criterion is to select these vectors such that the sum of squares of all Kn discrepancies is minimized. It is easily verified that the sum of squares of all elements a_{ij} of an $m \times n$ matrix $\mathbf{A}$ can be written as the trace of $\mathbf{A}'\mathbf{A}$:

$$\text{tr}\,\mathbf{A}'\mathbf{A} = \sum_{i=1}^{m} \sum_{j=1}^{n} a_{ij}^2$$

Therefore our objective is to minimize

$$(9.2) \quad \text{tr}\,(\mathbf{X} - \mathbf{pa}')'(\mathbf{X} - \mathbf{pa}') = \text{tr}\,\mathbf{X}'\mathbf{X} - \text{tr}\,\mathbf{ap}'\mathbf{X} - \text{tr}\,\mathbf{X}'\mathbf{pa}' + \text{tr}\,\mathbf{ap}'\mathbf{pa}'$$
$$= \text{tr}\,\mathbf{X}'\mathbf{X} - 2\mathbf{p}'\mathbf{Xa} + \mathbf{a}'\mathbf{a}$$

where use is made of $\text{tr}\,\mathbf{ap}'\mathbf{X} = \text{tr}\,\mathbf{p}'\mathbf{Xa} = \mathbf{p}'\mathbf{Xa}$ and similarly $\text{tr}\,\mathbf{ap}'\mathbf{pa}' = \text{tr}\,\mathbf{p}'\mathbf{pa}'\mathbf{a} = \mathbf{p}'\mathbf{pa}'\mathbf{a} = \mathbf{a}'\mathbf{a}$. We differentiate (9.2) with respect to $\mathbf{a}$ for given $\mathbf{p}$ and put the derivative equal to zero. This gives

$$(9.3) \qquad \mathbf{a} = \mathbf{X}'\mathbf{p}$$

which expresses the coefficient vector $\mathbf{a}$ in $\mathbf{p}$, whatever $\mathbf{p}$ may be. When substituting (9.3) into (9.2) we obtain $\text{tr}\,\mathbf{X}'\mathbf{X} - \mathbf{p}'\mathbf{XX}'\mathbf{p}$, which shows that our next task is to maximize $\mathbf{p}'\mathbf{XX}'\mathbf{p}$ for variations in $\mathbf{p}$ subject to (9.1). So we form the Lagrangian expression $\mathbf{p}'\mathbf{XX}'\mathbf{p} - \lambda(\mathbf{p}'\mathbf{p} - 1)$ and differentiate it with respect to $\mathbf{p}$. This gives $2\mathbf{XX}'\mathbf{p} - 2\lambda\mathbf{p}$, so that the condition on $\mathbf{p}$ becomes

$$(9.4) \qquad (\mathbf{XX}' - \lambda\mathbf{I})\mathbf{p} = \mathbf{0}$$

Hence, $\mathbf{p}$ is a characteristic vector of the $n \times n$ positive semidefinite matrix $\mathbf{XX}'$ corresponding to root λ. To find out which root is to be taken we premultiply (9.4) by $\mathbf{p}'$, which gives $\mathbf{p}'\mathbf{XX}'\mathbf{p} = \lambda\mathbf{p}'\mathbf{p} = \lambda$. Since our objective is to maximize $\mathbf{p}'\mathbf{XX}'\mathbf{p}$, we should take the largest root of $\mathbf{XX}'$.[14] Furthermore, by premultiplying (9.4) by $\mathbf{X}'$ we obtain

$$(9.5) \qquad (\mathbf{X}'\mathbf{X} - \lambda\mathbf{I})\mathbf{X}'\mathbf{p} = (\mathbf{X}'\mathbf{X} - \lambda\mathbf{I})\mathbf{a} = \mathbf{0}$$

in view of (9.3). Hence the coefficient vector $\mathbf{a}$ is a characteristic vector of the matrix $\mathbf{X}'\mathbf{X}$ corresponding to the largest root except that it is *not* normalized such that it has unit length (see Problem 9.1). Note also that (9.4) and (9.3) imply $\lambda\mathbf{p} = \mathbf{X}(\mathbf{X}'\mathbf{p}) = \mathbf{Xa}$ and, hence,

$$(9.6) \qquad \mathbf{p} = \frac{1}{\lambda}\mathbf{Xa}$$

The vector $\mathbf{p}$ thus derived gives the best linear description of the $\mathbf{X}$ columns in the LS sense. It is known as the *first principal component* of the K variables represented in $\mathbf{X}$. The addition "first" will become clear immediately; it will induce us to add a subscript 1 to $\mathbf{p}$, $\mathbf{a}$, and λ of (9.4) to (9.6).

[14] See Problem 9.2 for an analysis of the conditional maximum along the lines of the last two paragraphs of Section 1.8.

Other Principal Components

The matrix $\mathbf{X}$ is now approximated by $\mathbf{p}_1\mathbf{a}_1'$ and, therefore, the discrepancy matrix is $\mathbf{X} - \mathbf{p}_1\mathbf{a}_1'$. We may then ask whether this matrix of residual elements can in turn be described by another matrix of unit rank, $\mathbf{p}_2\mathbf{a}_2'$, so that we obtain $\mathbf{p}_1\mathbf{a}_1' + \mathbf{p}_2\mathbf{a}_2'$ as a more accurate approximation to $\mathbf{X}$. This question will be answered under the conditions

$$\text{(9.7)} \qquad \mathbf{p}_2'\mathbf{p}_2 = 1 \qquad \mathbf{p}_1'\mathbf{p}_2 = 0$$

the first of which is analogous to (9.1), while the second requires that the two principal components be orthogonal.[15] The procedure is precisely the same as before except that we should replace $\mathbf{X}$ by $\mathbf{X} - \mathbf{p}_1\mathbf{a}_1'$. So we minimize

$$\begin{aligned}\operatorname{tr}(\mathbf{X} - \mathbf{p}_1\mathbf{a}_1' - \mathbf{p}_2\mathbf{a}_2')'(\mathbf{X} - \mathbf{p}_1\mathbf{a}_1' - \mathbf{p}_2\mathbf{a}_2')&\\ = \operatorname{tr}(\mathbf{X} - \mathbf{p}_1\mathbf{a}_1')'(\mathbf{X} - \mathbf{p}_1\mathbf{a}_1') - 2\operatorname{tr}(\mathbf{X} - \mathbf{p}_1\mathbf{a}_1')'\mathbf{p}_2\mathbf{a}_2' + \operatorname{tr}\mathbf{a}_2\mathbf{p}_2'\mathbf{p}_2\mathbf{a}_2'&\\ = \operatorname{tr}(\mathbf{X} - \mathbf{p}_1\mathbf{a}_1')'(\mathbf{X} - \mathbf{p}_1\mathbf{a}_1') - 2\mathbf{a}_2'\mathbf{X}'\mathbf{p}_2 + \mathbf{a}_2'\mathbf{a}_2&\end{aligned}$$

where use has been made of (9.7) in the last step. Minimization with respect to $\mathbf{a}_2$ gives

$$\text{(9.8)} \qquad \mathbf{a}_2 = \mathbf{X}'\mathbf{p}_2$$

The function to be minimized for variations in $\mathbf{p}_2$ is then

$$\operatorname{tr}(\mathbf{X} - \mathbf{p}_1\mathbf{a}_1')'(\mathbf{X} - \mathbf{p}_1\mathbf{a}_1') - \mathbf{p}_2'\mathbf{X}\mathbf{X}'\mathbf{p}_2$$

so that $\mathbf{p}_2'\mathbf{X}\mathbf{X}'\mathbf{p}_2$ is to be maximized subject to (9.7). We construct the Lagrangian expression $\mathbf{p}_2'\mathbf{X}\mathbf{X}'\mathbf{p}_2 - \lambda_2(\mathbf{p}_2'\mathbf{p}_2 - 1) - \mu\mathbf{p}_1'\mathbf{p}_2$, differentiate it with respect to $\mathbf{p}_2$, and equate the result to zero:

$$\text{(9.9)} \qquad 2\mathbf{X}\mathbf{X}'\mathbf{p}_2 - 2\lambda_2\mathbf{p}_2 - \mu\mathbf{p}_1 = \mathbf{0}$$

We then premultiply by $\mathbf{p}_1'$, which gives $2\mathbf{p}_1'\mathbf{X}\mathbf{X}'\mathbf{p}_2 = \mu\mathbf{p}_1'\mathbf{p}_1 = \mu$. This implies $\mu = 0$ because $\mathbf{X}\mathbf{X}'\mathbf{p}_1 = \lambda_1\mathbf{p}_1$ [see (9.4)] and hence $\mathbf{p}_1'\mathbf{X}\mathbf{X}'\mathbf{p}_2 = \lambda_1\mathbf{p}_1'\mathbf{p}_2 = 0$. Therefore we can simplify (9.9) to

$$\text{(9.10)} \qquad (\mathbf{X}\mathbf{X}' - \lambda_2\mathbf{I})\mathbf{p}_2 = \mathbf{0}$$

which shows that $\mathbf{p}_2$ is a characteristic vector of $\mathbf{X}\mathbf{X}'$ corresponding to root λ_2. This vector should be orthogonal to the characteristic vector $\mathbf{p}_1$ which

[15] It can be shown that precisely the same second principal component is obtained when this orthogonality condition is not imposed. We shall not give a detailed proof but shall confine ourselves to stating that the basic reason is that (1) the first principal component is orthogonal to the columns of the discrepancy matrix $\mathbf{X} - \mathbf{p}_1\mathbf{a}_1'$, because $(\mathbf{X} - \mathbf{p}_1\mathbf{a}_1')'\mathbf{p}_1 = \mathbf{X}'\mathbf{p}_1 - \mathbf{a}_1 = \mathbf{0}$ follows from (9.3), and (2) if the second principal component is to give the best linear approximation of these columns in the LS sense, it must be orthogonal to any vector that is orthogonal to all of these columns.

Table 1.2

Sums of Squares and Products of Deviations from Means

x_1	x_2	x_3	x_4	x_5	x_6	x_7	x_8	x_9	x_{10}	x_{11}	x_{12}	x_{13}	x_{14}	x_{15}	x_{16}	x_{17}	Number of Variable
644.6	444.8	245.4	357.9	277.2	229.3	−109.8	105.6	65.7	94.2	129.4	101.8	−88.7	6.9	−25.5	−28.5	6.0	1
	328.5	195.8	239.4	174.2	139.3	−63.5	83.0	30.7	54.2	81.4	70.2	−57.2	0.4	−20.1	−19.9	1.2	2
		265.6	185.3	76.1	121.3	−56.4	72.2	−39.5	60.2	43.6	24.0	−23.5	−21.0	−11.2	−18.8	2.6	3
			232.4	159.2	163.9	−79.2	66.1	23.5	74.7	78.0	52.3	−48.1	−1.8	−10.7	−18.3	4.9	4
				138.6	116.8	−59.2	30.2	43.6	50.0	64.8	44.4	−42.5	8.2	−8.6	−11.1	5.8	5
					133.7	−69.8	31.9	21.0	64.5	59.1	29.4	−33.6	−1.4	−5.9	−12.8	7.4	6
						46.5	−15.6	−10.5	−35.8	−31.7	−12.0	17.7	1.2	6.7	7.1	−5.3	7
							45.5	− 2.8	14.2	15.6	17.2	−10.5	−4.3	−4.9	−6.4	−3.6	8
								41.3	7.3	18.0	14.0	−13.6	8.0	−0.4	−0.8	1.5	9
									33.7	26.8	10.5	−14.0	−2.3	−2.5	−6.4	4.5	10
										31.4	19.6	−19.7	2.5	−4.6	−5.9	3.4	11
											19.5	−14.3	3.8	−2.8	−3.2	−0.3	12
												13.7	−2.7	3.5	3.5	−1.7	13
													4.4	0.6	1.3	0.1	14
														4.4	1.7	−0.6	15
															2.1	−0.6	16
																1.9	17

Table 1.3

Correlation Coefficients Corresponding to Table 1.2

x_1	x_2	x_3	x_4	x_5	x_6	x_7	x_8	x_9	x_{10}	x_{11}	x_{12}	x_{13}	x_{14}	x_{15}	x_{16}	x_{17}	Number of Variable
1	.97	.59	.92	.93	.78	−.63	.62	.40	.64	.91	.91	−.94	.13	−.48	−.78	.17	1
	1	.66	.87	.82	.66	−.51	.68	.26	.52	.80	.88	−.85	.01	−.53	−.77	.05	2
		1	.75	.40	.64	−.51	.66	−.38	.64	.48	.33	−.39	−.61	−.33	−.80	.12	3
			1	.89	.93	−.76	.64	.24	.84	.91	.78	−.85	−.06	−.34	−.83	.24	4
				1	.86	−.74	.38	.58	.73	.98	.85	−.97	.33	−.35	−.66	.36	5
					1	−.88	.41	.28	.96	.91	.58	−.79	−.06	−.24	−.77	.47	6
						1	−.34	−.24	−.90	−.83	−.40	.70	.09	.47	.73	−.57	7
							1	−.07	.36	.41	.58	−.42	−.30	−.35	−.66	−.39	8
								1	.19	.50	.50	−.57	.60	−.03	−.09	.17	9
									1	.82	.41	−.65	−.19	−.21	−.77	.56	10
										1	.79	−.95	.21	−.40	−.73	.44	11
											1	−.87	.41	−.30	−.50	−.04	12
												1	−.35	.46	.66	−.34	13
													1	.14	.43	.03	14
														1	.55	−.22	15
															1	−.31	16
																1	17

corresponds to the largest root; at the same time, λ_2 should be as large as possible because the objective is to maximize $\mathbf{p}_2'\mathbf{XX}'\mathbf{p}_2 = \lambda_2$. Hence the second principal component $\mathbf{p}_2$ is a characteristic vector corresponding to the second largest root λ_2. We assume that λ_1 and λ_2 are different; the case of multiple positive roots of $\mathbf{XX}'$ is characterized by a lack of uniqueness of the principal components and will not be discussed here.

We can go on in this way by deriving r principal components, r being the rank of $\mathbf{XX}'$ (and of $\mathbf{X}$). The ith such component minimizes the sum of squares of the discrepancies that are left after the earlier components $\mathbf{p}_1, \ldots, \mathbf{p}_{i-1}$ have done their work, and the minimization takes place subject to the unit-length constraint $\mathbf{p}_i'\mathbf{p}_i = 1$ and the orthogonality constraints $\mathbf{p}_1'\mathbf{p}_i = \cdots = \mathbf{p}_{i-1}'\mathbf{p}_i = 0$. The result is that $\mathbf{p}_i$ is a characteristic vector of $\mathbf{XX}'$ corresponding to the ith largest root λ_i.

A Numerical Example

The principal components $\mathbf{p}_1, \mathbf{p}_2, \ldots$ can thus be determined by computing the matrix $\mathbf{XX}'$ and then finding its characteristic roots and vectors. One may also take $\mathbf{X}'\mathbf{X}$ instead of $\mathbf{XX}'$ and compute the characteristic vectors $\mathbf{a}_1, \mathbf{a}_2, \ldots$, after which the $\mathbf{p}$'s are computed from (9.6). Following the latter procedure, we obtain for the data of Table 1.1 the matrix of sums of squares and products given in Table 1.2. (Note that all 17 variables have been measured as deviations from the means. The corresponding correlation coefficients are given in Table 1.3 for comparison purposes.) The left-hand part of Table 1.4 contains the elements of the first three principal components together with the roots $\lambda_1, \lambda_2, \lambda_3$. These roots may be used to measure the relative importance of the corresponding components. The argument is based on the criterion used: the sum of squares of all Kn discrepancies. These discrepancies are of the form $\mathbf{X} - \mathbf{p}_1\mathbf{a}_1' - \cdots - \mathbf{p}_i\mathbf{a}_i'$ after the use of the ith component. Consequently, *before* any component is used the discrepancies are the elements of $\mathbf{X}$, and their sum of squares is tr $\mathbf{X}'\mathbf{X}$. The first principal component reduces this sum of squares to [see (9.2) to (9.4)]:

$$\begin{aligned}(9.11)\qquad \operatorname{tr}(\mathbf{X} - \mathbf{p}_1\mathbf{a}_1')'(\mathbf{X} - \mathbf{p}_1\mathbf{a}_1') &= \operatorname{tr}\mathbf{X}'\mathbf{X} - 2\mathbf{p}_1'\mathbf{X}\mathbf{a}_1 + \mathbf{a}_1'\mathbf{a}_1\\ &= \operatorname{tr}\mathbf{X}'\mathbf{X} - \mathbf{p}_1'\mathbf{XX}'\mathbf{p}_1\\ &= \operatorname{tr}\mathbf{X}'\mathbf{X} - \lambda_1\end{aligned}$$

It can be shown in the same way that the second principal component accounts for an additional reduction of the sum of squares of the discrepancies equal to λ_2, and so on. Thus, by dividing $\lambda_1, \lambda_2, \lambda_3$ by tr $\mathbf{X}'\mathbf{X}$ we obtain three ratios which can be regarded as measuring the degree to which the variation of the K variables is accounted for by the corresponding principal component. In this case the first component accounts for more than 80

Table 1.4

Three Principal Components and the Proportion of the Variance of Each Variable Accounted for by Each Component

Year	$\mathbf{p}_1$	$\mathbf{p}_2$	$\mathbf{p}_3$	Number of Variable	Proportion Accounted for by $\mathbf{p}_1$	$\mathbf{p}_2$	$\mathbf{p}_3$	Rest
1922	−.13	.33	.27	1	.97	.02	.01	.00
1923	.08	.28	.17	2	.91	.00	.09	.01
1924	.08	.14	.29	3	.50	.49	.00	.01
1925	.17	.21	.20	4	.95	.01	.03	.02
1926	.26	.07	.13	5	.83	.12	.04	.01
1927	.24	−.04	.16	6	.73	.01	.26	.01
1928	.27	−.03	.10	7	.50	.00	.34	.16
1929	.37	.09	−.08	8	.42	.10	.11	.37
1930	.14	−.52	−.00	9	.09	.72	.03	.16
1931	−.15	−.50	.13	10	.55	.03	.40	.02
1932	−.45	−.34	.21	11	.84	.06	.08	.02
1933	−.46	.16	11	12	.72	.14	.06	.08
1934	−.31	.16	− 18	13	.83	.13	.01	.03
1935	−.18	.14	− 30	14	.00	.75	.00	.25
1936	−.01	.12	− 47	15	.21	.00	.05	.74
1937	.12	.01	−.47	16	.71	.09	.01	.20
1938	−.02	−.09	−.27	17	.04	.01	.39	.56
λ_i	1605	211	121					
$\lambda_i/\text{tr}\,\mathbf{X}'\mathbf{X}$	.808	.106	.061					

percent of the total variation, the second for more than 10 percent, and the third for 6 percent. What remains for all other principal components is only $2\frac{1}{2}$ percent.

Analysis of Individual Variables

It is also interesting to consider the contributions of the three principal components to the "explanation" of the behavior of each of the 17 variables separately. The argument is as follows. Let $\mathbf{x}_h$ be one of the K columns of $\mathbf{X}$ (the observations on the hth variable) and consider the linear relation

$$\mathbf{x}_h = b_{1h}\mathbf{p}_1 + b_{2h}\mathbf{p}_2 + b_{3h}\mathbf{p}_3 + \text{discrepancy vector} \tag{9.12}$$

where the b's are coefficients that are still to be specified. Let us specify them according to the LS principle. Applying (7.8) we find

$$\begin{bmatrix} b_{1h} \\ b_{2h} \\ b_{3h} \end{bmatrix} = \begin{bmatrix} \mathbf{p}_1'\mathbf{p}_1 & \mathbf{p}_1'\mathbf{p}_2 & \mathbf{p}_1'\mathbf{p}_3 \\ \mathbf{p}_2'\mathbf{p}_1 & \mathbf{p}_2'\mathbf{p}_2 & \mathbf{p}_2'\mathbf{p}_3 \\ \mathbf{p}_3'\mathbf{p}_1 & \mathbf{p}_3'\mathbf{p}_2 & \mathbf{p}_3'\mathbf{p}_3 \end{bmatrix}^{-1} \begin{bmatrix} \mathbf{p}_1'\mathbf{x}_h \\ \mathbf{p}_2'\mathbf{x}_h \\ \mathbf{p}_3'\mathbf{x}_h \end{bmatrix} = \begin{bmatrix} \mathbf{p}_1'\mathbf{x}_h \\ \mathbf{p}_2'\mathbf{x}_h \\ \mathbf{p}_3'\mathbf{x}_h \end{bmatrix}$$

where the second equality sign is based on the unit-length condition $\mathbf{p}_i'\mathbf{p}_i = 1$ and the orthogonality condition $\mathbf{p}_i'\mathbf{p}_j = 0$, $i \neq j$. Now $\mathbf{p}_1'\mathbf{x}_h$ (and hence b_{1h}) is the hth element of the vector $\mathbf{p}_1'\mathbf{X} = \mathbf{a}_1'$; see (9.3). Therefore we can write (9.12) in the following specific form:

$$\mathbf{x}_h = a_{1h}\mathbf{p}_1 + a_{2h}\mathbf{p}_2 + a_{3h}\mathbf{p}_3 + \mathbf{v}_h \tag{9.13}$$

where a_{ih} is the hth element of the vector $\mathbf{a}_i$ and $\mathbf{v}_h$ is a discrepancy vector (whose length is minimized by the LS method).

If we premultiply each side of (9.13) by its own transpose we obtain

$$\begin{aligned}\mathbf{x}_h'\mathbf{x}_h &= a_{1h}^2\mathbf{p}_1'\mathbf{p}_1 + a_{2h}^2\mathbf{p}_2'\mathbf{p}_2 + a_{3h}^2\mathbf{p}_3'\mathbf{p}_3 + \mathbf{v}_h'\mathbf{v}_h \\ &\quad + 2(a_{1h}a_{2h}\mathbf{p}_1'\mathbf{p}_2 + \cdots + a_{1h}\mathbf{p}_1'\mathbf{v}_h + \cdots)\end{aligned}$$

The cross-product terms on the second line are all zero because of the orthogonality of the $\mathbf{p}$'s mutually and that of the $\mathbf{p}$'s and $\mathbf{v}_h$, $\mathbf{v}_h$ being an LS discrepancy vector which is orthogonal to the vectors of the regressors (the $\mathbf{p}$'s). Taking account of $\mathbf{p}_i'\mathbf{p}_i = 1$ we thus find

$$\mathbf{x}_h'\mathbf{x}_h = a_{1h}^2 + a_{2h}^2 + a_{3h}^2 + \mathbf{v}_h'\mathbf{v}_h \tag{9.14}$$

The sum of squares of the values taken by the hth variable can thus be decomposed into parts attributable to the first principal component (a_{1h}^2), the second (a_{2h}^2), the third (a_{3h}^2), and the rest ($\mathbf{v}_h'\mathbf{v}_h$). The results for our numerical example (in the "relative" form $a_{ih}^2/\mathbf{x}_h'\mathbf{x}_h$, $\mathbf{v}_h'\mathbf{v}_h/\mathbf{x}_h'\mathbf{x}_h$) are given in the last four columns of Table 1.4. They indicate that some of the variables are much more closely related to the second principal component than to the first (take x_9 and x_{14}). By adding the contributions of any given component to all K variables we obtain the λ's which refer to all these variables jointly:

$$\sum_{h=1}^{K} a_{ih}^2 = \mathbf{a}_i'\mathbf{a}_i = \mathbf{p}_i'\mathbf{X}\mathbf{X}'\mathbf{p}_i = \lambda_i\mathbf{p}_i'\mathbf{p}_i = \lambda_i \tag{9.15}$$

An Interpretation of the Three Principal Components

It is interesting to observe that the principal components of the present data allow a rather simple interpretation. We recall that the variables are all components of total income and total outlay of the United States. Consider then (1) total income, (2) the yearly change in total income, and (3) time. (The last variable is an ordinary linear trend which takes the value 1 in 1922, 2 in 1923, and so on.) The nine correlations of these three variables and the first three principal components are given in Table 1.5. It appears that the first component is very highly correlated with total income, that the second is highly correlated with the change in income, and that the third is rather highly correlated with time. The conclusion of the analysis is that the behavior

Table 1.5

Correlation Coefficients of Principal Components and Certain Economic Variables

Economic Variables	$\mathbf{p}_1$	$\mathbf{p}_2$	$\mathbf{p}_3$
Total income	.995	−.041	.057
Same, annual change	−.056	.948	−.124
Time	−.369	−.282	−.836

of the 17 variables during the period 1922–1938 can be described rather accurately by linear combinations of total income, of its change, and of a linear time trend.

However, the economic interpretation of principal components in general is no easy matter. In principle it is conceivable that there is a limited number of principal factors which dominate the behavior of economic variables, but there is no reason to assume that these factors satisfy the orthogonality condition $\mathbf{p}_i'\mathbf{p}_j = 0$. It just happened that in this example income, its change, and time have low correlations.

Principal Components Depend on the Origin and Scale of the Variables

The numerical results presented here are based on variables which are measured as deviations from the means. If the "natural" zeros are used instead of the means, one obtains different principal components. If the variables are standardized (measured as deviations from the means and subsequently divided by the standard deviations), the matrix $\mathbf{X}'\mathbf{X}$ becomes a matrix of correlation coefficients and the principal components are changed again. The latter procedure is often applied in psychology, where the variables frequently have no common unit of measurement; it was not applied here, since the variables are all in dollars per year. This dependence on the unit of measurement is obviously a weakness of the principal component technique. To show that there is such a dependence, it is sufficient to consider the case $K = 2$, so that $\mathbf{X}'\mathbf{X}$ is a 2×2 matrix, and to inspect the roots (5.3) of such a 2×2 matrix. It is also intuitively plausible. If a variable is measured in such small units that its numerical values dominate those of the other $K - 1$ variables, the first principal component will reflect the behavior of this particular variable rather closely; see Problem 9.3.

Problems

9.1 Let $\mathbf{X}$ be the matrix of observations on certain variables. Write $\mathbf{p}_i = (1/\lambda_i)\mathbf{X}\mathbf{a}_i$ for the ith principal component, where λ_i is a positive root of

$\mathbf{X}'\mathbf{X}$ (or of $\mathbf{XX}'$). Prove that the length of the weight vector $\mathbf{a}_i$ is $\sqrt{\lambda_i}$ if $\mathbf{p}_i$ has unit length.

9.2 To verify the second-order condition for the first principal component along the lines of the last two paragraphs of Section 1.8, recall that it is stated below eq. (9.3) that the problem is to maximize $\mathbf{p}_1'\mathbf{XX}'\mathbf{p}_1$ subject to $\mathbf{p}_1'\mathbf{p}_1 = 1$. (It is advantageous to use a subscript 1 here.) The Lagrangian function and the matrix of its second-order derivatives with respect to $\mathbf{p}_1$ and $\mathbf{p}_1'$ are then

$$F(\mathbf{p}_1, \lambda_1) = \mathbf{p}_1'\mathbf{XX}'\mathbf{p}_1 - \lambda_1(\mathbf{p}_1'\mathbf{p}_1 - 1)$$

(9.16)
$$\frac{\partial^2 F}{\partial \mathbf{p}_1\, \partial \mathbf{p}_1'} = 2(\mathbf{XX}' - \lambda_1\mathbf{I})$$

Prove that the second-order constrained maximum condition is

(9.17) $\quad \mathbf{q}'(\mathbf{XX}' - \lambda_1\mathbf{I})\mathbf{q} < 0 \quad$ for all $\quad \mathbf{q} \neq \mathbf{0} \quad$ satisfying $\quad \mathbf{p}_1'\mathbf{q} = 0$

where $\mathbf{q} = [q_\alpha] = [dp_{\alpha 1}]$, $dp_{\alpha 1}$ being an infinitesimal change in the αth element of $\mathbf{p}_1$. Prove that we may specify $\mathbf{q}'\mathbf{q} = 1$ without real loss of generality. Also prove that

$$\mathbf{q}'\mathbf{XX}'\mathbf{q} = \mathbf{q}'\left(\sum_{i=1}^{r} \lambda_i \mathbf{p}_i\mathbf{p}_i'\right)\mathbf{q} = \sum_{i=2}^{r} \lambda_i(\mathbf{p}_i'\mathbf{q})^2$$

where λ_i and $\mathbf{p}_i$ are the ith root and a corresponding characteristic vector, respectively, of $\mathbf{XX}'$ and r is the rank of this matrix. Conclude, using $\mathbf{q}'\mathbf{q} = 1$,

(9.18)
$$\mathbf{q}'(\mathbf{XX}' - \lambda_1\mathbf{I})\mathbf{q} = \sum_{i=2}^{r} \lambda_i(\mathbf{p}_i'\mathbf{q})^2 - \lambda_1$$

Finally, prove that $(\mathbf{p}_2'\mathbf{q})^2 + \cdots + (\mathbf{p}_r'\mathbf{q})^2 \leq 1$, and use this to prove that the second-order condition is satisfied when the largest root λ_1 of $\mathbf{XX}'$ is a simple root. [Hint for $\sum (\mathbf{p}_i'\mathbf{q})^2 \leq 1$: run an LS regression of $\mathbf{q}$ on $\mathbf{p}_2, \ldots, \mathbf{p}_r$ along the lines of eqs. (9.12) to (9.14).]

9.3 Consider the matrix $\mathbf{X}'\mathbf{X}$ of (9.5) and suppose that the first variable is measured in a different unit such that $x_{\alpha 1}$ becomes $cx_{\alpha 1}$. Prove that, if c is sufficiently large, the new matrix $\mathbf{X}'\mathbf{X}$ satisfies approximately $(1/c)^2\mathbf{X}'\mathbf{X} \approx (\sum x_{\alpha 1}^2)\mathbf{i}_1\mathbf{i}_1'$, where $\mathbf{i}_1$ is the first column of the $K \times K$ unit matrix. Next prove the following statements on the basis of this approximation: the new $\mathbf{X}'\mathbf{X}$ has unit rank, its (only) positive root is $c^2 \sum x_{\alpha 1}^2$, and $\mathbf{i}_1$ is a corresponding characteristic vector. Finally, conclude $\mathbf{a}_1 \approx \mathbf{i}_1$ and $\mathbf{p}_1' \approx [cx_{11} \cdots cx_{n1}]$, in both cases apart from a normalization factor.

CHAPTER 2

STATISTICAL TOOLS: INFERENCE AND DISTRIBUTION THEORY

There are several excellent statistics textbooks at the elementary level, among which MOOD and GRAYBILL (1963) and HOGG and CRAIG (1965) should be mentioned. More advanced are CRAMÉR (1946) and the three-volume edition of KENDALL and STUART (1963, 1967, 1966). GRAYBILL (1961) gives a convenient general statistical introduction to the theory of linear statistical models.

All sections of this chapter are recommended for an introductory course with the exception of certain subsections of Sections 2.6 and 2.9, which are optional.

2.1 Univariate Distributions[A]

A random variable X is, by definition, subject to a probability distribution.[1] This distribution is usually either discrete or continuous.

Discrete Univariate Distributions

When X has a discrete distribution, it takes a (possibly infinite) number of values $x_1, x_2, \ldots$ with probabilities $p_1, p_2, \ldots$:

[1] An equivalent expression for "X is a random variable" is "X is stochastic." The word variate is frequently used as a synonym for random variable.

$$\text{(1.1)} \qquad P[X = x_i] = p_i \qquad i = 1, 2, \ldots$$

In words: the probability is p_i that X takes the value x_i. The probabilities are constrained to be nonnegative and to add up to 1:

$$\text{(1.2)} \qquad \begin{aligned} p_i &\geq 0 \text{ for each } i \\ \sum p_i &= 1 \text{ (sum over all } i) \end{aligned}$$

The *mean* or *expectation* of X is defined as the weighted average of all the values which it can take, the weights being the corresponding probabilities:

$$\text{(1.3)} \qquad \mathscr{E}X = \sum_i p_i x_i$$

The mean is a special case of

$$\text{(1.4)} \qquad \mu'_k = \mathscr{E}(X^k) = \sum_i p_i x_i^k \qquad k = 1, 2, \ldots$$

which is the kth *order moment around zero*. The addition "around zero" serves to avoid confusion with the kth order moment around the mean:

$$\text{(1.5)} \qquad \mu_k = \mathscr{E}[(X - \mathscr{E}X)^k] = \sum_i p_i (x_i - \mathscr{E}X)^k \qquad k = 1, 2, \ldots$$

On comparing (1.3) and (1.4) we find $\mathscr{E}X = \mu'_1$. Usually the prime and the subscript of μ'_1 are deleted: $\mathscr{E}X = \mu$ and $\mu_k = \sum_i p_i(x_i - \mu)^k$.

The second-order moment around the mean is the *variance* of X, indicated by var X. The notation σ^2 is also frequently used, σ (the positive square root of σ^2) being the *standard deviation* of X. We have

$$\begin{aligned} \operatorname{var} X &= \sum_i p_i (x_i - \mathscr{E}X)^2 \\ &= \sum_i p_i [x_i^2 + (\mathscr{E}X)^2 - 2x_i \mathscr{E}X] \\ &= \sum_i p_i x_i^2 + (\mathscr{E}X)^2 \sum_i p_i - 2(\mathscr{E}X) \sum_i p_i x_i \\ &= \sum_i p_i x_i^2 - (\mathscr{E}X)^2 \end{aligned}$$

and hence

$$\text{(1.6)} \qquad \operatorname{var} X = \mathscr{E}(X^2) - (\mathscr{E}X)^2$$

In words: the variance of a random variable is equal to the second moment around zero minus the square of the mean. Note that when X takes an infinite number of values, the mean and the variance do not necessarily exist.

Binomial and Poisson

An example of a discrete distribution is the *binomial distribution:*

(1.7) $$P[X = i] = \binom{n}{i} p^i (1-p)^{n-i} \qquad i = 0, 1, \ldots, n$$

where $0 < p < 1$. This distribution has the following mean and variance:[2]

(1.8) $$\mathscr{E}X = np \qquad \text{var } X = np(1-p)$$

This distribution can serve as a model for random experiments of the following type. Let the outcome be either success (S) or failure (F) and consider n independent trials of the experiment. In each case the probability of success is p and hence the probability of failure is $1 - p$. For $n = 3$ the sequence of outcomes may be success-success-failure (SSF), the probability of which is $p^2(1 - p)$. In this case there are two successes in $n = 3$ trials. But $p^2(1 - p)$ is not the probability of obtaining two successes in three trials, since this result is also obtained by the sequences SFS and FSS. As a whole there are thus $\binom{3}{2} = 3$ possibilities, each of which has probability $p^2(1 - p)$. Since these possibilities are mutually exclusive, the probability of obtaining two successes in three trials is $\binom{3}{2}p^2(1 - p)$. The left-hand side of (1.7) can thus be interpreted as the chance that the number of successes (X) is equal to i, and the right-hand side specifies this chance under the condition that the number of trials is n, that the probability of success is p for each trial, and that the trials are independent.

A second example of a discrete distribution is

(1.9) $$P[X = i] = \frac{e^{-\lambda}\lambda^i}{i!} \qquad i = 0, 1, 2, \ldots$$

This is the *Poisson distribution* with parameter $\lambda > 0$. Note that the set of values taken by the random variable consists of all nonnegative integers, so that their number is infinite. (Also note that $0!$ is defined as 1.) The mean and variance can be shown to be both equal to λ:

(1.10) $$\mathscr{E}X = \lambda \qquad \text{var } X = \lambda$$

Continuous Univariate Distributions

The right-hand sides of (1.7) and (1.9) are functions of i, which are known as *probability mass functions.* When the random variable X is continuous

[2] In this and the following sections a number of moments of distributions will be given without proof. They will be derived in Section 2.5.

rather than discrete, our starting point is the *probability density function* $f(\ )$:[3]

$$\text{(1.11)} \qquad P[x < X \le x + dx] = f(x)\, dx$$

The density function is constrained to take nonnegative values and its total integral is unity:

$$\text{(1.12)} \qquad f(x) \ge 0 \quad (-\infty < x < \infty) \qquad \int_{-\infty}^{\infty} f(x)\, dx = 1$$

This is analogous to (1.2). As a matter of fact, the continuous analysis is a straightforward extension of the discrete analysis, the probabilities p_i being replaced by the density function (multiplied by the differential dx) and sums by integrals. Examples are the moments:

$$\text{(1.13)} \qquad \begin{aligned} \mu_k' &= \mathscr{E}(X^k) = \int_{-\infty}^{\infty} x^k f(x)\, dx \\ \mu_k &= \mathscr{E}[(X - \mathscr{E}X)^k] = \int_{-\infty}^{\infty} (x - \mu)^k f(x)\, dx \qquad (\mu = \mu_1') \end{aligned}$$

The mean and the variance are thus

$$\text{(1.14)} \qquad \mathscr{E}X = \int_{-\infty}^{\infty} x f(x)\, dx \qquad \operatorname{var} X = \int_{-\infty}^{\infty} (x - \mathscr{E}X)^2 f(x)\, dx$$

where $\mathscr{E}X$, μ, and μ_1' are all different expressions for the same first moment around zero, while the same is true for var X and μ_2 with respect to the variance.

Another important concept is the *cumulated distribution function* $F(\ )$, which specifies the chance that the random variable is at most equal to some given value:

$$\text{(1.15)} \qquad F(x) = P[X \le x] = \int_{-\infty}^{x} f(\xi)\, d\xi$$

Obviously, this function satisfies the following conditions:

$$\text{(1.16)} \qquad F(-\infty) = 0 \qquad F(\infty) = 1 \qquad \frac{dF}{dx} \ge 0 \quad (-\infty < x < \infty)$$

where $F(-\infty)$ and $F(\infty)$ should be interpreted as the limit of $F(x)$ for x approaching $-\infty$ and ∞, respectively.

[3] We should mention here for the purist that, strictly speaking, the distribution function (1.15) comes first and the density function (1.11) is derived from it by differentiation. A different order of treatment is chosen here because of the similar roles of the density function and the probability mass function.

The Uniform Distribution and the Cauchy Distribution

A random variable is said to be uniformly distributed over the range $[a, b]$ if its density function is

$$f(x) = \frac{1}{b-a} \quad \text{if } a \leq x \leq b \qquad (1.17)$$
$$0 \quad \text{elsewhere}$$

The mean and variance of this distribution are

$$\mathscr{E}X = \frac{1}{2}(a+b) \qquad \text{var } X = \frac{1}{12}(b-a)^2 \qquad (1.18)$$

Another example is the *Cauchy distribution*, which has the density function

$$f(x) = \frac{1}{\pi(1+x^2)} \qquad (-\infty < x < \infty) \qquad (1.19)$$

To find the mean we consider the following integral:

$$\begin{aligned} \int_a^b xf(x)\,dx &= \frac{1}{\pi}\int_a^b \frac{x\,dx}{1+x^2} \qquad (1.20) \\ &= \frac{1}{2\pi}\int_{a^2}^{b^2} \frac{dy}{1+y} \qquad (y = x^2) \\ &= \frac{1}{2\pi}[\log_e(1+b^2) - \log_e(1+a^2)] \end{aligned}$$

The expression on the third line does not converge to a finite limit when a approaches $-\infty$ and b approaches ∞, so that the mean of a Cauchy distribution does not exist.[4] It is easily seen that if the expectation of X fails to exist, this must also hold for the expectation of a higher power of X than the first. This applies in particular to the variance, which is equal to the second moment minus the square of the first.

The Normal Distribution; Skewness and Kurtosis

The density function of the normal distribution is

$$f(x) = \frac{1}{\sigma\sqrt{2\pi}} \exp\left\{-\frac{1}{2}\frac{(x-\mu)^2}{\sigma^2}\right\} \qquad (-\infty < x < \infty) \qquad (1.21)$$

[4] One may define the mean in the principal-value sense [i.e., one takes the limit of the integral (1.20) for a approaching $-\infty$ and b approaching ∞ subject to the constraint $a = -b$]. However, this definition has the disadvantage that it invalidates the theorem according to which the expectation of a sum of random variables is equal to the sum of the expectations; see Section 2.4 below.

where exp $\{k\}$ stands for e^k, while μ and σ^2 are the mean and the variance, respectively, as the notation indicates. All odd-order moments around the mean are zero. The even-order moments are given by

$$\mu_{2k} = \frac{\sigma^{2k}}{2^k} \frac{(2k)!}{k!} \qquad k = 1, 2, \ldots \tag{1.22}$$

The zero value of the odd-order moments around the mean is a general characteristic of symmetric distributions: $f(\mu + x) \equiv f(\mu - x)$ where μ is the mean. This is easily verified for the third-order moment:

$$\begin{aligned} \mathscr{E}[(X - \mu)^3] &= \int_{-\infty}^{\infty} (x - \mu)^3 f(x)\, dx \\ &= \int_{-\infty}^{\mu} (x - \mu)^3 f(x)\, dx + \int_{\mu}^{\infty} (x - \mu)^3 f(x)\, dx \\ &= \int_{-\infty}^{0} y^3 f(\mu + y)\, dy + \int_{0}^{-\infty} (-z^3) f(\mu - z)(-dz) \end{aligned}$$

where $y = x - \mu$ and $z = \mu - x$. It is immediately seen that the two integrals in the last line cancel each other out if the distribution is symmetric, provided, of course, that the third moment exists.

The ratio of the third moment around the mean to the third power of the standard deviation,

$$\frac{\mu_3}{\sigma^3} = \frac{\mathscr{E}[(X - \mu)^3]}{(\operatorname{var} X)^{\frac{3}{2}}} \tag{1.23}$$

is frequently used as a measure for the degree of nonsymmetry (skewness) of a distribution. For distributions with a long tail in positive direction it takes positive values (see Figure 2.1); for those with a long tail in the opposite direction it takes a negative value. Note that the ratio (1.23) is a dimensionless quantity because μ_3 has the same dimension as that of X^3 and σ the same as X (and hence σ^3 the same as X^3). Another ratio is

$$\frac{\mu_4}{\sigma^4} = \frac{\mathscr{E}[(X - \mu)^4]}{(\operatorname{var} X)^2} \tag{1.24}$$

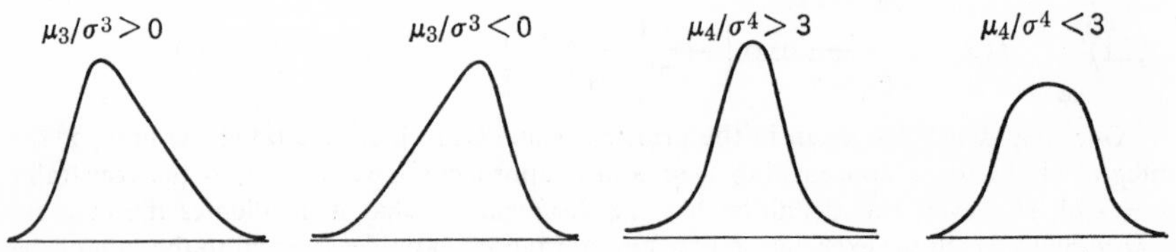

Fig. 2.1 Skewness and kurtosis.

which measures the kurtosis of the distribution. Its value is large when the distribution has long thick tails, which contribute more to the fourth moment than to the square of the second. Applying (1.22), we find $\mu_4/\sigma^4 = 3$ for the normal distribution, which is the "mesokurtic" value of the ratio (1.24).

Problems

1.1 (*Chebyshev's inequality*) For an arbitrary continuous distribution with finite variance σ^2, prove that the probability that the variate X deviates from the expectation μ by k times the standard deviation or more is at most equal to $1/k^2$:

$$\text{(1.25)} \qquad P[|X - \mu| \geq k\sigma] \leq \frac{1}{k^2} \qquad \text{for any} \quad k > 0$$

[*Hint.* Write $f(\ )$ for the density function and prove

$$\sigma^2 = \int_{-\infty}^{\infty} (x - \mu)^2 f(x)\, dx \geq \int_{-\infty}^{\mu-k\sigma} (x - \mu)^2 f(x)\, dx + \int_{\mu+k\sigma}^{\infty} (x - \mu)^2 f(x)\, dx$$

Next prove that the first integral after the $\geq$ sign is at least equal to $k^2\sigma^2 P[X \leq \mu - k\sigma]$, using the fact that $x \leq \mu - k\sigma$ and hence that $|x - \mu| \geq k\sigma$, and prove a similar result for the last integral.]

1.2 (*Continuation*) Prove the same result along similar lines for a discrete distribution with finite variance.

1.3 The third moment about the mean of the binomial distribution (1.7) is $\mu_3 = npq(q - p)$, where $q = 1 - p$. Evaluate the skewness coefficient (1.23) for this case, in particular its sign and its behavior when the number of trials (n) increases.

2.2 Multivariate Distributions[A]

Discrete Multivariate Distributions

Suppose we have a pair of random variables, X and Y, where X takes the values $x_1, x_2, \ldots$ and Y the values $y_1, y_2, \ldots$ in such a way that

$$\text{(2.1)} \qquad P[X = x_i, Y = y_j] = p_{ij}$$

This is a discrete bivariate distribution, the probabilities of which satisfy

$$\text{(2.2)} \qquad \begin{aligned} p_{ij} &\geq 0 && \text{for each pair } (i, j) \\ \sum_i \sum_j p_{ij} &= 1 && \text{(sum over all } i \text{ and } j) \end{aligned}$$

Such a bivariate distribution has two *marginal distributions*:

$$\text{(2.3)}\qquad \begin{aligned} \mathrm{P}[X = x_i] &= \sum_j \mathrm{P}[X = x_i,\, Y = y_j] = \sum_j p_{ij} = p_{i.} \quad \text{say} \\ \mathrm{P}[Y = y_j] &= \sum_i \mathrm{P}[X = x_i,\, Y = y_j] = \sum_i p_{ij} = p_{.j} \quad \text{say} \end{aligned}$$

The means and variances of the two random variables are those of the corresponding marginal distributions:

$$\text{(2.4)}\qquad \begin{aligned} \mathscr{E}X &= \sum_i p_{i.}x_i \qquad & \operatorname{var} X &= \sum_i p_{i.}(x_i - \mathscr{E}X)^2 \\ \mathscr{E}Y &= \sum_j p_{.j}y_j \qquad & \operatorname{var} Y &= \sum_j p_{.j}(y_j - \mathscr{E}Y)^2 \end{aligned}$$

There is also the *covariance*, which is a truly bivariate concept:

$$\text{(2.5)}\qquad \begin{aligned} \operatorname{cov}(X, Y) &= \sum_i \sum_j p_{ij}(x_i - \mathscr{E}X)(y_j - \mathscr{E}Y) \\ &= \mathscr{E}[(X - \mathscr{E}X)(Y - \mathscr{E}Y)] \end{aligned}$$

The covariance plays an important role in the analysis of linear combinations of random variables. This will be pursued in Section 2.4, where it will also be shown (Problem 4.2) that the covariance cannot exceed the geometric mean of the two variances in absolute value:

$$\text{(2.6)}\qquad -1 \le \frac{\operatorname{cov}(X, Y)}{\sqrt{\operatorname{var} X \operatorname{var} Y}} \le 1$$

The ratio between the two inequality signs is known as the correlation coefficient of the two random variables; it is usually indicated by ρ with appropriate subscripts (such as ρ_{XY}).

The extension to a larger number of variates is straightforward; it is a matter of adding a subscript to the probability p for each additional variable:

$$\mathrm{P}[X = x_i,\, Y = y_j,\, Z = z_k] = p_{ijk}$$

The Multinomial Distribution

An example of a discrete multivariate distribution is the multinomial distribution. It arises in the same experimental situation as that of the binomial distribution except that there are now k possible outcomes rather than two. Let the jth possibility have probability p_j, $j = 1, \ldots, k$, in each of the n trials, where $p_1 + p_2 + \cdots + p_k = 1$. Suppose that the trials are independent. Write X_j for the number of cases in which the jth possibility is realized; then

$$\text{(2.7)}\qquad \mathrm{P}[X_1 = i_1,\, X_2 = i_2, \ldots, X_k = i_k] = \frac{n!}{i_1!\, i_2! \cdots i_k!}\, p_1^{i_1} p_2^{i_2} \cdots p_k^{i_k}$$

where

$$\sum_{j=1}^{k} i_j = n$$

which, of course, reduces to the binomial distribution for $k = 2$. The means, variances, and covariances are

$$(2.8) \qquad \begin{aligned} \mathscr{E}X_j = np_j \qquad \text{var } X_j = np_j(1 - p_j) \qquad j = 1, \ldots, k \\ \text{cov }(X_j, X_h) = -np_jp_h \qquad j \neq h \end{aligned}$$

The Covariance Matrix

These first- and second-moment results can be written in elegant matrix form. We introduce a column vector $\mathbf{x}$ consisting of the k random variables $X_1, \ldots, X_k$. The expectation $\mathscr{E}\mathbf{x}$ is defined as the column vector of expectations $\mathscr{E}X_1, \ldots, \mathscr{E}X_k$. We postmultiply the random vector measured as a deviation from its expectation, $\mathbf{x} - \mathscr{E}\mathbf{x}$, by its own transpose:

$$(\mathbf{x} - \mathscr{E}\mathbf{x})(\mathbf{x} - \mathscr{E}\mathbf{x})' = \begin{bmatrix} X_1 - \mathscr{E}X_1 \\ X_2 - \mathscr{E}X_2 \\ \cdot \\ \cdot \\ \cdot \\ X_k - \mathscr{E}X_k \end{bmatrix} [X_1 - \mathscr{E}X_1 \quad X_2 - \mathscr{E}X_2 \cdots X_k - \mathscr{E}X_k]$$

We then take the expectation of each element of the product matrix, so that we obtain in the first row

$$\mathscr{E}[(X_1 - \mathscr{E}X_1)^2] = \text{var } X_1 \qquad \mathscr{E}[(X_1 - \mathscr{E}X_1)(X_2 - \mathscr{E}X_2)] = \text{cov }(X_1, X_2) \cdots$$

and, in the second row,

$$\mathscr{E}[(X_2 - \mathscr{E}X_2)(X_1 - \mathscr{E}X_1)] = \text{cov }(X_2, X_1) \qquad \mathscr{E}[(X_2 - \mathscr{E}X_2)^2] = \text{var } X_2 \cdots$$

and so on. If we define the expectation of a random matrix as the matrix of the expectations of the separate random elements, we obtain

(2.9)

$$\mathscr{E}[(\mathbf{x} - \mathscr{E}\mathbf{x})(\mathbf{x} - \mathscr{E}\mathbf{x})'] = \begin{bmatrix} \text{var } X_1 & \text{cov }(X_1, X_2) & \cdots & \text{cov }(X_1, X_k) \\ \text{cov }(X_2, X_1) & \text{var } X_2 & \cdots & \text{cov }(X_2, X_k) \\ \cdot & \cdot & & \cdot \\ \cdot & \cdot & & \cdot \\ \cdot & \cdot & & \cdot \\ \text{cov }(X_k, X_1) & \text{cov }(X_k, X_2) & \cdots & \text{var } X_k \end{bmatrix}$$

This is the variance-covariance matrix (*covariance matrix*, for short) of the random vector **x**. It is frequently indicated as $\mathscr{V}(\mathbf{x})$. Note that the variances are all on the diagonal and that the matrix is symmetric. The means, variances, and covariances of (2.8) can now be written in simple matrix form if we introduce a diagonal $k \times k$ matrix of probabilities and a k-element column vector consisting of units:

$$\text{(2.10)} \qquad \mathbf{P} = \begin{bmatrix} p_1 & 0 & \cdots & 0 \\ 0 & p_2 & \cdots & 0 \\ \cdot & \cdot & & \cdot \\ \cdot & \cdot & & \cdot \\ \cdot & \cdot & & \cdot \\ 0 & 0 & \cdots & p_k \end{bmatrix} \qquad \boldsymbol{\iota} = \begin{bmatrix} 1 \\ 1 \\ \cdot \\ \cdot \\ \cdot \\ 1 \end{bmatrix}$$

so that (2.8) amounts to

$$\text{(2.11)} \qquad \mathscr{E}\mathbf{x} = n\mathbf{P}\boldsymbol{\iota} \qquad \mathscr{V}(x) = n(\mathbf{P} - \mathbf{P}\boldsymbol{\iota}\boldsymbol{\iota}'\mathbf{P})$$

Continuous Multivariate Distributions

The case of continuous multivariate distributions is completely analogous. Our starting point is a random pair (X, Y) whose joint density function is defined as follows:

$$\text{(2.12)} \qquad \mathrm{P}[x < X \leq x + dx, y < Y \leq y + dy] = f(x, y)\, dx\, dy$$

This density function satisfies

$$\text{(2.13)} \qquad f(x, y) \geq 0 \quad (-\infty < x, y < \infty) \qquad \int_{-\infty}^{\infty}\int_{-\infty}^{\infty} f(x, y)\, dx\, dy = 1$$

and there are two marginal density functions:

$$\text{(2.14)} \qquad \begin{aligned} \mathrm{P}[x < X \leq x + dx] &= dx \int_{-\infty}^{\infty} f(x, y)\, dy = f_1(x)\, dx \quad \text{say} \\ \mathrm{P}[y < Y \leq y + dy] &= dy \int_{-\infty}^{\infty} f(x, y)\, dx = f_2(y)\, dy \quad \text{say} \end{aligned}$$

The means and variances are

$$\text{(2.15)} \qquad \begin{aligned} \mathscr{E}X &= \int_{-\infty}^{\infty} x f_1(x)\, dx \qquad \operatorname{var} X = \int_{-\infty}^{\infty} (x - \mathscr{E}X)^2 f_1(x)\, dx \\ \mathscr{E}Y &= \int_{-\infty}^{\infty} y f_2(y)\, dy \qquad \operatorname{var} Y = \int_{-\infty}^{\infty} (y - \mathscr{E}Y)^2 f_2(y)\, dy \end{aligned}$$

and the covariance is

$$\text{(2.16)} \qquad \operatorname{cov}(X, Y) = \int_{-\infty}^{\infty}\int_{-\infty}^{\infty} (x - \mathscr{E}X)(y - \mathscr{E}Y) f(x, y)\, dx\, dy$$

In addition, there is the cumulated distribution function of the joint distribution:

$$F(x, y) = \mathrm{P}[X \leq x, Y \leq y] = \int_{-\infty}^{x}\int_{-\infty}^{y} f(\xi, \eta)\, d\xi\, d\eta \tag{2.17}$$

as well as those of the marginal distributions:

$$\begin{aligned} F_1(x) &= \int_{-\infty}^{x} f_1(\xi)\, d\xi = F(x, \infty) \\ F_2(y) &= \int_{-\infty}^{y} f_2(\eta)\, d\eta = F(\infty, y) \end{aligned} \tag{2.18}$$

The Multinormal Distribution

As an example we take the multivariate normal distribution (also called multinormal distribution), the density function of which is

$$f(\mathbf{x}) = \frac{1}{(2\pi)^{k/2}\,|\boldsymbol{\Sigma}|^{\frac{1}{2}}} \exp\left\{-\frac{1}{2}(\mathbf{x} - \boldsymbol{\mu})'\,\boldsymbol{\Sigma}^{-1}\,(\mathbf{x} - \boldsymbol{\mu})\right\} \tag{2.19}$$

where $\mathbf{x}$ is a k-element column vector, $\boldsymbol{\mu}$ the column vector of means, $\boldsymbol{\Sigma}$ the covariance matrix, and $|\boldsymbol{\Sigma}|$ its determinant value:

$$\mathscr{E}\mathbf{x} = \boldsymbol{\mu} \qquad \mathscr{V}(\mathbf{x}) = \boldsymbol{\Sigma} \tag{2.20}$$

It is easily verified that (2.19) reduces to the one-dimensional normal density function (1.21) in the case $k = 1$. Also note that the exponent in (2.19) is a quadratic form whose matrix is equal to a multiple $-\frac{1}{2}$ of the inverse of the covariance matrix. A covariance matrix is necessarily positive semidefinite. Hence it should be positive definite in (2.19); otherwise $\boldsymbol{\Sigma}^{-1}$ does not exist. A proof of the semidefiniteness will be given in Section 2.4.

Problems

2.1 Prove that the density function of the bivariate normal distribution with means μ_1 and μ_2, variances σ_1^2 and σ_2^2, and covariance $\rho\sigma_1\sigma_2$ is of the form $e^{-A}/2\pi\sigma_1\sigma_2\sqrt{1-\rho^2}$, where

(2.21)

$$A = \frac{1}{2(1-\rho^2)}\left[\frac{(x_1-\mu_1)^2}{\sigma_1^2} + \frac{(x_2-\mu_2)^2}{\sigma_2^2} - \frac{2\rho(x_1-\mu_1)(x_2-\mu_2)}{\sigma_1\sigma_2}\right]$$

2.2 Consider the bivariate uniform distribution with the following density function:

$$(2.22)\quad f(x_1, x_2) = \begin{cases} \dfrac{1}{(b_1 - a_1)(b_2 - a_2)} & \text{if} \quad a_1 \leq x_1 \leq b_1 \\ & \text{and} \quad a_2 \leq x_2 \leq b_2 \\ 0 & \text{elsewhere} \end{cases}$$

Prove that the covariance is zero.

2.3 Conditional Distributions and Stochastic Independence[A]

Discrete Conditional Distributions

We return to the discrete bivariate distribution (2.1) and introduce the conditional probability that $X = x_i$, given $Y = y_j$:

$$\mathrm{P}[X = x_i,\ Y = y_j] = \mathrm{P}[X = x_i \mid Y = y_j]\,\mathrm{P}[Y = y_j]$$

the conditional probability just mentioned being the one immediately after the equality sign. Assuming that $Y = y_j$ holds true with positive probability ($p_{\cdot j} > 0$), we obtain

$$(3.1)\qquad \mathrm{P}[X = x_i \mid Y = y_j] = \frac{\mathrm{P}[X = x_i,\ Y = y_j]}{\mathrm{P}[Y = y_j]} = \frac{p_{ij}}{p_{\cdot j}}$$

Therefore, if $Y = y_j$, then X takes the values $x_1, x_2, \ldots$ with the probabilities $p_{1j}/p_{\cdot j}, p_{2j}/p_{\cdot j}, \ldots$. The mean of this distribution is the conditional expectation of X, given $Y = y_j$:

$$(3.2)\qquad \mathscr{E}(X \mid Y = y_j) = \frac{1}{p_{\cdot j}} \sum_i p_{ij} x_i$$

Notice that the mean of these conditional means over the Y distribution is equal to the unconditional mean $\mathscr{E}X$:

$$(3.3)\qquad \sum_j p_{\cdot j}\,\mathscr{E}(X \mid Y = y_j) = \sum_i \sum_j p_{ij} x_i = \sum_i p_{i\cdot} x_i = \mathscr{E}X$$

In the same way there is a variance of the conditional distribution of X, given $Y = y_j$, and so on. We also have the conditional distribution of Y, given $X = x_i$, the probabilities of which are of the following form:

$$(3.4)\qquad \mathrm{P}[Y = y_j \mid X = x_i] = \frac{\mathrm{P}[X = x_i,\ Y = y_j]}{\mathrm{P}[X = x_i]} = \frac{p_{ij}}{p_{i\cdot}} \qquad (p_{i\cdot} > 0)$$

and for which similar measures (mean, variance, etc.) can be derived.

Stochastic Independence

An important special case is that of stochastic independence of X and Y:

$$p_{ij} = p_{i.}\, p_{.j} \qquad \text{for all pairs } (i, j) \tag{3.5}$$

We then have $p_{ij}/p_{.j} = p_{i.}$ in (3.1), so that the conditional distribution of X, given $Y = y_j$ (any j for which $p_{.j} > 0$), coincides with the marginal distribution of X. We also have $p_{ij}/p_{i.} = p_{.j}$ in (3.4), so that the conditional distribution of Y, given $X = x_i$ (any i for which $p_{i.} > 0$), coincides with the marginal distribution of Y. Clearly, in the case of stochastic independence, any knowledge about X (such as $X = x_i$) is worthless for the formulation of probability statements on Y and vice versa. It is also easily verified that the two random variables then have zero covariance ("are uncorrelated"):

$$\sum_i \sum_j p_{ij}(x_i - \mathscr{E}X)(y_j - \mathscr{E}Y) = \sum_i p_{i.}(x_i - \mathscr{E}X) \sum_j p_{.j}(y_j - \mathscr{E}Y)$$

$$= (\mathscr{E}X - \mathscr{E}X)(\mathscr{E}Y - \mathscr{E}Y) = 0$$

In general the converse is not true: if X and Y are uncorrelated, they need not be independent.

Note further that the expectation of the product XY is equal to the product of the expectations if X and Y are independent:[5]

$$\mathscr{E}(XY) = \sum_i \sum_j p_{ij} x_i y_j = \sum_i p_{i.} x_i \sum_j p_{.j} y_j = \mathscr{E}X \mathscr{E}Y \tag{3.6}$$

Furthermore, if X and Y are independent, then any function of X such as X^2 is independent of any function of Y such as e^Y. Combining this with (3.6) we conclude that $\mathscr{E}(X^2 e^Y) = \mathscr{E}(X^2)\mathscr{E}(e^Y)$ if X and Y are indeed independent (and if the expectations exist).

Extension to Continuous Distributions

Conditional distributions and stochastic independence are defined similarly in the case of continuous distributions. We return to (2.12) and (2.14) and define:

$$\text{(3.7)} \quad \text{P}[x < X \le x + dx \mid Y = y]$$

$$= \frac{\text{P}[x < X \le x + dx,\, y < Y \le y + dy]}{\text{P}[y < Y \le y + dy]}$$

$$= \frac{f(x, y)}{f_2(y)}\, dx \qquad \text{provided} \qquad f_2(y) > 0$$

[5] In fact, uncorrelated (rather than independent) is sufficient for $\mathscr{E}(XY) = \mathscr{E}X\mathscr{E}Y$ (Problem 4.4 at the end of the next section).

Thus the ratio $f(x, y)/f_2(y)$ is the conditional density function of X given $Y = y$. In the same way $f(x, y)/f_1(x)$ is the conditional density function of Y given $X = x$. Stochastic independence is defined in terms of the following identity in x and y:

$$f(x, y) \equiv f_1(x)f_2(y) \tag{3.8}$$

and it is easily verified that the covariance (2.16) vanishes if (3.8) is true.

When we have a vector of an arbitrary number of random variables, these are said to be stochastically independent if the joint density function of the vector is identically equal to the product of all one-dimensional marginal density functions. [In the case of a discrete distribution: $p_{ijk} = p_{i..}p_{.j.}p_{..k}$ for all triples (i, j, k), where $p_{i..} = \sum_j \sum_k p_{ijk}$, $p_{.j.} = \sum_i \sum_k p_{ijk}$, $p_{..k} = \sum_i \sum_j p_{ijk}$, and similarly when there are four or more random variables.] All covariances vanish when the elements of a random vector are stochastically independent, so that the covariance matrix is then diagonal.

Independence in the Multinormal Case

Consider as an example the density function (2.19) of the multinormal distribution. If $\boldsymbol{\Sigma}$ is diagonal, then $|\boldsymbol{\Sigma}| = \sigma_1^2\sigma_2^2 \cdots \sigma_k^2$, where σ_i^2 is the variance of the ith component of $\mathbf{x}$. It is easily verified that the multivariate density function can then be written in the following form:

$$f(\mathbf{x}) = \prod_{i=1}^{k} \frac{1}{\sigma_i\sqrt{2\pi}} \exp\left\{-\frac{1}{2}\frac{(x_i - \mu_i)^2}{\sigma_i^2}\right\} \tag{3.9}$$

where x_i and μ_i are the ith elements of $\mathbf{x}$ and $\boldsymbol{\mu}$, respectively. The multivariate density function is thus equal to the product of k one-dimensional normal density functions. We conclude that in the case of normality, zero covariances guarantee stochastic independence. Again note that this does not hold for arbitrary distributions.

Let the normal vector $\mathbf{x}$ be partitioned as $[\mathbf{x}_1' \quad \mathbf{x}_2']'$ and write $\boldsymbol{\mu}_1$ and $\boldsymbol{\Sigma}_1$ for the mean vector and the covariance matrix, respectively, of $\mathbf{x}_1$ and similarly $\boldsymbol{\mu}_2$ and $\boldsymbol{\Sigma}_2$ for those of $\mathbf{x}_2$. Suppose that each element of $\mathbf{x}_1$ is uncorrelated with each element of $\mathbf{x}_2$. The covariance matrix $\boldsymbol{\Sigma}$ is then block-diagonal:

$$\boldsymbol{\Sigma} = \begin{bmatrix} \boldsymbol{\Sigma}_1 & \mathbf{0} \\ \mathbf{0} & \boldsymbol{\Sigma}_2 \end{bmatrix} \tag{3.10}$$

and the joint density function can be written as follows:

$$f(\mathbf{x}) = \prod_{h=1}^{2} \frac{1}{|\boldsymbol{\Sigma}_h|^{\frac{1}{2}}(2\pi)^{\frac{1}{2}k_h}} \exp\left\{-\frac{1}{2}(\mathbf{x}_h - \boldsymbol{\mu}_h)'\boldsymbol{\Sigma}_h^{-1}(\mathbf{x}_h - \boldsymbol{\mu}_h)\right\} \tag{3.11}$$

where k_1 and k_2 are the numbers of elements of $\mathbf{x}_1$ and $\mathbf{x}_2$, respectively ($k_1 + k_2 = k$). The k-dimensional density function is thus equal to the product of the density functions of $\mathbf{x}_1$ and $\mathbf{x}_2$, in which case these two *sub-vectors* are said to be stochastically independent. Of course, each element of $\mathbf{x}_1$ is then independent of each element of $\mathbf{x}_2$.

Problems

3.1 Prove that the bivariate uniform distribution of Problem 2.2 is characterized by stochastic independence.

3.2 Consider a random pair (X, Y) which takes the values (0, 1), (0, −1) and (2, 0) with probability $\frac{1}{3}$ each. Prove that X and Y have zero covariance (are uncorrelated) but that they are not stochastically independent.

2.4 The Algebra of Expectations[A]

Let (X, Y) be a random pair whose joint density function is given by (2.12). Consider an arbitrary linear combination, $\alpha X + \beta Y$, where α and β are fixed (nonstochastic) coefficients. Its expectation is

$$\begin{aligned}\mathscr{E}(\alpha X + \beta Y) &= \int_{-\infty}^{\infty}\int_{-\infty}^{\infty} (\alpha x + \beta y) f(x, y)\, dx\, dy \\ &= \alpha \int_{-\infty}^{\infty}\int_{-\infty}^{\infty} x f(x, y)\, dx\, dy + \beta \int_{-\infty}^{\infty}\int_{-\infty}^{\infty} y f(x, y)\, dx\, dy \\ &= \alpha \int_{-\infty}^{\infty} x f_1(x)\, dx + \beta \int_{-\infty}^{\infty} y f_2(y)\, dy \\ &= \alpha \mathscr{E} X + \beta \mathscr{E} Y\end{aligned}$$

We obtain the same result when the distribution of (X, Y) is discrete in accordance with (2.1):

$$\begin{aligned}\mathscr{E}(\alpha X + \beta Y) &= \sum_i \sum_j p_{ij}(\alpha x_i + \beta y_j) \\ &= \alpha \sum_i p_{i.} x_i + \beta \sum_j p_{.j} y_j \\ &= \alpha \mathscr{E} X + \beta \mathscr{E} Y\end{aligned}$$

More generally, a linear combination of random variables has an expectation which is equal to the same linear combination of the expectations of these variables:

$$\mathscr{E}(\mathbf{a}'\mathbf{x}) = \mathbf{a}'\mathscr{E}\mathbf{x} \tag{4.1}$$

where $\mathbf{x}$ is a column vector of random variables and $\mathbf{a}$ is a column vector of fixed coefficients. Of course, the proviso is that each element of $\mathbf{x}$ should have a finite expectation.

The same technique can be used to find the variance of $\mathbf{a}'\mathbf{x}$:

$$\begin{aligned}\text{(4.2)} \qquad \operatorname{var} \mathbf{a}'\mathbf{x} &= \mathscr{E}[(\mathbf{a}'\mathbf{x} - \mathbf{a}'\mathscr{E}\mathbf{x})^2] \\ &= \mathscr{E}[\mathbf{a}'(\mathbf{x} - \mathscr{E}\mathbf{x})(\mathbf{x} - \mathscr{E}\mathbf{x})'\mathbf{a}] \\ &= \mathbf{a}'\mathscr{E}[(\mathbf{x} - \mathscr{E}\mathbf{x})(\mathbf{x} - \mathscr{E}\mathbf{x})']\mathbf{a} \\ &= \mathbf{a}'\mathbf{V}\mathbf{a}\end{aligned}$$

where

$$\text{(4.3)} \qquad \mathbf{V} = \mathscr{E}[(\mathbf{x} - \mathscr{E}\mathbf{x})(\mathbf{x} - \mathscr{E}\mathbf{x})']$$

is the covariance matrix of $\mathbf{x}$. Notice that the second equality sign in (4.2) is based on the fact that $\mathbf{a}'\mathbf{x} - \mathbf{a}'\mathscr{E}\mathbf{x}$ is a scalar and, hence, equal to its own transpose. Also note that the third equality sign is based on the rule that the expectation of a linear combination of random variables is equal to the same combination of the expectations:

$$\mathscr{E}\left[\sum_i \sum_j a_i(x_i - \mathscr{E}x_i)(x_j - \mathscr{E}x_j)a_j\right] = \sum_i \sum_j a_i \mathscr{E}[(x_i - \mathscr{E}x_i)(x_j - \mathscr{E}x_j)]a_j$$

where the products $(x_i - \mathscr{E}x_i)(x_j - \mathscr{E}x_j)$ are the relevant random variables, x_i and a_i being the ith elements of $\mathbf{x}$ and $\mathbf{a}$, respectively.

The Covariance Matrix of Any Random Vector with Finite Variances Is Positive Semidefinite

The result (4.2) shows that the variance of a linear combination of random variables is equal to a quadratic form whose matrix is the covariance matrix of these variables and whose vector is the coefficient vector of the linear combination. (Again, the proviso is that the variances and covariances should be finite.) Since a variance is never negative, it follows that each covariance matrix must be positive semidefinite. A covariance matrix $\mathbf{V}$ is positive definite unless there exists an $\mathbf{a} \neq \mathbf{0}$ such that $\mathbf{a}'\mathbf{V}\mathbf{a} = 0$, which in view of (4.2) means that the variance of $\mathbf{a}'\mathbf{x}$ vanishes. Since a variance is defined as a weighted average with positive weights of the squares of the deviations from the expectation, the variance of $\mathbf{a}'\mathbf{x}$ vanishes if and only if $\mathbf{a}'\mathbf{x}$ equals $\mathbf{a}'\mathscr{E}\mathbf{x}$ with probability 1. The elements of the random vector $\mathbf{x}$ are said to be *linearly dependent* if an $\mathbf{a} \neq \mathbf{0}$ exists such that $\mathbf{a}'\mathbf{x}$ is a fixed number, and the covariance matrix of $\mathbf{x}$ is then singular (if $\mathbf{x}$ has finite variances—otherwise the covariance matrix is not defined). The multinomial distribution is an example. If we postmultiply the covariance matrix of (2.11) by $\boldsymbol{\iota}$, we obtain a zero column: $n\mathbf{P}\boldsymbol{\iota} - n\mathbf{P}\boldsymbol{\iota}(\boldsymbol{\iota}'\mathbf{P}\boldsymbol{\iota}) = \mathbf{0}$, since $\boldsymbol{\iota}'\mathbf{P}\boldsymbol{\iota}$ is the sum of all k probabilities and hence equal to unity. The random variables $X_1, \ldots, X_k$ of the multinomial distribution (2.7) must therefore be linearly dependent; indeed, they add up to n (the number of trials) with probability 1. It is also easily verified that the inequalities in (2.6) follow from the positive semidefiniteness of the covariance matrix; see Problem 4.2.

Problems

4.1 Describe in words the difference between the linear dependence of a set of random variables and the linear dependence of a set of vectors whose elements are fixed (nonstochastic) numbers. Also prove that if a set of random variables is linearly dependent and if they have finite variances, their covariance matrix consists of rows (and columns) that are linearly dependent in the second sense.

4.2 Prove inequality (2.6) by means of the nonnegativity of the variances of $X/\sigma_1 + Y/\sigma_2$ and of $X/\sigma_1 - Y/\sigma_2$, where σ_1 and σ_2 are the standard deviations of X and Y, respectively.

4.3 Prove $\text{cov}(X, Y) = \mathscr{E}[(X - \mathscr{E}X)Y] = \mathscr{E}[X(Y - \mathscr{E}Y)]$ when X and Y have finite variances. Conclude that when the covariance is computed as the expectation of the product of two random variables, it is sufficient to measure only one of them as a deviation from its mean.

4.4 Prove $\mathscr{E}(XY) = \mathscr{E}X\mathscr{E}Y + \text{cov}(X, Y)$ and conclude that $\mathscr{E}(XY) = \mathscr{E}X\mathscr{E}Y$ when X and Y are uncorrelated.

2.5 The Moment-Generating Function[A]

The moment-generating function of a random variable X is defined as

$$(5.1)\quad M_X(t) = \mathscr{E}(e^{tX}) = \sum_i p_i e^{tx_i} \qquad \text{if the distribution is discrete}$$

$$\int_{-\infty}^{\infty} e^{tx} f(x)\,dx \qquad \text{if the distribution is continuous}$$

Thus the moment-generating function is indeed a function, that of the variable t; specifically, it is equal to the expectation of the exponent of a multiple t of the random variable.[6] If we expand this exponent we obtain

$$(5.2)\qquad M_X(t) = \mathscr{E}\left[1 + tX + \frac{(tX)^2}{2!} + \cdots + \frac{(tX)^k}{k!} + \cdots\right]$$

$$= 1 + (\mathscr{E}X)t + \mathscr{E}(X^2)\frac{t^2}{2!} + \cdots + \mathscr{E}(X^k)\frac{t^k}{k!} + \cdots$$

[6] In more advanced treatments the moment-generating function is usually replaced by the *characteristic function*, which is defined as the expectation of the exponent of itX, where $i = \sqrt{-1}$ is the imaginary unit. This has the advantage that no problems of convergence of integrals arise, and, in fact, we shall use characteristic rather than moment-generating functions in Chapter 8 on asymptotic distribution theory. Here the simpler variant is preferred, but the reader should keep in mind that for certain distributions the moment-generating function is not defined for every value of t.

which shows that the kth order moment around zero of the random variable can be derived as the coefficient of $t^k/k!$ in the expansion of the moment-generating function (hence the name of this function). Now consider the first two derivatives of $M_X(t)$ as specified on the second line of (5.2):

$$\frac{d}{dt}M_X(t) = \mathscr{E}X + \mathscr{E}(X^2)t + \cdots + \mathscr{E}(X^k)\frac{t^{k-1}}{(k-1)!} + \cdots$$

$$\frac{d^2}{dt^2}M_X(t) = \mathscr{E}(X^2) + \mathscr{E}(X^3)t + \cdots + \mathscr{E}(X^k)\frac{t^{k-2}}{(k-2)!} + \cdots$$

Clearly the kth order moment around zero is also equal to the kth order derivative of the moment-generating function evaluated at $t = 0$. So there are two ways of using the moment-generating function to obtain the moments of a distribution.

Application to the Uniform Distribution

For the uniform distribution with density function (1.17) we have the following moment-generating function:

$$M_X(t) = \int_a^b \frac{e^{tx}}{b-a}\,dx = \frac{e^{bt} - e^{at}}{(b-a)t} \tag{5.3}$$

Expansion gives

$$\frac{1 + bt + \frac{1}{2}b^2t^2 + \frac{1}{6}b^3t^3 + \cdots - \left(1 + at + \frac{1}{2}a^2t^2 + \frac{1}{6}a^3t^3 + \cdots\right)}{(b-a)t}$$

$$= 1 + \frac{(b^2 - a^2)t^2}{2(b-a)t} + \frac{(b^3 - a^3)t^3}{6(b-a)t} + \cdots$$

$$= 1 + \frac{1}{2}(a+b)t + \frac{1}{3}(a^2 + ab + b^2)\frac{t^2}{2!} + \cdots$$

Hence the mean is $\frac{1}{2}(a + b)$ in accordance with (1.18). The coefficient of $t^2/2!$ is the second moment around zero. We subtract the square of the mean to find the variance:

$$\frac{1}{3}(a^2 + ab + b^2) - \left[\frac{1}{2}(a+b)\right]^2 = \frac{1}{12}(b-a)^2$$

which is in accordance with the variance of (1.18).

Application to the Univariate Normal Distribution

For the normal distribution (1.21) we have

$$M_X(t) = \frac{1}{\sigma\sqrt{2\pi}} \int_{-\infty}^{\infty} e^{tx} \exp\left\{-\frac{1}{2}\frac{(x-\mu)^2}{\sigma^2}\right\} dx$$

$$= \frac{1}{\sigma\sqrt{2\pi}} \int_{-\infty}^{\infty} \exp\left\{tx - \frac{1}{2}\frac{(x-\mu)^2}{\sigma^2}\right\} dx$$

The expression in curled brackets on the second line can be written as follows:

$$tx - \frac{1}{2}\frac{(x-\mu)^2}{\sigma^2} = -\frac{1}{2}\frac{(x-\mu)^2 - 2\sigma^2 tx}{\sigma^2}$$

$$= -\frac{1}{2}\frac{(x-\mu-\sigma^2 t)^2 - 2\mu\sigma^2 t - \sigma^4 t^2}{\sigma^2}$$

$$= -\frac{1}{2}\frac{(x-\mu-\sigma^2 t)^2}{\sigma^2} + \mu t + \frac{1}{2}\sigma^2 t^2$$

so that the moment-generating function of the normal distribution is

$$(5.4)\quad M_X(t) = \exp\left\{\mu t + \frac{1}{2}\sigma^2 t^2\right\} \frac{1}{\sigma\sqrt{2\pi}} \int_{-\infty}^{\infty} \exp\left\{-\frac{1}{2}\frac{(x-\mu-\sigma^2 t)^2}{\sigma^2}\right\} dx$$

$$= \exp\left\{\mu t + \frac{1}{2}\sigma^2 t^2\right\}$$

where the second equality sign is based on the fact that the multiple $1/\sigma\sqrt{2\pi}$ of the integral on the first line is equal to the total area below the normal density curve with mean $\mu + \sigma^2 t$ and variance σ^2, and hence equal to 1.

If we expand (5.4) we obtain

$$1 + \left(\mu t + \frac{1}{2}\sigma^2 t^2\right) + \frac{1}{2}\left(\mu t + \frac{1}{2}\sigma^2 t^2\right)^2 + \cdots = 1 + \mu t + (\sigma^2 + \mu^2)\frac{t^2}{2!} + \cdots$$

so that μ is indeed the mean, $\sigma^2 + \mu^2$ the second moment around zero, and hence σ^2 the variance. To verify the moments around the mean given in (1.22) we imagine that X is measured as a deviation from the mean. The new variable $X - \mu$ has the same normal distribution except that its mean is zero, so that the moment-generating function is simplified to

$$e^{\frac{1}{2}\sigma^2t^2} = 1 + \frac{1}{2}\sigma^2t^2 + \frac{1}{2!}\left(\frac{1}{2}\sigma^2t^2\right)^2 + \cdots$$

$$= 1 + \frac{\sigma^2}{2}\frac{2!}{1!}\frac{t^2}{2!} + \left(\frac{\sigma^2}{2}\right)^2\frac{4!}{2!}\frac{t^4}{4!} + \cdots$$

which leads directly to the result (1.22).

Application to the Binomial Distribution

The moment-generating function of the binomial distribution (1.7) is

(5.5)
$$M_X(t) = \sum_{i=0}^{n}\binom{n}{i}p^i(1-p)^{n-i}e^{ti}$$

$$= \sum_{i=0}^{n}\binom{n}{i}(pe^t)^i(1-p)^{n-i}$$

$$= (pe^t + 1 - p)^n$$

the last equality sign being based on the binomial expansion:

$$(A + B)^n = \sum_{i=0}^{n}\binom{n}{i}A^iB^{n-i}$$

To obtain the moments we apply the procedure of computing the derivatives:

$$\frac{d}{dt}M_X(t) = npe^t(pe^t + 1 - p)^{n-1}$$

$$\frac{d^2}{dt^2}M_X(t) = npe^t(pe^t + 1 - p)^{n-1} + n(n-1)p^2e^{2t}(pe^t + 1 - p)^{n-2}$$

$$= npe^t(pe^t + 1 - p)^{n-2}(npe^t + 1 - p)$$

the values of which at $t = 0$ are np and $np[(n-1)p + 1]$, respectively. It is immediately seen that this is in agreement with the mean and the variance given in (1.8).

Application to the Multinormal Distribution

When $\mathbf{x}$ is a k-element random vector, its moment-generating function is defined as

(5.6)
$$M_{\mathbf{x}}(\mathbf{t}) = \mathscr{E}(e^{\mathbf{t}'\mathbf{x}})$$

where $\mathbf{t}$ is the k-element column vector of arguments of this function. In the case of the multinormal distribution (2.19),

$$M_{\mathbf{x}}(\mathbf{t}) = \frac{1}{(2\pi)^{k/2}\,|\boldsymbol{\Sigma}|^{\frac{1}{2}}}\int_{-\infty}^{\infty}\cdots\int_{-\infty}^{\infty}\exp\left\{\mathbf{t}'\mathbf{x} - \frac{1}{2}(\mathbf{x}-\boldsymbol{\mu})'\boldsymbol{\Sigma}^{-1}(\mathbf{x}-\boldsymbol{\mu})\right\}dx_1\cdots dx_k$$

Since the expression in curled brackets can be written as

$$-\frac{1}{2}(\mathbf{x}-\boldsymbol{\mu}-\boldsymbol{\Sigma}\mathbf{t})'\boldsymbol{\Sigma}^{-1}(\mathbf{x}-\boldsymbol{\mu}-\boldsymbol{\Sigma}\mathbf{t}) + \boldsymbol{\mu}'\mathbf{t} + \frac{1}{2}\mathbf{t}'\boldsymbol{\Sigma}\mathbf{t}$$

we easily obtain

$$M_{\mathbf{x}}(\mathbf{t}) = \exp\left\{\boldsymbol{\mu}'\mathbf{t} + \frac{1}{2}\mathbf{t}'\boldsymbol{\Sigma}\mathbf{t}\right\} \tag{5.7}$$

which is the immediate generalization of (5.4). It can also be verified (see Problems 5.4 to 5.6) that the derivatives of $M_{\mathbf{x}}(\;)$ evaluated at $\mathbf{t} = \mathbf{0}$ yield the moments of the multivariate distribution and, in particular, that $\boldsymbol{\mu}$ and $\boldsymbol{\Sigma}$ are the mean vector and the covariance matrix of the multinormal distribution.

Other Applications

The above examples show that the moment-generating function can be a simple tool for the derivation of moments. Indeed, there are many distributions for which this tool is much more convenient than a direct evaluation of the moments. Also see Problems 5.2 and 5.7 for the Poisson and the multinomial distributions.

It is also possible to use the moment-generating function to obtain the moments of a *linear function* of the original random variable. Take $Y = \alpha_0 + \alpha_1 X$ where the α's are constants; then the moment-generating function of Y is

$$M_Y(t) = \mathscr{E}(e^{(\alpha_0+\alpha_1 X)t}) = e^{\alpha_0 t}\mathscr{E}(e^{(\alpha_1 t)X}) = e^{\alpha_0 t}M_X(\alpha_1 t) \tag{5.8}$$

If we expand this according to powers of t, we obtain

$$\left(1 + \alpha_0 t + \frac{1}{2}\alpha_0^2 t^2 + \cdots\right)\left[1 + (\alpha_1\mathscr{E}X)t + \alpha_1^2\mathscr{E}(X^2)\frac{t^2}{2!} + \cdots\right]$$

$$= 1 + (\alpha_0 + \alpha_1\mathscr{E}X)t + [\alpha_0^2 + 2\alpha_0\alpha_1\mathscr{E}X + \alpha_1^2\mathscr{E}(X^2)]\frac{t^2}{2!} + \cdots$$

Hence $\alpha_0 + \alpha_1\mathscr{E}X$ is the expectation of Y. Its variance is:

$$\alpha_0^2 + 2\alpha_0\alpha_1\mathscr{E}X + \alpha_1^2\mathscr{E}(X^2) - (\alpha_0 + \alpha_1\mathscr{E}X)^2 = \alpha_1^2[\mathscr{E}(X^2) - (\mathscr{E}X)^2]$$

$$= \alpha_1^2 \operatorname{var} X$$

The higher-order moments of Y can be derived similarly. A very simple case is that of *standardization*, which amounts to subtracting the mean from the random variable and dividing the difference by the standard deviation: $Y = (X - \mu)/\sigma$. The mean and the variance of Y are obviously equal to zero and to one, respectively. In the case of normality the density function becomes $(2\pi)^{-1/2}e^{-x^2/2}$, and a random variable which follows this distribution will be called a *standardized normal variate*.

The Moment-Generating Function of the Sum of Independent Variates

Let X and Y be independent random variables with moment-generating functions $M_X(\ )$ and $M_Y(\ )$. Consider their sum $Z = X + Y$ and its moment-generating function:

$$(5.9)\qquad M_Z(t) = \mathscr{E}(e^{tZ}) = \mathscr{E}(e^{t(X+Y)}) = \mathscr{E}(e^{tX}e^{tY}) = \mathscr{E}(e^{tX})\mathscr{E}(e^{tY}) = M_X(t)M_Y(t)$$

where the fourth equality sign is based on the fact that X and Y, and hence also e^{tX} and e^{tY}, are independent. We conclude that *the moment-generating function of the sum of two independent variates is equal to the product of the moment-generating functions of the latter*. This can be generalized and combined with the result obtained in the previous paragraph as follows. If $X_1, X_2, \ldots, X_k$ are independent, then the moment-generating function of

$$(5.10)\qquad Y = \alpha_0 + \alpha_1 X_1 + \alpha_2 X_2 + \cdots + \alpha_k X_k \qquad \text{(all } \alpha\text{'s constant)}$$

is of the following multiplicative form:

$$(5.11)\qquad M_Y(t) = e^{\alpha_0 t}M_{X_1}(\alpha_1 t)M_{X_2}(\alpha_2 t)\cdots M_{X_k}(\alpha_k t)$$

The Moment-Generating Function Determines the Distribution Uniquely

An important theorem, which will not be proved here, is the following: if the moment-generating functions $M_X(\ )$ and $M_Y(\ )$ of the random variables X and Y are identical for all values of the argument, $M_X(t) \equiv M_Y(t)$, then the distributions of X and Y are also identical.[7] The practical importance of this theorem is that we can use it to determine the distribution of a random variable as soon as we recognize the type of the moment-generating function. As an example we take $\mathbf{a}'\mathbf{x}$, a linear combination with fixed weights of the k elements of the random vector $\mathbf{x}$ which follows the

[7] It is actually sufficient that $M_X(t)$ and $M_Y(t)$ both exist and are equal for all t in some nondegenerate interval around zero. We shall make use of this property when discussing the moment-generating function of the chi-square distribution in eq. (6.3) below, where t has to be less than $\frac{1}{2}$.

multinormal distribution (2.19). The moment-generating function of $\mathbf{a}'\mathbf{x}$ is

$$(5.12)\qquad \mathscr{E}(e^{t(\mathbf{a}'\mathbf{x})}) = \mathscr{E}(e^{(t\mathbf{a})'\mathbf{x}})$$
$$= \exp\left\{\boldsymbol{\mu}'(t\mathbf{a}) + \frac{1}{2}(t\mathbf{a})'\boldsymbol{\Sigma}(t\mathbf{a})\right\}$$
$$= \exp\left\{(\mathbf{a}'\boldsymbol{\mu})t + \frac{1}{2}(\mathbf{a}'\boldsymbol{\Sigma}\mathbf{a})t^2\right\}$$

where the second equality sign is based on (5.6) and (5.7), the vector $\mathbf{t}$ of the latter equations corresponding to $t\mathbf{a}$ in the present derivation. But the expression on the third line in (5.12) is nothing but the moment-generating function of the univariate normal distribution with mean $\mathbf{a}'\boldsymbol{\mu}$ and variance $\mathbf{a}'\boldsymbol{\Sigma}\mathbf{a}$ [see (5.4)]. We conclude that *if* $\mathbf{x}$ *is multinormally distributed, any linear combination* $\mathbf{a}'\mathbf{x}$ *has a univariate normal distribution.* This can be generalized as follows. If $\mathbf{x}$ has a k-dimensional normal distribution with mean vector $\boldsymbol{\mu}$ and covariance matrix $\boldsymbol{\Sigma}$, then the vector $\mathbf{Ax}$ is multinormally distributed with mean vector $\mathbf{A}\boldsymbol{\mu}$ and covariance matrix $\mathbf{A}\boldsymbol{\Sigma}\mathbf{A}'$. Note that the existence of the inverse of this covariance matrix requires $\mathbf{A}$ to have full row rank.

Problems

5.1 Derive the third moment mentioned in Problem 1.3 from the moment-generating function (5.5).

5.2 Prove that the moment-generating function of the Poisson distribution with parameter λ is $M_X(t) = \exp[\lambda(e^t - 1)]$ and derive the moments given in eq. (1.10).

5.3 (*Continuation*) Prove that if $X_1, \ldots, X_n$ are Poisson distributed with parameters $\lambda_1, \ldots, \lambda_n$, and if they are independent, their sum follows the Poisson distribution with parameter $\lambda_1 + \cdots + \lambda_n$.

5.4 (*Multivariate moments*) Let $\mathbf{x}$ be a random vector with moment-generating function $M_{\mathbf{x}}(\mathbf{t})$, where $\mathbf{x}' = [X_1 \cdots X_k]$ and $\mathbf{t}' = [t_1 \cdots t_k]$. Apply the expansion of $\mathscr{E}(e^{\mathbf{t}'\mathbf{x}})$ to prove that $\mathscr{E}X_h$ is the coefficient of t_h, $\mathscr{E}(X_hX_i)$ that of $t_ht_i/2!$, $\mathscr{E}(X_hX_iX_j)$ that of $t_ht_it_j/3!$, and so on. Also, formulate the rule on (partial) derivatives evaluated at $\mathbf{t} = \mathbf{0}$.

5.5 (*First and second moments of the multinormal distribution*) Use the moment-generating function (5.7) to prove $\mathscr{E}\mathbf{x} = \boldsymbol{\mu}$, $\mathscr{E}(\mathbf{xx}') = \boldsymbol{\Sigma} + \boldsymbol{\mu\mu}'$, $\mathscr{V}(\mathbf{x}) = \boldsymbol{\Sigma}$ for the multinormal distribution (2.19).

5.6 (*Fourth moments of the bivariate normal distribution*) Let (X, Y) be bivariate normal with zero means. Prove $\mathscr{E}(X^3Y) = 3 \operatorname{var} X \operatorname{cov}(X, Y)$ and $\mathscr{E}(X^2Y^2) = \operatorname{var} X \operatorname{var} Y + 2[\operatorname{cov}(X, Y)]^2$.

5.7 (*First and second moments of the multinomial distribution*) Consider the multinomial expansion:

(5.13)

$$(A_1 + A_2 + \cdots + A_k)^n = \sum_{i_1=0}^{n} \sum_{i_2=0}^{n} \cdots \sum_{i_k=0}^{n} \frac{n!}{i_1!\, i_2! \cdots i_k!} A_1^{i_1} A_2^{i_2} \cdots A_k^{i_k}$$

where i_k is constrained to be equal to $n - i_1 - \cdots - i_{k-1}$. Use this expansion to prove that the moment-generating function of the multinomial distribution (2.7) is

$$M(t_1, \ldots, t_{k-1}) = (p_1 e^{t_1} + \cdots + p_{k-1} e^{t_{k-1}} + p_k)^n \qquad (5.14)$$

[No t_k is introduced for the variate X_k of (2.7) because X_k is simply equal to $n - X_1 - \cdots - X_{k-1}$.] Prove that this reduces to the binomial moment-generating function (5.5) for $k = 2$. Also, derive the means, variances, and covariances given in (2.8).

5.8 Prove the generalization, formulated at the end of the section, on linear combinations of normal variates.

2.6 Distributions Associated with the Normal[AB]

The Chi-Square Distribution[A]

Let $X_1, \ldots, X_k$ be independent standardized normal variates. The sum of their squares, $X_1^2 + \cdots + X_k^2$, can be shown to have the chi-square distribution with k degrees of freedom [indicated by $\chi^2(k)$], which has the following density function:

$$P[x < \chi^2(k) \le x + dx] = \frac{x^{(k-2)/2} e^{-x/2}}{2^{k/2}\Gamma(k/2)}\, dx \qquad 0 < x < \infty \qquad (6.1)$$

where

$$\Gamma(g) = \int_0^\infty x^{g-1} e^{-x}\, dx \qquad (6.2)$$

This gamma function satisfies $\Gamma(g) = (g - 1)\Gamma(g - 1)$ and $\Gamma(\frac{1}{2}) = \sqrt{\pi}$. In our applications the values of g are positive multiples of $\frac{1}{2}$; hence the relevant values of $\Gamma(g)$ are the following:

$$\Gamma(g) = (g-1)! \qquad \text{if } g \text{ is a positive integer}$$

$$\qquad\quad (g-1)(g-2)\cdots\left(\frac{1}{2}\right)\sqrt{\pi} \qquad \text{if } g + \frac{1}{2} \text{ is a positive integer}$$

The moment-generating function corresponding to the density function (6.1) is

$$M_{\chi^2(k)}(t) = (1 - 2t)^{-k/2} \qquad \left(t < \frac{1}{2}\right) \qquad (6.3)$$

and the mean and variance are

(6.4) $$\mathscr{E}[\chi^2(k)] = k \qquad \text{var}\,\chi^2(k) = 2k$$

The third and fourth moments around the mean are

(6.5) $$\mathscr{E}[\{\chi^2(k) - k\}^3] = 8k \qquad \mathscr{E}[\{\chi^2(k) - k\}^4] = 48k + 12k^2$$

Hence the skewness and kurtosis measures (1.23) and (1.24) are $\sqrt{(8/k)}$ and $3 + 12/k$, respectively. The positive value of the skewness coefficient reflects the tail of the density function in the direction of $+\infty$. However, when k increases more and more, the values converge to 0 and 3, respectively, which are the values of the normal distribution.

Suppose that we add two independent χ^2 variates, the first having m and the second n degrees of freedom. We conclude from (6.3) that the moment-generating function of this sum is

$$(1 - 2t)^{-m/2}(1 - 2t)^{-n/2} = (1 - 2t)^{-(m+n)/2}$$

which is the moment-generating function of the χ^2 distribution with $m + n$ degrees of freedom. Hence *the sum of two independent χ^2 variates also has the χ^2 distribution*, the number of degrees of freedom being equal to the sum of the degrees of freedom of the two original distributions. This can be generalized straightforwardly for the sum of any finite number of independent χ^2 variates.

Fisher's F Distribution[A]

Now consider the ratio rather than the sum of two independent χ^2 variates with m and n degrees of freedom, respectively. It can be shown that

(6.6) $$\frac{\frac{1}{m}\chi^2(m)}{\frac{1}{n}\chi^2(n)} = F(m, n)$$

is distributed as Fisher's F with m and n degrees of freedom, the density function of which is

(6.7) $$P[x < F(m, n) \leq x + dx]$$

$$= \frac{\Gamma\left(\frac{m+n}{2}\right)\left(\frac{m}{n}\right)^{m/2} x^{(m-2)/2}}{\Gamma\left(\frac{m}{2}\right)\Gamma\left(\frac{n}{2}\right)\left(1 + \frac{m}{n}x\right)^{(m+n)/2}} \qquad 0 < x < \infty$$

Student's t Distribution[A]

Suppose finally that X is a standardized normal variate, that Y^2 has a χ^2 distribution with k degrees of freedom, and that X and $Y = +\sqrt{Y^2}$ are independent. Then it can be shown that $X\sqrt{k}/Y$ is distributed as Student's t with k degrees of freedom, to be denoted by $t(k)$, the density function of which is

$$\text{(6.8)} \quad \mathrm{P}[x < t(k) \leq x + dx] = \frac{\Gamma\left(\frac{k+1}{2}\right)}{\sqrt{k\pi}\,\Gamma\left(\frac{k}{2}\right)\left(1 + \frac{x^2}{k}\right)^{(k+1)/2}}\,dx$$

$$-\infty < x < \infty$$

This is a symmetric distribution with the following mean and variance:

$$\text{(6.9)} \qquad \mathscr{E}[t(k)] = 0 \qquad \text{var } t(k) = \frac{k}{k-2} \qquad (k > 2)$$

The third-order moment vanishes because of the symmetry. The fourth-order moment is equal to $3k^2/(k-2)(k-4)$, so that the kurtosis measure (1.24) is equal to $3 + 6/(k-4)$. This exceeds 3, which indicates that the tails of the Student distribution are thicker than those of the normal distribution, but that the excess vanishes when k becomes larger and larger. Notice that the fourth-order moment exists only if $k > 4$.

Extensions[A]

The above results can be generalized slightly when $X_1, \ldots, X_k$ are independent normal variates with zero mean and variance σ^2. Their sum of squares divided by σ^2 is then distributed as $\chi^2(k)$, which is also expressed by saying that $X_1^2 + \cdots + X_k^2$ is distributed as $\sigma^2\chi^2(k)$. Obviously, if Y is distributed as $\sigma^2\chi^2(m)$ and Z as $\sigma^2\chi^2(n)$, and if they are independent, then nY/mZ is distributed as $F(m, n)$. Similarly, if X is normally distributed with zero mean and variance σ^2, and Y^2 is distributed as $\sigma^2\chi^2(k)$, and if they are independent, then $X\sqrt{k}/Y$ is distributed as $t(k)$.

A more important extension concerns the distribution of quadratic forms in normal variates. Write $\mathbf{x} = [X_1 \cdots X_k]'$, so that $\mathbf{x}'\mathbf{A}\mathbf{x}$ is a quadratic form in this vector. It can be shown that *if* $\mathbf{A}$ *is idempotent of rank r and if the elements of* $\mathbf{x}$ *are independent standardized normal variates, the quadratic form* $\mathbf{x}'\mathbf{A}\mathbf{x}$ *is distributed as* $\chi^2(r)$. Note that this distribution is determined completely by the rank of $\mathbf{A}$, so that it is independent of the number of elements of $\mathbf{x}$.

Since the unit matrix is idempotent, this result implies that $\mathbf{x}'\mathbf{x}$ is distributed as $\chi^2(k)$, which is equivalent to the statement made in the first paragraph of this section. The proof of the more general theorem requires a result derived in Section 1.5 and is given in the next subsection.

Proof of the Chi-square Distribution of Idempotent Quadratic Forms[B]

It is shown in the last subsection of Section 1.5 that if $\mathbf{A}$ is an idempotent $k \times k$ matrix of rank r, it has r unit latent roots and $k - r$ zero roots. Also, there exists a $k \times k$ orthogonal matrix $\mathbf{C}$ such that $\mathbf{C}'\mathbf{AC} = \mathbf{\Lambda}$, where $\mathbf{\Lambda}$ is a diagonal matrix containing the latent roots of $\mathbf{A}$ on the diagonal. It may be assumed without loss of generality that the first r diagonal elements of $\mathbf{\Lambda}$ are one and the last $k - r$ zero. Define $\mathbf{y} = \mathbf{C}'\mathbf{x}$ and consider

$$\mathbf{x}'\mathbf{Ax} = \mathbf{x}'(\mathbf{CC}')\mathbf{A}(\mathbf{CC}')\mathbf{x} = \mathbf{y}'(\mathbf{C}'\mathbf{AC})\mathbf{y} = \mathbf{y}'\mathbf{\Lambda y} \tag{6.10}$$

$$= [\mathbf{y}_1' \quad \mathbf{y}_2'] \begin{bmatrix} \mathbf{I} & \mathbf{0} \\ \mathbf{0} & \mathbf{0} \end{bmatrix} \begin{bmatrix} \mathbf{y}_1 \\ \mathbf{y}_2 \end{bmatrix} = \mathbf{y}_1'\mathbf{y}_1$$

where $\mathbf{y}_1$ is the subvector of $\mathbf{y}$ consisting of the first r elements. Now $\mathbf{y} = \mathbf{C}'\mathbf{x}$ is a vector of normal variates, since it is a linear function of the normal vector $\mathbf{x}$. The expectation is $\mathscr{E}\mathbf{y} = \mathbf{C}'\mathscr{E}\mathbf{x} = \mathbf{0}$ because $\mathscr{E}\mathbf{x} = \mathbf{0}$ by assumption; the covariance matrix is

$$\mathscr{V}(\mathbf{y}) = \mathscr{E}(\mathbf{C}'\mathbf{xx}'\mathbf{C}) = \mathbf{C}'\mathscr{E}(\mathbf{xx}')\mathbf{C} = \mathbf{C}'\mathbf{C} = \mathbf{I}$$

because $\mathscr{E}(\mathbf{xx}') = \mathbf{I}$ by assumption. Hence, $\mathbf{y}_1$ in (6.10) is an r-element vector of independent standardized normal variates, so that the sum of squares of these elements, $\mathbf{y}_1'\mathbf{y}_1$ in (6.10), has the χ^2 distribution with r degrees of freedom, which proves the theorem.

When Are Two Idempotent Quadratic Forms Independent?[A]

Let $\mathbf{x}'\mathbf{Ax}$ and $\mathbf{x}'\mathbf{Bx}$ be two idempotent quadratic forms, possibly with different ranks, and assume that the product of the two matrices is a zero matrix:[8]

$$\mathbf{AB} = \mathbf{BA} = \mathbf{0} \tag{6.11}$$

The quadratic form $\mathbf{x}'\mathbf{Ax} = \mathbf{x}'\mathbf{A}'\mathbf{Ax}$ is equal to the sum of the squares of the elements of $\mathbf{Ax}$ (see proposition I1 at the end of Section 1.5). The same holds true for $\mathbf{x}'\mathbf{Bx}$ and $\mathbf{Bx}$. Both $\mathbf{Ax}$ and $\mathbf{Bx}$ are normally distributed, and each

[8] The statements $\mathbf{AB} = \mathbf{0}$ and $\mathbf{BA} = \mathbf{0}$ are equivalent because the square $(k \times k)$ matrix $\mathbf{AB}$ is symmetric if it is a zero matrix, and hence $\mathbf{AB} = \mathbf{B}'\mathbf{A}' = \mathbf{BA}$, the idempotent matrices $\mathbf{A}$ and $\mathbf{B}$ being symmetric by assumption.

element of $\mathbf{Ax}$ is uncorrelated with each element of $\mathbf{Bx}$ because $\mathscr{E}(\mathbf{Axx'B'}) = \mathbf{A}\mathscr{E}(\mathbf{xx'})\mathbf{B} = \mathbf{AB} = \mathbf{0}$. We conclude from the last paragraph of Section 2.3 that the vectors $\mathbf{Ax}$ and $\mathbf{Bx}$ are then independent,[9] and so are the sums of squares of their elements, the quadratic forms $\mathbf{x'Ax}$ and $\mathbf{x'Bx}$. Thus, if $\mathbf{x}$ consists of independent standardized normal variates, the idempotent quadratic forms $\mathbf{x'Ax}$ and $\mathbf{x'Bx}$ are independent if (6.11) is true.[10]

When Is an Idempotent Quadratic Form Independent of a Linear Function?[A]

Let $\mathbf{x'Ax} = \mathbf{x'A'Ax}$ be an idempotent quadratic form and $\mathbf{Lx}$ a vector whose elements are linear in $\mathbf{x}$. It is easily seen along the lines of the previous paragraph that

$$\mathbf{LA} = \mathbf{0} \tag{6.12}$$

guarantees the independence of $\mathbf{Lx}$ and $\mathbf{Ax}$ (and hence of $\mathbf{Lx}$ and $\mathbf{x'Ax}$) when the elements of $\mathbf{x}$ are independent standardized normal variates.[11]

Problems

6.1 Derive the moments (6.4) of the chi-square distribution from the moment-generating function (6.3).

6.2 Prove that if X is distributed as $t(k)$, X^2 is distributed as $F(1, k)$.

6.3 Prove that condition (6.11) implies that each column of $\mathbf{B}$ is a characteristic vector of $\mathbf{A}$ corresponding to a zero root and that each column of $\mathbf{A}$ is a characteristic vector of $\mathbf{B}$ corresponding to a zero root. Similarly, prove that (6.12) implies that each row of $\mathbf{L}$ is a characteristic vector of $\mathbf{A}$ corresponding to a zero root. Do these characteristic vectors have unit length? (*Note*. Assume that these vectors are all nonzero.)

[9] Note that the vector $[(\mathbf{Ax})' \quad (\mathbf{Bx})']$ has a multinormal distribution with covariance matrix $\begin{bmatrix} \mathbf{A} & \mathbf{0} \\ \mathbf{0} & \mathbf{B} \end{bmatrix}$, which is singular in view of (6.11). Hence the joint density function of this vector cannot be written in the form (2.19). Nevertheless, the vectors $\mathbf{Ax}$ and $\mathbf{Bx}$ are independent, but we shall not pursue this further here. (See Section 6.9 for more details about singular multinormal distributions.)

[10] The independence result does not really require that $\mathbf{A}$ and $\mathbf{B}$ be idempotent, nor that the expectations of the $\mathbf{x}$ elements vanish. We have the following more general result. If $\mathbf{x}$ is normally distributed with density function (2.19), the quadratic forms $\mathbf{x'Ax}$ and $\mathbf{x'Bx}$ are independent if (and only if) $\mathbf{A\Sigma B} = \mathbf{0}$; see, for example, Theorem 4.21 of Graybill (1961, p. 88).

[11] This result does not require $\mathbf{A}$ to be idempotent; it may be any symmetric matrix. See, for example, Theorem 4.17 of Graybill (1961, p. 87).

6.4 Let $\mathbf{x}$ be a random vector that follows a multinormal distribution with zero mean vector and covariance matrix $\mathbf{\Sigma}$. Prove that the linear functions $\mathbf{a}'\mathbf{x}$ and $\mathbf{b}'\mathbf{x}$ are independent if and only if $\mathbf{a}'\mathbf{\Sigma}\mathbf{b} = 0$. Also prove that this condition amounts to orthogonality of the weight vectors $\mathbf{a}$ and $\mathbf{b}$ if the elements of $\mathbf{x}$ are standardized and independent.

2.7 Point Estimation[A]

Let X be a random variable with a certain probability distribution. Let $X_1, \ldots, X_n$ be n independent random variables each of which has the same distribution as X (in short, $X_1, \ldots, X_n$ are independently and identically distributed random variables). Then $(X_1, \ldots, X_n)$ is called a *random sample* of size n drawn from this distribution (or drawn from the population that is described by this distribution).

Statistic, Estimator, Estimate

Random samples enable us to draw statistical inferences about unknown parameters. Thus, let the distribution of X of the previous paragraph be continuous with density function $f(x \mid \theta)$, where θ is an unknown parameter which determines the distribution. The joint density function of the random sample is then

$$(7.1) \qquad \begin{aligned} &\mathrm{P}[x_1 < X_1 \le x_1 + dx_1, \ldots, x_n < X_n \le x_n + dx_n] \\ &\quad = f(x_1 \mid \theta) \cdots f(x_n \mid \theta)\, dx_1 \cdots dx_n \end{aligned}$$

Now suppose that a random sample $(X_1, \ldots, X_n)$ has been drawn, so that we have n numerical outcomes. The problem is: how can we use these data to obtain a numerical value for the unknown θ? The answer is that we formulate a certain function of the sample values which serves to approximate θ in some well-defined sense. This function is known as a *statistic.*

Table 2.1 serves as an example. It consists of 50 sample values, which may be interpreted as the percentage of income saved by 50 families with two children drawn at random from the income group between \$8000 and \$9000 per year.[12] We assume that these savings percentages are normally distributed with mean μ and unit variance. This μ is unknown and thus represents θ of (7.1). The joint density function of the random sample is

$$(7.2) \qquad \prod_{i=1}^{50} \frac{1}{\sqrt{2\pi}} \exp\left\{-\frac{1}{2}(x_i - \mu)^2\right\} = \frac{1}{(2\pi)^{25}} \exp\left\{-\frac{1}{2}\sum_{i=1}^{50}(x_i - \mu)^2\right\}$$

[12] The figures are obtained from random sampling numbers. One should expect that actual savings percentages are characterized by more dispersion than Table 2.1 indicates, and a numerically more realistic interpretation would be that of the average savings percentage of 10 (or perhaps 20) families drawn at random from each of the 50 states.

Table 2.1

A Random Sample of Savings Percentages

Number	Savings Percentage	Number	Savings Percentage	Number	Savings Percentage
1	10.11	18	10.21	35	8.97
2	9.11	19	8.67	36	10.35
3	10.99	20	11.70	37	9.18
4	10.50	21	9.08	38	11.76
5	9.05	22	11.73	39	9.32
6	10.81	23	10.66	40	9.12
7	9.72	24	8.31	41	9.86
8	8.36	25	12.13	42	10.77
9	8.56	26	7.80	43	8.39
10	10.01	27	11.57	44	9.33
11	10.24	28	8.15	45	10.58
12	10.46	29	7.76	46	8.94
13	10.02	30	9.85	47	10.51
14	7.91	31	9.55	48	9.76
15	12.08	32	9.97	49	8.40
16	9.20	33	11.01	50	10.29
17	10.27	34	11.19		

The problem, then, is: which statistic should be chosen to estimate μ? An obvious choice is the sample mean:

$$\bar{X} = \frac{1}{50}\sum_{i=1}^{50} X_i \tag{7.3}$$

where $X_1, \ldots, X_{50}$ are the savings percentages of the sample. We can regard $\bar{X}$ as a linear combination of a vector $\mathbf{x}' = [X_1 \cdots X_{50}]$ which follows a multinormal distribution with mean vector $[\mu \cdots \mu]$ and unit covariance matrix. (The diagonal units follow from the unit variances, the off-diagonal zeros from the independence of the sample elements.) We conclude from the results obtained at the end of Section 2.5 that $\bar{X}$ is also normally distributed, and that its mean is

$$\begin{bmatrix} \frac{1}{50} & \frac{1}{50} & \cdots & \frac{1}{50} \end{bmatrix} \begin{bmatrix} \mu \\ \mu \\ \cdot \\ \cdot \\ \cdot \\ \mu \end{bmatrix} = \mu \tag{7.4}$$

and that it has the following variance:

$$\begin{bmatrix} \frac{1}{50} & \frac{1}{50} & \cdots & \frac{1}{50} \end{bmatrix} \begin{bmatrix} 1 & 0 & \cdots & 0 \\ 0 & 1 & \cdots & 0 \\ \cdot & \cdot & & \cdot \\ \cdot & \cdot & & \cdot \\ \cdot & \cdot & & \cdot \\ 0 & 0 & \cdots & 1 \end{bmatrix} \begin{bmatrix} \frac{1}{50} \\ \frac{1}{50} \\ \cdot \\ \cdot \\ \cdot \\ \frac{1}{50} \end{bmatrix} = \frac{1}{50} \tag{7.5}$$

Thus we find that if we approximate μ by $\bar{X}$, we commit an error (usually called a *sampling error*) equal to $\bar{X} - \mu$ which is normally distributed with zero mean and variance $\frac{1}{50}$. In our case the value of $\bar{X}$ computed from Table 2.1 is 9.845. Our preference for this figure over any of the 50 of the table as an approximation of μ is, of course, motivated by the consideration that $\bar{X}$ has a much smaller variance around μ than any of the X_i. Note that the numerical value 9.845 is called an *estimate* of μ, whereas $\bar{X}$ [the function of the random sample $(X_1, \ldots, X_n)$ before the sample is specified numerically] is called an *estimator* of μ.

Unbiased Estimation; Sampling Distribution and Sampling Variance

In this example the expectation of the estimator ($\mathscr{E}\bar{X}$) coincides with the parameter which is estimated (μ), in which case the estimator is said to be *unbiased.* More generally, if $(X_1, \ldots, X_n)$ is a random sample drawn from a population which is determined by an unknown parameter θ, and if $\hat{\theta}(X_1, \ldots, X_n)$ is the statistic which is used as an estimator of θ, then $\hat{\theta}$ is said to be unbiased with respect to θ if

$$\mathscr{E}\hat{\theta} \equiv \theta \quad \text{or} \quad \mathscr{E}(\hat{\theta} - \theta) \equiv 0 \tag{7.6}$$

and in all other cases $\hat{\theta}$ is called biased. The first equation of (7.6) states that the expectation of $\hat{\theta}$ equals θ, whatever the value of θ may be; the second is an equivalent expression which states that the sampling error has zero mean.

It is easily seen that the sample mean $\bar{X}$ of a random sample $(X_1, \ldots, X_n)$ is unbiased with respect to the population mean μ (whenever μ exists), quite apart from the question of whether the distribution is normal or not:

$$\mathscr{E}\bar{X} = \mathscr{E}\left(\frac{1}{n}\sum_{i=1}^{n} X_i\right) = \frac{1}{n}\sum_{i=1}^{n} \mathscr{E}X_i = \frac{n\mu}{n} = \mu \tag{7.7}$$

The second equality sign is based on the rule that the expectation of a linear combination of random variables is equal to the same combination of their expectations, the third on the fact that the X_i's have the same distribution and hence the same mean μ. Also, if the variance σ^2 of the distribution is finite,

$$\text{(7.8)}\qquad \begin{aligned} \operatorname{var} \bar{X} &= \operatorname{var}\left(\frac{1}{n}\sum_{i=1}^{n} X_i\right) \\ &= \frac{1}{n^2}\left[\sum_{i=1}^{n} \operatorname{var} x_i + \sum_{i \neq j}\sum \operatorname{cov}(X_i, X_j)\right] \\ &= \frac{1}{n^2}(n\sigma^2 + 0) = \frac{\sigma^2}{n} \end{aligned}$$

where the second equality sign is based on (4.2) and the third on the independence of the X_i's, which implies that all covariances vanish. The variance of an estimator is usually called its *sampling variance*; the result σ^2/n is in accordance with the numerical result $\frac{1}{50}$ of (7.5) because the latter is based on $\sigma^2 = 1$, $n = 50$. Thus we find that it is possible to derive both the mean and the variance of $\bar{X}$ by specifying only the mean and the variance of the distribution from which the sample is drawn. To find the complete distribution of the estimator (known as its *sampling distribution*) we should know more about the distribution of the sample. For example, we found above that if the distribution of $(X_1, \ldots, X_n)$ is normal, the sampling distribution of $\bar{X}$ is also normal.

Extension of the Multiparameter Case

When we have a vector of unknown parameters, $\boldsymbol{\theta}$ with elements $\theta_1, \ldots, \theta_K$, the estimator is a K-element vector $\hat{\boldsymbol{\theta}}(X_1, \ldots, X_n)$ defined as a function of the sample in such a way that each element of $\hat{\boldsymbol{\theta}}$ is the estimator of the corresponding element of $\boldsymbol{\theta}$. The estimator is unbiased if $\mathscr{E}\hat{\boldsymbol{\theta}} \equiv \boldsymbol{\theta}$ or, equivalently, $\mathscr{E}(\hat{\boldsymbol{\theta}} - \boldsymbol{\theta}) \equiv \mathbf{0}$, which thus implies that *each* of the K separate estimators should be unbiased with respect to the corresponding element of the parameter vector. The K-dimensional extension of the sampling variance is the covariance matrix of $\hat{\boldsymbol{\theta}}$:

$$\text{(7.9)}\qquad \mathscr{V}(\hat{\boldsymbol{\theta}}) = \mathscr{E}[(\hat{\boldsymbol{\theta}} - \mathscr{E}\hat{\boldsymbol{\theta}})(\hat{\boldsymbol{\theta}} - \mathscr{E}\hat{\boldsymbol{\theta}})']$$

where $\mathscr{E}\hat{\boldsymbol{\theta}}$ can be replaced by $\boldsymbol{\theta}$ if the estimator is unbiased. The diagonal elements of $\mathscr{V}(\hat{\boldsymbol{\theta}})$ contain the sampling variances; the off-diagonal elements contain the sampling covariances.

The Maximum-Likelihood Method

There are several general methods for designing estimators. One is the "analogy method": estimate the population mean by the sample mean, the population variance by the sample variance, and so on. A second is the least-squares method but, since it will be pursued in detail in later chapters, there is no need to consider it here. A third is the maximum-likelihood method, which can be explained as follows. Let $(X_1, \ldots, X_n)$ be a random sample and let θ be the object of estimation. Then the joint density function of the sample evaluated at the sample values is

$$f(X_1 \mid \theta) \cdots f(X_n \mid \theta) = L(X_1, \ldots, X_n; \theta) \quad \text{say} \tag{7.10}$$

The product of the f's on the left specifies the probability density of obtaining the sample $(X_1, \ldots, X_n)$, given that θ is the parameter value. This product is rewritten as $L(\ )$ in (7.10), which is known as the *likelihood function*. The main reason for the introduction of this function is that the expression in (7.10) can also be regarded as a function of θ, given the sample. The likelihood function does precisely that, and this way of looking at the problem enables us to obtain a θ estimator, as will now be described.

Suppose that the sample has actually been drawn, so that we have data such as those in Table 2.1. Given these data, the value of the likelihood function depends on θ. The method of maximum likelihood proposes to use as an estimate of θ the function $\hat{\theta}(X_1, \ldots, X_n)$ which maximizes the value of the likelihood function:

$$L(X_1, \ldots, X_n; \hat{\theta}) \geq L(X_1, \ldots, X_n; \tilde{\theta}) \tag{7.11}$$

where $\tilde{\theta}(X_1, \ldots, X_n)$ is any other estimate of θ. The underlying intuitive idea is that one should prefer a parameter value that implies a large probability of the sample drawn rather than a parameter value that declares that the sample is less probable. Before the sample is drawn, the X's of (7.11) are random and, hence, the solution $\hat{\theta}(X_1, \ldots, X_n)$ of the maximum problem is also random; that solution is the maximum-likelihood estimator (in contrast to estimate). When the underlying distribution is not continuous but discrete, the approach is the same except that we have probabilities rather than densities in the left-hand side of (7.10).

As an example we take a random sample of size n from a normal distribution with mean μ (the unknown parameter) and unit variance. The likelihood function is

$$L(X_1, \ldots, X_n; \mu) = \frac{1}{(2\pi)^{n/2}} \exp\left\{-\frac{1}{2}\sum_{i=1}^{n}(X_i - \mu)^2\right\} \tag{7.12}$$

Maximizing $L(\ )$ is equivalent to maximizing its (natural) logarithm, since $\log L$ is a monotonically increasing function of L. So we maximize

$$-\frac{n}{2}\log 2\pi - \frac{1}{2}\sum_{i=1}^{n}(X_i - \mu)^2$$

with respect to μ, which gives $\hat{\mu} = \bar{X}$ for the maximum-likelihood estimator. Thus the estimator coincides with the sample mean.

Maximum-Likelihood Estimation of a Parameter Vector

This procedure can be generalized for the case of several unknown parameters, so that θ of (7.10) is a vector. An example is a random sample of size n from a normal population with unknown mean μ and unknown variance σ^2, for which the likelihood function is

$$L(X_1, \ldots, X_n; \mu, \sigma^2) = \frac{1}{(2\pi\sigma^2)^{n/2}} \exp\left\{-\frac{1}{2}\frac{\sum_{i=1}^{n}(X_i - \mu)^2}{\sigma^2}\right\} \tag{7.13}$$

Its logarithm is

$$\log L = -\frac{n}{2}\log 2\pi - \frac{n}{2}\log\sigma^2 - \frac{1}{2\sigma^2}\sum_{i=1}^{n}(X_i - \mu)^2$$

We compute the derivatives with respect to μ and σ^2 and equate them to zero:

$$\frac{\partial(\log L)}{\partial\mu} = \frac{1}{\sigma^2}\sum_{i=1}^{n}(X_i - \mu) = 0 \tag{7.14}$$

$$\frac{\partial(\log L)}{\partial\sigma^2} = -\frac{n/2}{\sigma^2} + \frac{\sum_{i=1}^{n}(X_i - \mu)^2}{2\sigma^4} = 0 \tag{7.15}$$

We conclude from (7.14) that the maximum-likelihood estimator of μ is the sample mean $\bar{X}$ as before. Substituting this solution into (7.15), we find that

$$\frac{1}{n}\sum_{i=1}^{n}(X_i - \bar{X})^2 \tag{7.16}$$

is the maximum-likelihood estimator of σ^2.[13] This estimator is not unbiased, which is proved as follows. We note that (7.16) is a fraction $1/n$ of the quadratic form $\mathbf{x}'\mathbf{A}\mathbf{x}$, where $\mathbf{x}' = [X_1 \cdots X_n]$ and $\mathbf{A} = \mathbf{I} - (1/n)\boldsymbol{\iota}\boldsymbol{\iota}'$ is the idempotent matrix which was defined in eq. (1.6) of Section 1.1. It was shown in eq. (1.18) of the same section that the trace of this matrix is $n - 1$; hence, given that the matrix is idempotent, its rank is also $n - 1$. Therefore, $\mathbf{x}'\mathbf{A}\mathbf{x}$ is

[13] For the second-order maximum condition, see Problem 7.1.

distributed as $\sigma^2\chi^2(n-1)$ and its expectation is $\sigma^2(n-1)$ [see (6.4)], so that $\sigma^2(n-1)/n$ is the expectation of $(1/n)\mathbf{x}'\mathbf{A}\mathbf{x}$.[14] This differs from σ^2, so that (7.16) is indeed a biased estimator of σ^2. But, at the same time, the result shows that

$$s^2 = \frac{1}{n-1}\sum_{i=1}^{n}(X_i - \bar{X})^2 \tag{7.17}$$

is an unbiased estimator of σ^2. Actually, the unbiasedness of s^2 is a general result which does not depend on the normality of the X_i's; see Problem 7.2.

It follows from (6.4) that the variance of $\mathbf{x}'\mathbf{A}\mathbf{x}$ is $2(n-1)\sigma^4$, so that the sampling variance of the variance estimator s^2 defined in (7.17) is $2\sigma^4/(n-1)$. We know from (7.8) that the variance of $\bar{X}$ is σ^2/n. Hence, if we take $[\bar{X} \quad s^2]$ as an (unbiased) estimator of the parameter vector $[\mu \quad \sigma^2]$, we have derived the diagonal elements of the following covariance matrix:

$$\mathscr{V}\begin{bmatrix}\bar{X}\\ s^2\end{bmatrix} = \begin{bmatrix}\sigma^2/n & 0\\ 0 & 2\sigma^4/(n-1)\end{bmatrix} \tag{7.18}$$

The zero off-diagonal elements indicate that $\bar{X}$ and s^2 are uncorrelated. This is true because *if the population is normal, the sample mean and the sample variance are independent* [which is stronger than the zero-correlation statement of (7.18)]. Proof: The sample mean $\bar{X}$ is obtained by premultiplying the column $[X_1 \cdots X_n]'$ by the row vector $\boldsymbol{\iota}'$, which consists of n unit elements; the idempotent matrix $\mathbf{A}$ obeys $\boldsymbol{\iota}'\mathbf{A} = \boldsymbol{\iota}' - (1/n)\boldsymbol{\iota}'\boldsymbol{\iota}\boldsymbol{\iota}' = \mathbf{0}$, so that condition (6.12) is satisfied.

Estimators Which Minimize Expected Loss

An estimator is not good or bad simply because it is obtained by means of the analogy method, the least-squares method, or the maximum-likelihood method. The quality of an estimator is to be judged in terms of the distribution of the deviations from the parameter value (the sampling errors) and the harm done (the loss inflicted) by these deviations. One criterion is unbiasedness, which implies that the deviations are zero on the average; but it is good not to attach too much importance to this criterion, since deviations of 100 and −100 cancel each other in exactly the same way as 1 and −1 do, whereas the former pair of deviations will normally be judged to be much more serious than the latter.

[14] Note that the chi-square distribution is based on the assumption that the X_i's have zero expectation, whereas it is assumed here that their expectation is μ. This does not make any difference, however, because the mean square (7.16) may also be regarded as the mean square of $Y_i - \bar{Y}$, where $Y_i = X_i - \mu$ and $\bar{Y} = (1/n)\sum Y_i$; and each Y_i obviously has zero expectation.

A more satisfactory approach is that of the so-called *loss function*, $l(\theta, \hat{\theta})$, which measures explicitly the loss inflicted when the true parameter value θ is estimated as $\hat{\theta}$. Since $\hat{\theta}$ depends on $(X_1, \ldots, X_n)$, the loss varies from sample to sample. The approach implies the selection of the estimator $\hat{\theta}(X_1, \ldots, X_n)$ for which the expected loss is as small as possible. A very popular loss function is the quadratic, $(\hat{\theta} - \theta)^2$, which leads to the estimator with a minimum second-order sampling moment around the true parameter. Notice that a minimal $\mathscr{E}[(\hat{\theta} - \theta)^2]$ does not imply that $\hat{\theta}$ is unbiased. This moment can be written as the sum of the variance and the square of the bias:

$$\mathscr{E}[(\hat{\theta} - \theta)^2] = \operatorname{var} \hat{\theta} + (\mathscr{E}\hat{\theta} - \theta)^2 \tag{7.19}$$

Although it is true that a nonzero bias implies a positive contribution to the second moment, it is conceivable that a biased estimator has a variance that is so much smaller than that of any unbiased estimator that this more than compensates for the positive term $(\mathscr{E}\hat{\theta} - \theta)^2$. On the other hand, it is found frequently that the "estimator" which minimizes the second moment around the parameter depends on other unknown parameters, so that it cannot be computed on the basis of the sample. Since it is also found frequently that this difficulty disappears when we impose unbiasedness (which implies that the second moment of the sampling error becomes the variance), this explains the rather prominent position of the unbiasedness criterion. The generalization of these ideas to vector estimation involves the covariance matrix and will be developed in the next chapter.

The quadratic loss function plays a very important role in statistics and econometrics. This does not mean that something is basically wrong with other loss functions. On the contrary, the quadratic has the property that numerically equal sampling errors of opposite sign are weighted equally, which is unattractive in several applications. Its prominent role stems partly from the fact that it provides a reasonable first approximation in many applications, and partly from its mathematical convenience. This convenience, in turn, is based on the fact that the expectation of a quadratic loss function can frequently be expressed easily in terms of a sampling variance or a matrix of sampling variances and covariances.

Standard Errors

In many cases it is not possible to determine the sampling variance of an estimator because this variance depends on unknown parameters itself. For example, we found in (7.8) that the variance of the sample mean $\bar{X}$ is σ^2/n, where σ^2 is the variance of the population from which the sample is drawn. We did find the numerical value $\frac{1}{50}$ for the sampling variance in (7.5) when discussing the data of Table 2.1, but this value was based on the assumption

$\sigma^2 = 1$. In the usual case of an unknown σ^2, one often replaces σ^2 by its unbiased estimator s^2 as defined in (7.17), so that s^2/n is then used as an unbiased estimator of the sampling variance of the sample mean $\bar{X}$. For the data of Table 2.1 we have $s^2 = 1.3461$ and $n = 50$; hence, $s^2/n = .02692$ and its square root is .164. This square root is known as the *standard error* of the estimate $\bar{X} = 9.845$. Thus the standard error is an estimate of the standard deviation of the sampling distribution of the estimator ($\bar{X}$ in this case). Note that it is not an unbiased estimate; see Problem 7.4.

Problems

7.1 Derive the 2×2 Hessian matrix of the logarithm of the likelihood function (7.13). Prove that it is diagonal with negative diagonal elements, and conclude that the solution is indeed a maximum.

7.2 Let $(X_1, \ldots, X_n)$ be a random sample from an arbitrary population with finite mean μ and variance σ^2. Prove that s^2 defined in (7.17) is unbiased for σ^2. [*Hint*. Write $X_i - \bar{X}$ in the form $X_i - \mu - (\bar{X} - \mu)$.]

7.3 Prove eq. (7.19) and generalize it for the case of a parameter vector $\boldsymbol{\theta}$.

7.4 Prove $\mathscr{E}s^2 = \text{var } s + (\mathscr{E}s)^2$ and use this to prove that if s^2 is an unbiased estimator of σ^2, s is biased with respect to σ. What is the sign of the bias $\mathscr{E}s - \sigma$?

7.5 Consider the multinomial distribution (2.7) and use the relative frequency of the jth outcome, $f_j = X_j/n$, as an estimator of the probability p_j, $j = 1, \ldots, k$. Write these frequencies in the form of a k-element vector $\mathbf{f}$; prove that $\mathbf{f}$ is unbiased and that its covariance matrix is $\mathscr{V}(\mathbf{f}) = n^{-1}(\mathbf{P} - \mathbf{P}\boldsymbol{\iota}\boldsymbol{\iota}'\mathbf{P})$, where $\mathbf{P}$ and $\boldsymbol{\iota}$ are defined in (2.10).

2.8 Interval Estimation (Confidence Intervals)[A]

In many cases one will want more than just one single numerical value as an approximation to the parameter θ. One may want an interval (a, b) so that there will be high confidence that θ lies in this interval. The estimator $\hat{\theta}(X_1, \ldots, X_n)$ of the previous section is a *point estimator* and its numerical value based on a particular sample is a *point estimate*; in this section we shall develop similar concepts for interval estimation.

Again suppose that we have a random sample $(X_1, \ldots, X_n)$ from a normal population with mean μ (unknown) and unit variance. We know from the previous section that the sample mean $\bar{X}$ is then normally distributed with mean μ and variance $1/n$. We also know from the table of the normal distribution that there is a .95 probability that a normal variate lies in the interval (mean $\pm 1.96 \times$ standard deviation). Hence

$$\text{(8.1)} \qquad \mathrm{P}\left[\mu - \frac{1.96}{\sqrt{n}} \leq \bar{X} \leq \mu + \frac{1.96}{\sqrt{n}}\right] = .95$$

By subtracting $\mu + \bar{X}$ we find that the double inequality within brackets is equivalent to

$$-\bar{X} - \frac{1.96}{\sqrt{n}} \leq -\mu \leq -\bar{X} + \frac{1.96}{\sqrt{n}}$$

which, in turn, is equivalent to

$$\bar{X} - \frac{1.96}{\sqrt{n}} \leq \mu \leq \bar{X} + \frac{1.96}{\sqrt{n}}$$

Hence (8.1) can also be written in the form

$$\text{(8.2)} \qquad \mathrm{P}\left[\bar{X} - \frac{1.96}{\sqrt{n}} \leq \mu \leq \bar{X} + \frac{1.96}{\sqrt{n}}\right] = .95$$

We thus have a *confidence interval* $(\bar{X} \pm 1.96\sqrt{n})$ for the parameter μ with *confidence coefficient* .95. This is precisely the interval (a, b) that we wanted to find at the beginning of this section, but we should be careful as to its interpretation. What is random between brackets in (8.2) is $\bar{X}$, not μ. Hence the interval (a, b) is random in the sense that its limits ($a = \bar{X} - 1.96/\sqrt{n}$ and $b = \bar{X} + 1.96/\sqrt{n}$) are random. Therefore it is preferable to read (8.2) as "The probability is .95 that the interval $(\bar{X} \pm 1.96/\sqrt{n})$ contains μ" rather than "The probability is .95 that μ lies in the interval $(\bar{X} \pm 1.96/\sqrt{n})$." If we construct confidence intervals with a .95 confidence coefficient a large number of times, we should expect that it will turn out in about 95 percent of all cases that the interval actually contains the parameter and, hence, in about 5 percent of all cases that the parameter lies outside the interval. We can raise the reliability of the procedure by raising the confidence coefficient, but this will also raise the width of the interval and hence reduce the precision of the statement. For example, if we want a .99 confidence coefficient in (8.2), we should replace 1.96 by 2.58 and thus increase the width of the confidence interval by more than 30 percent.

Confidence Intervals Based on the Student Distribution

The case (8.2) is very simple because the variance of the normal distribution is known. If the variance is an unknown parameter σ^2, the limits of the interval (8.2) are $\bar{X} \pm 1.96\sigma/\sqrt{n}$, which cannot be computed from the sample values. However, consider the following ratio:

$$\frac{(\bar{X} - \mu)\sqrt{n}}{\sqrt{(n-1)s^2}}\sqrt{n-1} = \frac{(\bar{X} - \mu)\sqrt{n}}{s} \tag{8.3}$$

The numerator $(\bar{X} - \mu)\sqrt{n}$ is normally distributed with zero mean and variance σ^2, since $\bar{X} - \mu$ follows the normal distribution with zero mean and variance σ^2/n. We found in the previous section that $(n-1)s^2$ is distributed as $\sigma^2\chi^2(n-1)$. We also found there that $\bar{X}$ and s^2 are independent. The conclusion is that the ratio (8.3) is distributed as $t(n-1)$. Using the table of the Student distribution with $n-1$ degrees of freedom, we can obtain limits $\pm t_{\alpha/2}(n-1)$ from

$$P[-t_{\alpha/2}(n-1) \leq t(n-1) \leq t_{\alpha/2}(n-1)] = 1 - \alpha \tag{8.4}$$

where $1 - \alpha$ is the confidence coefficient (e.g., .8, .9, .95, or .99). Thus the probability is $1 - \alpha$ that the ratio (8.3) is at most equal to $t_{\alpha/2}(n-1)$ in absolute value, which leads to a confidence interval for μ with confidence coefficient $1 - \alpha$.

As an illustrative example we take the data of Table 2.1, for which $n - 1 = 49$. The limits of the interval (8.4) are $\pm t_{.025}(49)$ if we choose a .95 confidence coefficient; we find $t_{.025}(49) = 2.0096$ from the table of the Student distribution. The interval for t of (8.3) is

$$-2.0096 \leq \frac{(\bar{X} - \mu)\sqrt{50}}{s} \leq 2.0096$$

or, equivalently,

$$\bar{X} - 2.0096\frac{s}{\sqrt{50}} \leq \mu \leq \bar{X} + 2.0096\frac{s}{\sqrt{50}}$$

If we substitute the observed values $\bar{X} = 9.845$ and $s^2 = 1.3461$ we obtain (9.52, 10.17) as the confidence interval for μ corresponding to the .95 confidence level.

Confidence Intervals Based on the Chi-square and the F Distributions

For σ^2, too, we can construct a confidence interval. We recall that $(n-1)s^2$ is distributed as $\sigma^2\chi^2(n-1)$ if the population from which the sample is drawn is normal. We then consider $(n-1)s^2/\sigma^2$ and apply the same argument to this ratio as we did in the previous paragraph with respect to the ratio (8.3), replacing the Student distribution by the chi-square distribution. Confidence intervals based on χ^2 and F as well as confidence regions for several parameters simultaneously will be discussed in the next chapter.

The Two-Sigma Rule

A very crude method of constructing confidence intervals is the twice-the-standard-error rule (often abbreviated as the two-sigma rule). It involves a confidence interval in which the standard deviation of the sampling distribution is approximated by the standard error (see the last paragraph of the previous section). In addition, the sampling distribution is supposed to be approximately normal, so that the factor 2 (≈ 1.96) corresponds to a .95 confidence coefficient. Of course, these approximations imply that the true confidence coefficient may deviate from the value just mentioned, and it would be wise to attach less confidence to the interval than this figure suggests.

Problems

8.1 Formulate a 95 percent confidence interval for σ^2 of Table 2.1, using $s^2 = 1.3461$, $\chi^2_{.025}(49) = 31.1$, and $\chi^2_{.975}(49) = 69.7$. Verify that $\sigma^2 = 1$ lies within the interval.

8.2 (*Continuation*) Suppose that $\sigma^2 = 1$ had been outside the interval. What would you conclude, given the knowledge that Table 2.1 is the result of a computer program for random normal sample numbers with mean 10 and unit variance?

2.9 Hypothesis Testing[AB]

Null Hypothesis and Alternative Hypothesis[A]

Parameter estimation is one area in the discipline of statistical inference; the testing of statistical hypotheses is another. Again suppose that a random sample $(X_1, \ldots, X_n)$ has been drawn from a normal population with mean μ and unit variance. We want to use this sample to decide whether it is true that $\mu = \mu_0$, where μ_0 is some given number. The equality $\mu = \mu_0$ is called the *null hypothesis* and is indicated by H_0. This hypothesis is tested against the *alternative hypothesis*, indicated by H_1, which may state that μ is equal to any real number other than μ_0; it may also amount to $\mu > \mu_0$ or $\mu < \mu_0$.

Test Statistic and Critical Region[A]

The usual procedure implies that one formulates a statistic, called *test statistic* in the present context, computes its value from the available sample, and decides to accept or reject H_0 on the basis of this value. In the example of the previous paragraph we may take the sample mean $\bar{X}$ as a test statistic.

If H_0 is true, $\bar{X}$ is distributed normally with mean μ_0 and variance $1/n$. If H_1 is true, $\bar{X}$ is also distributed normally with variance $1/n$ but with mean $\mu \neq \mu_0$. An obvious procedure is to accept H_0 if $\bar{X}$ is sufficiently close to μ_0 but to reject H_0 in favor of H_1 if this is not the case. Specifically, let H_1 imply that μ is any real number different from μ_0. We consider the interval $(\mu_0 \pm 1.96/\sqrt{n})$, which has a .95 probability of containing $\bar{X}$ if H_0 is true. When the observed $\bar{X}$ is either larger than $\mu_0 + 1.96/\sqrt{n}$ or smaller than $\mu_0 - 1.96/\sqrt{n}$, we reject H_0 in favor of H_1. The set of values $>\mu_0 + 1.96/\sqrt{n}$ and $<\mu_0 - 1.96/\sqrt{n}$ is called the *critical region* of the test statistic corresponding to the null hypothesis. If the observed value falls in this region, the null hypothesis is rejected; if this is not the case, the hypothesis is accepted. Note the intimate connection between hypothesis testing and interval estimation. The critical region for the test statistic $\bar{X}$ is the region outside the interval $(\mu_0 \pm 1.96/\sqrt{n})$, where μ_0 is the parameter value according to the null hypothesis, and the confidence interval (.95 confidence coefficient) for μ is $(\bar{X} \pm 1.96/\sqrt{n})$.

Errors of the First and of the Second Kind[A]

Obviously the test statistic may take a value in the critical region even if H_0 is true. In our example there is a .05 chance that $\bar{X}$ is not in $(\mu_0 + 1.96/\sqrt{n})$ when H_0 is true. There is also a positive probability that $\bar{X}$ falls in this interval when H_0 is not true (and hence H_1 is true). In both cases we commit errors. There is an *error of the first kind* when we reject H_0, though it is actually true; in our example the probability of the first-kind error is .05. We have an *error of the second kind* when H_0 is accepted though it is untrue. The probability of a second-kind error depends on the question of which specific hypothesis within the set described by H_1 is true. When the true μ differs very little from μ_0, the probability that $\bar{X}$ falls in $(\mu_0 \pm 1.96/\sqrt{n})$ will not be far below .95. But when μ_0 differs a great deal from the true μ, this probability will be much smaller.

Of course, one is interested in minimizing both kinds of error, but this is not really feasible. The conventional procedure implies that the probability of a first-kind error is fixed at a preassigned level, such as .05 in our example, in which case one is said to proceed at the 5 percent *significance level.* The limits of the corresponding interval $(\mu_0 \pm 1.96/\sqrt{n})$ are then called 5 percent *significance limits*. Preferably the test statistic chosen should be such that the probability of a second-kind error is minimized for each specific hypothesis which is part of the set of hypotheses described by H_1. However, there are not many cases in which such a "uniformly most powerful test" exists; nevertheless, there are satisfactory procedures based on the normal, Student, chi-square, and F distributions.

The Parameter Space; Simple and Composite Hypotheses[B]

A convenient way of visualizing hypothesis testing procedures is by means of the parameter space, usually indicated by Ω. In the case of one unknown parameter μ, which may in principle take any real value, we write this space as $\Omega = \{\mu; -\infty < \mu < \infty\}$. This amounts to a straight line, and the null hypothesis $\mu = \mu_0$ is a point on this line. When we have two unknown parameters, μ (any real value) and σ^2 (any positive real value), the parameter space is two-dimensional and it is indicated as follows:

$$\Omega = \{(\mu, \sigma^2); -\infty < \mu < \infty, 0 < \sigma^2 < \infty\} \tag{9.1}$$

If the null hypothesis H_0 states $\mu = \mu_0$ but specifies nothing about σ^2, then it is the following subspace ω of Ω:

$$\omega = \{(\mu, \sigma^2); \mu = \mu_0, 0 < \sigma^2 < \infty\} \tag{9.2}$$

In this case ω is represented by a straight line in the Ω plane. If H_0 had specified $\mu = \mu_0$, $\sigma^2 = \sigma_0^2$, it would have been represented by a single point in this plane, and the null hypothesis would then be said to be *simple*. The example (9.2) describes ω as a nondegenerate region in the parameter space, which is the case of a *composite* hypothesis. The alternative hypothesis H_1 is represented by the parameter subspace $\Omega - \omega$; this amounts to the half-plane (9.1) excluding the line (9.2) in our example. Alternative hypotheses are usually of the composite type, but there are exceptions. It is conceivable, for example, that one would want to test (μ_0, σ_0^2) against (μ_1, σ_1^2), and both H_0 and H_1 are then simple hypotheses.

The Likelihood Ratio Test[B]

A well-known method for testing a composite H_0 against a composite H_1 is the likelihood ratio test, which can be explained as follows for the case of random sampling from a normal population with unknown μ and σ^2 under the Ω, ω specification (9.1) and (9.2). At any point $(\mu, \sigma^2) \in \omega$ [that is, for any simple hypothesis which falls under H_0 as specified in (9.2)] the likelihood of the sample is

$$L(X_1, \ldots, X_n; \mu_0, \sigma^2) = \frac{1}{(2\pi\sigma^2)^{n/2}} \exp\left\{-\frac{1}{2}\frac{\sum_{i=1}^{n}(X_i - \mu_0)^2}{\sigma^2}\right\} \tag{9.3}$$

Given the sample $(X_1, \ldots, X_n)$ and the μ_0 specified by H_0, this expression still depends on the unspecified σ^2. But we can specify its maximum value for variations in σ^2 by differentiating the logarithm,

$$(9.4) \qquad -\frac{n}{2}\log 2\pi - \frac{n}{2}\log \sigma^2 - \frac{1}{2}\frac{\sum_{i=1}^{n}(X_i - \mu_0)^2}{\sigma^2}$$

with respect to σ^2. The solution for σ^2 is $(1/n)\sum (X_i - \mu_0)^2$. We substitute this into (9.3):

$$(9.5) \qquad L(\hat{\omega}) = \frac{e^{-n/2}}{\left[\frac{2\pi}{n}\sum_{i=1}^{n}(X_i - \mu_0)^2\right]^{n/2}}$$

where $L(\hat{\omega})$ stands for the maximum of $L(\ )$ when (μ, σ^2) is constrained to be located in ω.

If we do not impose this constraint, so that (μ, σ^2) may lie anywhere in Ω, the maximum value of $L(\ )$ will generally be larger. We then replace μ_0 by μ in (9.4) and differentiate with respect to both μ and σ^2. As we know from Section 2.7, this leads to $\bar{X}$ and $(1/n)\sum (X_i - \bar{X})^2$ as the solutions for μ and σ^2, respectively, so that the unconstrained maximum value $L(\hat{\Omega})$ becomes

$$(9.6) \qquad L(\hat{\Omega}) = \frac{e^{-n/2}}{\left[\frac{2\pi}{n}\sum_{i=1}^{n}(X_i - \bar{X})^2\right]^{n/2}}$$

The ratio of the two maxima,

$$(9.7) \qquad \lambda = \frac{L(\hat{\omega})}{L(\hat{\Omega})} = \left[\frac{\sum_{i=1}^{n}(X_i - \bar{X})^2}{\sum_{i=1}^{n}(X_i - \mu_0)^2}\right]^{n/2}$$

is known as the *likelihood ratio*. It is nonnegative and at most equal to 1 [since $L(\hat{\omega})$ is a maximum subject to the ω constraint]. In our example $\lambda = 1$ if and only if $\bar{X} = \mu_0$.

The likelihood ratio test principle states that H_0 is rejected if and only if λ is less than some critical number λ_0, $0 < \lambda_0 < 1$, which is determined by the significance level chosen before. In the case (9.7):

$$\frac{\sum_{i=1}^{n}(X_i - \bar{X})^2}{\sum_{i=1}^{n}(X_i - \mu_0)^2} < \lambda_0^{2/n}$$

Using

$$\sum_{i=1}^{n}(X_i - \mu_0)^2 = \sum_{i=1}^{n}(X_i - \bar{X})^2 + n(\bar{X} - \mu_0)^2$$

we can rewrite this inequality as

$$\frac{n(\bar{X}-\mu_0)^2}{s^2} > (n-1)(\lambda_0^{-2/n}-1)$$

or, equivalently,

$$\frac{\sqrt{n}\,|\bar{X}-\mu_0|}{s} > \sqrt{(n-1)(\lambda_0^{-2/n}-1)} \tag{9.8}$$

where $s^2 = \sum_i (X_i - \bar{X})^2/(n-1)$. Now $\sqrt{n}(\bar{X}-\mu_0)/s$ has a Student distribution with $n-1$ degrees of freedom if H_0 is true. Hence, in this case the likelihood ratio test of H_0 against H_1 may be based on the Student distribution. For example, if $n = 20$ and if we choose the 5 percent significance level, then we use the table of the Student distribution to find that $|t(19)| < 2.093$ holds with probability .975, so that 2.093 is the figure to be substituted for the right-hand side of (9.8).

Problems

9.1 Suppose that the data of Table 2.1 are known to be generated by a random normal sample number mechanism with (unknown) mean μ and unit variance. Use these data to test the null hypothesis $\mu = 10$ against the alternative $\mu \neq 10$. Choose your own level of significance.

9.2 Prove algebraically that the expression after the second equality sign of (9.7) is at most equal to 1.

CHAPTER 3

LEAST SQUARES AND THE STANDARD LINEAR MODEL

The problems with which we shall be concerned in this chapter can be explained and illustrated conveniently with the following example. We observe that the consumption of textiles per capita in the Netherlands in the years 1923 to 1931 was subject to an increasing trend, after which the development became more irregular during the later part of the 1930s. The relevant time series is shown in the first column of Table 3.1. We may then ask questions of the following type. First, given that classical demand theory indicates real income and relative prices as the variables that determine the consumption of various commodities, to what extent do statistical data show that these variables account for the variation of textile consumption over time? Second, can we estimate income and price elasticities from these data? Third, can we also test the hypothesis that, for example, the income elasticity is equal to 1 against the alternative hypothesis that it is larger than 1? Several of these questions and some others will be answered in this chapter, all sections of which are recommended for an introductory course with the exception of certain subsections of Sections 3.7 and 3.8, which are optional.

Table 3.1

Time Series Dealing with the Consumption of Textiles in the Netherlands, 1923–1939

Year	Volume of Textile Consumption per Capita[a] (1)	Real Income per Capita[a] (2)	Relative Price of Textiles[a] (3)	Logarithms of Columns (1)–(3) $\log_{10}$ (1) (4)	$\log_{10}$ (2) (5)	$\log_{10}$ (3) (6)
1923	99.2	96.7	101.0	1.99651	1.98543	2.00432
1924	99.0	98.1	100.1	1.99564	1.99167	2.00043
1925	100.0	100.0	100.0	2.00000	2.00000	2.00000
1926	111.6	104.9	90.6	2.04766	2.02078	1.95713
1927	122.2	104.9	86.5	2.08707	2.02078	1.93702
1928	117.6	109.5	89.7	2.07041	2.03941	1.95279
1929	121.1	110.8	90.6	2.08314	2.04454	1.95713
1930	136.0	112.3	82.8	2.13354	2.05038	1.91803
1931	154.2	109.3	70.1	2.18808	2.03862	1.84572
1932	153.6	105.3	65.4	2.18639	2.02243	1.81558
1933	158.5	101.7	61.3	2.20003	2.00732	1.78746
1934	140.6	95.4	62.5	2.14799	1.97955	1.79588
1935	136.2	96.4	63.6	2.13418	1.98408	1.80346
1936	168.0	97.6	52.6	2.22531	1.98945	1.72099
1937	154.3	102.4	59.7	2.18837	2.01030	1.77597
1938	149.0	101.6	59.5	2.17319	2.00689	1.77452
1939	165.5	103.8	61.3	2.21880	2.01620	1.78746

[a] Index base 1925 = 100.

3.1 The Two-Variable Case[A]

We start with the simple case of only two variables, say, income (x) and total consumption (y) of family households, which is illustrated in the three-dimensional Figure 3.1. Consider the set of families whose incomes in a certain year are all equal to x_1. In general the amounts that they spend will differ because income is not the only factor that determines consumption. Let us assume that these amounts can be described by a probability distribution. This is shown in Figure 3.1 by means of the density curve which is closest to the y-axis, the density itself being measured along the vertical axis.[1] Next, consider all families with income $x_2 > x_1$. One should expect (1) that the amount of consumption will again be subject to a probability distribution

[1] The continuous density curve should be regarded as an approximation to the true distribution of consumption, which is necessarily discrete when the number of families is finite.

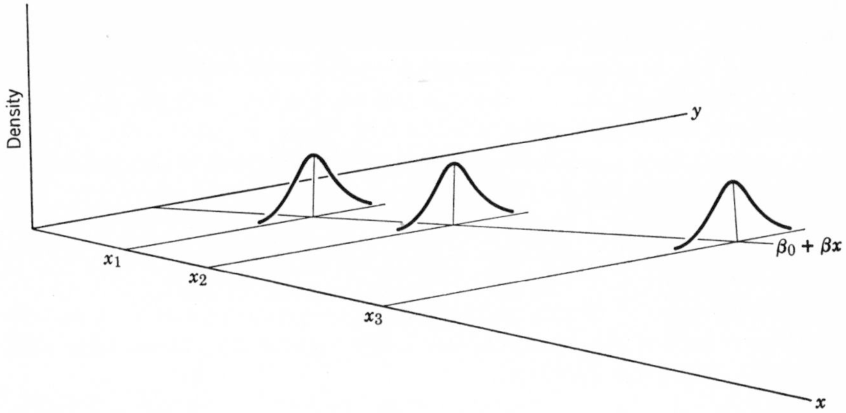

Fig. 3.1 Illustration of a consumption-income relation.

with a positive variance and (2) that the average consumption of this group will exceed that of the former because its income is larger.

A Linear Expectational Relation

Suppose that we specify n incomes $x_1, \ldots, x_n$ and that we draw independently one household at random from the population corresponding to each of these incomes. The idea of a larger average consumption corresponding to a larger income will now be made more specific. It is assumed that the conditional expectation of the household's consumption (y_α), given its income (x_α), is a linear function of x_α:

$$\mathscr{E}(y_\alpha \mid x_\alpha) = \beta_0 + \beta x_\alpha \tag{1.1}$$

This function is illustrated in Figure 3.1 by means of the straight line in the horizontal plane. Thus, as income varies, the average amount of consumption changes linearly with income.

Unbiased Least-Squares Estimation

The coefficients β_0 and β are unknown parameters, and their statistical estimation is one of our main objectives. Let us estimate them by b_0 and b, the constant term and the slope of the LS regression of y_α on x_α:

$$b = \frac{\sum_{\alpha=1}^{n}(x_\alpha - \bar{x})(y_\alpha - \bar{y})}{\sum_{\alpha=1}^{n}(x_\alpha - \bar{x})^2} \qquad b_0 = \bar{y} - b\bar{x} \tag{1.2}$$

where $\bar{x} = (1/n)\sum x_\alpha$ and $\bar{y} = (1/n)\sum y_\alpha$. It is easily shown that b is unbiased for β and b_0 for β_0 under the conditions of the previous paragraph. Recall that the numerator of the ratio in (1.2) can be written $\sum (x_\alpha - \bar{x})y_\alpha$, since in this kind of product sum it is sufficient to take only one of the two variables as a deviation from the average. Since we regard the incomes $x_1, \ldots, x_n$ as fixed conditioning factors, the expectation of this numerator can thus be written in view of (1.1):

$$\sum_{\alpha=1}^{n}(x_\alpha - \bar{x})(\beta_0 + \beta x_\alpha) = \beta\sum_{\alpha=1}^{n}(x_\alpha - \bar{x})x_\alpha = \beta\sum_{\alpha=1}^{n}(x_\alpha - \bar{x})^2$$

After dividing this by the denominator in (1.2), we obtain $\mathscr{E}b = \beta$, so that the LS slope estimator b is indeed unbiased. The proof of the unbiasedness of b_0 is equally simple (see Problem 1.1).

The Disturbance Formulation

Equation (1.1) can be written in the equivalent form

$$(1.3) \qquad y_\alpha = \beta_0 + \beta x_\alpha + \epsilon_\alpha \qquad \text{where} \qquad \mathscr{E}(\epsilon_\alpha \mid x_\alpha) = 0$$

The equivalence of (1.1) and (1.3) is easily proved by taking the conditional expectation (given x_α) of both sides of $y_\alpha = \beta_0 + \beta x_\alpha + \epsilon_\alpha$. The new formulation has the advantage that it clearly shows that y_α consists of two parts, one of which $(\beta_0 + \beta x_\alpha)$ is the component accounted for by income and the other (ϵ_α) is the component accounted for by all determining factors other than income. The ϵ's are known as the *disturbances* of eq. (1.3) and thus represent the combined effect on consumption of the determining factors which are not introduced explicitly. These factors are frequently called the *neglected variables*.

A Variance Condition

Next suppose that the conditional variance of y_α given x_α is a constant:

$$(1.4) \qquad \operatorname{var}(y_\alpha \mid x_\alpha) = \sigma^2$$

This conditional variance is thus completely independent of the level of income. The three density curves of Figure 3.1 illustrate this feature; they all have the same standard deviation (σ). The present assumption in conjunction with (1.1) implies that as income increases, the average amount of consumption changes but not its variance. Note that (1.4) can also be written as

$$(1.5) \qquad \operatorname{var}(\epsilon_\alpha \mid x_\alpha) = \sigma^2$$

because the disturbance ϵ_α is nothing but y_α measured as a deviation from its expectation $\beta_0 + \beta x_\alpha$, so that the two variances must indeed be identical.

The Sampling Variance of the LS Slope Estimator

Applying (1.3), we find the following expression for the sampling error of the LS slope coefficient b:

$$b - \beta = \frac{\sum_{\alpha=1}^{n}(x_\alpha - \bar{x})(\beta_0 + \beta x_\alpha + \epsilon_\alpha)}{\sum_{\alpha=1}^{n}(x_\alpha - \bar{x})^2} - \beta = \frac{\sum_{\alpha=1}^{n}(x_\alpha - \bar{x})\epsilon_\alpha}{\sum_{\alpha=1}^{n}(x_\alpha - \bar{x})^2} \tag{1.6}$$

The sampling error is thus a linear combination of the disturbances $\epsilon_1, \ldots, \epsilon_n$, the weights being $(x_1 - \bar{x})/A, \ldots, (x_n - \bar{x})/A$ where $A = \sum (x_\alpha - \bar{x})^2$. Note that these weights are all fixed numbers because the incomes are regarded as fixed.

To obtain the sampling variance of b we should square the sampling error,

$$(b - \beta)^2 = \frac{\sum_{\alpha=1}^{n}\sum_{\eta=1}^{n}(x_\alpha - \bar{x})(x_\eta - \bar{x})\epsilon_\alpha\epsilon_\eta}{\left[\sum_{\alpha=1}^{n}(x_\alpha - \bar{x})^2\right]^2} \tag{1.7}$$

and then take the expectation. The right-hand side of (1.7) is a linear combination of the n^2 disturbance products $\epsilon_\alpha\epsilon_\eta$ $(\alpha, \eta = 1, \ldots, n)$. For $\alpha \neq \eta$ we have such a product corresponding to two different observations. Recall that it was assumed that one household each is drawn *independently* from the populations corresponding to the incomes $x_1, \ldots, x_n$. This implies that ϵ_α and ϵ_η are independent for $\alpha \neq \eta$, so that the expectation of their product is equal to the product of the expectations and hence zero [see (1.3)]. For $\alpha = \eta$ the product becomes ϵ_α^2, the expectation of which is σ^2 [see (1.5)]. Therefore the expectation of the numerator of (1.7) is $\sigma^2 \sum (x_\alpha - \bar{x})^2$. Hence

$$\operatorname{var} b = \frac{\sigma^2}{\sum_{\alpha=1}^{n}(x_\alpha - \bar{x})^2} \tag{1.8}$$

Since the right-hand denominator of (1.8) may be written as n multiplied by the variance of the numbers $x_1, \ldots, x_n$, the sampling variance of the LS slope estimator b thus becomes smaller when the standard deviation σ of the disturbances is smaller, when the number of observations n is larger, and when the dispersion of the income values is larger. The first two statements imply that the slope is estimated with greater accuracy when the relation is less disturbed and when we have more observations; both implications ought to be intuitively obvious. The third statement is obvious, too. When the n incomes move closer to each other (less dispersion), the determination of the slope of the consumption-income line becomes more and more uncertain; in the limit, when all incomes are equal, the slope cannot be determined at all and the expression for the variance becomes infinite.

The variance of the constant term b_0 and the covariance of b_0 and b can be derived similarly; see Problems 1.2 and 1.3.

Problems

1.1 Prove that the expectation of $\bar{y}$ is equal to $\beta_0 + \beta\bar{x}$, and use this to prove that b_0 is unbiased for β_0.

1.2 Prove $b_0 - \beta_0 = \bar{\epsilon} - \bar{x}(b - \beta)$, where $\bar{\epsilon}$ is the average of $\epsilon_1, \ldots, \epsilon_n$. Square both sides and take the expectation to find

$$\text{(1.9)} \qquad \operatorname{var} b_0 = \frac{\sigma^2}{n} + \frac{\sigma^2\bar{x}^2}{\sum (x_\alpha - \bar{x})^2} = \frac{\sigma^2}{n}\frac{\sum x_\alpha^2}{\sum (x_\alpha - \bar{x})^2}$$

where all summations are over α from 1 through n.

1.3 (*Continuation*) Multiply the sampling errors of b_0 and b to find that their covariance is equal to $-\bar{x} \operatorname{var} b$, where $\operatorname{var} b$ is given in (1.8). Combine these results to obtain the following covariance matrix of b_0 and b:

$$\text{(1.10)} \qquad \mathscr{V}\begin{bmatrix} b_0 \\ b \end{bmatrix} = \frac{\sigma^2}{\sum (x_\alpha - \bar{x})^2}\begin{bmatrix} \frac{1}{n}\sum x_\alpha^2 & -\bar{x} \\ -\bar{x} & 1 \end{bmatrix}$$

Conclude that the constant-term and slope estimators are uncorrelated when the x-observations have a zero average.

3.2 The Assumptions of the Standard Linear Model[A]

The analysis of Section 3.1 will now be extended, in this and the next sections, to more general situations.

Four Assumptions Relating to the Textile Example

We return to the data in the first column of Table 3.1 and consider the following four assumptions, which are all directly comparable with similar assumptions made in the previous section.

(1) For each year α, $\alpha = 1923, \ldots, 1939$, the observed value of textile consumption per capita is the realization of a random variable. The distribution of this random variable describes in probabilistic form the set of

values which textile consumption could have taken in year α, whereas actually only one value is observed. Note that this assumption is not at all concerned with this particular numerical value; it deals only with the process which generates such a value.

(2) The distribution mentioned in the previous paragraph is such that the conditional expectation of the logarithm of textile consumption per capita in year α (to be written y_α), given real income per capita and the relative price of textile goods, is a linear function of the logarithm of real income per capita in that year ($x_{\alpha 1}$) and of the logarithm of the relative textile price in the same year ($x_{\alpha 2}$):

$$\mathscr{E}(y_\alpha \mid x_{\alpha 1}, x_{\alpha 2}) = \beta_0 + \beta_1 x_{\alpha 1} + \beta_2 x_{\alpha 2} \qquad (\alpha = 1923, \ldots, 1939) \tag{2.1}$$

where β_0, β_1, and β_2 are unknown parameters similar to β_0 and β of (1.1). Note that the present equation is log-linear, since y_α, $x_{\alpha 1}$, and $x_{\alpha 2}$ are the logarithms of textile consumption, income, and textile price, respectively, in year α.

(3) The conditional variance of y_α, given $x_{\alpha 1}$ and $x_{\alpha 2}$, is a constant:

$$\text{var}\,(y_\alpha \mid x_{\alpha 1}, x_{\alpha 2}) = \sigma^2 \qquad (\alpha = 1923, \ldots, 1939) \tag{2.2}$$

where σ^2 is an unknown positive parameter. This variance measures the extent to which textile consumption is affected by variables other than income and textile price (the neglected variables), which may include changes in fashion and in the distribution of income, prices of competing or complementary goods (such as footwear), and so on. The constancy of the variance implies that the variance of the combined effect of the neglected variables does not change over time.

(4) Introduce the disturbance formulation:

$$y_\alpha = \beta_0 + \beta_1 x_{\alpha 1} + \beta_2 x_{\alpha 2} + \epsilon_\alpha \tag{2.3}$$

In view of (2.1) and (2.2), each disturbance ϵ_α has (given $x_{\alpha 1}$ and $x_{\alpha 2}$) zero expectation and variance σ^2. In addition, we now also assume that they are independent, so that the value of $\epsilon_\alpha = y_\alpha - \mathscr{E}(y_\alpha \mid x_{\alpha 1}, x_{\alpha 2})$ in any year α is completely uninformative with respect to the distribution of the ϵ's in other years.

Economic Interpretation of the Textile Example

It follows from the logarithmic definition of y_α, $x_{\alpha 1}$, and $x_{\alpha 2}$ in (2.1) that β_1 and β_2 are the income elasticity and the price elasticity, respectively, of the demand for textile. More precisely, β_2 is the elasticity of the demand for textile with respect to the relative textile price under the condition of a constant real income. Notice that when the textile price goes up, while all other prices remain unchanged, real income decreases unless there is a compensating increase in money income.

Equation (2.1) contains only one relative price, which means that prices of competing or complementary products are assumed to play no important role. This assumption is made here to simplify the model and the analysis; at this stage there is no need to aim at generality. Further note that the same equation also determines the data requirements. We need real per capita income and the relative price of textile goods in each of the years 1923 to 1939. These are given in columns (2) and (3) of Table 3.1, and the logarithms (to the base 10) of the three variables in columns (4) through (6). The construction of these time series is as follows.

- ☐ The relative price of textiles is obtained by dividing a retail price index of clothing (used as a substitute for textiles generally) by a general cost of living index.
- ☐ Real income per capita is obtained by dividing total money income of private consumers by the product of the cost of living index and the population size.
- ☐ Textile consumption per capita is obtained by dividing the total money value of textile consumption by private consumers by the product of the retail price index of clothing and the population size.

The Dependent Variable and the Explanatory Variables

The model (1) to (4) for the textile example and the analogous model for the consumption-income relation of Section 3.1 are both special cases of the standard linear multiple regression model (or the *standard linear model*) which will now be described.

The starting point is always a variable whose behavior is to be described or explained in terms of other variables. This behavior may be a development over time, in which case the data usually consist of successive observations (in the textile example: the 17 annual observations 1923 to 1939). We may also have the cross-section case in which the data consist of observations on different households or firms. This applies to the example of Section 3.1 when we imagine that income-consumption data $(x_1, y_1), \ldots, (x_n, y_n)$ are available for n families.

The variable whose observed behavior is the object of analysis is called the variable "to be explained" or the *dependent variable*; in the textile case, the logarithm of textile consumption per capita. We are interested in the factors that determine this variable; in particular, we want to measure the effects of these factors on the dependent variable. But usually we do not know all of the determining factors and, even if we do know them, we usually do not have observations on all of these factors. The standard linear model divides the determining factors into two groups: those which are introduced explicitly as *explanatory variables* and those which are not introduced and are thereby neglected. In the textile example the explanatory variables are the logarithms of real income per capita and of the relative textile price.

The Expectation of the Dependent Variable

Write **y** for the vector of values of the dependent variable and **X** for the matrix of all values taken by the explanatory variables. The standard linear model assumes that the conditional expectation of **y** given **X** is a linear function of **X**.[2] For n observations and K explanatory variables this can be written

$$\mathscr{E}(\mathbf{y} \mid \mathbf{X}) = \mathbf{X}\boldsymbol{\beta} \quad \text{where} \quad [\mathbf{y} \quad \mathbf{X}] = \begin{bmatrix} y_1 & \vdots & x_{11} & \cdots & x_{1K} \\ y_2 & \vdots & x_{21} & \cdots & x_{2K} \\ \cdot & \vdots & \cdot & & \cdot \\ \cdot & \vdots & \cdot & & \cdot \\ \cdot & \vdots & \cdot & & \cdot \\ y_n & \vdots & x_{n1} & \cdots & x_{nK} \end{bmatrix} \quad \text{and} \quad \boldsymbol{\beta} = \begin{bmatrix} \beta_1 \\ \beta_2 \\ \cdot \\ \cdot \\ \cdot \\ \beta_K \end{bmatrix} \tag{2.4}$$

In the textile case the vector $\boldsymbol{\beta}$ consists of three components: β_0, β_1, β_2 in the notation of (2.1). The last two elements are the coefficients of two explanatory variables: the logarithm of real per capita income and of the relative price of textile goods. The coefficient β_0 is a constant term and can be interpreted as the coefficient of an explanatory variable which takes the unit value for each of the n observations [see the discussion of eq. (7.15) of Section 1.7]. Going back to Table 3.1, we conclude that **X** and **y** have 17 rows in the textile example, that the first column of **X** consists of 17 units, that the second and third are columns (5) and (6), respectively, of the table, and that column (4) is the vector of observed realizations corresponding to the random vector **y**.

The first basic assumption of the standard linear model is:

Assumption 3.1 (Expectation of dependent variable) *The observed values taken by the dependent variable are realizations of an n-element random vector* **y** *whose conditional expectation given* **X** *is specified in* (2.4), *where* **X** *is an observed* $n \times K$ *matrix of rank K consisting of values taken by K explanatory variables, while* $\boldsymbol{\beta}$ *is a column vector of K unknown parameters.*

Note that this assumption requires **X** to have full column rank. If the rank of **X** is less than K, the LS estimator of $\boldsymbol{\beta}$, which will be considered in the next section, does not exist. Indeed, it will be shown in Section 3.8 that $\boldsymbol{\beta}$ cannot

[2] In (1.1) and (2.1) we took as conditioning factors only the values of the explanatory variables of the same (αth) observation. However, the statistical analysis is simplified considerably when we extend this to all observations.

be estimated at all in that case except in a very limited sense. This is particularly clear for the example discussed in Section 3.1. Its matrix $\mathbf{X}$ consists of n rows $[1 \quad x_\alpha]$, where 1 refers to the constant term and x_α to the income of the αth household. This matrix has rank less than $K = 2$ if (and only if) all n incomes are equal, so that the second column of $\mathbf{X}$ is then a scalar multiple of the first. Clearly, it is impossible to estimate both the slope and the intercept of the straight line in the horizontal plane of Figure 3.1 when all incomes are equal.

The disturbance formulation is straightforward. Consider

$$\mathbf{y} = \mathbf{X}\boldsymbol{\beta} + \boldsymbol{\epsilon} \tag{2.5}$$

where $\boldsymbol{\epsilon}$ is the disturbance vector. On taking the expectation of both sides of (2.5) we obtain $\mathscr{E}(\boldsymbol{\epsilon} \mid \mathbf{X}) = \mathbf{0}$.

The Assumption of a Scalar Covariance Matrix

Assumption 3.1 corresponds to items (1) and (2) of the list of assumptions that we made at the beginning of this section when discussing the textile example. The following corresponds to items (3) and (4).

ASSUMPTION 3.2 (Scalar covariance matrix) *The conditional covariance matrix of* $\mathbf{y}$ *given* $\mathbf{X}$ *is a scalar matrix:*

$$\mathscr{V}(\mathbf{y} \mid \mathbf{X}) = \sigma^2\mathbf{I} \qquad (\sigma^2 < \infty) \tag{2.6}$$

where σ^2 *is an unknown positive parameter and* $\mathbf{I}$ *is the* $n \times n$ *unit matrix.*

The diagonal elements of the matrix equation (2.6) specify all variances to be equal to σ^2, and the off-diagonal elements declare all covariances to be zero; the corresponding equation for the disturbance vector is similar, $\mathscr{V}(\boldsymbol{\epsilon} \mid \mathbf{X}) = \sigma^2\mathbf{I}$. (Why?) Notice that these ϵ's are only assumed to be uncorrelated, not independent. In this respect the present assumption is (slightly) weaker than assumption (4) at the beginning of this section.

The Two Assumptions Combined

In many cases we shall have to use both Assumptions 3.1 and 3.2, and it will then be convenient to refer to only one assumption that covers both. This can be done by means of Assumption 3.3, which is based on the disturbance formulation.

ASSUMPTION 3.3 (Standard linear model) *The observed values taken by the dependent variable are realizations of an n-element random vector* $\mathbf{y}$ *which can be written as* $\mathbf{X}\boldsymbol{\beta} + \boldsymbol{\epsilon}$, *where* $\mathbf{X}$ *is an observed* $n \times K$ *matrix of rank* K *consisting of values taken by* K *explanatory variables,* $\boldsymbol{\beta}$ *is a column vector of* K *unknown parameters, and* $\boldsymbol{\epsilon}$ *is an* n*-element disturbance vector whose conditional mean vector and covariance matrix given* $\mathbf{X}$ *are* $\mathscr{E}(\boldsymbol{\epsilon} \mid \mathbf{X}) = \mathbf{0}$ *and* $\mathscr{V}(\boldsymbol{\epsilon} \mid \mathbf{X}) = \sigma^2\mathbf{I}$, σ^2 *being an unknown positive parameter and* $\mathbf{I}$ *the* $n \times n$ *unit matrix.*

Fixed or Random Values of the Explanatory Variables?

In the notation used in this and the previous sections we always indicated explicitly the values of the explanatory variables as conditioning factors of the expectations. This has the advantage that these values may actually be random rather than fixed numbers. Recall that we stipulated in Section 3.1 that the n incomes $x_1, \ldots, x_n$ are selected before we draw households at random. These x's are then fixed, but the analysis which follows is equally applicable on the basis of Assumptions 3.1 to 3.3 when $\mathbf{X}$ is a matrix consisting of random elements; the only thing which is needed is that $\mathbf{y}$ equals $\mathbf{X}\boldsymbol{\beta} + \boldsymbol{\epsilon}$ with $\mathscr{E}(\boldsymbol{\epsilon} \mid \mathbf{X}) = \mathbf{0}$ and $\mathscr{V}(\boldsymbol{\epsilon} \mid \mathbf{X}) = \sigma^2\mathbf{I}$, the observed $\mathbf{X}$ having full column rank. On the other hand, given that our assumptions are formulated conditionally on $\mathbf{X}$, nothing is lost when we regard this matrix as consisting of constant (nonstochastic) elements—just the values observed for each of the explanatory variables. We shall do so in what follows because it enables us to replace the rather cumbersome conditional notation $\mathscr{E}(\boldsymbol{\epsilon} \mid \mathbf{X})$, $\mathscr{V}(\boldsymbol{\epsilon} \mid \mathbf{X})$ by the simpler expressions $\mathscr{E}\boldsymbol{\epsilon}$, $\mathscr{V}(\boldsymbol{\epsilon})$.

Problems

2.1 Consider Assumptions 3.1 and 3.2 but modify the latter by specifying $\sigma^2 = 0$. How would you estimate $\boldsymbol{\beta}$ in that case? Describe the sampling distribution of the estimator.

2.2 Suppose that the matrices $\mathbf{X}$ and $\boldsymbol{\epsilon}$ of Assumption 3.3 are both random and continuously distributed. Prove that when $\mathbf{X}$ and $\boldsymbol{\epsilon}$ are stochastically independent, the conditional mean vector and covariance matrix of $\boldsymbol{\epsilon}$ given $\mathbf{X}$ are independent of $\mathbf{X}$ (which is in agreement with Assumption 3.3). Also prove that the independence condition is *not* implied by Assumption 3.3. (*Hint.* Consider the third and higher-order moments of the disturbances.)

3.3 The Least-Squares Estimation Method[A]

In Section 3.1 we used a simple LS regression to estimate the parameters of the expectational relationship between income and consumption. This procedure will be extended in this section, and the result will be applied to the textile data of Table 3.1.

Unbiasedness and Covariance Matrix of the LS Coefficient Estimator

In Section 1.7 we derived the coefficient vector that minimizes the length of the discrepancy vector $\mathbf{y} - \mathbf{Xb}$:

$$\mathbf{b} = (\mathbf{X}'\mathbf{X})^{-1}\mathbf{X}'\mathbf{y} \tag{3.1}$$

Recall that this vector is the unique solution of the minimization problem when $\mathbf{X}$ has full column rank.

The coefficient vector $\mathbf{b}$ will now be regarded as an estimator of the parameter vector $\boldsymbol{\beta}$ of (2.4), and we proceed to derive some of its properties. First, note that $\mathbf{b}$ is linear in $\mathbf{y}$, the matrix $(\mathbf{X}'\mathbf{X})^{-1}\mathbf{X}'$ consisting of constant elements. Second, the estimator is *unbiased*:

$$\mathscr{E}\mathbf{b} = \mathscr{E}[(\mathbf{X}'\mathbf{X})^{-1}\mathbf{X}'\mathbf{y}] = (\mathbf{X}'\mathbf{X})^{-1}\mathbf{X}'\mathscr{E}\mathbf{y} = (\mathbf{X}'\mathbf{X})^{-1}\mathbf{X}'\mathbf{X}\boldsymbol{\beta} = \boldsymbol{\beta} \tag{3.2}$$

where the third equality sign is based on (2.4) with $\mathscr{E}(\mathbf{y} \mid \mathbf{X})$ abbreviated as $\mathscr{E}\mathbf{y}$. Note that the unbiasedness property is independent of the question of whether Assumption 3.2 on the variances and covariances is fulfilled or not.

Using (2.5), we find for the sampling error

$$\mathbf{b} - \boldsymbol{\beta} = (\mathbf{X}'\mathbf{X})^{-1}\mathbf{X}'(\mathbf{X}\boldsymbol{\beta} + \boldsymbol{\epsilon}) - \boldsymbol{\beta} = (\mathbf{X}'\mathbf{X})^{-1}\mathbf{X}'\boldsymbol{\epsilon} \tag{3.3}$$

which shows that this error is the same function of the disturbance vector $\boldsymbol{\epsilon}$ as the estimator itself is of the vector $\mathbf{y}$. We postmultiply the sampling error by its own transpose:

$$(\mathbf{b} - \boldsymbol{\beta})(\mathbf{b} - \boldsymbol{\beta})' = (\mathbf{X}'\mathbf{X})^{-1}\mathbf{X}'\boldsymbol{\epsilon}\boldsymbol{\epsilon}'\mathbf{X}(\mathbf{X}'\mathbf{X})^{-1}$$

If we then take the expectation, we obtain the matrix of second-order moments of the sampling errors. Given the unbiasedness this is simply the covariance matrix of $\mathbf{b}$. Hence

$$\begin{aligned} \mathscr{V}(\mathbf{b}) &= (\mathbf{X}'\mathbf{X})^{-1}\mathbf{X}'\mathscr{E}(\boldsymbol{\epsilon}\boldsymbol{\epsilon}')\mathbf{X}(\mathbf{X}'\mathbf{X})^{-1} \\ &= \sigma^2(\mathbf{X}'\mathbf{X})^{-1}\mathbf{X}'\mathbf{X}(\mathbf{X}'\mathbf{X})^{-1} \\ &= \sigma^2(\mathbf{X}'\mathbf{X})^{-1} \end{aligned} \tag{3.4}$$

where use is made of $\mathscr{E}(\boldsymbol{\epsilon}\boldsymbol{\epsilon}') = \mathscr{V}(\boldsymbol{\epsilon}) = \sigma^2\mathbf{I}$. Thus we find that the covariance matrix of $\mathbf{b}$ is equal to precisely the same inverse matrix which occurs in (3.1), multiplied by the scalar σ^2. An immediate conclusion is that, given the values taken by the explanatory variables (i.e., given the matrix $\mathbf{X}$), the sampling variances and covariances decrease when the neglected variables play a smaller role in the sense that σ^2 is smaller.

We can summarize these results as follows.

THEOREM 3.1 (Existence and uniqueness of the LS coefficient estimator) *The LS coefficient vector* $\mathbf{b}$, *obtained by minimizing the length of the vector* $\mathbf{y} - \mathbf{Xb}$, *is given by* (3.1). *This vector exists and is unique if and only if* $\mathbf{X}$ *has full column rank.*

THEOREM 3.2 (Unbiasedness and covariance matrix of the LS coefficient estimator) *If Assumption* 3.1 *is true for given* $\mathbf{X}$, *the LS coefficient vector* $\mathbf{b}$ *is an unbiased estimator of* $\boldsymbol{\beta}$. *If Assumption* 3.2 *is also true, the covariance matrix of* $\mathbf{b}$ *is as specified in* (3.4).

The LS Residual Vector and the LS Variance Estimator

When attempting to compute the covariance matrix that is given in (3.4), we face the difficulty that σ^2 is as much an unknown parameter as the elements of $\boldsymbol{\beta}$ are. So we must estimate σ^2, the common variance of the n disturbances $\epsilon_1, \ldots, \epsilon_n$. These disturbances are not observable, however, since their vector $\boldsymbol{\epsilon}$ is equal to $\mathbf{y} - \mathbf{X}\boldsymbol{\beta}$ and $\boldsymbol{\beta}$ is unknown. We can make the situation clearer by formulating the following double dichotomy for the matrices that occur in $\mathbf{y} = \mathbf{X}\boldsymbol{\beta} + \boldsymbol{\epsilon}$.

	Stochastic	Nonstochastic
Observable	$\mathbf{y}$	$\mathbf{X}$
Not observable	$\boldsymbol{\epsilon}$	$\boldsymbol{\beta}$

It is to be understood, of course, that a random variable is interpreted here as observable when its realization is observable. For $\mathbf{y}$ this is true; for $\boldsymbol{\epsilon}$ it is not.

Under these circumstances we must use a substitute for $\boldsymbol{\epsilon} = \mathbf{y} - \mathbf{X}\boldsymbol{\beta}$ to estimate σ^2. An obvious choice is the discrepancy vector $\mathbf{y} - \mathbf{Xb}$, where $\mathbf{b}$ is the LS coefficient vector. This discrepancy vector will now be called the *LS residual vector* and will be denoted by $\mathbf{e}$. Its elements are $e_1, \ldots, e_n$, the LS residuals. The vector is defined as

(3.5) $$\mathbf{e} = \mathbf{y} - \mathbf{Xb} = \mathbf{y} - \mathbf{X}(\mathbf{X}'\mathbf{X})^{-1}\mathbf{X}'\mathbf{y} = \mathbf{My}$$

where

(3.6) $$\mathbf{M} = \mathbf{I} - \mathbf{X}(\mathbf{X}'\mathbf{X})^{-1}\mathbf{X}'$$

is the idempotent matrix that was introduced in eq. (7.19) of Section 1.7. Also recall that the vector $\mathbf{e}$ is orthogonal to each of the columns of $\mathbf{X}$:

(3.7) $$\mathbf{X}'\mathbf{e} = \mathbf{0}$$

The estimator of σ^2 is now derived from the sum of the squares of the LS residuals.

THEOREM 3.3 (Unbiasedness of the LS variance estimator) *Suppose that Assumption* 3.3 *is true for given* **X**;[3] *also suppose* $n > K$. *Then the statistic*

$$s^2 = \frac{\mathbf{e}'\mathbf{e}}{n-K} = \frac{\mathbf{y}'\mathbf{M}\mathbf{y}}{n-K} \tag{3.8}$$

is an unbiased estimator of σ^2, *and* $s^2(\mathbf{X}'\mathbf{X})^{-1}$ *is an unbiased estimator of the covariance matrix mentioned in Theorem* 3.2, **e** *and* **M** *being defined in* (3.5) *and* (3.6), *respectively.*

To prove the theorem we write

$$\mathbf{e} = \mathbf{M}\mathbf{y} = \mathbf{M}(\mathbf{X}\boldsymbol{\beta} + \boldsymbol{\epsilon}) = \mathbf{M}\boldsymbol{\epsilon} \tag{3.9}$$

where use is made of $\mathbf{MX} = \mathbf{0}$, which was proved in eq. (7.22) of Section 1.7. We conclude that the LS residual vector is equal to the same linear function of the true disturbance vector $\boldsymbol{\epsilon}$ as it is of **y**. The sum of squares of the elements of **e** is then

$$\mathbf{e}'\mathbf{e} = \boldsymbol{\epsilon}'\mathbf{M}'\mathbf{M}\boldsymbol{\epsilon} = \boldsymbol{\epsilon}'\mathbf{M}\boldsymbol{\epsilon} = \text{tr}\,\mathbf{M}\boldsymbol{\epsilon}\boldsymbol{\epsilon}' \tag{3.10}$$

The second equality sign is based on the idempotency of **M**, the third on the fact that $\boldsymbol{\epsilon}'\mathbf{M}\boldsymbol{\epsilon}$ is a scalar and hence equal to its own trace. We take the expectation and use the property that the trace of a square matrix is a linear operator on that matrix, so that the expectation of a trace is equal to the trace of the expectation:

$$\mathscr{E}(\mathbf{e}'\mathbf{e}) = \text{tr}\,\mathbf{M}\mathscr{E}(\boldsymbol{\epsilon}\boldsymbol{\epsilon}') = \sigma^2\,\text{tr}\,\mathbf{M} = (n-K)\sigma^2 \tag{3.11}$$

where the last step is based on eq. (7.21) of Section 1.7. The unbiasedness of s^2 defined in (3.8) follows immediately, while the unbiasedness of $s^2(\mathbf{X}'\mathbf{X})^{-1}$ with respect to the covariance matrix (3.4) then follows as a corollary.

Some comments on Theorem 3.3 are in order. First, we note that the sum of squares of the n residuals is not divided by their number (n), but by $n - K$, which is known as the number of *degrees of freedom* of the equation $\mathbf{y} = \mathbf{X}\boldsymbol{\beta} + \boldsymbol{\epsilon}$:[4] the number of observations minus the number of coefficients adjusted (one $\boldsymbol{\beta}$ element for each explanatory variable) or, equivalently, the excess of the number of rows of the **X** matrix over the number of columns. Second, it should be intuitively obvious that the sum of squares $\mathbf{e}'\mathbf{e}$ is, on the average, less than $n\sigma^2$ and that the difference tends to become larger when K increases [which is the "qualitative" interpretation of (3.11)]. The point is

[3] Whenever Assumptions 3.1 and 3.2 are both used, we shall formulate them as Assumption 3.3, which combines the two.

[4] The relationship with the degrees of freedom of Section 2.6 will become clear in Section 3.5, where the normality assumption is introduced.

that the LS estimation procedure is based on *minimizing* this sum of squares, and it stands to reason that we shall, on the average, be more successful in reducing the sum of squares when the number (K) of coefficients adjusted is larger. Third, the unbiasedness of the estimator (3.8) is the direct extension of the unbiasedness of s^2 defined in eq. (7.17) of Section 2.7, where only one coefficient (the mean μ estimated by $\bar{X}$) was adjusted; this is pursued in Problem 3.1. Fourth, it ought to be noted that the unbiasedness of s^2 of (3.8) requires the validity of Assumption 3.2, whereas this assumption is *not* needed for the unbiasedness of the coefficient vector **b**.

LS Estimation of the Demand Equation for Textile

The above development shows that the basic matrix for the LS estimation procedure is the observation matrix $[\mathbf{y} \quad \mathbf{X}]$ of the $K+1$ variables. In the textile case:

$$[\mathbf{y} \quad \mathbf{X}] = [\mathbf{y} \quad \boldsymbol{\iota} \quad \mathbf{x}_1 \quad \mathbf{x}_2] \tag{3.12}$$

where

$\mathbf{y}$ = the 17-element column vector of observations on the logarithm of textile consumption per capita

$\boldsymbol{\iota}$ = the 17-element column vector of units

$\mathbf{x}_1$ = the 17-element column vector of observations on the logarithm of real per capita income

$\mathbf{x}_2$ = the 17-element column vector of observations on the logarithm of the relative price of textile goods.

The LS method uses the observation matrix (3.12) exclusively in the form of the sums of squares and products of the variables:

$$\begin{bmatrix} \mathbf{y}' \\ \mathbf{X}' \end{bmatrix} [\mathbf{y} \quad \mathbf{X}] = \begin{bmatrix} \mathbf{y}'\mathbf{y} & \mathbf{y}'\mathbf{X} \\ \mathbf{X}'\mathbf{y} & \mathbf{X}'\mathbf{X} \end{bmatrix} \tag{3.13}$$

$$= \begin{array}{c} \\ \\ \\ \\ \\ \end{array} \begin{bmatrix} 76.65898 & 36.07631 & 72.59642 & 67.44192 \\ \hline 36.07631 & 17 & 34.20783 & 31.83389 \\ 72.59642 & 34.20783 & 68.84179 & 64.06457 \\ 67.44192 & 31.83389 & 64.06457 & 59.75950 \end{bmatrix} \begin{matrix} \mathbf{y}' \\ \boldsymbol{\iota}' \\ \mathbf{x}_1' \\ \mathbf{x}_2' \end{matrix}$$

$$\qquad\qquad \mathbf{y} \qquad\qquad \boldsymbol{\iota} \qquad\qquad \mathbf{x}_1 \qquad\qquad \mathbf{x}_2$$

We need the inverse of $\mathbf{X}'\mathbf{X}$:

$$(\mathbf{X}'\mathbf{X})^{-1} = \begin{bmatrix} 510.8912 & -254.2522 & .4167 \\ -254.2522 & 132.7044 & -6.8242 \\ .4167 & -6.8242 & 7.1106 \end{bmatrix} \tag{3.14}$$

after which the vector of LS point estimates of the coefficients is obtained easily:

$$\mathbf{b} = (\mathbf{X}'\mathbf{X})^{-1}\mathbf{X}'\mathbf{y} = \begin{bmatrix} 1.3742 \\ 1.1430 \\ -.8289 \end{bmatrix} \tag{3.15}$$

We also need the unbiased estimate of σ^2:

$$s^2 = \frac{1}{n-K}\mathbf{y}'\mathbf{M}\mathbf{y} = \frac{1}{14}[\mathbf{y}'\mathbf{y} - \mathbf{y}'\mathbf{X}(\mathbf{X}'\mathbf{X})^{-1}\mathbf{X}'\mathbf{y}] = .0001833 \tag{3.16}$$

so that the unbiased estimate of the covariance matrix of **b** is

$$s^2(\mathbf{X}'\mathbf{X})^{-1} = \begin{bmatrix} .093617 & -.046604 & .000077 \\ -.046604 & .024324 & -.001251 \\ .000077 & -.001251 & .001304 \end{bmatrix} \tag{3.17}$$

Combining (3.15) with the square roots of the diagonal elements of (3.17), we obtain

$$\begin{aligned} y_\alpha = \underset{(.31)}{1.37} + \underset{(.16)}{1.14}x_{\alpha 1} - \underset{(.04)}{.83}x_{\alpha 2} + e_\alpha \end{aligned} \tag{3.18}$$

where the numbers in parentheses below the point estimates are the corresponding standard errors. The LS regression equation (3.18) is the estimated variant of eq. (2.3).[5] There are three regression coefficients, one of which is a constant term and two are point estimates of elasticities. When real income per capita goes up by 1 percent, all other determining factors remaining constant (both the relative price of textile goods and the neglected variables represented by the disturbance), the textile consumption per capita will increase by a percentage that is estimated to be a little over 1.1, and the standard error of this estimate is slightly larger than .15 percent. When real income per capita increases by 1 percent and the relative price of textile goods decreases by 2 percent, the effect on textile consumption per capita is estimated as an increase of $1.1430 - 2(-.8289) \approx 2.8$ percent and the standard error of this estimate is

$$\sqrt{.024324 + 4(.001304) - 4(-.001251)} \approx .19 \text{ percent}$$

[5] Note that many decimal places are used in the intermediate steps (3.13) to (3.17) and only a few in the final result (3.18). This is a good general practice. In most cases economic data are not sufficiently accurate to make many decimal places in the final result meaningful, but the intermediate steps should be accurate in order to guarantee that the result presented will not be affected by rounding errors. This is of particular importance when the computations are more complicated, in which case double-precision programming routines are recommended.

The figures under the square root sign are the estimated sampling variances and covariance of the appropriate estimators, taken from (3.17). Again note that the effect is estimated under a ceteris paribus clause with respect to the neglected variables.

Practical Hints on Logarithms

Our logarithms are to the base 10, but this base has no effect on the coefficients β_1 and β_2 because we use the same base for all variables of the equation, both on the left and on the right. Therefore, as far as β_1 and β_2 are concerned, we may proceed as though our logarithms are natural logarithms, which facilitates the argument. We may then say that we assumed in the previous paragraph that a 1 percent increase is equivalent to a change of .01 in the natural logarithm or, more generally, that a $100x$ percent increase is equivalent to a change of x in the natural logarithm. This holds only approximately:

$$\log_e (1 + x) = x - \frac{1}{2}x^2 + \cdots \qquad (|x| < 1) \tag{3.19}$$

and the approximation error increases when x moves away from zero.[6]

The base of the logarithms *is* important for the constant term. If we write the equation in the original variables, not in their logarithms, we obtain

$$\begin{aligned} \text{textile consumption} &= 10^{1.3742}(\text{income})^{1.14}(\text{textile price})^{-.83} \\ &= 23.7(\text{income})^{1.14}(\text{textile price})^{-.83} \end{aligned} \tag{3.20}$$

which shows that the number 10 does play a crucial role.

Natural logarithms are more convenient than logarithms to any other base when we have a time series regression which is formulated in terms of *changes* in logarithms. Suppose, for example, that y_α in (2.3) stands for the change in the logarithm of textile consumption per capita and, similarly, $x_{\alpha 1}$ and $x_{\alpha 2}$ for the changes in the logarithms of, respectively, real income per capita and the relative price of textile goods:

$$\begin{aligned} \Delta[\log(\text{textile consumption})]_\alpha &= \text{constant term} \\ &\quad + \beta_1 \Delta[\log(\text{income})]_\alpha + \beta_2 \Delta[\log(\text{textile price})]_\alpha \end{aligned}$$

[6] For a convenient table transforming percentage changes into changes in the natural logarithms and vice versa, see Theil (1967, pp. 463–482).

where Δ is the first-difference operator: $\Delta z_\alpha = z_\alpha - z_{\alpha-1}$ for any variable z. Then take antilogs:

$$(3.21)\quad \frac{(\text{textile consumption})_\alpha}{(\text{textile consumption})_{\alpha-1}} = c^{\text{constant term}}$$
$$\times \left[\frac{(\text{income})_\alpha}{(\text{income})_{\alpha-1}}\right]^{\beta_1}\left[\frac{(\text{textile price})_\alpha}{(\text{textile price})_{\alpha-1}}\right]^{\beta_2}$$

where c stands for the base of the logarithms. Suppose then that income and textile price do not change from year $\alpha - 1$ to year α, so that the product on the second line of (3.21) is unity. Textile consumption does change, however, unless the constant term vanishes ($c^0 = 1$). If we choose natural logarithms ($c = e$), the ratio of textile consumption in year α to that in year $\alpha - 1$ becomes

$$e^{\text{constant term}} = 1 + \text{constant term} + \frac{1}{2}(\text{constant term})^2 + \cdots$$

That is, the constant term measures approximately the percentage change (divided by 100) of textile consumption which is not to be ascribed to income and price changes. The constant term thus plays the role of an autonomous trend term. [The word approximately in the previous sentence can be deleted if we replace the percentage change by the log-change (the change in the natural logarithm).] Note that in this discussion we disregarded the disturbances which represent the neglected variables. The reader is invited to extend the discussion, so that these variables are included.

Problems

3.1 Prove that the variance estimator defined in eq. (7.17) of Section 2.7 is equal to the LS variance estimator of Theorem 3.3 for the special case in which the right-hand side of $\mathbf{y} = \mathbf{X}\boldsymbol{\beta} + \boldsymbol{\epsilon}$ consists only of a constant term and a disturbance for each observation.

3.2 Estimate the effect on textile consumption per capita of a 10 percent increase in real income per capita and a 20 percent decrease in the relative price of textile goods, using the numerical data of this section. Do so both accurately and under the simplifying assumption that a $100x$ percent increase is approximately equal to a change of x in the natural logarithm. Also, derive the standard error of the estimate. The computations are to be carried out under a ceteris paribus clause on the neglected variables.

3.3 (*Continuation*) The ceteris paribus clause implies that the disturbances before and after the changes in income and textile price are required to be equal to their expected value (zero). True or false?

3.4 Prove that $\log_e (1 + x) \leq x$ holds for every real $x > -1$ and that the equality sign applies if and only if $x = 0$. [*Hint.* Consider the difference $\log_e (1 + x) - x$; prove that it vanishes for $x = 0$, and analyze the sign of its derivative with respect to x.]

3.5 Prove that under the assumptions of the standard linear model, the variance of the LS slope estimator of a simple regression is of the form $\sigma^2/\sum x_\alpha^2$ if there is no constant term and of the form $\sigma^2/\sum (x_\alpha - \bar{x})^2$ if there is such a term. Prove that the former variance is never larger than the latter, and argue along intuitive lines why this must be so.

3.6 Suppose that the equation $\mathbf{y} = \mathbf{X}\boldsymbol{\beta} + \boldsymbol{\epsilon}$ has a constant term (β_0), and partition: $\mathbf{X} = [\boldsymbol{\iota} \quad \mathbf{Z}]$, $\boldsymbol{\beta}' = [\beta_0 \quad \boldsymbol{\beta}_Z']$. Prove that under the conditions of the standard linear model the covariance matrix of the LS estimator of $\boldsymbol{\beta}_Z$ is equal to $\sigma^2(\mathbf{Z}'\mathbf{A}\mathbf{Z})^{-1}$, where $\mathbf{A} = \mathbf{I} - (1/n)\boldsymbol{\iota}\boldsymbol{\iota}'$. Also, derive the sampling variance of the estimator of β_0 in terms of σ^2, $\boldsymbol{\iota}$, $\mathbf{Z}$, and $\mathbf{A}$.

3.7 (*Continuation*) Let $y_\alpha = \beta_0 + \beta_1 x_{\alpha 1} + \beta_2 x_{\alpha 2} + \epsilon_\alpha$ be the basic equation (two explanatory variables plus a constant term). Prove that the sign of the covariance of the LS estimators of β_1 and β_2 is always opposite to the sign of

$$\sum_{\alpha=1}^{n} (x_{\alpha 1} - \bar{x}_1)(x_{\alpha 2} - \bar{x}_2)$$

where $\bar{x}_1$ and $\bar{x}_2$ are the means of the two explanatory variables.

3.4 Best Linear Unbiased Estimation and Prediction[A]

The Gauss-Markov Theorem

Consider the case of a simple regression without constant term, $y_\alpha = \beta x_\alpha + \epsilon_\alpha$, and the LS estimator $b = \sum x_\alpha y_\alpha / \sum x_\alpha^2$ of β. This b is a linear function of the random variables $y_1, \ldots, y_n$. We also know from Theorem 3.2 that it is an unbiased estimator. We shall now show that within the class of all such "linear unbiased" estimators the LS estimator is the one with minimum sampling variance. In fact, we shall prove the following more general theorem which deals with a parameter vector $\boldsymbol{\beta}$.

THEOREM 3.4 (Gauss-Markov theorem) *Suppose that Assumption* 3.3 *is true for given* $\mathbf{X}$. *Then the LS estimator* $\mathbf{b}$ *defined in* (3.1) *is best linear unbiased in the following sense. Any other estimator of* $\boldsymbol{\beta}$ *which is also linear in the vector* $\mathbf{y}$ *and unbiased has a covariance matrix which exceeds that of* $\mathbf{b}$ *by a positive semidefinite matrix.*

The proof is as follows. If an estimator of $\boldsymbol{\beta}$ is linear in $\mathbf{y}$, it can be written as $\mathbf{A}^*\mathbf{y}$, where $\mathbf{A}^*$ is a $K \times n$ matrix that does not depend on $\mathbf{y}$. We define $\mathbf{A} = \mathbf{A}^* - (\mathbf{X}'\mathbf{X})^{-1}\mathbf{X}'$, so that the estimator $\mathbf{A}^*\mathbf{y}$ becomes

$$\begin{aligned}(4.1)\qquad [\mathbf{A} + (\mathbf{X}'\mathbf{X})^{-1}\mathbf{X}']\mathbf{y} &= [\mathbf{A} + (\mathbf{X}'\mathbf{X})^{-1}\mathbf{X}'](\mathbf{X}\boldsymbol{\beta} + \boldsymbol{\epsilon})\\ &= (\mathbf{AX} + \mathbf{I})\boldsymbol{\beta} + [\mathbf{A} + (\mathbf{X}'\mathbf{X})^{-1}\mathbf{X}']\boldsymbol{\epsilon}\end{aligned}$$

The expectation of this estimator is $(\mathbf{AX} + \mathbf{I})\boldsymbol{\beta}$, which should be identically equal to $\boldsymbol{\beta}$ in order that the estimator be unbiased. This requires

$$(4.2)\qquad \mathbf{AX} = \mathbf{0}$$

The estimator is thus simplified to $\boldsymbol{\beta} + [\mathbf{A} + (\mathbf{X}'\mathbf{X})^{-1}\mathbf{X}']\boldsymbol{\epsilon}$, so that its sampling error is $[\mathbf{A} + (\mathbf{X}'\mathbf{X})^{-1}\mathbf{X}']\boldsymbol{\epsilon}$. Therefore the covariance matrix is

$$\begin{aligned}(4.3)\qquad &[\mathbf{A} + (\mathbf{X}'\mathbf{X})^{-1}\mathbf{X}']\mathscr{E}(\boldsymbol{\epsilon}\boldsymbol{\epsilon}')[\mathbf{A}' + \mathbf{X}(\mathbf{X}'\mathbf{X})^{-1}]\\ &= \sigma^2[\mathbf{A} + (\mathbf{X}'\mathbf{X})^{-1}\mathbf{X}'][\mathbf{A}' + \mathbf{X}(\mathbf{X}'\mathbf{X})^{-1}]\\ &= \sigma^2[\mathbf{AA}' + \mathbf{AX}(\mathbf{X}'\mathbf{X})^{-1} + (\mathbf{X}'\mathbf{X})^{-1}\mathbf{X}'\mathbf{A}' + (\mathbf{X}'\mathbf{X})^{-1}]\\ &= \sigma^2\mathbf{AA}' + \sigma^2(\mathbf{X}'\mathbf{X})^{-1}\end{aligned}$$

where use is made of (4.2) in the last step. If we compare the result with (3.4), we conclude that the covariance matrix of the competing estimator exceeds that of LS by $\sigma^2\mathbf{AA}'$, which is a positive semidefinite matrix.

Two Corollaries Based on the Gauss-Markov Theorem

The Gauss-Markov theorem is of such importance that it is appropriate to describe some of its implications more explicitly by means of two corollaries. For a third corollary, formulated in terms of the generalized variance of a vector estimator, see Problems 4.1 and 4.2.

COROLLARY 1 TO THEOREM 3.4 *Consider an arbitrary linear combination* $\mathbf{w}'\boldsymbol{\beta}$ (*with a fixed weight vector* $\mathbf{w}$) *of the elements of the parameter vector* $\boldsymbol{\beta}$; *also consider the corresponding combination* $\mathbf{w}'\mathbf{b}$ *of the LS estimator* $\mathbf{b}$. *Then, under the assumptions of* Theorem 3.4, *the sampling variance of* $\mathbf{w}'\mathbf{b}$ *is less than or equal to the sampling variance of the corresponding combination of any other linear unbiased estimator of* $\boldsymbol{\beta}$.

Using (4.3) we find that the latter variance is

$$\begin{aligned}(4.4)\qquad \mathbf{w}'[\sigma^2\mathbf{AA}' + \sigma^2(\mathbf{X}'\mathbf{X})^{-1}]\mathbf{w} &= \sigma^2(\mathbf{A}'\mathbf{w})'\mathbf{A}'\mathbf{w} + \sigma^2\mathbf{w}'(\mathbf{X}'\mathbf{X})^{-1}\mathbf{w}\\ &\geq \sigma^2\mathbf{w}'(\mathbf{X}'\mathbf{X})^{-1}\mathbf{w}\end{aligned}$$

which proves the corollary. Note its implication that the variance of each component b_h of the LS estimator is at most equal to the variance of any other linear unbiased estimator of β_h. (*Hint.* Choose **w** such that its hth element is 1 and all others 0.)

COROLLARY 2 TO THEOREM 3.4 *Under the assumptions of Theorem* 3.4 *the LS estimator of* $\boldsymbol{\beta}$ *minimizes the expected value of any positive semidefinite quadratic form in the sampling errors within the class of linear unbiased estimators.*

Write **Q** for the matrix of the quadratic form. For whatever estimator $\hat{\boldsymbol{\beta}}$ of $\boldsymbol{\beta}$ we have the following expression for the expectation of a quadratic form in the sampling errors:

$$\text{(4.5)} \qquad \begin{aligned} \mathscr{E}[(\hat{\boldsymbol{\beta}} - \boldsymbol{\beta})'\mathbf{Q}(\hat{\boldsymbol{\beta}} - \boldsymbol{\beta})] &= \mathscr{E}[\operatorname{tr} \mathbf{Q}(\hat{\boldsymbol{\beta}} - \boldsymbol{\beta})(\hat{\boldsymbol{\beta}} - \boldsymbol{\beta})'] \\ &= \operatorname{tr} \mathbf{Q}\mathscr{E}[(\hat{\boldsymbol{\beta}} - \boldsymbol{\beta})(\hat{\boldsymbol{\beta}} - \boldsymbol{\beta})'] \end{aligned}$$

The expectation on the second line is the covariance matrix of $\hat{\boldsymbol{\beta}}$ if this is an unbiased estimator. On substituting (4.3) we find for the expected value of the quadratic form:

$$\text{(4.6)} \qquad \begin{aligned} \sigma^2 \operatorname{tr} \mathbf{QAA}' + \sigma^2 \operatorname{tr} \mathbf{Q}(\mathbf{X}'\mathbf{X})^{-1} &= \sigma^2 \operatorname{tr} \mathbf{A}'\mathbf{QA} + \sigma^2 \operatorname{tr} \mathbf{Q}(\mathbf{X}'\mathbf{X})^{-1} \\ &\geq \sigma^2 \operatorname{tr} \mathbf{Q}(\mathbf{X}'\mathbf{X})^{-1} \end{aligned}$$

because $\mathbf{A}'\mathbf{QA}$ is symmetric and positive semidefinite if **Q** has these properties, and the trace of such a matrix is nonnegative. The expression on the second line in (4.6) is obviously the expectation of the quadratic form when the sampling errors are those of LS.

Theorem 3.4 and its corollaries show that the LS vector **b** has very strong optimum properties, but the qualifications are obvious. Assumption 3.3 has to be satisfied and, in addition, the optimality refers only to the class of linear unbiased estimators. An obvious question is what happens when we drop either the linearity or the unbiasedness restriction. It will appear in Section 8.4 that the LS coefficient vector retains its optimum property described in Theorem 3.4 when we impose only unbiasedness, not linearity, provided, however, that the random variation is normal. If only linearity is imposed, not unbiasedness, no useful result emerges. This is pursued in Problem 4.3, which shows that the resulting "optimal estimator" depends on unknown parameters.[7]

[7] Further results were obtained by STEIN (1956a, b, 1960) and JAMES and STEIN (1961), who proved the existence of a biased nonlinear estimator which has a smaller expected loss than that of LS, loss being defined in the familiar quadratic manner. These contributions are beyond the scope of this book.

Regression Prediction

Suppose that the standard linear model applies to $\mathbf{y} = \mathbf{X}\boldsymbol{\beta} + \boldsymbol{\epsilon}$, that $\boldsymbol{\beta}$ has been estimated by LS, and that we want to predict certain future values of the dependent variable.[8] We shall consider this prediction problem conditionally on the values of the explanatory variables. Specifically, consider an $m \times K$ matrix $\mathbf{X}_*$, each row consisting of values taken by the K explanatory variables. Our question is this. Given that these variables assume these values, what can be said about the corresponding values taken by the dependent variable? The answer is that if the assumptions of the standard linear model are still valid for these m (future) observations, the latter values form an m-element column vector $\mathbf{y}_*$ which satisfies

$$\mathbf{y}_* = \mathbf{X}_*\boldsymbol{\beta} + \boldsymbol{\epsilon}_* \tag{4.7}$$

where $\boldsymbol{\epsilon}_*$ is an m-element random vector with zero mean and covariance matrix $\sigma^2\mathbf{I}$ (of order $m \times m$). Two unknowns occur in the right-hand side, $\boldsymbol{\beta}$ and $\boldsymbol{\epsilon}_*$. If we are interested in the expectation of the future values, $\mathscr{E}\mathbf{y}_* = \mathbf{X}_*\boldsymbol{\beta}$, and use $\mathbf{b}$ to estimate $\boldsymbol{\beta}$, the estimator $\mathbf{X}_*\mathbf{b}$ is obviously unbiased and its covariance matrix is

$$\mathscr{E}[\mathbf{X}_*(\mathbf{b} - \boldsymbol{\beta})(\mathbf{b} - \boldsymbol{\beta})'\mathbf{X}_*'] = \sigma^2\mathbf{X}_*(\mathbf{X}'\mathbf{X})^{-1}\mathbf{X}_*' \tag{4.8}$$

It follows directly from Theorem 3.4 that if any other linear unbiased estimator of $\boldsymbol{\beta}$ is used to estimate $\mathbf{X}_*\boldsymbol{\beta}$, its covariance matrix exceeds (4.8) by a positive semidefinite matrix [see (4.3)]:

$$\begin{aligned}\mathscr{E}\{\mathbf{X}_*[\mathbf{A} + (\mathbf{X}'\mathbf{X})^{-1}\mathbf{X}']\boldsymbol{\epsilon}\boldsymbol{\epsilon}'[\mathbf{A}' + \mathbf{X}(\mathbf{X}'\mathbf{X})^{-1}]\mathbf{X}_*'\} &= \sigma^2\mathbf{X}_*\mathbf{A}(\mathbf{X}_*\mathbf{A})' \\ &\quad + \sigma^2\mathbf{X}_*(\mathbf{X}'\mathbf{X})^{-1}\mathbf{X}_*'\end{aligned}$$

Note that the matrix (4.8), in general, is not diagonal, so that the sampling errors of the estimators of the expectations of the separate future observations are usually correlated. This is not surprising, since these errors all result from the sampling error of the same $\mathbf{b}$.

Now consider the real prediction problem, which is concerned with $\mathbf{y}_*$ rather than its expectation. Let $\mathbf{X}_*\mathbf{b}$ be the predictor, so that the prediction error is

$$\mathbf{X}_*\mathbf{b} - \mathbf{y}_* = \mathbf{X}_*(\mathbf{b} - \boldsymbol{\beta}) - \boldsymbol{\epsilon}_* \tag{4.9}$$

This shows that the error consists of two parts, one of which deals with the sampling error of the LS coefficient estimator and the other with the neglect of

[8] The expression "prediction of future values" may suggest that the data have the form of time series. However, the analysis is equally applicable to cross-section data, for example, the case in which household expenditures are predicted from income and family size for households that were not included in the sample.

the future disturbances by the predictor. The predictor $\mathbf{X}_*\mathbf{b} = \mathbf{X}_*(\mathbf{X}'\mathbf{X})^{-1}\mathbf{X}'\mathbf{y}$ is obviously linear in $\mathbf{y}$. It is not unbiased in the sense that its expectation $(\mathbf{X}_*\boldsymbol{\beta})$ coincides with the predictand $\mathbf{y}_* = \mathbf{X}_*\boldsymbol{\beta} + \boldsymbol{\epsilon}_*$, but it is unbiased in the sense that the prediction error (4.9) has zero expectation. Equivalently, it is unbiased in the sense that the predictor $\mathbf{X}_*\mathbf{b}$ and the predictand $\mathbf{y}_*$ have identical expectations $(\mathbf{X}_*\boldsymbol{\beta})$. It is in this manner that we shall interpret the concept of unbiased prediction of random variables.

Furthermore, we assume that the elements of $\boldsymbol{\epsilon}_*$ are uncorrelated with those of $\boldsymbol{\epsilon}$:[9]

$$\mathscr{V}\begin{bmatrix}\boldsymbol{\epsilon}\\ \boldsymbol{\epsilon}_*\end{bmatrix} = \begin{bmatrix}\sigma^2\mathbf{I} & \mathbf{0}\\ \mathbf{0} & \sigma^2\mathbf{I}\end{bmatrix} = \sigma^2\mathbf{I} \tag{4.10}$$

The prediction error (4.9) then has the following covariance matrix:

$$\mathscr{E}[(\mathbf{X}_*\mathbf{b} - \mathbf{y}_*)(\mathbf{X}_*\mathbf{b} - \mathbf{y}_*)'] = \sigma^2[\mathbf{X}_*(\mathbf{X}'\mathbf{X})^{-1}\mathbf{X}_*' + \mathbf{I}] \tag{4.11}$$

This result shows that the covariance matrix of the prediction error (just as this error itself) consists of two parts, one of which $(\sigma^2\mathbf{I})$ concerns the future disturbances and the other the sampling error of $\mathbf{b}$.

We proceed to prove that the predictor $\mathbf{X}_*\mathbf{b}$ is "best" in the class of all linear unbiased predictors of $\mathbf{y}_*$ in the sense that the error vector of any such predictor has a covariance matrix that exceeds the matrix (4.11) by a positive semidefinite matrix. Since any linear predictor of $\mathbf{y}_*$ can be written as $[\mathbf{X}_*(\mathbf{X}'\mathbf{X})^{-1}\mathbf{X}' + \mathbf{B}]\mathbf{y}$, where $\mathbf{B}$ is some $m \times n$ matrix, its error vector is

$$\begin{aligned}&[\mathbf{X}_*(\mathbf{X}'\mathbf{X})^{-1}\mathbf{X}' + \mathbf{B}](\mathbf{X}\boldsymbol{\beta} + \boldsymbol{\epsilon}) - \mathbf{X}_*\boldsymbol{\beta} - \boldsymbol{\epsilon}_*\\ &\qquad = \mathbf{B}\mathbf{X}\boldsymbol{\beta} + [\mathbf{X}_*(\mathbf{X}'\mathbf{X})^{-1}\mathbf{X}' + \mathbf{B}]\boldsymbol{\epsilon} - \boldsymbol{\epsilon}_*\end{aligned}$$

This shows that $\mathbf{B}\mathbf{X} = \mathbf{0}$ should hold in order that the predictor be unbiased. The covariance matrix of the prediction error is then equal to σ^2 multiplied by $\mathbf{X}_*(\mathbf{X}'\mathbf{X})^{-1}\mathbf{X}_*' + \mathbf{B}\mathbf{B}' + \mathbf{I}$, which exceeds the matrix (4.11) by a positive semidefinite matrix. This result can be summarized as follows.

THEOREM 3.5 (Best linear unbiased prediction) *Suppose that Assumption* 3.3 *is true for given* $\mathbf{X}$. *Also suppose that the* K *explanatory variables take a given set of values arranged in an* $m \times K$ *matrix* $\mathbf{X}_*$ *and that the associated vector* $\mathbf{y}_*$ *obeys* (4.7), *where* $\boldsymbol{\epsilon}_*$ *is a random vector with zero mean satisfying* (4.10). *Then the predictor* $\mathbf{X}_*\mathbf{b}$ *of* $\mathbf{y}_*$, $\mathbf{b}$ *being the LS estimator defined in* (3.1), *is best linear unbiased, which is to be interpreted as follows. The prediction error of any other predictor of* $\mathbf{y}_*$ *which is also linear in* $\mathbf{y}$ *and unbiased (in the sense that the prediction error has zero mean) has a covariance matrix which exceeds the matrix* (4.11) *by a positive semidefinite matrix.*

[9] Note the different orders of the three unit matrices in (4.10)!

The two corollaries of Theorem 3.4, when applied to $\mathbf{X}_*\mathbf{b}$ and $\mathbf{y}_*$, refer to linear combinations of and quadratic forms in prediction errors. Their validity under this prediction interpretation will be obvious.

Historical Note

The least-squares method dates back to the early nineteenth century: LEGENDRE (1806), LAPLACE (1812), and GAUSS (1821–23). It is customary to refer to Theorem 3.4 as the Gauss-Markov theorem, but Gauss' work antedates that of MARKOV (1912) considerably. For further historical details, see WHITTAKER and ROBINSON (1944) and PLACKETT (1949).

The LS procedure can be extended substantially to handle weaker conditions than those which are discussed here. One of the main generalizations comes from AITKEN (1935), and is discussed in Section 6.1.[10]

Problems

4.1 Let $\boldsymbol{\Sigma}$ be the positive definite covariance matrix of a k-element random vector. The determinant of $\boldsymbol{\Sigma}$, $|\boldsymbol{\Sigma}|$, is known as the *generalized variance* of this vector.[11] Prove that it reduces to the ordinary variance for $k = 1$. Also prove that if each element of the random vector is multiplied by c, the generalized variance is multiplied by c^k.

4.2 (*Continuation*) Prove that under the assumptions of Theorem 3.4, the LS estimator $\mathbf{b}$ of $\boldsymbol{\beta}$ has a generalized variance that is less than or equal

[10] For a related contribution, see DAVID and NEYMAN (1938).

[11] For *sample* variances and covariances, this generalization has intuitive appeal. Let all variables be measured as deviations from their means. A single variable with observations $[x_1 \cdots x_n] = \mathbf{x}'$ has the geometric representation OX (see the figure below). Its var-

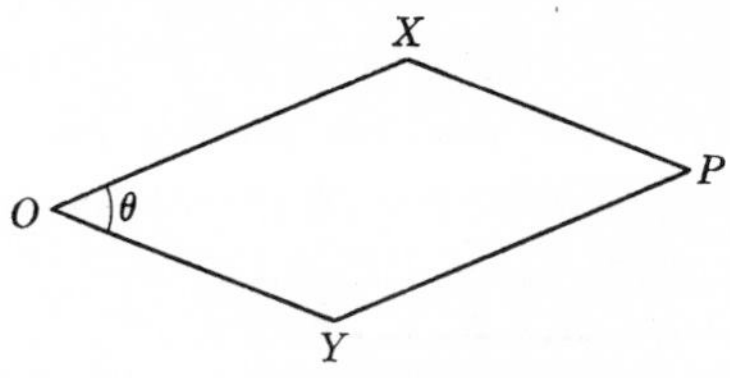

iance, apart from the factor $1/n$, equals $\mathbf{x}'\mathbf{x}$ or the square of the distance OX. For two variables with observation matrix $[\mathbf{x} \;\; \mathbf{y}]$ we generalize this one-dimensional distance to the two-dimensional area $OXPY$. It follows from Section 1.1, eq. (1.3) ff., that this area equals $(\mathbf{x}'\mathbf{x})^{\frac{1}{2}}(\mathbf{y}'\mathbf{y})^{\frac{1}{2}} \sin \theta$, which is the square root of the determinant of $\begin{bmatrix} \mathbf{x}'\mathbf{x} & \mathbf{x}'\mathbf{y} \\ \mathbf{y}'\mathbf{x} & \mathbf{y}'\mathbf{y} \end{bmatrix}$, i.e., the square root of the generalized variance (again, apart from $1/n$).

to the generalized variance of any other linear unbiased estimator. [*Hint*. Write $\mathbf{V}_0 = \sigma^2(\mathbf{X}'\mathbf{X})^{-1}$ and $\mathbf{V}$ for the covariance matrix (4.3), so that $\mathbf{V} - \mathbf{V}_0 = \sigma^2\mathbf{A}\mathbf{A}'$ (positive semidefinite). Introduce a nonsingular $\mathbf{P}$ such that $\mathbf{V}_0^{-1} = \mathbf{P}\mathbf{P}'$ and consider the determinantal equation

$$|\mathbf{V} - \mathbf{V}_0 - \lambda_h \mathbf{V}_0| = 0 \qquad h = 1, \ldots, K \tag{4.12}$$

Prove that λ_h is a latent root of $\mathbf{P}'(\mathbf{V} - \mathbf{V}_0)\mathbf{P}$ and use this to prove that $\lambda_h \geq 0$, $h = 1, \ldots, K$. Write (4.12) as $|\mathbf{V} - (1 + \lambda_h)\mathbf{V}_0| = 0$ and prove that $1 + \lambda_h$ is a root of $\mathbf{P}'\mathbf{V}\mathbf{P}$. Finally, prove $|\mathbf{P}'\mathbf{V}\mathbf{P}| = |\mathbf{V}|/|\mathbf{V}_0|$ and use the relation between roots and determinant to prove $|\mathbf{V}| \geq |\mathbf{V}_0|$.]

4.3 Consider the following linear "estimator" of $\boldsymbol{\beta}$:

$$\mathbf{A}_0\mathbf{y} = \boldsymbol{\beta}\boldsymbol{\beta}'\mathbf{X}'(\mathbf{X}\boldsymbol{\beta}\boldsymbol{\beta}'\mathbf{X}' + \sigma^2\mathbf{I})^{-1}\mathbf{y} \tag{4.13}$$

where the transformation matrix $\mathbf{A}_0 = \boldsymbol{\beta}\boldsymbol{\beta}'\mathbf{X}'(\mathbf{X}\boldsymbol{\beta}\boldsymbol{\beta}'\mathbf{X}' + \sigma^2\mathbf{I})^{-1}$ has unit rank. This "estimator" depends on $\boldsymbol{\beta}$ and σ^2 and, therefore, is useless. The meager consolation is that it is best linear under the conditions of the standard linear model. To prove this, consider any other linear estimator of $\boldsymbol{\beta}$, to be written in the form $(\mathbf{A}_0 + \mathbf{A})\mathbf{y}$, where $\mathbf{A}$ is an arbitrary $K \times n$ matrix. Prove that the sampling error of this estimator is

$$\begin{aligned}(\mathbf{A}_0 + \mathbf{A})\mathbf{y} - \boldsymbol{\beta} = {} & [\boldsymbol{\beta}\boldsymbol{\beta}'\mathbf{X}'(\mathbf{X}\boldsymbol{\beta}\boldsymbol{\beta}'\mathbf{X}' + \sigma^2\mathbf{I})^{-1}\mathbf{X} + \mathbf{A}\mathbf{X} - \mathbf{I}]\boldsymbol{\beta} \\ & + [\boldsymbol{\beta}\boldsymbol{\beta}'\mathbf{X}'(\mathbf{X}\boldsymbol{\beta}\boldsymbol{\beta}'\mathbf{X}' + \sigma^2\mathbf{I})^{-1} + \mathbf{A}]\boldsymbol{\epsilon}\end{aligned} \tag{4.14}$$

and also that the matrix of second-order sampling moments around $\boldsymbol{\beta}$ is

$$\begin{aligned} & \boldsymbol{\beta}\boldsymbol{\beta}'\mathbf{X}'(\mathbf{X}\boldsymbol{\beta}\boldsymbol{\beta}'\mathbf{X}' + \sigma^2\mathbf{I})^{-1}\mathbf{X}\boldsymbol{\beta}\boldsymbol{\beta}'\mathbf{X}'(\mathbf{X}\boldsymbol{\beta}\boldsymbol{\beta}'\mathbf{X}' + \sigma^2\mathbf{I})^{-1}\mathbf{X}\boldsymbol{\beta}\boldsymbol{\beta}' \\ & + \mathbf{A}\mathbf{X}\boldsymbol{\beta}\boldsymbol{\beta}'\mathbf{X}'(\mathbf{X}\boldsymbol{\beta}\boldsymbol{\beta}'\mathbf{X}' + \sigma^2\mathbf{I})^{-1}\mathbf{X}\boldsymbol{\beta}\boldsymbol{\beta}' \\ & + \boldsymbol{\beta}\boldsymbol{\beta}'\mathbf{X}'(\mathbf{X}\boldsymbol{\beta}\boldsymbol{\beta}'\mathbf{X}' + \sigma^2\mathbf{I})^{-1}\mathbf{X}\boldsymbol{\beta}\boldsymbol{\beta}'\mathbf{X}'\mathbf{A}' \\ & - 2\boldsymbol{\beta}\boldsymbol{\beta}'\mathbf{X}'(\mathbf{X}\boldsymbol{\beta}\boldsymbol{\beta}'\mathbf{X}' + \sigma^2\mathbf{I})^{-1}\mathbf{X}\boldsymbol{\beta}\boldsymbol{\beta}' \\ & + \mathbf{A}\mathbf{X}\boldsymbol{\beta}\boldsymbol{\beta}'\mathbf{X}'\mathbf{A}' - \mathbf{A}\mathbf{X}\boldsymbol{\beta}\boldsymbol{\beta}' - \boldsymbol{\beta}\boldsymbol{\beta}'\mathbf{X}'\mathbf{A}' \\ & + \boldsymbol{\beta}\boldsymbol{\beta}' + \sigma^2\boldsymbol{\beta}\boldsymbol{\beta}'\mathbf{X}'(\mathbf{X}\boldsymbol{\beta}\boldsymbol{\beta}'\mathbf{X}' + \sigma^2\mathbf{I})^{-2}\mathbf{X}\boldsymbol{\beta}\boldsymbol{\beta}' + \sigma^2\mathbf{A}\mathbf{A}' \\ & + \sigma^2\boldsymbol{\beta}\boldsymbol{\beta}'\mathbf{X}'(\mathbf{X}\boldsymbol{\beta}\boldsymbol{\beta}'\mathbf{X}' + \sigma^2\mathbf{I})^{-1}\mathbf{A}' + \sigma^2\mathbf{A}(\mathbf{X}\boldsymbol{\beta}\boldsymbol{\beta}'\mathbf{X}' + \sigma^2\mathbf{I})^{-1}\mathbf{X}\boldsymbol{\beta}\boldsymbol{\beta}'\end{aligned} \tag{4.15}$$

Prove that the sum of the four terms that do not contain $\mathbf{A}$ is equal to $[1 - \boldsymbol{\beta}'\mathbf{X}'(\mathbf{X}\boldsymbol{\beta}\boldsymbol{\beta}'\mathbf{X}' + \sigma^2\mathbf{I})^{-1}\mathbf{X}\boldsymbol{\beta}]\boldsymbol{\beta}\boldsymbol{\beta}'$, and that the sum of the terms involving $\mathbf{A}$ (and $\mathbf{A}'$) linearly is a zero matrix, so that the matrix of second-order moments is

$$[1 - \boldsymbol{\beta}'\mathbf{X}'(\mathbf{X}\boldsymbol{\beta}\boldsymbol{\beta}'\mathbf{X}' + \sigma^2\mathbf{I})^{-1}\mathbf{X}\boldsymbol{\beta}]\boldsymbol{\beta}\boldsymbol{\beta}' + \mathbf{A}(\mathbf{X}\boldsymbol{\beta}\boldsymbol{\beta}'\mathbf{X}' + \sigma^2\mathbf{I})\mathbf{A}' \tag{4.16}$$

Finally, prove that the second matrix in (4.16), which is of the second degree in the elements of $\mathbf{A}$, is positive semidefinite.

4.4 (*Continuation*) Consider the special case $y_\alpha = \beta x_\alpha + \epsilon_\alpha$ and prove that the "estimator" of β discussed in Problem 4.3 is

$$\hat{\beta} = \frac{\sum x_\alpha y_\alpha}{\dfrac{\sigma^2}{\beta^2} + \sum x_\alpha^2} \tag{4.17}$$

[*Hint*. Prove $(\mathbf{I} + k\mathbf{x}\mathbf{x}')^{-1} = \mathbf{I} - [k/(1 + k\mathbf{x}'\mathbf{x})]\mathbf{x}\mathbf{x}'$ for any scalar k and vector $\mathbf{x}$ satisfying $1 + k\mathbf{x}'\mathbf{x} \neq 0$.] Prove that $\hat{\beta}$ is biased toward zero. Prove also that its second-order sampling moment around β is

$$\mathscr{E}(\hat{\beta} - \beta)^2 = \frac{\sigma^2}{\dfrac{\sigma^2}{\beta^2} + \sum x_\alpha^2} \tag{4.18}$$

and, finally, prove that this is smaller than the variance of the LS estimator b.

4.5 Specify the orders of the four unit matrices in eqs. (4.10) and (4.11).

3.5 Point Estimation under the Normality Assumption[A]

In this and the next two sections we add to our assumptions the condition that $\mathbf{y}$ be multinormally distributed. This will enable us to obtain more specific results for estimation and hypothesis testing.

Maximum-Likelihood Estimators

The condition mentioned in the previous paragraph implies that $\mathbf{y}$ is multinormal with mean vector $\mathbf{X}\boldsymbol{\beta}$ and covariance matrix $\sigma^2\mathbf{I}$. The form of the distribution of $\mathbf{y}$ is thus specified completely, which enables us to derive maximum-likelihood estimators.

THEOREM 3.6 (Maximum-likelihood estimators) *Suppose that Assumption 3.3 is true for given* $\mathbf{X}$ *with the additional specification that the distribution of* $\mathbf{y}$ *(given* $\mathbf{X}$*) is n-variate normal. Then the maximum-likelihood estimator of* $\boldsymbol{\beta}$ *is equal to the LS estimator* $\mathbf{b}$ *and the maximum-likelihood estimator of* σ^2 *is equal to* $\mathbf{e}'\mathbf{e}/n$, *where* $\mathbf{e}$ *is the LS residual vector defined in* (3.5).

To prove the theorem we consider the likelihood function:

$$L(\mathbf{y}; \mathbf{X}\boldsymbol{\beta}, \sigma^2\mathbf{I}) = \frac{1}{(2\pi\sigma^2)^{n/2}} \exp\left\{-\frac{1}{2}\frac{(\mathbf{y} - \mathbf{X}\boldsymbol{\beta})'(\mathbf{y} - \mathbf{X}\boldsymbol{\beta})}{\sigma^2}\right\}$$

and its logarithm:

$$\log L = -\frac{n}{2}\log 2\pi - \frac{n}{2}\log \sigma^2 - \frac{1}{2}\frac{(\mathbf{y}-\mathbf{X}\boldsymbol{\beta})'(\mathbf{y}-\mathbf{X}\boldsymbol{\beta})}{\sigma^2} \tag{5.1}$$

which we differentiate with respect to $\boldsymbol{\beta}$ and σ^2:

$$\begin{aligned}\frac{\partial(\log L)}{\partial\boldsymbol{\beta}} &= -\frac{1}{2\sigma^2}\frac{\partial}{\partial\boldsymbol{\beta}}(\mathbf{y}'\mathbf{y} - 2\mathbf{y}'\mathbf{X}\boldsymbol{\beta} + \boldsymbol{\beta}'\mathbf{X}'\mathbf{X}\boldsymbol{\beta}) \\ &= \frac{1}{\sigma^2}(\mathbf{X}'\mathbf{y} - \mathbf{X}'\mathbf{X}\boldsymbol{\beta})\end{aligned} \tag{5.2}$$

$$\frac{\partial(\log L)}{\partial\sigma^2} = -\frac{n}{2\sigma^2} + \frac{1}{2\sigma^4}(\mathbf{y}-\mathbf{X}\boldsymbol{\beta})'(\mathbf{y}-\mathbf{X}\boldsymbol{\beta}) \tag{5.3}$$

If we equate the vector on the second line of (5.2) to zero, we obtain the LS estimator $(\mathbf{X}'\mathbf{X})^{-1}\mathbf{X}'\mathbf{y}$.[12] If we then substitute this result into (5.3) and put this derivative also equal to zero, we find that the maximum-likelihood estimator of σ^2 is equal to $\mathbf{e}'\mathbf{e}/n$, where $\mathbf{e}$ is the LS residual vector. This completes the proof except for the second-order conditions, which are examined in Problem 5.1. Note that both the result and the derivation are straightforward extensions of the analysis of Section 2.7 on the mean and the variance of a normal distribution.

Alternative Variance Estimators

We have obtained two different estimators of the variance: $\mathbf{e}'\mathbf{e}/n$ and $\mathbf{e}'\mathbf{e}/(n-K)$. A third will be obtained by considering an optimality criterion similar to that of Theorem 3.4. For this purpose we note that the estimator $s^2 = \mathbf{y}'\mathbf{M}\mathbf{y}/(n-K)$ is a quadratic form in $\mathbf{y}$, not a linear form as in the case of $\mathbf{b}$. So we consider the set of all quadratic estimators of σ^2, $\mathbf{y}'\mathbf{Q}\mathbf{y}$, where $\mathbf{Q}$ is some symmetric $n \times n$ matrix. Substituting $\mathbf{y} = \mathbf{X}\boldsymbol{\beta} + \boldsymbol{\epsilon}$ we obtain

$$\mathbf{y}'\mathbf{Q}\mathbf{y} = \boldsymbol{\beta}'\mathbf{X}'\mathbf{Q}\mathbf{X}\boldsymbol{\beta} + 2\boldsymbol{\beta}'\mathbf{X}'\mathbf{Q}\boldsymbol{\epsilon} + \boldsymbol{\epsilon}'\mathbf{Q}\boldsymbol{\epsilon} \tag{5.4}$$

so that the distribution of the σ^2 estimator depends on $\boldsymbol{\beta}$ unless

$$\mathbf{Q}\mathbf{X} = \mathbf{0} \tag{5.5}$$

which is a condition that will be imposed. Consider, then, the following theorem.

[12] It should be immediately obvious from the likelihood function that the maximum-likelihood estimator of $\boldsymbol{\beta}$ is identical with the LS estimator because $\boldsymbol{\beta}$ occurs exclusively in the exponent in the form of the squared length of $\mathbf{y} - \mathbf{X}\boldsymbol{\beta}$, multiplied by the negative constant $-\sigma^2/2$.

THEOREM 3.7 (Alternative variance estimators) *Suppose that Assumption 3.3 is true for given* **X** *with the additional specification that the distribution of* **y** *(given* **X**) *is n-variate normal; also suppose* $n > K$. *Then the LS estimator* s^2 *of* σ^2 *defined in* (3.8) *is best quadratic unbiased in the following sense. Any other estimator of* σ^2 *which is also unbiased and quadratic in* **y** *has a sampling variance larger than or equal to*

$$\text{var } s^2 = \frac{2\sigma^4}{n - K} \tag{5.6}$$

Under the same assumptions the estimator

$$s'^2 = \frac{\mathbf{e}'\mathbf{e}}{n - K + 2} \tag{5.7}$$

is best quadratic in the sense that any other σ^2 *estimator of the form* $\mathbf{y}'\mathbf{Q}\mathbf{y}$ *with* **Q** *satisfying* (5.5) *has a second-order sampling moment around* σ^2 *which is larger than or equal to*

$$\mathscr{E}(s'^2 - \sigma^2)^2 = \frac{2\sigma^4}{n - K + 2} \tag{5.8}$$

Moreover, under these assumptions

$$\mathscr{E}(s'^2 - \sigma^2) = -\frac{2\sigma^2}{n - K + 2} \tag{5.9}$$

gives the bias of s'^2.

The proof of this theorem is contained in Problems 5.2 to 5.5. It is interesting to observe that we need the additional normality assumption for the optimality of the variance estimator, whereas we did not need it for the optimality of **b**, in much the same way as the unbiasedness of s^2 does but that of **b** does not require Assumption 3.2. Note also that Theorem 3.7 imposes condition (5.5) explicitly only for s'^2, not for s^2, but it is easily seen that this condition has to be satisfied if we require (as we do for that part of the proof) that the estimator be unbiased: the expectation of the right-hand side of (5.4) involves $\boldsymbol{\beta}$ if $\mathbf{QX} \neq \mathbf{0}$, so that it cannot be identically equal to σ^2 when (5.5) is not satisfied.[13]

The results obtained indicate that there are at least three different ways of estimating σ^2. One may divide $\mathbf{e}'\mathbf{e}$ by n, which gives the maximum-likelihood estimator; one may also divide by $n - K$ and the result (the LS estimator s^2)

[13] The best quadratic unbiased property of s^2 was found by HSU (1938). For s'^2 see THEIL and SCHWEITZER (1961) and CORSTEN (1964). Reference is also made to related analyses for the variance of the univariate normal distribution by GOODMAN (1953, 1960) and EVANS (1964).

is best quadratic unbiased; or one may divide by $n - K + 2$ to obtain the best quadratic estimator. The last estimator is preferable from the standpoint of a quadratic loss criterion, but it is not in general use; we shall continue using s^2, primarily because it provides us with simpler expressions as will become clear in the next section. Nevertheless, it is interesting to observe that dropping the unbiasedness constraint leads to the estimator (5.7) which can actually be derived from the sample, although it must be admitted that the constraint (5.5) is required. We shall come back to this topic in Section 8.4.

The Complete Distribution of the Coefficient and Variance Estimators

THEOREM 3.8 (Joint distribution of the LS coefficient and variance estimators) *Suppose that Assumption* 3.3 *is true for given* $\mathbf{X}$ *with the additional specification that the distribution of* $\mathbf{y}$ *(given* $\mathbf{X}$*) is n-variate normal; also suppose* $n > K$. *Then the LS coefficient estimator* $\mathbf{b}$ *is normally distributed with mean vector* $\boldsymbol{\beta}$ *and covariance matrix* $\sigma^2(\mathbf{X}'\mathbf{X})^{-1}$, *and* $(n - K)s^2/\sigma^2$ *is distributed as* $\chi^2(n - K)$; *moreover,* $\mathbf{b}$ *and* s^2 *are distributed independently.*

The normality of $\mathbf{b} = (\mathbf{X}'\mathbf{X})^{-1}\mathbf{X}'\mathbf{y}$ follows from its linearity in $\mathbf{y}$, $\mathbf{X}$ being a matrix of constant elements. We have $(n - K)s^2 = \mathbf{y}'\mathbf{M}\mathbf{y} = \boldsymbol{\epsilon}'\mathbf{M}\boldsymbol{\epsilon}$, where $\mathbf{M}$ is an idempotent matrix of rank $n - K$; hence $(n - K)s^2$ is indeed distributed as $\sigma^2\chi^2(n - K)$,[14] the elements of $\boldsymbol{\epsilon}$ being independent random drawings from the same normal population with zero mean and variance σ^2. Furthermore, the matrix $\mathbf{M}$ of the quadratic form and the matrix $(\mathbf{X}'\mathbf{X})^{-1}\mathbf{X}'$ of $\mathbf{b} - \boldsymbol{\beta} = (\mathbf{X}'\mathbf{X})^{-1}\mathbf{X}'\boldsymbol{\epsilon}$ satisfy $(\mathbf{X}'\mathbf{X})^{-1}\mathbf{X}'\mathbf{M} = \mathbf{0}$ in view of eq. (7.22) of Section 1.7. We conclude from the last paragraph of Section 2.6 that $\mathbf{b}$ and s^2 are indeed independent.

Problems

5.1 Evaluate the Hessian matrix of $\log L$ defined in (5.1) at the point $(\mathbf{b}, \mathbf{e}'\mathbf{e}/n)$ and prove that it is negative definite. Compare the result with that of Problem 7.1 at the end of Section 2.7.

5.2 Let $X_1, \ldots, X_n$ be independent normal variates with zero mean and variance σ^2. Prove that $\mathscr{E}(X_iX_jX_hX_k)$ is nonzero only if the four indices are pairwise equal (including the case in which they are all equal). Also prove $\mathscr{E}(X_i^2X_j^2) = \sigma^4$ if $i \neq j$, $3\sigma^4$ if $i = j$.

5.3 (*Continuation*) Suppose that the elements of the disturbance vector $\boldsymbol{\epsilon}$ are independent normal variates with zero mean and variance σ^2, and

[14] Here it becomes clear that $n - K$ may be regarded as the number of degrees of freedom of our regression.

consider the quadratic form $\boldsymbol{\epsilon}'\mathbf{Q}\boldsymbol{\epsilon}$. Prove that its expectation is $\sigma^2 \operatorname{tr} \mathbf{Q}$ and that its second moment around zero is $\sigma^4(\operatorname{tr} \mathbf{Q})^2 + 2\sigma^4 \operatorname{tr} \mathbf{Q}^2$. Finally, prove that the second moment of $\boldsymbol{\epsilon}'\mathbf{Q}\boldsymbol{\epsilon}$ around σ^2 is

$$\mathscr{E}[(\boldsymbol{\epsilon}'\mathbf{Q}\boldsymbol{\epsilon} - \sigma^2)^2] = 2\sigma^4 \operatorname{tr} \mathbf{Q}^2 + \sigma^4(1 - \operatorname{tr} \mathbf{Q})^2 \tag{5.10}$$

5.4 (*Continuation*) Prove that the σ^2 estimator s'^2 defined in (5.7) is of the form $\boldsymbol{\epsilon}'\mathbf{Q}\boldsymbol{\epsilon}$ when $\mathbf{Q}$ is defined as $[1/(n - K + 2)]\mathbf{M}$. Consider any other estimator $\boldsymbol{\epsilon}'\mathbf{Q}\boldsymbol{\epsilon}$ and write $\mathbf{Q} = [1/(n - K + 2)]\mathbf{M} + \mathbf{B}$, where $\mathbf{B}$ is an arbitrary symmetric $n \times n$ matrix. Prove that condition (5.5) implies $\mathbf{BX} = \mathbf{0}$. Also prove that the second moment of this estimator around σ^2 is

$$\frac{2\sigma^4}{n - K + 2} + \sigma^4(\operatorname{tr} \mathbf{B})^2 + 2\sigma^4 \operatorname{tr} \mathbf{B}^2 \tag{5.11}$$

and prove—using the symmetry of $\mathbf{B}$—that the sum of the last two terms is positive when $\mathbf{B} \neq \mathbf{0}$. Finally, prove eqs. (5.8) and (5.9) directly by means of the relevant chi-square distribution. (Note that in the case $K = 1$ the estimator s'^2 is obtained by dividing the residual sum of squares by a number *larger* than n.)

5.5 (*Continuation*) To derive the best quadratic unbiased estimator, write it in the form $\boldsymbol{\epsilon}'\mathbf{Q}\boldsymbol{\epsilon}$, where $\mathbf{Q} = [1/(n - K)]\mathbf{M} + \mathbf{C}$. Prove that unbiasedness requires $\mathbf{CX} = \mathbf{0}$ and $\operatorname{tr} \mathbf{C} = 0$. Prove that its variance is equal to $2\sigma^4/(n - K) + 2\sigma^4 \operatorname{tr} \mathbf{C}^2$ and that $\operatorname{tr} \mathbf{C}^2 > 0$ except when $\mathbf{C} = \mathbf{0}$.

3.6 Confidence Intervals and Prediction Intervals under the Normality Assumption[A]

A Confidence Interval for the Variance

Since $(n - K)s^2/\sigma^2$ has a chi-square distribution with $n - K$ degrees of freedom, we can easily obtain a confidence interval for σ^2. Take the textile example, for which $n - K = 14$, and apply the 95 percent confidence coefficient. We have

$$P[5.63 \leq \chi^2(14) \leq 26.12] = .95$$

the probabilities of a value smaller than 5.63 and of a value larger than 26.12 both being equal to .025. We conclude that the following inequalities hold except for a .05 probability:

$$5.63 \leq \frac{14s^2}{\sigma^2} \leq 26.12$$

or, equivalently,

$$\frac{14s^2}{26.12} \leq \sigma^2 \leq \frac{14s^2}{5.63}$$

After substituting the value (3.16) for s^2 we obtain (.00010, .00046) as a confidence interval for σ^2 with .95 confidence coefficient. Note that this is not the shortest possible interval at the .95 confidence coefficient, since the χ^2 distribution is skew; see Problem 6.2.

A Confidence Interval for a Linear Function of the Coefficient Vector

Consider $\mathbf{w}'\boldsymbol{\beta}$, a linear function of the parameter vector $\boldsymbol{\beta}$ with fixed weights $w_1, \ldots, w_K$. We know that $\mathbf{w}'\mathbf{b} - \mathbf{w}'\boldsymbol{\beta}$ is normally distributed with zero mean and variance $\sigma^2\mathbf{w}'(\mathbf{X}'\mathbf{X})^{-1}\mathbf{w}$; hence the ratio

$$\frac{\mathbf{w}'\mathbf{b} - \mathbf{w}'\boldsymbol{\beta}}{\sigma\sqrt{\mathbf{w}'(\mathbf{X}'\mathbf{X})^{-1}\mathbf{w}}} \tag{6.1}$$

follows a standardized normal distribution. The variate (6.1) depends on the unknown σ; but $\mathbf{b}$ and s^2 are distributed independently, so that the same applies to the ratio (6.1) and $(n - K)s^2/\sigma^2$, which are functions of $\mathbf{b}$ and s^2, respectively. Since $(n - K)s^2/\sigma^2$ is distributed as $\chi^2(n - K)$, the ratio

$$\frac{\dfrac{\mathbf{w}'\mathbf{b} - \mathbf{w}'\boldsymbol{\beta}}{\sigma\sqrt{\mathbf{w}'(\mathbf{X}'\mathbf{X})^{-1}\mathbf{w}}}\sqrt{n - K}}{\sqrt{(n - K)s^2/\sigma^2}} = \frac{\mathbf{w}'\mathbf{b} - \mathbf{w}'\boldsymbol{\beta}}{s\sqrt{\mathbf{w}'(\mathbf{X}'\mathbf{X})^{-1}\mathbf{w}}} \tag{6.2}$$

follows the Student distribution with $n - K$ degrees of freedom. We shall apply this result to each of the three regression coefficients of the textile example at the .95 confidence level:

$$\mathrm{P}[-2.145 \leq t(14) \leq 2.145] = .95$$

The right-hand denominator in (6.2) becomes $s\sqrt{\mathbf{i}_h'(\mathbf{X}'\mathbf{X})^{-1}\mathbf{i}_h}$ in this case, where $\mathbf{i}_h$ is the hth column of the $K \times K$ unit matrix ($K = 3$ for the textile example). This is nothing but the square root of the hth diagonal element of $s^2(\mathbf{X}'\mathbf{X})^{-1}$, which is simply the relevant standard error in (3.18). Thus we obtain the following confidence intervals, each with .95 confidence coefficient:

$$\begin{aligned} .72 &\leq \beta_0 \leq 2.03 && \text{(constant term)} \\ .81 &\leq \beta_1 \leq 1.48 && \text{(income elasticity)} \\ -.91 &\leq \beta_2 \leq -.75 && \text{(price elasticity)} \end{aligned} \tag{6.3}$$

Confidence Regions for Several Parameters Simultaneously

We know from the general theory of interval estimation that if we construct confidence intervals with confidence coefficient .95 (say) a large number of times, we shall "miss" the parameter in about 5 percent of all cases. However, note that the underlying assumption implies that each interval statement is based on a different (independent) sample. This condition is obviously not satisfied by the three intervals in (6.3). Thus, if I_1 is the confidence interval for β_1 and I_2 the interval for β_2, both with confidence coefficient $1 - \alpha$, then each of the following two statements is true:

$$\mathrm{P}[\beta_1 \in I_1] = 1 - \alpha \qquad \mathrm{P}[\beta_2 \in I_2] = 1 - \alpha$$

However, it is not true that $\mathrm{P}[\beta_1 \in I_1, \beta_2 \in I_2]$ is equal to $(1 - \alpha)^2$ because of the lack of independence.

If one wants a confidence statement on two or more parameters simultaneously, one can proceed in at least two ways. We shall describe the simplest method for the case of two parameters, θ_1 and θ_2. Let I_1 be a confidence interval for θ_1 with confidence coefficient $1 - \alpha_1$ and, similarly, I_2 a confidence interval for θ_2 with confidence coefficient $1 - \alpha_2$:

$$\mathrm{P}[\theta_1 \in I_1] = 1 - \alpha_1 \qquad \mathrm{P}[\theta_2 \in I_2] = 1 - \alpha_2 \tag{6.4}$$

If we write $\notin$ for "not included in," we have

$$\begin{aligned}
\mathrm{P}[\theta_1 \in I_1, \theta_2 \in I_2] &= 1 - \mathrm{P}[\theta_1 \notin I_1, \theta_2 \in I_2] - \mathrm{P}[\theta_1 \in I_1, \theta_2 \notin I_2] \\
&\quad - \mathrm{P}[\theta_1 \notin I_1, \theta_2 \notin I_2] \\
&\geq 1 - \{\mathrm{P}[\theta_1 \notin I_1, \theta_2 \in I_2] + \mathrm{P}[\theta_1 \notin I_1, \theta_2 \notin I_2]\} \\
&\quad - \{\mathrm{P}[\theta_1 \in I_1, \theta_2 \notin I_2] + \mathrm{P}[\theta_1 \notin I_1, \theta_2 \notin I_2]\} \\
&= 1 - \mathrm{P}[\theta_1 \notin I_1] - \mathrm{P}[\theta_2 \notin I_2] = 1 - \alpha_1 - \alpha_2
\end{aligned} \tag{6.5}$$

This amounts to a *confidence region* for the two parameters jointly with a confidence coefficient at least equal to $1 - \alpha_1 - \alpha_2$. If we apply this to β_1 and β_2 of (6.3), we find that $.81 \leq \beta_1 \leq 1.48$, $-.91 \leq \beta_2 \leq -.75$ is a rectangular confidence region in the β_1, β_2-plane with a confidence coefficient $\geq .9$.

The second method does not lead to a simple rectangular region, but it has the advantage that the confidence coefficient can be determined exactly. Again, consider the income elasticity (β_1) and the price elasticity (β_2) of the textile example. Their LS estimators b_1, b_2 have a bivariate normal sampling distribution with means β_1, β_2 and covariance matrix $\sigma^2\mathbf{C}$, where $\mathbf{C}$ is the lower right-hand 2×2 submatrix of $(\mathbf{X}'\mathbf{X})^{-1}$ which is given in (3.14). Since $\mathbf{C}$ is symmetric and positive definite, there exists a nonsingular matrix $\mathbf{P}$

such that $\mathbf{C}^{-1} = \mathbf{P}'\mathbf{P}$.[15] We introduce

$$\begin{bmatrix} z_1 \\ z_2 \end{bmatrix} = \mathbf{P}\begin{bmatrix} b_1 - \beta_1 \\ b_2 - \beta_2 \end{bmatrix}$$

which is a random normal vector with zero mean and the following covariance matrix:

$$\mathscr{V}\begin{bmatrix} z_1 \\ z_2 \end{bmatrix} = \mathbf{P}\mathscr{V}\begin{bmatrix} b_1 - \beta_1 \\ b_2 - \beta_2 \end{bmatrix}\mathbf{P}' = \sigma^2\mathbf{PCP}' = \sigma^2\mathbf{PP}^{-1}(\mathbf{P}')^{-1}\mathbf{P}' = \sigma^2\mathbf{I}$$

We conclude that z_1/σ and z_2/σ are independent standardized normal variates. Hence the sum of squares of these z's,

$$z_1^2 + z_2^2 = [b_1 - \beta_1 \quad b_2 - \beta_2]\mathbf{P}'\mathbf{P}\begin{bmatrix} b_1 - \beta_1 \\ b_2 - \beta_2 \end{bmatrix} = [b_1 - \beta_1 \quad b_2 - \beta_2]\mathbf{C}^{-1}\begin{bmatrix} b_1 - \beta_1 \\ b_2 - \beta_2 \end{bmatrix} \tag{6.6}$$

is distributed as $\sigma^2\chi^2(2)$. We also recall that $(n - K)s^2$ is distributed as $\sigma^2\chi^2(n - K)$ and that $\mathbf{b}$ and s^2 are independent. It follows immediately that

$$\frac{1}{2s^2}[b_1 - \beta_1 \quad b_2 - \beta_2]\mathbf{C}^{-1}\begin{bmatrix} b_1 - \beta_1 \\ b_2 - \beta_2 \end{bmatrix} \tag{6.7}$$

is distributed as $F(2, n - K)$. Let F_α be a number such that the probability is α that this F ratio exceeds F_α. Then the confidence region for β_1 and β_2 is of the form

$$\mathrm{P}[a_{11}(b_1 - \beta_1)^2 + a_{22}(b_2 - \beta_2)^2 + 2a_{12}(b_1 - \beta_1)(b_2 - \beta_2) \leq F_\alpha] = 1 - \alpha \tag{6.8}$$

where $a_{hk} = c^{hk}/2s^2$, c^{hk} being the (h, k)th element of $\mathbf{C}^{-1}$ $(h, k = 1, 2)$. We substitute for $\mathbf{C}$ the lower right-hand 2×2 submatrix of (3.14) and for s^2 the value (3.16), which gives

$$a_{11} = 21.6 \qquad a_{22} = 403.5 \qquad a_{12} = 20.8 \tag{6.9}$$

Clearly, (6.8) defines a confidence region of the form of an ellipse with center at (b_1, b_2). We have $F_\alpha = 3.74$ for $1 - \alpha = .95$ and $F_\alpha = 6.51$ for $1 - \alpha = .99$ (2 degrees of freedom in the numerator, $n - K = 14$ in the denominator). The two ellipses are shown in Figure 3.2. Notice that $\mathbf{C}$ and hence also $[a_{hk}] = [c^{hk}/2s^2]$ are diagonal when b_1 and b_2 are uncorrelated. This implies $a_{12} = 0$, so that the axes of the ellipse are then parallel to the axes of the coordinate system. In Figure 3.2 we are fairly close to this situation, but

[15] See the last subsection of Section 1.4.

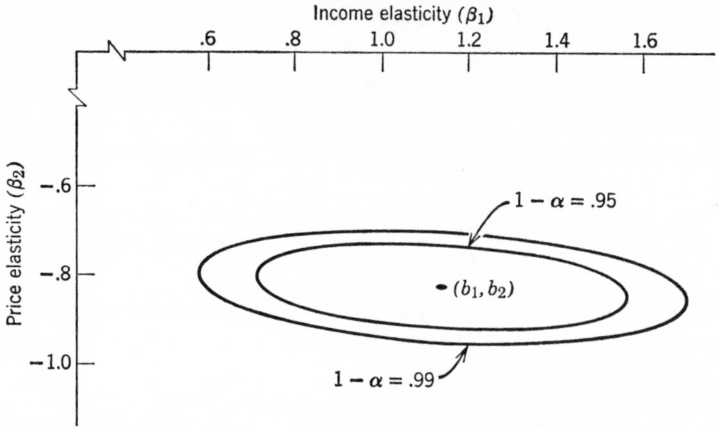

Fig. 3.2 Confidence regions for the income and price elasticities of the textile example.

one may also have confidence ellipses whose axes are far from parallel to those of the coordinate system.

The subject of simultaneous confidence intervals for several linear combinations has been pursued by SCHEFFÉ (1953, 1959) and TUKEY (1949). The most accessible text is MILLER (1966), particularly pp. 48–67 which deal with the Scheffé technique applied to linear regressions. Basically the technique amounts to the formulation of a simultaneous confidence region *for all possible sets* of q linear combinations of unknown coefficients, and the results are based on the F distribution with q and $n - K$ degrees of freedom. These confidence regions tend to be large; they are too pessimistic for the usual case in which the analyst is interested only in *one particular set* of q linear combinations.

Prediction Intervals

The confidence interval procedure can also be applied to obtain prediction intervals. We shall confine ourselves to the case of one single future observation, so that eq. (4.7) can be written as

$$y_* = \boldsymbol{\xi}'\boldsymbol{\beta} + \epsilon_* \tag{6.10}$$

where $\boldsymbol{\xi}'$ is a K-element row vector of given values taken by the explanatory variables. It follows from (4.11) that the variance of the prediction error $\boldsymbol{\xi}'\mathbf{b} - y_*$ is $\sigma^2[1 + \boldsymbol{\xi}'(\mathbf{X}'\mathbf{X})^{-1}\boldsymbol{\xi}]$. Hence, if the distribution of $[\boldsymbol{\epsilon}' \quad \epsilon_*]$ is $(n + 1)$-variate normal, the ratio

$$\frac{\boldsymbol{\xi}'\mathbf{b} - y_*}{\sigma\sqrt{1 + \boldsymbol{\xi}'(\mathbf{X}'\mathbf{X})^{-1}\boldsymbol{\xi}}} \tag{6.11}$$

follows a standardized normal distribution.[16] But $(n - K)s^2/\sigma^2$ is distributed as $\chi^2(n - K)$, and it is independent of the ratio (6.11) because s^2 and $\mathbf{b}$ are independent and the disturbance component ϵ_* of y_* is independent of $\boldsymbol{\epsilon}$ of the sample. Hence

$$(6.12)\qquad \frac{\dfrac{\boldsymbol{\xi}'\mathbf{b} - y_*}{\sigma\sqrt{1 + \boldsymbol{\xi}'(\mathbf{X}'\mathbf{X})^{-1}\boldsymbol{\xi}}}\sqrt{n - K}}{\sqrt{(n - K)s^2/\sigma^2}} = \frac{\boldsymbol{\xi}'\mathbf{b} - y_*}{s\sqrt{1 + \boldsymbol{\xi}'(\mathbf{X}'\mathbf{X})^{-1}\boldsymbol{\xi}}}$$

is distributed as $t(n - K)$. By using the limits

$$(6.13)\qquad P[-t_{\alpha/2} \leq t(n - K) \leq t_{\alpha/2}] = 1 - \alpha$$

we thus obtain the following prediction interval for y_*:

$$(6.14)\qquad P\Big[\boldsymbol{\xi}'\mathbf{b} - t_{\alpha/2}s\sqrt{1 + \boldsymbol{\xi}'(\mathbf{X}'\mathbf{X})^{-1}\boldsymbol{\xi}} \leq y_* \leq \boldsymbol{\xi}'\mathbf{b} + t_{\alpha/2}s\sqrt{1 + \boldsymbol{\xi}'(\mathbf{X}'\mathbf{X})^{-1}\boldsymbol{\xi}}\Big] = 1 - \alpha$$

Note that the prediction interval approach is entirely analogous to that of the confidence intervals with the following exception. The objective of a confidence interval is to find limits for a fixed parameter, but here we consider limits for a random variable. The double inequality in (6.14) is of the form $a \leq y_* \leq b$, and a, b, and y_* are all random. The double inequality of a confidence interval is of the form $a \leq \theta \leq b$ and only the limits (a and b) are random.

Application to the Demand for Textile

We shall illustrate this procedure for the textile example under the assumption that real per capita income and the relative price of textiles are equal to 105 and 65 (base 1925 = 100), respectively, which are approximate extrapolations for 1940.[17] Hence $\boldsymbol{\xi}' = [1 \quad 2.02119 \quad 1.81291]$, which gives $\boldsymbol{\xi}'(\mathbf{X}'\mathbf{X})^{-1}\boldsymbol{\xi} = .102$ on the basis of (3.14). This is the prediction error variance (apart from the factor σ^2) which is to be ascribed to the sampling errors of the coefficient estimators. We should add 1 (again apart from the factor σ^2) for the component of the prediction error variance that results from the neglect of the future disturbance. Our conclusion is that in this case only about 10 percent of the error variance of the prediction is due to the use of

[16] Note what this means. If we repeat the sampling and estimation procedure that led to $\mathbf{b}$, with $\mathbf{X}$ always the same, and also each time observing one new y_* for the same $\boldsymbol{\xi}$, then the ratio (6.11) is a standardized normal variate.

[17] The country was actually occupied by the Germans in that year, who thereby violated our assumption that the underlying process does not change.

b rather than **β** and, hence, about 90 percent to the zero value which is substituted for the disturbance.

The standard deviation of the prediction error is thus $\sigma\sqrt{1.102} \approx 1.050\sigma$. When substituting **b** of (3.15) and s of (3.16) and using a .95 confidence coefficient ($t_{.025} = 2.145$ for 14 degrees of freedom), we obtain (2.151, 2.212) as the prediction interval for the logarithm of textile consumption per capita. Taking antilogs, we find (142, 163) for the corresponding interval of textile consumption itself. Its limits should be compared with the figures of the first column of Table 3.1.

Prediction Based on a Simple Regression

It is instructive to consider the form of the interval in the simple case of one explanatory variable without constant term. Then **ξ** is a scalar, to be written x_*, so that the double inequality in (6.14) takes the form

$$(6.15)\quad bx_* - t_{\alpha/2}s\sqrt{1 + x_*^2/\sum x_\alpha^2} \le y_* \le bx_* + t_{\alpha/2}s\sqrt{1 + x_*^2/\sum x_\alpha^2}$$

where $\sum x_\alpha^2 = x_1^2 + \cdots + x_n^2$. The limits of y_* when viewed as functions of x_* are the two branches of the hyperbola which is shown in Figure 3.3. The straight line that passes through the origin is the regression line $y = bx$, which is determined from the sample (indicated by black dots). The regression line gives the point prediction bx_* for each value of x_*. It is easily verified that the width of the prediction interval takes the smallest value at $x_* = 0$

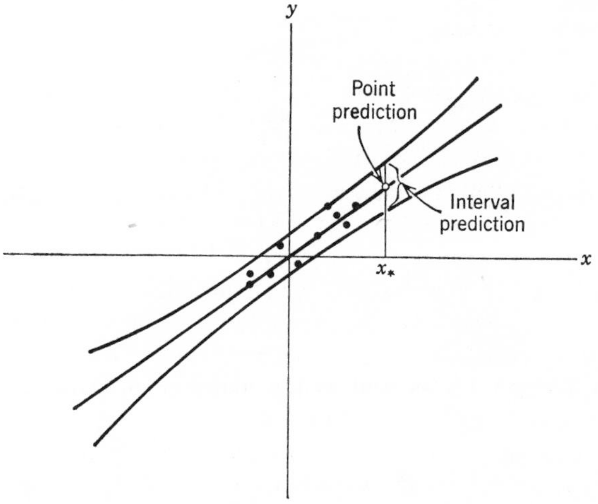

Fig. 3.3 Regression prediction for the case of one explanatory variable without constant term.

and that this minimum is equal to $2t_{\alpha/2}s$. Also see Problem 6.6 for the case of one explanatory variable plus a constant term.

Problems

6.1 Formulate a confidence interval for σ (rather than σ^2) on the basis of the results given in the first paragraph.

6.2 Consider $P[a_\eta \leq \chi^2(14)] = .025 - \eta$ and $P[\chi^2(14) \geq b_\eta] = .025 + \eta$. Use a table of the chi-square distribution to prove that if η takes a sufficiently small positive value, the width of the interval (a_η, b_η) is smaller than that of the confidence interval discussed in the first paragraph. (This shows that, owing to the skewness of the chi-square distribution, a shorter confidence interval at the same confidence level can be obtained by pushing the interval toward the origin.)

6.3 Illustrate the derivation (6.5) by means of a Venn diagram. Generalize the result for the case of an arbitrary number of parameters.

6.4 Generalize eq. (6.8) for the case of an arbitrary number of parameters. What is the form of the multidimensional confidence region?

6.5 Consider Figure 3.2 and draw a rectangular confidence region with confidence coefficient $\geq .95$ on the basis of the derivation (6.5). Compare it with the ellipse $(1 - \alpha = .95)$ and draw your conclusions.

6.6 Prove that the prediction error variance for a simple regression with a constant term is of the following form:

$$\sigma^2\left(1 + \frac{1}{n}\right) + \sigma^2 \frac{(x_* - \bar{x})^2}{\sum (x_\alpha - \bar{x})^2} \tag{6.16}$$

where $\bar{x}$ is the average of $x_1, \ldots, x_n$. Use this result to generalize the prediction interval for the case in which the regression includes a constant term. Make a diagram similar to Figure 3.3 and compare.

3.7 Hypotheses Testing under the Normality Assumption[AB]

In this section we shall develop testing procedures (1) for σ^2, (2) for one linear combination of the $\boldsymbol{\beta}$ components, (3) for the complete $\boldsymbol{\beta}$ vector, (4) for q components of this vector, and (5) for q linear combinations of the elements of this vector. Procedure (5) requires the constrained LS procedure described in Section 1.8 as well as the material on parameter spaces and likelihood ratio tests given in Section 2.9.

Testing a Hypothesis on the Variance[A]

Let $\sigma^2 = \sigma_0^2$ be the null hypothesis (H_0) and $\sigma^2 \neq \sigma_0^2$ the alternative hypothesis (H_1). We return to the beginning of Section 3.6, where a confidence interval was established for σ^2 based on the chi-square distribution with $n - K$ degrees of freedom of $(n - K)s^2/\sigma^2$. This becomes $(n - K)s^2/\sigma_0^2$ if H_0 is true, which can be computed from the sample. When we use a 100α percent significance level, we compute the significance limits a_α and b_α from

$$P[\chi^2(n - K) < a_\alpha] = P[\chi^2(n - K) > b_\alpha] = \frac{1}{2}\alpha$$

and reject H_0 in favor of H_1 if and only if the computed value of $(n - K)s^2/\sigma_0^2$ lies in the critical region, which consists of all values $< a_\alpha$ and $> b_\alpha$ (see Problem 7.1).

Testing a Linear Combination of the Coefficients[A]

Next consider H_0: $\mathbf{w}'\boldsymbol{\beta} = w_0$, where $\mathbf{w}$ is a known vector and w_0 a known scalar. Let $\mathbf{w}'\boldsymbol{\beta} \neq w_0$ be H_1. We conclude from (6.2) that

$$\frac{\mathbf{w}'\mathbf{b} - w_0}{s\sqrt{\mathbf{w}'(\mathbf{X}'\mathbf{X})^{-1}\mathbf{w}}} \tag{7.1}$$

is distributed as $t(n - K)$ if H_0 is true. Returning to our textile example, let our null hypothesis be that the income and price elasticities are equal except for the sign: $\beta_1 = -\beta_2$. Then the elements of $\mathbf{w}$ are 0, 1, and 1, and $w_0 = 0$. The numerator of the ratio (7.1) becomes $1.1430 + (-.8289) = .3141$, while the square of the denominator can be read directly from the matrix (3.17):

$$.024324 + .001304 + 2(-.001251) = .023126$$

so that we obtain $.3141/\sqrt{.023126} = 2.065$. This is less in absolute value than $t_{.025} = 2.145$, the 5 percent significance limit for 14 degrees of freedom. Hence we should accept H_0 if this is the significance level chosen. Note that we arrive at the opposite conclusion when the alternative hypothesis states $\beta_1 > -\beta_2$ instead of $\beta_1 \neq -\beta_2$. This is relevant when it is considered certain on a priori grounds that the absolute value of the price elasticity is not larger than the income elasticity. The critical region of the ratio (7.1) at the 5 percent significance level then consists of all values which exceed $t_{.05} = 1.761$ (for 14 degrees of freedom), and the observed value 2.065 falls in this region. The latter test is a one-tailed test, the former a two-tailed test.

Testing the Complete Coefficient Vector[A]

Our third H_0 is $\boldsymbol{\beta} = \boldsymbol{\beta}_0$, while $\boldsymbol{\beta}_0$ is a numerically specified K-element vector. An obvious testing procedure is a comparison of the sum of squares of the residuals which are implied by $\boldsymbol{\beta}_0$ and the minimum (LS) residual sum of squares. Recall eq. (7.24) of Section 1.7:

$$(7.2) \qquad (\mathbf{y} - \mathbf{X}\mathbf{z})'(\mathbf{y} - \mathbf{X}\mathbf{z}) = \mathbf{y}'\mathbf{M}\mathbf{y} + (\mathbf{z} - \mathbf{b})'\mathbf{X}'\mathbf{X}(\mathbf{z} - \mathbf{b})$$

where the left-hand side is the residual sum of squares associated with an arbitrary coefficient vector $\mathbf{z}$, while $\mathbf{y}'\mathbf{M}\mathbf{y}$ is the LS residual sum of squares. The latter quadratic form can also be written $\boldsymbol{\epsilon}'\mathbf{M}\boldsymbol{\epsilon}$. On substituting $\boldsymbol{\beta}_0$ for $\mathbf{z}$ we thus have

$$(7.3) \qquad (\mathbf{y} - \mathbf{X}\boldsymbol{\beta}_0)'(\mathbf{y} - \mathbf{X}\boldsymbol{\beta}_0) = \boldsymbol{\epsilon}'\mathbf{M}\boldsymbol{\epsilon} + (\mathbf{b} - \boldsymbol{\beta}_0)'\mathbf{X}'\mathbf{X}(\mathbf{b} - \boldsymbol{\beta}_0)$$

If H_0 is true, then $\mathbf{b} - \boldsymbol{\beta}_0 = \mathbf{b} - \boldsymbol{\beta} = (\mathbf{X}'\mathbf{X})^{-1}\mathbf{X}'\boldsymbol{\epsilon}$, so that the second quadratic form on the right is equal to $\boldsymbol{\epsilon}'\mathbf{X}(\mathbf{X}'\mathbf{X})^{-1}\mathbf{X}'\boldsymbol{\epsilon} = \boldsymbol{\epsilon}'(\mathbf{I} - \mathbf{M})\boldsymbol{\epsilon}$. Thus we can write (7.3) under H_0 as follows:

$$(7.4) \qquad (\mathbf{y} - \mathbf{X}\boldsymbol{\beta}_0)'(\mathbf{y} - \mathbf{X}\boldsymbol{\beta}_0) = \boldsymbol{\epsilon}'\mathbf{M}\boldsymbol{\epsilon} + \boldsymbol{\epsilon}'(\mathbf{I} - \mathbf{M})\boldsymbol{\epsilon}$$

The quadratic forms in the right-hand side are both idempotent and their matrices satisfy $\mathbf{M}(\mathbf{I} - \mathbf{M}) = \mathbf{M} - \mathbf{M}^2 = \mathbf{0}$, so that they are independent χ^2 variates. Since the rank of $\mathbf{M}$ is $n - K$ and that of $\mathbf{I} - \mathbf{M}$ is K, the ratio of $\boldsymbol{\epsilon}'(\mathbf{I} - \mathbf{M})\boldsymbol{\epsilon}/K$ to $\boldsymbol{\epsilon}'\mathbf{M}\boldsymbol{\epsilon}/(n - K)$ is distributed as $F(K, n - K)$ if H_0 is true. But $\boldsymbol{\epsilon}'\mathbf{M}\boldsymbol{\epsilon} = (n - K)s^2$ and $\boldsymbol{\epsilon}'(\mathbf{I} - \mathbf{M})\boldsymbol{\epsilon}$ is equal to the second quadratic form in the right-hand side of (7.3)—if H_0 is true; so we can equivalently state that the left-hand side of

$$(7.5) \qquad \frac{(\mathbf{b} - \boldsymbol{\beta}_0)'\mathbf{X}'\mathbf{X}(\mathbf{b} - \boldsymbol{\beta}_0)}{Ks^2} = \frac{(\mathbf{y} - \mathbf{X}\boldsymbol{\beta}_0)'(\mathbf{y} - \mathbf{X}\boldsymbol{\beta}_0) - (n - K)s^2}{Ks^2}$$

is distributed as $F(K, n - K)$ under H_0. The equality sign of (7.5) follows directly from (7.3). The right-hand numerator of (7.5) is simply the excess of the squared length of the residual vector implied by $\boldsymbol{\beta}_0$ over the squared length of the LS residual vector. The test statistic is equal to the ratio of this excess to K times the LS variance estimator. The null hypothesis is rejected when this ratio exceeds the relevant significance limit of the F ratio with K and $n - K$ degrees of freedom.

Testing a Subvector of the Coefficient Vector[A]

Testing $\boldsymbol{\beta} = \boldsymbol{\beta}_0$ presupposes a complete numerical specification of all elements of the parameter vector in the form $\boldsymbol{\beta}_0$. There are many cases in which the analyst does not want to go that far; for example, he may not want to specify a numerical value for the constant term simply because he is not interested in that term. So our fourth null hypothesis is $\boldsymbol{\beta}_1 = \boldsymbol{\beta}_{10}$, where $\boldsymbol{\beta}_1$ is a subvector of $\boldsymbol{\beta}$ consisting of q elements ($q < K$) and $\boldsymbol{\beta}_{10}$ is a numerically specified q-element vector. Without loss of generality we may assume (by interchanging the order of the explanatory variables if necessary) that $\boldsymbol{\beta}_1$ consists of the first q elements of $\boldsymbol{\beta}$, so that the basic equation can be written as

$$\text{(7.6)} \qquad \mathbf{y} = [\mathbf{X}_1 \quad \mathbf{X}_2]\begin{bmatrix} \boldsymbol{\beta}_1 \\ \boldsymbol{\beta}_2 \end{bmatrix} + \boldsymbol{\epsilon} = \mathbf{X}_1\boldsymbol{\beta}_1 + \mathbf{X}_2\boldsymbol{\beta}_2 + \boldsymbol{\epsilon}$$

where $\mathbf{X}_1$ consists of the first q columns of $\mathbf{X}$ and $\mathbf{X}_2$ of the last $K - q$ columns.

The present H_0 does not define a residual sum of squares directly, since only $\boldsymbol{\beta}_1$ is specified, not $\boldsymbol{\beta}_2$. However, we can take $\boldsymbol{\beta}_1 = \boldsymbol{\beta}_{10}$ and select for $\boldsymbol{\beta}_2$ the vector which minimizes the associated residual sum of squares. We can then compare the value of this minimum with the LS residual sum of squares, which is obviously never larger than this minimum (because of the constraint $\boldsymbol{\beta}_1 = \boldsymbol{\beta}_{10}$ which H_0 imposes and which LS does not impose). So we rewrite (7.6) as

$$\text{(7.7)} \qquad \mathbf{y} - \mathbf{X}_1\boldsymbol{\beta}_{10} = \mathbf{X}_2\boldsymbol{\beta}_2 + \boldsymbol{\epsilon}$$

which is correct if H_0 is true. The formulation (7.7) implies that the elements of $\mathbf{y} - \mathbf{X}_1\boldsymbol{\beta}_{10}$ are regarded as the values taken by a new dependent variable. (Note that these values are observable, given that $\boldsymbol{\beta}_{10}$ is known.) The LS estimator of $\boldsymbol{\beta}_2$ based on (7.7) is obtained by premultiplying the left-hand vector of that equation by $(\mathbf{X}_2'\mathbf{X}_2)^{-1}\mathbf{X}_2'$. Combining this with the value $\boldsymbol{\beta}_{10}$ of $\boldsymbol{\beta}_1$, we thus have the coefficient vector

$$\text{(7.8)} \qquad \mathbf{z} = \begin{bmatrix} \boldsymbol{\beta}_{10} \\ (\mathbf{X}_2'\mathbf{X}_2)^{-1} \;{}_2'(\mathbf{y} - \mathbf{X}_1\boldsymbol{\beta}_{10}) \end{bmatrix}$$

and we proceed to apply the decomposition (7.2) to this specification of $\mathbf{z}$ in the same way as we considered $\mathbf{z} = \boldsymbol{\beta}_0$ in (7.3). The algebraic details are rather lengthy; they are considered in Problems 7.3 and 7.4, but the result is simple and can be described as follows.

Define:

$$\text{(7.9)} \qquad \mathbf{M}_2 = \mathbf{I} - \mathbf{X}_2(\mathbf{X}_2'\mathbf{X}_2)^{-1}\mathbf{X}_2'$$

This matrix is analogous to $\mathbf{M} = \mathbf{I} - \mathbf{X}(\mathbf{X}'\mathbf{X})^{-1}\mathbf{X}'$; the only difference is that the first q columns of $\mathbf{X}$ are deleted. Obviously, $\mathbf{M}_2$ is an $n \times n$ idempotent matrix of rank $n - (K - q)$. It then turns out that the second quadratic form in the right-hand side of (7.2) under the present H_0 with $\mathbf{z}$ as specified in (7.8) is

$$\text{(7.10)} \qquad (\mathbf{b} - \mathbf{z})'\mathbf{X}'\mathbf{X}(\mathbf{b} - \mathbf{z}) = \boldsymbol{\epsilon}'\mathbf{N}\boldsymbol{\epsilon} \quad \text{where} \quad \mathbf{N} = \mathbf{M}_2\mathbf{X}_1(\mathbf{X}_1'\mathbf{M}_2\mathbf{X}_1)^{-1}\mathbf{X}_1'\mathbf{M}_2$$

The matrix $\mathbf{N}$ is idempotent:

$$\begin{aligned} \mathbf{N}^2 &= \mathbf{M}_2\mathbf{X}_1(\mathbf{X}_1'\mathbf{M}_2\mathbf{X}_1)^{-1}\mathbf{X}_1'\mathbf{M}_2^2\mathbf{X}_1(\mathbf{X}_1'\mathbf{M}_2\mathbf{X}_1)^{-1}\mathbf{X}_1'\mathbf{M}_2 \\ &= \mathbf{M}_2\mathbf{X}_1(\mathbf{X}_1'\mathbf{M}_2\mathbf{X}_1)^{-1}\mathbf{X}_1'\mathbf{M}_2\mathbf{X}_1(\mathbf{X}_1'\mathbf{M}_2\mathbf{X}_1)^{-1}\,\mathbf{X}_1'\mathbf{M} \\ &= \mathbf{M}_2 \;{}_1(\mathbf{X}_1'\mathbf{M}_2\mathbf{X}_1)^{-1}\mathbf{X}_1'\mathbf{M}_2 = \mathbf{N} \end{aligned}$$

The trace of $\mathbf{N}$ (and hence also its rank) is equal to q:

$$\operatorname{tr} \mathbf{N} = \operatorname{tr} (\mathbf{X}_1'\mathbf{M}_2\mathbf{X}_1)^{-1}\mathbf{X}_1'\mathbf{M}_2^2\mathbf{X}_1 = \operatorname{tr} (\mathbf{X}_1'\mathbf{M}_2\mathbf{X}_1)^{-1}\mathbf{X}_1'\mathbf{M}_2\mathbf{X}_1 = q$$

the expression before the last equality sign being the trace of the $q \times q$ unit matrix.

The conclusion is that under H_0 the quadratic form (7.10) is distributed as $\sigma^2\chi^2(q)$. We know that $\mathbf{y}'\mathbf{M}\mathbf{y}$ of (7.2) is distributed as $\sigma^2\chi^2(n - K)$. It can be shown that $\mathbf{MN} = \mathbf{0}$ (see Problem 7.5), so that the two quadratic forms are independent. Since the quadratic form (7.10) is, in view of (7.2), equal to the excess of the squared length of the present residual vector over that of LS, the ratio of this excess to qs^2 is thus distributed as $F(q, n - K)$ if H_0 is true. Notice that this result includes as a special case (for $q = K$) that of testing the complete vector $\boldsymbol{\beta}$.

Application to the Income and Price Elasticities of the Textile Example[A]

The discussion below eq. (7.1) showed that equality (except for sign) of the income and price elasticities is an acceptable hypothesis at the 5 percent significance level when the alternative is $\beta_1 \neq -\beta_2$. Let us specify this further by taking H_0: $\beta_1 = -\beta_2 = 1$. Equation (2.3) in the form (7.7) is then

$$y_\alpha - x_{\alpha 1} + x_{\alpha 2} = \beta_0 + \epsilon_\alpha \tag{7.11}$$

The left-hand side is the value in year α of the logarithm of the ratio of the total money value of textile consumption by private consumers to the total money income of private consumers. Thus our null hypothesis specifies that this ratio is completely independent of real income and the relative textile price.

In this case we have $n = 17$, $K = 3$, $q = 2$. The minimum residual sum of squares corresponding with (7.11) is simply $\sum (v_\alpha - \bar{v})^2$, where $v_\alpha = y_\alpha - x_{\alpha 1} + x_{\alpha 2}$ and $\bar{v} = \frac{1}{17}\sum v_\alpha$. The value of this minimum is .0074, which exceeds the LS value $(n - K)s^2$ as given in (3.16) by almost .005. The ratio of this excess to $qs^2 = 2s^2$ is larger than 10. The significance limit at the 1 percent level for $F(2, 14)$ is 6.51, and hence the null hypothesis is to be rejected at this significance level.[18]

Likelihood Ratio Tests[B]

It was shown at the end of Section 2.9 that a likelihood ratio test for the mean of a univariate normal distribution can be based on the Student distribution. A similar result holds for the testing of one element of the coefficient

[18] For another similar application of the F test (formulated in terms of the multiple correlation coefficient), see Section 4.6.

vector $\boldsymbol{\beta}$ (see Problem 7.7). Here we shall prove that the F test for the complete $\boldsymbol{\beta}$ vector may be regarded as a likelihood ratio test, too.

Consider again the likelihood function:

$$L(\mathbf{y}; \mathbf{X}\boldsymbol{\beta}, \sigma^2\mathbf{I}) = \frac{1}{(2\pi\sigma^2)^{n/2}} \exp\left\{-\frac{1}{2}\frac{(\mathbf{y}-\mathbf{X}\boldsymbol{\beta})'(\mathbf{y}-\mathbf{X}\boldsymbol{\beta})}{\sigma^2}\right\} \tag{7.12}$$

The number of unknown parameters is $K+1$: the K elements of $\boldsymbol{\beta}$ and σ^2. The parameter space Ω is thus $(K+1)$-dimensional and it is defined by the inequalities $-\infty < \beta_h < \infty$ $(h = 1, \ldots, K)$ and $0 < \sigma^2 < \infty$. If H_0 specifies $\boldsymbol{\beta} = \boldsymbol{\beta}_0$, the subspace ω corresponding to this null hypothesis is one-dimensional; it is determined by the vector equation $\boldsymbol{\beta} = \boldsymbol{\beta}_0$ and the inequality $0 < \sigma^2 < \infty$. When we are in ω, the logarithm of the likelihood function is

$$\log L(\mathbf{y}; \mathbf{X}\boldsymbol{\beta}_0, \sigma^2\mathbf{I}) = -\frac{n}{2}\log 2\pi - \frac{n}{2}\log\sigma^2 - \frac{1}{2}\frac{(\mathbf{y}-\mathbf{X}\boldsymbol{\beta}_0)'(\mathbf{y}-\mathbf{X}\boldsymbol{\beta}_0)}{\sigma^2}$$

which we maximize for variations in σ^2 by differentiation:

$$\frac{\partial(\log L)}{\partial\sigma^2} = -\frac{n}{2\sigma^2} + \frac{(\mathbf{y}-\mathbf{X}\boldsymbol{\beta}_0)'(\mathbf{y}-\mathbf{X}\boldsymbol{\beta}_0)}{2\sigma^4}$$

We equate this to zero and obtain $(1/n)(\mathbf{y}-\mathbf{X}\boldsymbol{\beta}_0)'(\mathbf{y}-\mathbf{X}\boldsymbol{\beta}_0)$ as the solution for σ^2. This is substituted into (7.12), where $\boldsymbol{\beta}$ is replaced by $\boldsymbol{\beta}_0$, which leads to the maximum value $L(\hat{\omega})$ of the likelihood function under the constraint H_0:

$$L(\hat{\omega}) = \frac{n^{n/2}e^{-n/2}}{(2\pi)^{n/2}[(\mathbf{y}-\mathbf{X}\boldsymbol{\beta}_0)'(\mathbf{y}-\mathbf{X}\boldsymbol{\beta}_0)]^{n/2}} \tag{7.13}$$

The unconstrained maximum $L(\hat{\Omega})$ of the likelihood function is obtained by differentiating the logarithm of the right-hand side of (7.2) with respect to both $\boldsymbol{\beta}$ and σ^2. We did this in the beginning of Section 3.5 and found that this leads to the LS estimator $\mathbf{b}$ of $\boldsymbol{\beta}$ and the estimator $\mathbf{e}'\mathbf{e}/n$ of σ^2, where $\mathbf{e} = \mathbf{y} - \mathbf{X}\mathbf{b}$. On substituting this into (7.12) we obtain

$$L(\hat{\Omega}) = \frac{n^{n/2}e^{-n/2}}{(2\pi)^{n/2}[(\mathbf{y}-\mathbf{X}\mathbf{b})'(\mathbf{y}-\mathbf{X}\mathbf{b})]^{n/2}} \tag{7.14}$$

so that the likelihood ratio $\lambda = L(\hat{\omega})/L(\hat{\Omega})$ becomes

$$\lambda = \left[\frac{(\mathbf{y}-\mathbf{X}\mathbf{b})'(\mathbf{y}-\mathbf{X}\mathbf{b})}{(\mathbf{y}-\mathbf{X}\boldsymbol{\beta}_0)'(\mathbf{y}-\mathbf{X}\boldsymbol{\beta}_0)}\right]^{n/2} \tag{7.15}$$

If we raise both sides of (7.15) to the power $-2/n$, the left-hand side becomes $\lambda^{-2/n}$ and the right-hand side becomes the ratio of the squared length of

$\mathbf{y} - \mathbf{X}\boldsymbol{\beta}_0$ to that of the LS residual vector $\mathbf{y} - \mathbf{Xb}$. This ratio is a simple function of the ratio (7.5) for which we showed that its distribution is $F(K, n-K)$ under H_0, and it is readily verified that small values of the likelihood ratio correspond to large values of the F ratio and vice versa, so that the two tests are equivalent.

Testing General Linear Constraints on the Coefficient Vector[B]

We conclude this section by applying the likelihood ratio principle to a set of general linear constraints on the parameter vector $\boldsymbol{\beta}$. (This includes all previous $\boldsymbol{\beta}$ tests as special cases.) So our last H_0 specifies that $\boldsymbol{\beta}$ satisfies

$$\mathbf{r} = \mathbf{R}\boldsymbol{\beta} \tag{7.16}$$

where $\mathbf{r}$ and $\mathbf{R}$ are given matrices of order $q \times 1$ and $q \times K$, respectively, the rank of $\mathbf{R}$ being q. [A smaller rank implies inconsistency or linear dependence of the constraints that are part of (7.16).] To find $L(\hat{\omega})$ for the present H_0 we have to maximize the likelihood function (7.12) subject to (7.16). It is easily seen that for any given value of σ^2, this function is maximized by the LS procedure. Hence the present $\boldsymbol{\beta}$ solution is found by LS subject to the linear constraint (7.16). This solution is given in eq. (8.9) of Section 1.8:

$$\mathbf{b}^* = \mathbf{b} + (\mathbf{X}'\mathbf{X})^{-1}\mathbf{R}'[\mathbf{R}(\mathbf{X}'\mathbf{X})^{-1}\mathbf{R}']^{-1}(\mathbf{r} - \mathbf{Rb}) \tag{7.17}$$

By substituting $\mathbf{b}^*$ in the logarithmic likelihood function, differentiating with respect to σ^2, and equating the result to zero, we find that the present σ^2 solution is equal to a fraction $1/n$ of the squared length of the residual vector associated with $\mathbf{b}^*$:

$$\frac{1}{n}(\mathbf{y} - \mathbf{Xb}^*)'(\mathbf{y} - \mathbf{Xb}^*) = \frac{n-K}{n}s^2 + \frac{1}{n}(\mathbf{r} - \mathbf{Rb})'[\mathbf{R}(\mathbf{X}'\mathbf{X})^{-1}\mathbf{R}']^{-1}(\mathbf{r} - \mathbf{Rb}) \tag{7.18}$$

the equality sign of which is based on eq. (8.10) of Section 1.8. By substituting $\mathbf{b}^*$ for $\boldsymbol{\beta}$ and the left-hand side of (7.18) for σ^2 in the likelihood function we obtain the following constrained maximum:

$$L(\hat{\omega}) = \frac{n^{n/2}e^{-n/2}}{(2\pi)^{n/2}[(\mathbf{y} - \mathbf{Xb}^*)'(\mathbf{y} - \mathbf{Xb}^*)]^{n/2}} \tag{7.19}$$

The likelihood ratio is thus

$$\lambda = \left[\frac{(\mathbf{y} - \mathbf{Xb})'(\mathbf{y} - \mathbf{Xb})}{(\mathbf{y} - \mathbf{Xb}^*)'(\mathbf{y} - \mathbf{Xb}^*)}\right]^{n/2} \tag{7.20}$$

which in view of (7.18) satisfies

$$\lambda^{-2/n} = 1 + \frac{(\mathbf{r} - \mathbf{Rb})'[\mathbf{R}(\mathbf{X}'\mathbf{X})^{-1}\mathbf{R}']^{-1}(\mathbf{r} - \mathbf{Rb})}{(n - K)s^2} \tag{7.21}$$

If $\mathbf{r} = \mathbf{R}\boldsymbol{\beta}$, then $\mathbf{r} - \mathbf{Rb} = -\mathbf{R}(\mathbf{X}'\mathbf{X})^{-1}\mathbf{X}'\boldsymbol{\epsilon}$, so that the quadratic form in the numerator on the right is $\boldsymbol{\epsilon}'\mathbf{X}(\mathbf{X}'\mathbf{X})^{-1}\mathbf{R}'[\mathbf{R}(\mathbf{X}'\mathbf{X})^{-1}\mathbf{R}']^{-1}\mathbf{R}(\mathbf{X}'\mathbf{X})^{-1}\mathbf{X}'\boldsymbol{\epsilon}$. It is easily verified that the matrix of this form is idempotent. Its rank and trace are equal to q:

$$\begin{aligned} \text{tr } &\mathbf{X}(\mathbf{X}'\mathbf{X})^{-1}\mathbf{R}'[\mathbf{R}(\mathbf{X}'\mathbf{X})^{-1}\mathbf{R}']^{-1}\mathbf{R}(\mathbf{X}'\mathbf{X})^{-1}\mathbf{X}' \\ &= \text{tr } [\mathbf{R}(\mathbf{X}'\mathbf{X})^{-1}\mathbf{R}']^{-1}\mathbf{R}(\mathbf{X}'\mathbf{X})^{-1}\mathbf{X}'\mathbf{X}(\mathbf{X}'\mathbf{X})^{-1}\mathbf{R}' = q \end{aligned} \tag{7.22}$$

the trace of the matrix on the second line being equal to the trace of the $q \times q$ unit matrix. It follows that the quadratic form in the right-hand numerator of (7.21) is distributed as $\sigma^2\chi^2(q)$ if H_0 is true. The denominator is distributed as $\sigma^2\chi^2(n - K)$ and it is independent of the numerator in view of

$$\mathbf{X}(\mathbf{X}'\mathbf{X})^{-1}\mathbf{R}'[\mathbf{R}(\mathbf{X}'\mathbf{X})^{-1}\mathbf{R}']^{-1}\mathbf{R}(\mathbf{X}'\mathbf{X})^{-1}\mathbf{X}'\mathbf{M} = \mathbf{0}$$

Therefore, if H_0 is true, the test statistic with the following two alternative expressions:

$$\frac{1}{qs^2}(\mathbf{r} - \mathbf{Rb})'[\mathbf{R}(\mathbf{X}'\mathbf{X})^{-1}\mathbf{R}']^{-1}(\mathbf{r} - \mathbf{Rb}) = \frac{1}{qs^2}(\mathbf{b} - \mathbf{b}^*)'\mathbf{X}'\mathbf{X}(\mathbf{b} - \mathbf{b}^*) \tag{7.23}$$

is distributed as $F(q, n - K)$. [The equivalence of the two expressions follows directly from (7.17).] Since this result involves the constrained LS estimator $\mathbf{b}^*$, which we have not yet met in any of the theorems of this chapter, we shall formulate it as a separate theorem.

THEOREM 3.9 (Testing linear constraints) *Suppose that Assumption* 3.3 *is true for given* $\mathbf{X}$ *with the additional specification that the distribution of* $\mathbf{y}$ *(given* $\mathbf{X}$*) is n-variate normal; also suppose* $n > K$. *Let the null hypothesis* H_0 *imply that the elements of* $\boldsymbol{\beta}$ *satisfy the constraint* (7.16), *where* $\mathbf{r}$ *and* $\mathbf{R}$ *are given matrices of order* $q \times 1$ *and* $q \times K$, *respectively, the rank of* $\mathbf{R}$ *being* q. *Then the test statistic* (7.23) *is distributed as* $F(q, n - K)$ *if* H_0 *is true, where* $\mathbf{b}^*$ *is the constrained LS estimator given in* (7.17), *while* $\mathbf{b}$ *and* s^2 *are the unconstrained LS estimators of* $\boldsymbol{\beta}$ *and* σ^2, *respectively.*

It is shown in Problem 7.8 that this theorem can be used to test the equality of two regressions.

The Income and Price Elasticities Reconsidered[B]

Theorem 3.9 can also be used to test the hypothesis $\beta_1 = -\beta_2 = 1$ for the income elasticity (β_1) and the price elasticity (β_2) of the demand for textile.

The constraint $\mathbf{r} = \mathbf{R}\boldsymbol{\beta}$ is then

$$\begin{bmatrix} 1 \\ -1 \end{bmatrix} = \begin{bmatrix} 0 & 1 & 0 \\ 0 & 0 & 1 \end{bmatrix} \begin{bmatrix} \beta_0 \\ \beta_1 \\ \beta_2 \end{bmatrix} \tag{7.24}$$

which implies that the constrained LS estimator (7.17) can be written as

$$\begin{aligned} \mathbf{b}^* - \mathbf{b} &= (\mathbf{X}'\mathbf{X})^{-1}\mathbf{R}'[\mathbf{R}(\mathbf{X}'\mathbf{X})^{-1}\mathbf{R}']^{-1} \begin{bmatrix} 1 - b_1 \\ -1 - b_2 \end{bmatrix} \\ &= (\mathbf{X}'\mathbf{X})^{-1}\mathbf{R}'\mathbf{C}^{-1} \begin{bmatrix} 1 - b_1 \\ -1 - b_2 \end{bmatrix} \end{aligned} \tag{7.25}$$

where $\mathbf{C} = \mathbf{R}(\mathbf{X}'\mathbf{X})^{-1}\mathbf{R}'$ is the lower right-hand 2×2 submatrix of $(\mathbf{X}'\mathbf{X})^{-1}$ which was introduced earlier in (6.6) and (6.7). On combining (7.23) and (7.25) we obtain for our test statistic:

$$\begin{aligned} &\frac{1}{qs^2}(\mathbf{b} - \mathbf{b}^*)'\mathbf{X}'\mathbf{X}(\mathbf{b} - \mathbf{b}^*) \\ &\quad = \frac{1}{2s^2}[1 - b_1 \quad -1 - b_2]\mathbf{C}^{-1}\mathbf{R}(\mathbf{X}'\mathbf{X})^{-1}\mathbf{R}'\mathbf{C}^{-1}\begin{bmatrix} 1 - b_1 \\ -1 - b_2 \end{bmatrix} \\ &\quad = \frac{1}{2s^2}[1 - b_1 \quad -1 - b_2]\mathbf{C}^{-1}\begin{bmatrix} 1 - b_1 \\ -1 - b_2 \end{bmatrix} \end{aligned}$$

which is a quadratic form with matrix $(1/2s^2)\mathbf{C}^{-1}$. But the four elements of this symmetric matrix are nothing but the a's of (6.9), so that the test statistic takes the following value:

$$\begin{aligned} &a_{11}(1 - b_1)^2 + a_{22}(-1 - b_2)^2 + 2a_{12}(1 - b_1)(-1 - b_2) \\ &\quad = 21.6(.1430)^2 + 403.5(-.1711)^2 + 2(20.8)(.1430)(-.1711) = 11.2 \end{aligned} \tag{7.26}$$

This result is in agreement with that obtained below (7.11), the value 11.2 being larger than the 1 percent significance point 6.51 of $F(2, 14)$. The derivation (7.26) has the virtue that it clearly shows that the specification $\beta_2 = -1$ for the price elasticity is mainly responsible for the rejection of the null hypothesis.

Problems

7.1 Test the hypothesis $\sigma = .01$ for the textile example against the alternative hypothesis $\sigma \neq .01$. Consider the 10, 5, and 2 percent significance levels. Also, test the same null hypothesis against the alternative hypothesis $\sigma > .01$ at the 5 percent level.

7.2 Test the hypothesis that the income elasticity of the demand for textile is twice the price elasticity apart from sign. Choose your own alternative hypothesis and your own significance level.

7.3 Use eq. (2.15) of Section 1.2 to prove that $(\mathbf{X}'\mathbf{X})^{-1}$ can be written as

$$(7.27) \quad \begin{bmatrix} \mathbf{X}_1'\mathbf{X}_1 & \mathbf{X}_1'\mathbf{X}_2 \\ \mathbf{X}_2'\mathbf{X}_1 & \mathbf{X}_2'\mathbf{X}_2 \end{bmatrix}^{-1}$$

$$= \begin{bmatrix} (\mathbf{X}_1'\mathbf{M}_2\mathbf{X}_1)^{-1} & -(\mathbf{X}_1'\mathbf{M}_2\mathbf{X}_1)^{-1}\mathbf{X}_1'\mathbf{X}_2(\mathbf{X}_2'\mathbf{X}_2)^{-1} \\ -(\mathbf{X}_2'\mathbf{X}_2)^{-1}\mathbf{X}_2'\mathbf{X}_1(\mathbf{X}_1'\mathbf{M}_2\mathbf{X}_1)^{-1} & (\mathbf{X}_2'\mathbf{X}_2)^{-1} + (\mathbf{X}_2'\mathbf{X}_2)^{-1}\mathbf{A}(\mathbf{X}_2'\mathbf{X}_2)^{-1} \end{bmatrix}$$

where $\mathbf{A} = \mathbf{X}_2'\mathbf{X}_1(\mathbf{X}_1'\mathbf{M}_2\mathbf{X}_1)^{-1}\mathbf{X}_1'\mathbf{X}_2$, $\mathbf{X}_1$ and $\mathbf{X}_2$ being defined in (7.6) and $\mathbf{M}_2$ in (7.9). Postmultiply the inverse (7.27) by the vector $\mathbf{X}'\mathbf{y}$, to be partitioned appropriately, to find

$$(7.28) \quad \mathbf{b}_1 = (\mathbf{X}_1'\mathbf{M}_2\mathbf{X}_1)^{-1}\mathbf{X}_1'\mathbf{M}_2\mathbf{y} \qquad \mathbf{b}_2 = (\mathbf{X}_2'\mathbf{X}_2)^{-1}\mathbf{X}_2'(\mathbf{y} - \mathbf{X}_1\mathbf{b}_1)$$

where $\mathbf{b}_1$ and $\mathbf{b}_2$ are subvectors of the LS coefficient vector $\mathbf{b}$ consisting of the first q and the last $K - q$ elements, respectively.

7.4 (*Continuation*) Prove under the null hypothesis $\boldsymbol{\beta}_1 = \boldsymbol{\beta}_{10}$:

$$(7.29) \qquad \mathbf{b} - \mathbf{z} = \begin{bmatrix} \mathbf{I} \\ -(\mathbf{X}_2'\mathbf{X}_2)^{-1}\mathbf{X}_2'\mathbf{X}_1 \end{bmatrix}(\mathbf{X}_1'\mathbf{M}_2\mathbf{X}_1)^{-1}\mathbf{X}_1'\mathbf{M}_2\boldsymbol{\epsilon}$$

where $\mathbf{z}$ is defined in (7.8) and $\mathbf{b}$ consists of the subvectors $\mathbf{b}_1$ and $\mathbf{b}_2$ given in (7.28). (*Hint.* Prove $\mathbf{M}_2\mathbf{X}_2 = \mathbf{0}$.) Then use (7.29) to prove (7.10).

7.5 (*Continuation*) Use (7.27) to prove:

$$(7.30) \qquad (\mathbf{X}'\mathbf{X})^{-1}\mathbf{X}' = \begin{bmatrix} (\mathbf{X}_1'\mathbf{M}_2\mathbf{X}_1)^{-1}\mathbf{X}_1'\mathbf{M}_2 \\ (\mathbf{X}_2'\mathbf{X}_2)^{-1}\mathbf{X}_2'[\mathbf{I} - \mathbf{X}_1(\mathbf{X}_1'\mathbf{M}_2\mathbf{X}_1)^{-1}\mathbf{X}_1'\mathbf{M}_2] \end{bmatrix}$$

Next, prove

$$(7.31) \quad \mathbf{X}(\mathbf{X}'\mathbf{X})^{-1}\mathbf{X}' = \mathbf{X}_2(\mathbf{X}_2'\mathbf{X}_2)^{-1}\mathbf{X}_2' + \mathbf{M}_2\mathbf{X}_1(\mathbf{X}_1'\mathbf{M}_2\mathbf{X}_1)^{-1}\mathbf{X}_1'\mathbf{M}_2$$

or, equivalently, $\mathbf{M} = \mathbf{M}_2 - \mathbf{N}$. Use this to prove $\mathbf{MN} = \mathbf{0}$.

7.6 In the lines below eq. (7.11) an interpretation is given of the left-hand side of that equation on the basis of the description of the data given in Section 3.2. Verify this interpretation.

7.7 Consider the null hypothesis $\beta_h = \beta_{h0}$ for some value of h ($h = 1, \ldots, K$). Use the derivation of Theorem 3.9 to show how the likelihood ratio principle leads to an F test with $q = 1$, and use Problem 6.2 at the end of Section 2.6 to prove that it is equivalent to the t test described in the third paragraph of this section. Compare it with the procedure described in the last paragraph of Section 2.9.

7.8 (*Testing the equality of two regressions*) Consider an equation for which both prewar and postwar data are available. Write $\mathbf{y}_1 = \mathbf{X}_1\boldsymbol{\beta}_1 + \boldsymbol{\epsilon}_1$ for the n_1 prewar observations and $\mathbf{y}_2 = \mathbf{X}_2\boldsymbol{\beta}_2 + \boldsymbol{\epsilon}_2$ for the n_2 postwar observations, where $\mathbf{X}_1$ and $\mathbf{X}_2$ are observation matrices of the same K explanatory variables, both with rank K. To test the null hypothesis $\boldsymbol{\beta}_1 = \boldsymbol{\beta}_2$ we combine these equations:

(7.32)

$$\begin{bmatrix} \mathbf{y}_1 \\ \mathbf{y}_2 \end{bmatrix} = \begin{bmatrix} \mathbf{X}_1 & \mathbf{0} \\ \mathbf{0} & \mathbf{X}_2 \end{bmatrix} \begin{bmatrix} \boldsymbol{\beta}_1 \\ \boldsymbol{\beta}_2 \end{bmatrix} + \begin{bmatrix} \boldsymbol{\epsilon}_1 \\ \boldsymbol{\epsilon}_2 \end{bmatrix} \qquad \mathscr{E}\begin{bmatrix} \boldsymbol{\epsilon}_1 \\ \boldsymbol{\epsilon}_2 \end{bmatrix} = \mathbf{0} \qquad \mathscr{V}\begin{bmatrix} \boldsymbol{\epsilon}_1 \\ \boldsymbol{\epsilon}_2 \end{bmatrix} = \sigma^2\mathbf{I}$$

Prove that the null hypothesis amounts to $\mathbf{R}\boldsymbol{\beta} = \mathbf{0}$, where $\mathbf{R} = [\mathbf{I} \quad -\mathbf{I}]$ and $\boldsymbol{\beta}' = [\boldsymbol{\beta}_1' \quad \boldsymbol{\beta}_2']$. Also prove that if $\boldsymbol{\epsilon}_1, \boldsymbol{\epsilon}_2$ is $(n_1 + n_2)$-variate normal and if the null hypothesis is true, the quadratic form

$$(7.33) \qquad (\mathbf{b}_1 - \mathbf{b}_0)'\mathbf{X}_1'\mathbf{X}_1(\mathbf{b}_1 - \mathbf{b}_0) + (\mathbf{b}_2 - \mathbf{b}_0)'\mathbf{X}_2'\mathbf{X}_2(\mathbf{b}_2 - \mathbf{b}_0)$$

is distributed as $\sigma^2\chi^2(K)$, where

$$(7.34) \quad \mathbf{b}_0 = (\mathbf{X}_1'\mathbf{X}_1 + \mathbf{X}_2'\mathbf{X}_2)^{-1}(\mathbf{X}_1'\mathbf{y}_1 + \mathbf{X}_2'\mathbf{y}_2) \qquad \mathbf{b}_i = (\mathbf{X}_i'\mathbf{X}_i)^{-1}\mathbf{X}_i'\mathbf{y}_i \qquad (i = 1, 2)$$

[*Hint*. This is the quadratic form $(\mathbf{b} - \mathbf{b}^*)'\mathbf{X}'\mathbf{X}(\mathbf{b} - \mathbf{b}^*)$ of (7.23).] Also prove that

$$(7.35) \qquad (\mathbf{y}_1 - \mathbf{X}_1\mathbf{b}_1)'(\mathbf{y}_1 - \mathbf{X}_1\mathbf{b}_1) + (\mathbf{y}_2 - \mathbf{X}_2\mathbf{b}_2)'(\mathbf{y}_2 - \mathbf{X}_2\mathbf{b}_2)$$

is distributed as $\sigma^2\chi^2(n_1 + n_2 - 2K)$. [*Hint*. This quadratic form corresponds to $(n - K)s^2$ in (7.23).] Finally, prove that the ratio of (7.33) to (7.35), multiplied by $(n_1 + n_2 - 2K)/K$, is distributed as $F(K, n_1 + n_2 - 2K)$ if the null hypothesis is true.

3.8 The Multicollinearity Problem[AB]

Linear Dependence of Explanatory Variables[A]

We know that the LS estimator **b** does not exist when the matrix **X**, contrary to our assumptions, has a rank less than K. The $K \times K$ matrix $\mathbf{X}'\mathbf{X}$ is then singular, so that the normal equations $\mathbf{X}'\mathbf{X}\mathbf{b} = \mathbf{X}'\mathbf{y}$ have no unique solution. Note that these equations are always consistent because the augmented matrix $[\mathbf{X}'\mathbf{X} \quad \mathbf{X}'\mathbf{y}]$ has the same rank as $\mathbf{X}'\mathbf{X}$. This follows from

$$(8.1) \qquad r(\mathbf{X}'\mathbf{X}) \leq r[\mathbf{X}'\mathbf{X} \quad \mathbf{X}'\mathbf{y}] = r(\mathbf{X}'[\mathbf{X} \quad \mathbf{y}]) \leq r(\mathbf{X}') = r(\mathbf{X}'\mathbf{X})$$

where $r(\ )$ stands for "rank of."

If the rank of $\mathbf{X}$ is less than K, the columns of $\mathbf{X}$ are linearly dependent, so that $\mathbf{Xc} = \mathbf{0}$ holds for some K-element vector $\mathbf{c} \neq \mathbf{0}$. Equivalently,

$$c_1 x_{\alpha 1} + \cdots + c_K x_{\alpha K} = 0 \qquad \alpha = 1, \ldots, n \tag{8.2}$$

for some set of c's not all zero. Therefore, in this case the observation matrix $[\mathbf{y} \quad \mathbf{X}]$ satisfies a second linear relation besides the basic equation $\mathbf{y} = \mathbf{X}\boldsymbol{\beta} + \boldsymbol{\epsilon}$ in which we are interested. This explains the term "multicollinearity" which is commonly used for this situation. A simple example is the case in which total consumption is described linearly in terms of total income, total wage income, and total nonwage income. Since the last two variables add up to total income, we have a case of linear dependence among the explanatory variables. Note that the basic equation $\mathbf{y} = \mathbf{X}\boldsymbol{\beta} + \boldsymbol{\epsilon}$ contains both the dependent variable and the explanatory variables, whereas the second relation (8.2) is confined to the latter variables.

Parameters Which Are Not Estimable[A]

Assume that (8.2) is true and that $c_1 \neq 0$, so that we may specify $c_1 = -1$ without loss of generality. Then (8.2) can be written as

$$\mathbf{x}_1 = c_2 \mathbf{x}_2 + \cdots + c_K \mathbf{x}_K \tag{8.3}$$

where $\mathbf{x}_1, \ldots, \mathbf{x}_K$ are the successive columns of $\mathbf{X}$. The expectation of $\mathbf{y}$ given $\mathbf{X}$ in this notation is

$$\mathbf{X}\boldsymbol{\beta} = \beta_1 \mathbf{x}_1 + \beta_2 \mathbf{x}_2 + \cdots + \beta_K \mathbf{x}_K \tag{8.4}$$

It follows from (8.3) that $\beta_1 \mathbf{x}_1 = (1 - \theta)\beta_1 \mathbf{x}_1 + \theta\beta_1(c_2 \mathbf{x}_2 + \cdots + c_K \mathbf{x}_K)$ holds for any real θ. Therefore the expectation (8.4) can be written equivalently as

$$\begin{aligned} \mathbf{X}\boldsymbol{\beta} &= (1 - \theta)\beta_1 \mathbf{x}_1 + (\beta_2 + \theta c_2 \beta_1)\mathbf{x}_2 + \cdots + (\beta_K + \theta c_K \beta_1)\mathbf{x}_K \\ &= \beta_1^* \mathbf{x}_1 + \beta_2^* \mathbf{x}_2 + \cdots + \beta_K^* \mathbf{x}_K \end{aligned} \tag{8.5}$$

where $\beta_1^* = (1 - \theta)\beta_1$ and $\beta_h^* = \beta_h + \theta c_h \beta_1$ for $h > 1$. The expression on the second line of (8.5) is of the form $\mathbf{X}\boldsymbol{\beta}^*$, where $\boldsymbol{\beta}^* = [\beta_1^* \cdots \beta_K^*]'$. It will be clear that, in general, $\boldsymbol{\beta} \neq \boldsymbol{\beta}^*$ for whatever $\theta \neq 0$ but, nevertheless, $\mathbf{X}\boldsymbol{\beta} = \mathbf{X}\boldsymbol{\beta}^*$ for any value of θ. In other words, if we say that $\mathbf{y}$ has an n-variate distribution with mean vector $\mathbf{X}\boldsymbol{\beta}$, we can equally well say that it has an n-variate distribution with mean vector $\mathbf{X}\boldsymbol{\beta}^*$. This clearly shows that no sample drawn from the $\mathbf{y}$ distribution will enable the analyst to discriminate between $\boldsymbol{\beta}$ and $\boldsymbol{\beta}^*$, and, therefore, the parameter vector is not estimable. This situation is frequently described by saying that the specifications $\mathscr{E}\mathbf{y} = \mathbf{X}\boldsymbol{\beta}$ and $\mathscr{E}\mathbf{y} = \mathbf{X}\boldsymbol{\beta}^*$ are *observationally equivalent*.

Linear Combinations of Parameters Which Are Estimable; Conditional Estimation[A]

The negative result obtained in the previous paragraph needs an amendment, because some of the β's or certain linear combinations of the β's may be estimable. Intuitively this can be seen as follows. Suppose that $\mathbf{X}$ has rank K and that we add a $(K+1)$st variable whose observations are identical with those of the Kth. Then the right-hand side of (8.4) may be written as

$$\beta_1 \mathbf{x}_1 + \beta_2 \mathbf{x}_2 + \cdots + (\beta_K + \beta_{K+1})\mathbf{x}_K \tag{8.6}$$

which shows that the vector $[\beta_1 \quad \beta_2 \quad \cdots \quad \beta_K + \beta_{K+1}]'$ has an LS estimator (since the matrix $[\mathbf{x}_1 \quad \mathbf{x}_2 \quad \cdots \quad \mathbf{x}_K]$ has full column rank by assumption). Although it is impossible to discriminate between β_K and β_{K+1}, we can thus estimate their sum and also $\beta_1, \ldots, \beta_{K-1}$. In fact, it will be shown in the next subsection that if a particular linear combination of the $\boldsymbol{\beta}$ elements is estimable, the LS procedure provides a best linear unbiased estimator.

The second amendment is that if $\mathbf{X}$ does not have full column rank, one may estimate in the following conditional manner. Consider the linear dependence (8.3) and suppose that we proceed under the condition that β_1 takes a given value β_{10}. Then subtract $\beta_{10}\mathbf{x}_1$ from both sides of $\mathbf{y} = \mathbf{X}\boldsymbol{\beta} + \boldsymbol{\epsilon}$:

$$\mathbf{y} - \beta_{10}\mathbf{x}_1 = \beta_2 \mathbf{x}_2 + \cdots + \beta_K \mathbf{x}_K + \boldsymbol{\epsilon} \tag{8.7}$$

We interpret the left-hand side as the vector of values taken by a new dependent variable and note that $[\mathbf{x}_2 \quad \cdots \quad \mathbf{x}_K]$ has full column rank if (8.3) is the only linear dependence. It is then possible to estimate $\beta_2, \ldots, \beta_K$ by LS, given the chosen value β_{10}. One may also vary β_{10} and formulate point estimators of $\beta_2, \ldots, \beta_K$ as functions of β_{10} as well as an estimator of the covariance matrix of these point estimators as a function of β_{10}; see Problem 8.1. In this limited (conditional) sense it is thus still possible to estimate a subset of the unknown parameters.

Best Linear Unbiased Estimators of Estimable Linear Combinations of Parameters[B]

Suppose that $\mathbf{X}$ does not (at least not necessarily) have full column rank and that we want to estimate $\mathbf{w}'\boldsymbol{\beta}$, where $\mathbf{w}$ is a given K-element vector. If the estimator is to be linear, it can be written as $\mathbf{k}'\mathbf{y}$, where $\mathbf{k}$ is a column vector consisting of n constant elements. The expectation of the estimator is $\mathbf{k}'\mathbf{X}\boldsymbol{\beta}$; hence, if it is to be an unbiased estimator of $\mathbf{w}'\boldsymbol{\beta}$, $\mathbf{k}$ should satisfy

$$\mathbf{X}'\mathbf{k} = \mathbf{w} \tag{8.8}$$

This means that the weight vector $\mathbf{w}'$ of $\mathbf{w}'\boldsymbol{\beta}$ must be a linear combination of the rows of $\mathbf{X}$. Note that this is always the case when $\mathbf{X}$ has full column rank because $\mathbf{k}$ can then be specified as $\mathbf{X}(\mathbf{X}'\mathbf{X})^{-1}\mathbf{w}$. However, condition (8.8) does imply a constraint on the linear combinations of the $\boldsymbol{\beta}$ elements that can be estimated unbiasedly when the explanatory variables are linearly dependent. To understand this, return to the case $\mathbf{X} = [\mathbf{x}_1 \quad \cdots \quad \mathbf{x}_K \quad \mathbf{x}_K]$ of (8.6). The transpose of $\mathbf{X}'\mathbf{k}$ is then

$$[\mathbf{k}'\mathbf{x}_1 \quad \cdots \quad \mathbf{k}'\mathbf{x}_K \quad \mathbf{k}'\mathbf{x}_K] \tag{8.9}$$

Condition (8.8) thus states that $\mathbf{w}'$ should be of the form (8.9) in order that the corresponding parameter combination can have an unbiased estimator. This combination is then

$$(\mathbf{k}'\mathbf{x}_1)\beta_1 + \cdots + (\mathbf{k}'\mathbf{x}_{K-1})\beta_{K-1} + (\mathbf{k}'\mathbf{x}_K)(\beta_K + \beta_{K+1}) \tag{8.10}$$

This becomes simply β_1 when we choose $\mathbf{k}$ so that

$$\begin{bmatrix} \mathbf{x}_1' \\ \cdot \\ \cdot \\ \cdot \\ \mathbf{x}_{K-1}' \\ \mathbf{x}_K' \end{bmatrix} \mathbf{k} = \mathbf{i}_1 \tag{8.11}$$

where $\mathbf{i}_1$ is the first column of the $K \times K$ unit matrix. It is always possible to find such a $\mathbf{k}$ because the coefficient matrix and the augmented matrix of the linear system (8.11) both have rank K if $[\mathbf{x}_1 \quad \cdots \quad \mathbf{x}_K]$ has full column rank. Thus β_1 can be estimated unbiasedly, and the same holds for $\beta_2, \ldots,$ β_{K-1} and $\beta_K + \beta_{K+1}$ [which is proved by putting $\mathbf{i}_2, \ldots, \mathbf{i}_{K-1}, \mathbf{i}_K$ in the right-hand side of (8.11)], and it is also possible to estimate any linear combination of $\beta_1, \ldots, \beta_{K-1}, \beta_K + \beta_{K+1}$ unbiasedly, but it is impossible to separate β_K and β_{K+1}.

If the weight vector $\mathbf{w}'$ of $\mathbf{w}'\boldsymbol{\beta}$ is indeed a linear combination of the rows of $\mathbf{X}$, a vector $\mathbf{k}$ satisfying (8.8) obviously exists, and the same is true for an unbiased estimator $\mathbf{k}'\mathbf{y}$ of $\mathbf{w}'\boldsymbol{\beta}$. This is stated more formally in the first part of the following theorem, which is due to C. R. Rao (1945).

Theorem 3.10 (Linearly dependent explanatory variables) *Suppose that Assumption 3.3 is true for given* $\mathbf{X}$ *except that* $\mathbf{X}$ *does not necessarily have full column rank. Then any linear combination* $\mathbf{w}'\boldsymbol{\beta}$ *of the elements of the parameter vector* $\boldsymbol{\beta}$ *can be estimated unbiasedly if the weight vector* $\mathbf{w}$ *satisfies* (8.8) *for some K-element vector* $\mathbf{k}$. *If this is true, the minimum-variance linear unbiased estimator of* $\mathbf{w}'\boldsymbol{\beta}$ *is* $\mathbf{w}'\mathbf{z}$, *where* $\mathbf{z}$ *is any solution of the normal equations* $\mathbf{X}'\mathbf{X}\mathbf{z} = \mathbf{X}'\mathbf{y}$, *and the estimator* $\mathbf{w}'\mathbf{z}$ *exists and is unique.*

To prove the second part of the theorem we note that the variance of the estimator $\mathbf{k}'\mathbf{y}$ is $\sigma^2\mathbf{k}'\mathbf{k}$. This variance is to be minimized for variations in $\mathbf{k}$ subject to the unbiasedness constraint (8.8). So we construct the Lagrangian function $\frac{1}{2}\mathbf{k}'\mathbf{k} - \boldsymbol{\lambda}'(\mathbf{X}'\mathbf{k} - \mathbf{w})$, where $\boldsymbol{\lambda}$ is a K-element vector of Lagrangian multipliers.[19] This is differentiated with respect to $\mathbf{k}$ and the vector of derivatives is put equal to zero:

$$\mathbf{k} = \mathbf{X}\boldsymbol{\lambda} \tag{8.12}$$

If we premultiply both sides by $\mathbf{X}'$ and use (8.8), we obtain

$$\mathbf{X}'\mathbf{X}\boldsymbol{\lambda} = \mathbf{w} \tag{8.13}$$

which is a system of K linear equations in the K elements of $\boldsymbol{\lambda}$. The equations are consistent because the rank of the augmented matrix $[\mathbf{X}'\mathbf{X} \quad \mathbf{w}]$ is equal to the rank of $\mathbf{X}'\mathbf{X}$:

$$r(\mathbf{X}'\mathbf{X}) \leq r[\mathbf{X}'\mathbf{X} \quad \mathbf{w}] = r[\mathbf{X}'\mathbf{X} \quad \mathbf{X}'\mathbf{k}] = r(\mathbf{X}'[\mathbf{X} \quad \mathbf{k}]) \leq r(\mathbf{X}') = r(\mathbf{X}'\mathbf{X})$$

the first equal sign of which is based on (8.8).

It follows from (8.12) and (8.13) that the minimum-variance linear unbiased estimator is of the form $\mathbf{k}'\mathbf{y} = \boldsymbol{\lambda}'\mathbf{X}'\mathbf{y}$, where $\boldsymbol{\lambda}$ is a solution of $\mathbf{X}'\mathbf{X}\boldsymbol{\lambda} = \mathbf{w}$. Consider then a solution $\mathbf{z}$ of the normal equations: $\mathbf{X}'\mathbf{X}\mathbf{z} = \mathbf{X}'\mathbf{y}$. Combining these equations with $\mathbf{k}'\mathbf{y} = \boldsymbol{\lambda}'\mathbf{X}'\mathbf{y}$, we obtain $\mathbf{k}'\mathbf{y} = \boldsymbol{\lambda}'\mathbf{X}'\mathbf{X}\mathbf{z} = \mathbf{w}'\mathbf{z}$, where the last step is based on (8.13). Hence $\mathbf{w}'\mathbf{z}$ is indeed a minimum-variance linear unbiased estimator of $\mathbf{w}'\boldsymbol{\beta}$. We know that $\mathbf{w}'\mathbf{z}$ exists because we proved in the first paragraph of this section that the normal equations are consistent. To prove the uniqueness of the estimator we consider any two solutions, $\mathbf{z}_1$ and $\mathbf{z}_2$, of the normal equations: $\mathbf{X}'\mathbf{X}\mathbf{z}_1 = \mathbf{X}'\mathbf{X}\mathbf{z}_2 = \mathbf{X}'\mathbf{y}$. This implies $\mathbf{X}'\mathbf{X}(\mathbf{z}_1 - \mathbf{z}_2) = \mathbf{0}$, and hence, after premultiplication of both sides by the transpose of $\mathbf{z}_1 - \mathbf{z}_2$,

$$(\mathbf{z}_1 - \mathbf{z}_2)'\mathbf{X}'\mathbf{X}(\mathbf{z}_1 - \mathbf{z}_2) = 0 \tag{8.14}$$

The left-hand side of (8.14) is the squared length of the vector $\mathbf{X}(\mathbf{z}_1 - \mathbf{z}_2)$, so that $\mathbf{X}\mathbf{z}_1 = \mathbf{X}\mathbf{z}_2$. We then use (8.13):

$$\mathbf{w}'\mathbf{z}_1 = \boldsymbol{\lambda}'\mathbf{X}'\mathbf{X}\mathbf{z}_1 = \boldsymbol{\lambda}'\mathbf{X}'\mathbf{X}\mathbf{z}_2 = \mathbf{w}'\mathbf{z}_2$$

which proves the uniqueness of the inner product of $\mathbf{w}$ and any solution of the normal equations.

If $\mathbf{X}$ has full column rank, the unique solution of (8.13) is $\boldsymbol{\lambda} = (\mathbf{X}'\mathbf{X})^{-1}\mathbf{w}$, so that (8.12) gives $\mathbf{k} = \mathbf{X}(\mathbf{X}'\mathbf{X})^{-1}\mathbf{w}$ and the estimator $\mathbf{k}'\mathbf{y}$ becomes $\mathbf{w}'\mathbf{b}$, where $\mathbf{b} = (\mathbf{X}'\mathbf{X})^{-1}\mathbf{X}'\mathbf{y}$ is the ordinary LS estimator. If $\mathbf{X}$ does not have full

[19] We confine ourselves to the first-order conditions; for the second-order conditions, see Problem 8.4.

column rank, $\boldsymbol{\lambda}$ is not unique. However, $\mathbf{k} = \mathbf{X}\boldsymbol{\lambda}$ is unique and so is $\mathbf{k}'\mathbf{y}$; see Problem 8.6.

Extreme versus Near-Extreme Multicollinearity[A]

The case (8.2) is that of "extreme" multicollinearity because it involves the existence of an *exact* linear relation among the explanatory variables. Such cases do occur in practice, but they are not as frequent as the situation of an almost exact linear relation. In time series regressions we may have wage income and nonwage income as explanatory variables, which will often move up and down almost proportionately. This may lead to an almost exact linear relation between these variables. We may have the same situation in a cross-section study when income and assets are explanatory variables, since families with large incomes also have, on the average, a large amount of assets. The possibility of an almost exact fulfillment of a linear relation of the type (8.2) increases when the number of explanatory variables is larger. Suppose, for example, that the age of the family head is a third explanatory variable besides income and assets. On the average, assets increase with income; but they also increase with the age of the family head, who has had more opportunities for saving because he is older. Thus, if $x_{\alpha 1}$ in (8.2) stands for the assets of the αth household, $x_{\alpha 2}$ for its income, and $x_{\alpha 3}$ for the age of the family head, it is highly conceivable that this equation holds fairly accurately when c_1, c_2, c_3 take appropriate values (the sign of c_1 being opposite to that of c_2 and c_3).

To show what is involved when we have an almost exact linear relation between the explanatory variables, we consider the following case of three observations and two explanatory variables (no constant term):

$$(8.15) \qquad \mathbf{X} = \begin{bmatrix} 10 & 10 \\ 0 & 0 \\ -9 & -10 \end{bmatrix} \qquad \text{implying} \qquad \mathbf{X}'\mathbf{X} = \begin{bmatrix} 181 & 190 \\ 190 & 200 \end{bmatrix}$$

Take $\sigma^2 = 1$, so that

$$(8.16) \qquad \mathscr{V}\begin{bmatrix} b_1 \\ b_2 \end{bmatrix} = \sigma^2(\mathbf{X}'\mathbf{X})^{-1} = \begin{bmatrix} 2 & -1.9 \\ -1.9 & 1.81 \end{bmatrix}$$

Compare this with

$$(8.17) \qquad \mathbf{X} = \begin{bmatrix} 10 & 10 \\ 0 & -10 \\ -9 & 0 \end{bmatrix} \qquad \text{implying} \qquad \mathbf{X}'\mathbf{X} = \begin{bmatrix} 181 & 100 \\ 100 & 200 \end{bmatrix}$$

The values taken by the explanatory variables are the same (so that the diagonal elements of $\mathbf{X}'\mathbf{X}$ are also the same) but the second and third observations on the second variable are interchanged, which leads to smaller off-diagonal elements of $\mathbf{X}'\mathbf{X}$. The covariance matrix is now (assuming $\sigma^2 = 1$ as before):

$$(8.18) \qquad \mathscr{V}\begin{bmatrix} b_1 \\ b_2 \end{bmatrix} = \begin{bmatrix} .00763 & -.00382 \\ -.00382 & .00691 \end{bmatrix}$$

which shows that the sampling variances and covariance are considerably closer to zero than in (8.16). In the two-variable case (without constant term) the variance of the LS coefficient estimator is $\sigma^2/\sum x_\alpha^2$, so that—given σ^2—the precision of the estimator is determined by the values taken by the explanatory variable. In the present case of two explanatory variables, these numerical values are the same for (8.15) and (8.17), but in (8.15) we have a situation close to extreme multicollinearity. It should be intuitively obvious that in such a situation it is hardly possible to estimate the parameters β_1 and β_2 with great precision. For when the first explanatory variable takes values that are almost exactly equal to some multiple of those of the second, the data do not really enable the analyst to distinguish the effects of these variables on the dependent variable; at least, these data do not enable him to do so with any real precision, and the standard errors of the coefficients will therefore be large.[20]

Two amendments are in order, similar to those of the case of extreme multicollinearity. First, we may apply the conditional estimation procedure along the lines of (8.7) and obtain smaller variances of the LS coefficients, given specified values of one or several elements of $\boldsymbol{\beta}$. This is pursued in Problem 8.7. Second, particular linear combinations of $\boldsymbol{\beta}$ elements may be estimated relatively precisely. Take $\beta_1 + \beta_2$ in the case (8.16). The standard deviation of the sampling distribution of $b_1 + b_2$ is

$$(8.19) \qquad \sqrt{2 + 1.81 + 2(-1.9)} = .1$$

which is considerably below the corresponding standard deviations of either b_1 or b_2. In the case (8.18) we have for the standard deviation of $b_1 + b_2$:

$$(8.20) \qquad \sqrt{.00763 + .00691 + 2(-.00382)} \approx .083$$

which is not very much smaller than the value (8.19). It is not difficult to understand why $b_1 + b_2$ has such a moderate standard deviation in eq. (8.19). Considering (8.15), we find that the values taken by the two variables are

[20] A more general result which expresses the sampling variance of an LS coefficient in terms of the degree of multicollinearity is given in Section 4.1; see eq. (1.9) of that section and the discussion below this equation.

almost the same: $x_{\alpha 1} \approx x_{\alpha 2}$, $\alpha = 1, 2, 3$. Therefore the basic equation can be approximated as follows:

$$
\begin{aligned}
(8.21) \qquad y_\alpha &= \beta_1 x_{\alpha 1} + \beta_2 x_{\alpha 2} + \epsilon_\alpha \\
&\approx (\beta_1 + \beta_2) x_{\alpha 1} + \epsilon_\alpha \qquad \alpha = 1, 2, 3
\end{aligned}
$$

Hence, if we are interested in $\beta_1 + \beta_2$, we have in effect the analysis of a simple regression on one explanatory variable, so that the multicollinearity problem is avoided, at least approximately. A relatively precise estimation of a particular combination of $\boldsymbol{\beta}$ elements may be important, but there is, of course, no guarantee that this is the combination in which the analyst is particularly interested.

The situation of multicollinearity (both extreme and near-extreme) implies for the analyst that he is asking more than his data are able to answer; only part of his questions admit a satisfactory answer. We note in conclusion that when there is near-extreme multicollinearity, the computations are to be carried out with considerable precision, since the matrix $\mathbf{X}'\mathbf{X}$ is then close to singularity.

Problems

8.1 Prove that the conditional estimators of $\beta_2, \ldots, \beta_K$ described below eq. (8.7) are linear functions of β_{10}. Partition $\mathbf{X} = [\mathbf{x}_1 \quad \mathbf{Z}]$ and prove that a conditionally unbiased estimator (the condition being $\beta_1 = \beta_{10}$) of the covariance matrix of these point estimators is $c(\mathbf{Z}'\mathbf{Z})^{-1}$, where

$$
(8.22) \qquad c = \frac{1}{n - K + 1} (\mathbf{y} - \beta_{10}\mathbf{x}_1)'[\mathbf{I} - \mathbf{Z}(\mathbf{Z}'\mathbf{Z})^{-1}\mathbf{Z}'](\mathbf{y} - \beta_{10}\mathbf{x}_1)
$$

8.2 (*Continuation*) Formulate a conditional confidence interval for β_2 as a function of β_{10} under the condition of normally distributed disturbances. Illustrate the result graphically and compare it with the diagram of Problem 6.6.

8.3 (*Continuation*) Extend the two previous problems for the case in which the rank of $\mathbf{X}$ is $K - 2$.

8.4 Apply the second-order constrained extremum conditions described in the last two paragraphs of Section 1.8 to prove that the estimator $\mathbf{w}'\mathbf{z}$ of Theorem 3.10 has minimum variance subject to the unbiasedness constraint.

8.5 Prove that the validity of Assumption 3.1 (except that $\mathbf{X}$ need not have full column rank) is sufficient for the statement made in the first part of Theorem 3.10.

8.6 Prove along lines similar to (8.14) that if $\boldsymbol{\lambda}_1$ and $\boldsymbol{\lambda}_2$ are two solutions of (8.13), they satisfy $\mathbf{X}\boldsymbol{\lambda}_1 = \mathbf{X}\boldsymbol{\lambda}_2$. Conclude that $\mathbf{k}$ of (8.12) is unique even if $\boldsymbol{\lambda}$ is not.

8.7 Specify $b_1 = b_2 = 1$ and construct a confidence ellipse for β_1 and β_2 on the basis of the covariance matrix (8.16); choose your own confidence coefficient. Use this picture to clarify why $\beta_1 + \beta_2$ is estimated so much more accurately that β_1 and β_2 separately. Also, construct for this numerical example a conditional confidence interval of β_2 given β_1 as a function of β_1, and compare the picture with that of Problem 8.2.

3.9 Limitations of the Standard Linear Model[A]

In this section we provide a brief summary of the limitations implied by the assumptions of the standard linear model, and we indicate the places in the text where these problems are considered in more detail.

(1) Linearity

Assumption 3.1 states that the expectation of $\mathbf{y}$ given $\mathbf{X}$ is linear in $\mathbf{X}$, but the linearity condition is actually rather weak. The textile example showed that the analyst can afford logarithms of variables. Polynomials can be handled in the same way; it is merely a matter of redefining variables. Take the following quadratic equation:

$$y = \beta_1 u + \beta_2 v + \beta_3 u^2 + \beta_4 v^2 + \beta_5 uv + \epsilon \tag{9.1}$$

where ϵ is a random disturbance with zero expectation. Define

$$x_1 = u \qquad x_2 = v \qquad x_3 = u^2 \qquad x_4 = v^2 \qquad x_5 = uv \tag{9.2}$$

Then (9.1) takes the simple linear form

$$y = \beta_1 x_1 + \beta_2 x_2 + \beta_3 x_3 + \beta_4 x_4 + \beta_5 x_5 + \epsilon \tag{9.3}$$

Qualitative determining factors can be handled by means of so-called *dummy variables*. For example, let the consumption of durables (y) be a linear function of wage income (x_1) and nonwage income (x_2). The intercept of this function is not the same in peace and war. When there is peace we have

$$y = \beta_0 + \beta_1 x_1 + \beta_2 x_2 + \epsilon \tag{9.4}$$

and, when there is war,

$$y = \beta_0' + \beta_1 x_1 + \beta_2 x_2 + \epsilon \tag{9.5}$$

One procedure consists of applying LS to peacetime and wartime observations separately, but this neglects the fact that we have the same slope parameters β_1 and β_2 in (9.4) and (9.5). Consider, then,

$$y = \beta_0 + \beta_1 x_1 + \beta_2 x_2 + \beta_3 x_3 + \epsilon \tag{9.6}$$

where

$$\beta_3 = \beta_0' - \beta_0 \qquad x_3 = \begin{cases} 0 & \text{for peacetime observations} \\ 1 & \text{for wartime observations} \end{cases} \tag{9.7}$$

It is easily seen that eq. (9.6) applies to peace as well as to war. The variable x_3, whose values are zero and one, is a dummy variable. To a large extent it is similar to another synthetic variable that was introduced earlier, the "unit variable," which serves to transform a constant term to a multiplicative coefficient.

We conclude that linearity is not as restrictive as it seemed in the first instance. What is needed is linearity of $\mathscr{E}\mathbf{y}$ in *known functions* of the determining variables. This may amount to these variables themselves or to their logarithms or squares and products and so on. We may also argue in the following way. When an expression is linear in a set of known functions of certain variables, it can be written as $\mathbf{a}'\mathbf{x}$, where the elements of $\mathbf{x}$ are the functions just mentioned. Clearly, $\mathbf{a}'\mathbf{x}$ is equally linear in the coefficient vector $\mathbf{a}$. Therefore we may say that the linearity assumption of the standard linear model amounts to *linearity of $\mathscr{E}\mathbf{y}$ in the unknown parameters $\beta_1, \ldots, \beta_K$*. An example that violates the linearity condition is

$$y = \alpha + \beta e^{\gamma x} + \epsilon \qquad (\mathscr{E}\epsilon = 0) \tag{9.8}$$

where α, β, and γ are unknown parameters. The right-hand side of (9.8) is linear in α and β but nonlinear in γ. It is also linear in $e^{\gamma x}$, which is a function of x; but it is an *unknown* function since γ is unknown. To test and estimate relations like (9.8) a nonlinear procedure is required. Such procedures will be considered in Sections 8.8, 11.8, and 11.9.

(2) *Does the Analyst Know All Relevant Explanatory Variables?*

Assumption 3.1 claims that the expectation of each y_α is equal to a linear combination of the values taken by a given set of K explanatory variables. But is the analyst really certain as to the variables that should be included in this set? Sometimes yes, more frequently no. What happens when the analyst proceeds as if one set is the correct set whereas actually a different set is the correct one? This is the subject of specification analysis, which is pursued in the first several sections of Chapter 11.

In practice one finds very often that the analyst *experiments* with a list of potential explanatory variables. He starts with a list of plausible variables, rejects those whose LS coefficients are not sufficiently significant and adds new variables, so that a new list is obtained. Then he applies LS to this new set of variables, rejects and adds again, and so on, until he finally arrives at a result which he prefers according to some criterion.

It would be wrong to say that experimentation as such is wrong, but it is true that the standard linear model supposes that it does not take place. This model implies that **X** is fixed and given, which is admittedly restrictive. Therefore, what is really needed is an extension of the theory which would allow for experimentation with different sets of explanatory variables. This subject is not particularly simple; it will be considered in Section 12.1.

(3) *Is the Analyst Completely Ignorant as to the Values of the Parameters?*

The parameter vector $\boldsymbol{\beta}$ is unknown, and it is assumed that its elements may take any real values. However, it frequently happens that the analyst does not like this idea, because he has certain prior notions about the values which some of the parameters should take. Returning to the textile example, we may well argue that it is known from previous analyses (or from introspection or any other source of information) that the income elasticity of the demand for textiles is of the order of 1 and that it is unlikely to be less than .5 or larger than 1.5. We may feel certain that the price elasticity is not positive. Note that this objection claims that we know *more* than the estimation procedure wants to admit, whereas the previous objection claims that we know *less* than Assumption 3.1 takes for granted.

The incorporation of prior information may take different forms. If it is known that the elements of $\boldsymbol{\beta}$ satisfy one or more linear equations, we may use constrained LS, which is pursued in more detail in Sections 6.8, 6.9, 7.3, and 7.7. Nonlinear equality constraints are analyzed in Sections 11.8 and 11.9. The case of linear inequality constraints is considered in Section 7.9. "Uncertain" prior constraints (such as "the income elasticity of the demand for textile goods is, in all likelihood, between .5 and 1.5") are analyzed and applied in Sections 7.8 and 10.6 and, from a Bayesian point of view, in Section 12.9.

(4) *Observational Errors*

The standard linear model operates conditionally on the values taken by the explanatory variables. But suppose that these values are subject to observational errors and that we declare such errors to be random. Then, if the true values are regarded as nonstochastic and if we formulate the matrix **X** in terms of the observed values, we cannot really assume that the **X** elements are nonstochastic. Note that observational errors in explanatory variables are particularly dangerous when the observed values are close to extreme multicollinearity. Suppose, for example, that the third observation on the first variable in (8.15) is subject to error. The observed value is -9, the true value is -10, so that the matrix of true values is

$$\begin{bmatrix} 10 & 10 \\ 0 & 0 \\ -10 & -10 \end{bmatrix} \tag{9.9}$$

If we knew the truth, we would realize that there is extreme multicollinearity and refrain from estimating β_1 and β_2. If we carry out the computations given in (8.16) and (8.19) in spite of this, we do obtain numerical results; but these are, of course, without any meaning if the (3, 1)st element of the true **X** is indeed -10.

It should also be noted that the concept of an observational error has to be interpreted liberally. It may happen that we need a certain explanatory variable on which no observations are available, so that we decide to use a substitute variable. An example is provided by the description of the textile data in Section 3.2, where it was mentioned that a price index of clothing is used as a substitute for the price index of textiles. There are no problems when the prices of clothing goods and of other textile goods move proportionally (why?), but, in general, this will not be exactly true. When there are deviations, they can be regarded as observational errors with respect to the index which we really need. If we assume these deviations to be random, they are effectively equivalent to random observational errors.

Another similar example is that of entrepreneurial profit expectations which act as an explanatory variable for investment decisions. Such anticipatory data are usually not available in numerical form, so that one may decide to use, say, the observed profit earnings of the year before. Even if these profit data are not subject to observational error themselves (which is an optimistic assumption), they are certainly not perfect with respect to profit expectations—and that is what counts for the investment equation.

The subject of errors in variables is a difficult one. It will be considered in Section 12.2.

(5) *Aggregation*

We just mentioned that a price index of clothing was used instead of a price index of textiles generally. Even if a textile price index were available, this question would arise: what kind of index is the correct index, if there is such an index? This leads to the problem of aggregation, which is discussed in several sections of Chapter 11. The economic theories which form the basis of our regressions are mostly of the microeconomic type, and an explicit treatment of the aggregation procedure is then appropriate.

(6) *Lagged Values of the Dependent Variable*

We face another difficulty with the assumption that the **X** elements are nonstochastic when lagged values of the dependent variable are among the explanatory variables of a time series regression. Suppose that consumption per capita (C) in year α depends linearly on that year's income per capita (Y) and the level of consumption per capita in the year before:

$$C_\alpha = \beta_0 + \beta_1 Y_\alpha + \beta_2 C_{\alpha-1} + \epsilon_\alpha \qquad (\epsilon_\alpha = \text{disturbance}) \tag{9.10}$$

Assumption 3.1 implies that the left-hand C_α, a value taken by the dependent variable, is random. But if we assume at the same time that all right-hand variables take fixed values, this must also apply to $C_{\alpha-1}$. That leads to a contradiction. Take $\alpha = 1$ and hence C_1, which is the first observation on the dependent variable and is therefore random, but which is also the second observation on one of the explanatory variables and thus nonstochastic. We have to weaken our assumptions in order to handle this situation. In fact, this can be done under appropriate conditions. The result, to be described in Section 8.7, is that the LS coefficient estimator has a distribution which approaches the familiar distribution with mean vector $\boldsymbol{\beta}$ and covariance matrix $\sigma^2(\mathbf{X}'\mathbf{X})^{-1}$ if the sample size (n) is sufficiently large.[21]

(7) *Systems of Simultaneous Equations*

Another difficulty of a similar kind owes its origin to the general interdependence which characterizes many economic phenomena. In the textile case we take the price level of textile goods of any year as fixed and ask what can be said about textile consumption, given this price level. But what happens when textile prices in turn depend on textile consumption, either directly or indirectly? It is then very difficult to maintain that the textile price level can be regarded as fixed and given with respect to textile consumption. In such a case we must declare this price level to be random and formulate a second equation describing it in terms of textile consumption (and possibly other determining factors as well). The addition of a second equation leads to a system of so-called simultaneous equations. This area is explored in Chapters 9 and 10.

[21] However, the situation is not nearly so satisfactory (even for large n) when the complication of lagged dependent values is combined with other complications, particularly that of correlated disturbances [see below under (9)].

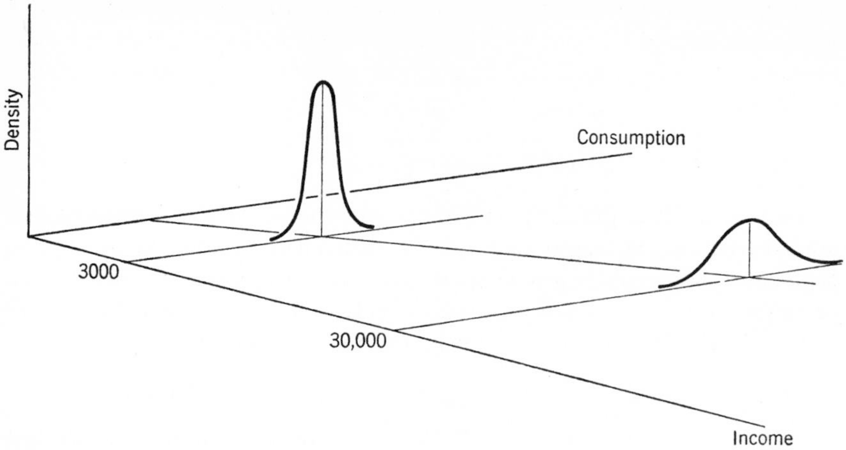

Fig. 3.4 Illustration of heteroscedastic disturbances.

(8) Heteroscedastic Disturbances

We proceed to Assumption 3.2, which deals with the covariance matrix $\mathscr{V}(\mathbf{y} \mid \mathbf{X}) = \mathscr{V}(\boldsymbol{\epsilon}) = \sigma^2\mathbf{I}$. The diagonal part of this matrix equation requires all the disturbances to have the same variance, which is also expressed by saying that they are assumed to be *homoscedastic* (from Greek ὁμοσ, equal, and σκεδαννυμι, to spread). Consider again the consumption-income relation of Section 3.1 and imagine that we do observe data on family households. It seems rather plausible that families with an annual income of \$3000 will have expenditures between \$2500 and \$3500 with very few exceptions, which amounts to a range of variation of \$1000, whereas families with an annual income of \$30,000 will have expenditures whose range of variation is much larger than \$1000. This is a case of *heteroscedastic* disturbances and it is illustrated in Figure 3.4, which should be compared with Figure 3.1 in Section 3.1. The subject of testing for heteroscedasticity is considered in Sections 5.1 and 5.4 and that of estimation under conditions of heteroscedasticity in Section 6.2.

(9) Correlated Disturbances

Finally, we consider the off-diagonal part of the matrix equation $\mathscr{V}(\boldsymbol{\epsilon}) = \sigma^2\mathbf{I}$, which requires the disturbances to be uncorrelated. Suppose that we have a time series regression based on successive annual data, so that the neglected variables whose effect is expressed by the disturbance also have the form of annual time series (although the relevant data may not be available). To simplify the analysis, assume that the disturbance is a linear combination of these variables:

$$\epsilon_\alpha = \sum_{i=1}^{N} c_i u_{\alpha i} \qquad \alpha = 1, \ldots, n \tag{9.11}$$

where $u_{\alpha i}$ is the αth value taken by the ith neglected variable, c_i its coefficient in the disturbance, and N the number of neglected variables. We take the c's as fixed but the u's as random with zero mean. (The effect of nonzero means of neglected variables on the dependent variable can be considered as being absorbed by the constant term of the equation.) For the covariance of two successive disturbances we then have

$$\mathscr{E}(\epsilon_\alpha \epsilon_{\alpha+1}) = \sum_{i=1}^{N}\sum_{j=1}^{N} c_i c_j \mathscr{E}(u_{\alpha i} u_{\alpha+1, j}) \tag{9.12}$$

Is this covariance zero as $\mathscr{V}(\boldsymbol{\epsilon}) = \sigma^2 \mathbf{I}$ requires? To answer this we consider those terms in the right-hand side of (9.12) for which $i = j$:

$$\sum_{i=1}^{N} c_i^2 \mathscr{E}(u_{\alpha i} u_{\alpha+1, i}) \tag{9.13}$$

This is a weighted sum with positive weights (c_i^2) of the covariances of successive values taken by the same variable. It frequently happens that, because of the inertia which characterizes many economic variables, a large value this year is followed by a rather large value next year. This suggests positive covariances and, hence, in view of the positive weights c_i^2, a positive value of the sum (9.13). It is more difficult to generalize about those terms in (9.12) for which $i \neq j$. Nevertheless, we should not be surprised to find positive covariances of successive disturbances ϵ_α and $\epsilon_{\alpha+1}$, which would amount to another violation of Assumption 3.2. This subject will be pursued from the standpoint of testing in Chapter 5 (particularly Sections 5.1 and 5.4) and from the standpoint of estimation in Chapter 6, in particular, Section 6.3.

Problems

9.1 When the time unit in a time series regression is less than a year, one frequently observes seasonal effects. For example, the supply of vegetables and the demand for soft drinks is different in different quarters of the year, quite apart from the effect of the usual explanatory variables. Let y_α be the consumption per capita of soft drinks, $x_{\alpha 1}$ real income per capita, and $x_{\alpha 2}$ the relative price of soft drinks. Let the time unit be a quarter and consider the following linear relation:

$$y_\alpha = \beta_0 + \beta_1 x_{\alpha 1} + \beta_2 x_{\alpha 2} + \beta_3 x_{\alpha 3} + \beta_4 x_{\alpha 4} + \beta_5 x_{\alpha 5} + \epsilon_\alpha \tag{9.14}$$

where

$x_{\alpha 3} = 1$ if α falls in the first quarter of any year; 0 otherwise
$x_{\alpha 4} = 1$ if α falls in the second quarter of any year; 0 otherwise
$x_{\alpha 5} = 1$ if α falls in the third quarter of any year; 0 otherwise

Why don't we introduce a separate dummy variable for the fourth quarter? What would happen if we did?

9.2 The C.E.S. (constant elasticity of substitution) production function is of the following form:

$$P = [\delta K^{-\rho} + (1 - \delta)L^{-\rho}]^{-1/\rho} \tag{9.15}$$

where P is output, K capital, L labor, and δ and ρ are parameters. Is it possible to transform the equation so that it becomes linear in the parameters?

9.3 Consider the **X** matrix (9.9). Use Theorem 3.10 to prove that the only linear combination of β_1 and β_2 that can be estimated unbiasedly is $\beta_1 + \beta_2$ (or any multiple of $\beta_1 + \beta_2$).

CHAPTER 4

PARTIAL AND MULTIPLE CORRELATION

There was one question raised in the opening paragraph of Chapter 3 that has not yet been answered. Given that classical demand theory indicates real income and relative prices as the variables that determine the consumption of various commodities, to what extent do statistical data show that these variables account for the variation of textile consumption over time? Another question may be added. Is it also possible to measure the contribution of each variable separately (real income and the relative textile price in this case) to the "explanation" of the behavior of the dependent variable? These questions will be answered in this chapter by means of correlation coefficients. The analysis will be largely descriptive, particularly the first several sections, in the same way that the LS method was introduced as a descriptive device in Section 1.7. Statistical models will play a more prominent role toward the end of the chapter. A more extensive treatment of partial and multiple correlation can be found in Chapter 27 of KENDALL and STUART (1967).

All sections of this chapter are recommended for an introductory course with the exception of the last two, which are optional.

4.1 The Coefficient of Multiple Correlation[A]

Our starting point is the LS regression equation

$$(1.1) \qquad y_\alpha = \sum_{h=1}^{K} b_h x_{\alpha h} + e_\alpha \qquad \alpha = 1, \ldots, n$$

It is clear that we can regard $\sum_h b_h x_{\alpha h}$ as the part of y_α that is accounted for by the explanatory variables and e_α as the "unexplained" (residual) part. We square both sides of the equation and sum over α:

$$(1.2) \qquad \sum_{\alpha=1}^{n} y_\alpha^2 = \sum_{\alpha=1}^{n}\left(\sum_{h=1}^{K} b_h x_{\alpha h}\right)^2 + \sum_{\alpha=1}^{n} e_\alpha^2 + 2\sum_{h=1}^{K} b_h \sum_{\alpha=1}^{n} x_{\alpha h} e_\alpha$$

$$= \sum_{\alpha=1}^{n}\left(\sum_{h=1}^{K} b_h x_{\alpha h}\right)^2 + \sum_{\alpha=1}^{n} e_\alpha^2$$

where the last equality sign is based on the fact that the sum over α of $x_{\alpha h} e_\alpha$ is the hth element of $\mathbf{X}'\mathbf{e} = \mathbf{0}$. Equation (1.2) shows that the sum of squares of the values taken by the dependent variable consists of two nonnegative parts, one part accounted for by the explanatory variables and a second which is the residual part. In matrix terms we obtain (1.2) by premultiplying each side of $\mathbf{y} = \mathbf{X}\mathbf{b} + \mathbf{e}$ by its own transpose:

$$(1.3) \qquad \mathbf{y}'\mathbf{y} = \mathbf{b}'\mathbf{X}'\mathbf{X}\mathbf{b} + \mathbf{e}'\mathbf{e} + 2\mathbf{b}'\mathbf{X}'\mathbf{e}$$

$$= \mathbf{b}'\mathbf{X}'\mathbf{X}\mathbf{b} + \mathbf{e}'\mathbf{e}$$

Within the framework of sums of squares and products, an obvious measure for the degree of variation of the dependent variable is indeed the sum of squares of its values, $\sum y_\alpha^2 = \mathbf{y}'\mathbf{y}$.[1] Comparing this sum of squares with (1.3), we conclude that a fraction R^2 of $\mathbf{y}'\mathbf{y}$ is accounted for by the explanatory variables and that a fraction $1 - R^2$ is residual in nature, where

$$(1.4) \qquad R^2 = \frac{\mathbf{b}'\mathbf{X}'\mathbf{X}\mathbf{b}}{\mathbf{y}'\mathbf{y}} \qquad 1 - R^2 = \frac{\mathbf{e}'\mathbf{e}}{\mathbf{y}'\mathbf{y}}$$

The coefficient R (the nonnegative square root of R^2) is known as the *multiple correlation coefficient* associated with the regression (1.1); its square (R^2) is sometimes called the coefficient of determination. Obviously, the closer R and R^2 are to 1, the better the performance of the explanatory variables.

[1] An even more obvious measure is the sum of squares of these values measured as deviations from the mean, $\sum (y_\alpha - \bar{y})^2$, but we prefer to work here with $\sum y_\alpha^2$ for reasons of notational simplicity. We shall come back to this point in Section 4.4.

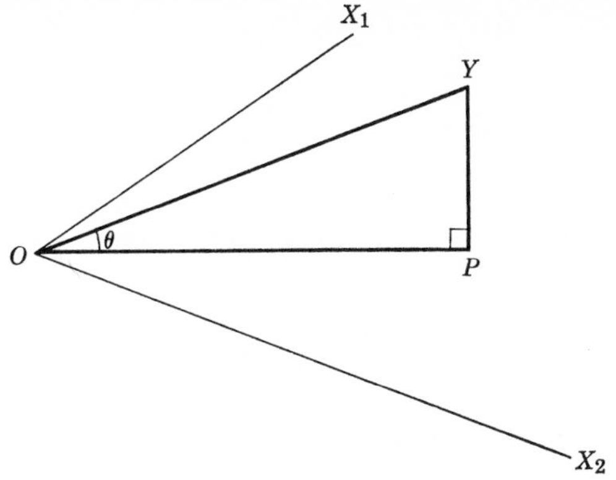

Fig. 4.1 A geometric picture of the multiple correlation coefficient.

A Geometric Picture of the Multiple Correlation Coefficient

Consider the n-dimensional Euclidean space which was introduced in Section 1.7 to illustrate the LS adjustment procedure. Figure 4.1 (for $n = 3$, $K = 2$) is similar to Figure 1.1*b* of that section. Recall that the vector $\mathbf{y}$ is represented by OY and $\mathbf{Xb}$ by OP. Hence, R defined in (1.4) is simply the ratio of the distance from O to P to the distance from O to Y, and hence equal to the cosine of the angle θ between the two vectors:

$$R = \frac{OP}{OY} = \cos\theta \tag{1.5}$$

where OP and OY are to be interpreted as distances (the lengths of the corresponding vectors). This result can be generalized for arbitrary K and n as follows: the multiple correlation coefficient R is equal to the cosine of the angle θ between the vector of the dependent variable and the K-dimensional subspace spanned by the vectors of the explanatory variables in the n-dimensional space.

Clearly, the smaller the angle θ, the larger the R and the closer the approximation of $\mathbf{y}$ by a linear combination of the $\mathbf{X}$ columns. Also note that extreme multicollinearity implies that the space spanned by the vectors of the explanatory variables is of a lower dimension than K. The relation between near-extreme multicollinearity and the sampling variances of the coefficient estimators will be considered at the end of this section.

Correlation Coefficients and the Variance of LS Coefficient Estimators

Additional insight is obtained when we express the multiple correlation coefficient in terms of the observation matrix $[\mathbf{y} \quad \mathbf{X}]$ and the corresponding matrix of sums of squares and products:

$$\mathbf{G} = \begin{bmatrix} \mathbf{y}'\mathbf{y} & \mathbf{y}'\mathbf{X} \\ \mathbf{X}'\mathbf{y} & \mathbf{X}'\mathbf{X} \end{bmatrix} \tag{1.6}$$

Under the conditions of the standard linear model the matrix $[\mathbf{y} \quad \mathbf{X}]$ and hence also $\mathbf{G}$ have rank $K + 1$ with unit probability, provided that $n > K$ and that the disturbances have a continuous distribution.[2] Thus, $\mathbf{G}$ has an inverse under these conditions, to be written $\mathbf{G}^{-1} = [g^{hk}]$, where $h, k = 0, 1, \ldots, K$, the index 0 referring to the dependent variable and $1, \ldots, K$ to the explanatory variables. We partition $\mathbf{G}^{-1}$ in the same way as $\mathbf{G}$ in (1.6) and apply eq. (2.15) of Section 1.2 to obtain the leading element g^{00} of $\mathbf{G}^{-1}$:

$$g^{00} = \frac{1}{\mathbf{y}'\mathbf{y} - \mathbf{y}'\mathbf{X}(\mathbf{X}'\mathbf{X})^{-1}\mathbf{X}'\mathbf{y}} = \frac{1}{\mathbf{y}'\mathbf{y} - \mathbf{b}'\mathbf{X}'\mathbf{X}\mathbf{b}} = \frac{1}{(1 - R^2)\mathbf{y}'\mathbf{y}} \tag{1.7}$$

Hence $1 - R^2$ is equal to the reciprocal of $g^{00}\mathbf{y}'\mathbf{y}$.

We now disregard $\mathbf{y}$ and imagine that we run a regression of one of the explanatory variables (say, the hth) on the $K - 1$ other explanatory variables. The relevant matrix of sums of squares and products is then no longer $\mathbf{G}$ but its submatrix $\mathbf{X}'\mathbf{X}$. Since g^{00} is the diagonal element of $\mathbf{G}^{-1}$ corresponding to $\mathbf{y}$, the analogous element in $(\mathbf{X}'\mathbf{X})^{-1}$ for the hth explanatory variable is $\mathbf{i}_h'(\mathbf{X}'\mathbf{X})^{-1}\mathbf{i}_h$, where $\mathbf{i}_h$ is the hth column of the $K \times K$ unit matrix. So the analogue of (1.7) is

$$\mathbf{i}_h'(\mathbf{X}'\mathbf{X})^{-1}\mathbf{i}_h = \frac{1}{(1 - P_h^2)\mathbf{x}_h'\mathbf{x}_h} \tag{1.8}$$

where $\mathbf{x}_h$ is the vector of values taken by the hth explanatory variable and P_h the multiple correlation coefficient corresponding to the regression of this variable on the $K - 1$ other explanatory variables.

It is instructive to compare this result with the sampling variance of b_h, the coefficient of the hth variable in the regression in which we are really interested. This is the (h, h)th element of $\mathscr{V}(\mathbf{b}) = \sigma^2(\mathbf{X}'\mathbf{X})^{-1}$, and hence in view of (1.8):

$$\text{var } b_h = \sigma^2\mathbf{i}_h'(\mathbf{X}'\mathbf{X})^{-1}\mathbf{i}_h = \frac{\sigma^2}{(1 - P_h^2)\mathbf{x}_h'\mathbf{x}_h} \qquad h = 1, \ldots, K \tag{1.9}$$

Recall that when there is only one explanatory variable and no constant term, the sampling variance of its coefficient estimator is equal to σ^2 divided by the

[2] *Proof.* Since $\mathbf{X}$ has rank K, the matrix $[\mathbf{y} \quad \mathbf{X}]$ can have a rank less than $K + 1$ only if $\mathbf{y}$ is a linear function of the columns of $\mathbf{X}$, which means that the LS residual vector is then zero. But this can happen only with zero probability when $n > K$ and when the disturbances have a continuous distribution (so that $\mathbf{e} = \mathbf{M}\boldsymbol{\epsilon}$ is also continuously distributed), because a nondegenerate continuous distribution assigns zero probability to any point.

sum of squares of the values taken by that variable. Clearly, this result is the same as (1.9) except that the sum of squares in (1.9) is multiplied by $1 - P_h^2$, P_h being the multiple correlation coefficient of the regression of the hth variable on the $K - 1$ other explanatory variables. But (1.4) states that $(1 - R^2)\mathbf{y}'\mathbf{y} = \mathbf{e}'\mathbf{e}$, so that by analogy $(1 - P_h^2)\mathbf{x}_h'\mathbf{x}_h$ must be the sum of squares of the residuals in that regression. We know that in a simple regression without constant term the precision with which the coefficient is estimated is (given σ^2 and n) higher when the explanatory variable takes larger absolute values. We conclude from (1.9) that what matters in the case of several variables is the absolute size of the residuals in the regression of the hth variable on the $K - 1$ other explanatory variables or, equivalently (less precisely but perhaps more clearly), what counts is the degree to which the behavior of the hth variable is "linearly independent" of that of the $K - 1$ other variables. If the multiple correlation P_h is unity, the column $\mathbf{x}_h$ can be written as a linear combination of the other columns of $\mathbf{X}$. We then have extreme multicollinearity and β_h is not estimable; the expression (1.9) for the variance is then infinite. If P_h is not far below unity, the multicollinearity is not extreme but it is nevertheless important, and the variance (1.9) takes a large value.

Problems

1.1 Prove that the expectation of the observation matrix $[\mathbf{y} \quad \mathbf{X}]$ has rank K under the conditions of the standard linear model. What is the implication for the inverse of $\mathbf{G}$ defined in (1.6) when $\mathbf{y}$ is replaced by $\mathscr{E}\mathbf{y}$?

1.2 Consider the variance $\sigma^2/\sum x_\alpha^2$ of the LS estimator of β of $y_\alpha = \beta x_\alpha + \epsilon_\alpha$. Prove that it is a special case of the variance (1.9) and indicate the nature of the case.

4.2 The Incremental Contributions of Explanatory Variables[A]

The results obtained in the previous section imply that R^2 as defined in (1.4) is a measure for the degree to which the behavior of the dependent variable is accounted for by the explanatory variables, and that $1 - R^2$ measures the residual component. This is an answer to the first question raised in the opening paragraph of this chapter. We now turn to the second question. Is it also possible to measure the contribution of each explanatory variable separately? Each such variable with nonzero coefficient makes a contribution, and intuition suggests that there are two main factors determining the size of this contribution: the absolute value of the coefficient and the degree of variation of this variable.

Two Unattractive Decompositions

It may seem at first glance that the question has a simple positive answer. The numerator of R^2 in (1.4), $\mathbf{b}'\mathbf{X}'\mathbf{X}\mathbf{b} = \mathbf{b}'\mathbf{X}'\mathbf{y}$, is equal to the sum over h of $b_h \sum_\alpha x_{\alpha h} y_\alpha$, so that the ratio

$$\text{(2.1)} \qquad \frac{b_h \sum_{\alpha=1}^{n} x_{\alpha h} y_\alpha}{\sum_{\alpha=1}^{n} y_\alpha^2}$$

can be regarded as the contribution of the hth explanatory variable to R^2, which in turn measures the total contribution of *all* explanatory variables. It is indeed true that the ratios (2.1) when summed over h give R^2, but the difficulty is that these ratios may be negative; see Problem 2.1. This destroys the usefulness of (2.1) as a measure for the merits of the hth explanatory variable.

Actually, it is not difficult to see that the decomposition of R^2 is two-dimensional rather than one-dimensional. The numerator $\mathbf{b}'\mathbf{X}'\mathbf{X}\mathbf{b}$ of R^2 is equal to the double sum over h and k of $b_h b_k \sum_\alpha x_{\alpha h} x_{\alpha k}$, so that we have K^2 ratios:

$$\text{(2.2)} \qquad \frac{b_h b_k \sum_{\alpha=1}^{n} x_{\alpha h} x_{\alpha k}}{\sum_{\alpha=1}^{n} y_\alpha^2} \qquad h, k = 1, \ldots, K$$

This ratio refers to only one variable when $h = k$, and it is positive in that case. For $h \neq k$ we deal with the interaction of two explanatory variables. The ratio (2.2) may then be negative, but it is perhaps not unreasonable to expect that for some pairs of explanatory variables the contribution of their interaction to R^2 is negative. However, a two-dimensional decomposition is much less convenient than a decomposition in one dimension, particularly when the components of the former are partly negative and large in absolute value.

The Incremental Contributions

We prefer to answer the question in "marginal" or "incremental" terms, that is, by measuring the increase of the squared multiple correlation resulting from the inclusion of the hth explanatory variable, given that the other $K - 1$ variables are used. Consider then first the situation in which the hth variable is not included, so that we run a regression of the dependent variable on $K - 1$ variables and obtain the LS coefficients

$$b_1^*, \ldots, b_{h-1}^*, b_{h+1}^*, \ldots, b_K^* \tag{2.3}$$

The corresponding multiple correlation coefficient is R_h, where the subscript refers to the excluded variable. It is determined from

$$R_h^2 \sum_{\alpha=1}^{n} y_\alpha^2 = \sum_{k \neq h} b_k^* \sum_{\alpha=1}^{n} x_{\alpha k} y_\alpha \tag{2.4}$$

and the incremental contribution of the hth variable is then $R^2 - R_h^2$. This is nonnegative because LS minimizes the residual sum of squares and hence maximizes the multiple correlation [see (1.4)], which implies that this correlation cannot be reduced when an additional coefficient (of the hth variable) is adjusted.

Note that b_k^* of (2.3) is, in general, not equal to the corresponding b_k ($k \neq h$) of the regression on all K variables. We do have this equality when the vector of values taken by the hth variable is orthogonal to the $K - 1$ vectors of the other explanatory variables. If that is the case, the incremental contribution of this variable (multiplied by $\sum y_\alpha^2$) is, in view of (2.4),

$$(R^2 - R_h^2) \sum_{\alpha=1}^{n} y_\alpha^2 = b_h \sum_{\alpha=1}^{n} x_{\alpha h} y_\alpha \tag{2.5}$$

This result holds for each $h = 1, \ldots, K$ when all columns of $\mathbf{X}$ are pairwise orthogonal, that is, when $\mathbf{X}'\mathbf{X}$ is a diagonal matrix. By summation over h we then obtain

$$\sum_{h=1}^{K} (R^2 - R_h^2) \sum_{\alpha=1}^{n} y_\alpha^2 = b_1 \sum_{\alpha=1}^{n} x_{\alpha 1} y_1 + \cdots + b_K \sum_{\alpha=1}^{n} x_{\alpha K} y_\alpha = R^2 \sum_{\alpha=1}^{n} y_\alpha^2$$

and hence

$$\sum_{h=1}^{K} (R^2 - R_h^2) = R^2 \tag{2.6}$$

Thus the sum of the incremental contributions of the K explanatory variables is equal to their total contribution R^2. Again note that this result presupposes pairwise orthogonality of all columns of $\mathbf{X}$. Also note that if this condition is satisfied, the ratios (2.1) are all positive and the ratios (2.2) for $h \neq k$ all vanish. Therefore it is not correct to say that the result (2.6) can be regarded as a positive point for the incremental contributions $R^2 - R_h^2$ relative to these ratios. The positive points of $R^2 - R_h^2$ are its simple interpretation and its nonnegativity.

A Geometric Picture of the Incremental Contributions

To show what is involved in the more general case in which there is not necessarily orthogonality we return to the n-dimensional space, which is displayed in Figure 4.2 for $n = 3$ and $K = 2$. When the first explanatory variable is excluded, we run a regression on the second, which amounts to a projection of the vector OY on the vector OX_2. This leads to the vector OP_1, so that R_1 becomes the cosine of the angle between the vectors OY and OX_2: $R_1 = OP_1/OY$. (It should be clear from the context whether a symbol such as OY stands for a vector or for its length.) Therefore the incremental contribution of the first explanatory variable is

$$R^2 - R_1^2 = \frac{(OP)^2}{(OY)^2} - \frac{(OP_1)^2}{(OY)^2} = \frac{(PP_1)^2}{(OY)^2} \tag{2.7}$$

where the second equality sign is based on the Pythagorian theorem. (The line PP_1 is perpendicular to OX_2 because it is located in the plane spanned by YP and YP_1, both of which are perpendicular to OX_2.) Similarly, we have for the marginal contribution of the second explanatory variable:

$$R^2 - R_2^2 = \frac{(OP)^2}{(OY)^2} - \frac{(OP_2)^2}{(OY)^2} = \frac{(PP_2)^2}{(OY)^2} \tag{2.8}$$

where OP_2 is the projection of OY on OX_1. By adding (2.7) and (2.8) we find that the total incremental contribution of the two explanatory variables is

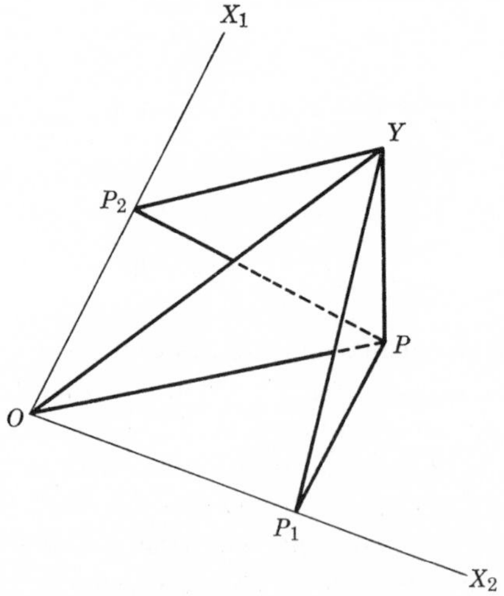

Fig. 4.2 A geometric picture of incremental contributions.

equal to the ratio of $(PP_1)^2 + (PP_2)^2$ to $(OY)^2$, which is equal to R^2 if and only if

$$(PP_1)^2 + (PP_2)^2 = (OP)^2 \tag{2.9}$$

This condition is satisfied when OP_1PP_2 is a rectangle, which implies that OX_1 and OX_2 are perpendicular, but otherwise it is not fulfilled. In general, therefore, the total incremental contribution of the explanatory variables [the left-hand side of (2.6)] differs from the total contribution R^2, and the difference may be of either sign.

Problems

2.1 Consider the following matrix of sums of squares and products:

$$\begin{bmatrix} \mathbf{y}'\mathbf{y} & \mathbf{y}'\mathbf{X} \\ \mathbf{X}'\mathbf{y} & \mathbf{X}'\mathbf{X} \end{bmatrix} = \left[\begin{array}{c|cc} 10 & 3 & 8 \\ \hline 3 & 10 & 5 \\ 8 & 5 & 10 \end{array}\right] \tag{2.10}$$

Verify that the ratio (2.1) is negative for $h = 1$. Also, compute the two-dimensional decomposition (2.2).

2.2 It is stated above eq. (2.5) that the coefficients (2.3) are equal to the corresponding LS coefficients of the regression on all K variables when the hth column of $\mathbf{X}$ is orthogonal to the $K - 1$ other columns. Prove this statement.

4.3 Partial Correlation Coefficients[A]

In the previous section we considered the regression of the dependent variable on $K - 1$ explanatory variables, with the hth excluded. Recall that in the discussion of eqs. (1.8) and (1.9) we considered the regression of the hth explanatory variable on the same $K - 1$ other variables. It is clear that these regressions are related, since they have the same variables in the right-hand side. In this section we shall investigate the correlation of the residuals of these two regressions. It leads to the theory of partial correlation, the basic idea of which can be formulated in terms of the following question. Given the observation that two variables are correlated, to what extent is this a result of a direct relation between them and to what extent is it caused by the fact that both are related linearly to another set of variables?[3] An obvious

[3] Note that this question is completely symmetric in the two variables, whereas their role in the standard linear model is not symmetric, one being the dependent variable and the other being one of the explanatory variables. However, this is not a serious objection to the approach followed in this section, which is descriptive rather than statistical.

approach, then, is to express both variables linearly in terms of that other group of variables and to see whether there is any correlation between the two sets of residuals.

A Geometric Approach

Let us start along geometric lines and consider Figure 4.3, which again deals with the case $n = 3$, $K = 2$. Take $h = 1$, so that the two regressions mentioned in the previous paragraph are both on the second explanatory variable whose vector is OX_2. The residual vector in the regression of the dependent variable is then YP_1 (perpendicular to OX_2) and the analogous residual vector in the regression of the first explanatory variable is X_1Q_1 (also perpendicular to OX_2). The correlation of the two sets of residuals is the cosine of the angle between these two vectors or, equivalently, the cosine of the angle ϕ between YP_1 and PP_1 because PP_1 and X_1Q_1 are parallel, both being located in the OX_1X_2-plane and perpendicular to OX_2. The square of the latter cosine is

$$r_1^2 = \frac{(PP_1)^2}{(YP_1)^2} = 1 - \frac{(YP)^2}{(YP_1)^2} = 1 - \frac{(OY)^2 - (OP)^2}{(OY)^2 - (OP_1)^2}$$

and hence, in view of (2.7), $1 - r_1^2 = (1 - R^2)/(1 - R_1^2)$. More generally:

$$(3.1) \qquad 1 - R^2 = (1 - R_h^2)(1 - r_h^2) \qquad h = 1, \ldots, K$$

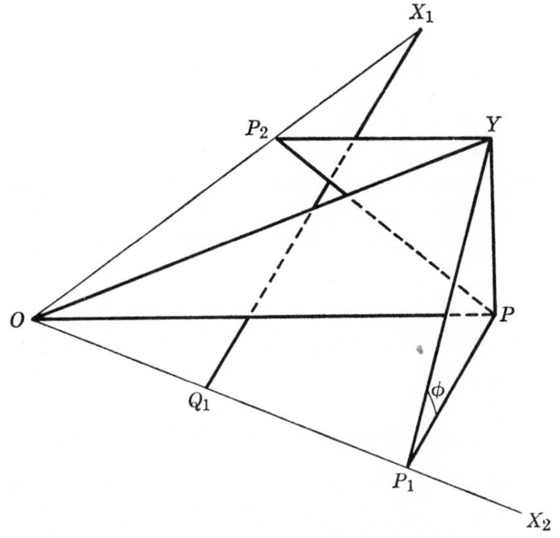

Fig. 4.3 The geometry of partial and multiple correlation.

where r_h is the *partial correlation coefficient* of the dependent variable and the hth explanatory variable, given the $K - 1$ other variables. As the geometric derivation clearly indicates, it is simply the ordinary correlation coefficient of the LS residuals of the two regressions of these two variables on the remaining $K - 1$ explanatory variables.

An Algebraic Approach

To prove (3.1) for general K and n we proceed algebraically. Take $h = 1$ and partition $\mathbf{X} = [\mathbf{x}_1 \quad \mathbf{W}]$, where $\mathbf{x}_1$ is the observation vector of the first explanatory variable. Write $\mathbf{N} = \mathbf{I} - \mathbf{W}(\mathbf{W}'\mathbf{W})^{-1}\mathbf{W}'$; it is then easily verified along the lines of LS algebra that $\mathbf{y}'\mathbf{N}\mathbf{y}$ and $\mathbf{x}_1'\mathbf{N}\mathbf{x}_1$ are the residual sums of squares of the two regressions and that $\mathbf{y}'\mathbf{N}\mathbf{x}_1$ is the sum of the products of these residuals. Hence

$$r_1 = \frac{\mathbf{y}'\mathbf{N}\mathbf{x}_1}{\sqrt{(\mathbf{y}'\mathbf{N}\mathbf{y})(\mathbf{x}_1'\mathbf{N}\mathbf{x}_1)}} \tag{3.2}$$

which implies

$$1 - r_1^2 = \frac{\mathbf{y}'\mathbf{N}\mathbf{y} - (\mathbf{y}'\mathbf{N}\mathbf{x}_1)^2/(\mathbf{x}_1'\mathbf{N}\mathbf{x}_1)}{\mathbf{y}'\mathbf{N}\mathbf{y}} \tag{3.3}$$

Next we use eq. (2.15) of Section 1.2 to partition $(\mathbf{X}'\mathbf{X})^{-1}$:

$$(\mathbf{X}'\mathbf{X})^{-1} = \begin{bmatrix} \mathbf{x}_1'\mathbf{x}_1 & \mathbf{x}_1'\mathbf{W} \\ \mathbf{W}'\mathbf{x}_1 & \mathbf{W}'\mathbf{W} \end{bmatrix}^{-1} \tag{3.4}$$

$$= \frac{1}{\mathbf{x}_1'\mathbf{N}\mathbf{x}_1} \begin{bmatrix} 1 & -\mathbf{x}_1'\mathbf{W}(\mathbf{W}'\mathbf{W})^{-1} \\ -(\mathbf{W}'\mathbf{W})^{-1}\mathbf{W}'\mathbf{x}_1 & \mathbf{x}_1'\mathbf{N}\mathbf{x}_1(\mathbf{W}'\mathbf{W})^{-1} + (\mathbf{W}'\mathbf{W})^{-1}\mathbf{W}'\mathbf{x}_1\mathbf{x}_1'\mathbf{W}(\mathbf{W}'\mathbf{W})^{-1} \end{bmatrix}$$

which gives

$$\mathbf{M} = \mathbf{I} - [\mathbf{x}_1 \quad \mathbf{W}](\mathbf{X}'\mathbf{X})^{-1}\begin{bmatrix} \mathbf{x}_1' \\ \mathbf{W}' \end{bmatrix} \tag{3.5}$$

$$= \mathbf{N} - \frac{1}{\mathbf{x}_1'\mathbf{N}\mathbf{x}_1}\mathbf{N}\mathbf{x}_1(\mathbf{N}\mathbf{x}_1)'$$

In turn, this implies

$$\frac{1 - R^2}{1 - R_1^2} = \frac{\mathbf{y}'\mathbf{M}\mathbf{y}}{\mathbf{y}'\mathbf{N}\mathbf{y}} = \frac{\mathbf{y}'\mathbf{N}\mathbf{y} - (\mathbf{y}'\mathbf{N}\mathbf{x}_1)^2/(\mathbf{x}_1'\mathbf{N}\mathbf{x}_1)}{\mathbf{y}'\mathbf{N}\mathbf{y}} \tag{3.6}$$

and a comparison of this result with (3.3) shows that the proof of (3.1) is complete.

Partial Correlation Coefficients Expressed in Terms of Student Test Statistics

Partial correlations can be obtained easily from the standard regression computations. First consider the variance estimator s^2 and apply (3.5):

$$(n - K)s^2 = \mathbf{y}'\mathbf{M}\mathbf{y} = \frac{(\mathbf{y}'\mathbf{N}\mathbf{y})(\mathbf{x}_1'\mathbf{N}\mathbf{x}_1) - (\mathbf{y}'\mathbf{N}\mathbf{x}_1)^2}{\mathbf{x}_1'\mathbf{N}\mathbf{x}_1} \tag{3.7}$$

Next consider the LS coefficient of $\mathbf{x}_1$, using the partitioned inverse (3.4):

$$\begin{aligned} b_1 &= \frac{1}{\mathbf{x}_1'\mathbf{N}\mathbf{x}_1}\begin{bmatrix}1 & -\mathbf{x}_1'\mathbf{W}(\mathbf{W}'\mathbf{W})^{-1}\end{bmatrix}\begin{bmatrix}\mathbf{x}_1'\mathbf{y} \\ \mathbf{W}'\mathbf{y}\end{bmatrix} \\ &= \frac{\mathbf{x}_1'\mathbf{y} - \mathbf{x}_1'\mathbf{W}(\mathbf{W}'\mathbf{W})^{-1}\mathbf{W}'\mathbf{y}}{\mathbf{x}_1'\mathbf{N}\mathbf{x}_1} = \frac{\mathbf{x}_1'\mathbf{N}\mathbf{y}}{\mathbf{x}_1'\mathbf{N}\mathbf{x}_1} \end{aligned} \tag{3.8}$$

Comparing this result with (3.2), we conclude that the partial correlation coefficient r_1 has the same sign as the corresponding regression coefficient b_1, this sign being equal to that of $\mathbf{y}'\mathbf{N}\mathbf{x}_1 = \mathbf{x}_1'\mathbf{N}\mathbf{y}$.

Finally, combine (1.9) and (3.4) to find

$$\text{var } b_1 = \sigma^2\mathbf{i}_1'(\mathbf{X}'\mathbf{X})^{-1}\mathbf{i}_1 = \frac{\sigma^2}{\mathbf{x}_1'\mathbf{N}\mathbf{x}_1} \tag{3.9}$$

and consider the ratio of b_1^2 to this variance: $(\mathbf{y}'\mathbf{N}\mathbf{x}_1)^2/\sigma^2\mathbf{x}_1'\mathbf{N}\mathbf{x}_1$. If we take the square root of this ratio and replace σ by s, we obtain the familiar Student statistic t_1 for testing the null hypothesis $\beta_1 = 0$:

$$t_1^2 = \frac{(\mathbf{y}'\mathbf{N}\mathbf{x}_1)^2}{s^2\mathbf{x}_1'\mathbf{N}\mathbf{x}_1} = \frac{(n - K)(\mathbf{y}'\mathbf{N}\mathbf{x}_1)^2}{(\mathbf{y}'\mathbf{N}\mathbf{y})(\mathbf{x}_1'\mathbf{N}\mathbf{x}_1) - (\mathbf{y}'\mathbf{N}\mathbf{x}_1)^2} = \frac{(n - K)r_1^2}{1 - r_1^2} \tag{3.10}$$

where the second equality sign is based on (3.7) and the third on (3.2). We then solve $t_1^2 = (n - K)r_1^2/(1 - r_1^2)$ and find that r_1 is equal to the ratio of t_1 to the square root of $t_1^2 + n - K$. More generally:

$$r_h = \frac{t_h}{\sqrt{t_h^2 + n - K}} \qquad h = 1, \ldots, K \tag{3.11}$$

Note that although (3.10) is formulated in terms of r_1^2, there is no uncertainty as to the sign of the square root in (3.11). This follows from the fact that the regression coefficient, the Student statistic, and the partial correlation coefficient all have the same sign (see the end of the previous paragraph).

The Relation Between Multiple and Partial Correlations and Incremental Contributions

The following relation follows directly from (3.1):

$$R^2 - R_{\bar{h}}^2 = r_h^2(1 - R_{\bar{h}}^2) \tag{3.12}$$

On the left is the incremental contribution of the hth explanatory variable. The equation states that this is equal to the product of two factors, both nonnegative and at most equal to 1; the first factor is the squared partial correlation of the hth variable and the dependent variable (given the $K - 1$ other variables) and the second is one minus the squared multiple correlation obtained when the hth variable is deleted. The first factor (r_h^2) implies that a large (absolute) value of the partial correlation with the dependent variable raises the incremental contribution of the hth variable. The second factor ($1 - R_{\bar{h}}^2$) states that this contribution is less when the $K - 1$ other variables account for a larger proportion of the behavior of the dependent variable, so that there is then less "room" for the hth variable.

Problems

3.1 Use Figure 4.3 to prove geometrically that the sign of the partial correlation coefficient r_h is the same as that of b_h (the hth element of the LS coefficient vector of the regression on all K variables). (*Hint.* In the figure, b_1 and r_1 are both positive, ϕ being an angle less than 90 degrees. If we multiply all observations on the first variable by some negative number, the new point X_1 is still on the line through O and P_2, but it is located to the left of the origin. Hence, b_1 changes its sign and the new ϕ is 180 degrees minus the old ϕ.)

3.2 Prove the derivations (3.4) and (3.5) as well as (3.10).

3.3 Prove $R^2 - R_{\bar{h}}^2 = (1 - R^2)t_h^2/(n - K)$.

4.4 Deviations from Means and Adjusted Correlation Coefficients[A]

Constant Terms and Deviations from Means

In equation (1.4) we defined $1 - R^2$ as $\mathbf{e}'\mathbf{e}/\mathbf{y}'\mathbf{y}$, the ratio of the second-order sample moment of the LS residuals to the second-order sample moment of the dependent variable, and both moments are moments around zero. In a considerable majority of cases, correlation coefficients are computed for regressions which contain constant terms. From an economic point of view, a constant term usually has little or no explanatory virtues. In that case something can be said in favor of the idea that eq. (1.1) should be replaced by

$$y_\alpha - \bar{y} = \sum_h b_h(x_{\alpha h} - \bar{x}_h) + e_\alpha \tag{4.1}$$

where $\bar{y}$ and $\bar{x}_h$ are averages. [There is no need to write $e_\alpha - \bar{e}$ for the residual part of (4.1) because $\bar{e} = 0$ when there is a constant term.] The constant term thus disappears, and the definition (1.4) of $1 - R^2$, if based on (4.1) rather than (1.1), is modified as follows:

$$1 - R_A^2 = \frac{\sum e_\alpha^2}{\sum (y_\alpha - \bar{y})^2} = \frac{\mathbf{e}'\mathbf{e}}{\mathbf{y}'\mathbf{A}\mathbf{y}} \qquad \text{where} \qquad \mathbf{A} = \mathbf{I} - \frac{1}{n}\boldsymbol{\iota}\boldsymbol{\iota}' \tag{4.2}$$

$\mathbf{A}$ being the idempotent matrix which was introduced in eq. (1.6) of Section 1.1 for the transformation to deviations from the mean. Note that R_A^2 is at most equal to R^2 of (1.4) because $\sum (y_\alpha - \bar{y})^2 \leq \sum y_\alpha^2$. This is the natural consequence of the fact that in (4.1) we do not recognize the constant term as a contributor to the "explanation" of the behavior of the dependent variable.

It is readily seen that if there is a constant term, the correlation results derived earlier in this chapter still apply under the new interpretation, provided we delete the constant term and measure all variables as deviations from their means. To prove this, we partition: $\mathbf{X} = [\boldsymbol{\iota} \;\; \mathbf{Z}]$, $\mathbf{b}' = [b_0 \;\; \mathbf{b}_Z']$, so that $\mathbf{y} = \mathbf{X}\mathbf{b} + \mathbf{e}$ becomes $\mathbf{y} = b_0\boldsymbol{\iota} + \mathbf{Z}\mathbf{b}_Z + \mathbf{e}$. Premultiply both sides by $\mathbf{A}$ of (4.2):

$$\begin{aligned} \mathbf{A}\mathbf{y} &= b_0\mathbf{A}\boldsymbol{\iota} + \mathbf{A}\mathbf{Z}\mathbf{b}_Z + \mathbf{A}\mathbf{e} \\ &= \mathbf{A}\mathbf{Z}\mathbf{b}_Z + \mathbf{e} \end{aligned} \tag{4.3}$$

because $\mathbf{A}\boldsymbol{\iota} = \mathbf{0}$ and $\mathbf{A}\mathbf{e} = \mathbf{e} - (1/n)\boldsymbol{\iota}\boldsymbol{\iota}'\mathbf{e} = \mathbf{e} - \bar{e}\boldsymbol{\iota} = \mathbf{e}$. Application of the R^2 definition (1.4) to $[\mathbf{A}\mathbf{y} \;\; \mathbf{A}\mathbf{Z}]$ rather than the original observation matrix $[\mathbf{y} \;\; \mathbf{X}]$ gives

$$R_A^2 = \frac{\mathbf{b}_Z'\mathbf{Z}'\mathbf{A}'\mathbf{A}\mathbf{Z}\mathbf{b}_Z}{\mathbf{y}'\mathbf{A}'\mathbf{A}\mathbf{y}} = \frac{\mathbf{b}_Z'\mathbf{Z}'\mathbf{A}\mathbf{Z}\mathbf{b}_Z}{\mathbf{y}'\mathbf{A}\mathbf{y}} \tag{4.4}$$

and the sum of this R_A^2 and $1 - R_A^2$ defined in (4.2) equals 1 as it should. This follows from

$$\mathbf{b}_Z'\mathbf{Z}'\mathbf{A}\mathbf{Z}\mathbf{b}_Z + \mathbf{e}'\mathbf{e} = (\mathbf{A}\mathbf{Z}\mathbf{b}_Z + \mathbf{e})'(\mathbf{A}\mathbf{Z}\mathbf{b}_Z + \mathbf{e}) = \mathbf{y}'\mathbf{A}\mathbf{y}$$

where the first equality sign is based on

$$\mathbf{e}'\mathbf{AZ} = \mathbf{e}'\mathbf{Z} = \mathbf{0} \tag{4.5}$$

the vector $\mathbf{e}'\mathbf{Z}$ being a subvector of $\mathbf{e}'\mathbf{X} = \mathbf{0}$.

The coefficient R_A is nothing but the simple correlation coefficient of the n pairs $(y_\alpha, \hat{y}_\alpha)$, where $\hat{y}_\alpha$ is the αth element of $\mathbf{Xb}$, the vector of the LS adjusted values corresponding to $\mathbf{y}$:

$$R_A = \frac{\sum_{\alpha=1}^{n}(y_\alpha - \bar{y})(\hat{y}_\alpha - \bar{y})}{\sqrt{\sum_{\alpha=1}^{n}(y_\alpha - \bar{y})^2 \sum_{\alpha=1}^{n}(\hat{y}_\alpha - \bar{y})^2}} \tag{4.6}$$

To prove this we note that $\mathbf{y}'\mathbf{AZb}_Z = \mathbf{b}_Z'\mathbf{Z}'\mathbf{AZb}_Z$ follows from (4.5). Hence, going back to (4.4):

$$R_A^2 = \frac{\mathbf{b}_Z'\mathbf{Z}'\mathbf{AZb}_Z}{\mathbf{y}'\mathbf{Ay}} = \frac{(\mathbf{y}'\mathbf{AZb}_Z)^2}{(\mathbf{y}'\mathbf{Ay})(\mathbf{b}_Z'\mathbf{Z}'\mathbf{AZb}_Z)}$$

On taking square roots we obtain (4.6), noting that $\hat{y}_\alpha - \bar{y}$ is the αth element of $\mathbf{AZb}_Z$. The $\hat{y}_\alpha$'s and the y_α's have the same average $\bar{y}$ because $e_\alpha = y_\alpha - \hat{y}_\alpha$, $\alpha = 1, \ldots, n$ have zero average when there is a constant term. Note further that although R_A can thus be interpreted as a simple correlation coefficient, it cannot be negative and, therefore, it is confined to the interval from zero to one rather than from minus one to plus one.

The development (4.3) to (4.5) showed that by deleting the constant term and measuring all variables as deviations from their means, we are able to obtain results for the multiple correlation coefficient which are completely analogous to the coefficient described in Section 4.1. The numerical value of the coefficient will never become larger by this modification; it usually becomes smaller. We also obtain completely analogous results for the incremental contributions of the explanatory variables (except that, obviously, there is now no such contribution of the constant-term variable). The reason is simply that these contributions are defined in terms of multiple correlation coefficients, $R^2 - R_h^2$, so that they are now of the form $R_A^2 - R_{Ah}^2$, where R_{Ah} is the multiple correlation corresponding to the regression (4.1) with $x_{\alpha h} - \bar{x}_h$ (rather than $y_\alpha - \bar{y}$) on the left and one variable deleted on the right. It will be clear that the orthogonality condition on the columns of $\mathbf{X}$ which underlies (2.6) now amounts to zero correlations of the explanatory variables in the sense

$$\sum_{\alpha=1}^{n}(x_{\alpha h} - \bar{x}_h)(x_{\alpha k} - \bar{x}_k) = 0 \quad \text{for all pairs } (h, k) \tag{4.7}$$

It will be equally clear that we also obtain completely analogous results for the partial correlation coefficients; see (3.1) and imagine that A subscripts are attached to R, R_h, and r_h.

In what follows *we shall*—unless otherwise stated—*apply correlation coefficients exclusively to regressions which contain a constant term, and these coefficients will be based on variables measured as deviations from their means.*[4] The relevant multiple correlation is thus R_A of (4.2), not R of (1.4). However, *we shall drop the A subscript to simplify the notation*, both for multiple and partial correlations and for incremental contributions. We thus write R for the R_A of (4.2) and forget about the R of (1.4). This should cause no confusion since only one type of correlation coefficient is used.

The Adjusted Multiple Correlation Coefficient

We know from Theorem 3.3 of Section 3.3 that the LS residual sum of squares has to be divided by $n - K$, not by n, in order to provide an unbiased estimator of σ^2 under the assumptions of the standard linear model. In addition, it is customary to divide $\sum (y_\alpha - \bar{y})^2$ by $n - 1$, not by n.[5] If we adopt both modifications, we obtain the adjusted multiple correlation coefficient $\bar{R}$, which is defined by

$$(4.8) \qquad 1 - \bar{R}^2 = \frac{\dfrac{1}{n-K}\displaystyle\sum_{\alpha=1}^{n} e_\alpha^2}{\dfrac{1}{n-1}\displaystyle\sum_{\alpha=1}^{n}(y_\alpha - \bar{y})^2} = \frac{n-1}{n-K}(1 - R^2)$$

[4] When the basic equation $\mathbf{y} = \mathbf{X}\boldsymbol{\beta} + \boldsymbol{\epsilon}$ of the standard linear model contains no constant term, there are two options for one minus the squared multiple correlation coefficient. One may divide $\mathbf{e}'\mathbf{e}/n$ (an estimator of the disturbance variance) either by $\mathbf{y}'\mathbf{y}/n$ (the sample second moment of the dependent variable) or by $\mathbf{y}'\mathbf{A}\mathbf{y}/n$ (the sample variance). The choice should be made dependent on whether the analyst wants to measure the performance of the regression in terms of the variance or the second moment around zero of his dependent variable. Note that the definition $1 - R^2 = \mathbf{e}'\mathbf{e}/\mathbf{y}'\mathbf{A}\mathbf{y}$ does not agree with the R^2 definition $\mathbf{b}'\mathbf{X}'\mathbf{X}\mathbf{b}/\mathbf{y}'\mathbf{A}\mathbf{y}$ nor with $R^2 = \mathbf{b}'\mathbf{X}'\mathbf{A}\mathbf{X}\mathbf{b}/\mathbf{y}'\mathbf{A}\mathbf{y}$ because $\mathbf{y}'\mathbf{y} \neq \mathbf{y}'\mathbf{A}\mathbf{y}$ in the first case and $\mathbf{e}'\mathbf{e} \neq \mathbf{e}'\mathbf{A}\mathbf{e}$ in the second (since there is no constant term). The use of $\mathbf{e}'\mathbf{A}\mathbf{e}$ is not recommended because this would eliminate a nonzero average of the residuals, and such a nonzero average should be regarded as part of the poorness of fit.

[5] This is done on the analogy of the unbiased estimator of the variance (see Problem 7.2 of Section 2.7). It will be clear, however, that there is no question of unbiasedness in this case, since the y_α's have different expectations.

or, equivalently,

$$\bar{R}^2 = R^2 - \frac{K-1}{n-K}(1 - R^2) \tag{4.9}$$

We have $\bar{R}^2 < R^2$ except when $K = 1$ or $\bar{R}^2 = 1$ (in which cases $\bar{R}^2 = R^2$). Note that $\bar{R}^2$ is not an unbiased estimator. Actually, this concept has no meaning in the present context, because a population analogue of R or $\bar{R}$ has not been defined here;[6] we use the multiple correlation coefficient simply as a descriptive measure. Nevertheless it is true that the correction (4.9) has some merit, because when the number of coefficients adjusted (K) is not very small compared with the number of observations (n), the mean square $\mathbf{e}'\mathbf{e}/n$ of the residuals tends to be on the low side and hence to give an overly optimistic picture of the performance of the explanatory variables. Further note that $\bar{R}^2$ may be negative; in that case the square root is usually not computed.

Application to the Textile Example

The procedure can now be summarized as follows. Consider a linear regression with an arbitrary number of explanatory variables plus a constant term. We have as many incremental contributions $R^2 - R_h^2$ as there are explanatory variables. Their sum is equal to R^2 if condition (4.7) is satisfied. This is usually not the case because explanatory variables normally have nonzero correlations. Therefore we shall call the discrepancy between the total contribution R^2 of these variables and their total incremental contribution, $\sum_h (R^2 - R_h^2)$, the *multicollinearity effect*. Finally, we subtract from R^2 the adjustment effect $R^2 - \bar{R}^2$ as given in (4.9) to obtain $\bar{R}^2$, which is our measure for the proportion of the variance of the dependent variable that is accounted for by the explanatory variables. The residual proportion is thus $1 - \bar{R}^2$.

[6] It is, of course, always possible to define a population analogue of R^2. Barten (1962) considered the basic equation $\mathbf{y} = \beta_0 \boldsymbol{\iota} + \mathbf{Z}\boldsymbol{\beta}_Z + \boldsymbol{\epsilon}$, where $\mathbf{Z}$ has $K - 1$ columns (K unknown coefficients, one of which is a constant term). He defined the population value of $1 - R^2$ as the ratio of σ^2 to $(1/n)\boldsymbol{\beta}_Z'\mathbf{Z}'\mathbf{A}\mathbf{Z}\boldsymbol{\beta}_Z + \sigma^2$ and proved that if the disturbances are normally distributed and if this ratio is estimated by

$$1 - \hat{R}^2 = (1 - R^2)\left[1 + \frac{K - (1 - R^2)(1 + 2R^2)}{n}\right]$$

where R on the right is R_A of (4.2), the bias is reduced to terms of the order $1/n^2$. He also provided a table which transforms R to $\hat{R}$.

We take the textile example of Section 3.3 to illustrate this procedure. Using the matrix (3.13) of that section, we obtain

$$n\sum_{\alpha=1}^{n}(y_\alpha - \bar{y})^2 = n\sum_{\alpha=1}^{n} y_\alpha^2 - \left(\sum_{\alpha=1}^{n} y_\alpha\right)^2$$

$$= 17 \times 76.65898 - (36.07631)^2$$

$$= 1.70243$$

$$n\sum_{\alpha=1}^{n}(x_{\alpha 1} - \bar{x}_1)(y_\alpha - \bar{y}) = n\sum_{\alpha=1}^{n} x_{\alpha 1}y_\alpha - \left(\sum_{\alpha=1}^{n} x_{\alpha 1}\right)\left(\sum_{\alpha=1}^{n} y_\alpha\right)$$

$$= 17 \times 72.59642 - 34.20783 \times 36.07631$$

$$= .04689$$

$$n\sum_{\alpha=1}^{n}(x_{\alpha 2} - \bar{x}_2)(y_\alpha - \bar{y}) = n\sum_{\alpha=1}^{n} x_{\alpha 2}y_\alpha - \left(\sum_{\alpha=1}^{n} x_{\alpha 2}\right)\left(\sum_{\alpha=1}^{n} y_\alpha\right)$$

$$= 17 \times 67.44192 - 31.83389 \times 36.07631$$

$$= -1.93664$$

We thus find for R^2, using (4.4) and $\mathbf{b}_Z'\mathbf{Z}'\mathbf{A}\mathbf{Z}\mathbf{b}_Z = \mathbf{b}_Z'\mathbf{Z}'\mathbf{A}\mathbf{y}$:

$$R^2 = \frac{b_1 \sum (x_{\alpha 1} - \bar{x}_1)(y_\alpha - \bar{y}) + b_2 \sum (x_{\alpha 2} - \bar{x}_2)(y_\alpha - \bar{y})}{\sum (y_\alpha - \bar{y})^2} \tag{4.10}$$

$$= \frac{1.1430 \times .04689 - .8289 \times (-1.93664)}{1.70243} = .97442$$

Using the point estimates b_1 and b_2 and their standard errors, we obtain for the squared Student statistics divided by the degrees of freedom:

$$\frac{t_h^2}{n - K} = \frac{(1.1430)^2}{14(.024324)} = 3.836 \quad \text{if} \quad h = 1 \tag{4.11}$$

$$\frac{(-.8289)^2}{14(.001304)} = 37.64 \quad \text{if} \quad h = 2$$

We multiply these two values by $1 - R^2 = .02558$ in accordance with Problem 3.3, which gives

$$R^2 - R_1^2 = .09815 \qquad R^2 - R_2^2 = .96305 \tag{4.12}$$

This shows that the incremental contribution of the logarithm of the relative textile price is almost ten times as large as that of the logarithm of real income per capita. The total incremental contribution is 1.06120, which indicates that this total may exceed 1. The multicollinearity effect is equal to

Table 4.1

Multiple Correlation and Incremental Contributions

Incremental contribution of income	$R^2 - R_1^2 =$	.098
Incremental contribution of textile price	$R^2 - R_2^2 =$	.963
Multicollinearity effect	$R^2 - \sum (R^2 - R_h^2) =$	−.087
		+
Total contribution of explanatory variables	$R^2 =$	.974
Adjustment effect	$R^2 - \bar{R}^2 =$	.004
		−
Proportion accounted for by explanatory variables	$\bar{R}^2 =$	.971

the difference between this figure and R^2, namely, −.08678, and the adjustment effect computed from (4.9) is $R^2 - \bar{R}^2 = (2/14)(.02558) = .00365$, which gives

$$\bar{R}^2 = .97076 \tag{4.13}$$

Thus, 97 percent of the variance of the dependent variable (the logarithm of textile consumption per capita) is accounted for by the two explanatory variables, and 3 percent is residual. Table 4.1 provides a convenient summary.

When Is a Multiple Correlation Coefficient Large or Small?

The evaluation of the numerical value of a multiple correlation coefficient is a matter of comparing this value with those of other coefficients obtained for similar regressions. It appears that, by and large, $\bar{R}$'s tend to be fairly close to 1 when the underlying data are characterized by a considerable degree of aggregation. In our numerical example we have aggregation over both individuals and commodities because the dependent variable covers all consumers in the Netherlands and all commodities in the important textile group. When we consider cross-section data and run a regression for textile expenditure by individual households, we should expect an $\bar{R}^2$ which is much smaller, say .5 or even less. When we run a regression for the expenditure on women's dresses by individual households, the $\bar{R}^2$ will generally be still smaller. The time period may also be important. A cross-section survey covering three months will usually produce lower $\bar{R}$'s than a survey that is carried out over a year. All these features reflect the fact that aggregation (over individuals, commodities, or time) tends to reduce the relative importance of neglected variables. Needless to say, this is not a rule without exceptions. The $\bar{R}$ of the textile example is on the high side and the adjustment effect is of minor numerical importance. This effect will be much larger when the unadjusted R^2 is smaller and when K is larger; see Problem 4.3.

Problems

4.1 Prove $\sum (\hat{y}_\alpha - \bar{y})^2 = R^2 \sum (y_\alpha - \bar{y})^2$, where the summations are over α from 1 through n.

4.2 Compute the partial correlation coefficients r_1 and r_2 for the textile example.

4.3 Find $\bar{R}^2$ for $n = 15$ and for the following combinations of K and R^2:

	$K = 2$	$K = 4$	$K = 6$
$R^2 = .9$			
$.7$			
$.5$			
$.3$			
$.1$			

4.4 Consider a variable which takes n values that are measured as deviations from their mean. Prove that this variable is never represented by a point located inside the positive orthant of the n-dimensional Euclidean space.

4.5 Some Useful Diagrams[A]

In the first three sections of this chapter we used the n-dimensional Euclidean space to describe the observation matrix $[\mathbf{y} \quad \mathbf{X}]$ geometrically. This number of dimensions corresponds to the number of rows of the matrix. An alternative geometric picture is obtained when the number of dimensions is equal to the number of columns of that matrix, $K + 1$, and when we measure each variable along one of the axes.[7] The number of points is then equal to the number of observations (n). It is easily seen that under the assumptions of the standard linear model, the n points representing the rows of $[\mathscr{E}\mathbf{y} \quad \mathbf{X}]$ are located in a K-dimensional hyperplane in this $(K + 1)$-dimensional space. The n observations are thus scattered in a random manner around this hyperplane. The LS procedure implies that we fit a K-dimensional plane through these n points in such a way that this plane contains the n points representing the rows of $[\hat{\mathbf{y}} \quad \mathbf{X}]$ where $\hat{\mathbf{y}} = \mathbf{Xb}$. It is also easily seen that when there is extreme multicollinearity, so that the rank of $\mathbf{X}$ is less than K, the points representing the rows of $[\mathscr{E}\mathbf{y} \quad \mathbf{X}]$ are located in a plane of fewer dimensions than K, and that this statement also applies to the points that represent the rows of $[\mathbf{Xz} \quad \mathbf{X}]$ for any value of the coefficient vector $\mathbf{z}$.

[7] When the equation has a constant term, so that $\mathbf{X}$ contains a column of units, the number of dimensions that are really relevant is K. This applies to the textile example ($K = 3$).

This illustrates geometrically why the parameter vector $\boldsymbol{\beta}$ cannot be estimated in the case of extreme multicollinearity.

The actual presentation of the $(K + 1)$-dimensional space is possible only when there are few variables. A substitute is a set of two-dimensional planes, one for each explanatory variable, with this variable measured along the horizontal axis and the dependent variable corrected for the effect of all other explanatory variables (as estimated by LS) along the vertical axis. If we take the hth explanatory variable, this leads to the following points:

$$\left(x_{\alpha h}, y_\alpha - \sum_{k \neq h} b_k x_{\alpha k}\right) \qquad \alpha = 1, \ldots, n$$

Such scatter diagrams are shown in Figure 4.4 for the textile example: on top for income after the price effect is eliminated from the consumption of textiles, and below for the textile price after elimination of the income effect.[8] Such scatter diagrams are very useful for visualizing the relationship analyzed and also for the analysis of nonlinearities. Figure 4.4 illustrates that in this case there is no evidence of nonlinearity. (Note that the variables have been measured as deviations from the average. Also note that the two diagrams do not have the same scales; why was this done?)

When the observations have a natural order (as in the case of successive time series observations), another useful diagram can be shown. We refer to Figure 4.5, which contains five lines, each describing the behavior of a variable over time. There are two lines on top, one for the logarithm of the observed textile consumption per capita (y_α, $\alpha = 1, \ldots, n$) and one for its computed value from the regression ($\hat{y}_\alpha$). The former variable is represented by the solid line, the latter by the dashed line. Below these two lines are the two components of the LS computed value: the logarithm of the relative price of textile goods multiplied by the estimated price elasticity (—.83) and the logarithm of real income per capita multiplied by the estimated income elasticity (1.14). The line at the bottom shows the LS residuals (the vertical distances between the two lines on top). Again note that the variables are all measured as deviations from the respective means.

Figure 4.5 is useful in several respects. First, it visualizes how closely the observed development of the dependent variable is approximated by the LS adjustment. In particular, it is worthwhile to inspect the turning points and to see whether the two top lines are similar in this respect. (In this example the agreement is satisfactory.) Second, it shows whether a particular change in a given year is the result of the behavior of one explanatory variable, or of the combined influence of several variables, or of residual effects. It shows

[8] It is frequently worthwhile to indicate for each point the year to which it refers, but this is not done here in order not to overburden the diagram.

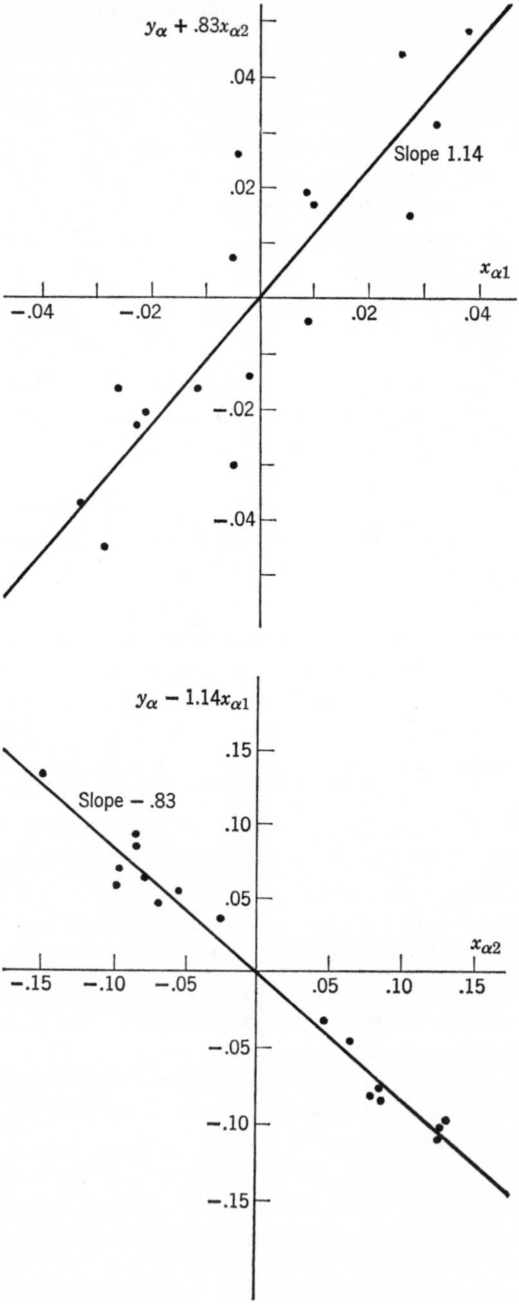

Fig. 4.4 Scatter diagrams for income and price of the textile example.

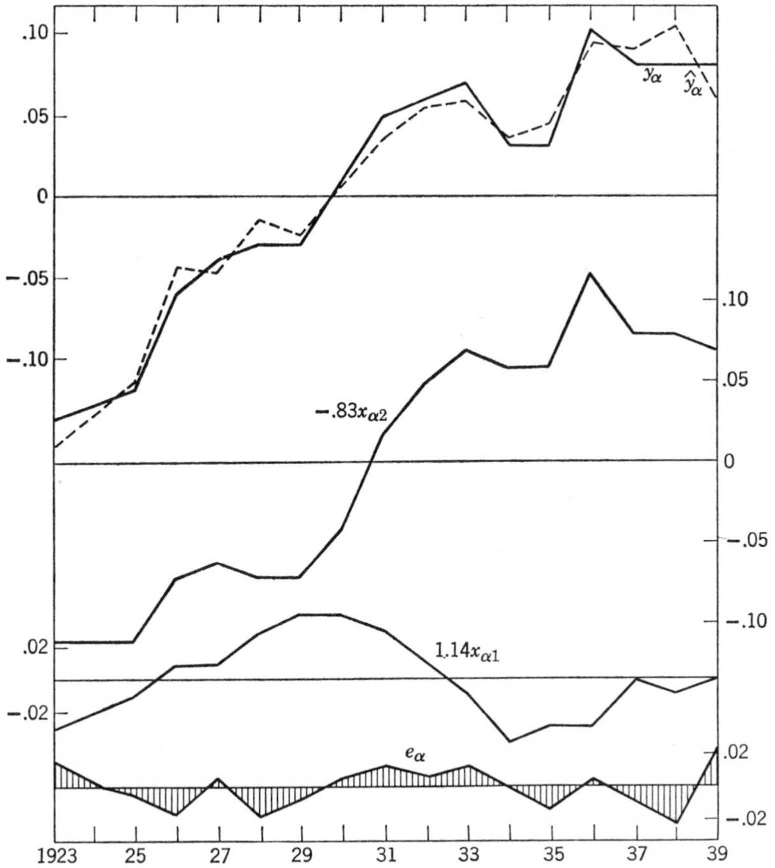

Fig. 4.5 Decomposition of the LS computed values of the dependent variable for the textile example.

also the variables that are more important. (In this case we have a dominance of the price variable over the income variable, which is in agreement with the larger incremental contribution of the former variable.) Third, the diagram allows a graphical inspection of the residuals. Are there any outliers? Does it seem realistic to assume that the disturbance variance is constant over time? Is there a large succession of residuals of the same sign that suggests that the zero covariance assumption is unrealistic? These questions will be considered from a more advanced point of view in the next chapter. In spite of the limited degree of sophistication, however, the visual advantages of such diagrams should not be underestimated.

Problems

5.1 Prove that if the scales of the two scatter diagrams of Figure 4.4 were the same, the vertical distance between each observation point and the upward sloping straight line in the diagram on the left would be equal to the vertical distance between some observation point and the downward sloping straight line on the right.

5.2 Suppose that we have a cross-section regression in which the observations are on U.S. cities rather than time series observations. Is it advisable to construct a diagram similar to Figure 4.5?

4.6 Multiple Correlation and Analysis of Variance[B]

Although R^2 has been introduced as a descriptive measure, it can be used for hypothesis testing in the framework of the standard linear model. The procedure is usually discussed from an analysis-of-variance point of view. Actually, it is a very special case of the test described in Theorem 3.9 of Section 3.7, and the only reason for its discussion here is to point out the relation between R^2 and the analysis of variance.

Consider the equation

$$y_\alpha = \beta_1 + \beta_2 x_{\alpha 2} + \cdots + \beta_K x_{\alpha K} \qquad \alpha = 1, \ldots, n \tag{6.1}$$

which contains K unknown parameters, one of which is a constant term. The problem is to test the null hypothesis H_0 that all multiplicative coefficients vanish. If it is true, all $K - 1$ explanatory variables are superfluous for this particular dependent variable, since the values of that variable then fluctuate randomly around the expectation β_1.

The standard linear model is applied with the additional specification of normality. If H_0 is true, then $\beta_2 = \cdots = \beta_K = 0$ and the constrained LS estimator of β_1 is obviously $\bar{y}$, the mean of the y_α's, so that the constrained LS estimator of the complete vector $\boldsymbol{\beta}$ is $\mathbf{b}^* = \bar{y}\mathbf{i}_1$, where $\mathbf{i}_1$ is the first column of the $K \times K$ unit matrix. We go back to the test statistic (7.23) of Theorem 3.9 in Section 3.7, to be written in the form

$$\frac{1}{qs^2}(\mathbf{b} - \mathbf{b}^*)'\mathbf{X}'\mathbf{X}(\mathbf{b} - \mathbf{b}^*) \tag{6.2}$$

which is distributed as $F(q, n - K)$ if H_0 is true, q being equal to $K - 1$ in this case. We conclude from $\mathbf{b}^* = \bar{y}\mathbf{i}_1$ that $\mathbf{X}\mathbf{b}^* = \bar{y}\mathbf{X}\mathbf{i}_1 = \bar{y}\boldsymbol{\iota}$ (the first column of $\mathbf{X}$ multiplied by the scalar $\bar{y}$). If we write $\hat{\mathbf{y}}$ for $\mathbf{Xb}$, we thus have

Table 4.2

Analysis of Variance

Source of Variation	Sum of Squares	Degrees of Freedom	Mean Square
Income and price[a]	$R^2 \sum (y_\alpha - \bar{y})^2 = .0972$	$K - 1 = 2$	.0486
Residual	$(1 - R^2) \sum (y_\alpha - \bar{y})^2 = .0029$	$n - K = 14$	.0002
Total	$\sum (y_\alpha - \bar{y})^2 = .1001$	$n - 1 = 16$	

[a] Logarithm of real income per capita and the logarithm of the relative price of textile goods.

$\mathbf{X}(\mathbf{b} - \mathbf{b}^*) = \hat{\mathbf{y}} - \bar{y}\boldsymbol{\iota}$, which is the vector of LS adjusted values corresponding to $\mathbf{y}$ measured as deviations from the mean. The test statistic (6.2) is nothing but the squared length of this vector divided by qs^2. This squared length is $\sum (\hat{y}_\alpha - \bar{y})^2 = R^2 \sum (y_\alpha - \bar{y})^2$, the equality sign being based on Problem 4.1. Since we have

$$s^2 = \frac{1}{n-K} \sum_{\alpha=1}^{n} e_\alpha^2 = \frac{1-R^2}{n-K} \sum_{\alpha=1}^{n} (y_\alpha - \bar{y})^2$$

we thus find after substituting $K - 1$ for q that the test statistic (6.2) in this case is

$$\frac{(n-K)R^2}{(K-1)(1-R^2)} \tag{6.3}$$

and that its distribution is $F(K - 1, n - K)$ if H_0 is true. Table 4.2 shows the result for the textile example in the form of an analysis-of-variance table. The F ratio is larger than 200, which is significant by any standard for 2 and 14 degrees of freedom. Given the results obtained earlier for this example, this should cause no surprise.

4.7 Regression and Correlation in the Multivariate Normal Model[B]

There exists a model, quite different from the standard linear model, in which correlations play a much more statistical than descriptive role. This is the multivariate normal model. Its applicability to economic problems is limited, however, and we shall therefore consider it only briefly. More details can be found in Chapter 10 of GRAYBILL (1961).

The Multivariate Normal Model

Imagine that the n rows of the matrix $[\mathbf{y} \quad \mathbf{X}]$ are independent random drawings from a $(K + 1)$-dimensional normal population with mean vector $[\mu_0 \quad \boldsymbol{\mu}']$ and covariance matrix

$$\begin{bmatrix} \sigma_{00} & \boldsymbol{\sigma}' \\ \boldsymbol{\sigma} & \boldsymbol{\Sigma} \end{bmatrix} \tag{7.1}$$

where μ_0 and σ_{00} are scalars (the mean and the variance of y_α for each α), while $\boldsymbol{\mu}$ and $\boldsymbol{\sigma}$ are K-element vectors and $\boldsymbol{\Sigma}$ is a $K \times K$ matrix. Obviously, $\boldsymbol{\mu}'$ and $\boldsymbol{\Sigma}$ are the mean vector and the covariance matrix of $[x_{\alpha 1} \quad \cdots \quad x_{\alpha K}]$ for each α, and $\boldsymbol{\sigma}'$ contains the covariances of each element of this vector and y_α. It is assumed that the elements of $[y_\alpha \quad x_{\alpha 1} \quad \cdots \quad x_{\alpha K}]$ are not linearly dependent, so that the covariance matrix (7.1) and its submatrix $\boldsymbol{\Sigma}$ are nonsingular.

To show how this model differs from the standard linear model, we consider the textile example with its three variables: the logarithms of textile consumption, of income, and of the textile price. In the standard linear model the first variable is dependent, the other two are explanatory; hence, there are two different kinds of variables. The present assumption, on the other hand, treats all variables symmetrically. (It is true that the notation is not symmetric, but this is a deliberate choice in view of the later derivations.) If we have symmetry, the philosophy of partial correlation is directly applicable.[9] However, note how unrealistic this assumption is for the textile case. There is no valid reason for assuming that the values taken by the logarithm of real income per capita and those taken by the logarithm of the relative price of textile goods follow the normal distribution. Also, it is unrealistic to assume that these values are independent over time. Sometimes a situation exists in which the assumption is satisfied more closely, but this is rather exceptional. Suppose, for example, that the logarithms of consumption and income of family households follow a bivariate normal distribution. If we then draw a random sample from this population, we have a case which satisfies our new assumption.[10]

A Conditional Distribution

Consider the conditional density function of y_α given $x_{\alpha 1}, \ldots, x_{\alpha K}$. This is found by dividing the density function of the joint distribution of all

[9] See the first paragraph of Section 4.3, particularly footnote 3 on p. 171.

[10] But note that the distribution can only be approximately normal because the population of families is finite.

$K + 1$ variates by the marginal density function of the last K variates. The $(K + 1)$-dimensional density function is of the form

$$\text{(7.2)} \qquad \text{constant} \times \exp\left\{-\frac{1}{2}\begin{bmatrix} u_0 - \mu_0 \\ \mathbf{u} - \boldsymbol{\mu} \end{bmatrix}'\begin{bmatrix} \sigma_{00} & \boldsymbol{\sigma}' \\ \boldsymbol{\sigma} & \boldsymbol{\Sigma} \end{bmatrix}^{-1}\begin{bmatrix} u_0 - \mu_0 \\ \mathbf{u} - \boldsymbol{\mu} \end{bmatrix}\right\}$$

and the K-dimensional density function:

$$\text{(7.3)} \qquad \text{constant} \times \exp\left\{-\frac{1}{2}(\mathbf{u} - \boldsymbol{\mu})'\boldsymbol{\Sigma}^{-1}(\mathbf{u} - \boldsymbol{\mu})\right\}$$

where u_0 is a scalar and $\mathbf{u}$ a K-element vector. Using the partitioned inverse of eq. (2.15) of Section 1.2, we find for the inverse in the exponent of (7.2):

$$\text{(7.4)} \qquad \frac{1}{\sigma_{00} - \boldsymbol{\sigma}'\boldsymbol{\Sigma}^{-1}\boldsymbol{\sigma}}\begin{bmatrix} 1 & -\boldsymbol{\sigma}'\boldsymbol{\Sigma}^{-1} \\ -\boldsymbol{\Sigma}^{-1}\boldsymbol{\sigma} & (\sigma_{00} - \boldsymbol{\sigma}'\boldsymbol{\Sigma}^{-1}\boldsymbol{\sigma})\boldsymbol{\Sigma}^{-1} + \boldsymbol{\Sigma}^{-1}\boldsymbol{\sigma}\boldsymbol{\sigma}'\boldsymbol{\Sigma}^{-1} \end{bmatrix}$$

so that the expression in braces of (7.2) can be written as a multiple $-\frac{1}{2}$ of

$$\frac{(u_0 - \mu_0)^2 - 2(u_0 - \mu_0)\boldsymbol{\sigma}'\boldsymbol{\Sigma}^{-1}(\mathbf{u} - \boldsymbol{\mu}) + [\boldsymbol{\sigma}'\boldsymbol{\Sigma}^{-1}(\mathbf{u} - \boldsymbol{\mu})]^2}{\sigma_{00} - \boldsymbol{\sigma}'\boldsymbol{\Sigma}^{-1}\boldsymbol{\sigma}}$$

$$+ (\mathbf{u} - \boldsymbol{\mu})'\boldsymbol{\Sigma}^{-1}(\mathbf{u} - \boldsymbol{\mu}) = \frac{[u_0 - \mu_0 - \boldsymbol{\sigma}'\boldsymbol{\Sigma}^{-1}(\mathbf{u} - \boldsymbol{\mu})]^2}{\sigma_{00} - \boldsymbol{\sigma}'\boldsymbol{\Sigma}^{-1}\boldsymbol{\sigma}} + (\mathbf{u} - \boldsymbol{\mu})'\boldsymbol{\Sigma}^{-1}(\mathbf{u} - \boldsymbol{\mu})$$

To obtain the ratio of (7.2) to (7.3) we simply subtract the expressions in braces. This gives

$$\text{(7.5)} \qquad \text{constant} \times \exp\left\{-\frac{1}{2}\frac{[u_0 - \mu_0 - \boldsymbol{\sigma}'\boldsymbol{\Sigma}^{-1}(\mathbf{u} - \boldsymbol{\mu})]^2}{\sigma_{00} - \boldsymbol{\sigma}'\boldsymbol{\Sigma}^{-1}\boldsymbol{\sigma}}\right\}$$

which is the density function of the univariate normal distribution whose mean and variance are $\mu_0 + \boldsymbol{\sigma}'\boldsymbol{\Sigma}^{-1}(\mathbf{u} - \boldsymbol{\mu})$ and $\sigma_{00} - \boldsymbol{\sigma}'\boldsymbol{\Sigma}^{-1}\boldsymbol{\sigma}$, respectively.

We have thus proved that if $[y_\alpha \;\; x_{\alpha 1} \;\; \cdots \;\; x_{\alpha K}]$ follows a $(K + 1)$-variate normal distribution with mean vector $[\mu_0 \;\; \boldsymbol{\mu}']$ and covariance matrix (7.1), the conditional distribution of y_α given $x_{\alpha 1}, \ldots, x_{\alpha K}$ is normal with mean

$$\text{(7.6)} \qquad \mathscr{E}(y_\alpha \mid x_{\alpha 1}, \ldots, x_{\alpha K}) = \mu_0 + \boldsymbol{\sigma}'\boldsymbol{\Sigma}^{-1}\begin{bmatrix} x_{\alpha 1} - \mu_1 \\ \cdot \\ \cdot \\ \cdot \\ x_{\alpha K} - \mu_K \end{bmatrix}$$

and variance

$$\text{(7.7)} \qquad \operatorname{var}(y_\alpha \mid x_{\alpha 1}, \ldots, x_{\alpha K}) = \sigma_{00} - \boldsymbol{\sigma}'\boldsymbol{\Sigma}^{-1}\boldsymbol{\sigma}$$

where $\mu_1, \ldots, \mu_K$ are the successive elements of $\boldsymbol{\mu}$. Equation (7.6) shows that the conditional expectation of y_α given $x_{\alpha 1}, \ldots, x_{\alpha K}$ is linear in the conditioning factors, which is analogous to Assumption 3.1 of the standard linear model (Section 3.2). Returning to the example of a bivariate normal distribution of the logarithms of income and consumption, we may conclude from this result that the expectation of the logarithm of consumption, given income, is a linear function of the logarithm of income. Since the assumption of bivariate normality is symmetric in the two variables, it is also true that the expectation of the logarithm of income, given consumption, is a linear function of the logarithm of consumption. One may dislike the latter statement from an economic point of view, but both statements are statistically valid because of the symmetry.

Equation (7.7) shows that the conditional variance of y_α, given $x_{\alpha 1}, \ldots, x_{\alpha K}$, is independent of α. Hence the homoscedasticity condition is satisfied by the conditional distribution. The same holds for the independence condition of the n random variables

$$(7.8) \qquad y_1 - \mathscr{E}(y_1 \mid x_{11}, \ldots, x_{1K}), \ldots, y_n - \mathscr{E}(y_n \mid x_{n1}, \ldots, x_{nK})$$

because the rows of $[\mathbf{y} \quad \mathbf{X}]$ are independent by assumption. This obviously implies that the random variables (7.8) are uncorrelated, which in conjunction with the homoscedasticity corresponds to Assumption 3.2 of the standard linear model. The appropriate conditional interpretation of the multivariate normal assumption thus leads to results which are quite close to the standard linear model.

The Multiple Correlation Coefficient in the Multinormal Model

The conditional variance $\sigma_{00} - \boldsymbol{\sigma}'\boldsymbol{\Sigma}^{-1}\boldsymbol{\sigma}$ of (7.7) has a considerable similarity to

$$(7.9) \qquad \frac{1}{n}[\mathbf{y}'\mathbf{A}\mathbf{y} - \mathbf{y}'\mathbf{A}\mathbf{X}(\mathbf{X}'\mathbf{A}\mathbf{X})^{-1}\mathbf{X}'\mathbf{A}\mathbf{y}] = (1 - R^2)\frac{1}{n}\sum_{\alpha=1}^{n}(y_\alpha - \bar{y})^2$$

where $\mathbf{A} = \mathbf{I} - (1/n)\boldsymbol{\iota}\boldsymbol{\iota}'$ is the transformation matrix for deviations from means. The reason is that $(1/n)\mathbf{y}'\mathbf{A}\mathbf{y}$ is the sample variance of the dependent variable, which corresponds to $\sigma_{00} = \text{var } y_\alpha$ of the present model, and that $(1/n)\mathbf{y}'\mathbf{A}\mathbf{X}$ contains the sample covariances of the dependent variable and the explanatory variables and hence corresponds to $\boldsymbol{\sigma}'$, and so on.[11]

[11] Note that we have K explanatory variables here, none of which is a constant-term variable, and that the use of the matrix $\mathbf{A}$ implies deviations from means throughout. This is in accordance with the fact that in (7.6) the x's are written as deviations from the corresponding μ's. [By subtracting μ_0 from both sides of (7.6) we also find that the conditional expectation of y_α is written as a deviation from the (unconditional) expectation μ_0.]

Thus the population analogue of (7.9) is $\sigma_{00} - \boldsymbol{\sigma}'\boldsymbol{\Sigma}^{-1}\boldsymbol{\sigma} = (1 - \mathrm{P}^2)\sigma_{00}$, where P (Greek rho) is the population coefficient of multiple correlation in the framework of the multivariate normal model. This gives

$$(7.10) \qquad 1 - \mathrm{P}^2 = \frac{\sigma_{00} - \boldsymbol{\sigma}'\boldsymbol{\Sigma}^{-1}\boldsymbol{\sigma}}{\sigma_{00}} \quad \text{or} \quad \mathrm{P}^2 = \frac{\boldsymbol{\sigma}'\boldsymbol{\Sigma}^{-1}\boldsymbol{\sigma}}{\sigma_{00}}$$

This P (the nonnegative square root of P^2) refers to the conditional distribution of y_α given $x_{\alpha 1}, \ldots, x_{\alpha K}$. In principle we can select any of the $K + 1$ variates and take the other K as a conditioning factor, which leads to as many as $K + 1$ population multiple correlation coefficients. However, this P corresponds to the R discussed in this chapter and, therefore, we shall confine ourselves to this particular one.

Within the framework of the multivariate normal model we may regard R^2 as an estimator of P^2. It was shown by WISHART (1931) that the expectation of the estimator can be approximated by

$$(7.11) \qquad \mathscr{E}R^2 \approx \mathrm{P}^2 + \frac{1}{n}(1 - \mathrm{P}^2)(K - 2\mathrm{P}^2)$$

where terms of order $1/n^2$ are neglected, and the variance by

$$(7.12) \qquad \operatorname{var} R^2 \approx \frac{n - K - 1}{n^2}(1 - \mathrm{P}^2)^2\left(4\mathrm{P}^2 \frac{n - K - 1}{n + 3} + \frac{2K}{n}\right)$$

where terms of order $1/n^3$ are neglected.[12] The expectation (7.11) implies $\mathscr{E}R^2 \approx K/n$ when y_α is uncorrelated with $x_{\alpha 1}, \ldots, x_{\alpha K}$ (i.e., when $\boldsymbol{\sigma} = \mathbf{0}$ and, hence, $\mathrm{P} = 0$). This result is intuitively understandable, since the LS minimization of $\sum e_\alpha^2$ is equivalent to the maximization of R^2, and a larger R^2 can be expected on the average when the number K of coefficients adjusted is larger. (This is basically the same as the bias of $\mathbf{e}'\mathbf{e}$ with respect to $n\sigma^2$.) Equation (7.12) indicates that the variance of R^2 is approximately equal to $4\mathrm{P}^2(1 - \mathrm{P}^2)^2/n$ when $\mathrm{P} > 0$ and to $2K/n^2$ when $\mathrm{P} = 0$. In the case $\mathrm{P} = 0$ the variance of R^2 is thus of the order of $1/n^2$, which is rather exceptional. We shall consider such order terms in more detail in Sections 8.1 to 8.3.

Problems

7.1 Since the multivariate normal model is symmetric in all variables, it is possible to run two different LS regressions in the two-variable case ($K = 1$): $y_\alpha = b_0 + bx_\alpha + e_\alpha$ and $x_\alpha = b_0' + b'y_\alpha + e_\alpha'$. Prove that these

[12] Note that these are the mean and the variance of the *unconditional* distribution of R^2, the x's being allowed to vary.

regressions are equivalent if and only if all observations (x_α, y_α) are located on a straight line in the x, y-plane. Also, prove that this can happen for $n > 2$ only with zero probability when the covariance matrix (7.1) is nonsingular.

7.2 Generalize eqs. (7.6) and (7.7) for the case in which there is an $n \times L$ matrix $\mathbf{Y}$ rather than a vector $\mathbf{y}$.

7.3 Consider three random variables X_1, X_2, X_3, and their correlation coefficients ρ_{12} (of X_1 and X_2), ρ_{13}, and ρ_{23}. Prove that ρ_{23} cannot lie outside the interval

$$\rho_{12}\rho_{13} \pm \sqrt{1 - \rho_{12}^2 - \rho_{13}^2 + \rho_{12}^2\rho_{13}^2} \tag{7.13}$$

[*Hint.* Write $\rho_{ii} = 1$ and consider the 3×3 matrix $[\rho_{ij}]$; what kind of matrix is this?] Use this result to prove that if X_1 is uncorrelated with X_2 and with X_3, no inference can be drawn from that fact as to the correlation of X_2 and X_3.

CHAPTER 5

THE STATISTICAL ANALYSIS OF DISTURBANCES

It was mentioned in Section 3.9 in the discussion under (8) and (9) that one should sometimes doubt the validity of Assumption 3.2 of Section 3.2 on the scalar covariance matrix, $\mathscr{V}(\boldsymbol{\epsilon}) = \sigma^2\mathbf{I}$. Therefore one will want to test whether this assumption is indeed acceptable. A major difficulty in this respect is the fact that $\boldsymbol{\epsilon}$ is not observable. The present chapter is devoted to the analysis and solution of this problem; as a by-product we shall also obtain a test against nonlinearity. It will be assumed throughout that the assumptions of the standard linear model are satisfied except that, obviously, Assumption 3.2 will sometimes play the role of a null hypothesis.

Section 5.1 is recommended for an introductory econometrics course; the material treated in the remainder of this chapter is mathematically more advanced.

5.1 The Least-Squares Residual Vector[A]

A rather natural substitute for the disturbance vector $\boldsymbol{\epsilon} = \mathbf{y} - \mathbf{X}\boldsymbol{\beta}$ is the LS residual vector

(1.1)
$$\mathbf{e} = \mathbf{y} - \mathbf{Xb} = \mathbf{My} \quad \text{where} \quad \mathbf{M} = \mathbf{I} - \mathbf{X}(\mathbf{X}'\mathbf{X})^{-1}\mathbf{X}'$$

This vector is easily computed and, indeed, it is a sound practice to compute it, since it enables the analyst to see whether he has overlooked some important determining factors. For example, let industrial output be the dependent variable of a production function and suppose that there was a strike in year α which reduced this output. This may be revealed by a large negative value of e_α, so that the analyst may then decide to introduce a dummy variable (equal to 1 in year α, 0 in all other years) for the effect of the strike on industrial output.[1]

The Best Linear Unbiasedness of the LS Residual Vector

The LS vector $\mathbf{e} = \mathbf{My} = \mathbf{M}(\mathbf{X}\boldsymbol{\beta} + \boldsymbol{\epsilon})$ can be written in the form $\mathbf{M}\boldsymbol{\epsilon}$ because $\mathbf{MX} = \mathbf{0}$ [see eq. (7.22) of Section 1.7].[2] If we use $\mathbf{e}$ to approximate the disturbance vector $\boldsymbol{\epsilon}$, the approximation error is the *LS error vector* $\mathbf{e} - \boldsymbol{\epsilon} = (\mathbf{M} - \mathbf{I})\boldsymbol{\epsilon}$. Notice that this approximation procedure is analogous to the prediction method described in Section 3.4. In both cases the analyst is interested in a random vector ($\mathbf{y}_*$ in Section 3.4, $\boldsymbol{\epsilon}$ here) and he uses another random vector ($\mathbf{X}_*\mathbf{b}$ or $\mathbf{e}$) as an approximation. We shall use this analogy by defining unbiasedness of a residual vector in the sense of a zero expectation of the error vector of the residual vector. (Recall that in the prediction case unbiasedness is defined as the case of zero expectation of the prediction error.) Equivalently, a residual vector is unbiased when its expectation is equal to the expectation of the corresponding vector of disturbances, namely, zero. It is readily seen that the LS residual vector is unbiased because $\mathscr{E}(\boldsymbol{\epsilon} - \mathbf{e}) = (\mathbf{M} - \mathbf{I})\mathscr{E}\boldsymbol{\epsilon} = \mathbf{0}$.

The vector $\mathbf{e} = \mathbf{My}$ is obviously linear in $\mathbf{y}$, so that $\mathbf{e}$ is a member of the class of linear unbiased residual vectors. The theorem which follows is a Gauss-Markov type theorem which declares $\mathbf{e}$ to be "best" in this class.

[1] Obviously, within the framework of the standard linear model it is preferable to take the strike immediately into account, because if we make the regression specification dependent on the results of a preliminary regression (without dummy), we face the difficulties described in Section 3.9 under (2). An alternative approach is to define the explanatory variables of the production function so that they handle the effect of the strike directly. This can be done by defining labor input as the number of man-hours actually worked and capital input as the capacity utilized (not including the unused capacity during the time of the strike).

[2] Note that $\mathbf{e} = \mathbf{M}\boldsymbol{\epsilon}$ implies that particular linear combinations of the disturbances are observable (in the sense that the realizations of these combinations are observable). It is true—see the opening paragraph of this chapter—that the complete vector $\boldsymbol{\epsilon}$ is not observable, but any linear combination $\mathbf{k}'\boldsymbol{\epsilon}$ is observable if $\mathbf{k}$ satisfies $\mathbf{k}'\mathbf{X} = \mathbf{0}$, because $\mathbf{k}'\mathbf{y} = \mathbf{k}'\boldsymbol{\epsilon}$ under that condition. In fact, the BLUS residuals discussed in Section 5.2 and later are $n - K$ such linear combinations chosen according to a certain optimality criterion.

THEOREM 5.1 (Best linear unbiasedness of the LS residual vector) *If Assumption* 3.3 *of Section* 3.2 *is true for given* $\mathbf{X}$, *the LS residual vector* $\mathbf{e}$ *defined in* (1.1) *is best linear unbiased in the following sense. The error vector of any other residual vector which is also linear in the vector* $\mathbf{y}$ *and unbiased (in the sense that its error vector has zero expectation) has a covariance matrix which exceeds that of* $\mathbf{e} - \boldsymbol{\epsilon}$ *by a positive semidefinite matrix. The latter covariance matrix is*

$$\mathscr{V}(\mathbf{e} - \boldsymbol{\epsilon}) = \sigma^2(\mathbf{I} - \mathbf{M}) \tag{1.2}$$

where $\mathbf{M}$ *is defined in* (1.1).

To prove the theorem we note that any linear residual vector can be written as $\mathbf{B}^*\mathbf{y}$, where $\mathbf{B}^*$ is an $n \times n$ matrix of constant elements. We define $\mathbf{B} = \mathbf{B}^* - \mathbf{M}$, so that the residual vector becomes

$$(\mathbf{B} + \mathbf{M})\mathbf{y} = (\mathbf{B} + \mathbf{M})(\mathbf{X}\boldsymbol{\beta} + \boldsymbol{\epsilon}) = \mathbf{B}\mathbf{X}\boldsymbol{\beta} + (\mathbf{B} + \mathbf{M})\boldsymbol{\epsilon} \qquad \text{(using } \mathbf{M}\mathbf{X} = \mathbf{0}\text{)}$$

The error of this residual vector is thus $\mathbf{B}\mathbf{X}\boldsymbol{\beta} + (\mathbf{B} + \mathbf{M} - \mathbf{I})\boldsymbol{\epsilon}$. In order that this vector have zero expectation whatever $\boldsymbol{\beta}$ may be, we should impose

$$\mathbf{B}\mathbf{X} = \mathbf{0} \tag{1.3}$$

so that the error vector becomes $(\mathbf{B} + \mathbf{M} - \mathbf{I})\boldsymbol{\epsilon}$. Its covariance matrix is

$$\begin{aligned}
(\mathbf{B} + \mathbf{M} - \mathbf{I})&\mathscr{E}(\boldsymbol{\epsilon}\boldsymbol{\epsilon}')(\mathbf{B} + \mathbf{M} - \mathbf{I})' \\
&= \sigma^2(\mathbf{B} + \mathbf{M} - \mathbf{I})(\mathbf{B} + \mathbf{M} - \mathbf{I})' \\
&= \sigma^2[\mathbf{B} - \mathbf{X}(\mathbf{X}'\mathbf{X})^{-1}\mathbf{X}'][\mathbf{B} - \mathbf{X}(\mathbf{X}'\mathbf{X})^{-1}\mathbf{X}']' \\
&= \sigma^2\mathbf{B}\mathbf{B}' + \sigma^2\mathbf{X}(\mathbf{X}'\mathbf{X})^{-1}\mathbf{X}' \\
&= \sigma^2\mathbf{B}\mathbf{B}' + \sigma^2(\mathbf{I} - \mathbf{M})
\end{aligned} \tag{1.4}$$

which proves the theorem. The second and fourth equality signs are based on (1.1), the third on (1.3).

It goes without saying that the corollaries formulated in Section 3.4 apply to the LS residual vector $\mathbf{e}$. Within the class of linear unbiased residual vectors, $\mathbf{w}'(\mathbf{e} - \boldsymbol{\epsilon})$ has the smallest variance, where $\mathbf{w}$ is any n-element vector of constant elements, and the quadratic form $(\mathbf{e} - \boldsymbol{\epsilon})'\mathbf{Q}(\mathbf{e} - \boldsymbol{\epsilon})$ has the smallest expectation for any $n \times n$ positive semidefinite $\mathbf{Q}$.

The Nonscalar Covariance Matrix of the LS Residual Vector

Despite its optimal property it is nevertheless true that the use of the LS residual vector for testing purposes is hampered by serious difficulties. This is owing to the fact that under the conditions of the standard linear model this vector does not have a scalar covariance matrix of the form $\sigma^2\mathbf{I}$.

THEOREM 5.2 (Nonscalar covariance matrix of the LS residual vector) *If Assumption* 3.3 *of Section* 3.2 *is true for given* $\mathbf{X}$, *the covariance matrix of the LS residual vector is*

$$\mathscr{V}(\mathbf{e}) = \sigma^2\mathbf{M} \tag{1.5}$$

which is a scalar matrix if and only if $n = K$, *in which case* $\mathbf{e} = \mathbf{0}$ *holds trivially with unit probability.*

The covariance matrix (1.5) follows directly from $\mathbf{e} = \mathbf{M}\boldsymbol{\epsilon}$ because $\mathscr{E}(\mathbf{ee}') = \mathbf{M}\mathscr{E}(\boldsymbol{\epsilon\epsilon}')\mathbf{M}' = \sigma^2\mathbf{MM}' = \sigma^2\mathbf{M}$. If $n = K$, the matrix $\mathbf{X}$ is square and, hence,

$$\mathbf{M} = \mathbf{I} - \mathbf{X}(\mathbf{X}'\mathbf{X})^{-1}\mathbf{X}' = \mathbf{I} - \mathbf{X}\mathbf{X}^{-1}(\mathbf{X}')^{-1}\mathbf{X}' = \mathbf{0}$$

This implies $\mathscr{V}(\mathbf{e}) = \mathbf{0}$, which proves the "if" part of the theorem, the square zero matrix being a scalar matrix. To prove the "only if" part we take as given that $\mathbf{M}$ is a scalar matrix, so that the rank of $\mathbf{M}$ is either 0 or n (depending on whether the scalar on the diagonal is zero or nonzero). But we know that the rank of $\mathbf{M}$ is $n - K$ and, hence, since $K > 0$, the only possibility is $n - K = 0$ or $n = K$, which completes the proof. It will be clear that the case $n = K$ (as many observations as $\boldsymbol{\beta}$ elements to be estimated) is not particularly interesting. We shall disregard this case implicitly when speaking about the nonscalar character of the covariance matrix of the LS residual vector.

We conclude from Theorem 5.2 that homoscedastic and uncorrelated disturbances do not at all guarantee that the LS residuals are homoscedastic and uncorrelated. This has serious implications for the possibility of testing properties of the distribution of the disturbance vector because test statistics based on t, χ^2, or F distributions do not in general have such distributions when they are formulated in terms of correlated random variables with different variances. In the remainder of this section we describe some tests based on LS residuals which avoid these difficulties. However, it will appear that a price must be paid to accomplish this.

A Test against Heteroscedasticity

Consider a time series regression whose disturbances are to be tested against the hypothesis that their variances are not constant but either increase or decrease over time. This is illustrated for 12 successive observations in Figure 5.1, which measures time along the horizontal axis and the squared disturbance along the vertical axis. In this case there is some evidence of an increasing variance. If the disturbances were indeed observable, one

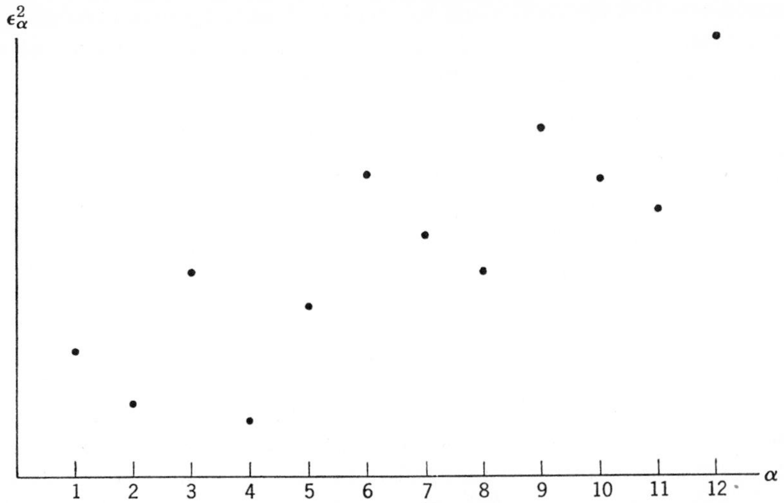

Fig. 5.1 A case of increasing variance of the disturbances.

could test the significance of this increase by means of the ratio

$$\frac{\epsilon_1^2 + \cdots + \epsilon_6^2}{\epsilon_7^2 + \cdots + \epsilon_{12}^2} \tag{1.6}$$

which is distributed as $F(6, 6)$ under the condition that the ϵ's are independently and normally distributed with zero mean and the same variance. The ratio (1.6) should take a sufficiently small value for the increase in the variance to be significant.

In actual fact, of course, we cannot observe the ϵ's, and it is then tempting to replace them by LS residuals. This leads to a second ratio:

$$\frac{e_1^2 + \cdots + e_6^2}{e_7^2 + \cdots + e_{12}^2} \tag{1.7}$$

The LS residuals are correlated, however, so that the numerator of (1.7) is not independent of the denominator. Therefore it is not permissible to conclude that the new ratio has an F distribution under the null hypothesis.

Goldfeld and Quandt (1965) proposed a ratio whose numerator and denominator are forced to be independent because they are derived separately.[3] Specifically, write the basic equation $\mathbf{y} = \mathbf{X}\boldsymbol{\beta} + \boldsymbol{\epsilon}$ for our 12 observations in partitioned form:

$$\begin{bmatrix} \mathbf{y}_A \\ \mathbf{y}_B \end{bmatrix} = \begin{bmatrix} \mathbf{X}_A \\ \mathbf{X}_B \end{bmatrix} \boldsymbol{\beta} + \begin{bmatrix} \boldsymbol{\epsilon}_A \\ \boldsymbol{\epsilon}_B \end{bmatrix} \tag{1.8}$$

[3] Also see Glejser (1969) for tests involving absolute values of the LS residuals.

in such a way that the vectors and matrices with subscript A refer to the first six observations and those with B subscripts to the last six. Then compute LS residuals for both sets of observations separately:

$$(1.9)\quad \begin{aligned} \mathbf{e}_A &= \mathbf{M}_A\mathbf{y}_A = \mathbf{M}_A\boldsymbol{\epsilon}_A \qquad \text{where} \qquad \mathbf{M}_A = \mathbf{I} - \mathbf{X}_A(\mathbf{X}_A'\mathbf{X}_A)^{-1}\mathbf{X}_A' \\ \mathbf{e}_B &= \mathbf{M}_B\mathbf{y}_B = \mathbf{M}_B\boldsymbol{\epsilon}_B \qquad \text{where} \qquad \mathbf{M}_B = \mathbf{I} - \mathbf{X}_B(\mathbf{X}_B'\mathbf{X}_B)^{-1}\mathbf{X}_B' \end{aligned}$$

The residual sums of squares $\mathbf{e}_A'\mathbf{e}_A$ and $\mathbf{e}_B'\mathbf{e}_B$ are independent, and both are distributed as $\sigma^2\chi^2(6 - K)$ when $\epsilon_1/\sigma, \ldots, \epsilon_{12}/\sigma$ are independent standardized normal variates.[4] Hence, their ratio:

$$(1.10)\qquad \frac{\mathbf{e}_A'\mathbf{e}_A}{\mathbf{e}_B'\mathbf{e}_B} = \frac{\mathbf{y}_A'\mathbf{M}_A\mathbf{y}_A}{\mathbf{y}_B'\mathbf{M}_B\mathbf{y}_B}$$

is distributed as $F(6 - K, 6 - K)$ under the null hypothesis. More generally, when we have n observations and when n is even,[5] the partitioning (1.8) leads to two sets of $\frac{1}{2}n$ observations each. For both sets the residual sums of squares are computed and their ratio (1.10) is then distributed as F with $\frac{1}{2}n - K$ degrees of freedom both in the numerator and in the denominator. A small (large) value of this ratio points to an increase (a decrease) of the disturbance variance over time.

Note that the total number of degrees of freedom on which the test is based is

$$(1.11)\qquad \frac{1}{2}n - K + \frac{1}{2}n - K = n - 2K$$

which is K below the number of degrees of freedom of the regression $(n - K)$. This illustrates the main weakness of the procedure as far as the power of the test is concerned. Its use of the LS residuals based on two separate subsets of the n observations implies that the analyst sacrifices twice the K degrees of freedom necessary to estimate the parameter vector $\boldsymbol{\beta}$. In fact, the ratio (1.10) has the F distribution even when the two subsets have different $\boldsymbol{\beta}$'s (see Problem 1.4). Thus it seems plausible that when it is assumed to be known that the two subsets have the same parameter vector, the power of the test can be improved by taking this knowledge into account. This problem is pursued in Section 5.4.

[4] *Proof.* When $\boldsymbol{\epsilon}$ is normally distributed with zero mean vector and covariance matrix $\sigma^2\mathbf{I}$, then $\mathbf{e}_A = \mathbf{M}_A\boldsymbol{\epsilon}_A$ and $\mathbf{e}_B = \mathbf{M}_B\boldsymbol{\epsilon}_B$ are also normally distributed with zero mean vectors and their covariance matrices are $\sigma^2\mathbf{M}_A$ and $\sigma^2\mathbf{M}_B$, respectively. Both $\mathbf{M}_A$ and $\mathbf{M}_B$ are idempotent matrices of rank $6 - K$, which proves that $\mathbf{e}_A'\mathbf{e}_A = \boldsymbol{\epsilon}_A'\mathbf{M}_A\boldsymbol{\epsilon}_A$ and $\mathbf{e}_B'\mathbf{e}_B = \boldsymbol{\epsilon}_B'\mathbf{M}_B\boldsymbol{\epsilon}_B$ are distributed as $\sigma^2\chi^2(6 - K)$. Furthermore, each element of $\mathbf{e}_A$ is uncorrelated with each element of $\mathbf{e}_B$ because $\mathscr{E}(\mathbf{e}_A\mathbf{e}_B') = \mathbf{M}_A\mathscr{E}(\boldsymbol{\epsilon}_A\boldsymbol{\epsilon}_B')\mathbf{M}_B' = \mathbf{M}_A\mathbf{0}\mathbf{M}_B' = \mathbf{0}$, and zero correlation implies independence because of the normality of $\mathbf{e}_A$ and $\mathbf{e}_B$.

[5] The case of odd n may be handled by omitting the middle observation.

Extensions and Modifications

The above test for homoscedasticity can also be applied when the alternative hypothesis states that the disturbance variance is, say, an increasing function of one of the explanatory variables. (Such a case was illustrated in Figure 3.4 in Section 3.9.) The procedure is then to rearrange the observations according to increasing values of that particular variable, after which they are partitioned in accordance with (1.8). The associated ratio (1.10) of the residual sums of squares should be sufficiently small in order that the alternative hypothesis be accepted.

Goldfeld and Quandt also considered a modification of their test which implies that a middle group of observations is omitted. Specifically, $\mathbf{e}_A$ is then the LS residual vector computed from the first $m < \frac{1}{2}n$ observations and $\mathbf{e}_B$ is computed from the last m, so that the middle $n - 2m$ observations are not used at all. This, of course, lowers the number of degrees of freedom on which the test is based and thereby reduces the power of the test. On the other hand, if the alternative hypothesis is true, the inclusion of the centrally located observations would cause $\mathbf{e}_A'\mathbf{e}_A$ and $\mathbf{e}_B'\mathbf{e}_B$ to be on the average closer to each other than they would be if these observations were not included,[6] and this effect works in the opposite direction. Some experimental studies suggest that the power of the test is improved by deleting a modest proportion of observations in the middle range.

The Durbin-Watson Test against Autocorrelation

Again consider a time series regression, and now suppose that the alternative hypothesis states that successive disturbances (ϵ_α and $\epsilon_{\alpha+1}$, $\alpha = 1, \ldots, n - 1$) are positively correlated. (This is frequently expressed by saying that the disturbances are then positively autocorrelated.) Our starting point is the following identity:

$$\mathscr{E}(\epsilon_{\alpha+1} - \epsilon_\alpha)^2 = \mathscr{E}\epsilon_{\alpha+1}^2 + \mathscr{E}\epsilon_\alpha^2 - 2\mathscr{E}(\epsilon_\alpha\epsilon_{\alpha+1}) \tag{1.12}$$

When successive disturbances are positively correlated, the left-hand expectation will be smaller than when they are uncorrelated because of the negative sign of $-2\mathscr{E}(\epsilon_\alpha\epsilon_{\alpha+1})$. To the extent that the LS residuals $e_1, \ldots, e_n$ are satisfactory approximations of the corresponding disturbances, we shall have

[6] This is easily made visually clear by means of Figure 5.1. If $\mathbf{e}_A$ refers to the first four observations rather than the first six and, similarly, $\mathbf{e}_B$ to the last four (rather than the last six), and if we neglect—for simplicity's sake—the distinction between residuals and disturbances in the figure, then the ratio $\mathbf{e}_A'\mathbf{e}_A/\mathbf{e}_B'\mathbf{e}_B$ is considerably reduced by this modification.

a similar result for $(e_{\alpha+1} - e_\alpha)^2$. These considerations lead to the Durbin-Watson statistic:

$$(1.13) \qquad d = \frac{\sum_{\alpha=1}^{n-1} (e_{\alpha+1} - e_\alpha)^2}{\sum_{\alpha=1}^{n} e_\alpha^2}$$

The null hypothesis is rejected in favor of the alternative hypothesis that the disturbances are positively autocorrelated when d takes a sufficiently small value. When the alternative hypothesis states that the disturbances are either positively or negatively autocorrelated, the critical region consists of both small and large values of d; this should be clear from the positive sign of $-2\mathscr{E}(\epsilon_\alpha \epsilon_{\alpha+1})$ in the case of negative autocorrelation.

It turns out that the dependence of d on the LS residuals $e_1, \ldots, e_n$ (rather than on the n disturbances) implies that its distribution involves the matrix $\mathbf{X}$ in a complicated manner. To avoid sizable computational procedures in the applications, DURBIN and WATSON (1950, 1951) formulated bounds (d_L, d_U) for each significance limit such that the limit lies in this interval whatever $\mathbf{X}$ may be. The procedure is then to reject the null hypothesis in favor of the alternative hypothesis of positive autocorrelation if $d < d_L$, to draw no conclusion if d falls in (d_L, d_U), and to declare the null hypothesis as acceptable if $d > d_U$. The bounds corresponding to the 5 and 1 percent significance levels are tabulated at the end of this book for $n = 15, 16, \ldots, 39, 40, 45, 50, \ldots, 100$ and $K = 2, \ldots, 6$. The underlying assumptions are those of the standard linear model including normality;[7] also, it is assumed that the regression contains a constant term, so that $K = 2$ means one explanatory variable plus a constant. For the textile example of Section 3.3 we obtain, using the LS residuals shown in column (1) of Table 5.2 in Section 5.4 below:

$$(1.14) \qquad d = \frac{(.0030 - .0142)^2 + \cdots + (.0216 + .0241)^2}{(n - K)s^2} = 1.93$$

where $n = 17$, $K = 3$, and s^2 is given in eq. (3.16) of Section 3.3. For this (n, K) combination we have $d_L = 1.02$ and $d_U = 1.54$ at the 5 percent

[7] Note that this also includes the assumption that the matrix $\mathbf{X}$ may be regarded as consisting of fixed elements, which excludes the presence of lagged values of the dependent variable $(y_{\alpha-1})$ among the explanatory variables. It can be shown (see Section 8.7) under appropriate conditions that the bounds d_L and d_U still apply to this case provided that n is sufficiently large, but the power of the test is then on the low side.

significance level; hence the null hypothesis, when tested against positive autocorrelation, is acceptable at this level.[8]

A difficulty in the application of the Durbin-Watson test is that the interval (d_L, d_U) of inconclusive tests is sometimes large, particularly when the number of observations is modest and when K is not very small. For example, for $n = 20$ and $K = 5$ we have $(d_L, d_U) = (.90, 1.83)$ at the 5 percent level and $(.68, 1.57)$ at the 1 percent level. In fact, a substantial proportion of the d's published in the literature are inconclusive at the conventional significance levels. There exists then the risk that such cases are regarded as falling under "no evidence against zero autocorrelation," whereas the use of the exact significance limit (which depends on the $\mathbf{X}$ matrix of the regression) might have indicated that there is positive autocorrelation. THEIL and NAGAR (1961) showed that the upper bound d_U is approximately equal to the true significance limit in all those cases in which the behavior of the explanatory variables is smooth in the sense that their first and second differences are small compared with the range of the corresponding variable itself. Many economic time series are characterized by considerable inertia, so that this condition is then at least approximately satisfied. The procedure thus simply amounts to adding the interval (d_L, d_U) to the critical region. However, note that the smoothness condition is not satisfied by dummy variables, which jump from zero to one and vice versa, nor by most of the regressions that are formulated in terms of the first differences of the original variables.

Durbin and Watson (1951) described an approximation method for obtaining conclusive results when d falls in (d_L, d_U), but there is little experience with this procedure. HENSHAW (1966) proposed to fit a beta distribution based on the first four moments of d; but this procedure appears to be rather laborious. Reference is also made to HANNAN (1960) and HANNAN and TERRELL (1968) for autocorrelation in time series regressions, and to ANSCOMBE (1961) and ANSCOMBE and TUKEY (1963) for LS residuals in more general contexts.

[8] A test (also one-tailed) against negative autocorrelation is obtained by replacing d by $4 - d$. This becomes clear by writing (1.13) as

$$d = \frac{\sum_{\alpha=1}^{n-1} e_{\alpha+1}^2}{\sum_{\alpha=1}^{n} e_\alpha^2} + \frac{\sum_{\alpha=1}^{n-1} e_\alpha^2}{\sum_{\alpha=1}^{n} e_\alpha^2} - 2\frac{\sum_{\alpha=1}^{n-1} e_\alpha e_{\alpha+1}}{\sum_{\alpha=1}^{n} e_\alpha^2}$$

which is approximately $1 + 1 - 2r = 2(1 - r)$ when n is not too small, r being the correlation coefficient of successive residuals. Replacing d by $4 - d \approx 2(1 + r)$ leads to significant values when r is negative and sufficiently large.

Problems

1.1 Prove that under the assumptions of the standard linear model, the variance of an LS residual e_α is at most equal to σ^2. Prove that the variance of e_α is equal to σ^2 if and only if the values taken by all explanatory variables vanish for the αth observation.

1.2 (*Continuation*) Suppose that the regression contains a constant term. Is it then possible for any LS residual to have a variance equal to σ^2?

1.3 It is stated below (1.7) that we cannot conclude that this ratio has an F distribution because of the dependence of the numerator and the denominator. Is this the only reason?

1.4 Replace eq. (1.8) by $\mathbf{y}_A = \mathbf{X}_A\boldsymbol{\beta}_A + \boldsymbol{\epsilon}_A$, $\mathbf{y}_B = \mathbf{X}_B\boldsymbol{\beta}_B + \boldsymbol{\epsilon}_B$. State the conditions under which the ratio (1.10) is distributed as $F(6 - K, 6 - K)$, and show in particular that $\boldsymbol{\beta}_A$ and $\boldsymbol{\beta}_B$ may be different vectors. Extend the result to the case in which $\mathbf{X}_A$ and $\mathbf{X}_B$ have different numbers of columns.

1.5 A time series regression based on 20 observations contains three explanatory variables plus a constant term. The Durbin-Watson statistic is computed to test the independence of the disturbances against positive autocorrelation at the 5 percent significance level; its value is 1.51. What is your conclusion? Answer the same question for the values 2.03, 1.41, and .67.

5.2 BLUS Residual Vectors[C]

The preceding section shows that LS residuals, although they have optimum properties, are not really convenient for testing the hypothesis $\mathscr{V}(\boldsymbol{\epsilon}) = \sigma^2\mathbf{I}$. An alternative procedure is to formulate tests based on residuals which, contrary to the LS residuals, do have a scalar covariance matrix when this hypothesis is true. This alternative is pursued in the remainder of this chapter; its advantage is that standard tests are straightforwardly applicable to such residuals. More specifically, the objective is to formulate a linear unbiased residual vector which is "best" in some sense but subject to the additional constraint that its covariance matrix be scalar (of the form $\sigma^2\mathbf{I}$). The procedure, which is described in this section (some of the proofs are given in Section 5.3), was developed by THEIL (1965b, 1968a). For related and additional contributions to this area, reference should be made to RAMSEY (1966, 1967), LEUSSINK (1966), PUTTER (1967), KOERTS (1967), and KOERTS and ABRAHAMSE (1968).

How Many Residuals Can Be Unbiased and Have a Scalar Covariance Matrix?

If the residual vector is to be linear, it can be written as $\mathbf{Cy}$, where $\mathbf{C}$ is a matrix of n columns not involving $\mathbf{y}$. This matrix should satisfy

$$\mathbf{CX} = \mathbf{0} \tag{2.1}$$

in order that the residual vector be unbiased because $\mathbf{Cy} = \mathbf{C}(\mathbf{X}\boldsymbol{\beta} + \boldsymbol{\epsilon})$ has the same expectation as the corresponding vector of disturbances (zero) if and only if $\mathbf{CX} = \mathbf{0}$. A linear unbiased residual vector thus has the form $\mathbf{C}\boldsymbol{\epsilon}$, so that its covariance matrix is

$$\mathscr{E}(\mathbf{C}\boldsymbol{\epsilon}\boldsymbol{\epsilon}'\mathbf{C}') = \sigma^2\mathbf{CC}' \tag{2.2}$$

which is a scalar matrix of the form $\sigma^2\mathbf{I}$ if and only if

$$\mathbf{CC}' = \mathbf{I} \tag{2.3}$$

This result is summarized in the first part of the following theorem.

THEOREM 5.3 (Linear unbiased residual vectors with a scalar covariance matrix) *If Assumption* 3.3 *of Section* 3.2 *is true for given* $\mathbf{X}$, *a necessary and sufficient condition in order that a residual vector be linear and unbiased and have a scalar covariance matrix* $\sigma^2\mathbf{I}$ *is that it can be written as* $\mathbf{Cy}$ *with* $\mathbf{C}$ *satisfying* (2.1) *and* (2.3). *The maximum number of rows of* $\mathbf{C}$ *is* $n - K$, *and* $\mathbf{I}$ *of* (2.3) *is at most of order* $(n - K) \times (n - K)$.

COROLLARY TO THEOREM 5.3 *Suppose that the assumptions of Theorem* 5.3 *are true. Then, if a residual vector is required to be linear and unbiased and to have a scalar covariance matrix* $\sigma^2\mathbf{I}$, *it can represent at most* $n - K$ *components of the disturbance vector* $\boldsymbol{\epsilon}$.

To prove the second part of the theorem, which leads to the corollary, we assume that $\mathbf{C}$ is of order $p \times n$, so that $\mathbf{Cy}$ represents p disturbances $(1 \le p \le n)$. Then $\mathbf{CC}'$ is of order $p \times p$, so that $\mathbf{I}$ in (2.3) is the unit matrix of that order. We see from (2.1) that the n columns of $\mathbf{C}$ are subject to K linear dependencies; hence the rank of $\mathbf{C}$ cannot exceed $n - K$. But the ranks of $\mathbf{C}$ and $\mathbf{CC}'$ are equal and the $p \times p$ unit matrix in (2.3) has full rank; therefore, $p \le n - K$.

It will appear from Theorem 5.4 below that $p = n - K$ is always possible when the matrix $\mathbf{X}$ has full column rank. Evidently, we must draw the conclusion that K disturbances will have to be disregarded when we insist on an unbiased residual vector with a scalar covariance matrix. It should be intuitively clear that this is unavoidable. Our starting point consists of n

uncorrelated random variables $\epsilon_1, \ldots, \epsilon_n$, but we have to sacrifice K degrees of freedom because of the unknown parameter vector $\boldsymbol{\beta}$. Therefore it should cause no surprise that the conditions $\mathbf{CX} = \mathbf{0}$ and $\mathbf{CC}' = \mathbf{I}$ (unbiasedness and a scalar covariance matrix) imply that only $n - K$ such residuals can be found. At first sight this may seem to be a disadvantage compared with the n LS residuals, but it will appear at the end of the next subsection that the situation with regard to the latter residuals is basically the same.

The Observation Matrix Partitioned

To simplify the discussion we shall first determine the best linear unbiased residual vector with a scalar covariance matrix for a given set of $n - K$ observations. We partition the observation matrix $[\mathbf{y} \quad \mathbf{X}]$ into two submatrices consisting of K and $n - K$ rows, respectively, in such a way that residuals will be derived corresponding to the latter rows. Without loss of generality it may be assumed (by interchanging the order of the observations if necessary) that the former set of K rows corresponds to the first K observations. The basic equation and its LS estimator then become

$$\text{(2.4)} \qquad \begin{matrix} K \text{ rows} \\ n-K \text{ rows} \end{matrix} \quad \begin{bmatrix} \mathbf{y}_0 \\ \mathbf{y}_1 \end{bmatrix} = \begin{bmatrix} \mathbf{X}_0 \\ \mathbf{X}_1 \end{bmatrix} \boldsymbol{\beta} + \begin{bmatrix} \boldsymbol{\epsilon}_0 \\ \boldsymbol{\epsilon}_1 \end{bmatrix} = \begin{bmatrix} \mathbf{X}_0 \\ \mathbf{X}_1 \end{bmatrix} \mathbf{b} + \begin{bmatrix} \mathbf{e}_0 \\ \mathbf{e}_1 \end{bmatrix}$$

where the matrices with subscript 0 all have K rows and those with subscript 1 have $n - K$ rows. Our objective is thus to find a linear unbiased residual vector with a scalar covariance matrix that corresponds to the $(n - K)$-element disturbance subvector $\boldsymbol{\epsilon}_1$.

It will be noted that $\mathbf{X}_0$ is a square $(K \times K)$ matrix. Since $\mathbf{X}$ has rank K, it is always possible to rearrange the observations so that $\mathbf{X}_0$ is nonsingular, and we shall make this assumption from now on. Also note that the orthogonality condition $\mathbf{X}'\mathbf{e} = \mathbf{0}$ on the LS residual vector can be written as $\mathbf{X}_0'\mathbf{e}_0 + \mathbf{X}_1'\mathbf{e}_1 = \mathbf{0}$ or, equivalently,

$$\text{(2.5)} \qquad \mathbf{e}_0 = -(\mathbf{X}_1\mathbf{X}_0^{-1})'\mathbf{e}_1$$

We conclude that the K-element subvector $\mathbf{e}_0$ of the LS residual vector is a known linear function of the complementary subvector $\mathbf{e}_1$. This means that $\mathbf{e}$ and $\mathbf{e}_1$ are equally informative with respect to the disturbance vector $\boldsymbol{\epsilon}$ and, hence, that the elements of $\mathbf{e}_0$ do not provide any information on $\boldsymbol{\epsilon}$ which is not contained in $\mathbf{e}_1$.

The Index Transformation of the Explanatory Variables

The matrix $\mathbf{X}_1\mathbf{X}_0^{-1}$ of (2.5) will play an important role in what follows, so that it is appropriate to discuss it here. Consider the special case of one explanatory variable (with values $x_1, \ldots, x_n$) and no constant term. Then $\mathbf{X}_1\mathbf{X}_0^{-1}$ is a column vector whose successive elements are $x_2/x_1, \ldots, x_n/x_1$, and the nonsingularity of $\mathbf{X}_0$ amounts to $x_1 \neq 0$. The variable is thus measured as a ratio or as a simple index (like "1952 = 100") and the first observation serves as the base of the index transformation. For $K > 1$ it may be argued that there is an index transformation in a generalized sense. The base then consists of K observations and all K explanatory variables are transformed simultaneously, not one by one as in the case of conventional index numbers. Consideration of

$$\text{(2.6)} \qquad \mathbf{X}\mathbf{X}_0^{-1} = \begin{bmatrix} \mathbf{X}_0 \\ \mathbf{X}_1 \end{bmatrix} \mathbf{X}_0^{-1} = \begin{bmatrix} \mathbf{I} \\ \mathbf{X}_1\mathbf{X}_0^{-1} \end{bmatrix}$$

shows that the first K observations (corresponding to the disturbance subvector $\boldsymbol{\epsilon}_0$ which will not be represented by our residuals) form the K-dimensional base of the generalized index transformation. The nonsingularity of $\mathbf{X}_0$ thus amounts to a nonsingular base of this transformation.

The BLUS Residual Vector for a Given Partitioning

Since $\mathbf{X}$ has rank K by assumption, the matrix $\mathbf{X}\mathbf{X}_0^{-1}$ of (2.6) also has rank K. Hence the symmetric $K \times K$ matrix $(\mathbf{X}\mathbf{X}_0^{-1})'\mathbf{X}\mathbf{X}_0^{-1}$ is positive definite and its inverse,

$$\text{(2.7)} \qquad [(\mathbf{X}\mathbf{X}_0^{-1})'\mathbf{X}\mathbf{X}_0^{-1}]^{-1} = [(\mathbf{X}_0')^{-1}\mathbf{X}'\mathbf{X}\mathbf{X}_0^{-1}]^{-1} = \mathbf{X}_0(\mathbf{X}'\mathbf{X})^{-1}\mathbf{X}_0'$$

is also symmetric and positive definite. Therefore the K roots of the matrix (2.7) are all positive and can thus be written as d_h^2, $h = 1, \ldots, K$. It will be shown in the next section that none of these K roots is larger than 1; they are either equal to 1 or less than 1 (but still positive). For the roots that are *less than one* we consider

$$\text{(2.8)} \qquad [\mathbf{X}_0(\mathbf{X}'\mathbf{X})^{-1}\mathbf{X}_0' - d_h^2\mathbf{I}]\mathbf{q}_h = \mathbf{0} \qquad h = 1, \ldots, H$$

where H ($\leq K$) is the number of roots < 1 and $\mathbf{q}_1, \ldots, \mathbf{q}_H$ are K-element characteristic vectors corresponding to the roots $d_1^2, \ldots, d_H^2$, all normalized in the conventional way (unit length and pairwise orthogonal).

Equations (2.4) and (2.8) define the concepts used in the following theorem which is concerned with the linear unbiased residual vector (with a scalar covariance matrix) that corresponds to $\boldsymbol{\epsilon}_1$ and that is "best" in a particular sense to be defined below. This vector will be called a BLUS residual vector, where B stands for best, L for linear, U for unbiased, and S for the scalar covariance matrix.

THEOREM 5.4 (BLUS residual vector expressed in terms of the LS residual vector) *Suppose that Assumption* 3.3 *of Section* 3.2 *is true for given* $\mathbf{X}$; *also suppose* $n > K$. *Consider the partitioning* (2.4) *and suppose that* $\mathbf{X}_0$ *is nonsingular. Also consider the roots* $d_1^2, \ldots, d_K^2$ *of the matrix* $\mathbf{X}_0(\mathbf{X}'\mathbf{X})^{-1}\mathbf{X}_0'$ *and define* d_h *as the positive square root of* d_h^2, $h = 1, \ldots, K$. *Finally, consider the K-element vectors* $\mathbf{q}_1, \ldots, \mathbf{q}_H$ *defined as characteristic vectors (corresponding to the H roots less than one) of this matrix. Then the* $(n - K)$-*element vector*

$$\hat{\boldsymbol{\epsilon}}_1 = \mathbf{e}_1 - \mathbf{X}_1\mathbf{X}_0^{-1}\left[\sum_{h=1}^{H} \frac{d_h}{1 + d_h} \mathbf{q}_h\mathbf{q}_h'\right]\mathbf{e}_0 \tag{2.9}$$

is the BLUS residual vector corresponding to the partitioning (2.4) *in the following sense. Given this partitioning and within the class of linear unbiased residual vectors with a scalar covariance matrix, this residual vector has a minimum expected squared length of the error vector. This minimum (the expected sum of the squares of the* $n - K$ *BLUS errors) is given by*

$$\mathscr{E}[(\hat{\boldsymbol{\epsilon}}_1 - \boldsymbol{\epsilon}_1)'(\hat{\boldsymbol{\epsilon}}_1 - \boldsymbol{\epsilon}_1)] = 2\sigma^2 \sum_{h=1}^{K}(1 - d_h) \tag{2.10}$$

and the sum of the squares of the $n - K$ *BLUS residuals themselves is identically equal to the sum of the squares of the n LS residuals*:

$$\hat{\boldsymbol{\epsilon}}_1'\hat{\boldsymbol{\epsilon}}_1 \equiv (n - K)s^2 \tag{2.11}$$

where $s^2 = \mathbf{e}'\mathbf{e}/(n - K)$ *is the LS variance estimator.*

This theorem will be proved in the next section along with several others. (The reader who is mainly interested in procedures rather than derivations may prefer to study Sections 5.4 and 5.5 before Section 5.3.) We conclude with three remarks.

(1) The optimality criterion of Theorem 5.4 is weaker than that of Theorem 5.1. The LS residuals considered in the latter theorem minimize in their class the expectation of a quadratic form in the errors for whatever positive semidefinite matrix of this form. In Theorem 5.4 this matrix has to be specified as $c\mathbf{I}$, where c is an arbitrary positive scalar.

(2) Theorem 5.4 is confined to one particular partitioning. There are, in general, many ways of dividing the n observations into two groups of K and $n - K$ observations, even when a nonsingularity condition is imposed on $\mathbf{X}_0$, in which case a choice must be made. This problem will be discussed in Section 5.4.

(3) The identity (2.11) should be regarded as a convenient check on the computation of $\hat{\boldsymbol{\epsilon}}_1$.

Problems

2.1 Is it the case that BLUS residuals always have zero sum when the equation contains a constant term? (*Hint.* Which condition of BLUS would be violated if that were the case?)

2.2 It is stated in remark (2) at the end of this section that there are, in general, many ways of dividing n observations into groups of K and $n - K$ subject to the nonsingularity of $\mathbf{X}_0$. State the necessary and sufficient condition under which there is exactly one way, given the assumptions of the standard linear model.

5.3 Properties of Three Families of Residual Vectors[C]

Theorem 5.5 below is concerned with the class of all linear unbiased residual vectors. In Theorems 5.6 and 5.7 we confine ourselves to those linear unbiased vectors which have a scalar covariance matrix. The remainder of the section is devoted to the case of a particular partitioning of the type (2.4).

Linear Unbiased Residual Vectors

THEOREM 5.5 (Linear unbiased residual vectors expressed in terms of $\mathbf{y}$, $\boldsymbol{\epsilon}$, and $\mathbf{e}$) *If Assumption* 3.1 *of Section* 3.2 *is true for given* $\mathbf{X}$, *any linear unbiased residual vector* $\mathbf{Cy}$ *is equal to the same linear function of the disturbance vector* $\boldsymbol{\epsilon}$ *and it is also equal to the same linear function of the LS residual vector* $\mathbf{e}$:

$$\mathbf{Cy} = \mathbf{C}\boldsymbol{\epsilon} = \mathbf{Ce} \tag{3.1}$$

First note that $\mathbf{Cy} = \mathbf{C}\boldsymbol{\epsilon}$ was already proved in the discussion below eq. (2.1). Next, consider

$$\mathbf{MC}' = [\mathbf{I} - \mathbf{X}(\mathbf{X}'\mathbf{X})^{-1}\mathbf{X}']\mathbf{C}' = \mathbf{C}' \tag{3.2}$$

where the second equality sign is based on $\mathbf{X}'\mathbf{C}' = \mathbf{0}$; see (2.1). We conclude that $\mathbf{Cy} = \mathbf{C}(\mathbf{My}) = \mathbf{Ce}$, which completes the proof of (3.1). Note that the condition $\mathscr{V}(\boldsymbol{\epsilon}) = \sigma^2\mathbf{I}$ has not been used; this is expressed in the theorem by the use of Assumption 3.1 rather than Assumption 3.3, and it should be compared with the analogous property of the LS coefficient vector $\mathbf{b}$ stated in Theorem 3.2 of Section 3.3.

Linear Unbiased Residual Vectors with a Scalar Covariance Matrix

THEOREM 5.6 (Existence of linear unbiased residual vectors with a scalar covariance matrix) *For any given matrix* **X** *of order* $n \times K$ *and rank* $K < n$ *there exists a matrix* **C** *of order* $(n - K) \times n$ *satisfying* (2.1) *and* (2.3). *Its rows are characteristic vectors of the matrix* **M** *corresponding to unit roots,* **M** *being defined in* (1.1), *and these rows have all unit length and are pairwise orthogonal.*

Since Theorem 5.3 of the previous section implies that the only thing needed for a linear unbiased residual vector with a scalar covariance matrix is a matrix **C** satisfying (2.1) and (2.3) by which the vector **y** can be premultiplied, this theorem ensures the existence of such residual vectors. Also, the fact that **C** of this theorem has $n - K$ rows ensures that the maximum mentioned in the second part of Theorem 5.3 can actually be attained. To prove Theorem 5.6 we write (3.2) in the equivalent form

$$(\mathbf{M} - \mathbf{I})\mathbf{C}' = \mathbf{0} \tag{3.3}$$

which shows that the columns of $\mathbf{C}'$ (the rows of **C**) are characteristic vectors of **M** corresponding to unit roots. Since **M** is an idempotent matrix of rank $n - K$, it has $n - K$ unit roots and hence as many corresponding characteristic vectors.[9] It follows directly from (2.3) that these vectors have unit length and are pairwise orthogonal.

THEOREM 5.7 (Length of linear unbiased residual vectors with a scalar covariance matrix—continuation of Theorem 5.6) *For any matrix* **C** *of order* $(n - K) \times n$ *satisfying* (2.1) *and* (2.3) *and for any n-element column vector* **y**, *the length of the vector* **Cy** *is identically equal to the length of* **My**.

To prove this theorem we note that the K roots of **M** that are not unity are all equal to zero. Let us write $\mathbf{F}'$ for an $n \times K$ matrix whose columns are characteristic vectors of **M** corresponding to these zero roots. As usual, the characteristic vectors are required to form an orthogonal matrix:

$$[\mathbf{C}' \quad \mathbf{F}']\begin{bmatrix}\mathbf{C}\\ \mathbf{F}\end{bmatrix} = \mathbf{I} \tag{3.4}$$

[9] Note that these vectors are not unique because of the multiplicity of the unit root [see the discussion preceding eq. (5.8) in Section 1.5]. In fact, this indeterminacy provides us with the opportunity to select one particular residual vector which is "best" (given the chosen base of the index transformation).

Recall the discussion of eqs. (5.5) to (5.8) in Section 1.5, which implies that if we postmultiply a symmetric matrix by a matrix of its characteristic vectors, we obtain the latter matrix postmultiplied by the diagonal matrix which contains the latent roots along the diagonal:

$$\text{(3.5)} \qquad \mathbf{M}[\mathbf{C}' \quad \mathbf{F}'] = [\mathbf{C}' \quad \mathbf{F}']\begin{bmatrix} \mathbf{I} & \mathbf{0} \\ \mathbf{0} & \mathbf{0} \end{bmatrix} = [\mathbf{C}' \quad \mathbf{0}]$$

where $\mathbf{I}$ of $\begin{bmatrix} \mathbf{I} & \mathbf{0} \\ \mathbf{0} & \mathbf{0} \end{bmatrix}$ is of order $(n - K) \times (n - K)$ and the lower right-hand $\mathbf{0}$ is of order $K \times K$. We now combine (3.4) and (3.5) as follows:

$$\mathbf{M} = \mathbf{MI} = \mathbf{M}[\mathbf{C}' \quad \mathbf{F}']\begin{bmatrix} \mathbf{C} \\ \mathbf{F} \end{bmatrix} = [\mathbf{C}' \quad \mathbf{0}]\begin{bmatrix} \mathbf{C} \\ \mathbf{F} \end{bmatrix}$$

which gives

$$\text{(3.6)} \qquad \mathbf{C}'\mathbf{C} = \mathbf{M}$$

Since the residual vector is $\mathbf{Cy}$, the sum of squares of its $n - K$ elements is therefore

$$\text{(3.7)} \qquad \mathbf{y}'\mathbf{C}'\mathbf{Cy} = \mathbf{y}'\mathbf{My}$$

which is precisely the same as the sum of squares of the n LS residuals. Note that this holds for *all* linear unbiased residual vectors with a scalar covariance matrix, not only for the BLUS vector.

BLUS Residual Vectors

We shall now prove Theorem 5.4 in a series of seven lemmas:[10]

LEMMA 1 *If* $\mathbf{X}' = [\mathbf{X}_0' \quad \mathbf{X}_1']$ *is a* $K \times n$ *matrix of rank* K *and if* $\mathbf{X}_0$ *is a nonsingular* $K \times K$ *matrix, then the latent roots* $d_1^2, \ldots, d_K^2$ *of the matrix* (2.7) *are positive and at most equal to one, and the number* H *of roots less than one is equal to the rank of* $\mathbf{X}_1$.

The inverse of the matrix (2.7) is

$$\text{(3.8)} \qquad \begin{aligned} (\mathbf{X}_0')^{-1}\mathbf{X}'\mathbf{X}\mathbf{X}_0^{-1} &= (\mathbf{X}_0')^{-1}(\mathbf{X}_0'\mathbf{X}_0 + \mathbf{X}_1'\mathbf{X}_1)\mathbf{X}_0^{-1} \\ &= \mathbf{I} + (\mathbf{X}_1\mathbf{X}_0^{-1})'\mathbf{X}_1\mathbf{X}_0^{-1} \\ &= \mathbf{I} + \mathbf{Z}'\mathbf{Z} \qquad \text{where} \quad \mathbf{Z} = \mathbf{X}_1\mathbf{X}_0^{-1} \end{aligned}$$

[10] In all lemmas the validity of Assumption 3.3 of Section 3.2 is assumed insofar as this is relevant.

Since the roots of the inverse are the reciprocals of the roots of the original matrix, we have $|\mathbf{I} + \mathbf{Z}'\mathbf{Z} - (1/d_h^2)\mathbf{I}| = 0$ or $|\mathbf{Z}'\mathbf{Z} - f_h\mathbf{I}| = 0$, where $f_h = (1 - d_h^2)/d_h^2$. We have $f_h \geq 0$ and hence $d_h^2 \leq 1$ because of the positive semi-definiteness of $\mathbf{Z}'\mathbf{Z}$. Since the ranks of $\mathbf{X}_1$, $\mathbf{Z}$ and $\mathbf{Z}'\mathbf{Z}$ are all equal, the number H of roots $f_h \neq 0$ (or $d_h^2 \neq 1$) is indeed equal to the rank of $\mathbf{X}_1$. Also note that we have

$$\left(\mathbf{Z}'\mathbf{Z} - \frac{1 - d_h^2}{d_h^2}\mathbf{I}\right)\mathbf{q}_h = \mathbf{0} \qquad h = 1, \ldots, H \tag{3.9}$$

because eq. (2.8) states that $\mathbf{q}_h$ is a characteristic vector of the matrix (2.7), and each such vector is also a characteristic vector of the inverse (3.8) of (2.7).

LEMMA 2 *Each linear unbiased residual vector corresponding to the* $(n - K)$-*element disturbance subvector* $\boldsymbol{\epsilon}_1$ *of* (2.4) *can be written as*

$$\mathbf{C}_0\mathbf{e}_0 + \mathbf{C}_1\mathbf{e}_1 = \mathbf{C}_1(\mathbf{I} + \mathbf{Z}\mathbf{Z}')\mathbf{e}_1 \tag{3.10}$$

where $\mathbf{C}_0$ *is of order* $(n - K) \times K$ *and* $\mathbf{C}_1$ *of order* $(n - K) \times (n - K)$. *The matrix* $\mathbf{C}_1$ *should satisfy*

$$\mathbf{C}_1(\mathbf{I} + \mathbf{Z}\mathbf{Z}')\mathbf{C}_1' = \mathbf{I} \tag{3.11}$$

in order that the residual vector have a scalar covariance matrix.

The left-hand side of (3.10) is equal to $\mathbf{Ce}$ of (3.1), where $\mathbf{C}$ is now an $(n - K) \times n$ matrix partitioned as $[\mathbf{C}_0 \quad \mathbf{C}_1]$. The unbiasedness condition (2.1) then becomes $\mathbf{C}_0\mathbf{X}_0 + \mathbf{C}_1\mathbf{X}_1 = \mathbf{0}$ or $\mathbf{C}_0 = -\mathbf{C}_1\mathbf{Z}$. Combining this with (2.5), to be written in the form $\mathbf{e}_0 = -\mathbf{Z}'\mathbf{e}_1$, we obtain (3.10) immediately. Condition (2.3) on the scalar covariance matrix is now $\mathbf{C}_0\mathbf{C}_0' + \mathbf{C}_1\mathbf{C}_1' = \mathbf{I}$, which is found to be equivalent to (3.11) by substituting $\mathbf{C}_0 = -\mathbf{C}_1\mathbf{Z}$.

LEMMA 3 *A matrix* $\mathbf{C}_1$ *satisfying* (3.11) *is* $\mathbf{C}_1 = \mathbf{PDP}'$, *where* $\mathbf{D}$ *is a diagonal matrix of order* $(n - K) \times (n - K)$ *whose successive diagonal elements are* $d_1 \leq d_2 \leq \cdots \leq d_H < 1, \ldots, 1$, *the* d*'s being positive square roots of the* d^2*'s defined in* (2.8), *and* $\mathbf{P}$ *is an orthogonal* $(n - K) \times (n - K)$ *matrix whose successive columns are characteristic vectors of* $\mathbf{I} + \mathbf{Z}\mathbf{Z}'$ *corresponding to the roots* $1/d_1^2, \ldots, 1/d_H^2, 1, \ldots, 1$.

Premultiplication of both sides of (3.9) by $\mathbf{Z}$ gives $(\mathbf{Z}\mathbf{Z}' - f_h\mathbf{I})\mathbf{Z}\mathbf{q}_h = \mathbf{0}$, where $f_h = (1 - d_h^2)/d_h^2$. This is equivalent to

$$\left(\mathbf{I} + \mathbf{Z}\mathbf{Z}' - \frac{1}{d_h^2}\mathbf{I}\right)\mathbf{Z}\mathbf{q}_h = \mathbf{0} \qquad h = 1, \ldots, H \tag{3.12}$$

which shows that the $(n - K) \times (n - K)$ matrix $\mathbf{I} + \mathbf{ZZ}'$ has H roots larger than 1. The other $n - K - H$ roots are equal to 1 because $|\mathbf{I} + \mathbf{ZZ}' - \lambda\mathbf{I}| = 0$ is satisfied by $\lambda = 1$ with multiplicity $n - K - H$, the order of $\mathbf{ZZ}'$ being $(n - K) \times (n - K)$ and its rank being H. (When $n - K = H$, the roots $1/d_1^2, \ldots, 1/d_H^2$ are obviously the only roots.) Hence,

$$\mathbf{I} + \mathbf{ZZ}' = \mathbf{PD}^{-2}\mathbf{P}' \tag{3.13}$$

where $\mathbf{P}$ and $\mathbf{D}$ are defined in the lemma. Equation (3.11) may then be written as $\mathbf{C}_1\mathbf{PD}^{-2}\mathbf{P}'\mathbf{C}_1' = \mathbf{I}$ and it is verified straightforwardly, using the orthogonality of $\mathbf{P}$, that $\mathbf{C}_1 = \mathbf{PDP}'$ satisfies this equation.

LEMMA 4 *The first H columns of $\mathbf{P}$ (corresponding to the roots $d_1, \ldots, d_H$) are of the form*

$$\mathbf{p}_h = \frac{d_h}{\sqrt{1 - d_h^2}}\mathbf{Zq}_h \qquad h = 1, \ldots, H \tag{3.14}$$

Equation (3.12) shows that $\mathbf{Zq}_h$ is a characteristic vector of $\mathbf{I} + \mathbf{ZZ}'$ corresponding to root $1/d_h^2$. Premultiplication of both sides of (3.9) by $\mathbf{q}_k'$, $k = 1, \ldots, H$ indicates that $\mathbf{Zq}_1, \ldots, \mathbf{Zq}_H$ are pairwise orthogonal, but that they do not have unit length. It is easily verified that $\mathbf{Zq}_h$ should be multiplied by $d_h/\sqrt{1 - d_h^2}$ to ensure that $\mathbf{p}_h'\mathbf{p}_h = 1$.

LEMMA 5 *The vector $\hat{\boldsymbol{\epsilon}}_1$ defined in* (2.9) *is a linear unbiased residual vector with a scalar covariance matrix and it is of the form* (3.10) *with $\mathbf{C}_1$ as specified in Lemma* 3.

It follows from Lemma 2 that if $\hat{\boldsymbol{\epsilon}}_1$ is indeed a linear unbiased residual vector with a scalar covariance matrix, it should be of the form $\mathbf{C}_1(\mathbf{I} + \mathbf{ZZ}')\mathbf{e}_1$ for some $\mathbf{C}_1$ satisfying (3.11). We conclude from Lemma 3 that $\mathbf{C}_1 = \mathbf{PDP}'$ does satisfy this condition. Using (2.5) in the form $\mathbf{e}_0 = -\mathbf{Z}'\mathbf{e}_1$, we write the right-hand side of (2.9) as

$$\left(\mathbf{I} + \mathbf{Z}\left[\sum_{h=1}^{H} \frac{d_h}{1 + d_h}\mathbf{q}_h\mathbf{q}_h'\right]\mathbf{Z}'\right)\mathbf{e}_1 \tag{3.15}$$

Therefore we must prove that $\mathbf{C}_1(\mathbf{I} + \mathbf{ZZ}')$ with $\mathbf{C}_1 = \mathbf{PDP}'$ is equal to the matrix by which $\mathbf{e}_1$ is premultiplied in (3.15). Application of (3.13) gives

$$\begin{aligned} \mathbf{C}_1(\mathbf{I} + \mathbf{ZZ}') &= \mathbf{PDP}'\mathbf{PD}^{-2}\mathbf{P}' = \mathbf{PD}^{-1}\mathbf{P}' = \mathbf{PP}' + \mathbf{P}(\mathbf{D}^{-1} - \mathbf{I})\mathbf{P}' \\ &= \mathbf{I} + \sum_{h=1}^{H}\left(\frac{1}{d_h} - 1\right)\mathbf{p}_h\mathbf{p}_h' \\ &= \mathbf{I} + \mathbf{Z}\left[\sum_{h=1}^{H}\left(\frac{1}{d_h} - 1\right)\frac{d_h^2}{1 - d_h^2}\mathbf{q}_h\mathbf{q}_h'\right]\mathbf{Z}' \end{aligned} \tag{3.16}$$

The fourth equality sign is based on the fact that all diagonal elements of $\mathbf{D}$ (and hence also of $\mathbf{D}^{-1}$) are 1 with the exception only of $d_1, \ldots, d_H$, so that $\mathbf{D}^{-1} - \mathbf{I}$ contains only H nonzero elements. The last equality sign follows from (3.14), and it is readily verified that the matrix in the last line in (3.16) is indeed the same as the matrix by which $\mathbf{e}_1$ is premultiplied in (3.15). Note that this also proves the identity (2.11), for we have shown that $\hat{\boldsymbol{\epsilon}}_1$ is linear unbiased with a scalar covariance matrix and we know from Theorem 5.7 that the length of any such residual vector is equal to that of the LS $\mathbf{e}$.

LEMMA 6 *The covariance matrix of the error vector of* $\hat{\boldsymbol{\epsilon}}_1$ *is*

$$\mathscr{V}(\hat{\boldsymbol{\epsilon}}_1 - \boldsymbol{\epsilon}_1) = 2\sigma^2 \sum_{h=1}^{H} (1 - d_h)\mathbf{p}_h\mathbf{p}_h' \tag{3.17}$$

It follows from (3.1) that $\hat{\boldsymbol{\epsilon}}_1$ can be written as $\mathbf{C}\boldsymbol{\epsilon} = \mathbf{C}_0\boldsymbol{\epsilon}_0 + \mathbf{C}_1\boldsymbol{\epsilon}_1 = -\mathbf{C}_1\mathbf{Z}\boldsymbol{\epsilon}_0 + \mathbf{C}_1\boldsymbol{\epsilon}_1 = \mathbf{C}_1(\boldsymbol{\epsilon}_1 - \mathbf{Z}\boldsymbol{\epsilon}_0)$, where $\mathbf{C}_0 = -\mathbf{C}_1\mathbf{Z}$ was proved below (3.11). Therefore the error vector is $\hat{\boldsymbol{\epsilon}}_1 - \boldsymbol{\epsilon}_1 = (\mathbf{C}_1 - \mathbf{I})\boldsymbol{\epsilon}_1 - \mathbf{C}_1\mathbf{Z}\boldsymbol{\epsilon}_0$ and its covariance matrix is

$$\begin{aligned} \mathscr{V}(\hat{\boldsymbol{\epsilon}}_1 - \boldsymbol{\epsilon}_1) &= \sigma^2(\mathbf{C}_1 - \mathbf{I})(\mathbf{C}_1 - \mathbf{I})' + \sigma^2\mathbf{C}_1\mathbf{Z}\mathbf{Z}'\mathbf{C}_1' \\ &= \sigma^2(\mathbf{C}_1\mathbf{C}_1' - \mathbf{C}_1 - \mathbf{C}_1' + \mathbf{I} + \mathbf{C}_1\mathbf{Z}\mathbf{Z}'\mathbf{C}_1') \\ &= \sigma^2[\mathbf{C}_1(\mathbf{I} + \mathbf{Z}\mathbf{Z}')\mathbf{C}_1' - \mathbf{C}_1 - \mathbf{C}_1' + \mathbf{I}] \\ &= \sigma^2(\mathbf{PDP}'\mathbf{PD}^{-2}\mathbf{P}'\mathbf{PDP}' - \mathbf{PDP}' - \mathbf{PDP}' + \mathbf{PP}') \\ &= 2\sigma^2\mathbf{P}(\mathbf{I} - \mathbf{D})\mathbf{P}' \end{aligned} \tag{3.18}$$

The expression on the last line is equal to the right-hand side of (3.17). Note that the expected sum of squares in the left-hand side of (2.10) is nothing other than the trace of $\mathscr{V}(\hat{\boldsymbol{\epsilon}}_1 - \boldsymbol{\epsilon}_1)$. Since tr $\mathbf{P}(\mathbf{I} - \mathbf{D})\mathbf{P}' = $ tr $(\mathbf{I} - \mathbf{D})\mathbf{P}'\mathbf{P} =$ tr $(\mathbf{I} - \mathbf{D}) = H - d_1 - \cdots - d_H = K - d_1 - \cdots - d_K$, this equation has been proved.

LEMMA 7 *If a residual vector corresponding to the partitioning* (2.4) *is constrained to be linear and unbiased and to have a scalar covariance matrix, the squared length of its error vector has an expectation at least equal to the BLUS value* (2.10).

Returning to (3.10), we write $\mathbf{C}_1(\mathbf{I} + \mathbf{Z}\mathbf{Z}')\mathbf{e}_1 = (\mathbf{PDP}' + \mathbf{A})(\mathbf{I} + \mathbf{Z}\mathbf{Z}')\mathbf{e}_1$ for the competing residual vector, where $\mathbf{PDP}'$ is the BLUS specification of $\mathbf{C}_1$ and $\mathbf{A}$ is an appropriate matrix of order $(n - K) \times (n - K)$. The constraint (3.11) then takes the form

$$(\mathbf{PDP}' + \mathbf{A})\mathbf{PD}^{-2}\mathbf{P}'(\mathbf{PDP}' + \mathbf{A})' = \mathbf{I} \tag{3.19}$$

where use is made of (3.13). This is equivalent to

$$(3.20) \qquad (\mathbf{I} + \mathbf{N})(\mathbf{I} + \mathbf{N})' = \mathbf{I} \qquad \text{where} \qquad \mathbf{N} = \mathbf{APD}^{-1}\mathbf{P}'$$

As in the proof of Lemma 6 we now write the residual vector as

$$\mathbf{C}_1(\boldsymbol{\epsilon}_1 - \mathbf{Z}\boldsymbol{\epsilon}_0) = (\mathbf{PDP}' + \mathbf{A})(\boldsymbol{\epsilon}_1 - \mathbf{Z}\boldsymbol{\epsilon}_0)$$

so that the error vector is $(\mathbf{PDP}' + \mathbf{A} - \mathbf{I})\boldsymbol{\epsilon}_1 - (\mathbf{PDP}' + \mathbf{A})\mathbf{Z}\boldsymbol{\epsilon}_0$. Its covariance matrix is

(3.21)

$$\begin{aligned}
&\sigma^2(\mathbf{PDP}' + \mathbf{A} - \mathbf{I})(\mathbf{PDP}' + \mathbf{A} - \mathbf{I})' + \sigma^2(\mathbf{PDP}' + \mathbf{A})\mathbf{ZZ}'(\mathbf{PDP}' + \mathbf{A})' \\
&= \sigma^2(\mathbf{PDP}' + \mathbf{A})(\mathbf{I} + \mathbf{ZZ}')(\mathbf{PDP}' + \mathbf{A})' + \sigma^2(\mathbf{I} - 2\mathbf{PDP}' - \mathbf{A} - \mathbf{A}') \\
&= \sigma^2(2\mathbf{I} - 2\mathbf{PDP}' - \mathbf{A} - \mathbf{A}')
\end{aligned}$$

where the last equality sign is based on (3.19) and (3.13). It follows from the orthogonality of $\mathbf{P}$ that the matrices on the last lines of (3.18) and (3.21) are equal for $\mathbf{A} = \mathbf{0}$ (as they should be). The excess of the covariance matrix of the error vector of this residual vector over $\mathscr{V}(\hat{\boldsymbol{\epsilon}}_1 - \boldsymbol{\epsilon}_1)$ is $-\sigma^2(\mathbf{A} + \mathbf{A}')$. Hence, in order to prove that BLUS minimizes the expected sum of squares of the errors, we must show that $\mathbf{A} + \mathbf{A}'$ has a nonpositive trace. Substitute $\mathbf{NPDP}'$ for $\mathbf{A}$ in accordance with (3.20):

$$\begin{aligned}
(3.22) \quad \operatorname{tr}(\mathbf{A} + \mathbf{A}') &= \operatorname{tr}\mathbf{NPDP}' + \operatorname{tr}\mathbf{PDP}'\mathbf{N}' = \operatorname{tr}\mathbf{NPDP}' + \operatorname{tr}\mathbf{N}'\mathbf{PDP}' \\
&= \operatorname{tr}(\mathbf{N} + \mathbf{N}')\mathbf{PDP}' = \operatorname{tr}(\mathbf{N} + \mathbf{N}')\mathbf{PE}^2\mathbf{P}' \\
&= \operatorname{tr}\mathbf{EP}'(\mathbf{N} + \mathbf{N}')\mathbf{PE}
\end{aligned}$$

where $\mathbf{E}$ is the diagonal matrix whose elements are the positive square roots of the corresponding elements of $\mathbf{D}$. Evidently, the last trace in (3.22) is the trace of a negative semidefinite matrix (and is thus nonpositive) when $\mathbf{N} + \mathbf{N}'$ is a negative semidefinite matrix. This is indeed the case because (3.20) can be written in the form $\mathbf{N} + \mathbf{N}' = -\mathbf{NN}'$. This completes the proof of Theorem 5.4. When some of the roots $d_1, \ldots, d_H$ are equal, the corresponding $\mathbf{q}$'s are not unique but the BLUS vector $\hat{\boldsymbol{\epsilon}}_1$ of (2.9) is unique; see Problem 3.4.

Problems

3.1 Prove that under Assumption 3.1 of Section 3.2 each linear unbiased residual vector is a zero vector when $n = K$. [*Hint.* Use eq. (3.2).]

3.2 Describe in words the difference between eqs. (3.6) and (2.3). In particular, discuss the orders and the ranks of the matrix products in the left-hand sides.

3.3 It is stated in footnote 10 on page 209 that the seven lemmas of this section are based on Assumption 3.3 of Section 3.2 insofar as this is relevant. Indicate for which lemmas the assumption is irrelevant, and justify your answer.

3.4 (*BLUS residuals and multiple roots*) To prove the uniqueness of $\hat{\boldsymbol{\epsilon}}_1$ as given in (2.9) when there are multiple roots among $d_1^2, \ldots, d_H^2$, consider a symmetric $n \times n$ matrix $\mathbf{A}$ with root λ of multiplicity s, so that $(\mathbf{A} - \lambda\mathbf{I})\mathbf{U} = \mathbf{0}$, where $\mathbf{U} = [\mathbf{u}_1 \cdots \mathbf{u}_s]$ is a matrix of characteristic vectors corresponding to λ. Assume that these vectors have unit length and are pairwise orthogonal: $\mathbf{U}'\mathbf{U} = \mathbf{I}$. [This condition is also imposed on $\mathbf{q}_1, \ldots, \mathbf{q}_H$ of (2.8) and (2.9).] Any other set of characteristic vectors can be expressed linearly in $\mathbf{u}_1, \ldots, \mathbf{u}_s$:

$$\mathbf{v}_i = \sum_{r=1}^{s} k_{ir}\mathbf{u}_r \qquad i = 1, \ldots, s \tag{3.23}$$

or $\mathbf{V} = \mathbf{U}\mathbf{K}'$ where $\mathbf{V} = [\mathbf{v}_1 \cdots \mathbf{v}_s]$ and $\mathbf{K} = [k_{ir}]$. Prove that the unit-length and pairwise orthogonality condition on $\mathbf{v}_1, \ldots, \mathbf{v}_s$ implies that $\mathbf{K}$ is orthogonal. Then prove $\mathbf{U}\mathbf{U}' = \mathbf{V}\mathbf{V}'$, and use this to prove that multiple roots among $d_1^2, \ldots, d_H^2$ do not impair the uniqueness of the BLUS vector.

3.5 In Theil (1968a) an attempt is made to prove that BLUS residuals satisfy the optimality criterion of Theorem 5.1 subject to the choice of the partitioning and the condition of a scalar covariance matrix. This requires that the matrix $\mathbf{A} + \mathbf{A}'$ in (3.21) be negative semidefinite. The argument is based on the assumption that one may regard $\mathbf{A}$ as symmetric without loss of generality, replacing it by $\mathbf{A}^* = \frac{1}{2}(\mathbf{A} + \mathbf{A}')$ if necessary. Prove that this argument is not correct, using the constraint (3.20) on $\mathbf{A}$.

5.4 Tests against Heteroscedasticity and Autocorrelation of Disturbances[C]

Theorem 5.4 provides us with a BLUS residual vector for any given partitioning of the type (2.4). In this section we shall use such residuals to test certain hypotheses, and the question thus arises as to which particular partitioning is to be chosen or, in the language used in the discussion around (2.6), which base is to be selected for the index transformation. We shall start with a simple case.

Testing against Heteroscedasticity

Again consider Figure 5.1 and assume that the associated parameter vector $\boldsymbol{\beta}$ contains $K = 2$ elements. As in Section 5.1, the alternative hypothesis states that the disturbance variances either increase or decrease over time.

Also recall that Goldfeld and Quandt found that it is advantageous from the standpoint of the power of the test to omit a number of observations in the middle range. In the BLUS case we have to omit observations because there are only $n - K$ which can be represented by the BLUS residual vector. Thus, a natural choice is the BLUS vector whose base consists of the middle K observations (the sixth and the seventh for $n = 12$ and $K = 2$), given that the two outer groups (the first five observations and the last five) are more informative when the alternative hypothesis states that the variance either increases or decreases over time. We thus compute the ratio:

$$\frac{\hat{\epsilon}_1^2 + \cdots + \hat{\epsilon}_5^2}{\hat{\epsilon}_8^2 + \cdots + \hat{\epsilon}_{12}^2} \tag{4.1}$$

which is distributed as $F(5, 5)$ under the null hypothesis that $\epsilon_1/\sigma, \ldots, \epsilon_{12}/\sigma$ are independent standardized normal variates.[11] Since this F distribution is an implication of this null hypothesis, we must certainly reject the latter in all those cases in which the implication is rejected [i.e., in all cases in which the observed ratio lies in the critical region of $F(5, 5)$]. Note that the ratio (4.1) is based on ten degrees of freedom and the earlier ratio (1.10) on only eight ($K = 2$).

Specifically, consider the following equation:

$$y_\alpha = \beta_1\alpha + \beta_2 \sin(\alpha/2) + \epsilon_\alpha \qquad \alpha = 1, \ldots, 20 \tag{4.2}$$

which amounts to a sine (measured in radians) superimposed on a linear trend. We specify $\beta_1 = 1$, $\beta_2 = 10$, and generate the ϵ's as random normal sampling numbers with zero mean and unit variance, the result of which is shown in column (2) of Table 5.1. Thus everything is known, which is not the usual situation, but it has the advantage that the various residuals can be compared with the ϵ's. Column (3) contains the LS residuals and column (4) shows the BLUS residuals whose base consists of the middle $K = 2$ observations (the tenth and the eleventh). They are computed from the LS residuals by means of (2.9) and (2.8), using

$$\mathbf{X}_0 = \begin{bmatrix} 10 & \sin 5 \\ 11 & \sin 5\tfrac{1}{2} \end{bmatrix} \qquad \mathbf{e}_0 = \begin{bmatrix} .093 \\ -1.497 \end{bmatrix}$$

which gives $d_1 = .0416$, $d_2 = .5081$, $\mathbf{q}_1' = [-.649 \quad .761]$, $\mathbf{q}_2' = [.761 \quad .649]$.[12]

[11] Note that the normality of the BLUS residuals follows from that of the disturbances because (2.9) expresses the BLUS vector linearly in terms of the LS residuals and the latter residuals are, in turn, linear functions of the disturbances ($\mathbf{e} = \mathbf{M}\boldsymbol{\epsilon}$).

[12] Note that $[\mathbf{q}_1 \quad \mathbf{q}_2]$ is a 2×2 orthogonal matrix in this case, which is basically determined by only one number; see eq. (5.8) of Section 1.5.

Table 5.1

An Example of Least-Squares and BLUS Residuals

Observation Number (α) (1)	Disturbance (ϵ_α) (2)	Residuals: LS (e_α) (3)	BLUS ($\hat{\epsilon}_\alpha$) (4)	(5)	(6)	(7)
1	1.046	1.019	1.062	.	.	.999
2	−.508	−.552	−.471	.	−.737	−.593
3	−1.630	−1.674	−1.563	−1.665	−1.903	−1.734
4	−.146	−.169	−.038	−.133	−.399	−.249
5	−.105	−.090	.053	−.014	−.279	−.188
6	−.357	−.291	−.143	−.168	−.413	−.407
7	−1.384	−1.264	−1.112	−1.091	−1.313	−1.398
8	.360	.527	.687	.744	.535	.375
9	−.992	−.794	−.619	−.542	−.762	−.965
10	−.116	.093	.	.366	.106	−.097
11	−1.698	−1.497	.	−1.217	−1.546	−1.707
12	−1.339	−1.160	−.886	−.882	−1.303	−1.390
13	1.827	1.978	2.295	2.250	1.729	1.727
14	−.959	−.831	−.473	−.563	−1.177	−1.103
15	.424	.541	.935	.816	.129	.250
16	.969	1.095	1.514	1.388	.657	.784
17	−1.141	−.986	−.551	−.660	−1.406	−1.316
18	−1.041	−.841	−.397	−.471	−1.207	−1.189
19	1.041	1.294	1.743	1.713	1.001	.
20	.535	.840	1.294	1.307	.	.
Sum of squares		20.52	20.52	20.52	20.52	20.52
d_1			.0416	.0023	.1377	.0950
d_2			.5081	.3105	.4456	.5628
$d_1 + d_2$			.5497	.3128	.5833	.6578

The positive sign of the d's indicates that $\mathbf{X}_0$ is nonsingular (as it should be). The F ratio is then

$$\frac{\frac{1}{9}[(1.062)^2 + \cdots + (-.619)^2]}{\frac{1}{9}[(-.886)^2 + \cdots + (1.294)^2]} = .404 \tag{4.3}$$

When applying the F distribution with nine degrees of freedom in the numerator and the denominator, we conclude that neither .404 nor its reciprocal is significant at the usual standards.

Selecting the Base of the Index Transformation

The previous subsection describes a simple method of selecting the base for a particular alternative hypothesis. Before formulating a general procedure for selecting such bases it should be stressed that the most satisfactory approach would be to use the base which maximizes the power of the test. This leads to considerable complications, however. First, there is the question of whether a base exists which maximizes the power for all individual hypotheses covered by the alternative hypothesis. Second, power involves the distribution of the relevant test statistic when the null hypothesis is not true, so that the BLUS residuals are then no longer uncorrelated and homoscedastic. Thus we face precisely the same difficulties as those which were described in Section 5.1 for the LS residuals under the null hypothesis. In order to keep the procedure manageable we shall have to use a simpler criterion, but it should be one that leads to a power which is not too far below the attainable maximum.

More specifically, in the case of testing against an increasing or decreasing variance of the disturbances, it seems indeed a priori reasonable to select the middle K observations as the base; however, there exists no unique set of middle K observations when $n - K$ is odd. This is the usual situation for other alternative hypotheses also. Take that of nonzero autocorrelation. When the alternative hypothesis makes a statement on *successive* disturbances—as is the case for autocorrelation—it seems a priori reasonable to use BLUS residuals corresponding to $n - K$ *successive* observations. This rule does not make the choice of the base unique, since we obtain such successive residuals by selecting any base consisting of the first m and the last $K - m$ observations, where m is a nonnegative integer $\leq K$. This leads to $K + 1$ possible bases, three in the case (4.2); the corresponding BLUS residuals are given in columns (5) to (7) of Table 5.1. Similarly, when we have an odd value of $n - K$ and when we test against an increasing or decreasing disturbance variance, one may argue that there are two sets of middle observations and thus two admissible bases. The F ratio is then based either on the $\frac{1}{2}(n - K - 1)$ first and the $\frac{1}{2}(n - K + 1)$ last observations or on the $\frac{1}{2}(n - K + 1)$ first and the $\frac{1}{2}(n - K - 1)$ last observations. Note that the degrees of freedom in the numerator and the denominator of such F ratios are no longer equal.

Thus the conclusion is that in both cases (autocorrelation and heteroscedasticity for odd $n - K$) a priori considerations of power lead to a substantial reduction of the number of base candidates: from $\binom{n}{K}$ to $K + 1$ in the case of autocorrelation and to 2 in that of heteroscedasticity. This is not enough, however, since we need exactly one base. The simplest choice is based on the optimality criterion of the BLUS residuals: select the base for which the expected sum of squares of the BLUS errors takes the smallest value. It follows from (2.10) that this expectation is a decreasing function of the sum of the d's. Thus, by choosing the base with the largest sum $d_1 + \cdots + d_K$ we minimize the expected sum of squares of the errors. Note that this minimum property applies, strictly speaking, only to the null hypothesis, whereas power refers to the alternative hypothesis. The use of this particular criterion is motivated by the presumption that if a BLUS vector is "best" under the null hypothesis, it will be at least "good" when this hypothesis is violated to a limited degree. Finally, note that bases which have one or more zero d's should be disregarded because they imply that $\mathbf{X}_0$ is a singular matrix.

The procedure may thus be summarized as follows.

(1) Formulate *a class of admissible bases* of the index transformation. This class is determined by the nature of the alternative hypothesis; the criterion is that the observations of the base should be less informative with respect to the alternative hypothesis than the other observations are. Thus, there are $K + 1$ admissible bases when the alternative hypothesis states $\mathscr{E}(\epsilon_\alpha \epsilon_{\alpha+1}) \neq 0$, and each of them leads to $n - K$ successive BLUS residuals.

(2) For each member of the class, compute $d_1, \ldots, d_K$ as the positive square roots of the latent roots of $\mathbf{X}_0(\mathbf{X}'\mathbf{X})^{-1}\mathbf{X}_0'$. Disregard those bases for which one or more roots vanish, because the base is then singular ($|\mathbf{X}_0| = 0$).[13] For all others compute the sum of the d's and select the base with the largest sum. The test statistic is based on $\hat{\boldsymbol{\epsilon}}_1$, to be computed from (2.9), corresponding to that particular base. This test statistic was the F ratio in the case of the alternative hypothesis considered in Figure 5.1.

Testing against Autocorrelation

We return to columns (5) to (7) of Table 5.1, which are concerned with nonzero autocorrelation as the alternative hypothesis. The last line of the table shows that column (7) has the largest sum of d's, corresponding to a base that consists of the last two observations; note that both d's are strictly positive for this base. The test against autocorrelation is exclusively based on the BLUS residuals of that column; columns (5) and (6) are superfluous except for their d's. [These d's are used to establish that column (7) is superior according to the criterion chosen.]

A well-known statistic for testing against autocorrelation of a series of random variables $X_1, \ldots, X_N$ is the *von Neumann ratio*, which is defined as

[13] In computational practice this means that one rejects a base whose smallest root is less than a given small number, for example, 10^{-6}.

the ratio of the mean square successive difference to the variance:

$$(4.4)\qquad Q = \frac{\dfrac{1}{N-1}\sum_{\alpha=1}^{N-1}(X_{\alpha+1}-X_\alpha)^2}{\dfrac{1}{N}\sum_{\alpha=1}^{N}(X_\alpha-\bar{X})^2} \qquad \text{where} \qquad \bar{X} = \frac{1}{N}\sum_{\alpha=1}^{N} X_\alpha$$

This ratio is obviously closely related to the Durbin-Watson statistic defined in (1.13). When it is sufficiently small (large), it points toward positive (negative) autocorrelation. Significance limits of Q have been computed by Miss B. I. HART (1942b) under the condition that $X_1, \ldots, X_N$ are independent normal variates with mean μ and variance σ^2. These limits are reproduced at the end of this book for $N \leq 60$. For $N > 60$ one may approximate the distribution of Q by a normal distribution with mean $2N/(N-1)$ and variance $4/N$.

The application of Q to BLUS residuals implies that one should interpret X_α as $\hat{\epsilon}_\alpha$ and N as $n - K$. Note, however, that X_α is supposed to have an unknown expectation (μ), whereas $\hat{\epsilon}_\alpha$ is known to have zero expectation. In the right-hand denominator of (4.4) we estimate μ by $\bar{X}$, but the fact that the expectation of $\hat{\epsilon}_\alpha$ is known to be zero suggests that one can just as well replace the sample variance in (4.4) by the mean square. This leads to the *modified von Neumann ratio* of $n - K$ successive BLUS residuals:

$$(4.5)\qquad Q' = \frac{\sum_{\alpha}(\hat{\epsilon}_{\alpha+1}-\hat{\epsilon}_\alpha)^2}{(n-K-1)s^2}$$

where the summation in the numerator is over all successive values of α (except the last) for which BLUS residuals are computed. The LS variance estimator s^2 has been substituted for the mean square of the BLUS residuals in the denominator; see (2.11). Significance limits of Q' for $n - K = 2, \ldots, 60$ have been derived by PRESS and BROOKS (1969) under the condition of independence and normality with zero mean and variance σ^2; they are also reproduced at the end of this book. For $n - K > 60$ a satisfactory approximation is obtained by using a normal distribution for Q' with mean 2 and variance $4/(n - K)$.

As an example we consider column (7) of Table 5.1, for which Q' takes the following value:

$$(4.6)\qquad Q' = \frac{(-.593 - .999)^2 + \cdots + (-1.189 + 1.316)^2}{17(20.52/18)} = 2.05$$

This is well above the 5 percent significance point (1.228) of Q' for $n - K = 18$ in the one-tailed test against positive autocorrelation, and also considerably below the 5 percent point (2.785) for the one-tailed test against negative autocorrelation.

Application to the Textile Example

Columns (1) to (3) of Table 5.2 deal with similar procedures for the textile example of Section 3.3. (The other columns of this table will be discussed in the next section.) We have $n = 17$, $K = 3$, so that $n - K$ is even and the choice of the base is unique when the alternative hypothesis states that the variance of the disturbances either increases or decreases over time. The corresponding BLUS vector is given in column (2) and the F ratio, similar to (4.3), is .678, which is far from significant for $F(7, 7)$. Column (3) is concerned with testing against autocorrelation. The admissible bases then consist of the

Table 5.2

Least-Squares and BLUS Residuals for the Textile Example

	LS (e_α)	BLUS ($\hat{\epsilon}_\alpha$)			
	(1)	(2)	(3)	(4)	(5)
1923	.0142	.0188	.	.0180	.
1924	.0030	.0069	.	.0064	.
1925	−.0026	.0005	−.0050	.0005	−.0050
1926	−.0142	−.0139	−.0155	−.0127	−.0138
1927	.0086	.0084	.0068	.0096	.0091
1928	−.0163	−.0180	−.0160	−.0157	−.0137
1929	−.0059	−.0080	−.0050	.	−.0027
1930	.0055	.	.0061	.	.0097
1931	.0135	.	.0117	.0122	.0170
1932	.0053	.	.0014	.0041	.0072
1933	.0129	.0112	.0071	.0118	.0133
1934	−.0004	.0008	−.0086	.	−.0034
1935	−.0131	−.0122	−.0207	−.0130	−.0156
1936	.0036	.0023	−.0052	.0019	.
1937	−.0116	−.0139	−.0174	−.0131	−.0109
1938	−.0241	−.0260	−.0302	−.0255	−.0237
1939	.0216	.0190	.	.0200	.0229
Sum of squares ($\times 10^6$)	2567	2567	2567	2567	2567
d_1		.038	.035	.093	.034
d_2		.229	.327	.382	.493
d_3		.677	.776	.712	.770
$d_1 + d_2 + d_3$		.945	1.138	1.187	1.296

first m and the last $3 - m$ observations with the following results for the d's:

	$m = 3$	$m = 2$	$m = 1$	$m = 0$
d_1	.003	.035	.065	.005
d_2	.093	.327	.456	.075
d_3	.894	.776	.595	.599
$d_1 + d_2 + d_3$	.990	1.138	1.116	.678

Hence, none of the d's vanishes and $m = 2$ gives the largest sum of d's, so that the base chosen consists of the first two observations plus the last. The modified von Neumann ratio computed from column (3) is 1.05, which is below the 5 percent significance limit of the one-tailed test against positive autocorrelation but above the 1 percent limit.

A Comparison with the Durbin-Watson Test

Since the Durbin-Watson test applied to LS residuals is computationally simpler than the BLUS-von Neumann procedure, it is appropriate to ask how much we gain by the extra effort. KOERTS and ABRAHAMSE (1968) considered this problem for the case in which successive disturbances are positively correlated. Their results indicate that although neither procedure is particularly powerful when the number of degrees of freedom is small and the disturbances are only moderately autocorrelated, the BLUS method rejects the null hypothesis in a substantially larger number of cases than its simpler rival. The frequency with which the Durbin-Watson statistic falls in the inclusive region (d_L, d_U) is quite large when $n - K$ is about 20 or less. The situation improves when $n - K$ increases, but the number of cases in which the Durbin-Watson procedure rejects the null hypothesis (as it should) continues to be lower than that of the other method unless $n - K$ is very large and the autocorrelation is substantial. More evidence will be needed, however, because these results are restricted to particular $\mathbf{X}$ matrices; also, more attention should be given to the selection of BLUS bases than the authors have done.

Problems

4.1 (*BLUS residuals and dummy variables*) Consider a time series regression based on two years of quarterly data. The transpose of the observation matrix $\mathbf{X}$ is

$$\text{(4.7)} \qquad \mathbf{X}' = \begin{bmatrix} 1 & 1 & 1 & 1 & 1 & 1 & 1 & 1 \\ 0 & 0 & 0 & 0 & 1 & 1 & 1 & 1 \\ x_1 & x_2 & x_3 & x_4 & x_5 & x_6 & x_7 & x_8 \end{bmatrix}$$

where the first row refers to the constant term and the second to a dummy variable (0 in the first year, 1 in the second). Prove that the base of the index transformation in the test against autocorrelation is either the first plus the last two observations or the first two plus the last one.

4.2 On the ground that the Durbin-Watson procedure is computationally simpler than the BLUS-von Neumann test, an analyst argues that he can avoid much of the additional computational work and still have a test equal in power to that of BLUS-von Neumann by proceeding as follows. First, he computes the value of the Durbin-Watson statistic and he draws his conclusions when it is less than d_L or larger than d_U. Second, if it falls in (d_L, d_U), he computes BLUS residuals and the modified von Neumann ratio and he decides on the significance of this ratio as described below (4.6). What is wrong with this procedure?

5.5 Tests against Nonlinearity[C]

A third alternative hypothesis besides heteroscedasticity and autocorrelation is nonlinearity in one or several explanatory variables. First consider the case of one explanatory variable and assume that the alternative hypothesis amounts to a quadratic relation:

$$y_\alpha = \beta_0 + \beta x_\alpha + \beta' x_\alpha^2 + \epsilon_\alpha \tag{5.1}$$

A straightforward approach is to run an LS regression of y_α on x_α and x_α^2 and to apply the t test to the β' estimate under the condition of normally distributed ϵ's. When there are several explanatory variables, say, two, we can apply the following quadratic specification:

$$y_\alpha = \beta_0 + \beta_1 x_{\alpha 1} + \beta_2 x_{\alpha 2} + \gamma_{11} x_{\alpha 1}^2 + \gamma_{22} x_{\alpha 2}^2 + \gamma_{12} x_{\alpha 1} x_{\alpha 2} + \epsilon_\alpha \tag{5.2}$$

and use the F test for the null hypothesis $\gamma_{11} = \gamma_{22} = \gamma_{12} = 0$. These procedures are straightforward applications of the general testing theory described in Section 3.7.

A Linearity Test Based on the von Neumann Ratio

In a number of cases one will prefer not to specify a particular algebraic form of the alternative specification such as (5.1) or (5.2), and BLUS residuals then provide a simple method of testing against nonlinearity. Consider Figure 5.2*a*, which measures one of the explanatory variables horizontally and the disturbances vertically. In this case there is an indication that ϵ_α is equal to a nonlinear function of $x_{\alpha h}$ plus a random variable with zero mean. One method of testing the significance of this nonlinearity is the

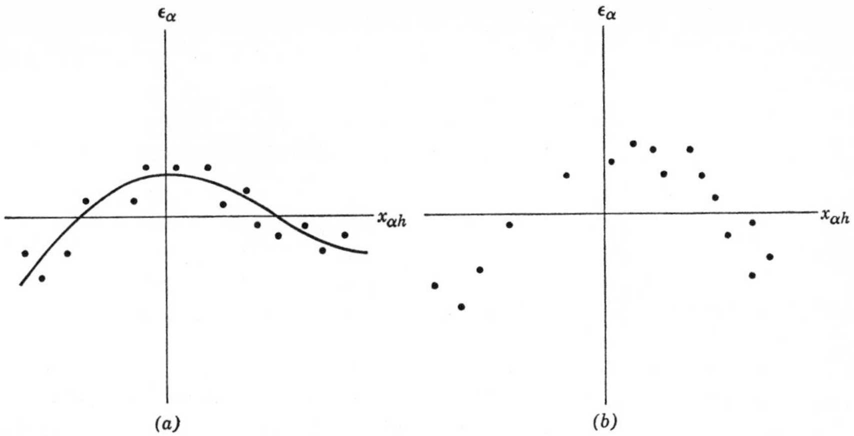

Fig. 5.2 Two cases of nonlinearity.

following.[14] If the curvilinearity is as indicated by the smooth curve that goes through the points of the left-hand diagram, then disturbances that correspond to nearly equal values of the explanatory variable concerned will, on the average, be rather close to each other in numerical value. Thus, if we rearrange the observations according to increasing values of this variable, $x_{1h} \leq x_{2h} \leq \cdots \leq x_{nh}$, the mean square successive difference of the n disturbances will be on the low side, so that the corresponding modified von Neumann ratio Q' will take a small value. A natural procedure is then to compute Q' for a set of $n - K$ BLUS residuals whose base consists of the first m and the last $K - m$ observations ($m = 0, 1, \ldots, K$), where "first" and "last" refer to the ranking just mentioned. The BLUS vector is again selected according to the criterion of the largest sum of d's subject to the constraint that none of them vanishes. The relevant significance limit of Q' is that of a one-tailed test against positive autocorrelation because a low value of Q' is indicative of nonlinearity in this ranking.

Application to the Textile Example

We take the textile example for a test against nonlinearity in the logarithm of income. Table 3.1 in the opening paragraph of Chapter 3 shows that the order of the observations according to increasing values of real per capita income is as follows (with 1934 abbreviated as 34): 34, 35, 23, 36, 24, 25, 38,

[14] The method described here was originally suggested by PRAIS and HOUTHAKKER (1955, pp. 52–53) in terms of LS residuals and the Durbin-Watson statistic. For another method (based on medians), see BROWN and MOOD (1951). Also see HILL (1962) and OLSHEN (1967).

33, 37, 39, (26, 27), 32, 31, 28, 29, 30, where (26, 27) indicates that the years 1926 and 1927 form a tie. The four admissible bases and their *d*'s are:[15]

	1934	1934	1934	1928
	1935	1935	1929	1929
	1923	1930	1930	1930
d_1	.021	.000	.093	.018
d_2	.437	.408	.382	.119
d_3	.717	.676	.712	.783
$d_1 + d_2 + d_3$	1.175	1.084	1.187	.919

The third base has the largest sum of *d*'s and none of the *d*'s of this base vanishes. The corresponding BLUS vector is shown in column (4) of Table 5.2. The modified von Neumann ratio based on the above ranking with 1926 preceding 1927 is 3.15; when 1927 precedes 1926 it becomes 2.85. Neither of these values is significant in a one-tailed test against positive autocorrelation.

In this example we have one tie, but when there are several it becomes cumbersome to consider all possible combinations. The analyst may then prefer to break the ties by means of a random selection procedure. Thus, instead of carrying out the computations both for (26, 27) and for (27, 26), he tosses an unbiased coin to decide which ranking he will choose, and he performs the test for this ranking only. See Problem 5.1 for a test against nonlinearity in the logarithm of the relative price of textile goods, which is characterized by two ties.

Testing against Convexity

The above BLUS-von Neumann procedure for testing linearity can be used when the alternative hypothesis is that of an arbitrary continuous relationship between the dependent and the *h*th explanatory variables. This should be contrasted with the much more specific alternative of a quadratic relation such as (5.1) or (5.2). Indeed, it is of great importance to reflect on the question of what kind of nonlinearity one has in mind as an alternative hypothesis.[16] This alternative may be more restrictive than that of a

[15] The smallest root of the second base as presented here is zero in three decimal places, but the fourth digit is 4 and, therefore, the root is positive.

[16] An analysis of the behavior of the dependent variable for extreme values of the explanatory variables is frequently useful. This may be illustrated by means of the following example from ZELLNER and SANKAR (1967). They considered consumption-income ratios (C/Y) for a number of countries in order to test the hypothesis that they are constant against the alternative that they depend on the level of real income per capita (Y). If the alternative is specified in the form of a linear consumption function, $C = \beta_0 + \beta Y$ with $\beta_0 > 0$, then C/Y exceeds 1 at low levels of Y (underdeveloped countries), which is occasionally but not

continuous relation but less restrictive than quadratic. For example, it may state that the dependence of the left-hand variable on the hth explanatory variable is either convex or concave. The procedure based on the modified von Neumann ratio may then be less powerful than is attainable. This is illustrated in Figure 5.2*b*; it shows that the observations which are most informative with respect to this alternative hypothesis are the outer observations (both on the far left and on the far right) plus the observations in the middle, since these two groups are represented by points which tend to be located on different sides of the horizontal axis if the relation is indeed convex or concave. This suggests computing BLUS residuals for the $\frac{1}{4}(n - K)$ observations on the far left, the $\frac{1}{2}(n - K)$ observations in the middle, and the $\frac{1}{4}(n - K)$ observations on the far right, so that the base of the index transformation is formed by the $\frac{1}{2}K$ observations immediately to the left of the middle and the $\frac{1}{2}K$ immediately to the right. One may then fit a parabola through the $n - K$ points and test its significance; for details see Problem 5.2.

Other Tests

The ranking according to increasing values of one of the explanatory variables can also be applied to test $\mathscr{V}(\boldsymbol{\epsilon}) = \sigma^2\mathbf{I}$ against the alternative hypothesis that the variance of the disturbances is an increasing (or decreasing) function of that variable; see Problems 5.3 and 5.4. In all such cases BLUS residuals can be used; the main problem is the formulation of a suitable class of admissible bases of the index transformation which enables the analyst to establish the validity of the alternative hypothesis if this hypothesis is indeed true.

Problems

5.1 The ranking of the observations of the textile example according to increasing values of the relative textile price is: 36, 38, 37, (33, 39), 34, 35, 32, 31, 30, 27, 28, (26, 29), 25, 24, 23. The d's of the relevant bases

---

permanently possible. If the alternative is $C = kY^\eta$ with $\eta < 1$, then C/Y increases indefinitely when Y converges to zero. The alternative chosen by the authors specifies the logit of the consumption-income ratio (the logarithm of the ratio of C/Y to $1 - C/Y$) as a decreasing linear function of log Y, which ensures that C/Y converges to 1 as Y approaches 0. A disadvantage of this specification is that C/Y converges to 0 when Y increases indefinitely, but this convergence is slow and not of great importance for the present range of per capita incomes.

for testing against nonlinearity in the logarithm of this price are as follows:

	1936	1936	1936	1925
	1938	1938	1924	1924
	1937	1923	1923	1923
d_1	.011	.110	.034	.003
d_2	.159	.560	.493	.093
d_3	.682	.606	.770	.894
$d_1 + d_2 + d_3$	.852	1.277	1.296	.990

Conclude that the third base is to be selected [see column (5) of Table 5.5]. Verify that there are four modified von Neumann ratios because of the two ties:

1933, 1939; 1926, 1929	$Q' = 1.26$
1933, 1939; 1929, 1926	$Q' = 1.34$
1939, 1933; 1926, 1929	$Q' = 1.32$
1939, 1933; 1929, 1926	$Q' = 1.40$

Draw your conclusions as to their significance.

5.2 (*Test against convexity*) Consider the testing procedure outlined in the second last subsection and write m_h and v_h for the mean and the variance, respectively, of the $n - K$ values $x_{\alpha h}$ for which BLUS residuals are computed. Also consider the parabola

$$\hat{\epsilon}_\alpha = \gamma[(x_{\alpha h} - m_h)^2 - v_h] + \eta_\alpha \tag{5.3}$$

Prove that under the assumptions of the standard linear model with the additional specification of normality, the coefficient γ vanishes and $\hat{\epsilon}_\alpha = \eta_\alpha$ is a normal variate with zero mean and variance σ^2 (independent over the $n - K$ values of α). Also prove $\gamma < 0$ in the case of Figure 5.2*b*. Next prove that the t test applied to the LS estimator of γ is based on the statistic

$$\frac{\sqrt{n-K-1}\,A_h}{\sqrt{(n-K)s^2B_h - A_h^2}} \quad \text{where} \quad \begin{aligned} A_h &= \sum (x_{\alpha h} - m_h)^2\hat{\epsilon}_\alpha - v_h \sum \hat{\epsilon}_\alpha \\ B_h &= \sum (x_{\alpha h} - m_h)^4 - (n-K)v_h^2 \end{aligned} \tag{5.4}$$

What is the number of degrees of freedom of this t ratio?

5.3 Let the alternative hypothesis be that the variance of the disturbances increases (or decreases) with increasing values of one of the explanatory variables. Formulate a testing procedure based on BLUS residuals and the F ratio.

5.4 (*Continuation*) More specifically, assume that the alternative hypothesis states that the variance of the disturbances increases linearly with the explanatory variable. Write $\hat{\epsilon}_\alpha^2 = \gamma_0 + \gamma_1 x_{\alpha h} + \eta'_\alpha$ and formulate a t test similar to that of Problem 5.2. Do you expect this test to be more powerful than that of Problem 5.3? Justify your answer.

5.6 Further Results on BLUS Residuals[C]

The objective of this section is to provide additional insight into the BLUS procedure, partly by describing how it works in some special cases and partly by the derivation of some general properties. We start with the latter.

A Principal Component Interpretation

The matrix $\mathbf{Z} = \mathbf{X}_1\mathbf{X}_0^{-1}$ of the values taken by the index-transformed explanatory variables is invariant under nonsingular linear transformations of the original variables. This follows from $\mathbf{X}_1\mathbf{A}(\mathbf{X}_0\mathbf{A})^{-1} = \mathbf{X}_1\mathbf{X}_0^{-1}$, where $\mathbf{A}$ is an arbitrary nonsingular $K \times K$ matrix. We also note that the first H columns of the orthogonal matrix $\mathbf{P}$ which are mentioned in Lemma 4 of Section 5.3 can be regarded as the principal components of the index-transformed variables. This is proved by combining (3.12) and (3.14), which gives

$$(6.1) \qquad \left(\mathbf{ZZ}' - \frac{1 - d_h^2}{d_h^2}\mathbf{I}\right)\mathbf{p}_h = \mathbf{0} \qquad h = 1, \ldots, H$$

and by comparing this result with eq. (9.4) of Section 1.9. [Note that the usual standardization procedure of principal component analysis (zero mean and unit mean square for each variable) is replaced here by the index transformation.] Furthermore, combine (3.9) and (3.14) to obtain the following result:

$$(6.2) \qquad \mathbf{q}_h = \frac{d_h^2}{1 - d_h^2}\mathbf{Z}'\mathbf{Z}\mathbf{q}_h = \frac{d_h}{\sqrt{1 - d_h^2}}\mathbf{Z}'\mathbf{p}_h \qquad h = 1, \ldots, H$$

Comparing this equation as well as (3.14) with eqs. (9.3) and (9.6) of Section 1.9, we conclude that $\mathbf{q}_h$ is—apart from a positive multiplicative scalar—the coefficient vector by which $\mathbf{Z}$ must be postmultiplied in order to provide the hth principal component.

The Case of One Explanatory Variable without Constant Term

When there is only one explanatory variable and no constant term, the matrix $\mathbf{Z} = \mathbf{X}_1\mathbf{X}_0^{-1}$ is a column vector and, therefore, it is equal to the single principal component $\mathbf{p}_1$ apart from a normalization constant. The matrix

$\mathbf{X}_0(\mathbf{X}'\mathbf{X})^{-1}\mathbf{X}_0'$ is a scalar, $x_1^2/\sum x_\alpha^2$ (assuming that we choose the first observation as the base), and there is only one root d_1 which is the positive square root of this scalar:

$$d_1 = \frac{|x_1|}{\sqrt{\sum_{\alpha=1}^{n} x_\alpha^2}} \tag{6.3}$$

The criterion of maximizing the sum of the d's thus amounts to maximizing d_1 and, hence, to the selection of the observation with the largest absolute x value as the base of the index transformation. We shall continue working with the first observation as the base for reasons of notational convenience.

The characteristic vector $\mathbf{q}_1$ of the 1×1 matrix $\mathbf{X}_0(\mathbf{X}'\mathbf{X})^{-1}\mathbf{X}_0'$ is simply 1. Hence eq. (2.9) takes the following form:

$$\begin{bmatrix} \hat{\epsilon}_2 \\ \cdot \\ \cdot \\ \cdot \\ \hat{\epsilon}_n \end{bmatrix} = \begin{bmatrix} e_2 \\ \cdot \\ \cdot \\ \cdot \\ e_n \end{bmatrix} - \begin{bmatrix} x_2/x_1 \\ \cdot \\ \cdot \\ \cdot \\ x_n/x_1 \end{bmatrix} \frac{|x_1|}{|x_1| + \sqrt{\sum x^2}}\, e_1 \tag{6.4}$$

where $\sum x^2$ stands for $x_1^2 + \cdots + x_n^2$. Writing $e_\alpha = y_\alpha - bx_\alpha$ with $b = \sum xy/\sum x^2$, we thus have for $\alpha = 2, \ldots, n$:

$$\begin{aligned} \hat{\epsilon}_\alpha &= y_\alpha - bx_\alpha - \frac{x_\alpha}{x_1}\left(\frac{|x_1|}{|x_1| + \sqrt{\sum x^2}}\right)(y_1 - bx_1) \\ &= y_\alpha - \left[\left(\frac{|x_1|}{|x_1| + \sqrt{\sum x^2}}\right)\frac{y_1}{x_1} + \left(\frac{\sqrt{\sum x^2}}{|x_1| + \sqrt{\sum x^2}}\right)b\right]x_\alpha \\ &= y_\alpha - \left(\frac{d_1}{1 + d_1}\frac{y_1}{x_1} + \frac{1}{1 + d_1}b\right)x_\alpha \end{aligned} \tag{6.5}$$

where the last equality sign is based on (6.3). This result can be simplified by the introduction of

$$b_1 = \frac{\sum xy - x_1 y_1}{\sum x^2 - x_1^2} \tag{6.6}$$

which is the LS coefficient obtained by disregarding the first (base) observation. Consider, then,

$$\begin{aligned} \frac{b}{1 + d_1} &= \frac{(\sum xy - x_1 y_1) + x_1 y_1}{(1 + d_1)\sum x^2} = \frac{b_1(\sum x^2 - x_1^2) + x_1 y_1}{(1 + d_1)\sum x^2} \\ &= b_1 \frac{(|x_1| + \sqrt{\sum x^2})(\sqrt{\sum x^2} - |x_1|)}{(1 + d_1)\sum x^2} + \frac{y_1}{x_1}\frac{x_1^2}{(1 + d_1)\sum x^2} \\ &= b_1(1 - d_1) + \frac{y_1}{x_1}\frac{d_1^2}{1 + d_1} \end{aligned}$$

Combining this with the last line of (6.5), we obtain

$$\hat{\epsilon}_\alpha = y_\alpha - \left[d_1 \frac{y_1}{x_1} + (1 - d_1)b_1\right]x_\alpha \qquad \alpha = 2, \ldots, n \tag{6.7}$$

Thus the BLUS residual is obtained from y_α by subtracting a multiple of x_α equal to a weighted average of y_1/x_1, which may be regarded as the LS coefficient estimator derived from the single base observation, and b_1 which is based on all other observations.

A still more special case is $x_\alpha = 1$, $\alpha = 1, \ldots, n$, so that $y_1, \ldots, y_n$ are uncorrelated random variables with the same but unknown mean and variance (the case of "a constant term with no explanatory variables"). We then have $b = \bar{y}$ (the average of the y_α's) and $d_1 = 1/\sqrt{n}$, so that (6.7) is simplified to

$$\hat{\epsilon}_\alpha = y_\alpha - \frac{1}{\sqrt{n}}\left[y_1 + (\sqrt{n} - 1)\frac{y_2 + \cdots + y_{n-1}}{n - 1}\right] \qquad \alpha = 2, \ldots, n \tag{6.8}$$

Here we subtract from y_α a weighted average of y_1 and the mean of the $n - 1$ other y's, the weights being $1/\sqrt{n}$ and $1 - 1/\sqrt{n}$.

A Case of Several Explanatory Variables

Now consider the general case of K explanatory variables but with the following restrictions. First, n/K is an integer. Second, the variables "repeat themselves" in the sense that $\mathbf{X}$ consists of n/K matrices all equal to $\mathbf{X}_0$:

$$\mathbf{X} = \begin{bmatrix} \mathbf{X}_0 \\ \mathbf{X}_0 \\ \cdot \\ \cdot \\ \cdot \\ \mathbf{X}_0 \end{bmatrix} \begin{matrix} \text{first set of } K \text{ rows} \\ \text{second set of } K \text{ rows} \\ \\ \\ \\ (n/K)\text{th set of } K \text{ rows} \end{matrix} \tag{6.9}$$

The first K observations will form the base. Since $\mathbf{X}'\mathbf{X} = (n/K)\mathbf{X}_0'\mathbf{X}_0$, the matrix $\mathbf{X}_0(\mathbf{X}'\mathbf{X})^{-1}\mathbf{X}_0'$ is $(K/n)\mathbf{I}$ and, hence, the d's are all equal:

$$d_h = \sqrt{\frac{K}{n}} \qquad \mathbf{q}_h = \mathbf{i}_h \qquad h = 1, \ldots, K \tag{6.10}$$

where $\mathbf{i}_h$ is the hth column of the $K \times K$ unit matrix. We then apply (2.9):

$$\hat{\boldsymbol{\epsilon}}_1 = \mathbf{e}_1 - \begin{bmatrix} \mathbf{I} \\ \vdots \\ \mathbf{I} \end{bmatrix} \frac{\sqrt{K/n}}{1 + \sqrt{K/n}} \mathbf{I}\mathbf{e}_0 = \mathbf{e}_1 - \frac{\sqrt{K}}{\sqrt{K} + \sqrt{n}} \begin{bmatrix} \mathbf{e}_0 \\ \vdots \\ \mathbf{e}_0 \end{bmatrix} \tag{6.11}$$

To express the $\mathbf{e}$'s in terms of the values of the dependent variable we partition the observation matrix as follows:

$$(6.12) \qquad [\mathbf{y} \quad \mathbf{X}] = \begin{bmatrix} \mathbf{y}_0 & \mathbf{X}_0 \\ \mathbf{y}_{(1)} & \mathbf{X}_0 \\ \vdots & \vdots \\ \mathbf{y}_{(p)} & \mathbf{X}_0 \end{bmatrix} \qquad \text{where} \qquad p = \frac{n}{K} - 1$$

The LS coefficient estimator $\mathbf{b} = (\mathbf{X}'\mathbf{X})^{-1}\mathbf{X}'\mathbf{y}$ can then be written as

$$\mathbf{b} = \frac{K}{n}\mathbf{X}_0^{-1}(\mathbf{X}_0')^{-1}[\mathbf{X}_0' \quad \mathbf{X}_0' \quad \cdots \quad \mathbf{X}_0'] \begin{bmatrix} \mathbf{y}_0 \\ \mathbf{y}_{(1)} \\ \vdots \\ \mathbf{y}_{(p)} \end{bmatrix} = \frac{K}{n}\mathbf{X}_0^{-1}\mathbf{y}_0 + \frac{K}{n}\mathbf{X}_0^{-1}\sum_{j=1}^{p}\mathbf{y}_{(j)}$$

so that

$$(6.13) \qquad \begin{aligned} \mathbf{e}_0 &= \mathbf{y}_0 - \mathbf{X}_0\mathbf{b} = \left(1 - \frac{K}{n}\right)\mathbf{y}_0 - \frac{K}{n}\sum_{j=1}^{p}\mathbf{y}_{(j)} \\ \mathbf{e}_{(i)} &= \mathbf{y}_{(i)} - \mathbf{X}_0\mathbf{b} = \mathbf{y}_{(i)} - \frac{K}{n}\mathbf{y}_0 - \frac{K}{n}\sum_{j=1}^{p}\mathbf{y}_{(j)} \qquad i = 1, \ldots, p \end{aligned}$$

where $\mathbf{e}_{(i)}$ is the ith K-element subvector of $\mathbf{e}_1$. If we write $\hat{\boldsymbol{\epsilon}}_{(i)}$ for the corresponding subvector of $\hat{\boldsymbol{\epsilon}}_1$, we obtain from (6.11) and (6.13) after some algebraic rearrangements:

$$(6.14) \qquad \begin{aligned} \hat{\boldsymbol{\epsilon}}_{(i)} &= \mathbf{y}_{(i)} - \sqrt{\frac{K}{n}}\,\mathbf{y}_0 - \frac{K}{\sqrt{n}(\sqrt{K} + \sqrt{n})}\sum_{j=1}^{p}\mathbf{y}_{(j)} \\ &= \mathbf{y}_{(i)} - \frac{1}{\sqrt{n}}\left[\sqrt{K}\,\mathbf{y}_0 + (\sqrt{n} - \sqrt{K})\frac{1}{p}\sum_{j=1}^{p}\mathbf{y}_{(j)}\right] \qquad i = 1, \ldots, p \end{aligned}$$

which is a generalization of (6.8). This is as it should be because (6.9) reduces to $x_\alpha = 1$, $\alpha = 1, \ldots, n$ in the case $K = 1$. Note that both the LS residuals (6.13) and the BLUS residuals (6.14) are completely determined by n, K, and the values of the dependent variable and, hence, they are independent of the matrix (6.9).

The BLUS Implied Coefficient Vector

Equation (6.7) suggests that there is a coefficient estimator that is implied by the BLUS residuals and that it is equal to the weighted average of y_1/x_1 and b_1 with d_1 and $1 - d_1$ as weights. In fact, a BLUS implied coefficient vector always exists for any given set of $n - K$ BLUS residuals. This is verified by substituting $\mathbf{y}_1 - \mathbf{X}_1\mathbf{b}$ for $\mathbf{e}_1$ in (2.9) and then writing this equation in the form $\hat{\boldsymbol{\epsilon}}_1 = \mathbf{y}_1 - \mathbf{X}_1\hat{\boldsymbol{\beta}}_1$, where

$$\hat{\boldsymbol{\beta}}_1 = \mathbf{b} + \mathbf{X}_0^{-1}\left[\sum_{h=1}^{H} \frac{d_h}{1 + d_h} \mathbf{q}_h\mathbf{q}_h'\right]\mathbf{e}_0 \tag{6.15}$$

It is easily verified that $\hat{\boldsymbol{\beta}}_1$ is a linear unbiased estimator of $\boldsymbol{\beta}$ under the assumptions of the standard linear model. The Gauss-Markov theorem then implies that $\mathscr{V}(\hat{\boldsymbol{\beta}}_1)$ exceeds $\mathscr{V}(\mathbf{b}) = \sigma^2(\mathbf{X}'\mathbf{X})^{-1}$ by a positive semidefinite matrix. The use of $\hat{\boldsymbol{\beta}}_1$ as an estimator of $\boldsymbol{\beta}$ cannot, therefore, be recommended, but the vector does serve a useful theoretical purpose for the analysis of the asymptotic behavior of BLUS residuals (see Section 8.3). For the relationship between $\hat{\boldsymbol{\beta}}_1$ and $\mathbf{b}$, see Problems 6.6 and 6.7.

An Efficiency Comparison of LS and BLUS Residuals

The main differences between BLUS and LS residuals are these. First, there are n LS residuals but only $n - K$ BLUS residuals. Second, the BLUS residuals have a scalar covariance matrix under the assumptions of the standard linear model, whereas this is not the case for the LS residuals. Third, the covariance matrix of the BLUS error vector exceeds that of LS by a positive semidefinite matrix. This follows directly from Theorem 5.1.

It was shown in the discussion below eq. (2.5) that the first difference is not really fundamental. The disappearance of K observations is obviously a practical disadvantage for BLUS, since in most cases it forces the analyst to consider several bases of the index transformation, but this disadvantage is becoming less important now that large-scale computing facilities are becoming more widespread. The real price to be paid for the advantage of a scalar covariance matrix is the third difference, which implies that the variance of each element of $\hat{\boldsymbol{\epsilon}}_1 - \boldsymbol{\epsilon}_1$ is at least as large as that of the corresponding element of $\mathbf{e}_1 - \boldsymbol{\epsilon}_1$, and usually larger.

A convenient scalar measure of this price is the ratio of the expected sums of squares of the two sets of errors. In the BLUS case this expected sum is given in (2.10). For the LS case our starting point is the covariance matrix $\sigma^2(\mathbf{I} - \mathbf{M}) = \sigma^2\mathbf{X}(\mathbf{X}'\mathbf{X})^{-1}\mathbf{X}'$ of the complete error vector $\mathbf{e} - \boldsymbol{\epsilon}$ given in (1.2). Therefore the covariance matrix of the subvector $\mathbf{e}_1 - \boldsymbol{\epsilon}_1$ is $\sigma^2\mathbf{X}_1(\mathbf{X}'\mathbf{X})^{-1}\mathbf{X}_1'$, so that the expected sum of squares of the errors is a multiple σ^2 of the trace of $\mathbf{X}_1(\mathbf{X}'\mathbf{X})^{-1}\mathbf{X}_1'$:

$$\begin{aligned} \text{tr } \mathbf{X}_1(\mathbf{X}'\mathbf{X})^{-1}\mathbf{X}_1' &= \text{tr } (\mathbf{X}'\mathbf{X})^{-1}\mathbf{X}_1'\mathbf{X}_1 = \text{tr } (\mathbf{X}'\mathbf{X})^{-1}(\mathbf{X}'\mathbf{X} - \mathbf{X}_0'\mathbf{X}_0) \\ &= \text{tr } [\mathbf{I} - (\mathbf{X}'\mathbf{X})^{-1}\mathbf{X}_0'\mathbf{X}_0] = K - \text{tr } \mathbf{X}_0(\mathbf{X}'\mathbf{X})^{-1}\mathbf{X}_0' \\ &= \sum_{h=1}^{K}(1 - d_h^2) \end{aligned} \tag{6.16}$$

Applying (2.10) and taking the ratio of the expected sums of squared errors, we thus obtain the following efficiency measure:

$$\text{(6.17)} \qquad \text{BLUS efficiency} = \frac{\mathscr{E}[(\mathbf{e}_1 - \boldsymbol{\epsilon}_1)'(\mathbf{e}_1 - \boldsymbol{\epsilon}_1)]}{\mathscr{E}[(\hat{\boldsymbol{\epsilon}}_1 - \boldsymbol{\epsilon}_1)'(\hat{\boldsymbol{\epsilon}}_1 - \boldsymbol{\epsilon}_1)]} = \frac{\sum_{h=1}^{K}(1 - d_h^2)}{2\sum_{h=1}^{K}(1 - d_h)}$$

In the one-variable case without constant term ($K = 1$) we have the d_1 of (6.3), which implies the following efficiency value:

$$\text{(6.18)} \qquad \frac{1}{2}(1 + d_1) = \frac{1}{2}\left(1 + \frac{|x_1|}{\sqrt{\sum x^2}}\right)$$

This confirms the idea that a large $|x_1|$ is desirable. In the case (6.9) all K roots d_h are equal to $\sqrt{(K/n)}$ [see (6.10)]. The BLUS efficiency is thus

$$\text{(6.19)} \qquad \frac{1}{2}\left(1 + \sqrt{\frac{K}{n}}\right) = \frac{\sqrt{K} + \sqrt{n}}{2\sqrt{n}}$$

This is .85 for $n/K = 2$, .79 for $n/K = 3$, .75 for $n/K = 4$, and it converges slowly to .5 when n increases indefinitely relative to K. Hence the BLUS efficiency decreases when the sample size is larger, which means that the performance of BLUS residuals as approximations of the disturbances declines when compared with the LS residuals. At the same time, however, the BLUS and LS errors themselves become smaller, so that efficiency is a matter of less concern for large n. This is a topic in the general area of asymptotic distribution theory, which will be discussed in Chapter 8.

Problems

6.1 Prove that the BLUS residuals given in eq. (6.7) can be written in the form

$$\text{(6.20)} \qquad \hat{\epsilon}_\alpha = \epsilon_\alpha - \left[\frac{d_1}{x_1^2}x_1\epsilon_1 + \frac{1 - d_1}{\sum x^2 - x_1^2}\left(\sum x\epsilon - x_1\epsilon_1\right)\right]x_\alpha$$

where $\sum x\epsilon$ stands for $x_1\epsilon_1 + \cdots + x_n\epsilon_n$. Use this result to prove directly that the residuals are uncorrelated and have variance σ^2. [*Hint.* First prove that the variance of the expression in square brackets is $2\sigma^2/(1 + d_1)\sum x^2$ and that the covariance of ϵ_α and this expression is $\sigma^2 x_\alpha/(1 + d_1)\sum x^2$.]

6.2 Consider a regression on one explanatory variable plus a constant term:

$$\text{(6.21)} \qquad y_\alpha = \beta_0 + \beta x_\alpha + \epsilon_\alpha = (\beta_0 + \beta\bar{x}) + \beta(x_\alpha - \bar{x}) + \epsilon_\alpha$$

where $\bar{x}$ is the average of $x_1, \ldots, x_n$. Write $X_\alpha = x_\alpha - \bar{x}$, take the first two observations as the base of the index transformation, and define $\mathbf{X}$ as the $n \times 2$ matrix whose first column consists of units and whose second column is $X_1, \ldots, X_n$. Prove that if $X_1 \neq X_2$,

$$\mathbf{Z} = \frac{1}{X_2 - X_1}\begin{bmatrix} X_2 - X_3 & -X_1 + X_3 \\ X_2 - X_4 & -X_1 + X_4 \\ \cdot & \cdot \\ \cdot & \cdot \\ \cdot & \cdot \\ X_2 - X_n & -X_1 + X_n \end{bmatrix} \tag{6.22}$$

Conclude that the index-transformed variables have unit sum. Next, prove

$$\mathbf{X}_0(\mathbf{X}'\mathbf{X})^{-1}\mathbf{X}_0' = \frac{1}{n\sigma_x^2}\begin{bmatrix} X_1^2 + \sigma_x^2 & X_1X_2 + \sigma_x^2 \\ X_1X_2 + \sigma_x^2 & X_2^2 + \sigma_x^2 \end{bmatrix} \tag{6.23}$$

where $\sigma_x^2 = (1/n) \sum X^2$. Find the trace and the determinant of this matrix with the following result:

$$d_1^2 + d_2^2 = \frac{X_1^2 + X_2^2 + 2\sigma_x^2}{n\sigma_x^2} \qquad d_1 d_2 = \frac{|X_1 - X_2|}{n\sigma_x} \tag{6.24}$$

and use this to prove

$$d_1 + d_2 = \frac{\sqrt{X_1^2 + X_2^2 + 2\sigma_x |X_1 - X_2| + 2\sigma_x^2}}{\sigma_x\sqrt{n}} \tag{6.25}$$

6.3 (*Continuation*) Suppose that the base consists of the ith and the jth observations rather than the first and the second, so that X_1 and X_2 are replaced by X_i and X_j, respectively ($X_i \neq X_j$). Arrange the observations according to increasing values of the explanatory variable: $X_1 \leq X_2 \leq \cdots \leq X_n$. Prove that the base which maximizes $d_1 + d_2$ consists of either the first and the last observations, or of the first two, or of the last two.

6.4 (*Continuation*) Prove that if the explanatory variable is a linear time trend ($X_1 = -m$, $X_2 = -m + 1, \ldots, X_n = m$, where $n = 2m + 1 =$ odd), the base which maximizes $d_1 + d_2$ consists of the first and the last observations. Prove that the squares of the corresponding roots are

$$d_1^2 = \frac{2}{n} \qquad d_2^2 = \frac{6(n-1)}{n(n+1)} \tag{6.26}$$

[*Hint*. Apply $1^2 + 2^2 + \cdots + m^2 = m(m+1)(2m+1)/6$; see Problem 7.1 of Section 1.7.]

6.5 Prove that in the case (6.9) the values taken by the explanatory variables in the base observations must form a matrix equal to $\mathbf{X}_0$. [*Hint.* Which condition is violated if we take, say, the first $K - 1$ rows of $\mathbf{X}$ plus the $(K + 1)$st row?] Note that this matrix $\mathbf{X}_0$ is not necessarily one of the n/K matrices $\mathbf{X}_0$ shown in (6.9); it may also consist, for example, of the first m rows of $\mathbf{X}$ plus the last $K - m$ $(m \leq K)$.

6.6 (*BLUS implied coefficient vector*) Assume that the submatrix $\mathbf{X}_1$ of $\mathbf{X}$ in (2.4) has full column rank, so that $H = K$ (Lemma 1 of Section 5.3) and $\mathbf{Q} = [\mathbf{q}_1 \cdots \mathbf{q}_K]$ is an orthogonal matrix. Define $\mathbf{D}_0$ as the $K \times K$ diagonal matrix which contains the roots $d_1, \ldots, d_K$ on the diagonal. Introduce the LS estimators of $\boldsymbol{\beta}$ derived from the base observations and from the $n - K$ other observations:

$$\mathbf{b}_0 = (\mathbf{X}_0'\mathbf{X}_0)^{-1}\mathbf{X}_0'\mathbf{y}_0 = \mathbf{X}_0^{-1}\mathbf{y}_0 \qquad \mathbf{b}_1 = (\mathbf{X}_1'\mathbf{X}_1)^{-1}\mathbf{X}_1'\mathbf{y}_1 \tag{6.27}$$

and note that this $\mathbf{b}_1$ is identical with b_1 of (6.6) for the special case discussed there. Prove that the LS estimator $\mathbf{b} = (\mathbf{X}'\mathbf{X})^{-1}\mathbf{X}'\mathbf{y}$ can be written as a weighted matrix average of $\mathbf{b}_0$ and $\mathbf{b}_1$:

$$\mathbf{b} = \mathbf{W}^2\mathbf{b}_0 + (\mathbf{I} - \mathbf{W}^2)\mathbf{b}_1 \qquad \text{where} \qquad \mathbf{W}^2 = (\mathbf{X}'\mathbf{X})^{-1}\mathbf{X}_0'\mathbf{X}_0 \tag{6.28}$$

Prove that $\mathbf{W}^2 = (\mathbf{X}'\mathbf{X})^{-1}\mathbf{X}_0'\mathbf{X}_0$ is satisfied by $\mathbf{W} = \mathbf{X}_0^{-1}\mathbf{Q}\mathbf{D}_0\mathbf{Q}'\mathbf{X}_0$. [*Hint.* Derive $\mathbf{X}_0(\mathbf{X}'\mathbf{X})^{-1}\mathbf{X}_0' = \mathbf{Q}\mathbf{D}_0^2\mathbf{Q}'$ from (2.8).] Next prove for $\hat{\boldsymbol{\beta}}_1$ defined in (6.15):

$$\hat{\boldsymbol{\beta}}_1 = \mathbf{b} + \mathbf{X}_0^{-1}\mathbf{Q}\mathbf{D}_0(\mathbf{I} + \mathbf{D}_0)^{-1}\mathbf{Q}'\mathbf{X}_0(\mathbf{b}_0 - \mathbf{b}) \tag{6.29}$$

making use of $\mathbf{e}_0 = \mathbf{y}_0 - \mathbf{X}_0\mathbf{b} = \mathbf{X}_0(\mathbf{b}_0 - \mathbf{b})$ and of the fact that diagonal matrices are commutative in multiplication, so that

$$\mathbf{D}_0(\mathbf{I} + \mathbf{D}_0)^{-1} = (\mathbf{I} + \mathbf{D}_0)^{-1}\mathbf{D}_0$$

Finally, use (6.28) to show that (6.29) can be simplified to

$$\hat{\boldsymbol{\beta}}_1 = \mathbf{W}\mathbf{b}_0 + (\mathbf{I} - \mathbf{W})\mathbf{b}_1 \tag{6.30}$$

and compare this result with that of $\mathbf{b}$ in (6.28).

6.7 (*Continuation*) Prove the following expressions for the sampling error of $\hat{\boldsymbol{\beta}}_1$:

$$\begin{aligned} \hat{\boldsymbol{\beta}}_1 - \boldsymbol{\beta} &= \mathbf{W}\mathbf{X}_0^{-1}\boldsymbol{\epsilon}_0 + (\mathbf{I} - \mathbf{W})(\mathbf{X}_1'\mathbf{X}_1)^{-1}\mathbf{X}_1'\boldsymbol{\epsilon}_1 \\ &= \mathbf{X}_0^{-1}\mathbf{Q}\mathbf{D}_0\mathbf{Q}'\boldsymbol{\epsilon}_0 + \mathbf{X}_0^{-1}\mathbf{Q}(\mathbf{I} - \mathbf{D}_0)\mathbf{Q}'\mathbf{X}_0(\mathbf{X}_1'\mathbf{X}_1)^{-1}\mathbf{X}_1'\boldsymbol{\epsilon}_1 \end{aligned} \tag{6.31}$$

Also prove the following expressions for the covariance matrix of $\hat{\boldsymbol{\beta}}_1$:

(6.32)

$$\begin{aligned} \mathscr{V}(\hat{\boldsymbol{\beta}}_1) &= \sigma^2\mathbf{X}_0^{-1}\mathbf{Q}[\mathbf{D}_0^2 + (\mathbf{I} - \mathbf{D}_0)\mathbf{Q}'\mathbf{X}_0(\mathbf{X}_1'\mathbf{X}_1)^{-1}\mathbf{X}_0'\mathbf{Q}(\mathbf{I} - \mathbf{D}_0)]\mathbf{Q}'(\mathbf{X}_0')^{-1} \\ &= 2\sigma^2\mathbf{X}_0^{-1}\mathbf{Q}\mathbf{D}_0^2(\mathbf{I} + \mathbf{D}_0)^{-1}\mathbf{Q}'(\mathbf{X}_0')^{-1} \end{aligned}$$

Next prove $\mathscr{V}(\mathbf{b}) = \sigma^2(\mathbf{X}'\mathbf{X})^{-1} = \sigma^2\mathbf{X}_0^{-1}\mathbf{Q}\mathbf{D}_0^2\mathbf{Q}'(\mathbf{X}_0')^{-1}$ for the covariance matrix of the LS estimator $\mathbf{b}$. Finally, prove for the ratio of the generalized variances:

$$\frac{|\mathscr{V}(\mathbf{b})|}{|\mathscr{V}(\hat{\boldsymbol{\beta}}_1)|} = \frac{1}{2}\prod_{h=1}^{K}(1 + d_h) \tag{6.33}$$

and conclude that $|\mathscr{V}(\mathbf{b})| < |\mathscr{V}(\hat{\boldsymbol{\beta}}_1)|$ holds under the assumptions made. (Note that the strict inequality sign applies here.)

6.8 Compute the BLUS efficiency for the trend regression of Problem 6.4 for $n = 3$, 5, 15, and 25, and prove that its limit is $\frac{1}{2}$ for n increasing indefinitely.

CHAPTER 6

GENERALIZED LEAST SQUARES AND LINEAR CONSTRAINTS

This chapter continues the discussion of Chapter 5 to the extent that items (8) and (9) of Section 3.9, which deal with the variances and covariances of the disturbances, are reexamined. It is also concerned with item (3) of that section, which deals with prior information on the coefficients. This combination may not seem obvious, but actually it is very convenient to generalize the LS method both with respect to the covariance matrix of the disturbances and also in the direction of linear a priori constraints on the coefficients. It should be noted that such generalizations lead us away from the standard linear model. Indeed, from this chapter on we shall successively replace the assumptions of Chapter 3 by other (more general) assumptions and we shall discuss methods that are appropriate in these new situations.

In the first five sections of this chapter we shall consider cases in which the disturbance covariance matrix is nonsingular. The extension to the singular case requires the concept of the generalized inverse of a matrix, which is introduced in Section 6.6. To avoid repetition, the use of linear constraints on the parameter vector is treated for the more general case only. Sections 6.1 to 6.4 are recommended for an introductory course,

Section 6.5 is optional, and the later sections are mathematically more advanced.

6.1 Aitken's Theorem[A]

A Nonscalar Disturbance Covariance Matrix

Consider the basic equation $\mathbf{y} = \mathbf{X}\boldsymbol{\beta} + \boldsymbol{\epsilon}$ of the standard linear model. Assumption 3.2 of Section 3.2 specifies $\mathscr{V}(\mathbf{y} \mid \mathbf{X}) = \sigma^2\mathbf{I}$, which is now modified as follows.

ASSUMPTION 6.1 (Nonscalar covariance matrix) *The conditional covariance matrix of* $\mathbf{y}$ *given* $\mathbf{X}$ *is*

$$\mathscr{V}(\mathbf{y} \mid \mathbf{X}) = \sigma^2\mathbf{V} \qquad (\sigma^2 < \infty) \tag{1.1}$$

where σ^2 is an unknown positive parameter and $\mathbf{V}$ *is a known symmetric positive definite $n \times n$ matrix whose trace is equal to n.*

This assumption is considerably weaker than its predecessor because it allows for heteroscedasticity (unequal diagonal elements of $\mathbf{V}$) as well as for positive or negative correlations of the disturbances (nonzero off-diagonal elements). The only cases that are excluded are those of infinite variances and of linearly dependent random variables, the first because $\sigma^2 < \infty$ and the second because it would imply a singular $\mathbf{V}$. The specification $\operatorname{tr} \mathbf{V} = n$ is not restrictive. What really counts is the covariance matrix $\sigma^2\mathbf{V}$, which remains unchanged when σ^2 is multiplied by $c > 0$ and $\mathbf{V}$ by $1/c$, so that $\operatorname{tr} \mathbf{V}$ is then also multiplied by $1/c$. Thus, by choosing c appropriately we can assign any positive value to $\operatorname{tr} \mathbf{V}$. Imposing $\operatorname{tr} \mathbf{V} = n$ is merely convenient; it is in line with the previous specification $\mathscr{V}(\mathbf{y} \mid \mathbf{X}) = \sigma^2\mathbf{I}$ because the $n \times n$ unit matrix also has the property that its trace is equal to n.

It *is* restrictive to assume that $\mathbf{V}$ is known, since this implies that all variances and covariances of the disturbances are supposed to be known except for a multiplicative constant (σ^2). This assumption is very unrealistic in many applications, and we shall have more to say about it in Section 6.2 and later.

A Linear Transformation of the Observation Matrix

It is still the case under Assumption 6.1 that the LS estimator $\mathbf{b}$ of $\boldsymbol{\beta}$ is unbiased when Assumption 3.1 of Section 3.2 is true (see the first part of Theorem 3.2 in Section 3.3), but this estimator is no longer "best" in the sense of the Gauss-Markov theorem. The simplest way to find an estimator that is best is by transforming the observation matrix $[\mathbf{y} \quad \mathbf{X}]$ so that the covariance matrix after the transformation is $\sigma^2\mathbf{I}$ rather than $\sigma^2\mathbf{V}$. This is straightforward. Since $\mathbf{V}$ is symmetric and positive definite, so is $\mathbf{V}^{-1}$ and, hence, there exists[1] a nonsingular $n \times n$ matrix $\mathbf{P}$ such that $\mathbf{P}'\mathbf{P} = \mathbf{V}^{-1}$. Premultiply both sides of $\mathbf{y} = \mathbf{X}\boldsymbol{\beta} + \boldsymbol{\epsilon}$ by $\mathbf{P}$:

$$\mathbf{P}\mathbf{y} = \mathbf{P}\mathbf{X}\boldsymbol{\beta} + \mathbf{P}\boldsymbol{\epsilon} \tag{1.2}$$

The new observation matrix is thus $[\mathbf{P}\mathbf{y} \quad \mathbf{P}\mathbf{X}]$ and the new disturbance vector is $\mathbf{P}\boldsymbol{\epsilon}$, which has zero expectation under Assumption 3.1 of Section 3.2. Its covariance matrix under Assumption 6.1 is

$$\mathscr{V}(\mathbf{P}\boldsymbol{\epsilon}) = \mathbf{P}\mathscr{E}(\boldsymbol{\epsilon}\boldsymbol{\epsilon}')\mathbf{P}' = \sigma^2\mathbf{P}\mathbf{V}\mathbf{P}' = \sigma^2\mathbf{P}(\mathbf{P}'\mathbf{P})^{-1}\mathbf{P}' = \sigma^2\mathbf{I} \tag{1.3}$$

where the third step is based on $\mathbf{P}'\mathbf{P} = \mathbf{V}^{-1}$ and the fourth on the nonsingularity of the square matrix $\mathbf{P}$. We conclude that the disturbance vector $\mathbf{P}\boldsymbol{\epsilon}$ has zero mean vector and a scalar covariance matrix.

GLS Estimation of the Coefficient Vector

Application of LS to (1.2) rather than to $\mathbf{y} = \mathbf{X}\boldsymbol{\beta} + \boldsymbol{\epsilon}$ leads to normal equations of the form $\mathbf{X}'\mathbf{P}'\mathbf{P}\mathbf{y} = \mathbf{X}'\mathbf{P}'\mathbf{P}\mathbf{X}\hat{\boldsymbol{\beta}}$, where $\hat{\boldsymbol{\beta}}$ is the LS estimator of $\boldsymbol{\beta}$ based on (1.2). Since $\mathbf{X}'\mathbf{P}'\mathbf{P}\mathbf{X}$ is positive definite when $\mathbf{X}$ has full column rank (why?) and $\mathbf{P}'\mathbf{P} = \mathbf{V}^{-1}$, the solution is

$$\hat{\boldsymbol{\beta}} = (\mathbf{X}'\mathbf{V}^{-1}\mathbf{X})^{-1}\mathbf{X}'\mathbf{V}^{-1}\mathbf{y} \tag{1.4}$$

which is known as the *generalized least-squares* (GLS) estimator of $\boldsymbol{\beta}$; its source is AITKEN (1935). We know that the covariance matrix of the LS estimator under the assumptions of the standard linear model is $\sigma^2(\mathbf{X}'\mathbf{X})^{-1}$. Since this model applies to the present case after the transformation, the covariance matrix of $\hat{\boldsymbol{\beta}}$ is thus $\sigma^2(\mathbf{X}'\mathbf{P}'\mathbf{P}\mathbf{X})^{-1}$ and hence:

$$\mathscr{V}(\hat{\boldsymbol{\beta}}) = \sigma^2(\mathbf{X}'\mathbf{V}^{-1}\mathbf{X})^{-1} \tag{1.5}$$

THEOREM 6.1 (Aitken's theorem) *Suppose that Assumption* 3.1 *of Section* 3.2 *and Assumption* 6.1 *are true for given* $\mathbf{X}$. *Then the GLS estimator* $\hat{\boldsymbol{\beta}}$ *defined in* (1.4) *is best linear unbiased in the following sense. Any other estimator of* $\boldsymbol{\beta}$ *which is also linear in the vector* $\mathbf{y}$ *and unbiased has a covariance matrix which exceeds that of* $\hat{\boldsymbol{\beta}}$, *given in* (1.5), *by a positive semidefinite matrix.*

Basically, this theorem does not need a separate proof because it follows from the Gauss-Markov theorem after the transformation. For the sake of clarity, however, we shall present a direct proof along the lines of the proof of the Gauss-Markov theorem given in Section 3.4.

[1] See the last subsection of Section 1.4.

Write $[(\mathbf{X}'\mathbf{V}^{-1}\mathbf{X})^{-1}\mathbf{X}'\mathbf{V}^{-1} + \mathbf{A}]\mathbf{y}$ for a linear estimator of $\boldsymbol{\beta}$, where $\mathbf{A}$ is a $K \times n$ matrix. By substituting $\mathbf{X}\boldsymbol{\beta} + \boldsymbol{\epsilon}$ for $\mathbf{y}$ and taking the expectation, we find that unbiasedness requires

$$\mathbf{AX} = \mathbf{0} \tag{1.6}$$

so that the sampling error is $[(\mathbf{X}'\mathbf{V}^{-1}\mathbf{X})^{-1}\mathbf{X}'\mathbf{V}^{-1} + \mathbf{A}]\boldsymbol{\epsilon}$. The covariance matrix is then

$$\begin{aligned}(1.7)\quad & [(\mathbf{X}'\mathbf{V}^{-1}\mathbf{X})^{-1}\mathbf{X}'\mathbf{V}^{-1} + \mathbf{A}]\mathscr{E}(\boldsymbol{\epsilon}\boldsymbol{\epsilon}')[(\mathbf{X}'\mathbf{V}^{-1}\mathbf{X})^{-1}\mathbf{X}'\mathbf{V}^{-1} + \mathbf{A}]' \\ &= \sigma^2[(\mathbf{X}'\mathbf{V}^{-1}\mathbf{X})^{-1}\mathbf{X}'\mathbf{V}^{-1} + \mathbf{A}]\mathbf{V}[\mathbf{V}^{-1}\mathbf{X}(\mathbf{X}'\mathbf{V}^{-1}\mathbf{X})^{-1} + \mathbf{A}'] \\ &= \sigma^2(\mathbf{X}'\mathbf{V}^{-1}\mathbf{X})^{-1} + \sigma^2\mathbf{AVA}' + \sigma^2(\mathbf{X}'\mathbf{V}^{-1}\mathbf{X})^{-1}\mathbf{X}'\mathbf{A}' + \sigma^2\mathbf{AX}(\mathbf{X}'\mathbf{V}^{-1}\mathbf{X})^{-1}\end{aligned}$$

The last two terms on the third line vanish in view of (1.6), so that the covariance matrix (1.7) exceeds $\mathscr{V}(\hat{\boldsymbol{\beta}})$ as specified in (1.5) by the positive semidefinite $\sigma^2\mathbf{AVA}'$.

GLS Minimizes a Quadratic Form in the Residual Vector

It is not true that the GLS coefficient vector $\hat{\boldsymbol{\beta}}$ minimizes the length of the residual vector; that property is reserved for the LS vector $\mathbf{b} = (\mathbf{X}'\mathbf{X})^{-1}\mathbf{X}'\mathbf{y}$. But it is true that $\hat{\boldsymbol{\beta}}$ minimizes this length after the $\mathbf{P}$ transformation, which means that we should not consider the length of $\mathbf{y} - \mathbf{X}\hat{\boldsymbol{\beta}}$ but the length of $\mathbf{P}(\mathbf{y} - \mathbf{X}\hat{\boldsymbol{\beta}})$, the square of which is

$$(\mathbf{y} - \mathbf{X}\hat{\boldsymbol{\beta}})'\mathbf{P}'\mathbf{P}(\mathbf{y} - \mathbf{X}\hat{\boldsymbol{\beta}}) = (\mathbf{y} - \mathbf{X}\hat{\boldsymbol{\beta}})'\mathbf{V}^{-1}(\mathbf{y} - \mathbf{X}\hat{\boldsymbol{\beta}}) \tag{1.8}$$

To prove that this quadratic form is minimized by GLS we write the normal equations $\mathbf{X}'\mathbf{V}^{-1}\mathbf{y} = \mathbf{X}'\mathbf{V}^{-1}\mathbf{X}\hat{\boldsymbol{\beta}}$ in the form

$$\mathbf{X}'\mathbf{V}^{-1}(\mathbf{y} - \mathbf{X}\hat{\boldsymbol{\beta}}) = \mathbf{0} \tag{1.9}$$

which enables us to derive the following identity for any K-element column vector $\mathbf{z}$:

$$\begin{aligned}(1.10)\quad (\mathbf{y} - \mathbf{Xz})'\mathbf{V}^{-1}(\mathbf{y} - \mathbf{Xz}) &= (\mathbf{y} - \mathbf{X}\hat{\boldsymbol{\beta}})'\mathbf{V}^{-1}(\mathbf{y} - \mathbf{X}\hat{\boldsymbol{\beta}}) \\ &\quad + (\mathbf{z} - \hat{\boldsymbol{\beta}})'\mathbf{X}'\mathbf{V}^{-1}\mathbf{X}(\mathbf{z} - \hat{\boldsymbol{\beta}})\end{aligned}$$

On the left we have a quadratic form (with $\mathbf{V}^{-1}$ as matrix) in the residual vector which is associated with the coefficient vector $\mathbf{z}$. The right-hand side indicates that it exceeds the corresponding quadratic form in the GLS residual vector $\mathbf{y} - \mathbf{X}\hat{\boldsymbol{\beta}}$ by a positive definite quadratic form. Thus, GLS minimizes a quadratic form in the residual vector with $\mathbf{V}^{-1}$ as matrix. It will be clear that (1.10) is the GLS extension of eq. (7.24) of Section 1.7.

Equation (1.9) takes the place of the orthogonality condition $\mathbf{X}'(\mathbf{y} - \mathbf{Xb}) = \mathbf{0}$ of the LS residual vector. Note that the presence of $\mathbf{V}^{-1}$ in (1.9) implies that it is *not* true, in general, that the GLS residuals have zero sum when the equation contains a constant term.

GLS Estimation of the Variance

The LS estimator s^2 of the variance is obtained by dividing the squared length of the LS residual vector by the number of degrees of freedom. In the GLS case we take the quadratic form (1.8) instead of the squared length:

$$\hat{\sigma}^2 = \frac{1}{n - K}(\mathbf{y} - \mathbf{X}\hat{\boldsymbol{\beta}})'\mathbf{V}^{-1}(\mathbf{y} - \mathbf{X}\hat{\boldsymbol{\beta}}) \tag{1.11}$$

This variance estimator is unbiased as stated in the following theorem.[2]

THEOREM 6.2 (Unbiasedness of the GLS variance estimator) *Suppose that Assumption* 3.1 *of Section* 3.2 *and Assumption* 6.1 *are true for given* $\mathbf{X}$; *also suppose* $n > K$. *Then the statistic* $\hat{\sigma}^2$ *defined in* (1.11) *is an unbiased estimator of the parameter* σ^2 *mentioned in Assumption* 6.1, $\hat{\boldsymbol{\beta}}$ *being given in* (1.4).

This theorem follows directly from Theorem 3.3 of Section 3.3, since $(n - K)\hat{\sigma}^2$ is equal to the squared length of the vector $\mathbf{Py} - \mathbf{PX}\hat{\boldsymbol{\beta}}$ in view of (1.8) and this vector is nothing but the LS residual vector corresponding to the observation matrix $[\mathbf{Py} \quad \mathbf{PX}]$.

Further Extensions

The above developments clearly show that if Assumption 3.2 of Section 3.2 is replaced by Assumption 6.1, the results of the standard linear model still apply when we replace the original observation matrix $[\mathbf{y} \quad \mathbf{X}]$ by $[\mathbf{Py} \quad \mathbf{PX}]$, where $\mathbf{P}$ is an $n \times n$ matrix which satisfies $\mathbf{P}'\mathbf{P} = \mathbf{V}^{-1}$. This may be used for hypothesis testing and for the construction of confidence intervals under the normality assumption. If $\mathbf{y}$ follows an n-variate normal distribution with mean vector $\mathbf{X}\boldsymbol{\beta}$ and covariance matrix $\sigma^2\mathbf{V}$, then $\hat{\boldsymbol{\beta}}$ is normal with mean vector $\boldsymbol{\beta}$ and covariance matrix $\sigma^2(\mathbf{X}'\mathbf{V}^{-1}\mathbf{X})^{-1}$, while $(n - K)\hat{\sigma}^2$ is distributed as $\sigma^2\chi^2(n - K)$ and $\hat{\boldsymbol{\beta}}$ and $\hat{\sigma}^2$ are independent. The normality of $\hat{\boldsymbol{\beta}}$ follows directly from its linearity in $\mathbf{y}$; the χ^2 distribution and the independence are proved easily by means of the $\mathbf{P}$ transformation.

There is one exception to this straightforward extension of the results of Chapter 3. If the disturbances are correlated ($\mathbf{V}$ being nondiagonal) and if the analyst wants to predict a future value of the dependent variable, then it is in principle possible that the disturbance component of that future value is

[2] The expression "variance estimator" implies that σ^2 of (1.1) is regarded as a variance. Note that it is not necessarily true that any of the n disturbances has a variance equal to σ^2 because this would imply that at least one diagonal element of $\mathbf{V}$ is equal to 1, which need not be the case. It is true, however, that σ^2 is always equal to the average of the n disturbance variances. This follows from the normalization rule tr $\mathbf{V} = n$.

correlated with the n disturbances of the sample. *This affects the prediction procedure of Sections* 3.4 *and* 3.6 *in a nontrivial way*. The subject will be discussed in Sections 6.7 to 6.9.

An interesting special case is that in which the disturbances all have the same variance and also the same covariance (the equicorrelated case). It turns out that if the equation contains a constant term, the GLS coefficient estimator is identical with the ordinary LS estimator and that the unbiased estimator of the covariance matrix of this estimator is simply $s^2(\mathbf{X}'\mathbf{X})^{-1}$—in spite of $\mathbf{V} \neq \mathbf{I}$—with the exception of the variance of the constant term estimator. This result, from McElroy (1967), is examined in Problems 1.6 to 1.8.[3] The following is an example of the equicorrelated case. Let each disturbance ϵ_α consist of a common part ζ_0 and a specific part ζ_α: $\epsilon_\alpha = \zeta_0 + \zeta_\alpha$, $\alpha = 1, \ldots, n$ in such a way that $[\zeta_1 \cdots \zeta_n]$ has zero mean vector and covariance matrix $\sigma_1^2\mathbf{I}$, while ζ_0 is a random variable with zero mean and variance σ_0^2 which is uncorrelated with $\zeta_1, \ldots, \zeta_n$. Then ϵ_α also has zero mean and its variance σ^2 is equal to $\sigma_0^2 + \sigma_1^2$, and the covariance $\rho\sigma^2$ of ϵ_α and ϵ_η for any pair (α, η), $\alpha \neq \eta$, is equal to σ_0^2. Hence $\rho = \sigma_0^2/(\sigma_0^2 + \sigma_1^2)$. A more complicated version of this model of disturbances consisting of a common part and a specific part was used by Balestra and Nerlove (1966) for the analysis of time series data on cross-sections.

Problems

1.1 Prove eq. (1.10).

1.2 Prove for the GLS residual vector: $\mathbf{y} - \mathbf{X}\hat{\boldsymbol{\beta}} = \mathbf{B}_1\boldsymbol{\epsilon}$, where

$$\mathbf{B}_1 = \mathbf{I} - \mathbf{X}(\mathbf{X}'\mathbf{V}^{-1}\mathbf{X})^{-1}\mathbf{X}'\mathbf{V}^{-1} \tag{1.12}$$

Next prove $\mathbf{B}_1'\mathbf{V}^{-1}\mathbf{B}_1 = \mathbf{B}_2$, where

$$\mathbf{B}_2 = \mathbf{V}^{-1} - \mathbf{V}^{-1}\mathbf{X}(\mathbf{X}'\mathbf{V}^{-1}\mathbf{X})^{-1}\mathbf{X}'\mathbf{V}^{-1} \tag{1.13}$$

Finally, prove $(n - K)\mathscr{E}\hat{\sigma}^2 = \sigma^2 \operatorname{tr} \mathbf{B}_2\mathbf{V} = \sigma^2(n - K)$. (This is the direct algebraic proof of Theorem 6.2, which does not rely on Theorem 3.3 of Section 3.3.)

1.3 (*Covariance matrices of residual vectors*) Prove that under the assumptions of Theorem 6.1 the covariance matrix of the GLS residual vector is

$$\mathscr{V}(\mathbf{y} - \mathbf{X}\hat{\boldsymbol{\beta}}) = \sigma^2[\mathbf{V} - \mathbf{X}(\mathbf{X}'\mathbf{V}^{-1}\mathbf{X})^{-1}\mathbf{X}'] \tag{1.14}$$

[3] For a similar result when there is no constant term (but based on only $n - 1$ observations), see C. R. Rao (1965a, p. 249, Problem 3). Also see Plackett (1960, p. 50), Watson (1967), and Kruskal (1968).

Also prove that under the same assumptions the covariance matrix of the LS residual vector $\mathbf{e} = \mathbf{y} - \mathbf{Xb}$ is $\mathscr{V}(\mathbf{e}) = \sigma^2\mathbf{MVM}$, where $\mathbf{b} = (\mathbf{X}'\mathbf{X})^{-1}\mathbf{X}'\mathbf{y}$ and $\mathbf{M} = \mathbf{I} - \mathbf{X}(\mathbf{X}')\mathbf{X}^{-1}\mathbf{X}'$.

1.4 (*Covariance matrices of error vectors of residual vectors*) Consider the error vector $\mathbf{y} - \mathbf{X}\hat{\boldsymbol{\beta}} - \boldsymbol{\epsilon}$ of the GLS residual vector. Prove that its covariance matrix is $\sigma^2\mathbf{X}(\mathbf{X}'\mathbf{V}^{-1}\mathbf{X})^{-1}\mathbf{X}'$ under the assumptions of Theorem 6.1. Next derive the covariance matrix of the error vector $\mathbf{e} - \boldsymbol{\epsilon}$ of the LS residual vector. Finally, state what can be said about the difference between these two matrices without using any algebra.

1.5 (*Deviations from means in the GLS case*) Suppose that the equation $\mathbf{y} = \mathbf{X}\boldsymbol{\beta} + \boldsymbol{\epsilon}$ contains a constant term and partition: $\mathbf{X} = [\boldsymbol{\iota} \quad \mathbf{Z}]$, $\boldsymbol{\beta}' = [\beta_0 \quad \boldsymbol{\beta}_Z']$. Prove that the estimator (1.4) can be written as

$$(1.15) \qquad \hat{\beta}_0 = \frac{1}{\boldsymbol{\iota}'\mathbf{V}^{-1}\boldsymbol{\iota}}\boldsymbol{\iota}'[\mathbf{V}^{-1}\mathbf{y} - (\mathbf{V}^{-1}\mathbf{Z})\,\hat{\boldsymbol{\beta}}_Z] \qquad \hat{\boldsymbol{\beta}}_Z = (\mathbf{Z}'\mathbf{N}\mathbf{Z})^{-1}\mathbf{Z}'\mathbf{N}\mathbf{y}$$

where $\mathbf{N} = \mathbf{V}^{-1} - (1/\boldsymbol{\iota}'\mathbf{V}^{-1}\boldsymbol{\iota})\mathbf{V}^{-1}\boldsymbol{\iota}\boldsymbol{\iota}'\mathbf{V}^{-1}$. Conclude from the equation for $\hat{\beta}_0$ that if $\mathbf{V}$ is normalized so that $\boldsymbol{\iota}'\mathbf{V}^{-1}\boldsymbol{\iota} = n$, the constant-term estimate is such that the GLS regression plane goes through the center of gravity of the observations, *provided* that the observation matrix $[\mathbf{y} \quad \mathbf{Z}]$ is first premultiplied by $\mathbf{V}^{-1}$. Note that, in general, $\boldsymbol{\iota}'\mathbf{V}^{-1}\boldsymbol{\iota} = n$ is different from the normalization rule $\operatorname{tr}\mathbf{V} = n$, but that the two rules are equivalent when $\mathbf{V} = \mathbf{I}$. Also prove $\mathbf{NVN} = \mathbf{N}$ and compare these results with the deviations-from-means analysis presented in Section 1.7.

1.6 (*GLS estimation in the equicorrelated case*) Suppose that the disturbances of $\mathbf{y} = \mathbf{X}\boldsymbol{\beta} + \boldsymbol{\epsilon}$ have constant variance σ^2 and pairwise equal correlation ρ. Prove that their covariance matrix is then $\sigma^2\mathbf{V}$, where $\mathbf{V} = (1 - \rho)\mathbf{I} + \rho\boldsymbol{\iota}\boldsymbol{\iota}'$, $\mathbf{I}$ being a unit matrix and $\boldsymbol{\iota}$ an n-element column vector of units. Also prove $\operatorname{tr}\mathbf{V} = n$ and

$$(1.16) \qquad \mathbf{V}^{-1} = \frac{1}{1-\rho}\left[\mathbf{I} - \frac{\rho}{1 + \rho(n-1)}\boldsymbol{\iota}\boldsymbol{\iota}'\right]$$

Conclude that GLS estimation of $\boldsymbol{\beta}$ falls under Theorem 6.1 if $0 \leq \rho < 1$.

1.7 (*Continuation*) Introduce $\alpha = \rho/[1 + \rho\{n - 1 - \boldsymbol{\iota}'\mathbf{X}(\mathbf{X}')\mathbf{X}^{-1}\mathbf{X}'\boldsymbol{\iota}\}]$ and prove successively:

$$(1.17) \qquad (\mathbf{X}'\mathbf{V}^{-1}\mathbf{X})^{-1} = (1 - \rho)[(\mathbf{X}'\mathbf{X})^{-1} + \alpha(\mathbf{X}'\mathbf{X})^{-1}\mathbf{X}'\boldsymbol{\iota}\boldsymbol{\iota}'\mathbf{X}(\mathbf{X}'\mathbf{X})^{-1}]$$

$$(1.18) \qquad (\mathbf{X}'\mathbf{V}^{-1}\mathbf{X})^{-1}\mathbf{X}'\mathbf{V}^{-1} = (\mathbf{X}'\mathbf{X})^{-1}\mathbf{X}' - \alpha[(\mathbf{X}'\mathbf{X})^{-1}\mathbf{X}'\boldsymbol{\iota}\boldsymbol{\iota}' - (\mathbf{X}'\mathbf{X})^{-1}\mathbf{X}'\boldsymbol{\iota}\boldsymbol{\iota}'\mathbf{X}(\mathbf{X}'\mathbf{X})^{-1}\mathbf{X}']$$

$$(1.19) \qquad \hat{\boldsymbol{\beta}} = \mathbf{b} - \alpha\boldsymbol{\iota}'(\mathbf{y} - \mathbf{X}\mathbf{b})(\mathbf{X}'\mathbf{X})^{-1}\mathbf{X}'\boldsymbol{\iota}$$

Use (1.19) to prove that $\hat{\boldsymbol\beta} = \mathbf{b}$ when the equation contains a constant term.

1.8 (*Continuation*) Assuming that the equation contains a constant term and that this is the first element of $\boldsymbol\beta$ (so that $\boldsymbol\iota$ is the first column of $\mathbf{X}$), prove $(\mathbf{X}'\mathbf{X})^{-1}\mathbf{X}'\boldsymbol\iota = \mathbf{i}_1$ and $\alpha = \rho/(1-\rho)$, where $\mathbf{i}_1$ is the first column of the $K \times K$ unit matrix. Also prove

$$(\mathbf{X}'\mathbf{V}^{-1}\mathbf{X})^{-1} = (1-\rho)(\mathbf{X}'\mathbf{X})^{-1} + \rho\mathbf{i}_1\mathbf{i}_1' \tag{1.20}$$

Next prove $(n-K)\hat\sigma^2 = \mathbf{e}'\mathbf{V}^{-1}\mathbf{e} = \mathbf{e}'\mathbf{e}/(1-\rho)$, where $\hat\sigma^2$ is defined in (1.11) and $\mathbf{e}$ is the LS residual vector. Combine this result with (1.20) to prove that the unbiased estimator of the covariance matrix of the GLS coefficient vector is

$$s^2\left[(\mathbf{X}'\mathbf{X})^{-1} + \frac{\rho}{1-\rho}\mathbf{i}_1\mathbf{i}_1'\right] \qquad \text{where} \qquad s^2 = \frac{\mathbf{e}'\mathbf{e}}{n-K} \tag{1.21}$$

and prove that this is identical with the LS estimated matrix $s^2(\mathbf{X}'\mathbf{X})^{-1}$ with the sole exception of the variance of the constant term. Conclude that in the equicorrelated case neither the GLS point estimates nor their estimated covariance matrix requires knowledge of ρ apart from this single exception (provided that a constant term is indeed present).

1.9 (*Continuation*) Again suppose that the equation contains a constant term and assume that ρ is unknown. Suppose that for the purpose of estimating ρ, the analyst uses the ratio of the mean product of the LS residuals to their mean square (on the grounds that the LS and GLS residuals are identical, given that the coefficient vectors are identical). Prove that this ratio satisfies

$$\frac{\dfrac{1}{n(n-1)}\sum\sum_{\alpha\neq\eta} e_\alpha e_\eta}{\dfrac{1}{n}\sum_{\alpha=1}^{n} e_\alpha^2} = -\frac{1}{n-1} \tag{1.22}$$

[*Hint*. Prove $\sum\sum_{\alpha\neq\eta} e_\alpha e_\eta = (\sum e_\alpha)^2 - \sum e_\alpha^2 = -\sum e_\alpha^2$.] Conclude that the distribution of this "estimator" of ρ does not involve ρ at all and, therefore, is useless.[4]

[4] To understand this unexpected result, consider the model described at the end of this section according to which ρ equals $\sigma_0^2/(\sigma_0^2+\sigma_1^2) = \sigma_0^2/\sigma^2$. Thus, to estimate ρ we have to estimate σ_0^2, and there can be little hope in estimating this variance when only one random variable (ζ_0) which has this variance is involved. Also note that if ρ cannot be estimated, the matrix (1.21) provides only a lower bound for the variance estimator of the constant term of the relation (given that $0 < \rho < 1$). This is not surprising under the conditions of this model because the constant term estimate is affected by ζ_0 whose variance σ_0^2 is completely unknown.

1.10 (*GLS and extreme multicollinearity*) Prove that neither $\hat{\boldsymbol{\beta}}$ nor $\mathbf{b}$ exists when the matrix $\mathbf{X}$ does not have full column rank.

6.2 Heteroscedasticity and Weighted Least Squares[A]

Consider the case in which the n disturbances are uncorrelated but have different variances: $\sigma_1^2, \ldots, \sigma_n^2$. This is the case of heteroscedasticity, and it falls directly under Assumption 6.1 when these variances are known (except possibly for a common multiplicative factor). The disturbance covariance matrix $\sigma^2\mathbf{V}$ is then diagonal and so is its inverse, and the diagonal elements of this inverse are $1/\sigma_1^2, \ldots, 1/\sigma_n^2$. It is readily verified that the $\mathbf{P}$ transformation of the previous section amounts to dividing the αth row of $[\mathbf{y} \quad \mathbf{X}]$ by σ_α:

$$(2.1) \qquad \frac{y_\alpha}{\sigma_\alpha} = \sum_{h=1}^{K} \beta_h \frac{x_{\alpha h}}{\sigma_\alpha} + \frac{\epsilon_\alpha}{\sigma_\alpha} \qquad \alpha = 1, \ldots, n$$

The application of LS to (2.1) thus implies that the values $y_\alpha, x_{\alpha 1}, \ldots, x_{\alpha K}$ of each observation are weighted inversely proportional to the standard deviation of the corresponding disturbance. Hence GLS is specialized here to *weighted least squares*, and the normal equations are of the form

$$(2.2) \qquad \sum_{\alpha=1}^{n} \frac{x_{\alpha h} y_\alpha}{\sigma_\alpha^2} = \hat{\beta}_1 \sum_{\alpha=1}^{n} \frac{x_{\alpha h} x_{\alpha 1}}{\sigma_\alpha^2} + \cdots + \hat{\beta}_K \sum_{\alpha=1}^{n} \frac{x_{\alpha h} x_{\alpha K}}{\sigma_\alpha^2}$$

where $h = 1, \ldots, K$.

The Case of Unknown Variances

When $\sigma_1^2, \ldots, \sigma_n^2$ are unknown, the mean vector and the covariance matrix of $\mathbf{y}$ given $\mathbf{X}$ depend on $K + n$ unknown parameters (K for $\boldsymbol{\beta}$ and n for the variances). It is clearly out of the question to estimate so many parameters from n observations. The only way out is to impose a simple model which describes the disturbance variances in terms of few (if any) additional unknown parameters. To illustrate this idea we consider the following example, which is based on the work of PRAIS and HOUTHAKKER (1955, pp. 55–56). Write y_α for the expenditure on tea of the αth household and suppose that it is a linear function of the household's income ($x_{\alpha 1}$) and the number of persons in the household ($x_{\alpha 2}$):

$$(2.3) \qquad y_\alpha = \beta_0 + \beta_1 x_{\alpha 1} + \beta_2 x_{\alpha 2} + \epsilon_\alpha \qquad \alpha = 1, \ldots, n$$

where ϵ_α is a random disturbance with zero expectation. First, suppose that the disturbance variance is proportional to the square of income: $\sigma_\alpha^2 = k x_{\alpha 1}^2$ for $\alpha = 1, \ldots, n$ and for some positive constant k. Dividing the values of the

αth observation by σ_α is thus equivalent to the following reformulation of (2.3):

$$\frac{y_\alpha}{x_{\alpha 1}} = \frac{\beta_0}{x_{\alpha 1}} + \beta_1 + \beta_2 \frac{x_{\alpha 2}}{x_{\alpha 1}} + \frac{\epsilon_\alpha}{x_{\alpha 1}} \tag{2.4}$$

The disturbances $\epsilon_1/x_{11}, \ldots, \epsilon_n/x_{n1}$ have a scalar covariance matrix ($k\mathbf{I}$) under our present condition, so that the assumptions of the standard linear model are satisfied by (2.4). The GLS procedure then amounts to an LS regression of $y_\alpha/x_{\alpha 1}$ (the proportion of income spent on tea) on the reciprocal of income and the reciprocal of income per household member.

The numerical data used by Prais and Houthakker did not support the hypothesis $\sigma_\alpha^2 = kx_{\alpha 1}^2$. Their large sample enabled them to eliminate (approximately) the effect of income and family size on the consumption of tea by dividing the households into family size groups and income brackets. For each income-family size combination they computed the mean and the variance of the amounts spent on tea, and they found that *the variance is approximately proportional to the square of the mean.* [Similar results were obtained by JØRGENSON (1965) for Danish data.] This variance corresponds to the disturbance variance σ_α^2 when the effects of income and family size are indeed eliminated, since σ_α^2 is the variance of y_α given $x_{\alpha 1}$ and $x_{\alpha 2}$; similarly, the mean corresponds to the expectation $\mathscr{E}y_\alpha$ of tea consumption given $x_{\alpha 1}$ and $x_{\alpha 2}$. This result suggests the following model:[5]

$$\sigma_\alpha^2 = c(\mathscr{E}y_\alpha)^2 \qquad \alpha = 1, \ldots, n \tag{2.5}$$

The application of LS to (2.1) under condition (2.5) is hampered by the fact that σ_α is unknown even though it does not depend on any other unknown parameters (except for the proportionality constant c):

$$\sigma_\alpha = \sqrt{c}(\beta_0 + \beta_1 x_{\alpha 1} + \beta_2 x_{\alpha 2}) \qquad \alpha = 1, \ldots, n \tag{2.6}$$

This follows directly from (2.5) and (2.3). Hence a regression of y_α/σ_α on $x_{\alpha 1}/\sigma_\alpha$ and $x_{\alpha 2}/\sigma_\alpha$ requires knowledge of the parameters β_0, β_1, and β_2 which we want to estimate. A direct application of the GLS procedure is thus impossible under the variance condition (2.5).

A Large-Sample Approximation

An approximate solution to this problem is the following two-step procedure. First, estimate the β's by LS applied to (2.3), thus ignoring the heteroscedasticity. Second, substitute the estimates thus obtained for the β's

[5] See also Section 12.4 for a similar proportionality between the disturbance variance and the square of the expectation of the dependent variable in the context of models with random coefficients.

in (2.6), which leads to an estimate $\hat{\sigma}_\alpha$ of σ_α (with unknown proportionality constant $\sqrt{c}$):

$$\frac{\hat{\sigma}_\alpha}{\sqrt{c}} = b_0 + b_1 x_{\alpha 1} + b_2 x_{\alpha 2} \qquad \alpha = 1, \ldots, n \tag{2.7}$$

after which LS is applied to the equation written in the form (2.1) with σ_α replaced by $\hat{\sigma}_\alpha$. This simply amounts to solving the normal equations (2.2) with $\hat{\sigma}_\alpha$ substituted for σ_α. It is readily verified that the unknown proportionality constant in the left-hand side of (2.7) is immaterial for the solution of these equations because it occurs in their left as well as right-hand sides in such a way that it cancels out.

We refer to Section 8.6 for an evaluation of this approximation method. It will turn out that under appropriate conditions, the estimator thus obtained has a distribution which is approximately the same as that of the weighted LS estimator based on the true σ_α's, provided that the sample is sufficiently large. In particular, one may then continue to use the covariance matrix given in (1.5) for the coefficient estimator based on the $\hat{\sigma}_\alpha$'s—as an approximation at least. The matrix (1.5) is, in the present case, equal to the inverse of

$$\mathbf{X}'\begin{bmatrix} \sigma_1^2 & 0 & \cdots & 0 \\ 0 & \sigma_2^2 & \cdots & 0 \\ \cdot & \cdot & & \cdot \\ \cdot & \cdot & & \cdot \\ \cdot & \cdot & & \cdot \\ 0 & 0 & \cdots & \sigma_n^2 \end{bmatrix}^{-1} \mathbf{X} = \begin{bmatrix} \sum \sigma_\alpha^{-2} & \sum \sigma_\alpha^{-2} x_{\alpha 1} & \sum \sigma_\alpha^{-2} x_{\alpha 2} \\ \sum \sigma_\alpha^{-2} x_{\alpha 1} & \sum \sigma_\alpha^{-2} x_{\alpha 1}^2 & \sum \sigma_\alpha^{-2} x_{\alpha 1} x_{\alpha 2} \\ \sum \sigma_\alpha^{-2} x_{\alpha 2} & \sum \sigma_\alpha^{-2} x_{\alpha 1} x_{\alpha 2} & \sum \sigma_\alpha^{-2} x_{\alpha 2}^2 \end{bmatrix} \tag{2.8}$$

When the σ's are replaced by $\hat{\sigma}$'s we obtain an approximate covariance matrix which can be computed from the sample. The square roots of the diagonal elements of this matrix are known as *asymptotic standard errors*, where "asymptotic" refers to the large-sample approximation; a more precise definition is given in Section 8.3.[6]

An Alternative Specification

Equation (2.3) can also be written in the form

$$y_\alpha = (\beta_0 + \beta_1 x_{\alpha 1} + \beta_2 x_{\alpha 2})(1 + \zeta_\alpha) \qquad \text{where} \qquad \zeta_\alpha = \frac{\epsilon_\alpha}{\mathscr{E} y_\alpha} \tag{2.9}$$

[6] Note that the calculation of this matrix requires the c that occurs in the left-hand side of (2.7), since we now need $\hat{\sigma}_\alpha$ completely (not only up to a multiplicative constant as in the solution of the normal equations). Since (2.5) implies that c may be regarded as the variance of the ratio $\epsilon_\alpha / \mathscr{E} y_\alpha$ for each α, one way of estimating c is by means of the mean square of $e'_\alpha/(y_\alpha - e'_\alpha)$, $\alpha = 1, \ldots, n$, where e'_α is the αth residual associated with the coefficient estimates.

It follows from (2.5) that the variance of ζ_α is independent of α. Let us extend assumption (2.5) so that the whole distribution of ζ_α is independent of α. Then write (2.9) in logarithmic form:

$$\log y_\alpha = \log(\beta_0 + \beta_1 x_{\alpha 1} + \beta_2 x_{\alpha 2}) + \log(1 + \zeta_\alpha) \tag{2.10}$$

Clearly, this formulation avoids the heteroscedasticity problem because the disturbances $\log(1 + \zeta_\alpha)$ cannot have different variances for different values of α if the distribution of ζ_α is the same for each α. Note, however, that we now have a new problem: the nonlinearity in the parameters $\beta_0, \beta_1, \beta_2$.[7] A necessary condition for the applicability of the standard linear model with $\log y$ as dependent variable is that the expectation of $\log y$ be equal to a known linear function of the unknown parameters. This condition is not fulfilled by (2.10), but it is conceivable that a double-log model such as

$$\mathscr{E}(\log y_\alpha) = \beta_0' + \beta_1' \log x_{\alpha 1} + \beta_2' \log x_{\alpha 2} \tag{2.11}$$

is realistic, in which case both the nonlinearity and the heteroscedasticity problems cease to exist. Of course, this simple solution fails if the expectation of $\log y_\alpha$ is not linear in the parameters.

The Variance of the LS Slope Estimator under Conditions of Heteroscedasticity

One may also decide to ignore the heteroscedasticity problem on the ground that it does not affect the unbiasedness of the LS estimator. However, the covariance matrix is no longer $\sigma^2(\mathbf{X}'\mathbf{X})^{-1}$. Using $(\mathbf{X}'\mathbf{X})^{-1}\mathbf{X}'\boldsymbol{\epsilon}$ for the sampling error of the LS estimator, we easily find for its covariance matrix:

$$\mathscr{V}(\mathbf{b}) = \sigma^2(\mathbf{X}'\mathbf{X})^{-1}\mathbf{X}'\mathbf{V}\mathbf{X}(\mathbf{X}'\mathbf{X})^{-1} \tag{2.12}$$

which exceeds $\mathscr{V}(\hat{\boldsymbol{\beta}}) = \sigma^2(\mathbf{X}'\mathbf{V}^{-1}\mathbf{X})^{-1}$ by a positive semidefinite matrix in view of Theorem 6.1. Therefore, LS is less than "best" in a heteroscedastic situation, and it is also true that the more complicated formula (2.12) replaces $\sigma^2(\mathbf{X}'\mathbf{X})^{-1}$ as the LS covariance matrix. To illustrate this result we consider a regression on one explanatory variable plus a constant term, which we write as follows:

$$y_\alpha = \beta_0 + \beta x_\alpha + \epsilon_\alpha = (\beta_0 + \beta\bar{x}) + \beta(x_\alpha - \bar{x}) + \epsilon_\alpha \tag{2.13}$$

where $\bar{x}$ is the mean of x_α, $\alpha = 1, \ldots, n$. We shall be interested in the estimation of β and treat $\beta_0 + \beta\bar{x}$ as the constant term. The observation matrix $[\mathbf{y} \quad \mathbf{X}]$ thus consists of n rows $[y_\alpha \quad 1 \quad X_\alpha]$, where $X_\alpha = x_\alpha - \bar{x}$.

[7] There is also the problem that the logarithm of $1 + \zeta_\alpha$ has nonzero expectation when ζ_α has zero expectation.

We then have

$$(2.14) \qquad \mathbf{X}'\mathbf{X} = \begin{bmatrix} n & 0 \\ 0 & \sum X_\alpha^2 \end{bmatrix} \qquad \sigma^2\mathbf{V} = \begin{bmatrix} \sigma_1^2 & 0 & \cdots & 0 \\ 0 & \sigma_2^2 & \cdots & 0 \\ \cdot & \cdot & & \cdot \\ \cdot & \cdot & & \cdot \\ \cdot & \cdot & & \cdot \\ 0 & 0 & \cdots & \sigma_n^2 \end{bmatrix}$$

where all summations—here as well as in the sequel of this paragraph—are over α from 1 through n. Using (2.14), we find for the covariance matrix of $\mathbf{b}$:

$$(2.15) \qquad \sigma^2(\mathbf{X}'\mathbf{X})^{-1}\mathbf{X}'\mathbf{V}\mathbf{X}(\mathbf{X}'\mathbf{X})^{-1} = \begin{bmatrix} \dfrac{1}{n^2}\sum \sigma_\alpha^2 & \dfrac{\sum \sigma_\alpha^2 X_\alpha}{n \sum X_\alpha^2} \\ \dfrac{\sum \sigma_\alpha^2 X_\alpha}{n \sum X_\alpha^2} & \dfrac{\sum \sigma_\alpha^2 X_\alpha^2}{(\sum X_\alpha^2)^2} \end{bmatrix}$$

The lower right-hand element of this matrix is the sampling variance of the LS estimator of the multiplicative coefficient. The "classical" expression is the corresponding element of $\sigma^2(\mathbf{X}'\mathbf{X})^{-1}$ and, hence, is equal to $\sigma^2/\sum X_\alpha^2$. Since tr $\mathbf{V} = n$ we have $n\sigma^2 = \sum \sigma_\alpha^2$ in view of (2.14), so that this expression can also be written as $\sum \sigma_\alpha^2/(n \sum X_\alpha^2)$. The difference between the two expressions is

$$(2.16) \qquad \frac{\sum \sigma_\alpha^2 X_\alpha^2}{(\sum X_\alpha^2)^2} - \frac{\sum \sigma_\alpha^2}{n \sum X_\alpha^2} = \frac{1}{\sum X_\alpha^2}\left(\frac{\sum \sigma_\alpha^2 X_\alpha^2}{\sum X_\alpha^2} - \frac{1}{n}\sum \sigma_\alpha^2\right)$$

The right-hand term in parentheses is the difference between a weighted and the unweighted average of the disturbance variances. The sampling variance of the LS estimator exceeds the value derived from $\sigma^2(\mathbf{X}'\mathbf{X})^{-1}$ when large disturbance variances correspond to large absolute X's. It is actually plausible that this will happen rather frequently in cross-section regressions. For example, let income be the explanatory variable, so that X_α is the income of the αth household measured as a deviation from the mean income. The income distribution is usually skew with a long tail on the right, which means that most of the largest absolute X's correspond to large incomes. The disturbances corresponding to large incomes have normally large variances, so that the difference (2.16) is then positive. We already know that the variance of the LS estimator exceeds the variance of the weighted LS estimator; so we now also find that in this particular case the former variance is underestimated when we apply the conventional expression $\sigma^2/\sum X_\alpha^2$.[8]

[8] For further details on corrections of the LS sampling variances under conditions of heteroscedasticity, see Theil (1951a) and also Prais (1953) and Prais and Houthakker (1955, pp. 55–58).

The Effect of Grouping

It sometimes happens that the original observations are homoscedastic (or approximately so), but that they are combined in groups of different sizes so that the grouped observations are heteroscedastic. For example, a survey may consist of so many individual observations that a detailed publication would be prohibitively expensive, and the published data may then consist of a limited number of group averages. For a rather extensive treatment of such cases, see PRAIS and AITCHISON (1954); a simple case is examined in Problem 2.5 below. See also J. S. CRAMER (1964) for the effect of grouping on the value of the multiple correlation coefficient.

Problems

2.1 Write $\sigma^2\mathbf{V}$ for the diagonal covariance matrix whose variances are given in (2.5):

$$\sigma^2\mathbf{V} = c\begin{bmatrix} (\mathscr{E}y_1)^2 & 0 & \cdots & 0 \\ 0 & (\mathscr{E}y_2)^2 & \cdots & 0 \\ \vdots & \vdots & & \vdots \\ 0 & 0 & \cdots & (\mathscr{E}y_n)^2 \end{bmatrix} \tag{2.17}$$

Prove that the normalization rule tr $\mathbf{V} = n$ implies that σ^2/c is equal to the average of $(\mathscr{E}y_1)^2, \ldots, (\mathscr{E}y_n)^2$.

2.2 Suppose that the specification (2.3) and (2.5) is simplified to that of one explanatory variable without constant term: $y_\alpha = \beta x_\alpha + \epsilon_\alpha$, $\mathscr{E}\epsilon_\alpha = 0$, var $\epsilon_\alpha = c(\mathscr{E}y_\alpha)^2$. Prove that the GLS estimator of β is equal to the average of the n ratios y_α/x_α and conclude that in this case no two-step procedure is necessary. Does this still hold when the equation has a constant term? Justify your answer.

2.3 Prove eq. (2.15).

2.4 To what extent must the conclusion reached below eq. (2.16) be modified when x_α stands for the *logarithm* of the income of the αth household? Justify your answer.

2.5 (*Grouping of observations*) Consider a linear regression on one explanatory variable without constant term and suppose that Assumption 3.3 of Section 3.2 is true for given $x_1, \ldots, x_n$. Suppose further that the n observations are divided into G groups $S_1, \ldots, S_G$ containing $n_1, \ldots, n_G$ observations ($\sum n_g = n$) and consider the group averages of the observations on the two variables:

$$\bar{x}_g = \frac{1}{n_g} \sum_{\alpha \in S_g} x_\alpha \qquad \bar{y}_g = \frac{1}{n_g} \sum_{\alpha \in S_g} y_\alpha \qquad g = 1, \ldots, G \tag{2.18}$$

Formulate the GLS procedure based on the G group observations $(\bar{x}_1, \bar{y}_1), \ldots, (\bar{x}_G, \bar{y}_G)$ and prove that it amounts to weighted LS with weights proportional to the number of observations in each group. Prove that the variance of the coefficient estimator is $\sigma^2/\sum n_g \bar{x}_g^2$ (sum over g from 1 through G) and also prove

$$\sum_{\alpha=1}^{n} x_\alpha^2 = \sum_{g=1}^{G} n_g \bar{x}_g^2 + \sum_{g=1}^{G} \left[\sum_{\alpha \in S_g} (x_\alpha - \bar{x}_g)^2 \right] \tag{2.19}$$

Use this equation to prove that the above sampling variance is larger than that of the LS estimator based on the original data except when the x-values within each group are all the same. To minimize the variance $\sigma^2/\sum n_g \bar{x}_g^2$, how would you form the groups $S_1, \ldots, S_G$ when their numbers $n_1, \ldots, n_G$ are given?[9]

6.3 Correlated Disturbances and Autoregressive Transformations[A]

We now turn to time series regressions and recall that it is frequently unrealistic to assume that the disturbances of such a regression are uncorrelated. It is clearly impossible to estimate all correlations because their number is $\frac{1}{2}n(n-1)$ when there are n observations, and a model that imposes a simple pattern is therefore in order.

An Autoregressive Process

The observations $\alpha = 1, \ldots, n$ are supposed to be arranged in the order of successive time periods. It will now be assumed that the disturbances are generated by a process which is described by the following equation:

$$\epsilon_\alpha = \rho \epsilon_{\alpha-1} + \zeta_\alpha \qquad |\rho| < 1 \tag{3.1}$$

where the ζ's are uncorrelated random variables with zero mean and variance σ_0^2. Equation (3.1) describes a so-called first-order autoregressive process; each ϵ_α is expressed linearly in terms of its own predecessor and a random term. (The addition "first order" refers to the fact that only the most recent predecessor plays a role; higher-order processes will be discussed in Section

[9] Note that the variance expression $\sigma^2/\sum n_g \bar{x}_g^2$ is not valid when the grouping criterion involves $y_1, \ldots, y_n$. When this is the case, the selection of the observations that fall under $S_1, \ldots, S_G$ involves a stochastic element, so that $\bar{x}_1, \ldots, \bar{x}_G$ become random even though $x_1, \ldots, x_n$ are all constants.

6.5.) The idea underlying such a process in this particular context is that the neglected variables which are represented by the disturbance move gradually over time. It is then plausible that successive disturbances (ϵ_α and $\epsilon_{\alpha+1}$) are positively correlated, that the correlation of more distant disturbances is closer to zero than that of ϵ_α and $\epsilon_{\alpha+1}$, and that the correlation converges toward zero when the distance in time becomes larger and larger. As we shall shortly see, this condition is satisfied when the disturbances are generated by the first-order process (3.1) with $0 < \rho < 1$.

The Mean and Covariance Matrix of the Disturbance Vector

By substituting $\rho\epsilon_{\alpha-2} + \zeta_{\alpha-1}$ for $\epsilon_{\alpha-1}$ in (3.1) we find that ϵ_α can be written as $\rho^2\epsilon_{\alpha-2} + \zeta_\alpha + \rho\zeta_{\alpha-1}$. We repeat this procedure s times:

$$\epsilon_\alpha = \rho^{s+1}\epsilon_{\alpha-s-1} + \zeta_\alpha + \rho\zeta_{\alpha-1} + \cdots + \rho^s\zeta_{\alpha-s}$$

When s increases indefinitely and $|\rho| < 1$ we obtain:

$$\epsilon_\alpha = \sum_{t=0}^{\infty} \rho^t\zeta_{\alpha-t} \qquad \alpha = 1, \ldots, n \tag{3.2}$$

The zero-mean assumption on the ζ's implies that ϵ_α has also zero mean. To find the variance we square the right-hand side of (3.2): $(\zeta_\alpha + \rho\zeta_{\alpha-1} + \cdots)^2$. After taking the expectation we obtain zero values for the product terms (with different time subscripts such as $2\rho\zeta_\alpha\zeta_{\alpha-1}$), while the expected square terms become

$$\mathscr{E}\zeta_\alpha^2 + \rho^2\mathscr{E}\zeta_{\alpha-1}^2 + \rho^4\mathscr{E}\zeta_{\alpha-2}^2 + \cdots = \frac{\sigma_0^2}{1-\rho^2}$$

This is the variance of ϵ_α. Since the expression is independent of α, we conclude that the disturbances are homoscedastic.

To find the covariance of ϵ_α and $\epsilon_{\alpha-k}$ we consider the product

$$(\zeta_\alpha + \rho\zeta_{\alpha-1} + \rho^2\zeta_{\alpha-2} + \cdots)(\zeta_{\alpha-k} + \rho\zeta_{\alpha-k-1} + \rho^2\zeta_{\alpha-k-2} + \cdots)$$

Assuming $k > 0$ we obtain for the expectation of this product

$$\rho^k\mathscr{E}\zeta_{\alpha-k}^2 + \rho^{k+2}\mathscr{E}\zeta_{\alpha-k-1}^2 + \rho^{k+4}\mathscr{E}\zeta_{\alpha-k-2}^2 + \cdots = \frac{\rho^k\sigma_0^2}{1-\rho^2}$$

Hence $\text{cov}(\epsilon_\alpha, \epsilon_{\alpha-k}) = \rho^k\sigma_0^2/(1-\rho^2)$ for $k > 0$. This expression is also valid for $k = 0$ because we just proved $\text{var}\,\epsilon_\alpha = \sigma_0^2/(1-\rho^2)$. For negative k write $g = -k$ and consider

$$\begin{aligned}\text{cov}(\epsilon_\alpha, \epsilon_{\alpha-k}) &= \text{cov}(\epsilon_\alpha, \epsilon_{\alpha+g}) = \text{cov}(\epsilon_{\alpha+g}, \epsilon_\alpha) \\ &= \text{cov}(\epsilon_{\alpha+g}, \epsilon_{\alpha+g-g}) = \frac{\rho^g\sigma_0^2}{1-\rho^2} = \frac{\rho^{|k|}\sigma_0^2}{1-\rho^2}\end{aligned}$$

where the second-last equality sign is based on the fact that the subscript $\alpha + g$ of the first ϵ exceeds that of the second by a positive number ($g > 0$), so that the result for positive k is applicable. We conclude that the exponent $|k|$ applies to the covariance of ϵ_α and $\epsilon_{\alpha-k}$ for positive, zero, and negative k. Hence,

$$\mathscr{E}(\epsilon_\alpha \epsilon_\eta) = \sigma_0^2 \frac{\rho^{|\alpha-\eta|}}{1-\rho^2} \qquad \alpha, \eta = 1, \ldots, n \tag{3.3}$$

which means that the successive lagged covariances of $(\epsilon_\alpha, \epsilon_{\alpha+1})$, $(\epsilon_\alpha, \epsilon_{\alpha+2})$, ... decline geometrically. Therefore we have the following covariance matrix:

$$\mathscr{E}(\epsilon\epsilon') = \sigma^2 \mathbf{V} \qquad \sigma^2 = \frac{\sigma_0^2}{1-\rho^2} \tag{3.4}$$

$$\mathbf{V} = \begin{bmatrix} 1 & \rho & \rho^2 & \cdots & \rho^{n-1} \\ \rho & 1 & \rho & \cdots & \rho^{n-2} \\ \rho^2 & \rho & 1 & \cdots & \rho^{n-3} \\ \cdot & \cdot & \cdot & & \cdot \\ \cdot & \cdot & \cdot & & \cdot \\ \cdot & \cdot & \cdot & & \cdot \\ \cdot & \cdot & \cdot & & \cdot \\ \rho^{n-1} & \rho^{n-2} & \rho^{n-3} & \cdots & 1 \end{bmatrix} \tag{3.5}$$

This result shows that the correlation coefficients of ϵ's whose time subscripts differ by 1 are all equal to ρ, that the correlations corresponding to a time difference of two periods are all equal to ρ^2, and so on. The correlation coefficient of ϵ_α and $\epsilon_{\alpha+k}$, $k > 0$, is known as the kth *order autocorrelation coefficient* of the ϵ's. Hence, if the ϵ's are generated by a first-order autoregressive process with $0 < \rho < 1$, their successive autocorrelation coefficients decline geometrically.

The matrix (3.5) is nonsingular and its inverse is the following $n \times n$ band matrix:

$$\mathbf{V}^{-1} = \frac{1}{1-\rho^2} \begin{bmatrix} 1 & -\rho & 0 & \cdots & 0 & 0 \\ -\rho & 1+\rho^2 & -\rho & \cdots & 0 & 0 \\ 0 & -\rho & 1+\rho^2 & \cdots & 0 & 0 \\ \cdot & \cdot & \cdot & & \cdot & \cdot \\ \cdot & \cdot & \cdot & & \cdot & \cdot \\ \cdot & \cdot & \cdot & & \cdot & \cdot \\ 0 & 0 & 0 & \cdots & 1+\rho^2 & -\rho \\ 0 & 0 & 0 & \cdots & -\rho & 1 \end{bmatrix} \tag{3.6}$$

Thus, all diagonal elements of $\mathbf{V}^{-1}$ are equal apart from the first and the last, while the off-diagonal elements whose row and column indices differ by 2 or more are all zero. This inverse can be written as the product of two simple triangular matrices, **P** and its transpose **P**′:

$$\text{(3.7)}\quad \mathbf{V}^{-1}=\mathbf{P}'\mathbf{P} \quad \text{where} \quad \mathbf{P}=\frac{1}{\sqrt{1-\rho^2}}\begin{bmatrix} \sqrt{1-\rho^2} & 0 & 0 & \cdots & 0 & 0 \\ -\rho & 1 & 0 & \cdots & 0 & 0 \\ 0 & -\rho & 1 & \cdots & 0 & 0 \\ \cdot & \cdot & \cdot & & \cdot & \cdot \\ \cdot & \cdot & \cdot & & \cdot & \cdot \\ \cdot & \cdot & \cdot & & \cdot & \cdot \\ 0 & 0 & 0 & \cdots & 1 & 0 \\ 0 & 0 & 0 & \cdots & -\rho & 1 \end{bmatrix}$$

Application of the GLS Method

The result just obtained indicates that the GLS procedure of Section 6.1 amounts to LS applied to the transformed observation matrix [**Py** **PX**], where **P** is given in (3.7). The first row of **P** implies that the basic equation for the first observation becomes[10]

$$\text{(3.8)}\qquad y_1\sqrt{1-\rho^2}=\sum_{h=1}^{K}\beta_h(x_{1h}\sqrt{1-\rho^2})+\epsilon_1\sqrt{1-\rho^2}$$

and for the $n-1$ other observations ($\alpha = 2,\ldots,n$):

$$\text{(3.9)}\qquad y_\alpha-\rho y_{\alpha-1}=\sum_{h=1}^{K}\beta_h(x_{\alpha h}-\rho x_{\alpha-1,h})+(\epsilon_\alpha-\rho\epsilon_{\alpha-1})$$

It is easy to verify directly that the n disturbances of eqs. (3.8) and (3.9) have a scalar covariance matrix. The disturbances of (3.9) are $\zeta_2,\ldots,\zeta_n$ of (3.1), which are uncorrelated and have variance σ_0^2, and the disturbance of (3.8) has also variance σ_0^2 in view of (3.3). Moreover, eq. (3.2) implies that the latter disturbance does not involve a ζ_α with $\alpha > 1$, and since all ζ's are uncorrelated by assumption, this disturbance is also uncorrelated with those of (3.9).[11]

[10] We disregard here, for simplicity's sake, the multiplicative factor $1/\sqrt{1-\rho^2}$ of **P**. This factor affects all elements of the covariance matrix of the transformed disturbance vector uniformly, so that the scalar character of this covariance matrix remains unchanged.

[11] Note that the disturbance of (3.8) has variance σ_0^2 only if the autoregressive process (3.1) has been operating during a long period of time [this variance is derived from (3.2) for $\alpha = 1$], whereas the corresponding property of the $n-1$ disturbances of (3.9) requires the operation of (3.1) for only one period each. If the first observation of the sample belongs to a period just after a major war, say, so that it is reasonable to assume that the process which generated the disturbances was affected, one may prefer to delete eq. (3.8) and to apply LS to the $n-1$ observations (3.9) only.

The subtraction procedure displayed in (3.9) is known as an *autoregressive transformation.* The values taken by each variable are replaced by a linear combination of successive values. In the present case we have a first-order autoregressive transformation because (3.9) contains only one observation [the ($\alpha - 1$)st] in addition to the αth for each variable.

What To Do When the Autoregressive Parameter Is Unknown

When ρ is known, the procedure is thus straightforward. In the absence of such knowledge it is sometimes assumed that ρ is not far below unity, in which case the approximation $\rho = 1$ in (3.9) leads to the *first-difference transformation*:

$$\Delta y_\alpha = \sum_{h=1}^{K} \beta_h \Delta x_{\alpha h} + \Delta \epsilon_\alpha \qquad \alpha = 2, \ldots, n \tag{3.10}$$

where $\Delta y_\alpha = y_\alpha - y_{\alpha-1}$, etc. This procedure was applied on a large scale by STONE (1954). Note that eq. (3.8) becomes $0 = 0$ for $\rho = 1$, which means that it is deleted.

One may also decide to use a two-step procedure based on an estimate of ρ. First, compute the n LS residuals $e_1, \ldots, e_n$, ignoring all complications of the covariance matrix $\sigma^2\mathbf{V}$. Then compute the ratio of the mean product of the successive residuals to the LS variance estimator:

$$\hat{\rho} = \frac{\dfrac{1}{n-1}\displaystyle\sum_{\alpha=1}^{n-1} e_\alpha e_{\alpha+1}}{\dfrac{1}{n-K}\displaystyle\sum_{\alpha=1}^{n} e_\alpha^2} = \frac{\displaystyle\sum_{\alpha=1}^{n-1} e_\alpha e_{\alpha+1}}{(n-1)s^2} \tag{3.11}$$

which is to be regarded as an estimator of ρ, and apply LS to (3.8) and (3.9) with ρ replaced by $\hat{\rho}$. Basically, this procedure is similar to that of the previous section where we replaced σ_α by $\hat{\sigma}_\alpha$ in (2.1). It will appear in Section 8.6 that the large-sample evaluation of the present approximation procedure is also similar, at least under certain conditions. One of these conditions is that the explanatory variables take nonstochastic values. If these values include those of a lagged dependent variable, so that this condition is violated, we have a different and less favorable result (see the last subsection of Section 8.7); we shall meet such cases in the next two sections.

The Variance of the LS Slope Estimator

As in the heteroscedasticity case, one may also decide to use LS and thus ignore the nonzero correlation complication. The estimator $\mathbf{b}$ of $\boldsymbol{\beta}$ is then unbiased and its covariance matrix is given in (2.12) where $\mathbf{V}$ is now the right-hand matrix of (3.5). To evaluate this covariance matrix we consider again, as we did at the end of the previous section, the case of one explanatory variable (measured as a deviation from its mean) plus a constant term. The matrix $\mathbf{X}'\mathbf{X}$ is thus the same as in (2.14), but $\mathbf{X}'\mathbf{V}\mathbf{X}$ is different. The lower right-hand element of this matrix is

$$(3.12)\quad [X_1 \quad X_2 \quad X_3 \quad \cdots \quad X_n]\begin{bmatrix} 1 & \rho & \rho^2 & \cdots & \rho^{n-1} \\ \rho & 1 & \rho & \cdots & \rho^{n-2} \\ \rho^2 & \rho & 1 & \cdots & \rho^{n-3} \\ \cdot & \cdot & \cdot & & \cdot \\ \cdot & \cdot & \cdot & & \cdot \\ \cdot & \cdot & \cdot & & \cdot \\ \rho^{n-1} & \rho^{n-2} & \rho^{n-3} & \cdots & 1 \end{bmatrix}\begin{bmatrix} X_1 \\ X_2 \\ X_3 \\ \cdot \\ \cdot \\ \cdot \\ X_n \end{bmatrix}$$

$$= [X_1 \quad X_2 \quad X_3 \quad \cdots \quad X_n]\begin{bmatrix} X_1 + \rho X_2 + \rho^2 X_3 + \cdots + \rho^{n-1} X_n \\ \rho X_1 + X_2 + \rho X_3 + \cdots + \rho^{n-2} X_n \\ \rho^2 X_1 + \rho X_2 + X_3 + \cdots + \rho^{n-3} X_n \\ \cdot \\ \cdot \\ \cdot \\ \rho^{n-1} X_1 + \rho^{n-2} X_2 + \rho^{n-3} X_3 + \cdots + X_n \end{bmatrix}$$

$$= \sum_{\alpha=1}^{n} X_\alpha^2 + 2\rho \sum_{\alpha=1}^{n-1} X_\alpha X_{\alpha+1} + 2\rho^2 \sum_{\alpha=1}^{n-2} X_\alpha X_{\alpha+2} + \cdots + 2\rho^{n-1} X_1 X_n$$

the last step of which is based on a collection of all terms with the same power of ρ. To obtain the sampling variance of the LS estimator of the multiplicative coefficient, we must divide this lower right-hand element of $\mathbf{X}'\mathbf{V}\mathbf{X}$ by the square of the corresponding element of the diagonal matrix $\mathbf{X}'\mathbf{X}$, which is $\sum X_\alpha^2$ [see (2.14)]. Taking account of the factor σ^2, we thus obtain for the variance of the LS multiplicative coefficient:

$$(3.13)\quad \frac{\sigma^2}{\sum_{\alpha=1}^{n} X_\alpha^2}\left[1 + 2\rho \frac{\sum_{\alpha=1}^{n-1} X_\alpha X_{\alpha+1}}{\sum_{\alpha=1}^{n} X_\alpha^2} + 2\rho^2 \frac{\sum_{\alpha=1}^{n-2} X_\alpha X_{\alpha+2}}{\sum_{\alpha=1}^{n} X_\alpha^2} + \cdots + 2\rho^{n-1} \frac{X_1 X_n}{\sum_{\alpha=1}^{n} X_\alpha^2}\right]$$

Since $\sigma^2/\sum X_\alpha^2$ is the classical expression for the sampling variance, we may conclude that the terms in square brackets form the correction factor which is to be applied to the expression. If ρ is such that ρ^2 and higher powers can be neglected, the correction factor is approximately equal to $1 + 2\rho r$, where r is the sample analogue of the first-order autocorrelation coefficient of the explanatory variable. For most economic time series this r is positive, since large values are usually followed by other large values and small values by other small values. If ρ is also positive, the correction factor is larger than 1, so that the classical LS variance expression [the relevant diagonal element of $\sigma^2(\mathbf{X}'\mathbf{X})^{-1}$] underestimates the true variability of the estimator. We note further that the higher powers of ρ are multiplied by ratios that are approximately equal to the sample analogues of the corresponding higher-order autocorrelation coefficients of the explanatory variable.

For more details on sampling variances and covariances under conditions of correlated disturbances, see WOLD (1953, Chapter 13) and LYTTKENS (1964). Reference should also be made to COCHRANE and ORCUTT (1949), ORCUTT and COCHRANE (1949), and ORCUTT and WINOKUR (1969).

The LS Variance Estimator Is Biased

The covariance matrix specification (3.4) and (3.5) does satisfy the homoscedasticity condition, since all n disturbance variances are equal to σ^2. Nevertheless, the LS estimator of this parameter is not unbiased, which is shown as follows. We have $\mathbf{e} = \mathbf{M}\boldsymbol{\epsilon}$ for the LS residual vector, where $\mathbf{M} = \mathbf{I} - \mathbf{X}(\mathbf{X}'\mathbf{X})^{-1}\mathbf{X}'$. The sum of squares of the elements of $\mathbf{e}$ is $\boldsymbol{\epsilon}'\mathbf{M}\boldsymbol{\epsilon} =$ tr $\mathbf{M}\boldsymbol{\epsilon}\boldsymbol{\epsilon}'$, the expectation of which is now

$$\sigma^2 \operatorname{tr} \mathbf{MV} = \sigma^2[\operatorname{tr} \mathbf{V} - \operatorname{tr} \mathbf{X}(\mathbf{X}'\mathbf{X})^{-1}\mathbf{X}'\mathbf{V}] = \sigma^2[n - \operatorname{tr} \mathbf{X}'\mathbf{VX}(\mathbf{X}'\mathbf{X})^{-1}]$$

The trace of $\mathbf{X}'\mathbf{VX}(\mathbf{X}'\mathbf{X})^{-1}$ is, in general, not equal to K. To evaluate it in a specific case we return to the one-variable regression (with constant term) of the previous subsection, so that $K = 2$ and $\mathbf{X}'\mathbf{VX}$ and $\mathbf{X}'\mathbf{X}$ are both 2×2 matrices. Since $\mathbf{X}'\mathbf{X}$ is diagonal [see (2.14)], the trace of $\mathbf{X}'\mathbf{VX}(\mathbf{X}'\mathbf{X})^{-1}$ is equal to the ratio of the first diagonal element of $\mathbf{X}'\mathbf{VX}$ to that of $\mathbf{X}'\mathbf{X}$ plus the ratio of the second diagonal element of $\mathbf{X}'\mathbf{VX}$ to that of $\mathbf{X}'\mathbf{X}$. The first diagonal element of $\mathbf{X}'\mathbf{VX}$ is examined in Problem 3.3; it turns out to be

$$n\frac{1+\rho}{1-\rho} - 2\rho\frac{1-\rho^n}{(1-\rho)^2} \tag{3.14}$$

The corresponding element of $\mathbf{X}'\mathbf{X}$ as given in (2.14) is n, so that the ratio is approximately $(1+\rho)/(1-\rho)$ when n is not too small. The second diagonal element of $\mathbf{X}'\mathbf{VX}$ was evaluated in (3.12) and the corresponding element of $\mathbf{X}'\mathbf{X}$ is $\sum X_\alpha^2$; their ratio is equal to $1 + 2\rho r$ if we use the approximation given below (3.13). On taking the sum of the two ratios we obtain

$$\operatorname{tr} \mathbf{X}'\mathbf{VX}(\mathbf{X}'\mathbf{X})^{-1} \approx \frac{1+\rho}{1-\rho} + 1 + 2\rho r = \frac{2}{1-\rho} + 2\rho r \tag{3.15}$$

This exceeds $K = 2$ when ρ and r are both positive. An example: $\rho = .5$, $r = .7$, which gives 4.7 for the value of the trace in (3.15). Thus $\mathbf{e}'\mathbf{e}/(n - 4.7)$ is approximately unbiased for σ^2 and $\mathbf{e}'\mathbf{e}/(n - 2)$ is biased toward zero. We concluded in the previous subsection that the covariance matrix expression $\sigma^2(\mathbf{X}'\mathbf{X})^{-1}$ is likely to understate the sampling variability of the LS coefficient. We now find that there will be an additional understatement when we replace σ^2 in $\sigma^2(\mathbf{X}'\mathbf{X})^{-1}$ by the conventional s^2. Also see Problem 3.4 for a comparison of the true variance of the LS estimator and that of the GLS estimator.

The bias of the σ^2 estimator for positive values of ρ and r is intuitively easy

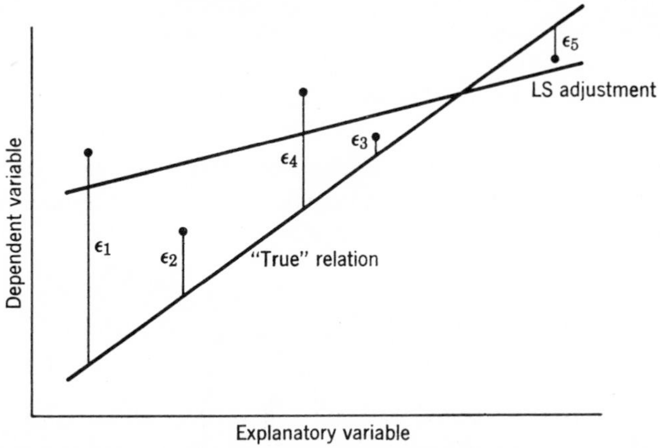

Fig. 6.1 Bias of the LS variance estimator under conditions of positive autocorrelation.

to understand when we use the following argument from JOHNSTON (1963, p. 189). Consider Figure 6.1, containing a scatter of points and two straight lines, one of which represents the equation in the true parameters and the other the LS estimate. The point on the far left is the first observation, the disturbance of which takes a positive value. If successive disturbances are positively correlated, the next disturbance is likely to be positive too. Also, if r is positive, the corresponding value of the explanatory variable is unlikely to be far from the first value. We may thus have a series of points fairly close to each other and above the "true" line, so that the LS fit through these points will underestimate the random variation of the observations around this true line.

Problems

3.1 Prove that $\mathbf{V}^{-1}$ of (3.6) is the inverse of the matrix (3.5). Also, prove that $\mathbf{V}^{-1}$ satisfies (3.7).

3.2 Prove that $\mathbf{V}$ of (3.5) satisfies the normalization rule $\operatorname{tr} \mathbf{V} = n$ but not the normalization rule $\boldsymbol{\iota}'\mathbf{V}^{-1}\boldsymbol{\iota} = n$ of Problem 1.5 when $\rho \neq 0$.

3.3 Prove that the expression (3.14) is equal to the leading element of $\mathbf{X}'\mathbf{V}\mathbf{X}$, where the αth row of $\mathbf{X}$ is $[1 \quad X_\alpha]$ and $\mathbf{V}$ is given in (3.5). (*Hint.* Prove that this element is equal to the sum of all elements of $\mathbf{V}$; add the diagonal elements of $\mathbf{V}$ and then the elements of the successive diagonals parallel to the main diagonal.)

3.4 (*Continuation*) For the same $\mathbf{X}$ and $\mathbf{V}$, prove that the matrix $(1 - \rho^2)\mathbf{X}'\mathbf{V}^{-1}\mathbf{X}$ is equal to

$$\begin{bmatrix} n(1-\rho)^2 + 2\rho(1-\rho) & \rho(1-\rho)(X_1 + X_n) \\ \rho(1-\rho)(X_1 + X_n) & (1+\rho^2)\sum_{\alpha=1}^{n} X_\alpha^2 - \rho^2(X_1^2 + X_n^2) - 2\rho \sum_{\alpha=1}^{n-1} X_\alpha X_{\alpha+1} \end{bmatrix}$$

Show that this 2×2 matrix is approximately diagonal when n is large and when X_1 and X_n do not dominate the other X's numerically. Also prove:

$$(3.16) \quad (1 - \rho^2)\mathbf{X}'\mathbf{V}^{-1}\mathbf{X} \approx n \begin{bmatrix} (1-\rho)^2 & 0 \\ 0 & (1 + \rho^2 - 2\rho r)\frac{1}{n}\sum_{\alpha=1}^{n} X_\alpha^2 \end{bmatrix}$$

where r is the sample analogue of the first-order autocorrelation coefficient of the explanatory variable. Prove on the basis of this approximation that the variance of the GLS slope coefficient is equal to the ratio of $\sigma^2(1 - \rho^2)$ to $(1 + \rho^2 - 2\rho r) \sum X_\alpha^2$. Compare this with the variance (3.13) of the LS coefficient, and prove that the ratio of the former variance to the latter is

$$(3.17) \qquad \frac{1 - \rho^2}{1 + \rho^2 + 2\rho^2 r(\rho - 2r)}$$

when the approximation described below (3.13) is applied. Tabulate this ratio for nine pairs (ρ, r), say, $\rho, r = .2, .4, .6$, and draw your conclusions. Be careful in your interpretation of cases with large ρ values.

6.4 A Class of Distributed Lag Models[A]

The concept of an autoregressive process is convenient for the solution of some of the problems that arise when one or more explanatory variables occur with several lags. This section and the next are devoted to problems dealing with lagged variables.

The Distributed Lag Concept

In a rather large number of cases the economic agent whose behavior is described by the equation does not react fully and immediately to changes, but he does so in a more gradual manner. For example, if a person receives a salary increase of \$1000, this may induce him to raise his consumption expenditures by \$500 this year, by another \$300 next year, and by another \$100 in the third year, so that the ultimate effect is an increase of \$900. The corresponding behavioral equation is $y_\alpha = .5x_\alpha + .3x_{\alpha-1} + .1x_{\alpha-2}$ (+ constant and disturbance), where x_α and y_α are income and consumption, respectively, in year α. If the equation were of the form $y_\alpha = .9x_{\alpha-1}$ (+ constant and disturbance), we would have the same ultimate effect but it would take place with a fixed lag of one year. Here, on the other hand, we have a *distributed lag* and the lag is distributed over three years. More generally, when we have more than one explanatory variable and when each of these occurs with various lags, the equation is of the following form:

$$(4.1) \quad y_\alpha = \beta_0 + \beta_1 x_{\alpha 1} + \beta_2 x_{\alpha-1,1} + \cdots + \beta_1' x_{\alpha 2} + \beta_2' x_{\alpha-1,2} + \cdots + \epsilon_\alpha$$

In principle there is no problem with respect to the estimation of an equation like (4.1). LS is best linear unbiased when the assumptions of the standard linear model are satisfied, and GLS has this property when these assumptions have to be modified in accordance with those of Section 6.1. In practice, however, we face the difficulty (1) that the number of β's occurring in an equation such as (4.1) may be rather large and (2) that we easily have a multicollinear situation. The latter statement is based on the fact that successive values taken by the same variable ($x_{\alpha h}$ and $x_{\alpha-1,h}$, $\alpha = 1, \ldots, n$) are frequently close to each other because of the inertia that characterizes many economic time series. Under these circumstances we should expect that the estimates obtained will be rather imprecise. As in the case of the two previous sections, the only answer is to impose a certain model, this time on the successive parameters $\beta_1, \beta_2, \ldots$ and $\beta_1', \beta_2', \ldots$. In this section we shall describe a very simple approach from Koyck (1954).

Koyck's Method

We start with the case of one explanatory variable which occurs in distributed-lag form: $y_\alpha = \beta_0 + \beta_1 x_\alpha + \beta_2 x_{\alpha-1} + \cdots + \epsilon_\alpha$. In most cases it is plausible that the multiplicative coefficients $\beta_1, \beta_2, \ldots$ converge in a rather regular manner toward zero from some critical value of the index onward. Specifically, suppose that the decline is of the geometric type and that it starts at the first lag: $\beta_2 = \lambda\beta_1, \beta_3 = \lambda^2\beta_1, \ldots$, where $0 < \lambda < 1$. The equation thus takes the following form:

$$y_\alpha = \beta_0 + \beta_1 x_\alpha + \lambda\beta_1 x_{\alpha-1} + \lambda^2\beta_1 x_{\alpha-2} + \cdots + \epsilon_\alpha \tag{4.2}$$

Also consider the same equation for the previous period ($\alpha - 1$) and multiply both sides by λ:

$$\lambda y_{\alpha-1} = \lambda\beta_0 + \lambda\beta_1 x_{\alpha-1} + \lambda^2\beta_1 x_{\alpha-2} + \cdots + \lambda\epsilon_{\alpha-1} \tag{4.3}$$

If we now subtract this equation from (4.2), we obtain a result that can be written as follows:

$$y_\alpha = (1 - \lambda)\beta_0 + \beta_1 x_\alpha + \lambda y_{\alpha-1} + (\epsilon_\alpha - \lambda\epsilon_{\alpha-1}) \tag{4.4}$$

This is an equation with the same dependent variable but with different right-hand variables. The original explanatory variable occurs here only in current form and, in addition, we have the lagged dependent variable on the right. The advantage of (4.4) is, of course, that we have only three unknown parameters against a much larger number in the original equation. Also, the estimation of (4.4) is not hampered by the multicollinearity problem of the successive values taken by the explanatory variable.

Therefore a natural way to proceed is to estimate the equation in the form (4.4) by running an LS regression on the current explanatory variable (x_α) and the lagged dependent variable ($y_{\alpha-1}$), including a constant term. The three regression coefficients can then be easily transformed to point estimates of the parameters of (4.2). However, there are several complications. First, when estimating the constant term β_0, the estimated constant term of (4.4) must be divided by one minus the estimated coefficient of $y_{\alpha-1}$. This division is obviously a nonlinear procedure, and at this stage we have no knowledge of the sampling theory of nonlinear functions. Second, one of the right-hand variables in (4.4) is the lagged dependent variable. As was argued in Section 3.9 under (6), we cannot really assume that the values of that variable are nonstochastic. Hence the observation matrix of the right-hand variables of (4.4) contains one random column. Third, if it is assumed that the ϵ's have a scalar covariance matrix, then the disturbances of (4.4) have a nonscalar covariance matrix. This is easily verified by computing the covariance of two successive disturbances of the latter equation:

$$\mathscr{E}[(\epsilon_\alpha - \lambda\epsilon_{\alpha-1})(\epsilon_{\alpha+1} - \lambda\epsilon_\alpha)] = -\lambda\mathscr{E}\epsilon_\alpha^2 = -\lambda\sigma^2$$

where σ^2 is the variance of ϵ_α. Also note that under the same assumption, the lagged dependent variable $y_{\alpha-1}$ in (4.4) is correlated with the corresponding disturbance of that equation:

$$\mathscr{E}[y_{\alpha-1}(\epsilon_\alpha - \lambda\epsilon_{\alpha-1})] = \mathscr{E}[\epsilon_{\alpha-1}(\epsilon_\alpha - \lambda\epsilon_{\alpha-1})] = -\lambda\mathscr{E}\epsilon_{\alpha-1}^2 = -\lambda\sigma^2$$

The first equality sign is based on (4.2) after α is replaced by $\alpha - 1$; the equation then states that $y_{\alpha-1}$ is equal to a nonstochastic expression plus the random $\epsilon_{\alpha-1}$.

Disturbances Generated by an Autoregressive Process

We must conclude that $y_{\alpha-1}$ is not only random but is also correlated with the corresponding disturbance $\epsilon_\alpha - \lambda\epsilon_{\alpha-1}$, at least when the successive ϵ's themselves are uncorrelated. In Section 8.8, where we shall elucidate this matter, we shall see that the nonzero correlation of $y_{\alpha-1}$ and $\epsilon_\alpha - \lambda\epsilon_{\alpha-1}$ is more serious than the mere fact that $y_{\alpha-1}$ is random. Here we confine ourselves to the simplest case. Suppose that the successive ϵ's are not uncorrelated but that they are generated by a first-order autoregressive process:

$$\epsilon_\alpha = \rho\epsilon_{\alpha-1} + \zeta_\alpha \qquad |\rho| < 1 \tag{4.5}$$

where the ζ's are uncorrelated random variables with zero mean and constant variance σ_0^2. Also suppose that ρ happens to be identical with λ of (4.4). Then the disturbance of (4.4) is simply ζ_α, which is uncorrelated with $y_{\alpha-1}$ because the random component of $y_{\alpha-1}$ is $\epsilon_{\alpha-1} = \zeta_{\alpha-1} + \rho\zeta_{\alpha-2} + \cdots$. Thus the nonzero correlation complication of $y_{\alpha-1}$ and $\epsilon_\alpha - \lambda\epsilon_{\alpha-1}$ disappears, but the randomness of $y_{\alpha-1}$ is still there. It will be shown in Section 8.8 that under appropriate conditions, and if the sample is large, the LS procedure applied to (4.4) is then not really affected by this randomness of $y_{\alpha-1}$. It should be admitted that the exact fulfillment of $\rho = \lambda$ is unlikely in any real situation, but procedures may be useful even when the underlying conditions are violated to a limited degree.

Two Nerlove Variants of Koyck's Transformation

Koyck's method amounts to a transformation of a basic equation with geometrically declining coefficients to another basic equation which contains $y_{\alpha-1}$ as one of the right-hand variables. NERLOVE (1958c) applied this approach for the specification of agricultural supply functions. He postulated that the farmers' acreage allotted to a certain crop in year α, to be denoted by y_α, depends linearly on the "expected normal price" of this crop in this year (p_α^*) and a random disturbance:

$$y_\alpha = \beta_0 + \beta p_\alpha^* + \epsilon_\alpha \tag{4.6}$$

He also postulated that farmers adjust the expected normal price from year $\alpha - 1$ to year α in proportion to the discrepancy between the observed price in year $\alpha - 1$ ($p_{\alpha-1}$) and the expected normal price in the same year:

$$p_\alpha^* - p_{\alpha-1}^* = \gamma(p_{\alpha-1} - p_{\alpha-1}^*) \qquad \text{where} \qquad 0 < \gamma \leq 1 \tag{4.7}$$

Equation (4.7) implies that p_α^* is a weighted average of $p_{\alpha-1}$ and $p_{\alpha-1}^*$ with weights γ and $1 - \gamma$, respectively. On substituting this weighted average for p_α^* in (4.6) and eliminating $p_{\alpha-1}^*, p_{\alpha-2}^*, \ldots$ successively, we obtain the following supply function:

$$(4.8) \quad y_\alpha = \beta_0 + \beta[\gamma p_{\alpha-1} + \gamma(1-\gamma)p_{\alpha-2} + \gamma(1-\gamma)^2 p_{\alpha-3} + \cdots] + \epsilon_\alpha$$

The Koyck transformation applied to this equation gives

$$(4.9) \qquad y_\alpha = \beta_0\gamma + \beta\gamma p_{\alpha-1} + (1-\gamma)y_{\alpha-1} + [\epsilon_\alpha - (1-\gamma)\epsilon_{\alpha-1}]$$

which is identical with (4.4) when we interpret γ as $1 - \lambda$ and $\beta\gamma p_{\alpha-1}$ as $\beta_1 x_\alpha$.

Nerlove also considered a second model which leads to a result that is almost identical with (4.9). Write y_α^* for the long-run equilibrium acreage that corresponds to the observed price $p_{\alpha-1}$ and suppose that it is a linear function of this price except for a disturbance:

$$(4.10) \qquad y_\alpha^* = \beta_0 + \beta p_{\alpha-1} + \epsilon_\alpha$$

Next suppose that the farmers adjust their actual acreage from year $\alpha - 1$ to year α in proportion to the discrepancy between y_α^* and the actual acreage in year $\alpha - 1$:

$$(4.11) \qquad y_\alpha - y_{\alpha-1} = \gamma(y_\alpha^* - y_{\alpha-1}) \qquad \text{where} \qquad 0 < \gamma \leq 1$$

This equation implies that y_α is a weighted average of y_α^* and $y_{\alpha-1}$ with weights γ and $1 - \gamma$, respectively, and (4.10) states that y_α^* is equal to $\beta_0 + \beta p_{\alpha-1} + \epsilon_\alpha$. Combining these results, we obtain

$$(4.12) \qquad y_\alpha = \beta_0\gamma + \beta\gamma p_{\alpha-1} + (1-\gamma)y_{\alpha-1} + \gamma\epsilon_\alpha$$

A comparison with (4.9) shows that only the disturbance terms are different. In the case of (4.12) it is not necessary to make the autoregressive assumption (4.5) with $\rho = \lambda$ in order that the disturbance covariance matrix be scalar; in fact, the disturbances of (4.12) have a scalar covariance matrix if and only if the ϵ's of the underlying equation (4.10) have this property. Needless to say, it is not satisfactory to prefer the model (4.10) and (4.11) to (4.6) and (4.7) on the ground that we can allow the disturbances to be uncorrelated and to have constant variance. What matters is what is true about the properties of the disturbances of the equation that is estimated, and this is a matter to be considered in every single instance.

Extensions

Koyck's method can be extended in a rather simple way in two different directions. The first extension is based on the consideration that it may be unrealistic to assume that the successive coefficients decline immediately, particularly when the time period is short (a quarter or a month or a week). One may then decide to proceed with a geometric decline which starts at the kth lag:

$$(4.13) \qquad y_\alpha = \beta_0 + \sum_{t=0}^{k-1} \beta_{t+1} x_{\alpha-t} + \lambda\beta_k x_{\alpha-k} + \lambda^2\beta_k x_{\alpha-k-1} + \cdots + \epsilon_\alpha$$

A subtraction procedure similar to (4.2), (4.3) and (4.4) gives

$$(4.14) \qquad y_\alpha = (1-\lambda)\beta_0 + \beta_1 x_\alpha + \sum_{t=1}^{k-1} (\beta_{t+1} - \lambda\beta_t) x_{\alpha-t} + \lambda y_{\alpha-1} + (\epsilon_\alpha - \lambda\epsilon_{\alpha-1})$$

This equation contains the current value and the first $k - 1$ lagged values of the explanatory variable, $x_\alpha, \ldots, x_{\alpha-k+1}$, besides the constant term and the lagged value of the dependent variable. It is analogous to (4.4) in all other respects, but it will be clear that there may still be a multicollinearity problem because of the k successive values of the x-variable. This is the price to be paid for this generalization.

The second extension deals with several explanatory variables, all of which occur in distributed lag form:

$$(4.15) \qquad y_\alpha = \beta_0 + \beta_1 x_{\alpha 1} + \lambda\beta_1 x_{\alpha-1,1} + \lambda^2\beta_1 x_{\alpha-2,1} + \cdots + \beta_2 x_{\alpha 2} + \lambda\beta_2 x_{\alpha-1,2} + \lambda^2\beta_2 x_{\alpha-2,2} + \cdots + \epsilon_\alpha$$

We apply the subtraction procedure and find

$$(4.16) \qquad y_\alpha = (1-\lambda)\beta_0 + \beta_1 x_{\alpha 1} + \beta_2 x_{\alpha 2} + \lambda y_{\alpha-1} + (\epsilon_\alpha - \lambda\epsilon_{\alpha-1})$$

which is very similar to (4.4).

Problems

4.1 To test the specification (4.2), formulate a procedure based on (4.13) and (4.14) under the condition that $\epsilon_\alpha - \lambda\epsilon_{\alpha-1}$ for $\alpha = 2, \ldots, n$ are independent normal variates with zero mean and constant variance. Disregard the complications related to the lagged dependent variable ($y_{\alpha-1}$).

4.2 Formulate a combination of the extensions (4.13) and (4.15) of the Koyck procedure (several explanatory variables and a geometric decline of the coefficients starting at the kth lag).

6.5 More Complicated Distributed Lag Models[B]

Different Geometric Declines for Different Explanatory Variables

It was assumed in (4.15) that the same λ applies to both explanatory variables. A more general specification contains different λ's for different variables:

$$(5.1)\qquad y_\alpha = \beta_0 + \beta_1 x_{\alpha 1} + \lambda_1\beta_1 x_{\alpha-1,1} + \lambda_1^2\beta_1 x_{\alpha-2,1} + \cdots$$
$$+ \beta_2 x_{\alpha 2} + \lambda_2\beta_2 x_{\alpha-1,2} + \lambda_2^2\beta_2 x_{\alpha-2,2} + \cdots + \epsilon_\alpha$$

We shift the equation one period backward, multiply it by λ_1, and subtract it from (5.1):

(5.2)

$$y_\alpha - \lambda_1 y_{\alpha-1} = (1-\lambda_1)\beta_0 + \beta_1 x_{\alpha 1} + \beta_2 x_{\alpha 2}$$
$$+ (\lambda_2 - \lambda_1)(\beta_2 x_{\alpha-1,2} + \lambda_2\beta_2 x_{\alpha-2,2} + \cdots) + (\epsilon_\alpha - \lambda_1\epsilon_{\alpha-1})$$

Next we apply precisely the same subtraction procedure to (5.2) with λ_1 replaced by λ_2. The result can be written as follows:

$$(5.3)\quad y_\alpha = (1-\lambda_1)(1-\lambda_2)\beta_0 + \beta_1(x_{\alpha 1} - \lambda_2 x_{\alpha-1,1}) + \beta_2(x_{\alpha 2} - \lambda_1 x_{\alpha-1,2})$$
$$+ (\lambda_1+\lambda_2)y_{\alpha-1} - \lambda_1\lambda_2 y_{\alpha-2} + [\epsilon_\alpha - (\lambda_1+\lambda_2)\epsilon_{\alpha-1} + \lambda_1\lambda_2\epsilon_{\alpha-2}]$$

This equation is analogous to the corresponding equations of the previous section to the extent that it has a finite number of terms. However, there are two new complications. The first is that the extension of condition (4.5) with $\rho = \lambda$ for the present case is

$$(5.4)\qquad \epsilon_\alpha = (\lambda_1+\lambda_2)\epsilon_{\alpha-1} - \lambda_1\lambda_2\epsilon_{\alpha-2} + \zeta_\alpha$$

where the ζ's are (as before) uncorrelated random variables with zero mean and constant variance. This is a second-order autoregressive process. The other complication is the fact that the total number of coefficients in (5.3) is seven (one constant term plus six multiplicative coefficients for $x_{\alpha 1}, x_{\alpha-1,1}, x_{\alpha 2}, x_{\alpha-1,2}, y_{\alpha-1}$, and $y_{\alpha-2}$) which are determined by only five basic parameters $(\beta_0, \beta_1, \beta_2, \lambda_1, \lambda_2)$. Hence one should estimate the seven coefficients under two constraints, but a major difficulty is that these constraints are nonlinear. An approximation procedure will be described in the paragraph below eq. (5.14).

It should be noted that neither complication arises when the second Nerlove variant (4.10) and (4.11) holds for several explanatory variables; see Problem 5.1.

The Pascal Distribution as a Lag Distribution

In the following discussion we shall confine ourselves mainly to the case of one explanatory variable which occurs with several lags; simple generalizations to a larger number of variables can frequently be made along the lines of (4.15) and (4.16). It will prove convenient to recognize that if all successive coefficients have the same sign, they can be regarded as probabilities of a discrete distribution (the *lag distribution*) multiplied by a positive or negative constant:

$$y_\alpha = \beta_0 + \beta \sum_{t=0}^{\infty} w_t x_{\alpha-t} + \epsilon_\alpha \tag{5.5}$$

where

$$\sum_{t=0}^{\infty} w_t = 1 \qquad w_t \geq 0 \qquad t = 0, 1, 2, \ldots \tag{5.6}$$

In the case (4.2) we have a geometric distribution, $w_t = (1 - \lambda)\lambda^t$ [and $\beta_1 = \beta(1 - \lambda)$], and an obvious question is whether one can generalize this distribution so that the result is nevertheless manageable. This would be important when one objects to an immediate decline of the coefficients, particularly when the specification (4.14) has the disadvantage of multicollinearity. One possibility, proposed by SOLOW (1960), is the Pascal distribution:

$$w_t = \frac{(r + t - 1)!}{(r - 1)!\, t!}(1 - \lambda)^r \lambda^t \qquad t = 0, 1, 2, \ldots \tag{5.7}$$

where r takes a positive integer value. For $r = 1$ we have the geometric distribution and for $r = 2$ we obtain

$$w_t = (1 - \lambda)^2 (t + 1)\lambda^t \qquad t = 0, 1, 2, \ldots \tag{5.8}$$

The successive w's for $r = 1$ and $r = 2$ are as follows:

	w_0	w_1	w_2	w_3	$\cdots$
$r = 1$	$1 - \lambda$	$(1 - \lambda)\lambda$	$(1 - \lambda)\lambda^2$	$(1 - \lambda)\lambda^3$	$\cdots$
$r = 2$	$(1 - \lambda)^2$	$2(1 - \lambda)^2\lambda$	$3(1 - \lambda)^2\lambda^2$	$4(1 - \lambda)^2\lambda^3$	$\cdots$

Evidently, for $r = 1$ the probabilities decline monotonically ($0 < \lambda < 1$), but for $r = 2$ they may increase to a certain maximum, after which they decline toward zero. Figure 6.2 illustrates two cases, $\lambda = .4$ and $\lambda = .6$. In the first case the probabilities decline monotonically; in the second there is a maximum at a lag of one period.

Estimates Based on a Simple Pascal Distribution

Suppose, then, that the lag structure (5.8) applies to eq. (5.5):

$$y_\alpha = \beta_0 + (1 - \lambda)^2 \beta(x_\alpha + 2\lambda x_{\alpha-1} + 3\lambda^2 x_{\alpha-2} + \cdots) + \epsilon_\alpha \tag{5.9}$$

Again, we write down the same equation for $y_{\alpha-1}$, multiply both sides by λ, and subtract the result from (5.9), which gives

(5.10)

$$y_\alpha - \lambda y_{\alpha-1} = (1 - \lambda)\beta_0 + (1 - \lambda)^2 \beta(x_\alpha + \lambda x_{\alpha-1} + \cdots) + (\epsilon_\alpha - \lambda\epsilon_{\alpha-1})$$

Next, apply the same subtraction procedure to (5.10) with the following result:

(5.11)

$$y_\alpha = (1 - \lambda)^2\beta_0 + (1 - \lambda)^2\beta x_\alpha + 2\lambda y_{\alpha-1} - \lambda^2 y_{\alpha-2} + (\epsilon_\alpha - 2\lambda\epsilon_{\alpha-1} + \lambda^2\epsilon_{\alpha-2})$$

Comparing this result with (5.3) for the special case $\lambda_1 = \lambda_2 = \lambda$, we find that they are identical except for the part dealing with the x-variables. As in (5.4), we have to assume that the ϵ's are generated by a second-order autoregressive process:

$$\epsilon_\alpha = 2\lambda\epsilon_{\alpha-1} - \lambda^2\epsilon_{\alpha-2} + \zeta_\alpha \tag{5.12}$$

if we want disturbances in (5.11) that have a scalar covariance matrix. Also, the number of coefficients in (5.11) is four, which exceeds the number of basic

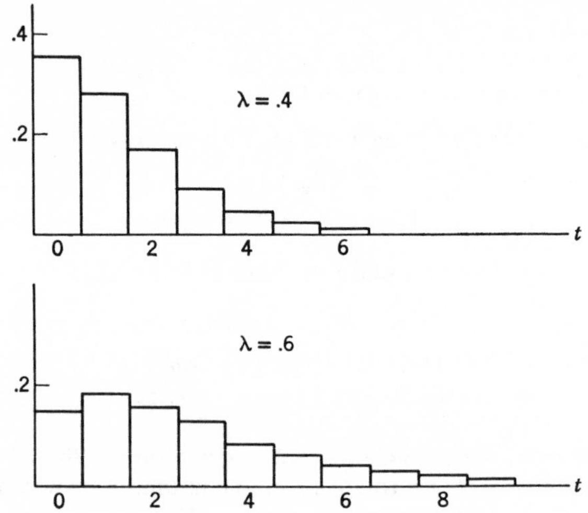

Fig. 6.2 Two Pascal distributions, $r = 2$.

parameters (β_0, β, λ). However, the excess is only one, not two as in (5.3), so that we may decide to proceed in the way now to be described.

GRILICHES and WALLACE (1965) estimated a number of alternative regressions for investment in U.S. manufacturing on the basis of quarterly data of the period 1948 to 1962. They included several explanatory variables besides investment lagged one and two quarters. [The formulation (5.11) is in terms of one x-variable, but the generalization along the lines of (4.15) and (4.16) is straightforward.] Three such variables are: capital stock at the beginning of the quarter, a stock price index (lagged two quarters), and an interest rate of industrial bonds (lagged two quarters). An LS regression of current investment on these variables as well as on investment lagged one quarter ($y_{\alpha-1}$) and investment lagged two quarters ($y_{\alpha-2}$) leads to the following coefficients (with standard errors in parentheses) of the last two variables:

$$y_{\alpha-1}:\ 1.150\ (.118) \qquad y_{\alpha-2}:\ -.331\ (.109) \tag{5.13}$$

When industrial production is introduced as a fourth explanatory variable, all coefficients change. In particular, for lagged investment:

$$y_{\alpha-1}:\ .877\ (.144) \qquad y_{\alpha-2}:\ -.126\ (.124) \tag{5.14}$$

Returning to (5.11), we find there that the coefficient of $y_{\alpha-1}$ is 2λ and that of $y_{\alpha-2}$ is $-\lambda^2$. The estimates (5.13) and (5.14) are not derived under the constraint that the two coefficients are determined by the same λ, so that we should not be surprised to find that no λ exists that reproduces both coefficients. But take $\lambda = .6$, which implies $2\lambda = 1.2$ and $-\lambda^2 = -.36$ in close agreement with the point estimates (5.13). Also, take $\lambda = .4$, which implies $2\lambda = .8$ and $-\lambda^2 = -.16$ in fairly close agreement with (5.14). This suggests the following linearization procedure. First, find a λ_0 which is such that $2\lambda_0$ and $-\lambda_0^2$ are in reasonable agreement with the point estimates of the coefficients of $y_{\alpha-1}$ and $y_{\alpha-2}$, respectively. Next, consider the identity $-\lambda^2 = \lambda_0^2 - 2\lambda_0\lambda - (\lambda - \lambda_0)^2$ and substitute the right-hand side for the coefficient $-\lambda^2$ in (5.11). The result can be written as follows:

$$\begin{aligned} y_\alpha - \lambda_0^2 y_{\alpha-2} = {} & (1-\lambda)^2\beta_0 + (1-\lambda)^2\beta x_\alpha + 2\lambda(y_{\alpha-1} - \lambda_0 y_{\alpha-2}) \\ & + [\epsilon_\alpha - 2\lambda\epsilon_{\alpha-1} + \lambda^2\epsilon_{\alpha-2} - (\lambda-\lambda_0)^2 y_{\alpha-2}] \end{aligned} \tag{5.15}$$

The expression on the first line contains $y_\alpha - \lambda_0^2 y_{\alpha-2}$ as the αth value of the dependent variable; it also contains a constant term, the current value of the explanatory variable, and $y_{\alpha-1} - \lambda_0 y_{\alpha-2}$ as the αth value of the second right-hand variable. The three right-hand coefficients correspond in number to the basic parameters (β_0, β, λ). The second line contains the disturbances as well as $y_{\alpha-2}$ multiplied by the squared difference of λ and λ_0. If λ_0 is sufficiently close to λ, we may decide to ignore this last term. Under the assumption of the second-order autoregressive process (5.12), we can then run an LS regression of the dependent variable of (5.15) on its two right-hand variables plus a constant term, from which point estimates of β_0, β, and λ may be derived. The standard errors of these estimates form a more complicated problem because β_0 and β are nonlinear functions of the coefficients of (5.15). The subject of asymptotic variances of nonlinear functions of random variables is pursued in Section 8.3.

Concluding Remarks

A comparison of the numerical results (5.13) and (5.14) shows that the introduction of an additional explanatory variable (industrial production in this case) may have a rather substantial impact on the lag picture. In particular, (5.14) indicates that the coefficient of $y_{\alpha-2}$ is not at all significantly different from zero, so that one may decide to drop that variable and to simplify the specification to that of the geometric lag distribution of (4.15) and (4.16). Indeed, one should expect that in a substantial number of cases, multicollinearity and autocorrelated disturbances are a serious impediment to lag analyses which are more refined than those of the previous section.

For an extensive treatment of lags, see GRILICHES (1967) and MALINVAUD (1966, Chapter 15), who describe specifications proposed by I. FISHER (1937), THEIL and STERN (1960), and JORGENSON (1966). The Theil-Stern specification corresponds to the Pascal distribution for $r = 2$, but it pays more explicit attention to the transition from a theoretical continuous lag distribution which is to be applied to noncontinuous data.

Problems

5.1 Consider the model (4.10) and (4.11) but suppose that a term $\beta' p'_{\alpha-1}$ is added to the right-hand side of (4.10), where $p'_{\alpha-1}$ stands for the price of a second crop in year $\alpha - 1$. Show that the corresponding extension of (4.12) has the same form as (4.16) except that the disturbance term does not involve $\epsilon_{\alpha-1}$.

5.2 Prove that the moment-generating function of the Pascal distribution (5.7) is

$$\mathscr{E}(e^{sX}) = \left(\frac{1-\lambda}{1-\lambda e^s}\right)^r \tag{5.16}$$

Use this result to prove that the mean and the variance are equal to $r\lambda/(1-\lambda)$ and $r\lambda/(1-\lambda)^2$, respectively, and apply this to the estimates (5.13) and (5.14) to find the average lags and the standard deviations of the lag distributions. [Use $r = 2$, $\lambda = .6$ for (5.13) and $r = 2$, $\lambda = .4$ for (5.14).]

6.6 The Generalized Inverse of a Matrix[C]

The remainder of this chapter is devoted to the case in which the disturbance covariance matrix is singular. To handle such cases it is convenient to work with the generalized inverse (also called the Moore-Penrose inverse) of a matrix. It will be shown in the next paragraph that for any $m \times n$ matrix $\mathbf{A}$ of rank r, there exists a unique generalized inverse, to be denoted by $\mathbf{A}^+$, which is determined by the following four conditions:

$$\mathbf{AA^+A} = \mathbf{A} \tag{6.1}$$

$$\mathbf{A^+AA^+} = \mathbf{A^+} \tag{6.2}$$

$$(\mathbf{AA^+})' = \mathbf{AA^+} \tag{6.3}$$

$$(\mathbf{A^+A})' = \mathbf{A^+A} \tag{6.4}$$

It follows from the left-hand multiplication in (6.1) that the order of $\mathbf{A}^+$ must be $n \times m$, that is, the order of the generalized inverse is the same as that of the transpose of the matrix. The ranks of $\mathbf{A}$ and $\mathbf{A}^+$ are equal. This follows from (6.1), which shows that the rank of $\mathbf{A}$ on the right is not larger than that of $\mathbf{A}^+$ on the left, and from (6.2), which shows that the rank of $\mathbf{A}^+$ cannot be larger than that of $\mathbf{A}$. Therefore $\mathbf{A}^+$ is an $n \times m$ matrix of rank r. It is a true generalization of the ordinary inverse $\mathbf{A}^{-1}$ of a nonsingular matrix $\mathbf{A}$, for if $\mathbf{A}^{-1}$ exists, it satisfies the four conditions: $\mathbf{AA^{-1}A} = \mathbf{A}$, $\mathbf{A^{-1}AA^{-1}} = \mathbf{A}^{-1}$, $\mathbf{AA}^{-1} = \mathbf{I} =$ symmetric, $\mathbf{A^{-1}A} = \mathbf{I} =$ symmetric.

Existence and Uniqueness of the Generalized Inverse

We shall first prove that if an $\mathbf{A}^+$ satisfying (6.1) to (6.4) exists, it is unique. Thus we assume that two matrices $\mathbf{B}$ and $\mathbf{C}$ both satisfy all four conditions and we prove by means of these conditions that $\mathbf{B}$ must be equal to $\mathbf{C}$:

$$\begin{aligned}\mathbf{B} &= \mathbf{BAB} = \mathbf{B}(\mathbf{AB})' = \mathbf{BB'A'} = \mathbf{BB'}(\mathbf{ACA})' = \mathbf{BB'A'C'A'}\\ &= \mathbf{B}(\mathbf{AB})'(\mathbf{AC})' = \mathbf{BABAC} = \mathbf{BAC} = \mathbf{BACAC} = (\mathbf{BA})'(\mathbf{CA})'\mathbf{C}\\ &= \mathbf{A'B'A'C'C} = (\mathbf{ABA})'\mathbf{C'C} = \mathbf{A'C'C} = (\mathbf{CA})'\mathbf{C} = \mathbf{CAC} = \mathbf{C}\end{aligned} \tag{6.5}$$

Next we have to prove that $\mathbf{A}^+$ exists. First, suppose that $\mathbf{A}$ is the $m \times n$ zero matrix. The generalized inverse is its transpose (the $n \times m$ zero matrix); this is verified straightforwardly by means of the four conditions (6.1) to (6.4). So we may confine ourselves in the sequel to an $m \times n$ matrix $\mathbf{A}$ with positive rank r. By premultiplying it by its own transpose we obtain $\mathbf{A'A}$, which is a symmetric positive semidefinite matrix of order $n \times n$ and rank $r > 0$. Write $\mathbf{D}$ for the $r \times r$ diagonal matrix whose diagonal elements are the positive latent roots of $\mathbf{A'A}$ and $[\mathbf{H} \quad \mathbf{K}]$ for an orthogonal $n \times n$ matrix whose columns are characteristic vectors of $\mathbf{A'A}$, $\mathbf{H}$ being an $n \times r$ submatrix of characteristic vectors corresponding to the r positive roots of $\mathbf{A'A}$. The orthogonality condition on $[\mathbf{H} \quad \mathbf{K}]$ can be expressed in two ways. Premultiplication of this matrix by its transpose and equating the product to the $n \times n$ unit matrix gives

$$\mathbf{H'H} = \mathbf{I} \qquad \mathbf{K'K} = \mathbf{I} \qquad \mathbf{H'K} = \mathbf{0} \tag{6.6}$$

Postmultiplication of $[\mathbf{H} \quad \mathbf{K}]$ by its transpose and equating the product to $\mathbf{I}$ gives

$$\mathbf{HH}' + \mathbf{KK}' = \mathbf{I} \tag{6.7}$$

Since the columns of $\mathbf{K}$ are characteristic vectors of $\mathbf{A}'\mathbf{A}$ corresponding to zero roots, we have $\mathbf{A}'\mathbf{AK} = \mathbf{0}$, which gives $(\mathbf{AK})'\mathbf{AK} = \mathbf{0}$ after premultiplication of both sides by $\mathbf{K}'$. This, in turn, implies $\mathbf{AK} = \mathbf{0}$ and hence $\mathbf{AKK}' = \mathbf{0}$, which in view of (6.7) implies

$$\mathbf{AHH}' = \mathbf{A} \tag{6.8}$$

Using these results, we can prove

$$\mathbf{A}'\mathbf{A} = \mathbf{HDH}' \qquad (\mathbf{A}'\mathbf{A})^+ = \mathbf{HD}^{-1}\mathbf{H}' \tag{6.9}$$

and

$$\mathbf{A}^+ = (\mathbf{A}'\mathbf{A})^+\mathbf{A}' = \mathbf{HD}^{-1}\mathbf{H}'\mathbf{A}' \tag{6.10}$$

The statement $\mathbf{A}'\mathbf{A} = \mathbf{HDH}'$ in (6.9) is nothing but the familiar diagonalization of the symmetric matrix $\mathbf{A}'\mathbf{A}$.[12] The generalized inverse statement in (6.9) is checked by means of the conditions (6.1) to (6.4). The symmetry conditions (6.3) and (6.4) refer to the product matrices $\mathbf{HDH}'\mathbf{HD}^{-1}\mathbf{H}' = \mathbf{HH}'$ and $\mathbf{HD}^{-1}\mathbf{H}'\mathbf{HDH}' = \mathbf{HH}'$, respectively, where use is made of $\mathbf{H}'\mathbf{H} = \mathbf{I}$ of (6.6). Obviously, both product matrices are indeed symmetric (they are identical in this case). It is readily verified that conditions (6.1) and (6.2) are also satisfied.

To check (6.10) we consider $\mathbf{AA}^+ = \mathbf{AHD}^{-1}\mathbf{H}'\mathbf{A}'$, which is symmetric in accordance with (6.3). Next consider

$$\mathbf{A}^+\mathbf{A} = \mathbf{HD}^{-1}\mathbf{H}'\mathbf{A}'\mathbf{A} = \mathbf{HD}^{-1}\mathbf{H}'\mathbf{HDH}' = \mathbf{HH}'$$

where use is made of (6.9) in the second step. The symmetry condition (6.4) is thus also fulfilled. By postmultiplying $\mathbf{A}^+\mathbf{A}$ by $\mathbf{A}^+ = \mathbf{HD}^{-1}\mathbf{H}'\mathbf{A}'$ we obtain

$$\mathbf{A}^+\mathbf{AA}^+ = \mathbf{HH}'\mathbf{HD}^{-1}\mathbf{H}'\mathbf{A}' = \mathbf{HD}^{-1}\mathbf{H}'\mathbf{A}' = \mathbf{A}^+$$

Finally, postmultiply $\mathbf{AA}^+ = \mathbf{AHD}^{-1}\mathbf{H}'\mathbf{A}'$ by $\mathbf{A}$:

$$\mathbf{AA}^+\mathbf{A} = \mathbf{AHD}^{-1}\mathbf{H}'\mathbf{A}'\mathbf{A} = \mathbf{AHD}^{-1}\mathbf{H}'\mathbf{HDH}' = \mathbf{AHH}' = \mathbf{A}$$

where use is made of (6.8) in the last step. We conclude that (6.10) does indeed provide the generalized inverse of $\mathbf{A}$.

[12] See eq. (5.7) of Section 1.5 and imagine that only r of the λ's of that equation are nonzero.

Applications

A special case is that of an $\mathbf{A}$ with full column rank, so that $\mathbf{A}'\mathbf{A}$ is nonsingular. It follows from (6.10) that $\mathbf{A}^+ = (\mathbf{A}'\mathbf{A})^{-1}\mathbf{A}'$, which may be checked directly as follows:

$$\mathbf{A}\mathbf{A}^+\mathbf{A} = \mathbf{A}(\mathbf{A}'\mathbf{A})^{-1}\mathbf{A}'\mathbf{A} = \mathbf{A}$$
$$\mathbf{A}^+\mathbf{A}\mathbf{A}^+ = (\mathbf{A}'\mathbf{A})^{-1}\mathbf{A}'\mathbf{A}(\mathbf{A}'\mathbf{A})^{-1}\mathbf{A}' = (\mathbf{A}'\mathbf{A})^{-1}\mathbf{A}' = \mathbf{A}^+$$
$$\mathbf{A}^+\mathbf{A} = (\mathbf{A}'\mathbf{A})^{-1}\mathbf{A}'\mathbf{A} = \mathbf{I} = \text{symmetric}$$
$$\mathbf{A}\mathbf{A}^+ = \mathbf{A}(\mathbf{A}'\mathbf{A})^{-1}\mathbf{A}' = \text{symmetric}$$

The usefulness of this result for LS estimation is immediately obvious, since we can now write the coefficient estimator in a simple form:

$$\mathbf{b} = (\mathbf{X}'\mathbf{X})^{-1}\mathbf{X}'\mathbf{y} = \mathbf{X}^+\mathbf{y} \tag{6.11}$$

Thus $\mathbf{b}$ is equal to the column vector $\mathbf{y}$ of values taken by the dependent variable premultiplied by the generalized inverse $\mathbf{X}^+$ of the $n \times K$ matrix of values taken by the explanatory variables. The notation $\mathbf{b} = \mathbf{X}^+\mathbf{y}$ is, of course, the immediate extension of $\mathbf{b} = \mathbf{X}^{-1}\mathbf{y}$ in the special case $n = K$.

The familiar idempotent matrix $\mathbf{M} = \mathbf{I} - \mathbf{X}(\mathbf{X}'\mathbf{X})^{-1}\mathbf{X}'$ can also be simplified:

$$\mathbf{M} = \mathbf{I} - \mathbf{X}\mathbf{X}^+ \tag{6.12}$$

It is easily seen that any idempotent matrix (like $\mathbf{M}$) is equal to its own generalized inverse. Substitute $\mathbf{A}$ for $\mathbf{A}^+$ in (6.1) and (6.2), then both equations amount to $\mathbf{A}^3 = \mathbf{A}$; similarly (6.3) and (6.4) require $\mathbf{A}^2$ to be symmetric, which is indeed true when $\mathbf{A}^2 = \mathbf{A}$, $\mathbf{A}' = \mathbf{A}$. (Recall that it is assumed implicitly that a matrix is symmetric when it is idempotent.) This result shows that idempotent matrices may be regarded as extensions of the scalar unit concept. Not only the squares and higher powers of such matrices are equal to the original matrix, but this is also true for the generalized inverse, in the same way that any positive or negative power of 1 is equal to 1.

Another special case of interest is that of an $m \times n$ matrix $\mathbf{A}$ which can be partitioned as follows:

$$\mathbf{A} = \begin{bmatrix} \mathbf{B} & \mathbf{0} \\ \mathbf{0} & \mathbf{0} \end{bmatrix} \tag{6.13}$$

where $\mathbf{B}$ is an $r \times r$ matrix of full rank, $r \leq m, n$. The generalized inverse is

$$\mathbf{A}^+ = \begin{bmatrix} \mathbf{B}^{-1} & \mathbf{0} \\ \mathbf{0} & \mathbf{0} \end{bmatrix} \tag{6.14}$$

[Note that the upper right zero matrix in (6.13) is of order $r \times (n - r)$, and that in (6.14) of order $r \times (m - r)$.] The check is again straightforward:

$$\mathbf{AA^+A} = \begin{bmatrix} \mathbf{B} & \mathbf{0} \\ \mathbf{0} & \mathbf{0} \end{bmatrix} \begin{bmatrix} \mathbf{B}^{-1} & \mathbf{0} \\ \mathbf{0} & \mathbf{0} \end{bmatrix} \begin{bmatrix} \mathbf{B} & \mathbf{0} \\ \mathbf{0} & \mathbf{0} \end{bmatrix} = \begin{bmatrix} \mathbf{B} & \mathbf{0} \\ \mathbf{0} & \mathbf{0} \end{bmatrix} = \mathbf{A}$$

$$\mathbf{A^+AA^+} = \begin{bmatrix} \mathbf{B}^{-1} & \mathbf{0} \\ \mathbf{0} & \mathbf{0} \end{bmatrix} \begin{bmatrix} \mathbf{B} & \mathbf{0} \\ \mathbf{0} & \mathbf{0} \end{bmatrix} \begin{bmatrix} \mathbf{B}^{-1} & \mathbf{0} \\ \mathbf{0} & \mathbf{0} \end{bmatrix} = \begin{bmatrix} \mathbf{B}^{-1} & \mathbf{0} \\ \mathbf{0} & \mathbf{0} \end{bmatrix} = \mathbf{A}^+$$

$$\mathbf{A^+A} = \begin{bmatrix} \mathbf{B}^{-1} & \mathbf{0} \\ \mathbf{0} & \mathbf{0} \end{bmatrix} \begin{bmatrix} \mathbf{B} & \mathbf{0} \\ \mathbf{0} & \mathbf{0} \end{bmatrix} = \begin{bmatrix} \mathbf{I} & \mathbf{0} \\ \mathbf{0} & \mathbf{0} \end{bmatrix} = \text{symmetric } (n \times n)$$

$$\mathbf{AA^+} = \begin{bmatrix} \mathbf{B} & \mathbf{0} \\ \mathbf{0} & \mathbf{0} \end{bmatrix} \begin{bmatrix} \mathbf{B}^{-1} & \mathbf{0} \\ \mathbf{0} & \mathbf{0} \end{bmatrix} = \begin{bmatrix} \mathbf{I} & \mathbf{0} \\ \mathbf{0} & \mathbf{0} \end{bmatrix} = \text{symmetric } (m \times m)$$

The generalized inverse of a singular symmetric positive semidefinite matrix can be computed easily when the characteristic vectors corresponding to the zero roots are known. Take the case of an $\mathbf{A}$ of order $n \times n$ and rank $n - 1$ and let $\mathbf{y}$ be a characteristic vector corresponding to the zero root:

$$\mathbf{Ay} = \mathbf{0} \qquad \mathbf{y'y} = 1 \tag{6.15}$$

Since $\mathbf{A}$ is positive semidefinite of rank $n - 1$, $\mathbf{A} + k\mathbf{yy}'$ is positive definite for any positive scalar k,[13] so that the latter matrix has an ordinary inverse. The generalized inverse of $\mathbf{A}$ can then be written as

$$\mathbf{A}^+ = (\mathbf{A} + k\mathbf{yy}')^{-1} - \frac{1}{k}\mathbf{yy}' \qquad (k > 0) \tag{6.16}$$

the proof of which is considered in Problem 6.11. A simple example:

$$\mathbf{A} = \begin{bmatrix} z & -z \\ -z & z \end{bmatrix} \quad \text{implying} \quad \mathbf{y} = \frac{1}{\sqrt{2}} \begin{bmatrix} 1 \\ 1 \end{bmatrix} \tag{6.17}$$

[13] For any n-element column vector $\mathbf{x} \neq \mathbf{0}$ we have $\mathbf{x'Ax} = 0$ or > 0 depending on whether or not a scalar c exists such that $\mathbf{x} = c\mathbf{y}$. If this scalar exists, then $k\mathbf{x'yy'x} = k(\mathbf{x'y})^2 = kc^2\mathbf{y'y} = kc^2 > 0$. By adding $\mathbf{x'Ax}$ and $k\mathbf{x'yy'x}$, we obtain a quadratic form in $\mathbf{x}$ with $\mathbf{A} + k\mathbf{yy}'$ as matrix, and it thus follows that this form is always positive. Note that $\mathbf{A} + k\mathbf{yy}'$ is also nonsingular for negative k; the matrix then has one negative and $n - 1$ positive roots and thus exclusively nonzero roots. The condition $k > 0$ in (6.16) may therefore be weakened to $k \neq 0$.

where z is an arbitrary nonzero number. The right-hand side of (6.16) is then

$$(6.18)\quad (\mathbf{A} + k\mathbf{yy}')^{-1} - \frac{1}{k}\mathbf{yy}' = \begin{bmatrix} z + \frac{1}{2}k & -z + \frac{1}{2}k \\ -z + \frac{1}{2}k & z + \frac{1}{2}k \end{bmatrix}^{-1} - \frac{1}{2k}\begin{bmatrix} 1 & 1 \\ 1 & 1 \end{bmatrix}$$

$$= \frac{1}{2kz}\begin{bmatrix} z + \frac{1}{2}k & z - \frac{1}{2}k \\ z - \frac{1}{2}k & z + \frac{1}{2}k \end{bmatrix} - \frac{1}{2kz}\begin{bmatrix} z & z \\ z & z \end{bmatrix}$$

$$= \frac{1}{4z}\begin{bmatrix} 1 & -1 \\ -1 & 1 \end{bmatrix}$$

The matrix on the last line is independent of k as it should be, since $\mathbf{A}^+$ is determined uniquely by $\mathbf{A}$, and $\mathbf{A}$ is independent of k. It is again a matter of straightforward substitution in (6.1) to (6.4) to verify that the solution found is indeed $\mathbf{A}^+$.

Problems

6.1 Check the conditions (6.1) and (6.2) for the generalized inverse in (6.9).

6.2 Specify the order of the unit and zero matrices which occur in (6.6) and (6.7).

6.3 Use eqs. (6.8) to (6.10) to prove $\mathbf{A}' = \mathbf{A}'\mathbf{A}\mathbf{A}^+ = \mathbf{A}^+\mathbf{A}\mathbf{A}'$.

6.4 Prove $(\mathbf{A}^+)^+ = \mathbf{A}$ (each matrix is the generalized inverse of its own generalized inverse) and $(\mathbf{A}')^+ = (\mathbf{A}^+)'$ (the transpose of a generalized inverse is equal to the generalized inverse of the transpose). Conclude that the generalized inverse of a symmetric matrix is also symmetric.

6.5 (*The generalized inverse of a singular symmetric matrix*) Let $\mathbf{A}$ be a symmetric $n \times n$ matrix of rank r with roots $\lambda_1, \ldots, \lambda_r, 0, \ldots, 0$. Let $\mathbf{x}_1, \ldots, \mathbf{x}_n$ be characteristic vectors of $\mathbf{A}$ corresponding to these successive roots:

$$(6.19)\quad \mathbf{A} = \sum_{i=1}^{r} \lambda_i \mathbf{x}_i \mathbf{x}_i' \qquad \mathbf{A}\mathbf{x}_i = \mathbf{0} \quad \text{for} \quad i = r+1, \ldots, n$$

Prove that $\mathbf{A}^+$ is a symmetric matrix with the same number of zero roots $(n - r)$ and that its r nonzero roots are the reciprocals of the nonzero roots of $\mathbf{A}$. Also prove under the condition that $\mathbf{x}_1, \ldots, \mathbf{x}_r$

have unit length and are pairwise orthogonal:

$$(6.20) \quad \mathbf{A}^+ = \sum_{i=1}^{r} \frac{1}{\lambda_i} \mathbf{x}_i\mathbf{x}_i' \qquad \mathbf{A}^+\mathbf{x}_i = \mathbf{0} \quad \text{for} \quad i = r+1, \ldots, n$$

and conclude that $\mathbf{x}_1, \ldots, \mathbf{x}_n$ are characteristic vectors of $\mathbf{A}^+$.

6.6 Prove $\mathbf{i}_k^+ = \mathbf{i}_k'$ and $\boldsymbol{\iota}^+ = (1/n)\boldsymbol{\iota}'$, where $\mathbf{i}_k$ is the kth column of the $n \times n$ unit matrix and $\boldsymbol{\iota}' = [1 \quad \cdots \quad 1]$ is a vector consisting of n unit elements.

6.7 Prove $(\mathbf{aa}')^+ = (1/\mathbf{a}'\mathbf{a})^2\mathbf{aa}'$ for any column vector $\mathbf{a} \neq \mathbf{0}$.

6.8 Prove that $\mathbf{AA}^+$ and $\mathbf{A}^+\mathbf{A}$ are idempotent matrices for any $\mathbf{A}$.

6.9 Generalize eqs. (6.13) and (6.14) for the case in which $\mathbf{B}$ has no (ordinary) inverse.

6.10 Let $\mathbf{A}$ be a singular square matrix. Prove

$$(6.21) \qquad \begin{bmatrix} \mathbf{A} & \mathbf{0} & \mathbf{0} \\ \mathbf{0} & \mathbf{A} & \mathbf{0} \\ \mathbf{0} & \mathbf{0} & \mathbf{A} \end{bmatrix}^+ = \begin{bmatrix} \mathbf{A}^+ & \mathbf{0} & \mathbf{0} \\ \mathbf{0} & \mathbf{A}^+ & \mathbf{0} \\ \mathbf{0} & \mathbf{0} & \mathbf{A}^+ \end{bmatrix}$$

6.11 Let $\mathbf{A}$ be a symmetric positive semidefinite $n \times n$ matrix of rank $n - 1$. Write $\lambda_1, \ldots, \lambda_{n-1}$ for its positive roots, $\mathbf{x}_1, \ldots, \mathbf{x}_{n-1}$ for corresponding characteristic vectors, and $\mathbf{y}$ for the vector corresponding to the zero root in accordance with (6.15). Prove that the roots of $\mathbf{A} + k\mathbf{yy}'$ are $\lambda_1, \ldots, \lambda_{n-1}, k$, that $\mathbf{x}_1, \ldots, \mathbf{x}_{n-1}, \mathbf{y}$ are corresponding characteristic vectors, and use Problem 6.5 to prove (6.16).

6.12 (*Continuation*) Extend (6.16) by proving that if $\mathbf{y}_1, \ldots, \mathbf{y}_{n-r}$ are characteristic vectors corresponding to the zero roots of a symmetric positive semidefinite matrix $\mathbf{A}$ of order $n \times n$ and rank r, then

$$(6.22) \qquad \mathbf{A}^+ = \left(\mathbf{A} + \sum_{i=1}^{n-r} k_i\mathbf{y}_i\mathbf{y}_i'\right)^{-1} - \sum_{i=1}^{n-r} \frac{1}{k_i} \mathbf{y}_i\mathbf{y}_i'$$

where $k_1, \ldots, k_{n-r}$ are arbitrary nonzero scalars.

6.13 Let $\mathbf{A}$ be nonsingular and $\mathbf{B}$ a matrix of full column rank. Define $\mathbf{C} = \mathbf{BAB}'$ and prove $\mathbf{B}'\mathbf{C}^+\mathbf{B} = \mathbf{A}^{-1}$. (*Hint.* Use $\mathbf{CC}^+\mathbf{C} = \mathbf{C}$, premultiply both sides of the equation by $\mathbf{B}'$ and postmultiply by $\mathbf{B}$; thereafter substitute $\mathbf{BAB}'$ for $\mathbf{C}$.)

6.7 A Singular Disturbance Covariance Matrix[C]

Linearly Dependent Disturbances

Suppose that we have data on the expenditures of N households of identical composition in a certain period and that we distinguish between three expenditure categories: food, durables, and the rest. Let us describe the expenditure on each category as a linear function of total expenditure except for random disturbances:

$$(7.1)\qquad \begin{aligned} (\text{food})_\alpha &= \beta_0 + \beta_1\,(\text{total expenditure})_\alpha + \epsilon_\alpha \\ (\text{durables})_\alpha &= \beta_0' + \beta_1'\,(\text{total expenditure})_\alpha + \epsilon_\alpha' \\ (\text{rest})_\alpha &= \beta_0'' + \beta_1''\,(\text{total expenditure})_\alpha + \epsilon_\alpha'' \end{aligned}$$

where the subscript α refers to the αth household. Adding the three equations gives a fourth which may be written as

$$(7.2)\qquad [1 - (\beta_1 + \beta_1' + \beta_1'')]\,(\text{total expenditure})_\alpha = (\beta_0 + \beta_0' + \beta_0'') + (\epsilon_\alpha + \epsilon_\alpha' + \epsilon_\alpha'')$$

If we take total expenditure as a variable whose values are nonstochastic, the right-hand side of (7.2) cannot be random either, so that $\epsilon_\alpha + \epsilon_\alpha' + \epsilon_\alpha''$ must be identically equal to its expectation (zero). Hence the disturbances are linearly dependent. The dependence can be removed by deleting one of the three equations (7.1), and it will indeed turn out that this is the appropriate procedure in this case (see Problems 7.3 and 7.4). On the other hand, linear dependence of disturbances may imply linear constraints on the parameter vector, and it is obviously undesirable to delete these. Therefore a more detailed analysis is appropriate.

A Singular Disturbance Covariance Matrix

If eq. (7.1) applies to N households, the complete disturbance vector contains $3N$ elements and hence its covariance matrix is of order $3N \times 3N$, but the rank of this matrix cannot be larger than $2N$ because of (7.2). To handle this situation we return to Assumption 6.1 with its $n \times n$ covariance matrix $\sigma^2\mathbf{V}$. This is now generalized so that $\mathbf{V}$ may be singular.

ASSUMPTION 6.2 (Singular covariance matrix) *The conditional covariance matrix of* $\mathbf{y}$ *given* $\mathbf{X}$ *is*

$$(7.3)\qquad \mathscr{V}(\mathbf{y} \mid \mathbf{X}) = \sigma^2\mathbf{V} \qquad (\sigma^2 < \infty)$$

where σ^2 *is an unknown positive parameter and* $\mathbf{V}$ *is a known symmetric positive semidefinite* $n \times n$ *matrix whose rank and trace are both equal to* n', *where* $0 < n' \leq n$.

This includes Assumption 6.1 as a special case for $n' = n$. The assumption on the trace of $\mathbf{V}$ is not restrictive; see the corresponding argument for $\text{tr}\,\mathbf{V} = n$ in the first subsection of Section 6.1, which applies here also.

Diagonalization of the Disturbance Covariance Matrix

Since $\mathbf{V}$ is symmetric and positive semidefinite of order $n \times n$ and rank n', it has $n - n'$ zero roots and n' positive roots. It will appear to be typographically advantageous to write the latter roots in the squared form λ_α^2 ($\alpha = 1, \ldots, n'$) and to define λ_α as the positive square root of λ_α^2. Therefore we have

$$\mathbf{VF} = \mathbf{F\Lambda}^2 \qquad \mathbf{VG} = \mathbf{0} \tag{7.4}$$

where $\mathbf{F}$ is an $n \times n'$ matrix whose columns are characteristic vectors of $\mathbf{V}$ corresponding to the positive roots, $\mathbf{\Lambda}$ is an $n' \times n'$ diagonal matrix with the λ's along the diagonal, and $\mathbf{G}$ is an $n \times (n - n')$ matrix whose columns are characteristic vectors of $\mathbf{V}$ corresponding to the zero roots. As in the case (6.6) and (6.7), we can express the orthogonality of $[\mathbf{F} \quad \mathbf{G}]$ in two ways:

$$\mathbf{F'F} = \mathbf{I} \qquad \mathbf{G'G} = \mathbf{I} \qquad \mathbf{F'G} = \mathbf{0} \tag{7.5}$$

$$\mathbf{FF'} + \mathbf{GG'} = \mathbf{I} \tag{7.6}$$

and $\mathbf{V}$ and its generalized inverse can be expressed in $\mathbf{F}$ and $\mathbf{\Lambda}$ as follows:

$$\mathbf{V} = \mathbf{F\Lambda}^2\mathbf{F}' \qquad \mathbf{V}^+ = \mathbf{F\Lambda}^{-2}\mathbf{F}' \tag{7.7}$$

The generalized inverse follows immediately from Problem 6.5; it may also be verified directly by means of the conditions (6.1) to (6.4).

LS after a Transformation

As in Section 6.1, it seems natural to apply the LS method after a transformation of the variables such that the disturbances have a scalar covariance matrix. For this purpose we premultiply both sides of $\mathbf{y} = \mathbf{X}\boldsymbol{\beta} + \boldsymbol{\epsilon}$ by $\mathbf{\Lambda}^{-1}\mathbf{F}'$:

$$\mathbf{\Lambda}^{-1}\mathbf{F}'\mathbf{y} = (\mathbf{\Lambda}^{-1}\mathbf{F}'\mathbf{X})\boldsymbol{\beta} + \mathbf{\Lambda}^{-1}\mathbf{F}'\boldsymbol{\epsilon} \tag{7.8}$$

which means that $[\mathbf{\Lambda}^{-1}\mathbf{F}'\mathbf{y} \quad \mathbf{\Lambda}^{-1}\mathbf{F}'\mathbf{X}]$ is the observation matrix after the transformation. Note that this matrix can indeed be computed because $\mathbf{\Lambda}$ and $\mathbf{F}$ are determined by $\mathbf{V}$, and $\mathbf{V}$ is known by assumption.[14] Also note that the new observation matrix contains n', not n, rows; basically, we disregard $n - n'$ observations whose disturbances are linearly dependent on those of the n' other observations, and it remains to be seen whether this neglect is acceptable.

[14] If $\mathbf{V}$ has multiple positive roots, $\mathbf{F}$ is not unique, but this is not of any importance since it will turn out that $\mathbf{F}$ occurs in the relevant expressions only in the forms $\mathbf{F\Lambda}^2\mathbf{F}' = \mathbf{V}$ and $\mathbf{F\Lambda}^{-2}\mathbf{F}' = \mathbf{V}^+$, which are unique.

The covariance matrix of the new disturbance vector $\boldsymbol{\Lambda}^{-1}\mathbf{F}'\boldsymbol{\epsilon}$ is indeed of the scalar type:

$$(7.9) \quad \mathscr{E}(\boldsymbol{\Lambda}^{-1}\mathbf{F}'\boldsymbol{\epsilon}\boldsymbol{\epsilon}'\mathbf{F}\boldsymbol{\Lambda}^{-1}) = \sigma^2\boldsymbol{\Lambda}^{-1}\mathbf{F}'\mathbf{V}\mathbf{F}\boldsymbol{\Lambda}^{-1} = \sigma^2\boldsymbol{\Lambda}^{-1}\mathbf{F}'\mathbf{F}\boldsymbol{\Lambda}^2\mathbf{F}'\mathbf{F}\boldsymbol{\Lambda}^{-1} = \sigma^2\mathbf{I}$$

where the second step is based on (7.7) and the third on (7.5); note that the unit matrix is of order $n' \times n'$. Thus let us apply LS to (7.8) in the formulation (6.11):

(7.10)
$$\hat{\boldsymbol{\beta}} = (\boldsymbol{\Lambda}^{-1}\mathbf{F}'\mathbf{X})^+\boldsymbol{\Lambda}^{-1}\mathbf{F}'\mathbf{y} = (\mathbf{X}'\mathbf{F}\boldsymbol{\Lambda}^{-2}\mathbf{F}'\mathbf{X})^{-1}\mathbf{X}'\mathbf{F}\boldsymbol{\Lambda}^{-2}\mathbf{F}'\mathbf{y} = (\mathbf{X}'\mathbf{V}^+\mathbf{X})^{-1}\mathbf{X}'\mathbf{V}^+\mathbf{y}$$

where the second equality sign is based on $\mathbf{A}^+ = (\mathbf{A}'\mathbf{A})^{-1}\mathbf{A}'$ (which involves the assumption that $\mathbf{A} = \boldsymbol{\Lambda}^{-1}\mathbf{F}'\mathbf{X}$ has full column rank), while the third is based on (7.7).

The First Rank Condition

The result (7.10) is the straightforward generalization of the Aitken estimator (1.4).[15] But is it true that $\boldsymbol{\Lambda}^{-1}\mathbf{F}'\mathbf{X}$ has full column rank? If so, is the estimator $\hat{\boldsymbol{\beta}}$ "best" in the familiar sense of the word? To answer the first question we note that the nonsingularity of $\boldsymbol{\Lambda}$ implies that $\boldsymbol{\Lambda}^{-1}\mathbf{F}'\mathbf{X}$ and $\mathbf{F}'\mathbf{X}$ have the same rank, so that the following assumption is involved.

ASSUMPTION 6.3 (First rank condition) *If* $\mathbf{F}$ *is an* $n \times n'$ *matrix whose columns are characteristic vectors of the matrix* $\mathbf{V}$ *defined in Assumption* 6.2 *corresponding to the* n' *positive roots, then the* $n' \times K$ *matrix* $\mathbf{F}'\mathbf{X}$ *has rank* K.

It is obvious that this assumption is needed, since $\boldsymbol{\beta}$ cannot be estimated from (7.8) if $\mathbf{F}'\mathbf{X}$ has a rank less than K. A necessary condition for the assumption to be satisfied is $n' \geq K$, but it is not sufficient. Take the case $n = 3$, $n' = 2$, $K = 1$, and

$$(7.11) \qquad \mathbf{X} = \begin{bmatrix} 0 \\ 0 \\ 1 \end{bmatrix} \qquad \mathbf{V} = \begin{bmatrix} 1 & 0 & 0 \\ 0 & 1 & 0 \\ 0 & 0 & 0 \end{bmatrix} \qquad \mathbf{F} = \begin{bmatrix} 1 & 0 \\ 0 & 1 \\ 0 & 0 \end{bmatrix}$$

The two positive roots of $\mathbf{V}$ are both equal to 1 and the two columns of $\mathbf{F}$ are corresponding characteristic vectors satisfying $\mathbf{F}'\mathbf{F} = \mathbf{I}$. Our $\mathbf{X}$ has full column rank ($K = 1$) but, nevertheless, $\mathbf{F}'\mathbf{X} = \mathbf{0}$, which violates Assumption

[15] We shall use the same symbol $\hat{\boldsymbol{\beta}}$ for the estimators (1.4) and (7.10) in order to avoid the number of different symbols becoming excessively large. It is to be understood that (7.10) provides the general form of the GLS coefficient estimator and that (1.4) is the special case for a nonsingular $\mathbf{V}$.

6.3. Note that (7.11) implies that the first two observations have disturbances with equal variance and that the explanatory variable takes zero values for these observations. Hence we have $y_\alpha = \epsilon_\alpha$ and var $\epsilon_\alpha = \sigma^2$ for $\alpha = 1$ and 2, which does not involve the unknown coefficient of the explanatory variable at all. Clearly, the estimation procedure (7.10), which is exclusively based on the first $n' = 2$ observations, breaks down in this case.

The Second Rank Condition

We now turn to the second question. Is $\hat{\boldsymbol{\beta}}$ "best" when it exists? We recall that by premultiplying $\mathbf{y} = \mathbf{X}\boldsymbol{\beta} + \boldsymbol{\epsilon}$ by $\boldsymbol{\Lambda}^{-1}\mathbf{F}'$ we reduced the number of observations from n to n'. We may also premultiply by $\mathbf{G}'$, which leads to $n - n'$ equations of the form $\mathbf{G}'\mathbf{y} = \mathbf{G}'\mathbf{X}\boldsymbol{\beta} + \mathbf{G}'\boldsymbol{\epsilon}$. The covariance matrix of $\mathbf{G}'\boldsymbol{\epsilon}$ is $\mathscr{E}(\mathbf{G}'\boldsymbol{\epsilon}\boldsymbol{\epsilon}'\mathbf{G}) = \sigma^2\mathbf{G}'\mathbf{V}\mathbf{G} = \mathbf{0}$ in view of (7.4), so $\mathbf{G}'\boldsymbol{\epsilon}$ is a random vector whose elements are all equal to their expectation (zero) with probability one. Hence,

$$\mathbf{G}'\mathbf{y} = \mathbf{G}'\mathbf{X}\boldsymbol{\beta} \text{ with unit probability} \tag{7.12}$$

which amounts to a linear constraint on $\boldsymbol{\beta}$ unless $\mathbf{G}'\mathbf{X} = \mathbf{0}$, in which case (7.12) becomes $\mathbf{0} = \mathbf{0}$. Note that $\mathbf{G}'\mathbf{X} = \mathbf{0}$ implies that the matrix $\mathbf{G}'\mathbf{X}$ has minimum (zero) rank, whereas Assumption 6.3 implies that $\mathbf{F}'\mathbf{X}$ has maximum rank (given the rank of $\mathbf{X}$). We shall first consider the case $\mathbf{G}'\mathbf{X} = \mathbf{0}$ and postpone treatment of $\mathbf{G}'\mathbf{X} \neq \mathbf{0}$ until the next section.

ASSUMPTION 6.4 (Second rank condition) *If* $\mathbf{G}$ *is an* $n \times (n - n')$ *matrix whose columns are characteristic vectors of the matrix* $\mathbf{V}$ *defined in Assumption* 6.2 *corresponding to the* $n - n'$ *zero roots, then the* $(n - n') \times K$ *matrix* $\mathbf{G}'\mathbf{X}$ *is a zero matrix.*

A Generalization of Aitken's Theorem

THEOREM 6.3 (Best linear unbiasedness of the unconstrained GLS coefficient estimator) *Suppose that Assumption* 3.1 *of Section* 3.2 *and Assumptions* 6.2 *through* 6.4 *are true for given* $\mathbf{X}$. *Then the GLS estimator*

$$\hat{\boldsymbol{\beta}} = (\mathbf{X}'\mathbf{V}^+\mathbf{X})^{-1}\mathbf{X}'\mathbf{V}^+\mathbf{y} \tag{7.13}$$

is best linear unbiased in the following sense. Any other estimator of $\boldsymbol{\beta}$ *which is also linear in the vector* $\mathbf{y}$ *and unbiased has a covariance matrix which exceeds*

$$\mathscr{V}(\hat{\boldsymbol{\beta}}) = \sigma^2(\mathbf{X}'\mathbf{V}^+\mathbf{X})^{-1} \tag{7.14}$$

by a positive semidefinite matrix.

This result is identical with that of Theorem 6.1 except that $\mathbf{V}^{-1}$ is replaced by $\mathbf{V}^+$. The proof is similar too. Write $[(\mathbf{X}'\mathbf{V}^+\mathbf{X})^{-1}\mathbf{X}'\mathbf{V}^+ + \mathbf{A}]\mathbf{y}$ for a linear estimator of $\boldsymbol{\beta}$, where $\mathbf{A}$ is a $K \times n$ matrix, and take the expectation to find that unbiasedness requires

$$\mathbf{AX} = \mathbf{0} \tag{7.15}$$

The sampling error is then $[(\mathbf{X}'\mathbf{V}^+\mathbf{X})^{-1}\mathbf{X}'\mathbf{V}^+ + \mathbf{A}]\boldsymbol{\epsilon}$ and the covariance matrix is

$$\begin{aligned}
&\sigma^2[(\mathbf{X}'\mathbf{V}^+\mathbf{X})^{-1}\mathbf{X}'\mathbf{V}^+ + \mathbf{A}]\mathbf{V}[\mathbf{V}^+\mathbf{X}(\mathbf{X}'\mathbf{V}^+\mathbf{X})^{-1} + \mathbf{A}'] \\
&\quad = \sigma^2(\mathbf{X}'\mathbf{V}^+\mathbf{X})^{-1}\mathbf{X}'\mathbf{V}^+\mathbf{V}\mathbf{V}^+\mathbf{X}(\mathbf{X}'\mathbf{V}^+\mathbf{X})^{-1} + \sigma^2\mathbf{AVA}' \\
&\qquad + \sigma^2(\mathbf{X}'\mathbf{V}^+\mathbf{X})^{-1}\mathbf{X}'\mathbf{V}^+\mathbf{VA}' + \sigma^2\mathbf{AVV}^+\mathbf{X}(\mathbf{X}'\mathbf{V}^+\mathbf{X})^{-1} \\
&\quad = \sigma^2[(\mathbf{X}'\mathbf{V}^+\mathbf{X})^{-1} + \mathbf{AVA}' + (\mathbf{X}'\mathbf{V}^+\mathbf{X})^{-1}\mathbf{X}'\mathbf{V}^+\mathbf{VA}' \\
&\qquad + \mathbf{AVV}^+\mathbf{X}(\mathbf{X}'\mathbf{V}^+\mathbf{X})^{-1}]
\end{aligned} \tag{7.16}$$

where use is made of $\mathbf{V}^+\mathbf{V}\mathbf{V}^+ = \mathbf{V}^+$ in the last step. Applying successively (7.7), (7.5), and (7.6), we find

$$\mathbf{V}^+\mathbf{V} = \mathbf{F}\boldsymbol{\Lambda}^{-2}\mathbf{F}'\mathbf{F}\boldsymbol{\Lambda}^2\mathbf{F}' = \mathbf{FF}' = \mathbf{I} - \mathbf{GG}' \tag{7.17}$$

and, hence,

$$\mathbf{X}'\mathbf{V}^+\mathbf{VA}' = \mathbf{X}'\mathbf{A}' - \mathbf{X}'\mathbf{GG}'\mathbf{A}' = \mathbf{0} - \mathbf{0} = \mathbf{0} \tag{7.18}$$

where the second equality sign is based on (7.15) and Assumption 6.4. Thus the last two terms on the last line of (7.16) vanish, so that the covariance matrix exceeds $\mathscr{V}(\hat{\boldsymbol{\beta}})$ as given in (7.14) by the positive semidefinite $\sigma^2\mathbf{AVA}'$.[16]

Unbiased Estimation of the Variance

THEOREM 6.4 (Unbiasedness of the unconstrained GLS variance estimator) *Suppose that Assumption* 3.1 *of Section* 3.2 *and Assumptions* 6.2 *through* 6.4 *are true for given* $\mathbf{X}$*; also suppose* $n' > K$*. Then the statistic*

$$\hat{\sigma}^2 = \frac{1}{n' - K}(\mathbf{y} - \mathbf{X}\hat{\boldsymbol{\beta}})'\mathbf{V}^+(\mathbf{y} - \mathbf{X}\hat{\boldsymbol{\beta}}) \tag{7.19}$$

is an unbiased estimator of the parameter σ^2 *defined in Assumption* 6.2, $\hat{\boldsymbol{\beta}}$ *being given in* (7.13).

[16] Note that this excess ($\sigma^2\mathbf{AVA}'$) may be a zero matrix for $\mathbf{A} \neq \mathbf{0}$ when $\mathbf{V}$ is singular. This suggests that there exists no unique best linear unbiased estimator of $\boldsymbol{\beta}$, but that is not true. Condition $\mathbf{AVA}' = \mathbf{0}$ is equivalent to $\mathscr{E}[\mathbf{A}\boldsymbol{\epsilon}(\mathbf{A}\boldsymbol{\epsilon})'] = \mathbf{0}$, which means that $\mathbf{A}\boldsymbol{\epsilon}$ is a zero vector with probability one. On combining this with (7.15) we conclude $\mathbf{Ay} = \mathbf{AX}\boldsymbol{\beta} + \mathbf{A}\boldsymbol{\epsilon} = \mathbf{0}$, and it then follows from the lines immediately below Theorem 6.3 that the best linear unbiased estimator of $\boldsymbol{\beta}$ must be of the form (7.13) even though $\mathbf{A}$ may be a nonzero matrix.

This theorem shows that if the disturbances and hence the observations are linearly dependent ($n' < n$), the number of degrees of freedom is found by subtracting K from the number of linearly independent observations, not from the total number of observations. We shall not prove this theorem here because a more general result will be derived in the next section from which this theorem follows immediately.

Best Linear Unbiased Prediction

Suppose, as we did in Section 3.4, that $\mathbf{y}_* = \mathbf{X}_*\boldsymbol{\beta} + \boldsymbol{\epsilon}_*$ is to be predicted, where $\mathbf{X}_*$ is a given $m \times K$ matrix of values of the K explanatory variables. The combined disturbance vector $\boldsymbol{\epsilon}$, $\boldsymbol{\epsilon}_*$ is supposed to have zero mean and the following covariance matrix:

$$\mathscr{V}\begin{bmatrix} \boldsymbol{\epsilon} \\ \boldsymbol{\epsilon}_* \end{bmatrix} = \sigma^2 \begin{bmatrix} \mathbf{V} & \mathbf{W} \\ \mathbf{W}' & \mathbf{V}_* \end{bmatrix} \qquad \text{where} \qquad \mathbf{G}'\mathbf{W} = \mathbf{0} \tag{7.20}$$

[The specification $\mathbf{G}'\mathbf{W} = \mathbf{0}$ is not a new condition but only the implication of (7.12): $\mathbf{G}'\mathbf{W} = \mathscr{E}(\mathbf{G}'\boldsymbol{\epsilon}\boldsymbol{\epsilon}_*') = \mathscr{E}(\mathbf{0}\boldsymbol{\epsilon}_*')$.] The LS predictor of $\mathbf{y}_*$ discussed in Section 3.4 is $\mathbf{X}_*\mathbf{b}$ and its immediate GLS extension is thus $\mathbf{X}_*\hat{\boldsymbol{\beta}}$. However, since this predictor neglects the disturbance component $\boldsymbol{\epsilon}_*$ of $\mathbf{y}_*$ and since $\boldsymbol{\epsilon}_*$ is correlated with $\boldsymbol{\epsilon}$ of the sample, it seems obvious that a better predictor can be obtained when the GLS residual vector $\mathbf{y} - \mathbf{X}\hat{\boldsymbol{\beta}}$ is taken into account. In fact, it can be proved that the predictor

$$\mathbf{X}_*\hat{\boldsymbol{\beta}} + \mathbf{W}'\mathbf{V}^+(\mathbf{y} - \mathbf{X}\hat{\boldsymbol{\beta}}) = (\mathbf{X}_* - \mathbf{W}'\mathbf{V}^+\mathbf{X})\hat{\boldsymbol{\beta}} + \mathbf{W}'\mathbf{V}^+\mathbf{y} \tag{7.21}$$

is superior, as stated in the following theorem which will be proved in the next section.

THEOREM 6.5 (Best linear unbiasedness of the unconstrained GLS predictor) *Suppose that Assumption* 3.1 *of Section* 3.2 *and Assumptions* 6.2 *through* 6.4 *are true for given* $\mathbf{X}$. *Also suppose that the K explanatory variables take a given set of values arranged in an $m \times K$ matrix* $\mathbf{X}_*$ *and that* $\mathbf{y}_* = \mathbf{X}_*\boldsymbol{\beta} + \boldsymbol{\epsilon}_*$ *holds for the associated vector of values of the dependent variable, where* $\boldsymbol{\epsilon}_*$ *is a random vector with zero mean satisfying* (7.20). *Then the predictor* (7.21) *of* $\mathbf{y}_*$ *is best linear unbiased in the sense that the prediction error of any other predictor of* $\mathbf{y}_*$ *which is also linear in* $\mathbf{y}$ *and unbiased has a covariance matrix which exceeds that of* (7.21) *by a positive semidefinite matrix.*

As an example we consider the autoregressive process $\epsilon_\alpha = \rho\epsilon_{\alpha-1} + \zeta_\alpha$ of Section 6.3. It is assumed that this equation holds for all values of α (including negative values) up to and including $\alpha = n + \tau$, that ρ is known and smaller than one in absolute value, and that the ζ's are uncorrelated random variables with zero mean and variance σ_0^2. It was shown by GOLDBERGER (1962) that, given $x_{n+\tau,1}, \ldots, x_{n+\tau,K}$, the best linear unbiased predictor of $y_{n+\tau}$ based on the observation matrix $[\mathbf{y} \quad \mathbf{X}]$ is

$$\sum_{h=1}^{K} \hat{\beta}_h x_{n+\tau,h} + \rho^{\tau}\left(y_n - \sum_{h=1}^{K} \hat{\beta}_h x_{nh}\right) \tag{7.22}$$

where $[\hat{\beta}_h]$ is the GLS coefficient vector. This result follows directly from Theorem 6.5 (see Problem 7.6). Note that the only GLS residual of the sample that occurs in (7.22) is the last (the nth).

Problems

7.1 Generalize Problems 1.2 to 1.4 at the end of Section 6.1 for the case of a singular $\mathbf{V}$.

7.2 Prove that the coefficient vector (7.13) minimizes a quadratic form in the residual vector with $\mathbf{V}^+$ as matrix.

7.3 Consider the following artificial attempt to raise the number of observations from n to $n + n^*$. Premultiply both sides of $\mathbf{y} = \mathbf{X}\boldsymbol{\beta} + \boldsymbol{\epsilon}$ by $\mathbf{H}$ of order $(n + n^*) \times n$ and rank n, so that we obtain $\mathbf{Hy} = \mathbf{HX}\boldsymbol{\beta} + \mathbf{H}\boldsymbol{\epsilon}$; for example, take $\mathbf{H}' = [\mathbf{I} \quad \mathbf{K}']$, which means that we add to the original n observations n^* linear combinations of these observations. Prove $\mathscr{V}(\mathbf{H}\boldsymbol{\epsilon}) = \sigma^2\mathbf{HVH}'$, where $\mathscr{V}(\boldsymbol{\epsilon}) = \sigma^2\mathbf{V}$, and assume $\mathbf{V}$ to be nonsingular. Prove that there exists an $(n + n^*) \times n^*$ matrix $\mathbf{G}$ such that (1) $\mathbf{G}'\mathbf{G} = \mathbf{I}$, (2) $\mathbf{G}'\mathbf{H} = \mathbf{0}$, and (3) this $\mathbf{G}$ may be regarded as the $\mathbf{G}$ of Assumption 6.4 when that assumption is applied to $\mathbf{Hy} = \mathbf{HX}\boldsymbol{\beta} + \mathbf{H}\boldsymbol{\epsilon}$. Then apply Theorem 6.3 to this equation and prove that the resulting GLS estimator of $\boldsymbol{\beta}$ is $(\mathbf{X}'\mathbf{V}^{-1}\mathbf{X})^{-1}\mathbf{X}'\mathbf{V}^{-1}\mathbf{y}$, that is, the Aitken estimator which is exclusively based on the original n observations (*Hint*. Use Problem 6.13 and interpret $\mathbf{A}$ as $\mathbf{V}$ and $\mathbf{B}$ as $\mathbf{H}$.) Why is it unnecessary to check the validity of Assumption 6.3?

7.4 (*Continuation*) Use this result to prove that if $\epsilon_\alpha + \epsilon'_\alpha + \epsilon''_\alpha = 0$ (for each α) is the only linear dependence of the disturbances of (7.1), the GLS technique applied to this demand equation system amounts to deleting the equation for one of the three commodity groups.

7.5 Interpret the result $\mathscr{V}(\mathbf{e}) = \sigma^2\mathbf{MVM}$ in the sense that the matrix $\mathbf{ee}'$ is an unbiased estimator of $\sigma^2\mathbf{MVM}$. This suggests that $\sigma^2\mathbf{V}$ can be estimated unbiasedly by $\mathbf{ee}'$ pre- and postmultiplied by the inverse of $\mathbf{M}$, but that is impossible because $\mathbf{M}$ is singular. So try the generalized inverse of $\mathbf{M}$, which is equal to $\mathbf{M}$ because $\mathbf{M}$ is idempotent. In other words, estimate $\sigma^2\mathbf{V}$ by $\mathbf{Mee'M}$ and apply Theorem 6.3 on the basis of this estimator of $\sigma^2\mathbf{V}$. Prove that the normal equations from which $\hat{\boldsymbol{\beta}}$ is to be solved are of the form $\mathbf{0}\hat{\boldsymbol{\beta}} = \mathbf{0}$, and draw your conclusions. (*Hint.* Simplify $\mathbf{Mee'M}$ and apply Problem 6.7.)

7.6 (*Prediction in the case of autocorrelated disturbances*) Prove that the expression (7.22) is the best linear unbiased predictor of $y_{n+\tau}$ as stated below Theorem 6.5. [*Hint.* Prove that $\mathbf{W'V^+}$ of eq. (7.21) is equal to $\rho^\tau \mathbf{i}_n'$, where $\mathbf{i}_n$ is the nth column of the $n \times n$ unit matrix.] Also prove that the error variance of the predictor is

$$\sigma^2(1 - \rho^{2\tau}) + \sigma^2(\boldsymbol{\xi}_\tau - \rho^\tau\boldsymbol{\xi}_0)'(\mathbf{X'V^{-1}X})^{-1}(\boldsymbol{\xi}_\tau - \rho^\tau\boldsymbol{\xi}_0) \tag{7.23}$$

where $\boldsymbol{\xi}_0' = [x_{n1} \cdots x_{nK}]$, $\boldsymbol{\xi}_\tau' = [x_{n+\tau,1} \cdots x_{n+\tau,K}]$, and $\mathbf{V}^{-1}$ is given in (3.6).

6.8 Constrained Generalized Least-Squares Estimation and Prediction[C]

It is easily seen that the analysis of the previous section does not cover the topic completely. Suppose that our observations are such that a subset is characterized by disturbances which vanish with unit probability:

$$\begin{bmatrix} \mathbf{y}_1 \\ \mathbf{y}_2 \end{bmatrix} = \begin{bmatrix} \mathbf{X}_1 \\ \mathbf{X}_2 \end{bmatrix} \boldsymbol{\beta} + \begin{bmatrix} \boldsymbol{\epsilon}_1 \\ \mathbf{0} \end{bmatrix}$$

The covariance matrix of the disturbances is then

$$\mathscr{V}\begin{bmatrix} \boldsymbol{\epsilon}_1 \\ \mathbf{0} \end{bmatrix} = \sigma^2\mathbf{V} = \sigma^2\begin{bmatrix} \mathbf{V}_1 & \mathbf{0} \\ \mathbf{0} & \mathbf{0} \end{bmatrix}$$

where $\sigma^2\mathbf{V}_1$ is the covariance matrix of $\boldsymbol{\epsilon}_1$. Assuming $\mathbf{V}_1$ to be nonsingular, we find from (6.13) and (6.14) that the generalized inverse of $\mathbf{V}$ is

$$\mathbf{V}^+ = \begin{bmatrix} \mathbf{V}_1^{-1} & \mathbf{0} \\ \mathbf{0} & \mathbf{0} \end{bmatrix}$$

The unconstrained GLS estimator (7.13) is then $\hat{\boldsymbol{\beta}} = (\mathbf{X}_1'\mathbf{V}_1^{-1}\mathbf{X}_1)^{-1}\mathbf{X}_1'\mathbf{V}_1^{-1}\mathbf{y}_1$, which is evidently completely independent of the observations $(\mathbf{X}_2, \mathbf{y}_2)$. To verify whether Theorem 6.3 is applicable we should analyze the validity of its assumptions. Therefore, consider

$$\begin{bmatrix} \mathbf{V}_1 & \mathbf{0} \\ \mathbf{0} & \mathbf{0} \end{bmatrix}\begin{bmatrix} \mathbf{0} \\ \mathbf{I} \end{bmatrix} = \mathbf{0}$$

which shows that the matrix $\mathbf{G}$ of Assumption 6.4 is, in the present case, equal to the second matrix on the left: $\mathbf{G}' = [\mathbf{0} \quad \mathbf{I}]$. [Note that $\mathbf{G'G} = \mathbf{I}$ as is required in (7.5).] We conclude:

$$\mathbf{G}'\mathbf{X} = [\mathbf{0} \quad \mathbf{I}]\begin{bmatrix} \mathbf{X}_1 \\ \mathbf{X}_2 \end{bmatrix} = \mathbf{X}_2$$

But Assumption 6.4 requires $\mathbf{G}'\mathbf{X} = \mathbf{0}$ and hence $\mathbf{X}_2 = \mathbf{0}$. If this is true, the subset of observations whose disturbances vanish with unit probability takes the form $\mathbf{y}_2 = \mathbf{0}$ (with the same probability). This does not involve $\boldsymbol{\beta}$, so that the constraint is ineffective. But if $\mathbf{X}_2 \neq \mathbf{0}$, Assumption 6.4 is violated and $\hat{\boldsymbol{\beta}}$ ceases to be best linear unbiased. This is illustrated dramatically by the case (7.11). We concluded in the discussion below that equation that $\hat{\boldsymbol{\beta}}$ does not exist at all. But the third observation is characterized by a zero disturbance; in fact, it is easily verified that the unknown parameter can be determined *exactly* and that it is equal to the third observation on the dependent variable.

The Third Rank Condition

We shall now extend the approach by generalizing Assumption 6.4 as follows.

ASSUMPTION 6.5 (Third rank condition) *If* $\mathbf{G}$ *is an* $n \times (n - n')$ *matrix whose columns are characteristic vectors of the matrix* $\mathbf{V}$ *defined in Assumption 6.2 corresponding to the* $n - n'$ *zero roots, then the* $(n - n') \times K$ *matrix* $\mathbf{G}'\mathbf{X}$ *has rank* $p < K$.

Our conclusion is that (7.12) is now a "real" constraint on the parameter vector $\boldsymbol{\beta}$ as soon as $p > 0$. The constraint consists of $n - n'$ linear equations, but it is possible that these are linearly dependent. Assumption 6.5 takes this possibility into account and postulates that the number of linearly independent constraints is p, which is less than K. The case $p = K$ is excluded because then there are enough linearly independent constraints to determine all components of $\boldsymbol{\beta}$ exactly from these constraints alone, so that there is no estimation problem in the real sense of the word. Note that we had this situation in the example (7.11). Also note that the present assumption contains Assumption 6.4 as a special case (for $p = 0$). Basically, the only restriction implied by Assumption 6.5 is thus the exclusion of the case $p = K$.

Linearly Independent Linear Constraints on the Coefficient Vector

It will prove convenient to work with linearly independent constraints.[17] This is performed easily by premultiplying both sides of (7.12) by a

[17] It is possible to formulate results based on constraints which are not linearly independent, but these are much more complicated; see GOLDMAN and ZELEN (1964). For related contributions, see CHIPMAN and M. M. RAO (1964a, b), RAYNER and PRINGLE (1967), and MITRA and C. R. RAO (1968). Some authors use so-called weak generalized inverses in their exposition, which satisfy only a subset of the four conditions (6.1) to (6.4). Such inverses are not unique.

$p \times (n - n')$ matrix $\mathbf{J}$ of full row rank. We shall specify $\mathbf{J}$ as the submatrix of the unit matrix of order $n - n'$ consisting of p appropriate rows, which simply means that we delete $n - n' - p$ equations of $\mathbf{G}'\mathbf{y} = \mathbf{G}'\mathbf{X}\boldsymbol{\beta}$ that depend linearly on the other p. The constraint thus takes the following form:

$$\mathbf{J}\mathbf{G}'\mathbf{y} = \mathbf{J}\mathbf{G}'\mathbf{X}\boldsymbol{\beta} \tag{8.1}$$

where $\mathbf{J}\mathbf{G}'\mathbf{X}$ is a $p \times K$ matrix of rank p.

So we have p linearly independent constraints on $\boldsymbol{\beta}$ which owe their existence to the structure of the covariance matrix $\sigma^2\mathbf{V}$ of the disturbances. Given that we have to handle such constraints anyway, it is worthwhile to consider other linear constraints as well. Suppose, for example, that we want to estimate the parameters of a Cobb-Douglas production function:

$$\log y_\alpha = \beta_0 + \beta_1 \log x_{\alpha 1} + \beta_2 \log x_{\alpha 2} + \cdots + \epsilon_\alpha \tag{8.2}$$

where the x's are inputs and y is output. If we impose constant returns to scale, the multiplicative parameters $\beta_1, \beta_2, \ldots$ add up to 1, which is a linear constraint on the parameter vector. Such a constraint can be used to eliminate one of the parameters. We can write, for example, $\beta_1 = 1 - \beta_2 - \beta_3 - \cdots$, so that (8.2) becomes

$$\begin{aligned} \log y - \log x_{\alpha 1} = \beta_0 &+ \beta_2(\log x_{\alpha 2} - \log x_{\alpha 1}) \\ &+ \beta_3(\log x_{\alpha 3} - \log x_{\alpha 1}) + \cdots + \epsilon_\alpha \end{aligned} \tag{8.3}$$

Thus the variables are changed, one parameter (β_1) has disappeared, and there is no longer a constraint. Therefore we can estimate (8.3) in the unconstrained manner.

On the other hand, one may argue that (8.3) treats variables and parameters in an asymmetric way and that it is more elegant to estimate (8.2) directly subject to $\beta_1 + \beta_2 + \cdots = 1$. This will be our attitude in this section.[18] We shall assume that there are $q - p$ linear constraints on the parameter vector $\boldsymbol{\beta}$ in addition to those of Assumption 6.5. Also, it will be assumed that the former constraints are linearly independent of the latter (which can be enforced, if necessary, by deleting a subset of the constraints). As a whole we thus have q linearly independent linear constraints:

> ASSUMPTION 6.6 (Linear constraints on the coefficient vector) *It is known that the parameter vector $\boldsymbol{\beta}$ is subject to $q - p$ linear constraints, $\mathbf{r}^* = \mathbf{R}^*\boldsymbol{\beta}$, where $\mathbf{r}^*$ and $\mathbf{R}^*$ are given matrices of order $(q - p) \times 1$ and $(q - p) \times K$,*

[18] It is also possible to interpret the constraint $\beta_1 + \beta_2 + \cdots = 1$ as an "observation" with zero disturbance; see Problem 8.1.

respectively. They can be combined with constraint (8.1) *as follows:*

$$\text{(8.4)} \qquad \mathbf{r} = \mathbf{R}\boldsymbol{\beta} \qquad \mathbf{r} = \begin{bmatrix} \mathbf{JG'y} \\ \mathbf{r}^* \end{bmatrix} \qquad \mathbf{R} = \begin{bmatrix} \mathbf{JG'X} \\ \mathbf{R}^* \end{bmatrix}$$

and the $q \times K$ *matrix* $\mathbf{R}$ *has rank* $q < K$.

The Constrained GLS Coefficient Vector

THEOREM 6.6 (Best linear unbiasedness of the constrained GLS coefficient estimator) *Suppose that Assumption* 3.1 *of Section* 3.2 *and Assumptions* 6.2, 6.3, 6.5, *and* 6.6 *are true for given* $\mathbf{X}$. *Then the constrained GLS estimator*

$$\text{(8.5)} \quad \hat{\boldsymbol{\beta}}^* = \hat{\boldsymbol{\beta}} + \mathbf{CR'}(\mathbf{RCR'})^{-1}(\mathbf{r} - \mathbf{R}\hat{\boldsymbol{\beta}}) \quad \textit{where} \quad \mathbf{C} = (\mathbf{X'V^+X})^{-1} \quad \textit{and} \quad \hat{\boldsymbol{\beta}} = \mathbf{CX'V^+y}$$

is best linear unbiased in the following sense. Any other estimator of $\boldsymbol{\beta}$ *which is also linear in the vectors* $\mathbf{y}$ *and* $\mathbf{r}$ *and unbiased has a covariance matrix which exceeds that of* $\hat{\boldsymbol{\beta}}^*$:

$$\text{(8.6)} \qquad \mathscr{V}(\hat{\boldsymbol{\beta}}^*) = \sigma^2[\mathbf{C} - \mathbf{CR'}(\mathbf{RCR'})^{-1}\mathbf{RC}]$$

by a positive semidefinite matrix. The $K \times K$ *covariance matrix* (8.6) *has rank* $K - q$.

It is clear that the relation between $\hat{\boldsymbol{\beta}}^*$ and $\hat{\boldsymbol{\beta}}$ is analogous to that between $\mathbf{b} = (\mathbf{X'X})^{-1}\mathbf{X'y}$ and $\mathbf{b}^*$, the constrained LS coefficient vector defined in eq. (8.9) of Section 1.8. In fact, if we have $\mathbf{V} = \mathbf{I}$ (the standard linear model), then $\mathbf{C} = (\mathbf{X'X})^{-1}$ and $\hat{\boldsymbol{\beta}} = \mathbf{b}$, $\hat{\boldsymbol{\beta}}^* = \mathbf{b}^*$. It is the case, both for $\mathbf{b}$ and $\mathbf{b}^*$ and for $\hat{\boldsymbol{\beta}}$ and $\hat{\boldsymbol{\beta}}^*$, that the difference between the constrained and the unconstrained coefficient vectors is equal to a linear function of a vector which measures the degree to which the latter coefficient vector fails to satisfy the constraint. Comparing (7.14) and (8.5), we conclude that the covariance matrix of $\hat{\boldsymbol{\beta}}$ can be written as $\sigma^2\mathbf{C}$. We see from (8.6) that this exceeds the covariance matrix of $\hat{\boldsymbol{\beta}}^*$ by a positive semidefinite matrix, which means that we gain in precision by taking the constraint into account. Note further that the linearity interpretation of $\hat{\boldsymbol{\beta}}^*$ amounts to an extension of the earlier interpretation. The estimator is not only linear in $\mathbf{y}$ but also in $\mathbf{r}$, the left-hand vector of the constraint. Reference is also made to Problem 8.2 for the theorem which states that $\hat{\boldsymbol{\beta}}^*$ minimizes, subject to this constraint, a quadratic form in the residuals with $\mathbf{V}^+$ as matrix.

Proof of Theorem 6.6

Consider the matrix

$$\mathbf{T} = \mathbf{C} - \mathbf{CR}'(\mathbf{RCR}')^{-1}\mathbf{RC} \tag{8.7}$$

which has the following properties:

$$\mathbf{T}' = \mathbf{T} \qquad \mathbf{TR}' = \mathbf{0} \qquad \mathbf{TC}^{-1}\mathbf{T} = \mathbf{T} \tag{8.8}$$

The estimator $\hat{\boldsymbol{\beta}}^*$ can be written as follows:

$$\begin{aligned} \hat{\boldsymbol{\beta}}^* &= \boldsymbol{\beta} + \mathbf{CX}'\mathbf{V}^+\boldsymbol{\epsilon} + \mathbf{CR}'(\mathbf{RCR}')^{-1}[\mathbf{R}\boldsymbol{\beta} - \mathbf{R}(\boldsymbol{\beta} + \mathbf{CX}'\mathbf{V}^+\boldsymbol{\epsilon})] \\ &= \boldsymbol{\beta} + [\mathbf{C} - \mathbf{CR}'(\mathbf{RCR}')^{-1}\mathbf{RC}]\mathbf{X}'\mathbf{V}^+\boldsymbol{\epsilon} \\ &= \boldsymbol{\beta} + \mathbf{TX}'\mathbf{V}^+\boldsymbol{\epsilon} \end{aligned} \tag{8.9}$$

from which we immediately see that $\hat{\boldsymbol{\beta}}^*$ is unbiased. Any other estimator that is also linear in $\mathbf{y}$ and $\mathbf{r}$ can be written as

$$\hat{\boldsymbol{\beta}}^* + \mathbf{Ay} + \mathbf{Br} = \hat{\boldsymbol{\beta}}^* + (\mathbf{AX} + \mathbf{BR})\boldsymbol{\beta} + \mathbf{A}\boldsymbol{\epsilon} \tag{8.10}$$

Therefore we conclude that

$$\mathbf{AX} + \mathbf{BR} = \mathbf{0} \tag{8.11}$$

should hold in order that the estimator be unbiased. Combining (8.9) through (8.11), we find that the sampling error of this estimator is $(\mathbf{TX}'\mathbf{V}^+ + \mathbf{A})\boldsymbol{\epsilon}$, so that its covariance matrix is

$$\begin{aligned} &\sigma^2(\mathbf{TX}'\mathbf{V}^+ + \mathbf{A})\mathbf{V}(\mathbf{TX}'\mathbf{V}^+ + \mathbf{A})' \\ &\qquad = \sigma^2(\mathbf{TC}^{-1}\mathbf{T} + \mathbf{TX}'\mathbf{V}^+\mathbf{VA}' + \mathbf{AVV}^+\mathbf{XT} + \mathbf{AVA}') \\ &\qquad = \sigma^2(\mathbf{T} + \mathbf{TX}'\mathbf{V}^+\mathbf{VA}' + \mathbf{AVV}^+\mathbf{XT} + \mathbf{AVA}') \end{aligned} \tag{8.12}$$

where use is made of (8.8) in the second step. Furthermore, since $\mathbf{V}^+\mathbf{V} = \mathbf{I} - \mathbf{GG}'$ [see (7.17)], we have

$$\begin{aligned} \mathbf{TX}'\mathbf{V}^+\mathbf{VA}' &= \mathbf{TX}'\mathbf{A}' - \mathbf{TX}'\mathbf{GG}'\mathbf{A}' \\ &= -\mathbf{TR}'\mathbf{B}' - \mathbf{TX}'\mathbf{GG}'\mathbf{A}' \\ &= -\mathbf{TX}'\mathbf{GG}'\mathbf{A}' \end{aligned} \tag{8.13}$$

the second equality sign being based on (8.11) and the third on (8.8). Now $\mathbf{JG}'\mathbf{X}$ is a submatrix of $\mathbf{R}$ [see (8.4)], so that $\mathbf{JG}'\mathbf{XT}$ is a submatrix of $\mathbf{RT}$ and hence $\mathbf{JG}'\mathbf{XT} = \mathbf{0}$ in view of (8.8). If the rank p of $\mathbf{G}'\mathbf{X}$ is equal to $n - n'$, then $\mathbf{J} = \mathbf{I}$, the unit matrix of order $n - n'$ [see the discussion above (8.1)], so that

$$\mathbf{G}'\mathbf{XT} = \mathbf{0} \tag{8.14}$$

If $p < n - n'$, the $n - n'$ rows of $\mathbf{G}'\mathbf{X}$ are linearly dependent and there are $n - n' - p$ rows of $\mathbf{G}'\mathbf{X}$ which are not rows of $\mathbf{JG}'\mathbf{X}$. However, the rows of $\mathbf{G}'\mathbf{X}$ which are not represented in $\mathbf{JG}'\mathbf{X}$ are linear combinations of those which are represented. Since the same is true for the rows of $\mathbf{G}'\mathbf{XT}$ and of $\mathbf{JG}'\mathbf{XT}$, it follows that (8.14) is true even if $p < n - n'$. Combining this result with (8.13), we conclude that the covariance matrix (8.12) is equal to $\sigma^2\mathbf{T}$ plus the positive semidefinite matrix $\sigma^2\mathbf{AVA}'$.

Finally, we have to prove that the covariance matrix (8.6) or, equivalently, $\mathbf{T}$, has rank $K - q$. For this purpose we write the symmetric positive definite matrix $\mathbf{C} = (\mathbf{X}'\mathbf{V}^+\mathbf{X})^{-1}$ in the form $\mathbf{NL}^2\mathbf{N}'$, where $\mathbf{L}^2$ is a diagonal matrix containing the latent roots of $\mathbf{C}$ on the diagonal and $\mathbf{N}$ is an orthogonal matrix. Using (8.7) we then obtain

$$\begin{aligned}(8.15)\qquad \mathbf{T} &= \mathbf{NL}^2\mathbf{N}' - \mathbf{NL}^2\mathbf{N}'\mathbf{R}'(\mathbf{RNL}^2\mathbf{N}'\mathbf{R}')^{-1}\mathbf{RNL}^2\mathbf{N}' \\ &= \mathbf{NL}[\mathbf{I} - \mathbf{LN}'\mathbf{R}'(\mathbf{RNL}^2\mathbf{N}'\mathbf{R}')^{-1}\mathbf{RNL}]\mathbf{LN}' \\ &= \mathbf{NL}[\mathbf{I} - \mathbf{H}(\mathbf{H}'\mathbf{H})^{-1}\mathbf{H}']\mathbf{LN}'\end{aligned}$$

where $\mathbf{H} = \mathbf{LN}'\mathbf{R}'$ is a $K \times q$ matrix of rank q. Now $\mathbf{T}$ has the same rank as the matrix in square brackets on the third line of (8.15) because it is obtained from that matrix by pre- and postmultiplication by nonsingular matrices. But $\mathbf{I} - \mathbf{H}(\mathbf{H}'\mathbf{H})^{-1}\mathbf{H}'$ is idempotent of rank $K - q$ and hence $\mathbf{T}$ has the same rank, which completes the proof.

The Constrained GLS Variance Estimator

THEOREM 6.7 (Unbiasedness of the constrained GLS variance estimator) *Suppose that Assumption* 3.1 *of Section* 3.2 *and Assumptions* 6.2, 6.3, 6.5, *and* 6.6 *are true for given* $\mathbf{X}$; *also suppose* $n' > K - q$. *Then the statistic*

$$(8.16)\qquad \hat{\sigma}^{*2} = \frac{1}{n' + q - K}(\mathbf{y} - \mathbf{X}\hat{\boldsymbol{\beta}}^*)'\mathbf{V}^+(\mathbf{y} - \mathbf{X}\hat{\boldsymbol{\beta}}^*)$$

is an unbiased estimator of the parameter σ^2 *defined in Assumption* 6.2, $\hat{\boldsymbol{\beta}}^*$ *being given in* (8.5).

This theorem indicates that the number q of linearly independent constraints is to be added to the number n' of linearly independent observations; it obviously contains Theorem 6.4 as a special case for $q = 0$. To prove the more general theorem we consider the residual vector

$$(8.17)\qquad \mathbf{y} - \mathbf{X}\hat{\boldsymbol{\beta}}^* = \boldsymbol{\epsilon} - \mathbf{X}(\hat{\boldsymbol{\beta}}^* - \boldsymbol{\beta}) = (\mathbf{I} - \mathbf{XTX}'\mathbf{V}^+)\boldsymbol{\epsilon} \quad \text{[see (8.9)]}$$

The transformation matrix after the second equality sign satisfies

$$(8.18)\qquad (\mathbf{I} - \mathbf{XTX}'\mathbf{V}^+)'\mathbf{V}^+(\mathbf{I} - \mathbf{XTX}'\mathbf{V}^+) = \mathbf{V}^+ - \mathbf{V}^+\mathbf{XTX}'\mathbf{V}^+$$

which is easily verified by means of $\mathbf{TX'V^+XT} = \mathbf{TC^{-1}T} = \mathbf{T}$ [see (8.8)]. Combining (8.17) and (8.18), we find for the quadratic form in the residual vector with $\mathbf{V}^+$ as matrix:

$$(8.19) \qquad (\mathbf{y} - \mathbf{X}\hat{\boldsymbol{\beta}}^*)'\mathbf{V}^+(\mathbf{y} - \mathbf{X}\hat{\boldsymbol{\beta}}^*) = \boldsymbol{\epsilon}'\mathbf{V}^+\boldsymbol{\epsilon} - \boldsymbol{\epsilon}'\mathbf{V}^+\mathbf{XTX'V}^+\boldsymbol{\epsilon}$$

The expectation of the second term on the right can be written as the trace of the matrix $\mathbf{TX'V^+}\mathscr{E}(\boldsymbol{\epsilon\epsilon}')\mathbf{V^+X} = \sigma^2\mathbf{TX'V^+VV^+X} = \sigma^2\mathbf{TX'V^+X} = \sigma^2\mathbf{TC}^{-1}$, which in view of (8.7) is equal to

$$(8.20) \quad \begin{aligned} \sigma^2 \operatorname{tr} [\mathbf{C} - \mathbf{CR}'(\mathbf{RCR}')^{-1}\mathbf{RC}]\mathbf{C}^{-1} &= \sigma^2[K - \operatorname{tr} \mathbf{CR}'(\mathbf{RCR}')^{-1}\mathbf{R}] \\ &= \sigma^2[K - \operatorname{tr} (\mathbf{RCR}')^{-1}\mathbf{RCR}'] \\ &= \sigma^2(K - q) \end{aligned}$$

The expectation of the first right-hand term in (8.19), $\boldsymbol{\epsilon}'\mathbf{V}^+\boldsymbol{\epsilon}$, is equal to σ^2 multiplied by $\operatorname{tr} \mathbf{V^+V} = \operatorname{tr} \mathbf{FF}' = \operatorname{tr} \mathbf{F'F} = n'$, where use is made of (7.17) in the first step and of (7.5) in the last. Combining this result with (8.20), we conclude that $\hat{\sigma}^{*2}$ defined in (8.16) is indeed an unbiased estimator of σ^2.

Constrained GLS Prediction

The constrained version of the GLS predictor (7.21) is

$$(8.21) \quad \mathbf{X}_*\hat{\boldsymbol{\beta}}^* + \mathbf{W'V}^+(\mathbf{y} - \mathbf{X}\hat{\boldsymbol{\beta}}^*) = (\mathbf{X}_* - \mathbf{W'V^+X})\hat{\boldsymbol{\beta}}^* + \mathbf{W'V^+y}$$

The following theorem is an extension of Theorem 6.5.

THEOREM 6.8 (Best linear unbiasedness of the constrained GLS predictor) *Suppose that Assumption* 3.1 *of Section* 3.2 *and Assumptions* 6.2, 6.3, 6.5, *and* 6.6 *are true for given* $\mathbf{X}$. *Also suppose that the K explanatory variables take a given set of values arranged in an $m \times K$ matrix* $\mathbf{X}_*$ *and that* $\mathbf{y}_* = \mathbf{X}_*\boldsymbol{\beta} + \boldsymbol{\epsilon}_*$ *holds for the associated vector of values of the dependent variable, where* $\boldsymbol{\epsilon}_*$ *is a random vector with zero mean satisfying* (7.20). *Then the predictor* (8.21) *is linear in* $\mathbf{y}$ *and* $\mathbf{r}$ *and unbiased and its prediction error has the following covariance matrix:*

$$(8.22) \quad \sigma^2[\mathbf{X}_*\mathbf{TX}_*' + \mathbf{V}_* - \mathbf{W}'(\mathbf{V}^+ - \mathbf{V^+XTX'V^+})\mathbf{W} - \mathbf{X}_*\mathbf{TX'V^+W} - \mathbf{W'V^+XTX}_*']$$

where $\mathbf{T}$ *is defined in* (8.7). *Also, the predictor* (8.21) *is best linear unbiased in the sense that the covariance matrix of the prediction error of any other linear unbiased predictor of* $\mathbf{y}_*$ *exceeds the matrix* (8.22) *by a positive semi-definite matrix.*

To prove this theorem we write a linear predictor of $\mathbf{y}_*$ in the form

$$(\mathbf{X}_* - \mathbf{W'V^+X})\hat{\boldsymbol{\beta}}^* + (\mathbf{W'V}^+ + \mathbf{P})\mathbf{y} + \mathbf{Qr}$$

where **P** and **Q** are matrices consisting of n and q columns, respectively. It is readily verified that the unbiasedness condition is

$$\mathbf{PX} + \mathbf{QR} = \mathbf{0} \tag{8.23}$$

Using (8.9), we find that the error vector of the predictor can then be written as the sum of four vectors:

(8.24)
$$\mathbf{X}_*\mathbf{TX}'\mathbf{V}^+\boldsymbol{\epsilon} + \mathbf{W}'(\mathbf{V}^+ - \mathbf{V}^+\mathbf{XTX}'\mathbf{V}^+)\boldsymbol{\epsilon} + \mathbf{P}\boldsymbol{\epsilon} - \boldsymbol{\epsilon}_* = \mathbf{a}_1 + \mathbf{a}_2 + \mathbf{a}_3 + \mathbf{a}_4$$

The covariance matrix of the error vector is $\sum\sum \mathscr{E}(\mathbf{a}_i\mathbf{a}_j')$, where the summations over i and j are from 1 through 4. The separate terms take the following values:

$$\mathscr{E}(\mathbf{a}_1\mathbf{a}_1') = \sigma^2\mathbf{X}_*\mathbf{TX}_*' \qquad \mathscr{E}(\mathbf{a}_2\mathbf{a}_3') = -\mathscr{E}(\mathbf{a}_4\mathbf{a}_3') = \sigma^2\mathbf{W}'\mathbf{P}'$$
$$\mathscr{E}(\mathbf{a}_1\mathbf{a}_2') = \mathscr{E}(\mathbf{a}_1\mathbf{a}_3') = \mathbf{0} \qquad \mathscr{E}(\mathbf{a}_3\mathbf{a}_3') = \sigma^2\mathbf{PVP}'$$
$$\mathscr{E}(\mathbf{a}_1\mathbf{a}_4') = -\sigma^2\mathbf{X}_*\mathbf{TX}'\mathbf{V}^+\mathbf{W} \qquad \mathscr{E}(\mathbf{a}_4\mathbf{a}_4') = \sigma^2\mathbf{V}_*$$
$$\mathscr{E}(\mathbf{a}_2\mathbf{a}_2') = -\mathscr{E}(\mathbf{a}_2\mathbf{a}_4') = \sigma^2\mathbf{W}'(\mathbf{V}^+ - \mathbf{V}^+\mathbf{XTX}'\mathbf{V}^+)\mathbf{W}$$

By adding the 16 terms $\mathscr{E}(\mathbf{a}_i\mathbf{a}_j')$ we obtain the matrix (8.22) plus $\sigma^2\mathbf{PVP}'$, which is positive semidefinite.

Problems

8.1 Consider the Cobb-Douglas function (8.2) and write the n observations in the form $\mathbf{y}_1 = \mathbf{X}_1\boldsymbol{\beta} + \boldsymbol{\epsilon}_1$, where the successive elements of the αth row of $[\mathbf{y}_1 \quad \mathbf{X}_1]$ are $\log y_\alpha$, 1, $\log x_{\alpha 1}, \ldots$. Write the constant-returns-to-scale constraint as $\mathbf{y}_2 = \mathbf{X}_2\boldsymbol{\beta}$, where $\mathbf{y}_2 = [1]$ and $\mathbf{X}_2 = [0 \quad 1 \quad 1 \quad \cdots]$. Show how the observations and the constraint can be combined to $\mathbf{y} = \mathbf{X}\boldsymbol{\beta} + \boldsymbol{\epsilon}$ and prove that the $(n + 1)$-element vector $\boldsymbol{\epsilon}$ has a singular covariance matrix. (This shows that it is not only true that a singular disturbance covariance matrix may imply a linear constraint on $\boldsymbol{\beta}$, but also that when a linear constraint is imposed which has nothing to do with the disturbances, it can be handled by enlarging a nonsingular covariance matrix so that it becomes singular.)

8.2 Form the Lagrangian expression $(\mathbf{y} - \mathbf{Xz})'\mathbf{V}^+(\mathbf{y} - \mathbf{Xz}) - \boldsymbol{\lambda}'(\mathbf{r} - \mathbf{Rz})$ and prove that $\hat{\boldsymbol{\beta}}^*$ defined in (8.5) minimizes a quadratic form in the residuals (with $\mathbf{V}^+$ as matrix) subject to the linear constraint. (*Hint.* See the derivation of the constrained LS coefficient vector in Section 1.8.)

8.3 Prove eqs. (8.8), (8.24), and the expressions for the matrices $\mathscr{E}(\mathbf{a}_i\mathbf{a}_j')$ given at the end of the section.

8.4 Verify algebraically that the error variance (7.23) is a special case of the matrix (8.22).

8.5 Prove that under the conditions of Theorem 6.6 the constrained best linear unbiased estimator of $\boldsymbol{\beta}$ is unique.

6.9 The Normal Distribution Theory of the Constrained Singular Case[C]

As in the case of the standard linear model, confidence and prediction intervals can be computed and tests can be applied when we know that the distribution of **y** given **X** is multinormal. This section describes the modifications required to make the results of the standard linear model applicable.

The Singular Normal Distribution

If a multinormal distribution has a singular covariance matrix, the corresponding density function cannot be written in the form of eq. (2.19) of Section 2.2. The situation can be illustrated geometrically for $n = 2$. We then have two random variables, say, y_1 and y_2, and the bivariate density function is represented by the familiar three-dimensional normal "mountain" when the covariance matrix is nonsingular. Next imagine that the correlation coefficient ρ of the distribution increases in absolute value, whereas the other parameters (the means and the variances) remain unchanged. The mountain is then elongated in one direction and shortened in the perpendicular direction. In the limit the mass of the distribution is completely concentrated on a straight line in the y_1, y_2-plane, so that the distribution has effectively become one-dimensional with a normal curve above this line as the density function. The density at any point in the y_1, y_2-plane which is not on the line is then zero.

There are no real complications in the singular case because the linear relation between the random variables which is implied by the singular covariance matrix may be used to eliminate a subset of these variates so that the remainder has a nonsingular covariance matrix. Alternatively, one may decide to retain the original variates, in which case the generalized inverse plays a useful role. For example, consider the model of Section 4.7 which implies that the n rows of the observation matrix $[\mathbf{y} \quad \mathbf{X}]$ are independent random drawings from a $(K + 1)$-dimensional normal population with covariance matrix

$$\begin{bmatrix} \sigma_{00} & \boldsymbol{\sigma}' \\ \boldsymbol{\sigma} & \boldsymbol{\Sigma} \end{bmatrix}$$

It was proved there that the conditional mean of y_α given $x_{\alpha 1}, \ldots, x_{\alpha K}$ is a linear function of the conditioning factors, that the conditional variance of y_α is a constant, and that both this mean and this variance depend on $\boldsymbol{\Sigma}^{-1}$. This result obviously breaks down when $\boldsymbol{\Sigma}$ is singular, but it was shown by

MARSAGLIA (1964) that the only modification which is then required is the replacement of $\mathbf{\Sigma}^{-1}$ by the generalized inverse $\mathbf{\Sigma}^{+}$.

The Transformation Approach

A simple procedure under the conditions of Theorems 6.3 and 6.4 is the application of a linear transformation which reduces the problem to that of the standard linear model. These theorems are based on $[\mathbf{\Lambda}^{-1}\mathbf{F}'\mathbf{y} \quad \mathbf{\Lambda}^{-1}\mathbf{F}'\mathbf{X}]$ as the observation matrix and on $\mathbf{\Lambda}^{-1}\mathbf{F}'\boldsymbol{\epsilon}$ as the associated disturbance vector [see (7.8)]. If $\boldsymbol{\epsilon}$ has a multinormal distribution with zero mean vector, so has $\mathbf{\Lambda}^{-1}\mathbf{F}'\boldsymbol{\epsilon}$, and it follows then from (7.9) that the n' elements of the latter vector are stochastically independent and have constant variance. Hence, premultiplication of $[\mathbf{y} \quad \mathbf{X}]$ by $\mathbf{\Lambda}^{-1}\mathbf{F}'$ is sufficient to apply the procedures of Sections 3.6 and 3.7, and the only thing that should be kept in mind is that this multiplication reduces the number of observations from n to n'. Also see Problem 9.1 for a prediction interval in the case of disturbances that are generated by a first-order autoregressive process.

The Elimination Approach

The assumptions of Theorems 6.3 and 6.4 exclude the presence of linear constraints on $\boldsymbol{\beta}$. The situation is different when there are such constraints because these were not imposed in Chapter 3. However, they can always be handled in the manner of eqs. (8.2) and (8.3) for the Cobb-Douglas production function, which implies that the constraints are used to eliminate some of the unknown parameters. As an example we take the constraint $\mathbf{r} = \mathbf{R}\boldsymbol{\beta}$ in the case of testing against positive correlation of successive disturbances. Since $\mathbf{R}$ has rank q, it is possible (by rearranging the elements of $\boldsymbol{\beta}$, if necessary) to partition $\mathbf{R}$ as $[\mathbf{R}_1 \quad \mathbf{R}_2]$, where $\mathbf{R}_2$ is a nonsingular $q \times q$ matrix. The constraint is then

$$\mathbf{r} = [\mathbf{R}_1 \quad \mathbf{R}_2]\begin{bmatrix}\boldsymbol{\beta}_1 \\ \boldsymbol{\beta}_2\end{bmatrix} \tag{9.1}$$

or $\boldsymbol{\beta}_2 = \mathbf{R}_2^{-1}(\mathbf{r} - \mathbf{R}_1\boldsymbol{\beta}_1)$, where $\boldsymbol{\beta}_2$ is the subvector of $\boldsymbol{\beta}$ consisting of the last q elements. The basic equation $\mathbf{y} = \mathbf{X}\boldsymbol{\beta} + \boldsymbol{\epsilon}$ can then be written as follows:

$$\mathbf{y} = [\mathbf{X}_1 \quad \mathbf{X}_2]\begin{bmatrix}\boldsymbol{\beta}_1 \\ \boldsymbol{\beta}_2\end{bmatrix} + \boldsymbol{\epsilon} = \mathbf{X}_1\boldsymbol{\beta}_1 + \mathbf{X}_2\mathbf{R}_2^{-1}(\mathbf{r} - \mathbf{R}_1\boldsymbol{\beta}_1) + \boldsymbol{\epsilon}$$

which amounts to

$$\mathbf{y} - \mathbf{X}_2\mathbf{R}_2^{-1}\mathbf{r} = (\mathbf{X}_1 - \mathbf{X}_2\mathbf{R}_2^{-1}\mathbf{R}_1)\boldsymbol{\beta}_1 + \boldsymbol{\epsilon} \tag{9.2}$$

Hence, $\boldsymbol{\beta}$ is reduced to its $(K - q)$-element subvector $\boldsymbol{\beta}_1$ and the observation matrix $[\mathbf{y} \quad \mathbf{X}]$ is changed to $[\mathbf{y} - \mathbf{X}_2\mathbf{R}_2^{-1}\mathbf{r} \quad \mathbf{X}_1 - \mathbf{X}_2\mathbf{R}_2^{-1}\mathbf{R}_1]$, but the disturbance vector remains the same. If we want to test the null hypothesis $\mathscr{E}(\boldsymbol{\epsilon\epsilon}') = \sigma^2\mathbf{I}$ against the alternative hypothesis of positive autocorrelation, we can apply the relevant BLUS procedure of Section 5.4 to eq. (9.2). If the null hypothesis is $\mathscr{E}(\boldsymbol{\epsilon\epsilon}') = \sigma^2\mathbf{V}$ rather than $\sigma^2\mathbf{I}$, we premultiply both sides of (9.2) by $\boldsymbol{\Lambda}^{-1}\mathbf{F}'$ and proceed as before.

The Complete Distribution of the Constrained Coefficient and Variance Estimators

It is also possible to proceed without transformations and eliminations. The basic theorem for the constrained case follows here; for the unconstrained case we simply put $q = 0$.

THEOREM 6.9 (Joint distribution of the constrained GLS coefficient and variance estimators) *Suppose that Assumption* 3.1 *of Section* 3.2 *and Assumptions* 6.2, 6.3, 6.5, *and* 6.6 *are true for given* $\mathbf{X}$ *with the additional specification that the distribution of* $\mathbf{y}$ (*given* $\mathbf{X}$) *is n-variate normal; also suppose* $n' > K - q$. *Then the constrained GLS coefficient estimator* $\hat{\boldsymbol{\beta}}^*$ *defined in* (8.5) *is normally distributed with mean vector* $\boldsymbol{\beta}$ *and covariance matrix* (8.6), *and* $(n' + q - K)\hat{\sigma}^{*2}/\sigma^2$ *with* $\hat{\sigma}^{*2}$ *defined in* (8.16) *is distributed as* $\chi^2(n' + q - K)$; *moreover*, $\hat{\boldsymbol{\beta}}^*$ *and* $\hat{\sigma}^{*2}$ *are distributed independently.*

The normality of $\hat{\boldsymbol{\beta}}^*$ follows from the fact that it is a linear function of $\mathbf{y}$, which has a multinormal distribution. (Note that the distribution of $\hat{\boldsymbol{\beta}}^*$ is singular when $q > 0$.) To find the distribution of $\hat{\sigma}^{*2}$ we consider the quadratic form (8.19) and apply (7.7):

$$(9.3) \quad \boldsymbol{\epsilon}'(\mathbf{V}^+ - \mathbf{V}^+\mathbf{X}\mathbf{T}\mathbf{X}'\mathbf{V}^+)\boldsymbol{\epsilon} = \boldsymbol{\epsilon}'(\mathbf{F}\boldsymbol{\Lambda}^{-2}\mathbf{F}' - \mathbf{F}\boldsymbol{\Lambda}^{-2}\mathbf{F}'\mathbf{X}\mathbf{T}\mathbf{X}'\mathbf{F}\boldsymbol{\Lambda}^{-2}\mathbf{F}')\boldsymbol{\epsilon}$$
$$= (\boldsymbol{\Lambda}^{-1}\mathbf{F}'\boldsymbol{\epsilon})'(\mathbf{I} - \boldsymbol{\Lambda}^{-1}\mathbf{F}'\mathbf{X}\mathbf{T}\mathbf{X}'\mathbf{F}\boldsymbol{\Lambda}^{-1})(\boldsymbol{\Lambda}^{-1}\mathbf{F}'\boldsymbol{\epsilon})$$

Hence, (8.19) can be written as a quadratic form in the vector $\boldsymbol{\Lambda}^{-1}\mathbf{F}'\boldsymbol{\epsilon}$, which consists of n' independent normal variates with zero mean and variance σ^2 under the assumptions of the theorem. To prove that the matrix of this form is idempotent it is sufficient to prove that this is true for $\boldsymbol{\Lambda}^{-1}\mathbf{F}'\mathbf{X}\mathbf{T}\mathbf{X}'\mathbf{F}\boldsymbol{\Lambda}^{-1}$, since the idempotency of $\mathbf{A}$ implies that of $\mathbf{I} - \mathbf{A}$ (see proposition I4 at the end of Section 1.5). This is verified as follows:

$$\boldsymbol{\Lambda}^{-1}\mathbf{F}'\mathbf{X}\mathbf{T}\mathbf{X}'\mathbf{F}\boldsymbol{\Lambda}^{-2}\mathbf{F}'\mathbf{X}\mathbf{T}\mathbf{X}'\mathbf{F}\boldsymbol{\Lambda}^{-1} = \boldsymbol{\Lambda}^{-1}\mathbf{F}'\mathbf{X}\mathbf{T}\mathbf{X}'\mathbf{V}^+\mathbf{X}\mathbf{T}\mathbf{X}'\mathbf{F}\boldsymbol{\Lambda}^{-1} \quad \text{[see (7.7)]}$$
$$= \boldsymbol{\Lambda}^{-1}\mathbf{F}'\mathbf{X}\mathbf{T}\mathbf{C}^{-1}\mathbf{T}\mathbf{X}'\mathbf{F}\boldsymbol{\Lambda}^{-1} \quad \text{[see (8.5)]}$$
$$= \boldsymbol{\Lambda}^{-1}\mathbf{F}'\mathbf{X}\mathbf{T}\mathbf{X}'\mathbf{F}\boldsymbol{\Lambda}^{-1} \quad \text{[see (8.8)]}$$

The rank of the idempotent matrix in the second line of (9.3) is equal to its trace, which is $n' + q - K$ (see Problem 9.2), and the χ^2 distribution mentioned in the theorem then follows immediately.

For the proof of the independence of $\hat{\boldsymbol{\beta}}^*$ and $\hat{\sigma}^{*2}$ we go back to (8.9) and write the sampling error of $\hat{\boldsymbol{\beta}}^*$ as follows:

$$\hat{\boldsymbol{\beta}}^* - \boldsymbol{\beta} = \mathbf{TX'V^+}\boldsymbol{\epsilon} = (\mathbf{TX'F\Lambda^{-1}})(\mathbf{\Lambda^{-1}F'}\boldsymbol{\epsilon}) \tag{9.4}$$

Comparing the last expression with the second line of (9.3), we conclude that one is a linear form and the other is an idempotent quadratic form in the vector $\mathbf{\Lambda^{-1}F'}\boldsymbol{\epsilon}$ of independent normal variates with zero mean and constant variance. We have

$$\begin{aligned}
\mathbf{TX'F\Lambda^{-1}(I - \Lambda^{-1}F'XTX'F\Lambda^{-1})} &= \mathbf{TX'F\Lambda^{-1} - TX'F\Lambda^{-2}F'XTX'F\Lambda^{-1}} \\
&= \mathbf{TX'F\Lambda^{-1} - TX'V^+XTX'F\Lambda^{-1}} \\
&= \mathbf{TX'F\Lambda^{-1} - TC^{-1}TX'F\Lambda^{-1}} \\
&= \mathbf{TX'F\Lambda^{-1} - TX'F\Lambda^{-1}} \\
&= \mathbf{0}
\end{aligned}$$

which proves the independence.

Problems

9.1 Prove that the error of the predictor (7.22) of $y_{n+\tau}$ is equal to

$$(\boldsymbol{\xi}_\tau - \rho^\tau \boldsymbol{\xi}_0)'(\hat{\boldsymbol{\beta}} - \boldsymbol{\beta}) - (\zeta_{n+\tau} + \rho\zeta_{n+\tau-1} + \cdots + \rho^{\tau-1}\zeta_{n+1}) \tag{9.5}$$

where $\boldsymbol{\xi}_0$ and $\boldsymbol{\xi}_\tau$ are defined in Problem 7.6. Prove that under the condition that the ζ's are normally distributed, the prediction error (9.5) and the GLS variance estimator $\hat{\sigma}^2$ are stochastically independent. Use this result to formulate a prediction interval similar to eq. (6.14) of Section 3.6.

9.2 Consider the developments below eq. (8.19) to prove that the trace of the matrix $\mathbf{I - \Lambda^{-1}F'XTX'F\Lambda^{-1}}$ is equal to $n' + q - K$.

CHAPTER 7

THE COMBINATION OF SEVERAL LINEAR RELATIONS

This chapter is a continuation of Chapter 6 in that the tools developed there are utilized here. The main subject matter is the combination of several equations which appear unrelated but are in fact related, either because their coefficients are partly the same or because their disturbances are correlated. In the latter case one can say that the variables that are neglected in the various equations are partly the same or at least correlated. In the last two sections we shall be concerned with prior constraints on the coefficients. The approaches described there will provide other tools to meet objection (3) of Section 3.9 in addition to the linear equality constraints considered in Sections 6.8 and 6.9.

Section 7.1 is recommended for an introductory econometrics course; it provides a convenient introduction to some of the concepts that are relevant for the simultaneous equation models of Chapter 9. Section 7.2, part of Section 7.3, and Sections 7.8 and 7.9 are optional, and the rest of the chapter is not recommended for an introductory course.

7.1 The Joint Generalized Least-Squares Estimation Technique[A]

Grunfeld's Investment Theory

Our starting point is an investment theory proposed by Y. GRUNFELD (1958). One of the variables which this theory regards as determinants of investment is expected profits. No data on the latter are available, so that a measurable substitute is needed. The variable that is taken for this purpose is the "market value of the firm," defined as the total value of the outstanding stock at end-of-year stock market quotations. Let us write F_α for the market value at the end of year α and also consider the "desired capital stock" at the same point of time, C_α^*, which is supposed to be an increasing linear function of F_α:

$$C_\alpha^* = c_0 + c_1 F_\alpha \tag{1.1}$$

Let C_α be the existing capital stock; then $C_\alpha^* - C_\alpha = c_0 + c_1 F_\alpha - C_\alpha$ is desired net investment. Assuming that a constant fraction q_1 of desired net investment is realized in a year, we thus obtain for net investment:

$$q_1(C_\alpha^* - C_\alpha) = q_1 c_0 + q_1 c_1 F_\alpha - q_1 C_\alpha \tag{1.2}$$

This is net investment during year $\alpha + 1$, since F_α, C_α, and C_α^* are values taken by stock variables at the end of year α.

The variable that is ultimately described by the theory is gross investment including maintenance and repairs. It is assumed that replacement investment plus maintenance and repairs equal a constant fraction q_2 of the existing capital stock C_α. This is to be added to (1.2), so that we obtain for gross investment in year $\alpha + 1$ (including maintenance and repairs):

$$\begin{aligned} I_{\alpha+1} &= q_1(C_\alpha^* - C_\alpha) + q_2 C_\alpha \\ &= q_1 c_0 + q_1 c_1 F_\alpha + (q_2 - q_1) C_\alpha \end{aligned} \tag{1.3}$$

Application to General Electric and Westinghouse

We shall apply this theory to annual data (see Table 7.1) on two corporations, General Electric and Westinghouse, during the period 1935–1954. On the assumptions of the standard linear model we apply LS with the following result:

$$\begin{array}{llll} \text{General Electric:} & I = & -10.0 + .027F_{-1} + .152C_{-1} & \bar{R}^2 = .671 \\ & & (31.4) \quad (.016) \qquad (.026) & \\ \text{Westinghouse:}^1 & I' = & -.5 + .053F'_{-1} + .092C'_{-1} & \bar{R}^2 = .714 \\ & & (8.0) \quad (.016) \qquad (.056) & \end{array} \tag{1.4}$$

where the subscript -1 stands for "lagged one year."

[1] Primes are added to the Westinghouse variables to distinguish them from those of General Electric. The same procedure is followed for the coefficients and the disturbances in eq. (1.5) below.

Table 7.1

Time Series Data on General Electric and Westinghouse

Year	General Electric			Westinghouse		
	I	F_{-1}	C_{-1}	I'	F'_{-1}	C'_{-1}
1935	33.1	1170.6	97.8	12.93	191.5	1.8
36	45.0	2015.8	104.4	25.90	516.0	.8
37	77.2	2803.3	118.0	35.05	729.0	7.4
38	44.6	2039.7	156.2	22.89	560.4	18.1
39	48.1	2256.2	172.6	18.84	519.9	23.5
1940	74.4	2132.2	186.6	28.57	628.5	26.5
41	113.0	1834.1	220.9	48.51	537.1	36.2
42	91.9	1588.0	287.8	43.34	561.2	60.8
43	61.3	1749.4	319.9	37.02	617.2	84.4
44	56.8	1687.2	321.3	37.81	626.7	91.2
1945	93.6	2007.7	319.6	39.27	737.2	92.4
46	159.9	2208.3	346.0	53.46	760.5	86.0
47	147.2	1656.7	456.4	55.56	581.4	111.1
48	146.3	1604.4	543.4	49.56	662.3	130.6
49	98.3	1431.8	618.3	32.04	583.8	141.8
1950	93.5	1610.5	647.4	32.24	635.2	136.7
51	135.2	1819.4	671.3	54.38	723.8	129.7
52	157.3	2079.7	726.1	71.78	864.1	145.5
53	179.5	2371.6	800.3	90.08	1193.5	174.8
54	189.6	2759.9	888.9	68.60	1188.9	213.5

Note. All variables are in millions of dollars at 1947 prices. The capital stock variables are measured as deviations from the capital stock in a year prior to the sample period. For further details, see Boot and De Wit (1960, p. 27).

This estimation procedure is completely straightforward, but the question arises whether this is all that can be said about the determinants of investment of these two corporations. Since General Electric and Westinghouse operate in the same branch of industry, it is conceivable that there are *common* factors that affect the investment decisions of *both* firms quite apart from a common development of the two explanatory variables, F_{-1}, F'_{-1}, and C_{-1}, C'_{-1}. Since these factors are neglected in the equation, they have to be analyzed in terms of disturbances. We must expect the disturbances of the General Electric investment equation to be correlated with those of the Westinghouse equation if there are indeed such common factors. (An indication in this direction is that the 20 General Electric LS residuals and the 20 Westinghouse LS residuals have a correlation coefficient of .73.) Whenever we have such a situation, the equations are only seemingly unrelated; one might say that they are disturbance-related.

Combining the Two Investment Equations

The following procedure, from ZELLNER (1962) and extended by ZELLNER and HUANG (1962) and ZELLNER (1963b), provides a convenient solution to our problem under appropriate conditions. We combine the 20 observations of General Electric and those of Westinghouse by means of a 40-element vector equation with a six-element coefficient vector:

$$
(1.5) \qquad \begin{bmatrix} I_1 \\ I'_1 \\ \cdot \\ \cdot \\ \cdot \\ I_{20} \\ I'_{20} \end{bmatrix} = \begin{bmatrix} 1 & F_0 & C_0 & 0 & 0 & 0 \\ 0 & 0 & 0 & 1 & F'_0 & C'_0 \\ \cdot & \cdot & \cdot & \cdot & \cdot & \cdot \\ \cdot & \cdot & \cdot & \cdot & \cdot & \cdot \\ \cdot & \cdot & \cdot & \cdot & \cdot & \cdot \\ 1 & F_{19} & C_{19} & 0 & 0 & 0 \\ 0 & 0 & 0 & 1 & F'_{19} & C'_{19} \end{bmatrix} \begin{bmatrix} q_1 c_0 \\ q_1 c_1 \\ q_2 - q_1 \\ q'_1 c'_0 \\ q'_1 c'_1 \\ q'_2 - q'_1 \end{bmatrix} + \begin{bmatrix} \epsilon_1 \\ \epsilon'_1 \\ \cdot \\ \cdot \\ \cdot \\ \epsilon_{20} \\ \epsilon'_{20} \end{bmatrix}
$$

The first, third, . . . , and thirty-ninth elements of the left-hand vector are investment values of General Electric, and the even-numbered elements refer to Westinghouse. We may write (1.5) in the familiar form $\mathbf{y} = \mathbf{X}\boldsymbol{\beta} + \boldsymbol{\epsilon}$, where $\mathbf{y}$ and $\boldsymbol{\epsilon}$ are 40-element vectors, $\boldsymbol{\beta}$ is a six-element vector, and $\mathbf{X}$ is of order 40×6. This $\mathbf{X}$ has full column rank if the observation matrices of the explanatory variables of the two individual investment equations have this property (see Problem 1.1). It is obvious that the elements of $\mathbf{X}$ are nonstochastic when the right-hand variables of (1.3) for both companies take fixed values. The properties of the disturbance vector of (1.5) then determine which estimation procedure is appropriate for the six-element coefficient vector.

Contemporaneous Covariances

If the assumptions of the standard linear model hold for both investment equations, the elements of the disturbance vector of (1.5) have zero mean but they do not have the same variance, since the variance of ϵ_α is, in general, not equal to that of ϵ'_α. In addition, we have three kinds of covariances. The first is $\mathscr{E}(\epsilon_\alpha \epsilon_\eta)$ and $\mathscr{E}(\epsilon'_\alpha \epsilon'_\eta)$ for $\alpha \neq \eta$, which concern disturbances of different years but of the same investment equation. These covariances are assumed to vanish in the standard linear model. The second kind is $\mathscr{E}(\epsilon_\alpha \epsilon'_\eta)$ for $\alpha \neq \eta$, which deals with disturbances both of different years and of different equations. It will be assumed that such covariances, too, are zero; this assumption is an extension of the zero correlation condition of the standard linear model. The third kind, finally, is $\mathscr{E}(\epsilon_\alpha \epsilon'_\alpha)$, which concerns disturbances of different equations but of the same year. This is a so-called *contemporaneous covariance.*[2] The condition that will be imposed on such a covariance can be explained conveniently in conjunction with that of the variances of ϵ_α and ϵ'_α:

$$(1.6) \qquad \mathscr{V}\begin{bmatrix} \epsilon_\alpha \\ \epsilon'_\alpha \end{bmatrix} = \begin{bmatrix} \operatorname{var} \epsilon_\alpha & \operatorname{cov}(\epsilon_\alpha, \epsilon'_\alpha) \\ \operatorname{cov}(\epsilon'_\alpha, \epsilon_\alpha) & \operatorname{var} \epsilon'_\alpha \end{bmatrix} = \begin{bmatrix} \sigma_{11} & \sigma_{12} \\ \sigma_{21} & \sigma_{22} \end{bmatrix}$$

The diagonal elements of this matrix are the variances, denoted here by σ_{11} and σ_{22}. This notation indicates that they are independent of α, which conforms with the homoscedasticity assumption for each investment equation separately. The off-diagonal elements in (1.6) are the contemporaneous covariance in year α, and the equation states that they are equal to σ_{12} $(= \sigma_{21})$ and thus also independent of α. This condition on the contemporaneous covariance amounts to an extension of homoscedasticity. It means that the disturbances ϵ_α and ϵ'_α of General Electric and Westinghouse, respectively, are random drawings from a bivariate population with zero mean vector and a constant covariance matrix.

The Joint GLS Coefficient Estimator

The above assumptions on the 40-element disturbance vector $\boldsymbol{\epsilon}$ of (1.5) imply that its covariance matrix is block-diagonal with 20 diagonal submatrices all equal to the matrix (1.6):

$$(1.7) \qquad \mathscr{V}(\boldsymbol{\epsilon}) = \begin{bmatrix} \boldsymbol{\Sigma} & \mathbf{0} & \cdots & \mathbf{0} \\ \mathbf{0} & \boldsymbol{\Sigma} & \cdots & \mathbf{0} \\ \cdot & \cdot & & \cdot \\ \cdot & \cdot & & \cdot \\ \cdot & \cdot & & \cdot \\ \mathbf{0} & \mathbf{0} & \cdots & \boldsymbol{\Sigma} \end{bmatrix} \qquad \text{where} \qquad \boldsymbol{\Sigma} = \begin{bmatrix} \sigma_{11} & \sigma_{12} \\ \sigma_{21} & \sigma_{22} \end{bmatrix}$$

The off-diagonal submatrices are all zero matrices because their elements are of the type $\mathscr{E}(\epsilon_\alpha \epsilon_\eta)$, $\mathscr{E}(\epsilon_\alpha \epsilon'_\eta)$ or $\mathscr{E}(\epsilon'_\alpha \epsilon'_\eta)$ for $\alpha \neq \eta$ and are hence covariances of either the first or the second kind discussed in the previous subsection.

It will be assumed that the random pair $(\epsilon_\alpha, \epsilon'_\alpha)$ is not characterized by linear dependence, so that $\boldsymbol{\Sigma}$ is nonsingular. (If there were such a linear dependence, a particular combination of the investment values of the two firms would be an *exact* linear function of F_{-1}, F'_{-1}, C_{-1}, and C'_{-1}, which is

[2] The expression "contemporaneous covariance" refers specifically to time series applications, but it is normally used in a more general context. See Problem 1.2 for a cross-section application.

not plausible.) The inverse of $\mathscr{V}(\boldsymbol{\epsilon})$ is then block-diagonal with $\boldsymbol{\Sigma}^{-1}$ in the diagonal blocks, and a natural estimator of the six-element parameter vector of (1.5) is the Aitken estimator defined in eq. (1.4) of Section 6.1:

$$\hat{\boldsymbol{\beta}} = (\mathbf{X}'\mathbf{V}^{-1}\mathbf{X})^{-1}\mathbf{X}'\mathbf{V}^{-1}\mathbf{y} \tag{1.8}$$

where $\mathbf{X}$ and $\mathbf{y}$ are now to be interpreted as explained below (1.5), while the matrix $\mathscr{V}(\boldsymbol{\epsilon})$ defined in (1.7) is to be substituted for the covariance matrix $\sigma^2\mathbf{V}$ of Section 6.1.

A difficulty in the computation of this Aitken estimator is that the matrix $\boldsymbol{\Sigma}$ in (1.7) is normally unknown. As in the analogous situations described in Sections 6.2 and 6.3, we replace $\boldsymbol{\Sigma}$ by an estimator; the corresponding coefficient estimator is known as the joint GLS estimator, to be denoted by $\mathbf{b}_J$, as will now be described for the investment equations.

Joint GLS Estimation of the Investment Equations

The estimator of $\boldsymbol{\Sigma}$ that will be used is the matrix of the mean squares and products of the two sets of LS residuals (e_α for General Electric and e'_α for Westinghouse):

$$\mathbf{S} = \frac{1}{20}\begin{bmatrix} \sum_{\alpha=1}^{20} e_\alpha^2 & \sum_{\alpha=1}^{20} e_\alpha e'_\alpha \\ \sum_{\alpha=1}^{20} e'_\alpha e_\alpha & \sum_{\alpha=1}^{20} e_\alpha'^2 \end{bmatrix} \tag{1.9}$$

The numerical value of the matrix of sums of squares and products of the LS residuals for the data of Table 7.1 is

$$20\mathbf{S} = \begin{bmatrix} 13216.6 & 3529.1 \\ 3529.1 & 1773.4 \end{bmatrix} \begin{matrix} \text{General Electric} \\ \text{Westinghouse} \end{matrix} \tag{1.10}$$

with the following inverse:

$$\frac{1}{20}\mathbf{S}^{-1} = 10^{-6}\begin{bmatrix} 161.46 & -321.31 \\ -321.31 & 1203.31 \end{bmatrix} \tag{1.11}$$

Consider the Aitken estimator $\hat{\boldsymbol{\beta}}$ of (1.8) and write it as the inverse of the 6×6 matrix

$$\mathbf{X}'(\sigma^2\mathbf{V})^{-1}\mathbf{X} \tag{1.12}$$

postmultiplied by the six-element vector $\mathbf{X}'(\sigma^2\mathbf{V})^{-1}\mathbf{y}$. We replace $(\sigma^2\mathbf{V})^{-1}$ in this vector and in the matrix (1.12) by the 40×40 block-diagonal matrix which contains $\mathbf{S}^{-1}$ defined in (1.11) in the diagonal blocks, interpret $\mathbf{X}$ and $\mathbf{y}$ as explained below eq. (1.5), and thus obtain a six-element coefficient estimate $\mathbf{b}_J$ which is the joint GLS estimate. It follows from the coefficient vector in (1.5) that the first three elements of $\mathbf{b}_J$ refer to the General Electric investment equation and the last three to that of Westinghouse. The result, which should be compared with the regressions (1.4), can be written as follows:

$$
\begin{aligned}
&\text{General Electric:} \quad I = \underset{(27.0)}{-27.7} + \underset{(.013)}{.038}F_{-1} + \underset{(.023)}{.139}C_{-1} \\
(1.13)\qquad &\\
&\text{Westinghouse:} \quad I' = \underset{(7.0)}{-1.3} + \underset{(.013)}{.058}F'_{-1} + \underset{(.049)}{.064}C'_{-1}
\end{aligned}
$$

where the figures in parentheses are asymptotic standard errors. It will be shown in Section 8.6 that under appropriate conditions and when the sample size n is sufficiently large, the distribution of the joint estimator $\mathbf{b}_J$ is approximately the same as that of $\hat{\boldsymbol{\beta}}$. The covariance matrix of $\hat{\boldsymbol{\beta}}$, which is equal to the inverse of the matrix (1.12) according to eq. (1.5) of Section 6.1, is then asymptotically applicable to $\mathbf{b}_J$. Also, we may then replace $(\sigma^2\mathbf{V})^{-1}$ in (2.12) by the block-diagonal matrix which contains $\mathbf{S}^{-1}$ rather than $\boldsymbol{\Sigma}^{-1}$ in the diagonal blocks, so that the inverse of (1.12) with $\boldsymbol{\Sigma}$ replaced by $\mathbf{S}$ provides an approximate covariance matrix. This matrix is shown in the middle part of Table 7.2; the asymptotic standard errors given in (1.13) are the square roots of the diagonal elements of this matrix. Note that this approximate covariance matrix is concerned with the covariance of every pair of elements of the estimator of the complete coefficient vector in (1.5), not just the covariances of the three coefficients of the General Electric equation plus those of the three coefficients of the Westinghouse equation. The upper right-hand 3×3 submatrix gives the approximate covariances of any General Electric coefficient and any Westinghouse coefficient.

The upper part of Table 7.2 contains the estimated covariance matrix of the LS estimates of the six coefficients. A comparison of the diagonal elements of the two matrices gives an impression of the gain obtained by applying the joint GLS rather than the LS method in this case. Note that the upper right-hand 3×3 submatrix of the first matrix in Table 7.2, which contains the covariances of the LS coefficients of different equations, was not considered in the LS theory of Chapter 3. However, it can be obtained easily as is shown in Problem 1.3.

The third covariance matrix in Table 7.2 (of the constrained estimates) will be discussed in Section 7.3.

Concluding Remarks

The matrix $\mathbf{S}$ is computed from (1.10) by dividing the right-hand matrix by $n = 20$, which means that no account is taken of the loss of degrees of

Table 7.2

Estimated Covariance Matrices of the Coefficients of Two Investment Equations[a]

General Electric			Westinghouse			
10^3	F_{-1}	C_{-1}	10^3	F'_{-1}	C'_{-1}	
Covariance matrix ($\times$ 10^6) *of LS estimates*						
836.7	−383.7	−146.7	144.3	−263.3	481.6	1000
	206.0	−40.2	−61.4	140.0	−379.3	F_{-1}
		561.6	−40.6	−20.7	636.4	C_{-1}
			54.6	−93.1	143.6	1000
				209.7	−555.4	F'_{-1}
					2674.2	C'_{-1}
Covariance matrix ($\times$ 10^6) *of joint estimates*						
730.8	−329.3	−146.3	127.0	−226.2	392.4	1000
	176.6	−34.0	−52.7	120.0	−324.7	F_{-1}
		530.6	−39.6	−16.9	594.7	C_{-1}
			48.4	−80.0	113.6	1000
				179.9	−474.5	F'_{-1}
					2390.4	C'_{-1}
Covariance matrix ($\times$ 10^6) *of constrained joint estimates*						
323.9	−108.1	−202.2	98.7	−108.1	−202.2	1000
	56.4	−3.6	−37.6	56.4	−3.6	F_{-1}
		522.8	−42.4	−3.6	522.8	C_{-1}
			33.3	−37.6	−42.4	1000
				56.4	−3.6	F'_{-1}
					522.8	C'_{-1}

[a] To obtain numerical results that are of the same order of magnitude, the constant terms are given here as coefficients of a variable that takes the value 1000 for each observation.

freedom caused by the adjustment of the six coefficients. In Section 7.4 we shall see that the problem of correcting for this loss is a difficult one.[3] Since the justification of the joint GLS method is based on the assumption of a large number of observations—for which such corrections have no appreciable effect—no correction for loss of degrees of freedom was applied

[3] See footnote 13 on page 322.

at all.[4] Note in this connection that the total number of observations used for the adjustment of the six coefficients is not 20 but 40.

To what extent does the joint GLS procedure lead to an important gain over LS? The first two covariance matrices of Table 7.2 provide an answer, but this is, of course, confined to the data of Table 7.1, while moreover the answer is imperfect owing to the fact that Table 7.2 contains only estimates of covariances. It will appear in the next section that there are two situations in which there is *no payoff at all* in combining equations in the form (1.5). One is the case in which the contemporaneous covariances are zero, so that $\mathbf{\Sigma}$ of (1.7) is a diagonal matrix. The other is the case in which the two equations have the same explanatory variables. This may seem to be true for the investment equations, but it is not true even though the variables carry the same names (F, market value of the firm, and C, capital stock). They are different because they refer to General Electric in one case and to Westinghouse in the other. But suppose that we have two demand equations, one for butter and one for margarine, both with real income per capita and the relative prices of butter and of margarine as explanatory variables. These variables are then identical for the two equations, and it will be shown in the next section that combining these equations in the manner of (1.5) simply leads to ordinary LS estimates.

Problems

1.1 Postmultiply the 40×6 matrix in the right-hand side of (1.5) by a nonzero column vector $[\mathbf{a}_1' \;\; \mathbf{a}_2']'$, where $\mathbf{a}_1$ and $\mathbf{a}_2$ consist of three elements each. [The nonzero condition implies that either $\mathbf{a}_1$ or $\mathbf{a}_2$ (or both) is nonzero.] Prove that the 40-element product vector can be a zero vector only if either the 20×3 observation matrix of the explanatory variables of General Electric or the corresponding matrix of Westinghouse fails to have full column rank.

1.2 Suppose that expenditure data on n households are available and write y_α for the amount spent on food by the αth household, y_α' for the amount spent on services, $x_{\alpha 1}$ for the household's income, and $x_{\alpha 2}$ for the number of persons in the household. Consider the equations

[4] The estimated variances and covariances of the LS estimates in the upper part of Table 7.2 are based on the mean squares of the LS residuals as the estimates of the disturbance variances σ_{11} and σ_{22} and on the mean product of these residuals as the estimate of the contemporaneous covariance σ_{12} (which is needed for the upper right-hand 3×3 submatrix as is evident from Problem 1.3). Thus, no correction for loss of degrees of freedom has been applied here either; this was done to make these figures comparable with the other variance and covariance estimates of the table. Note that the standard errors of the LS regressions (1.4) are based on degrees of freedom ($20 - 3 = 17$), so that their squares are equal to a multiple 20/17 of the diagonal elements of the upper matrix in Table 7.2.

$$\text{(1.14)} \qquad \begin{aligned} y_\alpha &= \beta_0 + \beta_1 x_{\alpha 1} + \beta_2 x_{\alpha 2} + \epsilon_\alpha \\ y'_\alpha &= \beta'_0 + \beta'_1 x_{\alpha 1} + \beta'_2 x_{\alpha 2} + \epsilon'_\alpha \end{aligned}$$

where ϵ_α and ϵ'_α are random disturbances with zero mean. Formulate in words the economic implications of the covariance matrix condition (1.6) for these disturbances. [Note that the equations (1.14) fall under the case of identical explanatory variables discussed in the last paragraph of this section.]

1.3 Write the investment equations of General Electric and of Westinghouse in the form $\mathbf{y}_j = \mathbf{X}_j\boldsymbol{\beta}_j + \boldsymbol{\epsilon}_j$, where $j = 1$ (General Electric) or $j = 2$ (Westinghouse), while $\mathbf{y}_1$, $\mathbf{y}_2$, $\boldsymbol{\epsilon}_1$, and $\boldsymbol{\epsilon}_2$ are 20-element vectors, $\boldsymbol{\beta}_1$ and $\boldsymbol{\beta}_2$ are three-element vectors, and $\mathbf{X}_1$ and $\mathbf{X}_2$ are 20×3 matrices. Postmultiply the sampling error of the LS estimator $\mathbf{b}_1$ of $\boldsymbol{\beta}_1$ by the transpose of the sampling error of the other LS vector and list the conditions under which the following result holds:

$$\text{(1.15)} \qquad \mathscr{E}[(\mathbf{b}_1 - \boldsymbol{\beta}_1)(\mathbf{b}_2 - \boldsymbol{\beta}_2)'] = \sigma_{12}(\mathbf{X}_1'\mathbf{X}_1)^{-1}\mathbf{X}_1'\mathbf{X}_2(\mathbf{X}_2'\mathbf{X}_2)^{-1}$$

where σ_{12} is the contemporaneous covariance. Conclude that the LS coefficients of different equations are uncorrelated when the disturbances are contemporaneously uncorrelated ($\sigma_{12} = 0$) or when the vectors of values taken by the explanatory variables of the first equation are orthogonal to those of the second.

7.2 An Extension Formulated in Terms of Kronecker Products[B]

The familiar basic equation $\mathbf{y} = \mathbf{X}\boldsymbol{\beta} + \boldsymbol{\epsilon}$ is actually a system of n equations, each of which is one linear equation for one observation. When we have several behavioral or technical equations which are to be estimated simultaneously, such as the two investment equations of the previous section, one may argue that we are dealing with a system of equation systems. The Kronecker product is a convenient tool for handling such supersystems.

The Kronecker Product of Two Matrices

Consider the $m \times n$ matrix $\mathbf{A} = [a_{ij}]$ and the $p \times q$ matrix $\mathbf{B}$. The Kronecker product of $\mathbf{A}$ and $\mathbf{B}$ (in that order) is defined as an $mp \times nq$ matrix which can be partitioned as follows:

$$\text{(2.1)} \qquad \mathbf{A} \otimes \mathbf{B} = \begin{bmatrix} a_{11}\mathbf{B} & a_{12}\mathbf{B} & \cdots & a_{1n}\mathbf{B} \\ a_{21}\mathbf{B} & a_{22}\mathbf{B} & \cdots & a_{2n}\mathbf{B} \\ \cdot & \cdot & & \cdot \\ \cdot & \cdot & & \cdot \\ \cdot & \cdot & & \cdot \\ a_{m1}\mathbf{B} & a_{m2}\mathbf{B} & \cdots & a_{mn}\mathbf{B} \end{bmatrix}$$

For example, when $m = 2$, $n = 3$, and $\mathbf{B}$ is the 2×2 unit matrix:

$$\mathbf{A} \otimes \mathbf{I} = \begin{bmatrix} a_{11} & 0 & a_{12} & 0 & a_{13} & 0 \\ 0 & a_{11} & 0 & a_{12} & 0 & a_{13} \\ a_{21} & 0 & a_{22} & 0 & a_{23} & 0 \\ 0 & a_{21} & 0 & a_{22} & 0 & a_{23} \end{bmatrix}$$

The Matrix Product of Two Kronecker Products

The (ordinary) matrix product of two Kronecker products, $\mathbf{A} \otimes \mathbf{B}$ and $\mathbf{C} \otimes \mathbf{D}$, can itself be written as a single Kronecker product of two matrix products:

$$(\mathbf{A} \otimes \mathbf{B})(\mathbf{C} \otimes \mathbf{D}) = \mathbf{AC} \otimes \mathbf{BD} \tag{2.2}$$

provided that $\mathbf{AC}$ and $\mathbf{BD}$ both exist. The verification is as follows:

$$(\mathbf{A} \otimes \mathbf{B})(\mathbf{C} \otimes \mathbf{D})$$

$$= \begin{bmatrix} a_{11}\mathbf{B} & a_{12}\mathbf{B} & \cdots & a_{1n}\mathbf{B} \\ a_{21}\mathbf{B} & a_{22}\mathbf{B} & \cdots & a_{2n}\mathbf{B} \\ \cdot & \cdot & & \cdot \\ \cdot & \cdot & & \cdot \\ \cdot & \cdot & & \cdot \\ a_{m1}\mathbf{B} & a_{m2}\mathbf{B} & \cdots & a_{mn}\mathbf{B} \end{bmatrix} \begin{bmatrix} c_{11}\mathbf{D} & c_{12}\mathbf{D} & \cdots & c_{1s}\mathbf{D} \\ c_{21}\mathbf{D} & c_{22}\mathbf{D} & \cdots & c_{2s}\mathbf{D} \\ \cdot & \cdot & & \cdot \\ \cdot & \cdot & & \cdot \\ \cdot & \cdot & & \cdot \\ c_{n1}\mathbf{D} & c_{n2}\mathbf{D} & \cdots & c_{ns}\mathbf{D} \end{bmatrix}$$

$$= \begin{bmatrix} \sum_j a_{1j}c_{j1}\mathbf{BD} & \sum_j a_{1j}c_{j2}\mathbf{BD} & \cdots & \sum_j a_{1j}c_{js}\mathbf{BD} \\ \sum_j a_{2j}c_{j1}\mathbf{BD} & \sum_j a_{2j}c_{j2}\mathbf{BD} & \cdots & \sum_j a_{2j}c_{js}\mathbf{BD} \\ \cdot & \cdot & & \cdot \\ \cdot & \cdot & & \cdot \\ \cdot & \cdot & & \cdot \\ \sum_j a_{mj}c_{j1}\mathbf{BD} & \sum_j a_{mj}c_{j2}\mathbf{BD} & \cdots & \sum_j a_{mj}c_{js}\mathbf{BD} \end{bmatrix} = \mathbf{AC} \otimes \mathbf{BD}$$

One immediate result is that when $\mathbf{A}$ and $\mathbf{B}$ are both square and nonsingular, the inverse of their Kronecker product is given by

$$(\mathbf{A} \otimes \mathbf{B})^{-1} = \mathbf{A}^{-1} \otimes \mathbf{B}^{-1} \tag{2.3}$$

since $(\mathbf{A} \otimes \mathbf{B})(\mathbf{A}^{-1} \otimes \mathbf{B}^{-1}) = \mathbf{AA}^{-1} \otimes \mathbf{BB}^{-1} = \mathbf{I} \otimes \mathbf{I} = \mathbf{I}$ follows directly from (2.2). (Why is $\mathbf{I} \otimes \mathbf{I} = \mathbf{I}$? What are the orders of these three unit matrices?) Another result is

$$(\mathbf{A}_1 \otimes \mathbf{B}_1)(\mathbf{A}_2 \otimes \mathbf{B}_2) \cdots (\mathbf{A}_N \otimes \mathbf{B}_N) = (\mathbf{A}_1\mathbf{A}_2 \cdots \mathbf{A}_N) \otimes (\mathbf{B}_1\mathbf{B}_2 \cdots \mathbf{B}_N) \tag{2.4}$$

This follows from (2.2) by postmultiplying both sides of that equation by another Kronecker product, say $\mathbf{E} \otimes \mathbf{F}$, and then generalizing the result for arbitrary N. The only condition for (2.4) to be true is that the products $\mathbf{A}_1 \cdots \mathbf{A}_N$ and $\mathbf{B}_1 \cdots \mathbf{B}_N$ both exist.

Other Properties of Kronecker Products

Other useful properties of Kronecker products, to be proved by the reader, are:

$$(\mathbf{A} \otimes \mathbf{B})' = \mathbf{A}' \otimes \mathbf{B}' \tag{2.5}$$

$$\mathbf{A} \otimes (\mathbf{B} + \mathbf{C}) = \mathbf{A} \otimes \mathbf{B} + \mathbf{A} \otimes \mathbf{C} \tag{2.6}$$

$$(\mathbf{B} + \mathbf{C}) \otimes \mathbf{A} = \mathbf{B} \otimes \mathbf{A} + \mathbf{C} \otimes \mathbf{A} \tag{2.7}$$

$$\mathbf{A} \otimes (\mathbf{B} \otimes \mathbf{C}) = (\mathbf{A} \otimes \mathbf{B}) \otimes \mathbf{C} \tag{2.8}$$

The determinant, trace, and rank of the Kronecker product of an $m \times m$ matrix $\mathbf{A}$ and an $n \times n$ matrix $\mathbf{B}$ can be derived easily by means of the characteristic roots and vectors of $\mathbf{A}$ and $\mathbf{B}$. Write $\lambda_1, \ldots, \lambda_m$ and $\mu_1, \ldots, \mu_n$ for the roots of the two matrices and $\mathbf{x}_1, \ldots, \mathbf{x}_m$ and $\mathbf{y}_1, \ldots, \mathbf{y}_n$ for corresponding characteristic vectors. Since $\mathbf{A}\mathbf{x}_i = \lambda_i \mathbf{x}_i$ and $\mathbf{B}\mathbf{y}_j = \mu_j \mathbf{y}_j$, we have

$$(\mathbf{A} \otimes \mathbf{B})(\mathbf{x}_i \otimes \mathbf{y}_j) = (\mathbf{A}\mathbf{x}_i) \otimes (\mathbf{B}\mathbf{y}_j) = (\lambda_i \mathbf{x}_i) \otimes (\mu_j \mathbf{y}_j) = \lambda_i \mu_j (\mathbf{x}_i \otimes \mathbf{y}_j) \tag{2.9}$$

which shows that the product $\lambda_i \mu_j$ of any pair of roots of the two matrices is a root of $\mathbf{A} \otimes \mathbf{B}$. There are mn such products, which is in accordance with the fact that $\mathbf{A} \otimes \mathbf{B}$ is square of that order. The vector $\mathbf{x}_i \otimes \mathbf{y}_j$ is a characteristic vector of $\mathbf{A} \otimes \mathbf{B}$ corresponding to the root $\lambda_i \mu_j$. Note that this is an mn-element column vector consisting of m subvectors, the kth subvector being the kth element of $\mathbf{x}_i$ multiplied by $\mathbf{y}_j$. The $mn \times mn$ matrix of these vectors is orthogonal when $[\mathbf{x}_1 \cdots \mathbf{x}_m]$ and $[\mathbf{y}_1 \cdots \mathbf{y}_n]$ are both orthogonal. This follows from

$$(\mathbf{x}_i \otimes \mathbf{y}_j)'(\mathbf{x}_i \otimes \mathbf{y}_j) = (\mathbf{x}_i' \otimes \mathbf{y}_j')(\mathbf{x}_i \otimes \mathbf{y}_j) = (\mathbf{x}_i'\mathbf{x}_i) \otimes (\mathbf{y}_j'\mathbf{y}_j) = 1 \tag{2.10}$$

and from an analogous result for the case in which the two $\mathbf{x}$ subscripts or the two $\mathbf{y}$ subscripts or both are not equal. For example, when we have $\mathbf{x}_1$ and $\mathbf{x}_2$, the product $\mathbf{x}_i'\mathbf{x}_i$ after the second equality sign becomes $\mathbf{x}_1'\mathbf{x}_2 = 0$, which proves that the characteristic vectors $\mathbf{x}_1 \otimes \mathbf{y}_j$ and $\mathbf{x}_2 \otimes \mathbf{y}_j$ are orthogonal.

Since the determinant of $\mathbf{A} \otimes \mathbf{B}$ is equal to the product of all mn roots, we have

$$\begin{aligned} |\mathbf{A} \otimes \mathbf{B}| &= \prod_{i=1}^{m} \prod_{j=1}^{n} \lambda_i \mu_j \\ &= \lambda_1^n (\mu_1 \mu_2 \cdots \mu_n) \lambda_2^n (\mu_1 \mu_2 \cdots \mu_n) \cdots \lambda_m^n (\mu_1 \mu_2 \cdots \mu_n) \\ &= \left(\prod_{i=1}^{m} \lambda_i^n\right)\left(\prod_{j=1}^{n} \mu_j^m\right) = |\mathbf{A}|^n \, |\mathbf{B}|^m \end{aligned} \tag{2.11}$$

Similarly for the trace:

$$\operatorname{tr}(\mathbf{A} \otimes \mathbf{B}) = \sum_{i=1}^{m} \sum_{j=1}^{n} \lambda_i \mu_j = \sum_{i=1}^{m} \lambda_i \sum_{j=1}^{n} \mu_j = (\operatorname{tr} \mathbf{A})(\operatorname{tr} \mathbf{B}) \tag{2.12}$$

The rank of $\mathbf{A} \otimes \mathbf{B}$ is equal to the rank of $\mathbf{A}$ multiplied by the rank of $\mathbf{B}$, so that the trace and the rank are subject to the same simple product rule.

To prove the theorem on the rank we write $\mathbf{A} \otimes \mathbf{B} = \mathbf{C}$ and conclude

$$\mathbf{A}' \otimes \mathbf{B}' = \mathbf{C}' \qquad \text{and} \qquad (\mathbf{A}'\mathbf{A}) \otimes (\mathbf{B}'\mathbf{B}) = \mathbf{C}'\mathbf{C}$$

from (2.5) and (2.2), respectively. Write λ_i^* for any of the roots of $\mathbf{A}'\mathbf{A}$ and μ_j^* for any of those of $\mathbf{B}'\mathbf{B}$. Since $\mathbf{C}'\mathbf{C}$ is symmetric, its rank is equal to the number of its nonzero roots $\lambda_i^*\mu_j^*$, which is, in turn, equal to the number of nonzero roots λ_i^* of $\mathbf{A}'\mathbf{A}$ multiplied by the number of nonzero roots μ_j^* of $\mathbf{B}'\mathbf{B}$. This product may be written as $r(\mathbf{A}'\mathbf{A})r(\mathbf{B}'\mathbf{B}) = r(\mathbf{A})r(\mathbf{B})$, where $r(\ )$ stands for "rank of." We thus have $r(\mathbf{C}) = r(\mathbf{C}'\mathbf{C}) = r(\mathbf{A})r(\mathbf{B})$, which proves the statement.

Kronecker multiplication of partitioned matrices is straightforward, too. For example:

$$\begin{bmatrix} \mathbf{A}_{11} & \mathbf{A}_{12} \\ \mathbf{A}_{21} & \mathbf{A}_{22} \end{bmatrix} \otimes \mathbf{B} = \begin{bmatrix} \mathbf{A}_{11} \otimes \mathbf{B} & \mathbf{A}_{12} \otimes \mathbf{B} \\ \mathbf{A}_{21} \otimes \mathbf{B} & \mathbf{A}_{22} \otimes \mathbf{B} \end{bmatrix} \tag{2.13}$$

which the reader is invited to verify.

The Combination of Several Linear Equations

Kronecker products will now be used for the formulation of estimators of the parameter vectors of several equations simultaneously. Let there be L such equations with the following combined observation matrix:

$$[\mathbf{y}_1 \quad \mathbf{X}_1 \quad \mathbf{y}_2 \quad \mathbf{X}_2 \quad \cdots \quad \mathbf{y}_L \quad \mathbf{X}_L]$$

which has n rows and $L(K + 1)$ columns. We write the equations in the form

$$\mathbf{y}_j = \mathbf{X}_j\boldsymbol{\beta}_j + \boldsymbol{\epsilon}_j \qquad j = 1, \ldots, L \tag{2.14}$$

where $\mathbf{y}_j$ is a column vector of n values taken by the dependent variable of the jth equation, $\mathbf{X}_j$ is an $n \times K_j$ matrix of values taken by the K_j explanatory variables of that equation, $\boldsymbol{\beta}_j$ is the corresponding parameter vector to be estimated, and $\boldsymbol{\epsilon}_j$ is a disturbance vector. In the investment example of the previous section we have $L = 2$, and for $j = 1$ (General Electric) we have an observation matrix $[\mathbf{y}_1 \quad \mathbf{X}_1]$ of order 20×4, the αth row of which is $[I_\alpha \quad 1 \quad F_{\alpha-1} \quad C_{\alpha-1}]$. For $j = 2$ (Westinghouse) the interpretation is analogous. Note that in this case we have $K_1 = K_2$ $(= 3)$, while moreover the corresponding columns of $\mathbf{X}_1$ and $\mathbf{X}_2$ refer to similar variables (C and C', F and F', etc.). In the present, more general, set-up this need not be the case.

Next we combine all L equations (2.14) in the following partitioned form:

$$\begin{bmatrix} \mathbf{y}_1 \\ \mathbf{y}_2 \\ \cdot \\ \cdot \\ \cdot \\ \mathbf{y}_L \end{bmatrix} = \begin{bmatrix} \mathbf{X}_1 & \mathbf{0} & \cdots & \mathbf{0} \\ \mathbf{0} & \mathbf{X}_2 & \cdots & \mathbf{0} \\ \cdot & \cdot & & \cdot \\ \cdot & \cdot & & \cdot \\ \cdot & \cdot & & \cdot \\ \mathbf{0} & \mathbf{0} & \cdots & \mathbf{X}_L \end{bmatrix} \begin{bmatrix} \boldsymbol{\beta}_1 \\ \boldsymbol{\beta}_2 \\ \cdot \\ \cdot \\ \cdot \\ \boldsymbol{\beta}_L \end{bmatrix} + \begin{bmatrix} \boldsymbol{\epsilon}_1 \\ \boldsymbol{\epsilon}_2 \\ \cdot \\ \cdot \\ \cdot \\ \boldsymbol{\epsilon}_L \end{bmatrix} \tag{2.15}$$

Note that this method of combining the L equations is not identical with that of (1.5). In (1.5) we start by taking the first-year observations of the two equations, next the second-year observations, and so on. In (2.15) we start by taking all n observations of the first equation ($j = 1$), next the n observations of the second equation, and so on. The order in which the Ln individual linear relations are taken up has, of course, no effect on the estimators of unknown parameters, but it does have notational implications. For example, the Ln-element disturbance vector in (2.15) does not have the block-diagonal form of (1.7), as we shall shortly see.

The system (2.15) consists of Ln separate equations containing as a whole $K_1 + \cdots + K_L$ unknown parameters. Define:

$$(2.16)\quad \mathbf{y} = \begin{bmatrix} \mathbf{y}_1 \\ \mathbf{y}_2 \\ \cdot \\ \cdot \\ \cdot \\ \mathbf{y}_L \end{bmatrix} \qquad \mathbf{X} = \begin{bmatrix} \mathbf{X}_1 & \mathbf{0} & \cdots & \mathbf{0} \\ \mathbf{0} & \mathbf{X}_2 & \cdots & \mathbf{0} \\ \cdot & \cdot & & \cdot \\ \cdot & \cdot & & \cdot \\ \cdot & \cdot & & \cdot \\ \mathbf{0} & \mathbf{0} & \cdots & \mathbf{X}_L \end{bmatrix} \qquad \boldsymbol{\beta} = \begin{bmatrix} \boldsymbol{\beta}_1 \\ \boldsymbol{\beta}_2 \\ \cdot \\ \cdot \\ \cdot \\ \boldsymbol{\beta}_L \end{bmatrix} \qquad \boldsymbol{\epsilon} = \begin{bmatrix} \boldsymbol{\epsilon}_1 \\ \boldsymbol{\epsilon}_2 \\ \cdot \\ \cdot \\ \cdot \\ \boldsymbol{\epsilon}_L \end{bmatrix}$$

so that (2.15) takes the familiar form $\mathbf{y} = \mathbf{X}\boldsymbol{\beta} + \boldsymbol{\epsilon}$. If each $\mathbf{X}_j$, $j = 1, \ldots, L$, consists of nonstochastic elements and has full column rank, $\mathbf{X}$ will have the same properties. If each $\boldsymbol{\epsilon}_j$ has zero mean vector, so has $\boldsymbol{\epsilon}$. We shall assume that the disturbances of each equation are homoscedastic and uncorrelated, which implies that $\mathscr{E}(\boldsymbol{\epsilon}_j\boldsymbol{\epsilon}_j') = \sigma_{jj}\mathbf{I}$, $j = 1, \ldots, L$, where σ_{jj} is the variance of the disturbances of the jth equation. Regarding the covariance matrix of the disturbances of two different equations:

$$\mathscr{E}(\boldsymbol{\epsilon}_j\boldsymbol{\epsilon}_l') = \begin{bmatrix} \mathscr{E}(\epsilon_{1j}\epsilon_{1l}) & \mathscr{E}(\epsilon_{1j}\epsilon_{2l}) & \cdots & \mathscr{E}(\epsilon_{1j}\epsilon_{nl}) \\ \mathscr{E}(\epsilon_{2j}\epsilon_{1l}) & \mathscr{E}(\epsilon_{2j}\epsilon_{2l}) & \cdots & \mathscr{E}(\epsilon_{2j}\epsilon_{nl}) \\ \cdot & \cdot & & \cdot \\ \cdot & \cdot & & \cdot \\ \cdot & \cdot & & \cdot \\ \mathscr{E}(\epsilon_{nj}\epsilon_{1l}) & \mathscr{E}(\epsilon_{nj}\epsilon_{2l}) & \cdots & \mathscr{E}(\epsilon_{nj}\epsilon_{nl}) \end{bmatrix}$$

note that the diagonal elements are contemporaneous covariances of the form $\mathscr{E}(\epsilon_{\alpha j}\epsilon_{\alpha l})$ and that the off-diagonal elements correspond to different observations. As in the previous section, we shall assume that the latter covariances vanish and that the former are constant in the sense of being independent of α; we shall denote these by σ_{jl}. Hence,

$$(2.17)\qquad \mathscr{E}(\boldsymbol{\epsilon}_j\boldsymbol{\epsilon}_l') = \sigma_{jl}\mathbf{I} \qquad j, l = 1, \ldots, L$$

which includes $\mathscr{E}(\boldsymbol{\epsilon}_j\boldsymbol{\epsilon}_j') = \sigma_{jj}\mathbf{I}$ as a special case. For the complete Ln-element vector $\boldsymbol{\epsilon}$ we then obtain

$$(2.18)\quad \mathscr{V}(\boldsymbol{\epsilon}) = \begin{bmatrix} \sigma_{11}\mathbf{I} & \sigma_{12}\mathbf{I} & \cdots & \sigma_{1L}\mathbf{I} \\ \sigma_{21}\mathbf{I} & \sigma_{22}\mathbf{I} & \cdots & \sigma_{2L}\mathbf{I} \\ \cdot & \cdot & & \cdot \\ \cdot & \cdot & & \cdot \\ \cdot & \cdot & & \cdot \\ \sigma_{L1}\mathbf{I} & \sigma_{L2}\mathbf{I} & \cdots & \sigma_{LL}\mathbf{I} \end{bmatrix} = \boldsymbol{\Sigma} \otimes \mathbf{I} \quad \text{where} \quad \boldsymbol{\Sigma} = [\sigma_{jl}]$$

The $L \times L$ matrix $\boldsymbol{\Sigma}$ is the covariance matrix of $[\epsilon_{\alpha 1} \ \cdots \ \epsilon_{\alpha L}]$ for any α. We shall assume that the contemporaneous disturbances of the L equations are not linearly dependent, so that $\boldsymbol{\Sigma}$ is positive definite.

The Aitken Coefficient Estimator

We proceed to estimate the complete $\boldsymbol{\beta}$ vector of (2.15) and (2.16) by GLS. We then need the inverse of the covariance matrix (2.18), which is $\boldsymbol{\Sigma}^{-1} \otimes \mathbf{I}$ in view of (2.3). Thus, using the notation (2.16), we obtain the following estimator of $\boldsymbol{\beta}$:

$$(2.19)\qquad \hat{\boldsymbol{\beta}} = [\mathbf{X}'(\boldsymbol{\Sigma}^{-1} \otimes \mathbf{I})\mathbf{X}]^{-1}\mathbf{X}'(\boldsymbol{\Sigma}^{-1} \otimes \mathbf{I})\mathbf{y}$$

with the following covariance matrix:

$$(2.20)\qquad \mathscr{V}(\hat{\boldsymbol{\beta}}) = [\mathbf{X}'(\boldsymbol{\Sigma}^{-1} \otimes \mathbf{I})\mathbf{X}]^{-1}$$

To interpret these expressions we write $\boldsymbol{\Sigma}^{-1} = [\sigma^{jl}]$, so that the matrix in square brackets becomes

$$(2.21)\quad \mathbf{X}'(\boldsymbol{\Sigma}^{-1} \otimes \mathbf{I})\mathbf{X}$$

$$= \begin{bmatrix} \mathbf{X}_1' & \mathbf{0} & \cdots & \mathbf{0} \\ \mathbf{0} & \mathbf{X}_2' & \cdots & \mathbf{0} \\ \cdot & \cdot & & \cdot \\ \cdot & \cdot & & \cdot \\ \cdot & \cdot & & \cdot \\ \mathbf{0} & \mathbf{0} & \cdots & \mathbf{X}_L' \end{bmatrix} \begin{bmatrix} \sigma^{11}\mathbf{I} & \sigma^{12}\mathbf{I} & \cdots & \sigma^{1L}\mathbf{I} \\ \sigma^{21}\mathbf{I} & \sigma^{22}\mathbf{I} & \cdots & \sigma^{2L}\mathbf{I} \\ \cdot & \cdot & & \cdot \\ \cdot & \cdot & & \cdot \\ \cdot & \cdot & & \cdot \\ \sigma^{L1}\mathbf{I} & \sigma^{L2}\mathbf{I} & \cdots & \sigma^{LL}\mathbf{I} \end{bmatrix} \begin{bmatrix} \mathbf{X}_1 & \mathbf{0} & \cdots & \mathbf{0} \\ \mathbf{0} & \mathbf{X}_2 & \cdots & \mathbf{0} \\ \cdot & \cdot & & \cdot \\ \cdot & \cdot & & \cdot \\ \cdot & \cdot & & \cdot \\ \mathbf{0} & \mathbf{0} & \cdots & \mathbf{X}_L \end{bmatrix}$$

$$= \begin{bmatrix} \sigma^{11}\mathbf{X}_1'\mathbf{X}_1 & \sigma^{12}\mathbf{X}_1'\mathbf{X}_2 & \cdots & \sigma^{1L}\mathbf{X}_1'\mathbf{X}_L \\ \sigma^{21}\mathbf{X}_2'\mathbf{X}_1 & \sigma^{22}\mathbf{X}_2'\mathbf{X}_2 & \cdots & \sigma^{2L}\mathbf{X}_2'\mathbf{X}_L \\ \cdot & \cdot & & \cdot \\ \cdot & \cdot & & \cdot \\ \cdot & \cdot & & \cdot \\ \sigma^{L1}\mathbf{X}_L'\mathbf{X}_1 & \sigma^{L2}\mathbf{X}_L'\mathbf{X}_2 & \cdots & \sigma^{LL}\mathbf{X}_L'\mathbf{X}_L \end{bmatrix}$$

To obtain $\hat{\boldsymbol{\beta}}$ we postmultiply the inverse of this matrix by the following vector:

$$\mathbf{X}'(\boldsymbol{\Sigma}^{-1} \otimes \mathbf{I})\mathbf{y} = \begin{bmatrix} \sum_{j=1}^{L} \sigma^{1j}\mathbf{X}_1'\mathbf{y}_j \\ \cdot \\ \cdot \\ \cdot \\ \sum_{j=1}^{L} \sigma^{Lj}\mathbf{X}_L' y_j \end{bmatrix} \tag{2.22}$$

The Case of Zero Contemporaneous Covariances

When the contemporaneous disturbances $\epsilon_{\alpha 1}, \ldots, \epsilon_{\alpha L}$ are pairwise uncorrelated, their covariance matrix $\boldsymbol{\Sigma}$ is diagonal. The matrix (2.21) is then block-diagonal with L diagonal blocks of the form $(1/\sigma_{jj})\mathbf{X}_j'\mathbf{X}_j$, so that its inverse is also block-diagonal with $\sigma_{jj}(\mathbf{X}_j'\mathbf{X}_j)^{-1}$ as typical diagonal block. This inverse is to be postmultiplied by the vector (2.22), the jth subvector of which is now simplified to $(1/\sigma_{jj})\mathbf{X}_j' y_j$. It is easily seen that the jth subvector of $\hat{\boldsymbol{\beta}}$ is then $\mathbf{b}_j = (\mathbf{X}_j'\mathbf{X}_j)^{-1}\mathbf{X}_j'\mathbf{y}_j$, the LS vector applied to the jth equation alone. Hence the estimator (2.19) implies no gain compared with LS when $\boldsymbol{\Sigma}$ is a diagonal matrix. When the L equations can be arranged in two (or more) groups such that the disturbances of each equation have a nonzero contemporaneous covariance only with those of the other equations of the same group, then the matrix $\boldsymbol{\Sigma}$ is block-diagonal. This is pursued in Problem 2.3, which shows that the estimation procedure (2.19) can then be performed separately for each group of equations.

The Case of Identical Explanatory Variables

When all L equations have exactly the same explanatory variables,[5] we have $\mathbf{X}_1 = \cdots = \mathbf{X}_L = \bar{\mathbf{X}}$ (say), so that the matrix $\mathbf{X}$ of (2.16) becomes

$$\mathbf{X} = \begin{bmatrix} \bar{\mathbf{X}} & \mathbf{0} & \cdots & \mathbf{0} \\ \mathbf{0} & \bar{\mathbf{X}} & \cdots & \mathbf{0} \\ \cdot & \cdot & & \cdot \\ \cdot & \cdot & & \cdot \\ \cdot & \cdot & & \cdot \\ \mathbf{0} & \mathbf{0} & \cdots & \bar{\mathbf{X}} \end{bmatrix} = \mathbf{I} \otimes \bar{\mathbf{X}} \tag{2.23}$$

[5] This applies to all variables including the constant-term variable if the latter is present. That is, if one of the L equations has a constant term, all L should have such a term, and if one of the equations has no constant term, none of them should have it.

Applying (2.5) and (2.4), we find that the matrix (2.21) can now be written as

$$\mathbf{X}'(\mathbf{\Sigma}^{-1} \otimes \mathbf{I})\mathbf{X} = (\mathbf{I} \otimes \bar{\mathbf{X}}')(\mathbf{\Sigma}^{-1} \otimes \mathbf{I})(\mathbf{I} \otimes \bar{\mathbf{X}}) = \mathbf{\Sigma}^{-1} \otimes (\bar{\mathbf{X}}'\bar{\mathbf{X}})$$

the inverse of which is $\mathbf{\Sigma} \otimes (\bar{\mathbf{X}}'\bar{\mathbf{X}})^{-1}$. We conclude that the $\hat{\boldsymbol{\beta}}$ vector of (2.19) can be simplified as follows:

$$(2.24) \quad \hat{\boldsymbol{\beta}} = [\mathbf{\Sigma} \otimes (\bar{\mathbf{X}}'\bar{\mathbf{X}})^{-1}](\mathbf{I} \otimes \bar{\mathbf{X}}')(\mathbf{\Sigma}^{-1} \otimes \mathbf{I})\mathbf{y}$$

$$= [\mathbf{I} \otimes (\bar{\mathbf{X}}'\bar{\mathbf{X}})^{-1}\bar{\mathbf{X}}']\mathbf{y}$$

$$= \begin{bmatrix} (\bar{\mathbf{X}}'\bar{\mathbf{X}})^{-1}\bar{\mathbf{X}}' & \mathbf{0} & \cdots & \mathbf{0} \\ \mathbf{0} & (\bar{\mathbf{X}}'\bar{\mathbf{X}})^{-1}\bar{\mathbf{X}}' & \cdots & \mathbf{0} \\ \vdots & \vdots & & \vdots \\ \mathbf{0} & \mathbf{0} & \cdots & (\bar{\mathbf{X}}'\bar{\mathbf{X}})^{-1}\bar{\mathbf{X}}' \end{bmatrix} \begin{bmatrix} \mathbf{y}_1 \\ \mathbf{y}_2 \\ \vdots \\ \mathbf{y}_L \end{bmatrix} = \begin{bmatrix} \mathbf{b}_1 \\ \mathbf{b}_2 \\ \vdots \\ \mathbf{b}_L \end{bmatrix}$$

where $\mathbf{b}_1, \ldots, \mathbf{b}_L$ are the LS coefficient vectors of each equation separately.

This result and that of the previous subsection imply that combining the L equations does not lead to any gain compared with LS when the contemporaneous covariances all vanish or when the L sets of explanatory variables are identical. Additional results will be provided in Section 7.4 for two-equation systems.

The Joint GLS Procedure

As in the case of Section 7.1, we face the difficulty that $\mathbf{\Sigma}$ is usually unknown. The two-step procedure proposed there starts with the estimation of $\mathbf{\Sigma}$ by the matrix of mean squares and products of the LS residuals:

$$(2.25) \qquad \mathbf{S} = \frac{1}{n}\begin{bmatrix} \mathbf{e}_1' \\ \vdots \\ \mathbf{e}_L' \end{bmatrix} [\mathbf{e}_1 \quad \cdots \quad \mathbf{e}_L]$$

where $\mathbf{e}_j = \mathbf{y}_j - \mathbf{X}_j\mathbf{b}_j$ is the LS residual vector of the jth equation. Next, we apply (2.19) with $\mathbf{\Sigma}$ replaced by $\mathbf{S}$:

$$(2.26) \qquad \mathbf{b}_J = [\mathbf{X}'(\mathbf{S}^{-1} \otimes \mathbf{I})\mathbf{X}]^{-1}\mathbf{X}'(\mathbf{S}^{-1} \otimes \mathbf{I})\mathbf{y}$$

This is the joint GLS estimator of the parameter vector $\boldsymbol{\beta}_1, \ldots, \boldsymbol{\beta}_L$. Note that the existence of $\mathbf{S}^{-1}$ requires $L \leq n$. It will be shown in Section 8.6 that under appropriate conditions, one of which requires n to be sufficiently large, $\mathbf{b}_J$ has approximately the same distribution as $\hat{\boldsymbol{\beta}}$ of (2.19) and that the estimator of the matrix (2.20),

$$[\mathbf{X}'(\mathbf{S}^{-1} \otimes \mathbf{I})\mathbf{X}]^{-1} \tag{2.27}$$

provides an approximate covariance matrix from which asymptotic standard errors can be computed. This is the extension of the procedure described in the previous section [see the discussion of eqs. (1.9) to (1.13)] for the case of L equations in the Kronecker product formulation.

Concluding Remarks

For the case of identical explanatory variables, reference should be made to GOLDBERGER (1964, pp. 201–212). This subject can be pursued in much greater detail; under the condition of normally distributed disturbances, it leads to the Wishart distribution of the matrix of sums of squares and products of the LS residuals—see ANDERSON (1958, Chapter 8).

TELSER (1964) and KMENTA and GILBERT (1968a) considered iterative and maximum-likelihood procedures for the estimation of $\boldsymbol{\beta}_1, \ldots, \boldsymbol{\beta}_L$. PARKS (1967) extended the joint estimation technique for the case in which the disturbances have nonzero lagged covariances. See also KAKWANI (1967) for conditions under which the joint GLS estimator of the coefficient vector is unbiased.

Problems

2.1 Prove eqs. (2.5) to (2.8). Conclude from (2.5) that if $\mathbf{A}$ and $\mathbf{B}$ are symmetric, $\mathbf{A} \otimes \mathbf{B}$ is also symmetric. Finally, prove $(\mathbf{A} \otimes \mathbf{B})^+ = \mathbf{A}^+ \otimes \mathbf{B}^+$ for any matrix pair $(\mathbf{A}, \mathbf{B})$ of arbitrary order.[6]

2.2 Prove that $\mathscr{V}(\boldsymbol{\epsilon})$ defined in (1.7) can be written $\mathbf{I} \otimes \boldsymbol{\Sigma}$ and specify the order of the unit matrix. Compare this result with (2.18).

2.3 (*Joint estimation for a block-diagonal* $\boldsymbol{\Sigma}$) Suppose that $\boldsymbol{\Sigma}$ is of the form

$$\boldsymbol{\Sigma} = \begin{bmatrix} \boldsymbol{\Sigma}_A & \mathbf{0} \\ \mathbf{0} & \boldsymbol{\Sigma}_B \end{bmatrix} \tag{2.28}$$

where $\boldsymbol{\Sigma}_A$ is $L_A \times L_A$ and $\boldsymbol{\Sigma}_B$ is $L_B \times L_B$ $(L_A + L_B = L)$. Describe in words the implication of this condition for the disturbances of the L equations. Write $\mathbf{X}_A$ for the upper left-hand submatrix of $\mathbf{X}$ given in (2.16) consisting of the first $L_A n$ rows and the first $K_1 + \cdots + K_{L_A}$ columns, and similarly $\mathbf{X}_B$ for the submatrix in the lower right-hand

[6] The last question is to be disregarded if Section 6.6 was omitted.

side, and $\mathbf{y}_A$ and $\mathbf{y}_B$ for the corresponding subvectors of $\mathbf{y}$. Prove:

$$(2.29) \qquad \mathbf{X}'(\mathbf{\Sigma}^{-1} \otimes \mathbf{I})\mathbf{X} = \begin{bmatrix} \mathbf{X}_A'(\mathbf{\Sigma}_A^{-1} \otimes \mathbf{I})\mathbf{X}_A & \mathbf{0} \\ \mathbf{0} & \mathbf{X}_B'(\mathbf{\Sigma}_B^{-1} \otimes \mathbf{I})\mathbf{X}_B \end{bmatrix}$$

$$(2.30) \qquad \mathbf{X}'(\mathbf{\Sigma}^{-1} \otimes \mathbf{I})\mathbf{y} = \begin{bmatrix} \mathbf{X}_A'(\mathbf{\Sigma}_A^{-1} \otimes \mathbf{I})\mathbf{y}_A \\ \mathbf{X}_B'(\mathbf{\Sigma}_B^{-1} \otimes \mathbf{I})\mathbf{y}_B \end{bmatrix}$$

and use these results to prove that the joint estimator $\hat{\boldsymbol{\beta}}$ consists of two subvectors, $\hat{\boldsymbol{\beta}}_A$ and $\hat{\boldsymbol{\beta}}_B$, where $\hat{\boldsymbol{\beta}}_A$ is the same function of $\mathbf{X}_A$, $\mathbf{y}_A$, and $\mathbf{\Sigma}_A$ (similarly for $\hat{\boldsymbol{\beta}}_B$) as $\hat{\boldsymbol{\beta}}$ is of $\mathbf{X}$, $\mathbf{y}$, and $\mathbf{\Sigma}$.

2.4 (*Continuation*) Indicate how the above result can be extended to the case of a block-diagonal $\mathbf{\Sigma}$ with three or more diagonal blocks. What can be said about the implied estimation procedure for blocks that consist of only one equation?

2.5 Consider the case $\mathbf{X}_1 = \cdots = \mathbf{X}_L = \bar{\mathbf{X}}$ (order $n \times K$), so that $\hat{\boldsymbol{\beta}}$ of (2.19) consists of L subvectors $\mathbf{b}_1, \ldots, \mathbf{b}_L$ which are LS coefficient vectors of the separate equations. Prove that the $KL \times KL$ covariance matrix of this $\hat{\boldsymbol{\beta}}$ consists of L^2 submatrices of order $K \times K$ which are all symmetric. Use this result to prove $\text{cov}(b_1, b_2') = \text{cov}(b_2, b_1')$, where the b's are the LS estimators of the β's of (1.14).

7.3 Linear Constraints on Coefficients of Different Equations[BC]

There are situations in which the analyst wants to test a hypothesis that involves coefficients of different equations. For example, in the investment case of Section 7.1 he may be interested in whether the coefficients of the market value of the firm are the same for General Electric and Westinghouse. In this section such tests will be formulated under the condition that the contemporaneous disturbances are independent random drawings from an L-dimensional normal population. The analyst may also want to estimate the six coefficients of the two equations subject to such a constraint, and therefore a constrained estimation procedure will also be developed. Part of the derivations are based on material discussed in Sections 6.7 and 6.8.

Formulation of the Constraints[B]

Consider the L equations (2.14), which are combined to $\mathbf{y} = \mathbf{X}\boldsymbol{\beta} + \boldsymbol{\epsilon}$, the four matrices of which are defined in (2.16). We shall be interested in testing the linear constraint

$$(3.1) \qquad \mathbf{r} = \mathbf{R}\boldsymbol{\beta}$$

where **r** is a known q-element vector and **R** a known matrix of full row rank and of order $q \times (K_1 + \cdots + K_L)$. For example, if the constraint amounts to pairwise equality of the multiplicative coefficients of the investment equations for General Electric and for Westinghouse [see (1.5)], then (3.1) takes the following form:

$$\begin{bmatrix} 0 \\ 0 \end{bmatrix} = \begin{bmatrix} 0 & 1 & 0 & 0 & -1 & 0 \\ 0 & 0 & 1 & 0 & 0 & -1 \end{bmatrix} \begin{bmatrix} q_1 c_0 \\ q_1 c_1 \\ q_2 - q_1 \\ q_1' c_0' \\ q_1' c_1' \\ q_2' - q_1' \end{bmatrix} \tag{3.2}$$

Testing under the Normality Condition[B]

The testing procedure will be based—after some modifications—on the statistic given in eq. (7.23) of Section 3.7:

$$\frac{1}{qs^2}(\mathbf{r} - \mathbf{Rb})'[\mathbf{R}(\mathbf{X}'\mathbf{X})^{-1}\mathbf{R}']^{-1}(\mathbf{r} - \mathbf{Rb}) \tag{3.3}$$

which is distributed as $F(q, n - K)$ under the following three conditions: (1) those of the standard linear model, (2) normality, and (3) the null hypothesis $\mathbf{r} = \mathbf{R}\boldsymbol{\beta}$. The proof was based on the consideration that under these conditions $(n - K)s^2/\sigma^2$ is distributed as $\chi^2(n - K)$, the quadratic form with $\mathbf{r} - \mathbf{Rb}$ as vector and $[\mathbf{R}(\mathbf{X}'\mathbf{X})^{-1}\mathbf{R}']^{-1}$ as matrix is distributed as $\sigma^2\chi^2(q)$, and this form is independent of s^2. Here, too, we shall assume normality as well as the validity of the null hypothesis (3.1), but the standard linear model has to be adapted. It will be shown later in this section that $(n - K)s^2$ is to be replaced by a quadratic form in the residual vector $\mathbf{y} - \mathbf{X}\hat{\boldsymbol{\beta}}$ which is, in general, not a diagonal form. Specifically, we shall prove that the quadratic form

$$(\mathbf{y} - \mathbf{X}\hat{\boldsymbol{\beta}})'(\boldsymbol{\Sigma}^{-1} \otimes \mathbf{I})(\mathbf{y} - \mathbf{X}\hat{\boldsymbol{\beta}}) \tag{3.4}$$

is distributed as $\chi^2(Ln - K_1 - \cdots - K_L)$, where $\hat{\boldsymbol{\beta}}$ is the estimator (2.19), that the quadratic form

$$(\mathbf{r} - \mathbf{R}\hat{\boldsymbol{\beta}})'\{\mathbf{R}[\mathbf{X}'(\boldsymbol{\Sigma}^{-1} \otimes \mathbf{I})\mathbf{X}]^{-1}\mathbf{R}'\}^{-1}(\mathbf{r} - \mathbf{R}\hat{\boldsymbol{\beta}}) \tag{3.5}$$

is distributed as $\chi^2(q)$, and that the forms (3.4) and (3.5) are independent.

The conclusion is that the test statistic (3.3) is to be modified to

$$\text{(3.6)} \qquad \frac{Ln - \sum_{j=1}^{L} K_j}{q} \times \frac{(\mathbf{r} - \mathbf{R}\hat{\boldsymbol{\beta}})'\{\mathbf{R}[\mathbf{X}'(\boldsymbol{\Sigma}^{-1} \otimes \mathbf{I})\mathbf{X}]^{-1}\mathbf{R}'\}^{-1}(\mathbf{r} - \mathbf{R}\hat{\boldsymbol{\beta}})}{(\mathbf{y} - \mathbf{X}\hat{\boldsymbol{\beta}})'(\boldsymbol{\Sigma}^{-1} \otimes \mathbf{I})(\mathbf{y} - \mathbf{X}\hat{\boldsymbol{\beta}})}$$

and that it has an F distribution with q and $Ln - K_1 - \cdots - K_L$ degrees of freedom if the null hypothesis (3.1) is true. See Problem 3.1 for the case in which all contemporaneous covariances vanish.

Application to the Investment Example[B]

If $\boldsymbol{\Sigma}$ is known up to a multiplicative scalar, the value of the statistic (3.6) can be computed without difficulty, but an approximation procedure is needed when this is not the case. We shall illustrate this for the investment example by testing the hypothesis (3.2) at the 5 percent significance level. We replace $\boldsymbol{\Sigma}$ by $\mathbf{S}$ of (2.25), so that the vector $\mathbf{r} - \mathbf{R}\hat{\boldsymbol{\beta}}$ becomes

$$\text{(3.7)} \qquad \mathbf{r} - \mathbf{R}\mathbf{b}_J = \begin{bmatrix} 0 \\ 0 \end{bmatrix} - \begin{bmatrix} -.0193 \\ .0751 \end{bmatrix} = \begin{bmatrix} .0193 \\ -.0751 \end{bmatrix}$$

the figures of which are based on the joint estimates given in (1.13). The matrix in curled brackets in (3.5) is

$$\text{(3.8)} \qquad \mathbf{R}[\mathbf{X}'(\mathbf{S}^{-1} \otimes \mathbf{I})\mathbf{X}]^{-1}\mathbf{R}' = \mathbf{R}\begin{bmatrix} s^{11}\mathbf{X}_1'\mathbf{X}_1 & s^{12}\mathbf{X}_1'\mathbf{X}_2 \\ s^{21}\mathbf{X}_2'\mathbf{X}_1 & s^{22}\mathbf{X}_2'\mathbf{X}_2 \end{bmatrix}^{-1}\mathbf{R}'$$

where $\mathbf{R}$ is the 2×6 matrix in the right-hand side of (3.2) and s^{jl} is the (j, l)th element of $\mathbf{S}^{-1}$. The right-hand inverse in (3.8) is the approximate covariance matrix of the joint estimator given in Table 7.2 of Section 7.1, and the 2×2 matrix (3.8) is then readily computed. Its inverse is

$$\text{(3.9)} \qquad \{\mathbf{R}[\mathbf{X}'(\mathbf{S}^{-1} \otimes \mathbf{I})\mathbf{X}]^{-1}\mathbf{R}'\}^{-1} = \begin{bmatrix} 9959.6 & 960.2 \\ 960.2 & 670.0 \end{bmatrix}$$

The numerical value of the quadratic form (3.5), based on (3.7) and (3.9), is 4.710. For the form (3.4) with $\boldsymbol{\Sigma}$ replaced by $\mathbf{S}$ we have

$$\text{(3.10)} \qquad (\mathbf{y} - \mathbf{X}\mathbf{b}_J)'(\mathbf{S}^{-1} \otimes \mathbf{I})(\mathbf{y} - \mathbf{X}\mathbf{b}_J) = \sum_{j=1}^{2}\sum_{l=1}^{2} s^{jl}(\mathbf{y}_j - \mathbf{X}_j\mathbf{b}_{Jj})'(\mathbf{y}_l - \mathbf{X}_l\mathbf{b}_{Jl})$$

where $\mathbf{y}_1$, $\mathbf{y}_2$, $\mathbf{b}_{J1}$, and $\mathbf{b}_{J2}$ are the subvectors of $\mathbf{y}$ and $\mathbf{b}_J$, respectively, corresponding to the two equations, while $\mathbf{X}_1$ and $\mathbf{X}_2$ are the 20×3 observation matrices of the two sets of explanatory variables. The numerical value of the quadratic form (3.10) is 38.87, so that the value of the test statistic is

$$\frac{2 \times 20 - 3 - 3}{2} \times \frac{4.710}{38.87} = 2.06 \tag{3.11}$$

The 5 percent significance limit of the F ratio with 2 degrees of freedom in the numerator and 34 degrees in the denominator is about 3.3. Thus, if we disregard the approximation of $\mathbf{\Sigma}$ by $\mathbf{S}$, we may consider the null hypothesis (3.2) acceptable. See Section 8.6 for a large-sample justification of this approximation.

Derivation of the Chi-Square Distributions and of the Independence[C]

Since each root of $\mathbf{\Sigma} \otimes \mathbf{I}$ is equal to a root of $\mathbf{\Sigma}$ multiplied by a root of $\mathbf{I}$, all roots of this Kronecker product are positive when $\mathbf{\Sigma}$ is nonsingular.[7] We write $\mathbf{\Lambda}^2$ for a positive definite diagonal matrix which contains these roots on the diagonal and define $\mathbf{\Lambda}$ as the matrix whose elements are the positive square roots of the corresponding elements of $\mathbf{\Lambda}^2$. Then there exists an orthogonal matrix $\mathbf{F}$ such that

$$\mathbf{\Sigma} \otimes \mathbf{I} = \mathbf{F\Lambda}^2\mathbf{F}' \tag{3.12}$$

This is exactly the same as $\mathbf{V} = \mathbf{F\Lambda}^2\mathbf{F}'$ of eq. (7.7) of Section 6.7 for the case of a nonsingular $\mathbf{V}$ except that the order of each of the three matrices occurring in the right-hand side of (3.12) is $Ln \times Ln$ and that σ^2 of the covariance matrix $\sigma^2\mathbf{V}$ of Chapter 6 should be interpreted as 1. These exceptions are not essential, however.[8] It follows from eq. (7.9) of Section 6.7 that the vector $\mathbf{\Lambda}^{-1}\mathbf{F}'\boldsymbol{\epsilon}$ has a unit covariance matrix for $\sigma^2 = 1$. Hence, if our present Ln-element disturbance vector $\boldsymbol{\epsilon}$ has a multinormal distribution, the vector $\mathbf{\Lambda}^{-1}\mathbf{F}'\boldsymbol{\epsilon}$ consists of Ln independent standardized normal variates. It is then a matter of straightforward algebra (see Problem 3.2) to verify that the quadratic form (3.4) can be written as

$$(\mathbf{\Lambda}^{-1}\mathbf{F}'\boldsymbol{\epsilon})'[\mathbf{I} - \mathbf{Z}(\mathbf{Z}'\mathbf{Z})^{-1}\mathbf{Z}'](\mathbf{\Lambda}^{-1}\mathbf{F}'\boldsymbol{\epsilon}) \qquad \text{where} \qquad \mathbf{Z} = \mathbf{\Lambda}^{-1}\mathbf{F}'\mathbf{X} \tag{3.13}$$

and that this is an idempotent quadratic form in the vector $\mathbf{\Lambda}^{-1}\mathbf{F}'\boldsymbol{\epsilon}$ of rank Ln (the order of the unit matrix) minus $K_1 + \cdots + K_L$ (the number of columns

[7] Since all roots of the unit matrix are equal to one, the Kronecker product has multiple roots, so that the matrix $\mathbf{F}$ of characteristic vectors considered in (3.12) below is not unique. This is of no concern, however, because any orthogonal matrix of characteristic vectors may be used.

[8] The specification $\sigma^2 = 1$ will, in general, contradict the rule that the trace of $\mathbf{V}$ is equal to its rank, but such normalization rules should be regarded as convenient rather than essential.

of **Z**). Hence its distribution under the normality condition is

$$\chi^2 (Ln - K_1 - \cdots - K_L).$$

Similarly it can be shown (see Problem 3.3) that the quadratic form (3.5) may be written as

$$(3.14) \qquad (\boldsymbol{\Lambda}^{-1}\mathbf{F}'\boldsymbol{\epsilon})'\mathbf{Z}(\mathbf{Z}'\mathbf{Z})^{-1}\mathbf{R}'[\mathbf{R}(\mathbf{Z}'\mathbf{Z})^{-1}\mathbf{R}']^{-1}\mathbf{R}(\mathbf{Z}'\mathbf{Z})^{-1}\mathbf{Z}'(\boldsymbol{\Lambda}^{-1}\mathbf{F}'\boldsymbol{\epsilon})$$

if the null hypothesis $\mathbf{r} = \mathbf{R}\boldsymbol{\beta}$ is indeed true, and that (3.14) is an idempotent quadratic form of rank q in the vector $\boldsymbol{\Lambda}^{-1}\mathbf{F}'\boldsymbol{\epsilon}$. The independence of the two forms is established by computing the product of their matrices, which appears to be a zero matrix.

Estimation under Constraints[C]

Suppose now that we accept constraint (3.1) and that we wish to impose it on the coefficient estimator. To solve this problem we simply return to the constrained estimator given in eq. (8.5) of Section 6.8:

$$(3.15) \qquad \hat{\boldsymbol{\beta}}^* = \hat{\boldsymbol{\beta}} + \mathbf{CR}'(\mathbf{RCR}')^{-1}(\mathbf{r} - \mathbf{R}\hat{\boldsymbol{\beta}})$$

and to its covariance matrix (8.6) of the same section:

$$(3.16) \qquad \mathscr{V}(\hat{\boldsymbol{\beta}}^*) = \sigma^2[\mathbf{C} - \mathbf{CR}'(\mathbf{RCR}')^{-1}\mathbf{RC}]$$

Here $\hat{\boldsymbol{\beta}}$ is the estimator (2.19), $\mathbf{C} = [\mathbf{X}'(\boldsymbol{\Sigma}^{-1} \otimes \mathbf{I})\mathbf{X}]^{-1}$, and $\sigma^2 = 1$. If we approximate $\boldsymbol{\Sigma}$ by $\mathbf{S}$, $(\mathbf{RCR}')^{-1}$ is simply the matrix (3.9) in the investment case and $\mathbf{r} - \mathbf{R}\hat{\boldsymbol{\beta}}$ is the vector (3.7). Their product is a two-element column vector, which is to be premultiplied by the 6×2 matrix $\mathbf{CR}'$ to provide the difference between the constrained and the unconstrained coefficient vectors. The result is:

$$(3.17) \qquad \begin{array}{llllll} \text{General Electric:} & I = & -23.0 & + .036F_{-1} & + .139C_{-1} \\ & & (18.0) & (.008) & (.023) \\ \text{Westinghouse:} & I' = & 6.9 & + .036F'_{-1} & + .139C'_{-1} \\ & & (5.8) & (.008) & (.023) \end{array}$$

The asymptotic standard errors in parentheses are computed as the square roots of the diagonal elements of the matrix (3.16) with $\sigma^2 = 1$, $\mathbf{C}^{-1} = \mathbf{X}'(\mathbf{S}^{-1} \otimes \mathbf{I})\mathbf{X}$. The complete estimated covariance matrix is shown in the last six lines of Table 7.2. A comparison of the multiplicative coefficients with the corresponding estimates in (1.13) shows that they have moved considerably toward the original General Electric coefficients. This is partly because of the relatively large standard error of the original Westinghouse C'_{-1} coefficient, which indicates that this point estimate is rather unstable. Also note that in this case the reduction of the standard errors caused by imposing the constraints is, on the average, larger than the difference between the standard errors of the LS and the corresponding joint estimates [compare the regressions (1.4) and the estimated equations (1.13)].

Problems

3.1 Prove that the quadratic form (3.4) is equal to the sum over j from 1 through L of $(n - K_j)s_j^2/\sigma_j^2$ when $\mathbf{\Sigma}$ is diagonal, s_j^2 being the LS estimator of the variance σ_j^2 of the jth equation. Next, partition $\mathbf{R} = [\mathbf{R}_1 \quad \cdots \quad \mathbf{R}_L]$, where $\mathbf{R}_j$ is of order $q \times K_j$, and prove that the matrix in curled brackets in (3.5) is equal to the sum over j of $\sigma_j^2\mathbf{R}_j(\mathbf{X}_j'\mathbf{X}_j)^{-1}\mathbf{R}_j'$ under the same condition. Finally, prove that if σ_j^2 is approximated by s_j^2 in the test statistic (3.6), this statistic is simplified to $1/q$ times the quadratic form (3.5) with $\sum_j s_j^2\mathbf{R}_j(\mathbf{X}_j'\mathbf{X}_j)^{-1}\mathbf{R}_j'$ as the matrix in curled brackets.

3.2 Prove $\mathbf{y} - \mathbf{X}\hat{\boldsymbol{\beta}} = \mathbf{F}\mathbf{\Lambda}[\mathbf{I} - \mathbf{Z}(\mathbf{Z}'\mathbf{Z})^{-1}\mathbf{Z}']\mathbf{\Lambda}^{-1}\mathbf{F}'\boldsymbol{\epsilon}$, where $\mathbf{F}$, $\mathbf{\Lambda}$, and $\mathbf{Z}$ are given in (3.12) and (3.13), and use this to prove that the quadratic forms (3.4) and (3.13) are identical.

3.3 Prove $\mathbf{r} - \mathbf{R}\hat{\boldsymbol{\beta}} = -\mathbf{R}(\mathbf{Z}'\mathbf{Z})^{-1}\mathbf{Z}'\mathbf{\Lambda}^{-1}\mathbf{F}'\boldsymbol{\epsilon}$ if the null hypothesis $\mathbf{r} = \mathbf{R}\boldsymbol{\beta}$ is true, and use this to prove that the quadratic forms (3.5) and (3.14) are identical under this condition. Consider (3.14) as a quadratic form in the vector $\mathbf{\Lambda}^{-1}\mathbf{F}'\boldsymbol{\epsilon}$ and prove that its matrix is idempotent of rank q as stated below (3.14). Also, prove the statement on independence made there.

3.4 Consider the estimated covariance matrix in the last six lines of Table 7.2 in Section 7.1. Verify which variances and covariances are pairwise equal and argue why this must be so.

7.4 Further Details on the Joint Estimation Procedure[C]

Additional insight into the joint GLS procedure is obtained when we use some concepts derived from canonical correlation theory. A brief account of this theory, insofar as it is of direct relevance for the joint GLS method, is given in the subsections that follow, after which we shall return to the main line of argument later in this section. Canonical correlation theory was developed by HOTELLING (1936); a more extensive account is given by ANDERSON (1958, Chapter 12).

The Canonical Correlation Concept

Suppose that we have L dependent and K explanatory variables and let $[\mathbf{Y} \quad \mathbf{X}]$ be their observation matrix, where $\mathbf{X}$ is $n \times K$ and $\mathbf{Y}$ is $n \times L$; it will be assumed here that both **X** and **Y** have full column rank. To what extent do the explanatory variables account for the behavior of the dependent variables?

We could answer this question for each dependent variable separately by computing L multiple correlation coefficients. However, the following approach, which treats all dependent variables simultaneously, will be more useful for our purposes. Imagine that the K columns of **X** are combined linearly to give the same number of column vectors $\boldsymbol{\xi}_1, \ldots, \boldsymbol{\xi}_K$ and that the L columns of **Y** are similarly combined to give L vectors $\boldsymbol{\eta}_1, \ldots, \boldsymbol{\eta}_L$ so that:

(1) Each of these $K + L$ columns has unit length;

(2) the $\boldsymbol{\xi}$'s are pairwise orthogonal and the $\boldsymbol{\eta}$'s are pairwise orthogonal;

(3) each $\boldsymbol{\xi}_i$ is orthogonal to each $\boldsymbol{\eta}_j$ except for the pairs of equal subscripts: $(\boldsymbol{\xi}_1, \boldsymbol{\eta}_1), (\boldsymbol{\xi}_2, \boldsymbol{\eta}_2), \ldots$. The $\boldsymbol{\xi}$'s and $\boldsymbol{\eta}$'s are selected in such a way that their inner products $\boldsymbol{\xi}_i'\boldsymbol{\eta}_i$, known as the *canonical correlation coefficients* of the two sets of variables, satisfy certain maximality conditions to be explained below. The number of such coefficients is equal to the smaller of the number of variables in the two sets, to be written min (K, L).

Consider, then, one particular pair $(\boldsymbol{\xi}_i, \boldsymbol{\eta}_i)$ and the corresponding canonical correlation $\boldsymbol{\xi}_i'\boldsymbol{\eta}_i = r_i$, say. Since $\boldsymbol{\xi}_i$ and $\boldsymbol{\eta}_i$ are linear combinations of the columns of **X** and **Y**, respectively, we can write them in the following form:

$$\boldsymbol{\xi}_i = \mathbf{X}\mathbf{h}_i \qquad \boldsymbol{\eta}_i = \mathbf{Y}\mathbf{k}_i \tag{4.1}$$

where $\mathbf{h}_i$ and $\mathbf{k}_i$ are column vectors of weights. The unit length condition implies

$$\boldsymbol{\xi}_i'\boldsymbol{\xi}_i = \mathbf{h}_i'\mathbf{X}'\mathbf{X}\mathbf{h}_i = 1 \qquad \boldsymbol{\eta}_i'\boldsymbol{\eta}_i = \mathbf{k}_i'\mathbf{Y}'\mathbf{Y}\mathbf{k}_i = 1 \tag{4.2}$$

and the canonical correlation coefficient is

$$r_i = \boldsymbol{\xi}_i'\boldsymbol{\eta}_i = \mathbf{h}_i'\mathbf{X}'\mathbf{Y}\mathbf{k}_i \tag{4.3}$$

The Largest Canonical Correlation Coefficient

We shall first derive the largest canonical correlation coefficient, to be indicated by the subscript $i = 1$. Thus, r_1 maximizes the function (4.3) subject to the constraints (4.2) with i interpreted as 1. Consider the Lagrangian expression

$$\mathbf{h}_1'\mathbf{X}'\mathbf{Y}\mathbf{k}_1 - \frac{1}{2}\lambda(\mathbf{h}_1'\mathbf{X}'\mathbf{X}\mathbf{h}_1 - 1) - \frac{1}{2}\mu(\mathbf{k}_1'\mathbf{Y}'\mathbf{Y}\mathbf{k}_1 - 1)$$

where λ and μ are Lagrangian multipliers. We differentiate the expression with respect to $\mathbf{h}_1$ and $\mathbf{k}_1$ and put the result equal to zero:

$$\mathbf{X}'\mathbf{Y}\mathbf{k}_1 - \lambda\mathbf{X}'\mathbf{X}\mathbf{h}_1 = \mathbf{0} \tag{4.4}$$

$$\mathbf{Y}'\mathbf{X}\mathbf{h}_1 - \mu\mathbf{Y}'\mathbf{Y}\mathbf{k}_1 = \mathbf{0} \tag{4.5}$$

Next we premultiply both sides of (4.4) by $\mathbf{h}_1'$ and those of (4.5) by $\mathbf{k}_1'$. Comparing the results with (4.2) and (4.3), we conclude

$$\lambda = \mu = r_1 \tag{4.6}$$

We now combine (4.4) and (4.6) to obtain $r_1\mathbf{h}_1 = (\mathbf{X}'\mathbf{X})^{-1}\mathbf{X}'\mathbf{Y}\mathbf{k}_1$ and combine this with (4.5):[9]

$$[(\mathbf{Y}'\mathbf{Y})^{-1}\mathbf{Y}'\mathbf{X}(\mathbf{X}'\mathbf{X})^{-1}\mathbf{X}'\mathbf{Y} - r_1^2\mathbf{I}]\mathbf{k}_1 = \mathbf{0} \tag{4.7}$$

We conclude that r_1^2 is a latent root of the matrix

$$(\mathbf{Y}'\mathbf{Y})^{-1}\mathbf{Y}'\mathbf{X}(\mathbf{X}'\mathbf{X})^{-1}\mathbf{X}'\mathbf{Y} \tag{4.8}$$

which shows immediately that r_1^2 contains the squared multiple correlation coefficient R^2 defined in eq. (1.4) of Section 4.1 as a special case:

$$R^2 = \frac{\mathbf{b}'\mathbf{X}'\mathbf{X}\mathbf{b}}{\mathbf{y}'\mathbf{y}} = (\mathbf{y}'\mathbf{y})^{-1}\mathbf{y}'\mathbf{X}(\mathbf{X}'\mathbf{X})^{-1}\mathbf{X}'\mathbf{y}$$

where $\mathbf{y}$ is the column vector of observations on the single dependent variable and $\mathbf{b} = (\mathbf{X}'\mathbf{X})^{-1}\mathbf{X}'\mathbf{y}$.[10] As in the case of R, r_1 is defined as the positive

[9] It is easily seen from (4.7) that r_1^2 must be real, nonnegative, and at most equal to 1. Premultiply the equation by $\mathbf{Y}'\mathbf{Y}$:

$$[\mathbf{Y}'\mathbf{X}(\mathbf{X}'\mathbf{X})^{-1}\mathbf{X}'\mathbf{Y} - r_1^2\mathbf{Y}'\mathbf{Y}]\mathbf{k}_1 = \mathbf{0} \tag{1}$$

Since $\mathbf{Y}'\mathbf{Y}$ is positive definite, so is $(\mathbf{Y}'\mathbf{Y})^{-1}$. Hence there exists a nonsingular $L \times L$ matrix $\mathbf{P}$ such that $\mathbf{P}'\mathbf{P} = (\mathbf{Y}'\mathbf{Y})^{-1}$. We thus have

$$|\mathbf{Y}'\mathbf{X}(\mathbf{X}'\mathbf{X})^{-1}\mathbf{X}'\mathbf{Y} - r_1^2\mathbf{P}^{-1}(\mathbf{P}')^{-1}| = 0$$

Premultiply both sides by $|\mathbf{P}|$ and postmultiply by $|\mathbf{P}'|$:

$$|\mathbf{P}\mathbf{Y}'\mathbf{X}(\mathbf{X}'\mathbf{X})^{-1}\mathbf{X}'\mathbf{Y}\mathbf{P}' - r_1^2\mathbf{I}| = 0$$

This shows that r_1^2 is a latent root of a symmetric and positive semidefinite matrix and hence that it is real and nonnegative. To prove that r_1^2 is at most equal to 1 we write (1) in the form:

$$[\mathbf{Y}'\mathbf{M}\mathbf{Y} - (1 - r_1^2)\mathbf{Y}'\mathbf{Y}]\mathbf{k}_1 = \mathbf{0} \qquad \text{where} \qquad \mathbf{M} = \mathbf{I} - \mathbf{X}(\mathbf{X}'\mathbf{X})^{-1}\mathbf{X}'$$

and apply exactly the same argument.

[10] Note that—as in Section 4.1—correlation coefficients are defined here in terms of the original values of the variables (including a constant-term variable if such a term is present), not in terms of deviations from the means. This is in contrast to the rules formulated below eq. (4.7) of Section 4.4. It is true that in most applications one computes canonical correlation coefficients for variables measured as deviations from their means, but there are few economic applications. Their treatment at this point is mainly motivated by the usefulness of canonical correlation coefficients in providing insight into the joint GLS procedure.

square root of r_1^2, and we should obviously take the largest latent root to obtain the largest canonical correlation coefficient.

We can simplify (4.7) by using generalized inverses:

$$(\mathbf{Y}^+\mathbf{X}\mathbf{X}^+\mathbf{Y} - r_1^2\mathbf{I})\mathbf{k}_1 = \mathbf{0} \tag{4.9}$$

Premultiplying both sides by $\mathbf{Y}$, we obtain $(\mathbf{Y}\mathbf{Y}^+\mathbf{X}\mathbf{X}^+ - r_1^2\mathbf{I})\mathbf{Y}\mathbf{k}_1 = \mathbf{0}$, which shows that $\boldsymbol{\eta}_1 = \mathbf{Y}\mathbf{k}_1$ is a characteristic vector of $\mathbf{Y}\mathbf{Y}^+\mathbf{X}\mathbf{X}^+$ corresponding to the root r_1^2. It follows from symmetry considerations that $\boldsymbol{\xi}_1$ is then a characteristic vector of $\mathbf{X}\mathbf{X}^+\mathbf{Y}\mathbf{Y}^+$ corresponding to the same root. So we have

$$(\mathbf{X}\mathbf{X}^+\mathbf{Y}\mathbf{Y}^+ - r_1^2\mathbf{I})\boldsymbol{\xi}_1 = \mathbf{0} \qquad (\mathbf{Y}\mathbf{Y}^+\mathbf{X}\mathbf{X}^+ - r_1^2\mathbf{I})\boldsymbol{\eta}_1 = \mathbf{0} \tag{4.10}$$

Other Canonical Correlation Coefficients

The second largest canonical correlation coefficient r_2 is obtained by maximizing (4.3) subject to (4.2) with $i = 2$ under the orthogonality constraints (2) and (3) mentioned in the third paragraph of this section: $\boldsymbol{\xi}_1'\boldsymbol{\xi}_2 = \boldsymbol{\eta}_1'\boldsymbol{\eta}_2 = \boldsymbol{\xi}_1'\boldsymbol{\eta}_2 = \boldsymbol{\xi}_2'\boldsymbol{\eta}_1 = 0$. The derivation is a straightforward extension of that of the largest canonical correlation coefficient; the result is that r_2^2 is the second largest latent root of the matrices $\mathbf{X}\mathbf{X}^+\mathbf{Y}\mathbf{Y}^+$ and $\mathbf{Y}\mathbf{Y}^+\mathbf{X}\mathbf{X}^+$ and that $\boldsymbol{\xi}_2$ and $\boldsymbol{\eta}_2$ are characteristic vectors of these respective matrices corresponding to this root. More generally, the ith largest canonical correlation coefficient is found by maximizing (4.3) subject to (4.2) and to the condition that both $\boldsymbol{\xi}_i$ and $\boldsymbol{\eta}_i$ be orthogonal to all earlier $\boldsymbol{\xi}$'s and $\boldsymbol{\eta}$'s. The successive canonical correlation coefficients can be found from

$$\left.\begin{aligned}(\mathbf{X}\mathbf{X}^+\mathbf{Y}\mathbf{Y}^+ - r_i^2\mathbf{I})\boldsymbol{\xi}_i = \mathbf{0}\\ (\mathbf{Y}\mathbf{Y}^+\mathbf{X}\mathbf{X}^+ - r_i^2\mathbf{I})\boldsymbol{\eta}_i = \mathbf{0}\end{aligned}\right\} \quad i = 1, 2, \ldots, \min(K, L) \tag{4.11}$$

The orthogonality of the $\boldsymbol{\xi}$'s and $\boldsymbol{\eta}$'s which correspond to different roots is pursued in Problem 4.3.

The Mean Square Canonical Correlation Coefficient

Canonical correlation theory supplies us with several coefficients $r_1^2, r_2^2, \ldots$ which jointly measure the extent to which two sets of variables are linearly related. It is frequently convenient to use one summary measure, for which purpose one can take the average of the r_i^2, to be called the mean square canonical correlation coefficient:[11]

$$\bar{r}^2 = \frac{1}{\min(K, L)} \sum_i r_i^2 = \frac{\operatorname{tr} \mathbf{X}\mathbf{X}^+\mathbf{Y}\mathbf{Y}^+}{\min(K, L)} = \frac{\operatorname{tr} \mathbf{Y}\mathbf{Y}^+\mathbf{X}\mathbf{X}^+}{\min(L, K)} \tag{4.12}$$

[11] The idea of taking the sum of the squares of all canonical correlation coefficients was conceived by HOOPER (1959), who also defined analogous partial correlation coefficients (1962). However, he did not divide the sum of the squared canonical correlations by the minimum of K and L as is done here.

This measure takes the minimum value (zero) when each column of $\mathbf{X}$ is orthogonal to each column of $\mathbf{Y}$ because $\mathbf{X}'\mathbf{Y} = \mathbf{0}$ implies $\mathbf{X}^{+}\mathbf{Y} = \mathbf{0}$. The maximum value (unity) is reached when each column of $\mathbf{X}$ is a linear combination of the $\mathbf{Y}$ columns or when each $\mathbf{Y}$ column is a linear combination of the $\mathbf{X}$ columns. To prove this we note that the matrix (4.8) is equal to the inverse of $\mathbf{Y}'\mathbf{Y}$ postmultiplied by $\mathbf{Y}'\mathbf{X}(\mathbf{X}'\mathbf{X})^{-1}\mathbf{X}'\mathbf{Y}$, the matrix of sums of squares and products of the LS computed values of the L dependent variables in their regressions on $\mathbf{X}$. This matrix is equal to $\mathbf{Y}'\mathbf{Y}$ if each column of $\mathbf{Y}$ is a linear function of the columns of $\mathbf{X}$ (zero LS residuals), so that (4.8) is then the $L \times L$ unit matrix. We conclude from (4.7) that we have L canonical correlation coefficients all equal to one in that case. Since K cannot be smaller than L,[12] we also have $\min(K, L) = L$ and hence $\bar{r}^2 = 1$. The argument for the case of $\mathbf{X}$ columns which depend linearly on the $\mathbf{Y}$ columns is completely analogous. Note also that $\bar{r}^2$ contains the single-equation R^2 as a special case [$L = 1$, which is equal to $\min(K, L)$ in that case].

Unbiased Estimation of the Contemporaneous Covariance Matrix

The only difference between $\hat{\boldsymbol{\beta}}$ of (2.19) and $\mathbf{b}_J$ of (2.26) is the use of the estimator $\mathbf{S}$ defined in (2.25). Note that $\mathbf{S}$ is not an unbiased estimator of $\boldsymbol{\Sigma}$. To verify this statement, consider the expectation of the inner product of two LS residual vectors:

$$\begin{aligned}(4.13)\qquad \mathscr{E}(\mathbf{e}_j'\mathbf{e}_l) &= \mathscr{E}\{\boldsymbol{\epsilon}_j'[\mathbf{I} - \mathbf{X}_j(\mathbf{X}_j'\mathbf{X}_j)^{-1}\mathbf{X}_j'][\mathbf{I} - \mathbf{X}_l(\mathbf{X}_l'\mathbf{X}_l)^{-1}\mathbf{X}_l']\boldsymbol{\epsilon}_l\} \\ &= \sigma_{jl}(\operatorname{tr}\mathbf{I} - \operatorname{tr}\mathbf{X}_j\mathbf{X}_j^{+} - \operatorname{tr}\mathbf{X}_l\mathbf{X}_l^{+} + \operatorname{tr}\mathbf{X}_j\mathbf{X}_j^{+}\mathbf{X}_l\mathbf{X}_l^{+}) \\ &= \sigma_{jl}(n - K_j - K_l + \operatorname{tr}\mathbf{X}_j\mathbf{X}_j^{+}\mathbf{X}_l\mathbf{X}_l^{+})\end{aligned}$$

Going back to (4.12), we define

$$(4.14)\qquad \bar{r}_{jl}^2 = \frac{\operatorname{tr}\mathbf{X}_j\mathbf{X}_j^{+}\mathbf{X}_l\mathbf{X}_l^{+}}{\min(K_j, K_l)}$$

This is the mean square canonical correlation of the explanatory variables in the jth and the lth equations. Combining (4.13) and (4.14), we find that the following estimator of σ_{jl} is unbiased:

$$\begin{aligned}(4.15)\qquad \hat{\sigma}_{jl} &= \frac{\mathbf{e}_j'\mathbf{e}_l}{n - K_j - K_l + \bar{r}_{jl}^2\min(K_j, K_l)} \\ &= \frac{\mathbf{e}_j'\mathbf{e}_l}{n - \max(K_j, K_l) - (1 - \bar{r}_{jl}^2)\min(K_j, K_l)}\end{aligned}$$

[12] It is assumed that $\mathbf{Y}$ has full column rank, so that the L columns of $\mathbf{Y}$ are linearly independent. They can then be linear functions of the K columns of $\mathbf{X}$ only if $K \geq L$.

For $j = l$ (the variance estimator) we obtain the familiar result that the residual sum of squares is to be divided by $n - K_j$; this follows directly from $\bar{r}_{jj}^2 = 1$. For $j \neq l$ our divisor is *at most* equal to the *smaller* of the values $n - K_j$ and $n - K_l$. When the columns of $\mathbf{X}_j$ are all orthogonal to the columns of $\mathbf{X}_l$, so that $\bar{r}_{jl}^2 = 0$, we have to divide by $n - K_j - K_l$, which is the lowest possible value. The bias of s_{jl} is evidently more important than that of s_{jj} and s_{ll} and it increases in importance as the explanatory variables of the two equations are less and less linearly related.

It should be noted that although $\hat{\mathbf{\Sigma}} = [\hat{\sigma}_{jl}]$ is an unbiased estimator of $\mathbf{\Sigma}$, $\hat{\mathbf{\Sigma}}^{-1}$ is not an unbiased estimator of $\mathbf{\Sigma}^{-1}$, and it is in the form of this inverse that $\mathbf{\Sigma}$ plays a role in (2.19).[13] Also note that $\hat{\mathbf{\Sigma}}$ is not necessarily positive definite (see Problem 4.5); therefore it is doubtful whether $\hat{\mathbf{\Sigma}}$ is really superior to $\mathbf{S}$.

Analysis of the Two-Equation Case

When there are two equations ($L = 2$), the covariance matrix (2.20) of the Aitken estimator $\hat{\boldsymbol{\beta}}$ can be written as

$$(4.16) \qquad \mathscr{V}(\hat{\boldsymbol{\beta}}) = \begin{bmatrix} \sigma^{11}\mathbf{X}_1'\mathbf{X}_1 & \sigma^{12}\mathbf{X}_1'\mathbf{X}_2 \\ \sigma^{21}\mathbf{X}_2'\mathbf{X}_1 & \sigma^{22}\mathbf{X}_2'\mathbf{X}_2 \end{bmatrix}^{-1}$$

Using the partitioned inverse (2.15) of Section 1.2, we find for the covariance matrix of the coefficient subvector $\hat{\boldsymbol{\beta}}_1$ corresponding to the first equation:

$$(4.17) \qquad \begin{aligned} \mathscr{V}(\hat{\boldsymbol{\beta}}_1) &= [\sigma^{11}\mathbf{X}_1'\mathbf{X}_1 - \sigma^{12}\mathbf{X}_1'\mathbf{X}_2(\sigma^{22}\mathbf{X}_2'\mathbf{X}_2)^{-1}\sigma^{21}\mathbf{X}_2'\mathbf{X}_1]^{-1} \\ &= \sigma_1^2(1 - \rho^2)[\mathbf{X}_1'\mathbf{X}_1 - \rho^2\mathbf{X}_1'\mathbf{X}_2(\mathbf{X}_2'\mathbf{X}_2)^{-1}\mathbf{X}_2'\mathbf{X}_1]^{-1} \end{aligned}$$

where $\sigma_{11} = \sigma_1^2$, $\sigma_{22} = \sigma_2^2$, $\sigma_{12} = \rho\sigma_1\sigma_2$. A comparison of this matrix will be made with the covariance matrix $\sigma_1^2(\mathbf{X}_1'\mathbf{X}_1)^{-1}$ of the LS estimator, based on the generalized variances.[14] Consider the identity

$$\begin{aligned} \mathbf{X}_1'\mathbf{X}_1 - \rho^2\mathbf{X}_1'\mathbf{X}_2(\mathbf{X}_2'\mathbf{X}_2)^{-1}\mathbf{X}_2'\mathbf{X}_1 &= \mathbf{X}_1'\mathbf{X}_1[\mathbf{I} - \rho^2(\mathbf{X}_1'\mathbf{X}_1)^{-1}\mathbf{X}_1'\mathbf{X}_2(\mathbf{X}_2'\mathbf{X}_2)^{-1}\mathbf{X}_2'\mathbf{X}_1] \\ &= \mathbf{X}_1'\mathbf{X}_1(\mathbf{I} - \rho^2\mathbf{X}_1^+\mathbf{X}_2\mathbf{X}_2^+\mathbf{X}_1) \end{aligned}$$

The generalized variance of $\hat{\boldsymbol{\beta}}_1$ can then be written as follows:

$$(4.18) \qquad |\mathscr{V}(\hat{\boldsymbol{\beta}}_1)| = |\sigma_1^2(\mathbf{X}_1'\mathbf{X}_1)^{-1}| \frac{(1 - \rho^2)^{K_1}}{|\mathbf{I} - \rho^2\mathbf{X}_1^+\mathbf{X}_2\mathbf{X}_2^+\mathbf{X}_1|}$$

Now $|\sigma_1^2(\mathbf{X}_1'\mathbf{X}_1)^{-1}|$ is the generalized variance of the LS estimator $\mathbf{b}_1$ and the determinant of $\mathbf{I} - \rho^2\mathbf{X}_1^+\mathbf{X}_2\mathbf{X}_2^+\mathbf{X}_1$ is equal to the product of the latent roots of

[13] This $\mathbf{\Sigma}^{-1}$ occurs in the covariance matrix (2.20) in an expression which is also inverted. This makes the problem of unbiased estimation of the matrix (2.20) highly intractable. See also the last two subsections of Section 12.7 below.

[14] For the generalized variance of a vector estimator (the determinant value of its covariance matrix) see Problems 4.1 and 4.2 at the end of Section 3.4.

this matrix. But every positive root r_i^2 of $|\mathbf{X}_1^+\mathbf{X}_2\mathbf{X}_2^+\mathbf{X}_1 - r_i^2\mathbf{I}| = 0$ is, in view of (4.11), a squared canonical correlation coefficient of the two sets of explanatory variables.[15] Since we can write this determinantal equation in the equivalent form

$$|\mathbf{I} - \rho^2\mathbf{X}_1^+\mathbf{X}_2\mathbf{X}_2^+\mathbf{X}_1 - (1 - \rho^2 r_i^2)\mathbf{I}| = 0 \tag{4.19}$$

we conclude that the determinant that occurs in the right-hand denominator of (4.18) is equal to the product over i of $1 - \rho^2 r_i^2$. Therefore our result can be written as follows:

$$\frac{|\mathscr{V}(\hat{\boldsymbol{\beta}}_1)|}{|\mathscr{V}(\mathbf{b}_1)|} = \prod_{i=1}^{K_1} \frac{1 - \rho^2}{1 - \rho^2 r_i^2} \tag{4.20}$$

where it is to be understood that if $K_2 < K_1$, $r_i^2 = 0$ for $i > K_2$.

The result (4.20) shows clearly that there is no gain for $\hat{\boldsymbol{\beta}}_1$ in the case of zero contemporaneous covariances ($\rho = 0$). It also shows that there is no gain either when all K_1 canonical correlation coefficients are equal to unity. This situation occurs when the two equations have the same explanatory variables, but that is more than is really needed; a sufficient condition is that each explanatory variable of the first equation can be expressed as a linear function of the explanatory variables of the second equation. The gain of $\hat{\boldsymbol{\beta}}_1$ is evidently large when the disturbances of the two equations are highly dependent [because a large absolute ρ forces the right-hand numerator $1 - \rho^2$ of (4.20) to be a small number] and when, at the same time, the explanatory variables are orthogonal or close to orthogonality (because small values of the canonical correlation coefficients r_i force the denominator $1 - \rho^2 r_i^2$ to be a number close to unity even if ρ^2 is large). It is interesting to consider this result from the viewpoint of the two sets of factors that determine the values taken by the dependent variable: those which are introduced explicitly in the equation as explanatory variables and those which are neglected and only represented by a random disturbance. The implication of (4.20) is that joint estimation of the parameters of two such equations is particularly useful when the first set of determining factors of the first equation shows a development that is largely unrelated to that of the second equation and when the random parts (the second set) are highly related.

An Exact Comparison of LS and Joint GLS Estimators under Conditions of Normality and Orthogonality

The previous subsection deals with $\hat{\boldsymbol{\beta}}$ which is based on $\boldsymbol{\Sigma}$, but $\boldsymbol{\Sigma}$ is usually unknown. We may then replace $\boldsymbol{\Sigma}$ by $\mathbf{S}$ to obtain $\mathbf{b}_J$ of (2.26), or we may use

[15] Substitute $\mathbf{Y}\mathbf{k}_i$ for $\boldsymbol{\eta}_i$ in the second equation of (4.11) and write the result in the form $\mathbf{Y}(\mathbf{Y}^+\mathbf{X}\mathbf{X}^+\mathbf{Y} - r_i^2\mathbf{I})\mathbf{k}_i = \mathbf{0}$. This is equivalent to (4.9) for the subscript i instead of 1 because of the linear independence of the columns of $\mathbf{Y}$.

$\hat{\boldsymbol{\Sigma}} = [\hat{\sigma}_{jl}]$ of (4.15) as an estimator of $\boldsymbol{\Sigma}$. However, this raises another problem. Suppose that $\boldsymbol{\Sigma}$ is in fact diagonal, so that LS applied to each equation separately is best linear unbiased. In general, S and $\hat{\boldsymbol{\Sigma}}$ will not be diagonal because of sampling errors. The joint estimator is then different from the LS estimator, and it seems plausible that replacing a true diagonal $\boldsymbol{\Sigma}$ by a nondiagonal estimator does not lead to a better coefficient estimator.[16] To what extent is this really serious? Intuitively, one should expect that even

Table 7.3

A Correction Factor for Some Values of ρ and $n - K_1 - K_2$

	$n - K_1 - K_2$						
$\lvert\rho\rvert$	10	15	20	25	30	35	∞
0	1.15	1.12	1.10	1.09	1.08	1.07	1.00
.1	1.14	1.11	1.09	1.08	1.07	1.06	.99
.2	1.11	1.07	1.05	1.04	1.03	1.03	.96
.3	1.05	1.02	1.00	.99	.98	.97	.91
.4	.97	.94	.92	.91	.90	.90	.84
.5	.87	.84	.82	.81	.81	.80	.75
.6	.74	.71	.70	.70	.69	.69	.64
.7	.59	.57	.56	.55	.55	.55	.51
.8	.42	.40	.40	.39	.39	.39	.36
.9	.22	.21	.21	.21	.20	.20	.19

if $\boldsymbol{\Sigma}$ is not diagonal but is such that the off-diagonal elements are sufficiently small, the LS procedure applied to the L equations separately may be preferable to the joint GLS procedure.

This problem was considered by ZELLNER (1963b) for the two-equation case under the orthogonality condition $\mathbf{X}_1'\mathbf{X}_2 = \mathbf{0}$ and the additional specification of normality. He proved that $\mathbf{b}_J$ is unbiased (in spite of the use of S rather than $\boldsymbol{\Sigma}$) and that the covariance matrix of its subvector of coefficients of the first equation can be obtained by multiplying the LS covariance matrix $\sigma_1^2(\mathbf{X}_1'\mathbf{X}_1)^{-1}$ by a scalar correction factor which is determined by $n - K_1 - K_2$ and the absolute value of ρ. If this correction factor exceeds 1, the joint estimation procedure is inferior to LS according to the quadratic criterion. Table 7.3 shows that this is the case when $|\rho|$ is sufficiently small. But when $|\rho|$ is of the order of .4 or larger, the joint procedure has a clear advantage,

[16] It may seem that $\mathbf{b}_J$ is definitely inferior on the basis of the Gauss-Markov criterion. However, this criterion cannot be easily applied here, since $\mathbf{b}_J$ is a nonlinear estimator owing to its dependence on S.

particularly when the number of observations is not small. When n increases indefinitely, the correction factor converges to $1 - \rho^2$ in accordance with (4.17) for $\mathbf{X}_1'\mathbf{X}_2 = \mathbf{0}$.

It should indeed be stressed that Table 7.3 is based on the orthogonality assumption $\mathbf{X}_1'\mathbf{X}_2 = \mathbf{0}$, which implies that the canonical correlation coefficients r_i of (4.20) all vanish. Recall from the discussion below that equation that this is the most favorable situation for the joint estimation technique as far as the behavior of the explanatory variables is concerned. Therefore, Table 7.3 gives an optimistic picture of the merits of this technique. This can be illustrated for the investment example. If we use the matrix (1.10) to estimate ρ, we obtain .73, so that the reduction factor is approximately .5 ($n = 20$, $K_1 = K_2 = 3$). Table 7.2 of Section 7.1 shows that there is indeed a reduction of the sampling variances, but it is certainly not that large. This is because the condition $\mathbf{X}_1'\mathbf{X}_2 = \mathbf{0}$ is not satisfied at all. Note that this condition cannot possibly be satisfied when both equations have constant terms, since one of the diagonal elements of $\mathbf{X}_1'\mathbf{X}_2$ is then $\boldsymbol{\iota}'\boldsymbol{\iota} = n$. Also note that Table 7.3 can only serve as a general indication because ρ is not really known; if ρ were known, the problem discussed here would cease to exist.

Problems

4.1 Prove directly (not by means of symmetry considerations) that $\boldsymbol{\xi}_1$ is a characteristic vector of the matrix $\mathbf{XX}^+\mathbf{YY}^+$ corresponding to the root r_1^2 as stated in (4.10).

4.2 Prove $\boldsymbol{\xi}_i'\mathbf{XX}^+ = \boldsymbol{\xi}_i'$ and use this to derive from (4.11) the following explicit expressions for the square of a canonical correlation coefficient:

$$r_i^2 = \boldsymbol{\xi}_i'\mathbf{Y}(\mathbf{Y}'\mathbf{Y})^{-1}\mathbf{Y}'\boldsymbol{\xi}_i = \boldsymbol{\eta}_i'\mathbf{X}(\mathbf{X}'\mathbf{X})^{-1}\mathbf{X}'\boldsymbol{\eta}_i \tag{4.21}$$

4.3 (*Continuation*) Premultiply both sides of the first equation of (4.11) by $\boldsymbol{\xi}_j'$ and prove that the result can be written as $\boldsymbol{\xi}_j'\mathbf{YY}^+\boldsymbol{\xi}_i = r_i^2\boldsymbol{\xi}_j'\boldsymbol{\xi}_i$. Take the same equation with subscript j rather than i and premultiply both sides by $\boldsymbol{\xi}_i'$. Subtract the two results and prove $\boldsymbol{\xi}_i'\boldsymbol{\xi}_j = 0$ when $r_i^2 \neq r_j^2$. (*Hint.* $\mathbf{YY}^+$ is symmetric.) Provide an analogous proof for $\boldsymbol{\eta}_i'\boldsymbol{\eta}_j = 0$ under the same condition. Finally, premultiply both sides of the first equation of (4.11) by $\boldsymbol{\eta}_j'$ and both sides of the second (with i replaced by j) by $\boldsymbol{\xi}_i'$ to prove $\boldsymbol{\xi}_i'\boldsymbol{\eta}_j = 0$ when $r_i^2 \neq r_j^2$.

4.4 Compare canonical correlation theory with the principal component analysis of Section 1.9. Explain in words the similarities and the differences.

4.5 As an example of an indefinite matrix $[\hat{\sigma}_{jl}] = \hat{\boldsymbol{\Sigma}}$ [see (4.15)], consider the following two-equation case with three observations:

$$\text{(4.22)} \quad \mathbf{X}_1 = \begin{bmatrix} 1 \\ 0 \\ 0 \end{bmatrix} \quad \mathbf{X}_2 = \begin{bmatrix} 1 & 0 \\ 0 & 1 \\ 0 & 0 \end{bmatrix} \quad \mathbf{y}_1 = \begin{bmatrix} a_1 \\ a_2 \\ a_3 \end{bmatrix} \quad \mathbf{y}_2 = \begin{bmatrix} b_1 \\ b_2 \\ b_3 \end{bmatrix}$$

Prove that the LS residual vectors are $\mathbf{e}_1' = [0 \quad a_2 \quad a_3]$ and $\mathbf{e}_2' = [0 \quad 0 \quad b_3]$ and that the matrix of their sums of squares and products is

$$\text{(4.23)} \qquad [\mathbf{e}_j'\mathbf{e}_l) = \begin{bmatrix} a_2^2 + a_3^2 & a_3 b_3 \\ a_3 b_3 & b_3^2 \end{bmatrix}$$

Prove that this matrix is positive semidefinite and that it is positive definite when a_2 and b_3 are both nonzero. Also prove that $\hat{\boldsymbol{\Sigma}}$ is indefinite when $|a_2| < |a_3|$.

4.6 Prove that the estimator (2.19) for $L = 2$ under the orthogonality condition $\mathbf{X}_1'\mathbf{X}_2 = \mathbf{0}$ consists of two subvectors $\hat{\boldsymbol{\beta}}_1$ and $\hat{\boldsymbol{\beta}}_2$:

$$\text{(4.24)} \qquad \hat{\boldsymbol{\beta}}_1 = \mathbf{b}_1 - \frac{\rho\sigma_1}{\sigma_2}\mathbf{X}_1^+\mathbf{y}_2 \qquad \hat{\boldsymbol{\beta}}_2 = \mathbf{b}_2 - \frac{\rho\sigma_2}{\sigma_1}\mathbf{X}_2^+\mathbf{y}_1$$

where $\mathbf{b}_1 = \mathbf{X}_1^+\mathbf{y}_1$ and $\mathbf{b}_2 = \mathbf{X}_2^+\mathbf{y}_2$ are the LS coefficient vectors and $\sigma_{11} = \sigma_1^2$, $\sigma_{22} = \sigma_2^2$, $\sigma_{12} = \rho\sigma_1\sigma_2$.

7.5 The Consumer's Allocation Problem: (1) Demand Equations in Infinitesimal Changes[C]

In this and the next two sections we present a more elaborate example of joint estimation and of linear constraints on the coefficients of different equations. We are concerned with the consumer's problem of how to allocate his income to N commodities, given the prices of these commodities and the level of his income. The particular model to be discussed is the Rotterdam model developed by BARTEN and THEIL; see, for example, Theil (1967, Chapters 6 and 7).[17] This section gives a brief outline of the model in infinitesimal changes; a more elaborate account is provided in Appendix A at the end of this book. The transition to finite changes as well as a set of data will be discussed in Section 7.6, and the estimation procedure [which is closely related to that of Barten (1965)] in Section 7.7. The model is further analyzed in Sections 11.6 to 11.9 and 12.7.

[17] Other similar models have been proposed by STONE (1954b), FRISCH (1959), and HOUTHAKKER (1960); for a comparative survey, see GOLDBERGER (1967). Also see POWELL (1966) and AYANIAN (1969).

Demand Equations in Money Income and Absolute Prices

Write $q_1, \ldots, q_N$ for the quantities bought and consumed and $u(q_1, \ldots, q_N)$ for the consumer's utility function. This function measures the satisfaction enjoyed by the consumer when he buys and consumes, in any given time period, q_1 units of the first commodity, q_2 units of the second, and so on. The consumer wishes to maximize this utility function subject to the budget constraint $\sum p_i q_i = m$, where $p_1, \ldots, p_N$ are the prices of the N commodities and m is total expenditure. (For the sake of convenience we shall refer to m as income in the sequel.) It is assumed that the p's and m are fixed positive numbers from the consumer's point of view. Then it can be shown that under appropriate conditions on the form of the utility function, there exists a unique set of optimal quantities $q_1^0, \ldots, q_N^0$ which maximize the utility function subject to the budget constraint for any set of given (positive) prices and income. Let us write the dependence of these optimal quantities on income and prices as follows:

$$q_i^0 = Q_i(m, p_1, \ldots, p_N) \qquad i = 1, \ldots, N \tag{5.1}$$

This is the demand function for the ith commodity. Our goal in this and the next sections will be to formulate and estimate such a system of N demand equations.

Demand Equations in Real Income and Absolute Prices

The formulation of the system is simplified by the recognition that the optimal quantities are not affected when income and prices are all multiplied by a positive factor k. This follows from the fact that the constraints $\sum p_i q_i = m$ and $\sum (kp_i)q_i = km$ are equivalent, and that the utility function does not involve income and prices at all. Hence we may write our demand functions in terms of income and prices divided by some price index. For our purposes the most convenient procedure is to formulate demand in terms of real income and the original (absolute) prices,

$$q_i^0 = q_i(\bar{m}, p_1, \ldots, p_N) \qquad i = 1, \ldots, N \tag{5.2}$$

where $\bar{m}$ is real income. At this stage we are not concerned with the appropriate index to be used to transform money income m to real income $\bar{m}$. In Section 11.6 we shall consider a demand model in which the prices are also deflated by an index.

The Substitution Effect of Price Changes

We proceed to a consideration of the derivatives of the N demand functions (5.2) with respect to the N prices. Note that these derivatives are not the same as those of the demand functions (5.1). If p_1 increases by dp_1, the optimal value of the ith quantity goes up by $(\partial Q_i/\partial p_1)\, dp_1$ according to (5.1); but the analogous expression $(\partial q_i/\partial p_1)\, dp_1$ based on (5.2) is different owing to the effect of a price change on real income. When we consider a price derivative of the demand equation (5.2), we implicitly assume that the price increase (dp_1) is compensated for by an increase in money income (m) so real income $(\bar{m})$ remains unchanged. In the language of classical demand theory, we confine ourselves to the *substitution effect* of a price change on the ith quantity when we consider a derivative $\partial q_i/\partial p_j$ of the demand function (5.2). Consider then the $N \times N$ matrix of these price derivatives,

$$\text{(5.3)} \qquad \frac{\partial \mathbf{q}}{\partial \mathbf{p}'} = \begin{bmatrix} \frac{\partial q_1}{\partial p_1} & \frac{\partial q_1}{\partial p_2} & \cdots & \frac{\partial q_1}{\partial p_N} \\ \frac{\partial q_2}{\partial p_1} & \frac{\partial q_2}{\partial p_2} & \cdots & \frac{\partial q_2}{\partial p_N} \\ \cdot & \cdot & & \cdot \\ \cdot & \cdot & & \cdot \\ \cdot & \cdot & & \cdot \\ \frac{\partial q_N}{\partial p_1} & \frac{\partial q_N}{\partial p_2} & \cdots & \frac{\partial q_N}{\partial p_N} \end{bmatrix}$$

where $\mathbf{q}$ and $\mathbf{p}$ on the left are N-element column vectors. It can be shown under mild regularity conditions on the utility function that the matrix $\partial \mathbf{q}/\partial \mathbf{p}'$ is symmetric and negative semidefinite of rank $N - 1$. The linear dependence that leads to the singularity of the matrix is $(\partial \mathbf{q}/\partial \mathbf{p}')\mathbf{p} = \mathbf{0}$ or, in scalar terms,

$$\text{(5.4)} \qquad \sum_{j=1}^{N} \frac{\partial q_i}{\partial p_j} p_j = 0 \qquad i = 1, \ldots, N$$

The left-hand side of this equation is the effect on q_i^0 of proportionate changes in all prices. We know from the discussion above eq. (5.2) that this effect is zero, as (5.4) states, when income m also moves proportionately. This condition is indeed satisfied because the procedure of taking partial price derivatives in (5.2) implies that real income $\bar{m}$ remains constant, which is possible only if money income m increases proportionately with the prices.

Demand Equations with the Quantity Component of a Value Share Change as Dependent Variable

Consider the following demand equation which is formulated in terms of infinitesimal changes in natural logarithms:[18]

$$\text{(5.5)} \qquad d(\log q_i) = \frac{\partial(\log q_i)}{\partial(\log m)} d(\log \bar{m}) + \sum_{j=1}^{N} \frac{\partial(\log q_i)}{\partial(\log p_j)} d(\log p_j)$$

[18] All logarithms in this and the next two sections are natural logarithms.

Note that we may use either $\partial(\log q_i)/\partial(\log m)$ or $\partial(\log q_i)/\partial(\log \bar{m})$ for the first right-hand derivative in this equation, since the partial-derivative procedure implies that prices are kept constant. Further note that the right-hand derivatives are all elasticities, either income or price elasticities. The latter are of the following form:

$$\frac{\partial(\log q_i)}{\partial(\log p_j)} = \frac{\partial q_i}{\partial p_j}\frac{p_j}{q_i}$$

The derivative $\partial q_i/\partial p_j$ is symmetric in i and j because of the symmetry of $\partial \mathbf{q}/\partial \mathbf{p}'$ defined in (5.3), but the corresponding elasticity is not symmetric in the two indices. We shall use this symmetry condition as a constraint on the parameters that will appear in the final version of the model, so that the specification (5.5) will have to be modified. This is performed easily by multiplying both sides of the equation by $w_i = p_i q_i/m$, which is the *value share* of the ith commodity (its share of total expenditure). The result is

$$(5.6)\qquad w_i\, d(\log q_i) = \left(\frac{p_i q_i}{m}\frac{\partial q_i}{\partial m}\frac{m}{q_i}\right) d(\log \bar{m}) + \sum_{j=1}^{N}\left(\frac{p_i q_i}{m}\frac{\partial q_i}{\partial p_j}\frac{p_j}{q_i}\right) d(\log p_j)$$

$$= p_i \frac{\partial q_i}{\partial m} d(\log \bar{m}) + \sum_{j=1}^{N}\frac{p_i p_j}{m}\frac{\partial q_i}{\partial p_j} d(\log p_j)$$

The coefficient of $d(\log p_j)$ is now evidently symmetric. To interpret the left-hand variable of (5.6), consider an infinitesimal change in the value share $w_i = p_i q_i/m$:

$$(5.7)\qquad dw_i = \frac{q_i}{m}dp_i + \frac{p_i}{m}dq_i - \frac{p_i q_i}{m^2}dm$$

$$= w_i\, d(\log p_i) + w_i\, d(\log q_i) - w_i\, d(\log m)$$

The second line gives a simple decomposition of the change in the value share in terms of changes attributable to the change in the ith price, the change in the ith quantity, and the change in income. Comparing this result with (5.6), we conclude that the left-hand variable of the latter equation is nothing but the quantity component of the change in the ith value share.

Marginal Value Shares and Price Coefficients

We obtain a more concise formulation of the demand equations when we introduce

$$(5.8)\qquad \mu_i = p_i \frac{\partial q_i}{\partial m} \qquad \pi_{ij} = \frac{p_i p_j}{m}\frac{\partial q_i}{\partial p_j}$$

so that (5.6) becomes

$$w_i\, d(\log q_i) = \mu_i\, d(\log \bar{m}) + \sum_{j=1}^{N} \pi_{ij}\, d(\log p_j) \tag{5.9}$$

The coefficient $\mu_i = p_i(\partial q_i/\partial m) = \partial(p_i q_i)/\partial m$ is the *marginal value share* of the ith commodity: the additional amount spent on that commodity when income increases by 1 dollar per unit of time. These marginal value shares satisfy the constraint

$$\sum_{i=1}^{N} \mu_i = 1 \tag{5.10}$$

which is verified by differentiating both sides of the constraint $\sum p_i q_i = m$ with respect to m. The price coefficients π_{ij} form an $N \times N$ matrix $[\pi_{ij}]$ which is equal to the positive multiple $1/m$ of the matrix $\mathbf{P}(\partial \mathbf{q}/\partial \mathbf{p}')\mathbf{P}$, where $\mathbf{P}$ is a diagonal $N \times N$ matrix with the (positive) prices $p_1, \ldots, p_N$ on the diagonal. Since $\partial \mathbf{q}/\partial \mathbf{p}'$ is symmetric and negative semidefinite of rank $N - 1$, $[\pi_{ij}]$ has the same properties:

(5.11) $[\pi_{ij}]$ is symmetric and negative semidefinite of rank $N - 1$

The cause of the singularity is

$$\sum_{j=1}^{N} \pi_{ij} = 0 \qquad i = 1, \ldots, N \tag{5.12}$$

which follows directly from (5.8) and (5.4).

7.6 The Consumer's Allocation Problem: (2) Demand Equations in Finite Changes[C]

In the previous section we developed a consumer demand model in infinitesimal changes, consisting of N equations (5.9) whose coefficients are subject to the constraints (5.10) to (5.12). However, the form of the data forces us to work with finite rather than infinitesimal changes, and for this purpose we introduce the following explicit time series notation. Write t for any year, which takes the values $1, \ldots, T$, where T is the total number of years for which the relevant data are available. Write D for the log-change operator; that is, if x is any variable and x_t its value in year t, then

$$Dx_t = \Delta(\log x_t) = \log x_t - \log x_{t-1} = \log \frac{x_t}{x_{t-1}} \tag{6.1}$$

The log-change has the simple property:

$$D(x_t^{\alpha} y_t^{\beta}) = \alpha \log \frac{x_t}{x_{t-1}} + \beta \log \frac{y_t}{y_{t-1}} = \alpha D x_t + \beta D y_t \tag{6.2}$$

where α and β are arbitrary constants.

The demand equations in finite (annual) changes are then as follows:

(6.3)
$$w_{it}^* Dq_{it} = \mu_i Dq_t + \sum_{j=1}^{N} \pi_{ij} Dp_{jt} + \epsilon_{it} \qquad i = 1, \ldots, n$$

where the μ's and π's are coefficients which are subject to the constraints (5.10) to (5.12). It is immediately clear that the price term in the right-hand side of (6.3) is a finite-change extension of the corresponding term in (5.9). The other terms in (6.3) are not so evident and will be explained in the following three subsections.

The Dependent Variables of the Finite-Change Equations

The finite-change analogue of $d(\log q_i)$ is Dq_{it}. The former change is multiplied by w_i in the left-hand side of (5.9), but in the finite case we face the problem that w_{it} and $w_{i,t-1}$ are equally likely candidates as multipliers, because the log-changes are symmetric in t and $t - 1$.[19] The simplest solution is their average:

(6.4)
$$w_{it}^* = \frac{w_{i,t-1} + w_{it}}{2}$$

which has the desirable properties of being positive and symmetric in t and $t - 1$ and of adding up to one when summed over i. The left-hand variable in (6.3) is thus

(6.5)
$$w_{it}^* Dq_{it} = \frac{w_{i,t-1} + w_{it}}{2} \log \frac{q_{it}}{q_{i,t-1}}$$

The Real-Income Terms of the Finite-Change Equations

The first right-hand term in the infinitesimal equation (5.9) is the marginal value share μ_i multiplied by the change in the logarithm of real income. In the finite-change equation (6.3) we multiply μ_i by

(6.6)
$$Dq_t = \sum_{i=1}^{N} w_{it}^* Dq_{it}$$

which is the sum of the left-hand variables of all N demand equations. It is also a weighted average of the N quantity log-changes of the individual commodities, the weights w_{it}^* being the corresponding value share averages of the years $t - 1$ and t. Therefore we shall interpret Dq_t as the log-change of

[19] More specifically, log-changes are symmetric in the two periods apart from sign: $\log (x_t/x_{t-1}) = -\log (x_{t-1}/x_t)$.

a volume index (quantity index) for all N commodities jointly or, equivalently, as the log-change in real income.

An alternative procedure would be to define real income as the ratio of money income to a price index. In fact, this is more in line with the discussion around eq. (5.2). Consider then a price index whose log-change is of the same form as that of the volume index in (6.6):

$$(6.7) \qquad Dp_t = \sum_{i=1}^{N} w_{it}^* Dp_{it}$$

The log-change in real income under the alternative interpretation is $Dm_t - Dp_t$, where $m_t = \sum_i p_{it}q_{it}$. In order that this be identical with the log-change (6.6) we should have $Dp_t + Dq_t = Dm_t$. Therefore, consider:

$$(6.8) \qquad \begin{aligned} Dp_t + Dq_t &= \sum_{i=1}^{N} w_{it}^*(Dp_{it} + Dq_{it}) = \sum_{i=1}^{N} w_{it}^* D(p_{it}q_{it}) \\ &= \sum_{i=1}^{N} w_{it}^* D(w_{it}m_t) = \sum_{i=1}^{N} w_{it}^* Dw_{it} + Dm_t \end{aligned}$$

where use is made of (6.2) in the second and fourth steps. We conclude that it is not true that $Dp_t + Dq_t$ equals Dm_t and that the discrepancy is $\sum_i w_{it}^* Dw_{it}$; hence the volume index (6.6) differs from money income divided by the price index (6.7). However, the difference is usually quite small. By expanding $Dw_{it} = \log (w_{it}/w_{i,t-1})$ we find

$$(6.9) \qquad \sum_{i=1}^{N} w_{it}^* Dw_{it} \approx \frac{1}{12} \sum_{i=1}^{N} w_{it}^* \left(\frac{w_{it} - w_{i,t-1}}{w_{it}^*}\right)^3$$

where the right-hand side is of the third order of smallness when the ratio of the difference between w_{it} and $w_{i,t-1}$ to their average w_{it}^* is small of the first order.[20]

The reason Dq_t is preferred to $Dm_t - Dp_t$ is that it guarantees that the sum of the demand disturbances ϵ_{it} over i is always zero, which is in accordance with the assumptions on the disturbances that will now be described.

The Disturbances of the Finite-Change Equations

The last term (ϵ_{it}) in (6.3) is the demand disturbance, which is regarded as the random effect of all variables other than income and prices. It is assumed that it has zero expectation, that the variances and contemporaneous

[20] For a more detailed analysis of the expressions of the type (6.9), see Sections 5.2 and 5.4 of Theil (1967). See also Section 6.B of the same volume in which it is shown that Dq_t and $Dm_t - Dp_t$ are approximations to the true index of real income evaluated at prices which are geometric means of those in t and $t - 1$, and that both approximations are accurate to the second order in the price and income log-changes.

covariances are constant over time, and that all other covariances vanish:

$$\mathscr{E}(\epsilon_{is}\epsilon_{jt}) = \begin{cases} \omega_{ij} & \text{if} \quad s = t \\ 0 & \text{if} \quad s \neq t \end{cases} \tag{6.10}$$

The $N \times N$ matrix $[\omega_{ij}]$ is the covariance matrix of $[\epsilon_{1t} \quad \cdots \quad \epsilon_{Nt}]$ for any t.

When we sum both sides of the demand equations (6.3) over i from 1 through N, we obtain Dq_t on the left in view of (6.6). On the right we get

$$\begin{aligned} Dq_t\sum_{i=1}^{N}\mu_i + \sum_{j=1}^{N} Dp_{jt}\sum_{i=1}^{N}\pi_{ij} + \sum_{i=1}^{N}\epsilon_{it} &= Dq_t + \sum_{j=1}^{N} Dp_{jt}\sum_{i=1}^{N}\pi_{ji} + \sum_{i=1}^{N}\epsilon_{it} \\ &= Dq_t + \sum_{i=1}^{N}\epsilon_{it} \end{aligned}$$

where the first equality sign is based on (5.10) and the symmetry of $[\pi_{ij}]$ stated in (5.11), while the second is based on (5.12). Summation of the demand equations thus gives $Dq_t = Dq_t + \sum_i \epsilon_{it}$, which implies that the sum of the N demand disturbances vanishes with unit probability. The same obviously holds for

$$\epsilon_{it}(\epsilon_{1t} + \cdots + \epsilon_{Nt}) \qquad i = 1, \ldots, N$$

We take the expectation to find

$$\sum_{j=1}^{N}\omega_{ij} = 0 \qquad i = 1, \ldots, N \tag{6.11}$$

which means that $[\omega_{ij}]$ cannot have a rank larger than $N - 1$. It will be assumed that the matrix has exactly this rank. If its rank were $N - 2$ or less, we could combine a subset of the N demand equations (6.3) linearly so that the corresponding linear combination of the left-hand variables is an exact linear function of Dq_t, $Dp_{1t}, \ldots, Dp_{Nt}$, which is not plausible.

Description of the Data

The demand model (6.3) will be applied in the next section to data on four commodity groups in the Netherlands for the period 1922–1963 (with the exception of the war years and the immediate postwar period during which there was rationing). These data, which are all on a per capita basis as far as consumption and income are concerned, are shown in Table 7.4.[21] The four groups are:

1. *Food* with a value share (w_{1t}) of about 30 percent on the average in the period as a whole.

[21] The data are obtained by aggregating smaller commodity groups. They have been taken from Theil (1967, pp. 160, 240) and were collected by A. P. Barten.

2. *Vice* (tobacco, beverages, confectionery, and ice cream) with an average value share of about 10 percent.

3. *Durables* (including clothing and footwear) with a value share average of about 25 percent.

4. *Remainder* (all other commodities and services) accounting for about 35 percent.

Table 7.4

Data on Food (1), Vice (2), Durables (3) and Remainder (4) for the Estimation of a System on Demand Equations, the Netherlands 1922–1963

	$w_{1t}^*Dq_{1t}$	$w_{2t}^*Dq_{2t}$	$w_{3t}^*Dq_{3t}$	$w_{4t}^*Dq_{4t}$	Dp_{1t}	Dp_{2t}	Dp_{3t}	Dp_{4t}
				Prewar				
1922–1923	.05	−.32	−.94	−.61	−4.75	−1.23	−9.65	−.82
1923–1924	−.37	.20	−.11	−.31	.57	.23	.41	−.13
1924–1925	−1.84	−.14	−.38	1.24	3.31	−.86	.51	−1.18
1925–1926	1.50	.81	1.07	−.15	−6.87	−6.37	−7.13	−.88
1926–1927	.79	−.02	1.28	.21	−3.59	−.34	−.55	.53
1927–1928	.63	.34	.58	1.21	.94	−.58	.08	.74
1928–1929	−.36	.19	.60	.96	−.16	−4.87	−.07	.25
1929–1930	.67	.18	1.47	1.57	−6.50	−1.21	−7.99	−1.31
1930–1931	.90	−.24	−.91	.36	−12.79	−2.26	−6.58	−2.83
1931–1932	.66	−.60	−.14	−.95	−14.73	−6.21	−11.76	−3.20
1932–1933	−1.04	−.22	.54	−.03	−1.11	−4.99	−7.83	−3.10
1933–1934	−.74	−.34	−1.73	−.19	.47	−1.57	−2.65	−2.27
1934–1935	.06	.02	−.52	−.65	−3.71	−5.42	−3.37	−2.87
1935–1936	−.40	.14	2.17	.99	−.97	−2.81	−9.19	−3.76
1936–1937	−.19	.10	−.52	−.46	6.93	1.20	7.24	2.05
1937–1938	.07	.27	−1.52	.36	4.21	.38	4.25	.02
1938–1939	1.30	.40	2.24	1.24	−1.28	.37	5.18	.31
				Postwar				
1949–1950	.56	.07	.51	.04	11.63	3.78	9.27	5.36
1950–1951	.56	−.18	−2.82	−.35	7.58	8.98	14.09	9.58
1951–1952	.16	.09	−.65	−.54	4.01	1.11	−9.48	3.77
1952–1953	1.55	.49	1.39	1.46	−1.25	−.61	−1.59	−.32
1953–1954	1.28	.38	3.08	.60	3.52	2.29	.86	6.59
1954–1955	.36	.27	3.07	1.90	1.27	.46	−.29	3.42
1955–1956	.89	.80	3.31	1.51	3.94	−.74	−.71	2.93
1956–1957	−.69	.30	−.03	−.15	4.74	6.96	.92	6.37
1957–1958	.69	−.15	−.85	−.37	−2.10	3.87	−.68	5.07
1958–1959	.44	.38	1.17	.93	1.83	−.17	−.07	1.24
1959–1960	.90	.41	2.77	1.41	−1.01	−.32	1.52	4.57
1960–1961	1.12	.60	1.97	.51	2.02	.47	.80	2.45
1961–1962	.65	.35	1.57	1.11	2.95	.83	.90	3.02
1962–1963	.89	.48	2.71	1.24	3.32	1.30	1.14	3.96

Note. All figures are to be divided by 100.

The first line of the table shows that the log-change of the price level of foods in 1923 from the level of 1922 is $-.0475$, which amounts to a decline of almost 5 percent. The first four columns contain the quantity components of the value share changes. Adding the four figures in each row gives, in view of (6.6), the log-change in real income. For example, if we take the first row, we obtain $.05 - .32 - .94 - .61 = -1.82$, which means that the 1923 level of real per capita income is almost 2 percent below that of 1922.

Problems

6.1 Prove for the log-change Dw_{it} in (6.9):

$$(6.12)\quad Dw_{it} = \log\left(1 + \frac{w_{it} - w_{i,t-1}}{2w_{it}^*}\right) - \log\left(1 - \frac{w_{it} - w_{i,t-1}}{2w_{it}^*}\right)$$

Expand the logarithms in the right-hand side and use the result to prove that the approximation (6.9) has an error term of the fifth degree.

6.2 Consider the sum of all numbers in the first four columns of Table 7.4 for the years 1922 through 1939. Show how this sum can be used to compute the percentage increase of real income per capita over this 17-year period.

7.7 The Consumer's Allocation Problem: (3) Testing and Estimation[C]

The discussion will start with the singularity of the covariance matrix $[\omega_{ij}]$, after which we shall consider the various constraints on the unknown parameters. We then present parameter estimates which are not derived subject to the symmetry constraints $\pi_{ij} = \pi_{ji}$; we test these constraints and thereafter consider estimates that satisfy them.

One of the Demand Equations May Be Deleted

Consider the sum of the first three demand equations (6.3):

$$(7.1)\qquad \sum_{i=1}^{3} w_{it}^* Dq_{it} = \left(\sum_{i=1}^{3}\mu_i\right) Dq_t + \sum_{j=1}^{4}\left(\sum_{i=1}^{3}\pi_{ij}\right) Dp_{jt} + \sum_{i=1}^{3}\epsilon_{it}$$

The left-hand side is equal to $Dq_t - w_{4t}^* Dq_{4t}$ in view of (6.6). The first term on the right is $(1 - \mu_4)Dq_t$ because of (5.10). For the coefficient of Dp_{jt}

we have

$$\sum_{i=1}^{3} \pi_{ij} = \sum_{i=1}^{3} \pi_{ji} = -\pi_{j4} = -\pi_{4j}$$

where the first and third steps are based on the symmetry of $[\pi_{ij}]$ and the second on (5.12). Since the disturbance sum in (7.1) is $-\epsilon_{4t}$ (because the four ϵ's have zero sum), we conclude that the sum of the first three demand equations can be written as

$$Dq_t - w_{4t}^* Dq_{4t} = (1 - \mu_4) Dq_t - \sum_{j=1}^{4} \pi_{4j} Dp_{jt} - \epsilon_{4t} \tag{7.2}$$

which is trivially equivalent to the fourth demand equation. In other words, this fourth equation is a redundant repetition of the first three. It follows directly from the result of Problems 7.3 and 7.4 at the end of Section 6.7 that we may simply delete this fourth equation.

General Discussion of the Constraints

The constraints (5.10) to (5.12) on the parameters may be conveniently divided into three groups. One is the negative semidefiniteness of $[\pi_{ij}]$, which can be formulated in determinantal form as follows:

$$\pi_{11} \leq 0 \qquad \begin{vmatrix} \pi_{11} & \pi_{12} \\ \pi_{21} & \pi_{22} \end{vmatrix} \geq 0 \qquad \begin{vmatrix} \pi_{11} & \pi_{12} & \pi_{13} \\ \pi_{21} & \pi_{22} & \pi_{23} \\ \pi_{31} & \pi_{32} & \pi_{33} \end{vmatrix} \leq 0 \tag{7.3}$$

This is a kth degree polynomial inequality for the kth order determinant. We shall consider these constraints only by verifying, in the last paragraph of this section, whether they are satisfied by the point estimates of the π's.[22]

The second group of constraints is that of the symmetry of $[\pi_{ij}]$:

$$\pi_{12} = \pi_{21} \qquad \pi_{13} = \pi_{31} \qquad \pi_{23} = \pi_{32} \tag{7.4}$$

and the third is that of the singularity of $[\pi_{ij}]$:

$$\begin{aligned} \pi_{11} + \pi_{12} + \pi_{13} + \pi_{14} &= 0 \\ \pi_{21} + \pi_{22} + \pi_{23} + \pi_{24} &= 0 \\ \pi_{31} + \pi_{32} + \pi_{33} + \pi_{34} &= 0 \end{aligned} \tag{7.5}$$

Note that the symmetry constraints $\pi_{i4} = \pi_{4i}$ are ineffective, because π_{4i} ceases to be a parameter of the demand system when the fourth demand

[22] The simplest case of a linear inequality (such as $\pi_{11} \leq 0$) will be considered in more detail in Section 7.9.

equation is deleted. The same is true for $\sum \pi_{4j} = 0$ and $\sum \mu_j = 1$ (sum over j from 1 through 4).

The constraints (7.5) will be imposed in all computations described below, but the symmetry constraints (7.4) will be tested and then imposed when the test shows that they are acceptable on the basis of our data. The estimates derived under (7.5) but not under (7.4) will be called the *unconstrained estimates* [even though they are forced to satisfy (7.5)]; the estimates derived under both sets of conditions will be called the *symmetry-constrained estimates.*

Unconstrained Estimation

Condition (7.5) can be written as $\pi_{i4} = -\pi_{i1} - \pi_{i2} - \pi_{i3}$, and it is readily verified that substitution of the right-hand side of this equation for π_{i4} gives (for $i = 1, 2, 3$):

$$w_{it}^* Dq_{it} = \mu_i Dq_t + \sum_{j=1}^{3} \pi_{ij}(Dp_{jt} - Dp_{4t}) + \epsilon_{it} \tag{7.6}$$

This means that the price of the fourth commodity is used as a deflator of the other prices: $Dp_{jt} - Dp_{4t} = D(p_{jt}/p_{4t})$. If we disregard the symmetry conditions (7.4), the three equations (7.6) fall under the case of identical explanatory variables. There are four such variables: Dq_t and $Dp_{jt} - Dp_{4t}$ for $j = 1$, 2 and 3, and there is no constant term. The disturbances are assumed to have zero mean, constant contemporaneous covariances, and zero lagged covariances [see (6.10)]. Therefore the LS estimator of each equation separately is best linear unbiased if we decide not to use the symmetry conditions (7.4). The results are shown in the first three lines of Table 7.5. The last element of each line is the point estimate of π_{i4} and its

Table 7.5

Constrained and Unconstrained GLS Estimates of the Demand Model

Commodity Group	μ_i	π_{ij}			
		Unconstrained estimates			
Food	.153(.033)	−.104(.025)	−.039(.049)	.044(.023)	.100(.045)
Vice	.086(.013)	.023(.010)	−.031(.019)	.002(.009)	.006(.018)
Durables	.490(.034)	.053(.026)	.015(.052)	−.047(.024)	−.022(.048)
Remainder	.271(.031)	.029(.024)	.055(.048)	.001(.022)	−.084(.044)
		Symmetry-constrained estimates			
Food	.179(.027)	−.107(.025)	.022(.009)	.043(.020)	.042(.020)
Vice	.088(.012)		−.027(.018)	.002(.009)	.003(.016)
Durables	.482(.028)			−.044(.024)	−.001(.017)
Remainder	.251(.027)				−.044(.027)

standard error. The point estimate is minus the sum of the estimates of π_{i1}, π_{i2}, and π_{i3} in view of (7.5); the standard error is computed from the sum of the estimated sampling variances and covariances of these estimates.[23] Since (7.2) represents the sum of the first three demand equations, we can derive the estimates and their standard errors of μ_4 and π_{4j} from μ_i and π_{ij} ($i = 1, 2, 3$), respectively. Equivalently, we can estimate the fourth demand equation in the form (7.6) for $i = 4$ directly (see Problem 7.2). Notice that the sum over i of the point estimates of μ_i and of π_{ij} (each j) is equal to unity and to zero, respectively.

Preliminary Discussion of the Symmetry Constraints

Since we want to test the symmetry constraints (7.4), it is appropriate to inspect the relevant point estimates and their standard errors of the unconstrained estimation procedure:

$$\begin{aligned} &\pi_{12}: \quad -.039\,(.049) \qquad &&\pi_{21}: \quad .023\,(.010) \\ &\pi_{13}: \quad .044\,(.023) \qquad &&\pi_{31}: \quad .053\,(.026) \\ &\pi_{23}: \quad .002\,(.009) \qquad &&\pi_{32}: \quad .015\,(.052) \end{aligned}$$

The point estimates are evidently not pairwise equal, but the standard errors are such that we cannot exclude a priori the possibility that the corresponding parameters are pairwise equal. To test this hypothesis we shall use the test statistic (3.6), which involves the unknown covariance matrix of the contemporaneous disturbances. We could replace this matrix by that of the mean squares and products of the LS residuals, as we did in Section 7.3 when applying the test to the investment example. Here we shall use a more refined approximation procedure, based on the following consideration. If we want to test some null hypothesis H_0 against some alternative hypothesis, our approach amounts to rejecting H_0 if and only if the observed sample is too improbable *when* H_0 *is true*. Therefore our probability statements should be based on the symmetry constraints (7.4), so it is preferable not to use the LS residuals but rather a set of residuals compatible with these constraints. The following paragraphs describe this procedure in detail.

Notation

If the hypothesis (7.4) is true, the constrained GLS estimator $\hat{\boldsymbol{\beta}}^*$ given in (3.15) is best linear unbiased. To formulate this estimator for the present

[23] The standard errors and estimated covariance matrices of this section are computed without any correction for loss of degrees of freedom. For the motivation see the last subsection of Section 7.1.

problem, we arrange the quantities occurring in (7.6) in the following four matrices:

$$(7.7)\quad \mathbf{y}_i = \begin{bmatrix} w_{i1}^* Dq_{i1} \\ w_{i2}^* Dq_{i2} \\ \cdot \\ \cdot \\ \cdot \\ w_{iT}^* Dq_{iT} \end{bmatrix} \qquad \boldsymbol{\beta}_i = \begin{bmatrix} \mu_i \\ \pi_{i1} \\ \pi_{i2} \\ \pi_{i3} \end{bmatrix} \qquad \boldsymbol{\epsilon}_i = \begin{bmatrix} \epsilon_{i1} \\ \epsilon_{i2} \\ \cdot \\ \cdot \\ \cdot \\ \epsilon_{iT} \end{bmatrix} \qquad i = 1, 2, 3$$

$$(7.8)\quad \bar{\mathbf{X}} = \begin{bmatrix} Dq_1 & Dp_{11} - Dp_{41} & Dp_{21} - Dp_{41} & Dp_{31} - Dp_{41} \\ Dq_2 & Dp_{12} - Dp_{42} & Dp_{22} - Dp_{42} & Dp_{32} - Dp_{42} \\ \cdot & \cdot & \cdot & \cdot \\ \cdot & \cdot & \cdot & \cdot \\ \cdot & \cdot & \cdot & \cdot \\ Dq_T & Dp_{1T} - Dp_{4T} & Dp_{2T} - Dp_{4T} & Dp_{3T} - Dp_{4T} \end{bmatrix}$$

The three demand equations (7.6) for all observations combined are then written as

$$(7.9)\quad \begin{bmatrix} \mathbf{y}_1 \\ \mathbf{y}_2 \\ \mathbf{y}_3 \end{bmatrix} = \begin{bmatrix} \bar{\mathbf{X}} & \mathbf{0} & \mathbf{0} \\ \mathbf{0} & \bar{\mathbf{X}} & \mathbf{0} \\ \mathbf{0} & \mathbf{0} & \bar{\mathbf{X}} \end{bmatrix} \begin{bmatrix} \boldsymbol{\beta}_1 \\ \boldsymbol{\beta}_2 \\ \boldsymbol{\beta}_3 \end{bmatrix} + \begin{bmatrix} \boldsymbol{\epsilon}_1 \\ \boldsymbol{\epsilon}_2 \\ \boldsymbol{\epsilon}_3 \end{bmatrix} \qquad \text{or} \qquad \mathbf{y} = \mathbf{X}\boldsymbol{\beta} + \boldsymbol{\epsilon}$$

where

$$(7.10)\quad \mathbf{y} = \begin{bmatrix} \mathbf{y}_1 \\ \mathbf{y}_2 \\ \mathbf{y}_3 \end{bmatrix} \qquad \mathbf{X} = \begin{bmatrix} \bar{\mathbf{X}} & \mathbf{0} & \mathbf{0} \\ \mathbf{0} & \bar{\mathbf{X}} & \mathbf{0} \\ \mathbf{0} & \mathbf{0} & \bar{\mathbf{X}} \end{bmatrix} \qquad \boldsymbol{\beta} = \begin{bmatrix} \boldsymbol{\beta}_1 \\ \boldsymbol{\beta}_2 \\ \boldsymbol{\beta}_3 \end{bmatrix} \qquad \boldsymbol{\epsilon} = \begin{bmatrix} \boldsymbol{\epsilon}_1 \\ \boldsymbol{\epsilon}_2 \\ \boldsymbol{\epsilon}_3 \end{bmatrix}$$

The $3T$-element disturbance vector has the following covariance matrix:

$$(7.11)\quad \mathscr{V}(\boldsymbol{\epsilon}) = \mathscr{V}\begin{bmatrix} \boldsymbol{\epsilon}_1 \\ \boldsymbol{\epsilon}_2 \\ \boldsymbol{\epsilon}_3 \end{bmatrix} = \begin{bmatrix} \omega_{11}\mathbf{I} & \omega_{12}\mathbf{I} & \omega_{13}\mathbf{I} \\ \omega_{21}\mathbf{I} & \omega_{22}\mathbf{I} & \omega_{23}\mathbf{I} \\ \omega_{31}\mathbf{I} & \omega_{32}\mathbf{I} & \omega_{33}\mathbf{I} \end{bmatrix} = \boldsymbol{\Omega} \otimes \mathbf{I}$$

where

$$(7.12)\quad \boldsymbol{\Omega} = \begin{bmatrix} \omega_{11} & \omega_{12} & \omega_{13} \\ \omega_{21} & \omega_{22} & \omega_{23} \\ \omega_{31} & \omega_{32} & \omega_{33} \end{bmatrix}$$

Note that $\boldsymbol{\Omega}$ is *not* the singular 4×4 covariance matrix of all four demand disturbances $\epsilon_{1t}, \epsilon_{2t}, \epsilon_{3t}, \epsilon_{4t}$. Instead, it is the leading 3×3 submatrix which refers to $\epsilon_{1t}, \epsilon_{2t}$, and ϵ_{3t} only. This submatrix is nonsingular. If it were singular, the 4 × 4 matrix would satisfy

$$(7.13)\qquad \begin{bmatrix} \omega_{11} & \omega_{12} & \omega_{13} & \omega_{14} \\ \omega_{21} & \omega_{22} & \omega_{23} & \omega_{24} \\ \omega_{31} & \omega_{32} & \omega_{33} & \omega_{34} \\ \omega_{41} & \omega_{42} & \omega_{43} & \omega_{44} \end{bmatrix} \begin{bmatrix} 1 & a_1 \\ 1 & a_2 \\ 1 & a_3 \\ 1 & 0 \end{bmatrix} = \mathbf{0}$$

where the three a's are not all equal to zero. If (7.13) is true, the rank of the 4 × 4 covariance matrix is at most 2 rather than 3, which contradicts our assumption that the rank of the $N \times N$ covariance matrix $[\omega_{ij}]$ is $N - 1$ ($N = 4$ in our case).

Testing for Symmetry

We have considered the unconstrained estimator of $\boldsymbol{\beta}$:

$$(7.14)\qquad \mathbf{b} = \begin{bmatrix} \mathbf{b}_1 \\ \mathbf{b}_2 \\ \mathbf{b}_3 \end{bmatrix} = \begin{bmatrix} (\bar{\mathbf{X}}'\bar{\mathbf{X}})^{-1}\bar{\mathbf{X}}'\mathbf{y}_1 \\ (\bar{\mathbf{X}}'\bar{\mathbf{X}})^{-1}\bar{\mathbf{X}}'\mathbf{y}_2 \\ (\bar{\mathbf{X}}'\bar{\mathbf{X}})^{-1}\bar{\mathbf{X}}'\mathbf{y}_3 \end{bmatrix}$$

and now proceed to consider the constraints (7.4), which we write as

$$(7.15)\qquad \mathbf{R}\boldsymbol{\beta} = \mathbf{0}$$

where

(7.16)

$$\mathbf{R} = \begin{array}{c} \begin{matrix} \mu_1 & \pi_{11} & \pi_{12} & \pi_{13} & \mu_2 & \pi_{21} & \pi_{22} & \pi_{23} & \mu_3 & \pi_{31} & \pi_{32} & \pi_{33} \end{matrix} \\ \begin{bmatrix} 0 & 0 & 1 & 0 & 0 & -1 & 0 & 0 & 0 & 0 & 0 & 0 \\ 0 & 0 & 0 & 1 & 0 & 0 & 0 & 0 & 0 & -1 & 0 & 0 \\ 0 & 0 & 0 & 0 & 0 & 0 & 0 & 1 & 0 & 0 & -1 & 0 \end{bmatrix} \end{array}$$

The constrained GLS estimator $\hat{\boldsymbol{\beta}}^*$ defined in (3.15) is then

$$(7.17)\qquad \hat{\boldsymbol{\beta}}^* = \mathbf{b} - \mathbf{C}\mathbf{R}'(\mathbf{R}\mathbf{C}\mathbf{R}')^{-1}\mathbf{R}\mathbf{b}$$

where $\mathbf{b}$ is given in (7.14), $\mathbf{R}$ in (7.15), and

$$(7.18)\qquad \mathbf{C} = [\mathbf{X}'(\boldsymbol{\Omega}^{-1} \otimes \mathbf{I})\mathbf{X}]^{-1} = \boldsymbol{\Omega} \otimes (\bar{\mathbf{X}}'\bar{\mathbf{X}})^{-1}$$

The second equality sign in (7.18) follows from $\mathbf{X} = \mathbf{I} \otimes \bar{\mathbf{X}}$, $\mathbf{I}$ being the 3 × 3 unit matrix [see (7.10)], and from the derivation immediately below (2.23).

Imagine, then, that as a first approximation, the variances and the contemporaneous covariances (the elements of $\boldsymbol{\Omega}$) are proportional to the sampling variances and covariances which emerge from random sampling from the following multinomial population. The proportions of this population are equal to the average value shares mentioned at the end of the previous section when the commodity groups were introduced (30 percent for food, 10 percent for vice, 25 percent for durables). Going back to eq. (2.8) of Section 2.2, we find that this amounts to the following $\boldsymbol{\Omega}$ approximation:

$$\boldsymbol{\Omega}_0 = k \begin{bmatrix} .30(1-.30) & -(.30)(.10) & -(.30)(.25) \\ -(.10)(.30) & .10(1-.10) & -(.10)(.25) \\ -(.25)(.30) & -(.25)(.10) & .25(1-.25) \end{bmatrix} \tag{7.19}$$

where k is a positive scalar which is irrelevant for our purposes. We then compute $\hat{\boldsymbol{\beta}}^*$ of (7.17) with $\mathbf{C}$ replaced by $\mathbf{C}_0$, which is the same function of $\boldsymbol{\Omega}_0$ as $\mathbf{C}$ is of $\boldsymbol{\Omega}$:

$$\hat{\boldsymbol{\beta}}_0 = \mathbf{b} - \mathbf{C}_0\mathbf{R}'(\mathbf{R}\mathbf{C}_0\mathbf{R}')^{-1}\mathbf{R}\mathbf{b} \qquad \text{where} \qquad \mathbf{C}_0 = \boldsymbol{\Omega}_0 \otimes (\bar{\mathbf{X}}'\bar{\mathbf{X}})^{-1} \tag{7.20}$$

Given this $\hat{\boldsymbol{\beta}}_0$, we compute a second approximation of $\boldsymbol{\Omega}$:

$$\hat{\omega}_{ij} = \frac{1}{T}(\mathbf{y}_i - \bar{\mathbf{X}}\hat{\boldsymbol{\beta}}_{0i})'(\mathbf{y}_j - \bar{\mathbf{X}}\hat{\boldsymbol{\beta}}_{0j}) \tag{7.21}$$

where $\hat{\boldsymbol{\beta}}_{0i}$ is the ith subvector of $\hat{\boldsymbol{\beta}}_0$. Since $\hat{\boldsymbol{\beta}}_0$ satisfies the symmetry constraints, we should expect that the implied $\hat{\omega}_{ij}$ will be a better estimator of ω_{ij} than the LS estimator if the null hypothesis is indeed true. The 3×3 matrix of these estimates is

$$\hat{\boldsymbol{\Omega}} = 10^{-4} \begin{bmatrix} .233 & .025 & -.136 \\ & .034 & -.040 \\ & & .249 \end{bmatrix} \begin{matrix} \text{Food} \\ \text{Vice} \\ \text{Durables} \end{matrix} \tag{7.22}$$

The test statistic (3.6) is now

$$\frac{3T-12}{3} \times \frac{\mathbf{b}'\mathbf{R}'\{\mathbf{R}[\boldsymbol{\Omega} \otimes (\bar{\mathbf{X}}'\bar{\mathbf{X}})^{-1}]\mathbf{R}'\}^{-1}\mathbf{R}\mathbf{b}}{(\mathbf{y}-\mathbf{X}\mathbf{b})'(\boldsymbol{\Omega}^{-1} \otimes \mathbf{I})(\mathbf{y}-\mathbf{X}\mathbf{b})} \approx (T-4)\frac{\mathbf{b}'\mathbf{R}'\{\mathbf{R}[\hat{\boldsymbol{\Omega}} \otimes (\bar{\mathbf{X}}'\bar{\mathbf{X}})^{-1}]\mathbf{R}'\}^{-1}\mathbf{R}\mathbf{b}}{(\mathbf{y}-\mathbf{X}\mathbf{b})'(\hat{\boldsymbol{\Omega}}^{-1} \otimes \mathbf{I})(\mathbf{y}-\mathbf{X}\mathbf{b})} \tag{7.23}$$

where the $\approx$ sign is based on $\boldsymbol{\Omega} \approx \hat{\boldsymbol{\Omega}}$. The denominator can be written as the double sum over i and j of $\hat{\omega}^{ij}(\mathbf{y}_i - \bar{\mathbf{X}}\mathbf{b}_i)'(\mathbf{y}_j - \bar{\mathbf{X}}\mathbf{b}_j)$, where $\hat{\omega}^{ij}$ is the (i, j)th element of $\hat{\boldsymbol{\Omega}}^{-1}$; its value is 90.0. The Kronecker product of $\hat{\boldsymbol{\Omega}}$ and $(\bar{\mathbf{X}}'\bar{\mathbf{X}})^{-1}$ in the numerator is the estimated matrix of the sampling variances and covariances of the 12 LS coefficients of the three equations. We premultiply this matrix by $\mathbf{R}$ and postmultiply by $\mathbf{R}'$, which gives a 3×3 matrix. The inverse of that matrix is postmultiplied by the vector $\mathbf{R}\mathbf{b}$ (consisting of the LS

Table 7.6

Estimated Covariance Matrix ($\times 10^6$) of the Unconstrained Estimates

μ_1	π_{11}	π_{12}	π_{13}	π_{14}	μ_2	π_{21}	π_{22}	π_{23}	π_{24}	μ_3	π_{31}	π_{32}	π_{33}	π_{34}	μ_4	π_{41}	π_{42}	π_{43}	π_{44}	
1112	13	924	−15	−922	117	1	98	−2	−97	−650	−8	−540	9	539	−580	−7	−482	8	481	μ_1
	636	−105	−291	−239		67	−11	−31	−25		−371	62	170	140		−331	55	152	125	π_{11}
		2561	−390	−2066			271	−41	−218			−1496	228	1207			−1336	203	1077	π_{12}
			555	126				59	13				−324	−73				−289	−66	π_{13}
				2180					230					−1273					−1137	π_{14}
					162	2	135	−2	−134	−191	−2	−159	3	158	−88	−1	−73	1	73	μ_2
						93	−15	−42	−35		−109	18	50	41		−51	8	23	19	π_{21}
							373	−57	−301			−440	67	355			−204	31	164	π_{22}
								81	18				−95	−22				−44	−10	π_{23}
									317					−374					−173	π_{24}
										1188	14	987	−16	−985	−347	−4	−289	5	288	μ_3
											679	−113	−311	−255		−198	33	91	75	π_{31}
												2736	−416	−2207			−800	122	645	π_{32}
													593	134				−173	−39	π_{33}
														2328					−680	π_{34}
															1016	12	844	−14	−842	μ_4
																580	−96	−266	−218	π_{41}
																	2339	−356	−1887	π_{42}
																		507	115	π_{43}
																			1990	π_{44}

Table 7.7

Estimated Covariance matrix (× 10^6) of the Symmetry-Constrained Estimates

μ_1	π_{11}	π_{12}	π_{13}	π_{14}	μ_2	π_{21}	π_{22}	π_{23}	π_{24}	μ_3	π_{31}	π_{32}	π_{33}	π_{34}	μ_4	π_{41}	π_{42}	π_{43}	π_{44}	
755	62	24	38	−125	79	24	−3	−4	−17	−431	38	−4	−60	26	−403	−125	−17	26	116	μ_1
	622	57	−333	−346	6	57	7	−31	−32	−33	−333	−31	179	185	−35	−346	−32	185	194	π_{11}
		84	−68	−74	4	84	−4	−43	−37	−15	−68	−43	55	55	−14	−74	−37	55	55	π_{12}
			381	20	1	−68	−7	55	20	−1	381	55	−315	−121	−38	20	20	−121	81	π_{13}
				400	−11	−74	5	19	49	49	20	19	80	−119	87	400	49	−119	−330	π_{14}
					152	4	112	−3	−113	−130	1	−3	−17	19	−101	−11	−113	19	104	μ_2
						84	−4	−43	−37	−15	−68	−43	55	55	−14	−74	−37	55	55	π_{21}
							315	−58	−253	−19	−7	−58	21	45	−90	5	−253	45	203	π_{22}
								81	21	9	55	81	−97	−38	−2	19	21	−38	−2	π_{23}
									269	24	20	21	21	−62	106	49	269	−62	−257	π_{24}
										807	−1	9	106	−114	−246	49	24	−114	40	μ_3
											381	55	−315	−121	−38	20	20	−121	81	π_{31}
												81	−97	−38	−2	19	21	−38	−2	π_{32}
													554	−142	−29	80	21	−142	40	π_{33}
														301	69	−119	−62	301	−119	π_{34}
															749	87	106	69	−261	μ_4
																400	49	−119	−330	π_{41}
																	269	−62	−257	π_{42}
																		301	−119	π_{43}
																			706	π_{44}

estimates of $\pi_{12} - \pi_{21}$, $\pi_{13} - \pi_{31}$, and $\pi_{23} - \pi_{32}$) and premultiplied by the transpose of this vector, which gives 2.26. Hence the value of the test statistic is

$$(T - 4)\frac{2.26}{90.0} = 27 \times (.0251) = .68 \tag{7.24}$$

If we accept the approximation $\mathbf{\Omega} \approx \hat{\mathbf{\Omega}}$, we may conclude that this statistic follows the F distribution with 3 degrees of freedom in the numerator and $3T - 12 = 81$ degrees of freedom in the denominator if the null hypothesis is true. The 5 percent significance limit is about 2.7 and, therefore, the result (7.24) is far from significant.

Constrained Estimation

We now impose the symmetry constraints and estimate $\boldsymbol{\beta}$ according to (7.17) with $\mathbf{C}$ approximated by $\hat{\mathbf{C}} = \hat{\mathbf{\Omega}} \otimes (\bar{\mathbf{X}}'\bar{\mathbf{X}})^{-1}$, and we use

$$\hat{\mathbf{C}} - \hat{\mathbf{C}}\mathbf{R}'(\mathbf{R}\hat{\mathbf{C}}\mathbf{R}')^{-1}\mathbf{R}\hat{\mathbf{C}}$$

as an approximate covariance matrix of this estimator in accordance with (3.16) for $\sigma^2 = 1$. The point estimates and their standard errors are given in the last four lines of Table 7.5. The complete estimated matrices of variances and covariances are presented in Tables 7.6 and 7.7 for the unconstrained and constrained estimates, respectively. Note that the submatrices of Table 7.6 are all symmetric in accordance with Problem 2.5. Also see Problem 7.5 for a convenient method to obtain the estimated sampling variances and covariances of the estimates which do not fall under the $\boldsymbol{\beta}_i$'s of (7.7).[24]

Two final questions. Do the estimates of the price coefficients in the last four lines of Table 7.5 form a negative semidefinite matrix of rank 3, as condition (5.11) requires? To answer this question we compute the latent roots of this matrix, which are 0, $-.033$, $-.043$, $-.146$; the answer is thus in the affirmative. Second question: Suppose that we do not use $\hat{\boldsymbol{\beta}}_{0i}$ but our final coefficient estimates (last four lines of Table 7.5) to estimate ω_{ij} in (7.21); is the resulting estimate of the covariance matrix close to the matrix (7.22) that we used to obtain the final coefficient estimates? In other words, do these estimates faithfully reproduce the estimated covariance matrix from which they are derived? The answer is provided by the following two matrices:

$$\begin{bmatrix} .233 & .025 & -.136 & -.122 \\ & .034 & -.040 & -.019 \\ & & .249 & -.073 \\ & & & .213 \end{bmatrix} \quad \text{and} \quad \begin{bmatrix} .234 & .027 & -.137 & -.125 \\ & .034 & -.041 & -.020 \\ & & .250 & -.072 \\ & & & .216 \end{bmatrix} \begin{matrix} \text{Food} \\ \text{Vice} \\ \text{Durables} \\ \text{Remainder} \end{matrix} \tag{7.25}$$

[24] The matrix $\hat{\mathbf{C}} = \hat{\mathbf{\Omega}} \otimes (\bar{\mathbf{X}}'\bar{\mathbf{X}})^{-1}$, with $\hat{\mathbf{\Omega}}$ as specified in (7.22), is used for the covariance matrix of the unconstrained estimates. Since the diagonal elements of $T\hat{\mathbf{\Omega}}$ are not exactly equal to the LS residual sums of squares for each demand equation separately there is no exact correspondence between the standard errors of these estimates in Table 7.5 and the variance estimates in Table 7.6.

The matrix on the left is $\hat{\boldsymbol{\Omega}}$ of (7.22) in enlarged 4×4 form and the matrix on the right is the estimated covariance matrix implied by the final coefficient estimates, in both cases apart from a factor 10^{-4}. The agreement is evidently close.

Problems

7.1 Under condition (7.5) the symmetry constraints (7.4) necessarily imply the validity of $\pi_{4i} = \pi_{i4}$ $(i < 4)$, where π_{4i} is defined as minus the sum of π_{1i}, π_{2i}, and π_{3i}. To prove this statement, check each of the following steps:

$$-\pi_{4i} = \pi_{1i} + \pi_{2i} + \pi_{3i} = \pi_{i1} + \pi_{i2} + \pi_{i3} = -\pi_{i4} \tag{7.26}$$

7.2 Prove that when the symmetry constraints (7.4) are disregarded, LS estimation of the fourth demand equation gives identically the same point estimators as the indirect estimation via the first three equations. [*Hint*. Define $\mathbf{y}_4$ similarly to $\mathbf{y}_1$, $\mathbf{y}_2$, $\mathbf{y}_3$ of (7.7) and $\mathbf{b}_4 = (\bar{\mathbf{X}}'\bar{\mathbf{X}})^{-1}\bar{\mathbf{X}}'\mathbf{y}_4$; write $\mathbf{x}_1$ for the first column of $\bar{\mathbf{X}}$ and prove $\mathbf{b}_1 + \mathbf{b}_2 + \mathbf{b}_3 = \mathbf{i}_1 - \mathbf{b}_4$, where $\mathbf{i}_1$ is the first column of the 4×4 unit matrix.]

7.3 Prove that the multinomial variance-covariance specification (7.19) in extended $N \times N$ form (4×4 in this case) has rank $N - 1$.

7.4 Prove that the denominator on the first line of (7.23) can be written as $\operatorname{tr} \boldsymbol{\Omega}^{-1}\mathbf{Y}'[\mathbf{I} - \bar{\mathbf{X}}(\bar{\mathbf{X}}'\bar{\mathbf{X}})^{-1}\bar{\mathbf{X}}']\mathbf{Y}$, where $\mathbf{Y} = [\mathbf{y}_1 \quad \mathbf{y}_2 \quad \mathbf{y}_3]$.

7.5 To obtain the variances and covariances of the coefficient estimators not represented in the $\boldsymbol{\beta}_i$'s of (7.7), consider

$$[\mu_4 - 1 \quad \pi_{14} \quad \pi_{24} \quad \pi_{34} \quad \pi_{41} \quad \pi_{42} \quad \pi_{43} \quad \pi_{44}]' = \mathbf{L}\boldsymbol{\beta} \tag{7.27}$$

and prove that $\mathbf{L}$ is the following 8×12 matrix:

$$\mathbf{L} = \begin{array}{c} \begin{array}{cccccccccccc} \mu_1 & \pi_{11} & \pi_{12} & \pi_{13} & \mu_2 & \pi_{21} & \pi_{22} & \pi_{23} & \mu_3 & \pi_{31} & \pi_{32} & \pi_{33} \end{array} \\ \begin{bmatrix} -1 & 0 & 0 & 0 & -1 & 0 & 0 & 0 & -1 & 0 & 0 & 0 \\ 0 & -1 & -1 & -1 & 0 & 0 & 0 & 0 & 0 & 0 & 0 & 0 \\ 0 & 0 & 0 & 0 & 0 & -1 & -1 & -1 & 0 & 0 & 0 & 0 \\ 0 & 0 & 0 & 0 & 0 & 0 & 0 & 0 & 0 & -1 & -1 & -1 \\ 0 & -1 & 0 & 0 & 0 & -1 & 0 & 0 & 0 & -1 & 0 & 0 \\ 0 & 0 & -1 & 0 & 0 & 0 & -1 & 0 & 0 & 0 & -1 & 0 \\ 0 & 0 & 0 & -1 & 0 & 0 & 0 & -1 & 0 & 0 & 0 & -1 \\ 0 & 1 & 1 & 1 & 0 & 1 & 1 & 1 & 0 & 1 & 1 & 1 \end{bmatrix} \end{array} \begin{array}{l} \\ \mu_4 - 1 \\ \pi_{14} \\ \pi_{24} \\ \pi_{34} \\ \pi_{41} \\ \pi_{42} \\ \pi_{43} \\ \pi_{44} \end{array}$$

Prove that the covariance matrices of the estimators of all 20 μ's and

π's in the unconstrained case and the constrained case are

$$\begin{bmatrix} \mathbf{I} \\ \mathbf{L} \end{bmatrix} \mathbf{C}[\mathbf{I} \quad \mathbf{L}'] \qquad \text{and} \qquad \begin{bmatrix} \mathbf{I} \\ \mathbf{L} \end{bmatrix} [\mathbf{C} - \mathbf{C}\mathbf{R}'(\mathbf{R}\mathbf{C}\mathbf{R}')^{-1}\mathbf{R}\mathbf{C}][\mathbf{I} \quad \mathbf{L}']$$

where **C** and **R** are given in (7.18) and (7.16), respectively.

7.8 Incomplete Extraneous Information and Mixed Estimation[B]

There are several situations in which there is extraneous information on some of the parameters of the equation. Consider the case of a time series demand regression for a certain commodity. If the logarithm of its consumption per capita is described by a linear function of the logarithm of income per capita and certain other variables, the coefficient of the income variable is the commodity's income elasticity. It may happen that we have an estimate of this elasticity from a cross-section analysis, which could help us to estimate the elasticity more accurately than is possible with the time series regression alone. Needless to say, it is not self-evident that we can identify the time series income elasticity and the cross-section elasticity, because the former measures the effect on consumption of a change in per capita income from level A to level B over time, whereas the latter deals with the transition from a family with income A to a family with income B. It is true that we correct for the effect of price changes in the time series case when these are among the explanatory variables; similarly, it is also true that we correct for the effect of family size in the cross-section case when this is an explanatory variable. Nevertheless, it is conceivable that a change in income has a lagged effect on consumption, which would be relevant for the time series regression. It is not relevant, however, for the cross-section case if we assume that the two families have had incomes A and B, respectively, over a sufficiently long period of time. In this case, therefore, we cannot identify the two income elasticities without further analysis.

An Unattractive Procedure

But suppose that there are no such difficulties, so that we can argue, before analyzing the data, that we have an estimate of one of our unknown parameters (the income elasticity in this case). Also suppose that the estimator is unbiased and that its sampling variance is known, or at least that an estimate of this variance is available. A generalization of this situation is the case in which this applies to a subvector $\boldsymbol{\beta}_2$ of the parameter vector, so that we can partition as follows:

$$\mathbf{y} = [\mathbf{X}_1 \quad \mathbf{X}_2] \begin{bmatrix} \boldsymbol{\beta}_1 \\ \boldsymbol{\beta}_2 \end{bmatrix} + \boldsymbol{\epsilon} \tag{8.1}$$

If an extraneous unbiased estimate $\tilde{\boldsymbol{\beta}}_2$ of $\boldsymbol{\beta}_2$ is available, the equation can be written in the form

$$(8.2) \qquad \mathbf{y} - \mathbf{X}_2\tilde{\boldsymbol{\beta}}_2 = \mathbf{X}_1\boldsymbol{\beta}_1 + (\boldsymbol{\epsilon} - \mathbf{X}_2\tilde{\boldsymbol{\epsilon}}) \qquad \text{where} \qquad \tilde{\boldsymbol{\epsilon}} = \tilde{\boldsymbol{\beta}}_2 - \boldsymbol{\beta}_2$$

which suggests that one should run a regression of a new left-hand variable (whose observations are arranged as elements of the vector $\mathbf{y} - \mathbf{X}_2\tilde{\boldsymbol{\beta}}_2$) on a smaller set of explanatory variables (whose observation matrix is $\mathbf{X}_1$). This procedure is pursued in Problem 8.1,[25] which shows that it is not an optimal procedure. In fact, there are situations in which the elements of the subvector $\mathbf{b}_1$ of the simple LS estimator, derived with disregard for the extraneous information on $\boldsymbol{\beta}_2$, have smaller variances than those of the LS coefficients of the regression based on (8.2). In other words, it is essential that we take the random nature of $\tilde{\boldsymbol{\beta}}_2$ into account.

A GLS Procedure

A more attractive procedure was suggested by Durbin (1953). It amounts to combining the two pieces of information symmetrically:

$$(8.3) \qquad \begin{bmatrix} \mathbf{y} \\ \tilde{\boldsymbol{\beta}}_2 \end{bmatrix} = \begin{bmatrix} \mathbf{X}_1 & \mathbf{X}_2 \\ \mathbf{0} & \mathbf{I} \end{bmatrix} \begin{bmatrix} \boldsymbol{\beta}_1 \\ \boldsymbol{\beta}_2 \end{bmatrix} + \begin{bmatrix} \boldsymbol{\epsilon} \\ \tilde{\boldsymbol{\epsilon}} \end{bmatrix}$$

and applying GLS to the equation system (8.3) as a whole. Comparing this system with the investment example of Section 7.1, we conclude that a similar situation prevails: several equations (here two, one with $\mathbf{y}$ and the other with $\tilde{\boldsymbol{\beta}}_2$ on the left), and each of these is linear in the unknown parameters. Of course, the economic interpretation of the two situations is not the same. In Section 7.1 we were equally interested in the two investment equations, whereas in the present case $\tilde{\boldsymbol{\beta}}_2 = \boldsymbol{\beta}_2 + \tilde{\boldsymbol{\epsilon}}$ is not more than an auxiliary relation which serves to estimate the parameters of (8.1) more accurately. It is conceivable, however, that the same statistical procedure is useful in both situations.

Mixed Estimation

We can extend the approach even further by considering any kind of extraneous information including introspection. As an example, let us return to the textile regression of Chapter 3 and suppose that the analyst argues as follows before actually computing the regression. "I consider unity to be the most plausible value of the income elasticity and I am willing to bet 20 to 1 that the elasticity is not outside the interval (.7, 1.3)." Applying the

[25] From Goldberger (1964, pp. 258–259).

two-sigma rule, one may argue that such a prior idea is equivalent to a point estimate of the elasticity equal to 1 with a standard error of .15. We can then combine this prior information with the sample data [$\mathbf{y}$ $\mathbf{X}$] in the manner of (8.3). This is the procedure of "mixed estimation," which originated with THEIL and GOLDBERGER (1961) and was extended by THEIL (1963). It implies that the analyst does not make the numerical values which he selects as parameter estimates dependent on the sample data only (that would be "pure" estimation), but that he combines sample and prior information by formulating the latter in terms of unbiased estimates and their covariance matrix. Essentially, the mixed estimation procedure consists of using the sample to modify one's prior judgments. It will be obvious that this method is a way to meet objection (3) of Section 3.9, which states that one frequently knows more than Assumption 3.1 of Section 3.2 is willing to admit.

We shall proceed under the assumption that prior unbiased estimators of q linear combinations of the parameters are available:

$$\text{(8.4)} \qquad \mathbf{r} = \mathbf{R}\boldsymbol{\beta} + \mathbf{v} \qquad \mathscr{E}\mathbf{v} = \mathbf{0} \qquad \mathscr{E}(\mathbf{v}\mathbf{v}') = \mathbf{V}_0$$

where $\mathbf{R}$ is a known $q \times K$ matrix of rank q and $\mathbf{V}_0$ is a known nonsingular covariance matrix. Under the procedure of mixed estimation we can interpret the elements of $\mathbf{r}$ as the best guesses of the corresponding elements of $\mathbf{R}\boldsymbol{\beta}$ and the diagonal elements of $\mathbf{V}_0$ as measures of uncertainty with respect to these guesses.[26] The off-diagonal elements of $\mathbf{V}_0$ deal with the interaction of the deviations from the best guesses; an example will be given in the next subsection. In many cases $\mathbf{r}$ will be an estimate of a subvector of $\boldsymbol{\beta}$, so that each row of $\mathbf{R}$ contains one unit element, all other elements being zero; note that this is actually true for (8.3). It need not always be true, however. For example, consider the Cobb-Douglas production function:

$$\text{(8.5)} \qquad \log y_\alpha = \beta_0 + \beta_1 \log x_{\alpha 1} + \beta_2 \log x_{\alpha 2} + \cdots + \epsilon_\alpha$$

where y_α is output in year α and the x's are inputs. Suppose that the analyst knows a priori that the assumption of constant returns to scale is at least approximately true. He can then declare unity to be a prior unbiased estimate of the sum $\beta_1 + \beta_2 + \cdots$ of the multiplicative coefficients and use .1 or .05 as the standard deviation of its distribution, depending on his confidence in the assumption of constant returns to scale in the particular case at hand. If he believes that increasing returns is slightly more realistic than decreasing returns, he may use, for example, a prior unbiased estimate of 1.1 with standard deviation .1. Clearly, the mixed estimation method is flexible.

To obtain the estimator, we combine (8.4) with $\mathbf{y} = \mathbf{X}\boldsymbol{\beta} + \boldsymbol{\epsilon}$ under the

[26] It is easily possible to extend the approach to the case in which the prior estimator $\mathbf{r}$ is not unbiased; see Problem 8.3.

condition $\mathscr{E}(\boldsymbol{\epsilon\epsilon}') = \sigma^2\mathbf{V}$ (nonsingular) and the assumption that prior and sample information are independent:

$$(8.6)\qquad \begin{bmatrix}\mathbf{y}\\ \mathbf{r}\end{bmatrix} = \begin{bmatrix}\mathbf{X}\\ \mathbf{R}\end{bmatrix}\boldsymbol{\beta} + \begin{bmatrix}\boldsymbol{\epsilon}\\ \mathbf{v}\end{bmatrix} \qquad \mathscr{E}\begin{bmatrix}\boldsymbol{\epsilon}\\ \mathbf{v}\end{bmatrix} = \mathbf{0} \qquad \mathscr{V}\begin{bmatrix}\boldsymbol{\epsilon}\\ \mathbf{v}\end{bmatrix} = \begin{bmatrix}\sigma^2\mathbf{V} & \mathbf{0}\\ \mathbf{0} & \mathbf{V}_0\end{bmatrix}$$

The best unbiased estimator of $\boldsymbol{\beta}$ which is linear in $\mathbf{y}$ and $\mathbf{r}$ is then obtained by applying Aitken's theorem to the specification (8.6). Since the covariance matrix of $(\boldsymbol{\epsilon}, \mathbf{v})$ is block-diagonal, its inverse is also block-diagonal with $(1/\sigma^2)\mathbf{V}^{-1}$ and $\mathbf{V}_0^{-1}$ in the diagonal blocks. It is then readily verified that the Aitken estimator is to be solved from the following normal equations:

$$(8.7)\qquad \left(\frac{1}{\sigma^2}\mathbf{X}'\mathbf{V}^{-1}\mathbf{X} + \mathbf{R}'\mathbf{V}_0^{-1}\mathbf{R}\right)\hat{\boldsymbol{\beta}} = \frac{1}{\sigma^2}\mathbf{X}'\mathbf{V}^{-1}\mathbf{y} + \mathbf{R}'\mathbf{V}_0^{-1}\mathbf{r}$$

and that the covariance matrix of $\hat{\boldsymbol{\beta}}$ is equal to the inverse of the $K \times K$ matrix on the left. Usually σ^2 is unknown, and we then approximate it by $\hat{\sigma}^2$ defined in eq. (1.11) of Section 6.1. This leads to the mixed estimator of $\boldsymbol{\beta}$:

$$(8.8)\qquad \mathbf{b}_M = \left(\frac{1}{\hat{\sigma}^2}\mathbf{X}'\mathbf{V}^{-1}\mathbf{X} + \mathbf{R}'\mathbf{V}_0^{-1}\mathbf{R}\right)^{-1}\left(\frac{1}{\hat{\sigma}^2}\mathbf{X}'\mathbf{V}^{-1}\mathbf{y} + \mathbf{R}'\mathbf{V}_0^{-1}\mathbf{r}\right)$$

and the matrix

$$(8.9)\qquad \left(\frac{1}{\hat{\sigma}^2}\mathbf{X}'\mathbf{V}^{-1}\mathbf{X} + \mathbf{R}'\mathbf{V}_0^{-1}\mathbf{R}\right)^{-1}$$

is then used as an approximate covariance matrix of $\mathbf{b}_M$.[27]

Application to the Textile Example

Consider the textile example of Chapter 3 and assume that there exists no prior knowledge of the constant term of the equation and of the variance σ^2 of the disturbances. The prior point estimates of the income and price elasticities are 1 and −.7, respectively, each with a standard deviation of .15. This amounts to a two-sigma range of (.7, 1.3) for the income elasticity and of (−1, −.4) for the price elasticity. Furthermore, the analyst argues that if his best guess overestimates the income sensitivity of the demand for textiles, the same should be true for the price sensitivity and vice versa, at least on the average. Given the opposite signs of the two elasticities this means that the prior covariance is negative. Let the prior specification in numerical form be:

$$(8.10)\qquad \mathbf{r} = \begin{bmatrix}1\\ -.7\end{bmatrix} \qquad \mathbf{R} = \begin{bmatrix}0 & 1 & 0\\ 0 & 0 & 1\end{bmatrix} \qquad \mathbf{V}_0 = \begin{bmatrix}.0225 & -.01\\ -.01 & .0225\end{bmatrix}$$

[27] See Mehta and Swamy (1969) for an exact procedure under the assumption that $\boldsymbol{\epsilon}$ and $\mathbf{v}$ are normally distributed. This procedure requires numerical integration. Also see Swamy and Mehta (1969).

where the first column of $\mathbf{R}$ (consisting of zeros) refers to the constant term. As in Section 3.3 we assume that the standard linear model applies to the sample data, so that $\sigma^2\mathbf{V}$ of (8.6) is simply $\sigma^2\mathbf{I}$, and σ^2 is estimated by $s^2 = .0001833$ [see eq. (3.16) of Section 3.3]. We find for the inverse in (8.8) and (8.9):

$$(8.11) \qquad \left(\frac{1}{s^2}\mathbf{X}'\mathbf{X} + \mathbf{R}'\mathbf{V}_0^{-1}\mathbf{R}\right)^{-1} = \begin{bmatrix} .04139 & -.01997 & -.00064 \\ -.01997 & .01069 & -.00082 \\ -.00064 & -.00082 & .00122 \end{bmatrix}$$

Next we postmultiply by $(1/s^2)\mathbf{X}'\mathbf{y} + \mathbf{R}'\mathbf{V}_0^{-1}\mathbf{r}$ and obtain the following result:

$$(8.12) \qquad \begin{array}{l} y_\alpha = 1.467 + 1.089x_{\alpha 1} - .821x_{\alpha 2} + e'_\alpha \\ \qquad\quad (.203) \quad (.103) \qquad (.035) \end{array}$$

where the figures in brackets are the square roots of the diagonal elements of the matrix (8.11). Comparing this result with that of Section 3.3, we conclude that the mixed estimation procedure leads to a slightly lower point estimate of the income elasticity (1.089 instead of 1.143) and to a rather considerable reduction of its standard error (.103 instead of .156), whereas the results for the price elasticity are virtually unchanged. These outcomes are intuitively understandable, for the standard error of the estimated income elasticity in Section 3.3 is relatively large and that of the estimated price elasticity is very small, but the standard deviations of the two prior estimates are both equal to .15. Thus it stands to reason that the mixed procedure leads to a larger gain in precision for the income elasticity than for the price elasticity.

Testing the Compatibility of Sample and Prior Information

An important question is whether the prior ideas are contradicted by the sample. Suppose, for example, that our analyst had a prior estimate of -2 with a standard deviation of .1 for the price elasticity of the demand for textile. Comparing this with the sample results in Section 3.3 (point estimate $-.829$, standard error .036), we would conclude strong disagreement.

The following is a natural procedure for testing the hypothesis that sample and prior information are not in conflict with each other. The prior information (8.4) states that $\mathbf{r} - \mathbf{R}\boldsymbol{\beta}$ is a random vector with zero mean and covariance matrix $\mathbf{V}_0$, and the sample supplies an estimator of $\boldsymbol{\beta}$. Consider

$$(8.13) \qquad \mathbf{r} - \mathbf{R}\hat{\boldsymbol{\beta}} = -\mathbf{R}(\hat{\boldsymbol{\beta}} - \boldsymbol{\beta}) + \mathbf{v}$$

where $\hat{\boldsymbol{\beta}} = (\mathbf{X}'\mathbf{V}^{-1}\mathbf{X})^{-1}\mathbf{X}'\mathbf{V}^{-1}\mathbf{y}$ is the GLS coefficient estimator based on the sample. Under assumption (8.6) the vector (8.13) has zero mean and the following covariance matrix:

$$(8.14) \qquad \mathscr{V}(\mathbf{r} - \mathbf{R}\hat{\boldsymbol{\beta}}) = \sigma^2\mathbf{R}(\mathbf{X}'\mathbf{V}^{-1}\mathbf{X})^{-1}\mathbf{R}' + \mathbf{V}_0$$

If, on the other hand, sample and prior information are in conflict with each other, so that assumption (8.6) is not true, one should expect that at least some of the elements of $\mathbf{r} - \mathbf{R}\hat{\boldsymbol{\beta}}$ are too large in absolute value to fit the description of zero mean and covariance matrix (8.14). Consider a quadratic form in $\mathbf{r} - \mathbf{R}\hat{\boldsymbol{\beta}}$ whose matrix is the inverse of the covariance matrix (8.14):

$$(8.15) \qquad (\mathbf{r} - \mathbf{R}\hat{\boldsymbol{\beta}})'[\sigma^2\mathbf{R}(\mathbf{X}'\mathbf{V}^{-1}\mathbf{X})^{-1}\mathbf{R}' + \mathbf{V}_0]^{-1}(\mathbf{r} - \mathbf{R}\hat{\boldsymbol{\beta}})$$

If $\boldsymbol{\epsilon}$ and $\mathbf{v}$ are normally distributed, this quadratic form is distributed as $\chi^2(q)$ under the null hypothesis (8.6) that sample and prior information are compatible with each other. To prove this statement we write the inverse of the covariance matrix (8.14) in the form $\mathbf{A}'\mathbf{A}$, where $\mathbf{A}$ is a nonsingular $q \times q$ matrix, so that the vector $\mathbf{A}(\mathbf{r} - \mathbf{R}\hat{\boldsymbol{\beta}})$ has a unit covariance matrix:[28]

$$\mathbf{A}\mathscr{E}[(\mathbf{r} - \mathbf{R}\hat{\boldsymbol{\beta}})(\mathbf{r} - \mathbf{R}\hat{\boldsymbol{\beta}})']\mathbf{A}' = \mathbf{A}(\mathbf{A}'\mathbf{A})^{-1}\mathbf{A}' = \mathbf{A}\mathbf{A}^{-1}(\mathbf{A}')^{-1}\mathbf{A}' = \mathbf{I}$$

Hence the elements of $\mathbf{A}(\mathbf{r} - \mathbf{R}\hat{\boldsymbol{\beta}})$ are q independent standardized normal variates. It is readily verified that the quadratic form (8.15) is nothing but the sum of the squares of these variates, and hence is distributed as $\chi^2(q)$ under the null hypothesis.

In the above example on the demand for textile we have $q = 2$ and $\mathbf{V} = \mathbf{I}$. This gives

$$(8.16) \qquad \mathbf{r} - \mathbf{R}\hat{\boldsymbol{\beta}} = \mathbf{r} - \mathbf{R}\mathbf{b} = \begin{bmatrix} 1 - 1.1430 \\ -.7 + .8289 \end{bmatrix} = \begin{bmatrix} -.1430 \\ .1289 \end{bmatrix}$$

We approximate σ^2 by $s^2 = .0001833$ and note that $s^2\mathbf{R}(\mathbf{X}'\mathbf{X})^{-1}\mathbf{R}'$ is simply the 2×2 matrix of estimated variances and covariance of the income and price elasticity estimators of Section 3.3. We then add $\mathbf{V}_0$ of (8.10), invert the sum, and compute the value of the quadratic form (8.15). The result is .86, which is well below the significance limit of the chi-square distribution with two degrees of freedom at any reasonable significance level.

The Specification of the Prior Covariances

The mixed estimation procedure requires a numerical specification of prior judgments in terms of all moments of the first and the second order. Usually the second-order cross-moments (the prior covariances) cause most of the difficulties except when the analyst feels that his prior point estimates are completely independent, in which case he is justified in using zero prior covariances. This is not the case in (8.10), where the prior covariance has been assigned a negative value. If it is felt to be very difficult to assign a particular numerical value to such a covariance, one may use alternative values to see whether the results are sensitive. Thus, consider the $\mathbf{V}_0$ of (8.10)

[28] Compare the analogous derivations in the second subsection of Section 6.1.

and suppose that the prior covariance is not positive. Alternative values of this covariance [with $\mathbf{r}$ and the diagonal elements of $\mathbf{V}_0$ as specified in (8.10)] give the following results for the mixed income and price elasticity estimates:

Prior covariance	*Income elasticity*	*Price elasticity*
0	1.066 (.108)	−.818 (.035)
−.005	1.078 (.107)	−.820 (.035)
−.01	1.089 (.103)	−.821 (.035)
−.015	1.100 (.094)	−.821 (.035)
−.02	1.113 (.070)	−.822 (.035)

In this case the point estimates are rather stable, but the standard error of the income elasticity estimate declines sharply when the prior covariance moves in the direction of perfect negative prior correlation.

Problems

8.1 Prove that under the conditions $\mathscr{E}(\boldsymbol{\epsilon\epsilon}') = \sigma^2\mathbf{I}$, $\mathscr{E}(\tilde{\boldsymbol{\epsilon}}\tilde{\boldsymbol{\epsilon}}') = \mathbf{V}_0$, $\mathscr{E}(\boldsymbol{\epsilon}\tilde{\boldsymbol{\epsilon}}') = \mathbf{0}$, the sampling error of the LS estimator of $\boldsymbol{\beta}_1$ corresponding to the formulation (8.2) is $(\mathbf{X}_1'\mathbf{X}_1)^{-1}\mathbf{X}_1'(\boldsymbol{\epsilon} - \mathbf{X}_2\tilde{\boldsymbol{\epsilon}})$ and also prove that its covariance matrix is

$$(8.17) \qquad \sigma^2(\mathbf{X}_1'\mathbf{X}_1)^{-1} + \mathbf{A}\mathbf{V}_0\mathbf{A}' \qquad \text{where} \qquad \mathbf{A} = (\mathbf{X}_1'\mathbf{X}_1)^{-1}\mathbf{X}_1'\mathbf{X}_2$$

Next apply eq. (2.15) of Section 1.2 to prove that the covariance matrix of the subvector corresponding to $\boldsymbol{\beta}_1$ of the ordinary LS estimator of $\boldsymbol{\beta}$ is

$$(8.18) \qquad \sigma^2[(\mathbf{X}_1'\mathbf{X}_1)^{-1} + \mathbf{A}(\mathbf{X}_2'\mathbf{M}_1\mathbf{X}_2)^{-1}\mathbf{A}'] \text{ where } \mathbf{M}_1 = \mathbf{I} - \mathbf{X}_1(\mathbf{X}_1'\mathbf{X}_1)^{-1}\mathbf{X}_1'$$

Conclude that the difference between the covariance matrices (8.17) and (8.18) is of the form $\mathbf{A}[\mathbf{V}_0 - \sigma^2(\mathbf{X}_2'\mathbf{M}_1\mathbf{X}_2)^{-1}]\mathbf{A}'$, and prove that this matrix may be either positive semidefinite, negative semidefinite, or indefinite.

8.2 What can be said about the sum of squares of the residuals e_α' of (8.12) in relation to the sum of squares of the LS residuals e_α?

8.3 Suppose that the statement $\mathscr{E}\mathbf{v} = \mathbf{0}$ in (8.4) is not true but that $\mathscr{E}(\mathbf{vv}') = \mathbf{V}_0$ is still true. Prove that the Aitken estimator $\hat{\boldsymbol{\beta}}$ obtained from (8.7) is biased but that the inverse of the $K \times K$ matrix in the left-hand side of this equation still gives its second-order moments around $\boldsymbol{\beta}$.

7.9 Inequality Constraints[B]

The constraints considered up to this point take the form of linear equations in unknown parameters; they are either exact linear equations or—as in the previous section—linear equations involving random variables. A third type is the linear inequality. For example, the analyst may feel sure that the elasticity of the demand for a commodity with respect to its own price cannot be positive. Or he may feel certain that the marginal propensity to consume cannot be larger than unity. When a consumption function contains both current income and income lagged one year, the analyst may require that the sum of the two corresponding coefficients be less than unity. More generally, consider an arbitrary set of linear inequality constraints on the parameter vector:

$$\mathbf{r} \leqq \mathbf{R}\boldsymbol{\beta} \tag{9.1}$$

where the inequality sign is to be interpreted in the sense that each element of $\mathbf{R}\boldsymbol{\beta}$ is at least equal to the corresponding element of $\mathbf{r}$. For example, if $K = 2$ and if $\beta_1 \geq 0$, $\beta_1 + \beta_2 \leq 1$ are the two inequality constraints, then (9.1) is specified as follows:

$$\begin{bmatrix} 0 \\ -1 \end{bmatrix} \leqq \begin{bmatrix} 1 & 0 \\ -1 & -1 \end{bmatrix} \begin{bmatrix} \beta_1 \\ \beta_2 \end{bmatrix}$$

LS and GLS under Linear Inequality Constraints

There are no particular difficulties in deriving point estimates subject to linear inequality constraints. Whether we apply LS or GLS, in both cases we minimize a positive definite quadratic form in the coefficient vector. This minimization subject to a set of linear inequality constraints on the coefficient vector is a matter of quadratic programming, for which several algorithms are available; see BOOT (1964) or HADLEY (1964, Chapter 7). We may also have linear equality constraints in addition to the inequalities; in this case, too, one can derive point estimates in a straightforward manner.

However, the sampling distribution of an estimator which is derived under an inequality constraint is drastically affected. This is easily shown for the case of one single (scalar) parameter β under the assumptions of the standard linear model including that of normality. Let the constraint be that of nonnegativity; the sampling distribution of the unconstrained LS estimator is then also normal (see Figure 7.1*a*), but the area to the left of the origin is replaced by a probability mass concentrated at the origin when the nonnegativity constraint is imposed (see Problem 9.1). The sampling distribution of

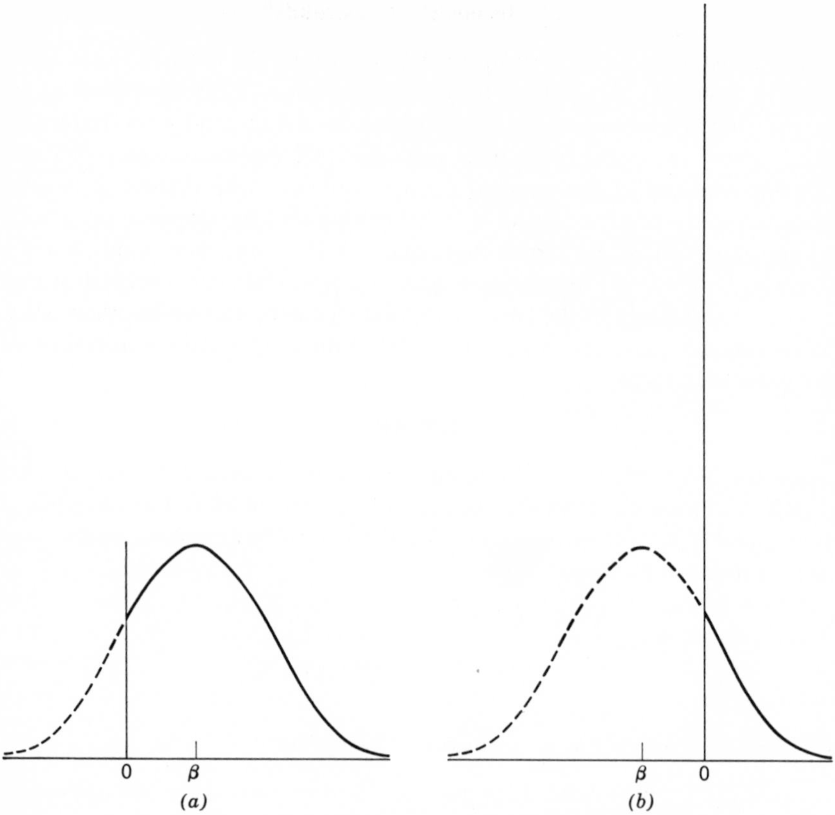

Fig 7.1 Distributions of estimators which are subject to inequality constraints.

the constrained estimator is thus of the mixed discrete-continuous type. It is immediately clear that this estimator is biased, and that the bias is positive when a lower bound is used (as in Figure 7.1) but negative when an upper bound is used. In the case of the left-hand diagram, mass is shifted in the direction of the parameter value β to be estimated. The constrained estimator may then be regarded as superior to the unconstrained estimator. This need not always be true, however. In Figure 7.1*b* the true value is on the left of the origin, so that the shift overshoots the mark. Nevertheless, even if this is the case, the constrained estimator may be superior, depending on the criterion chosen. Suppose, for example, that the mean square error $\mathscr{E}[(b - \beta)^2]$ is our criterion; then the contribution of the probability mass in the origin to this expected square will be less than that of the broken part of the density curve when β is not too far to the left of the origin.

A Flexible-Bound Procedure

Another procedure is based on the following "flexible bound." When the original (unconstrained) estimate violates the constraint, we take a weighted average of this estimate and of the bound with weights θ and $1 - \theta$, respectively, which are chosen in advance subject to $0 \leq \theta \leq 1$. This procedure indicates that the analyst does not have absolute confidence in the bound; he is merely suspicious when the unconstrained estimate is on the wrong side of it. Writing α for its value (to be interpreted as a lower bound for the sake of convenience), we thus have the following estimator of β:

$$b^{\dagger} = \begin{cases} b & \text{if } b \geq \alpha \\ \theta b + (1 - \theta)\alpha & \text{if } b < \alpha \end{cases} \tag{9.2}$$

The distribution of this flexible-bound estimator is continuous except for a jump at α. This is shown in Figure 7.2 for $\theta = \frac{1}{2}$; the two normal distributions are identical with those of Figure 7.1 if we put $\alpha = 0$. The present approach is obviously more cautious than that of the previous paragraph (for which $\theta = 0$), which is advantageous in the case of Figure 7.2*b* but disadvantageous in the other case. ZELLNER (1963a) analyzed the merits of the flexible-bound estimator relative to those of b on the base of the mean-square-error criterion; his main results are summarized in Table 7.8, which contains the second

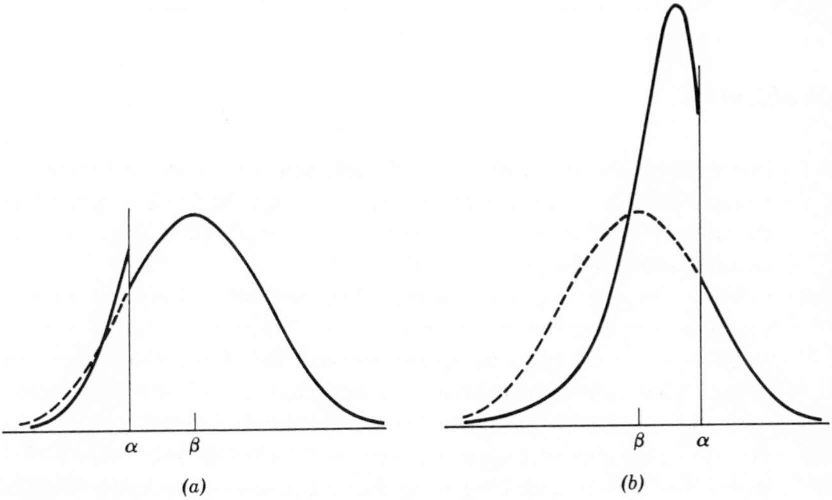

Fig. 7.2 Distributions of estimators which are subject to flexible bounds.

moment around β of the flexible-bound estimator measured as a fraction of the variance σ_b^2 of the unconstrained estimator b for certain values of θ and $(\beta - \alpha)/\sigma_b$. The figures indicate that if θ is not too small, the bound α may be rather far on the wrong side of β ($\beta - \alpha < 0$) before the second moment becomes larger than that of the unconstrained estimator.

Table 7.8

Mean Square Error of a Flexible-Bound Estimator Expressed as a Fraction of the Mean Square Error of the Unconstrained Estimator

$\frac{\beta - \alpha}{\sigma_b}$	$\theta = 0$	$\theta = .25$	$\theta = .5$	$\theta = .75$	$\theta = 1$
3	1.00	1.00	1.00	1.00	1
2.5	.99	.99	.99	1.00	1
2	.96	.97	.98	.99	1
1.5	.89	.91	.94	.97	1
1	.76	.80	.86	.93	1
.5	.59	.66	.74	.86	1
0	.50	.53	.62	.78	1
−.5	.66	.55	.57	.72	1
−1	1.24	.82	.64	.70	1
−1.5	2.36	1.42	.87	.74	1
−2	4.04	2.34	1.27	.82	1
−2.5	6.26	3.59	1.82	.96	1
−3	9.00	5.13	2.50	1.13	1

Problems

9.1 Prove that if the unconstrained LS coefficient illustrated in Figure 7.1 violates the nonnegativity constraint, the coefficient which minimizes the residual sum of squares subject to this constraint is zero (i.e., the solution satisfies the $\geq$ constraint in $=$ form).

9.2 Consider Figure 7.1*b* and suppose that the loss associated with a negative sampling error is measured by its square and that with a positive error by k times its square. Imagine that k becomes larger and larger; what can be said about the expected loss of the constrained estimator relative to that of the unconstrained estimator?

9.3 The two diagrams of Figure 7.1 have both a probability mass and a probability density measured along the vertical axis. Are the dimensions of mass and density the same?

CHAPTER 8

ASYMPTOTIC DISTRIBUTION THEORY

In the two previous chapters it was stated on several occasions that an estimator or a test statistic has approximately certain distribution properties when the sample is sufficiently large. In most of these cases it is difficult to derive the exact distribution of the statistic, but the difficulties disappear when the sample becomes larger and larger. There will obviously be approximation errors when the infinite-sample results are applied to samples of moderate size, as is frequently the case in the econometric practice.

This chapter develops the theory of approximate statistical inference for large samples. The best sources for the general statistical theory in this area are CRAMÉR (1946) and C. R. RAO (1965a). Section 8.1 and some subsections of Sections 8.2 and 8.9 are the parts of this chapter which are recommended for an introductory econometrics course, the remainder being of a more advanced nature.

8.1 Limits, Probability Limits, and Consistent Estimators[A]

Limits of Sequences

Consider a real sequence $a_1, a_2, \ldots, a_n, \ldots$, for example, $a_n = 3 + 1/n$ ($n = 1, 2, \ldots$). This sequence is said to have a limit equal to α when for any positive number δ (however small) there exists a number $N(\delta)$ such that the absolute difference $|a_n - \alpha|$ is less than δ for all $n > N(\delta)$. This is indicated as follows:

$$\lim_{n\to\infty} a_n = \alpha \tag{1.1}$$

In the case $a_n = 3 + 1/n$ there exists a limit and this is equal to 3, since for any given $\delta > 0$ the absolute difference $|a_n - 3| = 1/n$ is less than δ for whatever $n > N(\delta) = 1/\delta$. Note that not every sequence has a limit. Counter-examples are $\log n$ and $-n^2$, both of which diverge in either positive or negative direction when n increases indefinitely. Another counter-example is $(-1)^n$, which has no limit either but which is at least *bounded* in the sense that its absolute value is at most equal to a positive constant C (independent of n).

As an example in the area of statistical estimation, consider the maximum-likelihood estimator $(1/n)\sum(X_i - \bar{X})^2$ of the variance σ^2 of a normal distribution, which was formulated in eq. (7.16) of Section 2.7. We found there that the bias of this estimator is

$$\mathscr{E}\left[\frac{1}{n}\sum_{i=1}^{n}(X_i - \bar{X})^2\right] - \sigma^2 = \frac{n-1}{n}\sigma^2 - \sigma^2 = -\frac{\sigma^2}{n} \tag{1.2}$$

When we imagine that the sample size increases, the bias $-\sigma^2/n$ is a sequence with zero limit. Thus, although the maximum-likelihood estimator of σ^2 is biased for any finite sample size, the bias vanishes in the limit when n increases indefinitely.

The Order of Magnitude of a Sequence

Consider the sequence $a_n = 4 + n - 3n^2$. When n increases more and more, the terms 4 and n become small in absolute value compared with $-3n^2$ and, therefore, the last term is called the "leading term" of the sequence. This term determines the order of magnitude of the sequence. More formally, we say that the sequence a_n is at most of order n^k, written $O(n^k)$, when the sequence $n^{-k}a_n$ is bounded. For the above example take $k = 2$:

$$n^{-2}a_n = n^{-2}(4 + n - 3n^2) = \frac{4}{n^2} + \frac{1}{n} - 3$$

This converges to -3 as $n \to \infty$, so that it is certainly bounded; hence the sequence is $O(n^2)$. A related concept is "of smaller order than n^k," indicated by $o(n^k)$, which means that the sequence $n^{-k}a_n$ converges to zero. In our example $a_n = o(n^3)$, but also $a_n = o(n^{\frac{5}{2}})$ and $a_n = o(n^{10})$ for the same a_n. [Note that we may have $k = 0$; then $a_n = O(n^0) = O(1)$ means that the sequence is bounded, and $a_n = o(n^0) = o(1)$ that it has zero limit.] The algebra of sequences is rather straightforward. Take $a_n = 3n$ and $b_n = 1 + n^{-1}$; then $a_n + b_n = 3n + 1 + n^{-1}$ and $a_n b_n = 3n + 3$, which illustrates that if $a_n = O(n^h)$ and $b_n = O(n^k)$, then $a_n b_n = O(n^{h+k})$ and $a_n + b_n = O(n^g)$, where $g = \max(h, k)$.

Convergence in Probability of a Random Sequence

We now proceed to consider limit concepts within the purely statistical framework. Take a sequence of random variables $Y_1, Y_2, \ldots, Y_n, \ldots$ with distribution functions $F_1(\ ), F_2(\ ), \ldots, F_n(\ ), \ldots$. This sequence is said to *converge in probability* to a constant c if

$$(1.3) \qquad \lim_{n\to\infty} \mathrm{P}[|Y_n - c| > \epsilon] = 0 \quad \text{for any} \quad \epsilon > 0$$

The expression in brackets, $|Y_n - c| > \epsilon$, is an inequality which is either true or untrue. The probability that it is true is determined by the distribution function $F_n(\ )$ of Y_n, by c, and by ϵ. Thus, given c and the sequence of distributions, this probability forms a sequence $a_1(\epsilon), a_2(\epsilon), \ldots, a_n(\epsilon), \ldots$ depending parametrically on ϵ. Therefore the definition (1.3) amounts to the following. The sequence of random variables $Y_1, Y_2, \ldots$ converges in probability to the constant c if the limit of this sequence of probabilities is zero *for whatever positive value of* ϵ. The concept is illustrated in Figure 8.1 for a sequence of random variables with continuous distributions. The probability whose limit is considered in (1.3) is measured by the area below the density curve outside the interval $(c \pm \epsilon)$. Clearly, this area is smaller for $n = 50$ than for $n = 10$, and smaller again for $n = 250$.

As an example of convergence in probability to a constant, consider the sample mean $\bar{X}_n = (1/n) \sum X_i$ of a random sample $(X_1, \ldots, X_n)$ from an arbitrary population with finite mean μ and variance σ^2. (The subscript n of $\bar{X}_n$ serves to indicate explicitly that the underlying sample is of size n.) We know that the distribution of $\bar{X}_n$ has mean μ and variance σ^2/n. This is sufficient to guarantee that the sequence of random variables $\bar{X}_1, \bar{X}_2, \ldots, \bar{X}_n, \ldots$ (the sample means of successively large samples) converges in probability to the population mean μ. A simple proof is based on Chebyshev's inequality,[1] which states that for any random variable Z with finite mean μ and variance σ^2, the probability of a deviation from the mean equal to k times the standard deviation or more is at most equal to $1/k^2$:

$$(1.4) \qquad \mathrm{P}[|Z - \mu| \geq k\sigma] \leq \frac{1}{k^2} \quad \text{for any} \quad k > 0$$

[1] See Problem 1.1 at the end of Section 2.1.

In the case of $\bar{X}_n$ the mean is μ and the variance is σ^2/n, so that the inequality in brackets becomes $|\bar{X}_n - \mu| \geq k\sigma/\sqrt{n}$. By specifying $k = \epsilon\sqrt{n}/\sigma$ we thus obtain

$$\text{(1.5)} \qquad P[|X_n - \mu| \geq \epsilon] \leq \frac{\sigma^2}{n\epsilon^2} \quad \text{for any} \quad \epsilon > 0$$

Since $\sigma^2/n\epsilon^2$ converges to zero as $n \to \infty$ for whatever $\epsilon > 0$, we may conclude from the definition (1.3) that the sample mean $\bar{X}_n$ of a random sample

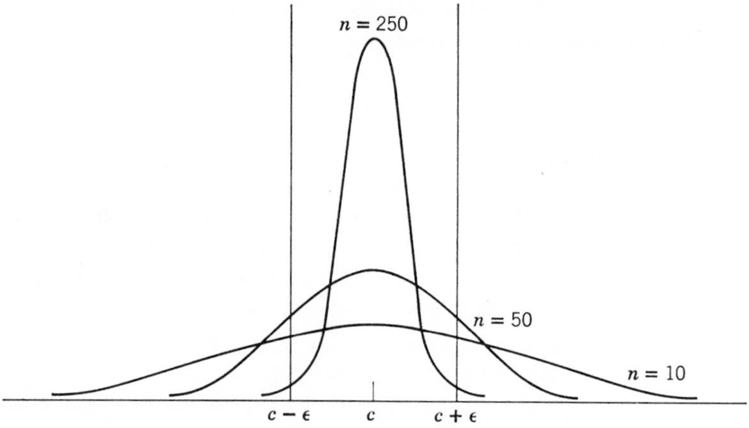

Fig. 8.1 Illustration of convergence in probability to a constant.

$(X_1, \ldots, X_n)$ from an arbitrary population with finite variance converges in probability to the mean μ of that population.

Khintchine's Theorem

The result of the previous paragraph is a special case of Khintchine's theorem, which may be formulated as follows. Let $X_1, \ldots, X_n$ be independent random variables, all having the same distribution with finite mean μ; then their average $\bar{X}_n$ converges in probability to μ as $n \to \infty$. Note that this theorem does not require the variance to be finite. See Problem 2.2 below for its proof, which requires a theorem that will be considered in the next section.

Probability Limits of Random Sequences

The notation (1.3) for convergence in probability is rather awkward. A more compact notation which is widely used is

$$\text{(1.6)} \qquad \operatorname*{plim}_{n\to\infty} Y_n = c$$

or in words: the *probability limit* (abbreviated as plim) of the random sequence is equal to c. This is fully equivalent to: "The sequence $Y_1, Y_2, \ldots$ converges in probability to c," but the term probability limit has the additional advantage (besides the compact notation to which it leads) that it stresses the difference with an ordinary limit. When $Y_1, Y_2, \ldots$ is a nonrandom sequence with limit c, we can be *certain* that $|Y_n - c|$ is less than any given positive number ϵ when n is sufficiently large. When $Y_1, Y_2, \ldots$ is a random sequence with probability limit c, we can only say that $|Y_n - c| < \epsilon$ is true with a *probability arbitrarily close to unity* when n is sufficiently large. But when the range of Y_n is infinite, there will always be a positive probability that $|Y_n - c|$ is larger than ϵ no matter how large n is. The ordinary limit is obviously a special case of the probability limit, so that all theorems concerning the latter apply to the former a fortiori.

Extensions

The concept of a probability limit can be extended straightforwardly to the case in which Y_n and c are vectors or matrices rather than scalars. Each element of Y_n then converges in probability to the corresponding element of c. Furthermore, if $g(\ )$ is a continuous function and if the probability limit of Y_n is equal to c as (1.6) states, then

$$\text{(1.7)} \qquad \operatorname*{plim}_{n\to\infty} g(Y_n) = g(\operatorname*{plim}_{n\to\infty} Y_n) = g(c)$$

In words: the probability limit of a random sequence, each term of which is a function $g(\ )$ of the corresponding term of another random sequence, is equal to the same function of the probability limit of the latter sequence, provided that this limit exists and the function is continuous. The proof is straightforward and can be outlined briefly as follows. If $g(\ )$ is continuous, its value is arbitrarily close to $g(c)$ when its argument Y_n is sufficiently close to c. But (1.6) guarantees that this condition is satisfied with a probability arbitrarily close to 1 when n is sufficiently large. Thus, $g(Y_n)$ is very close to $g(c)$ with increasing certainty as $n \to \infty$. Again, this result can be extended easily for continuous vector and matrix functions.

Consistent Estimators

Convergence in probability is a particularly important concept when the random sequence involved is an estimator based on successively larger samples ($n = 1, 2, \ldots$) and when the constant toward which this sequence converges is the corresponding unknown parameter. Specifically, let θ be a parameter characterizing some distribution and suppose that a random sample $(X_1, \ldots, X_n)$ is drawn from this population. A statistic $\hat{\theta}_n$ is used as an estimator of θ; the subscript n indicates the size of the sample on which the estimator is based. If $\hat{\theta}_n$ converges in probability to θ:

$$\lim_{n\to\infty} \mathrm{P}[|\hat{\theta}_n - \theta| > \epsilon] = 0 \quad \text{for any} \quad \epsilon > 0 \tag{1.8}$$

or, equivalently, if θ coincides with the probability limit of $\hat{\theta}_n$,

$$\operatorname*{plim}_{n\to\infty} \hat{\theta}_n = \theta \tag{1.9}$$

then $\hat{\theta}_n$ is said to be a *consistent estimator* of θ. Thus, going back to the sample mean $\bar{X}_n$ from a population with a finite variance, we proved that $\bar{X}_n$ converges in probability to the population mean μ; this is equivalent to saying that $\bar{X}_n$ is a consistent estimator of μ. Recall that we proved this by showing that the expectation of $\bar{X}_n$ is equal to μ and that its variance converges to zero. Therefore the following result, based on Chebyshev's inequality, generally holds. A sufficient condition for an estimator $\hat{\theta}_n$ to be consistent for θ is $\mathscr{E}\hat{\theta}_n = \theta$ (identically for all n and θ) and $\lim (\operatorname{var} \hat{\theta}_n) = 0$ as $n \to \infty$. Note that these are not necessary conditions. The estimator may be biased and still consistent if the bias converges to zero; see Problem 1.7. In some cases it is not even necessary that the variance exist for whatever finite n. Khintchine's theorem provides an example. If $X_1, \ldots, X_n$ are independently and identically distributed with finite mean μ, then the average $\bar{X}_n$ of the X_i's is a consistent estimator of μ. We shall return to the problem of the existence of variances of estimators for finite n in Section 8.3.

Consistency of LS Estimators under the Conditions of the Standard Linear Model

Consistency thus means that when the sample becomes larger and larger, there is only a very small chance that the estimator differs from the parameter by more than any given amount. It can be shown that under appropriate conditions, LS estimation in the standard linear model has this property:

THEOREM 8.1 (Consistency of LS coefficient and variance estimators) *Suppose that Assumption* 3.3 *of Section* 3.2 *is true for given* $\mathbf{X}$. *Then the LS vector* $\mathbf{b} = (\mathbf{X}'\mathbf{X})^{-1}\mathbf{X}'\mathbf{y}$ *is a consistent estimator of* $\boldsymbol{\beta}$ *if the matrix* $(1/n)\mathbf{X}'\mathbf{X}$ *converges to a positive definite matrix* $\mathbf{Q}$ *as* $n \to \infty$, *and the statistic* $s^2 = \mathbf{e}'\mathbf{e}/(n-K)$, *where* $\mathbf{e} = \mathbf{y} - \mathbf{X}\mathbf{b}$, *is a consistent estimator of* σ^2 *if the distribution of* $\mathbf{y}$ *(given* $\mathbf{X}$*) is n-variate normal.*

The consistency of $\mathbf{b}$ can be proved by means of Theorem 3.2 of Section 3.3, according to which this estimator has a K-dimensional distribution with mean vector $\boldsymbol{\beta}$ and covariance matrix $\sigma^2(\mathbf{X}'\mathbf{X})^{-1}$.[2] This matrix can be written as a scalar multiple σ^2/n of the inverse of $(1/n)\mathbf{X}'\mathbf{X}$. The latter matrix converges to $\mathbf{Q}$ as $n \to \infty$. Since the elements of an inverse are continuous functions of the elements of the original matrix (if this matrix has an inverse—but this is true by assumption), the inverse of $(1/n)\mathbf{X}'\mathbf{X}$ converges to $\mathbf{Q}^{-1}$. Hence,

$$\lim_{n\to\infty} \mathscr{V}(\mathbf{b}) = \lim_{n\to\infty} \left[\frac{\sigma^2}{n}\left(\frac{1}{n}\mathbf{X}'\mathbf{X}\right)^{-1}\right] = 0\mathbf{Q} = \mathbf{0} \tag{1.10}$$

because σ^2/n converges to zero. Therefore, all elements of $\mathbf{b}$ are unbiased and have variances that converge toward zero, so that Chebyshev's inequality may be used to establish their consistency with respect to the corresponding elements of $\boldsymbol{\beta}$.

To prove the consistency of s^2 under the normality condition, recall that the random variable $(n - K)s^2/\sigma^2$ is distributed as $\chi^2(n - K)$ according to Theorem 3.8 of Section 3.5; hence its mean is $n - K$ and its variance is $2(n - K)$, so that s^2 is an unbiased estimator of σ^2 with variance $2\sigma^4/(n - K)$. (See also Theorem 3.7 in Section 3.5.) Since this variance converges to zero as $n \to \infty$, s^2 is indeed consistent for σ^2, which completes the proof.

The Convergence Condition on the Moments of the Explanatory Variables

The condition $\lim n^{-1}\mathbf{X}'\mathbf{X} = \mathbf{Q}$ will be used on a large scale in the sequel.[3] We imagine that for each new observation, a new row is added to the matrix $\mathbf{X}$ and that the earlier rows remain intact in such a way that the K^2 elements of $\mathbf{X}'\mathbf{X}$ are $O(n)$. In addition, we exclude the possibility that the limit of $n^{-1}\mathbf{X}'\mathbf{X}$ is singular.

ASSUMPTION 8.1 (Convergence of $n^{-1}\mathbf{X}'\mathbf{X}$) *The matrix $n^{-1}\mathbf{X}'\mathbf{X}$ converges, as $n \to \infty$, to a positive definite $K \times K$ matrix $\mathbf{Q}$.*

The reader may think that this assumption is quite innocent, given that the available data are always finite in number and that the limiting procedure $n \to \infty$ is nothing but an abstract mathematical idea. However, the assumption does imply certain restrictions, which will be clear from the following examples.

[2] It would be more in conformity with the sequence notation to write $\mathbf{X}_n$ rather than $\mathbf{X}$, but we prefer not to deviate from the notation of the earlier chapters.

[3] Note that this condition is not needed for the consistency of s^2. On the other hand, if it is satisfied, we can replace the normality condition by the weaker condition of independently and identically distributed disturbances to obtain the same consistency result for s^2; see Theorem 8.2 in Section 8.3 below.

(1) Consider the simplest case $\mathbf{X}' = [1 \quad 1 \quad \cdots \quad 1]$—no slope coefficients, only a constant term. Then $(1/n)\mathbf{X}'\mathbf{X} = 1$, which trivially converges to a positive value (one) as $n \to \infty$. Evidently no difficulties arise in this case.

(2) Take a linear trend without constant term: $\mathbf{X}' = [1 \quad 2 \quad \cdots \quad n]$. Then $\mathbf{X}'\mathbf{X} = O(n^3)$, so that $(1/n)\mathbf{X}'\mathbf{X}$ does not converge to a finite limit. Nevertheless, the LS coefficient is consistent when the other assumptions of Theorem 8.1 are satisfied; see Problem 1.9.

(3) Again, take one explanatory variable and no constant term, but let the values of that variable be of the form $x_\alpha = (\frac{1}{2})^\alpha$: $x_1 = \frac{1}{2}$, $x_2 = \frac{1}{4}$, $x_3 = \frac{1}{8}, \ldots$. The sum of squares for n observations is $\sum x_\alpha^2 = [1 - (\frac{1}{4})^n]/3$, which is less than $\frac{1}{3}$ for any finite n and which converges to that value as $n \to \infty$. Hence the LS coefficient has a variance which is never smaller than $3\sigma^2$, no matter how large n is. Intuitively, the reason is clear. When we have one explanatory variable and no constant term, the precision with which the coefficient of that variable is estimated is determined (given σ^2) by the absolute values of this variable. Under the specification $x_\alpha = (\frac{1}{2})^\alpha$ these values converge to zero so rapidly that from a certain point onward, the contribution of all later observations to this precision is negligible.

(4) Suppose that we have two explanatory variables and assume that $x_{\alpha 2} = k x_{\alpha 1}$ holds for some k and for all α above a certain number N. When $(1/n) \sum x_{\alpha 1}^2$ converges to a finite positive limit, the matrix $(1/n)\mathbf{X}'\mathbf{X}$ converges to a singular $\mathbf{Q}$; see Problem 1.10. This is a case of "extreme multicollinearity in the limit."

"Constant in Repeated Samples"

The above examples illustrate that Assumption 8.1 requires that the mean squares and mean products of all explanatory variables converge to finite limits, and that these limits form a positive definite matrix.[4] When nothing is known about the behavior of the explanatory variables except the given observation matrix $\mathbf{X}$, a simple and convenient way of visualizing later values is the following. The matrix $\mathbf{X}$ contains the first n observations. Imagine, then, that all later observations on these variables are obtained in batches of n and that each such batch is identical with the original $\mathbf{X}$ matrix. For pn observations we thus have a $pn \times K$ matrix:

$$(1.11) \qquad \begin{bmatrix} \mathbf{X} \\ \mathbf{X} \\ \cdot \\ \cdot \\ \cdot \\ \mathbf{X} \end{bmatrix} \quad \begin{matrix} \text{first set of } n \text{ observations} \\ \text{second set of } n \text{ observations} \\ \\ \\ \\ p\text{th set of } n \text{ observations} \end{matrix}$$

[4] Note that the mean products include the means when the regression has a constant term.

If we premultiply this matrix by its own transpose and then multiply by the reciprocal of the number of observations (pn), we obtain

$$\frac{1}{pn}(\mathbf{X}'\mathbf{X} + \cdots + \mathbf{X}'\mathbf{X}) = \frac{1}{n}\mathbf{X}'\mathbf{X} \tag{1.12}$$

Here n and $\mathbf{X}$ are fixed; increasing the number of observations indefinitely amounts in this case to the limiting process $p \to \infty$. It follows that $\mathbf{Q}$ of Assumption 8.1 is now equal to the *fixed* matrix $(1/n)\mathbf{X}'\mathbf{X}$, so that this assumption is trivially fulfilled when the (fixed) matrix $\mathbf{X}$ has full column rank. This particular way of increasing the number of observations is sometimes indicated by saying that the explanatory variables are regarded as "constant in repeated samples." Note that this process cannot be applied to every type of variable. It applies trivially to the constant-term variable which takes the unit value for each observation, but it does not apply to a linear trend.

Problems

1.1 Prove that the sequence $a_n = (-1)^n + 2/n$ is bounded.

1.2 The following sequences are all $O(n^k)$ for some k; determine this k in each case. (1) $2 + 4n - n^2$; (2) $1 + 5\sqrt{n}$; (3) $2 - 5/\sqrt{n}$.

1.3 Consider two sequences: $a_n = O(n^h)$ and $b_n = o(n^k)$. Prove $a_n b_n = o(n^{h+k})$ and $a_n + b_n = O(n^h)$ if $h \geq k$, $o(n^k)$ if $h < k$.

1.4 Prove that the convergence in probability as defined in (1.3) can also be formulated in the following equivalent way. For any pair of positive numbers (δ, ϵ), however small, there exists a number $N(\delta, \epsilon)$ such that the probability that $|Y_n - c| > \epsilon$ is less than δ when $n > N(\delta, \epsilon)$.

1.5 Give a rigorous proof of (1.7) under the condition that plim $Y_n = c$ and that $g(\ )$ is continuous in an interval which contains c as an interior point.

1.6 Let $\mathbf{A}_1, \mathbf{A}_2, \ldots, \mathbf{A}_n, \ldots$ be a sequence of square random matrices of fixed order with probability limit $\mathbf{B}$. Prove plim $\mathbf{A}_n^{-1} = \mathbf{B}^{-1}$ if $\mathbf{B}$ is nonsingular.

1.7 Prove that $\hat{\theta}_n$ is consistent for θ if (1) $\hat{\theta}_n$ is biased but the bias converges to zero as $n \to \infty$ and (2) the variance of the estimator also converges to zero. [*Hint.* Write $\hat{\theta}_n - \theta = (\hat{\theta}_n - \mathscr{E}\hat{\theta}_n) + (\mathscr{E}\hat{\theta}_n - \theta)$ and prove plim $(a_n + b_n) =$ plim a_n + lim b_n, where $a_n = \hat{\theta}_n - \mathscr{E}\hat{\theta}_n$ is a random sequence with a finite probability limit and $b_n = \mathscr{E}\hat{\theta}_n - \theta$ is a nonrandom sequence with a finite limit.]

1.8 Prove that Assumption 8.1 may be replaced by the weaker condition lim $(\mathbf{X}'\mathbf{X})^{-1} = \mathbf{0}$ for the consistency of $\mathbf{b}$ (Theorem 8.1), and show that the latter condition is indeed weaker.

1.9 Consider example (2) below Assumption 8.1 (the linear trend without constant term) and prove that the variance of the LS coefficient under the assumptions of the standard linear model is $6\sigma^2/n(n+1)(2n+1)$. (*Hint.* See Problem 7.1 at the end of Section 1.7.) Also prove that this coefficient is a consistent estimator of the corresponding parameter. Next, take the case of a linear trend with constant term:

$$\mathbf{X}' = \begin{bmatrix} 1 & 1 & \cdots & 1 \\ 1 & 2 & \cdots & n \end{bmatrix} \tag{1.13}$$

and prove that this specification, too, violates Assumption 8.1. Derive the covariance matrix of the two LS coefficients and prove that it converges to the 2×2 zero matrix, thus establishing the consistency of these coefficients (given their unbiasedness under the assumptions of the standard linear model).

1.10 Consider the case of two explanatory variables (no constant term) and suppose that numbers k and N exist such that $x_{\alpha 2} = kx_{\alpha 1}$ holds for each $\alpha > N$. Find the matrix $\mathbf{Q}$ of Assumption 8.1 under the assumption that $(1/n)\sum x_{\alpha 1}^2$ converges to a positive limit, and prove that this $\mathbf{Q}$ is singular.

8.2 Limiting Distributions and the Central Limit Theorem[AC]

Limiting Distributions[A]

Consistency means only that there is high probability that the sampling error is very small when the sample is sufficiently large. The concept does not provide a statement on the size of the sampling error such as the standard error. For that purpose the analysis must be extended, and so we return to our sequence of random variables $Y_1, Y_2, \ldots$ with distribution functions $F_1(\ )$, $F_2(\ ), \ldots$. This sequence is said to *converge in distribution* to a random variable Y with distribution function $F(\ )$ if $F_n(x)$ converges to $F(x)$ as $n \to \infty$ for all continuity points of $F(\ )$. The distribution $F(\ )$ is called the *limiting distribution* of this sequence of random variables. Note that this definition includes, as a special case, convergence in probability to some constant c [see (1.3)]; the limiting distribution is then degenerate with all its mass concentrated at c. The concept is illustrated in Figure 8.2 for $F_{10}(\ )$, $F_{100}(\ )$, and the limiting distribution $F(\ )$. Clearly, $F_{100}(\ )$ is much closer to $F(\ )$ than $F_{10}(\ )$ is.

It will appear in the sections which follow that the asymptotic standard errors discussed in the two previous chapters refer to the standard deviations of limiting distributions associated with the estimators. It will also appear that if the sequence $F_1(\ ), F_2(\ ), \ldots$ converges to $F(\ )$ as outlined in the previous paragraph, the standard deviation (σ) of the limiting distribution $F(\ )$ is *not* necessarily identical with the limit of the sequence of standard deviations ($\sigma_1, \sigma_2, \ldots$) of the distributions $F_1(\ ), F_2(\ ), \ldots$. In fact, there is an important class of cases in which σ exists while $\sigma_1, \sigma_2, \ldots$ do not. These ideas will be pursued more systematically in Section 8.3.

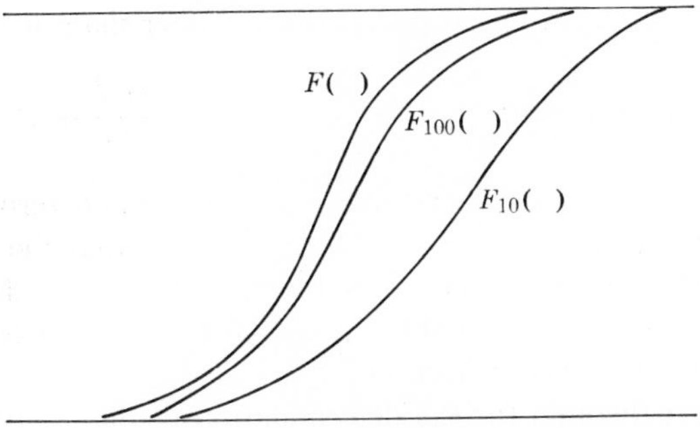

Fig. 8.2 Illustration of convergence in distribution.

Characteristic Functions and Their Role in the Determination of Limiting Distributions[C]

To derive the limiting distribution of a given sequence of distributions we return to Section 2.5, where we developed the moment-generating function $M(t) = \mathscr{E}(e^{tX})$ of a random variable X. The theorem that we shall need does not really hold for moment-generating functions, but it does hold for the characteristic function $\phi(t)$, which is defined as the expectation of e^{itX}, where $i = \sqrt{-1}$ is the imaginary unit:[5]

$$\phi(t) = \mathscr{E}(e^{itX}) \tag{2.1}$$

The evaluation of the characteristic function for a given distribution is straightforward when the moment-generating function is known; it is simply a matter of replacing t by it and of substituting -1 for i^2. Thus, on the basis of eqs. (5.4) and (5.7) of Section 2.5 we find for the characteristic function of the univariate normal distribution with mean μ and variance σ^2:

$$\phi(t) = \exp\left\{\mu it - \frac{1}{2}\sigma^2 t^2\right\} \tag{2.2}$$

and for the characteristic function of the multinormal distribution with mean

[5] See footnote 6 of Chapter 2 on p. 73.

vector $\boldsymbol{\mu}$ and covariance matrix $\boldsymbol{\Sigma}$:

$$\phi(\mathbf{t}) = \exp\left\{i\boldsymbol{\mu}'\mathbf{t} - \frac{1}{2}\mathbf{t}'\boldsymbol{\Sigma}\mathbf{t}\right\} \tag{2.3}$$

The characteristic function can also be used to generate moments. In the one-dimensional case the Taylor expansion given in the first paragraph of Section 2.5 is now according to powers of it, rather than of t:

$$\phi(t) = 1 + \mu it + \mu_2' \frac{(it)^2}{2!} + \cdots + \mu_k' \frac{(it)^k}{k!} + R_k \tag{2.4}$$

where $\mu, \mu_2', \mu_3', \ldots$ are the successive moments around zero; the last term (R_k) is a remainder term. It is also readily verified that the rule for linear functions of independent random variables which was derived for the moment-generating function holds equally for the characteristic function [see eqs. (5.10) and (5.11) of Section 2.5].

The important theorem for the determination of the limiting distribution of a sequence of random variables $Y_1, Y_2, \ldots$, based on the characteristic function, is as follows.[6] Let $\phi_1(t), \phi_2(t), \ldots$ be the sequence of characteristic functions of $Y_1, Y_2, \ldots$, and suppose that $\phi_n(t)$ converges to $\phi(t)$ as $n \to \infty$ for all t; then the sequence $Y_1, Y_2, \ldots$ converges in distribution to the limiting distribution whose characteristic function is $\phi(t)$, provided that $\phi(t)$ is continuous at $t = 0$. The procedure is thus as follows. Verify that the characteristic function $\phi_n(t)$ converges to a function $\phi(t)$ as $n \to \infty$ for all t, check the continuity of $\phi(t)$ at $t = 0$, and try to recognize the distribution which has this $\phi(t)$ as its characteristic function. That distribution is the limiting distribution of the sequence $Y_1, Y_2, \ldots$.

The Central Limit Theorem (Lindeberg-Lévy)[C]

The above procedure will now be illustrated for the average $\bar{X}_n$ of n independently and identically distributed random variables $X_1, \ldots, X_n$ with mean μ and variance σ^2. We measure each of these variables as a deviation from the mean; the characteristic function of $X_i - \mu$ can then be written as $1 - \frac{1}{2}\sigma^2 t^2 + R_2$ in view of (2.4). Next we divide $X_i - \mu$ by $\sigma\sqrt{n}$ and we recall that the kth order moment is then divided by $(\sigma\sqrt{n})^k$. The characteristic function of the ratio of $X_i - \mu$ to $\sigma\sqrt{n}$ thus becomes $1 - \frac{1}{2}t^2/n + o(n^{-1})$; the term $o(n^{-1})$ is based on the consideration that the remainder term R_2 is divided by $(\sigma\sqrt{n})^k$ with $k > 2$. Finally, we add the n ratios:

$$\sum_{i=1}^{n} \frac{X_i - \mu}{\sigma\sqrt{n}} = \frac{(\bar{X}_n - \mu)\sqrt{n}}{\sigma} \tag{2.5}$$

[6] For a proof see, for example, Cramér (1946, pp. 96–98).

Since the n ratios that are added are stochastically independent, the characteristic function of their sum (2.5), to be denoted by $\phi_n(t)$, is obtained by taking the product of the individual characteristic functions:

$$\phi_n(t) = \left[1 - \frac{1}{2}t^2/n + o(n^{-1})\right]^n \tag{2.6}$$

Then take natural logarithms on both sides and apply the familiar Taylor expansion of $\log(1 + x)$ for small $|x|$ (which amounts to a large n here):

$$\begin{aligned} \log \phi_n(t) &= n \log\left[1 - \frac{1}{2}t^2/n + o(n^{-1})\right] \\ &= -n\left[\frac{1}{2}t^2/n + o(n^{-1})\right] \to -\frac{1}{2}t^2 \quad \text{as} \quad n \to \infty \end{aligned} \tag{2.7}$$

We conclude that as $n \to \infty$ the characteristic function $\phi_n(t)$ of the random variable (2.5) converges, for all t, to $e^{-t^2/2}$, which is the characteristic function of the standardized normal distribution. Note that $e^{-t^2/2}$ is continuous at $t = 0$; this is part of the conditions mentioned above.

The preceding paragraph proves the *Lindeberg-Lévy variant* of the *central limit theorem*, which can be explained in words as follows. We already know that the sample mean $\bar{X}_n$ of a random sample from a *normal* population with mean μ and variance σ^2 is itself normally distributed with mean μ and variance σ^2/n; or, equivalently, that the random variable (2.5) follows a standardized normal distribution if the sampling takes place from a normal population. We now find that when we draw such a sample from *any* population with mean μ and variance σ^2 (both finite), the *limiting* distribution of (2.5) is of the standardized normal type. This is frequently expressed by saying that the sample mean $\bar{X}_n$ is *asymptotically normally distributed with mean μ and variance σ^2/n.* Note that the *limiting distribution* of $\bar{X}_n$ is degenerate with all its mass concentrated at μ. When we say that $\bar{X}_n$ is asymptotically normally distributed with mean μ and variance σ^2/n, we make a statement about the way in which the distribution of $\bar{X}_n$ behaves when approaching the degenerate distribution. Thus, even though $\bar{X}_n$ may not be normally distributed for any finite n, we can nevertheless make approximate statements on its distribution by acting as if it is normal with mean μ and variance σ^2/n, provided that n is large.

Extensions[C]

The vector generalization of the Lindeberg-Lévy theorem can be formulated as follows. Let $\mathbf{x}_1, \ldots, \mathbf{x}_n$ be independent random drawings from a k-dimensional population with finite mean vector $\boldsymbol{\mu}$ and finite covariance matrix $\mathbf{A}$; then the vector $n^{-\frac{1}{2}} \sum_i (\mathbf{x}_i - \boldsymbol{\mu})$ has a multinormal limiting distribution with zero mean vector and covariance matrix $\mathbf{A}$. Equivalently, the vector $\bar{\mathbf{x}} = (1/n) \sum \mathbf{x}_i$ is asymptotically normally distributed with mean vector $\boldsymbol{\mu}$ and covariance matrix $(1/n)\mathbf{A}$. The proof is a direct extension of that of the one-dimensional case.

A second generalization concerns the case in which $X_1, \ldots, X_n$ are still independent with common mean μ but otherwise have different distributions. We suppose that the distributions are continuous with density functions $f_i(\ )$ and finite variances σ_i^2, $i = 1, \ldots, n$. Write D_n for the standard deviation of $X_1 + \cdots + X_n$ (i.e., D_n is the positive square root of $\sigma_1^2 + \cdots + \sigma_n^2$) and consider the ratio

$$\frac{1}{D_n} \sum_{i=1}^{n} (X_i - \mu) \tag{2.8}$$

which reduces to (2.5) when the variances σ_i^2 are all equal. The ratio (2.8) can be shown to converge in distribution to a standardized normal variate if

$$\lim_{n \to \infty} \frac{1}{D_n^2} \sum_{i=1}^{n} \left[\int_{|x| > \epsilon D_n} (x - \mu)^2 f_i(x)\, dx \right] = 0 \tag{2.9}$$

for any given $\epsilon > 0$.[7] The implications of this condition are not immediately obvious, but it can be shown that it requires that $D_n \to \infty$ and $\sigma_n / D_n \to 0$ as $n \to \infty$. This means that the total variance D_n^2 of $X_1 + \cdots + X_n$ tends to infinity but that each component of this total variance contributes only a small fraction. Note that (2.9) implies $D_n \to \infty$, $\sigma_n / D_n \to 0$, but not vice versa.

This second generalization is of some importance for the distribution of the disturbances of our basic equations. If we imagine that these disturbances represent the combined influence of numerous neglected factors, and if we assume that these factors operate linearly and independently, then the disturbances are approximately normally distributed, provided that the number of these factors is sufficiently large and none dominates the others.

Five Propositions on Convergence in Probability and in Distribution[C]

Some important rules on convergence in probability and in distribution are listed below. The validity of these rules should be intuitively obvious; the proof of one of them is examined in Problem 2.5.[8]

(i) Let (X_n, Y_n), $n = 1, 2, \ldots$ be a sequence of pairs of random variables. If $X_n - Y_n$ converges in probability to zero and if Y_n has a limiting distribution, then X_n has also a limiting distribution and these two limiting distributions are identical.

[7] See, for example, Cramér (1937, pp. 57–61).

[8] For detailed proofs see C. R. Rao (1965a, pp. 101–106).

(ii) For the same sequence of pairs, suppose that Y_n has a limiting distribution and that X_n has zero probability limit. Then the product sequence $X_1Y_1, X_2Y_2, \ldots$ also has zero probability limit. (Obviously, if Y_n has no limiting distribution, for example, if Y_n is normally distributed with zero mean and variance kn, k being a constant independent of n, then the zero probability limit of X_n does not guarantee that $X_1Y_1, X_2Y_2, \ldots$ converges in probability to zero.)

(iii) For the same sequence of pairs, again suppose that Y_n converges in distribution to a random variable Y but now suppose that X_n converges in probability to a constant c (not necessarily zero). Then the sum sequence $X_n + Y_n$ converges in distribution to $c + Y$, the product sequence X_nY_n to cY [this includes rule (ii) as a special case], and the ratio sequence Y_n/X_n to Y/c if $c \neq 0$.

(iv) If $g(\ )$ is a continuous function and if X_n converges in distribution to X, then $g(X_n)$ converges in distribution to $g(X)$. [Note that here as well as in the following rule the *function* $g(\ )$ does not depend on n; only the distribution of the argument X_n does. Thus, $g(X_n) = nX_n^2$ is not a function covered by this rule.]

(v) If $g(\ )$ is a continuous function and if $X_n - Y_n$ converges in probability to zero and X_n in distribution to X, then $g(X_n) - g(Y_n)$ converges in probability to zero.

These rules are also valid when X_n and Y_n are sequences of random vectors or matrices and when $g(\ )$ is a vector or matrix function.

Problems

2.1 Describe how Figure 8.2 looks when the convergence in distribution degenerates to convergence in probability.

2.2 (*Proof of Khintchine's theorem*) Let $X_1, \ldots, X_n$ be independently and identically distributed with mean μ. Apply an argument similar to that of (2.5) and (2.6) to prove that the characteristic function of their average $\bar{X}_n$ is equal to the nth power of $1 + \mu it/n + o(n^{-1})$. Prove that this function converges to $e^{\mu it}$ for each t as $n \to \infty$, check its continuity at $t = 0$, and prove that $e^{\mu it}$ is the characteristic function of a (degenerate) random variable with mean μ and zero variance.

2.3 Consider the Cauchy distribution whose density function is equal to the reciprocal of $\pi[1 + (x - \mu)^2]$. Does it follow from Khintchine's theorem that the sample mean $\bar{X}_n$ of a random sample $(X_1, \ldots, X_n)$ from this distribution is a consistent estimator of μ?

2.4 (*Lyapunov's theorem*) Let $X_1, \ldots, X_n$ be independent random variables with means μ_i, variances σ_i^2, and third absolute moments

$\mathscr{E}(|X_i - \mu|^3) = c_i^3$, $i = 1, \ldots, n$, all of which are assumed to exist. Define C_n as the cube root of $c_1^3 + \cdots + c_n^3$. Lyapunov's theorem states that if $\lim (C_n/D_n) = 0$ as $n \to \infty$, where D_n is the positive square root of $\sigma_1^2 + \cdots + \sigma_n^2$, then the ratio (2.8) has a standardized normal limiting distribution. Questions:

(1) Prove that the limit of C_n/D_n is zero when the X's are identically distributed.

(2) Does it follow from (1) that Lyapunov's theorem contains the Lindeberg-Lévy theorem as a special case?

2.5 To prove rule (ii) in the last subsection on the product sequence $X_1 Y_1$, $X_2 Y_2, \ldots$, take two fixed positive numbers ϵ and k and write

$$\text{P}[|X_n Y_n| > \epsilon]$$

as the sum of:

$$\text{P}[|X_n Y_n| > \epsilon \quad \text{and} \quad |X_n| < \epsilon/k] \leq \text{P}[|Y_n| > k] \tag{2.10}$$

$$\text{P}[|X_n Y_n| > \epsilon \quad \text{and} \quad |X_n| \geq \epsilon/k] \leq \text{P}[|X_n| \geq \epsilon/k] \tag{2.11}$$

Conclude from the existence of a limiting distribution of Y_n that the right-hand side of (2.10) can be made arbitrarily small for sufficiently large n by choosing k sufficiently large. Conclude from the zero probability limit of X_n that the right-hand side of (2.11) converges to zero as $n \to \infty$ for any positive pair (ϵ, k)

8.3 Convergence in Probability and in Distribution: Applications and Further Extensions[C]

In this section we shall consider the asymptotic distributions of moments, of functions of moments, of functions of other statistics, and of the LS coefficients in the standard linear model. Other highlights are asymptotic standard errors and the distinction between the limits of the moments of a sequence of distributions and the moments of the corresponding limiting distribution.

The Asymptotic Distribution of a Sample Moment

Consider a random sample $(X_1, \ldots, X_n)$ from some univariate population; it will be assumed throughout that all population moments that appear to be relevant do exist. The sample moment and the population moment around zero of the hth order are $m_h' = n^{-1} \sum_i X_i^h$ and $\mu_h' = \mathscr{E}X_i^h$, respectively, and it is immediately clear that m_h' is an unbiased estimator of μ_h'. Consider, then, the expectation of the product of two sample moments:

$$(3.1)\quad \mathscr{E}(m_h'm_k') = \frac{1}{n^2}\sum_{i=1}^{n}\sum_{j=1}^{n}\mathscr{E}(X_i^hX_j^k) = \frac{1}{n^2}\sum_{i=1}^{n}\mathscr{E}X_i^{h+k} + \frac{1}{n^2}\sum_{i\neq j}\sum\mathscr{E}X_i^h\mathscr{E}X_j^k$$

$$= \frac{1}{n}\mu_{h+k}' + \frac{n-1}{n}\mu_h'\mu_k'$$

The covariance of m_h' and m_k' is thus

$$(3.2)\qquad \operatorname{cov}(m_h', m_k') = \mathscr{E}(m_h'm_k') - \mu_h'\mu_k' = \frac{1}{n}(\mu_{h+k}' - \mu_h'\mu_k')$$

and hence the variance of m_h' is $(\mu_{2h}' - \mu_h'^2)/n$.

Since $nm_h' = \sum_i X_i^h$ is the sum of n independent random variables $X_1^h, \ldots, X_n^h$, all of which have the same distribution with mean μ_h' and variance $\mu_{2h}' - \mu_h'^2$ (this variance is equal to that of m_h' in the special case $n = 1$), we may apply the Lindeberg-Lévy theorem to conclude that as $n \to \infty$, the distribution of

$$(3.3)\qquad \frac{\sum_{i=1}^{n}(X_i^h - \mu_h')}{\sqrt{(\mu_{2h}' - \mu_h'^2)n}} = \sqrt{n}\,\frac{m_h' - \mu_h'}{\sqrt{\mu_{2h}' - \mu_h'^2}}$$

converges to the standardized normal distribution. Thus, the sample moment m_h' is asymptotically normally distributed with mean μ_h' and variance $(\mu_{2h}' - \mu_h'^2)/n$. This result can be extended straightforwardly by means of the vector generalization of the Lindeberg-Lévy theorem in the following way. The joint distribution of any number of random variables $\sqrt{n}(m_h' - \mu_h')$, $h = 1, 2, \ldots$ converges to a limiting multinormal distribution with zero mean vector and covariances of the form $\mu_{h+k}' - \mu_h'\mu_k'$.

The Asymptotic Distribution of a Function of Sample Moments

Next, consider an arbitrary function $g(\ )$ of two sample moments with continuous derivatives of the first and second order in some neighborhood around the corresponding population moments. The function is assumed to be independent of n. It can be proved that the random variable

$$(3.4)\qquad \sqrt{n}[g(m_h', m_k') - g(\mu_h', \mu_k')]$$

has a normal limiting distribution with zero mean and a variance that may be described as follows. Apply a Taylor expansion:

$$(3.5)\quad g(m_h', m_k') - g(\mu_h', \mu_k') = \frac{\partial g}{\partial m_h'}(m_h' - \mu_h') + \frac{\partial g}{\partial m_k'}(m_k' - \mu_k') + R$$

where R is a remainder term and the derivatives $\partial g/\partial m_h'$ and $\partial g/\partial m_k'$ are both evaluated at the point (μ_h', μ_k'). Squaring both sides of (3.5) and taking the expectation, we obtain $\mathscr{E}[\{g(m_h', m_k') - g(\mu_h', \mu_k')\}^2]$ on the left, which is the variance of $g(m_h', m_k')$ if it is true (which need not be the case) that this $g(\ )$ is an unbiased estimator of $g(\mu_h', \mu_k')$. On the right we obtain, after squaring and taking the expectation and neglecting the remainder term:

$$(3.6)\quad \left(\frac{\partial g}{\partial m_h'}\right)^2 \text{var } m_h' + \left(\frac{\partial g}{\partial m_k'}\right)^2 \text{var } m_k' + 2\frac{\partial g}{\partial m_h'}\frac{\partial g}{\partial m_k'} \text{cov }(m_h', m_k')$$
$$= \left(\frac{\partial g}{\partial m_h'}\right)^2 \frac{\mu_{2h}' - \mu_h'^2}{n} + \left(\frac{\partial g}{\partial m_k'}\right)^2 \frac{\mu_{2k}' - \mu_k'^2}{n} + 2\frac{\partial g}{\partial m_h'}\frac{\partial g}{\partial m_k'}\frac{\mu_{h+k}' - \mu_h'\mu_k'}{n}$$

This procedure is, of course, not rigorous at all. However, it can be proved rigorously that $g(m_h', m_k')$ is asymptotically normally distributed with mean $g(\mu_h', \mu_k')$ and variance (3.6). Equivalently, the sequence (3.4) has a normal limiting distribution with zero mean and a variance equal to n times the expression (3.6). See Problems 3.1 to 3.3 for the proof, which is based on Cramér (1946, Section 28.4). The result can be extended straightforwardly to the case of p functions $g_1(\ ), \ldots, g_p(\ )$ depending on an arbitrary number of moments. Their asymptotic distribution is p-variate normal with a mean vector consisting of the corresponding population values and a covariance matrix determined by the leading terms of Taylor expansions. The only condition is that the p functions have continuous second-order derivatives in some region that contains the point of the population moments as an interior point.

Applications and Extensions

The asymptotic results described in the previous paragraph are particularly important because so many estimators and test statistics are functions of the moments $m_1', m_2', \ldots$ with continuous second-order derivatives. Examples are the moments about the mean such as the sample variance, the sample standard deviation, and so on; see Problems 3.4 and 3.5. But the result is basically even more general, since the arguments of the functions need not be moments. Whenever the arguments of $g(\ )$ are random variables which are asymptotically normally distributed with a mean vector equal to the corresponding population values and a covariance matrix whose elements are $O(1/n)$, then $g(\ )$ is also asymptotically normal if it has continuous second-order derivatives in the appropriate region; see Problems 3.6 and 3.7. This more general result is also important for the estimation of coefficients of the standard linear model and its extensions. If the estimators have the appropriate asymptotic normal distribution, any linear or nonlinear function of the estimators has also an asymptotic normal distribution if this function satisfies the condition on second-order derivatives. We shall come back to the standard linear model later in this section.

The Order of Magnitude of the Variance of an Asymptotic Distribution

It is clear from (3.6) that the variance of the asymptotic distribution of $g(m_h', m_k')$ is of the form c/n, where c is determined by the μ's and the g-derivatives evaluated at (μ_h', μ_k'). Hence c is independent of n. In general c will be positive, but $c = 0$ is possible when the μ's and the derivatives of $g(\ )$ take particular values. This means that the sequence (3.4) converges in probability to zero or, equivalently, that $g(m_h', m_k')$ is asymptotically normal with zero variance as far as the terms of order $1/n$ is concerned. In this case it may happen that the sequence

$$n^s[g(m_h', m_k') - g(\mu_h', \mu_k')] \tag{3.7}$$

for some $s > \frac{1}{2}$ has a nondegenerate limiting distribution, but this is not necessarily normal. Hence the procedure of approximating the distribution of $g(m_h', m_k')$ by a normal asymptotic distribution is guaranteed to work only if the latter has a positive variance of order $1/n$. If the variance is of a higher order of smallness, there may still be a normal limiting distribution with positive variance (see Problem 3.9), but such a limiting distribution may also be nonnormal. An example is that of R^2 in a multinormal population whose true multiple correlation vanishes. It follows from eq. (7.12) in Section 4.7 that var $R^2 = 2K/n^2 + o(n^{-2})$ in that case, which means that $n(R^2 - \mathscr{E}R^2)$ has a limiting distribution with positive variance, but this limiting distribution is not normal.

Limits of Moments and the Moments of a Limiting Distribution

It is of considerable importance to make a careful distinction between the moments of a limiting distribution and the limits of the moments of the corresponding sequence of distributions. If a sequence $F_1(\ ), F_2(\ ), \ldots$ converges to a limiting distribution $F(\ )$ and if *all* moments of the sequence exist and converge to finite limits, then it can be shown[9] that the limiting distribution, too, has finite moments of every order and that they are identical with the limits of the corresponding moments of the sequence. But it may happen that a limiting distribution exists with finite moments of every order and that, nevertheless, the moments of any member of the sequence do not exist at all. A very simple example is $X_n = Y + Z/n$, where Y has a normal

[9] See, for example, C. R. Rao (1965a, p. 101).

and Z a Cauchy distribution, neither of which depends on n. It follows from rule (i) at the end of Section 8.2 that the sequence $X_1, X_2, \ldots$ converges in distribution to Y, so that the limiting distribution is normal and has finite moments of every order. However, the expectation of X_n, which is equal to $\mathscr{E}Y$ plus $1/n$ times the expectation of Z, fails to exist because Z (a Cauchy variate) has no expectation. The same is obviously true for the higher moments of X_n, for whatever finite value of n.

As a second example, consider a discrete random variable which takes the zero value with positive probability; let the mean be $\mu \neq 0$ and the variance σ^2. Suppose that a random sample $(X_1, \ldots, X_n)$ is drawn from this population and that the reciprocal of the sample mean, $1/\bar{X}_n$, is used to estimate $1/\mu$. It is verified straightforwardly from the discussion around (3.4) to (3.6) that the limiting distribution of $\sqrt{n}(1/\bar{X}_n - 1/\mu)$ is normal with zero mean and variance σ^2/μ^4, so that $1/\bar{X}_n$ is asymptotically normal with mean $1/\mu$ and variance $\sigma^2/n\mu^4$. But $1/\bar{X}_n$ does not have a finite expectation for whatever finite n. This follows from the assumption that the zero value has positive probability, which implies for the sample that $X_1 = \cdots = X_n = 0$ and hence $\bar{X}_n = 0$ also have positive probability. If we then weight the values which $1/\bar{X}_n$ can take with their probabilities in order to obtain $\mathscr{E}(1/\bar{X}_n)$, we do not obtain a finite result. The nonexistence of this expectation can also be proved for sampling from a continuous population if $\bar{X}_n$ has positive density at zero (see Problem 3.8). Note that this applies to the normal distribution and to many other continuous distributions as well.

In what follows, when dealing with moments of distributions of statistics for large samples, we shall usually concentrate on the moments of the asymptotic distribution rather than the limits of the moments of the sequence of distributions. It cannot be denied that, for example, the second moment for a particular finite value of n is important when the analyst uses a quadratic criterion function and when this particular n is the size of the available sample. But when this moment does not exist, the criterion function is of limited use for finite n. The second moment of the asymptotic distribution exists under much more general conditions, so that it renders a more useful service when the sample is indeed large.

The above argument in favor of the use of moments of the asymptotic distribution is mainly pragmatic. There are many situations in which there is also a more fundamental reason to prefer these moments. Take the case of a random variable X which is necessarily positive because of economic considerations. Suppose that the analyst proceeds under the assumption that X follows a normal distribution with mean 6 and unit variance. This obviously violates the constraint $X > 0$, but the probability of a nonpositive value is so small that the analyst argues (justifiably) that there should be no reason for concern if this is his only specification error. Nevertheless, if our analyst is interested in the expectation of $1/X$, he must conclude that this expectation does not exist under the normality assumption because of the positive density at the origin ($X = 0$). Since the true density function takes the zero value at the origin, the nonexistence of $\mathscr{E}(1/X)$ is thus a spurious phenomenon caused by the seemingly innocent normal approximation of the X distribution. In the same way, if $\hat{\theta}_n$ is an estimator of a parameter θ based on a random sample $(X_1, \ldots, X_n)$, and if it appears that the variance of $\hat{\theta}_n$ is infinite, this is frequently because the distribution of the X_i's is slightly misspecified. No econometrician should exclude the possibility that his specifications are slightly in error. Therefore it is preferable in many cases not to rely on moments for finite n but to use the moments of the asymptotic distribution when n is large, since the latter are insensitive to such features as a positive value of the density function at the origin.

"*Asymptotic Unbiasedness*"

The distinction between limits of moments and the moments of a limiting distribution is also important for the concept of "asymptotic unbiasedness." One interpretation of this concept is the following. Consider again an estimator $\hat{\theta}_n$ of a parameter θ based on a random sample $(X_1, \ldots, X_n)$; then $\hat{\theta}_n$ is called an asymptotically unbiased estimator of θ when $\lim \mathscr{E}\hat{\theta}_n \equiv \theta$ as $n \to \infty$. It follows from (1.2) that the maximum-likelihood estimator of σ^2 considered there is asymptotically unbiased in this sense. However, $1/\bar{X}_n$ of the previous subsection is not an asymptotically unbiased estimator of $1/\mu$ because it has no expectation and the limit of the expectation is thus not defined. On the other hand, this estimator would be asymptotically unbiased if we decided (as some authors do) to define this concept in terms of the existence and zero mean of the limiting distribution of $\sqrt{n}(\hat{\theta}_n - \theta)$. But this would lead to confusion with the other definition and we shall therefore not use the term "asymptotically unbiased" at all.

Asymptotic Standard Errors

As in the case of finite-sample theory, it is frequently true that the variance of a limiting distribution depends on unknown parameters. For example, the variance of the asymptotic distribution of $1/\bar{X}_n$ is $\sigma^2/n\mu^4$, and both σ and μ are unknown. It is customary to replace these unknown parameters by consistent estimators, so that the variance of the limiting distribution is then estimated consistently if it is a continuous function of these parameters. Thus, if the population has finite moments up to the fourth order[10] and if $\mu \neq 0$,

[10] When σ^2 of σ^2/μ^4 is estimated by s^2, we may use Chebyshev's inequality to establish the consistency of s^2 if the variance of s^2 converges to zero. It appears from Problem 3.5 that this variance involves the fourth moment of the population.

then the variance σ^2/μ^4 of the limiting distribution of $\sqrt{n}(1/\bar{X}_n - 1/\mu)$ is estimated consistently by $s^2/\bar{X}_n^4$. The estimator of the variance of the asymptotic distribution of $1/\bar{X}_n$ is then $s^2/n\bar{X}_n^4$. By computing the positive square root, $s/\sqrt{n}\bar{X}_n^2$, we obtain the asymptotic standard error of the point estimate $1/\bar{X}_n$. More generally, if an estimator $\hat{\theta}_n$ of a parameter θ has an asymptotic distribution with mean θ and variance $O(1/n)$, we obtain an asymptotic standard error by dividing a consistent estimate of the standard deviation of the limiting distribution of $\sqrt{n}(\hat{\theta}_n - \theta)$ by $\sqrt{n}$.

Note carefully the difference between asymptotic standard errors and the ordinary standard errors. The latter are estimates of the standard deviations of sampling distributions; the former are estimates of the standard deviations of the asymptotic approximations of sampling distributions. Again note that an estimator may have an asymptotic standard error without having a variance for finite values of n.

Further Asymptotic Results for the Standard Linear Model

The remainder of this section is devoted to the following extension of Theorem 8.1.

THEOREM 8.2 (Additional asymptotic results for the standard linear model) *Suppose that Assumption* 3.3 *of Section* 3.2 *and Assumption* 8.1 *are both satisfied. Then, as $n \to \infty$, each LS residual e_α converges in distribution to the corresponding disturbance ϵ_α and the same holds for each BLUS residual $\hat{\epsilon}_\alpha$, provided that the K-dimensional base of the index transformation remains the same as $n \to \infty$. If, in addition, the disturbances $\epsilon_1, \ldots, \epsilon_n$ are independently and identically distributed, then the LS variance estimator s^2 is consistent for σ^2, and $\sqrt{n}(\mathbf{b} - \boldsymbol{\beta})$, $\mathbf{b}$ being the LS coefficient estimator, has a normal limiting distribution with zero mean vector and covariance matrix $\sigma^2\mathbf{Q}^{-1}$.*

The second part of the theorem shows that we may act as if the coefficient vector $\mathbf{b}$ has a multinormal distribution when the sample is sufficiently large, provided that the disturbances are independent random drawings from the same (but not necessarily normal) population.

The proof of Theorem 8.2 is given in the four subsections which follow.

Proof of the Convergence of the LS residuals

Theorem 5.1 of Section 5.1 states that the error vector $\mathbf{e} - \boldsymbol{\epsilon}$ of the LS residual vector has zero mean and covariance matrix $\sigma^2\mathbf{X}(\mathbf{X}'\mathbf{X})^{-1}\mathbf{X}'$. Hence,

$e_\alpha - \epsilon_\alpha$ has zero mean and the following variance:

$$(3.8) \qquad \text{var}\,(e_\alpha - \epsilon_\alpha) = \sigma^2[x_{\alpha 1} \quad \cdots \quad x_{\alpha K}](\mathbf{X}'\mathbf{X})^{-1}\begin{bmatrix} x_{\alpha 1} \\ \cdot \\ \cdot \\ \cdot \\ x_{\alpha K} \end{bmatrix}$$

which is a multiple σ^2/n of a quadratic form with $(n^{-1}\mathbf{X}'\mathbf{X})^{-1}$ as matrix and $[x_{\alpha 1} \quad \cdots \quad x_{\alpha K}]$ as vector. The matrix converges to $\mathbf{Q}^{-1}$ as $n \to \infty$, so that the quadratic form converges to a finite limit for any fixed $[x_{\alpha 1} \quad \cdots \quad x_{\alpha K}]$. The multiple σ^2/n thus guarantees that the variance of $e_\alpha - \epsilon_\alpha$ converges to zero as $n \to \infty$, and Chebyshev's inequality then shows that $e_\alpha - \epsilon_\alpha$ converges in probability to zero. Application of rule (i) at the end of Section 8.2 immediately proves that e_α converges in distribution to ϵ_α.

Proof of the Convergence of the BLUS Residuals

For the BLUS residual $\hat{\epsilon}_\alpha$ we return to eqs. (2.8) and (2.9) of Section 5.2 and to the BLUS coefficient vector $\hat{\boldsymbol{\beta}}_1$ defined in eq. (6.15) of Section 5.6. They imply:

$$(3.9) \qquad \hat{\epsilon}_\alpha = y_\alpha - [x_{\alpha 1} \quad \cdots \quad x_{\alpha K}]\hat{\boldsymbol{\beta}}_1 = \epsilon_\alpha - [x_{\alpha 1} \quad \cdots \quad x_{\alpha K}](\hat{\boldsymbol{\beta}}_1 - \boldsymbol{\beta})$$

where

$$(3.10) \qquad \hat{\boldsymbol{\beta}}_1 = \mathbf{b} + \mathbf{X}_0^{-1}\left[\sum_{h=1}^{H} \frac{d_h}{1 + d_h} \mathbf{q}_h\mathbf{q}_h'\right]\mathbf{e}_0$$

$\mathbf{X}_0$ being a nonsingular $K \times K$ matrix and $\mathbf{e}_0$ the corresponding K-element subvector of $\mathbf{e}$. The scalars $d_1, \ldots, d_H$ and the vectors $\mathbf{q}_1, \ldots, \mathbf{q}_H$ are defined by

$$(3.11) \qquad [\mathbf{X}_0(\mathbf{X}'\mathbf{X})^{-1}\mathbf{X}_0' - d_h^2\mathbf{I}]\mathbf{q}_h = \mathbf{0} \qquad h = 1, \ldots, H$$

The $\mathbf{q}$'s all have unit length and are pairwise orthogonal, and H is the number of roots d_h^2 of $\mathbf{X}_0(\mathbf{X}'\mathbf{X})^{-1}\mathbf{X}_0'$ which are less than one.

Under Assumption 8.1 the matrix $\mathbf{X}_0(\mathbf{X}'\mathbf{X})^{-1}\mathbf{X}_0'$ converges to the $K \times K$ zero matrix for any fixed matrix $\mathbf{X}_0$ (i.e., for any given choice of the base of the index transformation). Hence the roots d_h all converge to zero as $n \to \infty$. The $\mathbf{q}$'s will, in general, change when n increases, but their elements are bounded by the unit-length constraint. It follows that the matrix in brackets in (3.10) also converges to the $K \times K$ zero matrix. This matrix is premultiplied by the fixed $\mathbf{X}_0^{-1}$ and postmultiplied by the random $\mathbf{e}_0$ which converges in distribution to the corresponding disturbance subvector $\boldsymbol{\epsilon}_0$ (see the previous subsection). Application of rule (ii) of Section 8.2 then shows that this product and hence $\hat{\boldsymbol{\beta}}_1 - \mathbf{b}$ converge in probability to the K-element zero vector. Since the probability limit of $\mathbf{b}$ is $\boldsymbol{\beta}$ (Theorem 8.1), the probability limit of $\hat{\boldsymbol{\beta}}_1$ is also $\boldsymbol{\beta}$ in view of rule (i). It follows immediately from (3.9) and rule (i) that $\hat{\epsilon}_\alpha$ then converges to ϵ_α.

Proof of the Consistency of the LS Variance Estimator

The variance estimator s^2 can be written as follows:

$$s^2 = \frac{1}{n-K}\boldsymbol{\epsilon}'[\mathbf{I} - \mathbf{X}(\mathbf{X}'\mathbf{X})^{-1}\mathbf{X}']\boldsymbol{\epsilon} \tag{3.12}$$

$$= \frac{\boldsymbol{\epsilon}'\boldsymbol{\epsilon}}{n-K} - \frac{(\sqrt{1/n}\,\mathbf{X}'\boldsymbol{\epsilon})'(n^{-1}\mathbf{X}'\mathbf{X})^{-1}(\sqrt{1/n}\,\mathbf{X}'\boldsymbol{\epsilon})}{n-K}$$

It will be shown in the last paragraph of this section that $\sqrt{1/n}\mathbf{X}'\boldsymbol{\epsilon}$ has a normal limiting distribution with zero mean vector and covariance matrix $\sigma^2\mathbf{Q}$. This implies that the second term on the second line is asymptotically a fraction $1/(n-K)$ of a quadratic form in this normal vector with $\mathbf{Q}^{-1}$ as matrix. Thus, in the limit as $n \to \infty$, the quadratic form does not involve n, so that the division by $n - K$ guarantees that the second term on the second line of (3.12) converges in probability to zero. The first term can be written as $\boldsymbol{\epsilon}'\boldsymbol{\epsilon}/n$ multiplied by $n/(n-K)$. The multiplication factor converges to one and the convergence in probability of $\boldsymbol{\epsilon}'\boldsymbol{\epsilon}/n$ to σ^2 follows directly from Khintchine's theorem, since the disturbances and hence also their squares are independently and identically distributed, the latter having finite expectation σ^2.

Proof of the Asymptotic Normality of the LS Coefficient Vector

The normal limiting distribution of $\sqrt{1/n}\mathbf{X}'\boldsymbol{\epsilon}$ also implies the asymptotic normality of $\mathbf{b}$. This follows from the matrix generalization of rule (iii) of Section 8.2 (the convergence of X_nY_n in distribution to cY): the vector $\sqrt{n}(\mathbf{b} - \boldsymbol{\beta})$ is obtained from $\sqrt{1/n}\mathbf{X}'\boldsymbol{\epsilon}$ by premultiplication by $(n^{-1}\mathbf{X}'\mathbf{X})^{-1}$, which converges to $\mathbf{Q}^{-1}$, and its limiting distribution is thus normal with zero mean vector and covariance matrix $\sigma^2\mathbf{Q}^{-1}\mathbf{Q}\mathbf{Q}^{-1} = \sigma^2\mathbf{Q}^{-1}$.

The proof of the asymptotic normality of $\sqrt{1/n}\mathbf{X}'\boldsymbol{\epsilon}$ will be given along the lines of that of the Lindeberg-Lévy theorem. Write

$$\sqrt{1/n}\mathbf{X}' = \mathbf{C} = [\mathbf{c}_1 \quad \cdots \quad \mathbf{c}_n]$$

so that the transpose of $\mathbf{c}_\alpha$ is the following K-element row vector:

$$\mathbf{c}'_\alpha = \begin{bmatrix} \dfrac{x_{\alpha 1}}{\sqrt{n}} & \cdots & \dfrac{x_{\alpha K}}{\sqrt{n}} \end{bmatrix} \qquad \alpha = 1, \ldots, n \tag{3.13}$$

Since $\mathbf{CC}' = n^{-1}\mathbf{X}'\mathbf{X}$ converges to $\mathbf{Q}$, the elements of $\mathbf{CC}' = \mathbf{c}_1\mathbf{c}_1' + \cdots + \mathbf{c}_n\mathbf{c}_n'$ are obviously bounded, which implies that the K elements of $\mathbf{c}_n$ are $O(1/\sqrt{n})$. [If one element of $\mathbf{c}_n$ were $O(n^{p-\frac{1}{2}})$ with $p > 0$, then one element of $\mathbf{c}_n\mathbf{c}_n'$ would be $O(n^{2p-1})$ and the corresponding element of $\mathbf{CC}' = \mathbf{c}_1\mathbf{c}_1' + \cdots + \mathbf{c}_n\mathbf{c}_n'$ would be $O(n^{2p})$, which is not bounded.] The ϵ's are by assumption independently and identically distributed with zero mean and variance σ^2, so that the vector $\mathbf{c}_n\epsilon_n$ has zero mean and covariance matrix $\sigma^2\mathbf{c}_n\mathbf{c}_n' = O(n^{-1})$ and characteristic function $1 - \frac{1}{2}\sigma^2\mathbf{t}'\mathbf{c}_n\mathbf{c}_n'\mathbf{t} + o(n^{-1})$, while the vector

$$\frac{1}{\sqrt{n}}\mathbf{X}'\boldsymbol{\epsilon} = \mathbf{C}\boldsymbol{\epsilon} = \mathbf{c}_1\epsilon_1 + \cdots + \mathbf{c}_n\epsilon_n \tag{3.14}$$

has the following characteristic function:

$$\phi_n(t) = \prod_{\alpha=1}^{n}\left[1 - \frac{1}{2}\sigma^2\mathbf{t}'\mathbf{c}_\alpha\mathbf{c}_\alpha'\mathbf{t} + o(n^{-1})\right] \tag{3.15}$$

Take logarithms and expand for large n:

$$\log\phi_n(\mathbf{t}) = \sum_{\alpha=1}^{n}\log\left[1 - \frac{1}{2}\sigma^2\mathbf{t}'\mathbf{c}_\alpha\mathbf{c}_\alpha'\mathbf{t} + o(n^{-1})\right] \tag{3.16}$$

$$= -\frac{1}{2}\sigma^2\mathbf{t}'\left(\sum_{\alpha=1}^{n}\mathbf{c}_\alpha\mathbf{c}_\alpha'\right)\mathbf{t} + o(1) = -\frac{1}{2}\sigma^2\mathbf{t}'\left(\frac{1}{n}\mathbf{X}'\mathbf{X}\right)\mathbf{t} + o(1)$$

This converges to $-\frac{1}{2}\sigma^2\mathbf{t}'\mathbf{Q}\mathbf{t}$ and thus corresponds asymptotically to the multinormal distribution with zero mean vector and covariance matrix $\sigma^2\mathbf{Q}$. Note that $\exp\{-\frac{1}{2}\sigma^2\mathbf{t}'\mathbf{Q}\mathbf{t}\}$ is continuous at $\mathbf{t} = \mathbf{0}$ as is required.

Problems

3.1 Let $(X_1, \ldots, X_n)$ be a random sample from a population with finite moments of orders $2h$ and $2k$. Apply Chebyshev's inequality to the distribution of the hth sample moment to find:

$$\text{P}[|m_h' - \mu_h'| \geq \epsilon] \leq \frac{\mu_{2h}' - \mu_h'^2}{n\epsilon^2} \quad \text{for any} \quad \epsilon > 0 \tag{3.17}$$

Write Z for the set of points $(X_1, \ldots, X_n)$ satisfying both $|m_h' - \mu_h'| < \epsilon$ and $|m_k' - \mu_k'| < \epsilon$:

$$\text{P}(Z) = \text{P}[|m_h' - \mu_h'| < \epsilon \quad \text{and} \quad |m_k' - \mu_k'| < \epsilon] \tag{3.18}$$

$$\geq 1 - \text{P}[|m_h' - \mu_h'| \geq \epsilon] - \text{P}[|m_k' - \mu_k'| \geq \epsilon] \geq 1 - \frac{A_1}{n\epsilon^2}$$

where $A_1 = \mu'_{2h} - \mu'^2_h + \mu'_{2k} - \mu'^2_k$ (independent of ϵ and n). Specify $\epsilon = n^{-\frac{3}{8}}$, so that the inequality becomes $P(Z) \geq 1 - A_1 n^{-\frac{1}{4}}$.

3.2 (*Continuation*) Prove that the remainder term of (3.5) can be written as

$$(3.19)\quad R = \frac{1}{2}[g_{11}(m'_h - \mu'_h)^2 + g_{22}(m'_k - \mu'_k)^2 + 2g_{12}(m'_h - \mu'_h)(m'_k - \mu'_k)]$$

where the g_{ij}'s are second-order derivatives of $g(\ )$ evaluated at some point between (μ'_h, μ'_k) and (m'_h, m'_k). Next prove that if the sample falls in Z, so that $|m'_h - \mu'_h|$ and $|m'_k - \mu'_k|$ are smaller than ϵ, $|R\sqrt{n}|$ is at most equal to

(3.20)

$$\frac{1}{2}\sqrt{n}\,[|g_{11}|\,(m'_h - \mu'_h)^2 + |g_{22}|\,(m'_k - \mu'_k)^2 + 2|g_{12}|\,|m'_h - \mu'_h|\,|m'_k - \mu'_k|]$$
$$< \frac{1}{2}(|g_{11}| + |g_{22}| + 2|g_{12}|)\sqrt{n}\epsilon^2$$

Again, specify $\epsilon = n^{-\frac{3}{8}}$ and prove $|R\sqrt{n}| < A_2 n^{-\frac{1}{4}}$, where A_2 is the largest value of $\frac{1}{2}|g_{11}| + \frac{1}{2}|g_{22}| + |g_{12}|$ in the region Z. [Note that the existence of a finite largest value is guaranteed when the second-order derivatives of $g(\ )$ are continuous in the neighborhood of (μ'_h, μ'_k).]

3.3 (*Continuation*) Combine $|R\sqrt{n}| < A_2 n^{-\frac{1}{4}}$ (if the sample falls in Z) and $P(Z) \geq 1 - A_1 n^{-\frac{1}{4}}$ (Problem 3.1) to prove that $R\sqrt{n}$ converges in probability to zero as $n \to \infty$. Then use the appropriate rule of Section 8.2 to prove that the sequences

$$(3.21)\quad \sqrt{n}\,[g(m'_h, m'_k) - g(\mu'_h, \mu'_k)] \quad \text{and}$$
$$\frac{\partial g}{\partial m'_h}\sqrt{n}\,(m'_h - \mu'_h) + \frac{\partial g}{\partial m'_k}\sqrt{n}\,(m'_k - \mu'_k)$$

have the same limiting distribution if the second sequence has a limiting distribution. Finally, prove that this condition is satisfied and that the limiting distribution is as described below eq. (3.6).

3.4 Consider a random sample $(X_1, \ldots, X_n)$ from a population whose first four moments exist. Prove that as $n \to \infty$, the second-order sample moment about the mean, $(1/n)\sum (X_i - \bar{X})^2$, is asymptotically normally distributed with mean σ^2 and variance $(\mu_4 - \sigma^4)/n$, where σ^2 is the variance and μ_4 the fourth moment around the mean of the population. [*Hint*. Use $\mu'_3 = \mu_3 + 3\mu\sigma^2 + \mu^3$ and $\mu'_4 = \mu_4 + 4\mu\mu_3 + 6\mu^2\sigma^2 + \mu^4$, where μ is the population mean and μ'_3 and μ'_4 are moments around zero; see Kendall and Stuart (1963, p. 56).]

3.5 (*Continuation*) Prove that $s^2 = [1/(n-1)] \sum (X_i - \bar{X})^2$ has the same asymptotic distribution as the second-order sample moment about the mean and that the variance of this distribution is $2\sigma^4/n$ when the population is normal. Also prove that $s = \sqrt{s^2}$ has a normal asymptotic distribution with mean σ and variance $(\mu_4 - \sigma^4)/4n\sigma^2$. How can this variance be simplified when the population is normal?

3.6 Consider a sequence $\mathbf{y}_n = (Y_{n1}, \ldots, Y_{nK})$ of K-dimensional random variables and suppose that $\sqrt{n}(\mathbf{y}_n - \boldsymbol{\mu})$ has a K-dimensional normal limiting distribution with zero mean vector and finite positive definite covariance matrix $\boldsymbol{\Sigma}$. Also consider the sequence $g(\mathbf{y}_n)$, where $g(\ )$ is a function with continuous second-order derivatives in some region that contains $\boldsymbol{\mu}$ as an interior point. Extend the approach of Problems 3.1 to 3.3 to prove that the sequence $\sqrt{n}[g(\mathbf{y}_n) - g(\boldsymbol{\mu})]$ has a normal limiting distribution with zero mean and variance $\mathbf{g}'\boldsymbol{\Sigma}\mathbf{g}$, where $\mathbf{g}$ is the gradient of $g(\ )$ evaluated at $\boldsymbol{\mu}$.

3.7 (*Continuation*) Generalize this result for a p-element vector of functions with elements $g_1(\ ), \ldots, g_p(\ )$ to prove that the normal limiting distribution is p-dimensional with zero mean vector and covariance matrix $\mathbf{G}\boldsymbol{\Sigma}\mathbf{G}'$, where the (i, j)th element of $\mathbf{G}$ is the derivative of $g_i(\ )$ with respect to the jth argument evaluated at $\boldsymbol{\mu}$.

3.8 Let X be a random variable with continuous density function $f(\ )$ satisfying $f(0) > 0$. Prove that $1/X$ does not have a finite expectation. [*Hint*. Consider the following component of the total integral of $(1/x)f(x)$:

$$\int_0^\epsilon \frac{1}{x} f(x)\, dx \qquad (\epsilon > 0) \tag{3.22}$$

Use the continuity of $f(\ )$ to prove that ϵ can be chosen such that $f(x) > M > 0$ for every x satisfying $0 \leq x \leq \epsilon$ and conclude that the value of the integral (3.22) exceeds $M \displaystyle\int_0^\epsilon \frac{dx}{x} = M \lim_{a \to 0} \int_a^\epsilon \frac{dx}{x}$.]

3.9 Consider the linear trend (without constant term) of Problem 1.9 and assume that the disturbances are independently and identically distributed with zero mean and variance σ^2. Prove that $n^{\frac{3}{2}}(b - \beta)$ has a normal limiting distribution with zero mean and variance $3\sigma^2$. [*Hint*. Prove first:

$$n^{\frac{3}{2}}(b - \beta) = \frac{6\sqrt{n}}{(n+1)(2n+1)} \sum_{\alpha=1}^{n} \alpha\epsilon_\alpha \tag{3.23}$$

and conclude that $n^{\frac{3}{2}}(b - \beta)$ is equal to the sum of the following n independent random variables:

$$\frac{6\sqrt{n}}{(n+1)(2n+1)}\epsilon_1, \frac{6\sqrt{n}}{(n+1)(2n+1)}2\epsilon_2, \ldots, \frac{6\sqrt{n}}{(n+1)(2n+1)}n\epsilon_n$$

Next prove that the characteristic function of their sum is

$$\phi_n(t) = \prod_{\alpha=1}^{n} \left[1 - \frac{1}{2}\frac{36n}{(n+1)^2(2n+1)^2}\alpha^2\sigma^2t^2 + o(n^{-1})\right] \tag{3.24}$$

and prove $\log \phi_n(t) \to -\frac{3}{2}\sigma^2t^2$ as $n \to \infty$.]

8.4 The Cramér-Rao Inequality and the Information Matrix[C]

In this section we shall derive a lower bound for the sampling variance of an unbiased estimator in an important class of cases. This result is subsequently generalized for unbiased estimation of a parameter vector and applied to the LS coefficient and variance estimators under the conditions of the standard linear model. The analysis is confined to finite samples; asymptotic extensions will be considered in Section 8.5. For both sections reference should be made to Cramér (1946, Sections 32.3 and 33.3) and C. R. Rao (1965a, Section 5a.3).

Regularity Conditions

Consider a random sample $(X_1, \ldots, X_n)$ drawn from some population which is characterized by an unknown parameter θ. It is assumed that the distribution is continuous with density function $f(x; \theta)$, so that the joint density function of the sample is

$$f(x_1; \theta) \cdots f(x_n; \theta) = L(x_1, \ldots, x_n; \theta) \tag{4.1}$$

where $L(\ )$ is the likelihood function. For any fixed θ, this function is an n-dimensional density function, which implies

$$\int_{-\infty}^{\infty} \cdots \int_{-\infty}^{\infty} L(x_1, \ldots, x_n; \theta)\, dx_1 \cdots dx_n = 1 \tag{4.2}$$

It will be assumed that $f(\ )$ and hence also $L(\ )$ are twice differentiable with respect to θ; also, that the limits of integration in (4.2)—the range of the random variable—are independent of θ and that differentiation under the integration sign is permissible. These are the so-called regularity conditions, under which differentiation of both sides of (4.2) with respect to θ gives

$$\int_{-\infty}^{\infty} \cdots \int_{-\infty}^{\infty} \frac{\partial L(x_1, \ldots, x_n; \theta)}{\partial \theta}\, dx_1 \cdots dx_n = 0 \tag{4.3}$$

or, more compactly,

$$\int \frac{\partial L(x; \theta)}{\partial \theta}\, dx = 0 \tag{4.4}$$

where x stands for $x_1, \ldots, x_n$, dx for the product $dx_1 \cdots dx_n$, and the n integrals are represented by a single integral sign.

A Derivative of the Log-Likelihood of a Random Sample

It may be assumed without loss of generality that the integration in (4.3) and (4.4) is confined to the region of $(x_1, \ldots, x_n)$ for which $L(x; \theta)$ takes nonzero values. We can then write (4.4) in the form

$$\int \frac{\partial \log L(x; \theta)}{\partial \theta} L(x; \theta)\, dx = 0 \tag{4.5}$$

where log stands for natural logarithm.

The result (4.5) has a simple statistical interpretation. Write X for the random sample $(X_1, \ldots, X_n)$ for notational convenience. When we replace x by X in $L(x; \theta)$, we obtain the likelihood of the random sample, $L(X; \theta)$, which is obviously random itself. The derivative of the logarithm of this likelihood with respect to θ is then also random, and it follows immediately from (4.5) that the expectation of this derivative vanishes:

$$\mathscr{E}\left[\frac{\partial \log L(X; \theta)}{\partial \theta}\right] = 0 \tag{4.6}$$

Next we differentiate both sides of (4.5) with respect to θ:

$$\int \left[\frac{\partial^2 \log L(x; \theta)}{\partial \theta^2} L(x; \theta) + \frac{\partial \log L(x; \theta)}{\partial \theta} \frac{\partial L(x; \theta)}{\partial \theta}\right] dx$$
$$= \int \frac{\partial^2 \log L(x; \theta)}{\partial \theta^2} L(x; \theta)\, dx + \int \left[\frac{\partial \log L(x; \theta)}{\partial \theta}\right]^2 L(x; \theta)\, dx = 0$$

which can be written in the following more compact form:

$$\operatorname{var} \frac{\partial \log L(X; \theta)}{\partial \theta} = -\mathscr{E}\left[\frac{\partial^2 \log L(X; \theta)}{\partial \theta^2}\right] \tag{4.7}$$

In words: the variance of the derivative of the log-likelihood of the sample with respect to θ (recall that its expectation vanishes) is equal to minus the expectation of the second-order derivative of the same log-likelihood.

The Cramér-Rao Inequality

Now consider an estimator $t(X)$ of θ whose expectation,

$$\mathscr{E}[t(X)] = \int t(x) L(x; \theta)\, dx \tag{4.8}$$

exists and is a differentiable function of θ. (If the estimator is unbiased, this expectation is identically equal to θ, which is obviously differentiable.) We differentiate both sides of (4.8) with respect to θ:

$$\text{(4.9)} \qquad \frac{\partial \mathscr{E}[t(X)]}{\partial \theta} = \int t(x) \frac{\partial L(x;\theta)}{\partial \theta}\, dx = \int t(x) \frac{\partial \log L(x;\theta)}{\partial \theta} L(x;\theta)\, dx$$
$$= \operatorname{cov}\left[t(X), \frac{\partial \log L(X;\theta)}{\partial \theta}\right]$$

The first equality sign is based on the fact that $t(X)$ depends on the sample alone and, therefore, is independent of θ (although its distribution will, of course, depend on θ in general). The expression after the second equality sign is equal to the expectation of the product of $t(X)$ and the θ-derivative of the log-likelihood, which is their covariance because the latter random variable has zero mean.

We now use the fact that the square of a covariance is at most equal to the product of the corresponding variances:

$$\left(\frac{\partial \mathscr{E}[t(X)]}{\partial \theta}\right)^2 \leq \operatorname{var} t(X) \operatorname{var} \frac{\partial \log L(X;\theta)}{\partial \theta}$$
$$= -\operatorname{var} t(X) \mathscr{E}\left[\frac{\partial^2 \log L(X;\theta)}{\partial \theta^2}\right] \qquad \text{[see (4.7)]}$$

which can also be written as follows:

$$\text{(4.10)} \qquad \operatorname{var} t(X) \geq \frac{\left(\dfrac{\partial \mathscr{E}[t(X)]}{\partial \theta}\right)^2}{-\mathscr{E}\left[\dfrac{\partial^2 \log L(X;\theta)}{\partial \theta^2}\right]}$$

In the special case of an unbiased estimator this amounts to

$$\text{(4.11)} \qquad \operatorname{var} t(X) \geq \frac{1}{-\mathscr{E}\left[\dfrac{\partial^2 \log L(X;\theta)}{\partial \theta^2}\right]} \qquad \text{if} \qquad \mathscr{E}[t(X)] \equiv \theta$$

This is the *Cramér-Rao inequality* for the sampling variance of a regular unbiased estimator.[11] It is a very convenient inequality because it enables us to proceed as follows. As soon as we have found an unbiased estimator whose

[11] The word "regular" refers to the conditions listed between eqs. (4.2) and (4.3). Note that the right-hand side of the inequality can also be formulated in terms of the variance of the θ-derivative of the log-likelihood of the sample [see (4.7)]. However, the expectation of the second-order derivative is usually easier to evaluate.

variance is equal to minus the reciprocal of the expected second-order derivative of the log-likelihood of the sample, we know that we cannot find an unbiased estimator with a smaller variance. Hence, no further improvements are possible if we confine ourselves to unbiased estimators and if a minimum sampling variance is our goal. However, there are cases in which the lower bound of the Cramér-Rao inequality cannot be attained; an example will be given later [see the discussion below eq. (4.24)]. In such cases the inequality is obviously much less useful. On the other hand, when the sample size n increases indefinitely, the lower bound can be attained asymptotically under certain general assumptions as will be shown in the next section.

Application to the Normal Distribution with Unknown Mean and Known Variance

Let $X = (X_1, \ldots, X_n)$ be a random sample from a normal population with unknown mean μ (which is to be estimated) and unit variance. The likelihood of the sample is

$$L(X; \mu) = \frac{1}{(2\pi)^{n/2}} \exp\left\{-\frac{1}{2}\sum_{i=1}^{n}(X_i - \mu)^2\right\}$$

and its logarithm:

$$\log L = -\frac{n}{2}\log 2\pi - \frac{1}{2}\sum_{i=1}^{n}(X_i - \mu)^2 \tag{4.12}$$

The first-order derivative of $\log L$ with respect to μ is $\sum (X_i - \mu)$ and the second derivative is $-n$. According to (4.11), the minimum-variance bound of a regular unbiased estimator of μ is equal to minus the reciprocal of the expectation of the second derivative, which is $1/n$. (Note that in this special case the second-order derivative of the log-likelihood is not random but a constant.) This minimum is actually attained by the sample mean $\bar{X}$ because $\text{var } \bar{X} = 1/n$. Therefore, the sample mean is a minimum-variance unbiased estimator when sampling takes place from this normal population. (The regularity conditions are all satisfied by the normal distribution.)

A Vector Generalization Based on the Information Matrix

The extension of the Cramér-Rao inequality for the case of a column vector $\boldsymbol{\theta}$ of parameters $\theta_1, \ldots, \theta_K$ can be described as follows. Differentiation of the log-likelihood function with respect to θ_h along the lines of (4.4) and (4.5) gives

$$\int \frac{\partial \log L(x; \boldsymbol{\theta})}{\partial \theta_h} L(x; \boldsymbol{\theta})\, dx = 0 \qquad h = 1, \ldots, K \tag{4.13}$$

which implies that the column vector of derivatives with respect to $\boldsymbol{\theta}$ of the log-likelihood of the sample has zero expectation:

$$\mathscr{E}\left[\frac{\partial \log L(X;\boldsymbol{\theta})}{\partial \boldsymbol{\theta}}\right] = \mathbf{0} \tag{4.14}$$

Next differentiate both sides of (4.13) with respect to θ_k:

$$\int \frac{\partial^2 \log L(X;\boldsymbol{\theta})}{\partial \theta_h\, \partial \theta_k} L(x;\boldsymbol{\theta})\, dx + \int \frac{\partial \log L(x;\boldsymbol{\theta})}{\partial \theta_h} \frac{\partial \log L(x;\boldsymbol{\theta})}{\partial \theta_k} L(x;\boldsymbol{\theta})\, dx = 0$$

This holds for all pairs (h, k); the result can thus be written as

$$\mathscr{V}\left[\frac{\partial \log L(X;\boldsymbol{\theta})}{\partial \theta}\right] = -\mathscr{E}\left[\frac{\partial^2 \log L(X;\boldsymbol{\theta})}{\partial \boldsymbol{\theta}\, \partial \boldsymbol{\theta}'}\right] \tag{4.15}$$

Hence the covariance matrix of the $\boldsymbol{\theta}$-derivatives of the log-likelihood of the sample is equal to minus the matrix of the expectations of the second-order derivatives of this log-likelihood. This is the generalization of (4.7) for the multiparameter case. The right-hand matrix in (4.15) is known as the *information matrix*:

$$\mathbf{R}(\boldsymbol{\theta}) = -\mathscr{E}\left[\frac{\partial^2 \log L(X;\boldsymbol{\theta})}{\partial \boldsymbol{\theta}\, \partial \boldsymbol{\theta}'}\right] \tag{4.16}$$

We shall confine ourselves to the case in which the $\boldsymbol{\theta}$-derivatives of the log-likelihood of the random sample are not linearly dependent. This means that the covariance matrix in (4.15) and hence also $\mathbf{R}(\boldsymbol{\theta})$ are positive definite.

Next consider a vector estimator of $\boldsymbol{\theta}$, $\mathbf{t}(X)$ with elements $t_1(X), \ldots, t_K(X)$. Its expectation is

$$\mathscr{E}[\mathbf{t}(X)] = \int \mathbf{t}(x) L(x;\boldsymbol{\theta})\, dx \tag{4.17}$$

and the derivative of this expectation with respect to θ_h is

$$\frac{\partial \mathscr{E}[\mathbf{t}(X)]}{\partial \theta_h} = \int \mathbf{t}(x) \frac{\partial \log L(x;\boldsymbol{\theta})}{\partial \theta_h} L(x;\boldsymbol{\theta})\, d_x \tag{4.18}$$

$$= \begin{bmatrix} \operatorname{cov}\left\{t_1(X), \dfrac{\partial \log L(X;\boldsymbol{\theta})}{\partial \theta_h}\right\} \\ \cdot \\ \cdot \\ \cdot \\ \operatorname{cov}\left\{t_K(X), \dfrac{\partial \log L(X;\boldsymbol{\theta})}{\partial \theta_h}\right\} \end{bmatrix}$$

This is a column vector of covariances for each θ_h. If we combine all K such vectors in matrix form, we obtain

(4.19)
$$\frac{\partial \mathscr{E}[\mathbf{t}(X)]}{\partial \boldsymbol{\theta}'} = \mathscr{E}\left[\mathbf{t}(X)\frac{\partial \log L(X;\boldsymbol{\theta})}{\partial \boldsymbol{\theta}'}\right]$$

which is the matrix extension of (4.9). Note that when the vector estimator is unbiased, $\mathscr{E}[\mathbf{t}(X)] \equiv \boldsymbol{\theta}$, the left-hand side of (4.19) is the $K \times K$ unit matrix.

Now consider the $2K$-element random vector

$$\left[t_1(X) \cdots t_K(X) \quad \frac{\partial \log L(X;\boldsymbol{\theta})}{\partial \theta_1} \quad \cdots \quad \frac{\partial \log L(X;\boldsymbol{\theta})}{\partial \theta_K}\right]$$

and, in particular, its covariance matrix under the condition that $\mathbf{t}(X)$ is unbiased:

(4.20)
$$\mathscr{V}\begin{bmatrix} \mathbf{t}(X) \\ \dfrac{\partial \log L(X;\boldsymbol{\theta})}{\partial \boldsymbol{\theta}} \end{bmatrix} = \begin{bmatrix} \mathscr{V}[\mathbf{t}(X)] & \mathbf{I} \\ \mathbf{I} & \mathbf{R}(\boldsymbol{\theta}) \end{bmatrix}$$

where $\mathscr{V}[\mathbf{t}(X)]$ is the covariance matrix of the estimator, $\mathbf{R}(\boldsymbol{\theta})$ the information matrix or, equivalently, the covariance matrix of the $\boldsymbol{\theta}$-derivatives of the log-likelihood of the sample [see (4.15) and (4.16)], and $\mathbf{I}$ the unit matrix mentioned below eq. (4.19). Since the matrix (4.20) is a covariance matrix of a vector of random variables, it is necessarily positive semidefinite. Hence, for whatever K-element vector $\mathbf{a}$, we have

(4.21)
$$[\mathbf{a}' \quad -\mathbf{a}'\mathbf{R}(\boldsymbol{\theta})^{-1}]\begin{bmatrix} \mathscr{V}[\mathbf{t}(X)] & \mathbf{I} \\ \mathbf{I} & \mathbf{R}(\boldsymbol{\theta}) \end{bmatrix}\begin{bmatrix} \mathbf{a} \\ -\mathbf{R}(\boldsymbol{\theta})^{-1}\mathbf{a} \end{bmatrix} = \mathbf{a}'\{\mathscr{V}[\mathbf{t}(X)] - \mathbf{R}(\boldsymbol{\theta})^{-1}\}\mathbf{a} \geq 0$$

which shows that *the covariance matrix of a regular unbiased vector estimator exceeds the inverse of the information matrix by a positive semidefinite matrix.* This is the multidimensional generalization of the Cramér-Rao inequality. It is easily verified that this includes (4.11) as a special case for $K = 1$. Also see Problem 4.2 for K-dimensional biased estimators.

Application to the Normal Distribution with Unknown Mean and Variance

Our example is the normal distribution with $[\mu \quad \sigma^2]$ as the unknown parameter vector. The log-likelihood of the sample is

(4.22)
$$\log L(X;\mu,\sigma^2) = -\frac{n}{2}\log 2\pi - \frac{n}{2}\log\sigma^2 - \frac{1}{2\sigma^2}\sum_{i=1}^{n}(X_i - \mu)^2$$

and the matrix of its second-order derivatives with respect to μ and σ^2 is

$$\begin{bmatrix} \dfrac{\partial^2 \log L}{\partial \mu^2} & \dfrac{\partial^2 \log L}{\partial \mu\, \partial \sigma^2} \\ \dfrac{\partial^2 \log L}{\partial \sigma^2\, \partial \mu} & \dfrac{\partial^2 \log L}{\partial (\sigma^2)^2} \end{bmatrix} = \begin{bmatrix} -\dfrac{n}{\sigma^2} & -\dfrac{1}{\sigma^4}\sum_{i=1}^{n}(X_i-\mu) \\ -\dfrac{1}{\sigma^4}\sum_{i=1}^{n}(X_i-\mu) & \dfrac{n}{2\sigma^4} - \dfrac{1}{\sigma^6}\sum_{i=1}^{n}(X_i-\mu)^2 \end{bmatrix}$$

The information matrix is minus the expectation of this matrix:

(4.23)

$$\mathbf{R}(\mu, \sigma^2) = \begin{bmatrix} n/\sigma^2 & 0 \\ 0 & n/2\sigma^4 \end{bmatrix} \qquad \text{implying} \qquad \mathbf{R}(\mu, \sigma^2)^{-1} = \begin{bmatrix} \sigma^2/n & 0 \\ 0 & 2\sigma^4/n \end{bmatrix}$$

We know from eq. (7.18) of Section 2.7 that the sample mean $\bar{X}$ and the sample variance $s^2 = [1/(n-1)] \sum (X_i - \bar{X})^2$, which are unbiased estimators of μ and σ^2, respectively, have the following covariance matrix:

$$\mathscr{V}\begin{bmatrix} \bar{X} \\ s^2 \end{bmatrix} = \begin{bmatrix} \sigma^2/n & 0 \\ 0 & 2\sigma^4/(n-1) \end{bmatrix} \tag{4.24}$$

This exceeds the inverse of the information matrix by a positive semidefinite matrix. The difference between the two matrices is confined to the second diagonal element (the variance of the σ^2 estimator), which may suggest that there exists an unbiased σ^2 estimator with a smaller variance than that of s^2. Actually, however, this is *not* true, which provides an example of the case in which the Cramér-Rao bound cannot be attained. This result (which will not be proved here) means that the covariance matrix of any unbiased estimator of $[\mu \quad \sigma^2]$ has a covariance matrix which exceeds not only $\mathbf{R}(\mu, \sigma^2)^{-1}$ but also the matrix (4.24) by a positive semidefinite matrix.

Application to the Standard Linear Model under the Normality Assumption

We now turn to LS theory and consider the following theorem.

THEOREM 8.3 (Best unbiasedness of the LS coefficient and variance estimators under the normality condition) *Suppose that Assumption* 3.3 *of Section* 3.2 *is true for given* $\mathbf{X}$ *with the additional specification that the distribution of* $\mathbf{y}$ *(given* $\mathbf{X}$*) is n-variate normal; also suppose* $n > K$. *Then the LS estimator* $[\mathbf{b}' \quad s^2]$ *of* $[\boldsymbol{\beta}' \quad \sigma^2]$ *is best unbiased in the following sense. Any other estimator of* $[\boldsymbol{\beta}' \quad \sigma^2]$ *which is also unbiased has a covariance matrix which exceeds that of* $[\mathbf{b}' \quad s^2]$ *by a positive semidefinite matrix.*

A comparison with the Gauss-Markov theorem (Theorem 3.4 in Section 3.4) shows that as far as the LS coefficient vector **b** is concerned, we may delete the constraint "linear" of best linear unbiasedness *if the random variation is normal.*[12] Regarding the variance estimator s^2, recall that Theorem 3.7 in Section 3.5 is formulated under the normality condition and that it declares s^2 to be best quadratic unbiased. The present theorem implies that the constraint "quadratic" can simply be deleted.

For the Cramér-Rao verification of Theorem 8.3 we need the matrix of second-order derivatives of the log-likelihood function, which is obtained by taking the derivatives of the first-order derivatives given in eqs. (5.2) and (5.3) of Section 3.5. The result is

$$\begin{bmatrix} -\dfrac{1}{\sigma^2}\mathbf{X}'\mathbf{X} & -\dfrac{1}{\sigma^4}(\mathbf{X}'\mathbf{y}-\mathbf{X}'\mathbf{X}\boldsymbol{\beta}) \\ -\dfrac{1}{\sigma^4}(\mathbf{y}'\mathbf{X}-\boldsymbol{\beta}'\mathbf{X}'\mathbf{X}) & \dfrac{n}{2\sigma^4}-\dfrac{1}{\sigma^6}(\mathbf{y}-\mathbf{X}\boldsymbol{\beta})'(\mathbf{y}-\mathbf{X}\boldsymbol{\beta}) \end{bmatrix} \tag{4.25}$$

so that the inverse of the information matrix is

$$\mathbf{R}(\boldsymbol{\beta}, \sigma^2)^{-1} = \begin{bmatrix} \sigma^2(\mathbf{X}'\mathbf{X})^{-1} & \mathbf{0} \\ \mathbf{0} & 2\sigma^4/n \end{bmatrix} \tag{4.26}$$

The covariance matrix of $[\mathbf{b}' \quad s^2]$ under the normality condition follows directly from Theorem 3.8 in Section 3.5:

$$\mathscr{V}\begin{bmatrix} \mathbf{b} \\ s^2 \end{bmatrix} = \begin{bmatrix} \sigma^2(\mathbf{X}'\mathbf{X})^{-1} & \mathbf{0} \\ \mathbf{0} & 2\sigma^4/(n-K) \end{bmatrix} \tag{4.27}$$

The Cramér-Rao bound is thus attained by the coefficient estimator but not by the variance estimator. Nevertheless, as in the case of the univariate normal population with parameters μ and σ^2, it is not possible to find an unbiased σ^2 estimator with smaller variance; for a proof see C. R. Rao (1965a, pp. 257–259).

Problems

4.1 Derive the Cramér-Rao inequality for a univariate discrete distribution with probability mass function $P[X = x_i \mid \theta] = p_i(\theta)$, $i = 1, 2, \ldots$.

[12] See Anderson (1962) for the problem of best unbiasedness in nonnormal situations.

4.2 (*Cramér-Rao inequality for biased vector estimators*) Suppose that the vector estimator $\mathbf{t}(X)$ of $\boldsymbol{\theta}$ is biased in the sense that $\partial\mathscr{E}[\mathbf{t}(X)]/\partial\boldsymbol{\theta}' = \mathbf{H} \neq \mathbf{I}$. Prove along the lines of (4.19) to (4.21) that its covariance matrix $\mathscr{V}[\mathbf{t}(X)]$ exceeds $\mathbf{HR}(\boldsymbol{\theta})^{-1}\mathbf{H}'$ by a positive semidefinite matrix.

4.3 (*Aitken generalization of Theorem 8.3*) Formulate the Aitken variant of Theorem 8.3 (see Section 6.1) under the assumption that the disturbances are normally distributed. Derive the information matrix and prove that its inverse conforms with the covariance matrix of the GLS coefficient vector.

8.5 The Asymptotic Distribution of Maximum-Likelihood Estimators and of Likelihood Ratios[C]

In the previous section we differentiated with respect to the parameter θ, which means that we imagine that θ takes a number of alternative values. If we do so systematically, it becomes appropriate to use a special symbol, θ_0, say, for the true value of the parameter. We shall show in this section that the maximum-likelihood method yields an estimator which is not only consistent for θ_0 but also asymptotically normally distributed with mean θ_0 and a variance equal to the lower bound of the Cramér-Rao inequality. This property of the maximum-likelihood estimator is frequently described as *asymptotic efficiency*.

Some Fairly Weak Conditions

The above-mentioned theorem will be proved for a continuous distribution with density function $f(x;\theta)$ under the following conditions. First, the derivatives with respect to θ of $\log f(\ )$ exist up to the third order. This should hold for all values of x (apart possibly from a finite number of x-values) and for every θ belonging to an interval A that contains θ_0 as an interior point. Second, the assumptions underlying the zero value of the expectation in (4.6) are satisfied (which include the differentiability under the integration sign). Third, the θ-derivative of $\log f(X;\theta)$ evaluated at θ_0 has a positive and finite variance. Fourth, the third-order derivative of $\log f$ is bounded:

$$\left|\frac{\partial^3 \log f(x;\theta)}{\partial\theta^3}\right| < H(x) \qquad \text{for every } x \text{ and every } \theta \in A \tag{5.1}$$

and $H(\ )$ satisfies

$$\int H(x) f(x;\theta)\, dx < M \qquad \text{for every } \theta \in A \tag{5.2}$$

where M is a positive constant independent of θ. This means that the expectation of the random variable $H(X)$ is bounded, just as the third-order derivative of $f(x; \theta)$ with respect to θ.

Proof of the Consistency of the Maximum-Likelihood Estimator

Under our differentiability conditions the maximum-likelihood estimator is found by differentiating

$$\log L(X; \theta) = \sum_{i=1}^{n} \log f(X_i; \theta) \tag{5.3}$$

with respect to θ and equating the result to zero. [As in the previous section, X as an argument of $L(\ )$ stands for the sample $(X_1, \ldots, X_n)$.] Note that the resulting likelihood equation $\partial(\log L)/\partial\theta = 0$ may have several solutions; we shall consider here only one solution and return to the problem later in this section.

Apply a Taylor expansion to $\partial(\log f)/\partial\theta$ for some $\theta \in A$:

$$\begin{aligned}\frac{\partial \log f(X_i; \theta)}{\partial\theta} &= \left(\frac{\partial \log f(X_i; \theta)}{\partial\theta}\right)_{\theta_0} + (\theta - \theta_0)\left(\frac{\partial^2 \log f(X_i; \theta)}{\partial\theta^2}\right)_{\theta_0} \\ &\quad + \frac{1}{2}(\theta - \theta_0)^2\left(\frac{\partial^3 \log f(X_i; \theta)}{\partial\theta^3}\right)_{\theta^*} \\ &= \left(\frac{\partial \log f(X_i; \theta)}{\partial\theta}\right)_{\theta_0} + (\theta - \theta_0)\left(\frac{\partial^2 \log f(X_i; \theta)}{\partial\theta^2}\right)_{\theta_0} + \frac{1}{2}\zeta(\theta - \theta_0)^2 H(X_i)\end{aligned}$$

where θ^* is between θ_0 and θ (hence $\theta^* \in A$) and ζ is some number less than one in absolute value. We conclude from this equation and (5.3) that the likelihood equation $\partial(\log L)/\partial\theta = 0$ (after dividing both sides by n) can be written as

(5.4)
$$\frac{1}{n}\frac{\partial \log L(X; \theta)}{\partial\theta} = B_0(X) + (\theta - \theta_0)B_1(X) + \frac{1}{2}\zeta(\theta - \theta_0)^2 B_2(X) = 0$$

where the three B's are the following random variables:

$$\begin{aligned} B_0(X) &= \frac{1}{n}\sum_{i=1}^{n}\left(\frac{\partial \log f(X_i; \theta)}{\partial\theta}\right)_{\theta_0} \\ B_1(X) &= \frac{1}{n}\sum_{i=1}^{n}\left(\frac{\partial^2 \log f(X_i; \theta)}{\partial\theta^2}\right)_{\theta_0} \\ B_2(X) &= \frac{1}{n}\sum_{i=1}^{n} H(X_i)\end{aligned} \tag{5.5}$$

Under our assumptions each of the three B's is the average of n independently and identically distributed random variables with finite expectations, so that they converge in probability to these expectations according to Khintchine's theorem. In the case of $B_0(X)$ the expectation of each of the n components is zero:

$$\int \left(\frac{\partial \log f(X;\theta)}{\partial \theta}\right)_{\theta_0} f(x;\theta_0)\,dx = 0 \tag{5.6}$$

The validity of (5.6) follows directly from (4.5): take $n = 1$ in the latter equation, so that $L(\ )$ and $f(\ )$ become identical functions. Similarly, the expectation of each component of $B_1(X)$ is equal to $-k^2$, where k is the positive square root of

$$k^2 = -\int \left(\frac{\partial^2 \log f(x;\theta)}{\partial \theta^2}\right)_{\theta_0} f(x;\theta_0)\,dx \tag{5.7}$$
$$= \int \left(\frac{\partial \log f(x;\theta)}{\partial \theta}\right)_{\theta_0}^2 f(x;\theta_0)\,dx$$

the second equality sign of which is verified straightforwardly on the basis of (4.7) with $L(\ )$ replaced by $f(\ )$. Finally, each component $H(X_i)$ of $B_2(X)$ has an expectation between zero and M [cf. (5.2)], so that this expectation can be written as a nonnegative fraction of M. We may thus conclude:

$$\operatorname*{plim}_{n\to\infty} B_0(X) = 0 \qquad \operatorname*{plim}_{n\to\infty} B_1(X) = -k^2 \qquad \operatorname*{plim}_{n\to\infty} B_2(X) = \zeta' M \tag{5.8}$$

where $0 \le \zeta' < 1$.

Consider, then, the second member of (5.4) for $\theta = \theta_0 \pm \delta$, where δ is a small positive number:

$$B_0(X) \pm \delta B_1(X) + \frac{1}{2}\zeta\delta^2 B_2(X) \tag{5.9}$$

The first term converges in probability to zero as $n \to \infty$, the second to $\mp k^2\delta$, and the third to $\frac{1}{2}\zeta'' M\delta^2$, where $\zeta'' = \zeta\zeta'$ is a number less than 1 in absolute value. By choosing a sufficiently small δ and a sufficiently large n, we can ensure that the sum of the first and third terms of (5.9) is smaller in absolute value than the second with a probability arbitrarily close to one. Returning to (5.4), we conclude that the sign of the derivative $\partial(\log L)/\partial\theta$ is then determined by the second term, so that this derivative is positive (with arbitrarily high probability) for $\theta = \theta_0 - \delta$ and negative for $\theta = \theta_0 + \delta$. Since the second derivative $\partial^2(\log L)/\partial\theta^2$ exists, the likelihood equation $\partial(\log L)/\partial\theta = 0$ therefore has a root between the limits $\theta_0 \pm \delta$ with arbitrarily high probability for arbitrarily small δ when n is sufficiently large, which establishes the consistency of this root.

Proof of the Asymptotic Normality of the Maximum-Likelihood Estimator

Write $\hat{\theta} = \hat{\theta}(X)$ for this root of the likelihood equation and reformulate (5.4) as $(\hat{\theta} - \theta_0)[B_1(X) + \frac{1}{2}\zeta(\hat{\theta} - \theta_0)B_2(X)] = -B_0(X)$ or, equivalently,

$$k\sqrt{n}(\hat{\theta} - \theta_0) = \frac{\dfrac{1}{k\sqrt{n}}\displaystyle\sum_{i=1}^{n}\left(\frac{\partial \log f(X_i;\theta)}{\partial\theta}\right)_{\theta_0}}{-B_1(X)/k^2 - \dfrac{1}{2}\zeta(\hat{\theta} - \theta_0)B_2(X)/k^2} \tag{5.10}$$

It follows from (5.8) that $-B_1(X)/k^2$ converges in probability to 1. We also know from (5.8) that $B_2(X)$ converges in probability to a finite number, and we have just proved that $\hat{\theta} - \theta_0$ converges in probability to zero. Hence the right-hand denominator of (5.10) converges in probability to 1 as $n \to \infty$. As to the numerator, the n derivatives of $\log f(X_i; \theta)$ with respect to θ are independently and identically distributed with zero mean and finite variance k^2; see (5.6) and (5.7). It follows from the Lindeberg-Lévy theorem that the sum of these derivatives is asymptotically normally distributed with zero mean and variance k^2n, and hence that the right-hand numerator of (5.10) is asymptotically a standardized normal variate. We apply rule (iii) of Section 8.2 (the convergence of Y_n/X_n to Y/c, $c \neq 0$) to conclude that the right-hand ratio in (5.10) converges in distribution to a standardized normal variate also. Hence the distribution of the maximum-likelihood estimator $\hat{\theta}$ converges, as $n \to \infty$, to a normal distribution with mean θ_0 and a variance equal to the Cramér-Rao bound given in (4.11):

$$\frac{1}{k^2n} = \left(n \operatorname{var} \frac{\partial \log f(X_i;\theta)}{\partial\theta}\right)^{-1} = \left(\operatorname{var}\left[\sum_{i=1}^{n}\frac{\partial \log f(X_i;\theta)}{\partial\theta}\right]\right)^{-1} \tag{5.11}$$
$$= \left(\operatorname{var}\frac{\partial \log L(X;\theta)}{\partial\theta}\right)^{-1} = -\left(\mathscr{E}\left[\frac{\partial^2 \log L(X;\theta)}{\partial\theta^2}\right]\right)^{-1}$$

The first equality sign in (5.11) is based on the k^2 definition (5.7), the second on the independence of the θ-derivatives of $\log f(X_i; \theta)$, $i = 1, \ldots, n$, the third on (5.3), and the fourth on (4.7). Note that the derivatives of (5.11) are all evaluated at θ_0. In general, the asymptotic variance depends on θ_0, and replacing θ_0 by $\hat{\theta}_n$ then leads to asymptotic standard errors. Also note that it follows from the third assumption made at the beginning of this section that k^2 is a finite positive number, so that the variance (5.11) is $O(n^{-1})$.

Extensions

When there is a vector of parameters, say $\boldsymbol{\theta}_0$, then it can be shown under similar conditions that the vector estimator $\hat{\boldsymbol{\theta}}_n$ which is associated with the likelihood maximum is consistent and asymptotically normally distributed with mean vector $\boldsymbol{\theta}_0$ and covariance matrix $\mathbf{R}(\boldsymbol{\theta}_0)^{-1}$, the inverse of the information matrix, and the elements of the covariance matrix are $O(n^{-1})$. [A consistent estimator of $n\mathbf{R}(\boldsymbol{\theta}_0)^{-1}$ is $n\mathbf{R}(\hat{\boldsymbol{\theta}}_n)^{-1}$.] This result is in agreement with maximum-likelihood estimation of $\boldsymbol{\beta}$ and σ^2 in the standard linear model as will become clear from Problem 5.2.

As to the possibility that the likelihood equation $\partial(\log L)/\partial\theta = 0$ may have two or more solutions, it can be shown that if $\hat{\theta}_n$ and $\hat{\theta}'_n$ are two consistent roots of this equation, they are asymptotically equivalent in the sense that $\sqrt{n}(\hat{\theta}_n - \hat{\theta}'_n)$ converges in probability to zero. Furthermore, under certain additional conditions it can be proved that the global maximum of the likelihood function provides a consistent estimator with unit probability.

Minus Twice the Logarithm of a Likelihood Ratio Has Asymptotically a Chi-Square Distribution

Consider the following Taylor expansion:

$$\log L(X;\theta_0) - \log L(X;\hat{\theta}) = (\theta_0 - \hat{\theta})\left(\frac{\partial \log L(X;\theta)}{\partial\theta}\right)_{\hat{\theta}} + \frac{1}{2}(\theta_0 - \hat{\theta})^2\left(\frac{\partial^2 \log L(X;\theta)}{\partial\theta^2}\right)_{\theta^*}$$

where $\hat{\theta}$ is the maximum-likelihood estimator of θ_0 and θ^* is between θ_0 and $\hat{\theta}$. It follows from the likelihood equation $[\partial(\log L)/\partial\theta]_{\hat{\theta}} = 0$ that the first term on the right vanishes, so that the equation can be written as

$$(5.12) \qquad -2\log\frac{L(X;\theta_0)}{L(X;\hat{\theta})} = [\sqrt{n}\,(\hat{\theta} - \theta_0)]^2\,\frac{-1}{n}\left(\frac{\partial^2 \log L(X;\theta)}{\partial\theta^2}\right)_{\theta^*}$$

Consider then

$$(5.13) \qquad -\frac{1}{n}\left(\frac{\partial^2 \log L(X;\theta)}{\partial\theta^2}\right)_{\theta^*} = -\frac{1}{n}\sum_{i=1}^{n}\left(\frac{\partial^2 \log f(X_i;\theta)}{\partial\theta^2}\right)_{\theta^*}$$

The second-order derivatives appearing in this equation are all by assumption continuous in θ; and since $\hat{\theta}$ and hence θ^* converge in probability to θ_0, we may conclude that the right-hand side of (5.13) converges in distribution to minus the average of the same derivatives evaluated at θ_0. Application of Khintchine's theorem then shows that the left-hand term of (5.13) converges in probability to k^2 defined in (5.7). Now this term is multiplied in (5.12) by the square of $\sqrt{n}(\hat{\theta} - \theta)$, and we know from the discussion above eq.

(5.11) that the latter random variable has a normal limiting distribution with zero mean and variance $1/k^2$. We apply rule (iv) of Section 8.2 to conclude that the limiting distribution of its square is $(1/k^2)\chi^2(1)$. When this square is multiplied by a random variable which converges in probability to k^2, the limiting distribution of the product is $\chi^2(1)$ in view of rule (iii). But note that $L(X; \theta_0)/L(X; \hat{\theta})$ is nothing but the likelihood ratio for testing the null hypothesis $\theta = \theta_0$, the numerator being the likelihood of the sample when $\theta = \theta_0$ and the denominator the maximum value of the likelihood (the value associated with the maximum-likelihood estimator); see eq. (9.7) of Section 2.9 and the discussion around that equation. Since the left-hand side of (5.12) is $-2 \log_e \lambda$, where λ is the likelihood ratio, we have thus proved that, as $n \to \infty$, the distribution of $-2 \log_e \lambda$ converges to $\chi^2(1)$.

The vector generalization of this result can be stated as follows. Let $\boldsymbol{\theta}$ be a K-element vector and suppose that the null hypothesis implies that q elements ($q < K$) take certain given values. Then compute the maximum value of the likelihood under these q constraints and also with disregard for these constraints. The former maximum is indicated by $L(\hat{\omega})$, the latter by $L(\hat{\Omega})$; see again eq. (9.7) of Section 2.9. The likelihood ratio is then $L(\hat{\omega})/L(\hat{\Omega})$, and minus twice the logarithm of this ratio is asymptotically distributed as $\chi^2(q)$. See Problem 6.4 for a more explicit derivation in a special case.

Problems

5.1 Prove that assumptions (5.1) and (5.2) on the third-order derivative of $\log f(\;)$ are satisfied (1) if $f(\;)$ is the normal density function with mean θ and unit variance, and (2) if $f(\;)$ is the normal density function with zero mean and variance $\theta > 0$.

5.2 Assume that Assumption 3.3 of Section 3.2 and Assumption 8.1 are true with the additional specification that the distribution of $\mathbf{y}$ (given $\mathbf{X}$) is n-variate normal. Use eqs. (4.26) and (4.27) as well as the fact that the maximum-likelihood estimator $\mathbf{e}'\mathbf{e}/n$ of σ^2 is asymptotically equivalent to the LS estimator s^2 [in the sense that $\sqrt{n}(s^2 - \mathbf{e}'\mathbf{e}/n)$ converges in probability to zero] to prove that $\mathbf{b} - \boldsymbol{\beta}$, $\mathbf{e}'\mathbf{e}/n - \sigma^2$ has asymptotically a $(K + 1)$-dimensional normal distribution with zero mean vector and covariance matrix

$$\frac{1}{n}\begin{bmatrix} \sigma^2\mathbf{Q}^{-1} & \mathbf{0} \\ \mathbf{0} & 2\sigma^4 \end{bmatrix} \tag{5.14}$$

Also prove that this covariance matrix corresponds to the inverted information matrix.

8.6 Asymptotic Properties of Generalized Least-Squares Estimators[C]

The Case of a Known V *Matrix*

We return to Assumption 6.1 in Section 6.1, which states that the disturbance vector $\boldsymbol{\epsilon}$ of the basic equation $\mathbf{y} = \mathbf{X}\boldsymbol{\beta} + \boldsymbol{\epsilon}$ has covariance matrix $\sigma^2\mathbf{V}$, where $\mathbf{V}$ is a known nonsingular $n \times n$ matrix.[13] We derived in that section the GLS coefficient and variance estimators:

$$(6.1)\quad \hat{\boldsymbol{\beta}} = (\mathbf{X}'\mathbf{V}^{-1}\mathbf{X})^{-1}\mathbf{X}'\mathbf{V}^{-1}\mathbf{y} \qquad \hat{\sigma}^2 = \frac{1}{n-K}(\mathbf{y} - \mathbf{X}\hat{\boldsymbol{\beta}})'\mathbf{V}^{-1}(\mathbf{y} - \mathbf{X}\hat{\boldsymbol{\beta}})$$

by applying LS to the transformed observation matrix $[\mathbf{Py} \quad \mathbf{PX}]$, $\mathbf{P}$ being an $n \times n$ matrix which satisfies $\mathbf{P}'\mathbf{P} = \mathbf{V}^{-1}$. The justification of this procedure was that the transformed disturbance vector $\mathbf{P}\boldsymbol{\epsilon}$ has zero mean and a scalar covariance matrix.

Theorems 8.1 and 8.2 can be extended straightforwardly to this GLS case.[14]

(1) Theorem 8.1: If the moment matrix $(1/n)(\mathbf{PX})'\mathbf{PX} = (1/n)\mathbf{X}'\mathbf{V}^{-1}\mathbf{X}$ of the transformed explanatory variables converges to a positive definite matrix $\mathbf{Q}_V$ as $n \to \infty$:

$$(6.2)\qquad \lim_{n\to\infty} \frac{1}{n}\mathbf{X}'\mathbf{V}^{-1}\mathbf{X} = \mathbf{Q}_V \qquad |\mathbf{Q}_V| > 0$$

then the GLS vector $\hat{\boldsymbol{\beta}}$ is a consistent estimator of $\boldsymbol{\beta}$. If the distribution of $\mathbf{y}$ (given $\mathbf{X}$) is n-variate normal, the GLS variance estimator $\hat{\sigma}^2$ is consistent for σ^2. Both statements can be proved easily by means of the $\mathbf{P}$ transformation.

(2) Theorem 8.2: If (6.2) is true, each element of the GLS residual vector $\mathbf{y} - \mathbf{X}\hat{\boldsymbol{\beta}}$ converges in distribution to the corresponding element of the disturbance vector $\boldsymbol{\epsilon}$. If it is also true that the elements of the transformed disturbance vector $\mathbf{P}\boldsymbol{\epsilon}$ are independently and identically distributed, $\hat{\sigma}^2$ is a consistent estimator of σ^2 and $\sqrt{n}(\hat{\boldsymbol{\beta}} - \boldsymbol{\beta})$ has a normal limiting distribution with zero mean vector and covariance matrix $\sigma^2\mathbf{Q}_V^{-1}$. The latter condition is satisfied by the heteroscedasticity and autoregressive examples of Chapter 6 if $\zeta_1, \ldots, \zeta_n$ of eqs. (2.9) and (3.1) of Sections 6.2 and 6.3, respectively, are independently and identically distributed.

[13] We confine the analysis to the nonsingular case, but this is not a real restriction. If $\mathbf{V}$ has rank $n' < n$, we can delete $n - n'$ observations so that the remaining $n' \times n'$ submatrix of $\mathbf{V}$ is nonsingular. If the singularity of $\mathbf{V}$ implies linear constraints of $\boldsymbol{\beta}$ (the case of Section 6.8), these may be used to eliminate as many elements of $\boldsymbol{\beta}$.

[14] For Theorem 8.3 see Problem 4.3 above.

The Case of an Unknown V *Matrix*

There were several occasions in Chapters 6 and 7 on which it was stated that it is unrealistic to assume that $\mathbf{V}$ is a known matrix, and it was then replaced by an estimator, say $\hat{\mathbf{V}}_n$, where the subscript n refers to the size of the sample from which this estimator is derived. This leads to the following coefficient and variance estimators:

$$\text{(6.3)} \quad \hat{\boldsymbol{\beta}}_n = (\mathbf{X}'\hat{\mathbf{V}}_n^{-1}\mathbf{X})^{-1}\mathbf{X}'\hat{\mathbf{V}}_n^{-1}\mathbf{y} \qquad \hat{\sigma}_n^2 = \frac{1}{n-K}(\mathbf{y} - \mathbf{X}\hat{\boldsymbol{\beta}}_n)'\hat{\mathbf{V}}_n^{-1}(\mathbf{y} - \mathbf{X}\hat{\boldsymbol{\beta}}_n)$$

which should be compared with the estimators (6.1). How close are they to each other when n becomes larger and larger? It is sometimes stated that their difference converges in probability to zero when $\hat{\mathbf{V}}_n$ is a consistent estimator of $\mathbf{V}$, but a major complication is that these matrices increase in size when n increases. A more promising approach is based on the following theorem.

THEOREM 8.4 (Asymptotic distribution of GLS estimators based on an estimated disturbance covariance matrix) *Suppose that the assumptions of Theorem* 6.1 *of Section* 6.1 *are true except that* $\mathbf{V}$ *is an unknown matrix estimated by* $\hat{\mathbf{V}}_n$. *Suppose also that a square matrix* $\mathbf{P}$ *exists such that* (1) $\mathbf{P}'\mathbf{P} = \mathbf{V}^{-1}$ *and* (2) *the elements of* $\mathbf{P}\boldsymbol{\epsilon}$ *are independently and identically distributed. Then, if condition* (6.2) *and*

$$\text{(6.4)} \qquad \operatorname*{plim}_{n\to\infty} \frac{1}{n}\mathbf{X}'(\hat{\mathbf{V}}_n^{-1} - \mathbf{V}^{-1})\mathbf{X} = \mathbf{0}$$

$$\text{(6.5)} \qquad \operatorname*{plim}_{n\to\infty} \frac{1}{\sqrt{n}}\mathbf{X}'(\hat{\mathbf{V}}_n^{-1} - \mathbf{V}^{-1})\boldsymbol{\epsilon} = \mathbf{0}$$

are all satisfied, the estimator $\hat{\boldsymbol{\beta}}_n$ *defined in* (6.3) *is asymptotically equivalent with* $\hat{\boldsymbol{\beta}}$ *defined in* (6.1) *in the sense that* $\sqrt{n}(\hat{\boldsymbol{\beta}}_n - \hat{\boldsymbol{\beta}})$ *converges in probability to zero as* $n \to \infty$, *both coefficient estimators being asymptotically normally distributed with mean vector* $\boldsymbol{\beta}$ *and covariance matrix* $(\sigma^2/n)\mathbf{Q}_V^{-1}$. *If in addition*

$$\text{(6.6)} \qquad \operatorname*{plim}_{n\to\infty} \frac{1}{n}\boldsymbol{\epsilon}'(\hat{\mathbf{V}}_n^{-1} - \mathbf{V}^{-1})\boldsymbol{\epsilon} = 0$$

is also true, then $\hat{\sigma}_n^2$ *and* $\hat{\sigma}^2$ *defined in* (6.3) *and* (6.1), *respectively, are both consistent estimators of* σ^2.

To prove this theorem we consider the sampling error of $\hat{\boldsymbol{\beta}}_n$ multiplied by $\sqrt{n}$:

$$\sqrt{n}\,(\hat{\boldsymbol{\beta}}_n - \boldsymbol{\beta}) = \left(\frac{1}{n}\mathbf{X}'\hat{\mathbf{V}}_n^{-1}\mathbf{X}\right)^{-1}\frac{1}{\sqrt{n}}\mathbf{X}'\hat{\mathbf{V}}_n^{-1}\boldsymbol{\epsilon} \tag{6.7}$$

as well as the corresponding expression for $\hat{\boldsymbol{\beta}}$:

$$\sqrt{n}\,(\hat{\boldsymbol{\beta}} - \boldsymbol{\beta}) = \left(\frac{1}{n}\mathbf{X}'\mathbf{V}^{-1}\mathbf{X}\right)^{-1}\frac{1}{\sqrt{n}}\mathbf{X}'\mathbf{V}^{-1}\boldsymbol{\epsilon} \tag{6.8}$$

The expression in parentheses in the right-hand side of (6.8) converges to the nonsingular matrix $\mathbf{Q}_V$ when (6.2) is true. The corresponding expression in (6.7) has the same property under condition (6.4). The inverse of $(1/n)\mathbf{X}'\mathbf{V}^{-1}\mathbf{X}$ is postmultiplied by $\sqrt{1/n}\;\mathbf{X}'\mathbf{V}^{-1}\boldsymbol{\epsilon}$ in (6.8), and this vector has a normal limiting distribution with zero mean and covariance matrix $\sigma^2\mathbf{Q}_V$ when the elements of $\mathbf{P}\boldsymbol{\epsilon}$ are independently and identically distributed. (This is the GLS extension of the result proved in the last paragraph of Section 8.3.) The corresponding vector in (6.7) has the same property under condition (6.5). Hence $\hat{\boldsymbol{\beta}}_n$ and $\hat{\boldsymbol{\beta}}$ have the same asymptotic normal distribution if $\hat{\boldsymbol{\beta}}$ has the asymptotic distribution described in the last paragraph of the previous subsection. The covariance matrix of the corresponding limiting distribution is $\sigma^2\mathbf{Q}_V^{-1}$, which is estimated consistently by $\hat{\sigma}_n^2$ times the inverse of $(1/n)\mathbf{X}'\hat{\mathbf{V}}_n^{-1}\mathbf{X}$ if $\hat{\sigma}_n^2$ is consistent and if (6.4) is true. For the consistency of $\hat{\sigma}_n^2$ under condition (6.6) see Problem 6.3.

The subsections which follow serve to verify the conditions of Theorem 8.4 for a number of cases considered in Chapters 6 and 7. It will appear that this sometimes requires the existence of higher-order moments of disturbances and also of the explanatory variables in the limit as $n \to \infty$.

The Joint GLS Estimation Procedure

Consider the Aitken estimator $\hat{\boldsymbol{\beta}}$ defined in eq. (2.19) of Section 7.2. If we multiply its sampling error by $\sqrt{n}$, we obtain

$$\sqrt{n}\,(\hat{\boldsymbol{\beta}} - \boldsymbol{\beta}) = \left[\frac{1}{n}\mathbf{X}'(\boldsymbol{\Sigma}^{-1}\otimes\mathbf{I})\mathbf{X}\right]^{-1}\frac{1}{\sqrt{n}}\mathbf{X}'(\boldsymbol{\Sigma}^{-1}\otimes\mathbf{I})\boldsymbol{\epsilon} \tag{6.9}$$

The matrix in brackets on the right, which corresponds with $(1/n)\mathbf{X}'\mathbf{V}^{-1}\mathbf{X}$ in (6.8), consists of submatrices of the form $(\sigma^{jl}/n)\mathbf{X}_j'\mathbf{X}_l$. It is readily verified that this matrix converges to a nonsingular limit, as (6.2) requires, if the following conditions are satisfied:

$$\lim_{n\to\infty}\frac{1}{n}\mathbf{X}_j'\mathbf{X}_l = \mathbf{Q}_{jl} \qquad j, l = 1, \ldots, L \tag{6.10}$$

$$|\mathbf{Q}_{jj}| > 0 \qquad j = 1, \ldots, L \tag{6.11}$$

The condition on independence and identical distribution refers in this case to the vector $[\epsilon_{\alpha 1} \cdots \epsilon_{\alpha L}]$ of contemporaneous disturbances. It will be assumed that all n such vectors are independent random drawings from the same L-dimensional population with zero mean vector and covariance matrix $\mathbf{\Sigma}$. The result stated in the first subsection under (2) then implies that the left-hand vector in (6.9) has a normal limiting distribution with zero mean and a covariance matrix equal to the limit for $n \to \infty$ of the inverse of the matrix in square brackets in the right-hand side.

For the joint GLS estimator $\mathbf{b}_J$ given in eq. (2.26) of Section 7.2 we obtain

$$\text{(6.12)} \qquad \sqrt{n}\,(\mathbf{b}_J - \boldsymbol{\beta}) = \left[\frac{1}{n}\mathbf{X}'(\mathbf{S}^{-1} \otimes \mathbf{I})\mathbf{X}\right]^{-1} \frac{1}{\sqrt{n}}\mathbf{X}'(\mathbf{S}^{-1} \otimes \mathbf{I})\boldsymbol{\epsilon}$$

which shows that the matrix whose probability limit is considered in (6.4) now consists of submatrices of the form

$$\text{(6.13)} \qquad (s^{jl} - \sigma^{jl})\frac{1}{n}\mathbf{X}_j'\mathbf{X}_l \qquad j, l = 1, \ldots, L$$

Since $(1/n)\mathbf{X}_j'\mathbf{X}_l$ converges to $\mathbf{Q}_{jl}$ in view of (6.10), a sufficient condition for the matrices (6.13) to converge in probability to zero is that $\mathbf{S}$ be a consistent estimator of $\mathbf{\Sigma}$. The elements of $\mathbf{S}$ are mean squares and products of LS residuals:

$$\text{(6.14)} \qquad s_{jl} = \frac{1}{n}(\mathbf{y}_j - \mathbf{X}_j\mathbf{b}_j)'(\mathbf{y}_l - \mathbf{X}_l\mathbf{b}_l)$$

where $\mathbf{b}_j = (\mathbf{X}_j'\mathbf{X}_j)^{-1}\mathbf{X}_j'\mathbf{y}_j$ is the LS estimator of the parameter vector $\boldsymbol{\beta}_j$ of the jth equation. Under conditions (6.10) and (6.11) the sampling error $\mathbf{b}_j - \boldsymbol{\beta}_j$ converges in probability to zero, and hence s_{jl} converges in distribution to the average of the n disturbance products $\epsilon_{1j}\epsilon_{1l}, \ldots, \epsilon_{nj}\epsilon_{nl}$. Since the vectors of contemporaneous disturbances are by assumption independently and identically distributed with zero mean and covariance matrix $\mathbf{\Sigma}$, these products are independently and identically distributed with expectation σ_{jl}; hence Khintchine's theorem ensures that s_{jl} is consistent for σ_{jl}.

The vector in the left-hand side of (6.5) is, in this case, the probability limit of a vector of $K_1 + \cdots + K_L$ elements, the jth subvector of which is of the following form:

$$\text{(6.15)} \qquad (s^{j1} - \sigma^{j1})\frac{1}{\sqrt{n}}\mathbf{X}_j'\boldsymbol{\epsilon}_1 + \cdots + (s^{jL} - \sigma^{jL})\frac{1}{\sqrt{n}}\mathbf{X}_j'\boldsymbol{\epsilon}_L$$

Given that the elements of $\boldsymbol{\epsilon}_l$ are independently and identically distributed with zero mean and variance σ_{ll} and that $(1/n)\mathbf{X}_j'\mathbf{X}_j$ converges to $\mathbf{Q}_{jj}$, it can be proved along the lines of the last paragraph of Section 8.3 that the vector

$\sqrt{1/n}\,\mathbf{X}_j'\boldsymbol{\epsilon}_l$ has a normal limiting distribution with zero mean and covariance matrix $\sigma_{ll}\mathbf{Q}_{jj}$. The convergence of $\mathbf{S}^{-1} - \boldsymbol{\Sigma}^{-1}$ to zero then guarantees that the vector (6.15) also converges in probability to zero.

Testing Linear Constraints on Coefficients of Different Equations under the Normality Assumption

In Section 7.3 we developed an F test for the hypothesis $\mathbf{r} = \mathbf{R}\boldsymbol{\beta}$, where $\mathbf{r}$ and $\mathbf{R}$ have q rows, $\mathbf{R}$ has rank q, and $\boldsymbol{\beta}$ is the parameter vector of the previous subsection (consisting of $K_1 + \cdots + K_L$ elements). Under the assumption that $\epsilon_{\alpha 1}, \ldots, \epsilon_{\alpha L}$ is L-variate normal we considered two χ^2 variates, one being $\chi^2(q)$ if the null hypothesis is true:

$$(\mathbf{r} - \mathbf{R}\hat{\boldsymbol{\beta}})'\{\mathbf{R}[\mathbf{X}'(\boldsymbol{\Sigma}^{-1} \otimes \mathbf{I})\mathbf{X}]^{-1}\mathbf{R}'\}^{-1}(\mathbf{r} - \mathbf{R}\hat{\boldsymbol{\beta}}) \tag{6.16}$$

and the other having $Ln - K_1 - \cdots - K_L = N$ (say) degrees of freedom:

$$(\mathbf{y} - \mathbf{X}\hat{\boldsymbol{\beta}})'(\boldsymbol{\Sigma}^{-1} \otimes \mathbf{I})(\mathbf{y} - \mathbf{X}\hat{\boldsymbol{\beta}}) \tag{6.17}$$

The statistic is equal to the ratio of (6.16) to (6.17) multiplied by N/q, and its distribution is $F(q, N)$ if $\mathbf{r} = \mathbf{R}\boldsymbol{\beta}$ is true.

We replaced the unknown $\boldsymbol{\Sigma}$ by $\mathbf{S}$ [and hence also $\hat{\boldsymbol{\beta}}$ by $\mathbf{b}_J$; see (6.9) and (6.12)] in both (6.16) and (6.17). For (6.16) we thus use:

$$(\mathbf{r} - \mathbf{R}\mathbf{b}_J)'\{\mathbf{R}[\mathbf{X}'(\mathbf{S}^{-1} \otimes \mathbf{I})\mathbf{X}]^{-1}\mathbf{R}'\}^{-1}(\mathbf{r} - \mathbf{R}\mathbf{b}_J) \tag{6.18}$$

Since the quadratic form (6.16) is continuous in $\boldsymbol{\Sigma}$ and $\mathbf{S}$ is a consistent estimator, the substitute form (6.18) converges in distribution to (6.16), so that its limiting distribution is $\chi^2(q)$ under the null hypothesis and the normality condition.

By dividing the quadratic form (6.17) by the number of degrees of freedom (N), we obtain a ratio which converges in probability to 1 as n (and hence also N) increases indefinitely. This is so because the ratio is distributed as $(1/N)\chi^2(N)$ and hence has mean $N/N = 1$ and variance $2N/N^2 = 2/N$. Since the form (6.17) is a continuous function of $\boldsymbol{\Sigma}$, the corresponding fraction $1/N$ of the substitute form,

$$(\mathbf{y} - \mathbf{X}\mathbf{b}_J)'(\mathbf{S}^{-1} \otimes \mathbf{I})(\mathbf{y} - \mathbf{X}\mathbf{b}_J) \tag{6.19}$$

also converges in probability to 1.

The test statistic used in Section 7.3 is equal to the ratio of (6.18) to (6.19) multiplied by N/q. The two previous paragraphs show that its limiting distribution is $(1/q)\chi^2(q)$ under the null hypothesis and the normality condition. Instead of this limiting distribution we used $F(q, N)$. This makes no difference asymptotically, since $F(q, N)$ converges in distribution to $(1/q)\chi^2(q)$ as $N \to \infty$. For finite N the F approximation is more cautious than the χ^2

approximation because it gives a negative verdict on the null hypothesis in a smaller number of cases. This more cautious attitude is to be recommended, since the χ^2 procedure implies that the value of the quadratic form (6.19) may just as well be replaced by its expectation (N).

The Heteroscedasticity Case

We return to Section 6.2, in particular to its equation (2.9), which we write as follows:

$$y_\alpha = \beta_0 + \beta_1 x_{\alpha 1} + \beta_2 x_{\alpha 2} + (\mathscr{E} y_\alpha)\zeta_\alpha \qquad \alpha = 1, \ldots, n \tag{6.20}$$

where $\mathscr{E} y_\alpha = \beta_0 + \beta_1 x_{\alpha 1} + \beta_2 x_{\alpha 2}$ and $\zeta_1, \ldots, \zeta_n$ are n random variables which are now assumed to be independently and identically distributed with zero mean and variance c. This variance specification is in accordance with

$$\sigma_\alpha^2 = c(\mathscr{E} y_\alpha)^2 \qquad \text{[see eq. (2.5) of Section 6.2]} \tag{6.21}$$

The large-sample estimation procedure proposed in Section 6.2 may be briefly recapitulated as follows. First, estimate $\boldsymbol{\beta} = [\beta_0 \quad \beta_1 \quad \beta_2]'$ by LS. The estimator $\mathbf{b}$ is unbiased and its covariance matrix is

$$\mathscr{V}(\mathbf{b}) = (\mathbf{X}'\mathbf{X})^{-1}\mathbf{X}'(\sigma^2\mathbf{V})\mathbf{X}(\mathbf{X}'\mathbf{X})^{-1} \tag{6.22}$$

where $\mathbf{X}$ is the $n \times 3$ matrix whose αth row is $[1 \quad x_{\alpha 1} \quad x_{\alpha 2}]$ and $\sigma^2\mathbf{V}$ is the diagonal $n \times n$ matrix which contains the variances (6.21) on the diagonal. Therefore the typical element of $(\sigma^2/n)\mathbf{X}'\mathbf{V}\mathbf{X}$, apart from a proportionality factor (c), is equal to

$$\frac{1}{n}\sum_{\alpha=1}^{n} x_{\alpha h} x_{\alpha k} (\mathscr{E} y_\alpha)^2 = \frac{1}{n}\sum_{\alpha=1}^{n} x_{\alpha h} x_{\alpha k} (\beta_0 + \beta_1 x_{\alpha 1} + \beta_2 x_{\alpha 2})^2 \tag{6.23}$$

where $h, k = 0, 1, 2$. (The subscript $h = 0$ refers to the constant-term variable.) The expressions (6.23) converge to finite limits when the explanatory variables have finite fourth-order moments in the limit for $n \to \infty$. Since (6.22) states that the covariance matrix of $\mathbf{b}$ is equal to a fraction $1/n$ of $(\sigma^2/n)\mathbf{X}'\mathbf{V}\mathbf{X}$ pre- and postmultiplied by the inverse of $(1/n)\mathbf{X}'\mathbf{X}$, we may conclude that $\mathbf{b}$ is a consistent estimator of $\boldsymbol{\beta}$ when it is also true that the explanatory variables satisfy Assumption 8.1.

The vector $\mathbf{b}$ was used to estimate σ_α and the resulting sampling error may be written as follows:

$$\hat{\sigma}_\alpha - \sigma_\alpha = \sqrt{c}\,(\mathbf{b} - \boldsymbol{\beta})' \begin{bmatrix} 1 \\ x_{\alpha 1} \\ x_{\alpha 2} \end{bmatrix} \qquad \text{[see eq. (2.7) of Section 6.2]} \tag{6.24}$$

This shows that the consistency of **b** implies that of $\hat{\sigma}_\alpha$ for each α.[15] Condition (6.4) requires

$$\text{(6.25)} \qquad \underset{n\to\infty}{\text{plim}} \frac{1}{n}\sum_{\alpha=1}^{n} \frac{x_{\alpha h}x_{\alpha k}}{\hat{\sigma}_\alpha^2} = \lim_{n\to\infty} \frac{1}{n}\sum_{\alpha=1}^{n} \frac{x_{\alpha h}x_{\alpha k}}{\sigma_\alpha^2}$$

for each pair (h, k). This is true when the limit in the right-hand side exists. Since σ_α is proportional to $\mathscr{E}y_\alpha$, this requires that the three-element vector

$$\text{(6.26)} \qquad [1/\mathscr{E}y_\alpha \quad x_{\alpha 1}/\mathscr{E}y_\alpha \quad x_{\alpha 2}/\mathscr{E}y_\alpha] \qquad \alpha = 1, \ldots, n$$

have a finite second-order moment matrix in the limit for $n \to \infty$.

Condition (6.5) requires that the probability limits of these three expressions be zero:

$$\text{(6.27)} \qquad \frac{1}{\sqrt{n}}\sum_{\alpha=1}^{n}\left(\frac{1}{\hat{\sigma}_\alpha^2} - \frac{1}{\sigma_\alpha^2}\right)(x_{\alpha h}\mathscr{E}y_\alpha)\zeta_\alpha \qquad h = 0, 1, 2$$

The difference in parentheses is equal to $-(\hat{\sigma}_\alpha - \sigma_\alpha)(\hat{\sigma}_\alpha + \sigma_\alpha)$ divided by $\hat{\sigma}_\alpha^2\sigma_\alpha^2$ and is thus asymptotically equivalent to $-2(\hat{\sigma}_\alpha - \sigma_\alpha)/\sigma_\alpha^3$. We combine this with (6.24) to conclude that the expression (6.27) converges in distribution to

$$\text{(6.28)} \qquad -\frac{2\sqrt{c}}{\sqrt{n}}(\mathbf{b} - \boldsymbol{\beta})'\sum_{\alpha=1}^{n}\begin{bmatrix} 1/\sigma_\alpha \\ x_{\alpha 1}/\sigma_\alpha \\ x_{\alpha 2}/\sigma_\alpha \end{bmatrix}\left(\frac{x_{\alpha h}}{\sigma_\alpha}\right)\left(\frac{\mathscr{E}y_\alpha}{\sigma_\alpha}\right)\zeta_\alpha$$

$$= -\frac{2}{\sqrt{n}}(\mathbf{b} - \boldsymbol{\beta})'\sum_{\alpha=1}^{n}\begin{bmatrix} 1/\sigma_\alpha \\ x_{\alpha 1}/\sigma_\alpha \\ x_{\alpha 2}/\sigma_\alpha \end{bmatrix}\left(\frac{x_{\alpha h}}{\sigma_\alpha}\right)\zeta_\alpha$$

where the equality sign is based on (6.21). The expression on the second line is the inner product of $-2(\mathbf{b} - \boldsymbol{\beta})$ and $\sqrt{1/n}\,\mathbf{Z}_h'\boldsymbol{\zeta}$, where $\boldsymbol{\zeta} = [\zeta_1 \quad \cdots \quad \zeta_n]'$ and $\mathbf{Z}_h$ is the $n \times 3$ matrix whose αth row is

$$\text{(6.29)} \qquad \begin{bmatrix} \frac{x_{\alpha h}}{\sigma_\alpha^2} & \frac{x_{\alpha 1}x_{\alpha h}}{\sigma_\alpha^2} & \frac{x_{\alpha 2}x_{\alpha h}}{\sigma_\alpha^2} \end{bmatrix} = \frac{1}{c}\begin{bmatrix} \frac{x_{\alpha h}}{(\mathscr{E}y_\alpha)^2} & \frac{x_{\alpha 1}x_{\alpha h}}{(\mathscr{E}y_\alpha)^2} & \frac{x_{\alpha 2}x_{\alpha h}}{(\mathscr{E}y_\alpha)^2} \end{bmatrix}$$

The vector $\sqrt{1/n}\,\mathbf{Z}_h'\boldsymbol{\zeta}$ has a normal limiting distribution with zero mean and a covariance matrix equal to c (the variance of the ζ's) multiplied by the limit of $(1/n)\mathbf{Z}_h'\mathbf{Z}_h$, provided that this limit matrix exists. [Note that this proviso concerns the fourth-order moments of the variables considered in the vector

[15] Strictly speaking, $\hat{\sigma}_\alpha/\sqrt{c}$ is a consistent estimator of $\sigma_\alpha/\sqrt{c}$ because eq. (2.7) of Section 6.2 defines the $\hat{\sigma}$'s only up to a multiplicative factor. Recall, however, that the coefficient estimator is independent of c.

(6.26).] The consistency of **b** then guarantees that the inner product mentioned below (6.28), and hence also the expression (6.28), converge in probability to zero.

The Autoregressive Transformation

Next consider the case of Section 6.3, which is concerned with disturbances generated by an autoregressive process:

(6.30) $$\epsilon_\alpha = \rho\epsilon_{\alpha-1} + \zeta_\alpha \qquad |\rho| < 1$$

where the ζ's are random variables that will now be assumed to be independently and identically distributed with zero mean and variance σ_0^2.

The GLS procedure described in Section 6.3 amounts to the following reformulation of the basic equation $\mathbf{y} = \mathbf{X}\boldsymbol{\beta} + \boldsymbol{\epsilon}$. The equation corresponding to the first observation becomes

(6.31) $$y_1\sqrt{1-\rho^2} = \sum_{h=1}^{K}\beta_h(x_{1h}\sqrt{1-\rho^2}) + \epsilon_1\sqrt{1-\rho^2}$$

and the $n - 1$ other equations become

(6.32) $$y_\alpha - \rho y_{\alpha-1} = \sum_{h=1}^{K}\beta_h(x_{\alpha h} - \rho x_{\alpha-1,h}) + (\epsilon_\alpha - \rho\epsilon_{\alpha-1})$$

where $\alpha = 2, \ldots, n$. To simplify the exposition we shall disregard eq. (6.31). This makes no difference asymptotically because it involves only one observation out of n, and it has the advantage that it leads to more attractive algebraic expressions.

It will be assumed that ρ is replaced by a consistent estimator $\hat{\rho}$ in the $n - 1$ equations (6.32); the question of whether the particular $\hat{\rho}$ proposed in Section 6.3 actually is consistent will be considered in the next subsection. Condition (6.4) then amounts to the requirement that for each pair (h, k), the expression:

(6.33) $$\frac{1}{n-1}\sum_{\alpha=2}^{n}(x_{\alpha h} - \hat{\rho}x_{\alpha-1,h})(x_{\alpha k} - \hat{\rho}x_{\alpha-1,k})$$

converge in probability to the limit of the corresponding expression in the true ρ:

(6.34) $$\frac{1}{n-1}\sum_{\alpha=2}^{n} z_{\alpha h}z_{\alpha k} \qquad \text{where} \qquad z_{\alpha h} = x_{\alpha h} - \rho x_{\alpha-1,h}$$

This is true provided the mean product of $z_{\alpha h}z_{\alpha k}$ converges to a finite limit. We shall assume that this is the case and also that these limits form a nonsingular matrix, so that the GLS coefficient estimator based on the true ρ is asymptotically normally distributed [see the first subsection under (2)].

Condition (6.5) concerns the probability limit of a K-element vector of which the following expression is the hth element:

$$\frac{1}{\sqrt{n-1}}\sum_{\alpha=2}^{n}[(x_{\alpha h}-\hat{\rho}x_{\alpha-1,h})(\epsilon_\alpha-\hat{\rho}\epsilon_{\alpha-1})-(x_{\alpha h}-\rho x_{\alpha-1,h})(\epsilon_\alpha-\rho\epsilon_{\alpha-1})]$$

which is equal to

$$(6.35)\qquad -(\hat{\rho}-\rho)\left[\frac{1}{\sqrt{n-1}}\sum_{\alpha=2}^{n}x_{\alpha-1,h}\zeta_\alpha+\frac{1}{\sqrt{n-1}}\sum_{\alpha=2}^{n}z_{\alpha h}\epsilon_{\alpha-1} - \frac{\hat{\rho}-\rho}{\sqrt{n-1}}\sum_{\alpha=2}^{n}x_{\alpha-1,h}\epsilon_{\alpha-1}\right]$$

The first term in brackets has a normal limiting distribution with zero mean and a variance equal to σ_0^2 times the limit of the mean square of $x_{\alpha-1,h}$ (which is assumed to be finite). The multiplication by $\hat{\rho}-\rho$ before the brackets thus guarantees that the term converges in probability to zero. The second term inside the brackets is a random variable with zero mean and the following variance:

$$(6.36)\qquad \frac{1}{n-1}\sum_{\alpha=2}^{n}\sum_{\eta=2}^{n}z_{\alpha h}z_{\eta h}\mathscr{E}(\epsilon_{\alpha-1}\epsilon_{\eta-1})$$

$$=\frac{\sigma_0^2/(1-\rho^2)}{n-1}\sum_{\alpha=2}^{n}\sum_{\eta=2}^{n}\rho^{|\alpha-\eta|}z_{\alpha h}z_{\eta h}\qquad \text{[see eq. (3.3) of Section 6.3]}$$

$$=\frac{\sigma_0^2/(1-\rho^2)}{n-1}\sum_{\alpha=2}^{n}[z_{\alpha h}^2+\rho(z_{\alpha h}z_{\alpha+1,h}+z_{\alpha h}z_{\alpha-1,h}) + \rho^2(z_{\alpha h}z_{\alpha+2,h}+z_{\alpha h}z_{\alpha-2,h})+\cdots]$$

When n increases indefinitely, the expression after the second equality sign approaches a multiple $\sigma_0^2/(1-\rho^2)$ of the limit of the mean square of the z's plus 2ρ times the limit of the mean product of successive z's plus $\cdots$. Since such mean products cannot be larger than the mean square in absolute value—autocorrelation coefficients cannot lie outside the range $(-1, 1)$—the variance (6.36) for large n cannot exceed $\sigma_0^2/(1-\rho^2)$ times the limit of the mean square of the z's times

$$1+2\rho+2\rho^2+\cdots=1+\frac{2\rho}{1-\rho}$$

Therefore the second term in brackets of (6.35) is a random variable with zero mean and a bounded variance, so that the multiplication by $\hat{\rho}-\rho$ ensures that it converges in probability to zero. A similar argument may be used for the third term.

Consistent Estimation of the Autoregressive Parameter

The estimator of ρ proposed in eq. (3.11) of Section 6.3 is

$$\hat{\rho} = \frac{\dfrac{1}{n-1}\displaystyle\sum_{\alpha=1}^{n-1} e_\alpha e_{\alpha+1}}{\dfrac{1}{n-K}\displaystyle\sum_{\alpha=1}^{n} e_\alpha^2} = \frac{\displaystyle\sum_{\alpha=1}^{n-1} e_\alpha e_{\alpha+1}}{(n-1)s^2} \tag{6.37}$$

where $e_1, \ldots, e_n$ are the LS residuals and s^2 is the LS variance estimator. Each such residual is of the form

$$e_\alpha = \epsilon_\alpha - [x_{\alpha 1} \quad \cdots \quad x_{\alpha K}](\mathbf{b} - \boldsymbol{\beta}) \tag{6.38}$$

where $\mathbf{b}$ is the LS coefficient vector. This is an unbiased estimator of $\boldsymbol{\beta}$ with covariance matrix (6.22), but $\mathbf{X}'\mathbf{V}\mathbf{X}$ is now a matrix whose (h, k)th element is equal to the double sum over α and η of $\rho^{|\alpha-\eta|}x_{\alpha h}x_{\eta k}$. By applying an argument similar to that of eq. (6.36) and below, we find that $(1/n)\mathbf{X}'\mathbf{V}\mathbf{X}$ converges to a finite limit matrix. The estimator $\mathbf{b}$ is then consistent when Assumption 8.1 is also true.

In view of (6.38) this consistency implies that e_α converges in distribution to ϵ_α for each α. It then follows from (6.37) that $\hat{\rho}$ converges in distribution to the average of the n disturbance products $\epsilon_\alpha\epsilon_{\alpha+1}$ divided by $(\sum \epsilon_\alpha^2)/(n-K)$. If we replace $\epsilon_{\alpha+1}$ in the numerator by $\rho\epsilon_\alpha + \zeta_{\alpha+1}$ in accordance with (6.30), we obtain

$$\frac{\dfrac{1}{n-1}\displaystyle\sum_{\alpha=1}^{n-1} \epsilon_\alpha(\rho\epsilon_\alpha + \zeta_{\alpha+1})}{\dfrac{1}{n-K}\displaystyle\sum_{\alpha=1}^{n} \epsilon_\alpha^2} = \rho\,\frac{\dfrac{1}{n-1}\displaystyle\sum_{\alpha=1}^{n-1} \epsilon_\alpha^2}{\dfrac{1}{n-K}\displaystyle\sum_{\alpha=1}^{n} \epsilon_\alpha^2} + \frac{\dfrac{1}{n-1}\displaystyle\sum_{\alpha=1}^{n-1} \epsilon_\alpha\zeta_{\alpha+1}}{\dfrac{1}{n-K}\displaystyle\sum_{\alpha=1}^{n} \epsilon_\alpha^2} \tag{6.39}$$

The consistency of $\hat{\rho}$ is then established when it is proved that the second right-hand term converges in probability to zero and that the ratio by which ρ is multiplied converges in probability to one. This will be considered in the next section under the condition that the ζ's have a finite moment of the fourth order.[16] Note that it is *not* correct to say that the numerator and the denominator of the ratio by which ρ is multiplied in the right-hand side of (6.39) both converge to the variance of the ϵ's because of Khintchine's theorem. This theorem is not applicable because the ϵ's are not independent; see (6.30).

[16] See particularly footnote 17 on p. 411.

Problems

6.1 Prove statements (1) and (2) made in the first subsection. [Hint for the first part of (2): see Problem 1.4 of Section 6.1.]

6.2 Prove that the assumption that the n elements of $\mathbf{P}\boldsymbol{\epsilon}$ are independently and identically distributed with zero mean and variance σ^2 implies but is not implied by $\mathbf{P}'\mathbf{P} = \mathbf{V}^{-1}$. Conclude that the words "(1) $\mathbf{P}'\mathbf{P} = \mathbf{V}^{-1}$ and (2)" in the second sentence of Theorem 8.4 may be deleted.

6.3 (*Consistency of* $\hat{\sigma}_n^2$) Prove that $\hat{\sigma}_n^2$ defined in (6.3) can be written as

$$\hat{\sigma}_n^2 = \frac{1}{n-K}\boldsymbol{\epsilon}'\hat{\mathbf{V}}_n^{-1}\boldsymbol{\epsilon} - \frac{1}{n-K}\boldsymbol{\epsilon}'\hat{\mathbf{V}}_n^{-1}\mathbf{X}(\mathbf{X}'\hat{\mathbf{V}}_n^{-1}\mathbf{X})^{-1}\mathbf{X}'\hat{\mathbf{V}}_n^{-1}\boldsymbol{\epsilon} \tag{6.40}$$

Use this equation to prove the consistency of $\hat{\sigma}_n^2$ under the conditions stated in Theorem 8.4, and apply the result to the autoregressive case of eq. (6.30) and below.

6.4 Write F for N/q times the ratio of the quadratic forms (6.16) and (6.17), which is distributed as $F(q, N)$ under the null hypothesis $\mathbf{r} = \mathbf{R}\boldsymbol{\beta}$ and the normality condition. Also consider eq. (7.21) of Section 3.7 on the likelihood ratio λ and show that its extension for the multi-equation case considered here is $\lambda^{-2/Ln} = 1 + qF/N$. Take natural logarithms on both sides and prove that as n (and hence N) increases indefinitely, minus twice the logarithm of the likelihood ratio converges in distribution to $\chi^2(q)$.

8.7 Regressions on Lagged Values of the Dependent Variable[C]

Suppose that we have a time series equation of the following form:

$$y_\alpha = \sum_{g=1}^{G}\beta_g y_{\alpha-g} + \sum_{h=1}^{K-G}\beta_{G+h}x_{\alpha h} + \epsilon_\alpha \qquad \alpha = 1, \dots, n \tag{7.1}$$

On the right are G successive lagged values of the dependent variable, $y_{\alpha-1}, \dots, y_{\alpha-G}$, as well as $K - G$ "ordinary" explanatory variables whose values are $x_{\alpha 1}, \dots, x_{\alpha,K-G}$ for the αth observation. We can write this equation for all n observations combined in the familiar form $\mathbf{y} = \mathbf{X}\boldsymbol{\beta} + \boldsymbol{\epsilon}$ if we define $\mathbf{X}$ as the following $n \times K$ matrix:

(7.2)

$$\mathbf{X} = [\mathbf{X}_R \quad \mathbf{X}_F] = \left[\begin{array}{cccc|cccc} y_0 & y_{-1} & \cdots & y_{1-G} & x_{11} & x_{12} & \cdots & x_{1,K-G} \\ y_1 & y_0 & \cdots & y_{2-G} & x_{21} & x_{22} & \cdots & x_{2,K-G} \\ \cdot & \cdot & & \cdot & \cdot & \cdot & & \cdot \\ \cdot & \cdot & & \cdot & \cdot & \cdot & & \cdot \\ \cdot & \cdot & & \cdot & \cdot & \cdot & & \cdot \\ y_{n-1} & y_{n-2} & \cdots & y_{n-G} & x_{n1} & x_{n2} & \cdots & x_{n,K-G} \end{array}\right]$$

where $\mathbf{X}_F$ consists of $K - G$ fixed (nonstochastic) columns, while the G columns of $\mathbf{X}_R$ contain random elements. This randomness of the matrix $\mathbf{X}$ violates one of the basic assumptions of the standard linear model. Nevertheless, it is possible to justify the use of the LS method for large n under certain conditions, and this section describes this justification as well as its limitations. Note that it is still possible to treat the pre-sample values $y_0, \ldots, y_{1-G}$ as fixed. In fact, we shall do so in what follows by making the probability statements conditional on these values.

The Special Case of an Autoregressive Process

A major difficulty of the analysis is the dependence of the random variables $y_1, \ldots, y_n$. This dependence follows from eq. (7.1), which expresses each y_α in terms of previous values $y_{\alpha-1}, y_{\alpha-2}, \ldots$, and it is because of this that the proof of the main large-sample results of LS estimation of the parameters of this equation is too long and complicated to be given here. Therefore we start by considering the simplest case, $G = K = 1$:

$$(7.3) \qquad y_\alpha = \beta y_{\alpha-1} + \epsilon_\alpha \qquad \text{where} \qquad |\beta| < 1$$

which amounts to a first-order autoregressive process. It will be assumed that $\epsilon_1, \ldots, \epsilon_n$ are independently and identically distributed with zero mean and variance σ^2. The LS estimator of β is $b = \sum y_{\alpha-1}y_\alpha / \sum y_{\alpha-1}^2$ (summations over α from 1 through n). By substituting $\beta y_{\alpha-1} + \epsilon_\alpha$ for y_α in the numerator and multiplying by $\sqrt{n}$, we obtain

$$(7.4) \qquad \sqrt{n}\,(b - \beta) = \frac{\dfrac{1}{\sqrt{n}} \displaystyle\sum_{\alpha=1}^{n} y_{\alpha-1}\epsilon_\alpha}{\dfrac{1}{n} \displaystyle\sum_{\alpha=1}^{n} y_{\alpha-1}^2}$$

The numerator in the right-hand side can be shown to have a normal limiting distribution with zero mean and positive finite variance under appropriate conditions. To shorten the exposition we shall confine ourselves to proving in the next subsection that the expectation of this numerator vanishes for any finite n and that its variance converges to a positive finite limit as $n \to \infty$. Thereafter we shall prove that the denominator converges in probability to a positive limit.

Analysis of the Numerator

The zero value of the expectation of the right-hand numerator in (7.4) follows from the fact that $y_{\alpha-1}$ depends only on $\epsilon_{\alpha-1}, \epsilon_{\alpha-2}, \ldots$ (not on ϵ_α) and from the independence of the ϵ's. The variance of this numerator is equal to a fraction $1/n$ of the double sum ($\alpha, \eta = 1, \ldots, n$) of $\mathscr{E}(y_{\alpha-1}y_{\eta-1}\epsilon_\alpha\epsilon_\eta)$, so that it can be written as

$$\text{(7.5)} \qquad \frac{1}{n}\sum_{\alpha=1}^{n}\mathscr{E}(y_{\alpha-1}^2\epsilon_\alpha^2) + \frac{2}{n}\sum_{\alpha<\eta}\sum \mathscr{E}\epsilon_\eta \mathscr{E}(y_{\alpha-1}y_{\eta-1}\epsilon_\alpha) = \frac{\sigma^2}{n}\sum_{\alpha=1}^{n}\mathscr{E}y_{\alpha-1}^2$$

In the second term on the left the expectation of $y_{\alpha-1}y_{\eta-1}\epsilon_\alpha\epsilon_\eta$ is written as the product of two expectations. This is permissible because ϵ_η is independent of $y_{\alpha-1}, y_{\eta-1}$ and ϵ_α when $\eta > \alpha$. The equality sign in (7.5) follows from $\mathscr{E}\epsilon_\eta = 0$, from the independence of $y_{\alpha-1}^2$ and ϵ_α^2, and from $\mathscr{E}\epsilon_\alpha^2 = \sigma^2$.

The variance of our numerator is thus equal to a multiple σ^2 of the expectation of the average of $y_0^2, \ldots, y_{n-1}^2$. To evaluate this average we square both sides of (7.3) and sum over α from 1 through n:

$$\sum_{\alpha=1}^{n} y_\alpha^2 = \beta^2\sum_{\alpha=1}^{n} y_{\alpha-1}^2 + \sum_{\alpha=1}^{n}\epsilon_\alpha^2 + 2\beta\sum_{\alpha=1}^{n} y_{\alpha-1}\epsilon_\alpha$$

The left-hand term is equal to $\sum y_{\alpha-1}^2 - (y_0^2 - y_n^2)$. Therefore the equation can be written as

$$\text{(7.6)} \qquad \frac{1}{n}\sum_{\alpha=1}^{n} y_{\alpha-1}^2 = \frac{y_0^2 - y_n^2}{(1-\beta^2)n} + \frac{1}{(1-\beta^2)n}\sum_{\alpha=1}^{n}\epsilon_\alpha^2 + \frac{2\beta}{(1-\beta^2)n}\sum_{\alpha=1}^{n} y_{\alpha-1}\epsilon_\alpha$$

where use is made of $|\beta| < 1$ [see (7.3)]. Combining this result with (7.5), we conclude that the variance of our numerator is equal to a multiple σ^2 of the expectation of the right-hand side of (7.6). If we take the expectation of the three terms of this side, we obtain $\sigma^2/(1-\beta^2)$ for the second term and zero for the third. It will be shown in the next paragraph that the expectation of the first term converges to zero as $n \to \infty$, so that the variance of the numerator in (7.4) does indeed converge to a positive finite limit:

$$\text{(7.7)} \qquad \lim_{n\to\infty} \operatorname{var}\left(\frac{1}{\sqrt{n}}\sum_{\alpha=1}^{n} y_{\alpha-1}\epsilon_\alpha\right) = \frac{\sigma^4}{1-\beta^2}$$

To evaluate the expectation of the first right-hand term in (7.6), recall that y_0 is fixed, so that we need the conditional expected square of y_n, given y_0. By squaring both sides of

$$\text{(7.8)} \qquad y_n = \sum_{\alpha=0}^{n-1}\beta^\alpha\epsilon_{n-\alpha} + \beta^n y_0$$

we easily find

$$\text{(7.9)} \qquad \mathscr{E}(y_n^2 \mid y_0) = \sigma^2\frac{1-\beta^{2n}}{1-\beta^2} + \beta^{2n}y_0^2$$

It follows immediately that the first right-hand term in (7.6) has a conditional expectation (given y_0) which converges to zero as $n \to \infty$.

Analysis of the Denominator

The next paragraph will show that the right-hand denominator of (7.4) has the following probability limit:

$$\operatorname*{plim}_{n\to\infty} \frac{1}{n} \sum_{\alpha=1}^{n} y_{\alpha-1}^2 = \frac{\sigma^2}{1-\beta^2} \tag{7.10}$$

which is identical with the limit of the expectation of this denominator [see (7.6) and below]. Since the numerator has a normal limiting distribution with zero mean and variance (7.7)—note that we did not really prove this—$\sqrt{n}\,(b-\beta)$ thus has a normal limiting distribution with zero mean and the following variance:

$$\frac{\sigma^4}{1-\beta^2} \Big/ \left(\frac{\sigma^2}{1-\beta^2}\right)^2 = 1-\beta^2 \tag{7.11}$$

But (7.10) implies that $n\sigma^2/\sum y_{\alpha-1}^2$ converges in probability to $1-\beta^2$. Combining this with the variance (7.11) we conclude that $\sqrt{n}\,(b-\beta)$ has a normal limiting distribution with zero mean and a variance equal to the probability limit of $n\sigma^2/\sum y_{\alpha-1}^2$. If we then consider (7.3), we see that the classical LS formula for the variance of the β estimator gives $\sigma^2/\sum y_{\alpha-1}^2$, and the result obtained here thus indicates that this classical formula is asymptotically valid.

To prove (7.10) we go back to (7.6), which indicates that we have to derive the probability limits of the three terms on the right. The third term has zero expectation and a variance which converges to zero in view of (7.7); Chebyshev's inequality thus guarantees that it has zero probability limit. The second term is a multiple $1/(1-\beta^2)$ of the average of $\epsilon_1^2, \ldots, \epsilon_n^2$ and thus converges in probability to $\sigma^2/(1-\beta^2)$ in view of Khintchine's theorem. Apart from a factor $1/(1-\beta^2)$, the first term is equal to the difference between y_0^2/n, which converges to zero because y_0 is fixed, and y_n^2/n which converges in probability to zero when the disturbances have a finite fourth-order moment (see Problem 7.1). This completes the proof of (7.10).[17]

The General Case

Returning to the specification (7.1), we shall now state a more general result based on the following two assumptions:[18]

[17] This also proves that the right-hand side of (6.39) converges in probability to ρ under the conditions stated below that equation. Interpret $(y_\alpha, \beta, \epsilon_\alpha)$ of (7.3) as $(\epsilon_\alpha, \rho, \zeta_\alpha)$; then (7.10) implies that the ratio by which ρ is multiplied in (6.39) converges in probability to 1 when the ζ's have a finite fourth-order moment, and (7.7) in conjunction with the fact that the numerator of (7.4) has zero mean guarantees that the second right-hand term of (6.39) converges in probability to zero.

[18] The developments that follow go back to MANN and WALD (1943). More recent publications include KOOPMANS, RUBIN and LEIPNIK (1950), GRENANDER and ROSENBLATT (1957), and DURBIN (1960a).

ASSUMPTION 8.2 (Roots less than one in absolute value) *All G roots of the polynomial equation*

$$z^G - \beta_1 z^{G-1} - \beta_2 z^{G-2} - \cdots - \beta_G = 0 \tag{7.12}$$

where $\beta_1, \ldots, \beta_G$ *are defined in* (7.1), *have absolute values less than one.*

ASSUMPTION 8.3 (Convergence of moment matrices of "fixed" variables) *If* $K > G$, *then for each* $\eta = 0, 1, \ldots, G$ *the* $(K - G) \times (K - G)$ *matrix whose* (h, k)th *element is*

$$\frac{1}{n - \eta} \sum_{\alpha=1}^{n-\eta} x_{\alpha h} x_{\alpha+\eta, k} \qquad (h, k = 1, \ldots, K - G) \tag{7.13}$$

where $[x_{\alpha k}]$ *is defined in* (7.1), *converges to a finite matrix* $\bar{\mathbf{Q}}_\eta$ *as* $n \to \infty$, *and the limit matrix* $\bar{\mathbf{Q}}_0$ *is positive definite.*

Assumption 8.2 is a generalization of $|\beta| < 1$ of (7.3). [Take $G = 1$ in (7.12), so that this equation becomes $z - \beta = 0$ with root $z = \beta$, which has to be less than 1 in absolute value.] In the case $|\beta| \geq 1$ the equation "explodes" in the sense that the variance of y_n increases indefinitely with n [see (7.8) and (7.9)], and Assumption 8.2 is needed to prevent a similar phenomenon in the more general case (7.1).[19] Assumption 8.3 requires the convergence of mean squares and products of all explanatory variables other than the lagged values of the dependent variable. [Such variables are not present in (7.3).] Not only "current" mean squares and products are involved but also lagged versions with lags up to G periods, G being the largest lag of the dependent variable in (7.1).

THEOREM 8.5 (LS in the presence of lagged values of the dependent variable) *Consider eq.* (7.1) *in the form* $\mathbf{y} = \mathbf{X}\boldsymbol{\beta} + \boldsymbol{\epsilon}$ *with* $\mathbf{X}$ *as specified in* (7.2). *Suppose that Assumptions* 8.2 *and* 8.3 *are true, that* $\epsilon_1, \ldots, \epsilon_n$ *are independently and identically distributed with zero mean, positive variance* σ^2, *and finite moments of every order, and regard the pre-sample values* $y_0, \ldots, y_{1-G}$ *as constants. Then the LS estimators* $\mathbf{b} = (\mathbf{X}'\mathbf{X})^{-1}\mathbf{X}'\mathbf{y}$ *and* $s^2 = \mathbf{e}'\mathbf{e}/(n - K)$, *where* $\mathbf{e} = \mathbf{y} - \mathbf{X}\mathbf{b}$, *are consistent for* $\boldsymbol{\beta}$ *and* σ^2, *respectively. Also,* $(1/n)\mathbf{X}'\mathbf{X}$ *converges in probability to a finite positive definite matrix* $\mathbf{Q}$, $\sqrt{1/n}\,\mathbf{X}'\boldsymbol{\epsilon}$ *has a normal limiting distribution with zero mean vector and covariance matrix* $\sigma^2\mathbf{Q}$, *and* $\sqrt{n}(\mathbf{b} - \boldsymbol{\beta})$ *has a normal limiting distribution with zero mean vector and covariance matrix* $\sigma^2\mathbf{Q}^{-1}$. *If, in addition,* $\epsilon_1, \ldots, \epsilon_n$ *are normally distributed, and if* $\mathbf{t}$ *is any other consistent estimator of* $\boldsymbol{\beta}$,

[19] See RUBIN (1950a), WHITE (1958, 1959), ANDERSON (1959), and M. M. RAO (1961) or analyses of the explosive case.

then the covariance matrix of the limiting distribution of $\sqrt{n}(\mathbf{t} - \boldsymbol{\beta})$ *exceeds* $\sigma^2\mathbf{Q}^{-1}$ *by a positive semidefinite matrix.*

The main implication of this theorem is that under the conditions stated, lagged values of the dependent variable may be treated as "ordinary" explanatory variables when the sample is large. Also, in the case of normality we have the large-sample equivalent of Theorem 8.3. Note that the matrix $\mathbf{Q}$ defined in the theorem is not the limit but the probability limit of $(1/n)\mathbf{X}'\mathbf{X}$ because $\mathbf{X}$ is random.

However, the situation is not nearly so favorable (even for large n) when the conditions underlying the theorem are violated, in particular when the disturbances are dependent. Since the results listed below are all negative, no detailed proofs will be given; the proofs of many of these results can be found in MALINVAUD (1966, Section 14.5) or NERLOVE and WALLIS (1966).

Autocorrelated Disturbances Lead to Inconsistent LS Estimators

When $\mathbf{X}$ is a matrix of constant elements and the disturbances have zero mean, the LS coefficient vector $\mathbf{b}$ is unbiased even if the disturbances are correlated and it is also consistent when $(1/n)\mathbf{X}'\mathbf{X}$ and $(1/n)\mathbf{X}'\mathbf{V}\mathbf{X}$ both converge to appropriate limit matrices. This is not true when there are lagged values of the dependent variable among the explanatory variables. Consider the simple case (7.3) and assume that the disturbances are generated by

$$\epsilon_\alpha = \rho\epsilon_{\alpha-1} + \zeta_\alpha \qquad \text{where} \qquad |\rho| < 1 \tag{7.14}$$

Assume that $\zeta_1, \ldots, \zeta_n$ are independently and identically distributed with zero mean and finite moments of every order. Then it can be shown that the probability limit of the LS coefficient $b = \sum y_{\alpha-1}y_\alpha / \sum y_{\alpha-1}^2$ is

$$\operatorname*{plim}_{n\to\infty} b = \frac{\beta + \rho}{1 + \beta\rho} \tag{7.15}$$

so that b is not a consistent estimator of β as soon as $\rho \neq 0$. This should cause no surprise because $y_{\alpha-1}$ and ϵ_α in the right-hand numerator of (7.4) are correlated if $\rho \neq 0$, and this affects the analysis of LS estimation of eq. (7.3) drastically.

It is easily verified that the LS and BLUS residuals e_α and $\hat{\epsilon}_\alpha$ converge in distribution to the corresponding disturbance ϵ_α as $n \to \infty$ under the conditions of Theorem 8.5 (see Problem 7.2). But if the disturbances are correlated, the situation is quite different. Again take the case of (7.3) and (7.14). When

n increases indefinitely, the LS residual e_α converges in distribution to

$$(7.16) \qquad y_\alpha - y_{\alpha-1} \operatorname*{plim}_{n\to\infty} b = \epsilon_\alpha - \frac{\rho(1-\beta^2)}{1+\beta\rho}(\epsilon_{\alpha-1} + \beta\epsilon_{\alpha-2} + \cdots)$$

which differs from ϵ_α when $\rho \neq 0$.

Testing against Autocorrelation

Suppose one wants to estimate ρ by $\hat{\rho}$ defined in (6.37). It can be shown that this estimator, which is based on LS residuals, is not consistent:

$$(7.17) \qquad \operatorname*{plim}_{n\to\infty} \hat{\rho} = \rho \frac{\beta(\beta+\rho)}{1+\beta\rho}$$

The ratio in the right-hand side is less than 1 in absolute value because $\beta(\beta+\rho) < 1 + \beta\rho$ follows from $\beta^2 < 1$ and $\beta(\beta+\rho) > -(1+\beta\rho)$ follows from $\beta^2 + 2\beta\rho + 1 = (\beta+\rho)^2 + 1 - \rho^2 > 0$. Therefore, $\hat{\rho}$ converges in probability to a value smaller than $|\rho|$ and larger than $-|\rho|$, which means that the LS residuals show *less* autocorrelation than the disturbances do. This suggests that the Durbin-Watson statistic, which is based on these residuals, is asymptotically biased toward the acceptance of the null hypothesis of independence or, equivalently, that the power of this statistic is low in the presence of lagged values of the dependent variable. In fact, this was confirmed by sampling experiments conducted by MALINVAUD (1961b). It can be shown that the BLUS and LS coefficients have the same probability limit [see (3.10) and (3.11)], so that the von Neumann ratio based on BLUS residuals must be expected to be similar in this respect.

Consistent Estimation under Conditions of Autocorrelated Disturbances

When we subtract from (7.3) the same equation lagged one period and multiplied by ρ, $\rho y_{\alpha-1} = \beta\rho y_{\alpha-2} + \rho\epsilon_{\alpha-1}$, we obtain the following result when (7.14) is true:

$$(7.18) \qquad y_\alpha = (\beta+\rho)y_{\alpha-1} - \beta\rho y_{\alpha-2} + \zeta_\alpha$$

This equation satisfies the conditions of Theorem 8.5 when β and ρ are both less than one in absolute value (this is Assumption 8.2 for the present case), which justifies the use of LS with $y_{\alpha-1}$ and $y_{\alpha-2}$ as the two explanatory variables when n is large. Point estimates of β and ρ can then be obtained from the two regression coefficients, and the rule on continuous functions of random sequences provides asymptotic standard errors of these estimates (see Problem 7.4). Note, however, that eq. (7.18) is perfectly symmetric in β and ρ, so that it is impossible to conclude which estimate refers to β and which to ρ unless appropriate prior information is available. (For example, it may be known that β is negative and ρ positive.) This may seem surprising, but it is actually the simple consequence of the fact that as far as the generation of the observed y's by the basic random variables $\zeta_1, \ldots, \zeta_n$ is concerned, the process described by $y_\alpha = \beta y_{\alpha-1} + \epsilon_\alpha$, $\epsilon_\alpha = \rho\epsilon_{\alpha-1} + \zeta_\alpha$ is equivalent to that of $y_\alpha = \rho y_{\alpha-1} + \epsilon'_\alpha$, $\epsilon'_\alpha = \beta\epsilon'_{\alpha-1} + \zeta_\alpha$. Both pairs of equations lead to (7.18).

If we generalize (7.3) to $y_\alpha = \beta_1 y_{\alpha-1} + \beta_2 x_\alpha + \epsilon_\alpha$, where $x_1, \ldots, x_n$ are constants, and if the disturbances are generated by (7.14), then eq. (7.18) becomes

(7.19) $$y_\alpha = (\beta_1 + \rho)y_{\alpha-1} - \beta_1\rho y_{\alpha-2} + \beta_2 x_\alpha - \beta_2\rho x_{\alpha-1} + \zeta_\alpha$$

This equation is not symmetric in β_1 and ρ because the coefficient of $x_{\alpha-1}$ involves ρ and does not involve β_1. However, we now face the problem that an LS regression on the four variables on the right gives four coefficients, whereas there are only three basic parameters (β_1, β_2, ρ). When the ζ's are normally distributed, this can be handled by means of a procedure which will be described for a different model in the next section (see Problem 8.8).

The Combination of Lagged Dependent Variables and an Unknown Disturbance Covariance Matrix

It was shown in the previous section that under appropriate conditions, the GLS coefficient vector $\hat{\boldsymbol{\beta}}_n$ based on an estimator $\hat{\mathbf{V}}_n$ of $\mathbf{V}$ has the same asymptotic distribution as the vector $\hat{\boldsymbol{\beta}}$ which is based on the true $\mathbf{V}$. One of the conditions is that the matrix $\mathbf{X}$ consists of nonstochastic elements, and so the question arises: if $\mathbf{X}$ is of the form (7.2), so that it contains lagged values of the dependent variable, and if the disturbance covariance matrix is $\sigma^2\mathbf{V}$ rather than $\sigma^2\mathbf{I}$, is it then still true that $\hat{\boldsymbol{\beta}}_n$ based on $\hat{\mathbf{V}}_n$ has the same asymptotic distribution as $\hat{\boldsymbol{\beta}}$ based on $\mathbf{V}$? The answer is that this is not in general the case, even if a square matrix $\mathbf{P}$ satisfying $\mathbf{P}'\mathbf{P} = \mathbf{V}^{-1}$ exists such that the elements of $\mathbf{P}\boldsymbol{\epsilon}$ are independently and identically distributed.

Problems

7.1 Square both sides of (7.8) and prove:

(7.20) $$y_n^2 = \sum_{\alpha=0}^{n-1} \beta^{2\alpha}\epsilon_{n-\alpha}^2 + 2\sum_{\alpha=0}^{n-1}\sum_{\eta>\alpha} \beta^{\alpha+\eta}\epsilon_{n-\alpha}\epsilon_{n-\eta} + y_0^2\beta^{2n} + 2y_0\beta^n \sum_{\alpha=0}^{n-1}\beta^\alpha\epsilon_{n-\alpha}$$

Square both sides of this equation and prove:

(7.21) $$y_n^4 = \sum_{\alpha=0}^{n-1}\beta^{4\alpha}\epsilon_{n-\alpha}^4 + 6\sum_{\alpha=0}^{n-1}\sum_{\eta>\alpha}\beta^{2\alpha+2\eta}\epsilon_{n-\alpha}^2\epsilon_{n-\eta}^2 + y_0^4\beta^{4n}$$
$$+ 6y_0^2\beta^{2n}\sum_{\alpha=0}^{n-1}\beta^{2\alpha}\epsilon_{n-\alpha}^2 + 4y_0\beta^n\sum_{\alpha=0}^{n-1}\beta^{3\alpha}\epsilon_{n-\alpha}^3$$
$$+ \text{terms with zero expectation}$$

[*Hint.* When evaluating the square of the second right-hand term of (7.20), prove first that if a, b, c, and d are positive integers satisfying $a < b$, $c < d$, the product $\epsilon_{n-a}\epsilon_{n-b}\epsilon_{n-c}\epsilon_{n-d}$ has nonzero expectation only if $a = c$ and $b = d$.] Next take the expectation of (7.21) and prove that $\mathscr{E}(y_n^4 \mid y_0)$ converges to a finite limit as $n \to \infty$ if $|\beta| < 1$ and if the fourth moment of the disturbances is finite. Finally, use Chebyshev's inequality to prove that, given y_0, y_n^2/n has zero probability limit.

7.2 Prove that under the conditions of Theorem 8.5 (not necessarily including the normality of the disturbances), each LS residual e_α converges in distribution to the corresponding disturbance ϵ_α as $n \to \infty$. Prove the same result for the BLUS residual $\hat{\epsilon}_\alpha$ under the additional condition that the base of the index transformation remains the same as n increases. [*Hint.* Write

$$e_\alpha - \epsilon_\alpha = -[x_{\alpha 1} \quad \cdots \quad x_{\alpha K}](\mathbf{b} - \boldsymbol{\beta})$$

and

$$\hat{\epsilon}_\alpha - \epsilon_\alpha = -[x_{\alpha 1} \quad \cdots \quad x_{\alpha K}](\hat{\boldsymbol{\beta}}_1 - \boldsymbol{\beta})$$

Note that $\mathbf{X}$ is random but that Assumption 8.2 guarantees stability, $(1/n)\mathbf{X}'\mathbf{X}$ converging to $\mathbf{Q}$ as $n \to \infty$. Use (3.10) and (3.11) for the convergence of $\hat{\boldsymbol{\beta}}_1$.] Is it also true that under these conditions the BLUS residual vector has a scalar covariance matrix for finite n when $G > 0$? Justify your answer.

7.3 Prove that the Assumption 8.2 amounts to $|\beta|$, $|\rho| < 1$ in the case of (7.18) as stated below that equation. Similarly, prove that in the case of eqs. (5.4) and (5.12) of Section 6.5 it amounts to $|\lambda_1|$, $|\lambda_2| < 1$ and $|\lambda| < 1$, respectively.

7.4 Write a_1 and a_2 for the LS estimators of the coefficients of $y_{\alpha-1}$ and $y_{\alpha-2}$, respectively, in eq. (7.18). Write v_{11}, v_{22}, v_{12} for the estimated variances and covariance of their asymptotic distribution. Prove that the implied estimators of β and ρ are $\frac{1}{2}(a_1 \pm D)$,[20] where D is the positive square root of $a_1^2 + 4a_2$. Apply the result of Problem 3.7 to prove that these estimators are asymptotically normally distributed with a covariance matrix estimated by

$$\frac{1}{D^2}\begin{bmatrix} A_1 + v_{22} & a_2 v_{11} - a_1 v_{12} - v_{22} \\ a_2 v_{11} - a_1 v_{12} - v_{22} & A_2 + v_{22} \end{bmatrix}$$

where

$$A_1 = \tfrac{1}{4}(a_1 + D)^2 v_{11} + (a_1 + D)v_{12}$$
$$A_2 = \tfrac{1}{4}(a_1 - D)^2 v_{11} + (a_1 - D)v_{12}$$

[20] Recall from the discussion below eq. (7.18) that it is not possible to indicate whether $+$ or $-$ refers to β or to ρ.

The first row and column of this 2×2 matrix refer to the estimator $\frac{1}{2}(a_1 + D)$ and the second row and column to $\frac{1}{2}(a_1 - D)$. Describe the nature of this approximation of the covariance matrix.

8.8 Asymptotic Properties of Some Distributed Lag Estimators[C]

We now turn to the distributed-lag equation that was considered in Section 6.4:

$$(8.1) \qquad y_\alpha = \beta_0 + \beta(x_\alpha + \lambda x_{\alpha-1} + \lambda^2 x_{\alpha-2} + \cdots) + \epsilon_\alpha \qquad \alpha = 1, \ldots, n$$

or, equivalently,

$$(8.2) \qquad y_\alpha = (1 - \lambda)\beta_0 + \beta x_\alpha + \lambda y_{\alpha-1} + (\epsilon_\alpha - \lambda\epsilon_{\alpha-1}) \qquad \alpha = 1, \ldots, n$$

where λ is a number less than 1 in absolute value.

The Simplest Approach

The estimation procedure discussed in Section 6.4 below eq. (4.5) amounts to an LS regression of y_α on x_α and $y_{\alpha-1}$ in accordance with the present specification (8.2). It follows directly from Theorem 8.5 that if $\zeta_\alpha = \epsilon_\alpha - \lambda\epsilon_{\alpha-1}$, $\alpha = 1, \ldots, n$ are independently and identically distributed with zero mean and finite moments of every order, the LS estimators of $(1 - \lambda)\beta_0$, β, and λ are consistent and asymptotically normally distributed. Indeed, it was this particular case—an autoregressive process of the disturbances ϵ_α whose parameter coincides with λ of (8.1)—that was mentioned in particular in Section 6.4. These estimators are not consistent when the ϵ's are generated by $\epsilon_\alpha = \rho\epsilon_{\alpha-1} + \zeta_\alpha$ for $\rho \neq \lambda$ because the disturbance term of (8.2) is then $\zeta_\alpha + (\rho - \lambda)\epsilon_{\alpha-1}$ which is correlated with $y_{\alpha-1}$ in the right-hand side of that equation.

The remainder of this section is based on work done by DHRYMES (1969).[21] It will at first be assumed that the disturbances of the original equation (8.1) are independent normal variates. In the last subsection this will be generalized to ϵ's generated by a first-order autoregressive process.

A Numerical LS Estimation Procedure under the Normality Assumption

The basic idea, which is applicable to a large class of situations including distributed lag estimation, can be explained in the following terms. If the ϵ's

[21] For other contributions to this area, see KOYCK (1954), KLEIN (1958), NERLOVE (1958a, b, c), NERLOVE and ADDISON (1958), MUNDLAK (1961), MALINVAUD (1961a) and (1966, particularly p. 493), LIVIATAN (1963), HANNAN (1965), WAUD (1966), MORRISON (1967), and DHRYMES, KLEIN, and STEIGLITZ (1968).

of (8.1) are independent normal with zero mean and variance σ^2, the logarithm of the likelihood function is

$$(8.3) \qquad \log L = -\frac{n}{2}\log 2\pi - \frac{n}{2}\log \sigma^2 - \frac{1}{2\sigma^2}\sum_{\alpha=1}^{n}\epsilon_\alpha^2$$

where $\epsilon_\alpha = y_\alpha - \beta_0 - \beta(x_\alpha + \lambda x_{\alpha-1} + \lambda^2 x_{\alpha-2} + \cdots)$. The parameters β_0, β and λ thus appear exclusively in the third right-hand term, which shows immediately that the maximum-likelihood estimators of these parameters must be identical with the LS estimators. A difficulty is that ϵ_α is nonlinear in λ, so that the LS normal equations are nonlinear. Another difficulty is that (8.1) contains an infinite number of successive x's. When we succeed in solving these problems, we have LS estimators which are also maximum-likelihood estimators, and we may then conclude from the analysis of Section 8.5 that they are consistent and asymptotically normally distributed with a covariance matrix equal to the inverse of the information matrix.

To simplify the algebra, suppose that the constant term β_0 of (8.1) vanishes. (For the more general case, see Problem 8.7.) Then write the equation as follows:

$$(8.4) \qquad y_\alpha = \beta\sum_{t=0}^{\alpha-1}\lambda^t x_{\alpha-t} + \beta\lambda^\alpha\sum_{t=0}^{\infty}\lambda^t x_{-t} + \epsilon_\alpha$$

$$= \beta\sum_{t=0}^{\alpha-1}\lambda^t x_{\alpha-t} + \lambda^\alpha\theta + \epsilon_\alpha \qquad \text{where} \qquad \theta = \beta\sum_{t=0}^{\infty}\lambda^t x_{-t}$$

The second line shows that we can solve the problem of an infinite number of x's by introducing an additional unknown parameter θ, which may be interpreted as the expectation of the pre-sample value y_0 when this value is regarded as random. The nonlinearity problem is solved by first minimizing the residual sum of squares for a given fixed value of λ, after which the λ estimator is obtained by a numerical method. Thus, define $\mathbf{X}_\lambda$ as the $n \times 2$ matrix whose αth row is

$$(8.5) \qquad \begin{bmatrix} \lambda^\alpha & \sum_{t=0}^{\alpha-1}\lambda^t x_{\alpha-t} \end{bmatrix}$$

The conditional LS estimator of $[\theta \quad \beta]'$ given λ is $(\mathbf{X}_\lambda'\mathbf{X}_\lambda)^{-1}\mathbf{X}_\lambda'\mathbf{y}$, where $\mathbf{y}$ is the n-element column vector $[y_\alpha]$. The residual sum of squares is $\mathbf{y}'\mathbf{M}_\lambda\mathbf{y}$, where $\mathbf{M}_\lambda = \mathbf{I} - \mathbf{X}_\lambda(\mathbf{X}_\lambda'\mathbf{X}_\lambda)^{-1}\mathbf{X}_\lambda'$. Compute $\mathbf{y}'\mathbf{M}_\lambda\mathbf{y}$ as a function of λ over the permissible range of λ. (This range is from -1 to 1, but usually only from 0 to 1.) The LS estimator $\hat{\lambda}$ of λ is by definition the λ value for which $\mathbf{y}'\mathbf{M}_\lambda\mathbf{y}$ takes the smallest value, and the corresponding $(\mathbf{X}_{\hat\lambda}'\mathbf{X}_{\hat\lambda})^{-1}\mathbf{X}_{\hat\lambda}'\mathbf{y}$ gives $\hat{\theta}$ and $\hat{\beta}$.

To obtain the asymptotic covariance matrix of these estimators by means of the information matrix, we consider the logarithmic likelihood function:

$$(8.6)\quad \log L = -\frac{n}{2}\log 2\pi - \frac{n}{2}\log\sigma^2 - \frac{1}{2\sigma^2}\sum_{\alpha=1}^{n}\epsilon_\alpha^2$$

$$= -\frac{n}{2}\log 2\pi - \frac{n}{2}\log\sigma^2 - \frac{1}{2\sigma^2}\sum_{\alpha=1}^{n}\left[y_\alpha - \beta\sum_{t=0}^{\alpha-1}\lambda^t x_{\alpha-t} - \lambda^\alpha\theta\right]^2$$

The derivative with respect to σ^2 is $-n/2\sigma^2 + (1/2\sigma^4)\sum \epsilon_\alpha^2$. The second-order cross-derivative with respect to σ^2 and θ is then a multiple $1/\sigma^4$ of $\sum \epsilon_\alpha(\partial\epsilon_\alpha/\partial\theta)$. Since $\partial\epsilon_\alpha/\partial\theta = -\lambda^\alpha$ and is hence a constant, the expectation of this cross-derivative vanishes. This is also true for the cross-derivatives with respect to σ^2 and β and with respect to σ^2 and λ, since $\partial\epsilon_\alpha/\partial\beta$ and $\partial\epsilon_\alpha/\partial\lambda$ are constants too. Therefore the 4×4 information matrix is block-diagonal with a 3×3 block for θ, β, and λ and a 1×1 block for σ^2. There is then no need for analyzing derivatives of $\log L$ with respect to σ^2 when we are exclusively interested in the asymptotic covariance matrix of θ, β, and λ (the inverse of the 3×3 block). Note that we had exactly the same situation at the end of Section 8.4.

A second simplification is obtained by writing the third term of the second line of (8.6) as

$$-\frac{1}{2\sigma^2}\left(\mathbf{y} - \mathbf{X}_\lambda\begin{bmatrix}\theta\\ \beta\end{bmatrix}\right)'\left(\mathbf{y} - \mathbf{X}_\lambda\begin{bmatrix}\theta\\ \beta\end{bmatrix}\right)$$

where the subscript λ of $\mathbf{X}_\lambda$ stands for the true parameter value. It is obvious from this form that as far as θ and β are concerned, the standard linear model applies conditionally on λ. It follows from (4.25) that the leading 2×2 submatrix of the information matrix (corresponding to θ and β) is $(1/\sigma^2)\mathbf{X}_\lambda'\mathbf{X}_\lambda$. Three derivatives then remain, which are evaluated in Problems 8.2 and 8.3. Their expectations are:[22]

$$(8.7)\quad \mathscr{E}\left(\frac{\partial^2\log L}{\partial\lambda\,\partial\theta}\right) = -\frac{\beta}{\sigma^2}\sum_{\alpha=1}^{n}\lambda^\alpha\sum_{t=0}^{\alpha-1}t\lambda^{t-1}x_{\alpha-t} - \frac{\theta\lambda}{\sigma^2(1-\lambda^2)^2}\left[1 - \lambda^{2n} - n\lambda^{2n}(1-\lambda^2)\right]$$

$$(8.8)\quad \mathscr{E}\left(\frac{\partial^2\log L}{\partial\lambda\,\partial\beta}\right) = -\frac{1}{\sigma^2}\sum_{\alpha=1}^{n}\left(\sum_{t=0}^{\alpha-1}\lambda^t x_{\alpha-t}\right)\left(\beta\sum_{t=0}^{\alpha-1}t\lambda^{t-1}x_{\alpha-t} + \alpha\lambda^{\alpha-1}\theta\right)$$

$$(8.9)\quad \mathscr{E}\left(\frac{\partial^2\log L}{\partial\lambda^2}\right) = -\frac{1}{\sigma^2}\sum_{\alpha=1}^{n}\left(\beta\sum_{t=0}^{\alpha-1}t\lambda^{t-1}x_{\alpha-t} + \alpha\lambda^{\alpha-1}\theta\right)^2$$

[22] Note that the expression in square brackets on the second line of (8.7) converges to 1 as $n \to \infty$. It is recommended that this substitution be made because the terms of lower order suggest more accuracy than can be guaranteed.

This completes the specification of the nine relevant elements of the information matrix. They all depend on unknown parameters $(\theta, \beta, \lambda, \sigma^2)$, but by substituting the corresponding estimates we obtain an estimated information matrix and the inverse of this supplies asymptotic standard errors. For the σ^2 estimator we take the residual sum of squares divided by $n - 3$, which is obviously consistent.

An Example

To illustrate this procedure we consider

$$y_\alpha = \beta\left[\sin\frac{1}{2}\alpha + \lambda\sin\frac{1}{2}(\alpha - 1) + \cdots\right] + \epsilon_\alpha \tag{8.10}$$

or, equivalently,

$$y_\alpha = \beta\sin\frac{1}{2}\alpha + \lambda y_{\alpha-1} + (\epsilon_\alpha - \lambda\epsilon_{\alpha-1}) \tag{8.11}$$

where $\alpha = 1, \ldots, 20$, the number of observations being 20. We specify $\beta = 10$, $\lambda = .5$, and $y_0 = \epsilon_0 = 0$. The disturbances $\epsilon_1, \ldots, \epsilon_{20}$ are random normal numbers with zero mean and standard deviation 4, obtained by multiplying the disturbances of column (2) of Table 5.1 (Section 5.4) by 4. The equation then determines $y_1, \ldots, y_{20}$, so that the conditional LS estimate $(\mathbf{X}_\lambda'\mathbf{X}_\lambda)^{-1}\mathbf{X}_\lambda'\mathbf{y}$ can be computed for each λ, together with the sum of squares of the corresponding residuals. The results are shown in Table 8.1 for $\lambda = .01, .10, .20, \ldots, .90, .99$ with smaller intervals around the minimum. This minimum is approximately 332.2 and the associated $\hat{\lambda}$ in three decimal places is .474, while $\hat{\theta}$ and $\hat{\beta}$ are equal to 2.31 and 10.25, respectively. The asymptotic covariance matrix is computed straightforwardly from the information matrix, and the asymptotic standard errors are .073 (for $\hat{\lambda} = .474$), 8.57 (for $\hat{\theta} = 2.31$), and 1.27 (for $\hat{\beta} = 10.25$). The results for β and λ are in satisfactory agreement with the true values in spite of the fact that the sample is not particularly large.

One can obtain a more detailed impression of the behavior of the likelihood function by drawing contour lines of equal likelihood. This will be illustrated for λ and β only, since θ is not an interesting parameter from an economic point of view. Also, we shall draw contour lines of equal residual sum of squares rather than equal likelihood in order to obtain a direct link with the last column of Table 8.1; these geometric representations are, of course, equivalent under the normality assumption. Consider, then,

$$S(\lambda, \beta) = \min_{\theta}\sum_{\alpha=1}^{20}\left(y_\alpha - \beta\sum_{t=0}^{\alpha-1}\lambda^t\sin\frac{\alpha - t}{2} - \lambda^\alpha\theta\right)^2 \tag{8.12}$$

Table 8.1

Numerical Minimization of the Residual Sum of Squares

λ	Conditional Estimate of θ	Conditional Estimate of β	Residual Sum of Squares
.01	166.0180	15.178	678.70
.10	16.7340	14.255	597.51
.20	7.9648	13.221	504.88
.30	4.8314	12.169	417.51
.40	3.1702	11.087	351.34
.41	3.0428	10.977	346.85
.42	2.9200	10.866	342.89
.43	2.8012	10.755	339.48
.44	2.6859	10.643	336.68
.45	2.5735	10.531	334.52
.46	2.4637	10.418	333.05
.47	2.3559	10.305	332.32
.471	2.3453	10.293	332.28778
.472	2.3346	10.282	332.26449
.473	2.3239	10.271	332.24902
.474	2.3133	10.259	332.24171
.475	2.3026	10.248	332.24222
.476	2.2920	10.236	332.25089
.477	2.2814	10.225	332.26772
.478	2.2708	10.214	332.29288
.479	2.2602	10.202	332.32603
.48	2.2497	10.191	332.37
.49	2.1444	10.077	333.25
.50	2.0397	9.962	335.02
.60	.9079	8.790	413.95
.70	−.7642	7.590	646.51
.80	−3.3536	6.413	1075.46
.90	−6.1530	5.280	1654.32
.99	−6.8668	4.239	2154.63

which is the minimum sum of squares of the residuals, given λ and β. Figure 8.3 contains contour lines for this function in the λ, β-plane. The minimum is at $\hat{\lambda} = .474$, $\hat{\beta} = 10.25$, and the contour lines have approximately the form of ellipses. However, note that they are not concentric as they would be if eq. (8.4) were linear in the parameter λ (see Problem 8.6).

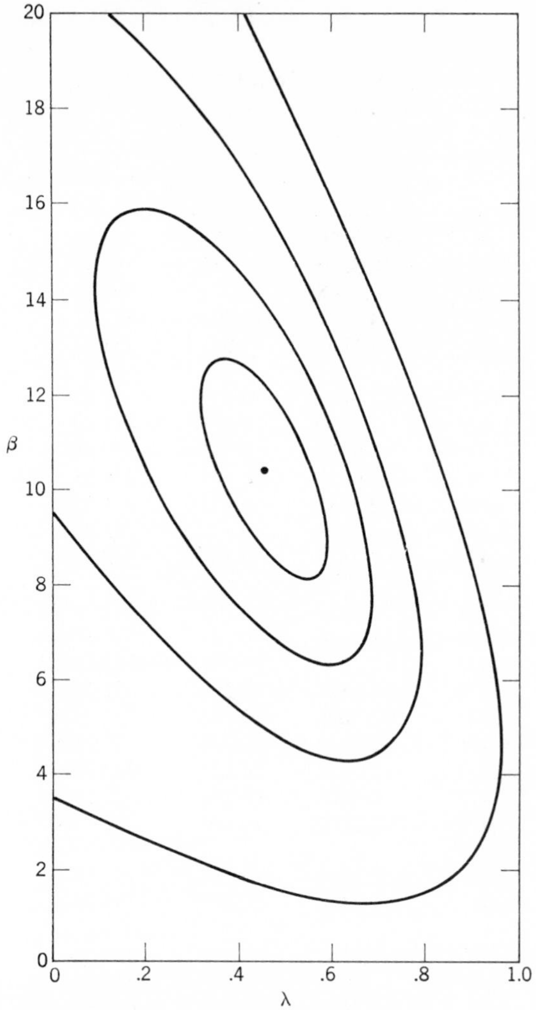

Fig. 8.3 Likelihood contours.

An Extension for the Case of Autocorrelated Disturbances

Suppose now that the disturbances of (8.1) are not independent but are generated by $\epsilon_\alpha = \rho\epsilon_{\alpha-1} + \zeta_\alpha$, where the ζ's are independent normal variates with zero mean and variance σ_0^2 and $|\rho| < 1$. The case $\rho = \lambda$ was considered in the second paragraph of this section. To handle the more general case we consider (8.4), multiply both sides by ρ, and lag the equation by one period:

$$\rho y_{\alpha-1} = \beta\rho\sum_{t=0}^{\alpha-2}\lambda^t x_{\alpha-1-t} + \beta\rho\lambda^{\alpha-1}\sum_{t=0}^{\infty}\lambda^t x_{\alpha-t} + \rho\epsilon_{\alpha-1} \tag{8.13}$$

$$= \beta(\rho/\lambda)\sum_{t=1}^{\alpha-1}\lambda^t x_{\alpha-t} + \rho\lambda^{\alpha-1}\theta + \rho\epsilon_{\alpha-1}$$

Subtract this from (8.4):

$$y_\alpha - \rho y_{\alpha-1} = \beta\left[x_\alpha + (\lambda - \rho)\sum_{t=1}^{\alpha-1}\lambda^{t-1}x_{\alpha-t}\right] + \lambda^{\alpha-1}(\lambda - \rho)\theta + \zeta_\alpha \tag{8.14}$$

The LS estimation procedure for θ and β is now conditional on both λ and ρ. So we define $\mathbf{X}_{\lambda\rho}$ as the $n \times 2$ matrix whose αth row is

$$\left[\lambda^{\alpha-1}(\lambda - \rho) \qquad x_\alpha + (\lambda - \rho)\sum_{t=1}^{\alpha-1}\lambda^{t-1}x_{\alpha-t}\right] \tag{8.15}$$

The αth element of the vector $\mathbf{y}_\rho$ of the dependent variable is now $y_\alpha - \rho y_{\alpha-1}$. The search for the minimum of the residual sum of squares is two-dimensional and these sums of squares take the form

$$\mathbf{y}_\rho'\mathbf{M}_{\lambda\rho}\mathbf{y}_\rho \qquad \text{where} \qquad \mathbf{M}_{\lambda\rho} = \mathbf{I} - \mathbf{X}_{\lambda\rho}(\mathbf{X}_{\lambda\rho}'\mathbf{X}_{\lambda\rho})^{-1}\mathbf{X}_{\lambda\rho}' \tag{8.16}$$

When the pair $(\hat{\lambda}, \hat{\rho})$ for which the quadratic form (8.16) is minimal has been found, we can proceed in a way similar to that described below eq. (8.6).[23] It will be clear that a simultaneous search in two dimensions requires a much larger computational effort than a search in one dimension, but it can be done with appropriate computer facilities.

Problems

8.1 Write a_0 and a_1 for the LS estimators of the constant term and of the coefficient of $y_{\alpha-1}$, respectively, in eq. (8.2). Write v_{00}, v_{11}, and v_{01}

[23] Note that the derivative of ζ_α of (8.14) with respect to ρ is not a constant but a linear function of the random variable $y_{\alpha-1}$. [See the discussion immediately below (8.6).] The second-order cross-derivative of $\log L$ with respect to σ_0^2 and ρ has, nevertheless, zero expectation because of the independence of ζ_α and $y_{\alpha-1}$. It should also be noted that it appears as if the function which Dhrymes minimizes is different from the one considered here, since he divides the minimum value (given λ and ρ) of the mean squared residual by $(1 - \rho^2)^{1/n}$. However, this makes no difference asymptotically because $(1 - \rho^2)^{1/n}$ converges to 1 as $n \to \infty$.

for the estimated variances and covariance of their asymptotic distribution. Prove that the implied estimator of β_0 is $a_0/(1 - a_1)$ and that the estimated variance of its asymptotic distribution is

$$\frac{v_{00}}{(1-a_1)^2} + \frac{2a_0 v_{01}}{(1-a_1)^3} + \frac{a_0^2 v_{11}}{(1-a_1)^4} \tag{8.17}$$

8.2 Prove that the first-order derivative of $\log L$ in (8.6) with respect to λ is

$$\frac{\partial \log L}{\partial \lambda} = \frac{1}{\sigma^2}\sum_{\alpha=1}^{n} \epsilon_\alpha \left(\beta \sum_{t=0}^{\alpha-1} t\lambda^{t-1} x_{\alpha-t} + \alpha\lambda^{\alpha-1}\theta\right) \tag{8.18}$$

Next derive the following second-order derivatives:

$$\frac{\partial^2 \log L}{\partial \lambda\, \partial \theta} = -\frac{1}{\sigma^2}\sum_{\alpha=1}^{n} \lambda^\alpha \left(\beta \sum_{t=0}^{\alpha-1} t\lambda^{t-1} x_{\alpha-t} + \alpha\lambda^{\alpha-1}\theta\right) + \frac{1}{\sigma^2}\sum_{\alpha=1}^{n} \alpha\lambda^{\alpha-1}\epsilon_\alpha \tag{8.19}$$

$$\frac{\partial^2 \log L}{\partial \lambda\, \partial \beta} = -\frac{1}{\sigma^2}\sum_{\alpha=1}^{n} \left(\sum_{t=0}^{\alpha-1} \lambda^t x_{\alpha-t}\right)\left(\beta \sum_{t=0}^{\alpha-1} t\lambda^{t-1} x_{\alpha-t} + \alpha\lambda^{\alpha-1}\theta\right) + \frac{1}{\sigma^2}\sum_{\alpha=1}^{n} \epsilon_\alpha \sum_{t=0}^{\alpha-1} t\lambda^{t-1} x_{\alpha-t} \tag{8.20}$$

$$\frac{\partial^2 \log L}{\partial \lambda^2} = -\frac{1}{\sigma^2}\sum_{\alpha=1}^{n} \left(\beta \sum_{t=0}^{\alpha-1} t\lambda^{t-1} x_{\alpha-t} + \alpha\lambda^{\alpha-1}\theta\right)^2 + \frac{1}{\sigma^2}\sum_{\alpha=1}^{n} \epsilon_\alpha \left[\beta \sum_{t=0}^{\alpha-1} t(t-1)\lambda^{t-2} x_{\alpha-t} + \alpha(\alpha-1)\lambda^{\alpha-2}\theta\right] \tag{8.21}$$

8.3 (*Continuation*) Derive the expectations (8.7) to (8.9). [*Hint*. For (8.7), use $\alpha\lambda^{2\alpha-1} = \frac{1}{2}\partial\lambda^{2\alpha}/\partial\lambda$.]

8.4 Prove that the minimum over λ of $\mathbf{y}'\mathbf{M}_\lambda\mathbf{y}$ divided by $n - 3$ is a consistent estimator of σ^2 [see the discussion below (8.5)]. Is it also an unbiased estimator?

8.5 (*Continuation*) Compare the minimum residual sum of squares in Table 8.1 with the variance of the disturbances that have been used. Apply a χ^2 test to verify whether they are in agreement, and describe the approximate nature of this test.

8.6 Consider the standard linear model $\mathbf{y} = \mathbf{X}\boldsymbol{\beta} + \boldsymbol{\epsilon}$. Prove that the locus of $\boldsymbol{\beta}$ values for which the residual sum of squares, $(\mathbf{y} - \mathbf{X}\boldsymbol{\beta})'(\mathbf{y} - \mathbf{X}\boldsymbol{\beta})$, is a constant is represented by a family of concentric ellipsoids in the K-dimensional $\boldsymbol{\beta}$ space. Next, write the equation in the form $\mathbf{y} = \mathbf{X}_1\boldsymbol{\beta}_1 + \mathbf{X}_2\boldsymbol{\beta}_2 + \boldsymbol{\epsilon}$, where $\mathbf{X}_1$ is of order $n \times K_1$ and $\mathbf{X}_2$ of order $n \times (K - K_1)$. Adjust $\boldsymbol{\beta}_2$ for any given $\boldsymbol{\beta}_1$ so that the residual sum of squares is minimized: $\hat{\boldsymbol{\beta}}_2 = (\mathbf{X}_2'\mathbf{X}_2)^{-1}\mathbf{X}_2'(\mathbf{y} - \mathbf{X}_1\boldsymbol{\beta}_1)$. [This is basically what we did in (8.12) when eliminating θ.] Prove that the locus of $\boldsymbol{\beta}_1$ values for which the residual sum of squares (after the conditional adjustment of $\boldsymbol{\beta}_2$ given $\boldsymbol{\beta}_1$) is a constant is algebraically of the form

$$(8.22)\quad (\mathbf{y} - \mathbf{X}_1\boldsymbol{\beta}_1)'\mathbf{M}_2(\mathbf{y} - \mathbf{X}_1\boldsymbol{\beta}_1) \quad \text{where} \quad \mathbf{M}_2 = \mathbf{I} - \mathbf{X}_2(\mathbf{X}_2'\mathbf{X}_2)^{-1}\mathbf{X}_2'$$

and geometrically a family of concentric ellipsoids in the K_1-dimensional $\boldsymbol{\beta}_1$ space.

8.7 If there is a constant term β_0 in (8.1), prove that the procedure (8.4) to (8.9) remains unchanged except for the following three modifications. First, β_0 is to be added to the right-hand side of (8.4) and θ is no longer $\mathscr{E}y_0$ (when y_0 is regarded as random) but $\mathscr{E}(y_0 - \beta_0)$. Second, the matrix $\mathbf{X}_\lambda$ is now of order $n \times 3$, its αth row is

$$(8.23)\quad \left[1 \quad \lambda^\alpha \quad \sum_{t=0}^{\alpha-1} \lambda^t x_{\alpha-t}\right]$$

and the successive elements of $(\mathbf{X}_\lambda'\mathbf{X}_\lambda)^{-1}\mathbf{X}_\lambda'\mathbf{y}$ are the conditional LS estimates (given λ) of β_0, θ, β, in that order. Third, the information matrix is now of order 5×5, the relevant submatrix (corresponding to β_0, θ, β and λ) is of order 4×4, the leading submatrix $(1/\sigma^2)\mathbf{X}_\lambda'\mathbf{X}_\lambda$ is of order 3×3, and the (1, 4)th element is

$$(8.24)\quad -\mathscr{E}\left(\frac{\partial^2 \log L}{\partial\beta_0\,\partial\lambda}\right) = \frac{\beta}{\sigma^2}\sum_{\alpha=1}^{n}\sum_{t=0}^{\alpha-1} t\lambda^{t-1}x_{\alpha-t} + \frac{\theta}{\sigma^2(1-\lambda)^2}\left[1 - \lambda^n - n\lambda^n(1-\lambda)\right]$$

The expression in brackets on the right converges to 1 as $n \to \infty$ (see footnote 22 on p. 419).

8.8 Write eq. (7.19) in the form

$$(8.25)\quad y_\alpha - \rho y_{\alpha-1} = \beta_1(y_{\alpha-1} - \rho y_{\alpha-2}) + \beta_2(x_\alpha - \rho x_{\alpha-1}) + \zeta_\alpha$$

Apply the procedure described in this section to (8.25) under the condition that $\zeta_1, \ldots, \zeta_n$ are independent normal variates with zero mean and variance σ^2.

8.9 Sampling Experiments and Higher-Order Approximations[AC]

When is a Sample Large Enough?[A]

The previous pages show that the use of LS and GLS can be justified in a number of cases which violate the basic assumptions of the standard linear model, provided the sample is large. This solves some problems, but not all. How large is large? It is gratifying to see that in a great many cases we can replace the statement that $\hat{\theta}_n$ is a consistent estimator of θ by the much stronger statement that $\hat{\theta}_n$ is asymptotically normally distributed with mean θ and a variance of order $1/n$ which can be estimated consistently, since this enables us to apply classical normal distribution theory, at least approximately. As stated in the beginning of Section 8.2, consistency of an estimator guarantees only that the sampling error converges in probability to zero as $n \to \infty$, and the use of a normal limiting distribution leads to considerable additional insight into the behavior of the sampling distribution before it becomes degenerate. But if we use the normal limiting distribution for testing and estimation purposes, we commit an approximation error when we do so for finite n. The only thing known about this error is that it converges to zero as $n \to \infty$. Basically, this leads us back to the objection raised at the beginning of Section 8.2, but now at a higher level of approximation. If mathematical difficulties prevent us from deriving the exact distribution of an estimator for any given finite n, we would be interested in a second-order approximation, which is perhaps not a normal distribution and perhaps has a different mean and variance. This is particularly true for econometric applications, which are frequently based on samples of limited size.

Sampling Experiments[A]

One way of extending our knowledge is the use of *sampling experiments* (also known as the "Monte Carlo method"). As an example, take the autoregressive process $y_\alpha = \beta y_{\alpha-1} + \epsilon_\alpha$, where the ϵ's are independent normal variates with zero mean and variance σ^2. Then specify β, σ^2, and y_0 numerically and use a table of random sampling numbers (or a computer which generates such numbers) to obtain a series of n disturbances. Each y_α can then be computed from $\beta y_{\alpha-1} + \epsilon_\alpha$ and hence also the LS estimate $b = \sum y_{\alpha-1}y_\alpha / \sum y_{\alpha-1}^2$. This procedure is repeated many times, in each case yielding an estimate of β. These estimates form an empirical distribution, which can be compared with the asymptotic normal distribution with mean β and variance $(1 - \beta^2)/n$ [cf. (7.11)].

As a slightly more complicated example, take the following equation analyzed by MALINVAUD (1961b):

$$y_\alpha = \beta_0 + \beta_1 y_{\alpha-1} + \beta_2 x_\alpha + \epsilon_\alpha \tag{9.1}$$

where the specifications are as follows: $\beta_0 = 0$, $\beta_1 = .6$, $\beta_2 = .4$; the ϵ's are independent normal variates with zero mean and a standard deviation equal to 6; and x_α, $\alpha = 1, \ldots, 20$, is the GNP of the United States in billions of dollars of 1939 purchasing power from 1929 ($\alpha = 1$) through 1948 ($\alpha = 20$)

except for some modifications for the war years 1942 to 1944. Each experimental sample thus consists of 20 observations and there are 100 samples as a whole, all based on the same specification of the β's and x's but on different random drawings for the ϵ's. In each case LS estimates were computed with the following result for the 100 estimates b_1 of β_1. They underestimate the true value in about three cases out of four; their average is .52, so that the bias $\mathscr{E}b_1 - \beta_1$ is estimated to be $.52 - .60 = -.08$ on the basis of these 100 samples; and the empirical distribution of the estimates is skew with a long tail in zero direction. If one computes confidence intervals of the form $(b_1 \pm 2.11 s_{b_1})$, where s_{b_1} is the asymptotic standard error of b_1 and 2.11 the t value corresponding to a 5 percent significance level, then the interval turns out to be on the left of the true value (.6) in 8 cases out of 100 but in no case on the right. These two frequencies should be compared with the theoretical value of $2\frac{1}{2}$ corresponding to the normal distribution. This suggests that a .95 confidence coefficient should actually be interpreted as a .92 confidence coefficient, but a much larger number of samples is obviously needed to warrant such a precise conclusion.

It will be clear that sampling experiments have an important disadvantage compared with the complete analytical evaluation of the sampling distribution. The results are specific for the chosen values of the parameters and the x-variables, so that a very large number of experiments is needed to obtain an adequate insight. However, the method does have merit in those cases where an exact analytical solution is difficult to obtain.

Higher-Order Approximations[C]

An alternative procedure is to derive analytically certain features of the sampling distribution, either exactly or at least to a higher degree of approximation than that of the asymptotic distribution. An example is the work done by HURWICZ (1950a) for the expectation of the LS estimator b of the autoregressive process $y_\alpha = \beta y_{\alpha-1} + \epsilon_\alpha$ (ϵ's normal). Taking $y_0 = 0$, he found for $n = 3$ that the ratio $\mathscr{E}b/\beta$ is between .75 and .8 when β is between 0 and 1. This amounts to a relative bias of at least 20 percent in zero direction when there are three observations. He also considered the mean of b for larger values of n under the assumption that the pre-sample value y_0 is random.[24] The result is that if β is not too far from zero, $\mathscr{E}b$ can be approximated by

$$\mathscr{E}b \approx \beta \frac{n^2 - 2n + 3}{n^2 - 1} \tag{9.2}$$

[24] The distribution of y_0 is taken to be normal with zero mean and variance $\sigma^2/(1 - \beta^2)$ in accordance with the limiting distribution of y_n for $n \to \infty$. In addition, y_0 and $\epsilon_1, \ldots, \epsilon_n$ are assumed to be independent.

Clearly, this again implies a bias in zero direction as soon as $n > 2$. If we multiply b by $(n^2 - 1)/(n^2 - 2n + 3)$, the estimator thus corrected is approximately unbiased. When applying this to the sampling experiment based on (9.1) with $n = 20$, we obtain an average of the corrected estimates equal to .57, which is closer to the true value .6 than the average .52 of the original estimates. Obviously, the result (9.2) is not directly applicable in this case, partly because $\beta_1 = .6$ is not close to zero, partly because (9.1) is a more complicated equation than the autoregressive process $y_\alpha = \beta y_{\alpha-1} + \epsilon_\alpha$.

A more systematic way of improving on the accuracy of large-sample approximations is by means of an expansion of the sequence of distribution functions $F_1(\ ), F_2(\ ), \ldots, F_n(\ ), \ldots$ in terms of a series. Reference should be made to D. L. WALLACE (1958), who describes several expansions including those of Edgeworth, Gram-Charlier, and Cornish-Fisher. For the theory of asymptotic expansions, see ERDÉLYI (1956).

CHAPTER 9

AN INFORMAL INTRODUCTION TO SIMULTANEOUS-EQUATION MODELS

The subject matter of this chapter is the point raised in Section 3.9 under (7), which is concerned with the general interdependence of economic phenomena and which leads to systems of simultaneous equations. Such systems are similar to the pair of investment equations considered in Section 7.1, but the degree to which the equations of this chapter are interrelated is greater owing to the fact that, in general, each equation has several dependent variables which also occur in the other equations.

The formal statistical analysis of equation systems is of the large-sample type and is postponed until Chapter 10. The major stress of the present chapter is on the economic interpretation and the operation of such systems and on illustrations and examples. All sections are recommended for an introductory course except Section 9.6, which is optional.

9.1 Endogenous and Exogenous Variables in a System of Simultaneous Equations[A]

Our starting point is a simple Keynesian model:

$$C_\alpha = \beta Y_\alpha + \epsilon_\alpha \tag{1.1}$$

$$C_\alpha + I_\alpha = Y_\alpha \tag{1.2}$$

where $\alpha = 1, \ldots, n$ refers to successive annual observations. The first equation is a macroeconomic consumption function which states that C_α, total consumption in year α, is proportional to total income earned in that year (Y_α) apart from a random disturbance (ϵ_α). The second equation is definitional in character and states that consumption plus investment (I) is equal to income in every year. It is our objective to estimate the proportionality constant β of the consumption function on the basis of n observations on these variables under the condition that the ϵ's are uncorrelated random variables with zero mean and constant variance.

To investigate the validity of the other assumptions of the standard linear model with respect to the consumption function, we should ask whether it is realistic to assume that the values taken by the explanatory variable, $Y_1, \ldots, Y_n$, are independent of the disturbances of that equation, so that we can operate conditionally on these values. Then subtract (1.1) from (1.2) to obtain $I_\alpha + \epsilon_\alpha = (1 - \beta) Y_\alpha$. Under the independence assumption of Y_α and ϵ_α this implies that I_α and ϵ_α are random variables with correlation -1 in their conditional distribution given Y_α. That is a very unattractive conclusion. Although it is possible that ϵ_α represents neglected factors which are correlated with investment, it is implausible that the correlation is perfect. It seems much more plausible to reject the conclusion, but this implies that we have to accept Y_α as a random variable which is not independent of ϵ_α, so that we are no longer operating under the conditions of the standard linear model.

Equation Systems; Endogenous and Exogenous Variables

The discussion of the preceding paragraph involves a disturbance in one equation and a variable (investment) which does not occur in that equation but in another. This suggests that the analysis should not be confined to individual equations but extended to a system of equations—in this case, a two-equation system. Such a system usually contains more variables than equations; in our example there are three variables (C, Y, I) and only two equations. Accordingly, the objective of an equation system is to describe a subset of its variables in terms of the other variables. The former variables are called *endogenous*, the latter *exogenous*. The intuitive background of this distinction is that the values of certain variables (the exogenous variables) are determined "from the outside," that is, in a way which is independent of the process described by the equation system, whereas the values of the other (endogenous) variables are determined, jointly and simultaneously, by the exogenous variables and the disturbances in the way prescribed by the equations of the system. (The term "simultaneously" should clarify why these equations are commonly known as simultaneous equations.) The statistical formalization of this idea is the assumption that the values of the exogenous variables are stochastically independent of the disturbances of the system. This assumption enables us to operate conditionally on the exogenous values, so that we may regard them as constants. This is analogous to the procedure applied to the explanatory variables of the standard linear model as described in the last paragraph of Section 3.2. However, there is the important difference that the equations of this chapter may have explanatory variables which are not exogenous and whose values are not independent of the disturbances. The previous paragraph provides an example of this situation.

Complete Systems of Structural Equations and the Reduced Form

Returning to the two-equation system (1.1) and (1.2), let us suppose that investment is an exogenous variable in this system and that consumption and income are two endogenous variables.[1] Under the assumption $\beta \neq 1$ we may then solve for the latter variables:

$$\begin{aligned} C_\alpha &= \frac{\beta}{1-\beta} I_\alpha + \frac{1}{1-\beta} \epsilon_\alpha \\ Y_\alpha &= \frac{1}{1-\beta} I_\alpha + \frac{1}{1-\beta} \epsilon_\alpha \end{aligned} \tag{1.3}$$

An equation system is said to be *complete* when it has as many endogenous variables as equations (both two in the example) and when it can be solved for these variables; we shall confine ourselves to complete systems from now on. The solution is called the *reduced form* of the system, and each equation of this form (one for C and one for Y in the example) is called a reduced-form equation. Such an equation describes one endogenous variable in terms of exogenous variables and disturbances. By contrast, the original equations are called *structural equations* because each of them serves to describe part of the structure of the economy. For example, the consumption function (1.1) describes the behavior of consumer households with respect to their purchases of commodities and services. [It should be admitted that the structural description of a definitional equation such as (1.2) is a little meager.]

The economic interpretation of structural equations is simpler and more direct than that of the reduced form. On the other hand, the reduced form is more convenient when one wants to calculate the effect of a change in an exogenous variable on the endogenous variables. For example, we see immediately from (1.3) that an increase in investment of one million dollars

[1] It is easy to criticize the assumption that I_α and ϵ_α are independent, but at this stage we have to sacrifice economic realism for the simplicity of the examples which serve to illustrate some fundamental concepts.

per year raises consumption and income by $\beta/(1 - \beta)$ and $1/(1 - \beta)$ million dollars per year, respectively. Also, it is important from a statistical point of view that the values $I_1, \ldots, I_n$ taken by the right-hand variable in (1.3) are assumed to be nonstochastic. This is in contrast to (1.1), where we have the random Y_α in the right-hand side. Hence the reduced form is in a sense closer to the standard linear model than the structural equations are. This explains why we shall meet the reduced form frequently in spite of the fact that our main statistical interest will be in the estimation of the parameters of the structural equations.

Problems

1.1 Prove that the basic equation of the standard linear model can be regarded as a complete one-equation system with the dependent variable as the endogenous variable and the explanatory variables as the exogenous variables. (Note that the reduced form is identical with the structural equation in this case.)

1.2 Prove that the two investment equations of Section 7.1 can be regarded as forming a two-equation system and that the separate equations are both structural and reduced-form equations when the market value of the firm and capital stock at the beginning of the year are taken as fixed. (Also see Problem 2.4.)

9.2 Jointly Dependent and Predetermined Variables in a Dynamic Equation System[A]

The Keynesian model (1.1) and (1.2) is actually too simple to give the real flavor of simultaneous-equation models. We can improve on this by discussing one of the models constructed by L. R. KLEIN (1950), the so-called Klein Model I, which is a favorite drilling ground of theoretical econometricians. It is a six-equation system based on annual data for the United States in the period between the two World Wars. Furthermore, it is dynamic in the sense that it is formulated in terms of variables belonging to different points or periods of time. As we shall see, this dynamic aspect calls for an extension of the endogenous-exogenous distinction.

The Behavioral Equations of Klein's Model I

One behavioral equation of the model is a consumption function:

$$C_\alpha = \beta_0 + \beta_1 P_\alpha + \beta_2 P_{\alpha-1} + \beta_3(W_\alpha + W'_\alpha) + \epsilon_\alpha \tag{2.1}$$

where C_α is aggregate consumption in year α, P_α total profits of that year, W_α the total wage bill paid by private industry in year α, and W'_α that year's government wage bill. Hence this equation describes aggregate consumption linearly in terms of the total wage bill of the same year ($W_\alpha + W'_\alpha$), of current profits (P_α), and of profits lagged one year ($P_{\alpha-1}$), apart from a random disturbance (ϵ_α). Note that all variables of the model are measured in billions (10^9) of dollars of 1934 purchasing power per year except when the contrary is mentioned explicitly.

Another behavioral equation is the investment function:

$$I_\alpha = \beta'_0 + \beta'_1 P_\alpha + \beta'_2 P_{\alpha-1} + \beta'_3 K_{\alpha-1} + \epsilon'_\alpha \tag{2.2}$$

where I_α is net investment in year α and K_α is the stock of capital goods at the end of the year. (The latter variable is measured in billions of 1934 dollars, not per year because it is a stock rather than a flow variable.) The presumption is that β'_3 is negative, which means that if the capital stock at the beginning of the year ($K_{\alpha-1}$) is larger, the addition to this stock in the form of net investment is reduced. The equation implies further that net investment reacts to profits both immediately and with a lag of one year, just as consumption does in eq. (2.1).

The third behavioral equation is a demand-for-labor function. This demand is measured by the (deflated) wage bill paid by private industry, so that the left-hand variable in year α is W_α:

$$W_\alpha = \beta''_0 + \beta''_1 X_\alpha + \beta''_2 X_{\alpha-1} + \beta''_3(\alpha - 1931) + \epsilon''_\alpha \tag{2.3}$$

Here X_α is the total production of private industry in year α. The equation thus states that the wage bill paid by this sector varies with total output, both current and with a one-year lag; moreover, that this wage bill is subject to a time trend. The latter feature is revealed by the fourth right-hand term, $\beta''_3(\alpha - 1931)$, where α should be regarded as time measured in calendar years. The author of the model ascribes this term to the increasing strength of the unions in the period between the wars, which led to wage increases (and hence to increases in the wage bill) wholly independent of the behavior of the other explanatory variables of the equation.

The Definitional Equations of Klein's Model I

Apart from the above behavioral equations there are the following identities:

$$\begin{aligned} X_\alpha &= C_\alpha + I_\alpha + G_\alpha \\ P_\alpha &= X_\alpha - W_\alpha - T_\alpha \\ K_\alpha &= K_{\alpha-1} + I_\alpha \end{aligned} \tag{2.4}$$

where G_α is government nonwage expenditure and T_α business taxes in year α. The first definition states that the production of the private sector is destined for either consumption or investment or the government. The second is a profit-and-loss account for the private sector as a whole; subtract from total output the amounts paid as wages and taxes, and what remains is total profits. The last equation simply states that net investment is equal to the change in capital stock.

Which Variables of the Model Are Exogenous?

The model (2.1) to (2.4) is a six-equation system in ten variables (C, P, W, W', I, K, X, α, G, T). Hence, in order to declare it complete, we should have exactly four exogenous variables. Therefore we should ask: which of these ten variables take values that are determined in a way that is independent of the operation of the economic system described by (2.1) to (2.4)? The most obvious case is time (α). Also, there are the three government variables: W' (government wage bill), T (taxes), G (government nonwage expenditure). If we imagine that these variables are indeed controlled by the government,[2] their values are fixed and given from the standpoint of the system described in eqs. (2.1) to (2.4). We then have four exogenous variables, while the following six are endogenous:

C	consumption
P	profits
W	wage bill paid by private industry
I	net investment
K	capital stock
X	total production of private industry

It should be added that it is frequently convenient to handle the constant terms of the equations (β_0, β_0', β_0'') by means of a variable which takes the unit value for each observation. This value is obviously nonstochastic, so

[2] It is not really satisfactory to say that the government controls a variable like tax revenue. It is preferable to say that the government controls the tax rates. This can be handled by the introduction of a seventh equation which describes tax revenue in terms of these rates and other determining variables, while tax revenue itself becomes endogenous. It is doubtful, however, whether such a refinement is appropriate for such a small and crude model as (2.1) to (2.4). See Section 9.9 for an attempt to attack this problem for a larger model. Also note that if the government follows a decision rule which links the controlled variables to the current behavior of the endogenous variables, the former variables cease to be exogenous. However, such a decision rule typically involves a reaction lag, and if this lag is one year or more, the controlled variables of an annual model such as (2.1) to (2.4) then fall under the predetermined category which is described later in this section. See Theil (1964) for details on such decision rules.

that under this interpretation there are five exogenous variables rather than four.

Extension of the Reduced-Form Concept When Lagged Endogenous Variables Are Present

In spite of the equality of the numbers of equations and of endogenous variables it is impossible to express each of these variables in terms of exogenous variables and disturbances only.[3] This is due to the presence of lagged values of the endogenous variables ($P_{\alpha-1}, K_{\alpha-1}, X_{\alpha-1}$). However, under general conditions it is possible to express each current endogenous variable in terms of (1) current exogenous variables, (2) lagged variables, and (3) disturbances. For example, if we apply this idea to total output in year α, we find after some algebra:

$$(2.5)\quad X_\alpha = \frac{\beta_0 + \beta_0' + \beta_0''(-\beta_1 + \beta_3 - \beta_1')}{D} \qquad \text{constant term}$$

$$+ \frac{\beta_3 W_\alpha' - (\beta_1 + \beta_1')T_\alpha + G_\alpha + \beta_3''(-\beta_1 + \beta_3 - \beta_1')(\alpha - 1931)}{D} \qquad \text{current exogenous}$$

$$+ \frac{(\beta_2 + \beta_2')P_{\alpha-1} + \beta_3' K_{\alpha-1} + \beta_2''(-\beta_1 + \beta_3 - \beta_1')X_{\alpha-1}}{D} \qquad \text{lagged endogenous}$$

$$+ \frac{\epsilon_\alpha + \epsilon_\alpha' + (-\beta_1 + \beta_3 - \beta_1')\epsilon_\alpha''}{D} \qquad \text{disturbances}$$

where

$$(2.6)\qquad D = 1 - (\beta_1 + \beta_1')(1 - \beta_1'') - \beta_3\beta_1''$$

The condition for the existence of this solution is $D \neq 0$ or, equivalently,

$$(2.7)\qquad (\beta_1 + \beta_1')(1 - \beta_1'') + \beta_3\beta_1'' \neq 1$$

The left-hand side of this inequality can be regarded as a weighted average of the marginal propensity to spend out of current profit income ($\beta_1 + \beta_1'$) and the marginal propensity to consume out of current wage income (β_3), the weights being $1 - \beta_1''$ and β_1'', respectively. The weight β_1'' is equal to the short-run change in the private wage bill induced by a unit increase in total private production; see (2.3).

[3] Specifically, it is not possible to express $C_\alpha, \ldots, X_\alpha$ in terms of the exogenous variables of the same year ($W_\alpha', T_\alpha, G_\alpha$, and α) and the disturbances of that year ($\epsilon_\alpha, \epsilon_\alpha', \epsilon_\alpha''$). It is possible, however, to express $C_\alpha, \ldots, X_\alpha$ in terms of exogenous variables and disturbances of year α *and earlier years*. This will be pursued in Section 9.7.

Equation (2.5) is an example of the new interpretation of the reduced form when structural equations contain lagged endogenous variables. These lagged variables, like the exogenous variables, have their place in the right-hand side of the reduced form. The justification is that while the exogenous variables are by assumption independent of the operation of the system, the lagged endogenous variables are at least independent of the *current* operation of the system if the vectors $[\epsilon_\alpha \quad \epsilon'_\alpha \quad \epsilon''_\alpha]$, $\alpha = 1, \ldots, n$ are stochastically independent. This is readily seen from (2.5) when we lag that equation by one period. The left-hand side then becomes $X_{\alpha-1}$, the αth value of a lagged endogenous variable. The first two lines on the right are constants. The fourth line contains disturbances in $\alpha - 1$, which are by assumption independent of the operation of the system in year α. The third line contains $P_{\alpha-2}$, $K_{\alpha-2}$, and $X_{\alpha-2}$, which are a fortiori independent of what happens in α.

Jointly Dependent and Predetermined Variables

The distinction between exogenous and endogenous variables on the one hand and that between current and lagged variables on the other hand calls for a simplification of the terminology. Consider the following double dichotomy:

	Endogenous variables	Exogenous variables
Current variables	Current endogenous	Current exogenous
Lagged variables	Lagged endogenous	Lagged exogenous

Current endogenous variables (C_α, P_α, W_α, I_α, K_α, X_α in Klein's Model I) are called *jointly dependent* variables. They are the left-hand variables of the reduced-form equations. (We shall usually delete the adverb "jointly" when considering only one such variable.) All other variables are called *predetermined*; they are either lagged or exogenous or both lagged and exogenous. For a lagged endogenous variable such as $P_{\alpha-1}$ the word predetermined should be interpreted in a temporal sense. For a current exogenous variable such as W'_α the word is to be interpreted in a causal sense, the values taken by the variable being determined "from the outside." For a lagged exogenous variable both interpretations apply. [In the model (2.1) to (2.4) there are no lagged exogenous variables.]

The function of the reduced form under the new interpretation is thus to describe the behavior of the jointly dependent variables in terms of the predetermined variables and the disturbances. This can be conveniently illustrated by means of a so-called *arrow scheme*, which is given in Figure 9.1 for the case of Klein's Model I. The jointly dependent variables are indicated by circles below the shaded area, the current exogenous variables by squares in that area, and all lagged variables (endogenous and exogenous) by circles above the area. Each structural equation is represented by a set of arrows pointing to the dependent variable that occurs in the left-hand side of the equation. For example, the consumption function (2.1) has four arrows, all pointing to C and originating from, respectively, P, P_{-1}, W, and W'. (The α subscript is deleted to obtain a simpler picture.) It should be clear that there cannot be any arrows pointing to variables inside or above the shaded area. In the latter case we would have a lagged variable dependent on a current

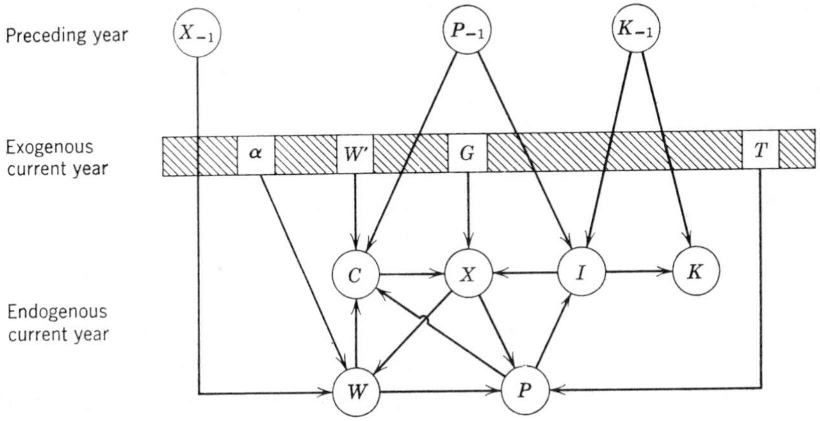

Fig. 9.1 Arrow scheme of Klein's Model I.

variable, which is absurd. In the former case an exogenous variable depends on an endogenous variable in the same period, which is equally absurd because the exogenous values are—by definition—determined independently of the mechanism described by the arrows.

Historical Note

The idea of a system of simultaneous economic relations is from TINBERGEN, who published a 24-equation system of the Dutch economy in 1936. The article has been translated into English in Tinbergen (1959, pp. 37–84). Among the well-known later models are Tinbergen's League of Nations study (1939) and the models of KLEIN (1950), KLEIN and GOLDBERGER (1955), and the Brookings model published in a monograph edited by DUESENBERRY, FROMM, KLEIN, and KUH (1965). The last model is the largest ever constructed. For a survey of these and other models, see NERLOVE (1966). Also see THEIL (1961, 1966) and STEKLER (1968) for evaluations of forecasts obtained from simultaneous-equation models.

The estimation method used for the earlier models was ordinary least-squares, applied to each structural equation separately. HAAVELMO (1943) was the first to consider the statistical implications of simultaneity. His article led to large-scale research activity in this area, particularly by the Cowles Commission for Research in Economics at The University of Chicago. Most of the results obtained there are summarized in two monographs, KOOPMANS (1950) and HOOD and KOOPMANS (1953).

Problems

2.1 Verify the dimensions of the coefficients of the investment equation (2.2):

β_0' billions of 1934 dollars per year
β_1' dimensionless
β_2' dimensionless
β_3' reciprocal of a year

Indicate the dimensions of the coefficients of eqs. (2.1) and (2.3).

2.2 Prove the reduced-form equation (2.5). [*Hint*. Start with the first definitional equation of (2.4) and then use the behavioral equations and the second definitional equation.]

2.3 Give your opinion of the following argument. "The total amount of investment this year depends on what entrepreneurs think profits will be next year. This is an example of a future variable (profits next year) which affects a current variable (investment this year). It is therefore possible that a lagged variable (investment last year) depends on a current variable (profits this year), contrary to the statement made at the end of the section."

2.4 Consider Problem 1.2 of the previous section, where capital stock at the beginning of the year is regarded as fixed. Compare this with the first subsection of Section 7.1 to conclude that one may object to this assumption when it is made for a series of successive years on the grounds that the change in capital stock is equal to net investment and that the latter variable is closely related to the dependent variable (gross investment including maintenance and repairs) of the investment equation. Next write I_α^N for net investment and I_α^G for gross investment in year α and derive the following equation system from eqs. (1.1) to (1.3) of Section 7.1:

$$I_\alpha^N = q_1c_0 + q_1c_1F_{\alpha-1} - q_1C_{\alpha-1} + \epsilon_\alpha \tag{2.8}$$

$$I_\alpha^G = I_\alpha^N + q_2C_{\alpha-1} + \epsilon_\alpha' \tag{2.9}$$

$$C_\alpha - C_{\alpha-1} = I_\alpha^N \tag{2.10}$$

where ϵ_α and ϵ'_α are random disturbances. Interpret I^N, I^G, and C as the three endogenous variables of the system and prove that the investment equations for General Electric and Westinghouse that were estimated in Section 7.1 can each be regarded as a reduced-form equation of this system:

(2.11) $$I_\alpha^G = q_1c_0 + q_1c_1F_{\alpha-1} + (q_2 - q_1)C_{\alpha-1} + (\epsilon_\alpha + \epsilon'_\alpha)$$

the two right-hand variables being predetermined because they are lagged.

9.3 Notation and Assumptions[A]

Notation for the System as a Whole

Before proceeding to the estimation of the parameters of a complete linear system in L jointly dependent variables and K predetermined variables, we should design a systematic notation. Write $y_{\alpha l}$ for the αth value of the lth dependent variable and $x_{\alpha k}$ for the corresponding value of the kth predetermined variable. The number of observations is n, each consisting of $K + L$ values:

(3.1) $$(y_{\alpha 1} \quad y_{\alpha 2} \quad \cdots \quad y_{\alpha L} \quad x_{\alpha 1} \quad x_{\alpha 2} \quad \cdots \quad x_{\alpha K}) \qquad \alpha = 1, \ldots, n$$

The x, y notation suggests that the predetermined variables are the extensions of the explanatory variables of the standard linear model and that the jointly dependent variables are the extensions of the single dependent variable of that model. This is indeed true to a large extent.

Since the system is complete by assumption, it consists of L structural equations, and the jth can be written as follows:

(3.2) $$\sum_{l=1}^{L} \gamma_{lj} y_{\alpha l} + \sum_{k=1}^{K} \beta_{kj} x_{\alpha k} = \epsilon_{\alpha j} \qquad \begin{array}{l} \alpha = 1, \ldots, n \\ j = 1, \ldots, L \end{array}$$

where $\epsilon_{\alpha j}$ is the disturbance of the αth observation and the jth equation and the β's and γ's are parameters to be estimated. We introduce the $n \times K$ matrix $\mathbf{X}$ and the $n \times L$ matrix $\mathbf{Y}$ of, respectively, the values taken by the predetermined variables and those taken by the jointly dependent variables:

(3.3)
$$\mathbf{X} = [x_{\alpha k}] = \begin{bmatrix} x_{11} & x_{12} & \cdots & x_{1K} \\ x_{21} & x_{22} & \cdots & x_{2K} \\ \cdot & \cdot & & \cdot \\ \cdot & \cdot & & \cdot \\ \cdot & \cdot & & \cdot \\ x_{n1} & x_{n2} & \cdots & x_{nK} \end{bmatrix} \qquad \mathbf{Y} = [y_{\alpha l}] = \begin{bmatrix} y_{11} & y_{12} & \cdots & y_{1L} \\ y_{21} & y_{22} & \cdots & y_{2L} \\ \cdot & \cdot & & \cdot \\ \cdot & \cdot & & \cdot \\ \cdot & \cdot & & \cdot \\ y_{n1} & y_{n2} & \cdots & y_{nL} \end{bmatrix}$$

Comparing this notation with (3.1), we see that the n observations consist of the successive rows of $[\mathbf{Y} \quad \mathbf{X}]$. Furthermore, we introduce the $n \times L$

matrix **E** of disturbances:

$$
(3.4) \qquad \mathbf{E} = [\epsilon_{\alpha j}] = \begin{bmatrix} \epsilon_{11} & \epsilon_{12} & \cdots & \epsilon_{1L} \\ \epsilon_{21} & \epsilon_{22} & \cdots & \epsilon_{2L} \\ \cdot & \cdot & & \cdot \\ \cdot & \cdot & & \cdot \\ \cdot & \cdot & & \cdot \\ \epsilon_{n1} & \epsilon_{n2} & \cdots & \epsilon_{nL} \end{bmatrix} = [\boldsymbol{\epsilon}_1 \quad \boldsymbol{\epsilon}_2 \quad \cdots \quad \boldsymbol{\epsilon}_L]
$$

where $\boldsymbol{\epsilon}_j$ is the jth column of **E** (corresponding to the jth equation). Finally, consider the $K \times L$ matrix **B** and the $L \times L$ matrix $\boldsymbol{\Gamma}$ of parameters:

(3.5)

$$
\mathbf{B} = [\beta_{kj}] = \begin{bmatrix} \beta_{11} & \beta_{12} & \cdots & \beta_{1L} \\ \beta_{21} & \beta_{22} & \cdots & \beta_{2L} \\ \cdot & \cdot & & \cdot \\ \cdot & \cdot & & \cdot \\ \cdot & \cdot & & \cdot \\ \beta_{K1} & \beta_{K2} & \cdots & \beta_{KL} \end{bmatrix} \qquad \boldsymbol{\Gamma} = [\gamma_{lj}] = \begin{bmatrix} \gamma_{11} & \gamma_{12} & \cdots & \gamma_{1L} \\ \gamma_{21} & \gamma_{22} & \cdots & \gamma_{2L} \\ \cdot & \cdot & & \cdot \\ \cdot & \cdot & & \cdot \\ \cdot & \cdot & & \cdot \\ \gamma_{L1} & \gamma_{L2} & \cdots & \gamma_{LL} \end{bmatrix}
$$

Note that $\boldsymbol{\Gamma}$ is square and that **Y** and **E** are of the same order ($n \times L$) because of the completeness of the system.

Using these matrices, we can write eq. (3.2) for all pairs (α, j) in the following compact form:

$$
(3.6) \qquad \mathbf{Y\Gamma} + \mathbf{XB} = \mathbf{E}
$$

For example, the Keynesian model (1.1) and (1.2) becomes

$$
(3.7) \qquad \begin{bmatrix} C_1 & Y_1 \\ C_2 & Y_2 \\ \cdot & \cdot \\ \cdot & \cdot \\ \cdot & \cdot \\ C_n & Y_n \end{bmatrix} \begin{bmatrix} 1 & 1 \\ -\beta & -1 \end{bmatrix} + \begin{bmatrix} I_1 \\ I_2 \\ \cdot \\ \cdot \\ \cdot \\ I_n \end{bmatrix} [0 \quad 1] = \begin{bmatrix} \epsilon_1 & 0 \\ \epsilon_2 & 0 \\ \cdot & \cdot \\ \cdot & \cdot \\ \cdot & \cdot \\ \epsilon_n & 0 \end{bmatrix}
$$

If we take any row (say, the αth) of such a matrix equation, we obtain all L structural equations corresponding to the αth observation. In the general case (3.6) we then have on the left:

$$
[y_{\alpha 1} \quad \cdots \quad y_{\alpha L}] \begin{bmatrix} \gamma_{11} & \cdots & \gamma_{1L} \\ \cdot & & \cdot \\ \cdot & & \cdot \\ \cdot & & \cdot \\ \gamma_{L1} & \cdots & \gamma_{LL} \end{bmatrix} + [x_{\alpha 1} \quad \cdots \quad x_{\alpha K}] \begin{bmatrix} \beta_{11} & \cdots & \beta_{1L} \\ \cdot & & \cdot \\ \cdot & & \cdot \\ \cdot & & \cdot \\ \beta_{K1} & \cdots & \beta_{KL} \end{bmatrix}
$$

and on the right $[\epsilon_{\alpha 1} \quad \cdots \quad \epsilon_{\alpha L}]$. Note that the second subscript of the elements of **B**, $\boldsymbol{\Gamma}$, and **E** is the number of the structural equation. Similarly, if we take any column (say, the jth) of the matrix equation (3.6), we obtain the jth structural equation for all n observations:

$$\begin{bmatrix} y_{11} & \cdots & y_{1L} \\ \cdot & & \cdot \\ \cdot & & \cdot \\ \cdot & & \cdot \\ y_{n1} & \cdots & y_{nL} \end{bmatrix} \begin{bmatrix} \gamma_{1j} \\ \cdot \\ \cdot \\ \cdot \\ \gamma_{Lj} \end{bmatrix} + \begin{bmatrix} x_{11} & \cdots & x_{1K} \\ \cdot & & \cdot \\ \cdot & & \cdot \\ \cdot & & \cdot \\ x_{n1} & \cdots & x_{nK} \end{bmatrix} \begin{bmatrix} \beta_{1j} \\ \cdot \\ \cdot \\ \cdot \\ \beta_{Kj} \end{bmatrix} = \begin{bmatrix} \epsilon_{1j} \\ \cdot \\ \cdot \\ \cdot \\ \epsilon_{nj} \end{bmatrix}$$

On the basis of this notation we formulate the assumptions that will be used in the derivations of this chapter. They will be extended in Section 10.1.

Completeness of the System

The matrix $\mathbf{\Gamma}$ is square because there are as many equations as jointly dependent variables. It is assumed to be nonsingular, so that the system can be solved for these variables:

$$\mathbf{Y} = -\mathbf{X}\mathbf{B}\mathbf{\Gamma}^{-1} + \mathbf{E}\mathbf{\Gamma}^{-1} \tag{3.8}$$

This is the reduced form for all n observations and all L jointly dependent variables.

Lagged Endogenous Variables Excluded

Current endogenous variables as explanatory variables represent one departure from the standard linear model; the presence of lagged endogenous variables implies another departure. Our statistical derivations will be simplified if we confine ourselves to the former and postpone treatment of the latter to Chapter 10. The reason is that if all predetermined variables are exogenous, we can maintain that the $n \times K$ matrix $\mathbf{X}$ consists of nonstochastic elements. It will also be assumed that this $\mathbf{X}$ has full column rank.

Means, Variances, and Covariances of Disturbances

The assumptions on the disturbance moments of the first and second order are basically the same as those which were made in Section 7.1. The expectations are supposed to vanish:

$$\mathscr{E}\boldsymbol{\epsilon}_j = \mathbf{0} \qquad j = 1, \ldots, L \tag{3.9}$$

where $\boldsymbol{\epsilon}_j$ is the jth column of the disturbance matrix $\mathbf{E}$ or, equivalently, the n-element disturbance vector of the jth structural equation. All lagged covariances, $\mathscr{E}(\epsilon_{\alpha j}\epsilon_{\eta l})$ for $\alpha \neq \eta$, are assumed to vanish[4] and all contemporaneous

[4] This condition is automatically satisfied by the disturbance vectors $[\epsilon_\alpha \;\; \epsilon'_\alpha \;\; \epsilon''_\alpha]$, $\alpha = 1, \ldots, n$ of Klein's Model I when they are stochastically independent. Recall that this independence condition was mentioned in the paragraph below eq. (2.7), which was concerned with the justification of the role of lagged endogenous variables as predetermined variables.

covariances, $\mathscr{E}(\epsilon_{\alpha j}\epsilon_{\alpha l})$, are supposed to be constant in the sense of being independent of α. We will write σ_{jl} for the covariance of $\epsilon_{\alpha j}$ and $\epsilon_{\alpha l}$, so that the disturbance variance of the jth structural equation is written σ_{jj}. The assumption on the second moments can then be compactly written as

$$\mathscr{E}(\boldsymbol{\epsilon}_j\boldsymbol{\epsilon}_l') = \sigma_{jl}\mathbf{I} \qquad j, l = 1, \ldots, L \tag{3.10}$$

The left-hand side contains the contemporaneous covariances $\mathscr{E}(\epsilon_{\alpha j}\epsilon_{\alpha l})$ on the diagonal and the right-hand side indicates that these are all equal to σ_{jl}. The off-diagonal elements on the left are all covariances which are not contemporaneous and, therefore, are equal to zero as $\sigma_{jl}I$ on the right confirms.

The σ's defined in (3.10) can be arranged in matrix form:

$$\boldsymbol{\Sigma} = [\sigma_{jl}] = \begin{bmatrix} \sigma_{11} & \sigma_{12} & \cdots & \sigma_{1L} \\ \sigma_{21} & \sigma_{22} & \cdots & \sigma_{2L} \\ \cdot & \cdot & & \cdot \\ \cdot & \cdot & & \cdot \\ \cdot & \cdot & & \cdot \\ \sigma_{L1} & \sigma_{L2} & \cdots & \sigma_{LL} \end{bmatrix} \tag{3.11}$$

which is the covariance matrix of $[\epsilon_{\alpha 1} \ \cdots \ \epsilon_{\alpha L}]$ for any value of α, as is easily verified. Therefore, $\boldsymbol{\Sigma}$ is symmetric and positive semidefinite. The only difference with the corresponding assumptions of Section 7.1 is that we do not exclude the possibility of a singular $\boldsymbol{\Sigma}$, since doing so would force us to consider only systems without definitional equations; see Problem 3.3.

Problems

3.1 Define the observation matrix $[\mathbf{Y} \ \ \mathbf{X}]$ of the variables of Klein's Model I as follows:

$$\mathbf{Y} = \begin{bmatrix} C_1 & P_1 & W_1 & I_1 & K_1 & X_1 \\ \cdot & \cdot & \cdot & \cdot & \cdot & \cdot \\ \cdot & \cdot & \cdot & \cdot & \cdot & \cdot \\ \cdot & \cdot & \cdot & \cdot & \cdot & \cdot \\ C_n & P_n & W_n & I_n & K_n & X_n \end{bmatrix} \tag{3.12}$$

$$\mathbf{X} = \begin{bmatrix} 1 & W_1' & T_1 & G_1 & -\frac{1}{2}(n-1) & P_0 & K_0 & X_0 \\ \cdot & \cdot & \cdot & \cdot & \cdot & \cdot & \cdot & \cdot \\ \cdot & \cdot & \cdot & \cdot & \cdot & \cdot & \cdot & \cdot \\ \cdot & \cdot & \cdot & \cdot & \cdot & \cdot & \cdot & \cdot \\ 1 & W_n' & T_n & G_n & \frac{1}{2}(n-1) & P_{n-1} & K_{n-1} & X_{n-1} \end{bmatrix} \tag{3.13}$$

The first column of $\mathbf{X}$ refers to the constant-term variable, the next four columns to the other exogenous variables, and the last three columns to the lagged endogenous variables. (Note that the fifth column corresponds to the linear trend, that this variable is measured as a deviation from the mean, and that it is assumed that n is odd.) Write the model in the form (3.6).

3.2 Consider the parameter matrices $\mathbf{B}$ and $\mathbf{\Gamma}$ of (3.7) to conclude that they contain six elements as a whole, only one of which is unknown. Do the same for Klein's Model I (see Problem 3.1) to conclude that the total number of elements of $\mathbf{B}$ and $\mathbf{\Gamma}$ is 84, the following of which are known: (1) 42 elements (all 1, 0, or -1) which are coefficients of definitional equations, (2) 26 zero elements which are coefficients of variables not occurring in a behavioral equation, (3) three unit elements which are coefficients of the left-hand variables (C_α, I_α, W_α) in the behavioral equations (2.1) to (2.3), and (4) one pair of equal elements because of the equality of the coefficients of W_α and W'_α in the consumption function (2.1). (This counts effectively as one known element because the coefficient of W'_α is known as soon as that of W_α is known or vice versa.) Conclude that only one seventh of the 84 elements of $\mathbf{B}$ and $\mathbf{\Gamma}$ are unknown.

3.3 Prove that the matrix $\mathbf{\Sigma}$ defined in (3.11) has one zero row and one zero column for each definitional equation. What can be said about the rank of $\mathbf{\Sigma}$ in the case of Klein's Model I?

3.4 Consider the L successive columns of the disturbance matrix $\mathbf{E\Gamma}^{-1}$ of the reduced form (3.8). Prove that under the assumptions of this section the disturbances of each of the L reduced-form equations have zero mean and constant contemporaneous covariances and zero lagged covariances. [*Hint*. Prove that the αth disturbance vector of the reduced form and the ηth have the following "cross" covariance matrix:

$$(3.14)\quad \mathscr{E}\left((\mathbf{\Gamma}')^{-1}\begin{bmatrix}\epsilon_{\alpha 1}\\ \cdot\\ \cdot\\ \cdot\\ \epsilon_{\alpha L}\end{bmatrix}[\epsilon_{\eta 1} \quad \cdots \quad \epsilon_{\eta L}]\mathbf{\Gamma}^{-1}\right) = \begin{matrix}(\mathbf{\Gamma}')^{-1}\mathbf{\Sigma}\mathbf{\Gamma}^{-1} & \text{if } \alpha = \eta\\ \mathbf{0} & \text{if } \alpha \neq \eta\end{matrix}$$

which shows that $(\mathbf{\Gamma}')^{-1}\mathbf{\Sigma}\mathbf{\Gamma}^{-1}$ is the contemporaneous covariance matrix of the reduced-form disturbances.]

9.4 The Identification Problem[A]

The notation (3.6) is compact and elegant, and it is very useful for the reduced form (3.8), but it is not really convenient when we want to estimate the parameters of one particular structural equation. The reason is that the parameter matrices $\mathbf{B}$ and $\mathbf{\Gamma}$ are "wasteful" in the sense that normally a large majority of their elements is known to be 1, 0, or −1. This is immediately evident from (3.7) and, in fact, Problem 3.2 shows that the fraction of unknown elements of $\mathbf{B}$ and $\mathbf{\Gamma}$ is only one seventh in the case of Klein's Model I and one sixth in that of the Keynesian model (1.1) and (1.2). Therefore we shall consider matters of notation prior to estimation. When attempting to estimate, however, we shall find that there is an identification problem to be solved prior to the estimation.

Notation for Individual Structural Equations

A considerable economy of notation for separate equations can be obtained, which is illustrated here for the investment function (2.2):

$$(4.1)\qquad \begin{bmatrix} I_1 \\ I_2 \\ \cdot \\ \cdot \\ \cdot \\ I_n \end{bmatrix} = \left[\begin{array}{c|ccc} P_1 & 1 & P_0 & K_0 \\ P_2 & 1 & P_1 & K_1 \\ \cdot & \cdot & \cdot & \cdot \\ \cdot & \cdot & \cdot & \cdot \\ \cdot & \cdot & \cdot & \cdot \\ P_n & 1 & P_{n-1} & K_{n-1} \end{array}\right] \left[\begin{array}{c} \beta_1' \\ \hline \beta_0' \\ \beta_2' \\ \beta_3' \end{array}\right] + \begin{bmatrix} \epsilon_1' \\ \epsilon_2' \\ \cdot \\ \cdot \\ \cdot \\ \epsilon_n' \end{bmatrix}$$

On the right is an $n \times 4$ matrix partitioned into two submatrices. The first submatrix contains the values of the explanatory jointly dependent variables, the second those of the explanatory predetermined variables. In the investment equation there is only one explanatory variable that falls under the jointly dependent category (P_α, current profits) and three which are predetermined ($1, P_{\alpha-1}, K_{\alpha-1}$). The $n \times 4$ matrix is postmultiplied by a 4-element parameter vector which is partitioned conformably. All elements of this vector are unknown, so that the waste mentioned in the previous paragraph is avoided completely.

All L structural equations can in principle be written in the form (4.1):[5]

$$(4.2)\qquad \mathbf{y}_j = \mathbf{Z}_j \boldsymbol{\delta}_j + \boldsymbol{\epsilon}_j \qquad j = 1, \ldots, L$$

The vector $\mathbf{y}_j$ on the left contains the n values C_α in (2.1), I_α in (2.2), and W_α in (2.3). The $n \times N_j$ matrix $\mathbf{Z}_j$ contains all values of the explanatory variables (both jointly dependent and predetermined), and the N_j-element vector $\boldsymbol{\delta}_j$ contains the unknown parameters, N_j being the number of variables in the right-hand side of the jth equation. The vector $\boldsymbol{\epsilon}_j$ (the jth column of $\mathbf{E}$) contains the disturbances of that equation.

[5] Note that in the case of a definitional equation the right-hand side of (4.2) is simply zero, all terms being put to the left of the equality sign, since such equations contain neither unknown parameters ($\boldsymbol{\delta}_j$) nor disturbances ($\boldsymbol{\epsilon}_j$). The problems discussed in this section do not arise in the case of definitional equations.

Perhaps the most obvious estimator of $\boldsymbol{\delta}_j$ is $(\mathbf{Z}_j'\mathbf{Z}_j)^{-1}\mathbf{Z}_j'\mathbf{y}_j$. However, it is not difficult to see that this LS estimator has its complications. Equation (4.2) does not satisfy the conditions of the standard linear model except when there are no jointly dependent variables in the right-hand side. In that special case the equation is said to be "in reduced form" because it describes the left-hand dependent variable exclusively in terms of predetermined variables and a disturbance; the estimation procedure to be described in Section 9.5 is then equivalent with LS (see Problem 5.2). But in all other cases we have to face the problem of the dependence of the disturbances on at least one explanatory variable, and it can be shown that the LS procedure applied to (4.2) leads to an estimator which does not have the property of consistency described in Section 8.1. Therefore it is worthwhile to consider other estimation methods.

Predetermined Variables as Instrumental Variables

Let us return temporarily to the standard linear model and premultiply both sides of its basic equation $\mathbf{y} = \mathbf{X}\boldsymbol{\beta} + \boldsymbol{\epsilon}$ by $\mathbf{X}'$ to obtain $\mathbf{X}'\mathbf{y} = \mathbf{X}'\mathbf{X}\boldsymbol{\beta} + \mathbf{X}'\boldsymbol{\epsilon}$. The vector $\mathbf{X}'\boldsymbol{\epsilon}$ is unknown, but it has zero expectation. If we estimate it to be zero, the equation becomes $\mathbf{X}'\mathbf{y} = \mathbf{X}'\mathbf{X}\mathbf{b}$, where $\mathbf{b}$ is the $\boldsymbol{\beta}$ estimator implied by this procedure; obviously, this $\mathbf{b}$ is the LS estimator. Now suppose that $\mathbf{X}'\boldsymbol{\epsilon}$ does not have zero expectation but that a matrix $\mathbf{W}$ consisting of n rows exists such that $\mathbf{W}'\boldsymbol{\epsilon}$ does have zero expectation. A similar procedure with $\mathbf{X}'$ replaced by $\mathbf{W}'$ leads to $\mathbf{W}'\mathbf{y} = \mathbf{W}'\mathbf{X}\hat{\boldsymbol{\beta}}$, and $\hat{\boldsymbol{\beta}}$ is an estimator which may be solved from these equations under certain conditions.

The procedure described in the previous paragraph is known as the method of *instrumental variables*, and the successive columns of $\mathbf{W}$ are the observations on these variables.[6] The main problem is which variables should be selected as instrumental variables. Consider then (4.2) and imagine that we use all K predetermined variables of the system as instrumental variables for the estimation of $\boldsymbol{\delta}_j$. So we premultiply both sides by $\mathbf{X}'$:

$$\mathbf{X}'\mathbf{y}_j = \mathbf{X}'\mathbf{Z}_j\boldsymbol{\delta}_j + \mathbf{X}'\boldsymbol{\epsilon}_j \tag{4.3}$$

and note that if $\mathbf{X}$ indeed consists of nonstochastic elements, $\mathbf{X}'\boldsymbol{\epsilon}_j$ has zero expectation. The instrumental-variable estimator $\mathbf{d}_j$ of $\boldsymbol{\delta}_j$ can then be solved from $\mathbf{X}'\mathbf{y}_j = \mathbf{X}'\mathbf{Z}_j\mathbf{d}_j$ if $\mathbf{X}'\mathbf{Z}_j$ is square and nonsingular:

$$\mathbf{d}_j = (\mathbf{X}'\mathbf{Z}_j)^{-1}\mathbf{X}'\mathbf{y}_j \qquad \text{if } \mathbf{X}'\mathbf{Z}_j \text{ is square and nonsingular} \tag{4.4}$$

The important issue is obviously whether $\mathbf{X}'\mathbf{Z}_j$ is indeed square and nonsingular. The matrix is of order $K \times N_j$, where K is the total number of predetermined variables in the system (the number of rows of $\mathbf{X}'$) and N_j is

[6] The instrumental variables technique goes back to REIERSØL (1941, 1945).

the number of parameters to be estimated in (4.2). It is readily verified that the procedure is not applicable to any of the behavioral equations of Klein's Model I, since $N_j < K = 8$ [see (3.13)] for each j. However, it does work for the consumption function of the Keynesian model (1.1) and (1.2), since $K = N_j = 1$. The estimator (4.4) of β is

$$b = \frac{\sum I_\alpha C_\alpha}{\sum I_\alpha Y_\alpha} \tag{4.5}$$

which should be compared with the LS estimator $\sum Y_\alpha C_\alpha / \sum Y_\alpha^2$. (All summations are over α from 1 through n.) Note that the nonsingularity condition of (4.4) amounts to $\sum I_\alpha Y_\alpha \neq 0$.

Some Simple Demand-and-Supply Examples

A necessary condition for the existence of the estimator (4.4) is $K = N_j$. The remainder of this section will show that it is of great importance for the estimation of the parameters of the jth equation to ascertain which of the three possibilities, $K \lesseqgtr N_j$, applies.

Consider the following simple demand and supply system:

$$q_\alpha = \beta_0 + \beta_1 p_\alpha + \epsilon_\alpha \qquad (j = 1, \text{demand}) \tag{4.6}$$

$$q_\alpha = \beta_0' + \beta_1' p_\alpha + \epsilon_\alpha' \qquad (j = 2, \text{supply}) \tag{4.7}$$

where q_α is the quantity bought and sold in year α, p_α is the price of the commodity in that year, and ϵ_α and ϵ_α' are random disturbances. The system is regarded as a complete two-equation system with two jointly dependent variables (price and quantity) and the constant-term variable as the only predetermined variable. Hence $K = 1$, $L = 2$. The number of parameters to be estimated is $N_1 = 2$ (demand) and $N_2 = 2$ (supply), so that K is smaller than both N's. This means that (4.3) consists of only one equation for two parameters, both for the demand and the supply equations. The procedure of (4.3) and (4.4) is therefore inapplicable, and Figure 9.2*a* illustrates why this must be so. The demand equation states that the observations are scattered randomly around the downward sloping demand line ($\beta_1 < 0$) and the supply equation states that they are scattered randomly around the upward sloping supply line ($\beta_1' > 0$). Hence the observations must be scattered around the point of intersection. Clearly, there is little hope that we can estimate the parameters of two lines in one plane when the observations all correspond to the intersection point apart from random deviations.

The preceding paragraph concerns a system for which $K < N_j$ holds for all its equations. Additional insight is obtained when the system (4.6) and

(4.7) is modified as follows:

(4.8) $$q_\alpha = \beta_0 + \beta_1 p_\alpha + \epsilon_\alpha \qquad (j = 1, \text{demand})$$

(4.9) $$q_\alpha = \beta_0' + \beta_1' p_\alpha + \beta_2' c_\alpha + \epsilon_\alpha' \qquad (j = 2, \text{supply})$$

where c_α is the price of a raw material in year α, assumed to be exogenous. Hence $K = 2$ in the present system, and $N_1 = 2$ (demand), $N_2 = 3$ (supply). Thus $K = N_1$ and $\mathbf{X}'\mathbf{Z}_1$ is square, so that $\mathbf{d}_1$ of (4.4) exists if $\mathbf{X}'\mathbf{Z}_1$ is also nonsingular. But $K < N_2$ as in the case of the previous paragraph, which suggests that the chances of estimating the parameters of the supply equation

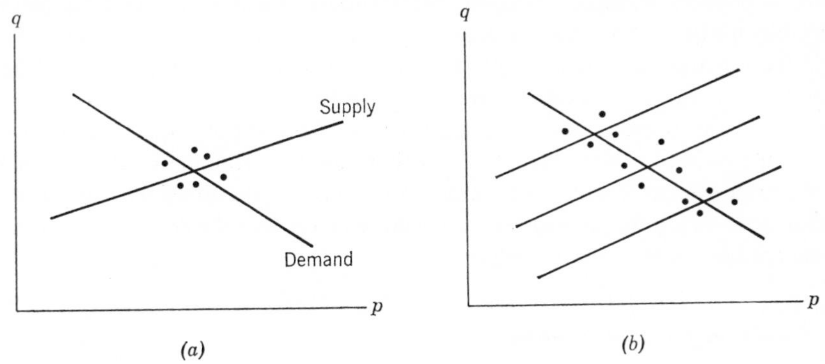

Fig. 9.2 Illustration of the identification problem.

have not improved. The situation is illustrated in Figure 9.2*b*, which contains the same demand line as that of Figure 9.2*a* but three different supply lines, each corresponding to one value of the raw material price *c*. For each such value, the observations must be scattered around the intersection point, but since the supply line shifts with different values of *c*, we obtain a series of intersection points along the demand line. In principle, this enables us to use the observations to estimate the parameters of the demand equation, but there is no evidence yet that we can use them for the estimation of the supply parameters.

A Comparison with Multicollinearity

Multiply both sides of (4.8) by θ and add the result to (4.9):

$$(1 + \theta)q_\alpha = \beta_0' + \theta\beta_0 + (\beta_1' + \theta\beta_1)p_\alpha + \beta_2' c_\alpha + \epsilon_\alpha' + \theta\epsilon_\alpha$$

Assume $\theta \neq -1$ and divide both sides by $1 + \theta$:

(4.10) $$q_\alpha = \frac{\beta_0' + \theta\beta_0}{1 + \theta} + \frac{\beta_1' + \theta\beta_1}{1 + \theta} p_\alpha + \frac{\beta_2'}{1 + \theta} c_\alpha + \frac{\epsilon_\alpha' + \theta\epsilon_\alpha}{1 + \theta}$$

This is an equation in precisely the same variables as those of the supply equation (4.9), but it is actually a mixture of (4.8) and (4.9) as soon as $\theta \neq 0$. The situation has a close resemblance to that of extreme multicollinearity discussed in Section 3.8. We found there that, when the explanatory variables of the standard linear model satisfy a second linear relation in addition to the basic equation $\mathbf{y} = \mathbf{X}\boldsymbol{\beta} + \boldsymbol{\epsilon}$ in which we are interested, the vector $\boldsymbol{\beta}$ ceases to be estimable. Here we have the same situation although with some minor but interesting differences. First, the second relation considered in Section 3.8 contains only explanatory variables, not the dependent variable, whereas in the system (4.8) and (4.9) both equations contain the same dependent variables. Second, the standard linear model of Chapter 3 specifies nothing about the nature of the second relation which prevents the first from being estimated, simply because that model takes the values of the explanatory variables as fixed and given, whereas we can be much more specific in the present case. The parameters of the supply equation are not estimable owing to the presence of another equation (the demand equation) in the same system. Third, we are making a comparison with extreme multicollinearity in which the second relation holds exactly, but the demand equation (4.8) contains a random disturbance.[7]

A Condition for Identification

The problem is evidently that eq. (4.8) contains no variable by which it is distinguished from (4.9). That destroys the estimability of the latter equation. When we have a three-equation system, there are three possibilities for the nonestimability of, say, the first equation: (1) the second equation contains no variables that do not occur in the first, (2) the third contains no variables not occurring in the first, and (3) there exists a linear combination of the second and third equations that contains no variables not occurring in the first equation. Clearly, the third possibility includes (1) and (2) as special cases in which the weight of either the third or the second equation in the linear combination is zero.

More generally, when we have a complete linear system of L equations, the parameters of the jth equation are not estimable when there exists a linear combination of the other $L - 1$ equations that does not contain any of the variables of the system which do not occur in the jth equation; or, to put it in more positive terms, the parameters of the jth equation are not estimable when there exists a linear combination of the other equations that contains

[7] The presence of a disturbance does make a difference, because it can be shown that the parameters of the supply equation may become estimable when certain properties of the disturbance distribution are known (for example, that ϵ_α and ϵ'_α are uncorrelated). This is considered in Section 10.2 below; here we assume that no such knowledge exists.

only the variables which do occur in the jth equation, and possibly fewer. In that case the jth equation is said to be *not identifiable* (or *underidentified*) in its system. The developments of the two previous subsections suggest that this is always the case when $K < N_j$ and hence that

(4.11) $$K \geq N_j$$

is a necessary condition in order that the jth equation can be identified in the system. It will appear in Section 10.2 that this is indeed correct. A necessary and sufficient condition for identifiability will be developed there in terms of the rank of a certain matrix. Condition (4.11) guarantees that this matrix is of such an order that it can have the required rank; therefore it is commonly known as the *order condition* of identifiability.

Note that $K \geq N_j$ is only a necessary, not a sufficient, condition for identifiability. This can be illustrated by means of the following three-equation system (with the observation subscripts deleted for notational simplicity):

(4.12) $$y_1 = \alpha_1 y_2 + \alpha_2 y_3 + \alpha_3 x_1 + \epsilon$$

(4.13) $$y_1 = \beta_2 y_3 + \beta_3 x_1 + \beta_4 x_2 + \beta_5 x_3 + \epsilon'$$

(4.14) $$y_1 = \gamma_1 y_2 + \gamma_3 x_1 + \gamma_4 x_2 + \gamma_5 x_3 + \epsilon''$$

where the x's are predetermined variables. Then $K = N_1 = 3$, which suggests that eq. (4.12) can be identified in the system (4.12) to (4.14). But suppose that it is known that the parameters β_4, γ_4, β_5, and γ_5 are subject to a proportionality of the form $\beta_4/\gamma_4 = \beta_5/\gamma_5$, and write c for this ratio (which may be known or unknown). For example, the economic theory that underlies the model may specify that the effects of changes in x_2 and x_3 in the last two equations are proportional. Multiplication of both sides of (4.14) by c and subtraction from (4.13) gives

$$(1 - c)y_1 = -c\gamma_1 y_2 + \beta_2 y_3 + (\beta_3 - c\gamma_3)x_1 + (\epsilon' - c\epsilon'')$$

which contains the same variables as those of (4.12), so that this equation is underidentified.

Just-Identified and Overidentified Equations

It will prove convenient to make a distinction between the case in which the equality sign holds in (4.11) and that in which the strict inequality sign applies. If the jth equation is identified and $K = N_j$, it is called *just-identified*; equation (4.4) then provides a simple estimation method when the square matrix $\mathbf{X}'\mathbf{Z}_j$ is nonsingular. The case of an identified equation whose N_j is smaller than K is that of an *overidentified* equation. An estimation procedure for its parameters is described in the next section.

Identifiability and the Size of the Equation System

The statistical estimation of the parameters of simultaneous equations has to be confined to identifiable equations. This restriction is less serious than it may seem because structural equations are usually overidentified except when the system is very small, as in (4.8) and (4.9). The reason is that the number K of predetermined variables tends to increase with the number of equations, whereas the number N_j of unknown parameters in any particular equation is typically three or four and usually at most six or seven. In Klein's Model I, for example, we have eight predetermined variables and only four unknown parameters in each of the three behavioral equations. The Klein-Goldberger model, which will be considered in Section 9.8, consists of about 20 equations and contains more than 30 predetermined variables, but the largest value of N_j is seven and the median value is only four. Even that model is not large by present-day standards; the Brookings model of the U.S. economy consists of well over 100 equations.[8]

Problems

4.1 Prove that none of the behavioral equations of Klein's Model I is in reduced form.

4.2 Prove that the estimator (4.4) of the parameters of the demand equation (4.8) in the system (4.8) and (4.9) is obtained by solving b_0 and b_1 from the equations

$$\sum q_\alpha = b_0 n \qquad + b_1 \sum p_\alpha \tag{4.15}$$

$$\sum c_\alpha q_\alpha = b_0 \sum c_\alpha + b_1 \sum c_\alpha p_\alpha \tag{4.16}$$

Also prove that the estimated demand line goes through the center of gravity of the n observations (p_α, q_α).

4.3 Prove that the demand and supply equations (4.8) and (4.9) are both

[8] It is, of course, possible to argue that the moderate values of N_j are the result of the analyst's desire not to overburden his equations with too many variables and unknown coefficients, and that a closer approximation to reality is obtained by including many more variables in each equation. This is the view adopted by LIU (1960); it implies that the dominance of overidentified equations is at least partly due to misspecification. However, although it may be realistic not to exclude the possibility of a certain influence of a great many more variables than the analyst typically introduces as explanatory variables, this does not necessarily mean that he will obtain better *coefficient estimators* by thus raising the number of variables in his equations. It will be shown in Section 11.1 (in a non-simultaneous framework) that there are situations in which better estimators are obtained by deleting a variable whose true coefficient is actually nonzero.

just-identified when $\beta_2 m_\alpha$ ($\beta_2 \neq 0$) is added to the right-hand side of the demand equation, where m_α is per capita income in year α.

9.5 The Two-Stage Least-Squares Estimation Method[A]

When the jth structural equation is overidentified, the K equations which form the vector equation (4.3) contain only $N_j < K$ unknown parameters. However, this is also true for the classical basic equation $\mathbf{y} = \mathbf{X}\boldsymbol{\beta} + \boldsymbol{\epsilon}$ when there are n observations and $K < n$ parameters are to be estimated. Since the disturbance vector $\mathbf{X}'\boldsymbol{\epsilon}$ of (4.3) has zero mean and covariance matrix $\mathscr{E}(\mathbf{X}'\boldsymbol{\epsilon}_j\boldsymbol{\epsilon}_j'\mathbf{X}) = \sigma_{jj}\mathbf{X}'\mathbf{X}$ under the conditions listed at the end of Section 9.3, it is tempting to apply the Aitken procedure of Section 6.1 to (4.3). The parameter vector is then $\boldsymbol{\delta}_j$, the observation matrix is $[\mathbf{X}'\mathbf{y}_j \quad \mathbf{X}'\mathbf{Z}_j]$, and the inverse of the disturbance covariance matrix is $(\sigma_{jj}\mathbf{X}'\mathbf{X})^{-1}$. Hence the Aitken estimator is

$$\mathbf{d}_j = [\mathbf{Z}_j'\mathbf{X}(\mathbf{X}'\mathbf{X})^{-1}\mathbf{X}'\mathbf{Z}_j]^{-1}\mathbf{Z}_j'\mathbf{X}(\mathbf{X}'\mathbf{X})^{-1}\mathbf{X}'\mathbf{y}_j \tag{5.1}$$

which reduces to the estimator (4.4) in the special case of a square and nonsingular matrix $\mathbf{X}'\mathbf{Z}_j$:

$$\mathbf{d}_j = (\mathbf{X}'\mathbf{Z}_j)^{-1}\mathbf{X}'\mathbf{X}(\mathbf{Z}_j'\mathbf{X})^{-1}\mathbf{Z}_j'\mathbf{X}(\mathbf{X}'\mathbf{X})^{-1}\mathbf{X}'\mathbf{y}_j = (\mathbf{X}'\mathbf{Z}_j)^{-1}\mathbf{X}'\mathbf{y}_j$$

It should be noted that Aitken's theorem is not fully applicable to eq. (4.3), since the observation matrix $\mathbf{X}'\mathbf{Z}_j$ on the right-hand variables contains random elements owing to the presence of jointly dependent variables in $\mathbf{Z}_j$. [See, for example, the first column of the $n \times 4$ matrix in the right-hand side of (4.1).] If the theorem were fully applicable, $\mathbf{d}_j$ would be an unbiased estimator of $\boldsymbol{\delta}_j$ and its covariance matrix would be a multiple σ_{jj} of the inverse of the matrix in brackets of (5.1). It will be shown in Section 10.3 that this result is asymptotically valid (for sufficiently large n) under appropriate conditions, and that

$$s_{jj}[\mathbf{Z}_j'\mathbf{X}(\mathbf{X}'\mathbf{X})^{-1}\mathbf{X}'\mathbf{Z}_j]^{-1} \tag{5.2}$$

may then be used as an approximate covariance matrix from which asymptotic standard errors can be computed by taking the square roots of the diagonal elements. The scalar s_{jj} before the brackets in (5.2) is an estimator of the disturbance variance σ_{jj}, defined as the mean square of the associated residuals:[9]

$$s_{jj} = \frac{1}{n}(\mathbf{y}_j - \mathbf{Z}_j\mathbf{d}_j)'(\mathbf{y}_j - \mathbf{Z}_j\mathbf{d}_j) \tag{5.3}$$

[9] No correction for loss of degrees of freedom is applied to s_{jj} because its known properties refer to large samples for which such corrections have no appreciable effect. This situation is analogous to that of the estimation of the contemporaneous covariance matrix discussed in the last subsection of Section 7.1.

The preceding paragraph summarizes the *two-stage least-squares* (abbreviated as 2SLS) estimation technique, which was developed by THEIL (1953a, b, 1961) and independently by BASMANN (1957). The remainder of this section is devoted to an alternative derivation of the 2SLS estimator (5.1), which will clarify its name, and to a numerical illustration.

Alternative Derivation of the 2SLS Estimator

We return to eq. (4.1) and note that the $n \times 4$ matrix $\mathbf{Z}_j$ on the right consists of two submatrices, one containing values of jointly dependent variables and the other consisting of predetermined values. Write $\mathbf{Y}_j$ for the first submatrix (of order $n \times L_j$) and $\mathbf{X}_j$ for the second (of order $n \times K_j$), where $L_j = 1$ and $K_j = 3$ in the case of (4.1). We partition the parameter vector $\boldsymbol{\delta}_j$ conformably, $\boldsymbol{\gamma}_j$ (the coefficients of the L_j explanatory variables which are jointly dependent) and $\boldsymbol{\beta}_j$ (the coefficients of the K_j predetermined explanatory variables):

$$(5.4) \qquad \mathbf{Z}_j = [\mathbf{Y}_j \quad \mathbf{X}_j] \qquad \boldsymbol{\delta}_j = \begin{bmatrix} \boldsymbol{\gamma}_j \\ \boldsymbol{\beta}_j \end{bmatrix} \qquad N_j = L_j + K_j$$

so that (4.2) can be written in the form

$$(5.5) \qquad \mathbf{y}_j = [\mathbf{Y}_j \quad \mathbf{X}_j]\begin{bmatrix} \boldsymbol{\gamma}_j \\ \boldsymbol{\beta}_j \end{bmatrix} + \boldsymbol{\epsilon}_j \qquad j = 1, \ldots, L$$

The notation (5.5) has the virtue that it distinguishes between the jointly dependent and the predetermined variables in the right-hand side. This is important because the former variables are the cause of the complications: they are random and correlated with the disturbance vector $\boldsymbol{\epsilon}_j$. To solve this problem, go back to the reduced form (3.8), which shows that $\mathscr{E}\mathbf{Y} = -\mathbf{X}\mathbf{B}\boldsymbol{\Gamma}^{-1}$, since $\mathscr{E}\mathbf{E} = \mathbf{0}$ and $\mathbf{X}$ is nonrandom. The matrix $\mathscr{E}\mathbf{Y}_j$ is then the submatrix of this $\mathscr{E}\mathbf{Y}$ which corresponds to those jointly dependent variables which occur in the right-hand side of (5.5). Next write this equation in the equivalent form

$$(5.6) \qquad \mathbf{y}_j = [\mathscr{E}\mathbf{Y}_j \quad \mathbf{X}_j]\begin{bmatrix} \boldsymbol{\gamma}_j \\ \boldsymbol{\beta}_j \end{bmatrix} + \boldsymbol{\epsilon}_j + (\mathbf{Y}_j - \mathscr{E}\mathbf{Y}_j)\boldsymbol{\gamma}_j$$

The observation matrix $[\mathscr{E}\mathbf{Y}_j \quad \mathbf{X}_j]$ is not stochastic because the randomness of $\mathbf{Y}_j$ is removed by the expectation operator. It is readily verified (see Problem 5.1) that the elements of the disturbance combination in (5.6) have zero mean and constant variance and are uncorrelated. An obvious estimation procedure is thus LS with $[\mathscr{E}\mathbf{Y}_j \quad \mathbf{X}_j]$ instead of $[\mathbf{Y}_j \quad \mathbf{X}_j]$ as the observation matrix of the explanatory variables.

The objection is, of course, that $\mathscr{E}\mathbf{Y}_j$, being a submatrix of $\mathscr{E}\mathbf{Y} = -\mathbf{XB\Gamma}^{-1}$, is unknown because it depends on unknown parameters. However, there is a simple albeit approximate solution for this problem. Estimate $\mathscr{E}\mathbf{Y}$ by applying LS to each of the reduced-form equations. This is the best linear unbiased approach given that $\mathbf{X}$ (the observation matrix of the right-hand variables in the reduced form) has full column rank and is nonrandom and given that the reduced-form disturbances have zero mean and constant variance and are uncorrelated over time (see Problem 3.4 above).[10] For example, take $\mathbf{y}_1$, the first column of $\mathbf{Y}$, which can be written as the sum of $\mathbf{X}(\mathbf{X}'\mathbf{X})^{-1}\mathbf{X}\mathbf{y}_1$ [$\mathbf{X}$ postmultiplied by the LS coefficient vector $(\mathbf{X}'\mathbf{X})^{-1}\mathbf{X}'\mathbf{y}_1$] and the LS residual vector of the first reduced-form equation, $\mathbf{u}_1 = \mathbf{My}_1$ where $\mathbf{M} = \mathbf{I} - \mathbf{X}(\mathbf{X}'\mathbf{X})^{-1}\mathbf{X}'$. For all L columns of $\mathbf{Y}$ we have

$$\begin{aligned}[\mathbf{y}_1 \quad \cdots \quad \mathbf{y}_L] &= [\mathbf{X}(\mathbf{X}'\mathbf{X})^{-1}\mathbf{X}'\mathbf{y}_1 \quad \cdots \quad \mathbf{X}(\mathbf{X}'\mathbf{X})^{-1}\mathbf{X}'\mathbf{y}_L] + [\mathbf{u}_1 \quad \cdots \quad \mathbf{u}_L] \\ &= \mathbf{X}(\mathbf{X}'\mathbf{X})^{-1}\mathbf{X}'[\mathbf{y}_1 \quad \cdots \quad \mathbf{y}_L] + [\mathbf{u}_1 \quad \cdots \quad \mathbf{u}_L]\end{aligned}$$

or, more compactly,

$$(5.7) \qquad \mathbf{Y} = \mathbf{XP} + \mathbf{U} \qquad \begin{aligned}&\text{where} \quad \mathbf{P} = (\mathbf{X}'\mathbf{X})^{-1}\mathbf{X}'\mathbf{Y}, \\ &\mathbf{U} = \mathbf{MY}, \qquad \mathbf{M} = \mathbf{I} - \mathbf{X}(\mathbf{X}'\mathbf{X})^{-1}\mathbf{X}'\end{aligned}$$

The LS estimator of $\mathscr{E}\mathbf{Y}$ is then $\mathbf{XP} = \mathbf{Y} - \mathbf{U}$ and that of $\mathscr{E}\mathbf{Y}_j$ is

$$(5.8) \quad \mathbf{XP}_j = \mathbf{Y}_j - \mathbf{U}_j \qquad \text{where} \qquad \mathbf{P}_j = (\mathbf{X}'\mathbf{X})^{-1}\mathbf{X}'\mathbf{Y}_j, \qquad \mathbf{U}_j = \mathbf{MY}_j$$

The *first stage* of 2SLS thus amounts to LS estimation of $\mathscr{E}\mathbf{Y}_j$, so that (5.6) is replaced by

$$(5.9) \qquad \mathbf{y}_j = [\mathbf{Y}_j - \mathbf{U}_j \quad \mathbf{X}_j]\begin{bmatrix}\boldsymbol{\gamma}_j \\ \boldsymbol{\beta}_j\end{bmatrix} + \boldsymbol{\epsilon}_j + \mathbf{U}_j\boldsymbol{\gamma}_j$$

The *second stage* is LS applied to (5.9) to obtain estimators $\mathbf{c}_j$, $\mathbf{b}_j$ of $\boldsymbol{\gamma}_j$, $\boldsymbol{\beta}_j$. This means that we have to solve the normal equations:

$$(5.10) \quad \begin{bmatrix}(\mathbf{Y}_j - \mathbf{U}_j)'\mathbf{y}_j \\ \mathbf{X}_j'\mathbf{y}_j\end{bmatrix} = \begin{bmatrix}(\mathbf{Y}_j - \mathbf{U}_j)'(\mathbf{Y}_j - \mathbf{U}_j) & (\mathbf{Y}_j - \mathbf{U}_j)'\mathbf{X}_j \\ \mathbf{X}_j'(\mathbf{Y}_j - \mathbf{U}_j) & \mathbf{X}_j'\mathbf{X}_j\end{bmatrix}\begin{bmatrix}\mathbf{c}_j \\ \mathbf{b}_j\end{bmatrix}$$

Note that $\mathbf{X}_j'\mathbf{U}_j$, which occurs in the off-diagonal blocks on the right, is a zero matrix because it is a submatrix of $\mathbf{X}'\mathbf{U}_j = \mathbf{X}'\mathbf{MY}_j = \mathbf{0}$ (since $\mathbf{MX} = \mathbf{0}$).

[10] One might think that the joint GLS approach applied to all L reduced-form equations simultaneously is superior, but this is not the case because all these equations have the same K predetermined variables as right-hand variables. The reduced form thus falls under the case of identical explanatory variables, for which the combined approach leads to results identical to those of LS as stated at the end of Section 7.1 and proved in Section 7.2.

Furthermore, using this result, we have

$$(5.11)\quad (\mathbf{Y}_j - \mathbf{U}_j)'(\mathbf{Y}_j - \mathbf{U}_j) = (\mathbf{Y}_j - \mathbf{U}_j)'\mathbf{X}\mathbf{P}_j = \mathbf{Y}_j'\mathbf{X}\mathbf{P}_j = \mathbf{Y}_j'(\mathbf{Y}_j - \mathbf{U}_j)$$
$$= \mathbf{Y}_j'\mathbf{Y}_j - \mathbf{Y}_j'\mathbf{U}_j = \mathbf{Y}_j'\mathbf{Y}_j - (\mathbf{X}\mathbf{P}_j + \mathbf{U}_j)'\mathbf{U}_j = \mathbf{Y}_j'\mathbf{Y}_j - \mathbf{U}_j'\mathbf{U}_j$$

Hence we may simplify (5.10) to

$$(5.12)\qquad \begin{bmatrix} (\mathbf{Y}_j - \mathbf{U}_j)'\mathbf{y}_j \\ \mathbf{X}_j'\mathbf{y}_j \end{bmatrix} = \begin{bmatrix} \mathbf{Y}_j'\mathbf{Y}_j - \mathbf{U}_j'\mathbf{U}_j & \mathbf{Y}_j'\mathbf{X}_j \\ \mathbf{X}_j'\mathbf{Y}_j & \mathbf{X}_j'\mathbf{X}_j \end{bmatrix} \begin{bmatrix} \mathbf{c}_j \\ \mathbf{b}_j \end{bmatrix}$$

This result shows that the only difference from the ordinary LS normal equations is the correction by means of LS reduced-form residuals of the sums of squares and products of the jointly dependent variables.

Proof of the Equivalence of the Two Approaches

We shall now show that the solution $\mathbf{c}_j$, $\mathbf{b}_j$ obtained from (5.12) is identical with the estimator $\mathbf{d}_j$ defined in (5.1). First consider

$$(5.13)\quad \mathbf{Z}_j'\mathbf{X}(\mathbf{X}'\mathbf{X})^{-1}\mathbf{X}' = \begin{bmatrix} \mathbf{Y}_j' \\ \mathbf{X}_j' \end{bmatrix}\mathbf{X}(\mathbf{X}'\mathbf{X})^{-1}\mathbf{X}' = \begin{bmatrix} \mathbf{P}_j'\mathbf{X}' \\ \mathbf{X}_j'\mathbf{X}(\mathbf{X}'\mathbf{X})^{-1}\mathbf{X}' \end{bmatrix} = \begin{bmatrix} \mathbf{Y}_j' - \mathbf{U}_j' \\ \mathbf{X}_j' \end{bmatrix}$$

The $\mathbf{X}_j$ part of the last equality sign is based on the fact that $\mathbf{X}_j'\mathbf{X}(\mathbf{X}'\mathbf{X})^{-1}$ is a submatrix of $\mathbf{X}'\mathbf{X}(\mathbf{X}'\mathbf{X})^{-1} = \mathbf{I}$ and thus consists of K_j rows of the $K \times K$ unit matrix; by postmultiplying these rows by $\mathbf{X}'$ we simply obtain $\mathbf{X}_j'$. Next we postmultiply the matrix (5.13) by $\mathbf{y}_j$:

$$(5.14)\qquad \mathbf{Z}_j'\mathbf{X}(\mathbf{X}'\mathbf{X})^{-1}\mathbf{X}'\mathbf{y}_j = \begin{bmatrix} (\mathbf{Y}_j - \mathbf{U}_j)'\mathbf{y}_j \\ \mathbf{X}_j'\mathbf{y}_j \end{bmatrix}$$

and also by $\mathbf{Z}_j$:

$$(5.15)\quad \mathbf{Z}_j'\mathbf{X}(\mathbf{X}'\mathbf{X})^{-1}\mathbf{X}'\mathbf{Z}_j = \begin{bmatrix} \mathbf{Y}_j' - \mathbf{U}_j' \\ \mathbf{X}_j' \end{bmatrix}[\mathbf{Y}_j \quad \mathbf{X}_j] = \begin{bmatrix} \mathbf{Y}_j'\mathbf{Y}_j - \mathbf{U}_j'\mathbf{U}_j & \mathbf{Y}_j'\mathbf{X}_j \\ \mathbf{X}_j'\mathbf{Y}_j & \mathbf{X}_j'\mathbf{X}_j \end{bmatrix}$$

In the last step we again used $\mathbf{U}_j'\mathbf{X}_j = \mathbf{0}$ and $\mathbf{U}_j'\mathbf{Y}_j = \mathbf{U}_j'\mathbf{U}_j$. A comparison of (5.14) and (5.15) with (5.12) and (5.1) shows that $\mathbf{d}_j$ is indeed identical with $[\mathbf{c}_j' \quad \mathbf{b}_j']'$.

The estimation equations (5.12) are $N_j = L_j + K_j$ in number, and the last K_j can be written as

$$(5.16)\qquad \mathbf{X}_j'(\mathbf{y}_j - \mathbf{Y}_j\mathbf{c}_j - \mathbf{X}_j\mathbf{b}_j) = \mathbf{0}$$

which means that the vector of values taken by each explanatory predetermined variable is orthogonal to the vector of 2SLS residuals. This property may be used to obtain an alternative expression for the variance estimator (5.3); see Problem 5.8.

2SLS Estimation of the Consumption Function of Klein's Model I

The 2SLS procedure will now be applied to the consumption function (2.1) of Klein's Model I, reproduced here for the sake of convenience:

$$C_\alpha = \beta_0 + \beta_1 P_\alpha + \beta_2 P_{\alpha-1} + \beta_3(W_\alpha + W'_\alpha) + \epsilon_\alpha \tag{5.17}$$

Since β_3 is multiplied by the sum of two variables, it is convenient to regard this sum as a separate variable. One of these (W) is endogenous and the other (W') is exogenous. This means that the sum $W_\alpha + W'_\alpha$ is random and dependent on ϵ_α, so that the sum variable ($W + W'$) should be considered endogenous. The consumption function can thus be written as $\mathbf{y}_1 = \mathbf{Z}_1\boldsymbol{\delta}_1 + \boldsymbol{\epsilon}_1$ [see (4.2) and (4.1)], the matrices of which are specified as follows:

(5.18)

$$\mathbf{y}_1 = \begin{bmatrix} C_1 \\ \cdot \\ \cdot \\ \cdot \\ C_{21} \end{bmatrix} \quad \mathbf{Z}_1 = \left[\begin{array}{cc:cc} P_1 & W_1 + W'_1 & 1 & P_0 \\ \cdot & \cdot & \cdot & \cdot \\ \cdot & \cdot & \cdot & \cdot \\ \cdot & \cdot & \cdot & \cdot \\ P_{21} & W_{21} + W'_{21} & 1 & P_{20} \end{array}\right] \quad \boldsymbol{\delta}_1 = \begin{bmatrix} \beta_1 \\ \beta_3 \\ \cdot\cdot \\ \beta_0 \\ \beta_2 \end{bmatrix} \quad \boldsymbol{\epsilon}_1 = \begin{bmatrix} \epsilon_1 \\ \cdot \\ \cdot \\ \cdot \\ \epsilon_{21} \end{bmatrix}$$

where the subscript 21 refers to the last of the 21 annual observations of the period 1921 to 1941, which are given in Table 9.1.[11] Note that in the notation (5.4), $\mathbf{Z}_1$ consists of two submatrices $\mathbf{Y}_1$ and $\mathbf{X}_1$, both of order 21 × 2. Also note that the second column of $\mathbf{X}_1$ consists of lagged values of an endogenous variable ($P_{\alpha-1}$). This means that the application is based on weaker assumptions than those listed in Section 9.3 (which require all columns of $\mathbf{X}$ to be nonstochastic); a justification will be provided in the next chapter.

Matrices of sums of squares and products, as far as these are needed for the 2SLS coefficient estimates of the consumption function, are given in Table 9.2: the symmetric 8 × 8 matrix $\mathbf{X}'\mathbf{X}$, the 2 × 8 matrix $\mathbf{Y}'_1\mathbf{X}$, and the 1 × 8 matrix $\mathbf{y}'_1\mathbf{X}$. Next we compute

$$\begin{bmatrix} \mathbf{Y}'_1\mathbf{Y}_1 - \mathbf{U}'_1\mathbf{U}_1 \\ \mathbf{y}'_1(\mathbf{Y}_1 - \mathbf{U}_1) \end{bmatrix} = \begin{bmatrix} \mathbf{Y}'_1\mathbf{X}(\mathbf{X}'\mathbf{X})^{-1}\mathbf{X}'\mathbf{Y}_1 \\ \mathbf{y}'_1\mathbf{X}(\mathbf{X}'\mathbf{X})^{-1}\mathbf{X}'\mathbf{Y}_1 \end{bmatrix} = \begin{bmatrix} 6285.300 & 15076.144 \\ 15076.144 & 37235.862 \\ \cdots & \cdots \\ 19507.721 & 48010.448 \end{bmatrix} \begin{matrix} P \\ W + W' \\ \\ C \end{matrix}$$

$$\qquad\qquad\qquad\qquad\qquad\qquad P \qquad\quad W + W'$$

[11] The data are reproduced from Klein (1950, p. 135). Government nonwage expenditure (G) is defined as Klein's variable G minus the government wage bill (W'). Klein's variable $Y + T - W_2$ is identical with our X.

Table 9.1

Time Series Data on the Variables of Klein's Model I

Year	C	P	W	I	K_{-1}	X	W'	G	T
1920	39.8	12.7	28.8	2.7	180.1	44.9	2.2	2.4	3.4
21	41.9	12.4	25.5	−.2	182.8	45.6	2.7	3.9	7.7
22	45.0	16.9	29.3	1.9	182.6	50.1	2.9	3.2	3.9
23	49.2	18.4	34.1	5.2	184.5	57.2	2.9	2.8	4.7
24	50.6	19.4	33.9	3.0	189.7	57.1	3.1	3.5	3.8
25	52.6	20.1	35.4	5.1	192.7	61.0	3.2	3.3	5.5
26	55.1	19.6	37.4	5.6	197.8	64.0	3.3	3.3	7.0
27	56.2	19.8	37.9	4.2	203.4	64.4	3.6	4.0	6.7
28	57.3	21.1	39.2	3.0	207.6	64.5	3.7	4.2	4.2
29	57.8	21.7	41.3	5.1	210.6	67.0	4.0	4.1	4.0
1930	55.0	15.6	37.9	1.0	215.7	61.2	4.2	5.2	7.7
31	50.9	11.4	34.5	−3.4	216.7	53.4	4.8	5.9	7.5
32	45.6	7.0	29.0	−6.2	213.3	44.3	5.3	4.9	8.3
33	46.5	11.2	28.5	−5.1	207.1	45.1	5.6	3.7	5.4
34	48.7	12.3	30.6	−3.0	202.0	49.7	6.0	4.0	6.8
35	51.3	14.0	33.2	−1.3	199.0	54.4	6.1	4.4	7.2
36	57.7	17.6	36.8	2.1	197.7	62.7	7.4	2.9	8.3
37	58.7	17.3	41.0	2.0	199.8	65.0	6.7	4.3	6.7
38	57.5	15.3	38.2	−1.9	201.8	60.9	7.7	5.3	7.4
39	61.6	19.0	41.6	1.3	199.9	69.5	7.8	6.6	8.9
1940	65.0	21.1	45.0	3.3	201.2	75.7	8.0	7.4	9.6
41	69.7	23.5	53.3	4.9	204.5	88.4	8.5	13.8	11.6

The left-hand column vector in (5.12) is thus

$$(5.19) \qquad \begin{bmatrix} (\mathbf{Y}_1 - \mathbf{U}_1)'\mathbf{y}_1 \\ \mathbf{X}_1'\mathbf{y}_1 \end{bmatrix} = \begin{bmatrix} 19507.721 \\ 48010.448 \\ \cdots\cdots \\ 1133.900 \\ 18929.370 \end{bmatrix} \begin{matrix} P \\ W + W' \\ \\ 1 \\ P_{-1} \end{matrix}$$

the last two elements of which are taken directly from Table 9.2. For the square matrix on the right in (5.12) we have

$$(5.20) \qquad \begin{bmatrix} \mathbf{Y}_1'\mathbf{Y}_1 - \mathbf{U}_1'\mathbf{U}_1 & \mathbf{Y}_1'\mathbf{X}_1 \\ \mathbf{X}_1'\mathbf{Y}_1 & \mathbf{X}_1'\mathbf{X}_1 \end{bmatrix}$$

$$= \begin{bmatrix} 6285.300 & 15076.144 & \vdots & 354.70 & 6070.13 \\ 15076.144 & 37235.862 & \vdots & 871.10 & 14617.95 \\ \cdots & \cdots & \cdots & \cdots & \cdots \\ 354.70 & 871.10 & \vdots & 21.00 & 343.90 \\ 6070.13 & 14617.95 & \vdots & 343.90 & 5956.29 \end{bmatrix} \begin{matrix} P \\ W + W' \\ \\ 1 \\ P_{-1} \end{matrix}$$

$$\begin{matrix} P & \quad W + W' & \quad 1 & \quad P_{-1} \end{matrix}$$

Table 9.2

Sums of Squares and Products for 2SLS Estimation of the Consumption Function (2.1)

1	W'	T	G	$\alpha - 1931$	P_{-1}	K_{-1}	X_{-1}	
				X′X				
21.00	107.50	142.90	100.70	.00	343.90	4210.40	1217.70	1
	626.87	789.27	573.32	238.00	1746.22	21683.18	6364.43	W'
		1054.95	756.84	176.00	2348.48	28766.25	8436.53	T
			596.43	183.70	1705.64	20342.96	6109.07	G
				770.00	−11.90	590.60	495.60	$\alpha - 1931$
					5956.29	69073.54	20542.22	P_{-1}
						846132.70	244984.77	K_{-1}
							72200.03	X_{-1}
				$\mathbf{Y}_1'\mathbf{X}$				
354.70	1821.11	2405.53	1756.94	18.90	6070.13	70946.78	21030.44	P
871.10	4670.94	6104.89	4451.71	698.90	14617.95	175153.74	51652.94	$W + W'$
				$\mathbf{y}_1'\mathbf{X}$				
1133.90	5977.33	7858.86	5656.35	577.70	18929.37	227767.38	66815.25	C

We then invert this matrix and postmultiply the inverse by the column (5.19), which gives the following estimate of the consumption function:

$$C = \underset{(1.3)}{16.6} + \underset{(.12)}{.02P} + \underset{(.11)}{.22P_{-1}} + \underset{(.04)}{.81(W + W')} \tag{5.21}$$

The figures in parentheses are standard errors computed according to (5.2), where

$$s_{11} = 1.0441 \tag{5.22}$$

is computed by means of formula (5.25) below. The application of this formula requires the following sums of squares and products which are not given in Table 9.2:

$$\begin{bmatrix} \mathbf{y}_1'\mathbf{y}_1 & \mathbf{y}_1'\mathbf{Y}_1 \\ \mathbf{Y}_1'\mathbf{y}_1 & \mathbf{Y}_1'\mathbf{Y}_1 \end{bmatrix} = \begin{bmatrix} 62166.63 & 19566.35 & 48054.11 \\ & 6347.25 & 15117.72 \\ & & 37275.87 \end{bmatrix} \begin{matrix} C \\ P \\ W + W' \end{matrix} \tag{5.23}$$

Problems

5.1 Consider the disturbance vector $\boldsymbol{\epsilon}_j + (\mathbf{Y}_j - \mathscr{E}\mathbf{Y}_j)\boldsymbol{\gamma}_j$ of eq. (5.6). Prove that under the conditions listed at the end of Section 9.3, its n elements have zero mean and constant variance and are uncorrelated. (*Hint.* Compare Problem 3.4.)

5.2 Prove that if the jth structural equation contains no jointly dependent variables in the right-hand side ($L_j = 0$), the 2SLS coefficient estimator is obtained by means of an LS regression on the explanatory variables.

5.3 (*Geometric interpretation of 2SLS*) Consider the n-dimensional Euclidean space with origin O. For each variable, measure the first observation along the first axis, the second along the second axis, and so on. Write $Y_1, \ldots, Y_{L_j}$ for the points corresponding to the jointly dependent variables occurring in the right-hand side of (5.5), $X_1, \ldots, X_{K_j}$ for the points associated with the matrix $\mathbf{X}_j$, and $X_{K_j+1}, \ldots, X_K$ for the points associated with the remaining columns of $\mathbf{X}$. Prove that the first stage of 2SLS amounts to defining Y_l^*, $l = 1, \ldots, L_j$, which is the projection of Y_l on the hyperplane through $O, X_1, \ldots, X_K$. Then prove that the second stage is a projection of the point associated with the vector $\mathbf{y}_j$ on the hyperplane through $O, Y_1^*, \ldots, Y_{L_j}^*, X_1, \ldots, X_{K_j}$. For $n = 3$, $K = 2$, $K_1 = L_1 = 1$ this is illustrated in Figure 9.3, where the point corresponding to $\mathbf{y}_j$ is indicated by Y. How can the 2SLS coefficients be read from the solid lines?

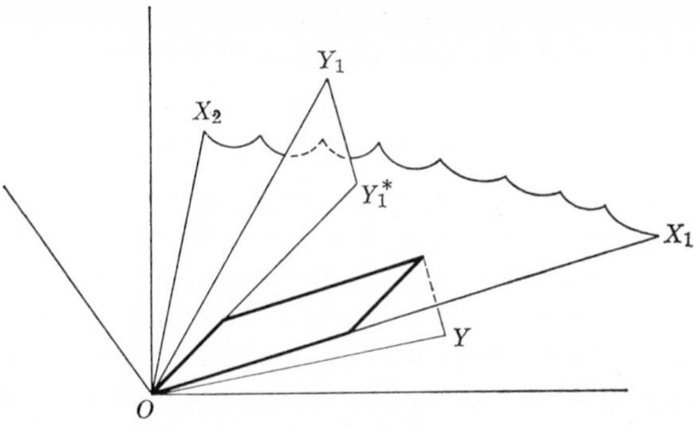

Fig. 9.3 Geometric illustration of 2SLS.

5.4 (*Continuation*) Prove that if the equation is just-identified (as in the case of Figure 9.3), the projections of the two stages are on the same hyperplane. Also prove that in the case of overidentification the second projection is on a plane of lower dimension (for example, if $K_1 = 0$, then OY is projected on the line OY_1^*). What happens in the under-identified case? (*Hint.* Take $K_1 = 2$ and consider the second-stage projection of OY on the plane spanned by O, Y_1^*, X_1, X_2; can this projection be decomposed uniquely?)

5.5 Arrange the variables so that those of $\mathbf{X}_j$ are the first K_j predetermined variables. Prove:

$$(5.24)\qquad [\mathbf{Y}_j - \mathbf{U}_j \quad \mathbf{X}_j] = \mathbf{X}\left[\mathbf{P}_j \;\middle|\; \begin{matrix}\mathbf{I}\\ \mathbf{0}\end{matrix}\right]$$

where $\mathbf{I}$ is of order $K_j \times K_j$ and $\mathbf{0}$ of order $(K - K_j) \times K_j$. Next prove that if $K < N_j$ (underidentification), the second stage of 2SLS is impossible owing to the insufficient rank of the observation matrix of the right-hand variables in (5.9).

5.6 (*Instrumental-variable interpretation of 2SLS*) Prove that the 2SLS coefficient estimator can be regarded as an instrumental-variable estimator with $[\mathbf{Y}_j - \mathbf{U}_j \quad \mathbf{X}_j]$ as the observation matrix on the instrumental variables. (*Hint.* Premultiply $\mathbf{y}_j = \mathbf{Y}_j\boldsymbol{\gamma}_j + \mathbf{X}_j\boldsymbol{\beta}_j + \boldsymbol{\epsilon}_j$ by the transpose of this matrix.)

5.7 Prove that the 2SLS residuals have zero sum when the equation contains a constant term.

5.8 Use eq. (5.16) to prove that the variance estimator s_{jj} of (5.3) can be written as

$$(5.25)\qquad ns_{jj} = [1 \quad -\mathbf{c}_j']\begin{bmatrix}\mathbf{y}_j'\mathbf{y}_j & \mathbf{y}_j'\mathbf{Y}_j\\ \mathbf{Y}_j'\mathbf{y}_j & \mathbf{Y}_j'\mathbf{Y}_j\end{bmatrix}\begin{bmatrix}1\\ -\mathbf{c}_j\end{bmatrix} - \mathbf{b}_j'\mathbf{X}_j'\mathbf{X}_j\mathbf{b}_j$$

5.9 The elements of the matrix (5.20) outside the leading 2×2 submatrix are given in only two decimal places. Why?

9.6 Recursive Systems[B]

We have an interesting special case when the L structural equations can be arranged in the following order. The first contains only one of the L jointly dependent variables. The second contains two, one in addition to the dependent variable of the first equation. The third equation contains three jointly dependent variables, one in addition to the two of the second equation, and so on. Using the notation (3.2), we can then write the system in the form:

$$
\begin{aligned}
&\gamma_{11}y_{\alpha 1} &&+ \sum_k \beta_{k1}x_{\alpha k} = \epsilon_{\alpha 1}\\
&\gamma_{12}y_{\alpha 1} + \gamma_{22}y_{\alpha 2} &&+ \sum_k \beta_{k2}x_{\alpha k} = \epsilon_{\alpha 2}\\
&\gamma_{13}y_{\alpha 1} + \gamma_{23}y_{\alpha 2} + \gamma_{33}y_{\alpha 3} &&+ \sum_k \beta_{k3}x_{\alpha k} = \epsilon_{\alpha 3}\\
&&&\quad\vdots\\
&\gamma_{1L}y_{\alpha 1} + \gamma_{2L}y_{\alpha 2} + \gamma_{3L}y_{\alpha 3} + \cdots + \gamma_{LL}y_{\alpha L} &&+ \sum_k \beta_{kL}x_{\alpha k} = \epsilon_{\alpha L}
\end{aligned}
\tag{6.1}
$$

This shows clearly that the matrix

$$
\mathbf{\Gamma}' = \begin{bmatrix}
\gamma_{11} & 0 & \cdots & 0\\
\gamma_{12} & \gamma_{22} & \cdots & 0\\
\cdot & \cdot & & \cdot\\
\cdot & \cdot & & \cdot\\
\cdot & \cdot & & \cdot\\
\gamma_{1L} & \gamma_{2L} & \cdots & \gamma_{LL}
\end{bmatrix}
\tag{6.2}
$$

is triangular in the sense that all elements above the diagonal are zero. (This also applies to $\mathbf{\Gamma}$ except that "above" should be replaced by "below.")

Furthermore, suppose that for each α, the L disturbances $\epsilon_{\alpha 1}, \ldots, \epsilon_{\alpha L}$ are stochastically independent, which implies a diagonal contemporaneous covariance matrix $\mathbf{\Sigma}$. It is easily seen that each equation of (6.1) is then completely unrelated to the equations by which it is preceded as far as the random components are concerned. The first equation is in reduced form because it contains only one dependent variable; the second equation implies that given the predetermined values $x_{\alpha 1}, \ldots, x_{\alpha K}$, $y_{\alpha 2}$ is determined by $\epsilon_{\alpha 2}$ and $y_{\alpha 1}$; but since the random component of $y_{\alpha 1}$ is $\epsilon_{\alpha 1}$ which is independent of $\epsilon_{\alpha 2}$, one would intuitively expect that $y_{\alpha 1}$ may be regarded as predetermined with respect to $y_{\alpha 2}$. This argument can be continued, step by step, for $y_{\alpha 3}, \ldots,$ $y_{\alpha L}$, and it suggests that the L-equation system (6.1) may be considered as L one-equation systems, each containing only one dependent variable. That particular variable is the y which does not occur in any of the previous equations, while all y's which do occur in the previous equations as well as the x's are all predetermined. This interpretation, in turn, suggests that each equation may be estimated by LS. Indeed, it will be shown in Section 10.7 that when we apply the maximum-likelihood method under the assumption of normally distributed disturbances, we obtain identically the same estimators as those of LS applied to each equation separately. The 2SLS procedure is unnecessary under these conditions.

The special case of a triangular $\mathbf{\Gamma}$ and a diagonal $\mathbf{\Sigma}$ is known as that of a *recursive* equation system. This is in contrast to an *interdependent* system, where either $\mathbf{\Gamma}$ is not triangular or $\mathbf{\Sigma}$ is not diagonal (or both). We have a *block-recursive* system when $\mathbf{\Gamma}$ is block-triangular (with square diagonal blocks) and when $\mathbf{\Sigma}$ is block-diagonal with conforming blocks:

(6.3)
$$\mathbf{\Gamma} = \begin{bmatrix} \mathbf{\Gamma}_{11} & \mathbf{\Gamma}_{12} & \mathbf{\Gamma}_{13} & \cdots & \mathbf{\Gamma}_{1r} \\ \mathbf{0} & \mathbf{\Gamma}_{22} & \mathbf{\Gamma}_{23} & \cdots & \mathbf{\Gamma}_{2r} \\ \mathbf{0} & \mathbf{0} & \mathbf{\Gamma}_{33} & \cdots & \mathbf{\Gamma}_{3r} \\ \cdot & \cdot & \cdot & & \cdot \\ \cdot & \cdot & \cdot & & \cdot \\ \cdot & \cdot & \cdot & & \cdot \\ \mathbf{0} & \mathbf{0} & \mathbf{0} & \cdots & \mathbf{\Gamma}_{rr} \end{bmatrix} \qquad \mathbf{\Sigma} = \begin{bmatrix} \mathbf{\Sigma}_{11} & \mathbf{0} & \mathbf{0} & \cdots & \mathbf{0} \\ \mathbf{0} & \mathbf{\Sigma}_{22} & \mathbf{0} & \cdots & \mathbf{0} \\ \mathbf{0} & \mathbf{0} & \mathbf{\Sigma}_{33} & \cdots & \mathbf{0} \\ \cdot & \cdot & \cdot & & \cdot \\ \cdot & \cdot & \cdot & & \cdot \\ \cdot & \cdot & \cdot & & \cdot \\ \mathbf{0} & \mathbf{0} & \mathbf{0} & \cdots & \mathbf{\Sigma}_{rr} \end{bmatrix}$$

In this case the L-equation system can be partitioned into r smaller equation systems, each of which is of the interdependent type as soon as it consists of more than one equation. Such an interdependent subsystem can be estimated by the 2SLS method if the equations are identifiable within their subsystem and if the zero correlations of the off-diagonal blocks of $\mathbf{\Sigma}$ can be replaced by the stronger assumption of independence. It will be clear that the computational procedure is greatly simplified when a large equation system is thus replaced by a number of smaller systems.

Wold's Criticism of Interdependent Systems

It was maintained by HERMAN WOLD, for some years at least, that an appropriate formulation of economic models necessarily leads to recursive systems, the main argument being that economic agents usually react after some lag. Suppose, for example, that demand reacts instantaneously to price changes but that the supply reacts after a week. Assuming that the market is always cleared, we have in the simplest linear case:

$$q_\alpha = \beta_0 + \beta_1 p_\alpha + \epsilon_\alpha \qquad \text{(demand)} \tag{6.4}$$

$$q_\alpha = \beta_0' + \beta_1' p_{\alpha-1} + \epsilon_\alpha' \qquad \text{(supply)} \tag{6.5}$$

where the observation subscript α measures time in weeks. The supply equation is in reduced form and the demand equation contains only one dependent variable (p_α) in addition to the q_α of the supply equation. The system is thus recursive when it is also true that ϵ_α and ϵ_α' are independent. We may then estimate the supply equation by an LS regression of q_α on $p_{\alpha-1}$ and the demand equation by an LS regression of p_α on q_α [not of q_α on p_α because q_α rather than p_α is predetermined by (6.5)!]. Obviously, this situation differs substantially from that of the interdependent supply and demand system (4.6) and (4.7).

The first counterargument is that the independence condition on ϵ_α and ϵ_α' is very restrictive, since it is certainly conceivable that the neglected factors which are represented by these two disturbances are correlated. Second, it is unlikely that successive disturbances such as ϵ_α and $\epsilon_{\alpha+1}$ are uncorrelated when their distance in time is only one week. The analysis is affected drastically when the disturbances are correlated over time, particularly when lagged endogenous variables are present. Third, it will frequently occur that weekly data are not available, so that the system (6.4) and (6.5) has to be reformulated in larger time units, and the new system need not be of the triangular type. For example, suppose that we have only biweekly data at our disposal, so that the observations are of the form

$$\begin{array}{lll} q_\alpha + q_{\alpha+1} & q_{\alpha+2} + q_{\alpha+3} & \cdots \text{(total quantity)} \\ \frac{1}{2}(p_\alpha + p_{\alpha+1}) & \frac{1}{2}(p_{\alpha+2} + p_{\alpha+3}) & \cdots \text{(average price)} \end{array} \tag{6.6}$$

It is clear from (6.5) that $q_\alpha + q_{\alpha+1}$ is not independent of the current price p_α. Hence, when we try to formulate a demand-and-supply model in terms of the observations (6.6), we should not expect to find a triangular $\mathbf{\Gamma}$ matrix. Indeed, the interdependence of an equation system is frequently a result of this kind of aggregation over time.

Although Wold's criticism of interdependent systems was exaggerated, it must be admitted that he contributed to a better understanding of the importance of recursive models.[12]

[12] See Wold (1954, 1956, 1959, 1964). See also F. M. Fisher (1967b) for an analysis of the view that simultaneous models are limiting approximations to nonsimultaneous models in which certain time lags converge to zero.

Problems

6.1 Verify whether the Keynesian model (1.1) and (1.2) is or is not recursive. Answer the same question for Klein's Model I.

6.2 Prove that completeness of the system in the block-recursive case (6.3) amounts to the nonsingularity of each of the matrices $\boldsymbol{\Gamma}_{11}, \ldots, \boldsymbol{\Gamma}_{rr}$.

9.7 The Final Form of an Equation System[A]

It was stated in the last paragraph of Section 9.1 that the reduced form is more convenient than the structural form for the calculation of the effects of exogenous changes on the behavior of the endogenous variables. But the reduced form is actually not good enough for this purpose when there are lagged endogenous variables, as we shall shortly see.

Derivation of the Final Form from the Reduced Form

Klein's Model I contains only one-year lags, no lags of two years or more. We shall confine ourselves to this simple case of one-period lags.[13] The following notation will be used in this section only: $\mathbf{y}_\alpha$ is the vector of endogenous variables in period α and $\mathbf{x}_\alpha$ is the vector of exogenous variables (excluding the constant-term variable) in the same period. Hence the reduced form is

$$\mathbf{y}_\alpha = \mathbf{d}_0 + \mathbf{D}_1\mathbf{y}_{\alpha-1} + \mathbf{D}_2\mathbf{x}_\alpha + \mathbf{D}_3\mathbf{x}_{\alpha-1} + \boldsymbol{\epsilon}_\alpha^* \tag{7.1}$$

where $\mathbf{d}_0$ is the L-element vector of constant terms in the reduced form, while $\mathbf{D}_1$, $\mathbf{D}_2$, and $\mathbf{D}_3$ are matrices of multiplicative reduced-form coefficients ($\mathbf{D}_1$ being square and $\mathbf{D}_2$ and $\mathbf{D}_3$ being of the same order) and $\boldsymbol{\epsilon}_\alpha^*$ is the L-element vector of reduced-form disturbances in period α (not to be confused with $\boldsymbol{\epsilon}_j$, which is the n-element vector of disturbances of the jth structural equation). In the case of Klein's Model I the vectors of variables are

$$\begin{aligned} \mathbf{y}_\alpha' &= [C_\alpha \quad P_\alpha \quad W_\alpha \quad I_\alpha \quad K_\alpha \quad X_\alpha] \\ \mathbf{x}_\alpha' &= [W_\alpha' \quad T_\alpha \quad G_\alpha \quad \alpha - 1931] \end{aligned} \tag{7.2}$$

The variables which occur with a one-year lag in this model are P, K, and X. None of these is exogenous, hence $\mathbf{D}_3 = \mathbf{0}$. Moreover, three columns of the 6×6 matrix $\mathbf{D}_1$ are zero because $C_{\alpha-1}$, $W_{\alpha-1}$, and $I_{\alpha-1}$ do not occur.

Equation (7.1) shows that the effect of an exogenous change on an endogenous variable in the *same* period is determined by the appropriate element

[13] For a simple extension to the case of lags exceeding one period, see footnote 20 on page 480.

of the matrix $\mathbf{D}_2$. The matrix $\mathbf{D}_3$ does not provide the effect one period later because of the indirect effect via the term $\mathbf{D}_1\mathbf{y}_{\alpha-1}$. This can be made explicit when we replace $\mathbf{y}_{\alpha-1}$ by the right-hand side of (7.1) lagged one period:

$$\begin{aligned} \mathbf{y}_\alpha &= \mathbf{d}_0 + \mathbf{D}_1(\mathbf{d}_0 + \mathbf{D}_1\mathbf{y}_{\alpha-2} + \mathbf{D}_2\mathbf{x}_{\alpha-1} + \mathbf{D}_3\mathbf{x}_{\alpha-2} + \boldsymbol{\epsilon}^*_{\alpha-1}) \\ &\quad + \mathbf{D}_2\mathbf{x}_\alpha + \mathbf{D}_3\mathbf{x}_{\alpha-1} + \boldsymbol{\epsilon}^*_\alpha \\ &= (\mathbf{I} + \mathbf{D}_1)\mathbf{d}_0 + \mathbf{D}_1^2\mathbf{y}_{\alpha-2} + \mathbf{D}_2\mathbf{x}_\alpha + (\mathbf{D}_1\mathbf{D}_2 + \mathbf{D}_3)\mathbf{x}_{\alpha-1} \\ &\quad + \mathbf{D}_1\mathbf{D}_3\mathbf{x}_{\alpha-2} + \boldsymbol{\epsilon}^*_\alpha + \mathbf{D}_1\boldsymbol{\epsilon}^*_{\alpha-1} \end{aligned}$$

By applying this substitution s times we obtain

$$\begin{aligned} (7.3)\quad \mathbf{y}_\alpha &= (\mathbf{I} + \mathbf{D} + \cdots + \mathbf{D}_1^s)\mathbf{d}_0 + \mathbf{D}_1^{s+1}\mathbf{y}_{\alpha-s-1} + \mathbf{D}_2\mathbf{x}_\alpha \\ &\quad + (\mathbf{D}_1\mathbf{D}_2 + \mathbf{D}_3)\mathbf{x}_{\alpha-1} + \cdots + \mathbf{D}_1^{s-1}(\mathbf{D}_1\mathbf{D}_2 + \mathbf{D}_3)\mathbf{x}_{\alpha-s} + \mathbf{D}_1^s\mathbf{D}_3\mathbf{x}_{\alpha-s-1} \\ &\quad + \boldsymbol{\epsilon}^*_\alpha + \mathbf{D}_1\boldsymbol{\epsilon}^*_{\alpha-1} + \cdots + \mathbf{D}_1^s\boldsymbol{\epsilon}^*_{\alpha-s} \end{aligned}$$

Assume that $\mathbf{D}_1^s$ converges to a zero matrix when s increases indefinitely,[14] so that the coefficient matrix of $\mathbf{x}_{\alpha-s-1}$ also converges to zero. In addition, the sum matrix $\mathbf{S} = \mathbf{I} + \cdots + \mathbf{D}_1^s$ then converges to $(\mathbf{I} - \mathbf{D}_1)^{-1}$; this is verified by subtracting $\mathbf{D}_1\mathbf{S} = \mathbf{D}_1 + \cdots + \mathbf{D}_1^{s+1}$ from the equation for $\mathbf{S}$, which gives $(\mathbf{I} - \mathbf{D}_1)\mathbf{S} = \mathbf{I} - \mathbf{D}_1^{s+1}$. So we have in the limit for $s \to \infty$:

$$(7.4)\quad \mathbf{y}_\alpha = (\mathbf{I} - \mathbf{D}_1)^{-1}\mathbf{d}_0 + \mathbf{D}_2\mathbf{x}_\alpha + \sum_{t=1}^{\infty}\mathbf{D}_1^{t-1}(\mathbf{D}_1\mathbf{D}_2 + \mathbf{D}_3)\mathbf{x}_{\alpha-t} + \sum_{t=0}^{\infty}\mathbf{D}_1^t\boldsymbol{\epsilon}^*_{\alpha-t}$$

This vector equation, which originated with Theil and Boot (1962), is known as the *final form* of the equation system. As a whole, therefore, there are three forms for the same economic model:

- ☐ The structural equations, which describe the economic relations in their elementary form.
- ☐ The reduced form, which describes the current endogenous variables in terms of current exogenous variables, lagged endogenous and exogenous variables, and disturbances.
- ☐ The final form, which describes the current endogenous variables in terms of current and lagged exogenous variables and disturbances. It is obtained by a repeated elimination of all lagged endogenous variables from the reduced form.

[14] A necessary and sufficient condition for this to be true is that all latent roots of $\mathbf{D}_1$ be less than one in absolute value. Since $\mathbf{D}_1$ is normally not symmetric, these roots may include conjugate complex pairs of the form $a \pm bi$ or $r(\cos\theta \pm i\sin\theta)$, the absolute value of which is defined as $\sqrt{(a^2 + b^2)} = r$. In the case of Klein's Model I, for example, $\mathbf{D}_1$ is of order 6×6 and three roots are zero; for the estimated version that will be considered below, one of the three other roots is .334 and the two remaining roots form a conjugate complex pair: .838(cos .435 $\pm$ i sin .435), all of which are less than one in absolute value.

Impact, Interim, and Total Multipliers

When there are no lagged endogenous variables in the system ($\mathbf{D}_1 = \mathbf{0}$), the reduced and the final forms are, of course, identical, but this is in general not true. In the case of (7.1) and (7.4) we have the following successive coefficient matrices of the final form:

$$\mathbf{D}_2 \quad \mathbf{D}_1\mathbf{D}_2 + \mathbf{D}_3 \quad \mathbf{D}_1(\mathbf{D}_1\mathbf{D}_2 + \mathbf{D}_3) \quad \mathbf{D}_1^2(\mathbf{D}_1\mathbf{D}_2 + \mathbf{D}_3) \quad \cdots \tag{7.5}$$

The elements of the first matrix ($\mathbf{D}_2$) describe the immediate (current) effect of exogenous changes and are known as the *impact multipliers* of the system. [The ordinary Keynesian multiplier of the model (1.1) and (1.2) is the coefficient $1/(1 - \beta)$ of the reduced form (1.3), which is obviously a special case of an impact multiplier and which explains the origin of the term.] The elements of the other matrices, $\mathbf{D}_1\mathbf{D}_2 + \mathbf{D}_3$, $\mathbf{D}_1(\mathbf{D}_1\mathbf{D}_2 + \mathbf{D}_3), \ldots,$ describe the effect during a given later period; they are known as the *interim multipliers*. The total effect of an exogenous change from now until the very end is found by adding all matrices of the sequence (7.5):

$$\begin{aligned} \mathbf{G} &= \mathbf{D}_2 + (\mathbf{I} + \mathbf{D}_1 + \mathbf{D}_1^2 + \cdots)(\mathbf{D}_1\mathbf{D}_2 + \mathbf{D}_3) \\ &= \mathbf{D}_2 + (\mathbf{I} - \mathbf{D}_1)^{-1}(\mathbf{D}_1\mathbf{D}_2 + \mathbf{D}_3) \\ &= (\mathbf{I} - \mathbf{D}_1)^{-1}[(\mathbf{I} - \mathbf{D}_1)\mathbf{D}_2 + \mathbf{D}_1\mathbf{D}_2 + \mathbf{D}_3] \\ &= (\mathbf{I} - \mathbf{D}_1)^{-1}(\mathbf{D}_2 + \mathbf{D}_3) \end{aligned} \tag{7.6}$$

The elements of $\mathbf{G}$ are the *total multipliers* of the system. The multiplier terminology is from GOLDBERGER (1959).

A numerical survey of all these multipliers for Klein's Model I is given in Table 9.3.[15] It shows, among other things, that a (nonsustained) one billion dollar increase in business taxes (T) in a given year leads to a decrease in total production of private industry (X) of nearly half a billion dollars in the same year, almost two billion in the next year, and so on. Note that the total multipliers for net investment are all zero. This is the implication of the finite values of the corresponding total multipliers for capital stock (see Problem 7.4). The table indicates that the lagged effects produced by the model are quite large and that successive impact and interim multipliers corresponding to the same pair of exogenous and endogenous variables need not have the same sign. This is illustrated in Figure 9.4, which shows the multipliers in the form of vertical distances from a horizontal time axis.

[15] The table contains only the effects of W', T, and G because the trend ($\alpha - 1931$) is less interesting. The numerical values are based on parameter estimates of the structural equations derived by means of the full-information maximum-likelihood method, which is discussed in Section 10.7.

Table 9.3

Impact, Interim, and Total Multipliers of Klein's Model I

Lag in Years	C	P	W	I	K	X	C	P	W	I	K	X	C	P	W	I	K	X
	Unit increase in W′						*Unit increase in T*						*Unit increase in G*					
0	1.34	.89	.65	.21	.21	1.54	−.19	−1.28	−.20	−.30	−.30	−.48	.67	1.12	.81	.26	.26	1.93
1	.94	.64	.90	.61	.81	1.54	−1.01	−1.03	−.88	−.89	−1.19	−1.91	1.17	.80	1.13	.76	1.02	1.93
2	.69	.32	.67	.31	1.12	.99	−1.01	−.57	−.95	−.52	−1.71	−1.52	.86	.40	.84	.38	1.40	1.24
3	.32	.03	.30	.02	1.14	.34	−.54	−.12	−.52	−.09	−1.80	−.63	.40	.04	.38	.02	1.42	.42
4	−.03	−.18	−.04	−.19	.95	−.22	−.03	.24	−.01	.25	−1.54	.23	−.03	−.23	−.04	−.24	1.18	−.27
5	−.27	−.30	−.28	−.31	.64	−.57	.37	.44	.38	.46	−1.09	.82	−.34	−.37	−.35	−.38	.80	−.72
6	−.39	−.33	−.40	−.33	.31	−.72	.59	.51	.60	.52	−.57	1.11	−.49	−.41	−.50	−.41	.39	−.90
7	−.41	−.29	−.41	−.29	.02	−.70	.64	.46	.65	.47	−.10	1.11	−.51	−.36	−.52	−.36	.03	−.87
8	−.35	−.21	−.35	−.21	−.19	−.55	.56	.34	.56	.35	.24	.91	−.43	−.26	−.43	−.26	−.23	−.69
9	−.24	−.11	−.24	−.11	−.30	−.35	.40	.20	.40	.20	.44	.60	−.30	−.14	−.30	−.14	−.37	−.44
10	−.12	−.03	−.12	−.02	−.32	−.14	.22	.06	.21	.06	.50	.28	−.15	−.03	−.15	−.03	−.40	−.18
11	−.01	.04	−.01	.04	−.28	.03	.05	−.05	.04	−.05	.45	−.00	−.02	.05	−.02	.05	−.35	.03
12	.06	.08	.06	.08	−.20	.14	−.08	−.11	−.08	−.12	.33	−.20	.08	.10	.08	.10	−.25	.18
13	.10	.09	.11	.09	−.11	.20	−.15	−.14	−.16	−.14	.19	−.30	.13	.11	.13	.12	−.13	.25
14	.12	.08	.12	.08	−.02	.20	−.18	−.13	−.18	−.14	.05	−.31	.14	.10	.14	.11	−.03	.25
15	.10	.06	.10	.06	.04	.16	−.16	−.10	−.16	−.10	−.05	−.27	.13	.08	.13	.08	.05	.21
16	.07	.04	.07	.04	.08	.11	−.12	−.06	−.12	−.06	−.11	−.19	.09	.05	.09	.05	.10	.14
17	.04	.01	.04	.01	.09	.05	−.07	−.02	−.07	−.02	−.14	−.10	.05	.01	.05	.01	.11	.06
18	.01	−.01	.01	−.01	.08	.00	−.02	.01	−.02	.01	−.13	−.01	.01	−.01	.01	−.01	.10	.00
19	−.01	−.02	−.01	−.02	.06	−.03	.02	.03	.02	.03	−.10	.05	−.02	−.03	−.02	−.03	.08	−.04
20	−.03	−.03	−.03	−.03	.04	−.05	.04	.04	.04	.04	−.06	.08	−.03	−.03	−.03	−.03	.04	−.07
Total multiplier	1.86	.77	1.09	0	4.10	1.86	−.57	−1.24	−.33	0	−6.56	−.57	1.32	.96	1.36	0	5.12	2.32

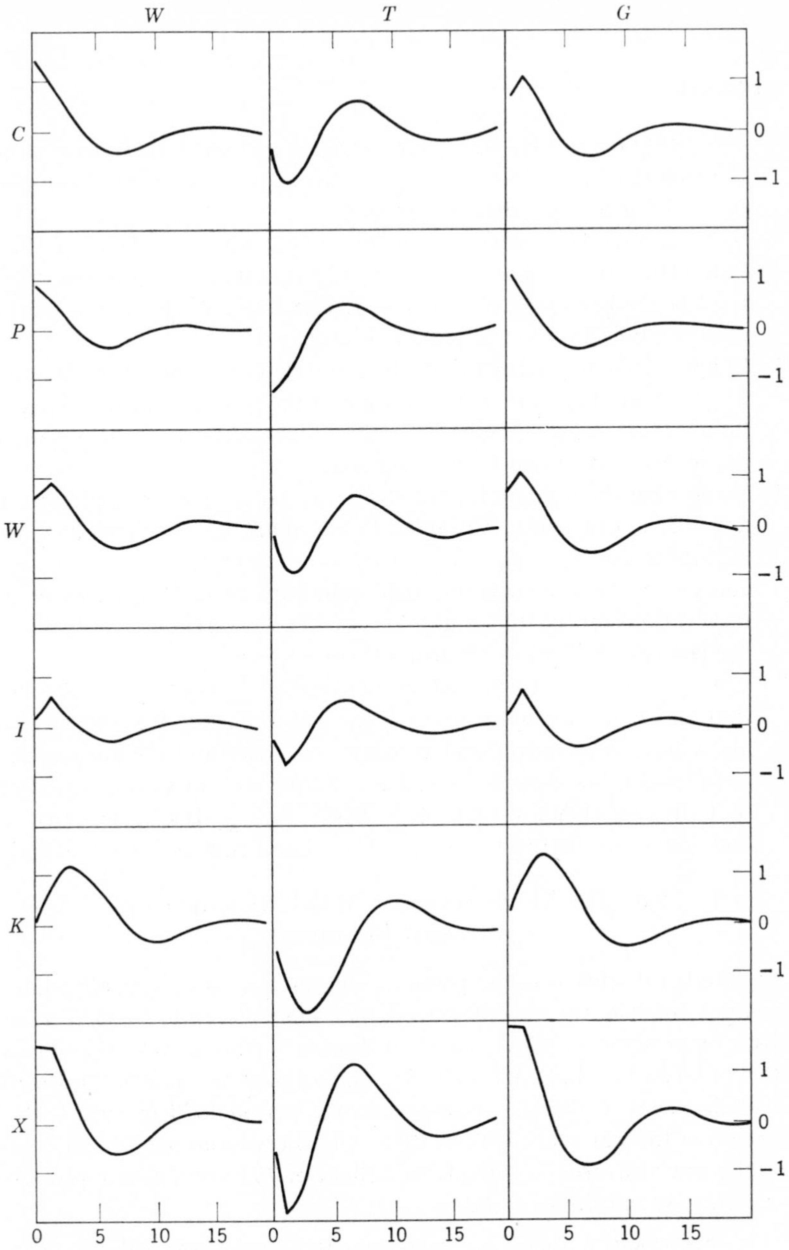

Fig. 9.4 The behavior of successive final-form coefficients of Klein's Model I.

Successive points have been connected by straight lines to obtain a clearer picture.[16]

Problems

7.1 Prove that the impact multipliers of Klein's Model I are independent of the structural parameters $\beta_2, \beta_2', \beta_2''$. Also prove that the interim multipliers do depend on these parameters.

7.2 Suppose that W' and G both increase by 1 billion dollars per year in year t from the level of year $t - 1$, and that they return to the original level at the beginning of year $t + 1$. Use Table 9.3 to obtain the total effect on consumption in years t through $t + 3$.

7.3 Suppose that W' increases by 1 billion dollars per year at the beginning of year t and that it remains constant at the new level (a sustained one-billion increase). Use Table 9.3 to find the successive annual changes in net investment caused by this increase.

7.4 Write γ for the total multiplier of K_α (capital stock at the end of year α) and some exogenous variable. Prove that the corresponding total multiplier for $I_\alpha = K_\alpha - K_{\alpha-1}$ (net investment) is $\gamma - \gamma = 0$. Also, analyze the two other definitional equations of (2.4) in terms of their implications for the total multipliers of W', T, and G, and verify whether the last row of Table 9.3 satisfies these implications.

7.5 Consider the final-form disturbance vector $\sum_t \mathbf{D}_1^t \boldsymbol{\epsilon}_{\alpha-t}^*$ in (7.4). Prove that under the conditions listed at the end of Section 9.3, these disturbances have zero means and constant variances and contemporaneous covariances, but that the lagged covariances do not vanish. Also prove that the covariance matrix of $\sum_t \mathbf{D}_1^t \boldsymbol{\epsilon}_{\alpha-t}^*$ and $\sum_t \mathbf{D}_1^t \boldsymbol{\epsilon}_{\eta-t}^*$ depends on α and η only in the form $|\alpha - \eta|$. [*Hint.* Use Problem 3.4 for $\mathscr{E}(\boldsymbol{\epsilon}_\alpha^* \boldsymbol{\epsilon}_\eta^{*\prime})$.]

9.8 The Klein-Goldberger Model: Description of Structural Equations[A]

The models discussed in the previous sections are all very small. Many of the larger models are economy-wide macromodels and, to give a more realistic impression of these, we shall discuss in this section the equation system published by L. R. KLEIN and A. S. GOLDBERGER in 1955. It describes the development of the U.S. economy in the period 1929 to 1952 with the exception of the war years 1942 to 1945. All observations are annual, and all variables are measured in billions of dollars of 1939 purchasing power per year except when otherwise stated.

[16] The lines indicate a damped oscillatory behavior. The damping is due to the roots having absolute value less than one, and the oscillation to their being complex roots; see footnote 14 on p. 464.

To simplify the comparison with Klein's Model I, we shall start with three behavioral equations (plus some identities) which are close to those of that model.

Consumption

The consumption function contains disposable wage income (W^*), disposable nonwage nonfarm income (P^*), and disposable farm income (R^*), which are defined as follows:[17]

$$W^* = W + W' - T_W \tag{8.1}$$

$$P^* = P - T_C - T_N - S_C \tag{8.2}$$

$$R^* = R_1 + R_2 - T_R \tag{8.3}$$

where W is the private wage bill, W' the government wage bill, T_W personal and payroll taxes (less transfers) associated with wage income, P nonwage nonfarm income, T_C corporate taxes, T_N nonwage nonfarm noncorporate taxes (less transfers), S_C corporate savings, R_1 farm income, R_2 farm subsidies, and T_R taxes (less transfers) associated with farm income. The consumption function is

$$\begin{aligned} C = &\underset{(9.66)}{-22.26} + \underset{(.06)}{.55W^*} + \underset{(.05)}{.41P^*} + \underset{(.04)}{.34R^*} \\ &+ \underset{(.075)}{.26C_{-1}} + \underset{(.025)}{.072(L_1)_{-1}} + \underset{(.10)}{.26N_P} \end{aligned} \tag{8.4}$$

The point estimate of the marginal propensity to consume out of wage income exceeds that out of nonwage nonfarm income, which in turn exceeds that out of farm income. The fourth variable, consumption lagged one year (C_{-1}), introduces a dynamic feature. When income goes up this year (any of the first three variables), this raises consumption in the same year; but an increase in consumption this year also implies an increase next year according to the C_{-1} term. The fifth term concerns a stock variable: L_1 stands for the liquid assets held by households at the end of the year (measured in billions of 1939 dollars). The positive coefficient indicates that a larger amount of assets at the beginning of the year leads to a higher level of consumption during the year. The last variable (N_P) is the midyear population in millions of persons. Its introduction is an attempt to correct for the fact that the other variables of the equation are not on a per capita basis.

[17] The notation used is that of Goldberger (1959) with few exceptions; the observation subscript α is deleted for notational simplicity. The point estimates of the coefficients of the behavioral equations and their asymptotic standard errors have been derived by means of the limited-information maximum-likelihood method, which is described in Section 10.4.

This consumption function is evidently more elaborate than the corresponding function (2.1) of Klein's Model I, since it distinguishes between three groups of income recipients rather than two and it contains liquid assets in addition to the income variables. On the other hand, it treats the lag structure of the effect of income changes in the same way for all three income groups, whereas (2.1) distinguishes between the lagged effect of wage income (which is zero) and that of nonwage income. Note that the coefficients of (8.4) are all individually significantly different from zero on the basis of the two-sigma rule.[18] As we shall shortly see, there are several equations for which this is not true.

Investment and Demand for Labor

In contrast to the investment function (2.2) of Klein's Model I, the corresponding function of the present model is concerned with *gross* investment (indicated by I):

$$(8.5)\qquad I = \underset{(4.74)}{-16.71} + \underset{(.18)}{.78}(P^* + S_C + R^* + D)_{-1} - \underset{(.067)}{.073}K_{-1} + \underset{(.11)}{.14}(L_2)_{-1}$$

The first explanatory variable is disposable nonwage income including disposable farm income $(P^* + R^*)$ plus corporate savings (S_C) plus depreciation (D). Hence this variable measures gross profit income after taxes. It occurs with a lag of one year; the term should be compared with $\beta_2' P_{-1}$ of the investment equation of Klein's Model I. The two other variables are stock variables, measured in billions of 1939 dollars per year: K_{-1}, capital stock at the beginning of the year, and $(L_2)_{-1}$, business liquid assets at the same point of time. Note that the point estimates of the coefficients of these two variables have signs that could be expected; also note, however, that neither estimate differs significantly from zero.

The demand-for-labor function is similar to (2.3):

$$(8.6)\qquad W = \underset{(1.46)}{-1.40} + \underset{(.07)}{.24}X + \underset{(.06)}{.24}X_{-1} + \underset{(.125)}{.29}(\alpha - 1929)$$

X being the value of total private production and α time measured in calendar years.

[18] Note that "sigma" (the standard deviation of the sampling distribution of the estimator) is approximated here by the asymptotic standard error. This approximation must be expected to be less accurate on the average than the standard error for the relevant finite number of observations (on the assumption that the estimator has a finite variance).

The Agricultural Sector

Since the consumption function makes a distinction between farm and nonfarm income, it is necessary to pay separate attention to the factors determining income development in the rural sector. Accordingly, the model contains an agricultural income equation which describes R_1 (farm income not including farm subsidies) in terms of certain variables which affect the farmers' prosperity. One of these is disposable nonfarm income ($W^* + P^*$), which measures the prosperity of the farmers' domestic customers; the other is an index of agricultural exports (F_R, base 1939 = 100). To take account of the terms of trade of agriculture, the income variables are multiplied by p/p_R, where p is a price index for the economy as a whole and p_R is an index of agricultural prices (both with base 1939 = 100). The equation runs as follows:

$$R_1 p/p_R = \underset{(2.12)}{-.36} + \underset{(.045)}{.054}(W^* + P^*)p/p_R \tag{8.7}$$
$$\qquad - \underset{(.043)}{.007}[(W^* + P^*)p/p_R]_{-1} + \underset{(.006)}{.012}F_R$$

The second agricultural equation relates the agricultural price index to the general price index:

$$p_R = \underset{(15.3)}{-131.2} + \underset{(.11)}{2.32}p \tag{8.8}$$

This equation is supposed to represent, among other things, the effect of the government support of agricultural prices. Note that the coefficient of p indicates that farm prices fluctuate much more than prices in general. Also note that the coefficients of the other agricultural equation (8.7) are statistically insignificant, with that of F_R as a marginal exception.

The Monetary Sector

The consumption function contains the liquid assets held by households, L_1. This variable is supposed to consist of transaction balances and idle balances, the former being proportional to disposable income and the latter a function of the long-term interest rate (i_L, measured as a percentage per year):

$$L_1 = .14(W^* + P^* + R^*) + \underset{(15.3)}{76.0}(i_L - 2)^{-.84} \tag{8.9}$$

The coefficient of the first variable (.14) is determined as the smallest ratio of deflated personal holdings of currency and checking accounts to deflated disposable income in the sample period. For the year of this smallest ratio (which is 1929) we have the largest velocity of money; the assumption is then that there were no idle balances in that year and that such balances in other years can be measured by the difference between L_1 and the first right-hand term in (8.9). The equation states that idle balances are a log-linear function of the long-term interest rate, measured as a percentage per year in excess of 2 percent. (The variable i_L fluctuated between 2.7 and 6.9 percent per year in the sample period.) Clearly, eq. (8.9) is nonlinear. The standard error of the point estimate $-.84$ of the exponent is .03.

The equation for business liquid assets, L_2 of the investment function (8.5), is

$$\begin{aligned} L_2 = -&.34 + .26W - 1.02i_S - .26\Delta p + .61(L_2)_{-1} \\ &(.99) \quad (.03) \qquad (.19) \qquad (.06) \qquad (.06) \end{aligned} \tag{8.10}$$

The first explanatory variable deals with the transactions motive for holding cash balances: the larger the operating expense (measured by the private wage bill W), the greater the need for cash. The second variable is the short-term rate of interest, i_S, measured as a percentage per year. The term indicates that when this interest rate goes up, there is a tendency to substitute securities for cash. The third variable, $\Delta p = p - p_{-1}$, is introduced to represent a speculation effect. When prices are on the increase, they are presumed to increase even further, so that it is disadvantageous to have a large amount of liquid assets. The fourth variable, with its large coefficient, indicates that L_2 is subject to a considerable inertia over time.

In the last two equations we introduced two new variables, the long-term and the short-term rates of interest. Their equations are as follows:

$$\begin{aligned} i_L = 2.58 &+ .44(i_S)_{-3} + .26(i_S)_{-5} \\ (.15) &\quad (.10) \qquad\quad (.09) \end{aligned} \tag{8.11}$$

$$100\,\frac{i_S - (i_S)_{-1}}{(i_S)_{-1}} = \underset{(7.8)}{11.2} - \underset{(.30)}{.67}L_B \tag{8.12}$$

The first equation relates the long-term rate of interest to the short-term rate with a considerable lag (3 and 5 years). The determination of these lags in this case is a matter of empirical manipulation, based on the criterion of a good fit. The second equation describes the annual percentage change in the short-term rate as a decreasing linear function of L_B, the excess reserves of banks as a percentage of total reserves. Thus, with large excess reserves, banks can easily lend and are forced to accept lower interest rates to dispose of these excesses.

Labor and Capital as Determinants of Output, Wages, and Depreciation

The model contains the following production function describing the output of the private sector (X) in terms of the inputs:

(8.13)

$$X = \underset{(7.3)}{-26.1} + \underset{(.18)}{2.17}[h(N_W - N_G) + N_E] + \underset{(.05)}{.16}\,\frac{K_{-1} + K}{2} + \underset{(.16)}{2.05}(\alpha - 1929)$$

The first explanatory variable represents labor input: N_W is the total number of employees, N_G is the number of government employees (both in millions of persons), h is an index of hours worked per person per year, and N_E is the number of self-employed (also in millions of persons). The assumption is that the last group always works a full period of time (i.e., $h = 1$ for the self-employed). The second variable represents the average capital input during the year, and the third the increasing efficiency of capital and labor resulting from a gradual technological change over time.

The variables N_W and N_E also act as determinants of the wage rate. The equation involved describes the annual change in the index of hourly wages, $\Delta w = w - w_{-1}$, in terms of the number of unemployed, the change in the price level one year earlier, and a linear time trend:

$$\Delta w = \underset{(4.85)}{4.11} - \underset{(.61)}{.74}(N_L - N_W - N_E) + \underset{(.28)}{.52}(\Delta p)_{-1} + \underset{(.24)}{.54}(\alpha - 1929) \tag{8.14}$$

Here N_L is the size of the labor force and, therefore, $N_L - N_W - N_E$ is the number of unemployed (millions of persons). If we accept the point estimates, the conclusion is that the wage rate goes up when there are fewer unemployed and when prices rose in the past year. In addition, the change in the wage rate is subject to an increasing linear trend, which amounts to a quadratic trend for the wage rate itself. Note, however, that not all of the point estimates are significant.

Regarding capital input in the production function (8.13), recall that the left-hand variable of the investment function (8.5) is gross investment, so that the change in capital stock is equal to $I - D$:

$$K = K_{-1} + I - D \tag{8.15}$$

where D is the depreciation variable which occurred earlier in (8.5). The following equation describes the behavior of D:

$$D = \underset{(.80)}{7.25} + \underset{(.01)}{.10}\,\frac{K_{-1} + K}{2} + \underset{(.008)}{.044}X \tag{8.16}$$

The first right-hand variable indicates that the amount of depreciation increases with the size of the capital stock, and the second shows that this amount increases when there is a high degree of capacity utilization as measured by a high level of output.

Imports

Imports form another input of a nation's economy. The model contains the following import equation:

$$(8.17) \qquad F_I = \underset{(.49)}{.32} + \underset{(.0084)}{.0060}(W^* + P^* + R^* + S_C)\frac{p}{p_F} + \underset{(.21)}{.81}(F_I)_{-1}$$

The first explanatory variable for the imports of goods and services (F_I) is deflated disposable income plus corporate savings (S_C), multiplied by p/p_F where p_F is an import price index. The money value of income is thus deflated by the import price level. Note that the coefficient of this variable has the "correct" sign but that it is not significant. Imports lagged one year appear to be a much more prominent explanatory variable; witness the significance of its coefficient. As in the similar case (8.10), one may conclude on the basis of the point estimate .81 that F_I is characterized by a considerable inertia over time.

Corporate Savings and Corporate Surplus

Corporate savings (S_C) is, by definition, equal to the change in corporate surplus (S_B):

$$(8.18) \qquad S_B = (S_B)_{-1} + S_C$$

The following equation describes the behavior of corporate savings:

(8.19)

$$S_C = \underset{(1.02)}{-3.53} + \underset{(.06)}{.72}(P_C - T_C) + \underset{(.25)}{.08}(P_C - T_C - S_C)_{-1} - \underset{(.019)}{.028}(S_B)_{-1}$$

The first explanatory variable is corporate profits (P_C) less corporate taxes (T_C). The second variable indicates that last year's profits affect current savings only insofar as they were not saved in that year. The last term states that a larger surplus at the beginning of the year reduces the addition during the year in the same way that a larger K_{-1} reduces investment according to (8.5).

For corporate profits we have a simple equation in terms of nonwage nonfarm income (P):

$$P_C = -7.60 + .68P \qquad (8.20)$$
$$\quad\ (.54)\quad (.02)$$

To a large extent this is an empirical equation, constructed mainly to maintain the completeness of the model.

Definitional Equations

The model contains eight identities, but five were considered previously: (8.1) to (8.3), (8.15) and (8.18). The other three are

$$X = C + I + G + F_E - F_I \qquad (8.21)$$

$$X = W + P + R_1 + R_2 + T_E + D \qquad (8.22)$$

$$p(W + W') = whN_W \qquad (8.23)$$

Equations (8.21) and (8.22) should be compared with the first and the second equation, respectively, of (2.4); G is government nonwage expenditure, F_E is exports of goods and services, and T_E is indirect taxes less subsidies.[19] The last equation equates the money value of the total wage bill with the product of the wage rate, the hours worked, and the number of employees.

Problems

8.1 In the discussion below eq. (8.10), it is stated that $(L_2)_{-1}$ has a large coefficient. But the coefficient of i_S is -1.02 and hence still larger in absolute value. What are your comments on this comparison?

8.2 Apply the two-sigma rule to delete all lagged variables which are not significant according to that criterion. Verify that this reduces the number of variables which occur in lagged form from 18 to 14.

9.9 The Klein-Goldberger Model: Miscellaneous Comments[A]

Table 9.4 summarizes the variables of the Klein-Goldberger model in the alphabetical order of their symbols. There are 42 variables as a whole (including time, $\alpha - 1929$, and the constant-term variable, which are not shown in the table). The first column contains the symbol of the variable, the second gives a brief description, and the next five specify the unit of measurement. The last column shows the equations in which the variable occurs.

[19] In Klein's Model I the net foreign balance $F_E - F_I$ is included in G; see the first equation of (2.4).

Table 9.4

Variables of the Klein-Goldberger Model

Symbol	Description	Unit: $\$10^9$/year[a]	Unit: 10^9 dollars[a]	Unit: 1939 = 100	Unit: 10^6 persons	Unit: %/year	Exogenous	Lags (Years)	Occurs in Equation:
C	Consumption	×						1	4, 21
D	Depreciation	×						1	5, 15, 16, 22
F_E	Exports	×					×		21
F_I	Imports	×						1	17, 21
F_R	Farm exports			×			×		7
G	Government nonwage expenditure	×					×		21
$100h$	Hours of work			×			×		13, 23
i_L	Long-term interest rate					×			9, 11
i_S	Short-term interest rate					×		1, 3, 5	10, 11, 12
I	Gross investment	×							5, 15, 21
K	Capital stock		×					1	5, 13, 15, 16
L_1	Household liquid assets		×					1	4, 9
L_2	Business liquid assets		×					1	5, 10
L_B	Percentage excess reserves[b]						×		12
N_E	Entrepreneurs				×		×		13, 14
N_G	Government employees				×		×		13
N_L	Labor force				×		×		14
N_P	Population				×		×		4
N_W	Employees				×				13, 14, 23
p	General price index			×				1, 2	7, 8, 10, 14, 17, 23
p_F	Import price index			×			×		17
p_R	Farm price index			×				1	7, 8
P	Nonwage nonfarm income	×							2, 20, 22
P^*	Disposable nonwage nonfarm income	×						1	2, 4, 5, 7, 9, 17
P_C	Corporate profits	×						1	19, 20
R^*	Disposable farm income	×						1	3, 4, 5, 9, 17
R_1	Farm income	×							3, 7, 22
R_2	Farm subsidies	×					×		3, 22
S_B	Corporate surplus		×					1	18, 19
S_C	Corporate savings	×						1	2, 5, 7, 18, 19
T_C	Corporate taxes	×					×	1	2, 19
T_E	Indirect taxes less subsidies	×					×		22
T_N	Nonwage nonfarm noncorporate taxes[c]	×					×		2
T_R	Farm taxes[c]	×					×		3
T_W	Wage taxes[c]	×					×		1
w	Wage rate[d]							1	14, 23
W	Private wage bill	×							1, 6, 10, 22, 23
W'	Government wage bill	×					×		1, 23
W^*	Disposable wage income	×						1	1, 4, 7, 9, 17
X	Output of private sector	×						1	6, 13, 16, 21, 22

[a] Dollars of 1939 purchasing power.
[b] Unit: percentage.
[c] Less transfers.
[d] Unit: 1939 = 122.1.

[The equation is indicated by its second number, so that eq. (8.4) becomes 4.] The second-last column specifies the lags of the variables; when a variable occurs in current form only, the cell is empty. There are only two variables which occur with a lag of more than one year: the short-term interest i_S in the long-term interest equation (8.11) and the price index p [in the form $(\Delta p)_{-1} = p_{-1} - p_{-2}$] in the wage rate equation (8.14). More than 40 percent of the variables do occur in lagged form (see also Problem 8.2 above).

The Size of the Model

The model as described in the previous section consists of 23 equations, but it is somewhat arbitrary to say that it is a 23-equation system. For example, consider the definitional equation (8.1); we may substitute $W + W' - T_W$ for W^* in all equations containing W^* and delete (8.1) from the system, so that a 22-equation system is obtained with one less endogenous variable (W^*). This applies to all definitional equations, none of which contains any unknown parameters. It is therefore preferable to measure the size of an equation system by the number of equations excluding the definitions. In the Klein-Goldberger case this number is 15. It will be clear, however, that the actual elimination of all definitions leads to very cumbersome expressions of the remaining equations, and this is the reason definitions are usually found in simultaneous equation models.

Exogenous and Endogenous Variables

It remains true that the Klein-Goldberger model *as presented in Section 9.8* is a 23-equation system. Therefore, if the model is complete, we should have exactly 23 endogenous variables. Consider, then, the following list of exogenous variables:

- ☐ Two variables are not listed in Table 9.4: time and the constant-term variable. These are obviously exogenous.
- ☐ Ten variables may be regarded as policy variables controlled by the government. Five are taxes: T_C, T_E, T_N, T_R, T_W. Three refer to government expenditure: G, R_2, and W'. There is also the number of government employees, N_G. Finally, the percentage of excess reserves (L_B) is regarded as controlled by the Federal Reserve Board.
- ☐ Three variables are considered determined by conditions abroad: exports (F_E), the index of farm exports (F_R), and the import price index (p_F).
- ☐ Four variables, finally, are regarded as exogenous because they are largely determined by gradual changes in the demographic and social environment: hours of work (h), the number of entrepreneurs (N_E), the labor force (N_L), and the population (N_P).

If we accept this list, the 23-equation system contains 23 endogenous variables and 19 exogenous variables. By adding the lagged variables of the second-last column of Table 9.4, we obtain $19 + 21 = 40$ predetermined variables as a whole.

It is easy to criticize the exogenous-endogenous distinction. For example, take exports (F_E). One may argue that this variable depends on the level of real income in the main importing countries and on the U.S. export price level in relation to the domestic price level of these countries. It is not plausible that the U.S. export price level is independent of the development of the U.S. economy. One could remedy this defect by introducing an export equation along the lines just described (which would make exports an endogenous variable) and by introducing another equation that describes the export price level in terms of its determining factors. The real incomes of the importing countries and their price levels are then new exogenous variables. Note, however, that in this case the transformation of an exogenous variable to an endogenous variable requires two equations and several new variables. If one prefers a model that is not too large, one will have to decide whether such an enlargement is worthwhile. The decision will depend on one's interest in foreign trade, which will, in turn, depend on the magnitude of this trade in relation to the domestic economy. This explains why Dutch models have stressed the foreign sector more than most American models; see, for example, THEIL (1966, Chapter 4).

Discussion of the Monetary Sector

The liquid assets equations (8.9) and (8.10) and the interest equations (8.11) and (8.12) form the monetary sector of the model; let us call the 19 other equations the real sector. Since W^*, P^*, and R^* occur in the right-hand side of (8.9) and W and Δp in the right-hand side of (8.10), the real sector affects the monetary sector; but the latter sector does not affect the former in the same year, since L_1, L_2, i_L, i_S occur in the real sector at most in lagged form. Hence there is no instantaneous feedback from the monetary sector to the real sector. But there is a lagged feedback because $(L_1)_{-1}$ and $(L_2)_{-1}$ occur in the consumption function (8.4) and in the investment function (8.5), respectively. It is easily seen that this feedback cannot be realistic. Consider the short-term interest equation (8.12) and suppose (for simplicity's sake) that its two point estimates coincide with the corresponding parameters and that its disturbances are negligible. Also suppose that the excess reserves L_B (an exogenous variable) remain constant at the level of 10 percent. Then the percentage change in the short-term interest rate is $4\frac{1}{2}$, year after year. When the short-term interest rate increases indefinitely, so does the long-term rate i_L in view of (8.11). Considering the negative effect of i_L on L_1 in (8.9) and of i_S on L_2 in (8.10), we conclude that the liquid assets held by households and by firms decrease continuously, which leads to a similar contraction of the real sector of the economy via the consumption function (8.4) and the investment equation (8.5). Obviously, the monetary sector of the model gives an inadequate picture of the phenomena which it serves to describe. In the following we shall disregard the liquid assets and interest equations by imposing

$$\Delta L_1 = \Delta L_2 = 0 \tag{9.1}$$

which means that L_1 and L_2 are regarded as exogenous variables fixed at a constant level. The interest rates i_L and i_S then disappear from the model.

Impact and Interim Multipliers for the Real Sector

On the basis of the model thus revised one can try to determine the effect of changes in the exogenous variables on the endogenous variables in successive years, similar to the procedure of Section 9.7 for Klein's Model I. However, several equations of the present model are nonlinear. This problem was solved by GOLDBERGER (1959) by linearization. For example, take the production function (8.13) in first differences:

(9.2)

$$\Delta X = 2.17\,\Delta[h(N_W - N_G)] + 2.17\,\Delta N_E + .08\,\Delta K_{-1} + .08\,\Delta K + 2.05$$

The first right-hand term is nonlinear in the variables h, N_W, and N_G. Consider, then, any two variables which take the values x and y in the present year and x_{-1} and y_{-1} in the previous year, as well as the following identity:

$$\Delta(xy) = A\,\Delta y + B\,\Delta x + (x - A)\,\Delta y + (y_{-1} - B)\,\Delta x$$

where A and B are arbitrary constants. When Δx and Δy are small and when $x - A$ and $y_{-1} - B$ are small in absolute value compared with A and B, respectively, we have $\Delta(xy) \approx A\,\Delta y + B\,\Delta x$. A convenient choice of A and B is the average of the x and the y observations, $\bar{x}$ and $\bar{y}$, say, so that we have $\Delta(xy) \approx \bar{x}\,\Delta y + \bar{y}\,\Delta x$; the condition on $x - A = x - \bar{x}$ and $y_{-1} - B = y_{-1} - \bar{y}$ is then that the deviations of the two variables from their means be small compared with the levels of these means. This procedure gives the following approximation to the first right-hand term in (9.2):

$$2.17\bar{h}(\Delta N_W - \Delta N_G) + 2.17(\bar{N}_W - \bar{N}_G)\,\Delta h$$

where $\bar{h}$, $\bar{N}_W$, and $\bar{N}_G$ are the averages of the three variables in the sample period.

Once the model is thus linearized, we can proceed along the lines of Section 9.7. The first four lines of Table 9.5 give impact and interim multipliers for one exogenous variable (G, government nonwage expenditure) and four endogenous variables: consumption (C), gross investment (I), the private wage bill (W), and nonwage nonfarm income (P)[20]. (The last four lines of the table will be discussed in the next subsection.) The results indicate that, as in the case of Klein's Model I (see Table 9.3 in Section 9.7), there are substantial lagged effects, and that the successive coefficients in each row do not all have the same sign.

Table 9.5

Impact and Interim Multipliers of Government Nonwage Expenditure for Some Selected Variables of the Klein-Goldberger Model

Endogenous Variable	Lag (years) 0	1	2	3	4	5	6
			Deflated tax yields exogenous				
C	.398	.619	.574	.418	.242	.086	−.035
I	0	.826	.533	.294	.112	−.024	−.117
W	.332	.674	.600	.422	.241	.086	−.034
P	.939	.590	.294	.078	−.075	−.176	−.234
			Deflated tax yields endogenous				
C	.238	.304	.188	.080	.023	−.001	−.010
I	0	.429	.086	−.011	−.019	−.016	−.014
W	.295	.468	.235	.076	.011	−.009	−.016
P	.724	.103	−.062	−.071	−.056	−.048	−.043

Impact and Interim Multipliers under Conditions of Endogenous Taxes

The first four lines of Table 9.5 are based on the assumption that the deflated tax yields T_C, T_E, T_N, T_R, and T_W are all exogenous, since they are presumed to be controlled by the government. Clearly, this assumption is not attractive; it is preferable to assume that the government controls the tax rates rather than the tax yields. Goldberger (1959) took this feature into account by postulating that these yields are approximately linear functions of the corresponding tax bases. For example, corporate tax yields are related

[20] The table is based on Goldberger (1959, pp. 87, 90). Note that the final-form analysis of Section 9.7 is confined to one-period lags, whereas there are longer lags here. This problem can be easily solved by the introduction of a new endogenous variable for each lagged endogenous variable. For example, to handle the price index lagged two years p_{-2} we introduce a variable "prices lagged," $p_L = p_{-1}$, so that p_{-2} can be replaced by $(p_L)_{-1}$ which has a one-year lag only. In each such case we have one additional endogenous variable (p_L here) and one additional equation ($p_L = p_{-1}$).

to corporate profits, indirect taxes to sales, etc. Consider the following relations in first differences:

$$\begin{aligned} \Delta T_C &= \gamma_1 \Delta P_C \\ \Delta T_E &= \gamma_2 \Delta(X + W' - T_E) \\ \Delta T_N &= \gamma_3 \Delta(P - T_C - S_C) \\ \Delta T_W &= \gamma_4 \Delta(W + W') \end{aligned} \tag{9.3}$$

and the following specification of the γ's:

$$\gamma_1 = .5 \qquad \gamma_2 = .1 \qquad \gamma_3 = .3 \qquad \gamma_4 = .15 \tag{9.4}$$

These numerical values correspond approximately to the marginal tax rates that were in effect in the United States in the years just following World War II.

Equation (9.3) implies that the four T's are now expressed in the variables of the model, so that they have become endogenous. [The variable T_R (farm taxes) is still kept exogenous because it is of minor numerical importance.] We can then find the effect of a change in government nonwage expenditure (G) in successive years on the basis of the model thus modified. The results for C, I, W, and P are shown on the last four lines of Table 9.5. Comparing these with the corresponding figures in the upper half of the table, we conclude that the effects of a change in G differ in magnitude. In each pairwise comparison the figure in the lower half of the table is closer to zero than the corresponding figure in the upper half. Moreover, on each line in the lower half the change in sign occurs earlier than on the corresponding line of the upper half.

Evidently, the addition of the four equations (9.3) leads to an entirely different model. In qualitative and intuitive terms, the difference is easy to understand. When government nonwage expenditure increases, this leads to an expansion of the economy, at least in the first few years. Thus, consumption, wages, profits, etc. all increase. In the upper half of Table 9.5 it is assumed that taxes (yields) on sales, wage income, etc. remain constant in spite of these increases; in the lower half we assume that the tax rates are unchanged, so that the tax yields increase. Obviously, the tax yield increases of the latter case imply a smaller expansion of the economy than does the former. Goldberger (1959, Section 6.2) computed some total multipliers of government nonwage expenditure for a slightly simplified version of the Klein-Goldberger model. He found the following values for the two cases:

	C	I	W	P
Taxes exogenous	1.26	.66	1.37	1.41
Taxes endogenous	.88	.46	1.13	.83

A Simulation Experiment

How well does the Klein-Goldberger model succeed in reproducing the oscillatory fluctuations known as business cycles? This question was raised by I. ADELMAN and F. L. ADELMAN (1959), who proceeded as follows. First, the model was simplified by deleting insignificant coefficients and in some other ways as well, and tax functions similar to (9.3) those of were added. Second, trends (mostly linear) were specified for the exogenous variables. Then the observed 1952 values of the variables were inserted as initial conditions, and the time path of all endogenous variables was traced, year by year, during 100 years through the year 2052. The monetary sector was suppressed for the reasons discussed above, but otherwise the model was applied in its original nonlinear form.

The result is that most of the endogenous variables behave according to a smooth and more or less linear trend. When a sizable sudden shock is

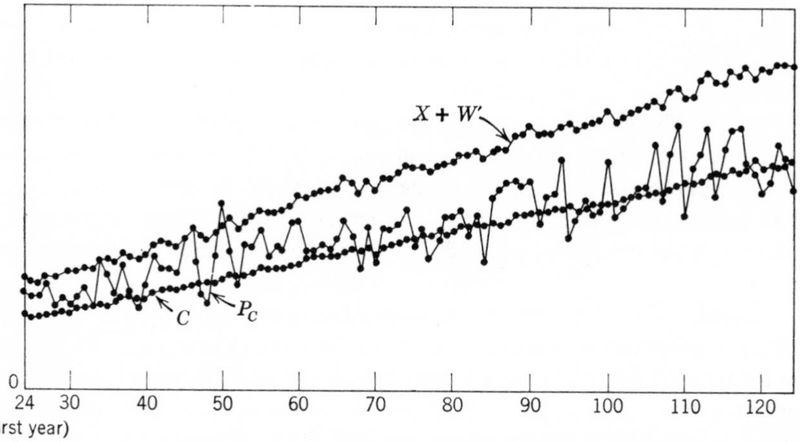

Fig. 9.5 Simulated time paths according to the Klein-Goldberger model.

inserted, this leads to some fluctuations but these dampen out rather rapidly. In this form, therefore, the model does not explain the business cycle phenomenon very adequately. However, any econometric model implies that period after period there are such shocks in the form of disturbances of structural equations; it may be that a time series of random shocks produces the kind of oscillatory fluctuations that are observed in reality. This was analyzed by the Adelmans, who added random normal error terms with zero mean to each structural equation; the standard deviations were evaluated from the observed standard deviations of the corresponding residuals of the sample period. Some results are shown in Figure 9.5 for gross national product ($X + W'$), consumption (C), and corporate profits (P_C). The results do seem to indicate that the model is capable of reproducing realistic oscillatory fluctuations when disturbances are added. Ultimately, this is because final-form disturbances are correlated over time even when the structural disturbances have zero lagged correlations; see Problems 7.5 and 9.5.[21]

In conclusion, we note that the previous paragraph is the only place in the discussion of this section where random effects enter into the picture. The final form describes the behavior of endogenous variables over time in terms of exogenous variables, both current and lagged, but also in terms of the disturbances of the structural equations, both current and lagged. In addition, the true coefficients of the final form are unknown and are derived from the coefficient estimates of the structural equations. Both here and in Section 9.7 we acted as if corresponding parameters and estimates coincide, but this is obviously not more than a simplifying assumption.

Problems

9.1 Suppose we eliminate all definitions from the Klein-Goldberger model (see the second paragraph of the section). How would this affect the last column of Table 9.4?

9.2 It was stated in Problem 8.2 that the Klein-Goldberger model contains 18 variables which occur in lagged form. But in this section (below the list of 19 exogenous variables) it is stated that there are 21 lagged variables. Is there any contradiction?

9.3 Prove that the investment equation (8.5) and the long-term interest equation (8.11) are in reduced form.

9.4 Why is it that the impact multipliers for investment are zero in Table 9.5? Why is it that the total multipliers for investment, contrary to those of Klein's Model I as shown in Table 9.3, are not zero?

9.5 Consider a one-equation system ($L = 1$), so that the (single) structural equation is in reduced form and the matrix $\mathbf{D}_1$ of (7.1) is a scalar, say, δ. Use a table of random normal sampling numbers to generate disturbances, compute the corresponding final-form disturbances for $\delta = .1$ and $\delta = .7$, and verify that the latter disturbances show oscillatory movements for $\delta = .7$ (but not for $\delta = .1$) which are similar in form to business cycle fluctuations.

[21] Reference should be made here to the pioneering article by SLUTZKY (1937) on the relationship between random shocks and oscillatory behavior.

CHAPTER **10**

STATISTICAL INFERENCE IN SIMULTANEOUS-EQUATION MODELS

This chapter examines the statistical analysis of systems of simultaneous equations, mainly for large samples. Section 10.2, parts of Sections 10.4 and 10.5, and Section 10.6 are optional for an introductory econometrics course.

10.1 Two Sets of Assumptions and Some Basic Convergence Results[C]

Our starting point may be formulated in terms of the concepts introduced in Section 9.3. The jth structural equation for the αth observation is then

$$(1.1) \qquad \sum_{l=1}^{L} \gamma_{lj} y_{\alpha l} + \sum_{k=1}^{K} \beta_{kj} x_{\alpha k} = \epsilon_{\alpha j} \qquad \begin{array}{l} \alpha = 1, \ldots, n \\ j = 1, \ldots, L \end{array}$$

and all L structural equations for all n observations combined are written in matrix form:

$$(1.2) \qquad \mathbf{Y\Gamma} + \mathbf{XB} = \mathbf{E}$$

The following two assumptions will be made throughout this chapter.

Assumption 10.1 (Completeness and linearity) *The n values taken by the L jointly dependent variables are the realizations of an $n \times L$ random matrix* $\mathbf{Y}$ *which satisfies*

(1.2), *where* $\mathbf{X}$ *is an* $n \times K$ *matrix of predetermined values,* $\mathbf{E}$ *an* $n \times L$ *matrix of disturbances, and* $\boldsymbol{\Gamma}$ *and* $\mathbf{B}$ *are unknown parameter matrices of order* $L \times L$ *and* $K \times L$*, respectively,* $\boldsymbol{\Gamma}$ *being nonsingular.*

ASSUMPTION 10.2 (Independence and identical distribution of the rows of the disturbance matrix) *The* n *rows of the* $n \times L$ *disturbance matrix* $\mathbf{E}$ *are independent random drawings from an* L*-dimensional population with zero mean vector and unknown but finite covariance matrix* $\boldsymbol{\Sigma}$.

It is readily verified that Assumption 10.2 implies the validity of the assumptions on means, variances, and covariances listed at the end of Section 9.3, $\boldsymbol{\Sigma}$ being the matrix of variances and contemporaneous covariances. Note that we assume here that the rows of $\mathbf{E}$ are independent, which is stronger than uncorrelated, and also that they are identically distributed. These stronger conditions will be needed for our proofs of the asymptotic results.

The Purely Exogenous Case

When all predetermined variables are exogenous, we need one assumption in addition to Assumptions 10.1 and 10.2. The second part of this assumption concerns the asymptotic behavior of the matrix $n^{-1}\mathbf{X}'\mathbf{X}$ and corresponds to Assumption 8.1 in Section 8.1.

ASSUMPTION 10.3 (Purely exogenous case) *The* $n \times K$ *matrix* $\mathbf{X}$ *of the values taken by the predetermined variables has rank* K *and consists of non-stochastic elements. The matrix* $n^{-1}\mathbf{X}'\mathbf{X}$ *converges, as* $n \to \infty$*, to a finite matrix:*

$$\lim_{n \to \infty} \frac{1}{n} \mathbf{X}'\mathbf{X} = \mathbf{Q} \tag{1.3}$$

and the $K \times K$ *limit matrix* $\mathbf{Q}$ *is positive definite.*

The Lagged Endogenous Case

When there are lagged endogenous variables in the system, we replace (1.2) by

$$\mathbf{Y}\boldsymbol{\Gamma} + \mathbf{X}_0\mathbf{B}_0 + \sum_{g=1}^{G} \mathbf{Y}_{-g}\mathbf{B}_g = \mathbf{E} \tag{1.4}$$

where G is the largest endogenous lag that occurs in the system, $\mathbf{Y}_{-1}, \ldots,$

$\mathbf{Y}_{-G}$ are $n \times L$ matrices of successive lagged endogenous values:

$$\mathbf{Y}_{-g} = \begin{bmatrix} y_{1-g,1} & y_{1-g,2} & \cdots & y_{1-g,L} \\ y_{2-g,1} & y_{2-g,2} & \cdots & y_{2-g,L} \\ \cdot & \cdot & & \cdot \\ \cdot & \cdot & & \cdot \\ \cdot & \cdot & & \cdot \\ y_{n-g,1} & y_{n-g,2} & \cdots & y_{n-g,L} \end{bmatrix} \qquad g = 1, \ldots, G \tag{1.5}$$

while $\mathbf{X}_0 = [x_{\alpha h}]$ is an $n \times (K - GL)$ matrix consisting of the nonstochastic values of all predetermined variables which are not lagged endogenous. The following two assumptions correspond to Assumptions 8.2 and 8.3 in Section 8.7.

Assumption 10.4 (Lagged endogenous case; roots less than one in absolute value) *All GL roots of the determinantal equation*

$$|z^G \boldsymbol{\Gamma} + z^{G-1}\mathbf{B}_1 + \cdots + \mathbf{B}_G| = 0 \tag{1.6}$$

where $\boldsymbol{\Gamma}, \mathbf{B}_1, \ldots, \mathbf{B}_G$ *are defined in* (1.4), *have absolute values less than one.*

Assumption 10.5 (Lagged endogenous case; convergence of moment matrices of exogenous variables) *If* $K > GL$, *then for each* $\eta = 0, 1, \ldots, G$ *the* $(K - GL) \times (K - GL)$ *matrix whose* (h, k)th *element is*

$$\frac{1}{n - \eta} \sum_{\alpha=1}^{n-\eta} x_{\alpha h} x_{\alpha+\eta,k} \qquad (h, k = 1, \ldots, K - GL) \tag{1.7}$$

where $[x_{\alpha h}] = \mathbf{X}_0$ *is defined in* (1.4), *converges to a finite matrix* $\bar{\mathbf{Q}}_\eta$ *as* $n \to \infty$, *and the limit matrix* $\bar{\mathbf{Q}}_0$ *is positive definite.*

In the special case of a one-period maximum lag ($G = 1$), eq. (1.6) takes the form $|z\boldsymbol{\Gamma} + \mathbf{B}_1| = 0$, so that each solution of z is a latent root of the reduced-form parameter matrix $-\mathbf{B}_1\boldsymbol{\Gamma}^{-1}$ of the lagged endogenous variables. Thus the assumption requires that all these roots be less than one in absolute value.[1] Actually, it may be argued that this special case includes Assumption 8.2 of Section 8.7 as a still more special case; see Problem 1.1.

Some Basic Convergence Results

Equation (1.4) can be written in the standard form $\mathbf{Y}\boldsymbol{\Gamma} + \mathbf{X}\mathbf{B} = \mathbf{E}$ when we define $\mathbf{X}$ and $\mathbf{B}$ as

$$\mathbf{X} = [\mathbf{X}_0 \quad \mathbf{Y}_{-1} \quad \cdots \quad \mathbf{Y}_{-G}] \qquad \mathbf{B}' = [\mathbf{B}_0' \quad \mathbf{B}_1' \quad \cdots \quad \mathbf{B}_G'] \tag{1.8}$$

[1] Note that these are also the roots of the matrix $\mathbf{D}_1$ of eq. (7.1) of Section 9.7; also see footnote 14 of Chapter 9 on p. 464.

This notation will enable us to treat the lagged endogenous case in a manner analogous to that of the purely exogenous case. It can be shown, as stated in the following theorem, that the random matrix $n^{-1}\mathbf{X}'\mathbf{X}$ converges in probability to a positive definite symmetric matrix, which will be written as $\mathbf{Q}$ on the analogy of (1.3).

THEOREM 10.1 (Two results on convergence in probability and in distribution) *Suppose either that Assumptions* 10.1 *through* 10.3 *are satisfied, or that Assumptions* 10.1, 10.2, 10.4 *and* 10.5 *are true and that the disturbance distribution of Assumption* 10.2 *has finite moments of every order. In the latter case, regard the pre-sample values* $y_{0j}, \ldots, y_{1-G,j}$ $(j = 1, \ldots, L)$ *as constants. Then, in both cases:*

$$(1.9)\quad \operatorname*{plim}_{n\to\infty} \frac{1}{n}\begin{bmatrix}\mathbf{X}'\\ \mathbf{Y}'\\ \mathbf{E}'\end{bmatrix}[\mathbf{X}\quad \mathbf{Y}\quad \mathbf{E}]$$

$$= \begin{bmatrix} \mathbf{Q} & -\mathbf{Q}\mathbf{B}\boldsymbol{\Gamma}^{-1} & \mathbf{0} \\ -(\mathbf{Q}\mathbf{B}\boldsymbol{\Gamma}^{-1})' & (\boldsymbol{\Gamma}')^{-1}(\mathbf{B}'\mathbf{Q}\mathbf{B} + \boldsymbol{\Sigma})\boldsymbol{\Gamma}^{-1} & (\boldsymbol{\Sigma}\boldsymbol{\Gamma}^{-1})' \\ \mathbf{0} & \boldsymbol{\Sigma}\boldsymbol{\Gamma}^{-1} & \boldsymbol{\Sigma} \end{bmatrix}$$

where $\mathbf{Q}$ *is the symmetric positive definite probability limit of* $n^{-1}\mathbf{X}'\mathbf{X}$*. Also, in both cases the KL-element vector,*

$$(1.10)\quad \frac{1}{\sqrt{n}}(\mathbf{I}\otimes\mathbf{X})'\boldsymbol{\epsilon} = \frac{1}{\sqrt{n}}\begin{bmatrix} \mathbf{X}' & \mathbf{0} & \cdots & \mathbf{0} \\ \mathbf{0} & \mathbf{X}' & \cdots & \mathbf{0} \\ \vdots & \vdots & & \vdots \\ \mathbf{0} & \mathbf{0} & \cdots & \mathbf{X}' \end{bmatrix}\begin{bmatrix}\boldsymbol{\epsilon}_1\\ \boldsymbol{\epsilon}_2\\ \vdots \\ \boldsymbol{\epsilon}_L\end{bmatrix} = \frac{1}{\sqrt{n}}\begin{bmatrix}\mathbf{X}'\boldsymbol{\epsilon}_1\\ \mathbf{X}'\boldsymbol{\epsilon}_2\\ \vdots \\ \mathbf{X}'\boldsymbol{\epsilon}_L\end{bmatrix}$$

where $\boldsymbol{\epsilon}_1, \ldots, \boldsymbol{\epsilon}_L$ *are the successive columns of the disturbance matrix* $\mathbf{E}$ *of* (1.2) *and* $\boldsymbol{\epsilon} = [\boldsymbol{\epsilon}_1' \quad \cdots \quad \boldsymbol{\epsilon}_L']'$*, has a normal limiting distribution with zero mean vector and covariance matrix* $\boldsymbol{\Sigma}\otimes\mathbf{Q}$.

In the lagged endogenous case, the normal limiting distribution of the vector (1.10) is an extension of the similar property of $\sqrt{1/n}\,\mathbf{X}'\boldsymbol{\epsilon}$ stated in Theorem 8.5 (Section 8.7); this will not be proved here.[2] In the purely exogenous case it is an extension of the result proved in the last paragraph of Section 8.3. Details are considered in Problem 1.2; here we confine ourselves to showing that the covariance matrix of the limiting distribution of the vector

[2] See KOOPMANS, RUBIN and LEIPNIK (1950, Section 3.3), MANN and WALD (1943), and MALINVAUD (1966, pp. 564–566).

(1.10) can easily be made plausible for the purely exogenous case. Each subvector $\sqrt{1/n}\,\mathbf{X}'\boldsymbol{\epsilon}_j$ of (1.10) has zero mean and covariance matrix $(\sigma_{jj}/n)\mathbf{X}'\mathbf{X}$, and the covariance matrix of each pair of subvectors, say $\sqrt{1/n}\,\mathbf{X}'\boldsymbol{\epsilon}_j$ and $\sqrt{1/n}\,\mathbf{X}'\boldsymbol{\epsilon}_l$, is $(\sigma_{jl}/n)\mathbf{X}'\mathbf{X}$. Hence the complete vector (1.10) has zero mean and covariance matrix $\boldsymbol{\Sigma} \otimes n^{-1}\mathbf{X}'\mathbf{X}$, the limit of which is $\boldsymbol{\Sigma} \otimes \mathbf{Q}$ in view of (1.3). This does not prove, of course, that $\boldsymbol{\Sigma} \otimes \mathbf{Q}$ is the covariance matrix of the limiting distribution, only that it is the limit of the covariance matrix for $n \to \infty$.

Given the limiting distribution of the vector (1.10) and $\text{plim}\, n^{-1}\mathbf{X}'\mathbf{X} = \mathbf{Q}$, one can prove (1.9) easily, using the reduced form $\mathbf{Y} = -\mathbf{XB\Gamma}^{-1} + \mathbf{E\Gamma}^{-1}$.

Problems

1.1 Consider eq. (7.1) of Section 8.7:

$$y_\alpha = \sum_{g=1}^{G} \beta_g y_{\alpha-g} + \sum_{h=1}^{K-G} \beta_{G+h} x_{\alpha h} + \epsilon_\alpha \tag{1.11}$$

and introduce $H - 1$ "synthetic endogenous variables," $y_\alpha^{(1)} = y_{\alpha-1}, \ldots, y_\alpha^{(G-1)} = y_{\alpha-G+1}$. Combine these definitions with (1.11) into a G-equation system:

$$\mathbf{y}_\alpha^* = \mathbf{D}_1\mathbf{y}_{\alpha-1}^* + \mathbf{D}_2\mathbf{x}_\alpha^* + \boldsymbol{\epsilon}_\alpha^* \tag{1.12}$$

where

$$\mathbf{y}_\alpha^* = [y_\alpha \quad y_\alpha^{(1)} \quad \cdots \quad y_\alpha^{(G-2)} \quad y_\alpha^{(G-1)}]'$$

$$\mathbf{y}_{\alpha-1}^* = [y_{\alpha-1} \quad y_{\alpha-1}^{(1)} \quad \cdots \quad y_{\alpha-1}^{(G-2)} \quad y_{\alpha-1}^{(G-1)}]'$$

$$= [y_{\alpha-1} \quad y_{\alpha-2} \quad \cdots \quad y_{\alpha-G+1} \quad y_{\alpha-G}]'$$

$$\mathbf{D}_1 = \begin{bmatrix} \beta_1 & \beta_2 & \beta_3 & \cdots & \beta_{G-1} & \beta_G \\ 1 & 0 & 0 & \cdots & 0 & 0 \\ 0 & 1 & 0 & \cdots & 0 & 0 \\ \cdot & \cdot & \cdot & & \cdot & \cdot \\ \cdot & \cdot & \cdot & & \cdot & \cdot \\ \cdot & \cdot & \cdot & & \cdot & \cdot \\ 0 & 0 & 0 & \cdots & 0 & 0 \\ 0 & 0 & 0 & \cdots & 1 & 0 \end{bmatrix}$$

$$\mathbf{x}_\alpha^* = \begin{bmatrix} x_{\alpha 1} \\ \cdot \\ \cdot \\ \cdot \\ x_{\alpha,K-G} \end{bmatrix} \qquad \mathbf{D}_2 = \begin{bmatrix} \beta_{G+1} & \cdots & \beta_K \\ \mathbf{0} & \cdots & \mathbf{0} \end{bmatrix} \qquad \boldsymbol{\epsilon}_\alpha^* = \begin{bmatrix} \epsilon_\alpha \\ \mathbf{0} \end{bmatrix}$$

the zero submatrices of $\mathbf{D}_2$ and $\boldsymbol{\epsilon}_\alpha^*$ being columns of $G - 1$ elements. Prove that Assumption 10.4 applied to (1.12) is equivalent to Assumption 8.2 applied to (1.11).

1.2 As in the last paragraph of Section 8.3, write $\mathbf{C} = [\mathbf{c}_1 \quad \cdots \quad \mathbf{c}_n]$ for $\sqrt{1/n}\,\mathbf{X}'$. Prove that the vector (1.10) can be written as

$$\sum_{\alpha=1}^{n} \begin{bmatrix} \mathbf{c}_\alpha \epsilon_{\alpha 1} \\ \cdot \\ \cdot \\ \cdot \\ \mathbf{c}_\alpha \epsilon_{\alpha L} \end{bmatrix}$$

and show that under Assumptions 10.1 to 10.3, the characteristic function of this vector is

$$\phi_n(\mathbf{t}) = \prod_{\alpha=1}^{n} \left[1 - \frac{1}{2} \mathbf{t}'(\boldsymbol{\Sigma} \otimes \mathbf{c}_\alpha \mathbf{c}_\alpha')\mathbf{t} + o(n^{-1}) \right]$$

Prove finally that $\log \phi_n(\mathbf{t})$ converges to $-\frac{1}{2}\mathbf{t}'(\boldsymbol{\Sigma} \otimes \mathbf{Q})\mathbf{t}$ as $n \to \infty$, and draw your conclusions.

1.3 Prove eq. (1.9), given plim $n^{-1}\mathbf{X}'\mathbf{X} = \mathbf{Q}$ and given the asymptotic normality of the vector (1.10). (Hint for $n^{-1}\mathbf{E}'\mathbf{E}$: Use Khintchine's theorem.)

1.4 Prove that the rank of the probability limit of $n^{-1}\mathbf{X}'\mathbf{Y}$ given in Theorem 10.1 is equal to the rank of the parameter matrix $\mathbf{B}$.

10.2 Conditions for Identification[B]

We may conclude from the reduced form $\mathbf{Y} = -\mathbf{X}\mathbf{B}\boldsymbol{\Gamma}^{-1} + \mathbf{E}\boldsymbol{\Gamma}^{-1}$ that if $\mathbf{X}$ consists of nonstochastic elements (the purely exogenous case), the expectation of the αth row of $\mathbf{Y}$ is equal to the corresponding row of $-\mathbf{X}\mathbf{B}\boldsymbol{\Gamma}^{-1}$ and that its covariance matrix is $(\boldsymbol{\Gamma}')^{-1}\boldsymbol{\Sigma}\boldsymbol{\Gamma}^{-1}$ (see Problem 3.4 of Section 9.3). Under the condition that the rows of $\mathbf{E}$ are stochastically independent, these statements are also valid for the lagged endogenous case, provided we consider the conditional distribution of the αth row of $\mathbf{Y}$, given the αth observation on each of the predetermined variables. We shall apply this conditional interpretation throughout this section, so that it will not be necessary to make a distinction between the two cases.

The Relative Abundance of Structural Parameters

Let us assume that the distribution of the rows of $\mathbf{E}$ is multivariate normal. (We shall come back to this assumption at the end of this section.) It is clear that the distribution of each row of $\mathbf{Y}$ is then completely determined by (1) its expectation, the corresponding row of $-\mathbf{X}\mathbf{B}\mathbf{\Gamma}^{-1}$, and hence (given $\mathbf{X}$) by the reduced-form parameter matrix $-\mathbf{B}\mathbf{\Gamma}^{-1}$, and (2) its covariance matrix $(\mathbf{\Gamma}')^{-1}\mathbf{\Sigma}\mathbf{\Gamma}^{-1}$. It follows immediately that *the observation matrix* $[\mathbf{X} \quad \mathbf{Y}]$ *does not enable us to draw any inference about the unknown parameters of the structural equations* (the elements of $\mathbf{B}$, $\mathbf{\Gamma}$, and $\mathbf{\Sigma}$) *except through* $-\mathbf{B}\mathbf{\Gamma}^{-1}$ *and* $(\mathbf{\Gamma}')^{-1}\mathbf{\Sigma}\mathbf{\Gamma}^{-1}$. The number of elements of each of these matrices is counted in Table 10.1, and the result shows that the total number of structural parameters exceeds the number of reduced-form parameters. Therefore, special conditions will be needed before we can identify the former parameters in terms of the latter. Note that the number $\frac{1}{2}L(L+1)$ for the elements of the two covariance matrices implies that each covariance is counted only once. Also note that we can reduce the number of unknown elements of $\mathbf{B}$, $\mathbf{\Gamma}$, and $\mathbf{\Sigma}$ by dividing both sides of each structural equation by the coefficient of one of its variables, so that this coefficient becomes 1, a known value. However, this is not sufficient to obtain equality of the two totals of Table 10.1; see Problem 2.1.

Table 10.1

Total Numbers of Structural and Reduced-Form Parameters

Structural Parameters		Reduced-Form Parameters	
Matrix	Number of Elements	Matrix	Number of Elements
$\mathbf{B}$	KL	$-\mathbf{B}\mathbf{\Gamma}^{-1}$	KL
$\mathbf{\Gamma}$	L^2	$(\mathbf{\Gamma}')^{-1}\mathbf{\Sigma}\mathbf{\Gamma}^{-1}$	$\frac{1}{2}L(L+1)$
$\mathbf{\Sigma}$	$\frac{1}{2}L(L+1)$		
Total	$\frac{1}{2}L(2K+3L+1)$	Total	$\frac{1}{2}L(2K+L+1)$

Identification by Means of Zero Restrictions on the Coefficients

To solve the identification problem we have to assume that Table 10.1 exaggerates what is unknown about $\mathbf{B}$, $\mathbf{\Gamma}$, and $\mathbf{\Sigma}$. The most important approach is based on the assumption that a sufficient number of parameters in each structural equation vanishes. For this purpose we write, as we did in Sections 9.4 and 9.5, the jth structural equation for all n observations combined as

$$\mathbf{y}_j = \mathbf{Z}_j\boldsymbol{\delta}_j + \boldsymbol{\epsilon}_j = [\mathbf{Y}_j \quad \mathbf{X}_j]\begin{bmatrix} \boldsymbol{\gamma}_j \\ \boldsymbol{\beta}_j \end{bmatrix} + \boldsymbol{\epsilon}_j \qquad (2.1)$$

the number of elements of $\boldsymbol{\beta}_j$, $\boldsymbol{\gamma}_j$, and $\boldsymbol{\delta}_j$ being K_j, L_j, and $N_j = K_j + L_j$, respectively. The specification (2.1) implies that it is assumed to be known that the jth equation contains only the following variables: (1) the dependent variable whose values form the vector $\mathbf{y}_j$, (2) at most L_j other dependent variables whose values form the matrix $\mathbf{Y}_j$, and (3) at most K_j predetermined variables whose values are arranged in the matrix $\mathbf{X}_j$. It follows that the only part of the matrix $\mathbf{Y}$ which occurs in (2.1) is its submatrix $[\mathbf{y}_j \quad \mathbf{Y}_j]$, and we may conclude from the first paragraph of this section that the distribution of each row of this submatrix is determined by the corresponding row of the right-hand side of the following equation:

(2.2) $$[\mathbf{y}_j \quad \mathbf{Y}_j] = [\mathbf{X}_j \quad \mathbf{X}_j^*]\begin{bmatrix} \boldsymbol{\pi}_j & \boldsymbol{\Pi}_j \\ \boldsymbol{\pi}_j^* & \boldsymbol{\Pi}_j^* \end{bmatrix} + \begin{matrix}\text{reduced-form} \\ \text{disturbances}\end{matrix}$$

where $\mathbf{X}_j^*$ is the $n \times (K - K_j)$ matrix of the values taken by the $K - K_j$ predetermined variables that are postulated to occur in the system but not in its jth equation, so that $[\mathbf{X}_j \quad \mathbf{X}_j^*] = \mathbf{X}$. (The notation used thus assumes that the K_j predetermined variables of the jth equation are the first K_j predetermined variables.) The column vectors $\boldsymbol{\pi}_j$ and $\boldsymbol{\pi}_j^*$ contain K_j and $K - K_j$ elements, respectively, $\boldsymbol{\Pi}_j$ is of order $K_j \times L_j$ and $\boldsymbol{\Pi}_j^*$ of order $(K - K_j) \times L_j$;[3] they are all submatrices of the reduced-form parameter matrix $-\mathbf{B}\boldsymbol{\Gamma}^{-1}$. The reduced-form disturbances in (2.2) form an $n \times (L_j + 1)$ matrix which is a submatrix of $\mathbf{E}\boldsymbol{\Gamma}^{-1}$.

One important difference between (2.1) and (2.2) is that the latter equation does and the former does not contain the variables whose values are arranged in $\mathbf{X}_j^*$. Thus, the structural equation whose parameters we want to identify and estimate is subject to certain restrictions which may help us to reach this goal. Let us then postmultiply both sides of (2.2) by the column vector $[1 \quad -\boldsymbol{\gamma}_j']'$, so that we obtain on the left $\mathbf{y}_j - \mathbf{Y}_j\boldsymbol{\gamma}_j$, which equals $\mathbf{X}_j\boldsymbol{\beta}_j + \boldsymbol{\epsilon}_j$ according to (2.1). Disregarding the disturbances, we obtain on the right after postmultiplication:

(2.3) $$[\mathbf{X}_j \quad \mathbf{X}_j^*]\begin{bmatrix} \boldsymbol{\pi}_j & \boldsymbol{\Pi}_j \\ \boldsymbol{\pi}_j^* & \boldsymbol{\Pi}_j^* \end{bmatrix}\begin{bmatrix} 1 \\ -\boldsymbol{\gamma}_j \end{bmatrix}$$

which must thus be equal to $\mathbf{X}_j\boldsymbol{\beta}_j$. The immediate conclusion is

(2.4) $$[\boldsymbol{\pi}_j \quad \boldsymbol{\Pi}_j]\begin{bmatrix} 1 \\ -\boldsymbol{\gamma}_j \end{bmatrix} = \boldsymbol{\beta}_j$$

(2.5) $$[\boldsymbol{\pi}_j^* \quad \boldsymbol{\Pi}_j^*]\begin{bmatrix} 1 \\ -\boldsymbol{\gamma}_j \end{bmatrix} = \mathbf{0}$$

[3] Note that the matrix $\mathbf{P}_j$ defined in eq. (5.8) of Section 9.5 is the LS estimator of $[\boldsymbol{\Pi}_j' \quad \boldsymbol{\Pi}_j^{*\prime}]'$.

Equation (2.4) expresses $\boldsymbol{\beta}_j$ in terms of $\boldsymbol{\gamma}_j$, given $\boldsymbol{\pi}_j$ and $\boldsymbol{\Pi}_j$; it does not imply any restrictions on the latter matrices. But (2.5) can also be written as $\boldsymbol{\pi}_j^* = \boldsymbol{\Pi}_j^*\boldsymbol{\gamma}_j$, which gives a unique solution for $\boldsymbol{\gamma}_j$ if and only if the rank of $\boldsymbol{\Pi}_j^*$ and that of $[\boldsymbol{\pi}_j^* \quad \boldsymbol{\Pi}_j^*]$ are both equal to L_j (see rule E2 of Section 1.3). In other words, if we want to identify the vectors $\boldsymbol{\gamma}_j$ and $\boldsymbol{\beta}_j$ in terms of the parameter matrix

$$\begin{bmatrix} \boldsymbol{\pi}_j & \boldsymbol{\Pi}_j \\ \boldsymbol{\pi}_j^* & \boldsymbol{\Pi}_j^* \end{bmatrix} \tag{2.6}$$

of the reduced form (2.2), then the L_j columns of $\boldsymbol{\Pi}_j^*$ should be linearly independent and $\boldsymbol{\pi}_j^*$ should be a linear function of these columns. Summarizing:

THEOREM 10.2 (Identification) *Let eq.* (2.1) *be one of the L equations which form the system* $\mathbf{Y\Gamma} + \mathbf{XB} = \mathbf{E}$. *A necessary and sufficient condition for its parameter vector to be expressed uniquely in terms of the reduced-form parameter matrix* (2.6) *is that the rank of* $\boldsymbol{\Pi}_j^*$ *and that of* $[\boldsymbol{\pi}_j^* \quad \boldsymbol{\Pi}_j^*]$ *be equal to* L_j (*the rank condition for identification*), *where* $\boldsymbol{\pi}_j^*$ *is the vector of reduced-form parameters of the left-hand dependent variable of* (2.1) *and* $\boldsymbol{\Pi}_j^*$ *is the matrix of reduced-form parameters of the* L_j *right-hand dependent variables, in both cases only insofar as these parameters belong to the* $K - K_j$ *predetermined variables that are excluded from* (2.1). *A necessary condition is* $K \geq K_j + L_j$ $(= N_j)$, *the order condition for identification.*

The order condition, which was discussed in Section 9.4, follows from the fact that $\boldsymbol{\Pi}_j^*$ and $[\boldsymbol{\pi}_j^* \quad \boldsymbol{\Pi}_j^*]$ cannot have rank L_j when the number of rows $(K - K_j)$ is less than L_j. This condition is obviously easier to apply than the rank condition because the latter is formulated in reduced-form parameters which are normally unknown, but it does not really guarantee that the equation is identifiable, since it is only a necessary, not a sufficient, condition.

Identification Conditions Formulated in Terms of Structural Parameters

Since the structural parameters generally have a simpler economic interpretation than the reduced-form parameters, it may be considered more convenient to formulate the rank condition in terms of $[\boldsymbol{\Gamma}' \quad \mathbf{B}']$. This can be done as follows. Consider the jth row of this matrix, which contains the parameters of the jth equation. Since this equation has one variable on the left and N_j variables on the right [see (2.1)], the jth row of $[\boldsymbol{\Gamma}' \quad \mathbf{B}']$ contains $K + L - (N_j + 1)$ elements which are prescribed to be zero. The columns of $[\boldsymbol{\Gamma}' \quad \mathbf{B}']$ which contain these zero elements form a submatrix of order $L \times (K + L - N_j - 1)$, and one of the rows of this submatrix obviously consists of zeros only; hence its rank is at most equal to $L - 1$. It can be shown (see Problem 2.2) that a necessary and sufficient condition for the identifiability of the parameters of the jth equation is that the rank be indeed equal to $L - 1$. Note that the condition that the number of columns of this matrix be larger than or equal to the required rank is

$$K + L - (N_j + 1) \geq L - 1 \tag{2.7}$$

which is equivalent to the order condition $K \geq N_j$. Also note that the rank condition of Theorem 10.2 deals with a parameter matrix of order $(K - K_j) \times (L_j + 1)$, which is generally much smaller than the matrix of structural parameters discussed here.

Identification in the Case of Linear Constraints

Theorem 10.2 can be extended straightforwardly to the case in which there are restrictions on structural parameters in the form of linear equations with known coefficients. One way is by elimination. For example, take the equation

$$y_{\alpha 1} = \gamma y_{\alpha 2} + \beta_1 x_{\alpha 1} + \beta_2 x_{\alpha 2} + \epsilon_\alpha \tag{2.8}$$

and let the restriction be $2\gamma + \beta_1 = 1$. Use this to eliminate β_1 from (2.8):

$$y_{\alpha 1} - x_{\alpha 1} = \gamma(y_{\alpha 2} - 2x_{\alpha 1}) + \beta_2 x_{\alpha 2} + \epsilon_\alpha \tag{2.9}$$

This is an equation in two jointly dependent variables (whose values are of the form $y_{\alpha 1} - x_{\alpha 1}$ and $y_{\alpha 2} - 2x_{\alpha 1}$) and only one predetermined variable. In other words, the constraint is used to reduce K_j of (2.8) from 2 to 1. It is also possible to formulate the rank condition of identification in terms of the original parameters with the constraints added (see Problem 2.3). The order condition becomes $K \geq N_j - q_j$, where q_j is the number of (linearly independent) linear constraints on the coefficients of the jth equation.

Other Methods of Identification

It was assumed in the second paragraph of this section that the disturbances are normally distributed. If this is not true, a negative verdict of the rank condition may have to be reversed. To show this we reconsider the demand and supply equations (4.8) and (4.9) of Section 9.4:

$$q_\alpha = \beta_0 + \beta_1 p_\alpha + \epsilon_\alpha \qquad \text{(demand)} \tag{2.10}$$

$$q_\alpha = \beta_0' + \beta_1' p_\alpha + \beta_2' c_\alpha + \epsilon_\alpha' \qquad \text{(supply)} \tag{2.11}$$

and their mixture (4.10) that contains the same variables as the supply equation:

$$q_\alpha = \frac{\beta_0' + \theta\beta_0}{1+\theta} + \frac{\beta_1' + \theta\beta_1}{1+\theta} p_\alpha + \frac{\beta_2'}{1+\theta} c_\alpha + \frac{\epsilon_\alpha' + \theta\epsilon_\alpha}{1+\theta} \tag{2.12}$$

If $(\epsilon_\alpha, \epsilon_\alpha')$ is a random drawing from a bivariate normal population, then the disturbance of (2.12) is also normally distributed. But if $(\epsilon_\alpha, \epsilon_\alpha')$ is not normal, the distribution of the disturbance of (2.12) and that of the supply disturbance ϵ_α' will generally be of different types, and it is conceivable that the supply equation (which fails to satisfy the rank condition) can be distinguished from (2.12) on the basis of this information.[4]

In the same way, when it is known that ϵ_α and ϵ_α' are uncorrelated (which amounts to a diagonal matrix $\boldsymbol{\Sigma}$ of order 2×2), then this may also be used to identify the parameters of the supply equation even when $(\epsilon_\alpha, \epsilon_\alpha')$ is normally distributed. The reason is that the disturbance of (2.12) is then uncorrelated with the demand disturbance ϵ_α if and only if $\theta = 0$; that is, if and only if the mixture (2.12) is no mixture at all but identical with the supply equation.[5] Note that a diagonal $\boldsymbol{\Sigma}$ implies that the total number of unknown structural parameters is overestimated in Table 10.1.

Identification based on restrictions on the disturbance distribution is attractive only when there exists a sufficient knowledge of the process which generates the disturbances. This is usually not the case.

Identification under Conditions of Nonzero Lagged Covariances of the Disturbances

When the rows of the disturbance matrix $\mathbf{E}$ are not stochastically independent, other considerations enter into the picture. This may be illustrated by the following example of a two-equation system, from KOOPMANS, RUBIN, and LEIPNIK (1950, pp. 109–110):

$$y_{\alpha 1} + \gamma y_{\alpha 2} = \epsilon_{\alpha 1} \tag{2.13}$$

$$y_{\alpha 1} + \beta_1 y_{\alpha-1,1} + \beta_2 y_{\alpha-1,2} = \epsilon_{\alpha 2} \tag{2.14}$$

Both equations are identifiable under the conditions of this section. However, when we lag the first equation, multiply both sides by θ, and add the result to (2.14), we obtain

$$y_{\alpha 1} + (\beta_1 + \theta) y_{\alpha-1,1} + (\beta_2 + \theta\gamma) y_{\alpha-1,2} = \epsilon_{\alpha 2} + \theta\epsilon_{\alpha-1,1} \tag{2.15}$$

which is an equation in the same variables as those of (2.14). This does not

[4] A similar argument can be used in the case of nonlinearity; see Problem 2.4.

[5] Note, however, that this procedure does not work when the demand equation fails to satisfy the rank condition of identification. This condition is fulfilled in the case (2.10) and (2.11); see Problem 2.5 for the case in which it is not fulfilled.

necessarily mean that eq. (2.14) is underidentified in the system (2.13) and (2.14). If $(\epsilon_{\alpha 1}, \epsilon_{\alpha 2})$, $\alpha = 1, \ldots, n$ are independent random pairs, then $(\epsilon_{\alpha 1}, \epsilon_{\alpha 2} + \theta\epsilon_{\alpha-1,1})$ are not independent as soon as $\theta \neq 0$:

$$\mathscr{E}\left(\begin{bmatrix} \epsilon_{\alpha 1} \\ \epsilon_{\alpha 2} + \theta\epsilon_{\alpha-1,1} \end{bmatrix}[\epsilon_{\alpha+1,1} \quad \epsilon_{\alpha+1,2} + \theta\epsilon_{\alpha 1}]\right) = \begin{bmatrix} 0 & \theta\sigma_{11} \\ 0 & \theta\sigma_{12} \end{bmatrix} \tag{2.16}$$

The independence of the pairs $(\epsilon_{\alpha 1}, \epsilon_{\alpha 2})$, $\alpha = 1, \ldots, n$ thus ensures that the system (2.13) and (2.14) is not observationally equivalent to the system consisting of (2.13) and (2.15) for $\theta \neq 0$. But equations (2.14) and (2.15) are indistinguishable when the independence is not assumed.

Also note that when there is no independence, we cannot really regard the lagged endogenous variables ($y_{\alpha-1,1}$ and $y_{\alpha-1,2}$) as predetermined because their values are no longer independent of the current operation of the equation system.[6] It should cause no surprise that this affects the identifiability of the equations of the system, since the order condition $K \geq N_j$ involves the total number of predetermined variables. On the other hand, when the left-hand side of (2.13) contains a term $\gamma' x_\alpha$, where x_α is the αth value taken by an exogenous variable, then the corresponding version of the mixture (2.15) contains a term in $x_{\alpha-1}$ and is thus distinguishable from (2.14). Reference is made to Chapter 6 of F. M. Fisher (1966a) for further details on identification under conditions of dependence over time.

Problems

2.1 Prove that when we divide both sides of each of the L structural equations by one of its (nonzero) coefficients, so that the coefficient of the corresponding variable becomes a known number, the total number of unknown structural parameters of Table 10.1 becomes $\frac{1}{2}L(2K + 3L - 1)$. Also prove that this exceeds the number of reduced-form parameters when the equation system contains two equations or more.

2.2 To prove the rank condition for the identification of the parameters of the first equation in terms of $[\mathbf{\Gamma}' \quad \mathbf{B}']$, partition this matrix as follows:

$$[\mathbf{\Gamma}' \quad \mathbf{B}'] = \left[\begin{array}{ccc:cc} 1 & -\boldsymbol{\gamma}_1' & \mathbf{0} & -\boldsymbol{\beta}_1' & \mathbf{0} \\ \mathbf{A}_1 & \mathbf{A}_2 & \mathbf{A}_3 & \mathbf{A}_4 & \mathbf{A}_5 \end{array}\right] \tag{2.17}$$

where $\mathbf{A}_1, \ldots, \mathbf{A}_5$ are matrices consisting of $L - 1$ rows and of 1, L_1, $L - L_1 - 1$, K_1, and $K - K_1$ columns, respectively. Premultiply

[6] See the paragraph below eq. (2.7) in Section 9.2.

both sides by $(\mathbf{\Gamma}')^{-1}$, so that we obtain on the left a matrix with $\mathbf{I}$ and $(\mathbf{B\Gamma}^{-1})'$ as submatrices. Prove that the equation thus obtained, as far as it refers to the $\mathbf{A}_3$ and $\mathbf{A}_5$ columns on the right, can be written as

$$(2.18) \qquad \begin{bmatrix} \mathbf{0} & -\boldsymbol{\pi}_1^{*\prime} \\ \hdashline \mathbf{0} & -\mathbf{\Pi}_1^{*\prime} \\ \mathbf{I} & -\mathbf{\Pi}_1^{**\prime} \end{bmatrix} = (\mathbf{\Gamma}')^{-1} \begin{bmatrix} \mathbf{0} & \mathbf{0} \\ \mathbf{A}_3 & \mathbf{A}_5 \end{bmatrix}$$

where the first $\mathbf{0}$ on the left is of order $1 \times (L - L_1 - 1)$, the second of order $L_1 \times (L - L_1 - 1)$, and $\mathbf{\Pi}_1^{**}$ is the $(K - K_1) \times (L - L_1 - 1)$ submatrix of the reduced-form parameter matrix corresponding to the predetermined variables not occurring in the first equation and the jointly dependent variables not occurring in that equation. Finally, prove that the rank of the partitioned matrix in the right-hand side of (2.18) is equal to $L - 1$ if and only if the rank of $[\boldsymbol{\pi}_1^* \quad \mathbf{\Pi}_1^*]$ is equal to L_1.

2.3 Suppose that the parameter vector of the jth equation is known to satisfy q_j linear constraints: $\mathbf{r}_j = \mathbf{R}_j\boldsymbol{\gamma}_j + \mathbf{Q}_j\boldsymbol{\beta}_j$, where $\mathbf{r}_j$, $\mathbf{R}_j$, $\mathbf{Q}_j$ are matrices of appropriate order consisting of known elements, the matrix $[\mathbf{R}_j \quad \mathbf{Q}_j]$ having full row rank. Prove that a necessary and sufficient condition for the identification of $\boldsymbol{\gamma}_j$, $\boldsymbol{\beta}_j$ is that the matrices

$$\begin{bmatrix} \mathbf{\Pi}_j & \mathbf{I} \\ \mathbf{\Pi}_j^* & \mathbf{0} \\ \mathbf{R}_j & \mathbf{Q}_j \end{bmatrix} \quad \text{and} \quad \begin{bmatrix} \boldsymbol{\pi}_j & \mathbf{\Pi}_j & \mathbf{I} \\ \boldsymbol{\pi}_j^* & \mathbf{\Pi}_j^* & \mathbf{0} \\ \mathbf{r}_j & \mathbf{R}_j & \mathbf{Q}_j \end{bmatrix}$$

both have rank N_j, and also prove that $K \geq N_j - q_j$ is a necessary condition. [*Hint.* Because of the q_j constraints, eq. (2.4) does imply restrictions in the present case.]

2.4 Let the price term $\beta_1 p_\alpha$ of (2.10) be replaced by $\beta_1 \log p_\alpha$. Prove that the supply equation (2.11) can then be distinguished from (2.12) when $\beta_1 \neq 0$.

2.5 Suppose that the demand equation (2.10) contains c_α in the right-hand side, so that it no longer satisfies the rank condition of identification.[7] Suppose that ϵ_α and ϵ_α' are uncorrelated and write σ and σ', respectively, for their standard deviations. Write the demand and supply equations for the αth observation as follows:

$$(2.19) \qquad \begin{bmatrix} q_\alpha/\sigma \\ q_\alpha/\sigma' \end{bmatrix} = \begin{bmatrix} \beta_0/\sigma \\ \beta_0'/\sigma' \end{bmatrix} + \begin{bmatrix} \beta_1/\sigma \\ \beta_1'/\sigma' \end{bmatrix} p_\alpha + \begin{bmatrix} \beta_2/\sigma \\ \beta_2'/\sigma' \end{bmatrix} c_\alpha + \begin{bmatrix} \epsilon_\alpha/\sigma \\ \epsilon_\alpha'/\sigma' \end{bmatrix}$$

[7] The assumption of a c_α occurring in the demand equation is not particularly attractive from an economic point of view. It is merely made to illustrate the statement made in footnote 5 on page 494.

Prove that the covariance matrix of the disturbance vector of (2.19) is the 2×2 unit matrix. Then premultiply both sides of (2.19) by an arbitrary 2×2 orthogonal matrix and prove that the covariance matrix of the disturbance vector after this transformation remains unchanged. Use this result to prove that the identification of the supply equation (2.11) on the basis of zero contemporaneous correlation of the disturbances requires that the demand equation satisfy the rank condition of identification.

10.3 Asymptotic Properties of the Two-Stage Least-Squares Estimator[C]

In this section we shall show that the 2SLS estimator of the parameter vector $\boldsymbol{\delta}_j$ of eq. (2.1):

$$\mathbf{d}_j = [\mathbf{Z}_j'\mathbf{X}(\mathbf{X}'\mathbf{X})^{-1}\mathbf{X}'\mathbf{Z}_j]^{-1}\mathbf{Z}_j'\mathbf{X}(\mathbf{X}'\mathbf{X})^{-1}\mathbf{X}'\mathbf{y}_j \tag{3.1}$$

is consistent and asymptotically normally distributed. We shall also prove certain results concerning the joint distribution of 2SLS estimators of different structural equations.

THEOREM 10.3 (2SLS consistency and asymptotic normality) *Suppose that the assumptions of Theorem* 10.1 *are satisfied and that the rank condition for identification holds for the jth equation*, (2.1), *its disturbance variance* σ_{jj} *being positive. Then the 2SLS estimator* $\mathbf{d}_j$ *defined in* (3.1) *is consistent for* $\boldsymbol{\delta}_j$ *and* $\sqrt{n}(\mathbf{d}_j - \boldsymbol{\delta}_j)$ *has a normal limiting distribution with zero mean vector and the following covariance matrix:*

$$\sigma_{jj} \operatorname*{plim}_{n\to\infty} [(n^{-1}\mathbf{Z}_j'\mathbf{X})(n^{-1}\mathbf{X}'\mathbf{X})^{-1}(n^{-1}\mathbf{X}'\mathbf{Z}_j)]^{-1} \tag{3.2}$$

Also, the statistic

$$s_{jj} = \frac{1}{n}(\mathbf{y}_j - \mathbf{Z}_j\mathbf{d}_j)'(\mathbf{y}_j - \mathbf{Z}_j\mathbf{d}_j) \tag{3.3}$$

is a consistent estimator of the variance σ_{jj}.

This theorem implies that asymptotic standard errors of the 2SLS estimates can be computed from the inverse of the matrix in brackets of (3.1), multiplied by s_{jj}. To prove it we substitute $\mathbf{Z}_j\boldsymbol{\delta}_j + \boldsymbol{\epsilon}_j$ for $\mathbf{y}_j$ in that equation, so that the sampling error of $\mathbf{d}_j$ can be written as

(3.4)
$$\mathbf{d}_j - \boldsymbol{\delta}_j = [(n^{-1}\mathbf{Z}_j'\mathbf{X})(n^{-1}\mathbf{X}'\mathbf{X})^{-1}(n^{-1}\mathbf{X}'\mathbf{Z}_j)]^{-1}(n^{-1}\mathbf{Z}_j'\mathbf{X})(n^{-1}\mathbf{X}'\mathbf{X})^{-1}(n^{-1}\mathbf{X}'\boldsymbol{\epsilon}_j)$$

The matrix $n^{-1}\mathbf{X}'\mathbf{Z}_j$ converges in probability to a finite limit because this is true for its submatrices $n^{-1}\mathbf{X}'\mathbf{Y}_j$ and $n^{-1}\mathbf{X}'\mathbf{X}_j$ in view of Theorem 10.1. Assuming that the columns of $\mathbf{X}_j$ are the first K_j columns of $\mathbf{X}$, we have

$$\text{(3.5)} \qquad \operatorname*{plim}_{n\to\infty} \frac{1}{n}\mathbf{X}'\mathbf{Z}_j = \operatorname*{plim}_{n\to\infty} \frac{1}{n}\mathbf{X}'\mathbf{X}\begin{bmatrix} \mathbf{\Pi}_j & \mathbf{I} \\ \mathbf{\Pi}_j^* & \mathbf{0} \end{bmatrix} = \mathbf{Q}\begin{bmatrix} \mathbf{\Pi}_j & \mathbf{I} \\ \mathbf{\Pi}_j^* & \mathbf{0} \end{bmatrix}$$

where $\mathbf{I}$ is of order $K_j \times K_j$ and $\mathbf{0}$ of order $(K - K_j) \times K_j$. The first equality sign is based on

$$\mathbf{Y}_j = [\mathbf{X}_j \quad \mathbf{X}_j^*]\begin{bmatrix} \mathbf{\Pi}_j \\ \mathbf{\Pi}_j^* \end{bmatrix} + \text{submatrix of } \mathbf{E\Gamma}^{-1}$$

and on plim $n^{-1}\mathbf{X}'\mathbf{E} = \mathbf{0}$. Since $\mathbf{Q}$ is nonsingular, the rank of plim $n^{-1}\mathbf{X}'\mathbf{Z}_j$ is therefore equal to that of the partitioned matrix occurring in (3.5), which is $K_j + L_j = N_j$ if $\mathbf{\Pi}_j^*$ has rank L_j (the rank condition for identification).

The inverse of the matrix in square brackets in (3.4) thus converges to a symmetric positive definite matrix of order $N_j \times N_j$:

$$\text{(3.6)} \quad \operatorname*{plim}_{n\to\infty} [(n^{-1}\mathbf{Z}_j'\mathbf{X})(n^{-1}\mathbf{X}'\mathbf{X})^{-1}(n^{-1}\mathbf{X}'\mathbf{Z}_j)]^{-1}$$
$$= \left[\left(\operatorname*{plim}_{n\to\infty} n^{-1}\mathbf{Z}_j'\mathbf{X}\right)\left(\operatorname*{plim}_{n\to\infty} n^{-1}\mathbf{X}'\mathbf{X}\right)^{-1}\left(\operatorname*{plim}_{n\to\infty} n^{-1}\mathbf{X}'\mathbf{Z}_j\right)\right]^{-1}$$

We conclude from (3.4) that as $n \to \infty$, the sampling error $\mathbf{d}_j - \boldsymbol{\delta}_j$ converges in probability to the limit matrix (3.6) postmultiplied successively by the probability limits of $n^{-1}\mathbf{Z}_j'\mathbf{X}$, of the inverse of $n^{-1}\mathbf{X}'\mathbf{X}$, and of $n^{-1}\mathbf{X}'\boldsymbol{\epsilon}_j$. The last limit is a zero vector because $\mathbf{X}'\boldsymbol{\epsilon}_j$ is one of the columns of $\mathbf{X}'\mathbf{E}$. Since all other probability limits are finite, the consistency of $\mathbf{d}_j$ follows immediately. To prove the consistency of s_{jj} we note that each element of $\mathbf{y}_j - \mathbf{Z}_j\mathbf{d}_j$ converges in distribution to the corresponding element of $\mathbf{y}_j - \mathbf{Z}_j\boldsymbol{\delta}_j = \boldsymbol{\epsilon}_j$ because plim $\mathbf{d}_j = \boldsymbol{\delta}_j$. Hence s_{jj} has asymptotically the same distribution as $\boldsymbol{\epsilon}_j'\boldsymbol{\epsilon}_j/n$, the average of n independently and identically distributed random variables $\epsilon_{1j}^2, \ldots, \epsilon_{nj}^2$ with finite expectation σ_{jj}. Application of Khintchine's theorem then leads to the required result.

To prove the asymptotic normality of $\mathbf{d}_j$, we write (3.4) as

$$\text{(3.7)} \qquad \sqrt{n}(\mathbf{d}_j - \boldsymbol{\delta}_j) = \mathbf{G}_j \frac{1}{\sqrt{n}} \mathbf{X}'\boldsymbol{\epsilon}_j$$

where

$$\text{(3.8)} \qquad \mathbf{G}_j = [(n^{-1}\mathbf{Z}_j'\mathbf{X})(n^{-1}\mathbf{X}'\mathbf{X})^{-1}(n^{-1}\mathbf{X}'\mathbf{Z}_j)]^{-1}(n^{-1}\mathbf{Z}_j'\mathbf{X})(n^{-1}\mathbf{X}'\mathbf{X})^{-1}$$

Since $\mathbf{G}_j$ converges in probability to a finite matrix $\bar{\mathbf{G}}_j$ (say), we may conclude that the limiting distribution of both sides of (3.7) is identical with that of $\bar{\mathbf{G}}_j\sqrt{1/n}\,\mathbf{X}'\boldsymbol{\epsilon}_j$, provided that the latter vector has a limiting distribution. But Theorem 10.1 implies that $\sqrt{1/n}\,\mathbf{X}'\boldsymbol{\epsilon}_j$ has a normal limiting distribution with zero mean vector and covariance matrix $\sigma_{jj}\mathbf{Q}$. Hence $\bar{\mathbf{G}}_j\sqrt{1/n}\,\mathbf{X}'\boldsymbol{\epsilon}_j$ and also (3.7) have a normal limiting distribution with zero mean vector and covariance matrix $\sigma_{jj}\bar{\mathbf{G}}_j\mathbf{Q}\bar{\mathbf{G}}_j'$, and this matrix is identical with (3.2) as is easily verified. This completes the proof of Theorem 10.3.

2SLS Estimation of Several Equations

Theorem 10.3 is confined to the estimation of only one of the L equations. It is, of course, possible to apply the 2SLS method to each equation, but some questions remain. How can we compute, for example, the asymptotic standard error of the sum of two coefficients of different equations? This is a relevant question when one wants to verify whether the marginal propensity to spend out of current profit income in Klein's Model I, $\beta_1 + \beta_1'$, is less than one [see eqs. (2.1) and (2.2) of Section 9.2]. This question cannot be answered on the basis of the covariance matrix (3.2), which deals with only one equation. Also, when handling each equation separately, we estimate the disturbance variances $\sigma_{11}, \ldots, \sigma_{LL}$ but not their covariances σ_{jl}, $j \neq l$. The answer is provided by:

THEOREM 10.4 (2SLS estimation of several equations) *Suppose that the assumptions of Theorem* 10.1 *are satisfied and that the rank condition for identification holds for the jth and the lth equations* ($j \neq l$), *their disturbance variances* σ_{jj} *and* σ_{ll} *being both positive. Then* $\sqrt{n}$ *times the sampling error of the 2SLS coefficient estimators of these equations,*

$$\sqrt{n}\,[(\mathbf{d}_j - \boldsymbol{\delta}_j)' \quad (\mathbf{d}_l - \boldsymbol{\delta}_l)']$$

has a normal limiting distribution with zero mean vector and the following covariance matrix:

$$\begin{bmatrix} \sigma_{jj}\mathbf{A}_{jj}^{-1} & \sigma_{jl}\mathbf{A}_{jj}^{-1}\mathbf{A}_{jl}\mathbf{A}_{ll}^{-1} \\ \sigma_{jl}\mathbf{A}_{ll}^{-1}\mathbf{A}_{lj}\mathbf{A}_{jj}^{-1} & \sigma_{ll}\mathbf{A}_{ll}^{-1} \end{bmatrix} \tag{3.9}$$

where

$$\mathbf{A}_{jl} = \operatorname*{plim}_{n\to\infty}\,(n^{-1}\mathbf{Z}_j'\mathbf{X})(n^{-1}\mathbf{X}'\mathbf{X})^{-1}(n^{-1}\mathbf{X}'\mathbf{Z}_l) \qquad j, l = 1, \ldots, L \tag{3.10}$$

Also, the statistic

$$s_{jl} = \frac{1}{n}(\mathbf{y}_j - \mathbf{Z}_j\mathbf{d}_j)'(\mathbf{y}_l - \mathbf{Z}_l\mathbf{d}_l) \tag{3.11}$$

is a consistent estimator of the covariance σ_{jl} *of the disturbance pairs* $(\epsilon_{\alpha j}, \epsilon_{\alpha l})$ *of the two equations.*

The proof of this theorem is a straightforward extension of that of Theorem

10.3 (see Problem 3.2). The implication is that the estimated asymptotic covariance matrix of $\mathbf{d}_j$ and $\mathbf{d}'_l$ is

$$(3.12)\quad s_{jl}[\mathbf{Z}'_j\mathbf{X}(\mathbf{X}'\mathbf{X})^{-1}\mathbf{X}'\mathbf{Z}_j]^{-1}\mathbf{Z}'_j\mathbf{X}(\mathbf{X}'\mathbf{X})^{-1}\mathbf{X}'\mathbf{Z}_l[\mathbf{Z}'_l\mathbf{X}(\mathbf{X}'\mathbf{X})^{-1}\mathbf{X}'\mathbf{Z}_l]^{-1}$$

$$= s_{jl}\begin{bmatrix}\mathbf{Y}'_j\mathbf{Y}_j - \mathbf{U}'_j\mathbf{U}_j & \mathbf{Y}'_j\mathbf{X}_j \\ \mathbf{X}'_j\mathbf{Y}_j & \mathbf{X}'_j\mathbf{X}_j\end{bmatrix}^{-1}\begin{bmatrix}\mathbf{Y}'_j\mathbf{Y}_l - \mathbf{U}'_j\mathbf{U}_l & \mathbf{Y}'_j\mathbf{X}_l \\ \mathbf{X}'_j\mathbf{Y}_l & \mathbf{X}'_j\mathbf{X}_l\end{bmatrix}\begin{bmatrix}\mathbf{Y}'_l\mathbf{Y}_l - \mathbf{U}'_l\mathbf{U}_l & \mathbf{Y}'_l\mathbf{X}_l \\ \mathbf{X}'_l\mathbf{Y}_l & \mathbf{X}'_l\mathbf{X}_l\end{bmatrix}^{-1}$$

where $\mathbf{U}_l = [\mathbf{I} - \mathbf{X}(\mathbf{X}'\mathbf{X})^{-1}\mathbf{X}']\mathbf{Y}_l$ is the matrix of LS reduced-form residuals corresponding to $\mathbf{Y}_l$. The expression on the second line of (3.12) is thus based on the notation introduced in Section 9.5.

Problems

3.1 Prove that $\sigma_{jj}\bar{\mathbf{G}}_j\mathbf{Q}\bar{\mathbf{G}}'_j$, $\bar{\mathbf{G}}_j$ being the probability limit of $\mathbf{G}_j$ defined in (3.8), is equal to the matrix (3.2) as stated below (3.8).

3.2 For the coefficient estimators of Theorem 10.4, prove

$$(3.13)\qquad \begin{bmatrix}\sqrt{n}(\mathbf{d}_j - \boldsymbol{\delta}_j) \\ \sqrt{n}(\mathbf{d}_l - \boldsymbol{\delta}_l)\end{bmatrix} = \begin{bmatrix}\mathbf{G}_j & \mathbf{0} \\ \mathbf{0} & \mathbf{G}_l\end{bmatrix}\begin{bmatrix}\sqrt{1/n}\,\mathbf{X}'\boldsymbol{\epsilon}_j \\ \sqrt{1/n}\,\mathbf{X}'\boldsymbol{\epsilon}_l\end{bmatrix}$$

where $\mathbf{G}_j$ is defined in (3.8) and $\mathbf{G}_l$ is defined analogously. Next prove that this vector has a normal limiting distribution with zero mean and covariance matrix (3.9).

3.3 Prove the equality sign of (3.12).

3.4 For $L = 2$, prove that the covariance matrix (3.9) includes as a special case the LS covariance matrix of Problem 1.3 of Section 7.1. Indicate the nature of this special case.

10.4 Limited-Information Maximum Likelihood and the *k*-Class[BC]

We now leave the 2SLS method temporarily to derive a maximum-likelihood estimator of the coefficient vector of (2.1). For that purpose, consider first the reduced form for all L jointly dependent variables:

$$(4.1)\qquad \mathbf{Y} = \mathbf{X}\boldsymbol{\Pi} + \mathbf{E}\boldsymbol{\Gamma}^{-1} \qquad \text{where} \qquad \boldsymbol{\Pi} = -\mathbf{B}\boldsymbol{\Gamma}^{-1}$$

or, in more explicit form,

(4.2)

$$[y_{\alpha 1} \quad \cdots \quad y_{\alpha L}] = [x_{\alpha 1} \quad \cdots \quad x_{\alpha K}]\boldsymbol{\Pi} + [\epsilon_{\alpha 1} \quad \cdots \quad \epsilon_{\alpha L}]\boldsymbol{\Gamma}^{-1} \qquad \alpha = 1, \ldots, n$$

If we assume that the disturbance distribution is L-variate normal, the conditional distribution of the left-hand row in (4.2), given $x_{\alpha 1}, \ldots, x_{\alpha K}$, is also L-variate normal, its mean vector is equal to the first row on the right, and its covariance matrix is

$$(\mathbf{\Gamma}')^{-1}\mathbf{\Sigma}\mathbf{\Gamma}^{-1} = \mathbf{\Omega} \quad \text{say} \tag{4.3}$$

Maximum-Likelihood Estimation of Reduced-Form Parameters[B]

We assume temporarily that $\mathbf{\Sigma}$, and hence also $\mathbf{\Omega}$, are nonsingular. The density function of the left-hand row in (4.2) is then equal to $(2\pi)^{-L/2}\,|\mathbf{\Omega}|^{-\frac{1}{2}}$ multiplied by the exponent of

$$-\frac{1}{2}([y_{\alpha 1} \quad \cdots \quad y_{\alpha L}] - [x_{\alpha 1} \quad \cdots \quad x_{\alpha K}]\mathbf{\Pi})\mathbf{\Omega}^{-1}\left(\begin{bmatrix} y_{\alpha 1} \\ \cdot \\ \cdot \\ \cdot \\ y_{\alpha L} \end{bmatrix} - \mathbf{\Pi}'\begin{bmatrix} x_{\alpha 1} \\ \cdot \\ \cdot \\ \cdot \\ x_{\alpha K} \end{bmatrix}\right)$$

$$= -\frac{1}{2}\operatorname{tr}\mathbf{\Omega}^{-1}\left(\begin{bmatrix} y_{\alpha 1} \\ \cdot \\ \cdot \\ \cdot \\ y_{\alpha L} \end{bmatrix} - \mathbf{\Pi}'\begin{bmatrix} x_{\alpha 1} \\ \cdot \\ \cdot \\ \cdot \\ x_{\alpha K} \end{bmatrix}\right)([y_{\alpha 1} \quad \cdots \quad y_{\alpha L}] - [x_{\alpha 1} \quad \cdots \quad x_{\alpha K}]\mathbf{\Pi})$$

Since the rows of the disturbance matrix are independent, the density function for all observations combined is obtained by multiplying the n separate density functions. Hence the logarithmic likelihood is found by summation:

$$\begin{aligned} &-\frac{1}{2}Ln\log 2\pi - \frac{1}{2}n\log|\mathbf{\Omega}| \\ &\quad -\frac{1}{2}\operatorname{tr}\mathbf{\Omega}^{-1}\sum_{\alpha=1}^{n}\left(\begin{bmatrix} y_{\alpha 1} \\ \cdot \\ \cdot \\ \cdot \\ y_{\alpha L} \end{bmatrix} - \mathbf{\Pi}'\begin{bmatrix} x_{\alpha 1} \\ \cdot \\ \cdot \\ \cdot \\ x_{\alpha K} \end{bmatrix}\right)([y_{\alpha 1} \quad \cdots \quad y_{\alpha L}] - [x_{\alpha 1} \quad \cdots \quad x_{\alpha K}]\mathbf{\Pi}) \\ &= -\frac{1}{2}Ln\log 2\pi - \frac{1}{2}n\log|\mathbf{\Omega}| - \frac{1}{2}\operatorname{tr}\mathbf{\Omega}^{-1}(\mathbf{Y} - \mathbf{X\Pi})'(\mathbf{Y} - \mathbf{X\Pi}) \end{aligned} \tag{4.4}$$

This shows that the maximum-likelihood estimator of $\mathbf{\Pi}$ is obtained by minimizing the trace term on the last line. The solution is $(\mathbf{X}'\mathbf{X})^{-1}\mathbf{X}'\mathbf{Y}$, the LS estimator of $\mathbf{\Pi}$. To prove that this is indeed the case we consider any other estimator, say, $(\mathbf{X}'\mathbf{X})^{-1}\mathbf{X}'\mathbf{Y} + \mathbf{A}$ where $\mathbf{A}$ is some $K \times L$ matrix. The trace is then

$$(4.5)\quad \operatorname{tr}\boldsymbol{\Omega}^{-1}[\mathbf{Y}-\mathbf{X}(\mathbf{X}'\mathbf{X})^{-1}\mathbf{X}'\mathbf{Y}-\mathbf{XA}]'[\mathbf{Y}-\mathbf{X}(\mathbf{X}'\mathbf{X})^{-1}\mathbf{X}'\mathbf{Y}-\mathbf{XA}] = \operatorname{tr}\boldsymbol{\Omega}^{-1}\mathbf{Y}'[\mathbf{I}-\mathbf{X}(\mathbf{X}'\mathbf{X})^{-1}\mathbf{X}']\mathbf{Y}+\operatorname{tr}\boldsymbol{\Omega}^{-1}\mathbf{A}'\mathbf{X}'\mathbf{XA}$$

The expression on the second line takes the smallest value for $\mathbf{A}=\mathbf{0}$ because $\operatorname{tr}\boldsymbol{\Omega}^{-1}\mathbf{A}'\mathbf{X}'\mathbf{XA} = \operatorname{tr}(\mathbf{XA})\boldsymbol{\Omega}^{-1}(\mathbf{XA})'$ is the trace of a positive semidefinite matrix and is thus nonnegative.[8]

Constrained Maximum-Likelihood Estimation[B]

Now consider the matrix $[\mathbf{y}_j \ \ \mathbf{Y}_j]$ of the values taken by the jointly dependent variables of (2.1). Since it is a submatrix of $\mathbf{Y}$, the corresponding logarithmic likelihood function is equal to (4.4) apart from the following modifications: replace L in the first right-hand term of (4.4) by $L_j + 1$, $\boldsymbol{\Omega}$ by its principal submatrix $\boldsymbol{\Omega}_j$ of order $(L_j+1)\times(L_j+1)$ corresponding to $[\mathbf{y}_j \ \ \mathbf{Y}_j]$,[9] $\mathbf{Y}$ by $[\mathbf{y}_j \ \ \mathbf{Y}_j]$, and $\boldsymbol{\Pi}$ by the partitioned matrix consisting of $\boldsymbol{\pi}_j$, $\boldsymbol{\pi}_j^*$, $\boldsymbol{\Pi}_j$, and $\boldsymbol{\Pi}_j^*$ that was introduced in (2.2). The resulting logarithmic likelihood function is thus

$$(4.6)\qquad -\frac{1}{2}(L_j+1)n\log 2\pi - \frac{1}{2}n\log|\boldsymbol{\Omega}_j| - \frac{1}{2}\operatorname{tr}\boldsymbol{\Omega}_j^{-1}\mathbf{D}_j'\mathbf{D}$$

where

$$(4.7)\qquad \mathbf{D}_j = [\mathbf{y}_j \ \ \mathbf{Y}_j] - \mathbf{X}\begin{bmatrix}\boldsymbol{\pi}_j & \boldsymbol{\Pi}_j\\ \boldsymbol{\pi}_j^* & \boldsymbol{\Pi}_j^*\end{bmatrix}$$

It is obvious that if there were nothing special, the maximum-likelihood estimators of $\boldsymbol{\pi}_j$, $\boldsymbol{\pi}_j^*$, $\boldsymbol{\Pi}_j$, and $\boldsymbol{\Pi}_j^*$ would be submatrices of $(\mathbf{X}'\mathbf{X})^{-1}\mathbf{X}'\mathbf{Y}$ in accordance with the result formulated below eq. (4.4). However, these parameter matrices must satisfy the constraints (2.4) and (2.5), which are reproduced here for the sake of convenience:

$$(4.8)\qquad [\boldsymbol{\pi}_j \ \ \boldsymbol{\Pi}_j]\begin{bmatrix}1\\ -\boldsymbol{\gamma}_j\end{bmatrix} = \boldsymbol{\beta}_j \qquad [\boldsymbol{\pi}_j^* \ \ \boldsymbol{\Pi}_j^*]\begin{bmatrix}1\\ -\boldsymbol{\gamma}_j\end{bmatrix} = \mathbf{0}$$

Recall that the first equation is not a real constraint; it will enable us to derive the maximum-likelihood estimator of $\boldsymbol{\beta}_j$ as soon as the $\boldsymbol{\gamma}_j$ estimator is

[8] Strictly speaking, we should maximize the logarithmic likelihood function (4.4) with respect to $\boldsymbol{\Pi}$ and $\boldsymbol{\Omega}$ simultaneously. However, the derivation shows that $\boldsymbol{\Pi} = (\mathbf{X}'\mathbf{X})^{-1}\mathbf{X}'\mathbf{Y}$ maximizes this function for whatever value of $\boldsymbol{\Omega}$.

[9] Note that we no longer have to assume that $\boldsymbol{\Sigma}$ is nonsingular because the nonsingularity of $\boldsymbol{\Omega}_j$ is guaranteed by the rank condition of identification: if $\boldsymbol{\Omega}_j$, the covariance matrix of the rows of $[\mathbf{y}_j \ \ \mathbf{Y}_j]$, is singular, then the jointly dependent variables of (2.1) obey an exact linear relation which destroys the identifiability of this equation.

obtained. But the second implies $\boldsymbol{\pi}_j^* = \boldsymbol{\Pi}_j^*\boldsymbol{\gamma}_j$, which is a real constraint as soon as the number of elements of $\boldsymbol{\pi}_j^*$ exceeds that of $\boldsymbol{\gamma}_j$; that is, as soon as the equation is overidentified ($K - K_j > L_j$ or, equivalently, $K > N_j$). We know that no estimation is possible when the equation is underidentified. When it is just-identified, the constraints (4.8) can be ignored and it is easily shown that unconditional maximization of (4.6) with respect to $\boldsymbol{\pi}_j$, $\boldsymbol{\pi}_j^*$, $\boldsymbol{\Pi}_j$, and $\boldsymbol{\Pi}_j^*$ followed by substitution of the solutions into (4.8) leads to the 2SLS estimator in the just-identified form of eq. (4.4) of Section 9.4; see Problem 4.2. But when the equation is overidentified, we have to maximize (4.6) subject to the constraint $\boldsymbol{\pi}_j^* = \boldsymbol{\Pi}_j^*\boldsymbol{\gamma}_j$. This can be done by means of the Lagrangian expression

(4.9) $$\frac{1}{2} n \log |\boldsymbol{\Omega}_j| + \frac{1}{2} \operatorname{tr} \boldsymbol{\Omega}_j^{-1}\mathbf{D}_j'\mathbf{D}_j - \boldsymbol{\lambda}'(\boldsymbol{\pi}_j^* - \boldsymbol{\Pi}_j^*\boldsymbol{\gamma}_j)$$

where $\boldsymbol{\lambda}$ is a $(K - K_j)$-element vector of Lagrangian multipliers.

The Limited-Information Maximum-Likelihood Estimator[B]

The coefficient estimator which is derived in the way described above is known as the "limited-information maximum-likelihood estimator." The expression "limited-information" refers to the fact that the estimator takes account of the absence of certain variables from the jth equation but not of the absence of any variables from any of the other $L - 1$ equations; this should be clear from the derivation of the constraints (2.4) and (2.5).[10] The actual derivation of this estimator is rather lengthy and is discussed in Appendix B.[11] The result can be summarized as follows. Define:

(4.10) $$\mathbf{M} = \mathbf{I} - \mathbf{X}(\mathbf{X}'\mathbf{X})^{-1}\mathbf{X}' \qquad \mathbf{M}_j = \mathbf{I} - \mathbf{X}_j(\mathbf{X}_j'\mathbf{X}_j)^{-1}\mathbf{X}_j'$$

Then $\mathbf{Y}'\mathbf{M}\mathbf{Y}$ and $\mathbf{Y}'\mathbf{M}_j\mathbf{Y}$ are two $L \times L$ matrices consisting of sums of squares and products of LS residuals, and they deal with the same set of dependent variables but with different sets of predetermined variables. In the case of $\mathbf{Y}'\mathbf{M}\mathbf{Y}$ the regressions are on all K predetermined variables of the system; in the case of $\mathbf{Y}'\mathbf{M}_j\mathbf{Y}$ they contain only the K_j predetermined variables of the jth equation. Submatrices of these two matrices enter into the following determinantal equation:

(4.11) $$\left| \begin{bmatrix} \mathbf{y}_j' \\ \mathbf{Y}_j' \end{bmatrix} \mathbf{M}_j [\mathbf{y}_j \quad \mathbf{Y}_j] - \mu \begin{bmatrix} \mathbf{y}_j' \\ \mathbf{Y}_j' \end{bmatrix} \mathbf{M} [\mathbf{y}_j \quad \mathbf{Y}_j] \right| = 0$$

[10] Note that the 2SLS method is similar in this respect; its estimator also disregards the fact that there may be other equations in the system which contain parameters that are prescribed to be zero. "Full-information" methods which handle restrictions on the coefficients of all L equations simultaneously are considered in Sections 10.5 to 10.7 below.

[11] For an alternative derivation (based on the least-variance-ratio principle), see CHRIST (1966, pp. 411–424).

The submatrices of $\mathbf{Y}'\mathbf{M}_j\mathbf{Y}$ and $\mathbf{Y}'\mathbf{M}\mathbf{Y}$ are both of order $(L_j + 1) \times (L_j + 1)$; they obviously refer to the jointly dependent variables of the jth equation. The determinantal equation thus has $L_j + 1$ solutions for the scalar μ, and it can be shown that they are all real and ≥ 1. The relevant root, as stated in the following theorem, which is from ANDERSON and RUBIN (1949, 1950), is the smallest.

THEOREM 10.5 (Limited-information maximum likelihood) *The estimator of the parameter vector* $\boldsymbol{\delta}_j$ *of eq.* (2.1) *which maximizes the logarithmic likelihood function* (4.6) *subject to the constraints* (4.8) *is*

$$\text{(4.12)} \qquad \begin{bmatrix} \mathbf{Y}_j'\mathbf{Y}_j - \mu\mathbf{U}_j'\mathbf{U}_j & \mathbf{Y}_j'\mathbf{X}_j \\ \mathbf{X}_j'\mathbf{Y}_j & \mathbf{X}_j'\mathbf{X}_j \end{bmatrix}^{-1} \begin{bmatrix} \mathbf{Y}_j' - \mu\mathbf{U}_j' \\ \mathbf{X}_j' \end{bmatrix} \mathbf{y}_j$$

where μ *is the smallest root of the determinantal equation* (4.11), *which is real and larger than or equal to one. The vector* (4.12) *exists if and only if eq.* (2.1) *satisfies the rank condition for identification.*

The k-Class[B]

The asymptotic properties of the maximum-likelihood estimator (4.12) can be described conveniently when we first introduce the following family of estimators of the parameter vector $\boldsymbol{\delta}_j$:

$$\text{(4.13)} \qquad (\mathbf{d}_j)_k = \begin{bmatrix} \mathbf{Y}_j'\mathbf{Y}_j - k\mathbf{U}_j'\mathbf{U}_j & \mathbf{Y}_j'\mathbf{X}_j \\ \mathbf{X}_j'\mathbf{Y}_j & \mathbf{X}_j'\mathbf{X}_j \end{bmatrix}^{-1} \begin{bmatrix} \mathbf{Y}_j' - k\mathbf{U}_j' \\ \mathbf{X}_j' \end{bmatrix} \mathbf{y}_j$$

where k is an arbitrary scalar which may be either random or nonstochastic. The family of estimators $(\mathbf{d}_j)_k$ of the vector $\boldsymbol{\delta}_j$ is known as the *k-class*, which is from THEIL (1953b, 1961).[12] It includes the limited-information maximum-likelihood estimator of Theorem 10.5 ($k = \mu$) and also the 2SLS estimator ($k = 1$) and the LS estimator obtained by regressing $\mathbf{y}_j$ on $\mathbf{Y}_j$ and $\mathbf{X}_j$ ($k = 0$). In the next subsection we shall derive certain asymptotic properties of this class of estimators, which will then be used to show that the limited-information maximum-likelihood estimator has an asymptotic distribution which is identical to that of the 2SLS estimator.

[12] Other families of estimators are the h-class and the double k-class; see THEIL (1961, pp. 353–354) and NAGAR (1962).

Asymptotic Properties of k-Class Estimators[C]

To find the sampling error of $(\mathbf{d}_j)_k$, consider the vector by which the inverse occurring in (4.13) is postmultiplied and substitute $[\mathbf{Y}_j \quad \mathbf{X}_j]\boldsymbol{\delta}_j + \boldsymbol{\epsilon}_j$ for $\mathbf{y}_j$:

$$
(4.14) \quad \begin{bmatrix} \mathbf{Y}_j' - k\mathbf{U}_j' \\ \mathbf{X}_j' \end{bmatrix}([\mathbf{Y}_j \quad \mathbf{X}_j]\boldsymbol{\delta}_j + \boldsymbol{\epsilon}_j)
$$

$$
= \begin{bmatrix} \mathbf{Y}_j'\mathbf{Y}_j - k\mathbf{U}_j'\mathbf{Y}_j & \mathbf{Y}_j'\mathbf{X}_j - k\mathbf{U}_j'\mathbf{X}_j \\ \mathbf{X}_j'\mathbf{Y}_j & \mathbf{X}_j'\mathbf{X}_j \end{bmatrix}\boldsymbol{\delta}_j + \begin{bmatrix} \mathbf{Y}_j' - k\mathbf{U}_j' \\ \mathbf{X}_j' \end{bmatrix}\boldsymbol{\epsilon}_j
$$

$$
= \begin{bmatrix} \mathbf{Y}_j'\mathbf{Y}_j - k\mathbf{U}_j'\mathbf{U}_j & \mathbf{Y}_j'\mathbf{X}_j \\ \mathbf{X}_j'\mathbf{Y}_j & \mathbf{X}_j'\mathbf{X}_j \end{bmatrix}\boldsymbol{\delta}_j + \begin{bmatrix} \mathbf{Y}_j' - k\mathbf{U}_j' \\ \mathbf{X}_j' \end{bmatrix}\boldsymbol{\epsilon}_j
$$

where the second equality sign is based on the fact that $\mathbf{U}_j'\mathbf{X}_j$ is a submatrix of $\mathbf{U}_j'\mathbf{X} = \mathbf{0}$ and on $\mathbf{U}_j'\mathbf{Y}_j = \mathbf{U}_j'[\mathbf{X}(\mathbf{X}'\mathbf{X})^{-1}\mathbf{X}'\mathbf{Y}_j + \mathbf{U}_j] = \mathbf{U}_j'\mathbf{U}_j$. Combining (4.13) and (4.14), we obtain the following expression for the sampling error:

$$
(4.15) \qquad (\mathbf{d}_j)_k - \boldsymbol{\delta}_j = \begin{bmatrix} \mathbf{Y}_j'\mathbf{Y}_j - k\mathbf{U}_j'\mathbf{U}_j & \mathbf{Y}_j'\mathbf{X}_j \\ \mathbf{X}_j'\mathbf{Y}_j & \mathbf{X}_j'\mathbf{X}_j \end{bmatrix}^{-1}\begin{bmatrix} \mathbf{Y}_j' - k\mathbf{U}_j' \\ \mathbf{X}_j' \end{bmatrix}\boldsymbol{\epsilon}_j
$$

The simplest derivation of the asymptotic properties of the k-class estimators is by means of a comparison with the 2SLS estimator. Consider the identity:

$$
\frac{1}{n}\begin{bmatrix} \mathbf{Y}_j'\mathbf{Y}_j - k\mathbf{U}_j'\mathbf{U}_j & \mathbf{Y}_j'\mathbf{X}_j \\ \mathbf{X}_j'\mathbf{Y}_j & \mathbf{X}_j'\mathbf{X}_j \end{bmatrix} = \frac{1}{n}\begin{bmatrix} \mathbf{Y}_j'\mathbf{Y}_j - \mathbf{U}_j'\mathbf{U}_j & \mathbf{Y}_j'\mathbf{X}_j \\ \mathbf{X}_j'\mathbf{Y}_j & \mathbf{X}_j'\mathbf{X}_j \end{bmatrix} - \frac{k-1}{n}\begin{bmatrix} \mathbf{U}_j'\mathbf{U}_j & \mathbf{0} \\ \mathbf{0} & \mathbf{0} \end{bmatrix}
$$

Since $n^{-1}\mathbf{U}_j'\mathbf{U}_j = n^{-1}\mathbf{Y}_j'\mathbf{M}\mathbf{Y}_j = n^{-1}\mathbf{Y}_j'\mathbf{Y}_j - (n^{-1}\mathbf{Y}_j'\mathbf{X})(n^{-1}\mathbf{X}'\mathbf{X})^{-1}(n^{-1}\mathbf{X}'\mathbf{Y}_j)$ converges to a finite probability limit in view of Theorem 10.1, it follows immediately that

$$
(4.16) \quad \operatorname*{plim}_{n\to\infty} \frac{1}{n}\begin{bmatrix} \mathbf{Y}_j'\mathbf{Y}_j - k\mathbf{U}_j'\mathbf{U}_j & \mathbf{Y}_j'\mathbf{X}_j \\ \mathbf{X}_j'\mathbf{Y}_j & \mathbf{X}_j'\mathbf{X}_j \end{bmatrix} = \operatorname*{plim}_{n\to\infty} \frac{1}{n}\begin{bmatrix} \mathbf{Y}_j'\mathbf{Y}_j - \mathbf{U}_j'\mathbf{U}_j & \mathbf{Y}_j'\mathbf{X}_j \\ \mathbf{X}_j'\mathbf{Y}_j & \mathbf{X}_j'\mathbf{X}_j \end{bmatrix}
$$

$$
= \operatorname*{plim}_{n\to\infty} (n^{-1}\mathbf{Z}_j'\mathbf{X})(n^{-1}\mathbf{X}'\mathbf{X})^{-1}(n^{-1}\mathbf{X}'\mathbf{Z}_j)
$$

provided that

$$
(4.17) \qquad \operatorname*{plim}_{n\to\infty} (k-1) = 0
$$

Under this condition the sampling error (4.15) has the same probability limit as

$$
(4.18) \qquad \left[\operatorname*{plim}_{n\to\infty} (n^{-1}\mathbf{Z}_j'\mathbf{X})(n^{-1}\mathbf{X}'\mathbf{X})^{-1}(n^{-1}\mathbf{X}'\mathbf{Z}_j)\right]^{-1} \frac{1}{n}\begin{bmatrix} \mathbf{Y}_j' - k\mathbf{U}_j' \\ \mathbf{X}_j' \end{bmatrix}\boldsymbol{\epsilon}_j
$$

if the vector (4.18) has indeed a probability limit. But this vector is equal to the 2SLS sampling error $\mathbf{d}_j - \boldsymbol{\delta}_j$ minus

$$(4.19) \qquad (k-1)\left[\operatorname*{plim}_{n\to\infty} (n^{-1}\mathbf{Z}_j'\mathbf{X})(n^{-1}\mathbf{X}'\mathbf{X})^{-1}(n^{-1}\mathbf{X}'\mathbf{Z}_j)\right]^{-1}\begin{bmatrix} n^{-1}\mathbf{U}_j'\boldsymbol{\epsilon}_j \\ \mathbf{0} \end{bmatrix}$$

The vector $n^{-1}\mathbf{U}_j'\boldsymbol{\epsilon}_j$ is a submatrix of

$$n^{-1}\mathbf{U}_j'\mathbf{E} = n^{-1}\mathbf{Y}_j'\mathbf{M}\mathbf{E} = n^{-1}\mathbf{Y}_j'\mathbf{E} - (n^{-1}\mathbf{Y}_j'\mathbf{X})(n^{-1}\mathbf{X}'\mathbf{X})^{-1}(n^{-1}\mathbf{X}'\mathbf{E})$$

which converges to a finite probability limit in view of Theorem 10.1. Since $k-1$ converges in probability to zero under condition (4.17), the vector (4.19) has the same property. The consistency of $(\mathbf{d}_j)_k$ under condition (4.17) then follows from the consistency of the 2SLS estimator (Theorem 10.3), which proves the first part of the following theorem.

THEOREM 10.6 (Consistency and asymptotic normality of k-class estimators) *Under the assumptions of Theorem* 10.3, *condition* (4.17) *is sufficient in order that the k-class estimator* $(\mathbf{d}_j)_k$ *defined in* (4.13) *be consistent for the parameter vector* $\boldsymbol{\delta}_j$ *of eq.* (2.1), *and the condition*

$$(4.20) \qquad \operatorname*{plim}_{n\to\infty} \sqrt{n}\,(k-1) = 0$$

is sufficient in order that $\sqrt{n}\,[(\mathbf{d}_j)_k - \boldsymbol{\delta}_j]$ *have the same limiting distribution as* $\sqrt{n}\,(\mathbf{d}_j - \boldsymbol{\delta}_j)$, *where* $\mathbf{d}_j$ *is the 2SLS estimator of* $\boldsymbol{\delta}_j$.

To prove the second part of the theorem, note that (4.16) implies that the vector $\sqrt{n}\,[(\mathbf{d}_j)_k - \boldsymbol{\delta}_j]$ has the same limiting distribution as

$$(4.21) \qquad \left[\operatorname*{plim}_{n\to\infty} (n^{-1}\mathbf{Z}_j'\mathbf{X})(n^{-1}\mathbf{X}'\mathbf{X})^{-1}(n^{-1}\mathbf{X}'\mathbf{Z}_j)\right]^{-1}\frac{1}{\sqrt{n}}\begin{bmatrix} \mathbf{Y}_j' - k\mathbf{U}_j' \\ \mathbf{X}_j' \end{bmatrix}\boldsymbol{\epsilon}_j$$

provided that the vector (4.21) does indeed have a limiting distribution. But this vector is equal to the 2SLS expression $\sqrt{n}\,(\mathbf{d}_j - \boldsymbol{\delta}_j)$ minus

$$(4.22) \qquad \sqrt{n}\,(k-1)\left[\operatorname*{plim}_{n\to\infty} (n^{-1}\mathbf{Z}_j'\mathbf{X})(n^{-1}\mathbf{X}'\mathbf{X})^{-1}(n^{-1}\mathbf{X}'\mathbf{Z}_j)\right]^{-1}\begin{bmatrix} n^{-1}\mathbf{U}_j'\boldsymbol{\epsilon}_j \\ \mathbf{0} \end{bmatrix}$$

By applying the argument given below eq. (4.19) we conclude that the vector (4.22) converges in probability to zero if (4.20) is true, which proves the theorem.

The Consistency and Asymptotic Normality of the Limited-Information Maximum-Likelihood Estimator[C]

Theorem 10.6 implies that when k converges in probability to 1 (the 2SLS value of k), the estimator is consistent; and when k converges to 1 sufficiently fast, the estimator has the same (normal) asymptotic distribution as the 2SLS estimator. Both conditions are violated by LS; indeed, simple examples can be given which show that this method may produce (and, in fact, usually does produce) an estimator whose probability limit differs from the parameter vector; see Problem 4.3. But the limited-information maximum-likelihood estimator (4.12) satisfies both conditions, so that it is consistent and has the same asymptotic distribution as the 2SLS estimator. This comes from the following result, proved by ANDERSON and RUBIN (1950): the limiting distribution of $n(\mu - 1)$, where μ is the smallest root of the determinantal equation (4.11), is χ^2 with $K - N_j$ degrees of freedom, so that $\sqrt{n}\,(\mu - 1)$ and certainly $\mu - 1$ converge in probability to zero. The proof of this theorem will not be given here.

Testing the Over-Identifying Restrictions[C]

The number of degrees of freedom of this limiting χ^2 distribution, $K - N_j$, may be regarded as the "degree of overidentification" of the jth structural equation. This distribution can also be used to test the overidentifying restrictions on this equation. More precisely, let the null hypothesis H_0 specify that the $K - N_j - 1$ variables which are postulated not to occur in the equation do have zero coefficients in that equation, and let the alternative hypothesis H_1 specify that at least one of these coefficients is not zero. Thus, H_1 states that H_0 declares too many variables to be absent from the equation. Under H_0 the test statistic $n(\mu - 1)$ is asymptotically distributed as $\chi^2(K - N_j)$. Under H_1 the residual sums of squares which are the diagonal elements of $[\mathbf{y}_j \quad \mathbf{Y}_j]'\mathbf{M}_j[\mathbf{y}_j \quad \mathbf{Y}_j]$ will be too large, because if H_1 is true, certain predetermined variables ought to be represented in $\mathbf{X}_j$ and hence in $\mathbf{M}_j$, but they are, in fact, not represented. This raises the value of μ in (4.11). Hence, H_0 is to be rejected in favor of H_1 if the observed μ exceeds the relevant significance limit of the χ^2 distribution with $K - N_j$ degrees of freedom.

Note that this procedure is only asymptotically valid.[13] BASMANN (1960b) carried out some sampling experiments and found that it rejects the null hypothesis too frequently when it is applied to samples of small or moderate

[13] Also note that it is only possible to test *over*identifying restrictions. Restrictions that are needed to identify an equation cannot be tested in the same way that coefficients of an underidentified equation cannot be estimated.

size. He proposed as an alternative test statistic the expression

$$(4.23) \qquad \frac{n-K}{K-N_j} \times \frac{(\mathbf{y}_j - \mathbf{Y}_j\mathbf{c}_j)'(\mathbf{M}_j - \mathbf{M})(\mathbf{y}_j - \mathbf{Y}_j\mathbf{c}_j)}{(\mathbf{y}_j - \mathbf{Y}_j\mathbf{c}_j)'\mathbf{M}(\mathbf{y}_j - \mathbf{Y}_j\mathbf{c}_j)}$$

$\mathbf{c}_j$ being the 2SLS estimator of the parameter subvector $\boldsymbol{\gamma}_j$, and he argued that this statistic has approximately the F distribution with $K - N_j$ and $n - K$ degrees of freedom. The available Monte Carlo evidence indicates that the performance of this procedure is superior to that of the χ^2 distribution applied to the root μ.

Problems

4.1 Prove that the trace on the second line of (4.4) is equal to the trace of $\boldsymbol{\Omega}^{-1}(\mathbf{Y} - \mathbf{X\Pi})'(\mathbf{Y} - \mathbf{X\Pi})$ as asserted in that equation. Also prove the equality sign of (4.5).

4.2 Prove that the estimators of $[\boldsymbol{\pi}_j' \quad \boldsymbol{\pi}_j^{*\prime}]'$ and $[\boldsymbol{\Pi}_j' \quad \boldsymbol{\Pi}_j^{*\prime}]'$ which minimize the trace of (4.6) are equal to $(\mathbf{X}'\mathbf{X})^{-1}\mathbf{X}'\mathbf{y}_j$ and $(\mathbf{X}'\mathbf{X})^{-1}\mathbf{X}'\mathbf{Y}_j$, respectively. Substitute these estimators into the constraints (2.4) and (2.5), to be written as

$$\begin{bmatrix} \boldsymbol{\Pi}_j & \mathbf{I} \\ \boldsymbol{\Pi}_j^* & \mathbf{0} \end{bmatrix} \begin{bmatrix} \boldsymbol{\gamma}_j \\ \boldsymbol{\beta}_j \end{bmatrix} = \begin{bmatrix} \boldsymbol{\pi}_j \\ \boldsymbol{\pi}_j^* \end{bmatrix}$$

and prove that the implied estimator of $[\boldsymbol{\gamma}_j' \quad \boldsymbol{\beta}_j']'$ is $(\mathbf{X}'\mathbf{Z}_j)^{-1}\mathbf{X}'\mathbf{y}_j$ if the matrix $\mathbf{X}'\mathbf{Z}_j = \mathbf{X}'[\mathbf{Y}_j \quad \mathbf{X}_j]$ is square and nonsingular.

4.3 Suppose that Assumptions 10.1 to 10.3 apply to the Keynesian model (1.1) and (1.2) of Section 9.1 with investment as the exogenous variable. Prove that the LS estimator $\sum C_\alpha Y_\alpha / \sum Y_\alpha^2$ of β has a probability limit which exceeds β by $(1 - \beta)\sigma^2/(q + \sigma^2)$, where σ^2 is the variance of the consumption disturbances and q is the limit of $n^{-1} \sum I_\alpha^2$.

4.4 (*Instrumental-variable interpretation of k-class estimators*) Prove that $(\mathbf{d}_j)_k$ defined in (4.13) is an instrumental-variable estimator and that the observation matrix of the instrumental variables is $[\mathbf{Y}_j - k\mathbf{U}_j \quad \mathbf{X}_j]$.

10.5 The Three-Stage Least-Squares Method[BC]

This section concerns an estimation technique, from ZELLNER and THEIL (1962), which handles the unknown coefficients of all structural equations at the same time. It may be regarded as a simultaneous equation extension of the joint GLS procedure described in Section 7.2.

Outline of the 3SLS Procedure[B]

We write the L structural equations for all n observations combined as follows:

$$\begin{bmatrix} \mathbf{y}_1 \\ \mathbf{y}_2 \\ \cdot \\ \cdot \\ \cdot \\ \mathbf{y}_L \end{bmatrix} = \begin{bmatrix} \mathbf{Z}_1 & \mathbf{0} & \cdots & \mathbf{0} \\ \mathbf{0} & \mathbf{Z}_2 & \cdots & \mathbf{0} \\ \cdot & \cdot & & \cdot \\ \cdot & \cdot & & \cdot \\ \cdot & \cdot & & \cdot \\ \mathbf{0} & \mathbf{0} & \cdots & \mathbf{Z}_L \end{bmatrix} \begin{bmatrix} \boldsymbol{\delta}_1 \\ \boldsymbol{\delta}_2 \\ \cdot \\ \cdot \\ \cdot \\ \boldsymbol{\delta}_L \end{bmatrix} + \begin{bmatrix} \boldsymbol{\epsilon}_1 \\ \boldsymbol{\epsilon}_2 \\ \cdot \\ \cdot \\ \cdot \\ \boldsymbol{\epsilon}_L \end{bmatrix} \quad \text{or} \quad \mathbf{y} = \mathbf{Z}\boldsymbol{\delta} + \boldsymbol{\epsilon} \tag{5.1}$$

where

$$\mathbf{y} = \begin{bmatrix} \mathbf{y}_1 \\ \mathbf{y}_2 \\ \cdot \\ \cdot \\ \cdot \\ \mathbf{y}_L \end{bmatrix} \quad \mathbf{Z} = \begin{bmatrix} \mathbf{Z}_1 & \mathbf{0} & \cdots & \mathbf{0} \\ \mathbf{0} & \mathbf{Z}_2 & \cdots & \mathbf{0} \\ \cdot & \cdot & & \cdot \\ \cdot & \cdot & & \cdot \\ \cdot & \cdot & & \cdot \\ \mathbf{0} & \mathbf{0} & \cdots & \mathbf{Z}_L \end{bmatrix} \quad \boldsymbol{\delta} = \begin{bmatrix} \boldsymbol{\delta}_1 \\ \boldsymbol{\delta}_2 \\ \cdot \\ \cdot \\ \cdot \\ \boldsymbol{\delta}_L \end{bmatrix} \quad \boldsymbol{\epsilon} = \begin{bmatrix} \boldsymbol{\epsilon}_1 \\ \boldsymbol{\epsilon}_2 \\ \cdot \\ \cdot \\ \cdot \\ \boldsymbol{\epsilon}_L \end{bmatrix} \tag{5.2}$$

It seems rather tempting to apply the joint estimation technique of Section 7.2 in order to estimate all

$$N = \sum_{j=1}^{L} N_j = \sum_{j=1}^{L} (K_j + L_j) \tag{5.3}$$

elements of the parameter vector $\boldsymbol{\delta}$ from the Ln-element vector equation (5.1). However, we then face the difficulty that $\mathbf{Z}$ contains the random matrices $\mathbf{Y}_1, \ldots, \mathbf{Y}_L$ which are not independent of the disturbance vector $\boldsymbol{\epsilon}$. A more promising approach is to premultiply both sides of (5.1) by the transpose of the $Ln \times KL$ Kronecker product

$$\mathbf{I} \otimes \mathbf{X} = \begin{bmatrix} \mathbf{X} & \mathbf{0} & \cdots & \mathbf{0} \\ \mathbf{0} & \mathbf{X} & \cdots & \mathbf{0} \\ \cdot & \cdot & & \cdot \\ \cdot & \cdot & & \cdot \\ \cdot & \cdot & & \cdot \\ \mathbf{0} & \mathbf{0} & \cdots & \mathbf{X} \end{bmatrix} \tag{5.4}$$

which gives

$$(\mathbf{I} \otimes \mathbf{X}')\mathbf{y} = (\mathbf{I} \otimes \mathbf{X}')\mathbf{Z}\boldsymbol{\delta} + (\mathbf{I} \otimes \mathbf{X}')\boldsymbol{\epsilon} \tag{5.5}$$

or, in partitioned form,

$$\begin{bmatrix} \mathbf{X}'\mathbf{y}_1 \\ \mathbf{X}'\mathbf{y}_2 \\ \cdot \\ \cdot \\ \cdot \\ \mathbf{X}'\mathbf{y}_L \end{bmatrix} = \begin{bmatrix} \mathbf{X}'\mathbf{Z}_1 & \mathbf{0} & \cdots & \mathbf{0} \\ \mathbf{0} & \mathbf{X}'\mathbf{Z}_2 & \cdots & \mathbf{0} \\ \cdot & \cdot & & \cdot \\ \cdot & \cdot & & \cdot \\ \cdot & \cdot & & \cdot \\ \mathbf{0} & \mathbf{0} & \cdots & \mathbf{X}'\mathbf{Z}_L \end{bmatrix} \begin{bmatrix} \boldsymbol{\delta}_1 \\ \boldsymbol{\delta}_2 \\ \cdot \\ \cdot \\ \cdot \\ \boldsymbol{\delta}_L \end{bmatrix} + \begin{bmatrix} \mathbf{X}'\boldsymbol{\epsilon}_1 \\ \mathbf{X}'\boldsymbol{\epsilon}_2 \\ \cdot \\ \cdot \\ \cdot \\ \mathbf{X}'\boldsymbol{\epsilon}_L \end{bmatrix} \tag{5.6}$$

Note that (5.6) consists of L equations of the form $\mathbf{X}'\mathbf{y}_j = \mathbf{X}'\mathbf{Z}_j\boldsymbol{\delta}_j + \mathbf{X}'\boldsymbol{\epsilon}_j$, which is eq. (4.3) of Section 9.4 from which we derived the 2SLS estimator in Section 9.5:

$$\mathbf{d}_j = [\mathbf{Z}_j'\mathbf{X}(\mathbf{X}'\mathbf{X})^{-1}\mathbf{X}'\mathbf{Z}_j]^{-1}\mathbf{Z}_j'\mathbf{X}(\mathbf{X}'\mathbf{X})^{-1}\mathbf{X}'\mathbf{y}_j \tag{5.7}$$

The estimator to be derived in this section will have the same relation to $\mathbf{d}_1, \ldots, \mathbf{d}_L$ as the joint GLS estimator of Section 7.2 has to the LS estimators of each equation separately.

The vector equation (5.6) consists of KL separate equations, and it contains $N = \sum N_j$ unknown parameters (the elements of $\boldsymbol{\delta}$). The former number (KL) exceeds the latter when all equations are identified and at least one of them is overidentified. The application of the joint estimation technique to (5.6) amounts to a "full information" technique, since the estimation of the $\boldsymbol{\delta}_j$ of *each* structural equation takes account of the restrictions on *all* equations. This follows from the fact that $\boldsymbol{\delta}_1, \ldots, \boldsymbol{\delta}_L$ contain only those parameters which are not prescribed to be zero; hence, all elements of the parameter matrix $[\boldsymbol{\Gamma}' \quad \mathbf{B}']$ that are postulated to vanish are simply deleted, not only those of the jth row corresponding to the jth equation.

As in the 2SLS derivation of Section 9.5, we proceed under the temporary assumption that all K predetermined variables are exogenous, so that $\mathbf{X}$ may be regarded as consisting of nonstochastic elements. The KL-element disturbance vector of (5.5) and (5.6) then has zero mean and covariance matrix $\boldsymbol{\Sigma} \otimes \mathbf{X}'\mathbf{X}$. By applying the rule

$$(\mathbf{A}_1 \otimes \mathbf{B}_1)(\mathbf{A}_2 \otimes \mathbf{B}_2)(\mathbf{A}_3 \otimes \mathbf{B}_3) = (\mathbf{A}_1\mathbf{A}_2\mathbf{A}_3) \otimes (\mathbf{B}_1\mathbf{B}_2\mathbf{B}_3)$$

one easily verifies that the Aitken procedure applied to (5.5) leads to the following estimator of $\boldsymbol{\delta}$:

$$(\mathbf{Z}'[\boldsymbol{\Sigma}^{-1} \otimes \mathbf{X}(\mathbf{X}'\mathbf{X})^{-1}\mathbf{X}']\mathbf{Z})^{-1}\mathbf{Z}'[\boldsymbol{\Sigma}^{-1} \otimes \mathbf{X}(\mathbf{X}'\mathbf{X})^{-1}\mathbf{X}']\mathbf{y} \tag{5.8}$$

Since $\boldsymbol{\Sigma}$ is normally unknown, we replace it by $\mathbf{S} = [s_{jl}]$, the matrix of mean squares and products of the 2SLS residuals. This leads to

$$\hat{\boldsymbol{\delta}} = (\mathbf{Z}'[\mathbf{S}^{-1} \otimes \mathbf{X}(\mathbf{X}'\mathbf{X})^{-1}\mathbf{X}']\mathbf{Z})^{-1}\mathbf{Z}'[\mathbf{S}^{-1} \otimes \mathbf{X}(\mathbf{X}'\mathbf{X})^{-1}\mathbf{X}']\mathbf{y} \tag{5.9}$$

which is known as the *three-stage least-squares* (3SLS) estimator. The first two stages are those of 2SLS, which provide the matrix $\mathbf{S}$; the third stage is GLS applied to (5.5) with $\boldsymbol{\Sigma}$ replaced by $\mathbf{S}$. The $N \times N$ inverse immediately to the right of the equality sign in (5.9) is an approximate covariance matrix of $\hat{\boldsymbol{\delta}}$ from which asymptotic standard errors can be computed by taking the square roots of the diagonal elements. It is worthwhile to note the similarity of the right-hand sides of (5.7) and (5.9).

The next subsection describes the asymptotic properties of the 3SLS estimator in more detail. It will turn out that the asymptotic covariance matrix of the 2SLS estimator $\mathbf{d}_j$ exceeds that of the corresponding subvector of $\hat{\boldsymbol{\delta}}$ by a positive semidefinite matrix. However, the 3SLS estimator provides no gain when the disturbance covariance matrix $\boldsymbol{\Sigma}$ is diagonal (which is similar to the joint GLS case) or when all structural equations are just-identified. The former statement is proved by noting that the Kronecker product of $\boldsymbol{\Sigma}^{-1}$ and $\mathbf{X}(\mathbf{X}'\mathbf{X})^{-1}\mathbf{X}'$ in (5.8) is block-diagonal when $\boldsymbol{\Sigma}$ is diagonal, which implies that the vector (5.8) simply consists of the 2SLS vectors $\mathbf{d}_1, \ldots, \mathbf{d}_L$. To prove the latter statement we need only note that if all equations are just-identified, the vector equation (5.6) consists of as many equations as there are $\boldsymbol{\delta}$ elements to be estimated; the estimator of $\boldsymbol{\delta}_j$ is then obviously $(\mathbf{X}'\mathbf{Z}_j)^{-1}\mathbf{X}'\mathbf{y}_j$, the 2SLS estimator in the just-identified case. Thus, the 3SLS procedure provides an asymptotic gain over 2SLS only when the structural disturbances have nonzero contemporaneous covariances and when at the same time at least some equations are overidentified. Certain simplifications are possible when the contemporaneous covariance matrix is block-diagonal and also when some equations are just-identified. These are pursued in Problems 5.1 to 5.4.

Asymptotic Properties of the 3SLS Estimator[C]

Some economy in notation is obtained by replacing the matrix product $(\mathbf{X}'\mathbf{X})^{-1}\mathbf{X}'$ by the generalized inverse $\mathbf{X}^+$. The 2SLS estimator (5.7) then becomes

$$\mathbf{d}_j = (\mathbf{Z}_j'\mathbf{X}\mathbf{X}^+\mathbf{Z}_j)^{-1}\mathbf{Z}_j'\mathbf{X}\mathbf{X}^+\mathbf{y}_j \tag{5.10}$$

and the 3SLS estimator (5.9):

$$\hat{\boldsymbol{\delta}} = [\mathbf{Z}'(\mathbf{S}^{-1} \otimes \mathbf{X}\mathbf{X}^+)\mathbf{Z}]^{-1}\mathbf{Z}'(\mathbf{S}^{-1} \otimes \mathbf{X}\mathbf{X}^+)\mathbf{y} \tag{5.11}$$

THEOREM 10.7 (3SLS estimation) *Suppose that the assumptions of Theorem* 10.1 *are satisfied and that the rank condition for identification holds for all equations of the system. For parts* (1) *and* (2) *below, also assume that the disturbance covariance matrix* $\boldsymbol{\Sigma}$ *is nonsingular.*

(1) *The estimator* $\hat{\boldsymbol{\delta}}$ *defined in* (5.11) *is consistent for the parameter vector* $\boldsymbol{\delta}$ *of* (5.1) *and* $\sqrt{n}(\hat{\boldsymbol{\delta}} - \boldsymbol{\delta})$ *has a normal limiting distribution with zero mean vector and the following covariance matrix:*

$$\operatorname*{plim}_{n\to\infty}\left[\frac{1}{n}\mathbf{Z}'(\boldsymbol{\Sigma}^{-1} \otimes \mathbf{X}\mathbf{X}^+)\mathbf{Z}\right]^{-1} = \begin{bmatrix} \sigma^{11}\mathbf{A}_{11} & \sigma^{12}\mathbf{A}_{12} & \cdots & \sigma^{1L}\mathbf{A}_{1L} \\ \sigma^{21}\mathbf{A}_{21} & \sigma^{22}\mathbf{A}_{22} & \cdots & \sigma^{2L}\mathbf{A}_{2L} \\ \vdots & \vdots & & \vdots \\ \sigma^{L1}\mathbf{A}_{L1} & \sigma^{L2}\mathbf{A}_{L2} & \cdots & \sigma^{LL}\mathbf{A}_{LL} \end{bmatrix}^{-1} \tag{5.12}$$

where $[\sigma^{jl}] = \mathbf{\Sigma}^{-1}$ *and* $\mathbf{A}_{jl}$ *is defined in* (3.10). *The covariance matrix* (5.12) *is estimated consistently by* $n[\mathbf{Z}'(\mathbf{S}^{-1} \otimes \mathbf{X}\mathbf{X}^{+})\mathbf{Z}]^{-1}$.

(2) *For each* $j = 1, \ldots, L$, *the covariance matrix of the limiting distribution of* $\sqrt{n}(\mathbf{d}_j - \boldsymbol{\delta}_j)$ *exceeds that of* $\sqrt{n}(\hat{\boldsymbol{\delta}}_j - \boldsymbol{\delta}_j)$ *by a positive semidefinite matrix, where* $\mathbf{d}_j$ *is the 2SLS estimator of* $\boldsymbol{\delta}_j$ *and* $\hat{\boldsymbol{\delta}}_j$ *is the subvector of* $\hat{\boldsymbol{\delta}}$ *corresponding to* $\boldsymbol{\delta}_j$.

(3) *If some of the L equations are identities with zero disturbances and no unknown parameters, so that* $\mathbf{\Sigma}$ *is singular, then parts* (1) *and* (2) *of this theorem are still valid for the remaining equations, provided that* $\mathbf{\Sigma}$ *is replaced by its principal submatrix corresponding to these equations and that this submatrix is nonsingular.*

Part (3) is concerned with the case in which some of the L equations, say the last $L - L'$, are identities with zero disturbances. Then $\mathbf{\Sigma}$ and $\mathbf{S}$ are singular, so that the estimator (5.11) fails to exist. However, the coefficients of such equations are generally known (they are usually 1, 0, or -1), which implies that these equations are then not represented in (5.1) at all. Thus, the 3SLS procedure simply deletes these identities and hence requires only that the covariance matrix of the disturbances $\epsilon_{\alpha 1}, \ldots, \epsilon_{\alpha L'}$ of the other equations be nonsingular.

To prove the consistency of $\hat{\boldsymbol{\delta}}$ we substitute $\mathbf{Z}\boldsymbol{\delta} + \boldsymbol{\epsilon}$ for $\mathbf{y}$ in (5.11) to find that, given that $\mathbf{S}$ converges in probability to $\mathbf{\Sigma}$ (Theorems 10.3 and 10.4), $\hat{\boldsymbol{\delta}} - \boldsymbol{\delta}$ converges in probability to the probability limit of

$$[n^{-1}\mathbf{Z}'(\mathbf{\Sigma}^{-1} \otimes \mathbf{X}\mathbf{X}^{+})\mathbf{Z}]^{-1} n^{-1}\mathbf{Z}'(\mathbf{\Sigma}^{-1} \otimes \mathbf{X}\mathbf{X}^{+})\boldsymbol{\epsilon} \tag{5.13}$$

provided that the vector (5.13) does indeed have a probability limit. The matrix in brackets in (5.13) consists of L^2 submatrices of which the (j, l)th is $\sigma^{jl}(n^{-1}\mathbf{Z}_j'\mathbf{X})(n^{-1}\mathbf{X}'\mathbf{X})^{-1}(n^{-1}\mathbf{X}'\mathbf{Z}_l)$, which has probability limit $\sigma^{jl}\mathbf{A}_{jl}$ in view of (3.10). [This proves the equality sign in (5.12).] Similarly, the vector by which the inverse of (5.13) is postmultiplied consists of L subvectors of the form $(j = 1, \ldots, L)$:

$$\sigma^{j1}(n^{-1}\mathbf{Z}_j'\mathbf{X})(n^{-1}\mathbf{X}'\mathbf{X})^{-1}(n^{-1}\mathbf{X}'\boldsymbol{\epsilon}_1) + \cdots + \sigma^{jL}(n^{-1}\mathbf{Z}_j'\mathbf{X})(n^{-1}\mathbf{X}'\mathbf{X})^{-1}(n^{-1}\mathbf{X}'\boldsymbol{\epsilon}_L)$$

which converge in probability to zero because the probability limits of $n^{-1}\mathbf{Z}_j'\mathbf{X}$ and $n^{-1}\mathbf{X}'\mathbf{X}$ are finite and that of $n^{-1}\mathbf{X}'\boldsymbol{\epsilon}_l$ is zero. It follows that the vector (5.13) converges in probability to zero as $n \to \infty$, which establishes the consistency of $\hat{\boldsymbol{\delta}}$.

For the proof of the asymptotic normality of $\hat{\boldsymbol{\delta}}$ we write

$$\sqrt{n}(\hat{\boldsymbol{\delta}} - \boldsymbol{\delta}) = \mathbf{G}\sqrt{1/n}(\mathbf{I} \otimes \mathbf{X}')\boldsymbol{\epsilon} \tag{5.14}$$

where

$$\mathbf{G} = [n^{-1}\mathbf{Z}'(\mathbf{S}^{-1} \otimes \mathbf{X}\mathbf{X}^{+})\mathbf{Z}]^{-1} n^{-1}\mathbf{Z}'(\mathbf{I} \otimes \mathbf{X})[\mathbf{S}^{-1} \otimes (n^{-1}\mathbf{X}'\mathbf{X})^{-1}] \tag{5.15}$$

It was shown in the previous paragraph that the $N \times N$ inverse immediately to the right of the equality sign converges in probability to a finite limit matrix. Since the same is true for $n^{-1}\mathbf{Z}_j'\mathbf{X}$ [and hence for $n^{-1}\mathbf{Z}'(\mathbf{I} \otimes \mathbf{X})$], for $\mathbf{S}^{-1}$, and for $n^{-1}\mathbf{X}'\mathbf{X}$, the matrix $\mathbf{G}$ also converges to a finite matrix, say $\bar{\mathbf{G}}$. The matrix $\mathbf{G}$ is postmultiplied in (5.14) by $\sqrt{1/n}\,(\mathbf{I} \otimes \mathbf{X}')\boldsymbol{\epsilon}$, which according to Theorem 10.1 has a normal limiting distribution with zero mean vector and covariance matrix $\boldsymbol{\Sigma} \otimes \mathbf{Q}$. Consequently, the vector (5.14) is also asymptotically normal with zero mean, and the covariance matrix of this limiting distribution is $\bar{\mathbf{G}}(\boldsymbol{\Sigma} \otimes \mathbf{Q})\bar{\mathbf{G}}'$. It is a matter of straightforward algebra to show that this covariance matrix is identical with (5.12).

The asymptotic superiority of 3SLS over 2SLS stated in part (2) of the theorem is ultimately a result of the optimality of the GLS method which underlies the joint estimation procedure. For a more explicit expression of the excess of the 2SLS asymptotic covariance matrix over the corresponding 3SLS matrix, see Problems 5.5 and 5.6.

Problems

5.1 Suppose that the disturbance covariance matrix $\boldsymbol{\Sigma}$ is block-diagonal. Prove along the lines of Problems 2.3 and 2.4 of Section 7.2 that the 3SLS method amounts to separate 3SLS estimation of two or more sets of structural equations.

5.2 Suppose that the first p equations are all overidentified and that the last $L - p$ are all just-identified, $\mathbf{X}'\mathbf{Z}_j$ being square and nonsingular for $j = p + 1, \ldots, L$. Separate eq. (5.6) for the two groups:

$$\begin{bmatrix} \mathbf{X}'\mathbf{y}_1 \\ \mathbf{X}'\mathbf{y}_2 \\ \cdot \\ \cdot \\ \cdot \\ \mathbf{X}'\mathbf{y}_p \end{bmatrix} = \begin{bmatrix} \mathbf{X}'\mathbf{Z}_1 & \mathbf{0} & \cdots & \mathbf{0} \\ \mathbf{0} & \mathbf{X}'\mathbf{Z}_2 & \cdots & \mathbf{0} \\ \cdot & \cdot & & \cdot \\ \cdot & \cdot & & \cdot \\ \cdot & \cdot & & \cdot \\ \mathbf{0} & \mathbf{0} & \cdots & \mathbf{X}'\mathbf{Z}_p \end{bmatrix} \begin{bmatrix} \boldsymbol{\delta}_1 \\ \boldsymbol{\delta}_2 \\ \cdot \\ \cdot \\ \cdot \\ \boldsymbol{\delta}_p \end{bmatrix} + \begin{bmatrix} \mathbf{X}'\boldsymbol{\epsilon}_1 \\ \mathbf{X}'\boldsymbol{\epsilon}_2 \\ \cdot \\ \cdot \\ \cdot \\ \mathbf{X}'\boldsymbol{\epsilon}_p \end{bmatrix}$$

$$\begin{bmatrix} \mathbf{X}'\mathbf{y}_{p+1} \\ \mathbf{X}'\mathbf{y}_{p+2} \\ \cdot \\ \cdot \\ \cdot \\ \mathbf{X}'\mathbf{Y}_L \end{bmatrix} = \begin{bmatrix} \mathbf{X}'\mathbf{Z}_{p+1} & \mathbf{0} & \cdots & \mathbf{0} \\ \mathbf{0} & \mathbf{X}'\mathbf{Z}_{p+2} & \cdots & \mathbf{0} \\ \cdot & \cdot & & \cdot \\ \cdot & \cdot & & \cdot \\ \cdot & \cdot & & \cdot \\ \mathbf{0} & \mathbf{0} & \cdots & \mathbf{X}'\mathbf{Z}_L \end{bmatrix} \begin{bmatrix} \boldsymbol{\delta}_{p+1} \\ \boldsymbol{\delta}_{p+2} \\ \cdot \\ \cdot \\ \cdot \\ \boldsymbol{\delta}_L \end{bmatrix} + \begin{bmatrix} \mathbf{X}'\boldsymbol{\epsilon}_{p+1} \\ \mathbf{X}'\boldsymbol{\epsilon}_{p+2} \\ \cdot \\ \cdot \\ \cdot \\ \mathbf{X}'\boldsymbol{\epsilon}_L \end{bmatrix}$$

Write these two vector equations as

$$\mathbf{y}_A = \mathbf{X}_A\boldsymbol{\delta}_A + \boldsymbol{\epsilon}_A \tag{5.16}$$

$$\mathbf{y}_B = \mathbf{X}_B\boldsymbol{\delta}_B + \boldsymbol{\epsilon}_B \tag{5.17}$$

where $\mathbf{y}_A$ and $\boldsymbol{\epsilon}_A$ are vectors of Kp elements and $\mathbf{X}_A$ is a matrix of order $Kp \times (N_1 + \cdots + N_p)$. Indicate the orders of $\boldsymbol{\delta}_A$, $\boldsymbol{\delta}_B$, $\mathbf{y}_B$, $\boldsymbol{\epsilon}_B$, and $\mathbf{X}_B$, and prove that $\mathbf{X}_B$ is nonsingular.

5.3 (*Continuation*) Partition the $L \times L$ matrix $\mathbf{S}^{-1}$:

$$\mathbf{S}^{-1} = \begin{bmatrix} \mathbf{S}_{AA} & \mathbf{S}_{AB} \\ \mathbf{S}_{BA} & \mathbf{S}_{BB} \end{bmatrix}^{-1} = \begin{bmatrix} \mathbf{S}^{AA} & \mathbf{S}^{AB} \\ \mathbf{S}^{BA} & \mathbf{S}^{BB} \end{bmatrix} \tag{5.18}$$

and prove that the 3SLS estimator is solved from the following equation:

$$\begin{bmatrix} \mathbf{X}_A' & \mathbf{0} \\ \mathbf{0} & \mathbf{X}_B' \end{bmatrix} \left(\begin{bmatrix} \mathbf{S}^{AA} & \mathbf{S}^{AB} \\ \mathbf{S}^{BA} & \mathbf{S}^{BB} \end{bmatrix} \otimes (\mathbf{X}'\mathbf{X})^{-1} \right) \begin{bmatrix} \mathbf{X}_A & \mathbf{0} \\ \mathbf{0} & \mathbf{X}_B \end{bmatrix} \begin{bmatrix} \hat{\boldsymbol{\delta}}_A \\ \hat{\boldsymbol{\delta}}_B \end{bmatrix} = \begin{bmatrix} \mathbf{X}_A' & \mathbf{0} \\ \mathbf{0} & \mathbf{X}_B' \end{bmatrix} \left(\begin{bmatrix} \mathbf{S}^{AA} & \mathbf{S}^{AB} \\ \mathbf{S}^{BA} & \mathbf{S}^{BB} \end{bmatrix} \otimes (\mathbf{X}'\mathbf{X})^{-1} \right) \begin{bmatrix} \mathbf{y}_A \\ \mathbf{y}_B \end{bmatrix} \tag{5.19}$$

Write (5.19) in the form of two vector equations:

$$\mathbf{X}_A'[\mathbf{S}^{AA} \otimes (\mathbf{X}'\mathbf{X})^{-1}]\mathbf{X}_A\hat{\boldsymbol{\delta}}_A + \mathbf{X}_A'[\mathbf{S}^{AB} \otimes (\mathbf{X}'\mathbf{X})^{-1}]\mathbf{X}_B\hat{\boldsymbol{\delta}}_B = \mathbf{X}_A'[\mathbf{S}^{AA} \otimes (\mathbf{X}'\mathbf{X})^{-1}]\mathbf{y}_A + \mathbf{X}_A'[\mathbf{S}^{AB} \otimes (\mathbf{X}'\mathbf{X})^{-1}]\mathbf{y}_B \tag{5.20}$$

$$\mathbf{X}_B'[\mathbf{S}^{BA} \otimes (\mathbf{X}'\mathbf{X})^{-1}]\mathbf{X}_A\hat{\boldsymbol{\delta}}_A + \mathbf{X}_B'[\mathbf{S}^{BB} \otimes (\mathbf{X}'\mathbf{X})^{-1}]\mathbf{X}_B\hat{\boldsymbol{\delta}}_B = \mathbf{X}_B'[\mathbf{S}^{BA} \otimes (\mathbf{X}'\mathbf{X})^{-1}]\mathbf{y}_A + \mathbf{X}_B'[\mathbf{S}^{BB} \otimes (\mathbf{X}'\mathbf{X})^{-1}]\mathbf{y}_B \tag{5.21}$$

Derive $(\mathbf{S}^{BB})^{-1}\mathbf{S}^{BA} = -\mathbf{S}_{BA}\mathbf{S}_{AA}^{-1}$ from eq. (2.15) of Section 1.2 and use this after premultiplication of (5.21) by $\mathbf{X}_B^{-1}[(\mathbf{S}^{BB})^{-1} \otimes (\mathbf{X}'\mathbf{X})](\mathbf{X}_B')^{-1}$ to find

$$\hat{\boldsymbol{\delta}}_B = \mathbf{X}_B^{-1}\mathbf{y}_B - \mathbf{X}_B^{-1}[(\mathbf{S}_{BA}\mathbf{S}_{AA}^{-1}) \otimes \mathbf{I}](\mathbf{y}_A - \mathbf{X}_A\hat{\boldsymbol{\delta}}_A) \tag{5.22}$$

or, equivalently, for each of the just-identified equations ($j = p + 1, \ldots, L$):

$$\hat{\boldsymbol{\delta}}_j = (\mathbf{X}'\mathbf{Z}_j)^{-1}\mathbf{X}'\mathbf{y}_j - (\mathbf{X}'\mathbf{Z}_j)^{-1}\sum_{l=1}^{p} c_{jl}\mathbf{X}'(\mathbf{y}_l - \mathbf{Z}_l\hat{\boldsymbol{\delta}}_l) \tag{5.23}$$

where $[c_{jl}] = \mathbf{S}_{BA}\mathbf{S}_{AA}^{-1}$. Conclude that the estimator $\hat{\boldsymbol{\delta}}_j$ of each just-identified equation differs from the 2SLS vector $(\mathbf{X}'\mathbf{Z}_j)^{-1}\mathbf{X}'\mathbf{y}_j$ by a vector which is a linear function of the 3SLS residuals of the over-identified equations.

5.4 (*Continuation*) Derive $\mathbf{S}^{AA} + \mathbf{S}^{AB}\mathbf{S}_{BA}\mathbf{S}_{AA}^{-1} = \mathbf{S}_{AA}^{-1}$ from eq. (2.15) of Section 1.2. Then substitute (5.22) into (5.20) to find

$$\mathbf{X}'[\mathbf{S}_{AA}^{-1} \otimes (\mathbf{X}'\mathbf{X})^{-1}]\mathbf{X}_A\hat{\boldsymbol{\delta}}_A = \mathbf{X}'[\mathbf{S}_{AA}^{-1} \otimes (\mathbf{X}'\mathbf{X})^{-1}]\mathbf{y}_A \tag{5.24}$$

Prove that this amounts to the application of 3SLS to the set of over-identified equations, ignoring all just-identified equations. Summarize the conclusions to be drawn from Problems 5.2 to 5.4.

5.5 Consider the two-equation case, for which the estimated asymptotic covariance matrix of the 3SLS estimator $\hat{\boldsymbol{\delta}}$ is

$$\begin{bmatrix} s^{11}\mathbf{Z}_1'\mathbf{X}(\mathbf{X}'\mathbf{X})^{-1}\mathbf{X}'\mathbf{Z}_1 & s^{12}\mathbf{Z}_1'\mathbf{X}(\mathbf{X}'\mathbf{X})^{-1}\mathbf{X}'\mathbf{Z}_2 \\ s^{21}\mathbf{Z}_2'\mathbf{X}(\mathbf{X}'\mathbf{X})^{-1}\mathbf{X}'\mathbf{Z}_1 & s^{22}\mathbf{Z}_2'\mathbf{X}(\mathbf{X}'\mathbf{X})^{-1}\mathbf{X}'\mathbf{Z}_2 \end{bmatrix}^{-1} \quad \text{where} \quad [s^{jl}] = \mathbf{S}^{-1}$$

as well as the corresponding matrix $s_{11}[\mathbf{Z}_1'\mathbf{X}(\mathbf{X}'\mathbf{X})^{-1}\mathbf{X}'\mathbf{Z}_1]^{-1}$ of the 2SLS estimator $\mathbf{d}_1$ of the first equation. Introduce $\mathbf{A}_j = \mathbf{X}(\mathbf{X}'\mathbf{X})^{-1}\mathbf{X}'\mathbf{Z}_j$ for $j = 1$ and 2, and give a statistical interpretation of $\mathbf{A}_j$. Prove that the two estimated asymptotic covariance matrices can be written as

$$(5.25) \qquad \begin{bmatrix} s^{11}\mathbf{A}_1'\mathbf{A}_1 & s^{12}\mathbf{A}_1'\mathbf{A}_2 \\ s^{21}\mathbf{A}_2'\mathbf{A}_1 & s^{22}\mathbf{A}_2'\mathbf{A}_2 \end{bmatrix}^{-1} \quad \text{and} \quad s_{11}(\mathbf{A}_1'\mathbf{A}_1)^{-1}$$

Apply eq. (2.15) of Section 1.2 to prove that the leading submatrix of the first inverse in (5.25), which is the estimated asymptotic covariance matrix of $\hat{\boldsymbol{\delta}}_1$, is equal to $\mathbf{D}^{-1}$, the inverse of

$$(5.26) \qquad \mathbf{D} = \frac{1}{s_1^2(1-r^2)}\mathbf{A}_1'\mathbf{A}_1 - \frac{r^2}{s_1^2(1-r^2)}\mathbf{A}_1'\mathbf{A}_2(\mathbf{A}_2'\mathbf{A}_2)^{-1}\mathbf{A}_2'\mathbf{A}_1$$

where $s_1^2 = s_{11}$, $s_2^2 = s_{22}$, $rs_1s_2 = s_{12}$. Also prove that when either $r = 0$ or the second equation is just-identified, $\mathbf{D}^{-1}$ is equal to the 2SLS matrix $s_{11}(\mathbf{A}_1'\mathbf{A}_1)^{-1}$. [*Hint:* Prove $\mathbf{A}_1'\mathbf{A}_2(\mathbf{A}_2'\mathbf{A}_2)^{-1}\mathbf{A}_2'\mathbf{A}_1 = \mathbf{A}_1'\mathbf{A}_1$ when $\mathbf{X}'\mathbf{Z}_2$ is square and nonsingular.]

5.6 (*Continuation*) Define $\mathbf{A}^* = \mathbf{A}_1'\mathbf{A}_1 - \mathbf{A}_1'\mathbf{A}_2(\mathbf{A}_2'\mathbf{A}_2)^{-1}\mathbf{A}_2'\mathbf{A}_1$ and prove that $\mathbf{A}^*$ is positive semidefinite. Also prove:

$$(5.27) \qquad \mathbf{D} = \frac{1}{s_1^2}\mathbf{A}_1'\mathbf{A}_1 + \frac{r^2}{s_1^2(1-r^2)}\mathbf{A}^*$$

and conclude that $\mathbf{D}$, the inverse of the 3SLS matrix of the first equation, exceeds the corresponding 2SLS inverse by a positive semidefinite matrix. Derive $|\mathbf{D}| \geq |(1/s_1^2)\mathbf{A}_1'\mathbf{A}_1|$ from (5.27) and draw your conclusions regarding the large-sample generalized variances of the 2SLS and the 3SLS estimators.

10.6 A Numerical Example; Mixed Three-Stage Least-Squares Estimation[B]

The 3SLS procedure will now be applied to the three behavioral equations of Klein's Model I described in Section 9.2. These equations are reproduced below for the sake of convenience:

$$C_\alpha = \beta_0 + \beta_1 P_\alpha + \beta_2 P_{\alpha-1} + \beta_3(W_\alpha + W'_\alpha) + \epsilon_\alpha \tag{6.1}$$

$$I_\alpha = \beta'_0 + \beta'_1 P_\alpha + \beta'_2 P_{\alpha-1} + \beta'_3 K_{\alpha-1} + \epsilon'_\alpha \tag{6.2}$$

$$W_\alpha = \beta''_0 + \beta''_1 X_\alpha + \beta''_2 X_{\alpha-1} + \beta''_3(\alpha - 1931) + \epsilon''_\alpha \tag{6.3}$$

In accordance with Theorem 10.7 (3) we delete the three identities and we treat the above equations as a three-equation system.

Sums of Squares and Products Needed

The observation matrix is given in Table 9.1 of Section 9.5, where we estimated the consumption function (6.1) according to the 2SLS method. Table 9.2 in the same section contains several elements of the matrix of sums of squares and products of the variables of the model, but more will be needed for the 3SLS procedure. To estimate the investment function (6.2) by 2SLS we need the eight product sums $\sum I_\alpha$, $\sum W'_\alpha I_\alpha, \ldots, \sum X_{\alpha-1} I_\alpha$ corresponding to the left-hand dependent variable and each of the eight predetermined variables. We also need similar product sums for the jointly dependent variables W and X of the demand-for-labor function (6.3). These are all given on the first three lines of Table 10.2.

Table 10.2

Sums of Squares and Products for 3SLS Estimation of Klein's Model I

	Elements of **Y′X**							
	1	W'	T	G	$\alpha - 1931$	P_{-1}	K_{-1}	X_{-1}
I	26.60	103.80	160.40	139.39	−105.60	625.33	5073.25	1831.12
W	763.60	4044.07	5315.62	3878.39	460.90	12871.73	153470.56	45288.51
X	1261.20	6654.45	8776.10	6392.17	655.80	21290.34	253183.59	74755.48

	Elements of **Y′Y**					
	C	P	W	$W + W'$	I	X
C	62166.63	19566.35	42076.78	48054.11	1679.01	69501.99
P		6347.25	13296.61	15117.72	726.10	22049.39
W			28560.86	32604.93	1217.92	47173.09
$W + W'$				37275.87	1321.72	53827.54
I					286.02	2104.42
X						77998.58

The typical element of the matrix **S** of mean squares and products of the 2SLS residuals may be written as

$$s_{jl} = \frac{1}{n}(\mathbf{y}_j - \mathbf{Y}_j\mathbf{c}_j - \mathbf{X}_j\mathbf{b}_j)'(\mathbf{y}_l - \mathbf{Y}_l\mathbf{c}_l - \mathbf{X}_l\mathbf{b}_l) \tag{6.4}$$

This shows that we need $\mathbf{y}'_j\mathbf{y}_l$, $\mathbf{y}'_j\mathbf{Y}_l$, and $\mathbf{Y}'_j\mathbf{Y}_l$ for all pairs (j, l), $j, l = 1, 2, 3$. The relevant elements of **Y′Y** are also given in Table 10.2. Note that W and

$W + W'$ enter as separate dependent variables, the first being needed for the demand-for-labor function and the second for the consumption function.[14]

2SLS Estimates

The 2SLS estimation of the investment and the demand-for-labor functions is completely analogous to that of the consumption function as described in Section 9.5. Therefore we confine ourselves to a presentation of point estimates and asymptotic standard errors in the first column of Table 10.3,

Table 10.3

2SLS and 3SLS Estimates of the Parameters of Klein's Model I

Equation	Variable	2SLS	3SLS	Mixed 3SLS
Consumption	1	16.55 (1.32)	16.44 (1.30)	16.77 (1.13)
	P	.0173 (.1180)	.1249 (.1081)	.0513 (.0125)
	P_{-1}	.2162 (.1073)	.1631 (.1004)	.2065 (.0310)
	$W + W'$	.8102 (.0402)	.7901 (.0379)	.7949 (.0259)
Investment	1	20.28 (7.54)	28.18 (6.79)	20.72 (4.57)
	P	.1502 (.1732)	−.0131 (.1619)	.1451 (.0330)
	P_{-1}	.6159 (.1628)	.7557 (.1529)	.6134 (.0603)
	K_{-1}	−.1578 (.0361)	−.1948 (.0325)	−.1593 (.0225)
Labor	1	1.50 (1.15)	1.80 (1.12)	1.53 (.97)
	X	.4389 (.0356)	.4005 (.0318)	.3985 (.0171)
	X_{-1}	.1467 (.0388)	.1813 (.0342)	.1880 (.0159)
	$\alpha - 1931$	.1304 (.0291)	.1497 (.0279)	.1559 (.0228)

[14] Also note that some of the elements of $\mathbf{Y'Y}$ in Table 10.2 were used in eq. (5.23) of Section 9.5 to obtain the 2SLS estimate of the variance of the consumption disturbances.

Table 10.4

Estimated Asymptotic Covariance Matrices (× 10^4) of the 2SLS and 3SLS Estimates of the Parameters of Klein's Model I

Consumption				Investment				Labor				
10	P	P_{-1}	$W + W'$	10	P	P_{-1}	K_{-1}	10	X	X_{-1}	$\alpha - 1931$	
						2SLS						
174.5	−15.3	−4.7	−32.7	211.2	−45.2	17.4	−8.0	−61.3	9.2	.7	2.8	10
	139.4	−95.7	−15.3	57.9	40.4	−31.1	−3.7	−.5	−18.1	18.9	6.6	P
		115.1	−5.3	20.4	−46.4	51.4	−1.3	32.8	11.8	−17.9	4.8	P_{-1}
			16.2	−82.1	12.8	−11.8	4.0	1.6	.5	−.8	−5.2	$W + W'$
				5689.2	−924.8	777.6	−269.0	36.9	13.4	−20.1	−32.1	10
					300.1	−257.7	41.9	−1.7	5.9	−5.9	4.8	P
						265.0	−38.7	−15.5	−3.3	6.1	−6.7	P_{-1}
							13.0	−.4	−.9	1.0	1.7	K_{-1}
								131.7	−6.7	−15.4	15.6	10
									12.7	−12.0	−3.1	X
										15.1	.5	X_{-1}
											8.5	$\alpha - 1931$
						3SLS						
170.2	−17.0	−5.6	−30.7	169.5	−43.0	15.3	−7.3	−61.5	9.9	−.0	3.4	10
	116.9	−80.6	−11.7	−15.7	60.9	−49.4	−.0	.8	−13.5	13.9	6.4	P
		100.9	−5.6	54.7	−59.0	63.4	−2.9	28.6	8.8	−14.0	4.4	P_{-1}
			14.4	−62.1	8.9	−8.6	3.0	2.8	−3.7	−.1	−5.2	$W + W'$
				4615.5	−732.2	604.5	−217.6	27.7	37.9	−44.8	−33.0	10
					262.1	−223.5	32.7	−1.7	.0	−.0	4.9	P
						233.9	−30.4	−14.8	1.8	.7	−6.6	P_{-1}
							10.6	.0	−2.1	2.1	1.8	K_{-1}
								124.5	−7.9	−12.9	14.1	10
									10.1	−9.1	−2.8	X
										11.7	.5	X_{-1}

Mixed 3SLS

128.0	−3.0	−10.7	−24.2	71.5	−6.0	−17.9	−1.5	−42.0	5.1	1.7	5.1	10
	1.6	1.3	.4	−7.3	2.4	.8	.0	.5	−.0	−.0	.3	P
		9.6	−1.7	−11.5	.9	11.1	−.4	2.1	−.1	−.2	1.0	P_{-1}
			6.7	−9.2	.1	−.4	.5	8.7	−1.2	−.3	−1.7	$W + W'$
				2089.1	−36.2	−17.7	−99.4	15.1	13.7	−16.6	−19.5	10
					10.9	−.7	.9	−3.0	.4	.1	−.2	P
						36.4	−2.0	−13.7	1.6	.7	−2.2	P_{-1}
							5.0	.7	−.8	.8	1.2	K_{-1}
								94.8	−9.4	−6.2	8.3	10
									2.9	−1.4	−1.3	X
										2.5	−.1	X_{-1}
											5.2	$\alpha - 1931$

and of the estimated asymptotic covariance matrix in the first 12 lines of Table 10.4. [The off-diagonal blocks are computed according to (3.12).] Using these results and $n = 21$, we apply (6.4) to obtain

$$\text{(6.5)} \qquad \mathbf{S} = \begin{bmatrix} 1.0441 & .4378 & -.3852 \\ & 1.3832 & .1926 \\ & & .4764 \end{bmatrix} \quad \begin{matrix} \text{consumption} \\ \text{investment} \\ \text{labor} \end{matrix}$$

which has the following inverse:

$$\text{(6.6)} \qquad \mathbf{S}^{-1} = \begin{bmatrix} 2.1615 & -.9829 & 2.1451 \\ & 1.2131 & -1.2852 \\ & & 4.3530 \end{bmatrix}$$

3SLS Estimates

We now proceed to the 3SLS estimator given in (5.9). This requires the inverse of a matrix consisting of $3 \times 3 = 9$ submatrices of the form

$$\text{(6.7)} \qquad s^{jl}\mathbf{Z}_j'\mathbf{X}(\mathbf{X}'\mathbf{X})^{-1}\mathbf{X}'\mathbf{Z}_l \qquad j, l = 1, 2, 3$$

where $\mathbf{Z}_j = [\mathbf{Y}_j \quad \mathbf{X}_j]$ is the observation matrix of the right-hand variables of the jth equation. This matrix consists of four columns for each j because all three equations happen to have four unknown parameters. Hence, all matrices (6.7) are of order 4×4 and the matrix in square brackets of (5.9) is of order 12×12. The inverse of the last matrix is the estimated asymptotic covariance matrix of the 3SLS estimates, which is presented in the middle part of Table 10.4. To obtain $\hat{\boldsymbol{\delta}}$ we should postmultiply the inverse of (5.9) by a 12-element column vector which consists of three subvectors of the form

$$\text{(6.8)} \qquad \sum_{l=1}^{3} s^{jl}\mathbf{Z}_j'\mathbf{X}(\mathbf{X}'\mathbf{X})^{-1}\mathbf{X}'\mathbf{y}_l \qquad j = 1, 2, 3$$

This leads to the 3SLS point estimates given in the second column of Table 10.3 along with the asymptotic standard errors (computed from the relevant diagonal elements of Table 10.4). A comparison with the 2SLS estimates shows that there are some differences, particularly for the coefficients of P and P_{-1} in the first two equations (which is due to the fact that the systematic reduced-form component of P is rather highly correlated with P_{-1}, so that the corresponding coefficients are not very stable). There is also some, but not much, reduction of the asymptotic standard errors compared with the 2SLS values.

On the basis of these results we can answer the question whether the capitalists' current marginal propensity to spend ($\beta_1 + \beta_1'$) is significantly less than 1. The sum of the 3SLS estimates $\hat{\beta}_1$ and $\hat{\beta}_1'$ is .1118 and its asymptotic standard error is

$$\frac{1}{100}\sqrt{116.9 + 262.1 + 2 \times 60.9} = .224 \tag{6.9}$$

where the figures under the square root sign are taken from Table 10.4. We conclude that $1 - .1118 = .8882$ is about four times the asymptotic standard error, which is significant by conventional standards.

Mixed 3SLS Estimation

If one knows that the structural parameters obey certain linear constraints, one may apply constrained 3SLS estimation. This leads to an estimator $\hat{\boldsymbol{\delta}}^*$ which differs from the unconstrained $\hat{\boldsymbol{\delta}}$ by a vector that describes the degree to which $\hat{\boldsymbol{\delta}}$ fails to satisfy the constraints; see Problem 6.3. Here we shall describe the procedure of mixed 3SLS estimation, which is essentially an extension of the ideas set forth in Section 7.8 in a nonsimultaneous context. Suppose that the analyst has the following prior ideas about certain parameters of Klein's Model I.

(1) He considers it likely on a priori grounds that the workers' marginal propensity to consume β_3 is between .7 and .8, and he sees it as almost certain that it is between .65 and .85. This will be regarded as equivalent to a point estimate of .75 with a standard error of .05.

(2) Consider the total (current plus lagged) marginal propensities of the capitalist group to consume and to invest, $\beta_1 + \beta_2$ and $\beta_1' + \beta_2'$. The analyst estimates (prior to the computations based on the sample) that the former should be roughly one-third of the latter. This will be formalized by declaring that $3(\beta_1 + \beta_2) - \beta_1' - \beta_2'$ is estimated to be zero with a standard error of .1.

(3) The analyst estimates (again, prior to the sample computations) that the capitalists react to income changes with an average lag of a little less than one year, both with respect to consumption and to investment, such that β_2 and β_2' are about four times as large as β_1 and β_1', respectively. Specifically, $4\beta_1 - \beta_2$ and $4\beta_1' - \beta_2'$ are estimated to be zero with standard errors equal to .05 and .15, respectively. These different standard errors reflect the different levels of β_1 and β_2 compared with β_1' and β_2' as the analyst sees them [see above under (2)]; since $\beta_1 + \beta_2$ is judged to be about one-third of $\beta_1' + \beta_2'$, the prior standard errors corresponding to $4\beta_1 - \beta_2$ and $4\beta_1' - \beta_2'$ measured as fractions of $\beta_1 + \beta_2$ and $\beta_1' + \beta_2'$, respectively, are of the same order of magnitude.

(4) The analyst guesses that the demand for labor reacts to changes in the output of private industry with an average lag of about four months, which means that β_1'' must be about one-half of β_2''. More precisely, $2\beta_1'' - \beta_2''$ is estimated to be zero with a standard error of .05.

It is assumed that the analyst has no prior ideas about the other parameters of the model. We can then summarize the prior point estimates by saying that the five-element vector

$$\begin{bmatrix} 0 & 0 & 1 & 0 & 0 & 0 & 0 \\ 3 & 3 & 0 & -1 & -1 & 0 & 0 \\ 4 & -1 & 0 & 0 & 0 & 0 & 0 \\ 0 & 0 & 0 & 4 & -1 & 0 & 0 \\ 0 & 0 & 0 & 0 & 0 & 2 & -1 \end{bmatrix} \begin{bmatrix} \beta_1 \\ \beta_2 \\ \beta_3 \\ \beta_1' \\ \beta_2' \\ \beta_1'' \\ \beta_2'' \end{bmatrix} \tag{6.10}$$

is estimated to be zero except for the top element whose estimate is .75. The prior standard errors, when squared, lead to the successive diagonal elements of the following covariance matrix:

$$\mathbf{V}_0 = 10^{-4} \begin{bmatrix} 25 & 0 & 0 & 0 & 0 \\ & 100 & 0 & 0 & 0 \\ & & 25 & 45 & 0 \\ & & & 225 & 0 \\ & & & & 25 \end{bmatrix} \tag{6.11}$$

The zero off-diagonal elements (with one exception) reflect that the prior estimates are regarded as independent. The exception refers to $4\beta_1 - \beta_2$ and $4\beta_1' - \beta_2'$. The analyst argues that if his prior estimate understates the average lag for consumption, it is more likely than not that he will also understate the average lag for investment. This is formalized by means of a positive covariance of 45×10^{-4}, which corresponds to a correlation coefficient of $45/\sqrt{25 \times 225} = .6$.

Following the line of argument of Section 7.8, we write the prior information in the form $\mathbf{r} = \mathbf{R}\boldsymbol{\delta} + \mathbf{v}$, $\mathscr{E}\mathbf{v} = \mathbf{0}$, $\mathscr{E}(\mathbf{vv}') = \mathbf{V}_0$, where $\mathbf{r}' = [.75 \quad 0 \quad \cdots \quad 0]$, $\mathbf{R}$ is the 5×7 matrix occurring in (6.10) with five zero columns added in appropriate places for those parameters on which no prior information is available, and $\mathbf{V}_0$ is as specified in (6.11). Proceeding along the lines of eqs. (8.8) and (8.9) of Section 7.8, we construct the matrix

$$\mathbf{Z}'[\mathbf{S}^{-1} \otimes \mathbf{X}(\mathbf{X}'\mathbf{X})^{-1}\mathbf{X}']\mathbf{Z} + \mathbf{R}'\mathbf{V}_0^{-1}\mathbf{R} \tag{6.12}$$

the inverse of which is the approximate covariance matrix of the mixed 3SLS estimator. (This inverse is given in the last 12 lines of Table 10.4.) We then postmultiply the inverse by the vector

$$\mathbf{Z}'[\mathbf{S}^{-1} \otimes \mathbf{X}(\mathbf{X}'\mathbf{X})^{-1}\mathbf{X}']\mathbf{y} + \mathbf{R}'\mathbf{V}_0^{-1}\mathbf{r} \tag{6.13}$$

which leads to the estimates themselves, given in the third column of Table 10.3.

The reader may disagree with some of the prior ideas used here, but this is the unavoidable consequence of their subjective nature. The main conclusion is that prior ideas can be incorporated easily. The analysis also shows—see the standard errors of Table 10.3—that their effect on the precision of the estimates may be much larger than the corresponding gain of pure 3SLS over 2SLS. See Problems 6.5 and 6.6 for a procedure to test the compatibility of the sample and prior information.

Problems

6.1 Verify that the only elements of the matrices $\mathbf{X}'\mathbf{X}$, $\mathbf{X}'\mathbf{Y}$, $\mathbf{Y}'\mathbf{Y}$ which are not needed for 3SLS estimation of Klein's Model I are those which involve the variable K (capital stock at the end of the year), and argue why this must be so. Also, prove that the 2SLS point estimates of the coefficients of none of the equations need any element of $\mathbf{Y}'\mathbf{Y}$.

6.2 It is stated below eq. (6.9) that four times the asymptotic standard error is significant by conventional standards. List the qualifications for this statement.

6.3 (*Constrained 3SLS estimation*) Suppose that the vector $\boldsymbol{\delta}$ of (5.1) is known to satisfy q linear constraints of the form $\mathbf{r} = \mathbf{R}\boldsymbol{\delta}$, where $\mathbf{r}$ and $\mathbf{R}$ are known matrices of appropriate order, $\mathbf{R}$ having full row rank. Consider the estimator

$$\hat{\boldsymbol{\delta}}^* = \hat{\boldsymbol{\delta}} + \mathbf{C}\mathbf{R}'(\mathbf{R}\mathbf{C}\mathbf{R}')^{-1}(\mathbf{r} - \mathbf{R}\hat{\boldsymbol{\delta}}) \tag{6.14}$$

where $\hat{\boldsymbol{\delta}}$ is defined in (5.11) and $\mathbf{C} = [\mathbf{Z}'(\mathbf{S}^{-1} \otimes \mathbf{X}\mathbf{X}^{+})\mathbf{Z}]^{-1}$. Prove that under the assumptions of Theorem 10.7, $\hat{\boldsymbol{\delta}}^*$ is consistent and that $\sqrt{n}(\hat{\boldsymbol{\delta}}^* - \boldsymbol{\delta})$ has a normal limiting distribution with zero mean vector and covariance matrix

$$\mathbf{H} - \mathbf{H}\mathbf{R}'(\mathbf{R}\mathbf{H}\mathbf{R}')^{-1}\mathbf{R}\mathbf{H} \qquad \text{where} \qquad \mathbf{H} = \operatorname*{plim}_{n\to\infty} (n\mathbf{C})$$

Conclude that the diagonal elements of $\mathbf{C} - \mathbf{C}\mathbf{R}'(\mathbf{R}\mathbf{C}\mathbf{R}')^{-1}\mathbf{R}\mathbf{C}$ provide the asymptotic standard errors of $\hat{\boldsymbol{\delta}}^*$.

6.4 Prove that the 5×7 matrix occurring in (6.10) has full row rank.

6.5 Let $\mathbf{v}$ of $\mathbf{r} = \mathbf{R}\boldsymbol{\delta} + \mathbf{v}$ (the uncertain prior information) be q-variate normal with zero mean and covariance matrix $\mathbf{V}_0$, the matrix $\mathbf{R}$ having full row rank. Use the normal limiting distribution of $\sqrt{n}(\hat{\boldsymbol{\delta}} - \boldsymbol{\delta})$ to prove that the quadratic form

$$(6.15) \quad (\mathbf{r} - \mathbf{R}\hat{\boldsymbol{\delta}})'[\mathbf{R}(\mathbf{Z}'\mathbf{A}\mathbf{Z})^{-1}\mathbf{R}' + \mathbf{V}_0]^{-1}(\mathbf{r} - \mathbf{R}\hat{\boldsymbol{\delta}}) \qquad \text{where} \quad \mathbf{A} = \mathbf{S}^{-1} \otimes \mathbf{X}(\mathbf{X}'\mathbf{X})^{-1}\mathbf{X}'$$

is approximately distributed as $\chi^2(q)$ when n is large.

6.6 (*Continuation*) The value of the quadratic form (6.15) in the case discussed at the end of the section is 2.97. Use this to test whether the sample and prior information are compatible with each other; choose your own level of significance.

10.7 Full-Information Maximum Likelihood[C]

In this section we shall discuss a maximum-likelihood method, from Koopmans, Rubin, and Leipnik (1950), which has a relation to 3SLS similar to that between the limited-information maximum-likelihood method and 2SLS. Our starting point is the logarithmic likelihood function (4.4), which is reproduced here for the sake of convenience:

$$(7.1) \quad -\frac{1}{2}Ln \log 2\pi - \frac{1}{2}n \log |\boldsymbol{\Omega}| - \frac{1}{2}\operatorname{tr} \boldsymbol{\Omega}^{-1}(\mathbf{Y} - \mathbf{X}\boldsymbol{\Pi})'(\mathbf{Y} - \mathbf{X}\boldsymbol{\Pi})$$

where it is assumed again that $\boldsymbol{\Sigma}$ and hence $\boldsymbol{\Omega}$ are nonsingular. Since we are interested in the set of structural parameters for all L equations, it is appropriate to express the reduced-form parameter matrices $\boldsymbol{\Pi}$ and $\boldsymbol{\Omega}$ in terms of $\boldsymbol{\Gamma}$ and $\mathbf{B}$ (or $\boldsymbol{\delta}$) and $\boldsymbol{\Sigma}$. Thus, applying $\boldsymbol{\Omega} = (\boldsymbol{\Gamma}')^{-1}\boldsymbol{\Sigma}\boldsymbol{\Gamma}^{-1}$ and $\mathbf{Y} - \mathbf{X}\boldsymbol{\Pi} = \mathbf{E}\boldsymbol{\Gamma}^{-1}$, we obtain for the trace in (7.1):

$$\begin{aligned}(7.2) \quad \operatorname{tr} \boldsymbol{\Omega}^{-1}(\mathbf{Y} - \mathbf{X}\boldsymbol{\Pi})'(\mathbf{Y} - \mathbf{X}\boldsymbol{\Pi}) &= \operatorname{tr} [(\boldsymbol{\Gamma}')^{-1}\boldsymbol{\Sigma}\boldsymbol{\Gamma}^{-1}]^{-1}(\mathbf{E}\boldsymbol{\Gamma}^{-1})'\mathbf{E}\boldsymbol{\Gamma}^{-1} \\ &= \operatorname{tr} \boldsymbol{\Gamma}\boldsymbol{\Sigma}^{-1}\mathbf{E}'\mathbf{E}\boldsymbol{\Gamma}^{-1} = \operatorname{tr} \boldsymbol{\Sigma}^{-1}\mathbf{E}'\mathbf{E} \\ &= \sum_{j=1}^{L}\sum_{l=1}^{L} \sigma^{jl}\boldsymbol{\epsilon}_j'\boldsymbol{\epsilon}_l \\ &= \sum_{j=1}^{L}\sum_{l=1}^{L} \sigma^{jl}(\mathbf{y}_j - \mathbf{Z}_j\boldsymbol{\delta}_j)'(\mathbf{y}_l - \mathbf{Z}_l\boldsymbol{\delta}_l)\end{aligned}$$

Substituting the double sum on the last line for the trace term as well as $|\boldsymbol{\Omega}| = |(\boldsymbol{\Gamma}')^{-1}\boldsymbol{\Sigma}\boldsymbol{\Gamma}^{-1}|$ into (7.1), we obtain the following expression for the log-likelihood function:

(7.3)

$$-\frac{1}{2}Ln \log 2\pi - \frac{1}{2}n \log |(\boldsymbol{\Gamma}')^{-1}\boldsymbol{\Sigma}\boldsymbol{\Gamma}^{-1}| - \frac{1}{2}\sum_{j=1}^{L}\sum_{l=1}^{L} \sigma^{jl}(\mathbf{y}_j - \mathbf{Z}_j\boldsymbol{\delta}_j)'(\mathbf{y}_l - \mathbf{Z}_l\boldsymbol{\delta}_l)$$

This expression will appear to be convenient in spite of the fact that the structural parameters enter into it in two different forms: as a matrix $(\boldsymbol{\Gamma})$ and in vector form $(\boldsymbol{\delta}_j)$.

Maximum-Likelihood Estimation of Recursive Systems

When the system is recursive, $\boldsymbol{\Sigma}$ is a diagonal matrix and the equations can be arranged such that $\boldsymbol{\Gamma}$ is triangular (see Section 9.6). When $\boldsymbol{\Gamma}$ thus has exclusively zero elements on one side of the diagonal, its determinant value is equal to the product of the diagonal elements $\gamma_{11}, \ldots, \gamma_{LL}$. But we can divide both sides of the jth equation by the parameter γ_{jj}, and if we do so for each equation, all diagonal elements of $\boldsymbol{\Gamma}$ become 1 and hence also $|\boldsymbol{\Gamma}| = 1$. In addition, since $\boldsymbol{\Sigma}$ is diagonal, its determinant $|\boldsymbol{\Sigma}|$ is equal to the product of $\sigma_{11}, \ldots, \sigma_{LL}$. By writing the determinant of the product matrix in the second term of (7.3) as the product of three determinants, we can then simplify the log-likelihood function to

$$(7.4) \qquad -\frac{1}{2} Ln \log 2\pi - \frac{1}{2} n \sum_{j=1}^{L} \log \sigma_{jj} - \frac{1}{2} \sum_{j=1}^{L} \frac{(\mathbf{y}_j - \mathbf{Z}_j\boldsymbol{\delta}_j)'(\mathbf{y}_j - \mathbf{Z}_j\boldsymbol{\delta}_j)}{\sigma_{jj}}$$

This is nothing but the sum of L log-likelihood functions corresponding to the individual structural equations $(j = 1, \ldots, L)$:

$$(7.5) \qquad -\frac{1}{2} n \log 2\pi - \frac{1}{2} n \log \sigma_{jj} - \frac{1}{2} \frac{(\mathbf{y}_j - \mathbf{Z}_j\boldsymbol{\delta}_j)'(\mathbf{y}_j - \mathbf{Z}_j\boldsymbol{\delta}_j)}{\sigma_{jj}}$$

It is obvious that maximizing (7.4) for variations in $\boldsymbol{\delta}_1, \ldots, \boldsymbol{\delta}_L$ and $\sigma_{11}, \ldots, \sigma_{LL}$ is equivalent to the maximization of each of the L functions (7.5) for variations in the corresponding $\boldsymbol{\delta}_j$ and σ_{jj} alone, and that this leads to the LS estimators:

$$(\mathbf{Z}_j'\mathbf{Z}_j)^{-1}\mathbf{Z}_j'\mathbf{y}_j \qquad \text{and} \qquad \mathbf{y}_j'[\mathbf{I} - \mathbf{Z}_j(\mathbf{Z}_j'\mathbf{Z}_j)^{-1}\mathbf{Z}_j']\mathbf{y}_j$$

of $\boldsymbol{\delta}_j$ and $(n - N_j)\sigma_{jj}$, respectively. When $\mathbf{Z}_j$ contains no observations on lagged y's, the standard linear model applies directly; when such observations are part of $\mathbf{Z}_j$, Theorem 8.5 (Section 8.7) provides similar results for large n. See Problem 7.2 for an extension of this result to block-recursive systems.

Full-Information Maximum Likelihood and Its Asymptotic Equivalence with 3SLS

In the more general case we have to maximize the function (7.3) as it stands. This problem was attacked by Koopmans, Rubin, and Leipnik (1950), and the resulting estimator is known as the full-information maximum-likelihood estimator. This estimator is only rarely used because it has to be solved from a very complicated set of estimation equations. The complications may be illustrated by differentiating $\log |\mathbf{\Gamma}|$, which is part of the second term of (7.3), with respect to γ_{jl} (one of the unknown elements of $\mathbf{\Gamma}$). The derivative is γ^{lj}, the (l, j)th element of $\mathbf{\Gamma}^{-1}$, which is obviously nonlinear in $\mathbf{\Gamma}$. Therefore, when we put the derivatives of (7.3) equal to zero, we obtain nonlinear equations.

It is a surprising result that although the maximum-likelihood estimation equations are complicated, the asymptotic covariance matrix of the full-information maximum-likelihood estimator takes a simple form. This follows from the following theorem, from ROTHENBERG and LEENDERS (1964), which will not be proved here.[15]

THEOREM 10.8 (Asymptotic efficiency of 3SLS) *Suppose that the assumptions of Theorem* 10.7 *are satisfied with the additional specification that the disturbance distribution of Assumption* 10.2 *is multinormal. Then the asymptotic covariance matrix of the 3SLS estimator* $\hat{\boldsymbol{\delta}}$ *defined in* (5.11) *is identical with the asymptotic covariance matrix of the full-information maximum-likelihood estimator of the same parameter vector, obtained by maximization of the logarithmic likelihood function* (7.3).

This result implies that the matrix (5.12) is the covariance matrix of the limiting distribution both of the 3SLS expression $\sqrt{n}(\hat{\boldsymbol{\delta}} - \boldsymbol{\delta})$ and also of the corresponding full-information maximum-likelihood expression. Since the maximum-likelihood method has the optimum property of a large-sample covariance matrix equal to the Cramér-Rao bound, the 3SLS method has the same property and is thus asymptotically efficient. The 3SLS technique is much simpler, however, and it is therefore to be preferred to the maximum-likelihood technique.

Linearized Maximum Likelihood

Theorem 10.8 presupposes the validity of all assumptions of Theorem 10.2, including Assumption 10.2 which implies that the covariance matrix $\mathbf{\Sigma}$ is unknown. But suppose that this matrix is known, either partly or completely; for example, let it be known that the disturbances of the first equation are uncorrelated with those of the second ($\sigma_{12} = 0$). It was proved by Rothenberg and Leenders that taking such knowledge into account when maximizing the function (7.3) leads to greater asymptotic efficiency for full-information maximum-likelihood compared with 3SLS. This suggests that the former estimator is preferable, but the computational difficulties remain. To solve this problem, Rothenberg and Leenders propose the following simpler

[15] Reference should also be made to related results obtained by MADANSKY (1964) and SARGAN (1964b).

procedure. Differentiate the function (7.3) with respect to $\boldsymbol{\delta}$ and write $\mathbf{f}(\boldsymbol{\delta})$ for the resulting gradient,[16] so that the maximum-likelihood estimator is to be found from the (nonlinear) equation $\mathbf{f}(\boldsymbol{\delta}) = \mathbf{0}$. Then select an estimator $\boldsymbol{\delta}_0$ which is easier to obtain and which is such that $\sqrt{n}\,(\boldsymbol{\delta}_0 - \boldsymbol{\delta})$ has a limiting distribution with zero mean vector and a finite covariance matrix; for example, the 2SLS vector $\boldsymbol{\delta}_0 = [\mathbf{d}_1' \quad \cdots \quad \mathbf{d}_L']'$. Next, replace $\mathbf{f}(\boldsymbol{\delta})$ by its linear Taylor approximation, so that the estimation equation becomes

$$\mathbf{f}(\boldsymbol{\delta}_0) + \mathbf{F}_0(\boldsymbol{\delta} - \boldsymbol{\delta}_0) = \mathbf{0} \tag{7.6}$$

where $\mathbf{F}_0$ is the Hessian matrix of the function (7.3) evaluated at $\boldsymbol{\delta}_0$. The solution is obviously $\boldsymbol{\delta}_0 - \mathbf{F}_0^{-1}\mathbf{f}(\boldsymbol{\delta}_0)$, which is known as the *linearized maximum-likelihood estimator*.[17] It can be shown that $\sqrt{n}$ times the sampling error of this estimator has the same limiting distribution as $\sqrt{n}$ times the sampling error of the full-information maximum-likelihood estimator, and also that minus the inverse of the Hessian matrix $\mathbf{F}_0$ provides an approximation to the large-sample covariance matrix of the estimator.

The linearization procedure avoids part of the computational difficulties of the full-information maximum-likelihood method, and the fact that both estimators have the same asymptotic distribution indicates that the former is to be preferred to the latter, at least when the sample is sufficiently large. However, the linearized maximum-likelihood method is still computationally much more complicated than the 3SLS procedure, and it leads to a gain in asymptotic efficiency only if prior knowledge of $\boldsymbol{\Sigma}$ is used. As stated earlier, it is exceptional to find situations in which such knowledge is available on firm grounds.

Problems

7.1 Verify the equality signs in (7.2), in particular the fourth.

7.2 Suppose that an equation system is block-recursive as described by eq. (6.3) of Section 9.6. Assume that the disturbance distribution of Assumption 10.2 is normal and prove that the log-likelihood function (7.3) is equal to the sum of r functions, one for each block. Conclude that full-information maximum-likelihood estimation takes place separately for each block.

[16] More precisely, they first differentiate (7.3) with respect to the unknown elements of $\boldsymbol{\Sigma}$, equate these derivatives to zero, and use these equations to eliminate the unknown $\boldsymbol{\Sigma}$ elements from (7.3). The resulting function is the so-called concentrated logarithmic likelihood function, and $\mathbf{f}(\boldsymbol{\delta})$ is the gradient of this function.

[17] This linearization procedure is essentially equivalent to the so-called method of scoring, details about which can be found in C. R. Rao (1965a, Section 5g).

10.8 The Choice of an Estimator for Simultaneous Equations[C]

The previous sections describe several alternative estimators of the same parameter vector. The obvious question is then which estimator is to be used in any specific case. The present section tries to answer this question to the limited extent that it is possible to do so, given the present state of the field.

Advantages of Full-Information Methods

The Rothenberg-Leenders results described in Section 10.7 imply that the 3SLS method is asymptotically efficient under certain conditions. In this respect it dominates the 2SLS method and all members of the k-class. In addition, when there are constraints involving coefficients of different structural equations, then a method which estimates these equations simultaneously is needed to handle these constraints. This applies both when these constraints are exact linear equations in the parameters and when they are random and describe uncertain prior information.

When prior knowledge exists about the covariance matrix $\mathbf{\Sigma}$, the full-information and the linearized maximum-likelihood estimators are asymptotically superior to 3SLS, and the linearized variant is then to be preferred because of its computational simplicity. Such knowledge is rare, however, and the 3SLS method is by far the most prominent full-information method both for this reason and because of its comparative simplicity.

Disadvantages of Full-Information Methods

The 3SLS estimator degenerates to a set of 2SLS estimators—one for each structural equation—when the covariance matrix $\mathbf{\Sigma}$ is, in fact, diagonal. One should expect that if $\mathbf{\Sigma}$ is not diagonal but is such that the contemporaneous correlations of the disturbances are modest, the gain in asymptotic efficiency of 3SLS will also be modest. In addition, since $\mathbf{\Sigma}$ is unknown and has to be estimated, the gain obtained by 3SLS will be reduced when the sample is actually of moderate size.[18] These are reasons why, if there are no constraints involving coefficients of different structural equations, the superiority of 3SLS over 2SLS should not be exaggerated.

The 3SLS method requires a much more detailed specification of the equation system than the 2SLS method does. For the latter method we need the list of all variables in the equation to be estimated plus the list of all predetermined variables of the system. The 3SLS method, on the other hand,

[18] Recall that this problem was considered in Section 7.4 in a nonsimultaneous context.

requires a specification of all zero elements of the parameter matrix $[\mathbf{\Gamma}' \quad \mathbf{B}']$, not only those of the row of that matrix which corresponds to one particular equation. If an element of such a row is postulated to vanish whereas it is actually nonzero, this affects the 2SLS estimators of the corresponding equation but not those of the other equations. However, in the case of 3SLS the point estimators of all equations are affected by such a specification error, which is obviously a disadvantage. The subject of specification errors will be considered in more detail in Section 11.2.

Another problem of 3SLS is that the matrix $\mathbf{S}$ consisting of mean squares and products of 2SLS residuals, which is used as an estimator of $\mathbf{\Sigma}$, is singular when $L > n$, so that the 3SLS estimator then fails to exist. This will happen when the model is large and the sample is not. One solution is to apply 3SLS to subsystems, which leads to a gain in asymptotic efficiency compared with 2SLS, but the gain is not as large as it would be if the 3SLS method had been applied to the system as a whole (see Problem 8.1). This particular solution is useful when there are linear constraints on the coefficients of different structural equations. The procedure is then to divide the system into subsystems in such a way that each pair of structural equations whose coefficients are related to each other are part of the same subsystem.

The Selection of a k-Class Estimator

Since the 3SLS method is more complicated than the limited-information estimators of the k-class, it is understandable that the latter are used on a larger scale.[19] All estimators of this class for which $\sqrt{n}\,(k-1)$ converges to zero as $n \to \infty$ have the same asymptotic distribution, so that simplicity should be the main consideration for the selection of such an estimator when the sample is indeed sufficiently large. The choice $k = 1$ (2SLS) is simpler than any other choice. In particular, it is simpler than the specification $k = \mu$ of the limited-information maximum-likelihood method, since it avoids the computation of the smallest root of the determinantal equation (4.11).[20]

[19] It should be noted, however, that considerations of computational difficulty are becoming less important now that powerful computational facilities are becoming more widespread.

[20] It is sometimes argued that the limited-information maximum-likelihood estimator is preferable to 2SLS because the former is symmetric in all $L_j + 1$ jointly dependent variables of the jth equation. (See Appendix B for this symmetry.) This is an irrelevant argument, however, because symmetry is not a virtue by itself; the quality of an estimator—given the criterion that one desires to use—is determined by the distribution of the estimator. In fact, symmetry may even be regarded as undesirable in the usual case where the structural equation is naturally associated with the endogenous variable which is determined by the decision makers whose behavior is described by the equation; see F. M. FISHER (1965c, p. 604).

A choice problem does arise when the sample is not large. The most satisfactory procedure would be to make the choice dependent on the exact distributions of the k-class estimators for finite n, and some progress in this direction has been made by BASMANN (1961, 1963a), BERGSTROM (1962), KABE (1963a, 1964), and RICHARDSON (1968). However, the results obtained by these authors refer only to particular (and very small) equation systems. A more general but approximate procedure was pursued by NAGAR (1959, 1961, 1962), who applied Taylor expansions to derive moments of k-class estimators of a higher order of approximation than that of the limiting distribution of $\sqrt{n}[(\mathbf{d}_j)_k - \boldsymbol{\delta}_j]$. One of his results is that the choice $k = 1 + (K - N_j - 1)/n$ leads to a zero bias of $(\mathbf{d}_j)_k$ to the order $1/n$. He also analyzed the second moments to the order $1/n^2$, but the results are more complicated than those of the first moments. A similar approach (with similar results) is that of the "small-sigma asymptotics" designed by KADANE (1969). This amounts to writing the disturbance covariance matrix in the form $\boldsymbol{\Sigma} = \sigma\mathbf{A}$, where σ is a scalar and $\mathbf{A}$ is a fixed matrix, and then analyzing the behavior of the distribution of the coefficient estimators when σ takes smaller and smaller values. These two approaches are not identical with the expansion of the distribution functions of the estimators that was mentioned in the last paragraph of Section 8.9; further analysis is needed to understand their relationships.

Some evidence of a different type is contained in Figure 10.1, which pictures k-class estimates as functions of k for four equations which are part of an equation system describing the operation of the U.S. food market.[21] The figure shows that the estimates of the coefficients of three of the four equations (the α's, β's, and δ's) "explode" for k values between 1 and 1.5. This is because the matrix that is to be inverted,

$$\begin{bmatrix} \mathbf{Y}_j'\mathbf{Y}_j - k\mathbf{U}_j'\mathbf{U}_j & \mathbf{Y}_j'\mathbf{X}_j \\ \mathbf{X}_j'\mathbf{Y}_j & \mathbf{X}_j'\mathbf{X}_j \end{bmatrix}$$

becomes singular for a k value between these limits. Since estimates close to the explosion point cannot be attractive, one should hesitate to choose a k larger than 1, such as $k = \mu$ of limited-information maximum likelihood.

Many efforts have been made to obtain additional insight into the behavior of simultaneous equation estimators by means of simulation experiments, several of which are described by JOHNSTON (1963, Chapter 10) and CHRIST (1966, pp. 477–481). On the whole, they confirm the idea that full-information

[21] The figure is taken from Theil (1961, p. 237) and is based on the model and data published by Girshick and Haavelmo (1953). The model consists of five equations, the third being in reduced form. This explains the absence of the γ's (the coefficients of the third equation) in Figure 10.1.

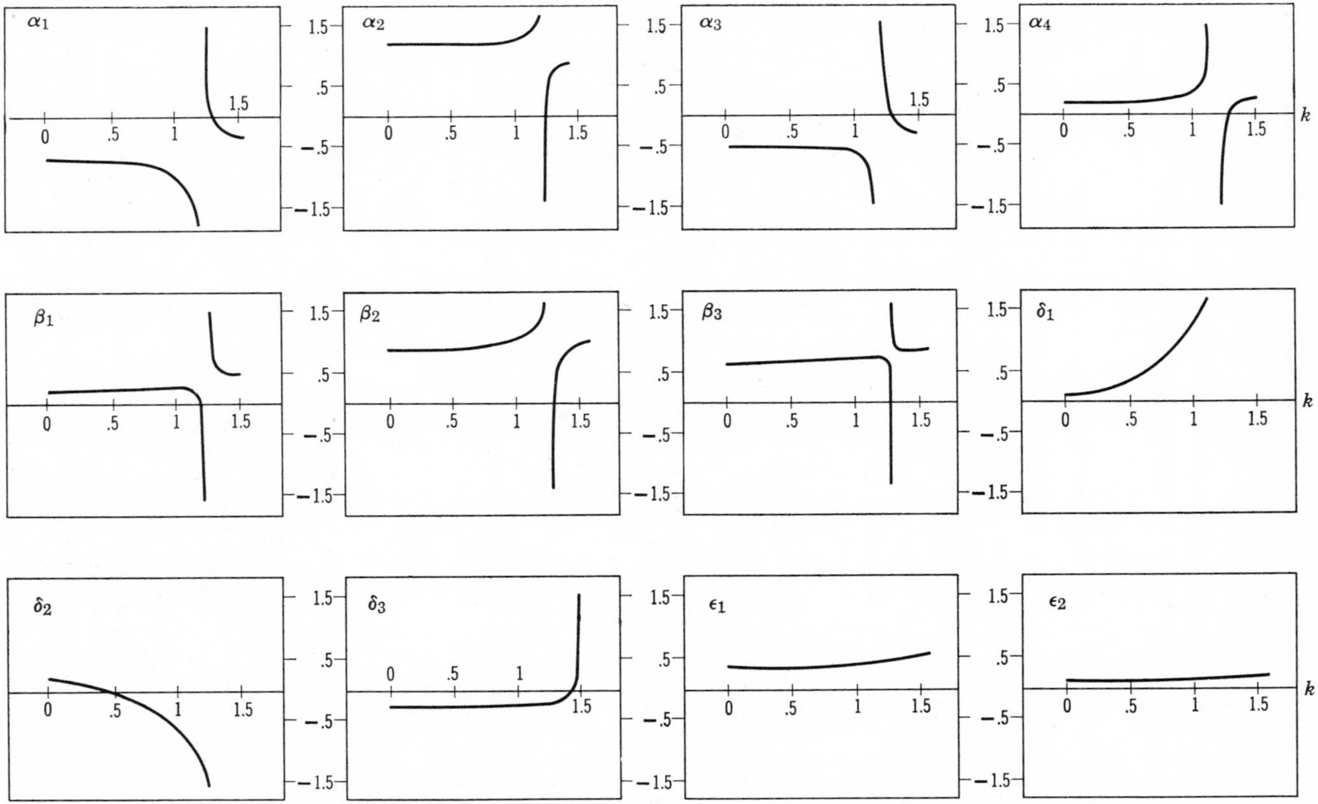

Fig. 10.1 The behavior of k-class estimates as functions of k.

methods are superior (even for moderately large n) when the model is specified correctly. The difference between 2SLS and limited-information maximum-likelihood is usually small, but when it is not small, the 2SLS estimates tend to be better on the average.[22] Also, the full-information methods may lose their superiority when the model is sufficiently misspecified.

The Problem of Undersized Samples

It was stated at the end of Section 9.4 that structural equations are usually overidentified except when the model is very small, the reason being that K (the total number of predetermined variables) typically exceeds the number of parameters to be estimated (N_j) in each of the structural equations. In fact, a major problem for the estimation of large and even of medium-sized models is that K is frequently too large rather than too small. The point is that $\mathbf{X}$, the observation matrix of the predetermined variables, cannot have a rank larger than n and thus fails to have full column rank when $n < K$. This is the problem of undersized samples, which is characterized by the serious implication that the 2SLS and 3SLS estimators do not exist, since they require the inverse of $\mathbf{X}'\mathbf{X}$.[23] The Klein-Goldberger model discussed in Sections 9.8 and 9.9 provides an example, since it contains more than 30 predetermined variables and is estimated from only 20 observations. Note that this is no problem at all from the standpoint of asymptotic theory. When n increases toward infinity, it will eventually exceed K by far, no matter how large K is. However, it is a problem for the existence of the estimator when $n < K$.

The solution proposed by Kloek and Mennes (1960) is to modify the first stage of 2SLS by running an LS regression of $\mathbf{Y}_j$ on a limited number of linear combinations of the K columns of $\mathbf{X}$ rather than on all K columns. Specifically, they suggest the use of principal components of predetermined variables. This method does have certain merits, but a disadvantage is its arbitrariness caused by the fact that the computation of principal components

[22] It should be noted that several Monte Carlo analysts have computed mean square errors of their estimates without verifying whether the corresponding second moment is finite. If this is not true, and if one computes a large number of estimates $\hat{\theta}_1, \hat{\theta}_2, \ldots$ of the same parameter θ, then the average of the squares $(\hat{\theta}_1 - \theta)^2, (\hat{\theta}_2 - \theta)^2, \ldots$ will increase indefinitely as the number of estimates increases. It is then better to describe the frequency distribution of Monte Carlo estimates by measures other than the moments such as the median and the quartiles. See Problem 8.2 for an example of a nonexisting moment.

[23] The situation is not better for the other consistent methods discussed in the previous sections, since they either require the inverse of $\mathbf{X}'\mathbf{X}$ or they are based on another estimator which is, in turn, based on this inverse. The latter statement applies, for example, to the linearized maximum-likelihood estimator if the vector $\boldsymbol{\delta}_0$ of eq. (7.6) consists of 2SLS estimators.

requires a certain normalization rule on the variables (such as a unit mean square).[24] Reference should be made to F. M. FISHER's (1965c) criticism of the Kloek-Mennes proposal and the alternative he suggests, which is based on causal orderings; however, this procedure is difficult to apply without extensive prior information on the equation system. A third approach, to be described in the next subsection, is heavily based on work done by SWAMY, MADDALA, and HOLMES (1969).

A GLS Approach for Undersized Samples

We return to the first paragraph of Section 9.5 and assume temporarily that the matrix $\mathbf{X}$ consists of nonstochastic elements. The disturbance vector $\mathbf{X}'\boldsymbol{\epsilon}_j$ of $\mathbf{X}'\mathbf{y}_j = \mathbf{X}'\mathbf{Z}_j\boldsymbol{\delta}_j + \mathbf{X}'\boldsymbol{\epsilon}_j$ then has covariance matrix $\sigma_{jj}\mathbf{X}'\mathbf{X}$ as before, but this matrix is singular when $\mathbf{X}$ fails to have full column rank. This suggests that it is appropriate to generalize the Aitken approach of Section 9.5 to the GLS approach of the singular disturbance covariance matrix developed in Section 6.7. The estimator of $\boldsymbol{\delta}_j$ then becomes

$$\text{(8.1)} \qquad \begin{aligned} \mathbf{d}_j &= [\mathbf{Z}_j'\mathbf{X}(\mathbf{X}'\mathbf{X})^+\mathbf{X}'\mathbf{Z}_j]^{-1}\mathbf{Z}_j'\mathbf{X}(\mathbf{X}'\mathbf{X})^+\mathbf{X}'\mathbf{y}_j \\ &= (\mathbf{Z}_j'\mathbf{X}\mathbf{X}^+\mathbf{Z}_j)^{-1}\mathbf{Z}_j'\mathbf{X}\mathbf{X}^+\mathbf{y}_j \end{aligned}$$

where the second equality sign is based on $\mathbf{X}^+ = (\mathbf{X}'\mathbf{X})^+\mathbf{X}'$ [see eq. (6.10) of Section 6.6]. It will be noted that the expression on the second line of (8.1) is identical with (5.10), so that it may be regarded as the general form of the 2SLS estimator both when $\mathbf{X}$ has full column rank and when $\mathbf{X}$ has less than full column rank.

It was stated in the first paragraph of Section 9.5 that Aitken's theorem is not fully applicable owing to the presence of $\mathbf{Y}_j$ as a submatrix of $\mathbf{Z}_j$. This qualification applies here also. In addition, we have to verify the validity of the two rank conditions under which the generalization of Aitken's theorem was derived in Section 6.7. These conditions are formulated in terms of characteristic vectors of the disturbance covariance matrix and the observation matrix of the right-hand variables. Hence we should compare the matrices $\mathbf{V}$ and $\mathbf{X}$ of Section 6.7 with $\mathbf{X}'\mathbf{X}$ and $\mathbf{X}'\mathbf{Z}_j$, respectively, of the present equation $\mathbf{X}'\mathbf{y}_j = \mathbf{X}'\mathbf{Z}_j\boldsymbol{\delta}_j + \mathbf{X}'\boldsymbol{\epsilon}_j$. So we write, similarly to eq. (7.4) of Section 6.7,

$$\text{(8.2)} \qquad \mathbf{X}'\mathbf{X}\mathbf{F} = \mathbf{F}\boldsymbol{\Lambda}^2 \qquad \mathbf{X}'\mathbf{X}\mathbf{G} = \mathbf{0}$$

where $\boldsymbol{\Lambda}^2$ is a diagonal matrix which contains the positive roots of $\mathbf{X}'\mathbf{X}$ on the

[24] Other sources of arbitrariness are the number of principal components to be used and the question of whether these components should refer to the set of all predetermined variables of the system or only to those which are excluded from the equation estimated. Also see AMEMYIA (1966b) for a more positive evaluation of the procedure.

diagonal and $[\mathbf{F} \quad \mathbf{G}]$ is an orthogonal $K \times K$ matrix, $\mathbf{F}$ consisting of columns which are characteristic vectors of $\mathbf{X}'\mathbf{X}$ corresponding to the positive roots, and $\mathbf{G}$ consisting of columns that are characteristic vectors of $\mathbf{X}'\mathbf{X}$ corresponding to the zero roots. The application of Assumption 6.3 to the present case implies that the matrix $\mathbf{F}'\mathbf{X}'\mathbf{Z}_j$ should have full column rank (i.e., rank N_j); if that is not the case, the matrix in brackets after the first equality sign in (8.1) has no (ordinary) inverse. It is readily verified that this condition is violated only if N_j exceeds the rank of $\mathbf{X}$, which is typically not the case.

Assumption 6.4 applied to the present situation implies that $\mathbf{G}'\mathbf{X}'\mathbf{Z}_j$ should be a zero matrix; if it is nonzero, the singularity of the covariance matrix $\sigma_{jj}\mathbf{X}'\mathbf{X}$ of the disturbance vector $\mathbf{X}'\boldsymbol{\epsilon}_j$ implies linear constraints on the parameter vector $\boldsymbol{\delta}_j$. Rearrange the predetermined variables so that the columns of $\mathbf{X}_j$ are the first K_j columns of $\mathbf{X}$ and consider

$$\text{(8.3)} \qquad \mathbf{X}'\mathbf{Z}_j = [\mathbf{X}'\mathbf{Y}_j \quad \mathbf{X}'\mathbf{X}_j] = \mathbf{X}'\mathbf{X}\begin{bmatrix} & \mathbf{I} \\ \mathbf{P}_j & \cdots \\ & \mathbf{0} \end{bmatrix}$$

which implies $\mathbf{X}'\mathbf{Y}_j = \mathbf{X}'\mathbf{X}\mathbf{P}_j$. If $\mathbf{X}$ has full column rank, then

$$\mathbf{P}_j = (\mathbf{X}'\mathbf{X})^{-1}\mathbf{X}'\mathbf{Y}_j$$

in accordance with eq. (5.8) of Section 9.5. If $\mathbf{X}$ fails to have full column rank, $\mathbf{P}_j$ is not uniquely determined by the LS normal equations $\mathbf{X}'\mathbf{Y}_j = \mathbf{X}'\mathbf{X}\mathbf{P}_j$, but solutions $\mathbf{P}_j$ do exist since these normal equations are never inconsistent (see the first paragraph of Section 3.8). Thus, taking any solution $\mathbf{P}_j$, we have

$$\text{(8.4)} \qquad \mathbf{G}'\mathbf{X}'\mathbf{Z}_j = \mathbf{G}'\mathbf{X}'\mathbf{X}\begin{bmatrix} & \mathbf{I} \\ \mathbf{P}_j & \cdots \\ & \mathbf{0} \end{bmatrix} = \mathbf{0}$$

because $\mathbf{G}'\mathbf{X}'\mathbf{X} = \mathbf{0}$ follows from (8.2). Assumption 6.4 is thus fulfilled, and we may therefore conclude that the estimator (8.1) for an $\mathbf{X}$ with rank less than K has exactly the same relation to the Aitken generalization of Section 6.7 as the original 2SLS estimator has to the original Aitken theorem.

The Approach Amounts to LS When the Sample Is Undersized

It will be shown in the next paragraph that the estimator (8.1) is identical with the LS estimator $(\mathbf{Z}_j'\mathbf{Z}_j)^{-1}\mathbf{Z}_j'\mathbf{y}_j$ when the number of observations does not exceed the number of columns of $\mathbf{X}$. This means that if we imagine that n increases from 1 to infinity, the estimator (8.1) coincides with that of LS as long as $n \leq K$ and that it coincides with the ordinary 2SLS estimator for $n > K$ when $\mathbf{X}$ has full column rank.

To prove that the vector (8.1) reduces to $(\mathbf{Z}_j'\mathbf{Z}_j)^{-1}\mathbf{Z}_j'\mathbf{y}_j$ when $n \leq K$, we note that $\mathbf{a}_1'\mathbf{X}\mathbf{X}^+\mathbf{a}_2 = \mathbf{a}_1'\mathbf{a}_2$ holds for any pair of n-element vectors $(\mathbf{a}_1, \mathbf{a}_2)$ under this condition. This is so because the ranks of $\mathbf{X}$ and of the augmented matrix $[\mathbf{X} \quad \mathbf{a}_i]$ are then equal, so that a solution $\mathbf{b}_i$ of $\mathbf{a}_i = \mathbf{X}\mathbf{b}_i$ exists $(i = 1, 2)$. Hence the LS regression of $\mathbf{a}_i$ on $\mathbf{X}$ has zero residuals. The proposition is then proved by means of the following steps:

$$\mathbf{a}_1'\mathbf{X}\mathbf{X}^+\mathbf{a}_2 = \mathbf{a}_1'\mathbf{X}(\mathbf{X}'\mathbf{X})^+\mathbf{X}'\mathbf{a}_2 = \mathbf{b}_1'\mathbf{X}'\mathbf{X}(\mathbf{X}'\mathbf{X})^+\mathbf{X}'\mathbf{X}\mathbf{b}_2 = \mathbf{b}_1'\mathbf{X}'\mathbf{X}\mathbf{b}_2 = \mathbf{a}_1'\mathbf{a}_2$$

where the third equality sign is based on $\mathbf{A}\mathbf{A}^+\mathbf{A} = \mathbf{A}$, which holds for any matrix $\mathbf{A}$. By interpreting $\mathbf{a}_1$ and $\mathbf{a}_2$ as the columns of $\mathbf{Z}_j$ or as $\mathbf{y}_j$, one easily verifies that the estimator (8.1) does indeed reduce to $(\mathbf{Z}_j'\mathbf{Z}_j)^{-1}\mathbf{Z}_j'\mathbf{y}_j$ under our condition.

So it turns out that the generalization (8.1) of the original 2SLS estimator is actually LS when the generalization is really needed. The asymptotic properties of this generalized estimator are obviously the same as those of ordinary 2SLS, but asymptotic properties are of limited relevance when the n of the available sample prevents the matrix $\mathbf{X}$ from having full column rank. The problem, then, is that the number of degrees of freedom available for LS estimation of the reduced form is not even positive, and it is clear what this means for the first stage of 2SLS (which is an attempt to remove the reduced-form disturbance component from the matrix $\mathbf{Y}_j$). It is not very clear, though, what conclusion should be drawn from this result. If the GLS approach (8.1) were fully applicable, the optimum properties of GLS would imply similar properties for LS applied to each structural equation when $n \leq K$. However, we know that the GLS approach is not fully applicable owing to the presence of $\mathbf{Y}_j$ as a submatrix of $\mathbf{Z}_j$; see the second paragraph of the previous subsection.

A Modified 2SLS Estimator for Undersized Samples

There are no obvious solutions in a case like this. A simple but approximate solution is the following modified 2SLS procedure. First stage: estimate each structural equation by LS and compute the reduced-form residual matrix $\hat{\mathbf{U}}$ which is implied by these structural coefficient estimates. Second stage: take the submatrix $\hat{\mathbf{U}}_j$ of $\hat{\mathbf{U}}$ which corresponds with $\mathbf{Y}_j$ and reestimate the jth structural equation by running an LS regression of $\mathbf{y}_j$ on $[\mathbf{Y}_j - \hat{\mathbf{U}}_j \quad \mathbf{X}_j]$. The use of $\hat{\mathbf{U}}$ has the advantage that this is a residual matrix which has been derived subject to all overidentifying restrictions on the structural equations. The LS residual matrix $\mathbf{U}$ does not have this advantage. It is, of course, true that $\hat{\mathbf{U}}$ does not converge in distribution to the reduced-form disturbance matrix $\mathbf{E}\Gamma^{-1}$ but, again, these convergence considerations are not particularly relevant in the present context. What is needed is an evaluation of the finite-sample properties of procedures such as this modified 2SLS approach, but these properties are presently unknown.

Iterative procedures may also be useful. For example, consider the reduced-form residual matrix $\mathbf{U}^{(2)}$ which is implied by the estimated coefficients of the second stage as described in the previous paragraph. A new estimate of the jth equation is obtained by running an LS regression of $\mathbf{y}_j$ on $[\mathbf{Y}_j - \mathbf{U}_j^{(2)} \quad \mathbf{X}_j]$, where $\mathbf{U}_j^{(2)}$ is the submatrix of $\mathbf{U}^{(2)}$ that corresponds to $\mathbf{Y}_j$. When this is done for each j, a new reduced-form residual matrix $\mathbf{U}^{(3)}$ is implied, and so forth. Such an iterative procedure requires the formulation of the conditions under which it converges and, if it converges, we need an evaluation of the finite-sample properties of the resulting estimator. Another iterative method was proposed by WOLD (1966a, b). It also consists of a series of LS regressions of $\mathbf{y}_j$ on $[\mathbf{Y}_j - \mathbf{U}_j^{(s)} \quad \mathbf{X}_j]$, $s = 1, 2, \ldots$. However, his $\mathbf{Y}_j - \mathbf{U}_j^{(1)}$ is a linear function of the values taken by the predetermined variables; the simplest example is $\mathbf{Y}_j - \mathbf{U}_j^{(1)} = \mathbf{0}$. Again, further results are needed before the merits of such procedures can be assessed.

Estimation of Reduced Form

The reduced-form coefficient estimator $(\mathbf{X}'\mathbf{X})^{-1}\mathbf{X}'\mathbf{Y}$ which is obtained in the first stage of 2SLS does not, in general, satisfy any of the overidentifying restrictions on the structural equations. An estimator with this property can be obtained by means of estimators of the structural coefficients. Such a procedure is worked out in Problems 8.3 and 8.4, which are based on GOLDBERGER, NAGAR, and ODEH (1961). Note that the procedure is based on an $\mathbf{X}$ with full column rank. Also see Problems 8.5 and 8.6 on reduced-form and final-form prediction.

Problems

8.1 (*3SLS as if $\boldsymbol{\Sigma}$ is block-diagonal*) Partition the disturbance covariance matrix:

$$\boldsymbol{\Sigma} = \begin{bmatrix} \boldsymbol{\Sigma}_{11} & \boldsymbol{\Sigma}_{12} & \cdots & \boldsymbol{\Sigma}_{1r} \\ \boldsymbol{\Sigma}_{21} & \boldsymbol{\Sigma}_{22} & \cdots & \boldsymbol{\Sigma}_{2r} \\ \vdots & \vdots & & \vdots \\ \boldsymbol{\Sigma}_{r1} & \boldsymbol{\Sigma}_{r2} & \cdots & \boldsymbol{\Sigma}_{rr} \end{bmatrix} \tag{8.5}$$

where all diagonal submatrices are square and nonsingular. Apply

3SLS to each of the r blocks separately:

$$\hat{\boldsymbol{\delta}}_{(i)} = [\mathbf{Z}'_{(i)}(\mathbf{S}_{ii}^{-1} \otimes \mathbf{X}\mathbf{X}^{+})\mathbf{Z}_{(i)}]^{-1}\mathbf{Z}'_{(i)}(\mathbf{S}_{ii}^{-1} \otimes \mathbf{X}\mathbf{X}^{+})\mathbf{y}_{(i)} \tag{8.6}$$

where $\mathbf{S}_{ii}$, $\mathbf{Z}_{(i)}$, and $\mathbf{y}_{(i)}$ are to be defined appropriately ($i = 1, \ldots, r$). Prove (under the assumptions of Theorem 10.7) the consistency and the asymptotic normality of this estimator and derive its asymptotic covariance matrix. Also prove that its asymptotic efficiency is *between* that of 2SLS and 3SLS, and that it is equal to that of 3SLS if $\mathbf{\Sigma}_{ij} = \mathbf{0}$ for all $i \neq j$, and equal to that of 2SLS if the diagonal blocks $\mathbf{\Sigma}_{11}, \ldots, \mathbf{\Sigma}_{rr}$ are diagonal matrices.

8.2 Consider the Keynesian model (1.1) and (1.2) of Section 9.1 and assume that Assumptions 10.1 to 10.3 are valid, investment being exogenous and the disturbances being normally distributed. Prove that the expectation of the 2SLS estimator of β does not exist. (*Hint*. See Problem 3.8 of Section 8.3.)

8.3 (*Reduced form estimation*) Write $\hat{\mathbf{\Pi}} = -\hat{\mathbf{B}}\hat{\mathbf{\Gamma}}^{-1}$ for the estimator of the reduced-form coefficient matrix $\mathbf{\Pi}$ which is implied by the estimator $[\hat{\mathbf{\Gamma}}' \quad \hat{\mathbf{B}}']$ of the structural coefficient matrix $[\mathbf{\Gamma}' \quad \mathbf{B}']$. Then define the KL-element column vector $\boldsymbol{\pi}$ whose jth subvector is equal to the jth column of $\mathbf{\Pi}$:

$$\boldsymbol{\pi}' = [\pi_{11} \quad \cdots \quad \pi_{K1} \quad \cdots \quad \pi_{1L} \quad \cdots \quad \pi_{KL}]$$

as well as the $(K + L)L$-element column vector $\boldsymbol{\alpha}$ whose jth subvector is equal to the transpose of the jth row of $[\mathbf{\Gamma}' \quad \mathbf{B}']$:

$$\boldsymbol{\alpha}' = [\gamma_{11} \quad \cdots \quad \gamma_{L1} \quad \beta_{11} \quad \cdots \quad \beta_{K1} \quad \cdots \quad \gamma_{1L} \quad \cdots \quad \gamma_{LL} \quad \beta_{1L} \quad \cdots \quad \beta_{KL}]$$

Prove that $\boldsymbol{\alpha}$ is equal to $-\boldsymbol{\delta}$ defined in (5.1) when those elements of $\boldsymbol{\alpha}$ are deleted that are postulated to be zero as well as those which are coefficients of the left-hand dependent variables of the structural equations given in (5.1). Assume that $\sqrt{n}\,(\hat{\boldsymbol{\alpha}} - \boldsymbol{\alpha})$, where $\hat{\boldsymbol{\alpha}}$ is the same function of $[\hat{\mathbf{\Gamma}}' \quad \hat{\mathbf{B}}']$ as $\boldsymbol{\alpha}$ is of $[\mathbf{\Gamma}' \quad \mathbf{B}']$, has a normal limiting distribution with zero mean vector and covariance matrix $\mathbf{V}_\alpha$.[25] Define $\hat{\boldsymbol{\pi}}$ analogously and prove that $\sqrt{n}\,(\hat{\boldsymbol{\pi}} - \boldsymbol{\pi})$ has a normal limiting distribution with zero mean vector and the following covariance matrix:

$$\mathbf{V}_\pi = \left(\frac{\partial \boldsymbol{\pi}}{\partial \boldsymbol{\alpha}'}\right)\mathbf{V}_\alpha\left(\frac{\partial \boldsymbol{\pi}}{\partial \boldsymbol{\alpha}'}\right)' \tag{8.7}$$

where $\partial\boldsymbol{\pi}/\partial\boldsymbol{\alpha}'$ is the $KL \times (K + L)L$ matrix of derivatives of $\boldsymbol{\pi}$ with respect to $\boldsymbol{\alpha}'$ evaluated at the point of the true $\boldsymbol{\alpha}$.

[25] Note that $\mathbf{V}_\alpha$ has as many zero rows (and columns) as there are fixed (zero or unit) elements in $\hat{\boldsymbol{\alpha}}$.

8.4 (*Continuation*) Write $\mathbf{\Pi} = -\mathbf{B\Gamma}^{-1}$ in scalar form:

$$\pi_{hj} = -\sum_{i=1}^{L} \beta_{hi}\gamma^{ij} \qquad \begin{matrix} h = 1, \ldots, K \\ j = 1, \ldots, L \end{matrix} \tag{8.8}$$

and prove $\partial\pi_{hj}/\partial\gamma_{gl} = \sum_i \beta_{hi}\gamma^{ig}\gamma^{lj} = -\pi_{hg}\gamma^{lj}$ as well as $\partial\pi_{hj}/\partial\beta_{kl} = 0$ if $h \neq k$ and $-\gamma^{lj}$ if $h = k$. Next prove that the derivative of the jth subvector of $\boldsymbol{\pi}$ (which is the jth column of $\mathbf{\Pi}$) with respect to the lth subvector of $\boldsymbol{\alpha}'$ (which is the lth row of $[\mathbf{\Gamma}' \quad \mathbf{B}']$) is

$$\left[\begin{array}{ccc|ccc} \dfrac{\partial\pi_{1j}}{\partial\gamma_{1l}} & \cdots & \dfrac{\partial\pi_{1j}}{\partial\gamma_{Ll}} & \dfrac{\partial\pi_{1j}}{\partial\beta_{1l}} & \cdots & \dfrac{\partial\pi_{1j}}{\partial\beta_{Kl}} \\ \cdot & & \cdot & \cdot & & \cdot \\ \cdot & & \cdot & \cdot & & \cdot \\ \cdot & & \cdot & \cdot & & \cdot \\ \dfrac{\partial\pi_{Kj}}{\partial\gamma_{1l}} & \cdots & \dfrac{\partial\pi_{Kj}}{\partial\gamma_{Ll}} & \dfrac{\partial\pi_{Kj}}{\partial\beta_{1l}} & \cdots & \dfrac{\partial\pi_{Kj}}{\partial\beta_{Kl}} \end{array}\right] = -\gamma^{lj}[\mathbf{\Pi} \quad \mathbf{I}] \tag{8.9}$$

Use this to prove

$$\frac{\partial\boldsymbol{\pi}}{\partial\boldsymbol{\alpha}'} = -(\mathbf{\Gamma}')^{-1} \otimes [\mathbf{\Pi} \quad \mathbf{I}] \tag{8.10}$$

where $\partial\boldsymbol{\pi}/\partial\boldsymbol{\alpha}'$ is the matrix occurring in the right-hand side of (8.7). Describe how asymptotic standard errors of the $\hat{\boldsymbol{\pi}}$ elements can be obtained from this result.

8.5 (*Reduced form prediction—continuation*) Use the subscript F for some future period for which conditional predictions of the values taken by the jointly dependent variables $(y_{F1}, \ldots, y_{FL})$ are to be made, given specified values of the predetermined variables $(x_{F1}, \ldots, x_{FK})$. Prove

$$\begin{bmatrix} y_{F1} \\ y_{F2} \\ \cdot \\ \cdot \\ \cdot \\ y_{FL} \end{bmatrix} = (\mathbf{\Gamma}')^{-1} \begin{bmatrix} \epsilon_{F1} \\ \epsilon_{F2} \\ \cdot \\ \cdot \\ \cdot \\ \epsilon_{FL} \end{bmatrix} \tag{8.11}$$

$$+ \begin{bmatrix} x_{F1} & \cdots & x_{FK} & 0 & \cdots & 0 & \cdots & 0 & \cdots & 0 \\ 0 & \cdots & 0 & x_{F1} & \cdots & x_{FK} & \cdots & 0 & \cdots & 0 \\ \cdot & & \cdot & \cdot & & \cdot & & \cdot & & \cdot \\ \cdot & & \cdot & \cdot & & \cdot & & \cdot & & \cdot \\ \cdot & & \cdot & \cdot & & \cdot & & \cdot & & \cdot \\ 0 & \cdots & 0 & 0 & \cdots & 0 & \cdots & x_{F1} & \cdots & x_{FK} \end{bmatrix} \boldsymbol{\pi}$$

where $\boldsymbol{\pi}$ is the KL-element vector introduced in Problem 8.3. Write $\mathbf{J}$ for the $L \times KL$ matrix in the right-hand side of (8.11) and assume that the disturbance distribution of Assumption 10.2 is L-variate normal. Let the left-hand vector of (8.11) be predicted by the right-hand side after $\boldsymbol{\pi}$ is replaced by $\hat{\boldsymbol{\pi}}$ of Problem 8.3 and the disturbances by zero. Prove that the prediction error vector is, for large n, approximately normally distributed with zero mean and covariance matrix $n^{-1}\mathbf{J}\mathbf{V}_{\pi}\mathbf{J}' + (\boldsymbol{\Gamma}')^{-1}\boldsymbol{\Sigma}\boldsymbol{\Gamma}^{-1}$, where $\mathbf{V}_{\pi}$ is given in (8.7).

8.6 (*Final form prediction—continuation*) Describe in general terms (without going into the algebra) how the result of the previous problem is to be extended when $y_{F1}, \ldots, y_{FL}$ must be predicted from the final form (as described in Section 9.7), given the time path of all exogenous variables up to and including period F.

CHAPTER 11

SPECIFICATION AND AGGREGATION ANALYSIS

Until now we usually acted as if the list of explanatory variables were known to be specified correctly and also as if there were no uncertainty with regard to the mathematical form of the relation. However, there are many cases in which there are doubts in either or both respects. Specification analysis is a tool which under appropriate conditions gives insight into the consequences of an erroneous specification of the basic relation. Aggregation theory is a related subject. These are the two main topics that are discussed in this chapter. Parts of Sections 11.1 and 11.2 are recommended for an introductory econometrics course; Sections 11.3 through 11.5 are optional, and the later sections are not recommended.

11.1 How Should a Relation Be Specified?[AB]

To make the discussion more specific we shall start with the problem of the mathematical form of a relation. It is sometimes argued that this form is not important as long as one is interested in small variations around the center of gravity of the observations, and in particular that the Taylor expansion may be used to justify the simple linear form. But there are situations in which the mathematical form is quite important, even for small changes, as the following example will illustrate.

A Monopolist Facing Two Alternative Demand Curves[A]

A monopolist produces one commodity, the total cost of which varies linearly with output. Hence the cost function is of the form $c_0 + cq$, where c_0 stands for fixed costs, c for marginal cost per unit of output, and q for output (which will be identified with sales). Gross revenue is thus pq, p being the price charged by the monopolist. Therefore his profit is

$$P = (p - c)q - c_0 \tag{1.1}$$

where q (sales) is a function of p. The monopolist's goal is to set p so that profit P is maximized. He is particularly interested in the answer to the following question: if marginal cost c rises by a given amount (because of wage increases or price rises of raw materials), how does this affect the profit-maximizing price?

To answer this question we differentiate P with respect to p:

$$\frac{\partial P}{\partial p} = q + (p - c)\frac{\partial q}{\partial p} \tag{1.2}$$

This derivative should be equated to zero and solved for p. Also, the second derivative should be negative: $\partial^2 P/\partial p^2 = 2\partial q/\partial p + (p - c)\partial^2 q/\partial p^2 < 0$. In view of (1.2), this can also be written as

$$2\frac{\partial q}{\partial p} + \frac{q}{-\partial q/\partial p}\frac{\partial^2 q}{\partial p^2} < 0 \quad \text{if} \quad \frac{\partial P}{\partial p} = 0 \tag{1.3}$$

These results indicate that the first two derivatives of the demand function are of crucial importance. Suppose, then, that we have at our disposal data on price and quantity over a number of successive years. Also suppose—to simplify the exposition—that there are no other important variables or other relations which exert a disturbing influence, so that the observations are as pictured in the figure opposite. It is seen that the data fit a linear relation and a constant-elasticity relation about equally well, which suggests that we

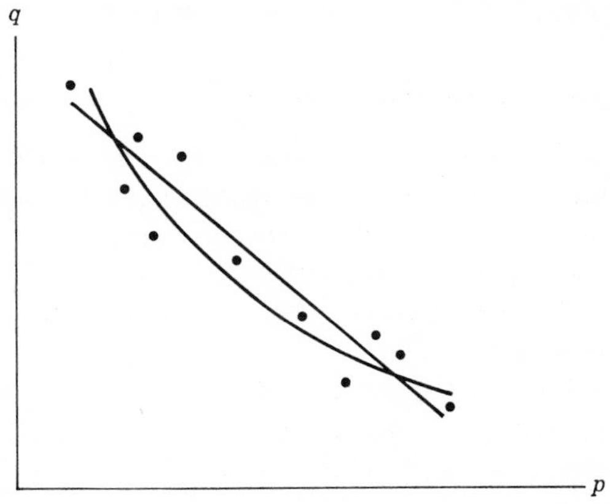

should answer the question asked by the monopolist under both conditions. First take the linear demand function:

$$q = \alpha + \beta p \qquad \alpha > 0, \quad \beta < 0 \tag{1.4}$$

When equating the derivative (1.2) to zero, we obtain the following profit-maximizing price:

$$p = \frac{\alpha}{-2\beta} + \frac{1}{2}c \tag{1.5}$$

and we note that condition (1.3) simply amounts to $\beta < 0$. The conclusion is that if marginal cost goes up by one dollar per unit of output, the price of the commodity should be raised by half a dollar when the demand equation is indeed linear. Note that this response to marginal cost changes is completely independent of the parameters α and β of the demand function.

Next consider the case of a constant-elasticity demand function:

$$q = Ap^{\eta} \qquad A > 0, \eta < 0 \tag{1.6}$$

where η is the price elasticity of demand. Again, we set the derivative (1.2) equal to zero and find as profit-maximizing price:

$$p = \frac{\eta}{\eta + 1} c \tag{1.7}$$

Condition (1.3) now amounts to $\eta < -1$ as is easily verified. This means that $\eta/(\eta + 1)$, the coefficient of c in (1.7), is larger than one. Thus, if the demand function is of the constant-elasticity type, a one dollar increase in marginal cost should induce the monopolist to raise his price by more than one dollar—more than twice the increase of the linear case. In addition, the response depends on the price elasticity η (which will usually be unknown) and it is therefore not independent of the parameters of the demand function, which is again different from the linear case.

The Specification Problem[A]

The above example shows that the mathematical form of a relation may have important consequences at the decision-making level. Therefore our problem is this: if we are interested in the behavior of a certain variable, how should the relation describing this behavior be specified? What should be the mathematical form and which variables should be selected as explanatory variables?

It is sometimes argued that economic theory should provide the appropriate knowledge in that respect, but this overestimates the power of economic theory in many cases. The problem is then to decide which of a number of alternative specifications is to be regarded as the correct one, after which the estimation of the unknown parameters takes place on the basis of this particular specification. Statistical testing procedures are therefore in order, but testing followed by subsequent estimation is characterized by difficulties about which we shall have more to say in Section 12.1. The exposition which follows is devoted to more limited aims: the residual-variance criterion for choosing among alternative specifications and the use of constraints on parameters which may be incorrect to a limited degree.

The Residual-Variance Criterion[A]

Let $\mathbf{y}$ be the vector of the dependent variable, and write $\mathbf{X}$ and $\mathbf{X}_0$ for the observation matrices of two competing sets of explanatory variables; they are of order $n \times K$ and $n \times K_0$, respectively, and they both have full column rank. The two specifications are assumed to be linear. Hence their residual-variance estimators are

$$(1.8) \qquad s^2 = \frac{1}{n-K}\mathbf{y}'\mathbf{M}\mathbf{y} \qquad s_0^2 = \frac{1}{n-K_0}\mathbf{y}'\mathbf{M}_0\mathbf{y}$$

where

$$(1.9) \qquad \mathbf{M} = \mathbf{I} - \mathbf{X}(\mathbf{X}'\mathbf{X})^{-1}\mathbf{X}' \qquad \mathbf{M}_0 = \mathbf{I} - \mathbf{X}_0(\mathbf{X}_0'\mathbf{X}_0)^{-1}\mathbf{X}_0'$$

It is assumed that both $\mathbf{X}$ and $\mathbf{X}_0$ consist of nonstochastic elements. Also, assume that $\mathbf{y} = \mathbf{X}\boldsymbol{\beta} + \boldsymbol{\epsilon}$, $\mathscr{E}\boldsymbol{\epsilon} = \mathbf{0}$, $\mathscr{V}(\boldsymbol{\epsilon}) = \sigma^2\mathbf{I}$ is the correct specification, so that $\mathscr{E}s^2 = \sigma^2$. Then consider the expectation of the residual sum of squares of the $\mathbf{X}_0$ specification:

$$\begin{aligned}\mathscr{E}(\mathbf{y}'\mathbf{M}_0\mathbf{y}) &= \boldsymbol{\beta}'\mathbf{X}'\mathbf{M}_0\mathbf{X}\boldsymbol{\beta} + 2\mathscr{E}(\boldsymbol{\beta}'\mathbf{X}'\mathbf{M}_0\boldsymbol{\epsilon}) + \mathscr{E}(\boldsymbol{\epsilon}'\mathbf{M}_0\boldsymbol{\epsilon}) \\ &= \boldsymbol{\beta}'\mathbf{X}'\mathbf{M}_0\mathbf{X}\boldsymbol{\beta} + 0 + (n-K_0)\sigma^2 \geq (n-K_0)\sigma^2\end{aligned}$$

Combining this result with $\mathscr{E}s^2 = \sigma^2$ and the s_0^2 definition given in (1.8), we obtain

$$(1.10) \qquad \mathscr{E}(s_0^2 - s^2) \geq 0$$

which means that, on the average, the residual-variance estimator of the incorrect specification exceeds that of the correct specification. This provides a justification for the selection of the specification with the smallest residual-variance estimate. Note that it is important to divide the residual sum of squares by the appropriate number of degrees of freedom ($n - K$ and $n - K_0$).

Limitations of the Residual-Variance Criterion[A]

The residual-variance criterion is used extensively, but it is far from being a perfect instrument. The expectation in the left-hand side of (1.10) is non-negative, but this does not prevent the wrong specification from being selected in a large minority of all cases. Also, the criterion obviously does not work when neither specification is correct. In addition, it stands to reason that if the analyst considers many alternative specifications and if he chooses the one with the smallest residual-variance estimate, this estimate will, on the average, be rather considerably below σ^2.

It should also be noted that the criterion can be applied in a straightforward manner only if the competing specifications have the same left-hand variable. This is not the case, for example, when one specification is linear in certain variables and the other linear in the logarithms of the same variables. The monopolist's problem falls under this category when it is assumed that the demand equations (1.4) and (1.6) are estimated by means of linear LS regressions of q on p and of $\log q$ on $\log p$, respectively.

As a specific numerical example, consider the demand equation for textiles introduced in Section 3.3. The specification adopted there is linear in the logarithms of textile consumption per capita, real income per capita, and the relative price of textile goods. Suppose we wish to compare it with a linear regression in these three variables themselves rather than their logarithms. In such a case one may take the logarithms of the calculated values of the latter (linear) regression, compute the sum of squares of their deviations from the observed values of the logarithm of textile consumption per capita, and compare this figure with the residual sum of squares of the log-linear regression. In the example of Section 3.3 this gives .00432 for the linear regression and .00257 for the log-linear case; hence the latter specification is preferable to the former on the basis of this criterion. Note, however, that this criterion is based on the performance of the regressions with respect to the *logarithm* of textile consumption per capita. It is conceivable that if our yardstick is textile consumption itself rather than its logarithm, the conclusion must be reversed. So we take the antilogs of the calculated values of the log-linear regression, compute the sum of squares of their deviations from the observed values of textile consumption per capita, and compare this figure with the residual sum of squares of the linear regression. This gives 433 for the linear specification and 277 for its log-linear competitor, so that the latter wins on both counts.

Note that by comparing these sums of squares of discrepancies we paid no attention to loss of degrees of freedom. This may be justified in this case by pointing out that the number of coefficients adjusted is the same for the two specifications. It is probably a good procedure always to divide the sum of squares of the discrepancies for each specification by the excess of the number of observations over the number of adjusted coefficients, but there exists no formal justification for this procedure (except, of course, when the discrepancies are the original LS residuals of the specification). The probabilistic evaluation of the procedure outlined in the previous paragraph is difficult anyway, and there are situations in which the two comparisons lead to opposite conclusions (see Problem 1.4).

Statistical procedures should not be regarded as the only tools for handling the selection problem. The analyst may be convinced on a priori grounds that one specification is more realistic than another, in which case he should feel justified in applying the former even if the latter has a slightly smaller residual-variance estimate. The real test is provided by prediction based on an independent set of data. It is not at all self-evident that selections that are exclusively based on the smallest residual-variance estimates lead to the best predictions.

Estimation Subject to Erroneous Constraints[B]

There may also be specification errors with respect to the constraints subject to which estimation takes place. Suppose that the basic equation is $\mathbf{y} = \mathbf{X}\boldsymbol{\beta} + \boldsymbol{\epsilon}$ and that it satisfies the assumptions of the standard linear model. Also suppose that the analyst estimates as if $\mathbf{r} = \mathbf{R}\boldsymbol{\beta}$, whereas actually $\mathbf{r} \neq \mathbf{R}\boldsymbol{\beta}$. The unconstrained LS estimator is $\mathbf{b} = (\mathbf{X}'\mathbf{X})^{-1}\mathbf{X}'\mathbf{y}$ and its covariance matrix is $\sigma^2(\mathbf{X}'\mathbf{X})^{-1}$. The constrained estimator according to eq. (8.9) of Section 1.8 is

$$(1.11)\quad \mathbf{b}^* = \mathbf{b} + (\mathbf{X}'\mathbf{X})^{-1}\mathbf{R}'\mathbf{A}^{-1}(\mathbf{r} - \mathbf{R}\mathbf{b}) \quad \text{where} \quad \mathbf{A} = \mathbf{R}(\mathbf{X}'\mathbf{X})^{-1}\mathbf{R}'$$

The sampling error of this estimator is obtained by subtracting $\boldsymbol{\beta}$ from both sides of the equation:

$$\begin{aligned}\mathbf{b}^* - \boldsymbol{\beta} &= (\mathbf{X}'\mathbf{X})^{-1}\mathbf{X}'\boldsymbol{\epsilon} + (\mathbf{X}'\mathbf{X})^{-1}\mathbf{R}'\mathbf{A}^{-1}[\mathbf{r} - \mathbf{R}\boldsymbol{\beta} - \mathbf{R}(\mathbf{X}'\mathbf{X})^{-1}\mathbf{X}'\boldsymbol{\epsilon}] \\ &= [\mathbf{I} - (\mathbf{X}'\mathbf{X})^{-1}\mathbf{R}'\mathbf{A}^{-1}\mathbf{R}](\mathbf{X}'\mathbf{X})^{-1}\mathbf{X}'\boldsymbol{\epsilon} + (\mathbf{X}'\mathbf{X})^{-1}\mathbf{R}'\mathbf{A}^{-1}(\mathbf{r} - \mathbf{R}\boldsymbol{\beta})\end{aligned}$$

Note that the expectation of $\mathbf{b}^* - \boldsymbol{\beta}$ does not vanish when $\mathbf{r} \neq \mathbf{R}\boldsymbol{\beta}$, so that the estimator is biased in that case. For the matrix of second-order moments around $\boldsymbol{\beta}$ we obtain

$$\begin{aligned}(1.12)\quad \mathscr{E}[(\mathbf{b}^* - \boldsymbol{\beta})(\mathbf{b}^* - \boldsymbol{\beta})'] &= \sigma^2(\mathbf{X}'\mathbf{X})^{-1} - \sigma^2(\mathbf{X}'\mathbf{X})^{-1}\mathbf{R}'\mathbf{A}^{-1}\mathbf{R}(\mathbf{X}'\mathbf{X})^{-1} \\ &\quad + (\mathbf{X}'\mathbf{X})^{-1}\mathbf{R}'\mathbf{A}^{-1}(\mathbf{r} - \mathbf{R}\boldsymbol{\beta})(\mathbf{r} - \mathbf{R}\boldsymbol{\beta})'\mathbf{A}^{-1}\mathbf{R}(\mathbf{X}'\mathbf{X})^{-1}\end{aligned}$$

Thus, this matrix is obtained from $\sigma^2(\mathbf{X}'\mathbf{X})^{-1}$, the covariance matrix of the unconstrained LS estimator, by first subtracting a positive semidefinite matrix and then adding another positive semidefinite matrix. When σ^2 is sufficiently small, the matrix which is subtracted will consist of such small elements that the second moments of the $\mathbf{b}^*$ elements may exceed those of $\mathbf{b}$. In that case imposing the incorrect constraint leads to estimators that are inferior (according to the quadratic criterion) to those of unconstrained LS. On the other hand, if the elements of $\mathbf{r} - \mathbf{R}\boldsymbol{\beta}$ are sufficiently close to zero, so that the constraint imposed is incorrect to only a limited degree, the matrix on the second line of (1.12) will consist of such small elements that the second moments of the $\mathbf{b}^*$ elements may be less than those of $\mathbf{b}$. Therefore it is not correct to say that imposing a constraint is wrong as soon as it is violated by the parameter vector.[1] If something is known about the order of magnitude of the elements of $\mathbf{r} - \mathbf{R}\boldsymbol{\beta}$, it is better to apply the mixed estimation approach described in Section 7.8, but if this is not the case it may be better to impose a slightly incorrect constraint (and compute point estimates as if it is correct) rather than to impose no constraint at all. This holds particularly in a case of multicollinearity; see Problem 1.5, where a simple case is worked out in some detail. Needless to say, the use of the conventional standard errors of such estimates [computed by neglecting the third right-hand term of (1.12)] implies that the variability of the estimator around the parameter vector is underestimated.

Problems

1.1 Prove that the second-order maximum condition for the monopolist in the constant-elasticity demand case is $\eta < -1$ as stated below eq. (1.7).

1.2 Is the residual-variance criterion identical with the criterion of maximum $\bar{R}^2$? Justify your answer and consider in particular the case in which the two competing specifications have different dependent variables (for example, y and $\log y$).

1.3 Consider the alternative of linearity versus log-linearity for the textile example of Section 3.3. The ratio of the sums of squares of the discrepancies is $433/277 = 1.56$ with respect to textile consumption and $(.00432)/(.00257) = 1.68$ with respect to the log of textile consumption. Both ratios are unfavorable for the linear specification, but the first is less unfavorable than the second. Explain in intuitive terms why such a difference should be expected.

1.4 Consider the following three pairs of observations:

$$(x_1, y_1) = (1, 1) \qquad (x_2, y_2) = (4, 1.87) \qquad (x_3, y_3) = (9, 3)$$

[1] Recall that we reached a similar conclusion in Section 7.9 in the discussion about the use of inequality constraints: even if the constraint is (slightly) incorrect, its use may nevertheless contribute to the quality of estimation and prediction.

Two alternative regressions are considered, linear and log-linear (logs to the base 10). Four sums of squares of discrepancies are given below; draw your own conclusions.

	Sum of squares ($\times 10^4$) of discrepancies from	
	y_α	$\log y_\alpha$
Linear regression	94.0	7.95
Log-linear regression	139.6	5.55

1.5 Consider the basic equation $y_\alpha = \beta_1 x_{\alpha 1} + \beta_2 x_{\alpha 2} + \epsilon_2$, $\alpha = 1, \ldots, n$, and suppose that the explanatory variables are measured so that both have unit mean square. Write ρ for their mean product and prove that under the assumptions of the standard linear model the covariance matrix of the LS estimators of β_1 and β_2 is

$$\sigma^2(\mathbf{X}'\mathbf{X})^{-1} = \frac{\sigma^2}{n(1-\rho^2)}\begin{bmatrix} 1 & -\rho \\ -\rho & 1 \end{bmatrix} \tag{1.13}$$

where $\sigma^2(\mathbf{X}'\mathbf{X})^{-1}$ on the left will now be interpreted as the first right-hand term of (1.12). Suppose that the analyst estimates under the constraint $\beta_1 = r$, so that $r = \mathbf{R}\boldsymbol{\beta}$ applies with $\mathbf{R} = [1 \quad 0]$, whereas actually $\beta_1 \neq r$. Prove that the second right-hand term of (1.12) is

$$-\sigma^2(\mathbf{X}'\mathbf{X})^{-1}\mathbf{R}'\mathbf{A}^{-1}\mathbf{R}(\mathbf{X}'\mathbf{X})^{-1} = \frac{-\sigma^2}{n(1-\rho^2)}\begin{bmatrix} 1 & -\rho \\ -\rho & \rho^2 \end{bmatrix} \tag{1.14}$$

and the third:

$$(\mathbf{X}'\mathbf{X})^{-1}\mathbf{R}'\mathbf{A}^{-1}(\mathbf{r} - \mathbf{R}\boldsymbol{\beta})(\mathbf{r} - \mathbf{R}\boldsymbol{\beta})'\mathbf{A}^{-1}\mathbf{R}(\mathbf{X}'\mathbf{X})^{-1} = (\beta_1 - r)^2\begin{bmatrix} 1 & -\rho \\ -\rho & \rho^2 \end{bmatrix} \tag{1.15}$$

Combine these results to find that the second moment of the constrained estimator of β_1 is $(\beta_1 - r)^2$. (This is, of course, an obvious result.) Conclude that this second moment is less than that of the unconstrained estimator when r is not too far from β_1, n not too large, σ^2 not too small, and ρ not too close to zero. Next prove that the second moment of the constrained estimator of β_2 is equal to $\sigma^2/n + \rho^2(\beta_1 - r)^2$, and show that this has a good chance of being smaller than the second moment of the unconstrained estimator when there is a sufficient degree of multicollinearity (ρ close to 1 or to -1).

11.2 Specification Analysis[AC]

Assume again, as in the analysis of the residual-variance criterion in the previous section, that the correct specification is

$$\mathbf{y} = \mathbf{X}\boldsymbol{\beta} + \boldsymbol{\epsilon} \qquad \mathscr{E}\boldsymbol{\epsilon} = \mathbf{0} \qquad (\mathbf{X} \text{ nonstochastic}) \tag{2.1}$$

and assume further that the analyst commits a specification error in the sense that he runs a regression on K_0 explanatory variables with observation matrix $\mathbf{X}_0$ rather than on the K right-hand variables of (2.1). There is obviously no specification error when $\mathbf{X} = \mathbf{X}_0$. But suppose that $\mathbf{X}_0$ is identical with $\mathbf{X}$ except that one column is deleted; then the specification is correct with the exception of the variable corresponding to this missing column. A variable may be omitted because the analyst is unaware of its role as a determining factor of the left-hand variable, or because he has no observations on this variable and decides to drop it, or because including the variable would lead to multicollinearity. Note that the first of these three alternatives includes the case in which the true form of the equation is quadratic in one of the variables whereas the analyst assumes it to be linear; the square of this variable is then omitted. It is also possible that $\mathbf{X}$ and $\mathbf{X}_0$ are of the same order and are identical except for one or two columns. This is the case, for example, when the variables corresponding to these columns are replaced by substitutes. Clearly, the approach is quite flexible.

Outline of Specification Analysis[A]

Specification analysis as developed by THEIL (1957) consists of a comparison of the expectation of the coefficient vector $\mathbf{b}_0$ of the incorrect regression and the parameter vector $\boldsymbol{\beta}$ of the correct specification. The coefficient vector is

$$\mathbf{b}_0 = (\mathbf{X}_0'\mathbf{X}_0)^{-1}\mathbf{X}_0'\mathbf{y} \tag{2.2}$$

We substitute $\mathbf{X}\boldsymbol{\beta} + \boldsymbol{\epsilon}$ for $\mathbf{y}$ and take the expectation under the assumption that both $\mathbf{X}$ and $\mathbf{X}_0$ consist of nonstochastic elements:

$$\mathscr{E}\mathbf{b}_0 = \mathscr{E}[(\mathbf{X}_0'\mathbf{X}_0)^{-1}\mathbf{X}_0'(\mathbf{X}\boldsymbol{\beta} + \boldsymbol{\epsilon})] = \mathbf{P}_0\boldsymbol{\beta} \qquad \text{where} \qquad \mathbf{P} = (\mathbf{X}_0'\mathbf{X}_0)^{-1}\mathbf{X}_0'\mathbf{X} \tag{2.3}$$

We conclude that there exists a simple linear relationship between the expectation of the coefficient vector of the regression used by the analyst and the unknown parameter vector $\boldsymbol{\beta}$. The transformation matrix is $\mathbf{P}_0$, which can be regarded as the coefficient matrix of the LS regression of the correct explanatory variables on those which are actually used:

$$\mathbf{X} = \mathbf{X}_0\mathbf{P}_0 + \text{matrix of residuals} \tag{2.4}$$

The regressions (2.4) are known as the *auxiliary regressions* of specification analysis. The extent to which this analysis is useful is determined by the analyst's knowledge of the elements of $\mathbf{P}_0$. The remainder of this section is devoted to examples illustrating this point.

An Omitted Variable[A]

Suppose that $\mathbf{X}_0$ is of order $n \times (K-1)$ and that it is identical with the $\mathbf{X}$ of the correct specification except that the last (Kth) column of $\mathbf{X}$ is deleted, so that one variable is omitted. It can be shown that this will, in general, affect the coefficients of all other variables. Write p_{hk} for the (h, k)th element of $\mathbf{P}_0$ and consider the hth element of $\mathscr{E}\mathbf{b}_0 = \mathbf{P}_0\boldsymbol{\beta}$:

$$(2.5) \qquad (\mathscr{E}\mathbf{b}_0)_h = \sum_{k=1}^{K} p_{hk}\beta_k = \beta_h + p_{hK}\beta_K \qquad h = 1, \ldots, K-1$$

where the second equality sign is based on the fact that the auxiliary regressions of the first $K-1$ columns of $\mathbf{X}$ on $\mathbf{X}_0$ lead to coefficients of the form $p_{hk} = 1$ if $h = k$, 0 if $h \neq k$. The auxiliary regressions are

$$(2.6) \qquad \begin{aligned} x_{\alpha 1} &= x_{\alpha 1} \\ &\vdots \\ x_{\alpha, K-1} &= x_{\alpha, K-1} \\ x_{\alpha K} &= p_{1K}x_{\alpha 1} + \cdots + p_{K-1,K}x_{\alpha, K-1} + \text{residual} \end{aligned}$$

We conclude from (2.5) that the expectation of the hth element of $\mathbf{b}_0$ exceeds the corresponding parameter β_h by $p_{hK}\beta_K$, which may be called the *specification bias* of this element. Assuming $\beta_K \neq 0$ (so that the $\mathbf{X}_0$ specification is indeed incorrect), we have a zero specification bias for this element if and only if p_{hK} vanishes, which according to (2.6) is a coefficient of the last (Kth) auxiliary regression. It is immediately evident that $p_{1K} = \cdots = p_{K-1,K} = 0$ holds if and only if the last column of $\mathbf{X}$ is orthogonal to all other columns of that matrix. When the equation has a constant term and when we measure the variables as deviations from their means, this condition amounts to zero correlations between the Kth variable and the others in the sense

$$(2.7) \qquad \sum_{\alpha=1}^{n}(x_{\alpha h} - \bar{x}_h)(x_{\alpha K} - \bar{x}_K) = 0$$

when $\bar{x}_h$ and $\bar{x}_K$ stand for the averages of $x_{\alpha h}$ and $x_{\alpha K}$, respectively, over $\alpha = 1, \ldots, n$. [The index h in (2.7) takes the values $2, \ldots, K-1$ if the first column of $\mathbf{X}$ corresponds to the constant term.] Note that even if this condition is fulfilled, so that none of the multiplicative coefficients is characterized by any specification bias, the constant term is, in general, affected by this bias (see Problem 2.1); but this will usually be regarded as less serious because of the limited interest which econometricians normally have in constant terms.

The zero-correlation criterion is unlikely to be fulfilled in most real-world situations. However, it happens rather frequently that one knows the direction of the deviation from this condition, in which case some interesting conclusions can be drawn. Two examples will be considered.

Omitting the Square of the Explanatory Variable[A]

Consider the quadratic relation

$$y_\alpha = \beta_0 + \beta_1 x_\alpha + \beta_2 x_\alpha^2 + \epsilon_\alpha \tag{2.8}$$

and suppose that the analyst acts as if it is linear. That is, he simply runs a linear regression of y_α on x_α (including a constant term). What can be said about the relation between the slope of this regression and the slope of the true functional form (2.8) at the center of gravity of the n observations? To simplify the expressions that follow, we assume (without real loss of generality) that the explanatory variable is measured as a deviation from its mean $\bar{x} = (1/n) \sum x_\alpha$. Applying (2.5) and (2.6), we conclude that we need the auxiliary regression of x_α^2 on x_α, which has $\sum x_\alpha^3 / \sum x_\alpha^2 = m_3/m_2$ as its multiplicative coefficient, where the m's are the moments of the x_α's around their mean. Inserting this into (2.5), we obtain

$$(\mathscr{E}\mathbf{b}_0)_1 = \beta_1 + \frac{m_3}{m_2}\beta_2 \tag{2.9}$$

for the expectation of the slope of the regression of y_α on x_α. Since the slope of (2.8) at the center of gravity ($\bar{x} = 0$) is equal to β_1, we may conclude that $\beta_2 m_3/m_2$ is the specification bias. The sign of this bias is evidently determined by the skewness of the distribution of the values taken by the explanatory variable. When the distribution is symmetric, the bias is zero; when it is positively skewed (with a long tail of large x_α's), the bias is positive if the slope of (2.8) increases with x (i.e., if $\beta_2 > 0$), negative in the opposite case, and so on. Note that in this special case the relevant coefficient of the auxiliary regression, m_3/m_2, can be computed directly from the data used for the incorrect regression.

Omitting an Input of a Cobb-Douglas Production Function[A]

Consider the Cobb-Douglas production function:

$$y_\alpha = A x_{\alpha 1}^{\beta_1} \cdots x_{\alpha K}^{\beta_K} e^{\epsilon_\alpha} \tag{2.10}$$

where y_α is output in year α, the x's are inputs, and ϵ_α is a random disturbance; the elasticities (the β's) are assumed to be all positive. Specify $A = 1$ for the sake of convenience and take logarithms of both sides of the equation:[2]

$$\log y_\alpha = \sum_{h=1}^{K} \beta_h \log x_{\alpha h} + \epsilon_\alpha \tag{2.11}$$

Assume now that we run a log-linear regression with the Kth input deleted. This implies that (2.5) applies to the $K - 1$ elasticity estimators corresponding to the included inputs. The coefficients p_{hK} are now derived from an auxiliary regression which is linear in the logs:

$$\log x_{\alpha K} = \sum_{h=1}^{K-1} p_{hK} \log x_{\alpha h} + \text{residual} \tag{2.12}$$

Next, assume that our real interest is in the returns to scale, measured by $E = \beta_1 + \cdots + \beta_K$ and estimated by $\hat{E} = (\mathbf{b}_0)_1 + \cdots + (\mathbf{b}_0)_{K-1}$. Using (2.5), we find the following value for the specification bias of the returns to scale:

$$\mathscr{E}(\hat{E} - E) = \beta_K\left(\sum_{h=1}^{K} p_{hK} - 1\right) \tag{2.13}$$

The specification bias is thus positive when the sum of the coefficients of the auxiliary regression (2.12) exceeds one, and negative in the opposite case. This regression in antilog form is a Cobb-Douglas type relation:

$$x_{\alpha K} = x_{\alpha 1}^{p_{1K}} \cdots x_{\alpha, K-1}^{p_{K-1,K}} e^r \qquad (r = \text{residual}) \tag{2.14}$$

Evidently, the specification bias of the returns to scale depends on how the excluded input changes in the sample when the other inputs are varied to scale. On the average, we shall overestimate if the excluded input varies more than proportionally with the included inputs, and we shall underestimate in the opposite case. Reference is made to GRILICHES (1957), who considered the effects of excluding managerial services as an input, of disregarding quality differences of the labor input, and of certain other exclusions as well.

The above results can be generalized straightforwardly to cases in which two or more explanatory variables are deleted or replaced by substitutes. It is also possible to obtain approximate results when the two specifications have different dependent variables, for example, when the correct specification requires a regression of $\log y_\alpha$ on certain variables whereas the specification used is linear in y_α itself. See Problems 2.2 to 2.5.

[2] Specifying $A = 1$ guarantees that the constant term of (2.11) vanishes. The same result can be obtained by expressing the logarithms as deviations from their means, but this would make the notation more cumbersome.

Extension to Simultaneous Equation Estimators[C]

Another extension concerns asymptotic distributions such as that of the 2SLS estimator. The effect of specification errors is then evaluated on the basis of the analysis of Chapters 8 and 10, and it is formulated in terms of probability limits rather than expectations. The following example is based on work done by F. M. Fisher (1961a, 1966b, 1967a). The equation system is $\mathbf{Y\Gamma} + \mathbf{XB} = \mathbf{E}$ and the true form of the jth equation is

$$\mathbf{y}_j = \mathbf{Y}_j\boldsymbol{\gamma}_j + \mathbf{X}_j\boldsymbol{\beta}_j + \zeta\mathbf{x} + \boldsymbol{\epsilon}_j \tag{2.15}$$

where $\mathbf{x}$ is a column vector consisting of n fixed elements and ζ is a nonzero constant. It is assumed that $(1/n)\mathbf{x}'\mathbf{x}$ converges to a finite positive limit as $n \to \infty$. The analyst commits a specification error by assuming $\zeta = 0$, and his 2SLS estimator is thus of the familiar form:

$$\mathbf{d}_j = \begin{bmatrix} \mathbf{Y}_j'\mathbf{Y}_j - \mathbf{U}_j'\mathbf{U}_j & \mathbf{Y}_j'\mathbf{X}_j \\ \mathbf{X}_j'\mathbf{Y}_j & \mathbf{X}_j'\mathbf{X}_j \end{bmatrix}^{-1} \begin{bmatrix} \mathbf{Y}_j' - \mathbf{U}_j' \\ \mathbf{X}_j' \end{bmatrix} \mathbf{y}_j \tag{2.16}$$

This estimator is not consistent when $\zeta \neq 0$. It is readily verified that the inconsistency, defined as the difference between the probability limit of $\mathbf{d}_j$ and $\boldsymbol{\delta}_j = [\boldsymbol{\gamma}_j' \quad \boldsymbol{\beta}_j']'$, is

(2.17)
$$\operatorname*{plim}_{n\to\infty} (\mathbf{d}_j - \boldsymbol{\delta}_j) = \zeta \operatorname*{plim}_{n\to\infty} n \begin{bmatrix} \mathbf{Y}_j'\mathbf{Y}_j - \mathbf{U}_j'\mathbf{U}_j & \mathbf{Y}_j'\mathbf{X}_j \\ \mathbf{X}_j'\mathbf{Y}_j & \mathbf{X}_j'\mathbf{X}_j \end{bmatrix}^{-1} \operatorname*{plim}_{n\to\infty} \frac{1}{n} \begin{bmatrix} (\mathbf{Y}_j - \mathbf{U}_j)'\mathbf{x} \\ \mathbf{X}_j'\mathbf{x} \end{bmatrix}$$

The inconsistency is thus proportional to ζ. Similar results can be obtained for other k-class estimators. Fisher considered in particular the problem of whether the 2SLS estimator is affected more (or less) by specification errors than the limited-information maximum-likelihood estimator is, but it appears not to be possible to make any strong general statements.

Full-information methods such as 3SLS can be analyzed along similar lines. It is obvious that the misspecification $\zeta = 0$ in (2.15) implies that, in general, all elements of the coefficient estimator (not only those which belong to the jth equation) lose the property of consistency. As stated in the second subsection of Section 10.8, this is one of the disadvantages of full-information estimation procedures. They do not quarantine specification errors as the limited-information estimators such as those of the k-class do.

Problems

2.1 Suppose that the zero-correlation condition (2.7) is satisfied and that the first columns of $\mathbf{X}$ and $\mathbf{X}_0$ consist of unit elements, thus representing the constant-term variable. Prove that the expectation of the constant term of the regression which is actually used is equal to $\beta_1 + p_{1K}\beta_K$, where p_{1K} is the average of the values $x_{1K}, \ldots, x_{nK}$ taken by the deleted variable.

2.2 (*A misspecified explanatory variable*) Suppose that $\mathbf{X}$ and $\mathbf{X}_0$ are both of order $n \times K$ and that they are identical except for the Kth column. Prove that (2.5) has to be modified to

$$(\mathscr{E}\mathbf{b}_0)_h = \begin{cases} \beta_h + p_{hK}\beta_K & h = 1, \ldots, K-1 \\ p_{KK}\beta_K & h = K \end{cases} \tag{2.18}$$

where the p's are the coefficients of the following auxiliary regression:

$$x_{\alpha K} = \sum_{h=1}^{K-1} p_{hK}x_{\alpha K} + p_{KK}x^*_{\alpha K} + \text{residual} \tag{2.19}$$

$x_{\alpha K}$ and $x^*_{\alpha K}$ being the (α, K)th elements of $\mathbf{X}$ and $\mathbf{X}_0$, respectively. Draw your conclusions on the specification bias along the lines of the discussion below eq. (2.6).

2.3 (*Two omitted variables*) Suppose that $\mathbf{X}_0$ is of order $n \times (K-2)$ and that it is identical with $\mathbf{X}$ except for the last two columns, which are deleted. Prove that the expectation of the coefficient vector of the incorrect specification is

$$(\mathscr{E}\mathbf{b}_0)_h = \beta_h + p_{h,K-1}\beta_{K-1} + p_{hK}\beta_K \qquad h = 1, \ldots, K-2 \tag{2.20}$$

where the p's are the coefficients of the following two auxiliary regressions:

$$x_{\alpha,K-1} = \sum_{h=1}^{K-2} p_{h,K-1}x_{\alpha h} + \text{residual} \qquad x_{\alpha K} = \sum_{h=1}^{K-2} p_{hK}x_{\alpha h} + \text{residual}$$

Draw your conclusions as to the specification bias and generalize the result for the case in which three variables are omitted.

2.4 (*Continuation*) Modify the result of the previous exercise along the lines of Problem 2.2 for the case in which $\mathbf{X}$ and $\mathbf{X}_0$ are of the same order but with two unequal columns, and for the case in which $\mathbf{X}_0$ is of order $n \times (K-1)$ but such that the $(K-1)$st column differs from the corresponding column of $\mathbf{X}$. Discuss the specification bias in both cases.

2.5 (*Specification analysis for different dependent variables*) Suppose that the true relationship between x and y is log-linear:

$$\log y_\alpha = \beta_0 + \beta \log x_\alpha + \epsilon_\alpha \qquad \alpha = 1, \ldots, n \tag{2.21}$$

where $\epsilon_1, \ldots, \epsilon_n$ are independent normal variates with zero mean and variance σ^2, while $x_1, \ldots, x_n$ are nonstochastic. Also suppose that the analyst proceeds as if the relation is linear and that he runs an LS regression of y on x (including a constant term); hence the dependent variables of the two specifications are different. Write the correct specification in constant-elasticity form, apply a Taylor expansion around $\bar{x}$, the mean of the n values $x_1, \ldots, x_n$:

(2.22)
$$\begin{aligned} y_\alpha &= e^{\beta_0} x_\alpha^\beta e^{\epsilon_\alpha} \\ &= e^{\beta_0}\left[\bar{x}^\beta + \beta\bar{x}^{\beta-1}(x_\alpha - \bar{x}) + \frac{1}{2}\beta(\beta-1)\bar{x}^{\beta-2}(x_\alpha - \bar{x})^2 + \cdots\right] e^{\epsilon_\alpha} \end{aligned}$$

and state the conditions under which this expansion converges for $\alpha = 1, \ldots, n$. Next, consider the multiplicative coefficient of the linear regression of y on x:

$$\begin{aligned} \text{(2.23)} \quad \frac{\sum (x_\alpha - \bar{x})y_\alpha}{\sum (x_\alpha - \bar{x})^2} &= e^{\beta_0}\bar{x}^\beta \frac{\sum (x_\alpha - \bar{x})e^{\epsilon_\alpha}}{\sum (x_\alpha - \bar{x})^2} \\ &\quad + \beta e^{\beta_0}\bar{x}^{\beta-1} \frac{\sum (x_\alpha - \bar{x})^2 e^{\epsilon_\alpha}}{\sum (x_\alpha - \bar{x})^2} \\ &\quad + \frac{1}{2}\beta(\beta-1)e^{\beta_0}\bar{x}^{\beta-2} \frac{\sum (x_\alpha - \bar{x})^3 e^{\epsilon_\alpha}}{\sum (x_\alpha - \bar{x})^2} \\ &\quad + \cdots \end{aligned}$$

where all summations are over $\alpha = 1, \ldots, n$. Use the moment-generating function of the normal distribution to prove $\mathscr{E}(e^{\epsilon_\alpha}) = e^{\sigma^2/2}$, and conclude that the expectation of the multiplicative coefficient of the incorrect specification is

$$\text{(2.24)} \quad \mathscr{E}\left[\frac{\sum (x_\alpha - \bar{x})y_\alpha}{\sum (x_\alpha - \bar{x})^2}\right] = e^{\beta_0}\bar{x}^{\beta-1}\left[\beta + \frac{1}{2}\beta(\beta-1)\frac{m_3}{m_2} + \cdots\right] e^{\sigma^2/2}$$

where the m's are moments of the n dimensionless numbers $(x_\alpha - \bar{x})/\bar{x}$:

$$\text{(2.25)} \quad m_r = \frac{1}{n}\sum_{\alpha=1}^{n}\left(\frac{x_\alpha - \bar{x}}{\bar{x}}\right)^r = \frac{(1/n)\sum (x_\alpha - \bar{x})^r}{\bar{x}^r}$$

Finally, define the expected value of y given $x = \bar{x}$:

$$\text{(2.26)} \quad \bar{y} = \mathscr{E}(e^{\beta_0}\bar{x}^\beta e^\epsilon) = e^{\beta_0}\bar{x}^\beta e^{\sigma^2/2}$$

and multiply the expected multiplicative coefficient of the incorrect specification by $\bar{x}/\bar{y}$ to obtain the expectation of the implied elasticity estimator at $\bar{x}$:

$$\frac{\bar{x}}{\bar{y}}\,\mathscr{E}\left[\frac{\sum (x_\alpha - \bar{x})y_\alpha}{\sum (x_\alpha - \bar{x})^2}\right] = \beta + \frac{1}{2}\,\beta(\beta - 1)\,\frac{m_3}{m_2} + \cdots \tag{2.27}$$

Compare this result with the true elasticity β and draw your conclusions as to the sign, size, and determinants of the specification bias.

2.6 (*Specification analysis for general linear unbiased estimation methods*) Suppose that the correct specification is $\mathbf{y} = \mathbf{X}\boldsymbol{\beta} + \boldsymbol{\epsilon}$, $\mathscr{E}\boldsymbol{\epsilon} = \mathbf{0}$, and that the analyst acts as if $\mathbf{X}_0$ is the matrix of values taken by the explanatory variables; both $\mathbf{X}$ and $\mathbf{X}_0$ consist of nonstochastic elements. Suppose further that the analyst applies an estimation method that would be linear and unbiased if the $\mathbf{X}_0$ specification were correct. Prove that the coefficient vector is then of the form $\mathbf{b}_0 = \mathbf{A}_0\mathbf{y}$ where $\mathbf{A}_0$ satisfies $\mathbf{A}_0\mathbf{X}_0 = \mathbf{I}$. Also prove $\mathscr{E}\mathbf{b}_0 = \mathbf{P}_0\boldsymbol{\beta}$ where $\mathbf{P}_0 = \mathbf{A}_0\mathbf{X}$; finally, prove that $\mathbf{P}_0$ is the coefficient matrix of the auxiliary regressions of $\mathbf{X}$ on $\mathbf{X}_0$, computed according to the *same* estimation method as that which is used for $\mathbf{b}_0$.

2.7 (*Specification analysis for simultaneous equations*) Consider the simple Keynesian model: $C_\alpha = \beta Y_\alpha + \epsilon_\alpha$, $C_\alpha + I_\alpha = Y_\alpha$ and suppose that the consumption function is misspecified because consumption depends linearly on profits (P_α) and wage income (W_α) with different coefficients. Hence the correct specification is

$$\begin{aligned} C_\alpha &= \beta_1 P_\alpha + \beta_2 W_\alpha + \epsilon'_\alpha \\ C_\alpha + I_\alpha &= Y_\alpha \\ P_\alpha + W_\alpha &= Y_\alpha \end{aligned} \tag{2.28}$$

Assume that ϵ'_α, $\alpha = 1, \ldots, n$ are independent normal variates with zero mean and variance σ^2, and also (for simplicity's sake) that wage income is an exogenous variable. Hence the correct specification amounts to a three-equation system in three endogenous variables (C, P, Y) and two exogenous variables (I, W). Prove that the reduced-form equation for P_α according to the correct specification is

$$P_\alpha = \frac{1}{1 - \beta_1}\,I_\alpha = \frac{1 - \beta_2}{1 - \beta_1}\,W_\alpha + \frac{1}{1 - \beta_1}\,\epsilon'_\alpha \tag{2.29}$$

Also prove that the probability limit of the 2SLS estimator of the propensity to consume β of the incorrect specification is

$$\operatorname*{plim}_{n\to\infty} \frac{\sum_{\alpha=1}^{n} I_\alpha C_\alpha}{\sum_{\alpha=1}^{n} I_\alpha Y_\alpha} = \frac{\beta_1 q_{II} + (\beta_2 - \beta_1) q_{IW}}{q_{II} + (\beta_2 - \beta_1) q_{IW}} \tag{2.30}$$

where

(2.31) $$q_{II} = \lim_{n \to \infty} \frac{1}{n} \sum_{\alpha=1}^{n} I_\alpha^2 \qquad q_{IW} = \mathrm{im}_{n \to \infty} \frac{1}{n} \sum_{\alpha=1}^{n} I_\alpha W_\alpha$$

which are assumed to satisfy $q_{II} + (\beta_2 - \beta_1)q_{IW} \neq 0$. Verify that the estimator of the propensity to consume is consistent if the two-equation model is the correct specification, that is, if $\beta_1 = \beta_2$.

2.8 (*Continuation*) Use the numerical example $q_{II} = 1$, $q_{IW} = -.5$, $\beta_1 = .4$, $\beta_2 = .8$ to show that the probability limit of the estimated propensity to consume of the incorrect specification does not necessarily lie between β_1 and β_2. Also prove that this probability limit may be negative for certain values of the q's and β's.

11.3 Linear Aggregation of Linear Economic Relations[B]

We now turn to an application of specification analysis, from THEIL (1954),[3] which must be treated separately because of its general nature. It is the subject of the aggregation of economic relations, and it can be described as follows. Most economic theories are microeconomic in nature in the sense that they are concerned with the behavior of individual family households or individual firms. On the other hand, econometric estimation and hypothesis testing are frequently based on data for groups of households and firms, and specification of the relationships involved is then of a macroeconomic character. For example, the theoretical starting point may be that of an individual household for which the consumption of sugar depends on the household's income, the price of sugar, and certain other characteristics; such a demand function may be derived from the theory of utility maximization. But the actual numerical specification of the demand function is usually based on data for *all* households in the country, and it is not self-evident that the individual demand functions can be combined to a simple demand function for the group of all households.

The Microrelations

Aggregation theory is concerned with the transformation of individual relations (microrelations) to a relation for the group as a whole (a macrorelation). We shall confine ourselves to linear relations in order to simplify the exposition. Imagine, then, that there are N economic agents, each characterized by a behavioral equation of the type

(3.1) $$y_i = X_i \beta_i + \epsilon_i \qquad i = 1, \ldots, N$$

where y_i and ϵ_i are n-element column vectors and X_i is of order $n \times K$, K being independent of i. It is thus assumed that each microequation has the

[3] The matrix presentation of this theory is from KLOEK (1961).

same number of explanatory variables. More specifically, we assume that for each pair of agents (i, j), any column of $[\mathbf{y}_i \quad \mathbf{X}_i]$ has the same interpretation as the corresponding column of $[\mathbf{y}_j \quad \mathbf{X}_j]$ except that it refers to a different agent. Thus, returning to the example of the previous paragraph, we may interpret the αth element of $\mathbf{y}_i$ as the consumption of sugar by the ith household in year α, and the first element of the αth row of $\mathbf{X}_i$ as 1 (corresponding to the constant term), the second element of that row as the household's income in year α, the third as the average price paid for sugar in that year, and so on. The parameter vectors $\boldsymbol{\beta}_1, \ldots, \boldsymbol{\beta}_N$ of the N households can then be arranged in a $K \times N$ matrix:

$$[\boldsymbol{\beta}_1 \quad \boldsymbol{\beta}_2 \quad \cdots \quad \boldsymbol{\beta}_N] = \begin{bmatrix} \beta_{11} & \beta_{12} & \cdots & \beta_{1N} \\ \beta_{21} & \beta_{22} & \cdots & \beta_{2N} \\ \vdots & \vdots & & \vdots \\ \beta_{K1} & \beta_{K2} & \cdots & \beta_{KN} \end{bmatrix} \tag{3.2}$$

The first row of this matrix consists of the constant terms of the N microrelations, the second of the N individual "marginal propensities to consume sugar," the third of the price coefficients, and so on.

The Macrovariables

We now introduce $K + 1$ macrovariables, defined simply as averages of the corresponding microvariables:

$$\bar{\mathbf{y}} = \frac{1}{N}\sum_{i=1}^{N} \mathbf{y}_i \qquad \bar{\mathbf{X}} = \frac{1}{N}\sum_{i=1}^{N} \mathbf{X}_i \tag{3.3}$$

In the above example $\bar{\mathbf{y}}$ is a column vector containing the average consumption of sugar per household for each of the n years. Similarly, the first column of $\bar{\mathbf{X}}$ consists of unit elements, the second contains income per household, the third the average price paid for sugar (averaged over all families), and so on. Our objective is to formulate a demand function which describes the behavior of sugar consumption per household. Therefore we combine (3.3) and (3.1) as follows:

$$\begin{aligned} \bar{\mathbf{y}} &= \frac{1}{N}\sum_{i=1}^{N} \mathbf{X}_i\boldsymbol{\beta}_i + \frac{1}{N}\sum_{i=1}^{N} \boldsymbol{\epsilon}_i \\ &= [(1/N)\mathbf{X}_1 \cdots (1/N)\mathbf{X}_N] \begin{bmatrix} \boldsymbol{\beta}_1 \\ \vdots \\ \boldsymbol{\beta}_N \end{bmatrix} + \frac{1}{N}\sum_{i=1}^{N} \boldsymbol{\epsilon}_i \end{aligned} \tag{3.4}$$

This is the correct specification of sugar consumption per household if we take the microrelations (3.1) as our starting point.

Aggregation

The right-hand side of (3.4) contains all *KN* explanatory microvariables: individual household incomes, the sugar price paid by each household, and so on. No analyst would regard it as attractive to work with so much detail; instead, he will prefer to replace (3.4) by a macrorelation which contains macrovariables on both sides of the equality sign. This would be very simple if the parameter vectors $\boldsymbol{\beta}_1, \ldots, \boldsymbol{\beta}_N$ were all equal (to $\boldsymbol{\beta}$, say) because (3.4) can then be written:

$$\bar{\mathbf{y}} = [(1/N)\mathbf{X}_1 \cdots (1/N)\mathbf{X}_N]\begin{bmatrix}\boldsymbol{\beta}\\ \cdot\\ \cdot\\ \cdot\\ \boldsymbol{\beta}\end{bmatrix} + \frac{1}{N}\sum_{i=1}^{N}\boldsymbol{\epsilon}_i \tag{3.5}$$

$$= \frac{1}{N}\sum_{i=1}^{N}\mathbf{X}_i\boldsymbol{\beta} + \frac{1}{N}\sum_{i=1}^{N}\boldsymbol{\epsilon}_i = \bar{\mathbf{X}}\boldsymbol{\beta} + \frac{1}{N}\sum_{i=1}^{N}\boldsymbol{\epsilon}_i$$

We thus obtain a simple linear relation in the macrovariables $[\bar{\mathbf{y}} \quad \bar{\mathbf{X}}]$; its coefficient vector is identical with that of the microrelations and its disturbances are equal to the averages of the microdisturbances corresponding to the same observations.

This simple result does not hold in the more usual case in which the parameter vectors $\boldsymbol{\beta}_1, \ldots, \boldsymbol{\beta}_N$ are not all equal. If one then runs an LS regression of $\bar{\mathbf{y}}$ on $\bar{\mathbf{X}}$, one commits a specification error of the type considered in the previous section. The LS coefficient vector is

$$\mathbf{b} = (\bar{\mathbf{X}}'\bar{\mathbf{X}})^{-1}\bar{\mathbf{X}}'\bar{\mathbf{y}} \tag{3.6}$$

To analyze the relationship between $\mathbf{b}$ and $\boldsymbol{\beta}_1, \ldots, \boldsymbol{\beta}_N$ we substitute the expression on the second line of (3.4) for $\bar{\mathbf{y}}$ and take the expectation under the assumption that $\mathscr{E}\boldsymbol{\epsilon}_i = \mathbf{0}$ and $\mathbf{X}_i$ is nonstochastic for $i = 1, \ldots, N$:[4]

$$\mathscr{E}\mathbf{b} = (\bar{\mathbf{X}}'\bar{\mathbf{X}})^{-1}\bar{\mathbf{X}}'[(1/N)\mathbf{X}_1 \cdots (1/N)\mathbf{X}_N]\begin{bmatrix}\boldsymbol{\beta}_1\\ \cdot\\ \cdot\\ \cdot\\ \boldsymbol{\beta}_N\end{bmatrix} = \sum_{i=1}^{N}\mathbf{B}_i\boldsymbol{\beta}_i \tag{3.7}$$

[4] We may also have random **X**'s and proceed conditionally on the observed values of these matrices, provided that the matrix $[\mathbf{X}_1 \quad \cdots \quad \mathbf{X}_N]$ is stochastically independent of $[\boldsymbol{\epsilon}_1 \quad \cdots \quad \boldsymbol{\epsilon}_N]$.

where

$$\mathbf{B}_i = (\bar{\mathbf{X}}'\bar{\mathbf{X}})^{-1}\bar{\mathbf{X}}'\frac{1}{N}\mathbf{X}_i \qquad i = 1, \ldots, N \tag{3.8}$$

The matrix $\mathbf{B}_i$ is the coefficient matrix of the auxiliary regressions whose left-hand variables are $1/N$ times the explanatory variables of the ith microrelation (3.1) and whose right-hand variables are those which are represented in $\bar{\mathbf{X}}$ defined in (3.3):

$$\frac{1}{N}\mathbf{X}_i = \bar{\mathbf{X}}\mathbf{B}_i + \mathbf{U}_i \qquad i = 1, \ldots, N \tag{3.9}$$

where $\mathbf{U}_i$ is the corresponding residual matrix:

$$\mathbf{U}_i = [\mathbf{I} - \bar{\mathbf{X}}(\bar{\mathbf{X}}'\bar{\mathbf{X}})^{-1}\bar{\mathbf{X}}']\frac{1}{N}\mathbf{X}_i \qquad i = 1, \ldots, N \tag{3.10}$$

Note that the auxiliary regressions (3.9) in scalar form are as follows:

$$\frac{1}{N}x_{\alpha hi} = \sum_{k=1}^{K} b_{khi}\bar{x}_{\alpha k} + u_{\alpha hi} \tag{3.11}$$

where $x_{\alpha hi}$, $\bar{x}_{\alpha h}$, and $u_{\alpha hi}$ are the (α, h)th elements of $\mathbf{X}_i$, $\bar{\mathbf{X}}$, and $\mathbf{U}_i$, respectively, and b_{khi} is the (k, h)th element of $\mathbf{B}_i$. Also note that the weight matrices $\mathbf{B}_1, \ldots, \mathbf{B}_N$ add up to the $K \times K$ unit matrix:

$$\sum_{i=1}^{N}\mathbf{B}_i = (\bar{\mathbf{X}}'\bar{\mathbf{X}})^{-1}\bar{\mathbf{X}}'\frac{1}{N}\sum_{i=1}^{N}\mathbf{X}_i = (\bar{\mathbf{X}}'\bar{\mathbf{X}})^{-1}\,\bar{\mathbf{X}}'\bar{\mathbf{X}} = \mathbf{I} \tag{3.12}$$

and that the sum of the residual matrices $\mathbf{U}_1, \ldots, \mathbf{U}_N$ is equal to the $n \times K$ zero matrix:

$$\sum_{i=1}^{N}\mathbf{U}_i = [\mathbf{I} - \bar{\mathbf{X}}(\bar{\mathbf{X}}'\bar{\mathbf{X}})^{-1}\bar{\mathbf{X}}']\frac{1}{N}\sum_{i=1}^{N}\mathbf{X}_i = [\mathbf{I} - \bar{\mathbf{X}}(\bar{\mathbf{X}}'\bar{\mathbf{X}})^{-1}\bar{\mathbf{X}}']\bar{\mathbf{X}} = \mathbf{0} \tag{3.13}$$

Corresponding and Noncorresponding Parameters

We conclude from (3.7) that each element of $\mathscr{E}\mathbf{b}$ depends on all elements of all microvectors $\boldsymbol{\beta}_1, \ldots, \boldsymbol{\beta}_N$. Thus the expectation of the LS coefficient of income per household depends not only on the microeconomic income coefficients but also on the microeconomic price coefficients. Since this result is rather disturbing, it is worthwhile to go into the matter more deeply.

Consider the parameter matrix (3.2) augmented by the vector $\mathscr{E}\mathbf{b}$:

$$[\boldsymbol{\beta}_1 \quad \cdots \quad \boldsymbol{\beta}_N \quad \mathscr{E}\mathbf{b}] = \begin{bmatrix} \beta_{11} & \cdots & \beta_{1N} & \mathscr{E}b_1 \\ \beta_{21} & \cdots & \beta_{2N} & \mathscr{E}b_2 \\ \cdot & & \cdot & \cdot \\ \cdot & & \cdot & \cdot \\ \cdot & & \cdot & \cdot \\ \beta_{K1} & \cdots & \beta_{KN} & \mathscr{E}b_K \end{bmatrix} \tag{3.14}$$

For each $\mathscr{E}b_h$, the hth element of $\mathscr{E}\mathbf{b}$, we shall call the parameters $\beta_{h1}, \ldots, \beta_{hN}$ of the same row the *corresponding microparameters*, and the parameters $\beta_{k1}, \ldots, \beta_{kN}$ of any other row the *noncorresponding microparameters*. Thus the N income microcoefficients are "corresponding" for the coefficient of income per household, and the N price coefficients and the N constant terms are noncorresponding. Similarly, the price coefficients of the N microrelations are corresponding for the price coefficient of the macrorelation and all other microcoefficients are noncorresponding for this coefficient.

Using this terminology, we should say that each element of $\mathscr{E}\mathbf{b}$ depends on corresponding as well as on noncorresponding microparameters. This becomes particularly clear when we write (3.7) in scalar form:

$$\mathscr{E}b_h = \sum_{i=1}^{N} b_{hhi}\beta_{hi} + \sum_{k \neq h}\left(\sum_{i=1}^{N} b_{hki}\beta_{ki}\right) \qquad h = 1, \ldots, K \tag{3.15}$$

The first right-hand term is a linear combination of the corresponding microparameters $\beta_{h1}, \ldots, \beta_{hN}$ with weights $b_{hh1}, \ldots, b_{hhN}$; the second concerns the noncorresponding microparameters $\beta_{k1}, \ldots, \beta_{kN}$ for each $k \neq h$ with weights $b_{hk1}, \ldots, b_{hkN}$. It follows from (3.12) that these weights obey the following sum rule:

$$\sum_{i=1}^{N} b_{hki} = 1 \quad \text{if} \quad h = k$$
$$0 \quad \text{if} \quad h \neq k \tag{3.16}$$

Hence the weights of the corresponding microparameters add up to one, whereas those of any set of noncorresponding microparameters (for any $k \neq h$) add up to zero.

Aggregation Bias

Note that the constant terms of the microrelations (if these relations have such terms) do not affect any of the multiplicative macrocoefficients. This follows from $b_{11i} = 1/N$, $b_{21i} = b_{31i} = \cdots = 0$, where the index 1 refers to the constant-term variable, and this, in turn, follows from (3.11) when we take $h = 1$, so that the left-hand side becomes $1/N$ for each α and i. Also note that although the weights $b_{hh1}, \ldots, b_{hhN}$ of the corresponding parameters add up to one, they are no ordinary weights because they are not necessarily nonnegative. If $b_{hhi} < 0$ for some i, the microparameter β_{hi} has a negative effect on the corresponding $\mathscr{E}b_h$. Since such a negative effect of corresponding microparameters is almost as awkward as a positive or negative effect of noncorresponding microparameters, there is some merit in writing eq. (3.15) as follows:

$$(3.17) \qquad \mathscr{E}b_h = \frac{1}{N}\sum_{i=1}^{N}\beta_{hi} + \sum_{i=1}^{N}\left(b_{hhi} - \frac{1}{N}\right)\beta_{hi} + \sum_{k\neq h}\left(\sum_{i=1}^{N} b_{hki}\beta_{ki}\right)$$

which expresses $\mathscr{E}b_h$ as a deviation from the arithmetic average of the corresponding microparameters $\beta_{h1}, \ldots, \beta_{hN}$.[5] This deviation may be called the *aggregation bias* of the macrocoefficient b_h.

Summary

The developments of this section may be briefly summarized as follows.

(1) The starting point consists of N linear microrelations in $K + 1$ variables, one for each economic agent. Corresponding variables are averaged and an LS regression is computed for the macrovariables thus defined. As in the case of specification analysis (of which the present analysis is a special case), the objective is to find the relationship between the expectation of the coefficient vector of this regression (the macroeconomic coefficient vector) and the underlying microparameters.

(2) The result formulated in eq. (3.17) expresses the expectation of the coefficient of the hth macrovariable as the average of the corresponding microparameters ($\beta_{h1}, \ldots, \beta_{hN}$) plus an aggregation bias for each of the K sets of microparameters—corresponding as well as noncorresponding. Regarding the latter ($k \neq h$), this bias is of the form $\sum_i b_{hki}\beta_{ki}$; and since $b_{hk1}, \ldots, b_{hkN}$ have zero sum and hence zero average in view of (3.16), we may regard this bias as the covariance of the two series

$$\begin{matrix} b_{hk1} & b_{hk2} & \cdots & b_{hkN} \\ \beta_{k1} & \beta_{k2} & \cdots & \beta_{kN} \end{matrix}$$

Hence the bias vanishes either when the N weights are equal[6] or when the N

[5] An alternative approach is to use a weighted average of $\beta_{h1}, \ldots, \beta_{hN}$, the weight of β_{hi} being proportional to the average of $x_{\alpha hi}$ over $\alpha = 1, \ldots, n$. This is, of course, attractive only if the explanatory microvariables take positive values.

[6] Note that equality of these N weights implies, in view of (3.16), that they are all equal to zero.

microparameters are equal[7] or when these weights and microparameters are uncorrelated.

(3) The aggregation bias resulting from the corresponding microparameters [the second right-hand term in (3.17)] can also be regarded as a covariance, namely, of the N pairs $(b_{hh1}, \beta_{h1}), \ldots, (b_{hhN}, \beta_{hN})$. This follows from the fact that the b's are measured as deviations from their average $1/N$. Recall that $b_{11i} = 1/N$ for each i if the subscript 1 refers to the constant-term variable. Hence the expectation of the constant term of the macrorelation is equal to the arithmetic average of the micro constant terms (except for the aggregation bias resulting from the multiplicative microparameters, which are noncorresponding with respect to the constant term).

In the next section we shall discuss an example based on these theoretical results. Extensions of the theory will be examined at the end of that section.

Problems

3.1 Suppose that the microrelations are log-linear rather than linear. What kind of macrovariables should be used for the theory of this section to be applicable to this case?

3.2 Suppose that the parameter vectors $\boldsymbol{\beta}_1, \ldots, \boldsymbol{\beta}_N$ of (3.1) are all equal (to $\boldsymbol{\beta}$, say). Prove that the matrix (3.2) can be written as $\boldsymbol{\beta}\boldsymbol{\iota}'$, where $\boldsymbol{\iota}$ is to be defined appropriately.

3.3 Consider N demand equations for N households, each of which describes the sugar consumption of a household linearly in terms of the household's real income and the relative price of sugar (except for a random disturbance). Suppose that the N income coefficients are equal and that the relative sugar prices paid by all households are all the same at any given point of time. Show that a macroeconomic demand equation for sugar consumption per household can be obtained by simple summation. What can be said about the aggregation bias of the macrocoefficients of this relation?

11.4 An Example of Aggregation[B]

This section examines an empirical study by Boot and de Wit (1960), which is based on Grunfeld's investment theory. This theory was described in Section 7.1; it led to the following equation:

$$I = \beta_0 + \beta_1 F_{-1} + \beta_2 C_{-1} + \epsilon \tag{4.1}$$

[7] Recall the analysis of the equal-parameter case $\beta_{k1} = \cdots = \beta_{kN}$ (all k) in the discussion of eq. (3.5) above.

where I is gross investment (including maintenance and repairs) in a certain year, F_{-1} the firm's market value (the total value of the outstanding stock) at the beginning of the year, C_{-1} capital stock at the same point of time, and ϵ a random disturbance with zero mean. This equation is applied to ten American corporations, listed in column (1) of Table 11.1, during the 20-year period 1935 to 1954.[8] Hence eq. (4.1) takes the following form when subscripts are added:

$$I_{\alpha i} = \beta_{0i} + \beta_{1i}F_{\alpha-1,i} + \beta_{2i}C_{\alpha-1,i} + \epsilon_{\alpha i} \tag{4.2}$$

where $\alpha = 1, \ldots, n$ $(= 20)$ and $i = 1, \ldots, N$ $(= 10)$. The LS point estimates of β_{1i} and β_{2i} are shown in columns (2) and (3) of Table 11.1.[9] Note that these are only estimates, whereas the decomposition (3.17) requires the true values of β_{1i} and β_{2i}. We shall proceed under the assumption that the estimates are equal to their parameters. This is undoubtedly unrealistic, but it enables us to proceed and to show at least the method of aggregation analysis.[10]

We construct three macrovariables: average investment, average market value, and average capital stock:

$$\bar{I}_\alpha = \frac{1}{N}\sum_{i=1}^{N} I_{\alpha i} \qquad \bar{F}_{\alpha-1} = \frac{1}{N}\sum_{i=1}^{N} F_{\alpha-1,i} \qquad \bar{C}_{\alpha-1} = \frac{1}{N}\sum_{i=1}^{N} C_{\alpha-1,i} \tag{4.3}$$

and obtain the following LS regression for investment per firm:[11]

$$\bar{I} = -33.2 + \underset{(.025)}{.099}\bar{F}_{-1} + \underset{(.020)}{.260}\bar{C}_{-1} \tag{4.4}$$

The problem is thus to establish the relationship between the multiplicative coefficients of this regression and the microcoefficients of columns (2) and

[8] The firms are listed according to decreasing values of average annual investment in the sample period. These averages are all between 40 and about 100 million dollars per year (of 1947 purchasing power) with three exceptions. General Motors has an average of approximately 600 million dollars per year, U.S. Steel of about 400 million, and the smallest company (Diamond Match) of about 3 million dollars per year. The data on two of the firms (General Electric and Westinghouse) were used in Section 7.1.

[9] The constant terms β_{0i} are not of great interest because they are affected by the fact that capital stock is measured as a deviation from its value in a year prior to the sample period.

[10] An alternative is the simulation approach. Choose numerical values for the microparameters and the explanatory microvariables, generate random sampling numbers for the microdisturbances, and derive the macrocoefficients as well as the decomposition (3.17) on the basis of these data.

[11] A more usual approach is to formulate an equation which describes total investment (rather than investment per firm) in terms of total market value and total capital stock. This is obtained by multiplying both sides of (4.4) by $N = 10$; it does not affect the multiplicative coefficients.

Table 11.1

Microparameters and Coefficients of Auxiliary Regressions for the Aggregation of the Investment Equations of Ten American Companies

Company (1)	β_{1i} (2)	β_{2i} (3)	b_{11i} (4)	b_{22i} (5)	b_{12i} (6)	b_{21i} (7)	b^*_{11i} (8)	b^*_{22i} (9)	b^*_{12i} (10)	b^*_{21i} (11)
General Motors Corporation	.119	.371	.4615	.3698	.0127	−.0622	1.152	1.574	.213	−.040
U.S. Steel Corporation	.175	.390	.1309	.0828	.0047	−.0729	.718	.776	.173	−.102
General Electric	.027	.152	.2077	.1581	−.0108	−.0770	1.158	1.090	−.293	−.109
Chrysler	.078	.316	.0720	.0580	.0108	−.0172	1.123	1.321	.965	−.069
Atlantic Refining	.162	.003	.0107	.1167	−.0062	.0345	.500	.662	−.138	.411
IBM	.131	.085	.0122	.0409	−.0004	.1208	.314	1.084	−.046	.794
Union Oil	.088	.123	.0121	.0759	−.0048	−.0029	.873	.665	−.165	−.054
Westinghouse	.053	.093	.0671	.0389	−.0037	.0657	1.082	1.253	−.469	.270
Goodyear Tire and Rubber	.075	.082	.0236	.0572	−.0025	.0146	.765	.530	−.091	.121
Diamond Match	.005	.437	.0021	.0016	.0002	−.0033	.327	.723	.440	−.130
Average							.801	.968	.059	.109
Standard deviation							.333	.346	.412	.301

(3) of Table 11.1. For this purpose we apply (3.17) for $h = 1$ (the coefficient of $\bar{F}_{-1}$) and $h = 2$ (the coefficient of $\bar{C}_{-1}$):[12]

$$\text{(4.5)} \qquad \begin{aligned} \mathscr{E}b_1 &= \bar{\beta}_1 + \sum_{i=1}^{N} \left(b_{11i} - \frac{1}{N}\right)\beta_{1i} + \sum_{i=1}^{N} b_{12i}\beta_{2i} \\ \mathscr{E}b_2 &= \bar{\beta}_2 + \sum_{i=1}^{N} \left(b_{22i} - \frac{1}{N}\right)\beta_{2i} + \sum_{i=1}^{N} b_{21i}\beta_{1i} \end{aligned}$$

where

$$\text{(4.6)} \qquad \bar{\beta}_h = \frac{1}{N}\sum_{i=1}^{N} \beta_{hi} \qquad h = 1, 2$$

The coefficients b_{hki} are derived from the following auxiliary regressions:

$$\text{(4.7)} \qquad \begin{aligned} \frac{1}{N} F_{\alpha-1,i} &= b_{01i} + b_{11i}\bar{F}_{\alpha-1} + b_{21i}\bar{C}_{\alpha-1} + u_{\alpha 1i} \\ \frac{1}{N} C_{\alpha-1,i} &= b_{02i} + b_{12i}\bar{F}_{\alpha-1} + b_{22i}\bar{C}_{\alpha-1} + u_{\alpha 2i} \end{aligned}$$

The multiplicative b's are shown in columns (4) to (7) of Table 11.1. The results indicate that the weights of the corresponding microparameters (b_{11i} and b_{22i}) are all positive and that the other weights (b_{12i} and b_{21i}) are about equally frequently positive and negative. The latter feature is not surprising in view of eq. (3.16). It is easy to see that if all micro F's move exactly proportionally over time, then $b_{01i} = b_{21i} = 0$ holds for each i, while b_{11i} is equal to the ratio of the average (over α) of $F_{\alpha-1,i}/N$ to the average of $\bar{F}_{\alpha-1}$. Consequently, when we divide b_{11i} and b_{21i} by this ratio, so that we obtain b^*_{11i} and b^*_{21i} (say), we should expect that they are close to 1 and to 0, respectively, when the proportionality condition is approximately true. A similar procedure can be applied to obtain b^*_{22i} and b^*_{12i} from the coefficients of the second equation of (4.7).[13] The b^*'s are presented in columns (8) to (11) of Table 11.1, and the results indicate that b^*_{11i} and b^*_{22i} are distributed around an average of a little less than one, and b^*_{12i} and b^*_{21i} around an average just exceeding zero, in all cases with a standard deviation of the order of .3 or .4. Thus, although there is a certain tendency toward a proportional development over time, it is not nearly an exact proportionality.

By combining the β_{hi}'s of columns (2) and (3) with the b_{hki}'s of columns (4) to (7), we can construct $\mathscr{E}b_1$ and $\mathscr{E}b_2$ using eq. (4.5). These two numbers are, of course, not equal to the point estimates of the regression (4.4); the

[12] Recall that the micro constant terms do not affect the multiplicative macrocoefficients.

[13] These b^*'s are obtained by dividing b_{22i} and b_{12i} by the ratio of the average of $C_{\alpha-1,i}/N$ to the average of $\bar{C}_{\alpha-1}$.

difference should be regarded as the deviation of the estimate from its expectation. The three components of the right-hand sides of (4.5) are shown in Table 11.2 along with these deviations. It is seen that the aggregation bias

Table 11.2

Aggregation Bias of LS Macrocoefficients

	Coefficient of	
	F_{-1}	C_{-1}
Average of corresponding microparameters	.0913	.2053
Aggregation bias:		
Corresponding microparameters	.0075	.0289
Noncorresponding microparameters	.0072	.0022
Deviation from expectation	−.0068	.0238
Total: Estimated coefficient	.0993	.2602

of the F_{-1} coefficient resulting from noncorresponding parameters is of the same order of magnitude (in absolute value) as the deviation from the expectation. However, this deviation is small compared with the standard error of the F_{-1} coefficient given in (4.4); hence, if this standard error is used to measure the precision of the estimate, it does not convey a grossly incorrect picture. The situation is different for the $\bar{C}_{-1}$ coefficient, which has a standard error of .020 in (4.4) and a total aggregation bias of .031;[14] but only a small part of this bias comes from noncorresponding parameters. Needless to say, this is only one case and there is no guarantee that the numerical results will be similar in other cases. It should also be remembered that the decompositions of Table 11.2 are conditional on the assumption that the LS estimates in columns (2) and (3) of Table 11.1 coincide with the corresponding microparameters.

Extensions of Aggregation Theory

The approach described in this section and its predecessor can be extended in several directions, some of which are pursued in Problems 4.1 to 4.6 below. One case is that of perfect aggregation (Problem 4.1), which basically proceeds

[14] The effect becomes even more pronounced when we replace the unweighted average $\bar{\beta}_2$ by the weighted average mentioned in footnote 5 on page 561, which is .1953. Then the expression $1/N$ in the second equation of (4.5) has to be replaced by the appropriate weight, which affects the aggregation bias due to the corresponding microparameters. The new value is .0389—almost twice the standard error.

along the lines of eq. (3.5); it avoids the problem of aggregation bias, but it does so at the expense of a presupposed knowledge of ratios of corresponding microparameters. Other examples are aggregation over several sets of households and commodities, aggregation over time, and the aggregation of a system of simultaneous microrelations to a smaller system of simultaneous macrorelations. In the last case parameters of noncorresponding microrelations also play a role; see Problems 4.5 and 4.6.

Problems

4.1 (*Perfect aggregation*) Write the microrelations (3.1) in scalar form:

$$y_{\alpha i} = \sum_{h=1}^{K} \beta_{hi} x_{\alpha hi} + \epsilon_{\alpha i} \tag{4.8}$$

and define the following macrovariables:

$$\bar{y}_\alpha = \frac{1}{N}\sum_{i=1}^{N} y_{\alpha i} \qquad x^*_{\alpha h} = \frac{1}{N\beta_h}\sum_{i=1}^{N} \beta_{hi} x_{\alpha hi} \qquad h = 1, \ldots, K \tag{4.9}$$

where $\beta_1, \ldots, \beta_K$ are arbitrary nonzero numbers. Prove

$$\bar{y}_\alpha = \sum_{h=1}^{K} \beta_h x^*_{\alpha h} + \frac{1}{N}\sum_{\alpha=1}^{N} \epsilon_{\alpha i} \tag{4.10}$$

and conclude that if explanatory macrovariables are defined as weighted (rather than arithmetic) averages of corresponding microvariables with weights proportional to their microparameters, a macroequation can be obtained by simple summation.

4.2 (*Aggregation over commodities*) Suppose that an entrepreneur uses N production factors and that his demand for each of these depends linearly on the level of production (assume for simplicity's sake that there is only one product) and on the price of the factor:

$$q_{\alpha i} = \beta_{0i} + \beta_{1i} Q_\alpha + \beta_{2i} p_{\alpha i} + \epsilon_{\alpha i} \tag{4.11}$$

where the q's and the p's are the inputs and their prices and Q is output. Define a fixed-weight input index and input price index:

$$\bar{q}_\alpha = \sum_{i=1}^{N} w_i q_{\alpha i} \qquad \bar{p}_\alpha = \sum_{i=1}^{N} w_i p_{\alpha i} \tag{4.12}$$

and run an LS regression of $\bar{q}_\alpha$ on Q_α and $\bar{p}_\alpha$. Prove that if the ϵ's have zero mean and if the Q's and p's are nonstochastic, the expectations of the two multiplicative macrocoefficients are

$$(4.13) \qquad \sum_{i=1}^{N} w_i(\beta_{1i} + \beta_{2i}c_{1i}) \qquad \sum_{i=1}^{N} w_i\beta_{2i}c_{2i}$$

where the c's are coefficients of the auxiliary regressions

$$(4.14) \qquad p_{\alpha i} = c_{0i} + c_{1i}Q_\alpha + c_{2i}\bar{p}_\alpha + \text{residual}$$

How can this result be simplified when the N prices move proportionally over time?

4.3 (*Aggregation over several sets of commodities or individuals*) Suppose that the ith production factor of Problem 4.2 can be supplied by N_i different suppliers and that the demand equations take the following form:

$$(4.15) \qquad q_{\alpha ij} = \beta_{0ij} + \beta_{1ij}Q_\alpha + \sum_{k=1}^{N_i} \beta_{2ijk}p_{\alpha ik} + \epsilon_{\alpha ij}$$

where $q_{\alpha ij}$ is the ith input bought in year α from supplier j and $p_{\alpha ik}$ the price charged by the kth supplier for this input in this year. Introduce the following fixed-weight indices:

$$(4.16) \qquad q_\alpha^* = \sum_{i=1}^{N}\sum_{j=1}^{N_i} w_{ij}q_{\alpha ij} \qquad p_\alpha^* = \sum_{i=1}^{N}\sum_{j=1}^{N_i} w_{ij}q_{\alpha ij}$$

and prove that if the ϵ's have zero mean and if the Q's and p's are nonstochastic, the expectations of the multiplicative coefficients of the regression of q_α^* on Q_α and p_α^* are

$$(4.17) \qquad \begin{gathered} \sum_{i=1}^{N}\sum_{j=1}^{N_i} w_{ij}\left(\beta_{1ij} + \sum_{k=1}^{N_i} \beta_{2ijk}\, d_{1ik}\right) \\ \sum_{i=1}^{N}\sum_{j=1}^{N_i}\sum_{k=1}^{N_i} w_{ij}\beta_{2ijk}\, d_{2ik} \end{gathered}$$

where the d's are coefficients of the auxiliary regressions

$$(4.18) \qquad p_{\alpha ik} = d_{0ik} + d_{1ik}Q_\alpha + d_{2ik}p_\alpha^* + \text{residual}$$

Can this result be simplified when the N_i prices of the ith input, for each $i = 1, \ldots, N$, move proportionally over time? What if *all* prices move proportionally?

4.4 (*Aggregation over time*)[15] Suppose that a variable y is generated by a first-order autoregressive process: $y_\alpha = \rho y_{\alpha-1} + \epsilon_\alpha$, where the ϵ's are independent normal variates with zero mean and variance σ^2, and $\alpha = 1, 2, \ldots$ measures time in six-month periods. Suppose further

[15] This problem requires material discussed in Section 8.7.

that the available data are in annual form, so that the analyst prefers to express $y_{\alpha+1} + y_\alpha$ in terms of $y_{\alpha-1} + y_{\alpha-2}$. Prove

$$(4.19)\quad y_{\alpha+1} + y_\alpha = \rho^2(y_{\alpha-1} + y_{\alpha-2}) + \epsilon_{\alpha+1} + (1 + \rho)\epsilon_\alpha + \rho\epsilon_{\alpha-1}$$

Also prove that an LS regression of $y_{\alpha+1} + y_\alpha$ on $y_{\alpha-1} + y_{\alpha-2}$ does *not* yield a consistent estimator of ρ^2 even if $|\rho| < 1$.

4.5 (*Aggregation of simultaneous equations*) Imagine that two commodities are supplied by one firm according to the following equations:

$$(4.20)\quad \begin{aligned} q_{\alpha 1} &= \beta_{01} + \beta_{11}p_{\alpha 1} + \beta_{21}p_{\alpha 2} + \beta_{31}c_\alpha + \epsilon_{\alpha 1} \\ q_{\alpha 2} &= \beta_{02} + \beta_{12}p_{\alpha 1} + \beta_{22}p_{\alpha 2} + \beta_{32}c_\alpha + \epsilon_{\alpha 2} \end{aligned}$$

where the q's are the quantities bought and sold of the two commodities, the p's their prices, and c the price of a raw material which is used for both. Suppose further that the commodities are bought by a consumer according to the following demand equations:

$$(4.21)\quad \begin{aligned} q_{\alpha 1} &= \gamma_{01} + \gamma_{11}p_{\alpha 1} + \gamma_{21}p_{\alpha 2} + \gamma_{31}m_\alpha + \epsilon'_{\alpha 1} \\ q_{\alpha 2} &= \gamma_{02} + \gamma_{12}p_{\alpha 1} + \gamma_{22}p_{\alpha 2} + \gamma_{32}m_\alpha + \epsilon'_{\alpha 2} \end{aligned}$$

where m is the consumer's income. An analyst introduces the average quantity and the average price as macrovariables:

$$(4.22)\quad q_\alpha = \frac{1}{2}(q_{\alpha 1} + q_{\alpha 2}) \qquad p_\alpha = \frac{1}{2}(p_{\alpha 1} + p_{\alpha 2})$$

and he postulates the following two-equation macromodel:

$$(4.23)\quad \begin{aligned} q_\alpha &= \beta_0 + \beta_1 p_\alpha + \beta_2 c_\alpha + \epsilon_\alpha \quad \text{(supply)} \\ q_\alpha &= \gamma_0 + \gamma_1 p_\alpha + \gamma_2 m_\alpha + \epsilon'_\alpha \quad \text{(demand)} \end{aligned}$$

Both the four-equation micromodel and the two-equation macromodel are regarded as complete systems with the prices and quantities as endogenous variables and m and c as exogenous variables; it is assumed that the reduced form of the microsystem exists. Prove along the following lines that the macrosystem is consistent with the microsystem.[16] (1) The reduced form of the microsystem expresses each of the four variables $p_{\alpha 1}$, $p_{\alpha 2}$, $q_{\alpha 1}$, $q_{\alpha 2}$ linearly in terms of m_α and c_α and the four microdisturbances; (2) by adding the reduced-form equations for $p_{\alpha 1}$ and $p_{\alpha 2}$ and similarly for $q_{\alpha 1}$ and $q_{\alpha 2}$ we obtain two linear stochastic equations expressing p_α and q_α in terms of m_α and c_α, which can be regarded as the reduced form of the macrosystem; (3) since the two

[16] Prove this only in general terms by commenting on the three statements which follow; the algebraic derivations [which lead to the results (4.24) and (4.25) of Problem 4.6] are rather tedious.

structural equations of the macrosystem are both just-identified, the reduced form of this system determines the coefficients of the structural equations uniquely.

4.6 (*Continuation*) If one carries out the procedure outlined above, one finds that γ_1 (the price coefficient of the macro demand equation) is equal to the ratio N/D, where

$$N = (\beta_{21}\beta_{32} - \beta_{22}\beta_{31})(\gamma_{11} + \gamma_{12}) + (\beta_{12}\beta_{31} - \beta_{11}\beta_{32})(\gamma_{22} + \gamma_{21}) + (\beta_{31} + \beta_{32})(\gamma_{11}\gamma_{22} - \gamma_{12}\gamma_{21}) \tag{4.24}$$

$$D = \beta_{31}(\gamma_{22} - \gamma_{12} - \beta_{22} + \beta_{12}) + \beta_{32}(\gamma_{11} - \gamma_{21} - \beta_{11} + \beta_{21}) \tag{4.25}$$

Conclude that a structural macrocoefficient may depend on the coefficients of noncorresponding microequations (the micro supply equations in this case). Substitute alternative numerical values for the microparameters to evaluate the sensitivity of N/D. [*Hint*. See Theil (1954), pp. 80–82.]

11.5 The Convergence Approach to the Aggregation Problem[B]

The appearance of noncorresponding microparameters as determining factors of macrocoefficients is a disturbing feature. Therefore it is worthwhile to see whether an alternative approach exists which sheds a more favorable light on the widespread practice of running regressions on aggregative data. Consider, then, the microrelations (3.1); sum both sides over $i = 1, \ldots, N$ and divide by N:

$$\begin{aligned} \bar{y}_\alpha &= \frac{1}{N}\sum_{i=1}^{N} \beta_{1i}x_{\alpha 1i} + \cdots + \frac{1}{N}\sum_{i=1}^{N} \beta_{Ki}x_{\alpha Ki} + \frac{1}{N}\sum_{i=1}^{N} \epsilon_{\alpha i} \\ &= \frac{\sum_{i=1}^{N} \beta_{1i}x_{\alpha 1i}}{\sum_{i=1}^{N} x_{\alpha 1i}}\bar{x}_{\alpha 1} + \cdots + \frac{\sum_{i=1}^{N} \beta_{Ki}x_{\alpha Ki}}{\sum_{i=1}^{N} x_{\alpha Ki}}\bar{x}_{\alpha K} + \frac{1}{N}\sum_{i=1}^{N} \epsilon_{\alpha i} \end{aligned} \tag{5.1}$$

It is assumed that $x_{\alpha hi} > 0$ holds for each triple (α, h, i), so that the denominators on the second line do not vanish.

The Random-Selection Assumption

Equation (5.1) can be regarded as a linear equation in $\bar{y}_\alpha, \bar{x}_{\alpha 1}, \ldots, \bar{x}_{\alpha K}$, but the coefficients are obviously not constant except when the explanatory microvariables corresponding to each h $(= 1, \ldots, K)$ move proportionally. Now suppose that we are engaged in a time series analysis of cross-section data on randomly selected households. This implies that the microparameters

β_{hi} are also random. Imagine that for each $i = 1, \ldots, N$, the K coefficients $\beta_{1i}, \ldots, \beta_{Ki}$ are a random drawing from a K-dimensional population with mean $\beta_1, \ldots, \beta_K$ and covariance matrix $[\sigma_{hk}]$. Assuming that the x's in (5.1) are nonstochastic (we shall return to this assumption in the next subsection), we conclude that the coefficients of $\bar{x}_{\alpha 1}, \ldots, \bar{x}_{\alpha K}$ on the second line of (5.1) are random with expectations $\beta_1, \ldots, \beta_K$ (independent of α) and that the covariance of the coefficients of $\bar{x}_{\alpha h}$ and $\bar{x}_{\alpha k}$ is

$$(5.2) \qquad \frac{\sum_{i=1}^{N}\sum_{j=1}^{N} x_{\alpha hi}x_{\alpha kj}\operatorname{cov}(\beta_{hi}, \beta_{kj})}{\left(\sum_{i=1}^{N} x_{\alpha hi}\right)\left(\sum_{i=1}^{N} x_{\alpha ki}\right)} = \frac{\sigma_{hk}}{N}\left[1 + \frac{\frac{1}{N}\sum_{i=1}^{N}(x_{\alpha hi} - \bar{x}_{\alpha h})(x_{\alpha ki} - \bar{x}_{\alpha k})}{\bar{x}_{\alpha h}\bar{x}_{\alpha k}}\right]$$

the equality sign being based on the independence of β_{hi} and β_{kj} for $i \neq j$. Note that the covariance (5.2) is not independent of α. This is because the coefficient of $\bar{x}_{\alpha h}$ on the second line of (5.1) is obtained by weighting $\beta_{h1}, \ldots, \beta_{hN}$ with weights that depend on α.

In particular, consider the variance of the $\bar{x}_{\alpha h}$ coefficient, which according to (5.2) is of the form $\sigma_{hh}(1 + c_{\alpha h}^2)/N$, where $c_{\alpha h}$ is the coefficient of variation (the standard deviation divided by the mean) of the N numbers $x_{\alpha h1}, \ldots, x_{\alpha hN}$. This coefficient $c_{\alpha h}$ may be larger for some observations (i.e., for some values of α), but there is no cogent reason for assuming that it will increase or decrease systematically when the number of households (N) increases. There is, of course, the trivial effect that $c_{\alpha h}$ will be larger for $N = 2$ than for $N = 1$ as soon as $x_{\alpha h1} \neq x_{\alpha h2}$, but that is not the real issue. The main point is whether $c_{\alpha h}$ is systematically larger (or smaller) for, say, $N = 10^5$ than for $N = 10^4$.

If we postulate that $c_{\alpha h}$ converges to a finite nonzero limit as N increases indefinitely, the variance of the $\bar{x}_{\alpha h}$ coefficient in (5.1), $\sigma_{hh}(1 + c_{\alpha h}^2)/N$, converges to zero. We found above that the expectation of this coefficient is β_h; application of Chebyshev's inequality then shows that the coefficient converges in probability to β_h. Therefore, for sufficiently large N, we can replace (5.1) by

$$(5.3) \qquad \bar{y}_\alpha \approx \sum_{h=1}^{K}\beta_h\bar{x}_{\alpha h} + \frac{1}{N}\sum_{i=1}^{N}\epsilon_{\alpha i}$$

The convergence in probability underlying this procedure will induce us to call it the *convergence approach* to the aggregation problem. It originated with THEIL (1968b).[17] Note that there is no problem of aggregation bias.

[17] The random-coefficient model for aggregation was used earlier by KLEIN (1953, pp. 211–226) and ZELLNER (1966), but they did not consider the convergence aspect. However, Zellner did prove that if the x's may be regarded as fixed, the expectations of the coefficients on the second line of (5.1) are equal to $\beta_1, \ldots, \beta_K$.

The Independence Assumption

It was assumed in the previous subsection that the x's which occur in (5.1) are nonstochastic. This assumption is not innocent at all. If we select households at random, not only the β_{hi}'s but also the $x_{\alpha hi}$'s become stochastic (the incomes of the households, the prices which they pay for sugar, etc.). This does not mean that we cannot treat the x's as fixed. It does mean, however, that if we do so, we operate conditionally on the x's and we assume implicitly that the conditional distribution of the β's given the x's is independent of these x's. Thus, the convergence approach is based on the assumption that over the set of individuals who are aggregated, there is stochastic independence of the factors determining their behavior (the x's) and the way in which they react to these factors (the β's). We may also put it this way. In order that the convergence approach be applicable in the sense that the macrocoefficients converge in probability to the expectations of the corresponding microcoefficients as $N \to \infty$, we should confine the aggregation to groups that satisfy the condition of independence of determining factors and reaction to these factors.

It is easily seen that we obtain different results when this condition is violated. Let $x_{\alpha 1i}$ of (5.1) be the income of the ith family in year α, so that the coefficient of $\bar{x}_{\alpha 1}$ can be written as $\sum_i \theta_{\alpha i}\beta_{1i}$, where $\theta_{\alpha i} = x_{\alpha 1i}/N\bar{x}_{\alpha 1}$ is the share of the ith family of total family income in that year. The $\bar{x}_{\alpha 1}$ coefficient is thus a weighted average of the income coefficients of the microrelations, the weights being equal to the corresponding income shares. This weighted average can be written as

$$\sum_{i=1}^{N} \theta_{\alpha i}\beta_{1i} = \frac{1}{N}\sum_{i=1}^{N} \beta_{1i} + \sum_{i=1}^{N} \left(\theta_{\alpha i} - \frac{1}{N}\right)\beta_i \tag{5.4}$$

which for large N is approximately equal to β_1 (the expectation of the β_{1i}'s) plus N times the covariance of the income shares and the income coefficients.[18] There is convergence toward β_1 when these shares and coefficients are stochastically independent, but not when they are correlated. To some degree, this covariance can be compared with the covariance components of the aggregation bias discussed at the end of Section 11.3. The comparability is limited, however, because the present covariance changes from observation to observation, whereas the analysis of Section 11.3 (including the aggregation bias) is based on the sample as a whole.

In conclusion, we note that the present aggregation analysis is confined to linear relations. Problem 5.2 below considers a simple nonlinear case; we

[18] The income shares are $O(N^{-1})$ and the income coefficients are $O(N^0) = O(1)$, so that N times their covariance is $O(1)$ and hence of the same order of magnitude as the first right-hand term in (5.4).

shall come back to the problem of aggregation under conditions of nonlinearity in Section 11.7.

The treatment of the aggregation problem in this and the two previous sections is by no means complete. Reference may be made to the monographs by GREEN (1964) and W. D. FISHER (1969) for other approaches to the problem. These approaches are mostly not of an econometric nature and are therefore outside the scope of this book.

Problems

5.1 Suppose that the coefficient of variation $c_{\alpha h}$ does not converge to a finite nonzero limit as $N \to \infty$ but that $c_{\alpha h} = O(N^k)$. Prove that the variance $\sigma_{hh}(1 + c_{\alpha h}^2)/N$ of the $\bar{x}_{\alpha h}$ coefficient still converges to zero when $k < \frac{1}{2}$.

5.2 Consider the following quadratic microrelations:

$$y_{\alpha i} = \beta_{0i} + \beta_{1i}x_{\alpha i} + \beta_{2i}x_{\alpha i}^2 + \epsilon_{\alpha i} \qquad i = 1, \ldots, N \tag{5.5}$$

Formulate the assumption on the distribution of the β's as well as the appropriate independence assumption in order that the following macrorelation be true for large N:

$$\bar{y}_\alpha \approx \beta_0 + \beta_1\bar{x}_{\alpha 1} + \beta_2\left[\bar{x}_\alpha^2 + \frac{1}{N}\sum_{i=1}^{N}(x_{\alpha i} - \bar{x}_\alpha)^2\right] + \frac{1}{N}\sum_{i=1}^{N}\epsilon_{\alpha i} \tag{5.6}$$

Give an interpretation of the term in square brackets.

11.6 The Consumer's Allocation Problem: (4) The Model in Relative Prices[C]

The remainder of this chapter is devoted to an application of some of the ideas developed in the earlier sections as well as in Chapters 7 and 8. To increase the economic content of the discussion we shall treat these problems in the context of the consumer's allocation problem which was considered in Sections 7.5 through 7.7. (These sections and also Appendix A should be read before proceeding to the material that follows.) The main objective of this and the next three sections is to re-specify the demand equation system of Section 7.7 so that it contains fewer unknown parameters. A complication will arise in that the new equations are nonlinear in their parameters.

The discussion of these demand systems is continued in Section 12.7, which is concerned with the goodness of fit of the demand equations; that section requires prior reading of Section 12.6.

Demand Equations in Absolute Prices

The basic demand equation in infinitesimal changes is eq. (5.6) of Section 7.5, reproduced here:

$$w_i\, d(\log q_i) = p_i \frac{\partial q_i}{\partial m}\, d(\log \bar{m}) + \sum_{j=1}^{N} \frac{p_i p_j}{m} \frac{\partial q_i}{\partial p_j}\, d(\log p_j) \tag{6.1}$$

where $\bar{m}$ stands for real income. Equation (A.16) of Appendix A defines the change in its natural logarithm in terms of money income and prices:

$$d(\log \bar{m}) = d(\log m) - \sum_{k=1}^{N} w_k\, d(\log p_k) \tag{6.2}$$

We write μ_i for the marginal value share $p_i(\partial q_i/\partial m)$ and π_{ij} for the price coefficient $(p_i p_j/m)(\partial q_i/\partial p_j)$. The finite-change equation corresponding to (6.1) is then eq. (6.3) of Section 7.6:

$$w_{it}^* Dq_{it} = \mu_i Dq_t + \sum_{j=1}^{N} \pi_{ij} Dp_{jt} + \epsilon_{it} \qquad \begin{array}{l} i = 1, \ldots, N \\ t = 1, \ldots, T \end{array} \tag{6.3}$$

The μ_i's and the π_{ij}'s are the unknown parameters; they are subject to the following constraints [see eqs. (5.10) to (5.12) of Section 7.5]:

$$\begin{array}{c} \sum_{i=1}^{N} \mu_i = 1 \qquad \sum_{j=1}^{N} \pi_{ij} = 0 \text{ for } i = 1, \ldots, N \\ [\pi_{ij}] \text{ is symmetric and negative semidefinite of rank } N - 1 \end{array} \tag{6.4}$$

The ϵ_{it}'s of (6.3) are random disturbances with zero mean, zero lagged covariances—$\mathscr{E}(\epsilon_{it}\epsilon_{jt'}) = 0$ whenever $t \neq t'$, and constant variances and contemporaneous covariances:

$$\mathscr{E}(\epsilon_{it}\epsilon_{jt}) = \omega_{ij} \qquad \begin{array}{r} i, j = 1, \ldots, N \\ t = 1, \ldots, T \end{array} \tag{6.5}$$

where $[\omega_{ij}]$ is an $N \times N$ positive semidefinite matrix of rank $N - 1$. The columns of this matrix add up to a zero column:

$$\sum_{j=1}^{N} \omega_{ij} = 0 \qquad i = 1, \ldots, N \tag{6.6}$$

The Number of Unknown Parameters

The total number of μ's and π's occurring in the N demand equations (6.3) is $N + N^2$, but (6.4) indicates that there is one linear constraint on the μ's, N such constraints on the π's in view of $\sum_j \pi_{ij} = 0$, and $\frac{1}{2}N(N - 1)$ symmetry constraints. The total number of free parameters is therefore $\frac{1}{2}(N + 2)(N - 1)$, which is 9 for $N = 4$. We did use four commodity groups in the application of Section 7.7, so that the total number of unknown parameters is not excessive in that case. But one can easily conceive of a larger number of commodity groups for which the number of unknown parameters indeed becomes excessively large. Therefore, if the analyst is interested in more detail, the specification (6.3) ceases to be attractive. We shall now describe another specification, based on relative rather than absolute prices, which leads to a substantial reduction in the number of unknown parameters under appropriate conditions.

Decomposition of the Substitution Effect

In eq. (5.3) of Section 7.5 we considered the $N \times N$ matrix of substitution effects of price changes, the (i, j)th element of which is $\partial q_i/\partial p_j$. It appears from eq. (A.17) of Appendix A that this substitution effect can be written as the sum of two terms:

$$\text{(6.7)} \qquad \frac{\partial q_i}{\partial p_j} = \lambda u^{ij} - \frac{\lambda}{\partial\lambda/\partial m}\frac{\partial q_i}{\partial m}\frac{\partial q_j}{\partial m} \qquad i, j = 1, \ldots, N$$

where λ is the marginal utility of income, $\partial\lambda/\partial m$ is its income derivative, and u^{ij} is the (i, j)th element of $\mathbf{U}^{-1}$, the inverse of the Hessian matrix of the utility function: $\mathbf{U} = [\partial^2 u/\partial q_i \partial q_j]$. It will be assumed that $\mathbf{U}$ is symmetric and negative definite (which guarantees that the utility function has a maximum subject to the budget constraint), so that $\mathbf{U}^{-1}$ has the same properties. Furthermore, it follows from eq. (A.19) of Appendix A that when we postmultiply this $\mathbf{U}^{-1}$ by the price vector, we obtain a multiple $(\partial\lambda/\partial m)^{-1}$ of the vector of income derivatives of the demand functions:

$$\text{(6.8)} \qquad \sum_{j=1}^{N} u^{ij} p_j = \frac{\partial q_i/\partial m}{\partial\lambda/\partial m} \qquad i = 1, \ldots, N$$

The marginal utility of income λ is not a constant but a function of income and prices, just as the optimal quantities $q_1^0, \ldots, q_N^0$. In fact, eqs. (6.7) and (6.8) both contain the income derivative of λ. The income elasticity of λ will play an important role in the further developments and, in particular, its reciprocal:

$$\text{(6.9)} \qquad \phi = \left(\frac{\partial\lambda}{\partial m}\frac{m}{\lambda}\right)^{-1}$$

This reciprocal of the income elasticity of the marginal utility of income will be indicated more briefly as the *income flexibility*. Intuitively, one would expect that an increase in income reduces its own marginal utility and hence that ϕ is negative. It will be shown in eq. (6.17) below that this is indeed the case when the Hessian matrix $\mathbf{U}$ is negative definite.

The first right-hand term of (6.7) is known as the *specific substitution effect* of the change in the jth price on the ith quantity, the second as the *general substitution effect*, and the sum of the two is the *total substitution effect*. The general substitution effect is concerned with the competition of all commodities for the consumer's dollar. If we take $\partial\lambda/\partial m < 0$ and consider the usual case of positive income derivatives of the demand functions, the general substitution effect of a price increase is always positive. The specific character of the specific substitution effect follows directly from the fact that the indices i and j really occur as a pair in λu^{ij}; they cannot be separated in contrast to the general substitution effect, which consists of a term in i multiplied by a similar term in j.

Preference Independence and Block-Independence

Now suppose that the utility function can be written as the sum of n functions, each containing the quantity of one commodity as the only argument:

$$u(\mathbf{q}) = \sum_{i=1}^{N} u_i(q_i) \tag{6.10}$$

The marginal utility of the ith commodity is then $\partial u_i/\partial q_i$, which depends only on q_i. Hence, $\partial^2 u/\partial q_i \partial q_j = 0$ whenever $i \neq j$, which means that the Hessian matrix $\mathbf{U}$ and its inverse are both diagonal. The independence of each marginal utility of the quantities of all other commodities will induce us to refer to the case (6.10) as that of *preference independence*.

The diagonal form of $\mathbf{U}$ and $\mathbf{U}^{-1}$ implies that the specific substitution effect in (6.7) vanishes except for $i = j$, which—as we shall shortly see—simplifies the price term of the demand equations substantially. But condition (6.10) is a serious restriction. In a large number of cases we can improve on this by imposing the following weaker constraint. Suppose that the N commodities can be grouped into a set of G mutually exclusive and exhaustive sets $S_1, \ldots, S_G$ containing $N_1, \ldots, N_G$ commodities ($\sum N_g = N$) and that the utility function can be written as

$$u(\mathbf{q}) = \sum_{g=1}^{G} u_g(\mathbf{q}_g) \tag{6.11}$$

where $\mathbf{q}_g$ is the vector of q_i's that fall under S_g. It is easily verified that the

Hessian matrix is then block-diagonal:

$$\mathbf{U} = \begin{bmatrix} \mathbf{U}_1 & \mathbf{0} & \cdots & \mathbf{0} \\ \mathbf{0} & \mathbf{U}_2 & \cdots & \mathbf{0} \\ \vdots & \vdots & & \vdots \\ \mathbf{0} & \mathbf{0} & \cdots & \mathbf{U}_G \end{bmatrix} \tag{6.12}$$

where $\mathbf{U}_g$ is the $N_g \times N_g$ Hessian matrix of $u_g(\ )$. This is the case of *block-independence*, the marginal utility $\partial u/\partial q_i$ being independent of q_j when the ith and the jth commodities belong to different sets ($i \in S_g$, $j \in S_h$, $g \neq h$). The inverse of $\mathbf{U}$ is then also block-diagonal with diagonal blocks $\mathbf{U}_1^{-1}, \ldots, \mathbf{U}_G^{-1}$, so that the specific substitution terms λu^{ij} in (6.7) can be nonzero only if i and j are members of the same set S_g.

Demand Equations in Relative Prices

We return to the demand equation (6.1) in infinitesimal changes. Consider in particular its price term and substitute the right-hand side of (6.7) for $\partial q_i/\partial p_j$:

$$\begin{aligned}(6.13)\qquad & \sum_{j=1}^{N} \frac{p_i p_j}{m}\left(\lambda u^{ij} - \frac{\lambda}{\partial\lambda/\partial m}\frac{\partial q_i}{\partial m}\frac{\partial q_j}{\partial m}\right) d(\log p_j) \\ &= \sum_{j=1}^{N} \frac{\lambda p_i p_j u^{ij}}{m}\, d(\log p_j) - \frac{\lambda/m}{\partial\lambda/\partial m}\mu_i \sum_{k=1}^{N} \mu_k\, d(\log p_k) \\ &= \sum_{j=1}^{N} \nu_{ij}\, d(\log p_j) - \phi\mu_i \sum_{k=1}^{N} \mu_k\, d(\log p_k) \\ &= \sum_{j=1}^{N} \nu_{ij}\left[d(\log p_j) - \sum_{k=1}^{N} \mu_k\, d(\log p_k)\right]\end{aligned}$$

The last two lines can be explained as follows. First, the price coefficients ν_{ij} of the specific substitution effects are defined as $\lambda p_i p_j u^{ij}/m$ or in matrix form:

$$[\nu_{ij}] = \frac{\lambda}{m}\mathbf{P}\mathbf{U}^{-1}\mathbf{P} \tag{6.14}$$

where $\mathbf{P}$ is the $n \times n$ diagonal matrix which contains the prices $p_1, \ldots, p_n$ on the diagonal. Since we assume that the p's, λ, and m are all positive and that $\mathbf{U}$ is symmetric and negative definite, the matrix $[\nu_{ij}]$ must have the latter properties too:

(6.15) $[\nu_{ij}]$ is symmetric and negative definite

Furthermore, ϕ which appears on the third line of (6.13) in the second term—

which is the general substitution term—is the income flexibility defined in (6.9). Finally, the last equality sign of (6.13) is based on

$$\sum_{j=1}^{N} \nu_{ij} = \phi\mu_i \qquad i = 1, \ldots, N \tag{6.16}$$

which follows directly from (6.8):

$$\sum_{j=1}^{N} \nu_{ij} = \frac{\lambda p_i}{m} \sum_{j=1}^{N} p_j u^{ij} = \frac{\lambda/m}{\partial\lambda/\partial m}\, p_i \frac{\partial q_i}{\partial m} = \phi\mu_i$$

Also note that a summation of both sides of (6.16) over i gives

$$\phi = \sum_{i=1}^{N} \sum_{j=1}^{N} \nu_{ij} < 0 \tag{6.17}$$

the inequality sign of which is based on the negative definiteness of $[\nu_{ij}]$.

We proceed to substitute the last line of (6.13) into the demand equation (6.1):

$$w_i\, d(\log q_i) = \mu_i\, d(\log \bar{m}) + \sum_{j=1}^{N} \nu_{ij} \left[d(\log p_j) - \sum_{k=1}^{N} \mu_k\, d(\log p_k) \right] \tag{6.18}$$

which corresponds to the following equation in finite changes:

$$w_{it}^* Dq_{it} = \mu_i Dq_t + \sum_{j=1}^{N} \nu_{ij} \left(Dp_{jt} - \sum_{k=1}^{N} \mu_k Dp_{kt} \right) + \epsilon_{it} \tag{6.19}$$

Comparing (6.19) and (6.3), we conclude that the present equation is formulated in relative prices, since a weighted average of the log-changes of all N prices is subtracted from Dp_{jt}. Note that the Dp_{jt} term itself represents the specific substitution effect and that the weighted average which is subtracted corresponds to the general substitution effect. Hence the latter effect acts as the deflator of the former. In particular, note that the weights of the weighted average are the *marginal* value shares, which is in contrast to the weights of the deflator of real income in (6.2). Finally, note that when all other prices remain constant, the effect of the log-change Dp_{jt} on the left-hand variable of (6.19) is

$$\nu_{ij} Dp_{jt} - \sum_{h=1}^{N} \nu_{ih}\mu_j Dp_{jt} = (\nu_{ij} - \phi\mu_i\mu_j) Dp_{jt}$$

This shows that the relation between the price coefficients of (6.3) and (6.19) is

$$\pi_{ij} = \nu_{ij} - \phi\mu_i\mu_j \qquad i, j = 1, \ldots, N \tag{6.20}$$

If $\nu_{ij} = \nu_{ji} > 0$ for some pair (i, j), an increase in the relative price of the ith (jth) commodity raises the demand for the jth (ith). The two commodities are then said to be each other's *specific substitutes*. If $\nu_{ij} = \nu_{ji} < 0$, they are called *complementary* in the same specific sense.

Demand Equations under Conditions of Preference Independence and Block-Independence

Now suppose that we have preference independence, so that **U** and $\mathbf{U}^{-1}$ are diagonal matrices. It follows directly from (6.14) that $\nu_{ij} = 0$ for all $i \neq j$, so that the N demand equations (6.19) are simplified to

$$w_{it}^* Dq_{it} = \mu_i Dq_t + \nu_{ii}\left(Dp_{it} - \sum_{k=1}^{N} \mu_k Dp_{kt}\right) + \epsilon_{it} \tag{6.21}$$

which means that each demand equation contains only one deflated price. The total number of unknown parameters is now $2N$ (the μ_i's and the ν_{ii}'s). There is one constraint on the μ_i's ($\sum \mu_i = 1$); there are N constraints of the form (6.16), which are now simplified to

$$\nu_{ii} = \phi\mu_i \qquad i = 1, \ldots, N \tag{6.22}$$

and constraint (6.15) is reduced to N inequality constraints: $\nu_{ii} < 0$, $i = 1, \ldots, n$. Taking account of the additional ϕ we thus have $2N - 1 - N + 1 = N$ free parameters when the inequality constraints are disregarded. This is a very drastic reduction compared with the number $\frac{1}{2}(N + 2)(N - 1)$ that was mentioned in the second subsection for the undeflated system (6.3). However, this result is obtained by imposing a very restrictive condition. One of the implications is that all marginal value shares must be positive. This follows directly from (6.22), which shows that μ_i is the ratio of two negative numbers, ν_{ii} and ϕ.

Next consider block-independence, which implies that **U**, $\mathbf{U}^{-1}$, and $[\nu_{ij}]$ are all block-diagonal with G diagonal blocks. The demand equation (6.19) now becomes

$$w_{it}^* Dq_{it} = \mu_i Dq_t + \sum_{j \in S_g} \nu_{ij}\left(Dp_{jt} - \sum_{k=1}^{N} \mu_k Dp_{kt}\right) + \epsilon_{it} \qquad \text{if } i \in S_g \tag{6.23}$$

Hence the demand equation for the ith commodity contains N_g relative prices when it belongs to set S_g. Condition (6.16) is now

$$\sum_{j \in S_g} \nu_{ij} = \phi\mu_i \qquad i \in S_g,\ g = 1, \ldots, G \tag{6.24}$$

and $[\nu_{ij}]$ contains G submatrices along the diagonal, each of which is symmetric and negative definite. The number of free parameters now depends on the number of sets and the number of commodities in each set; see Problem 6.2.

Is the Demand Model in Relative Prices Estimable?

It should be noted that the N demand equations (6.19) are not estimable unless conditions are imposed on the matrix $[\nu_{ij}]$ in addition to those of symmetry and negative definiteness, such as preference independence or block-independence. The simplest proof of this statement is based on (6.20), which shows that given any numerical specification of the π's and μ's of (6.3), the ν's of (6.19) can be varied arbitrarily by choosing an appropriate value of ϕ. Equivalently, the constraint (6.16) on $[\nu_{ij}]$ involves an additional unknown parameter (ϕ) which does not occur directly in (6.19), whereas the analogous constraint $\sum_j \pi_{ij} = 0$ on the price coefficients of the absolute price version involves no such additional unknown. As soon as there is one constraint on $[\nu_{ij}]$ in addition to symmetry and negative definiteness, such as $\nu_{12} = 0$, our data enable us in principle to estimate the relative price model. This model has fewer unknown parameters than the absolute price version if and only if there are two or more such constraints.

Problems

6.1 Use (6.20) as well as the constraints on the ν's and the μ's to prove that $[\pi_{ij}]$ is a singular matrix.

6.2 Consider the case of block-independence with G sets $S_1, \ldots, S_G$ containing $N_1, \ldots, N_G$ commodities each ($\sum N_g = N$). Prove that the number of free parameters of the N demand equations (6.23) is $\frac{1}{2}\sum_g N_g(N_g + 1)$. Also prove that given the total number of commodities (N) and the number of groups (G), this number of free parameters takes the smallest value, $\frac{1}{2}N(1 + N/G)$, when all groups contain the same number of commodities ($N_g = N/G$ for each g). Finally, prove that this minimum varies between N (for $G = N$) and $\frac{1}{2}N(N + 1)$ (for $G = 1$). Give an interpretation of these results.

6.3 (*Continuation*) The upper limit $\frac{1}{2}N(N + 1)$, which corresponds to the case in which the N commodities cannot be divided into two or more sets, exceeds by one the number $\frac{1}{2}(N + 2)(N - 1)$ of free parameters of (6.3). Verify that this is indeed true and explain how this is possible. (*Hint*. See the last subsection.)

11.7 The Consumer's Allocation Problem: (5) Aggregation over Consumers[C]

The analysis of the previous section is based on the idea that a consumer maximizes his utility function subject to his budget constraint. The approach is therefore microeconomic in nature, and an explicit treatment of the aggregation problem is appropriate. We shall proceed along the lines of

Section 11.5, but an extension of the approach outlined there is needed because of the nonlinearity of the price term of the demand equation (6.19).[19]

Outline of the Approach

The aggregation analysis of Section 11.5 shows that the disturbances of the equations play a purely passive role; they are simply averaged over the economic agents who are aggregated [see (5.3)]. Therefore there is not much difference between (6.19) and the infinitesimal demand equation (6.18); we shall prefer to use the latter because it is simpler for aggregation purposes. We indicate individual consumers by the subscript $c = 1, \ldots, C$, C being the total number of consumers, and proceed to formulate a random-selection model under certain simplifying conditions. The first is that all consumers pay the same price for each commodity at any given point of time. (This can be weakened to proportional rather than identical prices as will become clear in Problem 7.1 below.) Equation (6.18) then becomes for the cth consumer:

$$(7.1) \qquad w_{ic}d(\log q_{ic}) = \mu_{ic}\left[d(\log m_c) - \sum_{k=1}^{N} w_{kc}d(\log p_k)\right] + \sum_{j=1}^{N} \nu_{ijc}\left[d(\log p_j) - \sum_{k=1}^{N} \mu_{kc}d(\log p_k)\right]$$

where use is made of (6.2) for the real income term. We indicate per capita concepts by capitals:

$$(7.2) \qquad Q_i = \frac{1}{C}\sum_{c=1}^{C} q_{ic} \qquad M = \frac{1}{C}\sum_{c=1}^{C} m_c = \sum_{i=1}^{N} p_i Q_i \qquad W_i = \frac{p_i Q_i}{M}$$

and consider a weighted average of the left-hand sides of the C demand equations (7.1), the weights being the shares of the individual consumers of total income:

$$(7.3) \qquad \frac{1}{CM}\sum_{c=1}^{C} m_c w_{ic} d(\log q_{ic}) = \frac{p_i}{CM}\sum_{c=1}^{C} dq_{ic} = \frac{p_i}{M}\, dQ_i = W_i d(\log Q_i)$$

Hence this particular weighted average of the left-hand sides of the micro demand equations is equal to the analogous expression in per capita concepts.

In the remainder of this section we shall aggregate the right-hand sides of the demand equations in a similar manner under certain conditions on the distribution of the microcoefficients.

[19] When the theory is applied to the four commodity groups of Section 7.7, we have not only aggregation over consumers but also aggregation over commodities. The latter type is examined in Problem 7.6 for the block-independence case.

The Distribution of the Microcoefficients

We assume that for each c the income flexibility $\phi_c = \sum\sum \nu_{ijc}$, the N marginal value shares $\mu_{1c}, \ldots, \mu_{Nc}$, and the N^2 price coefficients ν_{11c}, $\nu_{12c}, \ldots, \nu_{NNc}$ are a random drawing from a $(1 + N + N^2)$-dimensional population with means $\phi, \mu_1, \ldots, \mu_N, \nu_{11}, \nu_{12}, \ldots, \nu_{NN}$. It is also assumed that the restrictions on the coefficients derived in the previous section apply to every consumer: $\sum_i \mu_{ic} = 1$, $[\nu_{ijc}]$ is symmetric and negative definite, and

$$\sum_{j=1}^{N} \nu_{ijc} = \phi_c \mu_{ic} \qquad i = 1, \ldots, N \tag{7.4}$$

Furthermore, we assume that the same restrictions apply to expectations of the microcoefficients. Thus, by taking the expectations of both sides of $\sum_i \mu_{ic} = 1$ we obtain $\sum_i \mu_i = 1$; similarly $[\nu_{ij}]$ is symmetric and negative definite. The case of (7.4) does involve a real restriction, however, because if we take the expectations of both sides of that equation, we obtain $\sum_j \nu_{ij} = \phi\mu_i$ only if the microeconomic income flexibility ϕ_c is uncorrelated with the marginal value shares $\mu_{1c}, \ldots, \mu_{Nc}$ in the population of consumers. In order to keep the model manageable, we shall impose the slightly stronger condition that the $(1 + N + N^2)$-dimensional distribution of the microcoefficients is such that the income flexibility is independent of the marginal value shares (see Problem 7.4). Note that this additional condition is ultimately a result of the nonlinearity of the constraint (7.4).

The marginal value shares $\mu_{1c}, \ldots, \mu_{Nc}$ must have nonzero covariances because their sum is equal to one. We shall write $[V_{ij}]$ for their covariance matrix:

$$\mathscr{E}[(\mu_{ic} - \mu_i)(\mu_{jc} - \mu_j)] = V_{ij} \qquad i, j = 1, \ldots, N \quad c = 1, \ldots, C \tag{7.5}$$

The sum of the columns of $[V_{ij}]$ is obviously a zero column:

$$\sum_{j=1}^{N} V_{ij} = 0 \qquad i = 1, \ldots, N \tag{7.6}$$

Aggregating the Real-Income Terms

We return to the demand equation (7.1) and recall that we weighted the left-hand variable with the income share m_c/CM in (7.3). Consider, then, the corresponding weighted average of the money income terms:

$$\frac{1}{CM}\sum_{c=1}^{C} m_c \mu_{ic} d(\log m_c) = \frac{1}{CM}\sum_{c=1}^{C} \mu_{ic} dm_c$$

and also the weighted average of the associated deflator terms for the kth price:

$$-\frac{1}{CM}\sum_{c=1}^{C} m_c\mu_{ic}w_{kc}d(\log p_k) = -\frac{dp_k}{CM}\sum_{c=1}^{C}\mu_{ic}q_{kc}$$

Combine these two results to obtain the following real income term of the aggregated demand equation:

$$(7.7)\quad \frac{1}{CM}\sum_{c=1}^{C}\mu_{ic}\left(dm_c - \sum_{k=1}^{N} q_{kc}dp_k\right)$$
$$= \frac{\mu_i}{CM}\sum_{c=1}^{C}\left(dm_c - \sum_{k=1}^{N} q_{kc}dp_k\right) + \frac{1}{CM}\sum_{c=1}^{C}(\mu_{ic}-\mu_i)\left(dm_c - \sum_{k=1}^{N} q_{kc}dp_k\right)$$
$$= \mu_i\left[d(\log M) - \sum_{k=1}^{N} W_k d(\log p_k)\right] + \frac{1}{CM}\sum_{c=1}^{C}(\mu_{ic}-\mu_i)\left(dm_c - \sum_{k=1}^{N} q_{kc}dp_k\right)$$
$$= \mu_i d(\log \bar{M}) + \frac{1}{CM}\sum_{c=1}^{C}(\mu_{ic}-\mu_i)\, d\bar{m}_c$$

If we assume that the real income change $d\bar{m}_c$ is independent of the marginal value shares $\mu_{1c}, \ldots, \mu_{Nc}$ and operate conditionally on the income changes, the second term on the last line is a random variable with zero mean and the following variance:

$$(7.8)\qquad \frac{1}{C^2M^2}\sum_{c=1}^{C}\sum_{d=1}^{C} d\bar{m}_c d\bar{m}_d \operatorname{cov}(\mu_{ic}, \mu_{id}) = \frac{V_{ii}}{C^2M^2}\sum_{c=1}^{C}(d\bar{m}_c)^2$$

Here $(1/C)\sum (d\bar{m}_c)^2$ is the mean square of the changes in the real incomes of the individual consumers. It is reasonable to assume that this mean square does not increase systematically when the number of consumers increases. Since the variance (7.8) is obtained from the mean square by multiplication by V_{ii}/CM^2, we may ignore it when C is sufficiently large. The real income term (7.7) of the aggregated demand equation thus becomes $\mu_i d(\log \bar{M})$, which is the straightforward macroeconomic analogue of the corresponding term in (7.1).

Aggregating the Price Terms

The weighted average of the specific substitution effects over all consumers is

$$(7.9)\quad \frac{1}{CM}\sum_{c=1}^{C} m_c\nu_{ijc}d(\log p_j) = \nu_{ij}d(\log p_j) + \frac{d(\log p_j)}{CM}\sum_{c=1}^{C} m_c(\nu_{ijc}-\nu_{ij})$$

It is easily verified that under reasonably realistic conditions, the second right-hand term converges to zero relative to the first as C increases; see Problem 7.3.

The general substitution effect is slightly more complicated owing to its nonlinearity in the parameters. First, note that this effect for the change in the kth price can be written as $-\phi_c \mu_{ic} \mu_{kc} d(\log p_k)$ in view of (7.4). In the aggregated demand equation this expression is multiplied by m_c/CM and then summed over c. The result is thus

$$(7.10) \quad -\frac{1}{CM}\sum_{c=1}^{C} m_c \phi_c \mu_{ic} \mu_{kc} d(\log p_k) = -\phi(\mu_i \mu_k + V_{ik}) d(\log p_k) - \frac{d(\log p_k)}{CM}\sum_{c=1}^{C} m_c[\phi_c \mu_{ic} \mu_{kc} - \phi(\mu_i \mu_k + V_{ik})]$$

where $\phi(\mu_i \mu_k + V_{ik})$ stands for the expectation of $\phi_c \mu_{ic} \mu_{kc}$ over consumers in accordance with (7.5) and the independence of ϕ_c and $\mu_{1c}, \ldots, \mu_{Nc}$. The term on the second line is similar to the second right-hand term of (7.9). We assume that it converges to zero as $C \to \infty$, so that the left-hand side of (7.10) then converges to the first term on the right.

The Aggregated Demand Equations

Collecting our results, which start with (7.3) and end with (7.10), we conclude that the macroequation takes the following form in the limit for $C \to \infty$:

$$(7.11) \quad W_i d(\log Q_i) = \mu_i d(\log \bar{M}) + \sum_{j=1}^{N} \nu_{ij}\left[d(\log p_j) - \sum_{k=1}^{N} \mu_k d(\log p_k)\right] - \phi \sum_{k=1}^{N} V_{ik} d(\log p_k)$$

where the component $-\phi \mu_i \mu_k d(\log p_k)$ of the general substitution term (7.10) has been combined with the specific substitution term (after applying $\sum_j \nu_{ij} = \phi \mu_i$), while the variance component $-\phi V_{ik} d(\log p_k)$ is shown separately.

Obviously, this variance component is a considerable nuisance when our goal is to estimate only a limited number of parameters. Taking account of the symmetry of $[V_{ij}]$ and of constraint (7.6), we must conclude that this term leads to $\frac{1}{2}N(N-1)$ additional unknown free parameters in the system as a whole. Also, there are rather good reasons for believing that this term is relatively unimportant. Take the case of preference independence: the price term in the first line of (7.11) is then simplified to $\nu_{ii} = \phi \mu_i$ multiplied by the logarithmic change in the (deflated) price of the ith commodity. The corresponding price term on the second line has $-\phi V_{ii}$ as coefficient, so that the ratio of the latter coefficient to the former is $-V_{ii}/\mu_i$. The μ_i's are fractions of 1, and even if the standard deviation of the μ_{ic}'s around μ_i is of the same order of magnitude as μ_i itself, the variance V_{ii} will be small compared with μ_i. One procedure is to neglect the variance component of the general substitution effect altogether, but it is more elegant to design for this component a plausible model which is based on a limited number of parameters.

A Simple Model for the Variance Component of the General Substitution Effect

As a preliminary model we consider

$$(7.12) \qquad V_{ij} = \begin{cases} \theta\mu_i(1-\mu_i) & \text{if} \quad i=j \\ -\theta\mu_i\mu_j & \text{if} \quad i\neq j \end{cases}$$

where θ is an unknown positive fraction. This specification implies that the variances and covariances of the individual marginal value shares are proportional to the variances and covariances which emerge from random sampling from a multinomial urn whose proportions are the expected marginal shares $\mu_1, \ldots, \mu_N$ [see eq. (2.8) of Section 2.2]. To ensure that the variances are positive we have to assume that μ_i is positive for each i, and each covariance V_{ij} $(i \neq j)$ is then negative. The variance V_{ii} is an increasing function of μ_i up to $\mu_i = \frac{1}{2}$ and the coefficient of variation $\sqrt{V_{ii}}/\mu_i$ is a decreasing function of μ_i. This seems reasonable because larger relative differences between the μ_{ic}'s must be expected on the average when the commodity has a smaller average μ_i.

Consider the last term of (7.11) under condition (7.12):

$$(7.13) \qquad \phi\theta\mu_i\sum_{k=1}^{N}\mu_k d(\log p_k) - \phi\theta\mu_i d(\log p_i) = -\phi\theta\mu_i\left[d(\log p_i) - \sum_{k=1}^{N}\mu_k d(\log p_k)\right]$$

and suppose that the conditions of preference independence apply to all microequations (7.1), so that $\nu_{ij} = 0$ for $i \neq j$ and $\nu_{ii} = \phi\mu_i$. Combining (7.11) and (7.13), we obtain the following demand equation:

$$(7.14) \qquad W_i d(\log Q_i) = \mu_i d(\log \bar{M}) + \phi(1-\theta)\mu_i\left[d(\log p_i) - \sum_{k=1}^{N}\mu_k d(\log p_k)\right]$$

which shows that the role of ϕ in the original specification is now taken over by $\phi(1-\theta)$. The first conclusion is that ϕ and θ cannot be identified separately on the basis of the observations, since they occur only in this combined form. The second is that if $\theta > 0$ and if we estimate ϕ as if $\theta = 0$, we tend to underestimate the absolute value of ϕ. It is unlikely, however, that the effect is numerically very important. Three pairs of values μ_i, $\sqrt{V_{ii}}$ are shown below, all of which correspond to $\theta = .04$, so that $\phi(1 - \theta)$ underestimates ϕ by only 4 percent. The underestimation will obviously be larger when the V_{ii}'s are larger, but it does not seem plausible on a priori grounds that they are much larger than the values specified here.

$\mu_i = .01$	$\sqrt{V_{ii}} = .02$	$\theta = .04$
.1	.06	.04
.5	.1	.04

Of course, the result (7.14) applies only under conditions of preference independence. If these conditions are not satisfied, the aggregated demand equations implied by assumption (7.12) are rather complicated. Suppose, however, that we modify this assumption as follows:

$$V_{ij} = \theta\left(\frac{1}{\phi} v_{ij} - \mu_i\mu_j\right) \tag{7.15}$$

This is equivalent to (7.12) when there is preference independence, so that the result (7.14) still holds under that condition. The present assumption implies that the covariance of the marginal value shares of two commodities consists of two parts, one of which $(-\theta\mu_i\mu_j)$ is concerned with the general substitution effect and the other with the specific substitution effect. The original formulation (7.12) takes only the general effect into account, but it is not difficult to argue that the specific effect should also play a role. Take two commodities, say, beef A and beef B (of about the same quality), which are specific substitutes in the sense that their v_{ijc} is positive for each consumer. Since the two kinds of beef satisfy almost identical needs, there is little to choose between them. Therefore one should not be surprised to find that when incomes increase, many consumers spend comparatively much of their additional income on beef A and comparatively little on beef B, while at the same time another large group of consumers proceeds in exactly the opposite way. This amounts to a negative covariance of the marginal value shares of the two kinds of beef over the set of all consumers, which is reflected by the negative specific component $\theta v_{ij}/\phi$ of the covariance (7.15).

The last term of (7.11) under condition (7.15) becomes

$$-\theta\sum_{j=1}^{N} v_{ij}d(\log p_j) + \phi\theta\mu_i\sum_{k=1}^{N}\mu_k d(\log p_k) \tag{7.16}$$

$$= -\theta\sum_{j=1}^{N} v_{ij}\left[d(\log p_j) - \sum_{k=1}^{N}\mu_k d(\log p_k)\right]$$

so that the aggregated demand equation is simplified to

$$(7.17) \qquad W_i d(\log Q_i) = \mu_i d(\log \bar{M}) + (1-\theta)\sum_{j=1}^{N} \nu_{ij}\left[d(\log p_j) - \sum_{k=1}^{N}\mu_k d(\log p_k)\right]$$

the interpretation of which is analogous to that of (7.14). The coefficients of the deflated prices are thus equal to a fraction $1 - \theta$ of the expectations of the ν_{ijc}'s.

Problems

7.1 Suppose that the price paid by consumer c for the ith commodity is of the form $A_c p_i$, A_c being a positive constant, so that the prices paid by different consumers for the same commodity are not identical but merely proportional. Prove that eq. (7.1) then still holds when the value shares $w_{1c}, \ldots, w_{Nc}$ are interpreted as the ratios of $p_1 q_{1c}, \ldots, p_N q_{Nc}$ to m_c/A_c, that is, when each consumer's money income is proportionally adjusted so that the associated prices for each commodity become identical. Note that this adjustment amounts to an income increase (decrease) for a consumer who pays low (high) prices; also note that M of (7.2) becomes the average over c of m_c/A_c.

7.2 Specify a number of alternative but—in your view—reasonably realistic values for μ_i, V_{ii}, C, and other relevant quantities to verify whether the first term on the last line of (7.7) is indeed normally large in absolute value compared with the second.

7.3 Prove that under the conditions stated in the text, the second right-hand term in (7.9) is a random variable with zero mean and the following standard deviation: when measured as a fraction of the first right-hand term (which is supposed to be nonzero), this standard deviation is equal to $k_{ij}\sqrt{(1 + k^2)/C}$, where k is the coefficient of variation of the distribution of incomes and k_{ij} is the coefficient of variation of the distribution of ν_{ijc}, $c = 1, \ldots, C$. Draw your own conclusions.

7.4 Prove that the expectation of $\phi_c \mu_{ic} \mu_{kc}$ in (7.10) is not equal to the product of the expectations of ϕ_c and $\mu_{ic}\mu_{kc}$ if ϕ_c is uncorrelated with but not independent of μ_{ic} and μ_{kc}. [*Hint*. Prove first that cov $(X, Y) = 0$, cov $(X, Y^2) \neq 0$ is possible by using Problem 3.2 of Section 2.3.]

7.5 Prove that the covariance specification (7.15) can be written as $[V_{ij}] = \theta[\phi^{-1}\mathbf{N} - (\phi^{-1}\mathbf{N})\iota\iota'(\phi^{-1}\mathbf{N})]$, where $\mathbf{N} = [\nu_{ij}]$. Compare this with eq. (2.11) of Section 2.2 to conclude that (7.15) is a "nondiagonal" extension of the covariance matrix of the multinomial urn. [*Hint*. $\phi^{-1}\mathbf{N}$ is a positive definite matrix whose elements add up to one, just as **P** of eq. (2.11) of Section 2.2.]

7.6 (*Aggregation over commodities*) Consider the block-independent system (6.23) and define the log-change of the volume index of the set S_g as

$$(7.18) \qquad DQ_{gt} = \sum_{i \in S_g} \frac{w_{it}^*}{W_{gt}^*} Dq_{it} \qquad \text{where} \qquad W_{gt}^* = \sum_{i \in S_g} w_{it}^*$$

Add the demand equations (6.23) over $i \in S_g$:

$$(7.19) \quad W_{gt}^* DQ_{gt} = M_g Dq_t + \sum_{i \in S_g} \sum_{j \in S_g} \nu_{ij} \left(Dp_{jt} - \sum_{k=1}^{N} \mu_k Dp_{kt} \right) + E_{gt}$$

where

$$(7.20) \qquad M_g = \sum_{i \in S_g} \mu_i \qquad \text{and} \qquad E_{gt} = \sum_{i \in S_g} \epsilon_{it}$$

are the marginal value share of S_g and the tth disturbance of its demand equation, respectively. Prove

$$(7.21) \quad \sum_{i \in S_g} \sum_{j \in S_g} \nu_{ij} \left(Dp_{jt} - \sum_{k=1}^{N} \mu_k Dp_{kt} \right) = \phi M_g \left(DP_{gt} - \sum_{k=1}^{N} \mu_k Dp_{kt} \right)$$

where DP_{gt} is the log-change of a price index of S_g, marginally weighted:

$$(7.22) \qquad DP_{gt} = \sum_{i \in S_g} \frac{\mu_i}{M_g} Dp_{it}$$

Combine (7.19) and (7.21):

$$(7.23) \quad W_{gt}^* DQ_{gt} = M_g Dq_t + \phi M_g \left(DP_{gt} - \sum_{k=1}^{N} \mu_k Dp_{kt} \right) + E_{gt}$$

and conclude that in the block-independence case, summation of all demand equations of each of the G blocks leads to a G-equation system that has the preference-independence form (6.21) and (6.22).

7.7 (*Continuation*) The definition (7.22) presupposes that M_g does not vanish. Which condition guarantees that M_g is strictly positive?

11.8 The Consumer's Allocation Problem: (6) Estimation under Conditions of Block-Independence[C]

Preliminary

The objective of this section is to apply the demand system (7.17) to the data on the four commodity groups which were discussed in Sections 7.6 and

7.7. For that purpose we need the finite-change variant of (7.17), which will be written as follows for the case of block-independent preferences:

$$w_{it}^{*}Dq_{it} = \mu_i Dq_t + \sum_{j\in S_g} \nu_{ij}\left(Dp_{jt} - \sum_{k=1}^{N}\mu_k Dp_{kt}\right) + \epsilon_{it} \qquad \text{if } i \in S_g \tag{8.1}$$

The notation used in (8.1) involves two minor inconsistencies with that of the previous section, which we shall accept in order to avoid the overburdening of the analysis by additional symbols. First, all variables refer to per capita concepts, which is in contrast to the use of capitals for such symbols in the previous section. However, the notation chosen has the advantage of being in accordance with that of Sections 7.6 and 7.7. Second, the price coefficient ν_{ij} in (8.1) is to be regarded as a fraction $1 - \theta$ of the expectation of the ν_{ijc}'s, whereas we used ν_{ij} in Section 11.7 for the expectation itself. On the other hand, the parameter μ_i is—as in the previous section—the expectation of the μ_{ic}'s.

The constraints on the parameters of (8.1) are

$$\sum_{i=1}^{N} \mu_i = 1 \tag{8.2}$$

$$[\nu_{ij}] \text{ is symmetric and negative definite} \tag{8.3}$$

$$\sum_{j\in S_g} \nu_{ij} = \phi\mu_i \qquad \text{for} \qquad i \in S_g,\ g = 1,\ldots, G \tag{8.4}$$

where ϕ is a fraction $1 - \theta$ of the expectation of the ϕ_c's.

Two Alternative Specifications of Block-Independence

The first four lines of Table 11.3 reproduce the symmetry-constrained point estimates and their asymptotic standard errors of Table 7.5 of Section 7.7. These estimates enable us to obtain an idea of whether preference independence is a realistic assumption for our data. Consider then eq. (6.20), which shows that $\pi_{ij} = -\phi\mu_i\mu_j$ whenever $i \neq j$ if there is indeed preference independence. Since the μ_i's are positive under this condition and ϕ is negative, all off-diagonal π's should then be positive. The table shows that this is true for the estimates of π_{12}, π_{13}, π_{14} (all corresponding to food), but that those of the three other off-diagonal π's are all virtually zero. In particular, the value of $\pi_{34} = -\phi\mu_3\mu_4$ (corresponding to durables and remainder) should be larger than those of all other off-diagonal π's because μ_3 and μ_4 are the two largest μ's; but its point estimate is actually negative (although certainly not significantly negative). If we take the point estimates as our criterion, we must conclude that π_{34} represents the most serious violation of the preference

Table 11.3

Alternative Estimates of Marginal Value Shares and of Coefficients of Absolute Prices

Commodity Group	μ_i	π_{ij}			
			Absolute price version		
Food	.179(.027)	−.107(.025)	.022(.009)	.043(.020)	.042(.020)
Vice	.088(.012)		−.027(.018)	.002(.009)	.003(.016)
Durables	.482(.028)			−.044(.024)	−.001(.017)
Remainder	.251(.027)				−.044(.027)
			Extended variant		
Food	.183(.027)	−.115(.025)	.012(.004)	.068(.015)	.035(.008)
Vice	.088(.012)		−.026(.015)	.009(.009)	.005(.015)
Durables	.482(.029)			−.069(.018)	−.008(.019)
Remainder	.247(.027)				−.031(.026)
			Simple variant		
Food	.183(.027)	−.083(.019)	.009(.003)	.049(.012)	.025(.006)
Vice	.085(.011)		−.043(.010)	.023(.005)	.012(.003)
Durables	.483(.029)			−.068(.018)	−.004(.018)
Remainder	.249(.026)				−.033(.018)

independence conditions, and that the triple $(\pi_{23}, \pi_{24}, \pi_{34})$ is the next serious violation. Therefore we shall specify the demand system (8.1) in two alternative ways. The simple variant postulates block-independence for three blocks: food, vice, and durables/remainder, so that the only off-diagonal ν_{ij} which is allowed to be nonzero is ν_{34} $(\equiv \nu_{43})$. The extended variant uses only two blocks: food and nonfood (≡ vice/durables/remainder), so that $\nu_{12} = \nu_{13} = \nu_{14} = 0$ and all other price coefficients are left free.

Elimination of the Constraints

It was shown in Section 7.7 that one of the four demand equations (that of remainder, say) may be deleted. We shall use the constraints (8.4) to eliminate the parameters $\nu_{ii} = \phi\mu_i - \sum_{j\neq i}\nu_{ij}$, so that the price term of (8.1) becomes

$$\begin{aligned}(8.5)\quad &\Big(\phi\mu_i - \sum_{j\neq i}\nu_{ij}\Big)\Big(Dp_{it} - \sum_{k=1}^{4}\mu_k Dp_{kt}\Big) + \sum_{j\neq i}\nu_{ij}\Big(Dp_{jt} - \sum_{k=1}^{4}\mu_k Dp_{kt}\Big)\\ &= \phi\mu_i\Big(Dp_{it} - \sum_{k=1}^{4}\mu_k Dp_{kt}\Big) + \sum_{j\neq i}\nu_{ij}(Dp_{jt} - Dp_{it})\\ &= \phi\mu_i\Big[Dp_{it} - Dp_{4t} - \sum_{k=1}^{3}\mu_k(Dp_{kt} - Dp_{4t})\Big] + \sum_{j\neq i}\nu_{ij}(Dp_{jt} - Dp_{it})\end{aligned}$$

where the last equality sign is based on $\mu_4 = 1 - \sum_{k\neq 4}\mu_k$.

Combining (8.1) and (8.5), we obtain

$$(8.6)\qquad w_{it}^{*}Dq_{it} = \mu_i Dq_t + \phi\mu_i\left[Dp_{it} - Dp_{4t} - \sum_{k=1}^{3}\mu_k(Dp_{kt} - Dp_{4t})\right] + \sum_{j\neq i}\nu_{ij}(Dp_{jt} - Dp_{it}) + \epsilon_{it}$$

These are three demand equations ($i = 1, 2, 3$) whose coefficients are all free except for the symmetry of $[\nu_{ij}]$.[20] The number of free parameters is five for the simple variant (ϕ, μ_1, μ_2, μ_3, ν_{34}) and seven for the extended variant (ν_{23} and ν_{24} in addition to these five). The symmetry-constrained absolute-price version has three free μ's plus six free π's. Therefore, both new variants economize on the number of coefficients, but the extended variant is only half as effective in this regard as the simple variant.

The Estimation Procedure

The estimation of the demand equations (8.6) would be a straightforward application of the procedure described in Section 7.7 if the right-hand side were linear in the unknown parameters, but this is not true for the second term. To solve this problem, define

$$(8.7)\qquad A_{it}(\boldsymbol{\mu}) = \mu_i\left[Dp_{it} - Dp_{4t} - \sum_{k=1}^{3}\mu_k(Dp_{kt} - Dp_{4t})\right]$$

so that (8.6) can be written as

$$(8.8)\qquad w_{it}^{*}Dq_{it} = \mu_i Dq_t + \phi A_{it}(\boldsymbol{\mu}) + \sum_{j\neq i}\nu_{ij}(Dp_{jt} - Dp_{it}) + \epsilon_{it}$$

This would be linear in the parameters if $A_{it}(\boldsymbol{\mu})$ were known. That is not the case, but we shall approximate it by $A_{it}(\hat{\boldsymbol{\mu}})$, where $\hat{\boldsymbol{\mu}}$ is the symmetry-constrained estimator of the vector of marginal value shares defined in Section 7.7. Thus, by substituting the corresponding estimates—given in the first column and the first four rows of Table 11.3—we effectively linearize the demand equations, so that we can proceed as in Section 7.7. The large-sample justification of this procedure will be outlined in the next section.

In the case of the simple variant we can write eq. (8.8) for $i = 1, 2$, and 3 as

$$(8.9)\qquad \begin{bmatrix} w_{1t}^{*}Dq_{1t} \\ w_{2t}^{*}Dq_{2t} \\ w_{3t}^{*}Dq_{3t} \end{bmatrix} = \begin{bmatrix} Dq_t & 0 & 0 & A_{1t}(\boldsymbol{\mu}) & 0 \\ 0 & Dq_t & 0 & A_{2t}(\boldsymbol{\mu}) & 0 \\ 0 & 0 & Dq_t & A_{3t}(\boldsymbol{\mu}) & Dp_{4t} - Dp_{3t} \end{bmatrix} \begin{bmatrix} \mu_1 \\ \mu_2 \\ \mu_3 \\ \phi \\ \nu_{34} \end{bmatrix} + \begin{bmatrix} \epsilon_{1t} \\ \epsilon_{2t} \\ \epsilon_{3t} \end{bmatrix}$$

[20] The negative definiteness of $[\nu_{ij}]$ will be handled separately in a way similar to that of the negative semidefiniteness of $[\pi_{ij}]$ in Section 7.7; see footnote 22 on page 594.

or more simply as

$$\mathbf{y}_t = \mathbf{X}_t\boldsymbol{\beta} + \boldsymbol{\epsilon}_t \tag{8.10}$$

where $\mathbf{y}_t$ is the three-element vector on the left, $\mathbf{X}_t$ the 3×5 matrix on the right, $\boldsymbol{\beta}$ the five-element parameter vector, and $\boldsymbol{\epsilon}_t$ the three-element disturbance vector. For the extended variant we have the same $\mathbf{y}_t$ and $\boldsymbol{\epsilon}_t$ but $\mathbf{X}_t$ and $\boldsymbol{\beta}$ are different, as is shown in the following partitioned matrix:

$$\begin{bmatrix} \boldsymbol{\beta}' \\ \mathbf{X}_t \end{bmatrix} = \left[\begin{array}{ccccccc} \mu_1 & \mu_2 & \mu_3 & \phi & \nu_{23} & \nu_{24} & \nu_{34} \\ \hdashline Dq_t & 0 & 0 & A_{1t}(\boldsymbol{\mu}) & 0 & 0 & 0 \\ 0 & Dq_t & 0 & A_{2t}(\boldsymbol{\mu}) & Dp_{3t} - Dp_{2t} & Dp_{4t} - Dp_{2t} & 0 \\ 0 & 0 & Dq_t & A_{3t}(\boldsymbol{\mu}) & Dp_{2t} - Dp_{3t} & 0 & Dp_{4t} - Dp_{3t} \end{array}\right] \tag{8.11}$$

Note that the $\mathbf{X}_t$ definition is such that the symmetry constraint $\nu_{ij} = \nu_{ji}$ is built in.

The GLS estimator of $\boldsymbol{\beta}$ based on T observations is then

$$\left(\sum_{t=1}^{T} \mathbf{X}_t'\boldsymbol{\Omega}^{-1}\mathbf{X}_t\right)^{-1} \sum_{t=1}^{T} \mathbf{X}_t'\boldsymbol{\Omega}^{-1}\mathbf{y}_t \tag{8.12}$$

where $\boldsymbol{\Omega}$ is the 3×3 covariance matrix whose elements ω_{ij} $(i, j = 1, 2, 3)$ are defined in (6.5), and the covariance matrix of this estimator is

$$\left(\sum_{t=1}^{T} \mathbf{X}_t'\boldsymbol{\Omega}^{-1}\mathbf{X}_t\right)^{-1} \tag{8.13}$$

Both $\mathbf{X}_t$ [which depends on $\boldsymbol{\mu}$ via $A_{it}(\boldsymbol{\mu})$] and $\boldsymbol{\Omega}$ are not really known. For $\boldsymbol{\Omega}$ we shall use the leading 3×3 submatrix of the second matrix in (7.25) of Section 7.7, which is the estimated disturbance covariance matrix implied by the symmetry-constrained coefficient estimates of that section. For $A_{it}(\boldsymbol{\mu})$ in $\mathbf{X}_t$ we shall use $A_{it}(\hat{\boldsymbol{\mu}})$ as indicated above. When these substitutions are made, point estimates can be obtained from (8.12) and asymptotic standard errors from the diagonal elements of the matrix (8.13). They are shown in columns (1) and (3) of Table 11.4.

Given the new point estimates of the marginal value shares and the new estimate of $\boldsymbol{\Omega}$ which is implied by the new coefficient estimates, we can repeat this procedure to obtain a second estimate of $\boldsymbol{\beta}$. Although this does not lead to any gain in asymptotic efficiency, it is nevertheless interesting to see whether the second estimates differ substantially from the first; in particular also whether a repeated (iterative) application of this procedure leads to

Table 11.4

Coefficient Estimates of the Demand Model in Relative Prices

	Extended Variant		Simple Variant	
	No Iteration (1)	After Convergence (2)	No Iteration (3)	After Convergence (4)
μ_1	.183(.027)	.183(.027)	.183(.027)	.183(.027)
μ_2	.088(.012)	.088(.012)	.085(.010)	.085(.011)
μ_3	.482(.028)	.482(.029)	.483(.028)	.483(.029)
ϕ	−.78(.14)	−.77(.14)	−.55(.10)	−.56(.11)
ν_{23}	−.024(.010)	−.023(.010)		
ν_{24}	−.012(.016)	−.012(.016)		
ν_{34}	−.103(.026)	−.100(.026)	−.070(.022)	−.071(.023)

convergence and, if so, whether the values after convergence are close to the corresponding values in columns (1) and (3) of Table 11.4. Columns (2) and (4) provide the answer; the figures in parentheses are the square roots of the diagonal elements of the matrix (8.13) after convergence. The results indicate that the differences are only slight. Table 11.5 presents the alternative

Table 11.5

Alternative Estimates of the Variances and Contemporaneous Covariances of the Demand Disturbances[a]

	Absolute price version							
Food	.234	.027	−.137	−.125				
Vice		.034	−.041	−.020				
Durables			.250	−.072				
Remainder				.216				
	Extended variant							
	No iteration				*After convergence*			
Food	.248	.030	−.146	−.132	.247	.030	−.146	−.131
Vice		.035	−.044	−.021		.035	−.044	−.021
Durables			.256	−.066			.256	−.066
Remainder				.220				.219
	Simple variant							
	No iteration				*After convergence*			
Food	.248	.026	−.145	−.130	.247	.027	−.145	−.129
Vice		.039	−.046	−.020		.040	−.046	−.020
Durables			.257	−.067			.258	−.067
Remainder				.217				.216

[a] All figures are to be multiplied by 10^{-4}.

estimates of the disturbance covariance matrix $[\omega_{ij}]$ in extended 4×4 form, and it shows that the differences are comparatively minor. Intuitively, one would guess that the estimates of the variances (ω_{ii}) should be smaller on the average for the absolute price version than for the present extended variant, and smaller for the latter than for the simple variant, because the number of coefficients adjusted decreases in that order. The diagonal elements in Table 11.5 corroborate this, but the effect is evidently small.

The Three Specifications Compared

We return to Table 11.3, which contains the estimates of the marginal value shares and of the coefficients of the absolute prices for all three specifications: the absolute price version and the two variants of the relative price version.[21] The results show that the point estimates of the marginal value shares and also their asymptotic standard errors are virtually the same for all three specifications. Indeed, the constraints of block-independence are primarily effective with respect to the estimation of the price coefficients; a comparison of corresponding asymptotic standard errors for the absolute price version and the simple variant shows that the difference is substantial in several cases. The extended variant occupies an intermediate position.

Table 11.4 compares the two variants of the relative price version. The difference between the two is that the simple variant assumes the validity of the constraint $\nu_{23} = \nu_{24} = 0$, which is not imposed by the other variant. If we assume that the disturbance distribution is normal, we can apply an F test to verify whether the null hypothesis $\nu_{23} = \nu_{24} = 0$ is true. This is pursued in Problems 8.1 and 8.2, which show that this hypothesis is acceptable at the 5 percent level. Considerations of simplicity may then induce us to prefer the simple variant to its rival. The negative value of ν_{34} indicates a specific complementarity relationship between durables and remainder, which has a great deal of plausibility because many durable goods need electricity, fuel, maintenance, repairs, and insurance, all of which are part of remainder.

Table 11.6 contains the estimates of the relative price coefficients (ν_{ij}) in matrix form, together with their asymptotic standard errors.[22] The estimates of the simple variant are all closer to zero than the corresponding values of the other variant with the exception of ν_{22}.

[21] The π_{ij} estimates of the two variants of the relative price version are derived by means of eq. (6.20). The estimates for these two specifications are those obtained after convergence, both in Tables 11.3 and 11.6 and in later tables.

[22] It is immediately evident from the table that the point estimates of the simple variant form a negative definite matrix. For the extended variant it is sufficient to consider the latent roots of the 3×3 submatrix in the lower right-hand corner, which are $-.295$, $-.032$, and $-.030$.

Table 11.6

Estimates of the Coefficients of Relative Prices

		Extended variant		
Food	−.141(.034)	0	0	0
Vice		−.032(.015)	−.023(.010)	−.012(.016)
Durables			−.246(.047)	−.100(.026)
Remainder				−.078(.035)
		Simple variant		
Food	−.102(.025)	0	0	0
Vice		−.047(.011)	0	0
Durables			−.197(.041)	−.071(.023)
Remainder				−.067(.025)

Table 11.4 reveals that the ϕ estimates of the two variants are rather different. If we take the estimate of the simple variant and reduce it slightly to take account of the aggregation result of the previous section, we may conclude that the expected value of the income flexibility across consumers is of the order of $-\frac{1}{2}$, which corresponds to an income elasticity of the marginal utility of income in the neighborhood of -2. The elasticity implied by the ϕ estimate of the extended variant is smaller in absolute value.

Problems

8.1 Consider eq. (1.10) of Section 6.1:

$$(8.14)\quad (\mathbf{y}-\mathbf{X}\mathbf{z})'\mathbf{V}^{-1}(\mathbf{y}-\mathbf{X}\mathbf{z}) = (\mathbf{y}-\mathbf{X}\hat{\boldsymbol{\beta}})'\mathbf{V}^{-1}(\mathbf{y}-\mathbf{X}\hat{\boldsymbol{\beta}}) + (\mathbf{z}-\hat{\boldsymbol{\beta}})'\mathbf{X}'\mathbf{V}^{-1}\mathbf{X}(\mathbf{z}-\hat{\boldsymbol{\beta}})$$

and interpret $\hat{\boldsymbol{\beta}}$ as the vector (8.12) corresponding to the extended variant. Prove that the extension of (8.14) for the case of this section is

$$(8.15)\quad \sum_{t=1}^{T}(\mathbf{y}_t-\mathbf{X}_t\mathbf{z})'\boldsymbol{\Omega}^{-1}(\mathbf{y}_t-\mathbf{X}_t\mathbf{z}) = \sum_{t=1}^{T}(\mathbf{y}_t-\mathbf{X}_t\hat{\boldsymbol{\beta}})'\boldsymbol{\Omega}^{-1}(\mathbf{y}_t-\mathbf{X}_t\hat{\boldsymbol{\beta}}) + (\mathbf{z}-\hat{\boldsymbol{\beta}})'\left(\sum_{t=1}^{T}\mathbf{X}_t'\boldsymbol{\Omega}^{-1}\mathbf{X}_t\right)(\mathbf{z}-\hat{\boldsymbol{\beta}})$$

Next interpret $\mathbf{z}$ as the GLS estimator obtained under the constraint $\nu_{23} = \nu_{24} = 0$, so that $\mathbf{z}$ is the vector (8.12) for the simple variant but with two zeros inserted in appropriate places. Write R_S for the left-hand side of (8.15) and R_E for the first term on the right, and prove that if the null hypothesis $\nu_{23} = \nu_{24} = 0$ is true and if $(\epsilon_{1t}, \epsilon_{2t}, \epsilon_{3t})$ are independent random drawings from a three-variate normal distribution with zero means and a nonsingular covariance matrix $\mathbf{\Omega}$, $R_S - R_E$ is distributed as $\chi^2(2)$. Finally, prove that R_E is distributed as $\chi^2(3T - 7)$ and that R_E and $R_S - R_E$ are stochastically independent under the same conditions. (*Hint*. Extend the analysis of the fourth subsection of Section 3.7.)

8.2 (*Continuation*) The estimators actually used in this section involve approximations of $\mathbf{\Omega}$ and $\mathbf{X}_t$, so that eq. (8.15) fails to hold exactly. When applying columns (2) and (4) of Table 11.4 for $\hat{\boldsymbol{\beta}}$ and $\mathbf{z}$, respectively, and the relevant estimates of the extended variant after convergence for $\mathbf{\Omega}$ and for $\boldsymbol{\mu}$ of $A_{it}(\boldsymbol{\mu})$ in $\mathbf{X}_t$, we find that (8.15) in numerical form becomes $98.2 \approx 93.0 + 5.5$. Use $R_E = 93.0$ and specify $R_S - R_E$ in two alternative ways: 5.5 and $98.2 - 93.0 = 5.2$. Apply the F test to verify that neither specification leads to rejection of the null hypothesis at the 5 percent level, using 3.1 for the 5 percent limit of $F(2, 86)$. (See Problem 9.2 for an asymptotic justification of this procedure.)

8.3 Table 11.4 shows that the ν_{24} estimate of the extended variant is not at all significantly different from zero. Suppose that the analyst decides to impose $\nu_{24} = 0$ and to leave both ν_{23} and ν_{34} free. Can this specification be interpreted in terms of block-independence for particular subsets of the four commodities?

11.9 The Consumer's Allocation Problem: (7) Asymptotic Evaluation of the Estimation Procedure[C]

The estimation procedure of the previous section is joint GLS except for the complication of an $\mathbf{X}_t$ matrix which depends on unknown parameters via $A_{it}(\boldsymbol{\mu})$. The large-sample justification of this procedure will rely on the analysis of Section 8.6 and, therefore, the main objective of the present section is to outline how the joint GLS results presented there have to be modified to handle this complication.

Assumptions

In the present case condition (6.2) of Section 8.6 amounts to the assumption that as $T \to \infty$, the matrix $(1/T)\sum_t \mathbf{X}_t'\mathbf{\Omega}^{-1}\mathbf{X}_t$ converges to a nonsingular limit matrix, where $\mathbf{X}_t$ is as indicated in (8.9) and (8.11) for the two variants. This involves the assumption of finite limits of the second-order moments of log-changes in real income and relative prices. In addition, we assume that the disturbance triples $(\epsilon_{1t}, \epsilon_{2t}, \epsilon_{3t})$ are independent random drawings from a three-dimensional population with zero means and a nonsingular covariance matrix. It follows directly from the results stated in the first subsection of Section 8.6 that under these conditions the estimator (8.12) is consistent and asymptotically normally distributed with mean vector $\boldsymbol{\beta}$ and covariance matrix (8.13).

Asymptotic Properties of the Coefficient Estimator

We proceed to consider the asymptotic properties of the estimator which was actually used as described below (8.13). Write $\hat{\boldsymbol{\Omega}}$ for the $\boldsymbol{\Omega}$ estimator which is implied by the symmetry-constrained coefficient vector of Section 7.7 and $\hat{\mathbf{X}}_t$ for the $\mathbf{X}_t$ matrix after the $A_{it}(\boldsymbol{\mu})$ of the fourth column is replaced by $A_{it}(\hat{\boldsymbol{\mu}})$, where $\hat{\boldsymbol{\mu}}$ is the subvector of the symmetry-constrained coefficient estimator which concerns the marginal value shares. We shall show that a replacement of $(\boldsymbol{\Omega}, \mathbf{X}_t)$ in the estimator (8.12) by this $(\hat{\boldsymbol{\Omega}}, \hat{\mathbf{X}}_t)$ does not affect its asymptotic distribution. For the corresponding property of the successive estimators in the iterations, see Problem 9.1.

Since eq. (8.7) defines $A_{it}(\boldsymbol{\mu})$ as a continuous function of $\boldsymbol{\mu}$, the consistency of $\hat{\boldsymbol{\mu}}$ guarantees that $A_{it}(\hat{\boldsymbol{\mu}})$ converges in probability to the A_{it} of the true $\boldsymbol{\mu}$ as $T \to \infty$ for each pair (i, t). Hence, plim $\hat{\mathbf{X}}_t = \mathbf{X}_t$ for each t. We also have plim $\hat{\boldsymbol{\Omega}} = \boldsymbol{\Omega}$, so that $\hat{\mathbf{X}}_t'\hat{\boldsymbol{\Omega}}^{-1}\hat{\mathbf{X}}_t$ converges in probability to $\mathbf{X}_t'\boldsymbol{\Omega}^{-1}\mathbf{X}_t$ for each t. Therefore

$$\text{(9.1)} \qquad \operatorname*{plim}_{T\to\infty} \frac{1}{T}\sum_{t=1}^{T} \hat{\mathbf{X}}_t'\hat{\boldsymbol{\Omega}}^{-1}\hat{\mathbf{X}}_t = \lim_{T\to\infty} \frac{1}{T}\sum_{t=1}^{T} \mathbf{X}_t'\boldsymbol{\Omega}^{-1}\mathbf{X}_t$$

The estimation procedure described below (8.13) implies that $\sqrt{T}$ times the sampling error of our coefficient estimator is equal to

$$\text{(9.2)} \qquad \left(\frac{1}{T}\sum_{t=1}^{T} \hat{\mathbf{X}}_t'\hat{\boldsymbol{\Omega}}^{-1}\hat{\mathbf{X}}_t\right)^{-1} \frac{1}{\sqrt{T}}\sum_{t=1}^{T} \hat{\mathbf{X}}_t'\hat{\boldsymbol{\Omega}}^{-1}\boldsymbol{\epsilon}_t$$

It follows from (9.1) that the matrix in parentheses converges in probability to the limit of the corresponding expression without hats. It will be shown in the next subsection that the vector by which its inverse is postmultiplied is asymptotically normally distributed with zero mean and covariance matrix (9.1). It then follows immediately that our estimator has the same asymptotic distribution as that of the vector (8.12). Also, (9.1) implies that the probability limit of the inverse of $(1/T)\sum_t \hat{\mathbf{X}}_t'\hat{\boldsymbol{\Omega}}^{-1}\hat{\mathbf{X}}_t$ is the covariance matrix of the associated limiting distribution, so that asymptotic standard errors may be obtained by taking the square roots of the diagonal elements of the inverse of $\sum_t \hat{\mathbf{X}}_t'\hat{\boldsymbol{\Omega}}^{-1}\hat{\mathbf{X}}_t$.

Proof of the Asymptotic Normality

The results given in the first subsection of Section 8.6 imply that under our conditions the vector $\sqrt{1/T}\sum_t \mathbf{X}_t'\boldsymbol{\Omega}^{-1}\boldsymbol{\epsilon}_t$ is asymptotically normally distributed with zero mean and a covariance matrix equal to the limit of $(1/T)\sum_t \mathbf{X}_t'\mathbf{\Omega}^{-1}\mathbf{X}_t$. Hence, to prove that the vector $\sqrt{1/T}\sum_t \hat{\mathbf{X}}_t'\hat{\mathbf{\Omega}}^{-1}\boldsymbol{\epsilon}_t$ of (9.2) has the same limiting distribution it is sufficient to show that the difference between the two vectors:

$$\frac{1}{\sqrt{T}}\sum_{t=1}^{T}(\hat{\mathbf{X}}_t'\hat{\mathbf{\Omega}}^{-1} - \mathbf{X}_t'\mathbf{\Omega}^{-1})\boldsymbol{\epsilon}_t \tag{9.3}$$

converges in probability to zero as $T \to \infty$. Consider then, for the sake of definiteness, the simple variant (8.9). [The treatment of the extended variant (8.11) is completely analogous.] The vector (9.3) thus consists of five elements, the first three of which are of the following form:

$$\sum_{j=1}^{3}(\hat{\omega}^{ij} - \omega^{ij})\frac{1}{\sqrt{T}}\sum_{t=1}^{T} Dq_t\epsilon_{jt} \qquad i = 1, 2, 3 \tag{9.4}$$

The fourth element of (9.3) is

$$\begin{aligned}\frac{1}{\sqrt{T}}\sum_{t=1}^{T}\sum_{i=1}^{3}\sum_{j=1}^{3}[A_{it}(\hat{\boldsymbol{\mu}})\hat{\omega}^{ij} - A_{it}(\boldsymbol{\mu})\omega^{ij}]\epsilon_{jt} &= \sum_{i=1}^{3}\sum_{j=1}^{3}(\hat{\mu}_i\hat{\omega}^{ij} - \mu_i\omega^{ij})\frac{1}{\sqrt{T}}\sum_{t=1}^{T}(Dp_{it} - Dp_{4t})\epsilon_{jt} \\ &\quad - \sum_{i=1}^{3}\sum_{j=1}^{3}\sum_{k=1}^{3}(\hat{\mu}_i\hat{\mu}_k\hat{\omega}^{ij} - \mu_i\mu_k\omega^{ij})\frac{1}{\sqrt{T}}\sum_{t=1}^{T}(Dp_{kt} - Dp_{4t})\epsilon_{jt}\end{aligned} \tag{9.5}$$

and the fifth:

$$\sum_{j=1}^{3}(\hat{\omega}^{3j} - \omega^{3j})\frac{1}{\sqrt{T}}\sum_{t=1}^{T}(Dp_{4t} - Dp_{3t})\epsilon_{jt} \tag{9.6}$$

It is readily seen that these five elements all involve random variables of the form $\sqrt{1/T}\sum_t x_t\epsilon_{jt}$, where x_t is either Dq_t or $Dp_{ht} - Dp_{kt}$ for some subscript pair (h, k). Our assumptions imply that such a random variable converges in distribution to a normal variate with zero mean and a variance equal to ω_{jj} multiplied by the limit of $(1/T)\sum_t x_t^2$, and this limit is a finite number under each interpretation of x_t. Since all these random variables are multiplied by expressions which converge in probability to zero (such as $\hat{\omega}^{ij} - \omega^{ij}$ and $\hat{\mu}_i\hat{\omega}^{ij} - \mu_i\omega^{ij}$), the vector (9.3) does indeed converge in probability to a zero vector as $T \to \infty$.

Additional Asymptotic Variances and Covariances

The estimated asymptotic covariance matrix $(\sum_t \hat{\mathbf{X}}_t'\hat{\mathbf{\Omega}}^{-1}\hat{\mathbf{X}}_t)^{-1}$ confines itself to the coefficients which occur in the three equations (8.8) for $i = 1, 2, 3$. This excludes the marginal value share of the fourth commodity, which is related to the three other μ's by the linear equation

$$\mu_4 = 1 - \mu_1 - \mu_2 - \mu_3 \tag{9.7}$$

It also excludes the ν's with equal subscripts. These can be derived by means of a nonlinear equation:

$$\nu_{ii} = \phi\mu_i - \sum_{j \neq i} \nu_{ij} \qquad i = 1, 2, 3, 4 \tag{9.8}$$

In addition, we need the nonlinear equation (6.20):

$$\pi_{ij} = \nu_{ij} - \phi\mu_i\mu_j \qquad i, j = 1, 2, 3, 4 \tag{9.9}$$

to obtain the asymptotic standard errors of the π_{ij} estimates which are given in Table 11.3.

Each of the left-hand coefficients in eqs. (9.7) to (9.9) is a function of the elements of $\boldsymbol{\beta}$ with continuous second-order derivatives. Hence we may apply the result formulated in the third subsection of Section 8.3 to conclude that their estimators are asymptotically normally distributed with means equal to the corresponding parameters and with variances and covariances which are determined by the first-order derivatives of these functions. For example, in the case of the extended variant we have for ν_{44}:

$$\nu_{44} = \phi\mu_4 - \nu_{24} - \nu_{34} = \phi(1 - \mu_1 - \mu_2 - \mu_3) - \nu_{24} - \nu_{34}$$

The derivative of ν_{44} with respect to μ_i is thus $-\phi$ for $i = 1, 2, 3$; the derivatives with respect to ϕ, ν_{23}, ν_{24}, and ν_{34} are μ_4, 0, -1 and -1, respectively. The complete matrix of all derivatives for all left-hand coefficients in (9.7) to (9.9), to be written as **D**, is shown in Table 11.7. If we indicate by **V** the

Table 11.7

Derivatives of Derived Parameters

	μ_1	μ_2	μ_3	ϕ	ν_{23}	ν_{24}	ν_{34}
μ_4	-1	-1	-1	0	0	0	0
ν_{11}	ϕ	0	0	μ_1	0	0	0
ν_{22}	0	ϕ	0	μ_2	-1	-1	0
ν_{33}	0	0	ϕ	μ_3	-1	0	-1
ν_{44}	$-\phi$	$-\phi$	$-\phi$	μ_4	0	-1	-1
π_{11}	$\phi(1 - 2\mu_1)$	0	0	$\mu_1(1 - \mu_1)$	0	0	0
π_{22}	0	$\phi(1 - 2\mu_2)$	0	$\mu_2(1 - \mu_2)$	-1	-1	0
π_{33}	0	0	$\phi(1 - 2\mu_3)$	$\mu_3(1 - \mu_3)$	-1	0	-1
π_{44}	$-\phi(1 - 2\mu_4)$	$-\phi(1 - 2\mu_4)$	$-\phi(1 - 2\mu_4)$	$\mu_4(1 - \mu_4)$	0	-1	-1
π_{12}	$-\phi\mu_2$	$-\phi\mu_1$	0	$-\mu_1\mu_2$	0	0	0
π_{13}	$-\phi\mu_3$	0	$-\phi\mu_1$	$-\mu_1\mu_3$	0	0	0
π_{14}	$\phi(\mu_1 - \mu_4)$	$\phi\mu_1$	$\phi\mu_1$	$-\mu_1\mu_4$	0	0	0
π_{23}	0	$-\phi\mu_3$	$-\phi\mu_2$	$-\mu_2\mu_3$	1	0	0
π_{24}	$\phi\mu_2$	$\phi(\mu_2 - \mu_4)$	$\phi\mu_2$	$-\mu_2\mu_4$	0	1	0
π_{34}	$\phi\mu_3$	$\phi\mu_3$	$\phi(\mu_3 - \mu_4)$	$-\mu_3\mu_4$	0	0	1

Table 11.8

Estimated Asymptotic Covariance Matrix ($\times 10^6$) for the Extended Variant

μ_1	μ_2	μ_3	μ_4	$\phi/10$	ν_{11}	ν_{22}	ν_{33}	ν_{44}	ν_{23}	ν_{24}	ν_{34}	π_{11}	π_{22}	π_{33}	π_{44}	π_{12}	π_{13}	π_{14}	π_{23}	π_{24}	π_{34}	
751	91	−443	−399	−3	−582	−70	330	304	−2	−1	−5	−370	−57	11	155	64	218	88	3	−10	−232	μ_1
	154	−140	−105	−1	−72	−7	89	174	−2	−110	14	−46	14	−11	135	28	15	3	46	−88	−50	μ_2
		820	−237	−1	337	88	−538	263	3	15	−100	213	69	71	174	−49	−47	−117	7	−27	−31	μ_3
			741	6	317	−11	119	−740	1	96	91	203	−25	−70	−463	−43	−186	26	−57	125	313	μ_4
				200	369	25	571	133	95	57	299	301	9	106	14	−33	−178	−90	9	14	63	$\phi/10$
					1123	100	793	12	175	105	552	835	61	185	−94	−109	−494	−233	15	33	294	ν_{11}
						236	30	162	−47	−162	70	72	233	37	143	−10	−36	−26	−54	−170	53	ν_{22}
							2232	424	219	184	711	694	−2	510	120	−57	−458	−179	−26	85	−26	ν_{33}
								1198	70	−248	−53	52	175	309	836	23	31	−107	95	−294	−435	ν_{44}
									102	30	134	143	−54	2	12	−16	−84	−43	61	9	22	ν_{23}
										267	49	86	−181	63	−247	−25	−49	−13	−34	240	19	ν_{24}
											673	450	49	−57	−201	−47	−280	−124	5	−7	332	ν_{34}
												630	42	153	−55	−80	−372	−178	13	26	207	π_{11}
													234	27	160	−3	−20	−19	−48	−182	41	π_{22}
														317	218	−18	−79	−56	−43	33	−195	π_{33}
															652	27	70	−42	68	−255	−355	π_{44}
																14	46	21	5	−15	−33	π_{12}
																	231	96	−6	−20	−146	π_{13}
																		61	−12	9	−29	π_{14}
																			74	−31	−26	π_{23}
																				229	17	π_{24}
																					367	π_{34}

Table 11.9

Estimated Asymptotic Covariance Matrix ($\times 10^6$) for the Simple Variant

μ_1	μ_2	μ_3	μ_4	$\phi/10$	ν_{11}	ν_{22}	ν_{33}	ν_{44}	ν_{34}	π_{11}	π_{22}	π_{33}	π_{44}	π_{12}	π_{13}	π_{14}	π_{23}	π_{24}	π_{34}	
752	81	−440	−393	−2	−421	−47	236	216	−3	−268	−39	7	109	44	158	65	2	−7	−167	μ_1
	122	−141	−62	15	−18	−55	126	47	24	−7	−45	16	21	14	−5	−2	20	11	−30	μ_2
		826	−245	−7	232	73	−385	225	−106	145	60	73	162	−34	−28	−83	4	−30	−49	μ_3
			699	−6	207	29	21	−489	86	129	24	−96	−292	−24	−125	19	−26	26	246	μ_4
				124	228	98	402	112	200	186	90	110	34	−18	−111	−57	−48	−25	48	$\phi/10$
					650	205	603	85	367	488	186	197	1	−57	−290	−141	−88	−41	181	ν_{11}
						114	274	70	158	163	102	85	17	−23	−91	−48	−52	−27	58	ν_{22}
							1674	508	482	517	257	530	265	−39	−330	−148	−151	−67	−49	ν_{33}
								643	−91	91	66	367	438	−2	−18	−71	−23	−41	−326	ν_{44}
									541	299	145	−40	−192	−29	−188	−83	−81	−35	309	ν_{34}
										372	148	162	12	−42	−221	−108	−72	−34	131	π_{11}
											91	79	17	−20	−84	−44	−46	−24	52	π_{22}
												313	273	−15	−88	−59	−38	−26	−188	π_{33}
													336	2	16	−30	−1	−18	−288	π_{44}
														6	24	12	10	5	−19	π_{12}
															137	60	43	17	−92	π_{13}
																37	19	13	−20	π_{14}
																	25	12	−30	π_{23}
																		8	−3	π_{24}
																			311	π_{34}

covariance matrix of the limiting distribution of $\sqrt{n}(\hat{\boldsymbol{\beta}} - \boldsymbol{\beta})$, where $\hat{\boldsymbol{\beta}}$ is the coefficient estimator used in the previous section (with seven elements for the extended variant), the matrix

$$\begin{bmatrix} \mathbf{I} \\ \mathbf{D} \end{bmatrix} \mathbf{V} [\mathbf{I} \quad \mathbf{D}'] \tag{9.10}$$

provides the variances and covariances of the limiting distribution of $\sqrt{T}$ times the sampling errors of all coefficient estimators including those which correspond with the left-hand parameters in (9.7) to (9.9). It is to be understood that the matrix $\mathbf{D}$ in (9.10) is evaluated at the point of the true values of the parameters. By substituting consistent estimates we obtain $\hat{\mathbf{D}}$, and

$$\begin{bmatrix} \mathbf{I} \\ \hat{\mathbf{D}} \end{bmatrix} \left(\sum_{t=1}^{T} \hat{\mathbf{X}}_t' \hat{\boldsymbol{\Omega}}^{-1} \hat{\mathbf{X}}_t \right)^{-1} [\mathbf{I} \quad \hat{\mathbf{D}}'] \tag{9.11}$$

is then the estimated asymptotic covariance matrix of the complete vector of all coefficient estimators. Its order is 22×22 for the extended variant, 20×20 for the simple variant. (In the case of the latter variant we delete the ν_{23} and ν_{24} columns of Table 11.7.) The two estimated asymptotic covariance matrices are shown in Tables 11.8 and 11.9. They both refer to the estimates obtained after convergence, so that $\hat{\mathbf{D}}$ is obtained by substituting columns (2) and (4) of Table 11.4 into the entries of Table 11.7, and the asymptotic standard errors shown in the previous section are the square roots of the diagonal elements of Tables 11.8 and 11.9. It is interesting to observe that in both cases the ϕ estimator is almost uncorrelated with the estimators of the marginal value shares. Also note that the covariances of the ν_{ij} estimators are predominantly positive. Since ϕ is equal to the sum of all ν_{ij}'s, this leads to a larger variance of the ϕ estimator than would be obtained if the ν_{ij} estimators were uncorrelated.

Problems

9.1 Carefully read the proof of the asymptotic distribution in the second and third subsections to verify that consistency is the only property of $\hat{\boldsymbol{\Omega}}$ and $\hat{\boldsymbol{\mu}}$ which is actually needed. Use this to prove that the second, third, ... estimators of the iteration have the same asymptotic distribution as the first.

9.2 Prove that under the conditions stated in the first subsection with the additional condition of normality, the two alternative F tests of Problem 8.2 are both asymptotically valid.

9.3 Check the matrix of derivatives presented in Table 11.7.

CHAPTER 12

FRONTIERS OF ECONOMETRICS

This chapter consists of a number of sections most of which have little in common except that several of them describe problems that are difficult to solve adequately, so that satisfactory solutions are not always available. Most of the sections are optional for an introductory econometrics course.

12.1 Regression Strategies[B]

It was stated in the second subsection of Section 11.1 that there are certain difficulties when the analyst performs one or several tests for the selection of a particular specification of his relation and then uses the same data to estimate the parameters of the specification selected. No special problems arise when these two successive steps are based on independent sets of data. Indeed, a plea can be made to divide the available observations into *three* parts, the first of which is used for the choice of the specification, the second for the estimation, and the third for conditional prediction based on the estimated equation in order to verify whether the method actually works. In most cases, however, the analyst feels that the number of observations is such that he would do three poor jobs if he actually followed this advice, and he decides to use the *same* set of data for the selection of the specification as well as for the estimation. This affects the sampling distribution of the estimators. To illustrate this, consider the quadratic specification $y_\alpha = \beta_0 + \beta_1 x_\alpha + \beta_2 x_\alpha^2 + \epsilon_\alpha$ and suppose that the correct specification is linear ($\beta_2 = 0$). If the null hypothesis $\beta_2 = 0$ is verified by means of the t test at the 5 percent significance level (say), the correct specification is rejected with probability .05. The estimators of this specification have the familiar normal sampling distribution only if the specification is used 100 percent of the time, not 95 percent, and so it is obvious that the sampling distribution is indeed affected by the two-step procedure.

The problem gains in importance when the procedure is applied on a larger scale with more than just two steps. Consider the following situation. The analyst knows that the dependent variable is affected by K explanatory variables, but several of these may actually be redundant because their coefficients may be zero. He is confident, however, that the first K^* variables have nonzero coefficients, and his confidence in this respect is less for the $(K^* + 1)$st variable, still less for the $(K^* + 2)$nd, and so on. How should he proceed? In the next two subsections we shall consider two different lines of action.

Extending the Set of Explanatory Variables

The "hard core" of the first K^* explanatory variables is always retained. The first step is a regression on the first $K^* + 1$ variables and a test of the hypothesis that the coefficient of the last variable [the $(K^* + 1)$st] is zero. If this hypothesis is accepted, he deletes this variable and he also disregards the variables numbered $K^* + 2, \ldots, K$ because he has even less confidence in the relevance of these variables than in the rejected $(K^* + 1)$st variable. Thus his final product consists of a regression on the first K^* variables only. If the hypothesis is rejected, he runs a regression on the first $K^* + 2$ variables and tests whether the coefficient of the $(K^* + 2)$nd variable is zero, and so on. The final result is a regression on the first $K^* + p$ variables, where p (a nonnegative integer at most equal to $K - K^*$) is such that the $(K^* + 1)$st, $\ldots$, $(K^* + p)$th variables have significant coefficients in the successive regression attempts, whereas this is not the case for the $(K^* + p + 1)$st variable.

Reducing the Set of Explanatory Variables

Next take the case in which we start from the set of all K variables and then reduce the size of this set step by step. If the regression on all K variables leads to a significant coefficient of the last (Kth) variable, this regression is the final outcome. Otherwise this variable is deleted and a new regression on $K - 1$ variables is computed. It is accepted when the $(K - 1)$st variable has a significant coefficient but rejected in favor of a regression on the first $K - 2$ variables in the opposite case, and so on. If all variables numbered $K, K - 1, \ldots, K^* + 1$ are rejected in this way, the regression which is finally accepted is that on the first K^* variables, all of which are retained. The result of this procedure is a regression on the first $K - q$ variables, where q (a nonnegative integer at most equal to $K - K^*$) is such that the Kth, . . . , $(K - q + 1)$st variables have insignificant coefficients in the successive regression attempts, whereas the $(K - q)$th variable does have a significant coefficient in attempt number $q + 1$.

The Concept of a Regression Strategy

Any form of dynamic decision making in which each successive decision is made dependent on the information available at the time when the decision has to be made is called a *strategy*. The two regression procedures described above fall under this heading, since each new computation is made dependent on the result of its predecessor; hence these procedures may be called regression strategies. Such strategies are becoming increasingly popular because of the availability of computer programs by which they are carried out automatically. At the theoretical level, however, there are still formidable unsolved problems. What is the best regression strategy? What is the best significance level at each step? Which criterion should be chosen for "best"? The answer to such questions involves the sampling distribution of the coefficients appearing in a strategy, which presents a very complicated problem. LARSON and BANCROFT (1963a, b)[1] analyzed the bias and the second moment of a conditional prediction of a value taken by the dependent variable for both regression strategies described above. They assumed that all K explanatory variables take nonstochastic values and that the disturbances are independent normal variates with zero mean and variance σ^2. It appears that the bias and the second moment of the prediction depend on the unknown true values of the coefficients and on σ^2, so that these results cannot be applied easily. Given the present state of the art, the most sensible procedure is to interpret confidence coefficients and significance limits liberally when confidence intervals and test statistics are computed from the final regression of a regression strategy in the conventional way. That is, a 95

[1] Other useful references in this general area include Bancroft (1944, 1964, 1965), Huntsberger (1955), Bozivich, Bancroft, and Hartley (1956), Kale and Bancroft (1967), Srivastava and Bancroft (1967), and Sawa (1968). Draper and Smith (1966, Chapter 6) discuss several types of regression strategies, but the sampling variability of the coefficients obtained is not considered from the point of view of a strategy.

percent confidence coefficient may actually be an 80 percent confidence coefficient and a 1 percent significance level may actually be a 10 percent level.

Not Every Two-Step Regression Procedure is a Regression Strategy

Two-step regression procedures were discussed in earlier chapters on several occasions. In Section 6.2, for example, we considered a problem of heteroscedasticity and proposed the following solution. First, estimate the equation by LS and estimate each disturbance variance σ_α^2 by $\hat{\sigma}_\alpha^2$, using the LS coefficient vector. Then, as the next step, apply weighted LS to the equation (in accordance with Aitken's theorem) but with σ_α^2 replaced by $\hat{\sigma}_\alpha^2$. Similarly, in Section 6.3 we considered a problem of correlated disturbances and proposed the following two-step procedure. First, compute a set of LS residuals, ignoring the nonzero autocorrelation. Second, estimate the first-order autocorrelation coefficient by means of these residuals and estimate the equation by LS after transforming the observations by means of the estimated autocorrelation coefficient.

The essential point for both cases is that the final result *always* consists of the regression computed in the second step. The question of whether the computation of the second step is to be carried out or not is thus not made dependent on the outcome of the first step, and this means that these regression procedures are not regression strategies. We do have a true strategy for the second example when the analyst proceeds as follows. He is not sure about whether or not the disturbances are autocorrelated, so he decides to test this by means of one of the procedures described in Chapter 5. If the null hypothesis of independence cannot be rejected at the 5 percent level, he accepts as his final result the LS regression based on the observations in their original form. If the hypothesis is rejected, he uses the regression based on the transformed observations as described in the previous paragraph. Clearly, this procedure leads to two distinct regression results, each of which has a positive probability of being accepted as the final outcome.

Problems

1.1 Consider the adjusted multiple correlation coefficient $\bar{R}$ defined in eq. (4.8) of Section 4.4. Define an analogous adjusted coefficient $\bar{R}_h$ for the regression in which the hth explanatory variable is deleted, taking account of the fact that this regression has $n - K + 1$ degrees of freedom. Prove that *any* regression strategy which at each step deletes the variable with the algebraically smallest value of $\bar{R}^2 - \bar{R}_h^2$ is identical with the corresponding strategy which at each step deletes the variable with the smallest squared partial correlation coefficient $r_{h\cdot}^2$. (*Hint.* Consider the ratio of $1 - \bar{R}^2$ to $1 - \bar{R}_{h\cdot}^2$.)

1.2 In the last subsection two examples are discussed and for one of them a strategy variant is described. Do this also for the other example.

12.2 Errors in the Variables[B]

The standard linear model assumes that neglected determining factors are the only cause of the fact that the explanatory variables do not fully account for the observed behavior of the left-hand variable. Essentially the same explanation is given by the extensions of this model that were developed in Chapter 6 and later. However, there may be other causes such as observational errors. Suppose, for example, that $\mathbf{y} = \mathbf{X}\boldsymbol{\beta} + \boldsymbol{\epsilon}$ with the $\mathbf{X}$ elements nonstochastic and $\mathscr{E}\boldsymbol{\epsilon} = \mathbf{0}$ is the correct specification, but that the last (Kth) explanatory variable is measured with error. The matrix of the actual observations on the explanatory variables is then not $\mathbf{X}$ but $\mathbf{X}_0$ (say), which differs from $\mathbf{X}$ as far as the Kth column is concerned. What can be done in such a case?

An Approach Based on Specification Analysis

Assume that $\mathbf{X}_0$ has rank K and that the observational errors may be regarded as nonstochastic, so that $\mathbf{X}_0$ consists of nonstochastic elements (just as $\mathbf{X}$ does). We may then conclude from Problem 2.2 of Section 11.2 that the expectation of the coefficient estimator $\mathbf{b}_0 = (\mathbf{X}_0'\mathbf{X}_0)^{-1}\mathbf{X}_0'\mathbf{y}$ is given by

$$(\mathscr{E}\mathbf{b}_0)_h = \begin{cases} \beta_h + p_{hK}\beta_K & h = 1, \dots, K-1 \\ p_{KK}\beta_K & h = K \end{cases} \tag{2.1}$$

where p_{hK} is the (h, K)th element of $\mathbf{P}_0 = (\mathbf{X}_0'\mathbf{X}_0)^{-1}\mathbf{X}_0'\mathbf{X}$, the coefficient matrix of the auxiliary regressions of $\mathbf{X}$ on $\mathbf{X}_0$. (Note that $\mathbf{P}_0$ is equal to the $K \times K$ unit matrix except for the Kth column.) The relevant auxiliary regression is

$$x_{\alpha K} = \sum_{h=1}^{K-1} p_{hK}x_{\alpha h} + p_{KK}x_{\alpha K}^* + \text{residual} \tag{2.2}$$

where $x_{\alpha K}$ is the αth true value of the Kth variable and $x_{\alpha K}^*$ the corresponding observed value. We conclude that if the vector of true values of this variable is orthogonal to the $K - 1$ vectors of all other variables, the coefficients of the latter variables are not subject to any specification bias. In general, however, there will be such a bias. The coefficient of the Kth variable is always subject to bias except when $p_{KK} = 1$.

Random Observational Errors

In the previous paragraph we assumed that the observational errors are nonstochastic, but most errors-in-variables models proceed under the condition that they are random. We start with the following simple case. Two variables are known to be exactly proportional:

$$y_\alpha = \beta x_\alpha \qquad \alpha = 1, \ldots, n \tag{2.3}$$

but their values are measured with error. The observed values are x_α^* and y_α^* and the errors are ξ_α and η_α:

$$x_\alpha^* = x_\alpha + \xi_\alpha \qquad y_\alpha^* = y_\alpha + \eta_\alpha \tag{2.4}$$

Therefore the relation between the observed values is not exact but subject to error:

$$y_\alpha^* = \beta x_\alpha^* + (\eta_\alpha - \beta\xi_\alpha) \qquad \alpha = 1, \ldots, n \tag{2.5}$$

It will be assumed that $\xi_1, \ldots, \xi_n$ and $\eta_1, \ldots, \eta_n$ are $2n$ independent variates with zero mean and variance $\sigma_{\xi\xi}$ and $\sigma_{\eta\eta}$, respectively.

This is the classical errors-in-variables model for the two-variable case without constant term. Note that the nonrandomness of the proportionality (2.3) excludes any influence on y_α of neglected determining factors. Thus it appears that the model is not realistic for most econometric applications, but it is easily seen that this is not so. When we add a random disturbance ϵ_α to the right-hand side of (2.3), the term in parentheses in (2.5) becomes $\epsilon_\alpha + \eta_\alpha - \beta\xi_\alpha$, which means that in the presence of disturbances the observational error η_α of (2.5) should be interpreted as including the disturbance ϵ_α.

The Inconsistency of LS Coefficient Estimators

Consider the LS estimator of β which is based on the n observations (x_α^*, y_α^*):

$$b = \frac{\sum x_\alpha^* y_\alpha^*}{\sum x_\alpha^{*2}} = \beta + \frac{\sum (x_\alpha + \xi_\alpha)(\eta_\alpha - \beta\xi_\alpha)}{\sum (x_\alpha + \xi_\alpha)^2} \tag{2.6}$$

where all summations are over α from 1 through n. Now assume that the n true values $x_1, \ldots, x_n$ are nonstochastic and that $(1/n) \sum x_\alpha^2$ converges, as $n \to \infty$, to a finite positive limit σ_{xx}. The following result is derived in Problem 2.3:

$$\operatorname*{plim}_{n\to\infty} b = \beta - \frac{\beta\sigma_{\xi\xi}}{\sigma_{xx} + \sigma_{\xi\xi}} = \beta \frac{\sigma_{xx}}{\sigma_{xx} + \sigma_{\xi\xi}} \tag{2.7}$$

This shows that b is inconsistent as soon as $\sigma_{\xi\xi} \neq 0$. The probability limit of

b has the same sign as β but it is closer to zero, and the magnitude of the inconsistency is determined by the ratio of the error variance $\sigma_{\xi\xi}$ to σ_{xx}, the limit of the mean square of the true values of the explanatory variable.

This result can be made intuitively clearer by means of Figure 12.1, which contains a point P representing the true values (x_α, y_α) of the αth observation as well as a point P^* which represents the corresponding observed values. When ξ_α is nonzero, the observation P^* is not located on a vertical straight line through P. Recall that the LS method estimates the linear relationship by minimizing the sum of the squared residuals in vertical direction; that is, the discrepancies are measured in the direction of the y axis. This is indeed an obvious procedure when the observation P^* lies on a vertical line above or below the corresponding point P on the line $y = \beta x$, but it is evidently less obvious when the explanatory variable is subject to error ($\xi_\alpha \neq 0$) and that is basically the source of the difficulty.

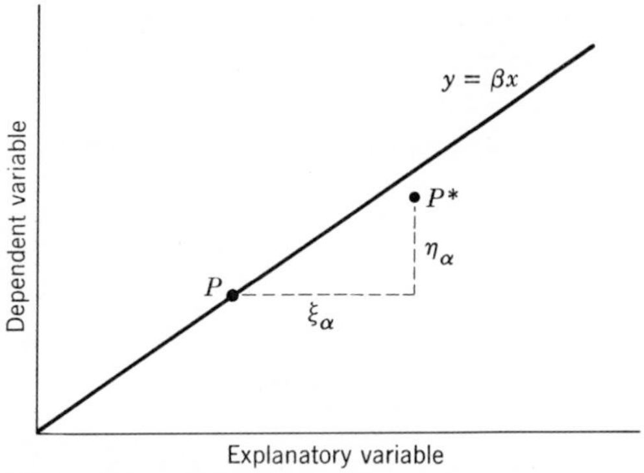

Fig. 12.1 Illustration of the inconsistency of the LS estimator when the explanatory variable is subject to error.

Attempts to Solve the Problem

The obvious question now is whether a more attractive estimator can be obtained. Under the condition that the ξ's and η's are normally distributed, one can apply the maximum-likelihood method provided that the ratio $\sigma_{\eta\eta}/\sigma_{\xi\xi}$ of the error variances is known, but this proviso is usually not fulfilled; and even if it is, the resulting estimators of β, $\sigma_{\xi\xi}$, and $\sigma_{\eta\eta}$ are not all three consistent. This may seem surprising in view of the general theorem which states that maximum-likelihood estimators are consistent under certain weak conditions. The cause of the trouble is the fact that the true values $x_1, \ldots, x_n$ act like n unknown parameters which increase in number when the sample becomes larger and larger. This violates these weak conditions. One may also use the method of instrumental variables, but the choice of an appropriate set of such variables remains a problem. For an extensive treatment of these and other procedures, none of which is really simple in application, see KENDALL and STUART (1967, Chapter 29) and MALINVAUD (1966, Chapter 10).

An approximate but simple procedure consists of a correction of the mean square of the observed values of the explanatory variable for its error component. Again consider (2.6) and imagine that we subtract from the denominator, $\sum x_\alpha^{*2}$, n times an estimate $\hat{\sigma}_{\xi\xi}$ of the error variance $\sigma_{\xi\xi}$. It is assumed that this estimate is an enlightened guess based on an evaluation of the quality of the x_α^* data. We also assume that $\hat{\sigma}_{\xi\xi}$ is stochastically independent of the ξ's and η's, so that we can operate conditionally on $\hat{\sigma}_{\xi\xi}$. The new estimator of β is thus

$$(2.8) \qquad b' = \frac{\frac{1}{n}\sum x_\alpha^* y_\alpha^*}{\frac{1}{n}\sum x_\alpha^{*2} - \hat{\sigma}_{\xi\xi}}$$

$$= \frac{\beta\frac{1}{n}\sum(x_\alpha + \xi_\alpha)^2 + \frac{1}{n}\sum(x_\alpha + \xi_\alpha)(\eta_\alpha - \beta\xi_\alpha)}{\frac{1}{n}\sum(x_\alpha + \xi_\alpha)^2 - \hat{\sigma}_{\xi\xi}}$$

It appears from Problem 2.3 below that the probability limit of this estimator is

$$(2.9) \qquad \operatorname*{plim}_{n\to\infty} b' = \beta\frac{\sigma_{xx}}{\sigma_{xx} + \sigma_{\xi\xi} - \hat{\sigma}_{\xi\xi}}$$

This shows that the inconsistency of b' is of minor importance when the error $\hat{\sigma}_{\xi\xi} - \sigma_{\xi\xi}$ of the variance estimate is small in absolute value compared with σ_{xx}. The approach can be extended (see Problem 2.4) to the general case of K explanatory variables, all of which are measured with error. The correction then involves all second-order moments of these errors.

Wald's Method of Fitting Straight Lines

WALD (1940) proposed the following procedure for estimating the slope of a simple regression with constant term under conditions of random observational errors of the explanatory variable. He divides the n observations into two groups, one consisting of the $\frac{1}{2}n$ observations with the largest values of the explanatory variable and the other containing the smallest values of this variable.[2] The division into groups is shown by the vertical dashed line in Figure 12.2. The slope of the straight line which connects the centers of gravity of the two groups (indicated by small circles in the figure) is the estimator of β.[3] (The line through the crosses will be discussed in the next paragraph.) If the observational errors of the explanatory variables are so small that the grouping according to the observed values is identical (with probability 1) to that according to the corresponding true values, this slope is a consistent estimator of β. However, this condition is very strong;

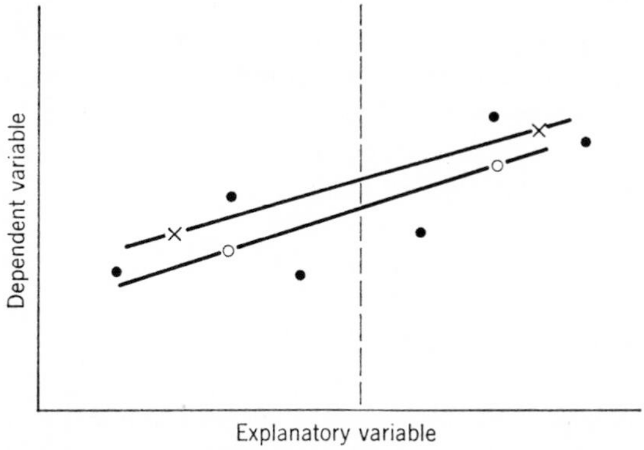

Fig. 12.2 Slope estimation based on observation groups.

it requires that the range of the random errors be finite and sufficiently small. Therefore the estimator is of limited value when the explanatory variable is indeed subject to error. See NEYMAN and SCOTT (1951).

Nevertheless, Wald's method is of practical importance when the explanatory variable is free of observational errors, because it is computationally very simple. The slope estimator is linear and unbiased under the conditions of the standard linear model, so that its variance cannot be smaller than the variance of the LS slope estimator under these conditions. The difference of the two variances depends on the values taken by the explanatory variables. This problem was analyzed by NAIR and SHRIVASTAVA (1942), BARTLETT

[2] When n is odd, the middle observation is deleted. To simplify the exposition, we assume that there are no ties in the ranking according to increasing values of the explanatory variable.

[3] The constant term estimator of this procedure is found by the condition that the regression line go through the center of gravity of all n observations (not shown in the figure). Therefore the regression line is not the line connecting the two circles but a parallel line which goes through this gravity center. The same is true for the line through the points indicated by crosses in the figure, to be discussed in the next paragraph.

(1949), THEIL and VAN IJZEREN (1956), and GIBSON and JOWETT (1957a). The result is that for a wide range of distributions of the x values (including rectangular, skew, and symmetric unimodal distributions), the best procedure is to divide the observations into three groups rather than two, with the outer groups containing about 30 percent of the observations each, and to use the slope of the straight line which connects the centers of gravity of the outer groups as the estimator of β. This is illustrated in Figure 12.2 by means of crosses. Note that this slope estimator does not use the observations of the middle group at all.[4] Deleting observations has, of course, a negative effect on the precision of the estimator, but this is more than compensated for by the fact that its denominator (the horizontal distance between the crosses) becomes larger.[5] It appears that under the conditions of the standard linear model, the variance of this estimator exceeds that of the LS estimator by about 20 or 25 percent depending on the distribution of the x's. Also see GIBSON and JOWETT (1957b) and HOOPER and THEIL (1958) for an extension of the approach to multiple regression.

A Reformulation of the Specification

It is sometimes possible to modify a specification in a plausible way such that the errors-in-variables problem is avoided. The above paragraphs indicate that this problem is indeed difficult to solve, so that it is worthwhile to avoid it if at all possible.[6] As an example we take FRIEDMAN's (1957) theory of the consumption function, which in its simplest form can be explained as follows. The consumer's income is considered to consist of two components, one of which is "permanent" and the other "transitory." By definition, the transitory component is that part of income which the consumer regards as accidental; his decisions as to the amount of consumption are determined by the other (permanent) component. Write x_α for the permanent component of income per capita in year α and y_α for consumption per capita, and assume that they are proportional except for a random disturbance: $y_\alpha = \beta x_\alpha + \epsilon_\alpha$. Permanent income cannot be measured, however. Observed income per capita, to be denoted by x_α^*, differs from permanent income x_α by $\xi_\alpha = x_\alpha^* - x_\alpha$, the transitory component, which is assumed to be a random variable. Thus, the relation formulated in terms of

[4] But the constant term estimator uses all n observations (see the previous footnote).

[5] Recall a similar phenomenon described in Section 5.1, where the power of the Goldfeld-Quandt test appears to increase when observations in the middle range are deleted.

[6] Also note that errors in explanatory variables are dangerous in a near-multicollinear situation. The coefficient estimates may then be affected drastically even when the errors are small; see subsection (4) of Section 3.9.

observed income is

$$y_\alpha = \beta x_\alpha^* + (\epsilon_\alpha - \beta \xi_\alpha) \tag{2.10}$$

which is identical with (2.5) except that the disturbance ϵ_α takes the role of the error η_α. Basically, we have the same statistical problem.

One may object to the probabilistic formulation of this model in two respects. First, the proportionality relation $y_\alpha = \beta x_\alpha + \epsilon_\alpha$ combined with the assumption that the ϵ's have constant variance implies that the disturbances play a smaller role in years with a high per capita permanent income than in low-income years. This is particularly relevant when the equation is applied to a long period in which income per capita is subject to a sizable upward trend. We can meet this objection by specifying the relation in multiplicative form:

$$y_\alpha = \beta x_\alpha e^{\epsilon'_\alpha} \qquad \text{or} \qquad \log y_\alpha = \log \beta + \log x_\alpha + \epsilon'_\alpha \tag{2.11}$$

Second, if we assume that the transitory income component $\xi_\alpha = x_\alpha^* - x_\alpha$ has a constant variance, it will also play a relatively smaller role in the high-income years. This difficulty, too, can be met by specifying that the decomposition is multiplicative. Write $x_\alpha^* = x_\alpha(1 + T_\alpha)$, where T_α is the transitory component of income measured as a fraction of permanent income. If we take logarithms on both sides and write ξ'_α for the natural logarithm of $1 + T_\alpha$, we obtain

$$\log x_\alpha^* = \log x_\alpha + \xi'_\alpha \tag{2.12}$$

and, combining this with (2.11),

$$\log \frac{y_\alpha}{x_\alpha^*} = \log \beta + (\epsilon'_\alpha - \xi'_\alpha) \tag{2.13}$$

where the left-hand variable is the logarithm of the observed consumption-income ratio. If we assume that ϵ'_α and ξ'_α have zero means, constant variances, and constant contemporaneous covariance [$\mathscr{E}(\epsilon'_\alpha \xi'_\alpha)$ independent of α], and that they are uncorrelated over time [$\mathscr{E}(\epsilon'_\alpha \epsilon'_\eta) = \mathscr{E}(\epsilon'_\alpha \xi'_\eta) = \mathscr{E}(\xi'_\alpha \xi'_\eta) = 0$ for all $\alpha \neq \eta$], the standard linear model applies directly to (2.13). We actually have a very special and simple case because the left-hand random variables of (2.13) for $\alpha = 1, \ldots, n$ are uncorrelated variates with the same mean and the same variance. As is easily verified, the LS estimator of $\log \beta$ is equal to the average of the n logarithms of y_α / x_α^*; the implied estimator of β is then the geometric mean of the observed consumption-income ratios. There may be reasonable doubt about the assumption that ϵ'_α and ξ'_α are uncorrelated over time, but this aspect can also be handled, at least under certain conditions; see Problems 2.6 and 2.7.

Problems

2.1 (*Observational errors in the dependent variable only*) Suppose that the observation matrix **X** of the explanatory variables is known without error but that the dependent variable is subject to error: $\eta_1, \ldots, \eta_n$. Formulate conditions on the η's and the disturbances $\epsilon_1, \ldots, \epsilon_n$ under which the standard linear model is applicable to the observation matrix $[\mathbf{y}^* \quad \mathbf{X}]$, where $\mathbf{y}^*$ is the vector of observations on the dependent variable.

2.2 (*Continuation*) Consider a system of simultaneous linear equations and suppose that the exogenous variables are all measured without error but that the endogenous variables are subject to error. Is it possible to extend the convenient result of the previous problem (1) when the endogenous variables do not occur in lagged form in the system, (2) when there are such lags?

2.3 Derive the following probability limits under the conditions stated below (2.5) and (2.6):

$$\text{(2.14)} \qquad \begin{aligned} \operatorname*{plim}_{n\to\infty} \frac{1}{n} \sum_{\alpha=1}^{n} (x_\alpha + \xi_\alpha)(\eta_\alpha - \beta\xi_\alpha) &= -\beta\sigma_{\xi\xi} \\ \operatorname*{plim}_{n\to\infty} \frac{1}{n} \sum_{\alpha=1}^{n} (x_\alpha + \xi_\alpha)^2 &= \sigma_{xx} + \sigma_{\xi\xi} \end{aligned}$$

Use these results to prove (2.7) and (2.9).

2.4 Prove that the estimation procedure (2.8) may be generalized to the K-element vector $(\mathbf{X}'\mathbf{X} - n\hat{\mathbf{\Sigma}})^{-1}\mathbf{X}'\mathbf{y}$, where $\hat{\mathbf{\Sigma}}$ is an estimate of the second-order moment matrix of the errors in the K explanatory variables.

2.5 Consider Figure 12.2 and write $\bar{x}_L$ for the average of the $\frac{1}{2}n$ largest values of the explanatory variable and, similarly, $\bar{x}_S$ for the average of the $\frac{1}{2}n$ smallest values. Prove that the variance of Wald's slope estimator is $4\sigma^2/n(\bar{x}_L - \bar{x}_S)^2$ under the conditions of the standard linear model.

2.6 Formulate a procedure, based on BLUS residuals, to test the null hypothesis that $\epsilon'_\alpha - \xi'_\alpha$ of (2.13) is independent over time against the alternative hypothesis of positive autocorrelation. [*Hint*. See eq. (6.8) of Section 5.6.]

2.7 (*Continuation*) Suppose that the null hypothesis is rejected and that the analyst concludes that a first-order autoregressive process,

$$\text{(2.15)} \qquad \epsilon'_\alpha - \xi'_\alpha = \rho(\epsilon'_{\alpha-1} - \xi'_{\alpha-1}) + \zeta_\alpha \qquad (0 < \rho < 1)$$

is a better approximation, the ζ's being independent random drawings from a population with zero mean and constant variance. Suppose that ρ is estimated by $\hat{\rho}$ defined in eq. (3.11) of Section 6.3 and that we apply the transformation (3.8) and (3.9) of the same section to (2.13), using the estimate $\hat{\rho}$:

$$\sqrt{1-\hat{\rho}^2}\log\frac{y_1}{x_1^*} = \sqrt{1-\hat{\rho}^2}\log\beta + \sqrt{1-\hat{\rho}^2}\,(\epsilon_1' - \xi_1') \tag{2.16}$$

$$\log\frac{y_\alpha}{x_\alpha^*} - \hat{\rho}\log\frac{y_{\alpha-1}}{x_{\alpha-1}^*} = (1-\hat{\rho})\log\beta + \hat{\zeta}_\alpha \qquad \alpha = 2, \ldots, n \tag{2.17}$$

where $\hat{\zeta}_\alpha = \zeta_\alpha - (\hat{\rho} - \rho)(\epsilon_{\alpha-1}' - \xi_{\alpha-1}')$. Prove that the resulting LS estimator of $\log\beta$ is

$$\frac{m + \dfrac{\hat{\rho}}{(1-\hat{\rho})n}\left(\log\dfrac{y_1}{x_1^*} + \log\dfrac{y_n}{x_n^*}\right)}{1 + \dfrac{2\hat{\rho}}{(1-\hat{\rho})n}} \tag{2.18}$$

where m is the average of $\log(y_1/x_1^*), \ldots, \log(y_n/x_n^*)$. Conclude that this result, when compared with the geometric-mean estimator described at the end of this section, implies a simple end-effect correction of the order $1/n$.

12.3 Robust and Distribution-Free Procedures[B]

Robustness

The confidence interval and testing procedures described in the earlier chapters are all based on the normality assumption. It is true that normality is an important case and that it can sometimes be justified by the central limit theorem, but it is equally true that the assumption is made in many cases in which it does not really hold. How serious are the consequences? To what extent is a test "robust" (insensitive to departures from the assumptions under which it is derived)?

It appears that, by and large, tests which concern first moments (such as t tests for elements of the parameter vector $\boldsymbol{\beta}$ of the expectation $\mathbf{X}\boldsymbol{\beta}$ in the standard linear model) are relatively insensitive to departures from normality, whereas tests concerning second moments such as F tests are much less robust; see KENDALL and STUART (1967, pp. 465–466). BOX and WATSON (1962) considered in particular F tests under the conditions of the standard linear model. Their main conclusion is that the robustness of these tests is largely determined by the question of whether or not the values taken by the explanatory variables form approximately a normal distribution. (Their distribution cannot be exactly normal, of course, since it is necessarily discrete.) The F tests are robust when this condition is satisfied. If, on the other hand, the histogram of these values differs considerably from the normal density, the F tests are also considerably affected by deviations of the disturbance distribution from the normal.

Distribution-Free Inference

If a random variable is not normally distributed, it can sometimes be made normal, or at least approximately so, by applying a transformation. This will often lead to other difficulties, however.[7] An alternative procedure is to design a test which is valid for a wide class of distributions, say, all continuous distributions. Such a test does not depend on the normality assumption at all and, therefore, its robustness is guaranteed. Tests of this kind are called distribution-free because they are independent of a particular form of the underlying distribution.

Two such methods are discussed below, both from THEIL (1950),[8] for testing and interval estimation of the slope β of the relation $y_\alpha = \beta_0 + \beta x_\alpha + \epsilon_\alpha$, $\alpha = 1, \ldots, n$. These methods will also give us the opportunity to discuss rank correlation coefficients, which are the distribution-free analogue of the ordinary product-moment correlation coefficient. The first of the two distribution-free regression procedures, which is developed in the next two subsections, is based on the following conditions: (1) the values $x_1, \ldots, x_n$ are fixed and (2) the disturbances $\epsilon_1, \ldots, \epsilon_n$ are either (2a) independently, identically, and continuously distributed or (2b) they are independently, symmetrically, and continuously distributed around the same median.[9] Hence it is indeed the case that no particular form of the distribution (such as the normal one) is assumed. Also note that nothing is assumed about the mean and the variance of the disturbances. The approach is thus applicable

[7] An example is provided by eq. (2.9) of Section 6.2: if $\epsilon_1, \ldots, \epsilon_n$ are not independently and normally distributed with zero mean and the same variance but $\zeta_\alpha = \epsilon_\alpha / \mathscr{E} y_\alpha$, $\alpha = 1, \ldots, n$ do satisfy this condition, one may apply the logarithmic transformation shown in eq. (2.10) of that section. The difficulty, then, is the nonlinearity in the unknown parameters. This may be solved by the numerical LS procedure described in Section 8.8, but that is attractive only when very few unknown parameters are involved.

[8] Reference should also be made to ADICHIE (1967a, b) and SEN (1968).

[9] These conditions can be weakened slightly. The crucial condition is eq. (3.2) below, and conditions (2a) and (2b) are both sufficient but not necessary for (3.2). Also, there may be random observational errors in the explanatory variable, provided the ranking according to increasing observed values of that variable coincides with the ranking according to increasing true values with probability one. This proviso is even more restrictive than the corresponding condition on Wald's method, which requires that the division of the observations into two groups never be affected by the observational errors (see the previous section).

even when these moments fail to exist. Finally, note that condition (2b) allows the disturbances to have different dispersions.

A Comparison of Slopes

Arrange the observations according to increasing values of the explanatory variable and delete the middle observation when n is odd. Write $m = \frac{1}{2}n$ and consider the slope of the straight line (see Figure 12.3) which connects the αth observation with the $(m + \alpha)$th:

$$(3.1) \qquad h_\alpha = \frac{y_\alpha - y_{m+\alpha}}{x_\alpha - x_{m+\alpha}} = \beta + \frac{\epsilon_\alpha - \epsilon_{m+\alpha}}{x_\alpha - x_{m+\alpha}} \qquad \alpha = 1, \ldots, m$$

The independence of the ϵ's implies that $h_1, \ldots, h_m$ are also independently

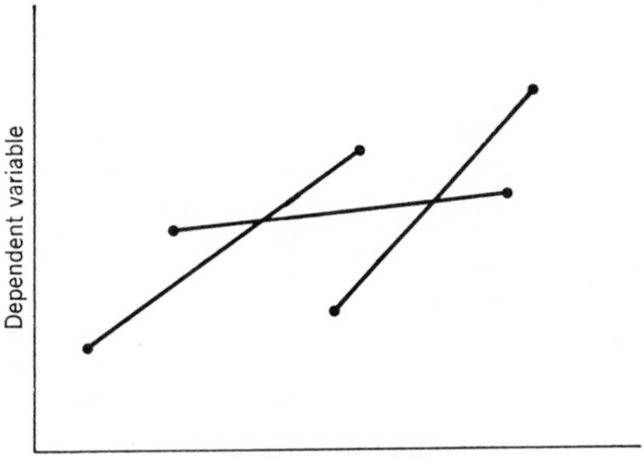

Fig. 12.3 A comparison of $\frac{1}{2}n$ slopes.

distributed. It will be shown in the next subsection that $\epsilon_\alpha - \epsilon_{m+\alpha}$ has zero median:

$$(3.2) \qquad P[\epsilon_\alpha - \epsilon_{m+\alpha} < 0] = P[\epsilon_\alpha - \epsilon_{m+\alpha} > 0] = \frac{1}{2}$$

so that $h_1, \ldots, h_m$ have median β in view of (3.1). It follows that the number of h's less than β follows the binomial distribution with parameter $\frac{1}{2}$. Thus, when the h's are rearranged in increasing order:

$$(3.3) \qquad h_{(1)} \leq h_{(2)} \leq \cdots \leq h_{(m)}$$

we have the following result:

$$(3.4) \qquad P[h_{(r)} \leq \beta \leq h_{(m-r+1)}] = 1 - 2^{1-m} \sum_{\alpha=0}^{r-1} \binom{m}{\alpha}$$

This amounts to a confidence interval with limits $h_{(r)}$ and $h_{(m-r+1)}$ and a confidence coefficient given in the right-hand side of the equation. Equivalently, if we want to test the null hypothesis $\beta = \bar{\beta}$ at the significance level corresponding to this right-hand side, we should reject it if and only if $\bar{\beta}$ is less than $h_{(r)}$ or larger than $h_{(m-r+1)}$. Table 12.1 gives a numerical illustration, taken from THEIL (1951b), for a linear relation between income and

Table 12.1

The Slope Method Applied to Consumption-Income Relationships

r	Confidence Coefficient	Confidence Interval: Lower Limit	Confidence Interval: Upper Limit
	White-collar workers ($m = 103$)		
39	.990	.84	1.01
40	.982	.85	1.00
41	.970	.86	1.00
42	.952	.87	1.00
43	.924	.87	1.00
	Blue-collar workers ($m = 139$)		
55	.989	.87	.965
56	.983	.87	.96
57	.973	.87	.96
58	.959	.88	.96
59	.938	.885	.95
60	.911	.89	.94
	Farm laborers ($m = 20$)		
5	.988	.64	1.045
6	.959	.65	1.04

total expenditure for three groups of families who participated in a Dutch budget survey conducted in 1935–1936. The expression on the right in (3.4) has been tabulated by VAN WIJNGAARDEN (1950).

Proof of the Lemma on Medians

To prove (3.2) we start with the case of condition (2a), which is illustrated in Figure 12.4*a*. The axes refer to the two disturbances, and it is imagined that their joint density function is measured vertically in the third dimension. Under condition (2a) this joint density is symmetric around the line $\epsilon_\alpha = \epsilon_{m+\alpha}$ because of the independence and the identical distribution of the two disturbances. Thus, when P_1P_2 is perpendicular to the line $\epsilon_\alpha = \epsilon_{m+\alpha}$ and when P_1 and P_2 are at opposite sides of this line but at equal distance from it, the joint density at P_1 must be equal to the joint density at P_2. Since $\epsilon_\alpha - \epsilon_{m+\alpha}$ is negative when we are above the line and positive when we are below, these two possibilities thus have equal probability. This probability is $\frac{1}{2}$ because the continuity of the disturbance distribution guarantees that the line $\epsilon_\alpha = \epsilon_{m+\alpha}$ itself has zero probability.

For the case (2b) we consider Figure 12.4*b* under the condition that the disturbance distributions have zero median. (When the median takes any other value we can apply the same argument after subtracting this value from ϵ_α

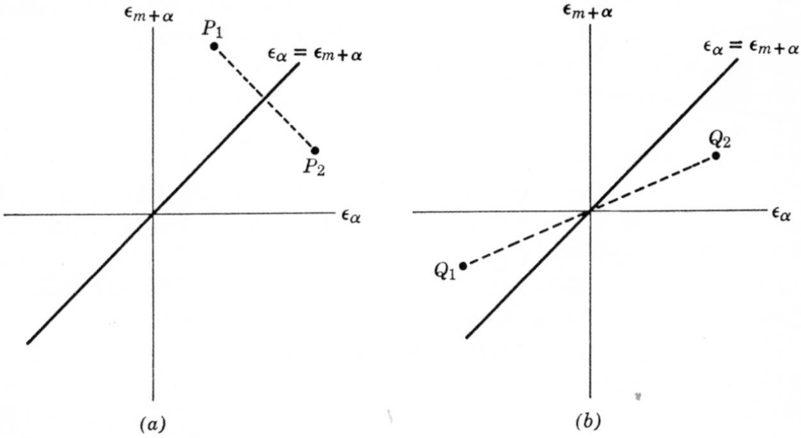

Fig. 12.4 The lemma on medians.

and $\epsilon_{m+\alpha}$.) The joint density is now symmetric around the origin because of the independence and the symmetry of the two marginal distributions: $f(x, y) \equiv f(-x, -y)$, where $f(\ )$ is the joint density function of the two ϵ's. The argument of the points P_1 and P_2 may now be applied to Q_1 and Q_2 (at equal distance from the origin) with the same result.

Tests Based on Rank Correlation Coefficients

Figure 12.3 suggests a simple linearity test against the alternative that the relation between the two variables is convex or concave. If the null hypothesis is true, the successive slopes $h_1, \ldots, h_m$ will not show any appreciable trend, but they will tend either to increase or to decrease when the alternative hypothesis is true. An obvious comparison is then between the ranking of the slopes according to increasing values of the explanatory variable and that according to increasing values of the slopes themselves. For example, take $m = 5$ and $h_1 = .61$, $h_2 = .75$, $h_3 = .50$, $h_4 = 1.09$, and $h_5 = .81$. Then the two rankings are the following permutations of the first five integers:

$$\begin{matrix} 1 & 2 & 3 & 4 & 5 \\ 2 & 3 & 1 & 5 & 4 \end{matrix} \tag{3.5}$$

The numbers on the first line form the ranking according to increasing values of the explanatory variable, and those on the second line form the ranking according to increasing slopes. To test the linearity hypothesis one may compute the correlation coefficient of the five pairs of numbers given in (3.5). This coefficient, known as Spearman's rank correlation coefficient, is symmetrically distributed with zero mean and variance $1/(m-1)$ under the null hypothesis that all $m!$ permutations are equally probable.

An alternative procedure consists of counting the number of inversions of the two permutations. In (3.5) we have three inversions for the second ranking compared with the first: 2-1, 3-1, and 5-4. The number of such inversions, v, say, ranges from 0 to $\frac{1}{2}m(m-1)$; in the case of (3.5) the first limit is reached when the second ranking is 1, 2, 3, 4, 5 and the second limit when this ranking is 5, 4, 3, 2, 1. Thus, $1 - 4v/m(m-1)$ may be regarded as another rank correlation coefficient which ranges from -1 to 1. Its distribution under the above null hypothesis is symmetric with zero mean and variance $2(2m+5)/9m(m-1)$. The exact distribution for $m = 4, 5, \ldots, 10$ has been tabulated by KENDALL (1962), whose work in this area contributed much to its popularity. For $m > 10$ a normal approximation may be used with little loss of accuracy. For proofs and additional details, see Kendall and Stuart (1967, Chapter 31).

A Comparison of All Possible Slopes

We return to the slope method described in the third subsection and consider now the slopes of the straight lines through all pairs of points:

$$H_{\alpha\eta} = \frac{y_\alpha - y_\eta}{x_\alpha - x_\eta} = \beta + \frac{\epsilon_\alpha - \epsilon_\eta}{x_\alpha - x_\eta} \qquad \alpha < \eta \tag{3.6}$$

For $\eta = m + \alpha$ we have $H_{\alpha\eta} = h_\alpha$ defined in (3.1). The present number of slopes is $\frac{1}{2}n(n-1)$, and they are obviously not independent, but they can nevertheless be used to obtain a confidence interval for β under conditions (1) and (2a). [Condition (2b) is not applicable here.] The argument is as follows. When the observations are arranged in the order of increasing x values in (3.6), so that $x_\alpha < x_\eta$ in view of $\alpha < \eta$, the sign of $H_{\alpha\eta} - \beta$ is always opposite to that of $\epsilon_\alpha - \epsilon_\eta$. Imagine, then, that we reject the null hypothesis $\beta = \bar{\beta}$ if and only if the ranking of the observations according to increasing x values has a significant correlation with the ranking according to increasing values of the disturbances implied by the null hypothesis. This idea is illustrated in Figure 12.5 for $n = 4$ and for a case of positive correlation between the two rankings. The picture suggests that $\bar{\beta}$ must be lower than the true slope.[10] If a slope is selected which is sufficiently larger than $\bar{\beta}$, the corresponding steeper line will reduce the rank correlation.

We shall measure the rank correlation by means of the number of inversions as described in the previous subsection. That number is equal to the number of pairs (α, η) in (3.6) for which $\epsilon_\alpha > \epsilon_\eta$ because $\alpha < \eta$ is specified there and this implies $x_\alpha < x_\eta$. We found above that $H_{\alpha\eta} < \beta$ if and only if

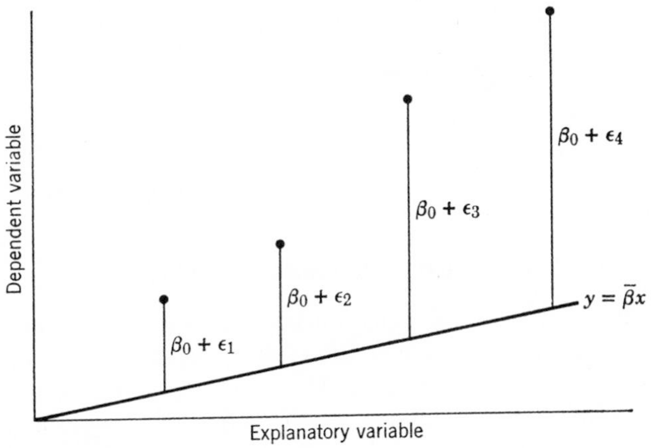

Fig. 12.5 Rank correlation between disturbances and explanatory variable.

$\epsilon_\alpha > \epsilon_\eta$. Hence the number of $H_{\alpha\eta}$'s smaller than β is distributed as the number of inversions. So we rearrange the H's according to increasing magnitude:

$$H_{(1)} \leq H_{(2)} \leq \cdots \leq H_{(N)} \quad \text{where} \quad N = \frac{1}{2}n(n-1) \tag{3.7}$$

and formulate a confidence interval of the form

$$\mathrm{P}[H_{(r)} \leq \beta \leq H_{(N-r+1)}] = 1 - 2p(n, r) \tag{3.8}$$

where $p(n, r)$ is the probability that there are fewer than r inversions for two permutations of the first n integers, the first being $1, 2, \ldots, n$ and the second random such that all $n!$ permutations are equally probable. This probability can be determined for any pair (n, r) from Kendall's table or the normal approximation mentioned in the previous subsection.

[10] Note that the line implied by the null hypothesis is drawn through the origin, so that the vertical distances of the observations from this line include the constant term (β_0) as well as the disturbances.

Problems

3.1 For $m = 15$ we have the following slopes $h_1, \ldots, h_{15}$, arranged according to increasing values of the explanatory variable:

(1) .16	(4) .37	(7) .50	(10) .12	(13) .78
(2) −.39	(5) −.12	(8) .40	(11) .37	(14) .68
(3) .14	(6) .18	(9) .38	(12) .25	(15) .13

Apply the rank test based on inversions to verify whether there is any evidence that the relation is convex or concave. Use the normal approximation of the distribution of the number of inversions and take your own level of significance.

3.2 For $n = 6$ we have $\frac{1}{2}n(n-1) = 15$ slopes $H_{\alpha\eta}$. Interpret the 15 numerical values of the previous problem now as $H_{\alpha\eta}$'s and formulate a confidence interval based on (3.8). Use Kendall's table for $p(n, r)$.

12.4 Models with Random Coefficients[B]

In the analysis of the basic equation $\mathbf{y} = \mathbf{X}\boldsymbol{\beta} + \boldsymbol{\epsilon}$ and its various extensions, it was always assumed that the right-hand variables affect the left-hand variable with fixed coefficients. This is a restrictive assumption and a plea can be made for randomness. For example, if a right-hand variable increases by one unit, all other factors remaining constant, the left-hand variable may respond with a random increase with a certain mean and a positive variance.[11] Such models will be considered in this section.

Assumptions for a Simple Case

Consider the simplest case of two variables with no constant term. Write y_α for the change in the dependent variable in year α and suppose that it is proportional to the change in the explanatory variable in that year, written x_α, except for a random disturbance. (To simplify the notation we use no Δ operator to indicate changes.) It is assumed that the proportionality "constant" fluctuates randomly from one observation to the next. Hence the basic equation is of the following form:

$$y_\alpha = b_\alpha x_\alpha + \epsilon_\alpha \qquad \alpha = 1, \ldots, n \tag{4.1}$$

[11] In the aggregation analysis of Section 11.5 we also worked with random coefficients, but it should be stressed that this is an entirely different matter. The randomness considered there is based on the random selection of the economic agent whose behavior is described by the equation. *Given* that a particular agent is selected, the coefficients of the corresponding equation cease to be random.

The objective is to estimate the mean β of b_α, its variance σ_1^2, and the disturbance variance σ_0^2. The b_α's are thus assumed to be homoscedastic and to have the same mean. To simplify the analysis we shall also assume that $\epsilon_1, \ldots, \epsilon_n, b_1, \ldots, b_n$ are all uncorrelated:

$$\mathscr{E}\begin{bmatrix}\epsilon_\alpha \\ b_\alpha\end{bmatrix} = \begin{bmatrix}0 \\ \beta\end{bmatrix} \qquad \mathscr{V}\begin{bmatrix}\epsilon_\alpha \\ b_\alpha\end{bmatrix} = \begin{bmatrix}\sigma_0^2 & 0 \\ 0 & \sigma_1^2\end{bmatrix} \qquad \alpha = 1, \ldots, n \tag{4.2}$$

$$\mathscr{E}\left(\begin{bmatrix}\epsilon_\alpha \\ b_\alpha - \beta\end{bmatrix}[\epsilon_\eta \quad b_\eta - \beta]\right) = \mathbf{0} \quad \text{for} \quad \alpha \neq \eta \tag{4.3}$$

An LS and a GLS Approach

Write (4.1) in the form $y_\alpha = \beta x_\alpha + \epsilon_\alpha^*$, where $\epsilon_\alpha^* = (b_\alpha - \beta)x_\alpha + \epsilon_\alpha$, and consider the LS coefficient b as an estimator of the expectation β of the random b_α's:

$$b = \frac{\sum x_\alpha y_\alpha}{\sum x_\alpha^2} = \beta + \frac{\sum x_\alpha \epsilon_\alpha^*}{\sum x_\alpha^2} = \beta + \frac{\sum x_\alpha^2(b_\alpha - \beta) + \sum x_\alpha \epsilon_\alpha}{\sum x_\alpha^2} \tag{4.4}$$

where all summations are over α from 1 through n. This estimator is unbiased, it is linear in $y_1, \ldots, y_n$, and it has the following variance:

$$\text{var } b = \frac{\sigma_0^2}{\sum x_\alpha^2} + \frac{\sigma_1^2 \sum x_\alpha^4}{(\sum x_\alpha^2)^2} \tag{4.5}$$

but it is not best linear unbiased because ϵ_α^*, $\alpha = 1, \ldots, n$ are uncorrelated random variables with zero mean and variances of the form $\sigma_0^2 + \sigma_1^2 x_\alpha^2$. This means that we are basically in a heteroscedastic situation as far as the estimation of β is concerned. Aitken's theorem suggests the use of

$$\left(\sum_{\alpha=1}^{n} \frac{x_\alpha y_\alpha}{\sigma_0^2 + \sigma_1^2 x_\alpha^2}\right) \Bigg/ \left(\sum_{\alpha=1}^{n} \frac{x_\alpha^2}{\sigma_0^2 + \sigma_1^2 x_\alpha^2}\right) \tag{4.6}$$

as the estimator of β, the variance of which is equal to the reciprocal of its own denominator. The difficulty is obviously that σ_0^2 and σ_1^2 in (4.6) are unknown. Therefore we shall consider an approximation procedure similar to that of Section 6.2.

An Approximative GLS Approach

To estimate σ_0^2 and σ_1^2 we consider the LS residuals:

$$\begin{aligned} e_\alpha &= y_\alpha - b x_\alpha \\ &= (b_\alpha - \beta)x_\alpha - (b - \beta)x_\alpha + \epsilon_\alpha \end{aligned} \tag{4.7}$$

Consider in particular the variance of (say) the first residual, using (4.4) and (4.5):

$$\begin{aligned}\text{var } e_1 &= x_1^2 \text{ var } b_1 + x_1^2 \text{ var } b + \text{var } \epsilon_1 - 2x_1^2 \text{ cov } (b_1, b) \\ &\quad + 2x_1 \text{ cov } (b_1, \epsilon_1) - 2x_1 \text{ cov } (b, \epsilon_1) \\ &= \sigma_1^2 x_1^2 + \frac{\sigma_0^2 x_1^2}{\sum x_\alpha^2} + \frac{\sigma_1^2 x_1^2 \sum x_\alpha^4}{(\sum x_\alpha^2)^2} + \sigma_0^2 - 2\frac{\sigma_1^2 x_1^4}{\sum x_\alpha^2} + 0 - 2\frac{\sigma_0^2 x_1^2}{\sum x_\alpha^2} \\ &= \sigma_0^2\left[1 - \frac{x_1^2}{\sum x_\alpha^2}\right] + \sigma_1^2 x_1^2 \left[1 - 2\frac{x_1^2}{\sum x_\alpha^2} + \frac{\sum x_\alpha^4}{(\sum x_\alpha^2)^2}\right]\end{aligned}$$

Thus, the variance of the αth residual is

$$\text{var } e_\alpha = \sigma_0^2 P_\alpha + \sigma_1^2 Q_\alpha \tag{4.8}$$

with P_α and Q_α defined as the following known functions of the known x's:

$$P_\alpha = 1 - \frac{x_\alpha^2}{\sum x^2} \qquad Q_\alpha = x_\alpha^2\left[1 - 2\frac{x_\alpha^2}{\sum x^2} + \frac{\sum x^4}{(\sum x^2)^2}\right] \tag{4.9}$$

where $\sum x^2$ stands for $x_1^2 + \cdots + x_n^2$ (similarly for $\sum x^4$).

Since e_α has zero expectation, the left-hand side of (4.8) is the expectation of e_α^2, so that we can write this equation in the form

$$e_\alpha^2 = \sigma_0^2 P_\alpha + \sigma_1^2 Q_\alpha + f_\alpha \quad \text{where} \quad \mathscr{E} f_\alpha = 0 \tag{4.10}$$

with f_α defined as the deviation of e_α^2 from its own expectation. Given that P_α and Q_α are known, the formulation (4.10) suggests that σ_0^2 and σ_1^2 can be estimated by running a regression of e_α^2 on P_α and Q_α with f_α treated as a disturbance. To find out which regression method is appropriate we need the covariance matrix of f_α, which will now be derived under the condition that b_α and ϵ_α (and hence also e_α) are normally distributed; this assumption will simplify the results drastically. So consider the variance of f_α:

$$\begin{aligned}\text{var } f_\alpha &= \mathscr{E}(e_\alpha^2 - \mathscr{E} e_\alpha^2)^2 = \mathscr{E} e_\alpha^4 - (\mathscr{E} e_\alpha^2)^2 = 2(\mathscr{E} e_\alpha^2)^2 \\ &= 2(\sigma_0^2 P_\alpha + \sigma_1^2 Q_\alpha)^2\end{aligned} \tag{4.11}$$

where the third step is based on the fact that the fourth moment about the mean of a normal variate is equal to three times the square of the variance. The problem of the covariance of two different f's, $\mathscr{E}(f_\alpha f_\eta)$ for $\alpha \neq \eta$, is considered in Problems 4.1 to 4.3. It turns out that they are small compared with the variances and that it is asymptotically correct to neglect them. In other words, we shall proceed as if the disturbances $f_1, \ldots, f_n$ of (4.10) are uncorrelated random variables with zero mean and variances of the form (4.11). But this is precisely the heteroscedastic situation described in detail in

Section 6.2 [see eq. (2.5) of that section] because the variance (4.11) is proportional to the square of the expectation of the dependent variable in (4.10). Therefore we shall follow the procedure of Section 6.2 to obtain estimates of σ_0^2 and σ_1^2, after which these estimates will be used to estimate β along the lines of (4.6).

A Numerical Illustration

Following THEIL and MENNES (1959), who developed the procedure, we shall use British import and export price data and define x_α as the percentage change in the import price index and y_α as the percentage change in the export price index. Equation (4.1) thus implies that the latter change is a random multiple of the former change plus a random disturbance. The sample ($n = 65$) consists of annual observations of the period 1870 to 1952 excluding war periods.

The first step consists of an LS regression of squared LS residuals on P_α and Q_α in accordance with (4.10), which leads to preliminary estimates s_0^2 and s_1^2 of σ_0^2 and σ_1^2, respectively:

$$\begin{bmatrix} \sum P_\alpha e_\alpha^2 \\ \sum Q_\alpha e_\alpha^2 \end{bmatrix} = \begin{bmatrix} \sum P_\alpha^2 & \sum P_\alpha Q_\alpha \\ \sum P_\alpha Q_\alpha & \sum Q_\alpha^2 \end{bmatrix} \begin{bmatrix} s_0^2 \\ s_1^2 \end{bmatrix} \tag{4.12}$$

This gives $s_0^2 = 11.5$ and $s_1^2 = .044$ for the British price data. Next apply weighted LS to (4.10), the weight of the αth observation being the reciprocal of the standard deviation of f_α. This standard deviation follows from (4.11), and we substitute s_0^2 for σ_0^2 and s_1^2 for σ_1^2:

$$\begin{bmatrix} \sum w_\alpha P_\alpha e_\alpha^2 \\ \sum w_\alpha Q_\alpha e_\alpha^2 \end{bmatrix} = \begin{bmatrix} \sum w_\alpha P_\alpha^2 & \sum w_\alpha P_\alpha Q_\alpha \\ \sum w_\alpha P_\alpha Q_\alpha & \sum w_\alpha Q_\alpha^2 \end{bmatrix} \begin{bmatrix} \hat\sigma_0^2 \\ \hat\sigma_1^2 \end{bmatrix} \tag{4.13}$$

where

$$w_\alpha = \frac{1}{2}(s_0^2 P_\alpha + s_1^2 Q_\alpha)^{-2} \tag{4.14}$$

The solutions are $\hat\sigma_0^2 = 9.7$ and $\hat\sigma_1^2 = .075$ for our sample. The inverse of the 2×2 matrix in the right-hand side of (4.13) is an approximate covariance matrix, and the square roots of the diagonal elements of this inverse provide asymptotic standard errors: 2.4 for $\hat\sigma_0^2$ and .033 for $\hat\sigma_1^2$.

Finally, we estimate β by weighted LS as the ratio (4.6) with σ_0^2, σ_1^2 replaced by $\hat\sigma_0^2$, $\hat\sigma_1^2$, which gives $\hat\beta = .855$ with asymptotic standard error .078 (determined as the square root of the reciprocal of the denominator). The LS estimate b of β is .795 and its standard error [determined from (4.5) with σ_0^2, σ_1^2 replaced by $\hat\sigma_0^2$, $\hat\sigma_1^2$] is .098; hence the LS estimate of β is below the weighted LS estimate and its standard error is larger. If we accept the three point estimates ($\hat{\beta}$, $\hat{\sigma}_0^2$, and $\hat{\sigma}_1^2$), we may conclude that the percentage change in the export price level is subject to an additive disturbance with zero mean and standard deviation $\hat{\sigma}_0 = 3.1$, and that it is affected by percentage changes in the import price level on the basis of a random multiplicative coefficient whose expectation is $\hat{\beta} = .855$ and whose standard deviation is $\hat{\sigma}_1 = .27$.

The Goodness of Fit of the Regression of the Squared Residuals

The unknown parameters σ_0^2 and σ_1^2 are constrained to be nonnegative, but the normal equations (4.12) and (4.13) do not exclude negative solutions as estimates. Indeed, one should expect that negative solutions will be rather frequent unless the sample is quite large, because the regression associated with these normal equations is characterized by a poor fit and thus leads to estimators with considerable sampling variability. To prove that the fit is poor, write (4.10) in the form $e_\alpha^2 = \mathscr{E}e_\alpha^2 + f_\alpha$, square both sides, take the expectation, and average the result over the n observations:

(4.15)
$$\frac{1}{n}\sum_{\alpha=1}^{n}\mathscr{E}e_\alpha^4 = \frac{1}{n}\sum_{\alpha=1}^{n}(\mathscr{E}e_\alpha^2)^2 + \frac{1}{n}\sum_{\alpha=1}^{n}\mathscr{E}f_\alpha^2$$

It follows from (4.11) that under the normality condition, the second term on the right is twice as large as the first. Hence the systematic part of (4.10), $\sigma_0^2 P_\alpha + \sigma_1^2 Q_\alpha$, accounts for only one-third of the behavior of the dependent variable ($e_1^2, \ldots, e_n^2$) as measured by the second-moment expression in the left-hand side of (4.15).[12] Therefore a rather considerable number of observations will be needed to estimate σ_0^2 and σ_1^2 with reasonable precision.

Extensions and Other Estimation Methods

The procedure can be extended to the general case of K explanatory variables with random coefficients $b_{\alpha 1}, \ldots, b_{\alpha K}$ for the αth observation. The expectations of these coefficients are $\beta_1, \ldots, \beta_K$ and their covariance matrix $[\sigma_{hk}]$ is by its nature constrained to be positive semidefinite. Such a specification has K unknown β's, $\frac{1}{2}K(K+1)$ unknown variances and covariances of the form σ_{hk}, and an unknown disturbance variance. Clearly, a sizable sample is needed if all these parameters are to be estimated with any degree of precision. A relatively substantial reduction of the number of unknowns is obtained when $b_{\alpha 1}, \ldots, b_{\alpha K}$ are postulated to be uncorrelated, but the

[12] This amounts to a population value of R^2 equal to $\frac{1}{3}$ if we define this on the basis of moments around zero (rather than around the mean). The observed R^2 corresponding to the LS estimate of (4.10) is .37 for the import-export price example, which is a satisfactory agreement.

number of parameters is still as large as $2K + 1$ (instead of the $K + 1$ of the standard linear model); in addition, there are K nonnegativity constraints, $\sigma_{hh} \geq 0$ for $h = 1, \ldots, K$. Reference is made to the original article by Theil and Mennes (1959) and also to an article by HILDRETH and HOUCK (1968) in which a quadratic programming approach is proposed to ensure that the variance estimates will be nonnegative.

The first authors who considered models with random coefficients were HURWICZ (1950b) and RUBIN (1950b). Rubin applied the maximum-likelihood method, but the solution appears to be complicated. Reference should also be made to articles by C. R. RAO (1965b), SWAMY and MADDALA (1968), and ROSENBERG (1967).

Problems

4.1 Use eq. (4.7) to derive the following covariance of the LS residuals e_α and e_η ($\alpha \neq \eta$):

$$(4.16) \qquad \mathscr{E}(e_\alpha e_\eta) = -\frac{x_\alpha x_\eta}{\sum x^2}\left[\sigma_0^2 + \sigma_1^2\left(x_\alpha^2 + x_\eta^2 - \frac{\sum x^4}{\sum x^2}\right)\right]$$

Next apply Problem 5.6 of Section 2.5 to prove that the covariance of f_α and f_η is equal to twice the square of the covariance (4.16). Finally, combine this result with (4.11) to prove that if $(1/n)\sum x_\alpha^2$ and $(1/n)\sum x_\alpha^4$ both converge to finite positive limits as $n \to \infty$, the correlation of f_α and f_η is $O(n^{-2})$.

4.2 (*Continuation*) Write $\mathbf{D}$ for the $n \times n$ diagonal matrix whose αth diagonal element is $\sqrt{2}(\sigma_0^2 P_\alpha + \sigma_1^2 Q_\alpha)$ and show that the weighted LS estimator of $[\sigma_0^2 \quad \sigma_1^2]'$ described below (4.11) is of the form

$$(4.17) \qquad (\mathbf{X}'\mathbf{D}^{-2}\mathbf{X})^{-1}\mathbf{X}'\mathbf{D}^{-2}\mathbf{y}$$

where $[\mathbf{y} \quad \mathbf{X}]$ is the $n \times 3$ matrix whose αth row is $[e_\alpha^2 \vdots P_\alpha \quad Q_\alpha]$. Also prove that the covariance matrix of $f_1, \ldots, f_n$ can be written as $\mathbf{D}(\mathbf{I} + n^{-2}\mathbf{G})\mathbf{D}$, where $n^{-2}\mathbf{G}$ is a symmetric matrix with zeros on the diagonal and the correlation coefficients of the f's elsewhere, and conclude from the previous problem that $g_{\alpha\eta}$, the (α, η)th element of $\mathbf{G}$, converges to a finite limit as $n \to \infty$ for any pair (α, η). Finally, prove that the estimator (4.17) is unbiased, that its covariance matrix can be written as the sum of two matrices:

$$(4.18) \quad (\mathbf{X}'\mathbf{D}^{-2}\mathbf{X})^{-1} + (\mathbf{X}'\mathbf{D}^{-2}\mathbf{X})^{-1}\left(\frac{1}{n^2}\mathbf{X}'\mathbf{D}^{-1}\mathbf{G}\mathbf{D}^{-1}\mathbf{X}\right)(\mathbf{X}'\mathbf{D}^{-2}\mathbf{X})^{-1}$$

and that under the limit conditions stated at the end of the previous problem, the four elements of the first matrix are $O(n^{-1})$ and those of the second are $O(n^{-2})$. [*Hint.* Prove that the (h, k)th element of the matrix $n^{-2}\mathbf{X}'\mathbf{D}^{-1}\mathbf{G}\mathbf{D}\mathbf{X}$ is

$$\frac{1}{n^2}\sum_{\alpha=1}^{n}\sum_{\eta=1}^{n}\frac{g_{\alpha\eta}x_{\alpha h}x_{\eta k}}{2(\sigma_0^2P_\alpha+\sigma_1^2Q_\alpha)(\sigma_0^2P_\eta+\sigma_1^2Q_\eta)}=O(1) \tag{4.19}$$

where $x_{\alpha h}$ is either P_α or Q_α.]

4.3 (*Continuation*) The derivations of the previous problem, which shows that it is asymptotically correct to use $(\mathbf{X}'\mathbf{D}^{-2}\mathbf{X})^{-1}$ as the covariance matrix of the weighted LS estimators of σ_0^2 and σ_1^2, are based on the use of the diagonal matrix $\mathbf{D}^2$ as an approximate covariance matrix of $f_1, \ldots, f_n$. Note that this is a fixed matrix, not a random estimator of the true disturbance covariance matrix as in the cases analyzed in Section 8.6. But if we replace σ_0^2 and σ_1^2 in the diagonal elements of $\mathbf{D}$ by s_0^2 and s_1^2, as is done in (4.13) and (4.14), we have a situation of the type considered in Section 8.6. Analyze this situation and describe the conditions under which the limiting distribution of $\hat{\sigma}_0^2$ and $\hat{\sigma}_1^2$ is in accordance with the asymptotic standard errors described below (4.14).

12.5 Probit Analysis and Logit Analysis[B]

There are several situations in which the dependent variable has a dichotomous character. For example, the analyst may be interested in the factors which determine the question of whether a family buys a car in a certain year. These factors are then the explanatory variables and what they try to explain is whether "buy" or "not buy" is the event which actually takes place.

A Dummy Variable as Dependent Variable

When explanatory variables are dichotomous, we can represent them by dummy variables; see subsection (1) of Section 3.9. Hence it seems worthwhile to try the same approach for the dependent variable. Suppose, then, that the question of whether or not the αth family buys a car is determined by its income (x_α) except for random effects. Define $y_\alpha = 1$ if the family actually buys a car and $y_\alpha = 0$ if it does not, and consider the linear equation

$$y_\alpha = \beta_0 + \beta x_\alpha + \epsilon_\alpha \tag{5.1}$$

where ϵ_α is a random disturbance.

It is easily seen that (5.1) cannot be an attractive specification. The systematic part of the right-hand side, $\beta_0 + \beta x_\alpha$, may be larger than 1 and smaller than 0 (depending on the value of income), whereas y_α cannot lie outside these limits. In fact, y_α takes only two values (0 and 1), which means that the disturbance ϵ_α given x_α can also take only two values: $-(\beta_0 + \beta x_\alpha)$ and $1 - (\beta_0 + \beta x_\alpha)$. If ϵ_α is to have zero expectation for whatever value of x_α, it should take the former value with probability $1 - (\beta_0 + \beta x_\alpha)$ and the latter with probability $\beta_0 + \beta x_\alpha$. But we just showed that $\beta_0 + \beta x_\alpha$ may be negative or larger than one, so it seems that the approach is not very promising.[13]

Conditional Probabilities and Their Transformations

Returning temporarily to the standard linear model, suppose that y_α of (5.1) is the amount spent by the αth household on a certain commodity and that this model is applicable to this equation. Then (5.1) states that the conditional distribution of y_α given x_α has mean $\beta_0 + \beta x_\alpha$ and variance σ^2. Nothing is specified about the actual amount spent by a particular household; the model is merely concerned with the set of all households with income x_α and, therefore, it is entirely probabilistic.

The situation in the case of car purchase is basically the same. There is no way of knowing whether a particular person will buy a car when his income is x_α. In a case like this we are interested in the *conditional probability* of car purchase, given that the income is equal to x_α, and in the way in which this conditional probability varies when income takes different values. This is completely analogous to the case of the previous paragraph, which is concerned with the conditional distribution of the amount spent, given income, and in the way in which this conditional distribution varies when income varies.

The object of the analysis is thus a probability, which implies that we have to face the problem that this is a quantity which is confined to the interval from zero to one. Since this aspect is awkward in regression-type situations, there is some merit in applying a monotonic transformation to the probability as is shown in Figure 12.6. The probability p is measured along the horizontal axis and its transformation along the vertical axis. When p increases from 0 to 1, its transform increases from $-\infty$ to ∞ and thus avoids the problem of a finite range. There are infinitely many transformations with this property, but two are more popular than others: the probit and the logit transformations.

[13] It is possible, however, to work with a dependent dummy variable when one formulates a model in which the explanatory variable is random and subject to appropriate conditional distributions given "buy" and "not buy." This approach is related to that of Section 4.7 where the explanatory variables are also random. See WARNER (1963, 1967) for the case in which these conditional distributions are normal.

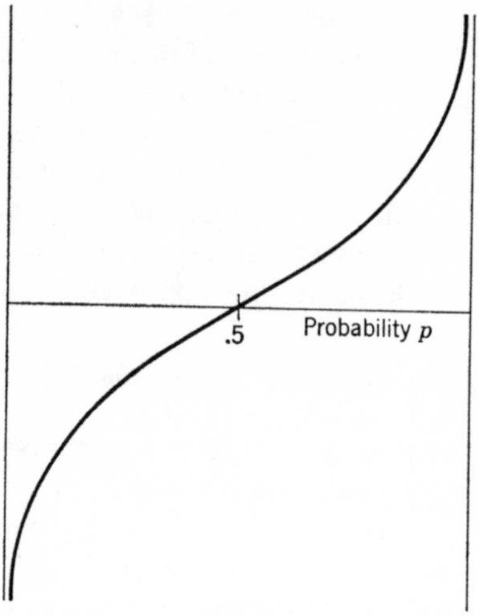

Fig. 12.6 Monotonic transformation of a probability to the range $(-\infty, \infty)$.

Probit Analysis

Write $F(\ )$ for the cumulated distribution function of a standardized normal variate and define y implicitly by $F(y) = p$, where p is the probability of Figure 12.6. The transformation used in probit analysis is $y = F^{-1}(p)$, $F^{-1}(\ )$ being the inverse function corresponding to $F(\ )$, and it is readily seen that this transformation has the general form indicated in the figure and that its curve intersects the horizontal axis at $p = .5$.

Probit analysis originated in biology, and its application in that area can be justified on the following grounds. An analyst is interested in the effect of some drug on the survival of a large number of insects. One possibility is that each insect survives until a certain critical dosage is reached and that they all die as soon as this limit is surpassed; but that is an extreme case. It is much more plausible that the critical level varies from one insect to the other according to a certain distribution. When there are many independent factors determining the critical level for each insect, the central limit theorem may be used to justify the choice of the normal distribution. Thus, when p is the proportion of insects killed, the analyst applies the probit transformation $y = F^{-1}(p)$ and he then proceeds to express y linearly in terms of the dosage of the drug.

Returning to the example of car purchase, we have family income as the variable which takes the role of the drug of the insect case. The assumption is thus that the critical level at which a family decides to buy a car varies from one family to the other, and that the distribution of these critical levels is of the normal type. Write $p(x)$ for the conditional probability of car purchase given that income equals x; then the probit specification is

$$p(x) = F(\beta_0 + \beta x) = \frac{1}{\sqrt{2\pi}} \int_{-\infty}^{\beta_0+\beta x} e^{-\xi^2/2}\, d\xi \tag{5.2}$$

or, equivalently,

$$F^{-1}(p(x)) = \beta_0 + \beta x \tag{5.3}$$

To estimate the parameters β_0 and β one can apply the maximum-likelihood method. Let $x_1, \ldots, x_n$ be the given income values of the sample and suppose that we arrange the observations such that the first n' families are the buyers and the last $n - n'$ families are the nonbuyers. The logarithmic likelihood function can then be written as

$$\sum_{\alpha=1}^{n'} \log p(x_\alpha) + \sum_{\alpha=n'+1}^{n} \log [1 - p(x_\alpha)] \tag{5.4}$$

where each $p(x_\alpha)$ is of the form (5.2) and is thus a function of β_0 and β. By differentiating (5.4) with respect to these parameters and equating the derivatives to zero, one obtains nonlinear equations from which estimates can be derived numerically by an iterative procedure. For details, see FINNEY's monograph (1964).

Extensions

The approach can be generalized to the case of two or more explanatory variables. For example, the probability of a car purchase may depend on the household's income as well as on the age of the present car. Write $x_{\alpha 1}$ and $x_{\alpha 2}$ for the values taken by these two variables for the αth household; then the conditional probability $p(x_{\alpha 1}, x_{\alpha 2})$ is equal to the third member of (5.2) after $\beta_0 + \beta_1 x_{\alpha 1} + \beta_2 x_{\alpha 2}$ is substituted for the upper limit of the integration. The idea is thus that the conditional probability that a family will buy a car, given its value $x_{\alpha 1}$ and $x_{\alpha 2}$, is identical with the probability that a standardized normal variate is less than $\beta_0 + \beta_1 x_{\alpha 1} + \beta_2 x_{\alpha 2}$.

Another extension, proposed by TOBIN (1958), concerns a half-way dichotomous situation in which the analyst is not only interested in the question of whether a family buys a car, but also in the amount spent on the car when the family does buy. This amount is thus either positive or zero, and the analysis concerns both this dichotomy and the distribution of the amount when it is positive. The approach is based on a specification in which the dependent variable (the amount spent on the car) is equated to a linear combination of explanatory variables with unknown coefficients plus a normally distributed disturbance, provided that this linear combination plus disturbance is positive; otherwise the dependent variable takes the zero value. As in the case of probit analysis, Tobin suggests the maximum-likelihood method to estimate the unknown coefficients.

Logit Analysis

The theoretical background of probit analysis is rather complicated, and the justification of the normality assumption in this particular context is not very strong in econometric applications. Therefore it is worthwhile to consider another approach, that of logit analysis, which performs a transformation of the type in Figure 12.6 more directly. The simplest starting point is the odds in favor of car purchase, defined as the ratio $p/(1-p)$ where p is the purchase probability. The odds may be regarded as a monotonic transformation of p with range from 0 to ∞. This is still restrictive because negative values are excluded. Suppose, however, that we describe the odds as a log-linear function of income:

$$\log \frac{p_\alpha}{1-p_\alpha} = \beta_0 + \beta \log x_\alpha \tag{5.5}$$

where p_α is the probability that the αth family will buy a car, given that its income is equal to x_α. The parameter β is simply the income elasticity of the odds in favor of a car purchase. Note that it is also equal to minus the income elasticity of the odds against a car purchase. This is because interchanging p_α and $1-p_\alpha$ leaves both sides of (5.5) unchanged except for sign.

The left-hand side of (5.5) is known as the *logit* of a car purchase.[14] It is a transformation of the probability of the type illustrated in Figure 12.6: $-\infty$ at $p=0$, 0 at $p=.5$, ∞ at $p=1$. The logit owes its name to the relationship with the logistic function, which is seen more clearly when (5.5) is solved for p_α:

$$p_\alpha = \frac{1}{1+e^{-\beta_0-\beta\log x_\alpha}} = \frac{1}{1+e^{-\beta_0}x_\alpha^{-\beta}}.$$

It will also be clear that the approach can be extended straightforwardly when more explanatory variables are needed (the price of new cars, the age of the present car, etc.). This is merely a matter of adding more terms in the right-hand side of (5.5).

Regarding the estimation of the parameters of (5.5), consider first the case in which the sample consists of n_1 families with income x_1, n_2 families with income x_2, and so on. For each of these groups, one can then replace the

[14] The term logit is from Berkson, who contributed extensively to this subject (1944, 1946, 1949, 1953, 1955).

probability in the left-hand side of the equation by the observed relative frequency of car purchase and estimate β_0 and β by the weighted LS method. An example will be given in the next subsection. When the incomes of the families are different, one may group the observations in income brackets and neglect the income differences within groups when these are not too large. See THEIL (1967, Sections 3.7–3.8) for a description of this procedure and a simulation experiment.[15]

A Linear Logit Relation for Production Plan Revisions

The following example, taken from Theil (1967, Sections 3.2 and 3.5), has two explanatory variables which are both dummy variables in the sense that they take only two values each. It is concerned with revisions of production plans of entrepreneurs who participated in a survey conducted by the *Ifo-Institut für Wirtschaftsforschung*. These entrepreneurs state at the beginning of each month whether they plan to raise their production in that month (to be indicated by +), or to keep the rate of production unchanged (0), or to lower it (−). One month later they state whether they did raise the production (+), or kept it unchanged (0), or lowered it (−). We shall say that the plan was carried out when the plan-realization sequence is ++, 00 or −−. When the sequence is 0+, −0 or −+, the realization amounts to a higher rate of production than was anticipated, which will be indicated by saying that there is a positive plan revision. A negative revision is any of the sequences 0−, +0 or +−. The problem is: what are the factors which determine such revisions and how large is the influence of each of these factors?

The survey also contains data on expected and actual rates of orders received. For these variables we have similar sign sequences. For example, 0− means that no change in the rate of orders received was anticipated but that one month later a decrease was reported. This is a case of negative surprise on orders received; +0 and +− are the two other cases which fall under this category, 0+, −0, and −+ are those of positive surprise, and ++, 00, and −− those of no surprise.

It stands to reason that when there is a positive surprise on orders received, this will raise the probability of a positive production plan revision. Also, this probability may be affected by the entrepreneur's appraisal of his inventory of finished goods. The survey asks him to state whether this inventory is too small, "normal," or too large. If it is considered too large, one would expect the probability of a positive production plan revision to be reduced.

[15] One may also use a maximum-likelihood procedure; see, for example, CRAGG and UHLER (1969).

Thus our objective is to describe the probability of a positive or negative production plan revision in terms of the surprise on orders received and the appraisal of the inventory of finished goods. For simplicity's sake, imagine that we eliminate all cases in which either the production plan was carried out, or there was no surprise on orders received, or the inventories were considered normal. Then our three variables take only two values each, to be indicated as follows:

$X = X_1$: positive production plan revision
X_2: negative revision
$Y = Y_1$: positive surprise on orders received
Y_2: negative surprise
$Z = Z_1$: inventories are considered too small
Z_2: inventories are considered too large

We are interested in the conditional probability of a positive production plan revision, given a particular (Y, Z) combination:

$$P_{jk} = \mathrm{P}[X = X_1 \mid Y = Y_j, Z = Z_k] \qquad j, k = 1, 2 \tag{5.6}$$

and the corresponding conditional probability of a negative plan revision is then $1 - P_{jk}$. Our linear logit relation is

$$\log \frac{P_{jk}}{1 - P_{jk}} = \beta_0 + \beta_j + \gamma_k \qquad j, k = 1, 2 \tag{5.7}$$

Without loss of generality we can put $\beta_1 = \gamma_1 = 0$, in which case β_0 stands for the logit of a positive plan revision under the conditions $Y = Y_1$ and $Z = Z_1$ (a positive surprise on orders received and inventories which are considered too small), $\beta_0 + \beta_2$ for the logit under condition (Y_2, Z_1), and $\beta_0 + \gamma_2$ and $\beta_0 + \beta_2 + \gamma_2$ for the logits under the conditions (Y_1, Z_2) and (Y_2, Z_2), respectively.

The data consist of 379 observations. The first line of Table 12.2 shows

Table 12.2

Production Plan Revisions Determined by Surprises on Orders Received and the Appraisal of Inventory

	(Y_1, Z_1)	(Y_1, Z_2)	(Y_2, Z_1)	(Y_2, Z_2)	Total
Total number of cases	89	82	43	164	379
Number of positive revisions	68	50	14	19	151
Relative frequency	.76	.60	.33	.12	.40

how they are divided over the four pairs of values taken by the explanatory variables. The second line gives the numbers of positive production plan revisions, and the third shows the relative frequencies of this event. As could be anticipated, this frequency takes the largest value under condition (Y_1, Z_1) and the smallest value under condition (Y_2, Z_2) with those of conditions (Y_1, Z_2) and (Y_2, Z_1) occupying an intermediate position. When replacing the probabilities in the left-hand side of (5.7) by these frequencies and adding error terms to the right-hand side, we obtain four equations which can be arranged in vector form:

$$\begin{bmatrix} \log(68/21) \\ \log(50/33) \\ \log(14/29) \\ \log(19/145) \end{bmatrix} = \begin{bmatrix} 1 & 0 & 0 \\ 1 & 0 & 1 \\ 1 & 1 & 0 \\ 1 & 1 & 1 \end{bmatrix} \begin{bmatrix} \beta_0 \\ \beta_2 \\ \gamma_2 \end{bmatrix} + \begin{bmatrix} \epsilon_{11} \\ \epsilon_{12} \\ \epsilon_{21} \\ \epsilon_{22} \end{bmatrix} \tag{5.8}$$

This is of the familiar form $\mathbf{y} = \mathbf{X\beta} + \boldsymbol{\epsilon}$ with $\mathbf{y}$ a four-element vector and $\mathbf{X}$ of order 4×3. Regarding the distribution of the ϵ's, we shall proceed under the assumption that the relative frequencies on the third line of Table 12.2 are based on independent samples from binomial populations. This implies that the ϵ's are independent, too. Their means and variances are examined in Problem 5.1, where it turns out that the large-sample expectation and variance of ϵ_{jk} are zero and $1/n_{jk}f_{jk}(1 - f_{jk})$, respectively, where n_{jk} is the relevant number in the first row of Table 12.2 and f_{jk} the corresponding relative frequency in the third row.[16] We thus apply weighted LS to the four observations arranged in (5.8) with weights proportional to the reciprocal of the approximate standard deviation of ϵ_{jk}. This leads to the following estimates and asymptotic standard errors:

$$\hat{\beta}_0 = 1.30(.22) \qquad \hat{\beta}_2 = -2.23(.26) \qquad \hat{\gamma}_2 = -.98(.26) \tag{5.9}$$

This result indicates that the effect of the surprise on orders received (β_2) is larger than that of the inventory evaluation (γ_2). By substituting the point estimates (5.9) into the logit formula (5.7), we can obtain the implied estimates of P_{jk}:

(5.10)

(Y_1, Z_1)	(Y_1, Z_2)	(Y_2, Z_1)	(Y_2, Z_2)
.79	.58	.28	.13

A comparison with the relative frequencies of Table 12.2 shows that the agreement is reasonably close.

[16] It is to be understood that the logarithms of (5.7) and (5.8) are natural logarithms.

Problems

5.1 Write f_{jk} for the relative frequency corresponding to P_{jk} defined in (5.6) and assume that it is based on a random sample of size n_{jk} from a binomial population with probability P_{jk} of success, where $0 < P_{jk} < 1$. Define the logit and its estimator:

$$L_{jk} = \log \frac{P_{jk}}{1 - P_{jk}} \qquad \hat{L}_{jk} = \log \frac{f_{jk}}{1 - f_{jk}} \tag{5.11}$$

Apply the results of Section 8.3 to prove that $\sqrt{n_{jk}}(\hat{L}_{jk} - L_{jk})$ approaches, as $n_{jk} \to \infty$, a normal limiting distribution with zero mean and variance $1/P_{jk}(1 - P_{jk})$. Use this to prove that the asymptotic standard error of $\hat{L}_{jk}$ is equal to the reciprocal of the square root of $n_{jk}f_{jk}(1 - f_{jk})$.

5.2 The specification (5.7) involves three unknown parameters $(\beta_0, \beta_2, \gamma_2)$ which are used to summarize the four relative frequencies of Table 12.2. That is a very modest reduction. Consider the case in which Y and Z take n_Y and n_Z values, respectively. Prove that the number of relative frequencies is then $n_Y n_Z$ and the number of unknown parameters $n_Y + n_Z - 1$, and verify that this amounts to a much more substantial reduction when $n_Y, n_Z > 2$. Extend this result to the case of an arbitrary number of explanatory variables.

12.6 Univariate Informational Measures[B]

In this and the next two sections we continue the analysis of factors that determine probabilities. Their subject is information theory, an area that originated with SHANNON (1948); for econometric applications in addition to those considered below, see THEIL (1967). It should be stressed at the outset that although the basic concepts of this theory are conventionally formulated in terms of probabilities, it actually covers the much wider area of decompositions of given totals in terms of nonnegative parts. This is shown in the first subsection of Section 12.7.

The Information Concept

Consider an arbitrary event E whose probability is p. Suppose that at some point of time we receive a reliable message stating that E occurred. The problem is: can we measure in any reasonable way the amount of information conveyed by such a message? Proceeding along intuitive lines, we may say that if p is close to 1 ($p = .98$, say), only little information is received because it was practically certain that E would take place before the message was received. But suppose that $p = .01$, so that it is virtually certain that E will not occur. If in spite of this E did occur, the message stating this causes considerable surprise and hence contains a great deal of information.

These intuitive arguments suggest that if we want to measure the information received from a message in terms of the probability p prior to its arrival, we should choose a decreasing function. The choice is

$$h(p) = \log \frac{1}{p} \tag{6.1}$$

which decreases from ∞ (infinite surprise and hence infinite information if the probability before the message is zero) to 0 (zero information when the probability is one). The function is illustrated in Figure 12.7. The unit of

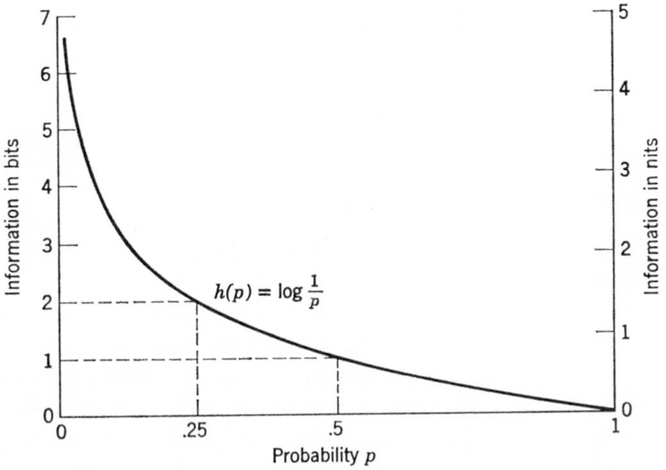

Fig. 12.7 Information measured in bits and in nits.

information is determined by the base of the logarithm. Frequently 2 is used as the base, which implies a unit value of the information when the message refers to a 50–50 event: $h(\frac{1}{2}) = 1$. Information is then said to be measured in binary digits, usually abbreviated as *bits*. When natural logarithms are used, the information unit is a *nit*. The left-hand vertical scale of Figure 12.7 measures information in bits, the other vertical scale in nits.

The Additivity of Information

The function (6.1) is one choice out of many decreasing functions. This particular choice is motivated by the convenient property of additivity.

Indeed, in this and the next two sections we shall add, subtract, and take weighted averages of information values on a large scale. To show what is meant by additivity, consider two events A and B as well as their joint, conditional, and unconditional probabilities. These are connected by

$$\text{(6.2)} \qquad \mathrm{P}[A \text{ and } B] = \mathrm{P}[A]\ \mathrm{P}[B \mid A] = \mathrm{P}[B]\ \mathrm{P}[A \mid B]$$

Now assume that we are first informed that A occurred, so that the information received is $\log(1/\mathrm{P}[A])$. Given this message, the probability that B will occur is $\mathrm{P}[B \mid A]$. Next assume that we are informed that B also occurred. The total information received from the two messages is

$$\text{(6.3)} \qquad \log \frac{1}{\mathrm{P}[A]} + \log \frac{1}{\mathrm{P}[B \mid A]} = \log \frac{1}{\mathrm{P}[A \text{ and } B]}$$

That is, the total information is equal to the information that would have been received if the message had stated immediately that both A and B occurred. Note that we have the same result when the first message refers to B and the second to A:

$$\text{(6.4)} \qquad \log \frac{1}{\mathrm{P}[B]} + \log \frac{1}{\mathrm{P}[A \mid B]} = \log \frac{1}{\mathrm{P}[A \text{ and } B]}$$

The conclusion is that if we measure information in accordance with (6.1), the total amount of information received is independent of the order in which the messages arrive. The only thing that matters is the set of probabilities $\mathrm{P}[A]$, $\mathrm{P}[B]$, $\mathrm{P}[A \mid B]$, $\mathrm{P}[B \mid A]$. Indeed, it can be shown that if we start with certain axioms, the information function must necessarily be of the form (6.1). One of these axioms states that the probability p of the event prior to the message should be the only determinant of the information content of the message; the axiom that is mainly responsible for the logarithmic form (6.1) is the one concerned with additivity. Details about such axioms are provided by KOOPMAN and KIMBALL (1959); for a more informal summary see THEIL (1967, Section 1.3).[17]

The Entropy of a Distribution

It will be noted that the information received from the message which states that E occurred is not the same as the information of the message associated with the complementary event. The latter information is $h(1-p) = \log[1/(1-p)]$. It should be obvious that the two values are not the same unless $p = \frac{1}{2}$, for if $p = .99$ (say), we are not at all surprised to hear later

[17] It will be obvious that the word "information" as it is used here does not have the same meaning as it has in the information matrix of Section 8.4. There is some similarity, however, as was stressed by KULLBACK (1967).

that E did occur, whereas the opposite message causes a great deal of surprise.[18]

As far as event E is concerned, the information to be received is thus either $h(p)$ or $h(1-p)$ and we do not know which as long as the message of occurrence or non-occurrence has not been received. But we can compute the *expected information content* of this message prior to its arrival. Since E will occur with probability p and not-E with probability $1-p$, the information received will be $h(p)$ with the former probability and $h(1-p)$ with the

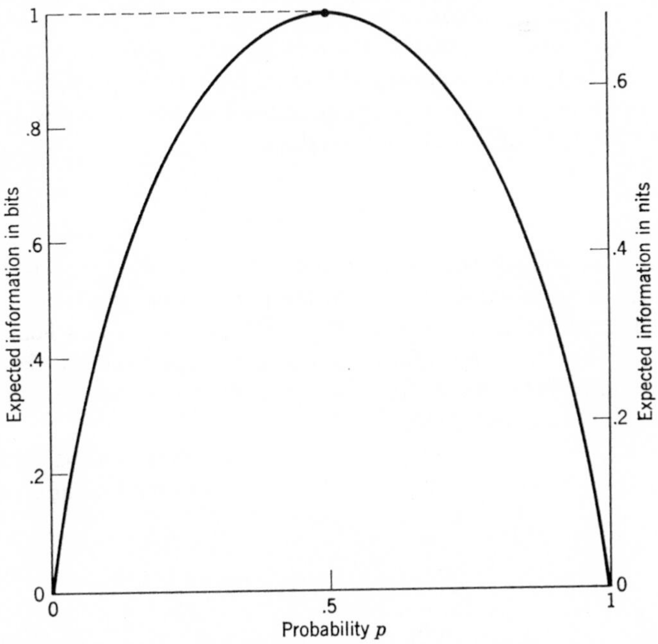

Fig. 12.8 The entropy for two alternatives (E and not-E).

latter. Hence the expected information content is

$$H = ph(p) + (1-p)h(1-p) \tag{6.5}$$
$$= p \log \frac{1}{p} + (1-p) \log \frac{1}{1-p}$$

[18] It is interesting to note that the logit introduced in the previous section is equal to the difference between these complementary information values:

$$\log \frac{p}{1-p} = h(1-p) - h(p)$$

See also Problem 6.5 for another relation between the logit and informational concepts.

which is also known as the *entropy* of any distribution which assigns probabilities p and $1 - p$ to the two different points.[19] Obviously, this entropy is symmetric in p and $1 - p$ and hence also in E and not-E. The function (6.5) is shown in Figure 12.8; it reaches a maximum at $p = .5$, and the value of the maximum is 1 bit.

Extension to Several Events

More generally, let there be N events $E_1, \ldots, E_N$ with probabilities $p_1, \ldots, p_N$. It is certain that exactly one of these events will occur, so that the p's add up to one. If E_i occurs, the message which states this has information content $h(p_i)$. Since the probability of E_i is p_i, the expected information of the message on the occurrence of one of these events (or, equivalently, the entropy of the distribution whose probabilities are $p_1, \ldots, p_N$) is

$$H = \sum_{i=1}^{N} p_i h(p_i) = \sum_{i=1}^{N} p_i \log \frac{1}{p_i} \tag{6.6}$$

The entropy is nonnegative because it is obtained by weighting the nonnegative information values $h(p_i)$ with the nonnegative p_i's. The zero value can indeed be attained, namely, when $p_i = 1$ for some i and hence $p_j = 0$ for each $j \neq i$.[20] Hence, no information is to be expected from the message when it is known beforehand that one of the N alternatives has unit probability—which is a natural result.

The largest value of the entropy can be derived by maximizing the function (6.6) subject to the constraint $\sum p_i = 1$. So we form the Lagrangian expression

$$-\sum_{i=1}^{N} p_i \log p_i - \mu\left(\sum_{i=1}^{N} p_i - 1\right) \tag{6.7}$$

where μ is a Lagrangian multiplier. We differentiate (6.7) with respect to p_i and put the result equal to zero, which gives $-1 - \log p_i - \mu = 0$.[21] This shows that all p_i's must be equal and hence equal to $1/N$, which in turn implies that the maximum entropy value is $\log N$. Note further that this maximum increases when we imagine that the number of possible outcomes (N) increases. These results are also natural. When there are three possibilities with probabilities .98, .01, .01, there is little uncertainty as to the

[19] The term entropy has its origin in physics. The concept plays a central role in the second law of thermodynamics.

[20] Note that $p_j \log (1/p_j)$ is of the form $0 \times \infty$ if $p_j = 0$. It is conventional to replace this indeterminate value by the limit of this function for $p_j \to 0$, which is zero; see Problem 6.1.

[21] This holds under the assumption that natural logarithms are used. The use of other logarithms implies that -1 in the left-hand side of this equation is replaced by a different number, but that does not affect the result.

question of what will happen, so that little information is to be expected from the message which states what actually happened. But when the probabilities are .34, .33, .33, there is a great deal of uncertainty and hence much information to be expected. When we have five possibilities rather than three, each of which has a probability of .2, there is even more uncertainty and hence more information to be expected. These examples also show that uncertainty and expected information are two sides of the same coin. Uncertainty prevails prior to the message, and information is received when the message arrives; the more uncertainty prior to the message, the larger the amount of information which it conveys, at least on the average. Therefore the entropy (6.6), originally introduced here as the expected information of the message that states which of the N possible outcomes is realized, may also be regarded as a measure of the uncertainty associated with a distribution whose probabilities are $p_1, \ldots, p_N$.

Prior and Posterior Probabilities

Returning to the case of one single event E with probability p, suppose that a message is received which—contrary to the messages considered up to now—does not state with certainty whether or not E took place; rather, it states that the odds in favor of E have changed so that the new probability is q, some number between 0 and 1. This is a generalization of the original problem formulated at the beginning of this section, where the message stated that E took place with certainty and hence $q = 1$. We shall call the original probability p (before the message came in) the prior probability of E. After the message is received, this probability is no longer relevant; the new value is q, to be called the posterior probability of E.

The problem is again: can we measure in any reasonable way the amount of information conveyed by this message—this time the message transforming prior p to posterior q? The following extension of the original information definition is straightforward and intuitively appealing. Suppose that it ultimately turns out that E does take place, so that the chain of successive probabilities is $p \to q \to 1$. We are interested in the information associated with the link $p \to q$ of this chain. Given the prior probability p, the information content of the message which states with certainty that E did occur ($p \to 1$) is $h(p)$; given the posterior probability q, the information content of this message ($q \to 1$) is $h(q)$. The change from $h(p)$ to $h(q)$ is a result of the message which transforms prior p to posterior q, and since information is an additive measure, a natural way of defining the information received from this message is by taking the difference: $h(p) - h(q) = \log (q/p)$. Its value is zero when $p = q$, which is as it should be because $p = q$ implies that the odds favoring E are simply unchanged. The value is $\log (1/p)$

for $q = 1$ and thus includes—as it should—the special case in which the message states with certainty that E occurred. The value is negative when $q < p$, which may seem surprising but which becomes understandable when it is recalled that E is supposed to occur at the end. A message which states that E has become less probable rather than more probable thus has a negative information value when E ultimately takes place.

It remains true, however, that $\log (q/p)$ defines the information of the message which transforms prior p to posterior q only under the condition that the event occurs at the end. But this partial definition is sufficient to obtain the expected information of the message. To show this, consider the more general situation of a complete system of N mutually exclusive events:

	E_1	E_2	$\cdots$	E_N
prior	p_1	p_2	$\cdots$	p_N
posterior	q_1	q_2	$\cdots$	q_N

If it turns out that E_i ultimately takes place, the information received from the message which transforms the p's to the q's is $\log (q_i/p_i)$. Since this message states that the probability of E_i is q_i, the expected information is

$$I(q:p) = \sum_{i=1}^{N} q_i \log \frac{q_i}{p_i} \tag{6.8}$$

where q and p on the left stand for the sets of probabilities $q_1, \ldots, q_N$ and $p_1, \ldots, p_N$, respectively.

The information expectation $I(q:p)$ takes the zero value, as it should, when the two sets of probabilities are pairwise equal: $p_i = q_i$ for each i. It can be shown (see Problem 6.2) that it is positive as soon as there are pairwise differences. When the corresponding p's and q's are not too far from each other, we have the following approximate result when natural logarithms are used (see Problem 6.3):

$$I(q:p) \approx \frac{1}{2} \sum_{i=1}^{N} q_i \left(\frac{p_i - q_i}{q_i}\right)^2 = \frac{1}{2} \sum_{i=1}^{N} \frac{(p_i - q_i)^2}{q_i} \tag{6.9}$$

The expression in the middle indicates that, as a first approximation, the information expectation is equal to one-half of a weighted average of the squares of the relative deviations between corresponding prior and posterior probabilities, the weights being the latter probabilities. The third expression of (6.9) indicates that $I(q:p)$ is approximately proportional to the chi-square with the q's as the theoretical probabilities and the p's as the observed frequencies.

Note that the information expectation $I(q:p)$ may be infinitely large. This follows from (6.8) by specifying $q_i > p_i = 0$ for some i. The prior probabilities then specify that E_i has zero chance, and the message states that this is raised to a positive level. Hence the probability is raised by a factor "infinity," and we are also "infinitely surprised" by the message. Note further that if the message states that one of the outcomes, E_i say, has unit probability (and hence all others have zero probability), the expected information becomes $\log(1/p_i)$, which is in accordance with the basic definition (6.1), as it should indeed be.

Aggregation Properties

One of the attractive features of informational measures is the simplicity of their aggregation properties. Consider the events $E_1, \ldots, E_N$ with their prior and posterior probabilities (the p's and the q's) and suppose that they are combined into $G \leq N$ sets of events, $S_1, \ldots, S_G$, in such a way that each E_i belongs to exactly one S_g, where $g = 1, \ldots, G$. What is the relationship between $I(q:p)$ and the corresponding expression after aggregation?

To answer this question we define

$$P_g = \sum_{i \in S_g} p_i \qquad Q_g = \sum_{i \in S_g} q_i \qquad g = 1, \ldots, G \tag{6.10}$$

which are the prior and posterior probabilities, respectively, of the union of events in the set S_g. The expression $Q_1 \log(Q_1/P_1) + \cdots + Q_G \log(Q_G/P_G)$ is thus the information expectation (6.8) after aggregation. Consider, then,

$$\begin{aligned} I(q:p) &= \sum_{i=1}^{N} q_i \log \frac{q_i}{p_i} \\ &= \sum_{g=1}^{G} Q_g \sum_{i \in S_g} \frac{q_i}{Q_g} \left(\log \frac{Q_g}{P_g} + \log \frac{q_i/Q_g}{p_i/P_g} \right) \\ &= \sum_{g=1}^{G} Q_g \log \frac{Q_g}{P_g} + \sum_{g=1}^{G} Q_g \sum_{i \in S_g} \frac{q_i}{Q_g} \log \frac{q_i/Q_g}{p_i/P_g} \end{aligned} \tag{6.11}$$

Note that p_i/P_g and q_i/Q_g for $i \in S_g$, $g = 1, \ldots, G$ are conditional probabilities of E_i given S_g. The second term on the last line of (6.11) is thus a weighted average (with the Q's as weights) of information expectations which refer to these conditional probabilities. Therefore we can write this equation more clearly and concisely as follows:

$$I(q:p) = I_0(q:p) + \sum_{g=1}^{G} Q_g I_g(q:p) \tag{6.12}$$

where

$$\begin{aligned} I_0(q:p) &= \sum_{g=1}^{G} Q_g \log \frac{Q_g}{P_g} \\ I_g(q:p) &= \sum_{i \in S_g} \frac{q_i}{Q_g} \log \frac{q_i/Q_g}{p_i/P_g} \qquad g = 1, \ldots, G \end{aligned} \tag{6.13}$$

The result (6.12) thus implies that the total information expectation $I(q{:}p)$ is equal to the between-group information expectation $I_0(q{:}p)$ plus a weighted average of the within-group information expectations $I_1(q{:}p), \ldots, I_G(q{:}p)$ with weights equal to the posterior probabilities $Q_1, \ldots, Q_G$ of the groups.

Problems

6.1 Use L'Hôpital's rule to prove that $x \log x$ converges to zero as $x \to 0$.

6.2 Suppose that the posterior probabilities $q_1, \ldots, q_N$ are all positive[22] and define $a_i = (p_i - q_i)/q_i$. Prove $I(q{:}p) = \sum_i q_i f(a_i)$, where $f(x) = x - \log(1 + x)$. Use this result to prove $I(q{:}p) \geq 0$ and $= 0$ if and only if $p_i = q_i$ for each i. (*Hint.* See Problem 3.4 of Section 3.3.)

6.3 (*Continuation*) Prove $I(q{:}p) = -\sum_i q_i \log(1 + a_i)$ and expand the logarithm in a Taylor series to verify that the approximation (6.9) contains the leading quadratic term. What is the convergence condition for this expansion?

6.4 (*Disaggregation of the entropy*) Consider the events $E_1, \ldots, E_N$ and the sets of events $S_1, \ldots, S_G$ of the last subsection. Prove the following entropy decomposition for their prior probabilities:

$$H = H_0 + \sum_{g=1}^{G} P_g H_g \tag{6.14}$$

where H is defined in (6.6) and

$$H_0 = \sum_{g=1}^{G} P_g \log \frac{1}{P} \qquad H_g = \sum_{i \in S_g} \frac{p_i}{P_g} \log \frac{P_g}{p_i} \qquad g = 1, \ldots, G \tag{6.15}$$

Interpret this result.

6.5 Let the entropy (6.5) be measured in nits. Prove that its derivative with respect to p is minus the logit corresponding to p.

12.7 The Consumer's Allocation Problem: (8) Informational Measures of Goodness of Fit[BC]

Extension to General Decompositions[B]

The scene will now be changed by the assumption that there is an analyst who is interested in a set of proportions (nonnegative numbers which add up to one) or in several sets of proportions. Here are some examples.

(1) Students at some school are distinguished by race, a certain proportion being black and another proportion (the remainder) white. The entropy of

[22] When $p_i > q_i = 0$ for some i, one may apply a limiting process ($q_i \to 0$) with the same result.

this racial distribution as illustrated in Figure 12.8 is a simple measure for the degree to which the school is integrated: the minimum is zero (only one race is represented) and the maximum is 1 bit (the 50–50 distribution). See THEIL and FINIZZA (1967).

(2) This school, along with several others, is part of a school district. Let the racial composition of the student body of the district as a whole be p (the black proportion) and $1 - p$ (the white proportion). Write q and $1 - q$ for the corresponding proportions of our particular school. Then the information expectation,

$$q \log \frac{q}{p} + (1 - q) \log \frac{1 - q}{1 - p} \tag{7.1}$$

is a measure for the extent to which the racial composition of this school differs from that of the district as a whole. See also Problem 7.1 for an aggregative measure describing the extent to which the schools of the district tend to serve the needs of only one race.

(3) Let $p_1, \ldots, p_N$ be the market shares of the firms of an industry. Then the entropy (6.6) is an inverse measure of industrial concentration: zero when one firm has a 100 percent share, the maximum value ($\log N$) when all N firms have equal shares, and this maximum increases when N becomes larger. Furthermore, Problem 6.4 shows that this inverse concentration measure lends itself to a simple disaggregation, which is a useful property in case the analyst decides to divide the industry into more homogeneous subindustries.

(4) Consider the states of the United States and write p's for their shares of the national population (state population divided by the national population) and q's for their shares of total personal income (total personal income of the state divided by total personal income of the nation). Then the expression (6.8) is a measure for the degree of income inequality among the states: zero when the population and income shares are all pairwise equal—which implies that all states have the same per capita income—and positive as soon as the per capita incomes differ. Furthermore, the aggregation analysis in the last subsection of Section 12.6 shows that if we combine the states into regions, there is a simple decomposition which describes the income inequality at the state level as the sum of two components, one of which deals with regional income inequality and the other with the inequality of the states within each region. See also Problems 7.2 and 7.3 for an extension of this inequality measure for the case of individual and continuous income distributions.

(5) Suppose that the analyst wants to predict a set of proportions, for example, the shares of N commodities of total expenditure. Write $q_1, \ldots, q_N$ for the observed shares and $p_1, \ldots, p_N$ for the predictions. Then $I(q:p)$ as defined in (6.8) is an inverse measure of the accuracy of these predictions: zero when each prediction p_i coincides with the corresponding q_i, and

positive otherwise. The information expectation $I(q:p)$ may thus be regarded as a measure of badness of fit, and it is accordingly called the *information inaccuracy* of the decomposition forecast $p_1, \ldots, p_N$, given the observed realizations $q_1, \ldots, q_N$.

In Section 12.6 we treated the p's and q's strictly as probabilities. The above examples show, whoever, that the measures developed there can also be usefully employed when the p's and q's are racial shares, market shares, population shares, income shares, and predicted and observed expenditure shares of commodities. Basically, we depart from the original "information" interpretation, and the theory of Section 12.6 is thus extended to "decomposition mathematics." The entropy (6.6) has become a measure for the degree to which the given total is subdivided into parts: zero when there is no subdivision at all, a maximum of log N when all N parts are of equal size, and this maximum increases with N. Similarly, the information expectation (6.8) has become a measure for the degree to which a decomposition $p_1, \ldots, p_N$ differs from another decomposition $q_1, \ldots, q_N$. The main virtue of these measures is their additivity and the simplicity of their aggregation properties.

The remainder of this section is devoted to an application of the information inaccuracy concept to the demand equation systems that are discussed in Sections 7.5 to 7.7 and 11.6 to 11.9.

Demand Predictions of Value Shares[C]

Recall that the discussion in Section 11.8 concerns three alternative specifications for a system of four demand equations: the absolute price version and two variants of the relative price version. The problem to be examined here is that of measuring the goodness of fit of these equations. One could compute an R^2 for each equation, but this neglects the fact that all four equations are estimated simultaneously. Also, recall that the dependent variables of these equations are the quantity components of changes in value shares. This will provide us with an opportunity to compute an information inaccuracy value for the demand system as a whole. Specifically, consider eq. (5.7) of Section 7.5:

$$dw_i = w_i d(\log p_i) + w_i d(\log q_i) - w_i d(\log m) \tag{7.2}$$

and imagine that for finite changes the three successive terms on the right are replaced by $w_{it}^* Dp_{it}$, $w_{it}^* Dq_{it}$, $-w_{it}^*(Dp_t + Dq_t)$, where $Dp_t = \sum_i w_{it}^* Dp_{it}$.[23] After rearranging the terms, we thus have for Δw_{it}, the change in the value

[23] This Dp_t is the price index log-change defined in eq. (6.7) of Section 7.6. One could also substitute $w_{it}^* Dm_t$ for $w_i d(\log m)$ in the finite-change equation (7.3) below, but this would have the disadvantage that the sum over i of the right-hand side of that equation is not equal to the corresponding sum of the left-hand side, which is zero for each pair (i, t); see Problem 7.4.

share from year $t - 1$ to year t:

$$\Delta w_{it} = w_{it}^* Dq_{it} + w_{it}^*(Dp_{it} - Dp_t) - w_{it}^* Dq_t \tag{7.3}$$

The first right-hand term in (7.3) is the dependent variable of the ith demand equation. The other terms refer to changes in relative prices and real income, which are taken as given by demand theory. Thus, our demand equations supply conditional predictions, given the log-changes in real income and relative prices, both of $w_{it}^* Dq_{it}$ and also, via (7.3), of Δw_{it}. By adding the prediction of Δw_{it} to the observed $w_{i,t-1}$, we obtain $\hat{w}_{it}$, the implied prediction of w_{it}, and the information inaccuracy,

$$I_t = \sum_{i=1}^{4} w_{it} \log \frac{w_{it}}{\hat{w}_{it}} \tag{7.4}$$

is then a simple measure for the degree to which the $\hat{w}$'s of the four commodity groups are inaccurate as predictors of the observed value shares of year t. Note that $\hat{w}_{it}$ may be computed from w_{it} by simply subtracting the tth residual of the ith demand equation. This follows from the fact that the prediction of $w_{it}^* Dq_{it}$ of (7.3) is equal to the right-hand side of the demand equation with the disturbance deleted and the parameters replaced by their point estimates.[24]

The first three lines of Table 12.3 contain the average information inaccuracies over the sample period as a whole as well as over the prewar and postwar components of this period for the three alternative demand specifications.[25] The other figures are based on simple extrapolations which will now be discussed.

A Comparison with Naive Predictions[C]

A very simple prediction method is the no-change extrapolation of the value shares: $\Delta w_{it} = 0$ for each i and t. This implies

$$\hat{w}_{it} = w_{i,t-1} \tag{7.5}$$

[24] Note that when we take the second and third terms in the right-hand side of (7.3) as given, we implicitly assume that w_{it}^* is known. This is not really correct because w_{it}^* is the average of $w_{i,t-1}$ and w_{it}, and w_{it} is the object of prediction. One could replace w_{it}^* in these two terms by $w_{i,t-1}$ or proceed by iteration: first apply this replacement, which gives a prediction of w_{it}, then use for w_{it}^* the average of this prediction and $w_{i,t-1}$, and so on. However, the variability of $Dp_{it} - Dp_t$ and Dq_t in the two terms is considerably larger than that of w_{it}^*, and these alternative procedures will therefore lead to practically the same numerical results as those obtained here.

[25] The figures of the relative price version are based on the estimates obtained after convergence. The observed shares w_{it} are taken from Theil (1967, p. 175). They are given there in four decimal places, so that their sum may deviate from 1 by 10^{-4}. It is recommended that these numbers be divided by their sum, so that the ratios add up to 1 exactly.

Table 12.3

Average Information Inaccuracies (in 10^{-6} Nits) for Demand Predictions and Extrapolations

Period	Absolute Price Version	Relative Price Version: Extended Variant	Relative Price Version: Simple Variant	Extrapolations: (7.5)	Extrapolations: (7.8) $\theta = .4$
			All commodity groups		
All observations	139	143	145	406	290
Prewar	145	143	149	370	250
Postwar	132	143	141	451	340
			Food		
All observations	56	59	59	126	88
Prewar	46	45	54	103	69
Postwar	69	76	65	153	111
			Vice		
All observations	20	20	23	33	23
Prewar	23	23	21	22	23
Postwar	15	17	25	46	22
			Durables		
All observations	69	70	71	268	216
Prewar	68	66	68	222	164
Postwar	69	75	75	323	279
			Remainder		
All observations	47	47	47	136	70
Prewar	62	63	64	170	85
Postwar	28	28	26	94	53

This no-change extrapolation for value shares can, in view of (7.3), be based on a demand equation which equates $w_{it}^* Dq_{it}$ to

$$w_{it}^* Dq_t - w_{it}^*(Dp_{it} - Dp_t) \tag{7.6}$$

This, in turn, amounts to the assumption that each commodity has unitary income elasticity and an elasticity with respect to its own deflated price equal to -1, all other prices being irrelevant except for their role as deflators.[26] Since it is plausible that an own-price elasticity of -1 is on the large side, there is some merit in considering the family of demand equations which equate $w_{it}^* Dq_{it}$ to

$$w_{it}^* Dq_t - \theta w_{it}^*(Dp_{it} - Dp_t) \tag{7.7}$$

[26] Note that the deflator $Dp_t = \sum_i w_{it}^* Dp_{it}$ in (7.6) uses the w_{it}^*'s as weights, whereas the price term of the demand equations in relative prices is based on the marginal shares (the μ's) as weights. See also Problem 7.6.

where θ is some number between zero and one. A comparison with (7.3) shows that the implied prediction of w_{it} is

$$\hat{w}_{it} = w_{i,t-1} + (1-\theta)w_{it}^*(Dp_{it} - Dp_t) \tag{7.8}$$

The average information inaccuracy for the prediction (7.8) was computed for $\theta = 0, .1, .2, \ldots, 1$, and it turns out that the smallest value for the sample as a whole is attained at $\theta = .4$. The last column of Table 12.3 contains the corresponding numerical results.

The first three rows of the table indicate that the fit of the three demand specifications is almost equally good and that there is not much difference between the prewar and postwar periods in this regard. They also indicate that these demand equations are considerably superior to the no-change extrapolation (7.5) as far as fit is concerned. The prediction (7.8) for $\theta = .4$ implies a considerable improvement, but its average information inaccuracy is still about twice as large as those of the demand specifications.

Evaluation for Individual Commodity Groups[C]

The lines of the table below the third are concerned with the prediction of the shares of the four commodity groups separately. Take the ith share in year t and let $\hat{w}_{it}$ be its prediction. Then the information inaccuracy which refers to this share and its complement is

$$I_{it} = w_{it} \log \frac{w_{it}}{\hat{w}_{it}} + (1 - w_{it}) \log \frac{1 - w_{it}}{1 - \hat{w}_{it}} \tag{7.9}$$

Since $1 - w_{it}$ is the combined share of all commodities other than the ith, we have $I_{it} \le I_t$ for each pair (i, t). This follows from (6.12) because this equation implies $I_0(q:p) \le I(q:p)$ in view of the nonnegativity of the within-group expression $\sum Q_g I_g(q:p)$. The figures on the last 12 lines of Table 12.3 corroborate this inequality, since they are all smaller than the corresponding figure on the first three lines. Except for this scale factor these outcomes are similar to those of the four commodity groups jointly; only vice provides an exception because of the comparatively good performance of the extrapolations.

Correction for Loss of Degrees of Freedom[C]

The average information inaccuracies of the three demand equations are not fully comparable because their estimation involves the adjustment of different numbers of coefficients. The following procedure, which is similar to the substitution of $\bar{R}^2$ for R^2 (see Section 4.4), provides a simple although approximate correction. Since corresponding predicted and observed value shares are close to each other, we can apply the quadratic approximation (6.9) with little loss of accuracy. The average information inaccuracy then becomes

$$(7.10) \qquad \frac{1}{2T}\sum_{t=1}^{T}\left[\sum_{i=1}^{4}\frac{(\hat{w}_{it}-w_{it})^2}{w_{it}}\right]=\frac{1}{2T}\sum_{t=1}^{T}\left[\sum_{i=1}^{4}\frac{e_{it}^2}{w_{it}}\right]$$

where e_{it} is the tth residual of the ith demand equation.[27] One should expect that, on the average, the square of this residual underestimates the variance ω_{ii} of the corresponding disturbance ϵ_{it}. The reason is that the estimation procedure is basically GLS applied to $n = 3T$ observations with K unknown coefficients ($K = 9$ for the absolute price version, 7 for the extended variant, and 5 for the simple variant), and Theorem 6.2 of Section 6.1 then suggests the use of the multiplicative factor $3T/(3T - K)$ for unbiased estimation. If we apply this to each e_{it}^2 in the right-hand side of (7.10), the procedure in effect amounts to multiplying the average information inaccuracies in the first row and the first three columns of Table 12.3 by $3T/(3T - K)$. This gives

$$(7.11) \qquad \frac{93}{84}\,139.1 = 154 \qquad \frac{93}{86}\,143.3 = 155 \qquad \frac{93}{88}\,145.4 = 154$$

These outcomes suggest that there is no real difference between the three demand specifications as far as fit is concerned, and hence that one may just as well use the simple variant with $K = 5$ instead of the absolute price version with $K = 9$.

The next subsection describes the correction procedure in more detail; it will turn out that its justification is a little more complicated than that of unbiased estimation of the variances ω_{ii}. Before turning to that topic, it is appropriate to stress that the procedure of using the same data for testing and estimation, which was discussed in Section 12.1, has been applied repeatedly to the present body of data. In Section 7.7 we tested the symmetry of the matrix $[\pi_{ij}]$ of the price coefficients, after which we re-estimated subject to this symmetry constraint. In Section 11.8 we inspected these estimates to see whether preference independence is an acceptable hypothesis. The answer was negative and we came up with two alternative hypotheses of block-independence. We also tested these two hypotheses against each other (see Problems 8.1 and 8.2 of Section 11.8). It was suggested at the end of the second-last subsection of Section 12.1 that numerical results derived from formulas for one-step procedures be interpreted liberally when the procedure actually consists of several steps which are all performed on the same set of data. It is probably good to apply the correction (7.11) anyway, but it should be taken with a grain of salt.

[27] Recall that it was stated below eq. (7.4) that the demand prediction $\hat{w}_{it}$ may be calculated as $w_{it} - e_{it}$.

Derivation of the Correction^{C}

Write $\mathbf{e}_t = [e_{1t} \quad e_{2t} \quad e_{3t}]'$ for the residual vector which corresponds to the disturbance vector $\boldsymbol{\epsilon}_t$ of eq. (8.10) of Section 11.8.[28] That equation also shows that $\mathbf{e}_t$ equals $\boldsymbol{\epsilon}_t - \mathbf{X}_t(\hat{\boldsymbol{\beta}} - \boldsymbol{\beta})$, where $\hat{\boldsymbol{\beta}}$ is the coefficient estimator corresponding to this residual vector. Take $t = 1$ for notational simplicity and consider the product $\mathbf{e}_1\mathbf{e}_1'$:

$$(7.12) \quad \mathbf{e}_1\mathbf{e}_1' = \boldsymbol{\epsilon}_1\boldsymbol{\epsilon}_1' + \mathbf{X}_1(\hat{\boldsymbol{\beta}} - \boldsymbol{\beta})(\hat{\boldsymbol{\beta}} - \boldsymbol{\beta})'\mathbf{X}_1' - \mathbf{X}_1(\hat{\boldsymbol{\beta}} - \boldsymbol{\beta})\boldsymbol{\epsilon}_1' - \boldsymbol{\epsilon}_1(\hat{\boldsymbol{\beta}} - \boldsymbol{\beta})'\mathbf{X}_1'$$

Our first objective is the expectation of $\mathbf{e}_1\mathbf{e}_1'$. For the first term on the right we have simply $\mathscr{E}(\boldsymbol{\epsilon}_1\boldsymbol{\epsilon}_1') = \boldsymbol{\Omega}$. The other terms involve $\hat{\boldsymbol{\beta}}$; their expectations will be derived on the basis of the asymptotic distribution of this estimator as described in Section 11.9. The second term then becomes the asymptotic covariance matrix of $\hat{\boldsymbol{\beta}}$ pre- and postmultiplied by $\mathbf{X}_1$ and $\mathbf{X}_1'$, respectively:

$$(7.13) \qquad \mathbf{X}_1\left(\sum_{t=1}^{T}\mathbf{X}_t'\boldsymbol{\Omega}^{-1}\mathbf{X}_t\right)^{-1}\mathbf{X}_1'$$

For the third term in (7.12) recall that $\sqrt{T}(\hat{\boldsymbol{\beta}} - \boldsymbol{\beta})$ converges in distribution to the vector

$$(7.14) \qquad \left(\frac{1}{T}\sum_{t=1}^{T}\mathbf{X}_t'\boldsymbol{\Omega}^{-1}\mathbf{X}_t\right)^{-1}\frac{1}{\sqrt{T}}\sum_{t=1}^{T}\mathbf{X}_t'\boldsymbol{\Omega}^{-1}\boldsymbol{\epsilon}_t$$

The sampling error $\hat{\boldsymbol{\beta}} - \boldsymbol{\beta}$ is premultiplied by $-\mathbf{X}_1$ in the third term and postmultiplied by $\boldsymbol{\epsilon}_1'$. If we perform this postmultiplication on the vector (7.14) and take the expectation, we obtain

$$\left(\frac{1}{T}\sum_{t=1}^{T}\mathbf{X}_t'\boldsymbol{\Omega}^{-1}\mathbf{X}_t\right)^{-1}\frac{1}{\sqrt{T}}\sum_{t=1}^{T}\mathbf{X}_t'\boldsymbol{\Omega}^{-1}\mathscr{E}(\boldsymbol{\epsilon}_t\boldsymbol{\epsilon}_1') = \sqrt{T}\left(\sum_{t=1}^{T}\mathbf{X}_t'\boldsymbol{\Omega}^{-1}\mathbf{X}_t\right)^{-1}\mathbf{X}_1'\boldsymbol{\Omega}^{-1}\boldsymbol{\Omega}$$

$$= \sqrt{T}\left(\sum_{t=1}^{T}\mathbf{X}_t'\boldsymbol{\Omega}^{-1}\mathbf{X}_t\right)^{-1}\mathbf{X}_1'$$

If we then premultiply by $-\mathbf{X}_1$ and take out the factor $\sqrt{T}$ we obtain precisely the same matrix as that of (7.13) except for sign. [We must divide by $\sqrt{T}$ because the vector (7.14) is not the asymptotic equivalent of $\hat{\boldsymbol{\beta}} - \boldsymbol{\beta}$ but of $\sqrt{T}(\hat{\boldsymbol{\beta}} - \boldsymbol{\beta})$.] It is readily verified that we obtain the same result for the fourth right-hand term in (7.12), so that the result is

$$(7.15) \qquad \mathscr{E}_{\infty}(\mathbf{e}_1\mathbf{e}_1') = \boldsymbol{\Omega} - \mathbf{X}_1\left(\sum_{t=1}^{T}\mathbf{X}_t'\boldsymbol{\Omega}^{-1}\mathbf{X}_t\right)^{-1}\mathbf{X}_1'$$

[28] The exposition which follows is confined to the demand specifications in relative prices. See Problem 7.8 for the absolute price version.

where $\mathscr{E}_\infty$ indicates that the expectation is based on the asymptotic distribution of $\hat{\boldsymbol{\beta}}$.

We may repeat the above derivation for $t = 2, \ldots, T$ and take the average with the following result:

$$(7.16) \qquad \frac{1}{T}\sum_{t=1}^{T}\mathscr{E}_\infty(\mathbf{e}_t\mathbf{e}_t') = \boldsymbol{\Omega} - \frac{1}{T}\sum_{s=1}^{T}\mathbf{X}_s\left(\sum_{t=1}^{T}\mathbf{X}_t'\boldsymbol{\Omega}^{-1}\mathbf{X}_t\right)^{-1}\mathbf{X}_s'$$

This indicates that if we accept the asymptotic approximation of the $\hat{\boldsymbol{\beta}}$ distribution, the true disturbance covariance matrix $\boldsymbol{\Omega}$ exceeds the expectation of its estimator $(1/T)\sum_t \mathbf{e}_t\mathbf{e}_t'$ by a positive semidefinite matrix. Therefore it is reasonable to modify this estimator in an upward direction, but it is out of the question to obtain unbiased estimators of all elements of $\boldsymbol{\Omega}$ by applying a single multiplicative correction to the matrix $(1/T)\sum_t \mathbf{e}_t\mathbf{e}_t'$. The following procedure describes a more modest but at least feasible objective.

If we postmultiply the $\boldsymbol{\Omega}$ estimator by $\boldsymbol{\Omega}^{-1}$, the expectation of the product matrix is a unit matrix when the estimator is unbiased. In our case this unit matrix would be of order 3×3, in which case its trace is equal to 3. When we use the $\boldsymbol{\Omega}$ estimator $(1/T)\sum_t \mathbf{e}_t\mathbf{e}_t'$, we certainly do not obtain a unit matrix after postmultiplication by $\boldsymbol{\Omega}^{-1}$ and taking the expectation, but we can at least apply a multiplicative adjustment so that the trace of the expected product matrix is equal to 3. To show this we postmultiply both sides of (7.16) by $\boldsymbol{\Omega}^{-1}$, which gives for the right-hand side:

$$(7.17) \qquad \mathbf{I} - \frac{1}{T}\sum_{s=1}^{T}\mathbf{X}_s\left(\sum_{t=1}^{T}\mathbf{X}_t'\boldsymbol{\Omega}^{-1}\mathbf{X}_t\right)^{-1}\mathbf{X}_s'\boldsymbol{\Omega}^{-1}$$

the trace of which is

$$(7.18) \qquad 3 - \frac{1}{T}\operatorname{tr}\left[\left(\sum_{t=1}^{T}\mathbf{X}_t'\boldsymbol{\Omega}^{-1}\mathbf{X}_t\right)^{-1}\sum_{s=1}^{T}\mathbf{X}_s'\boldsymbol{\Omega}^{-1}\mathbf{X}_s\right] = 3 - \frac{K}{T}$$

where K is the number of rows of $\mathbf{X}_t'$. The multiplication factor which ensures that the expected product of the $\boldsymbol{\Omega}$ estimator and $\boldsymbol{\Omega}^{-1}$ have trace 3 is thus

$$(7.19) \qquad \frac{3}{3 - K/T} = \frac{3T}{3T - K}$$

which is the factor that was used in (7.11).

Problems

7.1 (*Integration in schools and school districts*) Let a school district consist of n schools and write w_i for the ith school population measured as a fraction of the district's student body. Write p for the proportion of black students in the district as a whole (hence $1 - p$ for the white proportion) and q_i for the population of black students in the ith school. Prove $p = \sum_i w_i q_i$. Next consider the informational measure (7.1) for the extent to which the racial composition of the ith school differs from that of the district (add a subscript i to q) and take a weighted average of these measures over all schools with weights equal to their student shares:

$$\bar{I} = \sum_{i=1}^{n} w_i \left[q_i \log \frac{q_i}{p} + (1 - q_i) \log \frac{1 - q_i}{1 - p} \right] \tag{7.20}$$

Prove $\bar{I} = H_D - \sum_i w_i H_i$, where H_D is the district's racial entropy and H_i is the racial entropy of the ith school:

$$H_D = p \log \frac{1}{p} + (1 - p) \log \frac{1}{1 - p} \tag{7.21}$$

$$H_i = q_i \log \frac{1}{q_i} + (1 - q_i) \log \frac{1}{1 - q_i} \qquad i = 1, \ldots, n \tag{7.22}$$

Write $\bar{I} = H_D - \sum_i w_i H_i$ in the form $\sum_i w_i H_i = H_D - \bar{I}$. Use this to prove that the average racial entropy of the schools (i.e., the weighted average with the w's as weights) is never larger than the racial entropy of the district. Also conclude that $\bar{I}$ may be regarded as a measure for the degree to which segregation in schools exists above and beyond the level implied by the racial composition of the district.

7.2 (*Income inequality at the individual level*) Write N for the number of persons in a country, so that the population share of the ith individual is simply $1/N$. Write z_i for this person's income and m for average income. Prove that the informational inequality measure described in the first subsection under (4) at this individual level is of the following form:

$$\sum_{i=1}^{N} \frac{z_i}{Nm} \log \frac{z_i}{m} \tag{7.23}$$

7.3 (*Inequality for continuous income distributions*) Approximate the discrete income distribution of Problem 7.2 by a continuous distribution with density function $f(\ )$. Prove that the number of persons who earn an income between $z - \frac{1}{2}\,dz$ and $z + \frac{1}{2}\,dz$ is $Nf(z)\,dz$, and use this to prove that the income inequality measure based on (7.23) is

$$\int_0^{\infty} \left(\frac{z}{m} \log \frac{z}{m} \right) f(z)\,dz = \mathscr{E}\left(\frac{z}{\mathscr{E}z} \log \frac{z}{\mathscr{E}z} \right) \tag{7.24}$$

where $\mathscr{E}$ stands for the expectation operator corresponding to the income distribution. In particular, when the income distribution is lognormal,

$$f(z) = \frac{1}{(\sigma\sqrt{2\pi})z} \exp\left\{-\frac{1}{2}\frac{(\log z - \mu)^2}{\sigma^2}\right\} \qquad 0 < z < \infty \tag{7.25}$$

prove that the expression (7.24) is equal to $\frac{1}{2}\sigma^2$ (use natural logarithms).

7.4 Suppose that $w_{it}^* Dm_t$ is substituted for $w_i d(\log m)$ in the finite-change variant of (7.2). Prove that the sum over i of the right-hand side of (7.3), thus modified, is equal to the expression $\sum_i w_{it}^* Dw_{it}$, which is discussed below eq. (6.8) of Section 7.6.

7.5 Prove that the sum over i of the predictions (7.8) is equal to one for each t and for any value of θ.

7.6 (*Continuation*) Suppose that the deflator $Dp_t = \sum_k w_{kt}^* Dp_{kt}$ in (7.8) is replaced by $\sum_k \mu_k Dp_{kt}$, where μ_k is the marginal value share of the kth commodity. Is it then still true that the sum over i of $\hat{w}_{it}$ equals one?

7.7 Use eq. (7.15) to prove $\mathscr{E}_\infty e_{it}^2 \leq \omega_{ii}$ for each pair (i, t). When does the equality sign apply?

7.8 Prove that the basic equation of the symmetry-constrained variant of the absolute price version can be written as $\mathbf{y}_t = \mathbf{X}_t \boldsymbol{\beta} + \boldsymbol{\epsilon}_t$, where $\mathbf{y}_t$ and $\boldsymbol{\epsilon}_t$ are as described in eqs. (8.9) and (8.10) of Section 11.8, while $[\boldsymbol{\beta} \quad \mathbf{X}_t]'$ is the following matrix:

$$\begin{bmatrix} \mu_1 & \mu_2 & \mu_3 & \pi_{11} & \pi_{22} & \pi_{33} & \pi_{12} & \pi_{13} & \pi_{23} \\ \cdots & \cdots & \cdots & \cdots & \cdots & \cdots & \cdots & \cdots & \cdots \\ Dq_t & 0 & 0 & Dp'_{1t} & 0 & 0 & Dp'_{2t} & Dp'_{3t} & 0 \\ 0 & Dq_t & 0 & 0 & Dp'_{2t} & 0 & Dp'_{1t} & 0 & Dp'_{3t} \\ 0 & 0 & Dq_t & 0 & 0 & Dp'_{3t} & 0 & Dp'_{1t} & Dp'_{2t} \end{bmatrix}$$

where $Dp'_{it} = Dp_{it} - Dp_{4t}$ for $i = 1, 2, 3$. Then inspect each step of the last subsection to verify that the trace result (7.18) also applies to this case.

12.8 Multivariate Informational Measures[C]

Bivariate Information Theory: Three Unconditional Entropies

Consider a bivariate probability distribution with probabilities p_{ij}, $i = 1, \ldots, N_1$ and $j = 1, \ldots, N_2$. A convenient interpretation is that of N_1 messages sent $(X_1, \ldots, X_{N_1})$ and N_2 messages received $(Y_1, \ldots, Y_{N_2})$, so that p_{ij} stands for the probability that the messages sent and received are X_i and Y_j, respectively. Following the definition (6.6), we write[29]

$$H(X, Y) = \sum_i \sum_j p_{ij} \log \frac{1}{p_{ij}} \tag{8.1}$$

[29] It is to be understood that the summations are always over the entire range of the relevant subscript: $i = 1, \ldots, N_1$ and $j = 1, \ldots, N_2$.

for the joint entropy of the two-dimensional distribution; X and Y on the left stand for $X_1, \ldots, X_{N_1}$ and $Y_1, \ldots, Y_{N_2}$, respectively. This joint entropy may be regarded as a measure for the uncertainty regarding the message sent and the message received.

We introduce the marginal probabilities

$$(8.2)\quad p_{i.} = \sum_j p_{ij} \quad (i = 1, \ldots, N_1) \qquad p_{.j} = \sum_i p_{ij} \quad (j = 1, \ldots, N_2)$$

as well as the entropies of the two marginal distributions:

$$(8.3)\qquad H(X) = \sum_i p_{i.} \log \frac{1}{p_{i.}} \qquad H(Y) = \sum_j p_{.j} \log \frac{1}{p_{.j}}$$

The marginal entropy $H(X)$ describes the uncertainty as to the message sent and $H(Y)$ performs the same role for the message received.

Bivariate Information Theory: The Expected Mutual Information

To establish the relationship between the three entropies $H(X)$, $H(Y)$, and $H(X, Y)$, we introduce

$$(8.4)\qquad h_{ij} = \log \frac{p_{ij}}{p_{i.}p_{.j}} \qquad \begin{array}{l} i = 1, \ldots, N_1 \\ j = 1, \ldots, N_2 \end{array}$$

which is known as the *mutual information* between the message sent X_i and the message received Y_j. Each h_{ij} vanishes in the special case of stochastic independence of the messages sent and received. The mutual information h_{ij} is positive when, given that X_i was sent, Y_j is more frequently the message received than the independence pattern implies, and it is negative in the opposite case.

Next consider the average of all mn mutual information values with the p_{ij}'s as weights, known as the *expected mutual information*:

$$(8.5)\qquad I_{XY} = \sum_i \sum_j p_{ij} \log \frac{p_{ij}}{p_{i.}p_{.j}}$$

This I_{XY} is nonnegative, for it is nothing but the expected information of the message which transforms mn "prior" probabilities $p_{i.}p_{.j}$ to the "posterior" probabilities p_{ij}; see definition (6.8) and note that the present prior and posterior probabilities are indeed nonnegative and add up to one when summed over i and j as they should be. We have $I_{XY} = 0$ if and only if the messages sent and the messages received are stochastically independent. In fact, I_{XY} may be used as a measure of the degree to which the probability array $[p_{ij}]$ is characterized by dependence rather than independence. This is most easily seen by means of the approximation (6.9), which implies that if the elements of the pair $(p_{i.}p_{.j}, p_{ij})$ are not too far from each other, I_{XY} is approximately proportional to

$$\frac{1}{2}\sum_i\sum_j p_{ij}\left(\frac{p_{i.}p_{.j} - p_{ij}}{p_{ij}}\right)^2$$

Now consider the right-hand side of (8.5):

$$\sum_i\sum_j p_{ij}\log\frac{p_{ij}}{p_{i.}p_{.j}} = \sum_i\sum_j p_{ij}\log\frac{1}{p_{i.}} + \sum_i\sum_j p_{ij}\log\frac{1}{p_{.j}} - \sum_i\sum_j p_{ij}\log\frac{1}{p_{ij}}$$

$$= \sum_i p_{i.}\log\frac{1}{p_{i.}} + \sum_j p_{.j}\log\frac{1}{p_{.j}} - \sum_i\sum_j p_{ij}\log\frac{1}{p_{ij}}$$

$$= H(X) + H(Y) - H(X, Y)$$

or, equivalently,

$$H(X, Y) = H(X) + H(Y) - I_{XY} \tag{8.6}$$

Since I_{XY} is nonnegative this means that the joint entropy is at most equal to the sum of the two marginal entropies:

$$H(X, Y) \leq H(X) + H(Y) \tag{8.7}$$

The equality sign applies if and only if there is independence $(I_{XY} = 0)$. As soon as there is dependence, the sum of the marginal entropies exceeds the joint entropy. This result can be further clarified by the introduction of conditional entropies.

Bivariate Information Theory: Conditional Entropies

Consider the ratio $p_{ij}/p_{i.}$, which is the conditional probability that Y_j is the message received when it is given that X_i is the message sent. Take a fixed X_i and let Y_j vary over the set of messages received. The entropy of the resulting distribution is

$$H_{X_i}(Y) = \sum_j \frac{p_{ij}}{p_{i.}}\log\frac{p_{i.}}{p_{ij}} \tag{8.8}$$

where the subscript X_i on the left indicates the conditioning event.

Equation (8.8) defines the conditional entropy of the messages received, given that X_i is the message sent. Now consider a weighted average of these N_1 conditional entropies for $i = 1, \ldots, N_1$ with weights equal to the probabilities $p_{1.}, \ldots, p_{N_1.}$ of the conditioning events:

$$H_X(Y) = \sum_i p_{i.}H_{X_i}(Y) = \sum_i\sum_j p_{ij}\log\frac{p_{i.}}{p_{ij}} \tag{8.9}$$

This is known as the *average conditional entropy* of the messages received, given the messages sent. The conditional entropy (8.8) measures the uncertainty of the message received when it is known that X_i has been sent. In eq. (8.9) we average these uncertainties over the set of all messages sent.

The expression after the second equality sign in (8.9) can be rewritten as follows:

$$\sum_i \sum_j p_{ij} \log \frac{p_{i.}}{p_{ij}} = \sum_i \sum_j p_{ij} \log \frac{1}{p_{ij}} - \sum_i p_{i.} \log \frac{1}{p_{i.}}$$

or, equivalently,

$$H_X(Y) = H(X, Y) - H(X) \tag{8.10}$$

In words: The average conditional entropy of the messages received, given the messages sent, is equal to the excess of the joint entropy over the univariate entropy of the conditioning factor (i.e., of the messages sent). Combining (8.10) with (8.6) and (8.7), we obtain

$$I_{XY} = H(Y) - H_X(Y) \qquad H_X(Y) \leq H(Y) \tag{8.11}$$

The expected mutual information I_{XY} is thus equal to the excess of the unconditional entropy of the messages received over the corresponding average conditional entropy. Also, since I_{XY} is nonnegative, the latter entropy cannot be larger than the former. This result ought to be intuitively obvious. It means that the uncertainty as to the message received when it is known which message is sent is on the average at most equal to the uncertainty which prevails when this knowledge is not available. Note that this holds indeed only *on the average*; an *individual* conditional entropy may well be larger than the unconditional entropy. To illustrate this point, consider the following 2 × 2 table:

	Y_1	Y_2	
X_1	$p_{11} = \frac{1}{4}$	$p_{12} = \frac{1}{4}$	$p_{1.} = \frac{1}{2}$
X_2	$p_{21} = \frac{1}{2}$	$p_{22} = 0$	$p_{2.} = \frac{1}{2}$
	$p_{.1} = \frac{3}{4}$	$p_{.2} = \frac{1}{4}$	

The unconditional entropy of Y is

$$H(Y) = \frac{3}{4} \log \frac{4}{3} + \frac{1}{4} \log 4 = .81 \text{ bit}$$

The conditional entropies of Y given $X = X_1$ and $X = X_2$ are 1 bit and zero, respectively, so that $H_X(Y) = \frac{1}{2}(1) + \frac{1}{2}(0) = \frac{1}{2}$ bit. This is indeed smaller than $H(Y) = .81$ bit, but the first conditional entropy (given $X = X_1$) is larger than $H(Y)$.[30]

Since $H_X(Y)$ is obtained by averaging the nonnegative conditional entropies $H_{X_i}(Y)$ with nonnegative weights, it must be nonnegative itself. This means, in view of (8.10), that the marginal entropy $H(X)$ is at most equal to the joint entropy $H(X, Y)$. The two are equal if and only if $H_X(Y) = 0$, which amounts to $H_{X_i}(Y) = 0$ for each i for which $p_{i.} > 0$. In other words, the joint entropy exceeds the marginal entropy $H(X)$ unless it is certain what value Y will take when the X value is given, for whatever X value having positive probability.

In the above paragraphs we took the messages sent as the conditioning factors, but one can take instead the messages received; this leads to completely analogous results. See Problem 8.1.

A Multivariate Extension

The analysis can be generalized to the case of several variables in addition to X and Y. The interpretation of messages sent and received is then no longer applicable, but this is not a matter of any real concern. Specifically, consider the case of only three variables, X, Y, and Z, in order to avoid a larger number of indices than three; the further extension will appear to be straightforward. As an example we take the case in which the analyst is interested in the ownership of cars among families with equal incomes. X stands for car ownership; X_1 means no car, X_2 one car, and X_3 more than one car. The explanatory variables are Y whose values indicate different forms of marital status and Z which indicates whether the family lives in a large city, a suburb, a small town, or in a rural area. The question is: to what extent do Y and Z account for the observed type of car ownership among the families? Or, equivalently, to what degree is the uncertainty as to the type of car ownership reduced when the marital status and the residence type of the family is known? It will be shown how this question can be answered by means of conditional entropies.

Write p_{ijk} for the joint probability of $X = X_i$, $Y = Y_j$, $Z = Z_k$. As before, probabilities of marginal distributions will be indicated by a dot at the place of the index over which summation takes place. Examples are

$$p_{.jk} = \sum_i p_{ijk} \qquad p_{..k} = \sum_i \sum_j p_{ijk}$$

[30] Also see footnote 32 on page 663.

The uncertainty as to the type of car ownership is measured by the univariate entropy of X:

(8.12) $$H(X) = \sum_i p_{i..} \log \frac{1}{p_{i..}}$$

When the marital status of the family is known to be $Y = Y_j$, the uncertainty of X is measured by its conditional entropy given Y_j:

$$H_{Y_j}(X) = \sum_i \frac{p_{ij.}}{p_{.j.}} \log \frac{p_{.j.}}{p_{ij.}}$$

On the average, when the marital status is known, the uncertainty of X is thus measured by its average conditional entropy given Y:

(8.13) $$H_Y(X) = \sum_i \sum_j p_{ij.} \log \frac{p_{.j.}}{p_{ij.}}$$

The expressions (8.12) and (8.13) are completely analogous to the corresponding expressions in (8.3) and (8.9), respectively, so that we may conclude from the discussion below (8.11) that the average conditional entropy (8.13) is at most equal to the marginal entropy (8.12) and that the difference between the two is a measure of the degree to which marital status accounts for the type of car ownership. Similarly, the average conditional entropy of X given Z,

(8.14) $$H_Z(X) = \sum_i \sum_k p_{i.k} \log \frac{p_{..k}}{p_{i.k}}$$

is also at most equal to $H(X)$ and the difference $H(X) - H_Z(X)$ measures the extent to which the residence type accounts for the type of car ownership. Note that the entropies (8.13) and (8.14) may be determined from unconditional entropies as follows:

(8.15) $$H_Y(X) = H(X, Y) - H(Y) \qquad H_Z(X) = H(X, Z) - H(Z)$$

which is analogous to (8.10); see Problem 8.2.

The discussion of the previous paragraph treats each explanatory factor (Y and Z) in isolation. Now suppose that it is given that $Y = Y_j$ and $Z = Z_k$. The relevant conditional entropy of X is then

(8.16) $$H_{Y_jZ_k}(X) = \sum_i \frac{p_{ijk}}{p_{.jk}} \log \frac{p_{.jk}}{p_{ijk}}$$

The weighted average of these entropies with weights equal to the probabilities $p_{.jk}$ of the relevant conditions is

(8.17) $$H_{YZ}(X) = \sum_i \sum_j \sum_k p_{ijk} \log \frac{p_{.jk}}{p_{ijk}}$$

which is the average conditional entropy of X given Y and Z. It is easily seen that this entropy may be determined from two unconditional entropies in a way similar to (8.15):

$$H_{YZ}(X) = H(X, Y, Z) - H(Y, Z) \tag{8.18}$$

In addition, it can be proved that $H_{YZ}(X)$ never exceeds the left-hand entropies of (8.15) in which one of the two conditioning factors is deleted:

$$H_{YZ}(X) \leq H_Y(X) \qquad H_{YZ}(X) \leq H_Z(X) \tag{8.19}$$

This result is intuitively understandable because the left-hand entropy involves an additional condition which should lead to a lower (at least not larger) level of uncertainty with respect to X. To prove (8.19) we consider the difference between $H_Y(X)$ and $H_{YZ}(X)$:

$$\begin{aligned} H_Y(X) - H_{YZ}(X) &= \sum_i \sum_j p_{ij.} \log \frac{p_{.j.}}{p_{ij.}} - \sum_i \sum_j \sum_k p_{ijk} \log \frac{p_{.jk}}{p_{ijk}} \\ &= \sum_i \sum_j \sum_k p_{ijk} \log \frac{p_{ijk}}{p_{ij.}p_{.jk}/p_{.j.}} \geq 0 \end{aligned} \tag{8.20}$$

The inequality sign follows from the fact that the triple sum on the second line is the information expectation of the message which transforms the prior probabilities $p_{ij.}p_{.jk}/p_{.j.}$ to the posterior probabilities p_{ijk}. (Note that these prior probabilities do indeed add up to one when summed over i, j, and k.) The entropy difference (8.20) vanishes if and only if the logarithm on the second line is equal to $\log 1 = 0$ for each subscript combination. This amounts to

$$\frac{p_{ijk}}{p_{.jk}} = \frac{p_{ij.}}{p_{.j.}} \qquad \text{for all triples } (i, j, k) \tag{8.21}$$

which means that the conditional probability $P[X = X_i \mid Y = Y_j, Z = Z_k]$ is independent of the condition $Z = Z_k$. In words: given $Y = Y_j$, the chance of $X = X_i$ is the same whatever value Z may take. Thus, when Y is given, knowledge of Z does not lead to any reduction of the uncertainty of X. It stands to reason that $H_Y(X)$ and $H_{YZ}(X)$ are equal in that case. The analogous assertion on $H_Z(X)$ in (8.19) is proved and interpreted similarly.

Application to Production Plan Revisions

We return to the last subsection of Section 12.5, where X is used for the sign of the production plan revision, Y for that of the surprise on orders received, and Z for the inventory appraisal. The last two variables are assumed to take fixed values. This means that the joint probabilities of their two-dimensional marginal distribution, which are written as $p_{.jk}$ in the notation of the previous subsection ($j, k = 1, 2$), are obtained by dividing the figures in the first row of Table 12.2 by their sum:

$$(8.22) \qquad p_{.11} = \frac{89}{379} \qquad p_{.12} = \frac{83}{379} \qquad p_{.21} = \frac{43}{379} \qquad p_{.22} = \frac{164}{379}$$

The conditional probability of a positive production plan revision given (Z_j, Y_k) is denoted by P_{jk} in (5.6). Hence the probabilities of the three-dimensional distribution are obtained from

$$(8.23) \qquad p_{1jk} = p_{.jk}P_{jk} \qquad p_{2jk} = p_{.jk}(1 - P_{jk}) \qquad j, k = 1, 2$$

To specify these probabilities numerically we shall substitute for P_{jk} the figures on the third line of Table 12.2. This means that the p_{ijk}'s are simply the observed relative frequencies of the three-dimensional distribution.[31]

Since the unconditional probability $p_{1..}$ of a positive plan revision is .40, the univariate entropy of the plan revisions is

$$(8.24) \qquad H(X) = .40 \log \frac{1}{.40} + .60 \log \frac{1}{.60} = .97 \text{ bit}$$

This is just below 1 bit, the entropy value of a 50–50 distribution. The difference of .03 bit may be regarded as a measure for the reduction in uncertainty caused by our knowledge that the probability of a positive plan revision is .40 rather than $\frac{1}{2}$.

When the surprise on orders received is given, we know still more. The average conditional entropy $H_Y(X)$ measures the average uncertainty which still prevails when this surprise is known:

$$(8.25) \qquad H_Y(X) = \sum_{i=1}^{2} \sum_{j=1}^{2} p_{ij.} \log \frac{p_{.j.}}{p_{ij.}} = .75 \text{ bit}$$

This is less than the entropy (8.24), and the difference reflects the reduced uncertainty caused by the knowledge of the surprise on orders received. Similarly,

$$(8.26) \qquad H_Z(X) = \sum_{i=1}^{2} \sum_{k=1}^{2} p_{i.k} \log \frac{p_{..k}}{p_{i.k}} = .89 \text{ bit}$$

This indicates that knowledge of the inventory appraisal reduces the uncertainty with respect to the sign of the production plan revision but not as much as knowledge of the surprise on orders received does. Given the estimates (5.9) of the linear logit specification, this should come as no

[31] An alternative procedure is to substitute for P_{jk} the estimates (5.10) of the linear logit specification. In the present case the numerical results of the two methods will be close to each other because the estimates (5.10) are close to the corresponding values on the third line of Table 12.2.

surprise. Finally, when both Y and Z are introduced as explanatory variables, we obtain

$$H_{YZ}(X) = \sum_{i=1}^{2} \sum_{j=1}^{2} \sum_{k=1}^{2} p_{ijk} \log \frac{p_{.jk}}{p_{ijk}} = .67 \text{ bit} \tag{8.27}$$

which is indeed below both $H_Y(X)$ and $H_Z(X)$.

Statistical Estimation of Informational Measures

The example discussed in the previous subsection is one in which certain probabilities are unknown and must be estimated from a sample. Informational measures based on a random sample are obviously also random, and the question then arises of how they are distributed around the corresponding population values. Some work, but not much, has been done by various authors in this area. We give here a brief summary based on a survey article by LUCE (1960, pp. 45–48).

Consider the one-dimensional entropy (6.6) and suppose that it is estimated by $\hat{H}$, which is the same function of the observed relative frequencies $f_1, \ldots, f_N$ as H is of the p's. Under the assumption that the f's are based on a random sample of size n from a multinomial population with probabilities $p_1, \ldots, p_N$, $\hat{H}$ is asymptotically ($n \rightarrow \infty$) normally distributed with mean H and the following variance:

$$\frac{1}{n} \sum_{i=1}^{N} p_i(\log p_i + H)^2 \tag{8.28}$$

Since the square in (8.28) is also the square of $(-\log p_i - H)$, this asymptotic variance is nothing but a fraction $1/n$ of the "variance of information." This follows from the fact that $-\log p_i = \log (1/p_i)$ is (by definition) information and H is expected information.

When the sample is not large, it has been suggested that $(N - 1)/2n$ be added to $\hat{H}$ to obtain an entropy estimator whose bias is reduced to the order n^{-2}. (This correction presupposes that entropy is measured in nits.) A similar procedure has been proposed to correct the estimator of the expected mutual information (8.5).

Three Kinds of Statistics for Three Kinds of Variables

The use of informational measures is particularly appropriate when the variables are qualitative rather than quantitative. The modal value (the outcome with the largest probability) may then be used as a measure of central tendency, the entropy as a measure of dispersion, and the expected mutual information as a measure of dependence. These three should be compared respectively with the mean, the variance, and the covariance (or the correlation coefficient) of the more conventional type of statistics. There is an intermediate situation in which the variables are "ordinal" in the sense that their values have a natural ordering but no more than that. Examination grades (A, B, C, D, F) fall under this heading. It is possible, of course, to compute a "grade average" by assigning numerical values to A, B, . . . , F, but this is essentially arbitrary. The median is a more appropriate measure of central tendency for this class of variables, and the rank correlation based on the number of inversions (see Section 12.3) is an appropriate measure of dependence.

Pursuing this line of thought a little further, we should note that the difference between the average conditional entropies $H_Y(X)$ and $H_{YZ}(X)$ is conceptually related to the partial correlation coefficient of X and Z given Y. Consider eq. (3.1) of Section 4.3 for the regression of the dependent variable X on the explanatory variables Y and Z and write it as follows:

$$1 - R^2_{X.YZ} = (1 - r^2_{XY})(1 - r^2_{XZ.Y}) \tag{8.29}$$

where $R_{X.YZ}$ is the multiple correlation coefficient associated with this regression, r_{XY} is the correlation coefficient of X and Y, and $r_{XZ.Y}$ is the partial correlation coefficient of X and Z given Y. We may regard the left-hand side of (8.29) as a measure of the uncertainty of X given knowledge of both Y and Z, so that it performs conceptually the same role as $H_{YZ}(X)$.[32] The first factor on the right, $1 - r^2_{XY}$, measures the uncertainty of X given Y only and thus corresponds with $H_Y(X)$. It follows from (8.29) that this factor is equal to the left-hand side if and only if the partial correlation $r_{XZ.Y}$ of X and Z given Y is zero, that is, if and only if Z contributes nothing to a reduction of the residual variance when Y is used as an explanatory variable. In exactly the same way, the entropy $H_{YZ}(X)$ which corresponds to the left-hand side of (8.29) is equal to the entropy $H_Y(X)$ which corresponds to the first factor on the right if and only if condition (8.21) is true. This, as we saw, implies that knowledge of Z does not reduce the uncertainty as to X when Y is known. Therefore the entropy difference $H_Y(X) - H_{YZ}(X)$ performs essentially the same role as the second factor of (8.29), $1 - r^2_{XZ.Y}$.

Note that the entropy difference has an additive character whereas the right-hand side of (8.29) is the product of two factors. This distinction is a result of the additivity of the information measure.

[32] Note that $1 - R^2_{X.YZ}$ is a measure for the uncertainty of X given Y and Z *on the average* (in the mean square sense). This is so because the expression is equal to the ratio of the mean square deviation of the X values from the regression plane to the mean square of the X values themselves. It may well be that there is an individual observation for which the squared deviation of its X value from that plane is larger than the square of this X value, in which case it can be argued that for this particular observation there is an increase in uncertainty when we operate conditionally on Y and Z. This is completely analogous to the corresponding situation for entropies discussed below (8.11).

Problems

8.1 Define the conditional entropy of the messages sent, $X_1, \ldots, X_{N_1}$, given that the message received is Y_j. Next define $H_Y(X)$, the average conditional entropy of the messages sent, given the messages received, by means of weights which are equal to the probabilities of the latter messages. Derive relationships involving $H_Y(X)$ similar to (8.10) and (8.11). Finally, prove $H(Y) \leq H(X, Y)$ and show that the equality sign applies if and only if it is certain which message was sent when it is known which message is received, for any message received which has positive probability.

8.2 Define $H(X, Y)$ and $H(X, Z)$ in terms of the probabilities p_{ijk} and prove (8.15).

8.3 Prove $H_Y(X) - H_{YZ}(X) = H_Y(Z) - H_{XY}(Z)$. Interpret this result and show that the interpretation is analogous to that of $r_{XZ.Y} = r_{ZX.Y}$.

8.4 Apply the analysis of Section 8.3 to derive the asymptotic distribution of the entropy estimator $\hat{H}$ which is described in the discussion leading to (8.28).

12.9 Bayesian Inference[B]

The method of Bayesian inference differs from the inference procedures described in Sections 2.7 to 2.9 in that it does not consider parameters as fixed unknown quantities. It proceeds under the assumption that the analyst has certain prior judgments about the values of these parameters and that these judgments can be expressed in probabilistic form. Specifically, the parameters are regarded as random variables and the analyst is supposed to be able to assess a prior probability distribution for these parameters which expresses these prior ideas numerically.[33] The most authoritative treatment of this line of thought is that of SAVAGE (1954); a more elementary exposition has been given by PRATT, RAIFFA, and SCHLAIFER (1964). The approach has some similarities with the mixed estimation procedure described in Section 7.8, and that section should be read before the material which follows.

Prior and Posterior Probability Distributions

Let $X = (X_1, \ldots, X_n)$ be a random sample drawn from a population with a continuous distribution which is determined by an unknown parameter

[33] The terms "prior" and "posterior" were used in the three previous sections for messages which transform probabilities. The interpretation used in this section is much more specific: prior means "before the sample of observations is available" and posterior means "after the sample has been incorporated."

vector $\boldsymbol{\theta}$. Write $p(\boldsymbol{\theta})$ for the prior density function which the analyst desires to use to express his prior judgments about $\boldsymbol{\theta}$. Write $p(X, \boldsymbol{\theta})$ for the joint density function of the sample and the parameter vector.[34] We apply the ordinary rules for conditional density functions:

$$p(X, \boldsymbol{\theta}) = p(\boldsymbol{\theta})p(X \mid \boldsymbol{\theta}) = p(X)p(\boldsymbol{\theta} \mid X) \tag{9.1}$$

which gives

$$p(\boldsymbol{\theta} \mid X) = \frac{p(\boldsymbol{\theta})p(X \mid \boldsymbol{\theta})}{p(X)} \qquad \text{if } p(X) > 0 \tag{9.2}$$

This is Bayes' theorem for continuous random variables. The function $p(\boldsymbol{\theta} \mid X)$ on the left is the conditional density function of the parameter vector given the sample. It is obtained by combining the observations and the prior judgments, and it is therefore called the *posterior density function* of the parameter vector. This density function is used in the Bayesian approach to make probability statements about $\boldsymbol{\theta}$. The right-hand numerator in (9.2) is the product of the prior density function of $\boldsymbol{\theta}$ and the conditional density function of X given $\boldsymbol{\theta}$. The latter density, when interpreted as a function of $\boldsymbol{\theta}$ for given X, is nothing but the likelihood function $L(X; \boldsymbol{\theta})$. Since $p(X)$ in the denominator is simply a constant when we operate conditionally on the sample—the left-hand side of (9.2) shows that this is the case for the posterior density function—we thus have the following result: *the posterior density function is proportional to the product of the prior density function and the likelihood function*. This enables us to obtain the posterior density function, since the proportionality constant can be found by means of the condition that the total integral of the density function be equal to one.

Application to the Normal Distribution with Known Variance

Let X be a random sample drawn from a normal distribution with unknown mean μ and known variance σ^2. Suppose that the analyst postulates that μ is normally distributed with prior mean μ_0 and prior variance σ_0^2:

$$p(\mu) = \frac{1}{\sigma_0\sqrt{2\pi}} \exp\left\{-\frac{1}{2}\frac{(\mu - \mu_0)^2}{\sigma_0^2}\right\} \tag{9.3}$$

The likelihood of the sample is

$$L(X; \mu, \sigma^2) = \frac{1}{(2\pi\sigma^2)^{n/2}} \exp\left\{-\frac{1}{2}\frac{\sum_{i=1}^{n}(X_i - \mu)^2}{\sigma^2}\right\} \tag{9.4}$$

[34] In what follows we use the symbol $p(\ )$ for density functions in general and we indicate by means of the arguments which particular density function is considered.

Write $\bar{X} = (1/n) \sum X_i$ and $s^2 = [1/(n-1)] \sum (X_i - \bar{X})^2$ for the sample mean and the sample variance, respectively. Consider

$$\sum_{i=1}^{n} (X_i - \mu)^2 = \sum_{i=1}^{n} [X_i - \bar{X} + (\bar{X} - \mu)]^2 = (n-1)s^2 + n(\bar{X} - \mu)^2$$

Substituting the third member for $\sum (X_i - \mu)^2$ in (9.4), we obtain

$$L(X; \mu, \sigma^2) = \frac{\exp\left\{-\frac{1}{2}(n-1)s^2/\sigma^2\right\}}{(2\pi\sigma^2)^{n/2}} \exp\left\{-\frac{1}{2}\frac{(\bar{X} - \mu)^2}{\sigma^2/n}\right\} \tag{9.5}$$

The ratio immediately to the right of the equality sign is a given number when σ^2 is known. Therefore we may write

$$L(X; \mu, \sigma^2) \propto \exp\left\{-\frac{1}{2}\frac{(\bar{X} - \mu)^2}{\sigma^2/n}\right\} \tag{9.6}$$

where $\propto$ stands for "is proportional to." This notation is useful because of the frequent occurrence of proportionality relations in Bayesian analysis.

We obtain the posterior density function of μ by multiplying the prior density function (9.3) by the likelihood function:

$$\begin{aligned} p(\mu \mid X, \sigma^2) &\propto \exp\left\{-\frac{1}{2}\left[\frac{(\mu - \mu_0)^2}{\sigma_0^2} + \frac{(\bar{X} - \mu)^2}{\sigma^2/n}\right]\right\} \\ &\propto \exp\left\{-\frac{1}{2}\left(\frac{1}{\sigma_0^2} + \frac{1}{\sigma^2/n}\right)\left(\mu - \frac{(\sigma^2/n)\mu_0 + \sigma_0^2\bar{X}}{\sigma_0^2 + \sigma^2/n}\right)^2\right\} \end{aligned} \tag{9.7}$$

where the second proportionality is based on the completion of the square of μ:

$$\begin{aligned} &\frac{(\mu - \mu_0)^2}{\sigma_0^2} + \frac{(\bar{X} - \mu)^2}{\sigma^2/n} \\ &\quad = \frac{\mu^2(\sigma_0^2 + \sigma^2/n) - 2\mu(\bar{X}\sigma_0^2 + \mu_0\sigma^2/n)}{\sigma_0^2(\sigma^2/n)} + \text{constant}^{35} \\ &\quad = \left(\frac{1}{\sigma_0^2} + \frac{1}{\sigma^2/n}\right)\left(\mu^2 - 2\mu\frac{(\sigma^2/n)\mu_0 + \sigma_0^2\bar{X}}{\sigma_0^2 + \sigma^2/n}\right) + \text{constant} \\ &\quad = \left(\frac{1}{\sigma_0^2} + \frac{1}{\sigma^2/n}\right)\left(\mu - \frac{(\sigma^2/n)\mu_0 + \sigma_0^2\bar{X}}{\sigma_0^2 + \sigma^2/n}\right)^2 + \text{constant} \end{aligned}$$

The result (9.7) shows that the posterior distribution of μ is normal with the following mean:

$$\frac{(\sigma^2/n)\mu_0 + \sigma_0^2\bar{X}}{\sigma_0^2 + \sigma^2/n} = \frac{(\sigma_0^2)^{-1}\mu_0 + (\sigma^2/n)^{-1}\bar{X}}{(\sigma_0^2)^{-1} + (\sigma^2/n)^{-1}} \tag{9.8}$$

[35] Constant in the sense that the terms do not involve μ.

and the following variance:

$$\frac{1}{(\sigma_0^2)^{-1} + (\sigma^2/n)^{-1}} \tag{9.9}$$

The posterior mean of μ is thus a weighted average of the prior mean μ_0 and the sample mean $\bar{X}$, the weights being proportional to the reciprocals of the corresponding variances. The posterior variance (9.9) of μ is equal to the reciprocal of the sum of the reciprocal variances; it is thus smaller than both, as could be expected.

Bayesian Estimation

In the Bayesian approach the posterior distribution contains all information provided by the sample and by the analyst's prior judgments, so that this distribution may be regarded as the final product of the analysis. It is conceivable, however, that the analyst prefers to replace the posterior distribution by a small number of measures for central tendency, dispersion, and so on. Such a measure of central tendency of the posterior distribution, which is the Bayesian variant of the point estimate of a parameter, may be the mode of the distribution (if it is unimodal) or its expectation (if the expectation exists). But it is more in the spirit of Bayesian thinking to formulate a loss function and to minimize expected loss. The approach is as follows.

Write $\hat{\boldsymbol{\theta}} = \hat{\boldsymbol{\theta}}(X)$ for the Bayesian estimator of $\boldsymbol{\theta}$. The analysis is based on the posterior distribution $p(\boldsymbol{\theta} \mid X)$ and is thus conditional on X, so that $\hat{\boldsymbol{\theta}}$ is fixed. On the other hand, $\boldsymbol{\theta}$ is regarded as random because parameters are treated as random variables in the Bayesian approach. Both features differ from the approach of Section 2.7, where parameters are regarded as fixed and estimators as random. Then formulate a loss function $l(\boldsymbol{\theta}, \hat{\boldsymbol{\theta}})$ and minimize expected loss by varying $\hat{\boldsymbol{\theta}}$:

$$\min_{\hat{\boldsymbol{\theta}}} \int l(\boldsymbol{\theta}, \hat{\boldsymbol{\theta}}) p(\boldsymbol{\theta} \mid X)\, d\boldsymbol{\theta} \tag{9.10}$$

where $d\boldsymbol{\theta}$ stands for the product $d\theta_1\, d\theta_2 \cdots$ and the integration is extended over all values of $\theta_1, \theta_2, \ldots$ for which $p(\boldsymbol{\theta} \mid X)$ is positive. The approach presupposes that a finite minimum exists.

As an example, take the case of a loss function which is a quadratic form in the estimation error $\hat{\boldsymbol{\theta}} - \boldsymbol{\theta}$ with positive semidefinite matrix $\mathbf{Q}$. Write $\mathscr{E}$ for the expectation operator associated with the posterior distribution and consider

$$\begin{aligned} &\mathscr{E}[(\hat{\boldsymbol{\theta}} - \boldsymbol{\theta})'\mathbf{Q}(\hat{\boldsymbol{\theta}} - \boldsymbol{\theta})] \\ &= \mathscr{E}[\{\hat{\boldsymbol{\theta}} - \mathscr{E}\boldsymbol{\theta} - (\boldsymbol{\theta} - \mathscr{E}\boldsymbol{\theta})\}'\mathbf{Q}\{\hat{\boldsymbol{\theta}} - \mathscr{E}\boldsymbol{\theta} - (\boldsymbol{\theta} - \mathscr{E}\boldsymbol{\theta})\}] \\ &= (\hat{\boldsymbol{\theta}} - \mathscr{E}\boldsymbol{\theta})'\mathbf{Q}(\hat{\boldsymbol{\theta}} - \mathscr{E}\boldsymbol{\theta}) + \mathscr{E}[(\boldsymbol{\theta} - \mathscr{E}\boldsymbol{\theta})'\mathbf{Q}(\boldsymbol{\theta} - \mathscr{E}\boldsymbol{\theta})] \end{aligned} \tag{9.11}$$

where the last equality is based on

$$\mathscr{E}[(\boldsymbol{\theta} - \mathscr{E}\boldsymbol{\theta})'\mathbf{Q}(\hat{\boldsymbol{\theta}} - \mathscr{E}\boldsymbol{\theta})] = \mathbf{0}\mathbf{Q}(\hat{\boldsymbol{\theta}} - \mathscr{E}\boldsymbol{\theta}) = 0$$

the estimator $\hat{\boldsymbol{\theta}} = \hat{\boldsymbol{\theta}}(X)$ being fixed from the point of view of the posterior density $p(\boldsymbol{\theta} \mid X)$. Since the second term on the last line of (9.11) does not involve $\hat{\boldsymbol{\theta}}$, the expected loss is minimized by minimizing the first term. It follows immediately from the positive semidefiniteness of $\mathbf{Q}$ that $\hat{\boldsymbol{\theta}} = \mathscr{E}\boldsymbol{\theta}$ leads to the minimum. This amounts to the mean of the posterior distribution as the choice of the estimator. In particular, when $c(\hat{\mu} - \mu)^2$ is the loss function selected for the case of the previous subsection, c being a positive constant, then the estimator of μ which minimizes expected loss is the mean (9.8) of the posterior distribution.

The analysis can be extended to confidence intervals. Again consider the normal posterior density function of μ with mean (9.8) and variance (9.9). By adding and subtracting a multiple 1.96 of the square root of the variance to and from the mean, we obtain an interval that contains μ with .95 probability according to the posterior distribution. This is the Bayesian version of a confidence interval. Note that the limits of this interval are fixed because these are based on the sample X which is a conditioning factor for the posterior distribution, whereas the parameter μ is random. This is different from the confidence interval approach of Section 2.8, where the parameter is fixed and the limits of the interval are random. In the same way, if one wants to test the hypothesis that μ is less than a constant k, one can do so by computing the probability of $\mu < k$ according to the posterior distribution. This is in contrast to the analysis of Section 2.9, where it is not appropriate to speak about the probability that a hypothesis is true.

Diffuse Prior Distributions

In the example of the normal distribution with mean μ we made the restrictive assumption that the variance σ^2 is known. When it is unknown, the analyst has to formulate a prior density $p(\mu, \sigma^2)$ on the two parameters jointly. Now suppose that the analyst claims that he knows very little or nothing about one or both parameters—a situation which is frequently realistic with respect to the variance σ^2. The user of the mixed estimation procedure of Section 7.8 will say that there is no problem for him because he uses uncertain prior information only to the extent that such information is really available. In the Bayesian approach this is not possible, since a prior distribution for all parameters is needed in order to obtain the posterior distribution.

In this case a Bayesian would argue that it is not really true that the analyst knows nothing about the parameter, but that the prior judgment is vague by comparison to the information which is promised by the forthcoming sample. Therefore the analyst must choose a prior distribution which expresses his vagueness appropriately. This leads to the subject of "diffuse" or "uninformative" prior distributions, for which uniform distributions are used on a large scale.[36] Imagine, for example, that the mean μ of the normal distribution is considered a priori to be uniformly distributed over an interval $(-A, A)$ and assume that A takes larger and larger values. This amounts to a prior density of μ which is a constant in the interval $(-\infty, \infty)$.[37] This density, the Bayesian would argue, is not taken as a literal expression of the analyst's judgments on μ, but it is a device to indicate that in the μ interval for which the likelihood function takes appreciable values, there is not much variation in the prior density. This device is used to ensure that the sample evidence will be accorded overwhelming weight in the determination of the posterior distribution.

In principle, one could also apply a uniform density to the variance σ^2 of the normal distribution, but this must, of course, be restricted to the interval $(0, \infty)$. However, a uniform distribution of σ^2 implies a nonuniform distribution of the standard deviation σ. This asymmetry can be avoided by postulating that the natural logarithm of σ^2 has a uniform prior distribution, because $\log \sigma = \frac{1}{2} \log \sigma^2$ has constant prior density when $\log \sigma^2$ has this property. Thus, when postulating that μ and $\log \sigma$ have constant prior densities and also that they are independent a priori, we have the following joint prior density function:

$$p(\mu, \sigma)\, d\mu\, d\sigma \propto \frac{d\mu\, d\sigma}{\sigma} \qquad \begin{array}{r} -\infty < \mu < \infty \\ 0 < \sigma < \infty \end{array} \tag{9.12}$$

By multiplying this function by the likelihood function (9.5), we obtain the joint posterior density function of μ and σ:

$$p(\mu, \sigma \mid X) \propto \frac{1}{\sigma^{n+1}} \exp\left\{-\frac{1}{2}\frac{(n-1)s^2 + n(\bar{X}-\mu)^2}{\sigma^2}\right\} \tag{9.13}$$

If the analyst is interested in μ but not in σ he computes the marginal posterior density function of μ, which is obtained by integrating $p(\mu, \sigma \mid X)$ with

[36] One way of generating uninformative distributions is by maximizing the entropy (as a measure of uncertainty). Take the entropy which is defined in (6.6) as minus the sum of $p_i \log p_i$ or, equivalently, as minus the expectation of the logarithm of the probability; for continuous distributions this is modified to minus the expectation of the logarithm of the density. It can be shown that out of all continuous distributions with finite range (a, b), the uniform distribution over this range has maximum entropy.

[37] Note that this is an "improper" density function because the constant density $1/2A$ in the interval $(-A, A)$ converges to zero as $A \to \infty$ We shall not discuss this problem.

respect to σ:

$$(9.14)\quad p(\mu \mid X) = \int_0^\infty p(\mu, \sigma \mid X)\, d\sigma$$

$$\propto \int_0^\infty \frac{1}{\sigma^{n+1}} \exp\left\{-\frac{1}{2}\frac{(n-1)s^2 + n(\bar{X}-\mu)^2}{\sigma^2}\right\} d\sigma$$

$$\propto \left(1 + \frac{[(\bar{X}-\mu)/(s/\sqrt{n})]^2}{n-1}\right)^{-n/2} \qquad \text{(see Problem 9.2)}$$

The last line indicates that the posterior distribution of μ is such that the ratio of $\bar{X} - \mu$ to $s/\sqrt{n}$ follows the Student distribution with $n - 1$ degrees of freedom [see eq. (6.8) of Section 2.6]. Recall eq. (8.3) of Section 2.8 and the discussion below that equation; the analysis presented there led to the same algebraic result, but again note that in the present case μ is regarded as random and $\bar{X}$ and s as fixed, whereas precisely the opposite is true for the case of Section 2.8.

This example also illustrates the fact that in a number of applications the Bayesian approach, given an appropriate mathematical expression of diffuseness, leads to the same expressions as those of Section 2.7 to 2.9. In fact, this similarity extends to a wide range, but by no means all, of the best-known statistical techniques. The interpretation of the result always differs, as noted above, in that what is regarded as a random variable in one approach is regarded as a fixed number in the other.

A Bayesian Interpretation of the Mixed Estimation Technique

Consider the basic equation of the standard linear model, $\mathbf{y} = \mathbf{X}\boldsymbol{\beta} + \boldsymbol{\epsilon}$, and assume that $\mathbf{X}$ has full column rank and that it consists of nonstochastic elements. Also, assume that the elements of $\boldsymbol{\epsilon}$ are independent random drawings from a normal population with zero mean and variance σ^2. Our objective is to analyze the mixed estimation procedure of Section 7.8 from a Bayesian point of view. The approach outlined there amounts to the use of a q-element vector $\mathbf{r}$, which is a prior unbiased estimator of $\mathbf{R}\boldsymbol{\beta}$, $\mathbf{R}$ being a given matrix of full row rank. This is written in the form $\mathbf{r} = \mathbf{R}\boldsymbol{\beta} + \mathbf{v}$, and the vector $\mathbf{v}$ thus has zero expectation because of the unbiasedness of $\mathbf{r}$. Furthermore, it was assumed in Section 7.8 that $\mathbf{v}$ has a known nonsingular covariance matrix $\mathbf{V}_0$. If this is the case, a simple linear transformation suffices to obtain an error vector with a unit covariance matrix. Write $\mathbf{V}_0^{-1} = \mathbf{P}'\mathbf{P}$, where $\mathbf{P}$ is a nonsingular $q \times q$ matrix; then the error vector $\mathbf{Pv}$ of $\mathbf{Pr} = \mathbf{PR}\boldsymbol{\beta} + \mathbf{Pv}$ has zero mean and covariance matrix $\mathbf{PV}_0\mathbf{P}' = \mathbf{P}(\mathbf{P}'\mathbf{P})^{-1}\mathbf{P}' = \mathbf{I}$. Therefore we can assume without real loss of generality that the error vector $\mathbf{v}$ of the prior estimator $\mathbf{r}$ has a unit covariance matrix.

The sample and prior information can thus be combined as follows:

$$(9.15)\qquad \begin{bmatrix}\mathbf{y}\\ \mathbf{r}\end{bmatrix} = \begin{bmatrix}\mathbf{X}\\ \mathbf{R}\end{bmatrix}\boldsymbol{\beta} + \begin{bmatrix}\boldsymbol{\epsilon}\\ \mathbf{v}\end{bmatrix} \qquad \mathscr{E}\begin{bmatrix}\boldsymbol{\epsilon}\\ \mathbf{v}\end{bmatrix} = \mathbf{0} \qquad \mathscr{V}\begin{bmatrix}\boldsymbol{\epsilon}\\ \mathbf{v}\end{bmatrix} = \begin{bmatrix}\sigma^2\mathbf{I} & \mathbf{0}\\ \mathbf{0} & \mathbf{I}\end{bmatrix}$$

which is precisely the same as eq. (8.6) of Section 7.8 except that the matrices $\mathbf{V}$ and $\mathbf{V}_0$ of that equation are specified here as unit matrices. Normality will be assumed throughout; hence the elements of the enlarged disturbance vector $[\boldsymbol{\epsilon}' \quad \mathbf{v}']$ are independent normal variates with zero mean and variance σ^2 for the first n elements and unit variance for the last q.

When applying Bayesian analysis to the uncertain prior information described in the previous paragraph, we face the problem that $\mathbf{r} = \mathbf{R}\boldsymbol{\beta} + \mathbf{v}$ is concerned with only q linear combinations of the K elements of $\boldsymbol{\beta}$, while nothing is stated about the variance σ^2. To solve this problem in a reasonably simple way we shall proceed in the following manner, which amounts to an adapted version of a result obtained by TIAO and ZELLNER (1964a)[38]. We act as if eq. (9.15) is concerned with sample information, so that the prior uncertain constraint $\mathbf{r} = \mathbf{R}\boldsymbol{\beta} + \mathbf{v}$ is treated as if it refers to a second sample which is independent of the sample with observation matrix $[\mathbf{y} \quad \mathbf{X}]$. In addition, given that the original prior information is now incorporated in the sample, we assume that the $\boldsymbol{\beta}$ elements and $\log \sigma$ are uniformly and independently distributed a priori:

$$(9.16)\qquad p(\boldsymbol{\beta}, \sigma) \propto \frac{1}{\sigma} \qquad \begin{matrix} -\infty < \beta_h < \infty \quad (h = 1, \ldots, K)\\ 0 < \sigma < \infty \end{matrix}$$

The likelihood of the sample (9.15), given fixed values of $\mathbf{X}$ and $\mathbf{R}$, is

(9.17)

$$L(\mathbf{y}, \mathbf{r}; \boldsymbol{\beta}, \sigma^2) \propto \frac{1}{\sigma^n} \exp\left\{-\frac{1}{2\sigma^2}(\mathbf{y} - \mathbf{X}\boldsymbol{\beta})'(\mathbf{y} - \mathbf{X}\boldsymbol{\beta}) - \frac{1}{2}(\mathbf{r} - \mathbf{R}\boldsymbol{\beta})'(\mathbf{r} - \mathbf{R}\boldsymbol{\beta})\right\}$$

The joint posterior density function of $\boldsymbol{\beta}$ and σ, $p(\boldsymbol{\beta}, \sigma \mid \mathbf{y}, \mathbf{r})$, is obtained by multiplying the functions (9.16) and (9.17), so that it is proportional to the right-hand side of (9.17) except that $1/\sigma^n$ before the exponent is to be replaced by $1/\sigma^{n+1}$. Integration with respect to σ then gives $p(\boldsymbol{\beta} \mid y, r)$, the posterior density function of $\boldsymbol{\beta}$. The result is given without proof:

$$(9.18)\qquad p(\boldsymbol{\beta} \mid \mathbf{y}, \mathbf{r}) \propto \left[1 + \frac{(\boldsymbol{\beta} - \mathbf{b})'\mathbf{X}'\mathbf{X}(\boldsymbol{\beta} - \mathbf{b})}{(n - K)s^2}\right]^{-n/2} \times \exp\left\{-\frac{1}{2}(\mathbf{r} - \mathbf{R}\boldsymbol{\beta})'(\mathbf{r} - \mathbf{R}\boldsymbol{\beta})\right\}$$

[38] Also see SUZUKI (1964).

where $\mathbf{b} = (\mathbf{X}'\mathbf{X})^{-1}\mathbf{X}'\mathbf{y}$ is the LS coefficient estimator and s^2 the corresponding variance estimator. The density function (9.18) is not very manageable analytically, but it can be evaluated by means of numerical methods. More interesting for our purpose is the following approximation, which is based on an expansion of the first factor on the right:

$$(9.19)\qquad p(\boldsymbol{\beta} \mid \mathbf{y}, \mathbf{r}) \propto \exp\left\{-\frac{1}{2}(\boldsymbol{\beta} - \mathbf{b}_M)'\left(\frac{1}{s^2}\mathbf{X}'\mathbf{X} + \mathbf{R}'\mathbf{R}\right)(\boldsymbol{\beta} - \mathbf{b}_M)\right\}$$

where

$$(9.20)\qquad \mathbf{b}_M = \left(\frac{1}{s^2}\mathbf{X}'\mathbf{X} + \mathbf{R}'\mathbf{R}\right)^{-1}\left(\frac{1}{s^2}\mathbf{X}'\mathbf{y} + \mathbf{R}'\mathbf{r}\right)$$

is nothing but the mixed estimator of $\boldsymbol{\beta}$ defined in eq. (8.8) of Section 7.8 (take unit matrices for $\mathbf{V}$ and $\mathbf{V}_0$ in that equation, so that $\hat{\sigma}^2$ becomes the LS variance estimator s^2). Thus the result is that, approximately, the parameter vector $\boldsymbol{\beta}$ is a posteriori normally distributed with an expectation equal to the mixed estimator $\mathbf{b}_M$ and a covariance matrix equal to the inverse of $(1/s^2)\mathbf{X}'\mathbf{X} + \mathbf{R}'\mathbf{R}$, that is, precisely the same matrix as that of (8.9) of Section 7.8 which is used there as an approximate covariance matrix of $\mathbf{b}_M$.

Extensions to Multi-Equation Systems

The Bayesian approach can be extended to many other areas that are discussed in this book including the multi-equation systems that are examined in Chapters 7, 9, and 10. When there are L equations and when $\boldsymbol{\Sigma}$ is the contemporaneous covariance matrix, a prior distribution has to be formulated which involves all elements of this $L \times L$ matrix in addition to the elements of the coefficient vectors. Usually little is known about $\boldsymbol{\Sigma}$ a priori, so that a diffuse prior distribution is needed. A convenient choice is $p(\boldsymbol{\Sigma}) \propto |\boldsymbol{\Sigma}|^{-(L+1)/2}$, which reduces to $p(\sigma) \propto 1/\sigma$ in the case $L = 1$.[39] There are

[39] As an example, take the demand model in relative prices as given in eq. (8.1) of Section 11.8 and assume, for simplicity's sake, that there is preference independence, so that $\nu_{ij} = 0$ for $i \neq j$ and $\nu_{ii} = \phi\mu_i$. Delete the last (Nth) equation; the unknown parameters are then $\mu_1, \ldots, \mu_{N-1}$, ϕ, and the elements of the $(N-1) \times (N-1)$ disturbance covariance matrix $\boldsymbol{\Omega}$. Assume that the vector $[\mu_1 \ \cdots \ \mu_{N-1}]$, the scalar ϕ and the matrix $\boldsymbol{\Omega}$ are a priori independent, so that the joint prior density function can be written as the product of three functions. Assume further that diffuse priors are needed for ϕ and $\boldsymbol{\Omega}$. A convenient choice is

$$p(-\phi) \propto 1/(-\phi) \qquad p(\boldsymbol{\Omega}) \propto |\boldsymbol{\Omega}|^{-N/2}$$

which corresponds to a uniform prior for $\log(-\phi)$ and to the covariance matrix prior mentioned in the text. For the prior of the marginal value shares an informative distribution would be more appropriate.

various ways of justifying this particular choice, but it is true, of course, that such generalizations are obtained at the cost of a reduced intuitive appeal.

DRÈZE (1962) suggested a Bayesian variant of identification analysis. The approach which was considered in particular in Sections 9.4 and 10.2 is based on constraints which imply that certain variables are absent from certain equations. Drèze's proposal is to formulate such constraints in the form of a prior distribution. Coefficients are then not constrained to be zero, but it is postulated that their distribution has most of its mass concentrated in a small interval around zero.

For other contributions to Bayesian inference in econometrics, see CHETTY (1968a, b), DRÈZE (1968), GEISSER (1965), RAIFFA and SCHLAIFER (1961, Chapter 13), ROTHENBERG (1963, 1968), TIAO and ZELLNER (1964b), and ZELLNER and TIAO (1964).

Problems

9.1 Explain in words the difference between the random character of the coefficients which is assumed in this section and the randomness of the coefficients considered in Sections 11.5 and 12.4.

9.2 Define $c = (n-1)s^2 + n(\bar{X} - \mu)^2$ and $\xi = c/2\sigma^2$. Prove that the integral on the second line of (9.14) is equal to the following integral and verify the proportionality relations thereafter:

$$(9.21)\quad c^{-n/2}\int_0^\infty (2\xi)^{(n-2)/2}e^{-\xi}\,d\xi \propto c^{-n/2}$$

$$= [(n-1)s^2 + n(\bar{X}-\mu)^2]^{-n/2} \propto \left[1 + \frac{n(\bar{X}-\mu)^2/s^2}{n-1}\right]^{-n/2}$$

APPENDIX

A. Elements of Consumer Demand Theory

Preliminary

Write **p** and **q** for the N-element column vectors of prices and quantities, respectively, so that the utility function becomes $u = u(\mathbf{q})$ and the budget constraint $\mathbf{p}'\mathbf{q} = m$. It is assumed that **p** and m are given from the consumer's point of view. To maximize $u(\mathbf{q})$ subject to $\mathbf{p}'\mathbf{q} = m$ we form the Lagrangian expression

$$u(\mathbf{q}) - \lambda(\mathbf{p}'\mathbf{q} - m) \tag{A.1}$$

where λ is a Lagrangian multiplier. Then differentiate (A.1) with respect to q_i and equate the result to zero:

$$\frac{\partial u}{\partial q_i} = \lambda p_i \qquad i = 1, \ldots, N \tag{A.2}$$

These N proportionalities of the marginal utilities of the commodities and the corresponding prices plus the budget constraint are equal in number to the N unknown optimal quantities plus the associated value of λ, which is known as the marginal utility of income. It is assumed that the utility function has continuous second-order derivatives in the relevant region, so that the Hessian matrix $\mathbf{U} = [\partial^2 u/\partial q_i \partial q_j]$ at the point of the constrained maximum is symmetric. It is also assumed that **U** is negative definite, which is a sufficient condition for the existence of a utility maximum. Finally, it is assumed that the marginal utilities as well as the values of the optimal quantities are all positive.

The objective is to evaluate the derivatives of the demand equations (5.1) of Section 7.5 in money income and absolute prices:

$$q_i^0 = Q_i(m, p_1, \ldots, p_N) \qquad i = 1, \ldots, N \tag{A.3}$$

as well as those of the demand equations (5.2) of the same section in real income and absolute prices:

$$q_i^0 = q_i(\bar{m}, p_1, \ldots, p_N) \qquad i = 1, \ldots, N \tag{A.4}$$

and to clarify the relationship between real income $\bar{m}$ and $m, p_1, \ldots, p_N$.

The Fundamental Matrix Equation

Differentiate both sides of the budget constraint $\mathbf{p}'\mathbf{q} = m$ with respect to m:

$$\mathbf{p}'\mathbf{q}_m = 1 \tag{A.5}$$

where $\mathbf{q}_m = [\partial Q_i/\partial m]$ is the vector of income derivatives of the N demand functions (A.3). Similarly, by differentiating the budget constraint with respect to p_k, we obtain

$$\sum_{i=1}^{N} p_i \frac{\partial Q_i}{\partial p_k} + q_k = 0$$

If we repeat this for all prices, we can write the result in matrix form:

$$\mathbf{p}'\mathbf{Q}_p + \mathbf{q}' = \mathbf{0} \tag{A.6}$$

where $\mathbf{Q}_p = [\partial Q_i/\partial p_j]$ is the matrix of price derivatives of the N demand equations (A.3) with respect to the N prices.

We proceed to handle the N proportionalities (A.2) in the same way. First, differentiate them with respect to income:

$$\sum_{j=1}^{N} \frac{\partial^2 u}{\partial q_i\, \partial q_j} \frac{\partial Q_j}{\partial m} = p_i \frac{\partial \lambda}{\partial m} \qquad i = 1, \ldots, N$$

or in matrix form:

$$\mathbf{U}\mathbf{q}_m = \lambda_m \mathbf{p} \tag{A.7}$$

where $\lambda_m = \partial\lambda/\partial m$. Next, differentiate (A.2) with respect to the kth price:

$$\sum_{j=1}^{N} \frac{\partial^2 u}{\partial q_i\, \partial q_j} \frac{\partial Q_j}{\partial p_k} = \begin{cases} p_i \dfrac{\partial \lambda}{\partial p_k} & \text{if } k \neq i \\[2ex] p_i \dfrac{\partial \lambda}{\partial p_i} + \lambda & \text{if } k = i \end{cases}$$

or in matrix form

$$\text{(A.8)} \qquad \mathbf{U}\mathbf{Q}_p = \mathbf{p}\boldsymbol{\lambda}_p' + \lambda\mathbf{I}$$

where $\boldsymbol{\lambda}_p$ is the column vector of price derivatives of the marginal utility of income and $\mathbf{I}$ the $N \times N$ unit matrix.

The results (A.5) to (A.8) can be combined in the following partitioned form:

$$\text{(A.9)} \qquad \begin{bmatrix} \mathbf{U} & \mathbf{p} \\ \mathbf{p}' & 0 \end{bmatrix} \begin{bmatrix} \mathbf{q}_m & \mathbf{Q}_p \\ -\lambda_m & -\boldsymbol{\lambda}_p' \end{bmatrix} = \begin{bmatrix} \mathbf{0} & \lambda\mathbf{I} \\ 1 & -\mathbf{q}' \end{bmatrix}$$

This equation, from BARTEN (1964), is known as the fundamental matrix equation of consumer demand theory.

Solving the Fundamental Matrix Equation

We apply eq. (2.15) of Section 1.2 to obtain the inverse of the bordered Hessian matrix in the left-hand side of (A.9):

$$\begin{bmatrix} \mathbf{U} & \mathbf{p} \\ \mathbf{p}' & 0 \end{bmatrix}^{-1} = \frac{1}{\mathbf{p}'\mathbf{U}^{-1}\mathbf{p}} \begin{bmatrix} (\mathbf{p}'\mathbf{U}^{-1}\mathbf{p})\mathbf{U}^{-1} - \mathbf{U}^{-1}\mathbf{p}(\mathbf{U}^{-1}\mathbf{p})' & \mathbf{U}^{-1}\mathbf{p} \\ (\mathbf{U}^{-1}\mathbf{p})' & -1 \end{bmatrix}$$

Premultiplication of both sides of (A.9) by this inverse gives the following solution for the income derivatives $\mathbf{q}_m$ and λ_m and for the price derivative $\mathbf{Q}_p$:

$$\text{(A.10)} \qquad \begin{aligned} \mathbf{q}_m &= \frac{1}{\mathbf{p}'\mathbf{U}^{-1}\mathbf{p}}\mathbf{U}^{-1}\mathbf{p} \qquad\qquad \lambda_m = \frac{1}{\mathbf{p}'\mathbf{U}^{-1}\mathbf{p}} \\ \mathbf{Q}_p &= \lambda\mathbf{U}^{-1} - \frac{\lambda}{\mathbf{p}'\mathbf{U}^{-1}\mathbf{p}}\mathbf{U}^{-1}\mathbf{p}(\mathbf{U}^{-1}\mathbf{p})' - \frac{1}{\mathbf{p}'\mathbf{U}^{-1}\mathbf{p}}\mathbf{U}^{-1}\mathbf{p}\mathbf{q}' \end{aligned}$$

The expression for $\mathbf{q}_m$ can be simplified by substituting λ_m for the reciprocal of $\mathbf{p}'\mathbf{U}^{-1}\mathbf{p}$, which gives

$$\text{(A.11)} \qquad \mathbf{q}_m = \lambda_m\mathbf{U}^{-1}\mathbf{p}$$

Similarly, by making this substitution and by replacing the vector $\mathbf{U}^{-1}\mathbf{p}$ by $(1/\lambda_m)\mathbf{q}_m$, we obtain for $\mathbf{Q}_p$:

$$\text{(A.12)} \qquad \mathbf{Q}_p = \lambda\mathbf{U}^{-1} - \frac{\lambda}{\lambda_m}\mathbf{q}_m\mathbf{q}_m' - \mathbf{q}_m\mathbf{q}'$$

which shows that the price derivatives of the demand equations (A.3) consist of three terms.

Real Income and the Income Effect of Price Changes

Equation (A.12) in scalar form is as follows:

$$\text{(A.13)} \qquad \frac{\partial Q_i}{\partial p_j} = \lambda u^{ij} - \frac{\lambda}{\partial\lambda/\partial m}\frac{\partial Q_i}{\partial m}\frac{\partial Q_j}{\partial m} - \frac{\partial Q_i}{\partial m}q_j \qquad i, j = 1, \ldots, N$$

where u^{ij} is the (i, j)th element of $\mathbf{U}^{-1}$. The last term on the right is the income effect of a price increase dp_j on the ith quantity: if p_j increases by dp_j, the commodity basket that was originally optimal becomes more expensive and an income compensation equal to $q_j dp_j$ is needed to enable the consumer to buy this basket in the new price situation. If he receives this compensation, he faces two changes: a price increase dp_j and an income increase $dm = q_j dp_j$. It follows from (A.13) that their combined effect on the ith quantity is

$$\text{(A.14)} \qquad \left(\frac{\partial Q_i}{\partial p_j} + \frac{\partial Q_i}{\partial m}q_j\right) dp_j = \left(\lambda u^{ij} - \frac{\lambda}{\partial\lambda/\partial m}\frac{\partial Q_i}{\partial m}\frac{\partial Q_j}{\partial m}\right) dp_j$$

The left-hand side of (A.14) is the effect of dp_j on q_i when real income is held constant. Suppose now that all prices change infinitesimally, so that their combined income effect is $q_1 dp_1 + \cdots + q_N dp_N$. When the actual change in money income is dm, the change in real income is

$$\text{(A.15)} \qquad d\bar{m} = dm - \sum_{k=1}^{N} q_k dp_k$$

This equation specifies only the change in real income and thus leaves its level undefined. If we define this level equal to that of money income (m), we obtain after dividing both sides of (A.15) by m:

$$\text{(A.16)} \qquad d(\log \bar{m}) = d(\log m) - \sum_{k=1}^{N} w_k d(\log p_k)$$

This result provides a specification of the real income term in the demand equations (5.6) and (5.9) of Section 7.5.

The Total Substitution Effect of Price Changes

It was stated below (A.14) that the left-hand side of that equation measures the effect of dp_j on the ith quantity when real income is held constant. Hence this expression is equal to dp_j multiplied by the derivative of the demand equation (A.4) with respect to p_j:

$$\text{(A.17)} \qquad \frac{\partial q_i}{\partial p_j} = \lambda u^{ij} - \frac{\lambda}{\partial\lambda/\partial m}\frac{\partial q_i}{\partial m}\frac{\partial q_j}{\partial m}$$

The income derivatives in the right-hand side may be written as either $\partial q_i/\partial m$ or $\partial Q_i/\partial m$ because (A.3) and (A.4) describe the ith quantity as the same function of income when the prices are held constant.

It is immediately evident from (A.17) that $[\partial q_i/\partial p_j]$ is a symmetric matrix. To prove that it is negative semidefinite of rank $N - 1$ we go back to (A.10), which shows that $\partial \mathbf{q}/\partial \mathbf{p}'$ can be written as a (positive) multiple λ of the matrix

$$\mathbf{A} = \mathbf{U}^{-1} - \frac{1}{\mathbf{p}'\mathbf{U}^{-1}\mathbf{p}} \mathbf{U}^{-1}\mathbf{p}(\mathbf{U}^{-1}\mathbf{p})'$$

The quadratic form $\mathbf{x}'\mathbf{A}\mathbf{x}$, where $\mathbf{x}$ is an arbitrary N-element vector, is of the following form:

$$\mathbf{x}'\mathbf{A}\mathbf{x} = \frac{1}{\mathbf{p}'\mathbf{U}^{-1}\mathbf{p}} [(\mathbf{x}'\mathbf{U}^{-1}\mathbf{x})(\mathbf{p}'\mathbf{U}^{-1}\mathbf{p}) - (\mathbf{x}'\mathbf{U}^{-1}\mathbf{p})^2]$$

The expression in square brackets vanishes if a scalar c exists such that $\mathbf{x} = c\mathbf{p}$, and it is positive when no such scalar exists.[1] Therefore, given that $\mathbf{p}'\mathbf{U}^{-1}\mathbf{p}$ before the brackets is negative, the matrix $\mathbf{A}$ and hence also $\partial \mathbf{q}/\partial \mathbf{p}'$ are negative semidefinite of rank $N - 1$.

Three Constraints on Income and Price Derivatives

The matrices which occur in (A.11) and (A.12) are subject to three constraints. One is (A.5), which states that the weighted sum of the elements of $\mathbf{q}_m$ of (A.11) is equal to 1 when the corresponding prices are chosen as weights. Another concerns the first matrix which appears in the right-hand side of (A.12):

(A.18) $\lambda \mathbf{U}^{-1}$ is symmetric and negative definite

The third follows from (A.11):

$$\text{(A.19)} \qquad \lambda \mathbf{U}^{-1}\left(\frac{\lambda_m}{\lambda}\mathbf{p}\right) = \mathbf{q}_m$$

which means that if we postmultiply the first right-hand matrix of (A.12) by the price vector, we obtain a scalar multiple of the vector of income derivatives of the demand equations.

[1] This is easily proved by means of Schwarz' inequality after writing $\mathbf{U}^{-1} = \mathbf{B}'\mathbf{B}$ for a nonsingular $\mathbf{B}$.

B. Derivation of the Limited-Information Maximum-Likelihood Estimator

Preliminary

The Lagrangian expression to be considered is given in eq. (4.9) of Section 10.4:

$$\text{(B.1)} \qquad \frac{1}{2} n \log |\mathbf{\Omega}_j| + \frac{1}{2} \operatorname{tr} \mathbf{\Omega}_j^{-1}\mathbf{D}_j'\mathbf{D}_j - \boldsymbol{\lambda}'(\boldsymbol{\pi}_j^* - \mathbf{\Pi}_j^*\boldsymbol{\gamma}_j)$$

where $\mathbf{D}_j$ is a reduced-form disturbance matrix defined in eq. (4.7) of the same section:

$$\text{(B.2)} \qquad \mathbf{D}_j = [\mathbf{y}_j \quad \mathbf{Y}_j] - \mathbf{X}\begin{bmatrix} \boldsymbol{\pi}_j & \mathbf{\Pi}_j \\ \boldsymbol{\pi}_j^* & \mathbf{\Pi}_j^* \end{bmatrix}$$

The following derivatives will be needed:

$$\text{(B.3)} \qquad \frac{\partial\left(\frac{1}{2} \operatorname{tr} \mathbf{\Omega}_j^{-1}\mathbf{D}_j'\mathbf{D}_j\right)}{\partial \mathbf{D}_j} = \mathbf{D}_j\mathbf{\Omega}_j^{-1}$$

$$\text{(B.4)} \qquad \frac{\partial\left(\frac{1}{2} \operatorname{tr} \mathbf{\Omega}_j^{-1}\mathbf{D}_j'\mathbf{D}_j\right)}{\partial \begin{bmatrix} \boldsymbol{\pi}_j & \mathbf{\Pi}_j \\ \boldsymbol{\pi}_j^* & \mathbf{\Pi}_j^* \end{bmatrix}} = -\mathbf{X}'\mathbf{D}_j\mathbf{\Omega}_j^{-1}$$

$$\text{(B.5)} \qquad \frac{\partial(\boldsymbol{\lambda}'\boldsymbol{\pi}_j^* - \boldsymbol{\lambda}'\mathbf{\Pi}_j^*\boldsymbol{\gamma}_j)}{\partial \begin{bmatrix} \boldsymbol{\pi}_j & \mathbf{\Pi}_j \\ \boldsymbol{\pi}_j^* & \mathbf{\Pi}_j^* \end{bmatrix}} = \begin{bmatrix} \mathbf{0} & \mathbf{0} \\ \boldsymbol{\lambda} & -\boldsymbol{\lambda}\boldsymbol{\gamma}_j' \end{bmatrix}$$

By computing the derivatives of (B.1) with respect to $\boldsymbol{\pi}_j$, $\boldsymbol{\pi}_j^*$, $\mathbf{\Pi}_j$, and $\mathbf{\Pi}_j^*$ and equating the result to zero, we obtain

$$\text{(B.6)} \qquad \mathbf{X}'\mathbf{D}_j\mathbf{\Omega}_j^{-1} + \begin{bmatrix} \mathbf{0} & \mathbf{0} \\ \boldsymbol{\lambda} & -\boldsymbol{\lambda}\boldsymbol{\gamma}_j' \end{bmatrix} = \mathbf{0}$$

Similarly, by differentiating (B.1) with respect to $\boldsymbol{\lambda}$ and $\boldsymbol{\gamma}_j$ and equating the results to zero, we find

$$\text{(B.7)} \qquad \boldsymbol{\pi}_j^* - \mathbf{\Pi}_j^*\boldsymbol{\gamma}_j = \mathbf{0} \qquad \mathbf{\Pi}_j^{*\prime}\boldsymbol{\lambda} = \mathbf{0}$$

Notation

It will prove convenient to handle all $L_j + 1$ jointly dependent variables of our equation symmetrically. Suppose, then, that this equation is the first of the system, so that we may put $j = 1$, and introduce

$$\text{(B.8)} \qquad \mathbf{Y}_0 = [\mathbf{y}_1 \quad \mathbf{Y}_1] \qquad \begin{bmatrix} \mathbf{\Pi}_0 \\ \mathbf{\Pi}_0^* \end{bmatrix} = \begin{bmatrix} \boldsymbol{\pi}_1 & \mathbf{\Pi}_1 \\ \hdashline \boldsymbol{\pi}_1^* & \mathbf{\Pi}_1^* \end{bmatrix} \qquad \boldsymbol{\gamma}_0 = \begin{bmatrix} -1 \\ \boldsymbol{\gamma}_1 \end{bmatrix}$$

Our equation $\mathbf{y}_1 = \mathbf{Y}_1\boldsymbol{\gamma}_1 + \mathbf{X}_1\boldsymbol{\beta}_1 + \boldsymbol{\epsilon}_1$ thus takes the form

$$\text{(B.9)} \qquad \mathbf{Y}_0\boldsymbol{\gamma}_0 + \mathbf{X}_1\boldsymbol{\beta}_1 + \boldsymbol{\epsilon}_1 = \mathbf{0}$$

which is indeed symmetric in all $L_1 + 1$ jointly dependent variables of this equation. It is readily verified that the determinantal equation (4.11) of Section 10.4 is now simplified to

$$\text{(B.10)} \qquad |\mathbf{Y}_0'\mathbf{M}_1\mathbf{Y}_0 - \mu\mathbf{Y}_0'\mathbf{M}\mathbf{Y}_0| = 0$$

The reduced-form disturbance matrix $\mathbf{D}_1$ of (B.2) is now

$$\text{(B.11)} \qquad \mathbf{D}_1 = \mathbf{Y}_0 - \mathbf{X}_1\mathbf{\Pi}_0 - \mathbf{X}_1^*\mathbf{\Pi}_0^*$$

where $\mathbf{X}_1^*$ is the observation matrix of the $K - K_1$ predetermined variables which are excluded from the first equation. Then postmultiply both sides of (B.6) for $j = 1$ by $\mathbf{\Omega}_1$ and write the result in the form of two matrix equations:

$$\text{(B.12)} \qquad \mathbf{X}_1'\mathbf{Y}_0 - \mathbf{X}_1'\mathbf{X}_1\mathbf{\Pi}_0 - \mathbf{X}_1'\mathbf{X}_1^*\mathbf{\Pi}_0^* = \mathbf{0}$$

$$\text{(B.13)} \qquad \mathbf{X}_1^{*\prime}\mathbf{Y}_0 - \mathbf{X}_1^{*\prime}\mathbf{X}_1\mathbf{\Pi}_0 - \mathbf{X}_1^{*\prime}\mathbf{X}_1^*\mathbf{\Pi}_0^* - \boldsymbol{\lambda}\boldsymbol{\gamma}_0'\mathbf{\Omega}_1 = \mathbf{0}$$

In the same way, the expression $\boldsymbol{\lambda}'(\boldsymbol{\pi}_j^* - \mathbf{\Pi}_j^*\boldsymbol{\gamma}_j)$ in (B.1) is now simplified to $-\boldsymbol{\lambda}'\mathbf{\Pi}_0^*\boldsymbol{\gamma}_0$, so that the first equation of (B.7) becomes $\mathbf{\Pi}_0^*\boldsymbol{\gamma}_0 = \mathbf{0}$ and the second [which is now obtained by differentiating (B.1) for $j = 1$ with respect to $\boldsymbol{\gamma}_0$] becomes $\mathbf{\Pi}_0^{*\prime}\boldsymbol{\lambda} = \mathbf{0}$. To indicate that we have estimators rather than parameters in these equations, we replace the $\mathbf{\Pi}$'s by $\mathbf{P}$'s and $\boldsymbol{\gamma}_0$ by $\mathbf{c}_0$ in what follows. The two equations just derived thus take the following form:

$$\text{(B.14)} \qquad \mathbf{P}_0^*\mathbf{c}_0 = \mathbf{0} \qquad \mathbf{P}_0^{*\prime}\boldsymbol{\lambda} = \mathbf{0}$$

and eq. (B.12) enables us to express $\mathbf{P}_0$ in terms of $\mathbf{P}_0^*$:

$$\text{(B.15)} \qquad \mathbf{P}_0 = (\mathbf{X}_1'\mathbf{X}_1)^{-1}\mathbf{X}_1'(\mathbf{Y}_0 - \mathbf{X}_1^*\mathbf{P}_0^*)$$

By substituting this result into (B.13)—with the $\mathbf{\Pi}$'s replaced by $\mathbf{P}$'s—we obtain

$$\mathbf{X}_1^{*\prime}(\mathbf{Y}_0 - \mathbf{X}_1^*\mathbf{P}_0^*) - \mathbf{X}_1^{*\prime}\mathbf{X}_1(\mathbf{X}_1'\mathbf{X}_1)^{-1}\mathbf{X}_1'(\mathbf{Y}_0 - \mathbf{X}_1^*\mathbf{P}_0^*) - \boldsymbol{\lambda}\mathbf{c}_0'\mathbf{\Omega}_1 = \mathbf{0}$$

or, equivalently,

$$\mathbf{X}_1^{*\prime}\mathbf{M}_1\mathbf{Y}_0 - \mathbf{X}_1^{*\prime}\mathbf{M}_1\mathbf{X}_1^*\mathbf{P}_0^* - \boldsymbol{\lambda}\mathbf{c}_0'\mathbf{\Omega}_1 = \mathbf{0}$$

This gives

$$\mathbf{P}_0^* = (\mathbf{X}_1^{*\prime}\mathbf{M}_1\mathbf{X}_1^*)^{-1}(\mathbf{X}_1^{*\prime}\mathbf{M}_1\mathbf{Y}_0 - \boldsymbol{\lambda}\mathbf{c}_0'\boldsymbol{\Omega}_1) \tag{B.16}$$

Estimation of the Reduced-Form Covariance Matrix

The result (B.16) indicates that the covariance matrix $\boldsymbol{\Omega}_1$ enters into the estimation equations in an essential way. This is in sharp contrast to the case of the logarithmic likelihood estimator (4.4) of Section 10.4, which is maximized by the $\boldsymbol{\Pi}$ estimator $(\mathbf{X}'\mathbf{X})^{-1}\mathbf{X}'\mathbf{Y}$ for whatever value of $\boldsymbol{\Omega}$. Here it is no longer sufficient to minimize (B.1) for variations in the coefficients; we must also consider variations in the reduced-form disturbance covariance matrix. The simplest procedure is to compute the derivative of (B.1) for $j = 1$ with respect to $\boldsymbol{\Omega}_1^{-1}$:

$$\frac{\partial\left(\frac{1}{2}n \log |\boldsymbol{\Omega}_1|\right)}{\partial \boldsymbol{\Omega}_1^{-1}} + \frac{\partial\left(\frac{1}{2}\operatorname{tr} \boldsymbol{\Omega}_1^{-1}\mathbf{D}_1'\mathbf{D}_1\right)}{\partial \boldsymbol{\Omega}_1^{-1}} = -\frac{1}{2}n\boldsymbol{\Omega}_1 + \frac{1}{2}\mathbf{D}_1'\mathbf{D}_1 \tag{B.17}$$

which shows that the maximum-likelihood estimator of $\boldsymbol{\Omega}_1$, to be written $\hat{\boldsymbol{\Omega}}_1$, is equal to the matrix of mean squares and products of the reduced-form maximum-likelihood residuals:

$$\hat{\boldsymbol{\Omega}}_1 = \frac{1}{n}\hat{\mathbf{D}}_1'\hat{\mathbf{D}}_1 \tag{B.18}$$

where $\hat{\mathbf{D}}_1$ is equal to $\mathbf{D}_1$ of (B.11) except that the $\boldsymbol{\Pi}$'s in the right-hand side are replaced by $\mathbf{P}$'s:

$$\begin{aligned} \hat{\mathbf{D}}_1 &= \mathbf{Y}_0 - \mathbf{X}_1\mathbf{P}_0 - \mathbf{X}_1^*\mathbf{P}_0^* \\ &= \mathbf{Y}_0 - \mathbf{X}_1^*\mathbf{P}_0^* - \mathbf{X}_1(\mathbf{X}_1'\mathbf{X}_1)^{-1}\mathbf{X}_1'(\mathbf{Y}_0 - \mathbf{X}_1^*\mathbf{P}_0^*) \qquad \text{[see (B.15)]} \\ &= \mathbf{M}_1(\mathbf{Y}_0 - \mathbf{X}_1^*\mathbf{P}_0^*) \end{aligned} \tag{B.19}$$

Next we postmultiply both sides of (B.16) by $\mathbf{c}_0$ and use (B.14) to obtain the following solution for the vector of Lagrangian multipliers:

$$\boldsymbol{\lambda} = \frac{1}{\mathbf{c}_0'\hat{\boldsymbol{\Omega}}_1\mathbf{c}_0}\mathbf{X}_1^{*\prime}\mathbf{M}_1\mathbf{Y}_0\mathbf{c}_0 \tag{B.20}$$

Substitute this into (B.16):

$$\mathbf{P}_0^* = (\mathbf{X}_1^{*\prime}\mathbf{M}_1\mathbf{X}_1^*)^{-1}\mathbf{X}_1^{*\prime}\mathbf{M}_1\mathbf{Y}_0\left(\mathbf{I} - \frac{1}{\mathbf{c}_0'\hat{\boldsymbol{\Omega}}_1\mathbf{c}_0}\mathbf{c}_0\mathbf{c}_0'\hat{\boldsymbol{\Omega}}_1\right) \tag{B.21}$$

from which it is readily verified that $\mathbf{P}_0^*\mathbf{c}_0 = \mathbf{0}$ holds as (B.14) requires.

Combine this with (B.19):

$$\text{(B.22)} \qquad \hat{\mathbf{D}}_1 = [\mathbf{M}_1 - \mathbf{M}_1\mathbf{X}_1^*(\mathbf{X}_1^{*\prime}\mathbf{M}_1\mathbf{X}_1^*)^{-1}\mathbf{X}_1^{*\prime}\mathbf{M}_1]\mathbf{Y}_0 + \frac{1}{\mathbf{c}_0'\hat{\mathbf{\Omega}}_1\mathbf{c}_0}\mathbf{M}_1\mathbf{X}_1^*(\mathbf{X}_1^{*\prime}\mathbf{M}_1\mathbf{X}_1^*)^{-1}\mathbf{X}_1^{*\prime}\mathbf{M}_1\mathbf{Y}_0\mathbf{c}_0\mathbf{c}_0'\hat{\mathbf{\Omega}}_1$$
$$= \mathbf{M}\mathbf{Y}_0 + \frac{1}{\mathbf{c}_0'\hat{\mathbf{\Omega}}_1\mathbf{c}_0}(\mathbf{M}_1 - \mathbf{M})\mathbf{Y}_0\mathbf{c}_0\mathbf{c}_0'\hat{\mathbf{\Omega}}_1$$

The second equality sign is based on

$$\text{(B.23)} \quad \mathbf{M}_1 - \mathbf{M} = \mathbf{X}(\mathbf{X}'\mathbf{X})^{-1}\mathbf{X}' - \mathbf{X}_1(\mathbf{X}_1'\mathbf{X}_1)^{-1}\mathbf{X}_1'$$
$$= [\mathbf{X}_1 \quad \mathbf{X}_1^*]\begin{bmatrix} \mathbf{X}_1'\mathbf{X}_1 & \mathbf{X}_1'\mathbf{X}_1^* \\ \mathbf{X}_1^{*\prime}\mathbf{X}_1 & \mathbf{X}_1^{*\prime}\mathbf{X}_1^* \end{bmatrix}^{-1}\begin{bmatrix} \mathbf{X}_1' \\ \mathbf{X}_1^{*\prime} \end{bmatrix} - \mathbf{X}_1(\mathbf{X}_1'\mathbf{X}_1)^{-1}\mathbf{X}_1'$$
$$= \mathbf{M}_1\mathbf{X}_1^*(\mathbf{X}_1^{*\prime}\mathbf{M}_1\mathbf{X}_1^*)^{-1}\mathbf{X}_1^{*\prime}\mathbf{M}_1$$

The last step follows from the partitioned inversion procedure of eq. (2.15) of Section 1.2. (Basically, the derivation is identical with that of Problems 7.3 to 7.5 of Section 3.7.)

The matrices $\mathbf{M}$, $\mathbf{M}_1$ and $\mathbf{M}_1 - \mathbf{M}$ are all idempotent. Also, the product of $\mathbf{M}$ and $\mathbf{M}_1 - \mathbf{M}$ is a zero matrix:

$$\mathbf{M}(\mathbf{M}_1 - \mathbf{M}) = \mathbf{M}_1(\mathbf{M}_1 - \mathbf{M}) - (\mathbf{M}_1 - \mathbf{M})^2 = \mathbf{M}_1 - \mathbf{M} - (\mathbf{M}_1 - \mathbf{M}) = \mathbf{0}$$

Using these properties, we conclude from (B.18) and (B.22):

$$\text{(B.24)} \qquad \hat{\mathbf{\Omega}}_1 = \frac{1}{n}\mathbf{Y}_0'\mathbf{M}\mathbf{Y}_0 + \frac{\mathbf{c}_0'\mathbf{Y}_0'(\mathbf{M}_1 - \mathbf{M})\mathbf{Y}_0\mathbf{c}_0}{n(\mathbf{c}_0'\hat{\mathbf{\Omega}}_1\mathbf{c}_0)^2}\hat{\mathbf{\Omega}}_1\mathbf{c}_0\mathbf{c}_0'\hat{\mathbf{\Omega}}_1$$

which shows that $\hat{\mathbf{\Omega}}_1$ exceeds $(1/n)\mathbf{Y}_0'\mathbf{M}\mathbf{Y}_0$, the unconstrained maximum-likelihood estimator of $\mathbf{\Omega}_1$, by a positive semidefinite matrix. This is the natural consequence of the fact that the likelihood function is maximized subject to constraints.

Equation (B.24) provides no explicit solution for $\hat{\mathbf{\Omega}}_1$, since it contains this matrix in the right-hand side also. So we postmultiply both sides of this equation by $\mathbf{c}_0$:

$$\hat{\mathbf{\Omega}}_1\mathbf{c}_0 = \frac{1}{n}\mathbf{Y}_0'\mathbf{M}\mathbf{Y}_0\mathbf{c}_0 + \frac{\mathbf{c}_0'\mathbf{Y}_0'(\mathbf{M}_1 - \mathbf{M})\mathbf{Y}_0\mathbf{c}_0}{n(\mathbf{c}_0'\hat{\mathbf{\Omega}}_1\mathbf{c}_0)}\hat{\mathbf{\Omega}}_1\mathbf{c}_0$$

which implies the following solution for the vector $\hat{\mathbf{\Omega}}_1\mathbf{c}_0$:

$$\text{(B.25)} \qquad \hat{\mathbf{\Omega}}_1\mathbf{c}_0 = \frac{1}{n(1-\alpha)}\mathbf{Y}_0'\mathbf{M}\mathbf{Y}_0\mathbf{c}_0$$

where

$$\alpha = \frac{\mathbf{c}_0'\mathbf{Y}_0'(\mathbf{M}_1 - \mathbf{M})\mathbf{Y}_0\mathbf{c}_0}{n(\mathbf{c}_0'\hat{\mathbf{\Omega}}_1\mathbf{c}_0)} \geq 0 \tag{B.26}$$

Also, pre- and postmultiplying (B.24) by $\mathbf{c}_0'$ and $\mathbf{c}_0$, respectively, and premultiplying (B.25) by $\mathbf{c}_0'$, we find:

$$\begin{aligned} \mathbf{c}_0'\hat{\mathbf{\Omega}}_1\mathbf{c}_0 &= \frac{1}{n}\,\mathbf{c}_0'\mathbf{Y}_0'\mathbf{M}_1\mathbf{Y}_0\mathbf{c}_0 \\ &= \frac{1}{n(1-\alpha)}\,\mathbf{c}_0'\mathbf{Y}_0'\mathbf{M}\mathbf{Y}_0\mathbf{c}_0 \end{aligned} \tag{B.27}$$

The equivalence of the two right-hand expressions in (B.27) implies

$$\alpha = 1 - \frac{\mathbf{c}_0'\mathbf{Y}_0'\mathbf{M}\mathbf{Y}_0\mathbf{c}_0}{\mathbf{c}_0'\mathbf{Y}_0'\mathbf{M}_1\mathbf{Y}_0\mathbf{c}_0} \tag{B.28}$$

This result in conjunction with (B.26) indicates that α lies between zero and one.

Consider now the ratio which occurs in the second term on the right of (B.24):

$$\begin{aligned} \frac{\mathbf{c}_0'\mathbf{Y}_0'(\mathbf{M}_1 - \mathbf{M})\mathbf{Y}_0\mathbf{c}_0}{n(\mathbf{c}_0'\hat{\mathbf{\Omega}}_1\mathbf{c}_0)^2} &= \frac{\alpha}{\mathbf{c}_0'\hat{\mathbf{\Omega}}_1\mathbf{c}_0} && \text{[see (B.26)]} \\ &= \frac{n\alpha(1-\alpha)}{\mathbf{c}_0'\mathbf{Y}_0'\mathbf{M}\mathbf{Y}_0\mathbf{c}_0} && \text{[see (B.27)]} \end{aligned}$$

Combining this result with (B.24) and (B.25), we obtain the following solution for $\hat{\mathbf{\Omega}}_1$:

$$\hat{\mathbf{\Omega}}_1 = \frac{1}{n}\,\mathbf{Y}_0'\mathbf{M}\mathbf{Y}_0 + \frac{\alpha}{n(1-\alpha)\mathbf{c}_0'\mathbf{Y}_0'\mathbf{M}\mathbf{Y}_0\mathbf{c}_0}\,\mathbf{Y}_0'\mathbf{M}\mathbf{Y}_0\mathbf{c}_0(\mathbf{Y}_0'\mathbf{M}\mathbf{Y}_0\mathbf{c}_0)' \tag{B.29}$$

The Determinantal Equation and Its Smallest Root

We have $\mathbf{P}_0^{*\prime}\boldsymbol{\lambda} = \mathbf{0}$ in view of (B.14). Application of (B.20) and (B.21) shows that this amounts to

$$\left(\mathbf{I} - \frac{1}{\mathbf{c}_0'\hat{\mathbf{\Omega}}_1\mathbf{c}_0}\hat{\mathbf{\Omega}}_1\mathbf{c}_0\mathbf{c}_0'\right)\mathbf{Y}_0'\mathbf{M}_1\mathbf{X}_1^*(\mathbf{X}_1^{*\prime}\mathbf{M}_1\mathbf{X}_1^*)^{-1}\mathbf{X}_1^{*\prime}\mathbf{M}_1\mathbf{Y}_0\mathbf{c}_0 = \mathbf{0}$$

which can be simplified in view of (B.23):

$$\left(\mathbf{I} - \frac{1}{\mathbf{c}_0'\hat{\mathbf{\Omega}}_1\mathbf{c}_0}\hat{\mathbf{\Omega}}_1\mathbf{c}_0\mathbf{c}_0'\right)\mathbf{Y}_0'(\mathbf{M}_1 - \mathbf{M})\mathbf{Y}_0\mathbf{c}_0 = \mathbf{0} \tag{B.30}$$

Apply (B.25) and (B.27):

$$\frac{1}{\mathbf{c}_0'\hat{\mathbf{\Omega}}_1\mathbf{c}_0}\hat{\mathbf{\Omega}}_1\mathbf{c}_0 = \frac{1}{\mathbf{c}_0'\mathbf{Y}_0'\mathbf{M}\mathbf{Y}_0\mathbf{c}_0}\mathbf{Y}_0'\mathbf{M}\mathbf{Y}_0\mathbf{c}_0$$

Substitute this into (B.30):

$$\mathbf{Y}_0'(\mathbf{M}_1 - \mathbf{M})\mathbf{Y}_0\mathbf{c}_0 - \frac{\mathbf{c}_0'\mathbf{Y}_0'(\mathbf{M}_1 - \mathbf{M})\mathbf{Y}_0\mathbf{c}_0}{\mathbf{c}_0'\mathbf{Y}_0'\mathbf{M}\mathbf{Y}_0\mathbf{c}_0}\mathbf{Y}_0'\mathbf{M}\mathbf{Y}_0\mathbf{c}_0 = \mathbf{0}$$

Application of (B.28) shows that this equation can be simplified to

$$\left(\mathbf{Y}_0'\mathbf{M}_1\mathbf{Y}_0 - \frac{1}{1-\alpha}\mathbf{Y}_0'\mathbf{M}\mathbf{Y}_0\right)\mathbf{c}_0 = \mathbf{0} \tag{B.31}$$

The result indicates that the matrix in parentheses must be singular. It also shows that the reciprocal of $1 - \alpha$ corresponds to μ of (B.10). Hence, in view of (B.28):

$$\mu = \frac{\mathbf{c}_0'\mathbf{Y}_0'\mathbf{M}_1\mathbf{Y}_0\mathbf{c}_0}{\mathbf{c}_0'\mathbf{Y}_0'\mathbf{M}\mathbf{Y}_0\mathbf{c}_0} \tag{B.32}$$

The determinantal equation $|\mathbf{Y}_0'\mathbf{M}_1\mathbf{Y}_0 - (1-\alpha)^{-1}\mathbf{Y}_0'\mathbf{M}\mathbf{Y}_0| = 0$ has $L_1 + 1$ roots. To find which root is to be used we recall that the function to be minimized is $\frac{1}{2}n \log|\mathbf{\Omega}_1| + \frac{1}{2}\operatorname{tr}\mathbf{\Omega}_1^{-1}\mathbf{D}_1'\mathbf{D}_1$. It follows from (B.18) that the second term is equal to $\frac{1}{2}(L_1 + 1)n$ for each of the $L_1 + 1$ solutions. Hence we must select the solution for which the determinant of $\hat{\mathbf{\Omega}}_1$ as given in (B.29) takes the smallest value. Note that this equation involves $\mathbf{c}_0$ and that (B.31) determines this vector only up to a multiplicative scalar. We shall use this freedom to normalize $\mathbf{c}_0$ so that $\mathbf{c}_0'\mathbf{Y}_0'\mathbf{M}\mathbf{Y}_0\mathbf{c}_0 = 1$. (This normalization is different from that used in the text, where the coefficients of one of the jointly dependent variables is put equal to -1.) We write $\mu_2, \ldots, \mu_{L_1+1}$ for the other roots of the determinantal equation and assume that they are all distinct. Also write $\mathbf{g}_1 = \mathbf{c}_0, \mathbf{g}_2, \ldots, \mathbf{g}_{L_1+1}$ for corresponding characteristic vectors, all normalized so that $\mathbf{g}_i'\mathbf{Y}_0'\mathbf{M}\mathbf{Y}_0\mathbf{g}_i = 1$. The distinctness of the roots implies $\mathbf{g}_i'\mathbf{Y}_0'\mathbf{M}\mathbf{Y}_0\mathbf{g}_k = 0$ for $i \neq k$, and hence

$$\mathbf{G}'\mathbf{Y}_0'\mathbf{M}\mathbf{Y}_0\mathbf{G} = \mathbf{I} \tag{B.33}$$

where $\mathbf{G}$ is a square matrix of order $L_1 + 1$ whose ith column is $\mathbf{g}_i$. Then consider (B.29) for the kth root (μ_k), taking account of the normalization and of the fact that this root is equal to the reciprocal of $1 - \alpha$:

$$n\hat{\mathbf{\Omega}}_1 = \mathbf{Y}_0'\mathbf{M}\mathbf{Y}_0 + (\mu_k - 1)\mathbf{Y}_0'\mathbf{M}\mathbf{Y}_0\mathbf{g}_k(\mathbf{Y}_0'\mathbf{M}\mathbf{Y}_0\mathbf{g}_k)'$$

Pre- and postmultiply both sides by $\mathbf{G}'$ and $\mathbf{G}$, respectively:

(B.34) $$n\mathbf{G}'\hat{\mathbf{\Omega}}_1\mathbf{G} = \mathbf{I} + (\mu_k - 1)\mathbf{i}_k\mathbf{i}_k'$$

The unit matrix on the right follows directly from (B.33); the second term follows from the fact that $\mathbf{G}'\mathbf{Y}_0'\mathbf{M}\mathbf{Y}_0\mathbf{g}_k$ is equal to the kth column of the unit matrix of order $L_1 + 1$ in view of (B.33), which is indicated here by $\mathbf{i}_k$.

The right-hand matrix of (B.34) is equal to a unit matrix except that the kth diagonal element is μ_k rather than 1. Hence its determinant value is μ_k. The determinant of the matrix on the left is equal to the product of $|n\hat{\mathbf{\Omega}}_1|$ and $|\mathbf{G}|^2$, so that $|n\hat{\mathbf{\Omega}}_1| = \mu_k|\mathbf{G}|^{-2}$. Taking determinants on both sides of (B.33), we obtain $|\mathbf{G}|^2|\mathbf{Y}_0'\mathbf{M}\mathbf{Y}_0| = 1$. Hence

(B.35) $$|n\hat{\mathbf{\Omega}}_1| = \mu_k\,|\mathbf{Y}_0'\mathbf{M}\mathbf{Y}_0|$$

which shows that we should take the smallest root of the determinantal equation.

The Limited-Information Maximum-Likelihood Estimator as a Member of the k-Class

Consider the first constraint of eq. (4.8) of Section 10.4 for $j = 1$ and write it in the form $\mathbf{\Pi}_0\boldsymbol{\gamma}_0 + \boldsymbol{\beta}_1 = \mathbf{0}$. Then apply (B.15) and (B.14) to prove

(B.36) $$\text{estimator of } \boldsymbol{\beta}_1 = -(\mathbf{X}_1'\mathbf{X}_1)^{-1}\mathbf{X}_1'\mathbf{Y}_0\mathbf{c}_0$$

We define $\mathbf{u}_1 = \mathbf{M}\mathbf{y}_1$, the column vector of LS reduced-form residuals corresponding to the left-hand variable of the first structural equation (in the original normalization). It is easily verified that $\mathbf{U}_1'\mathbf{y}_1 = \mathbf{U}_1'\mathbf{u}_1$. Then we write the normal equations from which the k-class estimator is solved [see eq. (4.13) of Section 10.4] as follows:

(B.37) $$(\mathbf{Y}_1'\mathbf{Y}_1 - k\mathbf{U}_1'\mathbf{U}_1)(\mathbf{c}_1)_k + \mathbf{Y}_1'\mathbf{X}_1(\mathbf{b}_1)_k = \mathbf{Y}_1'\mathbf{y}_1 - k\mathbf{U}_1'\mathbf{u}_1$$

(B.38) $$\mathbf{X}_1'\mathbf{Y}_1(\mathbf{c}_1)_k + \mathbf{X}_1'\mathbf{X}_1(\mathbf{b}_1)_k = \mathbf{X}_1'\mathbf{y}_1$$

where $(\mathbf{c}_1)_k$ and $(\mathbf{b}_1)_k$ are subvectors of $(\mathbf{d}_1)_k$. Define $(\mathbf{c}_0)_k = [-1 \quad (\mathbf{c}_1)_k']'$ as the k-class estimator of $\boldsymbol{\gamma}_0$. It is then immediately clear that the $\boldsymbol{\beta}_1$ estimator defined in (B.36) satisfies (B.38), so that what remains to be proved is that $\mathbf{c}_0$ as defined in (B.31) is a subvector of a k-class estimator. For this purpose, write (B.37) in the following form:

(B.39) $$(\mathbf{Y}_1'\mathbf{Y}_0 - k\mathbf{U}_1'\mathbf{U}_0)(\mathbf{c}_0)_k + \mathbf{Y}_1'\mathbf{X}_1(\mathbf{b}_1)_k = \mathbf{0} \text{ where } \mathbf{U}_0 = [\mathbf{u}_1 \quad \mathbf{U}_1]$$

We have $(\mathbf{b}_1)_k = -(\mathbf{X}_1'\mathbf{X}_1)^{-1}\mathbf{X}_1'\mathbf{Y}_0(\mathbf{c}_0)_k$ in view of (B.38). Substitution into (B.39) gives

$$[\mathbf{Y}_1'\mathbf{Y}_0 - k\mathbf{U}_1'\mathbf{U}_0 - \mathbf{Y}_1'\mathbf{X}_1(\mathbf{X}_1'\mathbf{X}_1)^{-1}\mathbf{X}_1'\mathbf{Y}_0](\mathbf{c}_0)_k = \mathbf{0} \tag{B.40}$$

The matrix in square brackets can be written as $\mathbf{Y}_1'\mathbf{M}_1\mathbf{Y}_0 - k\mathbf{U}_1'\mathbf{U}_0 = \mathbf{Y}_1'\mathbf{M}_1\mathbf{Y}_0 - k\mathbf{Y}_1'\mathbf{M}\mathbf{Y}_0$, so that (B.40) may be simplified to

$$(\mathbf{Y}_1'\mathbf{M}_1\mathbf{Y}_0 - k\mathbf{Y}_1'\mathbf{M}\mathbf{Y}_0)(\mathbf{c}_0)_k = \mathbf{0} \tag{B.41}$$

which for $k = \mu = (1 - \alpha)^{-1}$ consists of the $L_1 + 1$ equations of (B.31) except the first. Since the limited-information maximum-likelihood estimator $\mathbf{c}_0$ satisfies all $L_1 + 1$ equations, it certainly satisfies the L_1 of (B.41).

BIBLIOGRAPHY

Adelman, I., and F. L. Adelman (1959). "The Dynamic Properties of the Klein-Goldberger Model." *Econometrica*, **27**, pp. 596–625.

Adichie, J. N. (1967a). "Asymptotic Efficiency of a Class of Non-parametric Tests for Regression Parameters." *Annals of Mathematical Statistics*, **38**, pp. 884–893.

Adichie, J. N. (1967b). "Estimates of Regression Parameters Based on Rank Tests." *Annals of Mathematical Statistics*, **38**, pp. 894–904.

Aitchison, J., and J. A. C. Brown (1957). *The Lognormal Distribution*. Cambridge University Press.

Aitken, A. C. (1935). "On Least Squares and Linear Combination of Observations." *Proceedings of the Royal Society of Edinburgh*, **55**, pp. 42–48.

Allen, R. G. D. (1965). *Mathematical Economics*. Second edition (first edition, 1956). London: Macmillan & Co., Ltd.

Alt, F. L. (1942). "Distributed Lags." *Econometrica*, **10**, pp. 113–128.

Amemiya, T. (1966a). "Specification Analysis in the Estimation of Parameters of a Simultaneous Equation Model with Autoregressive Residuals." *Econometrica*, **34**, pp. 283–306.

Amemiya, T. (1966b). "On the Use of Principal Components of Independent Variables in Two-Stage Least-Squares Estimation." *International Economic Review*, **7**, pp. 283–303.

Amemiya, T., and W. A. Fuller (1967). "A Comparative Study of Alternative Estimators in a Distributed Lag Model." *Econometrica*, **35,** pp. 509–529.

Anderson, T. W. (1958). *An Introduction to Multivariate Statistical Analysis*. New York: John Wiley and Sons, Inc.

Anderson, T. W. (1959). "On Asymptotic Distributions of Estimates of Parameters of Stochastic Difference Equations." *Annals of Mathematical Statistics*, **30,** pp. 676–687.

Anderson, T. W. (1962). "Least Squares and Best Unbiased Estimates." *Annals of Mathematical Statistics*, **33,** pp. 266–272.

Anderson, T. W., and H. Rubin (1949). "Estimation of the Parameters of a Single Equation in a Complete System of Stochastic Equations." *Annals of Mathematical Statistics*, **20,** pp. 46–63.

Anderson, T. W., and H. Rubin (1950). "The Asymptotic Properties of Estimates of the Parameters of a Single Equation in a Complete System of Stochastic Equations." *Annals of Mathematical Statistics*, **21,** pp. 570–582.

Anscombe, F. J. (1961). "Examination of Residuals." *Proceedings of the Fourth Berkeley Symposium on Mathematical Statistics and Probability*, Vol. I, edited by J. Neyman, pp. 1–36. Berkeley and Los Angeles: University of California Press.

Anscombe, F. J., and J. W. Tukey (1963). "The Examination and Analysis of Residuals." *Technometrics*, **5,** pp. 141–160.

Ayanian, R. (1969). "A Comparison of Barten's Estimated Demand Elasticities with Those Obtained Using Frisch's Method." *Econometrica*, **37,** pp. 79–94.

Balestra, P., and M. Nerlove (1966). "Pooling Cross Section and Time Series Data in the Estimation of a Dynamic Model: The Demand for Natural Gas." *Econometrica*, **34,** pp. 585–612.

Bancroft, T. A. (1944). "On Biases in Estimation Due to the Use of Preliminary Tests of Significance." *Annals of Mathematical Statistics*, **15,** pp. 190–204.

Bancroft, T. A. (1964). "Analysis and Inference for Incompletely Specified Models Involving the Use of Preliminary Test(s) of Significance." *Biometrics*, **20,** pp. 427–442.

Bancroft, T. A. (1965). "Inference for Incompletely Specified Models in Physical Sciences." *Bulletin of the International Statistical Institute*, **41,** (1), pp. 497–514.

Barten, A. P. (1962). "Note on Unbiased Estimation of the Squared Multiple Correlation Coefficient." *Statistica Neerlandica*, **16,** pp. 151–163.

Barten, A. P. (1964). "Consumer Demand Functions under Conditions of Almost Additive Preferences." *Econometrica*, **32,** pp. 1–38.

Barten, A. P. (1965). "Evidence on the Slutsky Conditions for Demand Equations." *Review of Economics and Statistics*, **49,** pp. 77–84.

Barten, A. P., and S. J. Turnovsky (1966). "Some Aspects of the Aggregation Problem for Composite Demand Equations." *International Economic Review*, **7,** pp. 231–259.

Bartlett, M. S. (1949). "Fitting a Straight Line When Both Variables Are Subject to Error." *Biometrics*, **5**, pp. 207–212.

Basmann, R. L. (1957). "A Generalized Classical Method of Linear Estimation of Coefficients in a Structural Equation." *Econometrica*, **25**, pp. 77–83.

Basmann, R. L. (1959). "The Computation of Generalized Classical Estimates of Coefficients in a Structural Equation." *Econometrica*, **27**, pp. 72–81.

Basmann, R. L. (1960a). "On the Asymptotic Distribution of Generalized Linear Estimators." *Econometrica*, **28**, pp. 97–107.

Basmann, R. L. (1960b). "On Finite Sample Distributions of Generalized Classical Linear Identifiability Test Statistics." *Journal of the American Statistical Association*, **55**, pp. 650–659.

Basmann, R. L. (1961). "A Note on the Exact Finite Sample Frequency Functions of Generalized Classical Linear Estimators in Two Leading Over-identified Cases." *Journal of the American Statistical Association*, **56**, pp. 619–636.

Basmann, R. L. (1963a). "A Note on the Exact Finite Sample Frequency Functions of Generalized Classical Linear Estimators in a Leading Three Equation Case." *Journal of the American Statistical Association*, **58**, pp. 161–171.

Basmann, R. L. (1963b). "The Causal Interpretation of Non-Triangular Systems of Economic Relations." *Econometrica*, **31**, pp. 439–448. This article is followed by a reply by R. H. Strotz and H. O. A. Wold on pp. 449–450 and by a rejoinder on pp. 451–453.

Basmann, R. L. (1963c). "Remarks Concerning the Application of Exact Finite Sample Distribution Functions of GCL Estimators in Econometric Statistical Inference." *Journal of the American Statistical Association*, **58**, pp. 943–976. Corrections in **59** (1964), p. 1296.

Basmann, R. L. (1965a). "A Tchebychev Inequality for the Convergence of a Generalized Classical Linear Estimator, Sample Size Being Fixed." *Econometrica*, **33**, pp. 608–618.

Basmann, R. L. (1965b). "A Note on the Statistical Testability of 'Explicit Causal Chains' Against the Class of 'Interdependent' Models." *Journal of the American Statistical Association*, **60**, pp. 1080–1093.

Bentzel, R., and B. Hansen (1954). "On Recursiveness and Interdependency in Economic Models." *Review of Economic Studies*, **22**, pp. 153–168.

Bentzel, R., and H. Wold (1946). "On Statistical Demand Analysis from the Viewpoint of Simultaneous Equations." *Skandinavisk Aktuarietidskrift*, **29**, pp. 95–114.

Bergstrom, A. R. (1962). "The Exact Sampling Distributions of Least Squares and Maximum Likelihood Estimators of the Marginal Propensity to Consume." *Econometrica*, **30**, pp. 480–490.

Bergstrom, A. R. (1966). "Nonrecursive Models as Discrete Approximations to Systems of Stochastic Differential Equations." *Econometrica*, **34**, pp. 173–182.

Berkson, J. (1944). "Application of the Logistic Function to Bio-assay." *Journal of the American Statistical Association*, **39**, pp. 357–365.

Berkson, J. (1946). "Approximation of Chi-square by 'Probits' and by 'Logits'." *Journal of the American Statistical Association*, **41**, pp. 70–74.

Berkson, J. (1949). "Minimum χ^2 and Maximum Likelihood Solution in Terms of a Linear Transform, with Particular Reference to Bio-assay." *Journal of the American Statistical Association*, **44**, pp. 273–278.

Berkson, J. (1950). "Are There Two Regressions?" *Journal of the American Statistical Association*, **45**, pp. 164–180.

Berkson, J. (1953). "A Statistically Precise and Relatively Simple Method of Estimating the Bio-assay with Quantal Response, Based on the Logistic Function." *Journal of the American Statistical Association*, **48**, pp. 565–599.

Berkson, J. (1955). "Maximum Likelihood and Minimum χ^2 Estimates of the Logistic Function." *Journal of the American Statistical Association*, **50**, pp. 130–162.

Birch, M. W. (1964). "A Note on the Maximum Likelihood Estimation of a Linear Structural Relationship." *Journal of the American Statistical Association*, **59**, pp. 1175–1178.

Birkhoff, G., and S. Mac Lane (1965). *A Survey of Modern Algebra*. Third edition (first edition, 1941). New York: The Macmillan Company.

Blumenthal, T. (1965). "A Test of the Klein-Shinkai Econometric Model of Japan." *International Economic Review*, **6**, pp. 211–228.

Blyth, C. R. (1959). "Note on Estimating Information." *Annals of Mathematical Statistics*, **30**, pp. 71–79.

Boot, J. C. G. (1964). *Quadratic Programming*. Chicago: Rand McNally and Company. Amsterdam: North-Holland Publishing Company.

Boot, J. C. G., and G. M. de Wit (1960). "Investment Demand: An Empirical Contribution to the Aggregation Problem." *International Economic Review*, **1**, pp. 3–30.

Box, G. E. P., and D. R. Cox (1964). "An Analysis of Transformations." *Journal of the Royal Statistical Society*, Series B, **26**, pp. 211–252.

Box, G. E. P., and G. S. Watson (1962). "Robustness to Non-normality in Regression Tests." *Biometrika*, **49**, pp. 93–106.

Bozivich, H., T. A. Bancroft, and H. O. Hartley (1956). "Power of Analysis of Variance Test Procedures for Certain Incompletely Specified Models, I." *Annals of Mathematical Statistics*, **27**, pp. 1017–1043.

Brennan, M. J., Jr. (1965). *Preface to Econometrics: An Introduction to Quantitative Methods in Economics*. Second edition (first edition, 1960). Cincinnati, Ohio: Southwestern Publishing Company.

Brown, G. W., and A. M. Mood (1951). "On Median Tests for Linear Hypotheses." *Proceedings of the Second Berkeley Symposium on Mathematical Statistics and Probability*, pp. 159–166. Berkeley and Los Angeles: University of California Press.

Brown, T. M. (1954). "Standard Errors of Forecast of a Complete Econometric Model." *Econometrica*, **22**, pp. 178–192.

Brown, T. M. (1959). "Simplified Full Maximum Likelihood and Comparative Structural Estimates." *Econometrica*, **27**, pp. 638–653.

Brown, T. M. (1960). "Simultaneous Least Squares: A Distribution Free Method of Equation System Structure Estimation." *International Economic Review*, **1**, pp. 173–191.

Brown, T. M. (1963). "Structure Estimation for Nonlinear Systems of Simultaneous Equations." *International Economic Review*, **4**, pp. 117–133.

Brown, T. M. (1967). "Simultaneous Least Squares and Invariance under Changes of Units of Measurement." *International Economic Review*, **8**, pp. 97–102.

Champernowne, D. G. (1948). "Sampling Theory Applied to Autoregressive Sequences." *Journal of the Royal Statistical Society*, Series B, **10**, pp. 204–231.

Champernowne, D. G. (1960). "An Experimental Investigation of the Robustness of Certain Procedures for Estimating Means and Regression Coefficients." *Journal of the Royal Statistical Society*, Series A, **123**, pp. 398–412.

Chernoff, H., and N. Divinsky (1953). "The Computation of Maximum-Likelihood Estimates of Linear Structural Equations." Chapter X of Hood and Koopmans (1953).

Chetty, V. K. (1968a). "Pooling of Time Series and Cross Section Data." *Econometrica*, **36**, pp. 279–290.

Chetty, V. K. (1968b). "Bayesian Analysis of Haavelmo's Models." *Econometrica*, **36**, pp. 582–602.

Chipman, J. S. (1964). "On Least Squares with Insufficient Observations." *Journal of the American Statistical Association*, **59**, pp. 1078–1111.

Chipman, J. S. (1968). "Specification Problems in Regression Analysis." *Proceedings of the Symposium on Theory and Application of Generalized Inverses of Matrices*, edited by T. L. Boullion and P. L. Odell, pp. 114–176. Lubbock, Texas: Texas Technological College.

Chipman, J. S., and M. M. Rao (1964a). "The Treatment of Linear Restrictions in Regression Analysis." *Econometrica*, **32**, pp. 198–209.

Chipman, J. S., and M. M. Rao (1964b). "Projections, Generalized Inverses, and Quadratic Forms." *Journal of Mathematical Analysis and Applications*, **9**, pp. 1–11.

Chow, G. C. (1960). "Tests for Equality between Sets of Coefficients in Two Linear Regressions." *Econometrica*, **28**, pp. 591–605.

Chow, G. C. (1964). "A Comparison of Alternative Estimators for Simultaneous Equations." *Econometrica*, **32**, pp. 532–553.

Chow, G. C. (1968). "Two Methods of Computing Full-information Maximum Likelihood Estimates in Simultaneous Stochastic Equations." *International Economic Review*, **9**, pp. 100–112.

Christ, C. (1951). "A Test of an Econometric Model for the United States, 1921–1947." *Conference on Business Cycles*, pp. 35–107. New York: National Bureau of Economic Research, Inc.

Christ, C. F. (1956). "Aggregate Econometric Models: A Review Article." *American Economic Review*, **46,** pp. 385–408.

Christ, C. F. (1957). "On Econometric Models of the U.S. Economy." *Income and Wealth*, Series VI, edited by M. Gilbert and R. Stone, pp. 1–23. London: Bowes and Bowes.

Christ, C. F. (1960). "Simultaneous Equation Estimation: Any Verdict Yet?" *Econometrica*, **28,** pp. 835–845.

Christ, C. F. (1966). *Econometric Models and Methods.* New York: John Wiley and Sons, Inc.

Cochrane, D., and G. H. Orcutt (1949). "Application of Least Squares Regression to Relationships Containing Autocorrelated Error Terms." *Journal of the American Statistical Association*, **44,** pp. 32–61.

Conlisk, J. (1969). "The Equilibrium Covariance Matrix of Dynamic Econometric Models." *Journal of the American Statistical Association*, **64,** pp. 277–279.

Corsten, L. C. A. (1964). "A Different Solution of a Problem Posed by Theil and Schweitzer." *Statistica Neerlandica*, **18,** pp. 15–18.

Cragg, J. G. (1966). "On the Sensitivity of Simultaneous-Equations Estimators to the Stochastic Assumptions of the Models." *Journal of the American Statistical Association*, **61,** pp. 136–151.

Cragg, J. G. (1967). "On the Relative Small-sample Properties of Several Structural-equation Estimators." *Econometrica*, **35,** pp. 89–110.

Cragg, J. G. (1968): "Some Effects of Incorrect Specification on the Small-sample Properties of Several Simultaneous-equation Estimators." *International Economic Review*, **9,** pp. 63–86.

Cragg, J. G., and R. S. Uhler (1969). "The Demand for Automobiles." Discussion Paper No. 27, Department of Economics, University of British Columbia.

Cramér, H. (1937). *Random Variables and Probability Distributions.* Cambridge University Press.

Cramér, H. (1946). *Mathematical Methods of Statistics.* Princeton University Press.

Cramer, J. S. (1964). "Efficient Grouping, Regression and Correlation in Engel Curve Analysis." *Journal of the American Statistical Association*, **59,** pp. 233–250.

Cramer, J. S. (1969). *Empirical Econometrics.* Amsterdam: North-Holland Publishing Company.

Cronholm, J. N. (1963). "A General Method of Obtaining Exact Sampling Probabilities of the Shannon-Wiener Measure of Information $\hat{H}$." *Psychometrika*, **28,** pp. 405–413.

Daniels, H. E. (1956). "The Approximate Distribution of Serial Correlation Coefficients." *Biometrika*, **43,** pp. 169–185.

David, F. N., and J. Neyman (1938). "Extension of the Markoff Theorem on Least Squares." *Statistical Research Memoirs*, **2,** pp. 105–116.

Dhrymes, P. J. (1969). "Efficient Estimation of Distributed Lags with Autocorrelated Errors." *International Economic Review*, **10,** pp. 47–67.

Dhrymes, P. J., L. R. Klein, and K. Steiglitz (1968). "Estimation of Distributed Lags." Discussion Paper No. 77, Department of Economics, University of Pennsylvania.

Draper, N. R., and H. Smith (1966). *Applied Regression Analysis.* New York: John Wiley and Sons, Inc.

Drèze, J. (1962). "The Bayesian Approach to Simultaneous Equations Estimation." O.N.R. Research Memorandum 67, The Technology Institute, Northwestern University.

Drèze, J. (1968). "Limited Information Estimation from a Bayesian Viewpoint." Report 6816, Center for Operations Research and Econometrics, University of Louvain.

Duesenberry, J. S., G. Fromm, L. R. Klein, and E. Kuh (editors) (1965). *The Brookings Quarterly Econometric Model of the United States.* Chicago: Rand McNally and Company. Amsterdam: North-Holland Publishing Company.

Durand, D. (1954). "Joint Confidence Regions for Multiple Regression Coefficients." *Journal of the American Statistical Association*, **49,** pp. 130–146.

Durbin, J. (1953). "A Note on Regression When There is Extraneous Information about One of the Coefficients." *Journal of the American Statistical Association* **48,** pp. 799–808.

Durbin, J. (1957). "Testing for Serial Correlation in Systems of Simultaneous Regression Equations." *Biometrika*, **44,** pp. 370–377.

Durbin, J. (1960a). "Estimation of Parameters in Time-Series Regression Models." *Journal of the Royal Statistical Society*, Series B, **22,** pp. 139–153.

Durbin, J. (1960b). "The Fitting of Time-Series Models." *Review of the International Statistical Institute*, **28,** pp. 233–244.

Durbin, J., and G. S. Watson (1950). "Testing for Serial Correlation in Least Squares Regression, I." *Biometrika*, **37,** pp. 409–428.

Durbin, J., and G. S. Watson (1951). "Testing for Serial Correlation in Least Squares Regression, II." *Biometrika*, **38,** pp. 159–178.

Eicker, F. (1963). "Asymptotic Normality and Consistency of the Least Squares Estimators for Families of Linear Regressions." *Annals of Mathematical Statistics*, **34,** pp. 447–456.

Eisenpress, H. (1962). "Note on the Computation of Full-Information Maximum-Likelihood Estimates of Coefficients of a Simultaneous System." *Econometrica*, **30,** pp. 343–348.

Eisenpress, H., and J. Greenstadt (1966). "The Estimation of Nonlinear Econometric Systems." *Econometrica*, **34,** pp. 851–861.

Erdélyi, A. (1956). *Asymptotic Expansions.* New York: Dover Publications, Inc.

Evans, I. G. (1964). "Bayesian Estimation of the Variance of a Normal Distribution." *Journal of the Royal Statistical Society*, Series B, **26,** pp. 63–68.

Ezekiel, M., and K. A. Fox (1959). *Methods of Correlation and Regression Analysis.* Third edition (first edition, 1930). New York: John Wiley and Sons, Inc.

Finney, D. J. (1964). *Probit Analysis.* Second edition (first edition, 1947). Cambridge University Press.

Fisher, F. M. (1959). "Generalizations of the Rank and Order Conditions for Identifiability." *Econometrica*, **27**, pp. 431–447.

Fisher, F. M. (1961a). "On the Cost of Approximate Specification in Simultaneous Equation Estimation." *Econometrics*, **29**, pp. 139–170.

Fisher, F. M. (1961b). "Identifiability Criteria in Nonlinear Systems." *Econometrica*, **29**, pp. 574–590.

Fisher, F. M. (1963). "Uncorrelated Disturbances and Identifiability Criteria." *International Economic Review*, **4**, pp. 134–152.

Fisher, F. M. (1965a). "Identifiability Criteria in Nonlinear Systems: A Further Note." *Econometrica*, **33**, pp. 197–205.

Fisher, F. M. (1965b). "Near-Identifiability and the Variances of the Disturbance Terms." *Econometrica*, **33**, pp. 409–419.

Fisher, F. M. (1965c). "Dynamic Structure and Estimation in Economy-wide Econometric Models." Chapter 15 of Duesenberry, Fromm, Klein, and Kuh (1965).

Fisher, F. M. (1966a). *The Identification Problem in Econometrics.* New York: McGraw-Hill Book Company.

Fisher, F. M. (1966b). "The Relative Sensitivity to Specification Error of Different *k*-Class Estimators." *Journal of the American Statistical Association*, **61**, pp. 345–356.

Fisher, F. M. (1966c). "Restrictions on the Reduced Form and the Rank and Order Conditions." *International Economic Review*, **7**, pp. 77–82.

Fisher, F. M. (1967a). "Approximate Specification and the Choice of a *k*-Class Estimator." *Journal of the American Statistical Association*, **62**, pp. 1265–1276.

Fisher, F. M. (1967b). "A Correspondence Principle for Simultaneous Equation Models." Department of Economics Working Paper No. 9, Massachusetts Institute of Technology.

Fisher, I. (1937). "Note on a Short-cut Method for Calculating Distributed Lags." *Bulletin de l'Institut International de Statistique*, **29** (troisième livraison), pp. 323–328.

Fisher, W. D. (1961). "A Note on Curve Fitting with Minimum Deviations by Linear Programming." *Journal of the American Statistical Association*, **56**, pp. 359–362.

Fisher, W. D. (1962a). "Estimation in the Linear Decision Model." *International Economic Review*, **3**, pp. 1–29.

Fisher, W. D. (1962b). "Optimal Aggregation in Multi-equation Prediction Models." *Econometrica*, **30**, pp. 744–769.

Fisher, W. D. (1969). *Clustering and Aggregation in Economics.* Baltimore: The Johns Hopkins Press.

Fox, K. A. (1958). *Econometric Analysis for Public Policy.* Ames, Iowa: The Iowa State College Press.

Fox, K. A. (1968). *Intermediate Economic Statistics.* New York: John Wiley and Sons, Inc.

Friedman, M. (1957). *A Theory of the Consumption Function.* Princeton University Press.

Frisch, R. (1934). *Statistical Confluence Analysis by Means of Complete Regression Systems.* Oslo: Universitets Økonomiske Institutt.

Frisch, R. (1959). "A Complete Scheme for Computing All Direct and Cross Demand Elasticities in a Model with Many Sectors." *Econometrica,* **27,** pp. 177–196.

Gauss, K. F. (1821–23). *Theoria Combinationis Observationum Erroribus Minimis Obnoxiae.* French translation by J. Bertrand under the title *Méthode des moindres carrés.* Paris: Mallet-Bachelier, 1855.

Geisser, S. (1965). "Bayesian Estimation in Multivariate Analysis." *Annals of Mathematical Statistics,* **36,** pp. 150–159.

Gibson, W. M., and G. H. Jowett (1957a). "Three-Group Regression Analysis. Part I: Simple Regression Analysis." *Applied Statistics,* **6,** pp. 114–122.

Gibson, W. M., and G. H. Jowett (1957b). "Three-Group Regression Analysis. Part II: Multiple Regression Analysis." *Applied Statistics,* **6,** pp. 189–197.

Girshick, M. A. and T. Haavelmo (1953). "Statistical Analysis of the Demand for Food: Examples of Simultaneous Estimation of Structural Equations." Chapter V of Hood and Koopmans (1953). Also in *Econometrica,* **15** (1947), pp. 79–110.

Glejser, H. (1969). "A New Test for Heteroscedasticity." *Journal of the American Statistical Association,* **64,** pp. 316–323.

Goldberger, A. S. (1959). *Impact Multipliers and Dynamic Properties of the Klein-Goldberger Model.* Amsterdam: North-Holland Publishing Company.

Goldberger, A. S. (1961). "Stepwise Least Squares: Residual Analysis and Specification Error." *Journal of the American Statistical Association,* **56,** pp. 998–1000.

Goldberger, A. S. (1962). "Best Linear Unbiased Prediction in the Generalized Linear Regression Model." *Journal of the American Statistical Association,* **57,** pp. 369–375.

Goldberger, A. S. (1964). *Econometric Theory.* New York: John Wiley and Sons, Inc.

Goldberger, A. S. (1965). "An Instrumental Variable Interpretation of *k*-Class Estimation." Econometric Annual of the *Indian Economic Journal,* **13,** pp. 424–431.

Goldberger, A. S. (1967). "Functional Form and Utility: A Review of Consumer Demand Theory." Systems Formulation, Methodology and Policy Workshop Paper 6703, Social Systems Research Institute, University of Wisconsin.

Goldberger, A. S. (1968). "The Interpretation and Estimation of Cobb-Douglas Functions." *Econometrica*, **36,** pp. 464–472.

Goldberger, A. S., and D. B. Jochems (1961). "Note on Stepwise Least Squares." *Journal of the American Statistical Association*, **56,** pp. 105–110.

Goldberger, A. S., A. L. Nagar, and H. S. Odeh (1961). "The Covariance Matrices of Reduced-form Coefficients and of Forecasts for a Structural Econometric Model." *Econometrica*, **29,** pp. 556–573.

Goldfeld, S. M., and R. E. Quandt (1965). "Some Tests for Homoscedasticity." *Journal of the American Statistical Association*, **60,** pp. 539–547.

Goldfeld, S. M., and R. E. Quandt (1968). "Nonlinear Simultaneous Equations: Estimation and Prediction." *International Economic Review*, **9,** pp. 113–136.

Goldman, A. J., and M. Zelen (1964). "Weak Generalized Inverses and Minimum Variance Linear Unbiased Estimation." *Journal of Research of the National Bureau of Standards*, Series B: Mathematics and Mathematical Physics, **68B,** pp. 151–172.

Goldman, S. M., and H. Uzawa (1964). "A Note on Separability in Demand Analysis." *Econometrica*, **32,** pp. 387–398.

Goodman, L. A. (1953). "A Simple Method for Improving Some Estimators." *Annals of Mathematical Statistics*, **24,** pp. 114–117.

Goodman, L. A. (1960). "A Note on the Estimation of Variance." *Sankhya*, **22,** pp. 221–228.

Gorman, W. M. (1959). "Separable Utility and Aggregation." *Econometrica*, **27,** pp. 469–481. This article is followed by a reply by R. H. Strotz on pp. 482–488 and by a rejoinder on p. 489.

Granger, C. W. J., in association with M. Hatanaka (1964). *Spectral Analysis of Economic Time Series.* Princeton: Princeton University Press.

Graybill, F. A. (1961). *An Introduction to Linear Statistical Models.* Volume I. New York: McGraw-Hill Book Company, Inc.

Graybill, F. A. (1969). *Introduction to Matrices with Applications in Statistics.* Belmont, California: Wadsworth Publishing Company, Inc.

Green, H. A. J. (1964). *Aggregation in Economic Analysis.* Princeton University Press.

Grenander, U. (1954). "On the Estimation of Regression Coefficients in the Case of an Autocorrelated Disturbance." *Annals of Mathematical Statistics*, **25,** pp. 252–272.

Grenander, U., and M. Rosenblatt (1957). *Statistical Analysis of Stationary Time Series.* New York: John Wiley and Sons. Stockholm: Almqvist and Wiksell.

Griliches, Z. (1957). "Specification Bias in Estimates of Production Functions." *Journal of Farm Economics*, **39,** pp. 8–20.

Griliches, Z. (1961). "A Note on Serial Correlation Bias in Estimates of Distributed Lags." *Econometrica*, **29,** pp. 65–73.

Griliches, Z. (1967). "Distributed Lags: A Survey." *Econometrica*, **35**, pp. 16–49.

Griliches, Z., and N. Wallace (1965). "The Determinants of Investment Revisited." *International Economic Review*, **6**, pp. 311–329.

Grunfeld, Y. (1958). "The Determinants of Corporate Investment." Unpublished Ph.D. thesis, The University of Chicago.

Grunfeld, Y., and Z. Griliches (1960). "Is Aggregation Necessarily Bad?" *Review of Economics and Statistics*, **42**, pp. 1–13.

Gurland, J. (1954). "An Example of Autocorrelated Disturbances in Linear Regression." *Econometrica*, **22**, pp. 218–227.

Haavelmo, T. (1943). "The Statistical Implications of a System of Simultaneous Equations." *Econometrica*, **11**, pp. 1–12.

Haavelmo, T. (1944). "The Probability Approach in Econometrics." Supplement to *Econometrica*, **12.**

Hadley, G. (1961). *Linear Algebra.* Reading, Mass.: Addison-Wesley Publishing Company, Inc.

Hadley, G. (1964). *Nonlinear and Dynamic Programming.* Reading, Mass.: Addison-Wesley Publishing Company, Inc.

Halmos, P. R. (1958). *Finite-Dimensional Vector Spaces.* Second edition (first edition, 1942). Princeton, N.J.: D. Van Nostrand Company, Inc.

Halperin, M. (1961). "Fitting of Straight Lines and Prediction When Both Variables Are Subject to Error." *Journal of the American Statistical Association*, **56,** pp. 657–669.

Halperin, M. (1964). "Interval Estimation in Linear Regression When Both Variables Are Subject to Error." *Journal of the American Statistical Association*, **59,** pp. 1112–1120.

Hannan, E. J. (1957). "Testing for Serial Correlation in Least Squares Regression." *Biometrika*, **44,** pp. 57–66.

Hannan, E. J. (1960). *Times Series Analysis.* London: Methuen and Company, Ltd. New York: John Wiley and Sons, Inc.

Hannan, E. J. (1965). "The Estimation of Relationships Involving Distributed Lags." *Econometrica*, **33,** pp. 206–224.

Hannan, E. J., and R. D. Terrell (1968). "Testing for Serial Correlation after Least Squares Regression." *Econometrica*, **36,** pp. 133–150.

Hart, B. I. (1942a). "Tabulation of the Probabilities for the Ratio of the Mean Square Successive Difference to the Variance." *Annals of Mathematical Statistics*, **13,** pp. 207–214.

Hart, B. I. (1942b). "Significance Levels for the Ratio of the Mean Square Successive Difference to the Variance." *Annals of Mathematical Statistics*, **13,** pp. 445–447.

Hartley, H. O., and A. Booker (1965). "Nonlinear Least Squares Estimation." *Annals of Mathematical Statistics*, **36,** pp. 638–650.

Heady, E. O., and J. L. Dillon (1961). *Agricultural Production Functions.* Ames, Iowa: Iowa State University Press.

Henshaw, R. C., Jr. (1966). "Testing Single-equation Least Squares Regression Models for Autocorrelated Disturbances." *Econometrica*, **34,** pp. 646–660.

Hicks, J. R. (1946). *Value and Capital.* Second edition (first edition, 1939). London: Oxford University Press.

Hildreth, C. (1960). "Simultaneous Equations: Any Verdict Yet?" *Econometrica*, **28,** pp. 846–854.

Hildreth, C. (1969). "Asymptotic Distribution of Maximum Likelihood Estimators in a Linear Model with Autoregressive Disturbances." *Annals of Mathematical Statistics*, **40,** pp. 583–594.

Hildreth, C., and J. P. Houck (1968). "Some Estimators for a Linear Model with Random Coefficients." *Journal of the American Statistical Association*, **63,** pp. 584–595.

Hill, B. M. (1962). "A Test of Linearity versus Convexity of a Median Regression Curve." *Annals of Mathematical Statistics*, **33,** pp. 1096–1123.

Hoch, I. (1962). "Estimation of Production Function Parameters Combining Time-series and Cross-section Data." *Econometrica*, **30,** pp. 34–53.

Hogg, R. V., and A. T. Craig (1965). *Introduction to Mathematical Statistics*, Second edition (first edition, 1959). New York: The Macmillan Company.

Hood, W. C., and T. C. Koopmans (editors) (1953). *Studies in Econometric Method.* New York: John Wiley and Sons, Inc.

Hooper, J. W. (1959). "Simultaneous Equations and Canonical Correlation Theory." *Econometrica*, **27,** pp. 245–256.

Hooper, J. W. (1962). "Partial Trace Correlations." *Econometrica*, **30,** pp. 324–331.

Hooper, J. W., and H. Theil (1958). "The Extension of Wald's Method of Fitting Straight Lines to Multiple Regression." *Review of the International Statistical Institute*, **26,** pp. 37–47.

Hooper, J. W., and A. Zellner (1961). "The Error of Forecast for Multivariate Regression Models." *Econometrica*, **29,** pp. 544–555.

Hotelling, H. (1936). "Relations between Two Sets of Variates." *Biometrika*, **28,** pp. 321–377.

Houthakker, H. S. (1960). "Additive Preferences." *Econometrica*, **28,** pp. 244–257.

Houthakker, H. S. (1965). "A Note on Self-Dual Preferences." *Econometrica*, **33,** pp. 797–801.

Hsu, P. L. (1938). "On the Best Unbiassed Quadratic Estimate of the Variance." *Statistical Research Memoirs*, Vol. II, pp. 91–104.

Huntsberger, D. V. (1955). "A Generalization of a Preliminary Testing Procedure for Pooling Data." *Annals of Mathematical Statistics*, **26,** pp. 734–743.

Hurwicz, L. (1950a). "Least-squares Bias in Time Series." Chapter XV of Koopmans (1950).

Hurwicz, L. (1950b). "Systems with Nonadditive Disturbances." Chapter XVIII of Koopmans (1950).

Hymans, S. A. (1968). "Simultaneous Confidence Intervals in Econometric Forecasting." *Econometrica*, **36**, pp. 18–30.

Ijiri, Y. (1968). "The Linear Aggregation Coefficient as the Dual of the Linear Correlation Coefficient." *Econometrica*, **36**, pp. 252–259.

James, W., and C. Stein (1961), "Estimation with Quadratic Loss." *Proceedings of the Fourth Berkeley Symposium on Mathematical Statistics and Probability*, Vol. I, pp. 361–379. Berkeley and Los Angeles: University of California Press.

Jenkins, G. M. (1954). "Tests of Hypotheses in the Linear Autoregressive Model: I. Null Hypothesis Distributions in the Yule Scheme." *Biometrika*, **41**, pp. 405–419.

Jenkins, G. M. (1956). "Tests of Hypotheses in the Linear Autoregressive Model: II. Null Distributions for Higher Order Schemes: Non-null Distributions." *Biometrika*, **43**, pp. 186–199.

Jennrich, R. I. (1969). "Asymptotic Properties of Non-linear Least Squares Estimators." *Annals of Mathematical Statistics*, **40**, pp. 633–643.

Johnston, J. (1960). *Statistical Cost Analysis.* New York: McGraw-Hill Book Company, Inc.

Johnston, J. (1963). *Econometric Methods.* New York: McGraw-Hill Book Company, Inc.

Jorgenson, D. W. (1964). "Minimum Variance, Linear, Unbiased Seasonal Adjustment of Economic Time Series." *Journal of the American Statistical Association*, **59**, pp. 681–724.

Jorgenson, D. W. (1966). "Rational Distributed Lag Functions." *Econometrica*, **34**, pp. 135–149.

Jorgenson, D. W. (1967). "Seasonal Adjustment of Data for Econometric Analysis." *Journal of the American Statistical Association*, **62**, pp. 137–140.

Jørgenson, E. (1965). *Income-Expenditure Relations of Danish Wage and Salary Earners.* Copenhagen: The Statistical Department.

Judge, G. G., and T. Takayama (1966). "Inequality Restrictions in Regression Analysis." *Journal of the American Statistical Association*, **61**, pp. 166–181.

Kabe, D. G. (1963a). "A Note on the Exact Distributions of the GCL Estimators in Two Leading Over-Identified Cases." *Journal of the American Statistical Association*, **58**, pp. 535–537.

Kabe, D. G. (1963b). "Stepwise Multivariate Linear Regression." *Journal of the American Statistical Association*, **58**, pp. 770–773.

Kabe, D. G. (1964). "On the Exact Distributions of the GCL Estimators in a Leading Three-equation Case. *Journal of the American Statistical Association*, **59**, pp. 881–894.

Kadane, J. B. (1969). "Comparison of k-Class Estimators When the Disturbances Are Small." Cowles Foundation Discussion Paper No. 269, Yale University.

Kadiyala, K. R. (1968). "A Transformation Used to Circumvent the Problem of Autocorrelation." *Econometrica*, **36**, pp. 93–96.

Kakwani, N. C. (1965). "Note on the Unbiased Estimation of the Third Moment of the Residual in Regression Analysis." *Econometrica*, **33**, pp. 434–436.

Kakwani, N. C. (1967). "The Unbiasedness of Zellner's Seemingly Unrelated Regression Equations Estimators." *Journal of the American Statistical Association*, **62**, pp. 141–142.

Kakwani, N. C. (1968). "Note on the Unbiasedness of a Mixed Regression Estimator." *Econometrica*, **36**, pp. 610–611.

Kale, B. K., and T. A. Bancroft (1967). "Inference for Some Incompletely Specified Models Involving Normal Approximations to Discrete Data." *Biometrics*, **23**, pp. 335–348.

Kaufman, G. M. (1969). "Conditional Prediction and Unbiasedness in Structural Equations." *Econometrica*, **37**, pp. 44–49.

Kendall, M. G. (1962). *Rank Correlation Methods*. Third edition (first edition, 1948) New York: Hafner Publishing Company.

Kendall, M. G., and A. Stuart (1963, 1967, 1966). *The Advanced Theory of Statistics*. Three-volume edition. Volume 1, second edition 1963 (first edition, 1958). Volume 2, second edition 1967 (first edition, 1961). Volume 3, 1966. New York: Hafner Publishing Company.

Klein, L. R. (1950). *Economic Fluctuations in the United States*, 1921–1941. New York: John Wiley and Sons, Inc.

Klein, L. R. (1953). *A Textbook of Econometrics*. Evanston: Row, Peterson and Company.

Klein, L. R. (1955). "On the Interpretation of Theil's Method of Estimating Economic Relationships." *Metroeconomica*, **7**, pp. 147–153.

Klein, L. R. (1958). "The Estimation of Distributed Lags." *Econometrica*, **26**, pp. 553–565.

Klein, L. R. (1960a). "The Efficiency of Estimation in Econometric Models." *Essays in Economics and Econometrics* (A Volume in Honor of Harold Hotelling), edited by R. W. Pfouts, pp. 216–232. Chapel Hill: The University of North Carolina Press.

Klein, L. R. (1960b). "Single Equation vs. Equation System Methods of Estimation in Econometrics." *Econometrica*, **28**, pp. 866–871.

Klein, L. R. (1962). *An Introduction to Econometrics*. Englewood Cliffs, N.J.: Prentice-Hall, Inc.

Klein, L. R. (1968). *An Essay on the Theory of Economic Prediction*. Helsinki: The Academic Book Store.

Klein, L. R., R. J. Ball, A. Hazlewood, and P. Vandome (1961). *An Econometric Model of the United Kingdom*. Oxford: Basil Blackwell.

Klein, L. R., and A. S. Goldberger (1955). *An Econometric Model of the United States, 1929–1952.* Amsterdam: North-Holland Publishing Company.

Klein, L. R., and M. Nakamura (1962). "Singularity in the Equation Systems of Econometrics: Some Aspects of the Problem of Multicollinearity." *International Economic Review*, **3**, pp. 274–299.

Klein, L. R., and Y. Shinkai (1963). "An Econometric Model of Japan, 1930–59." *International Economic Review*, **4**, pp. 1–28.

Kloek, T. (1961). "Note on Convenient Matrix Notations in Multivariate Statistical Analysis and in the Theory of Linear Aggregation." *International Economic Review*, **2**, pp. 351–360.

Kloek, T., and L. B. M. Mennes (1960). "Simultaneous Equations Estimation Based on Principal Components of Predetermined Variables." *Econometrica*, **28**, pp. 45–61.

Kmenta, J., and R. F. Gilbert (1968a). "Small Sample Properties of Alternative Estimators of Seemingly Unrelated Regressions." *Journal of the American Statistical Association*, **63**, pp. 1180–1200.

Kmenta, J., and R. F. Gilbert (1968b). "Estimation of Seemingly Unrelated Regressions with Autocorrelated Disturbances." Econometrics Workshop Paper No. 6805, Michigan State University.

Koerts, J. (1967). "Some Further Notes on Disturbance Estimates in Regression Analysis." *Journal of the American Statistical Association*, **62**, pp. 169–183.

Koerts, J., and A. P. J. Abrahamse (1968). "On the Power of the BLUS Procedure." *Journal of the American Statistical Association*, **63**, pp. 1227–1236.

Konijn, H. S. (1958). "A Restatement of the Conditions for Identifiability in Complete Systems of Linear Difference Equations." *Metroeconomica*, **10**, pp. 182–190.

Konijn, H. S. (1962). "Identification and Estimation in a Simultaneous Equations Model with Errors in the Variables." *Econometrica*, **30**, pp. 79–87.

Koopman, B. O., and G. E. Kimball (1959). "Information Theory." Chapter 9 of *Notes on Operations Research.* Cambridge, Mass.: The M.I.T. Press.

Koopmans, T. (1937). *Linear Regression Analysis of Economic Time Series.* Haarlem: De Erven F. Bohn N.V.

Koopmans, T. (1941). "The Logic of Econometric Business-Cycle Research." *Journal of Political Economy*, **49**, pp. 157–181.

Koopmans, T. (1945). "Statistical Estimation of Simultaneous Economic Relations." *Journal of the American Statistical Association*, **40**, pp. 448–466.

Koopmans, T. C. (1949). "Identification Problems in Economic Model Construction." *Econometrica*, **17**, pp. 125–144.

Koopmans, T. C. (editor) (1950). *Statistical Inference in Dynamic Economic Models.* New York: John Wiley and Sons, Inc.

Koopmans, T. C., and W. C. Hood (1953). "The Estimation of Simultaneous Linear Economic Relationships." Chapter VI of Hood and Koopmans (1953).

Koopmans, T. C., and O. Reiersøl (1950). "The Identification of Structural Characteristics." *Annals of Mathematical Statistics*, **21**, pp. 165–181.

Koopmans, T. C., H. Rubin, and R. B. Leipnik (1950). "Measuring the Equation Systems of Dynamic Economics." Chapter II of Koopmans (1950).

Koyck, L. M. (1954). *Distributed Lags and Investment Analysis*. Amsterdam: North-Holland Publishing Company.

Kruskal, W. (1968). "When Are Gauss-Markov and Least Squares Estimators Identical? A Coordinate-free Approach." *Annals of Mathematical Statistics*, **39**, pp. 70–75.

Kuh, E. (1959). "The Validity of Cross-Sectionally Estimated Behavior Equations in Time Series Applications." *Econometrica*, **27**, pp. 197–214.

Kullback, S. (1967). "The Two Concepts of Information." *Journal of the American Statistical Association*, **62**, pp. 685–686.

Ladd, G. W. (1956). "Effects of Shocks and Errors in Estimation: An Empirical Comparison." *Journal of Farm Economics*, **38**, pp. 485–495.

Ladd, G. W. (1964). "Regression Analysis of Seasonal Data." *Journal of the American Statistical Association*, **59**, pp. 402–421.

Lancaster, T. (1966). "A Note on an 'Errors in Variables' Model." *Journal of the American Statistical Association*, **61**, pp. 128–135.

Lancaster, T. (1968). "Grouping Estimators on Heteroscedastic Data." *Journal of the American Statistical Association*, **63**, pp. 182–191.

Laplace, P. S. (1812). *Théorie analytique des probabilités*. Reprinted as Volume 7 of *Oeuvres de Laplace* (1847). Paris: Imprimerie Royale.

Larson, H. J., and T. A. Bancroft (1963a). "Sequential Model Building for Prediction in Regression Analysis, I." *Annals of Mathematical Statistics*, **34**, pp. 462–479.

Larson, H. J., and T. A. Bancroft (1963b). "Biases in Prediction by Regression for Certain Incompletely Specified Models." *Biometrika*, **50**, pp. 391–402.

Legendre, A. M. (1806). *Nouvelles méthodes pour la détermination des orbites des comètes*. Paris: Courcier.

Leser, C. E. V. (1961) "Commodity Group Expenditure Functions for the United Kingdom, 1948–1957." *Econometrica*, **29**, pp. 24–32.

Leser, C. E. V. (1966a). *Econometric Techniques and Problems*. London: Charles Griffin and Company, Ltd.

Leser, C. E. V. (1966b). "The Role of Macroeconomic Models in Short-Term Forecasting." *Econometrica*, **34**, pp. 862–872.

Leussink, A. B. (1966). "A Reconsideration of the BLUS Problem." Report 6605, Econometric Institute of the Netherlands School of Economics.

Lewis, T. O., and P. L. Odell (1966). "A Generalization of the Gauss-Markov Theorem." *Journal of the American Statistical Association*, **61**, pp. 1063–1066.

Lindley, D. V. (1947). "Regression Lines and the Linear Functional Relationship." *Journal of the Royal Statistical Society*, **9**, pp. 218–244.

Liu, T. C. (1960). "Underidentification, Structural Estimation, and Forecasting." *Econometrica*, **28,** pp. 855–865.

Liu, T. C. (1963). "An Exploratory Quarterly Econometric Model of Effective Demand in the Postwar U.S. Economy." *Econometrica*, **31,** pp. 301–348.

Liviatan, N. (1961). "Errors in Variables and Engel Curve Analysis." *Econometrica*, **29,** pp. 336–362.

Liviatan, N. (1963). "Consistent Estimation of Distributed Lags." *International Economic Review*, **4,** pp. 44–52.

Lovell, M. C. (1963). "Seasonal Adjustment of Economic Time Series and Multiple Regression Analysis." *Journal of the American Statistical Association*, **58,** pp. 993–1010.

Lovell, M. C. (1966). "Alternative Axiomatizations of Seasonal Adjustment." *Journal of the American Statistical Association*, **61,** pp. 800–802.

Luce, R. D. (1960). "The Theory of Selective Information and Some of Its Behavioral Applications." *Developments in Mathematical Psychology*, edited by R. D. Luce, Part I. Glencoe, Ill.: The Free Press.

Lyttkens, E. (1964). "Standard Errors of Regression Coefficients by Autocorrelated Residuals." Chapter 4 of Wold (1964).

McElroy, F. W. (1967). "A Necessary and Sufficient Condition that Ordinary Least-squares Estimators Be Best Linear Unbiased." *Journal of the American Statistical Association*, **62,** pp. 1302–1304.

Madansky, A. (1959). "The Fitting of Straight Lines When Both Variables Are Subject to Error." *Journal of the American Statistical Association*, **54,** pp. 173–205.

Madansky, A. (1964). "On the Efficiency of Three-stage Least-squares Estimation." *Econometrica*, **32,** pp. 51–56.

Maeshiro, A. (1966). "A Simple Mathematical Relationship among *k*-Class Estimators." *Journal of the American Statistical Association*, **61,** pp. 368–373.

Malinvaud, E. (1961a). "The Estimation of Distributed Lags: A Comment." *Econometrica*, **29,** pp. 430–433.

Malinvaud, E. (1961b). "Estimation et prévision dans les modèles économiques autorégressifs." *Review of the International Statistical Institute*, **29** (2), pp. 1–32.

Malinvaud, E. (1966). *Statistical Methods of Econometrics*. English translation of *Méthodes statistiques de l'économétrie*, published by Dunod, Paris, in 1964. Chicago: Rand McNally & Company. Amsterdam: North-Holland Publishing Company.

Mandel, J. (1958). "A Note on Confidence Intervals in Regression Problems." *Annals of Mathematical Statistics*, **29,** pp. 903–907.

Mann, H. B., and A. Wald (1943). "On the Statistical Treatment of Linear Stochastic Difference Equations." *Econometrica*, **11,** pp. 173–220.

Markov, A. A. (1912). *Wahrscheinlichkeitsrechnung*. German translation by H. Liebmann of the second Russian edition. Leipzig: B. G. Teubner.

Marsaglia, G. (1964). "Conditional Means and Covariances of Normal Variables with Singular Covariance Matrix." *Journal of the American Statistical Association*, **59**, pp. 1203–1204.

Marschak, J. (1947). "Economic Structure, Path Policy, and Prediction." *American Economic Review*, **37**, pp. 81–84.

Marschak, J. (1953). "Economic Measurements for Policy and Prediction." Chapter I of Hood and Koopmans (1953).

Marschak, J., and W. H. Andrews, Jr. (1944). "Random Simultaneous Equations and the Theory of Production." *Econometrica*, **12**, pp. 143–205.

Mehta, J. S., and P. A. V. B. Swamy (1969). "The Finite Sample Distribution of Theil's Mixed Regression Estimator and a Related Problem." Discussion Paper No. 37, Department of Economics, State University of New York at Buffalo.

Meyer, J. R., and E. Kuh, (1957). *The Investment Decision*. Cambridge, Mass.: Harvard University Press.

Meyer, J. R., and H. L. Miller, Jr. (1954). "Some Comments on the 'Simultaneous Equations Approach'." *Review of Economics and Statistics*, **36**, pp. 88–92.

Miller, R. G., Jr. (1966). *Simultaneous Statistical Inference*. New York: McGraw-Hill Book Company, Inc.

Mitra, S. K., and C. R. Rao (1968). "Some Results in Estimation and Tests of Linear Hypotheses under the Gauss-Markoff Model." *Sankhya*, Series A, **30**, pp. 281–290.

Mood, A. M., and F. A. Graybill (1963). *Introduction to the Theory of Statistics*. Second edition (first edition, 1950). New York: McGraw-Hill Book Company, Inc.

Moore, H. L. (1914). *Economic Cycles: Their Law and Cause*. New York: The Macmillan Company.

Morrison, J. L., Jr. (1967). "Small Sample Properties of Selected Distributed Lag Estimators." Discussion Paper No. 42, Department of Economics, University of Pennsylvania.

Mundlak, Y. (1961). "Aggregation over Time in Distributed Lag Models." *International Economic Review*, **2**, pp. 154–163.

Mundlak, Y. (1967). "Long-run Coefficients and Distributed Lag Analysis: A Reformulation." *Econometrica*, **35**, pp. 278–293.

Nagar, A. L. (1959). "The Bias and Moment Matrix of the General *k*-Class Estimators of the Parameters in Simultaneous Equations." *Econometrica*, **27**, pp. 575–595.

Nagar, A. L. (1960). "A Monte Carlo Study of Alternative Simultaneous Equation Estimators." *Econometrica*, **28**, pp. 573–590.

Nagar, A. L. (1961). "A Note on the Residual Variance Estimation in Simultaneous Equations." *Econometrica*, **29**, pp. 238–243.

Nagar, A. L. (1962). "Double *k*-Class Estimators of Parameters in Simultaneous Equations and Their Small Sample Properties." *International Economic Review*, **3**, pp. 168–188.

Nagar, A. L., and Y. P. Gupta (1968). "The Bias of Liviatan's Consistent Estimator in a Distributed Lag Model." *Econometrica*, **36**, pp. 337–342.

Nagar, A. L., and N. C. Kakwani (1964). "The Bias and Moment Matrix of a Mixed Regression Estimator." *Econometrica*, **32**, pp. 174–182.

Nagar, A. L., and N. C. Kakwani (1966). "Note on the Bias of a Mixed Simultaneous Equation Estimator." *International Economic Review*, **7**, pp. 65–71.

Nair, K. R., and K. S. Banerjee (1943). "A Note on Fitting of Straight Lines if Both Variables are Subject to Error." *Sankhya*, **6**, p. 331.

Nair, K. R., and M. P. Shrivastava (1942). "On a Simple Method of Curve Fitting." *Sankhya*, **6**, pp. 121–132.

Nakamura, M. (1960). "A Note on the Consistency of Simultaneous Least Squares Estimation." *International Economic Review*, **1**, pp. 192–197.

Neiswanger, W. A., and T. A. Yancey (1959). "Parameter Estimates and Autonomous Growth." *Journal of the American Statistical Association*, **54**, pp. 389–402.

Nerlove, M. (1958a). *Distributed Lags and Demand Analysis for Agricultural and Other Commodities*. Washington, D.C.: U.S. Department of Agriculture, Agriculture Handbook No. 141.

Nerlove, M. (1958b). "Distributed Lags and Estimation of Long-run Supply and Demand Elasticities: Theoretical Considerations." *Journal of Farm Economics*, **40**, pp. 301–311.

Nerlove, M. (1958c). *The Dynamics of Supply: Estimation of Farmers' Response to Price*. Baltimore: Johns Hopkins Press.

Nerlove, M. (1964). "Spectral Analysis of Seasonal Adjustment Procedures." *Econometrica*, **32**, pp. 241–286.

Nerlove, M. (1965a). *Estimation and Identification of Cobb-Douglas Production Functions*. Chicago: Rand McNally and Company. Amsterdam: North-Holland Publishing Company.

Nerlove, M. (1965b). "Two Models of the British Economy: A Fragment of a Critical Survey." *International Economic Review*, **6**, pp. 127–181.

Nerlove, M. (1966). "A Tabular Survey of Macro-econometric Models." *International Economic Review*, **7**, pp. 127–175.

Nerlove, M., and W. Addison (1958). "Statistical Estimation of Long-run Elasticities of Supply and Demand." *Journal of Farm Economics*, **40**, pp. 861–880.

Nerlove, M., and K. F. Wallis (1966). "Use of the Durbin-Watson Statistic in Inappropriate Situations." *Econometrica*, **34**, pp. 235–238.

Neumann, J. von (1941). "Distribution of the Ratio of the Mean Square Successive Difference to the Variance." *Annals of Mathematical Statistics*, **12**, pp. 367–395.

Neumann, J. von (1942). "A Further Remark Concerning the Distribution of the Ratio of the Mean Square Successive Difference to the Variance." *Annals of Mathematical Statistics*, **13**, pp. 86–88.

Neyman, J. (1951). "Existence of Consistent Estimates of the Directional Parameter in a Linear Structural Relation between Two Variables." *Annals of Mathematical Statistics*, **22**, pp. 497–512.

Neyman, J., and E. L. Scott (1948). "Consistent Estimates Based on Partially Consistent Observations." *Econometrica*, **16**, pp. 1–32.

Neyman, J., and E. L. Scott (1951). "On Certain Methods of Estimating the Linear Structural Relation." *Annals of Mathematical Statistics*, **22**, pp. 352–361. [Correction in **23** (1952), p. 135.]

Oi, W. Y. (1969). "On the Relationship among Different Members of the *k*-Class." *International Economic Review*, **10**, pp. 36–46.

Olshen, R. A. (1967). "Sign and Wilcoxon Tests for Linearity." *Annals of Mathematical Statistics*, **38**, pp. 1759–1769.

Orcutt, G. H., and D. Cochrane (1949). "A Sampling Study of the Merits of Autoregressive and Reduced Form Transformations in Regression Analysis." *Journal of the American Statistical Association*, **44**, pp. 356–372.

Orcutt, G. H., and H. S. Winokur, Jr. (1969). "First Order Autoregression: Inference, Estimation, and Prediction." *Econometrica*, **37**, pp. 1–14.

Parks, R. W. (1967). "Efficient Estimation of a System of Regression Equations When Disturbances Are Both Serially and Contemporaneously Correlated." *Journal of the American Statistical Association*, **62**, pp. 500–509.

Pearce, I. F. (1961). "An Exact Method of Consumer Demand Analysis." *Econometrica*, **29**, pp. 499–516.

Phillips, A. W. (1956). "Some Notes on the Estimation of Time-Forms of Reactions in Interdependent Dynamic Systems." *Economica*, **23**, pp. 99–113.

Plackett, R. L. (1949). "A Historical Note on the Method of Least Squares." *Biometrika*, **36**, pp. 458–460.

Plackett, R. L. (1960). *Principles of Regression Analysis*. Oxford University Press.

Powell, A. (1966). "A Complete System of Consumer Demand Equations for the Australian Economy Fitted by a Model of Additive Preferences." *Econometrica*, **34**, pp. 661–675.

Prais, S. J. (1953). "A Note on Heteroscedastic Errors in Regression Analysis." *Review of the International Statistical Institute*, **21**, pp. 28–29.

Prais, S. J., and J. Aitchison (1954). "The Grouping of Observations in Regression Analysis." *Review of the International Statistical Institute*, **22**, pp. 1–22.

Prais, S. J., and H. S. Houthakker (1955). *The Analysis of Family Budgets*. Cambridge University Press.

Pratt, J. W., H. Raiffa, and R. Schlaifer (1964). "The Foundations of Decision under Uncertainty: An Elementary Exposition." *Journal of the American Statistical Association*, **59**, pp. 353–375.

Press, S. J. (1969). "On Serial Correlation." *Annals of Mathematical Statistics*, **40**, pp. 188–196.

Press, S. J., and R. B. Brooks (1969). "Testing for Serial Correlation in Regression." Report No. 6911, Center for Mathematical Studies in Business and Economics, The University of Chicago.

Putter, J. (1967). "Orthonormal Bases of Error Spaces and Their Use for Investigating the Normality and Variances of Residuals." *Journal of the American Statistical Association*, **62**, pp. 1022–1036.

Quandt, R. E. (1958). "The Estimation of the Parameters of a Linear Regression System Obeying Two Separate Regimes." *Journal of the American Statistical Association*, **53**, pp. 873–880.

Quandt, R. E. (1960). "Tests of the Hypothesis that a Linear Regression System Obeys Two Separate Regimes." *Journal of the American Statistical Association*, **55**, pp. 324–330.

Quandt, R. E. (1965). "On Certain Small Sample Properties of k-Class Estimators." *International Economic Review*, **6**, pp. 92–104.

Quenouille, M. H. (1957). *The Analysis of Multiple Time-series*. London: Charles Griffin and Company, Ltd.

Radner, R. (1958). "Minimax Estimation for Linear Regressions." *Annals of Mathematical Statistics*, **29**, pp. 1244–1250.

Raiffa, H. and R. Schlaifer (1961). *Applied Statistical Decision Theory*. Boston: Division of Research, Graduate School of Business Administration, Harvard University.

Ramsey, J. B. (1966). "Tests for Specification Errors in Classical Linear Least Squares Regression Analysis." Econometrics Workshop Paper No. 6601, Michigan State University.

Ramsey, J. B. (1967). "Models, Specification Error, and Inference: A Discussion of Some Problems in Econometric Methodology." Econometrics Workshop Paper No. 6714, Michigan State University.

Rao, C. R. (1945). "Generalisation of Markoff's Theorem and Tests of Linear Hypotheses." *Sankhya*, **7**, pp. 9–16.

Rao, C. R. (1965a). *Linear Statistical Inference and Its Applications*. New York: John Wiley and Sons, Inc.

Rao, C. R. (1965b). "The Theory of Least-Squares When the Parameters Are Stochastic and Its Application to the Analysis of Growth Curves." *Biometrika*, **52**, pp. 447–458.

Rao, M. M. (1961). "Consistency and Limit Distributions of Estimators of Parameters in Explosive Stochastic Difference Equations." *Annals of Mathematical Statistics*, **32**, pp. 195–218.

Rao, P., and Z. Griliches (1969). "Small-sample Properties of Several Two-stage Regression Methods in the Context of Auto-correlated Errors." *Journal of the American Statistical Association*, **64**, pp. 253–272.

Rayner, A. A., and R. M. Pringle (1967). "A Note on Generalized Inverses in the Linear Hypothesis Not of Full Rank." *Annals of Mathematical Statistics*, **38**, pp. 271–273.

Reiersøl, O. (1941). "Confluence Analysis by Means of Lag Moments and Other Methods of Confluence Analysis." *Econometrica*, **9**, pp. 1–24.

Reiersøl, O. (1945). "Confluence Analysis by Means of Instrumental Sets of Variables." *Arkiv for Mathematik, Astronomi och Fysik*, **32A** (4) (119 pages).

Reiersøl, O. (1950). "Identifiability of a Linear Relation between Variables Which Are Subject to Error." *Econometrica*, **18**, pp. 375–389.

Richardson, D. H. (1968). "The Exact Distribution of a Structural Coefficient Estimator." *Journal of the American Statistical Association*, **63**, pp. 1214–1226.

Rosenberg, B. (1967). "Regression in the Presence of Stochastically Varying Parameters." Mimeographed report, School of Business Administration, University of California at Berkeley.

Rosenblatt, M. (1956). "Some Regression Problems in Time Series Analysis." *Proceedings of the Third Berkeley Symposium on Mathematical Statistics and Probability*, Vol. I, edited by J. Neyman, pp. 165–186. Berkeley and Los Angeles: University of California Press.

Rothenberg, T. (1963). "A Bayesian Analysis of Simultaneous Equation Systems." Report 6315, Econometric Institute of the Netherlands School of Economics, Rotterdam.

Rothenberg, T. (1968). "The Value of Structural Information: A Bayesian Approach." Report 6814, Center for Operations Research and Econometrics, University of Louvain.

Rothenberg, T. J., and C. T. Leenders (1964). "Efficient Estimation of Simultaneous Equation Systems." *Econometrica*, **32**, pp. 57–76.

Roy, S. N. (1957). *Some Aspects of Multivariate Analysis*. New York: John Wiley and Sons, Inc. Calcutta: Indian Statistical Institute.

Rubin, H. (1950a). "Consistency of Maximum-Likelihood Estimates in the Explosive Case." Chapter XIV of Koopmans (1950).

Rubin, H. (1950b). "Note on Random Coefficients." Chapter XIX of Koopmans (1950).

Ruble, W. L. (1968). "Improving the Computation of Simultaneous Stochastic Linear Equations Estimates." Agricultural Economics Report No. 116, Michigan State University.

Rutemiller, H. C., and D. A. Bowers (1968). "Estimation in a Heteroscedastic Regression Model." *Journal of the American Statistical Association*, **63**, pp. 552–557.

Samuelson, P. A. (1965). "Using Full Duality to Show that Simultaneously Additive Direct and Indirect Utilities Implies Unitary Price Elasticity of Demand." *Econometrica*, **33**, pp. 781–796.

Sargan, J. D. (1958). "The Estimation of Economic Relationships Using Instrumental Variables." *Econometrica*, **26**, pp. 393–415.

Sargan, J. D. (1961). "The Maximum Likelihood Estimation of Economic Relationships with Autoregressive Residuals." *Econometrica*, **29**, 414–426.

Sargan, J. D. (1964a). "Wages and Prices in the United Kingdom: A Study in Econometric Methodology." *Econometric Analysis for National Economic*

Planning, edited by P. E. Hart, G. Mills, and J. K. Whitaker (1964), pp. 25–54. London: Butterworth and Co., Ltd.

Sargan, J. D. (1964b). "Three-stage Least-squares and Full Maximum Likelihood Estimates." *Econometrica*, **32**, pp. 77–81.

Savage, L. J. (1954). *The Foundations of Statistics*. New York: John Wiley and Sons, Inc. London: Chapman and Hall, Ltd.

Sawa, T. (1968). "Selection of Variables in Regression Analysis." *Quarterly Review of Economics*, **19**, pp. 53–63.

Scheffé, H. (1953). "A Method for Judging All Contrasts in the Analysis of Variance." *Biometrika*, **40**, pp. 87–104.

Scheffé, H. (1959). *The Analysis of Variance*. New York: John Wiley and Sons, Inc.

Schultz, H. (1938). *The Theory and Measurement of Demand*. Chicago: The University of Chicago Press.

Sclove, S. L. (1968). "Improved Estimators for Coefficients in Linear Regression." *Journal of the American Statistical Association*, **63**, pp. 596–606.

Sen, P. K. (1968). "Estimates of the Regression Coefficient Based on Kendall's Tau." *Journal of the American Statistical Association*, **63**, pp. 1379–1389.

Sewell, W. P. (1969). "Least Squares, Conditional Predictions, and Estimator Properties." *Econometrica*, **37**, pp. 39–43.

Shannon, C. E. (1948). "A Mathematical Theory of Communication." *Bell System Technical Journal*, **27**, pp. 379–423, 623–656.

Shannon, C. E., and W. Weaver (1949). *The Mathematical Theory of Communication*. Urbana, Ill.: The University of Illinois Press.

Simon, H. A. (1953). "Causal Ordering and Identifiability." Chapter III of Hood and Koopmans (1953).

Slutzky, E. (1937). "The Summation of Random Causes as the Source of Cyclic Processes." *Econometrica*, **5**, pp. 105–146. The article originally appeared in Russian in 1927.

Solow, R. M. (1960). "On a Family of Lag Distributions." *Econometrica*, **28**, pp. 393–406. (Errata on p. 735.)

Srivastava, S. R., and T. A. Bancroft (1967). "Inferences Concerning a Population Correlation Coefficient from One or Possibly Two Samples Subsequent to a Preliminary Test of Significance." *Journal of the Royal Statistical Society*, Series B, **29**, pp. 282–291.

Stein, C. (1956a). "Inadmissibility of the Usual Estimator for the Mean of a Multivariate Normal Distribution." *Proceedings of the Third Berkeley Symposium on Mathematical Statistics and Probability*, Vol. I, pp. 197–206. Berkeley and Los Angeles: University of California Press.

Stein, C. (1956b). "The Admissibility of Hotelling's T^2-Test." *Annals of Mathematical Statistics*, **27**, pp. 616–623.

Stein, C. (1960). "Multiple Regression." Chapter 37 of *Contributions to Probability and Statistics: Essays in Honor of Harold Hotelling*, edited by I. Olkin, S.

Ghurye, W. Hoeffding, W. G. Madow, and H. B. Mann (1960). Stanford: Stanford University Press.

Stekler, H. O. (1968). "Forecasting with Econometric Models: An Evaluation." *Econometrica*, **36,** pp. 437–463.

Stone, R. (1947). "On the Interdependence of Blocks of Transactions." Supplement to the *Journal of the Royal Statistical Society*, **9,** pp. 1–45.

Stone, R. (1954a). *The Measurement of Consumer's Expenditure and Behavior in the United Kingdom, 1920–1938.* Volume I. Cambridge University Press.

Stone, R. (1954b). "Linear Expenditure Systems and Demand Analysis: An Application to the Pattern of British Demand." *The Economic Journal*, **64,** pp. 511–527.

Strotz, R. H. (1957). "The Empirical Implications of a Utility Tree." *Econometrica*, **25,** pp. 269–280.

Strotz, R. H. (1960). "Interdependence as a Specification Error." *Econometrica*, **28,** pp. 428–442.

Strotz, R. H., and H. O. A. Wold (1960). "Recursive vs. Nonrecursive Systems: An Attempt at Synthesis." *Econometrica*, **28,** pp. 417–427.

Summers, R. (1965). "A Capital Intensive Approach to the Small Sample Properties of Various Simultaneous Equation Estimators." *Econometrica*, **33,** pp. 1–41.

Suzuki, Y. (1964). "On the Use of Some Extraneous Information in the Estimation of the Coefficients of Regression." *Annals of the Institute of Statistical Mathematics*, **16,** pp. 161–173.

Swamy, P. A. V. B., and G. S. Maddala (1968). "Tests of Random Coefficient vs. Fixed Coefficient Models Based on the Likelihood Ratio Principle." Department of Economics Workshop Paper No. 35, State University of New York at Buffalo.

Swamy, P. A. V. B., G. S. Maddala, and J. Holmes (1969). "Use of Undersized Samples in the Estimation of Simultaneous Equation Systems." Mimeographed report.

Swamy, P. A. V. B., and J. S. Mehta (1969). "On Theil's Mixed Regression Estimator." *Journal of the American Statistical Association*, **64,** pp. 273–276.

Telser, L. G. (1964). "Iterative Estimation of a Set of Linear Regression Equations." *Journal of the American Statistical Association*, **59,** pp. 845–862.

Theil, H. (1950). "A Rank-Invariant Method of Linear and Polynomial Regression Analysis." *Proceedings of the Royal Netherlands Academy of Sciences*, **53,** pp. 386–392, 521–525, 1397–1412.

Theil, H. (1951a). "Estimates and Their Sampling Variance of Parameters of Certain Heteroscedastic Distributions." *Review of the International Statistical Institute*, **19,** pp. 141–147.

Theil, H. (1951b). "Verdelingsvrije methoden in de regressieanalyse van twee variabelen." *Statistica Neerlandica*, **5,** pp. 97–117.

Theil, H. (1953a). "Repeated Least-Squares Applied to Complete Equation Systems." The Hague: Central Planning Bureau (mimeographed).

Theil, H. (1953b). "Estimation and Simultaneous Correlation in Complete Equation Systems." The Hague: Central Planning Bureau (mimeographed).

Theil, H. (1954). *Linear Aggregation of Economic Relations*. Amsterdam: North-Holland Publishing Company.

Theil, H. (1957). "Specification Errors and the Estimation of Economic Relationships." *Review of the International Statistical Institute*, **25**, pp. 41–51.

Theil, H. (1959). "The Aggregation Implications of Identifiable Structural Macrorelations." *Econometrica*, **27**, pp. 14–29.

Theil, H. (1961). *Economic Forecasts and Policy*. Second edition (first edition, 1958). Amsterdam: North-Holland Publishing Company.

Theil, H. (1963). "On the Use of Incomplete Prior Information in Regression Analysis." *Journal of the American Statistical Association*, **58**, pp. 401–414.

Theil, H. (1964). *Optimal Decision Rules for Government and Industry*. Chicago: Rand McNally and Company. Amsterdam: North-Holland Publishing Company.

Theil, H. (1965a). "The Information Approach to Demand Analysis." *Econometrica*, **33**, pp. 67–87.

Theil, H. (1965b). "The Analysis of Disturbances in Regression Analysis." *Journal of the American Statistical Association*, **60**, pp. 1067–1079.

Theil, H. (1966). *Applied Economic Forecasting*. Chicago: Rand McNally and Company. Amsterdam: North-Holland Publishing Company.

Theil, H. (1967). *Economics and Information Theory*. Chicago: Rand McNally and Company. Amsterdam: North-Holland Publishing Company.

Theil, H. (1968a). "A Simplification of the BLUS Procedure for Analyzing Regression Disturbances." *Journal of the American Statistical Association*, **63**, pp. 242–251.

Theil, H. (1968b). "Consistent Aggregation of Micromodels with Random Coefficients." Report 6816, Center for Mathematical Studies in Business and Economics, The University of Chicago.

Theil, H., and J. C. G. Boot (1962). "The Final Form of Econometric Equation Systems." *Review of the International Statistical Institute*, **30**, pp. 136–152.

Theil, H., J. C. G. Boot, and T. Kloek (1965). *Operations Research and Quantitative Economics*. New York: McGraw-Hill Book Company, Inc.

Theil, H., and A. J. Finizza (1967). "An Informational Approach to the Measurement of Racial Segregation in Schools." Report 6712, Center for Mathematical Studies in Business and Economics, The University of Chicago.

Theil, H., and A. S. Goldberger (1961). "On Pure and Mixed Statistical Estimation in Economics." *International Economic Review*, **2**, pp. 65–78.

Theil, H., and J. van IJzeren (1956). "On the Efficiency of Wald's Method of Fitting Straight Lines." *Review of the International Statistical Institute*, **24**, pp. 17–26.

Theil, H., and L. B. M. Mennes (1959). "Conception stochastique de coefficients multiplicateurs dans l'adjustement linéaire des séries temporelles." *Publications de l'Institut de Statistique de l'Université de Paris*, **8**, pp. 211–227.

Theil, H., and A. L. Nagar (1961). "Testing the Independence of Regression Disturbances." *Journal of the American Statistical Association*, **56**, pp. 793–806.

Theil, H., and A. Schweitzer (1961). "The Best Quadratic Estimator of the Residual Variance in Regression Analysis." *Statistica Neerlandica*, **15**, pp. 19–23.

Theil, H., and R. M. Stern (1960). "A Simple Unimodal Lag Distribution." *Metroeconomica*, **12**, pp. 111–119.

Thornber, H. (1967). "Finite Sample Monte Carlo Studies: An Autoregressive Illustration." *Journal of the American Statistical Association*, **62**, pp. 801–818.

Tiao, G. C., and A. Zellner (1964a). "Bayes's Theorem and the Use of Prior Knowledge in Regression Analysis." *Biometrika*, **51**, pp. 219–230.

Tiao, G. C., and A. Zellner (1964b). "On the Bayesian Estimation of Multivariate Regression." *Journal of the Royal Statistical Society*, Series B, **26**, pp. 277–285.

Tinbergen, J. (1939). *Statistical Testing of Business-Cycle Theories*. Volume 1: *A Method and Its Application to Investment Activity*. Volume 2: *Business Cycles in the United States of America, 1919–1932*. Geneva: League of Nations.

Tinbergen, J. (1951a). *Econometrics*. London: George Allen and Unwin, Ltd.

Tinbergen, J. (1951b). *Business Cycles in the United Kingdom, 1870–1914*. Amsterdam: North-Holland Publishing Company.

Tinbergen, J. (1959). *Selected Papers*, edited by L. H. Klaassen, L. M. Koyck, and J. H. Witteveen. Amsterdam: North-Holland Publishing Company.

Tinsley, P. A. (1967). "An Application of Variable Weight Distributed Lags." *Journal of the American Statistical Association*, **62**, pp. 1277–1289.

Tintner, G. (1952). *Econometrics*. New York: John Wiley and Sons, Inc.

Tobin, J. (1958). "Estimation of Relationships for Limited Dependent Variables." *Econometrica*, **26**, pp. 24–36.

Toro-Vizcarrondo, C., and T. D. Wallace (1968). "A Test of the Mean Square Error Criterion for Restrictions in Linear Regression." *Journal of the American Statistical Association*, **63**, 558–572.

Tukey, J. W. (1949). "Comparing Individual Means in the Analysis of Variance." *Biometrics*, **5**, pp. 99–114.

Ueno, H., and S. Kinoshita (1968). "A Simulation Experiment for Growth with a Long-term Model of Japan." *International Economic Review*, **9**, pp. 14–48.

Valavanis, S. (1959). *Econometrics: An Introduction to Maximum Likelihood Methods*. New York: McGraw-Hill Book Company, Inc.

Wagner, H. M. (1958). "A Monte Carlo Study of Estimates of Simultaneous Linear Structural Equations." *Econometrica*, **26**, pp. 117–133.

Wagner, H. M. (1962). "Non-linear Regression with Minimal Assumptions." *Journal of the American Statistical Association*, **57**, pp. 572–578.

Wald, A. (1940). "The Fitting of Straight Lines if Both Variables Are Subject to Error." *Annals of Mathematical Statistics*, **11**, pp. 284–300.

Wald, A. (1948a). "Asymptotic Properties of the Maximum Likelihood Estimate of an Unknown Parameter of a Discrete Stochastic Process." *Annals of Mathematical Statistics*, **19**, pp. 40–46.

Wald, A. (1948b). "Estimation of a Parameter When the Number of Unknown Parameters Increases Indefinitely with the Number of Observations." *Annals of Mathematical Statistics*, **19**, pp. 220–227.

Wallace, D. L. (1958). "Asymptotic Approximations to Distributions." *Annals of Mathematical Statistics*, **29**, pp. 635–654.

Wallace, T. D., and A. Hussain (1969). "The Use of Error Components Models in Combining Cross Section with Time Series Data." *Econometrica*, **37**, pp. 55–72.

Wallis, W. A. (1951). "Tolerance Intervals for Linear Regression." *Proceedings of the Second Berkeley Symposium on Mathematical Statistics and Probability*, pp. 43–51. Berkeley and Los Angeles: University of California Press.

Walters, A. A. (1963). "Production and Cost Functions: An Econometric Survey." *Econometrica*, **31**, pp. 1–66.

Warner, S. L. (1963). "Multivariate Regression of Dummy Variates under Normality Assumptions." *Journal of the American Statistical Association*, **58**, pp. 1054–1063.

Warner, S. L. (1967). "Asymptotic Variances for Dummy Variate Regression under Normality Assumptions." *Journal of the American Statistical Association*, **62**, pp. 1305–1314.

Watson, G. S. (1955). "Serial Correlation in Regression Analysis. I." *Biometrika*, **42**, pp. 327–341.

Watson, G. S. (1967). "Linear Least Squares Regression." *Annals of Mathematical Statistics*, **38**, pp. 1679–1699.

Watson, G. S., and E. J. Hannan (1956). "Serial Correlation in Regression Analysis. II." *Biometrika*, **43**, pp. 436–445.

Waud, R. (1966). "Small Sample Bias Due to Misspecification in the 'Partial Adjustment' and 'Adaptive Expectations' Models." *Journal of the American Statistical Association*, **61**, pp. 1130–1152.

Waud, R. N. (1968). "Misspecification in the 'Partial Adjustment' and 'Adaptive Expectations' Models." *International Economic Review*, **9**, pp. 204–217.

White, J. S. (1958). "The Limiting Distribution of the Serial Correlation Coefficient in the Explosive Case." *Annals of Mathematical Statistics*, **29**, pp. 1188–1197.

White, J. S. (1959). "The Limiting Distribution of the Serial Correlation Coefficient in the Explosive Case, II." *Annals of Mathematical Statistics*, **30**, pp. 831–834.

Whittaker, E. T., and G. Robinson (1944). *The Calculus of Observations*. Fourth edition (first edition, 1924). London: Blackie and Son Limited.

Wijngaarden, A. van (1950). "Table of the Cumulative Symmetric Binomial Distribution." *Proceedings of the Royal Netherlands Academy of Sciences*, **53**, pp. 857–868.

Wishart, J. (1931). "The Mean and Second Moment Coefficient of the Multiple Correlation Coefficient, in Samples from a Normal Population." *Biometrika*, **22**, pp. 353–367.

Wold, H., in association with L. Juréen (1953). *Demand Analysis*. New York: John Wiley and Sons, Inc.

Wold, H. (1954). "Causality and Econometrics." *Econometrica*, **22**, pp. 162–177.

Wold, H. (1956). "Causal Inference from Observational Data: A Review of Ends and Means." *Journal of the Royal Statistical Society*, Series A, **119**, pp. 28–50.

Wold, H. (1959). "Ends and Means in Econometric Model Building." *Probability and Statistics: The Harold Cramér Volume*, edited by U. Grenander, pp. 355–434. New York: John Wiley and Sons, Inc. Stockholm: Almqvist and Wiksell.

Wold, H. (1960). "A Generalization of Causal Chain Models." *Econometrica*, **28**, pp. 443–463.

Wold, H. (editor) (1964). *Econometric Model Building: Essays on the Causal Chain Approach*. Amsterdam: North-Holland Publishing Company.

Wold, H. (1966a). "A Fix-point Theorem with Econometric Background." *Arkiv för Matematik*, **6**, pp. 209–240.

Wold, H. (1966b). "Nonlinear Estimation by Iterative Least Squares Procedures." *Research Papers in Statistics*, edited by F. N. David, pp. 411–444. New York: John Wiley and Sons, Inc.

Wold, H., and P. Faxér (1957). "On the Specification Error in Regression Analysis." *Annals of Mathematical Statistics*, **28**, pp. 265–267.

Wolfowitz, J. (1952). "Consistent Estimators of the Parameters of a Linear Structural Relation." *Skandinavisk Aktuarietidskrift*, **35**, pp. 132–151.

Wolfowitz, J. (1954). "Estimation of the Components of Stochastic Structures." *Proceedings of the National Academy of Sciences*, **40**, pp. 602–606.

Working, E. J. (1927). "What Do Statistical 'Demand Curves' Show?" *Quarterly Journal of Economics*, **41**, pp. 212–235.

Working, H. (1925). "The Statistical Determination of Demand Curves." *Quarterly Journal of Economics*, **39**, pp. 503–543.

Yule, G. U. (1921). "On the Time-correlation Problem, with Especial Reference to the Variate-difference Correlation Method." *Journal of the Royal Statistical Society*, **84**, pp. 497–526.

Zarembka, P. (1968). "Functional Form in the Demand for Money." *Journal of the American Statistical Association*, **63**, pp. 502–511.

Zellner, A. (1961). "Econometric Estimation with Temporally Dependent Disturbance Terms." *International Economic Review*, **2**, pp. 164–178.

Zellner, A. (1962). "An Efficient Method of Estimating Seemingly Unrelated

Regressions and Tests for Aggregation Bias." *Journal of the American Statistical Association*, **57**, pp. 348–368.

Zellner, A. (1963a). "Decision Rules for Economic Forecasting." *Econometrica*, **31**, pp. 111–130.

Zellner, A. (1963b). "Estimators for Seemingly Unrelated Regression Equations: Some Exact Finite Sample Results." *Journal of the American Statistical Association*, **58**, pp. 977–992.

Zellner, A. (1966). "On the Aggregation Problem: A New Approach to a Troublesome Problem." Report 6628, Center for Mathematical Studies in Business and Economics, The University of Chicago.

Zellner, A. (editor) (1968). *Readings in Economic Statistics and Econometrics*. Boston: Little, Brown and Company, Inc.

Zellner, A., and Chetty, V. K. (1965). "Prediction and Decision Problems in Regression Models from the Bayesian Point of View." *Journal of the American Statistical Association*, **60**, pp. 608–616.

Zellner, A., and D. S. Huang (1962). "Further Properties of Efficient Estimators for Seemingly Unrelated Regression Equations." *International Economic Review*, **3**, pp. 300–313.

Zellner, A., J. Kmenta, and J. Drèze (1966). "Specification and Estimation of Cobb-Douglas Production Function Models." *Econometrica*, **34**, pp. 784–795.

Zellner, A., and T. H. Lee (1965). "Joint Estimation of Relationships Involving Discrete Random Variables." *Econometrica*, **33**, pp. 382–394.

Zellner, A., and U. Sankar (1967). "On Errors in the Variables." Report 6703, Center for Mathematical Studies in Business and Economics, The University of Chicago.

Zellner, A., and H. Theil (1962). "Three-stage Least Squares: Simultaneous Estimation of Simultaneous Equations." *Econometrica*, **30**, pp. 54–78.

Zellner, A., and G. C. Tiao (1964). "Bayesian Analysis of the Regression Model with Autocorrelated Errors." *Journal of the American Statistical Association*, **59**, pp. 763–778.

Zyskind, G. (1963). "A Note on Residual Analysis." *Journal of the American Statistical Association*, **58**, pp. 1125–1132.

Zyskind, G. (1967). "On Canonical Forms, Non-negative Covariance Matrices and Best and Simple Least Squares Linear Estimators in Linear Models." *Annals of Mathematical Statistics*, **38**, pp. 1092–1109.

TABLES

The t Distribution and the Normal Distribution[a]

Degrees of Freedom \ Pb	.25 .5	.1 .2	.05 .1	.025 .05	.01 .02	.005 .01
1	1.000	3.078	6.314	12.706	31.821	63.657
2	.816	1.886	2.920	4.303	6.965	9.925
3	.765	1.638	2.353	3.182	4.541	5.841
4	.741	1.533	2.132	2.776	3.747	4.604
5	.727	1.476	2.015	2.571	3.365	4.032
6	.718	1.440	1.943	2.447	3.143	3.707
7	.711	1.415	1.895	2.365	2.998	3.499
8	.706	1.397	1.860	2.306	2.896	3.355
9	.703	1.383	1.833	2.262	2.821	3.250
10	.700	1.372	1.812	2.228	2.764	3.169
11	.697	1.363	1.796	2.201	2.718	3.106
12	.695	1.356	1.782	2.179	2.681	3.055
13	.694	1.350	1.771	2.160	2.650	3.012
14	.692	1.345	1.761	2.145	2.624	2.977
15	.691	1.341	1.753	2.131	2.602	2.947
16	.690	1.337	1.746	2.120	2.583	2.921
17	.689	1.333	1.740	2.110	2.567	2.898
18	.688	1.330	1.734	2.101	2.552	2.878
19	.688	1.328	1.729	2.093	2.539	2.861
20	.687	1.325	1.725	2.086	2.528	2.845
21	.686	1.323	1.721	2.080	2.518	2.831
22	.686	1.321	1.717	2.074	2.508	2.819
23	.685	1.319	1.714	2.069	2.500	2.807
24	.685	1.318	1.711	2.064	2.492	2.797
25	.684	1.316	1.708	2.060	2.485	2.787
26	.684	1.315	1.706	2.056	2.479	2.779
27	.684	1.314	1.703	2.052	2.473	2.771
28	.683	1.313	1.701	2.048	2.467	2.763
29	.683	1.311	1.699	2.045	2.462	2.756
30	.683	1.310	1.697	2.042	2.457	2.750
40	.681	1.303	1.684	2.021	2.423	2.704
60	.679	1.296	1.671	2.000	2.390	2.660
120	.677	1.289	1.658	1.980	2.358	2.617
(Normal) ∞	.674	1.282	1.645	1.960	2.326	2.576

Source. This table is abridged from E. S. Pearson and H. O. Hartley, *Biometrika Tables for Statisticians*, Vol. I (1954), p. 138, with kind permission of the Syndics of the Cambridge University Press, publishers for the Biometrika Society.

[a] The smaller probability shown at the head of each column is the area in one tail; the larger probability is the area in both tails. Example: With 20 degrees of freedom, a t value larger than 1.725 has a .05 probability and a t value exceeding 1.725 in absolute value has a .1 probability.

The χ^2 Distribution[a]

Degrees of Freedom \ Pb	.995	.990	.975	.950	.900
1	$392704 \cdot 10^{-10}$	$157088 \cdot 10^{-9}$	$982069 \cdot 10^{-9}$	$393214 \cdot 10^{-8}$	.0157908
2	.0100251	.0201007	.0506356	.102587	.210720
3	.0717212	.114832	.215795	.351846	.584375
4	.206990	.297110	.484419	.710721	1.063623
5	.411740	.554300	.831211	1.145476	1.61031
6	.675727	.872085	1.237347	1.63539	2.20413
7	.989265	1.239043	1.68987	2.16735	2.83311
8	1.344419	1.646482	2.17973	2.73264	3.48954
9	1.734926	2.087912	2.70039	3.32511	4.16816
10	2.15585	2.55821	3.24697	3.94030	4.86518
11	2.60321	3.05347	3.81575	4.57481	5.57779
12	3.07382	3.57056	4.40379	5.22603	6.30380
13	3.56503	4.10691	5.00874	5.89186	7.04150
14	4.07468	4.66043	5.62872	6.57063	7.78953
15	4.60094	5.22935	6.26214	7.26094	8.54675
16	5.14224	5.81221	6.90766	7.96164	9.31223
17	5.69724	6.40776	7.56418	8.67176	10.0852
18	6.26481	7.01491	8.23075	9.39046	10.8649
19	6.84398	7.63273	8.90655	10.1170	11.6509
20	7.43386	8.26040	9.59083	10.8508	12.4426
21	8.03366	8.89720	10.28293	115913	13.2396
22	8.64272	9.54249	10.9823	12.3380	14.0415
23	9.26042	10.19567	11.6885	13.0905	14.8479
24	9.88623	10.8564	12.4011	13.8484	15.6587
25	10.5197	11.5240	13.1197	14.6114	16.4734
26	11.1603	12.1981	13.8439	15.3791	17.2919
27	11.8076	12.8786	14.5733	16.1513	18.1138
28	12.4613	13.5648	15.3079	16.9279	18.9392
29	13.1211	14.2565	16.0471	17.7083	19.7677
30	13.7867	14.9535	16.7908	18.4926	20.5992
40	20.7065	22.1643	24.4331	26.5093	29.0505
50	27.9907	29.7067	32.3574	34.7642	37.6886
60	35.5346	37.4848	40.4817	43.1879	46.4589
70	43.2752	45.4418	48.7576	51.7393	55.3290
80	51.1720	53.5400	57.1532	60.3915	64.2778
90	59.1963	61.7541	65.6466	69.1260	73.2912
100	67.3276	70.0648	74.2219	77.9295	82.3581

[a] The probability shown at the head of the column is the area in the right-hand tail. Example: With 4 degrees of freedom, a χ^2 value larger than 7.78 has a .1 probability.

.750	.500	.250	.100	.050	.025	.010	.005
.1015308	.454937	1.32330	2.70554	3.84146	5.02389	6.63490	7.87944
.575364	1.38629	2.77259	4.60517	5.99147	7.37776	9.21034	10.5966
1.212534	2.36597	4.10835	6.25139	7.81473	9.34840	11.3449	12.8381
1.92255	3.35670	5.38527	7.77944	9.48773	11.1433	13.2767	14.8602
2.67460	4.35146	6.62568	9.23635	11.0705	12.8325	15.0863	16.7496
3.45460	5.34812	7.84080	10.6446	12.5916	14.4494	16.8119	18.5476
4.25485	6.34581	9.03715	12.0170	14.0671	16.0128	18.4753	20.2777
5.07064	7.34412	10.2188	13.3616	15.5073	17.5346	20.0902	21.9550
5.89883	8.34283	11.3887	14.6837	16.9190	19.0228	21.6660	23.5893
6.73720	9.34182	12.5489	15.9871	18.3070	20.4831	23.2093	25.1882
7.58412	10.3410	13.7007	17.2750	19.6751	21.9200	24.7250	26.7569
8.43842	11.3403	14.8454	18.5494	21.0261	23.3367	26.2170	28.2995
9.29906	12.3398	15.9839	19.8119	22.3621	24.7356	27.6883	29.8194
10.1653	13.3393	17.1170	21.0642	23.6848	26.1190	29.1413	31.3193
11.0365	14.3389	18.2451	22.3072	24.9958	27.4884	30.5779	32.8013
11.9122	15.3385	19.3688	23.5418	26.2962	28.8454	31.9999	34.2672
12.7919	16.3381	20.4887	24.7690	27.5871	30.1910	33.4087	35.7185
13.6753	17.3379	21.6049	25.9894	28.8693	31.5264	34.8053	37.1564
14.5620	18.3376	22.7178	27.2036	30.1435	32.8523	36.1908	38.5822
15.4518	19.3374	23.8277	28.4120	31.4104	34.1696	37.5662	39.9968
16.3444	20.3372	24.9348	29.6151	32.6705	35.4789	38.9321	41.4010
17.2396	21.3370	26.0393	30.8133	33.9244	36.7807	40.2894	42.7956
18.1373	22.3369	27.1413	32.0069	35.1725	38.0757	41.6384	44.1813
19.0372	23.3367	28.2412	33.1963	36.4151	39.3641	42.9798	45.5585
19.9393	24.3366	29.3389	34.3816	37.6525	40.6465	44.3141	46.9278
20.8434	25.3364	30.4345	35.5631	38.8852	41.9232	45.6417	48.2899
21.7494	26.3363	31.5284	36.7412	40.1133	43.1944	46.9630	49.6449
22.6572	27.3363	32.6205	37.9159	41.3372	44.4607	48.2782	50.9933
23.5666	28.3362	33.7109	39.0875	42.5569	45.7222	49.5879	52.3356
24.4776	29.3360	34.7998	40.2560	43.7729	46.9792	50.8922	53.6720
33.6603	39.3354	45.6160	51.8050	55.7585	59.3417	63.6907	66.7659
42.9421	49.3349	56.3336	63.1671	67.5048	71.4202	76.1539	79.4900
52.2938	59.3347	66.9814	74.3970	79.0819	83.2976	88.3794	91.9517
61.6983	69.3344	77.5766	85.5271	90.5312	95.0231	100.425	104.215
71.1445	79.3343	88.1303	96.5782	101.879	106.629	112.329	116.321
80.6247	89.3342	98.6499	107.565	113.145	118.136	124.116	128.299
90.1332	99.3341	109.141	118.498	124.342	129.561	135.807	140.169

Source. This table is abridged from E. S. Pearson and H. O. Hartley, *Biometrika Tables for Statisticians*, Vol. I (1954), pp. 130–131, with kind permission of the Syndics of the Cambridge University Press, publishers for the Biometrika Society.

5% and 1% Points for the Distribution of F (5% roman, 1% boldface)[a]

Degrees of Freedom n_2	Degrees of Freedom n_1: 1	2	3	4	5	6	7	8	9	10	11	12	14	16	20	24	30	40	50	75	100	200	500	∞
1	161	200	216	225	230	234	237	239	241	242	243	244	245	246	248	249	250	251	252	253	253	254	254	254
	4052	**4999**	**5403**	**5625**	**5764**	**5859**	**5928**	**5981**	**6022**	**6056**	**6082**	**6106**	**6142**	**6169**	**6203**	**6234**	**6258**	**6286**	**6302**	**6323**	**6334**	**6352**	**6361**	**6366**
2	18.51	19.00	19.16	19.25	19.30	19.33	19.36	19.37	19.38	19.39	19.40	19.41	19.42	19.43	19.44	19.45	19.46	19.47	19.47	19.48	19.49	19.49	19.50	19.50
	98.49	**99.00**	**99.17**	**99.25**	**99.30**	**99.33**	**99.34**	**99.36**	**99.38**	**99.40**	**99.41**	**99.42**	**99.43**	**99.44**	**99.45**	**99.46**	**99.47**	**99.48**	**99.48**	**99.49**	**99.49**	**99.49**	**99.50**	**99.50**
3	10.13	9.55	9.28	9.12	9.01	8.94	8.88	8.84	8.81	8.78	8.76	8.74	8.71	8.69	8.66	8.64	8.62	8.60	8.58	8.57	8.56	8.54	8.54	8.53
	34.12	**30.82**	**29.46**	**28.71**	**28.24**	**27.91**	**27.67**	**27.49**	**27.34**	**27.23**	**27.13**	**27.05**	**26.92**	**26.83**	**26.69**	**26.60**	**26.50**	**26.41**	**26.35**	**26.27**	**26.23**	**26.18**	**26.14**	**26.12**
4	7.71	6.94	6.59	6.39	6.26	6.16	6.09	6.04	6.00	5.96	5.93	5.91	5.87	5.84	5.80	5.77	5.74	5.71	5.70	5.68	5.66	5.65	5.64	5.63
	21.20	**18.00**	**16.69**	**15.98**	**15.52**	**15.21**	**14.98**	**14.80**	**14.66**	**14.54**	**14.45**	**14.37**	**14.24**	**14.15**	**14.02**	**13.93**	**13.83**	**13.74**	**13.69**	**13.61**	**13.57**	**13.52**	**13.48**	**13.46**
5	6.61	5.79	5.41	5.19	5.05	4.95	4.88	4.82	4.78	4.74	4.70	4.68	4.64	4.60	4.56	4.53	4.50	4.46	4.44	4.42	4.40	4.38	4.37	4.36
	16.26	**13.27**	**12.06**	**11.39**	**10.97**	**10.67**	**10.45**	**10.27**	**10.15**	**10.05**	**9.96**	**9.89**	**9.77**	**9.68**	**9.55**	**9.47**	**9.38**	**9.29**	**9.24**	**9.17**	**9.13**	**9.07**	**9.04**	**9.02**
6	5.99	5.14	4.76	4.53	4.39	4.28	4.21	4.15	4.10	4.06	4.03	4.00	3.96	3.92	3.87	3.84	3.81	3.77	3.75	3.72	3.71	3.69	3.68	3.67
	13.74	**10.92**	**9.78**	**9.15**	**8.75**	**8.47**	**8.26**	**8.10**	**7.98**	**7.87**	**7.79**	**7.72**	**7.60**	**7.52**	**7.39**	**7.31**	**7.23**	**7.14**	**7.09**	**7.02**	**6.99**	**6.94**	**6.90**	**6.88**
7	5.59	4.74	4.35	4.12	3.97	3.87	3.79	3.73	3.68	3.63	3.60	3.57	3.52	3.49	3.44	3.41	3.38	3.34	3.32	3.29	3.28	3.25	3.24	3.23
	12.25	**9.55**	**8.45**	**7.85**	**7.46**	**7.19**	**7.00**	**6.84**	**6.71**	**6.62**	**6.54**	**6.47**	**6.35**	**6.27**	**6.15**	**6.07**	**5.98**	**5.90**	**5.85**	**5.78**	**5.75**	**5.70**	**5.67**	**5.65**
8	5.32	4.46	4.07	3.84	3.69	3.58	3.50	3.44	3.39	3.34	3.31	3.28	3.23	3.20	3.15	3.12	3.08	3.05	3.03	3.00	2.98	2.96	2.94	2.93
	11.26	**8.65**	**7.59**	**7.01**	**6.63**	**6.37**	**6.19**	**6.03**	**5.91**	**5.82**	**5.74**	**5.67**	**5.56**	**5.48**	**5.36**	**5.28**	**5.20**	**5.11**	**5.06**	**5.00**	**4.96**	**4.91**	**4.88**	**4.86**
9	5.12	4.26	3.86	3.63	3.48	3.37	3.29	3.23	3.18	3.13	3.10	3.07	3.02	2.98	2.93	2.90	2.86	2.82	2.80	2.77	2.76	2.73	2.72	2.71
	10.56	**8.02**	**6.99**	**6.42**	**6.06**	**5.80**	**5.62**	**5.47**	**5.35**	**5.26**	**5.18**	**5.11**	**5.00**	**4.92**	**4.80**	**4.73**	**4.64**	**4.56**	**4.51**	**4.45**	**4.41**	**4.36**	**4.33**	**4.31**
10	4.96	4.10	3.71	3.48	3.33	3.22	3.14	3.07	3.02	2.97	2.94	2.91	2.86	2.82	2.77	2.74	2.70	2.67	2.64	2.61	2.59	2.56	2.55	2.54
	10.04	**7.56**	**6.55**	**5.99**	**5.64**	**5.39**	**5.21**	**5.06**	**4.95**	**4.85**	**4.78**	**4.71**	**4.60**	**4.52**	**4.41**	**4.33**	**4.25**	**4.17**	**4.12**	**4.05**	**4.01**	**3.96**	**3.93**	**3.91**
11	4.84	3.98	3.59	3.36	3.20	3.09	3.01	2.95	2.90	2.86	2.82	2.79	2.74	2.70	2.65	2.61	2.57	2.53	2.50	2.47	2.45	2.42	2.41	2.40
	9.65	**7.20**	**6.22**	**5.67**	**5.32**	**5.07**	**4.88**	**4.74**	**4.63**	**4.54**	**4.46**	**4.40**	**4.29**	**4.21**	**4.10**	**4.02**	**3.94**	**3.86**	**3.80**	**3.74**	**3.70**	**3.66**	**3.62**	**3.60**
12	4.75	3.88	3.49	3.26	3.11	3.00	2.92	2.85	2.80	2.76	2.72	2.69	2.64	2.60	2.54	2.50	2.46	2.42	2.40	2.36	2.35	2.32	2.31	2.30
	9.33	**6.93**	**5.95**	**5.41**	**5.06**	**4.82**	**4.65**	**4.50**	**4.39**	**4.30**	**4.22**	**4.16**	**4.05**	**3.93**	**3.86**	**3.78**	**3.70**	**3.61**	**3.56**	**3.49**	**3.46**	**3.41**	**3.38**	**3.36**

13	4.67	3.80	3.41	3.18	3.02	2.92	2.84	2.77	2.72	2.67	2.63	2.60	2.55	2.51	2.46	2.42	2.38	2.34	2.32	2.28	2.26	2.24	2.22	2.21
	9.07	**6.70**	**5.74**	**5.20**	**4.86**	**4.62**	**4.44**	**4.30**	**4.19**	**4.10**	**4.02**	**3.96**	**3.85**	**3.78**	**3.67**	**3.59**	**3.51**	**3.42**	**3.37**	**3.30**	**3.27**	**3.21**	**3.18**	**3.16**
14	4.60	3.74	3.34	3.11	2.96	2.85	2.77	2.70	2.65	2.60	2.56	2.53	2.48	2.44	2.39	2.35	2.31	2.27	2.24	2.21	2.19	2.16	2.14	2.13
	8.86	**6.51**	**5.56**	**5.03**	**4.69**	**4.46**	**4.28**	**4.14**	**4.03**	**3.94**	**3.86**	**3.80**	**3.70**	**3.62**	**3.51**	**3.43**	**3.34**	**3.26**	**3.21**	**3.14**	**3.11**	**3.06**	**3.02**	**3.00**
15	4.54	3.68	3.29	3.06	2.90	2.79	2.70	2.64	2.59	2.55	2.51	2.48	2.43	2.39	2.33	2.29	2.25	2.21	2.18	2.15	2.12	2.10	2.08	2.07
	8.68	**6.36**	**5.42**	**4.89**	**4.56**	**4.32**	**4.14**	**4.00**	**3.89**	**3.80**	**3.73**	**3.67**	**3.56**	**3.48**	**3.36**	**3.29**	**3.20**	**3.12**	**3.07**	**3.00**	**2.97**	**2.92**	**2.89**	**2.87**
16	4.49	3.63	3.24	3.01	2.85	2.74	2.66	2.59	2.54	2.49	2.45	2.42	2.37	2.33	2.28	2.24	2.20	2.16	2.13	2.09	2.07	2.04	2.02	2.01
	8.53	**6.23**	**5.29**	**4.77**	**4.44**	**4.20**	**4.03**	**3.89**	**3.78**	**3.69**	**3.61**	**3.55**	**3.45**	**3.37**	**3.25**	**3.18**	**3.10**	**3.01**	**2.96**	**2.89**	**2.86**	**2.80**	**2.77**	**2.75**
17	4.45	3.59	3.20	2.96	2.81	2.70	2.62	2.55	2.50	2.45	2.41	2.38	2.33	2.29	2.23	2.19	2.15	2.11	2.08	2.04	2.02	1.99	1.97	1.96
	8.40	**6.11**	**5.18**	**4.67**	**4.34**	**4.10**	**3.93**	**3.79**	**3.68**	**3.59**	**3.52**	**3.45**	**3.35**	**3.27**	**3.16**	**3.08**	**3.00**	**2.92**	**2.86**	**2.79**	**2.76**	**2.70**	**2.67**	**2.65**
18	4.41	3.55	3.16	2.93	2.77	2.66	2.58	2.51	2.46	2.41	2.37	2.34	2.29	2.25	2.19	2.15	2.11	2.07	2.04	2.00	1.98	1.95	1.93	1.92
	8.28	**6.01**	**5.09**	**4.58**	**4.25**	**4.01**	**3.85**	**3.71**	**3.60**	**3.51**	**3.44**	**3.37**	**3.27**	**3.19**	**3.07**	**3.00**	**2.91**	**2.83**	**2.78**	**2.71**	**2.68**	**2.62**	**2.59**	**2.57**
19	4.38	3.52	3.13	2.90	2.74	2.63	2.55	2.48	2.43	2.38	2.34	2.31	2.26	2.21	2.15	2.11	2.07	2.02	2.00	1.96	1.94	1.91	1.90	1.88
	8.18	**5.93**	**5.01**	**4.50**	**4.17**	**3.94**	**3.77**	**3.63**	**3.52**	**3.43**	**3.36**	**3.30**	**3.19**	**3.12**	**3.00**	**2.92**	**2.84**	**2.76**	**2.70**	**2.63**	**2.60**	**2.54**	**2.51**	**2.49**
20	4.35	3.49	3.10	2.87	2.71	2.60	2.52	2.45	2.40	2.35	2.31	2.28	2.23	2.18	2.12	2.08	2.04	1.99	1.96	1.92	1.90	1.87	1.85	1.84
	8.10	**5.85**	**4.94**	**4.43**	**4.10**	**3.87**	**3.71**	**3.56**	**3.45**	**3.37**	**3.30**	**3.23**	**3.13**	**3.05**	**2.94**	**2.86**	**2.77**	**2.69**	**2.63**	**2.56**	**2.53**	**2.87**	**2.44**	**2.42**
21	4.32	3.47	3.07	2.84	2.68	2.57	2.49	2.42	2.37	2.32	2.28	2.25	2.20	2.15	2.09	2.05	2.00	1.96	1.93	1.89	1.87	1.84	1.82	1.81
	8.02	**5.78**	**4.87**	**4.37**	**4.04**	**3.81**	**3.65**	**3.51**	**3.40**	**3.31**	**3.24**	**3.17**	**3.07**	**2.99**	**2.88**	**2.80**	**2.72**	**2.63**	**2.58**	**2.51**	**2.47**	**2.42**	**2.38**	**2.36**
22	4.30	3.44	3.05	2.82	2.66	2.55	2.47	2.40	2.35	2.30	2.26	2.23	2.18	2.13	2.07	2.03	1.98	1.93	1.91	1.87	1.84	1.81	1.80	1.78
	7.94	**5.72**	**4.82**	**4.31**	**3.99**	**3.76**	**3.59**	**3.45**	**3.35**	**3.26**	**3.18**	**3.12**	**3.02**	**2.94**	**2.83**	**2.75**	**2.67**	**2.58**	**2.53**	**2.46**	**2.42**	**2.37**	**2.33**	**2.31**
23	4.28	3.42	3.03	2.80	2.64	2.53	2.45	2.38	2.32	2.28	2.24	2.20	2.14	2.10	2.04	2.00	1.96	1.91	1.88	1.84	1.82	1.79	1.77	1.76
	7.88	**5.66**	**4.76**	**4.26**	**3.94**	**3.71**	**3.54**	**3.41**	**3.30**	**3.21**	**3.14**	**3.07**	**2.97**	**2.89**	**2.78**	**2.70**	**2.62**	**2.53**	**2.48**	**2.41**	**2.37**	**2.32**	**2.28**	**2.26**
24	4.26	3.40	3.01	2.78	2.62	2.51	2.43	2.36	2.30	2.26	2.22	2.18	2.13	2.09	2.02	1.98	1.94	1.89	1.86	1.82	1.80	1.76	1.74	1.73
	7.82	**5.61**	**4.72**	**4.22**	**3.90**	**3.67**	**3.50**	**3.36**	**3.25**	**3.17**	**3.09**	**3.03**	**2.93**	**2.85**	**2.74**	**2.66**	**2.58**	**2.49**	**2.44**	**2.36**	**2.33**	**2.27**	**2.23**	**2.21**
25	4.24	3.38	2.99	2.76	2.60	2.49	2.41	2.34	2.28	2.24	2.20	2.16	2.11	2.06	2.00	1.96	1.92	1.87	1.84	1.80	1.77	1.74	1.72	1.71
	7.77	**5.57**	**4.68**	**4.18**	**3.86**	**3.63**	**3.46**	**3.32**	**3.21**	**3.13**	**3.05**	**2.99**	**2.89**	**2.81**	**2.70**	**2.62**	**2.54**	**2.45**	**2.40**	**2.32**	**2.29**	**2.23**	**2.19**	**2.17**
26	4.22	3.37	2.98	2.74	2.59	2.47	2.39	2.32	2.27	2.22	2.18	2.15	2.10	2.05	1.99	1.95	1.90	1.85	1.82	1.78	1.76	1.72	1.70	1.69
	7.72	**5.53**	**4.64**	**4.14**	**3.82**	**3.59**	**3.42**	**3.29**	**3.17**	**3.09**	**3.02**	**2.96**	**2.86**	**2.77**	**2.66**	**2.58**	**2.50**	**2.41**	**2.36**	**2.28**	**2.25**	**2.19**	**2.15**	**2.13**
27	4.21	3.35	2.96	2.73	2.57	2.46	2.37	2.30	2.25	2.20	2.16	2.13	2.08	2.03	1.97	1.93	1.88	1.84	1.80	1.76	1.74	1.71	1.68	1.67
	7.68	**5.49**	**4.60**	**4.11**	**3.79**	**3.56**	**3.39**	**3.26**	**3.14**	**3.06**	**2.98**	**2.93**	**2.83**	**2.74**	**2.63**	**2.55**	**2.47**	**2.38**	**2.33**	**2.25**	**2.21**	**2.16**	**2.12**	**2.10**

5% and 1% Points for the Distribution of F (5% roman, 1% boldface)[a] (continued)

Degrees of Freedom n_2	Degrees of Freedom n_1: 1	2	3	4	5	6	7	8	9	10	11	12	14	16	20	24	30	40	50	75	100	200	500	∞
28	4.20 **7.64**	3.34 **5.45**	2.95 **4.57**	2.71 **4.07**	2.56 **3.76**	2.44 **3.53**	2.36 **3.36**	2.29 **3.23**	2.24 **3.11**	2.19 **3.03**	2.15 **2.95**	2.12 **2.90**	2.06 **2.80**	2.02 **2.71**	1.96 **2.60**	1.91 **2.52**	1.87 **2.44**	1.81 **2.35**	1.78 **2.30**	1.75 **2.22**	1.72 **2.18**	1.69 **2.13**	1.67 **2.09**	1.65 **2.06**
29	4.18 **7.60**	3.33 **5.42**	2.93 **4.54**	2.70 **4.04**	2.54 **3.73**	2.43 **3.50**	2.35 **3.33**	2.28 **3.20**	2.22 **3.08**	2.18 **3.00**	2.14 **2.92**	2.10 **2.87**	2.05 **2.77**	2.00 **2.68**	1.94 **2.57**	1.90 **2.49**	1.85 **2.41**	1.80 **2.32**	1.77 **2.27**	1.73 **2.19**	1.71 **2.15**	1.68 **2.10**	1.65 **2.06**	1.64 **2.03**
30	4.17 **7.56**	3.32 **5.39**	2.92 **4.51**	2.69 **4.02**	2.53 **3.70**	2.42 **3.47**	2.34 **3.30**	2.27 **3.17**	2.21 **3.06**	2.16 **2.98**	2.12 **2.90**	2.09 **2.84**	2.04 **2.74**	1.99 **2.66**	1.93 **2.55**	1.89 **2.47**	1.84 **2.38**	1.79 **2.29**	1.76 **2.24**	1.72 **2.16**	1.69 **2.13**	1.66 **2.07**	1.64 **2.03**	1.62 **2.01**
32	4.15 **7.50**	3.30 **5.34**	2.90 **4.46**	2.67 **3.97**	2.51 **3.66**	2.40 **3.42**	2.32 **3.25**	2.25 **3.12**	2.19 **3.01**	2.14 **2.94**	2.10 **2.86**	2.07 **2.80**	2.02 **2.70**	1.97 **2.62**	1.91 **2.51**	1.86 **2.42**	1.82 **2.34**	1.76 **2.25**	1.74 **2.20**	1.69 **2.12**	1.67 **2.08**	1.64 **2.02**	1.61 **1.98**	1.59 **1.96**
34	4.13 **7.44**	3.28 **5.29**	2.88 **4.42**	2.65 **3.93**	2.49 **3.61**	2.38 **3.38**	2.30 **3.21**	2.23 **3.08**	2.17 **2.97**	2.12 **2.89**	2.08 **2.82**	2.05 **2.76**	2.00 **2.66**	1.95 **2.58**	1.89 **2.47**	1.84 **2.38**	1.80 **2.30**	1.74 **2.21**	1.71 **2.15**	1.67 **2.08**	1.64 **2.04**	1.61 **1.98**	1.59 **1.94**	1.57 **1.91**
36	4.11 **7.39**	3.26 **5.25**	2.86 **4.38**	2.63 **3.89**	2.48 **3.58**	2.36 **3.35**	2.28 **3.18**	2.21 **3.04**	2.15 **2.94**	2.10 **2.86**	2.06 **2.78**	2.03 **2.72**	1.98 **2.62**	1.93 **2.54**	1.87 **2.43**	1.82 **2.35**	1.78 **2.26**	1.72 **2.17**	1.69 **2.12**	1.65 **2.04**	1.62 **2.00**	1.59 **1.94**	1.56 **1.90**	1.55 **1.87**
38	4.10 **7.35**	3.25 **5.21**	2.85 **4.34**	2.62 **3.86**	2.46 **3.54**	2.35 **3.32**	2.26 **3.15**	2.19 **3.02**	2.14 **2.91**	2.09 **2.82**	2.05 **2.75**	2.02 **2.69**	1.96 **2.59**	1.92 **2.51**	1.85 **2.40**	1.80 **2.32**	1.76 **2.22**	1.71 **2.14**	1.67 **2.08**	1.63 **2.00**	1.60 **1.97**	1.57 **1.90**	1.54 **1.86**	1.53 **1.84**
40	4.08 **7.31**	3.23 **5.18**	2.84 **4.31**	2.61 **3.83**	2.45 **3.51**	2.34 **3.29**	2.25 **3.12**	2.18 **2.99**	2.12 **2.88**	2.07 **2.80**	2.04 **2.73**	2.00 **2.66**	1.95 **2.56**	1.90 **2.49**	1.84 **2.37**	1.79 **2.29**	1.74 **2.20**	1.69 **2.11**	1.66 **2.05**	1.61 **1.97**	1.59 **1.94**	1.55 **1.88**	1.53 **1.84**	1.51 **1.81**
42	4.07 **7.27**	3.22 **5.15**	2.83 **4.29**	2.59 **3.80**	2.44 **3.49**	2.32 **3.26**	2.24 **3.10**	2.17 **2.96**	2.11 **2.86**	2.06 **2.77**	2.02 **2.70**	1.99 **2.64**	1.94 **2.54**	1.89 **2.46**	1.82 **2.35**	1.78 **2.26**	1.73 **2.17**	1.68 **2.08**	1.64 **2.02**	1.60 **1.94**	1.57 **1.91**	1.54 **1.85**	1.51 **1.80**	1.49 **1.78**
44	4.06 **7.24**	3.21 **5.12**	2.82 **4.26**	2.58 **3.78**	2.43 **3.46**	2.31 **3.24**	2.23 **3.07**	2.16 **2.94**	2.10 **2.84**	2.05 **2.75**	2.01 **2.68**	1.98 **2.62**	1.92 **2.52**	1.88 **2.44**	1.81 **2.32**	1.76 **2.24**	1.72 **2.15**	1.66 **2.06**	1.63 **2.00**	1.58 **1.92**	1.56 **1.88**	1.52 **1.82**	1.50 **1.78**	1.48 **1.75**
46	4.05 **7.21**	3.20 **5.10**	2.81 **4.24**	2.57 **3.76**	2.42 **3.44**	2.30 **3.22**	2.22 **3.05**	2.14 **2.92**	2.09 **2.82**	2.04 **2.73**	2.00 **2.66**	1.97 **2.60**	1.91 **2.50**	1.87 **2.42**	1.80 **2.30**	1.75 **2.22**	1.71 **2.13**	1.65 **2.04**	1.62 **1.98**	1.57 **1.90**	1.54 **1.86**	1.51 **1.80**	1.48 **1.76**	1.46 **1.72**
48	4.04 **7.19**	3.19 **5.08**	2.80 **4.22**	2.56 **3.74**	2.41 **3.42**	2.30 **3.20**	2.21 **3.04**	2.14 **2.90**	2.08 **2.80**	2.03 **2.71**	1.99 **2.64**	1.96 **2.58**	1.90 **2.48**	1.86 **2.40**	1.79 **2.28**	1.74 **2.20**	1.70 **2.11**	1.64 **2.02**	1.61 **1.96**	1.56 **1.88**	1.53 **1.84**	1.50 **1.78**	1.47 **1.73**	1.45 **1.70**
50	4.03 **7.17**	3.18 **5.06**	2.79 **4.20**	2.56 **3.72**	2.40 **3.41**	2.29 **3.18**	2.20 **3.02**	2.13 **2.88**	2.07 **2.78**	2.02 **2.70**	1.98 **2.62**	1.95 **2.56**	1.90 **2.46**	1.85 **2.39**	1.78 **2.26**	1.74 **2.18**	1.69 **2.10**	1.63 **2.00**	1.60 **1.94**	1.55 **1.86**	1.52 **1.82**	1.48 **1.76**	1.46 **1.71**	1.44 **1.68**

55	4.02	3.17	2.78	2.54	2.38	2.27	2.18	2.11	2.05	2.00	1.97	1.93	1.88	1.83	1.76	1.72	1.67	1.61	1.58	1.52	1.50	1.46	1.43	1.41
	7.12	**5.01**	**4.16**	**3.68**	**3.37**	**3.15**	**2.98**	**2.85**	**2.75**	**2.66**	**2.59**	**2.53**	**2.43**	**2.35**	**2.23**	**2.15**	**2.06**	**1.96**	**1.90**	**1.82**	**1.78**	**1.71**	**1.66**	**1.64**
60	4.00	3.15	2.76	2.52	2.37	2.25	2.17	2.10	2.04	1.99	1.95	1.92	1.86	1.81	1.75	1.70	1.65	1.59	1.56	1.50	1.48	1.44	1.41	1.39
	7.08	**4.98**	**4.13**	**3.65**	**3.34**	**3.12**	**2.95**	**2.82**	**2.72**	**2.63**	**2.56**	**2.50**	**2.40**	**2.32**	**2.20**	**2.12**	**2.03**	**1.93**	**1.87**	**1.79**	**1.74**	**1.68**	**1.63**	**1.60**
65	3.99	3.14	2.75	2.51	2.36	2.24	2.15	2.08	2.02	1.98	1.94	1.90	1.85	1.80	1.73	1.68	1.63	1.57	1.54	1.49	1.46	1.42	1.39	1.37
	7.04	**4.95**	**4.10**	**3.62**	**3.31**	**3.09**	**2.93**	**2.79**	**2.70**	**2.61**	**2.54**	**2.47**	**2.37**	**2.30**	**2.18**	**2.09**	**2.00**	**1.90**	**1.84**	**1.76**	**1.71**	**1.64**	**1.60**	**1.56**
70	3.98	3.13	2.74	2.50	2.35	2.23	2.14	2.07	2.01	1.97	1.93	1.89	1.84	1.79	1.72	1.67	1.62	1.56	1.53	1.47	1.45	1.40	1.37	1.35
	7.01	**4.92**	**4.08**	**3.60**	**3.29**	**3.07**	**2.91**	**2.77**	**2.67**	**2.59**	**2.51**	**2.45**	**2.35**	**2.28**	**2.15**	**2.07**	**1.98**	**1.88**	**1.82**	**1.74**	**1.69**	**1.62**	**1.56**	**1.53**
80	3.96	3.11	2.72	2.48	2.33	2.21	2.12	2.05	1.99	1.95	1.91	1.88	1.82	1.77	1.70	1.65	1.60	1.54	1.51	1.45	1.42	1.38	1.35	1.32
	6.96	**4.88**	**4.04**	**3.56**	**3.25**	**3.04**	**2.87**	**2.74**	**2.64**	**2.55**	**2.48**	**2.41**	**2.32**	**2.24**	**2.11**	**2.03**	**1.94**	**1.84**	**1.78**	**1.70**	**1.65**	**1.57**	**1.52**	**1.49**
100	3.94	3.09	2.70	2.46	2.30	2.19	2.10	2.03	1.97	1.92	1.88	1.85	1.79	1.75	1.68	1.63	1.57	1.51	1.48	1.42	1.39	1.34	1.30	1.28
	6.90	**4.82**	**3.98**	**3.51**	**3.20**	**2.99**	**2.82**	**2.69**	**2.59**	**2.51**	**2.43**	**2.36**	**2.26**	**2.19**	**2.06**	**1.98**	**1.89**	**1.79**	**1.73**	**1.64**	**1.59**	**1.51**	**1.46**	**1.43**
125	3.92	3.07	2.68	2.44	2.29	2.17	2.08	2.01	1.95	1.90	1.86	1.83	1.77	1.72	1.65	1.60	1.55	1.49	1.45	1.39	1.36	1.31	1.27	1.25
	6.84	**4.78**	**3.94**	**3.47**	**3.17**	**2.95**	**2.79**	**2.65**	**2.56**	**2.47**	**2.40**	**2.33**	**2.23**	**2.15**	**2.03**	**1.94**	**1.85**	**1.75**	**1.68**	**1.59**	**1.54**	**1.46**	**1.40**	**1.37**
150	3.91	3.06	2.67	2.43	2.27	2.16	2.07	2.00	1.94	1.89	1.85	1.82	1.76	1.71	1.64	1.59	1.54	1.47	1.44	1.37	1.34	1.29	1.25	1.22
	6.81	**4.75**	**3.91**	**3.44**	**3.14**	**2.92**	**2.76**	**2.62**	**2.53**	**2.44**	**2.37**	**2.30**	**2.20**	**2.12**	**2.00**	**1.91**	**1.83**	**1.72**	**1.66**	**1.56**	**1.51**	**1.43**	**1.37**	**1.33**
200	3.89	3.04	2.65	2.41	2.26	2.14	2.05	1.98	1.92	1.87	1.83	1.80	1.74	1.69	1.62	1.57	1.52	1.45	1.42	1.35	1.32	1.26	1.22	1.19
	6.76	**4.71**	**3.88**	**3.41**	**3.11**	**2.90**	**2.73**	**2.60**	**2.50**	**2.41**	**2.34**	**2.28**	**2.17**	**2.09**	**1.97**	**1.88**	**1.79**	**1.69**	**1.62**	**1.53**	**1.48**	**1.39**	**1.33**	**1.28**
400	3.86	3.02	2.62	2.39	2.23	2.12	2.03	1.96	1.90	1.85	1.81	1.78	1.72	1.67	1.60	1.54	1.49	1.42	1.38	1.32	1.28	1.22	1.16	1.13
	6.70	**4.66**	**3.83**	**3.36**	**3.06**	**2.85**	**2.69**	**2.55**	**2.46**	**2.37**	**2.29**	**2.23**	**2.12**	**2.04**	**1.92**	**1.84**	**1.74**	**1.64**	**1.57**	**1.47**	**1.42**	**1.32**	**1.24**	**1.19**
1000	3.85	3.00	2.61	2.38	2.22	2.10	2.02	1.95	1.89	1.84	1.80	1.76	1.70	1.65	1.58	1.53	1.47	1.41	1.36	1.30	1.26	1.19	1.13	1.08
	6.66	**4.62**	**3.80**	**3.34**	**3.04**	**2.82**	**2.66**	**2.53**	**2.43**	**2.34**	**2.26**	**2.20**	**2.09**	**2.01**	**1.89**	**1.81**	**1.71**	**1.61**	**1.54**	**1.44**	**1.38**	**1.28**	**1.19**	**1.11**
∞	3.84	2.99	2.60	2.37	2.21	2.09	2.01	1.94	1.88	1.83	1.79	1.75	1.69	1.64	1.57	1.52	1.46	1.40	1.35	1.28	1.24	1.17	1.11	1.00
	6.64	**4.60**	**3.78**	**3.32**	**3.02**	**2.80**	**2.64**	**2.51**	**2.41**	**2.32**	**2.24**	**2.18**	**2.07**	**1.99**	**1.87**	**1.79**	**1.69**	**1.59**	**1.52**	**1.41**	**1.36**	**1.25**	**1.15**	**1.00**

Source. This table is reproduced from *Statistical Methods*, 4th edition, with the permission of the author, George W. Snedecor, and his publisher, The Collegiate Press, Ames, Iowa.

[a] The number of degrees of freedom in the numerator and the denominator are n_1 and n_2, respectively. Example: With 5 degrees of freedom in the numerator and 20 in the denominator, an F value larger than 2.71 has .05 probability and a value exceeding 4.10 has .01 probability. Also, an F value exceeding $1/4.56 = .219$ has .95 probability with the same degrees of freedom. The figure .219 represents the lower 5 percent point of the distribution; it is obtained by taking the reciprocal of the F ratio and interchanging the degrees of freedom in the numerator and the denominator.

Lower and Upper Bounds of the 5% Points of the Durbin-Watson Test Statistic[a]

	$K=2$		$K=3$		$K=4$		$K=5$		$K=6$	
n	d_L	d_U	d_L	d_U	d_L	d_U	d_L	d_U	d_L	d_U
15	1.08	1.36	.95	1.54	.82	1.75	.69	1.97	.56	2.21
16	1.10	1.37	.98	1.54	.86	1.73	.74	1.93	.62	2.15
17	1.13	1.38	1.02	1.54	.90	1.71	.78	1.90	.67	2.10
18	1.16	1.39	1.05	1.53	.93	1.69	.82	1.87	.71	2.06
19	1.18	1.40	1.08	1.53	.97	1.68	.86	1.85	.75	2.02
20	1.20	1.41	1.10	1.54	1.00	1.68	.90	1.83	.79	1.99
21	1.22	1.42	1.13	1.54	1.03	1.67	.93	1.81	.83	1.96
22	1.24	1.43	1.15	1.54	1.05	1.66	.96	1.80	.86	1.94
23	1.26	1.44	1.17	1.54	1.08	1.66	.99	1.79	.90	1.92
24	1.27	1.45	1.19	1.55	1.10	1.66	1.01	1.78	.93	1.90
25	1.29	1.45	1.21	1.55	1.12	1.66	1.04	1.77	.95	1.89
26	1.30	1.46	1.22	1.55	1.14	1.65	1.06	1.76	.98	1.88
27	1.32	1.47	1.24	1.56	1.16	1.65	1.08	1.76	1.01	1.86
28	1.33	1.48	1.26	1.56	1.18	1.65	1.10	1.75	1.03	1.85
29	1.34	1.48	1.27	1.56	1.20	1.65	1.12	1.74	1.05	1.84
30	1.35	1.49	1.28	1.57	1.21	1.65	1.14	1.74	1.07	1.83
31	1.36	1.50	1.30	1.57	1.23	1.65	1.16	1.74	1.09	1.83
32	1.37	1.50	1.31	1.57	1.24	1.65	1.18	1.73	1.11	1.82
33	1.38	1.51	1.32	1.58	1.26	1.65	1.19	1.73	1.13	1.81
34	1.39	1.51	1.33	1.58	1.27	1.65	1.21	1.73	1.15	1.81
35	1.40	1.52	1.34	1.58	1.28	1.65	1.22	1.73	1.16	1.80
36	1.41	1.52	1.35	1.59	1.29	1.65	1.24	1.73	1.18	1.80
37	1.42	1.53	1.36	1.59	1.31	1.66	1.25	1.72	1.19	1.80
38	1.43	1.54	1.37	1.59	1.32	1.66	1.26	1.72	1.21	1.79
39	1.43	1.54	1.38	1.60	1.33	1.66	1.27	1.72	1.22	1.79
40	1.44	1.54	1.39	1.60	1.34	1.66	1.29	1.72	1.23	1.79
45	1.48	1.57	1.43	1.62	1.38	1.67	1.34	1.72	1.29	1.78
50	1.50	1.59	1.46	1.63	1.42	1.67	1.38	1.72	1.34	1.77
55	1.53	1.60	1.49	1.64	1.45	1.68	1.41	1.72	1.38	1.77
60	1.55	1.62	1.51	1.65	1.48	1.69	1.44	1.73	1.41	1.77
65	1.57	1.63	1.54	1.66	1.50	1.70	1.47	1.73	1.44	1.77
70	1.58	1.64	1.55	1.67	1.52	1.70	1.49	1.74	1.46	1.77
75	1.60	1.65	1.57	1.68	1.54	1.71	1.51	1.74	1.49	1.77
80	1.61	1.66	1.59	1.69	1.56	1.72	1.53	1.74	1.51	1.77
85	1.62	1.67	1.60	1.70	1.57	1.72	1.55	1.75	1.52	1.77
90	1.63	1.68	1.61	1.70	1.59	1.73	1.57	1.75	1.54	1.78
95	1.64	1.69	1.62	1.71	1.60	1.73	1.58	1.75	1.56	1.78
100	1.65	1.69	1.63	1.72	1.61	1.74	1.59	1.76	1.57	1.78

Source. This table is taken from Durbin and Watson (1951) with the kind permission of *Biometrika*, the publisher, and the authors.

[a] The value of K at the head of each pair of columns is the number of elements of the parameter vector, and it is assumed that one of these elements is a constant term. See Section 5.1 for details.

Lower and Upper Bounds of the 1% Points of the Durbin-Watson Test Statistic

	K = 2		K = 3		K = 4		K = 5		K = 6	
n	d_L	d_U	d_L	d_U	d_L	d_U	d_L	d_U	d_L	d_U
15	.81	1.07	.70	1.25	.59	1.46	.49	1.70	.39	1.96
16	.84	1.09	.74	1.25	.63	1.44	.53	1.66	.44	1.90
17	.87	1.10	.77	1.25	.67	1.43	.57	1.63	.48	1.85
18	.90	1.12	.80	1.26	.71	1.42	.61	1.60	.52	1.80
19	.93	1.13	.83	1.26	.74	1.41	.65	1.58	.56	1.77
20	.95	1.15	.86	1.27	.77	1.41	.68	1.57	.60	1.74
21	.97	1.16	.89	1.27	.80	1.41	.72	1.55	.63	1.71
22	1.00	1.17	.91	1.28	.83	1.40	.75	1.54	.66	1.69
23	1.02	1.19	.94	1.29	.86	1.40	.77	1.53	.70	1.67
24	1.04	1.20	.96	1.30	.88	1.41	.80	1.53	.72	1.66
25	1.05	1.21	.98	1.30	.90	1.41	.83	1.52	.75	1.65
26	1.07	1.22	1.00	1.31	.93	1.41	.85	1.52	.78	1.64
27	1.09	1.23	1.02	1.32	.95	1.41	.88	1.51	.81	1.63
28	1.10	1.24	1.04	1.32	.97	1.41	.90	1.51	.83	1.62
29	1.12	1.25	1.05	1.33	.99	1.42	.92	1.51	.85	1.61
30	1.13	1.26	1.07	1.34	1.01	1.42	.94	1.51	.88	1.61
31	1.15	1.27	1.08	1.34	1.02	1.42	.96	1.51	.90	1.60
32	1.16	1.28	1.10	1.35	1.04	1.43	.98	1.51	.92	1.60
33	1.17	1.29	1.11	1.36	1.05	1.43	1.00	1.51	.94	1.59
34	1.18	1.30	1.13	1.36	1.07	1.43	1.01	1.51	.95	1.59
35	1.19	1.31	1.14	1.37	1.08	1.44	1.03	1.51	.97	1.59
36	1.21	1.32	1.15	1.38	1.10	1.44	1.04	1.51	.99	1.59
37	1.22	1.32	1.16	1.38	1.11	1.45	1.06	1.51	1.00	1.59
38	1.23	1.33	1.18	1.39	1.12	1.45	1.07	1.52	1.02	1.58
39	1.24	1.34	1.19	1.39	1.14	1.45	1.09	1.52	1.03	1.58
40	1.25	1.34	1.20	1.40	1.15	1.46	1.10	1.52	1.05	1.58
45	1.29	1.38	1.24	1.42	1.20	1.48	1.16	1.53	1.11	1.58
50	1.32	1.40	1.28	1.45	1.24	1.49	1.20	1.54	1.16	1.59
55	1.36	1.43	1.32	1.47	1.28	1.51	1.25	1.55	1.21	1.59
60	1.38	1.45	1.35	1.48	1.32	1.52	1.28	1.56	1.25	1.60
65	1.41	1.47	1.38	1.50	1.35	1.53	1.31	1.57	1.28	1.61
70	1.43	1.49	1.40	1.52	1.37	1.55	1.34	1.58	1.31	1.61
75	1.45	1.50	1.42	1.53	1.39	1.56	1.37	1.59	1.34	1.62
80	1.47	1.52	1.44	1.54	1.42	1.57	1.39	1.60	1.36	1.62
85	1.48	1.53	1.46	1.55	1.43	1.58	1.41	1.60	1.39	1.63
90	1.50	1.54	1.47	1.56	1.45	1.59	1.43	1.61	1.41	1.64
95	1.51	1.55	1.49	1.57	1.47	1.60	1.45	1.62	1.42	1.64
100	1.52	1.56	1.50	1.58	1.48	1.60	1.46	1.63	1.44	1.65

Source. This table is taken from Durbin and Watson (1951) with the kind permission of *Biometrika*, the publisher, and the authors.

5%, 1%, and .1% Points of the Von Neumann Ratio[a]

Number of Observations	5%	1%	.1%	5%	1%	.1%
	One-tailed test against positive correlation			*One-tailed test against negative correlation*		
4	1.0406	.8341	.7864	4.2927	4.4992	4.5469
5	1.0255	.6724	.5201	3.9745	4.3276	4.4799
6	1.0682	.6738	.4361	3.7318	4.1262	4.3639
7	1.0919	.7163	.4311	3.5748	3.9504	4.2356
8	1.1228	.7575	.4612	3.4486	3.8139	4.1102
9	1.1524	.7974	.4973	3.3476	3.7025	4.0027
10	1.1803	.8353	.5351	3.2642	3.6091	3.9093
11	1.2962	.8706	.5717	3.1938	3.5294	3.8283
12	1.2301	.9033	.6062	3.1335	3.4603	3.7574
13	1.2521	.9336	.6390	3.0812	3.3996	3.6944
14	1.2725	.9618	.6702	3.0352	3.3458	3.6375
15	1.2914	.9880	.6999	2.9943	3.2977	3.5858
16	1.3090	1.0124	.7281	2.9577	3.2543	3.5386
17	1.3253	1.0352	.7548	2.9247	3.2148	3.4952
18	1.3405	1.0566	.7801	2.8948	3.1787	3.4552
19	1.3547	1.0766	.8040	2.8675	3.1456	3.4182
20	1.3680	1.0954	.8265	2.8425	3.1151	3.3840
21	1.3805	1.1131	.8477	2.8195	3.0869	3.3523
22	1.3923	1.1298	.8677	2.7982	3.0607	3.3228
23	1.4035	1.1456	.8866	2.7784	3.0362	3.2953
24	1.4141	1.1606	.9045	2.7599	3.0133	3.2695
25	1.4241	1.1748	.9215	2.7426	2.9919	3.2452
26	1.4336	1.1883	.9378	2.7264	2.9718	3.2222
27	1.4426	1.2012	.9535	2.7112	2.9528	3.2003
28	1.4512	1.2135	.9687	2.6969	2.9348	3.1794
29	1.4594	1.2252	.9835	2.6834	2.9177	3.1594
30	1.4672	1.2363	.9978	2.6707	2.9016	3.1402

[a] See Section 5.4 for details.

5%, 1%, and .1% Points of the Von Neumann Ratio

Number of Observations	5%	1%	.1%	5%	1%	.1%
	One-tailed test against positive correlation			*One-tailed test against negative correlation*		
31	1.4746	1.2469	1.0115	2.6587	2.8864	3.1219
32	1.4817	1.2570	1.0245	2.6473	2.8720	3.1046
33	1.4885	1.2667	1.0369	2.6365	2.8583	3.0882
34	1.4951	1.2761	1.0488	2.6262	2.8451	3.0725
35	1.5014	1.2852	1.0603	2.6163	2.8324	3.0574
36	1.5075	1.2940	1.0714	2.6068	2.8202	3.0429
37	1.5135	1.3025	1.0822	2.5977	2.8085	3.0289
38	1.5193	1.3108	1.0927	2.5889	2.7973	3.0154
39	1.5249	1.3188	1.1029	2.5804	2.7865	3.0024
40	1.5304	1.3266	1.1128	2.5722	2.7760	2.9898
41	1.5357	1.3342	1.1224	2.5643	2.7658	2.9776
42	1.5408	1.3415	1.1317	2.5567	2.7560	2.9658
43	1.5458	1.3486	1.1407	2.5494	2.7466	2.9545
44	1.5506	1.3554	1.1494	2.5424	2.7376	2.9436
45	1.5552	1.3620	1.1577	2.5357	2.7289	2.9332
46	1.5596	1.3684	1.1657	2.5293	2.7205	2.9232
47	1.5638	1.3745	1.1734	2.5232	2.7125	2.9136
48	1.5678	1.3802	1.1807	2.5173	2.7049	2.9044
49	1.5716	1.3856	1.1877	2.5117	2.6977	2.8956
50	1.5752	1.3907	1.1944	2.5064	2.6908	2.8872
51	1.5787	1.3957	1.2010	2.5013	2.6842	2.8790
52	1.5822	1.4007	1.2075	2.4963	2.6777	2.8709
53	1.5856	1.4057	1.2139	2.4914	2.6712	2.8630
54	1.5890	1.4107	1.2202	2.4866	2.6648	2.8553
55	1.5923	1.4156	1.2264	2.4819	2.6585	2.8477
56	1.5955	1.4203	1.2324	2.4773	2.6524	2.8403
57	1.5987	1.4249	1.2383	2.4728	2.6465	2.8331
58	1.6019	1.4294	1.2442	2.4684	2.6407	2.8260
59	1.6051	1.4339	1.2500	2.4640	2.6350	2.8190
60	1.6082	1.4384	1.2558	2.4596	2.6294	2.8120

Source. This table is taken from Hart (1942b) by kind permission of the *Annals of Mathematical Statistics*, publisher.

5%, 1%, and .1% Points of the Modified Von Neumann Ratio[a]

Degrees of Freedom	5%	1%	.1%	5%	1%	.1%
	One-tailed test against positive autocorrelation			*One-tailed test against negative autocorrelation*		
2	.025	.001	.000	3.975	3.999	4.000
3	.252	.052	.005	4.142	4.427	4.493
4	.474	.170	.037	3.827	4.295	4.496
5	.598	.292	.095	3.571	4.076	4.378
6	.701	.386	.163	3.413	3.881	4.233
7	.790	.464	.228	3.299	3.731	4.095
8	.861	.537	.285	3.206	3.618	3.973
9	.922	.601	.339	3.131	3.524	3.871
10	.975	.657	.390	3.069	3.445	3.784
11	1.020	.708	.438	3.016	3.378	3.710
12	1.060	.753	.482	2.970	3.319	3.645
13	1.096	.795	.523	2.930	3.268	3.587
14	1.128	.832	.561	2.895	3.222	3.535
15	1.157	.866	.597	2.863	3.181	3.488
16	1.183	.898	.630	2.835	3.144	3.445
17	1.207	.927	.661	2.809	3.110	3.406
18	1.228	.954	.691	2.785	3.079	3.370
19	1.249	.979	.718	2.764	3.051	3.337
20	1.267	1.003	.744	2.744	3.025	3.306
21	1.285	1.024	.769	2.725	3.000	3.277
22	1.301	1.045	.792	2.708	2.978	3.250
23	1.316	1.064	.814	2.692	2.957	3.225
24	1.330	1.082	.834	2.677	2.937	3.201
25	1.344	1.100	.854	2.663	2.918	3.179
26	1.356	1.116	.873	2.650	2.901	3.157
27	1.368	1.131	.891	2.638	2.884	3.137
28	1.380	1.146	.908	2.626	2.868	3.118
29	1.390	1.160	.925	2.615	2.854	3.100
30	1.400	1.173	.940	2.605	2.839	3.083

[a] See Section 5.4 for details.

Degrees of Freedom	5%	1%	.1%	5%	1%	.1%
	One-tailed test against positive autocorrelation			*One-tailed test against negative autocorrelation*		
31	1.410	1.186	.955	2.595	2.826	3.066
32	1.419	1.198	.970	2.585	2.813	3.051
33	1.428	1.209	.984	2.576	2.801	3.036
34	1.437	1.221	.997	2.567	2.789	3.021
35	1.445	1.231	1.010	2.559	2.778	3.007
36	1.452	1.241	1.022	2.551	2.767	2.994
37	1.460	1.251	1.034	2.544	2.757	2.982
38	1.467	1.261	1.045	2.536	2.747	2.969
39	1.474	1.270	1.057	2.529	2.738	2.957
40	1.480	1.279	1.067	2.522	2.729	2.946
41	1.487	1.287	1.078	2.516	2.720	2.935
42	1.493	1.295	1.088	2.510	2.711	2.925
43	1.499	1.303	1.097	2.504	2.703	2.914
44	1.504	1.311	1.107	2.498	2.695	2.904
45	1.510	1.318	1.116	2.492	2.687	2.895
46	1.515	1.325	1.125	2.487	2.680	2.885
47	1.520	1.332	1.133	2.482	2.673	2.876
48	1.525	1.339	1.142	2.477	2.666	2.868
49	1.530	1.346	1.150	2.472	2.659	2.859
50	1.535	1.352	1.158	2.467	2.653	2.851
51	1.540	1.358	1.165	2.462	2.646	2.843
52	1.544	1.364	1.173	2.458	2.640	2.835
53	1.548	1.370	1.180	2.453	2.634	2.828
54	1.552	1.376	1.187	2.449	2.628	2.820
55	1.557	1.381	1.194	2.445	2.623	2.813
56	1.561	1.387	1.201	2.441	2.617	2.806
57	1.564	1.392	1.207	2.437	2.612	2.799
58	1.568	1.397	1.214	2.433	2.606	2.793
59	1.572	1.402	1.220	2.429	2.601	2.786
60	1.575	1.407	1.226	2.426	2.596	2.780

Source. This table is taken from Press and Brooks (1969) with kind permission of the authors.

INDEX